The J2EE™ Tutorial

Second Edition

The Java™ Series

Lisa Friendly, Series Editor
Tim Lindholm, Technical Editor
Alan Sommerer, Technical Editor
Ken Arnold, Technical Editor of The Jini™ Technology Series
Jim Inscore, Technical Editor of The Java™ Series, Enterprise Edition   **www.javaseries.com**

Eric Armstrong, Stephanie Bodoff, Debbie Carson, Maydene Fisher, Dale Green, Kim Haase
The Java™ Web Services Tutorial

Ken Arnold, James Gosling, David Holmes
The Java™ Programming Language, Third Edition

Cynthia Bloch, Annette Wagner
MIDP 2.0 Style Guide for the Java™ 2 Platform, Micro Edition

Joshua Bloch
Effective Java™ Programming Language Guide

Mary Campione, Kathy Walrath, Alison Huml
The Java™ Tutorial, Third Edition: A Short Course on the Basics

Mary Campione, Kathy Walrath, Alison Huml,Tutorial Team
The Java™ Tutorial Continued: The Rest of the JDK™

Patrick Chan
The Java™ Developers Almanac 1.4, Volume 1

Patrick Chan
The Java™ Developers Almanac 1.4, Volume 2

Patrick Chan, Rosanna Lee
The Java™ Class Libraries, Second Edition, Volume 2: java.applet, java.awt, java.beans

Patrick Chan, Rosanna Lee, Doug Kramer
The Java™ Class Libraries, Second Edition, Volume 1: java.io, java.lang, java.math, java.net, java.text, java.util

Patrick Chan, Rosanna Lee, Doug Kramer
The Java™ Class Libraries, Second Edition, Volume 1: Supplement for the Java™ 2 Platform, Standard Edition, v1.2

Kirk Chen, Li Gong
Programming Open Service Gateways with Java™ Embedded Server

Zhiqun Chen
Java Card™ Technology for Smart Cards: Architecture and Programmer's Guide

Maydene Fisher, Jon Ellis, Jonathan Bruce
JDBC™ API Tutorial and Reference, Third Edition

Li Gong, Gary Ellison, Mary Dageforde
Inside Java™ 2 Platform Security, Second Edition: Architecture, API Design, and Implementation

James Gosling, Bill Joy, Guy Steele, Gilad Bracha
The Java™ Language Specification, Second Edition

Doug Lea
Concurrent Programming in Java™, Second Edition: Design Principles and Patterns

Rosanna Lee, Scott Seligman
JNDI API Tutorial and Reference: Building Directory-Enabled Java™ Applications

Sheng Liang
The Java™ Native Interface: Programmer's Guide and Specification

Tim Lindholm, Frank Yellin
The Java™ Virtual Machine Specification, Second Edition

Roger Riggs, Antero Taivalsaari, Jim Van Peursem, Jyri Huopaniemi, Mark Patel, Aleksi Uotila
Programming Wireless Devices with the Java™ 2 Platform, Micro Edition, Second Edition

Sun Microsystems, Inc.
Java™ Look and Feel Design Guidelines: Advanced Topics

Kathy Walrath, Mary Campione, Alison Huml, Sharon Zakhour
The JFC Swing Tutorial, Second Edition: A Guide to Constructing GUIs

Seth White, Maydene Fisher, Rick Cattell, Graham Hamilton, Mark Hapner
JDBC™ API Tutorial and Reference, Second Edition: Universal Data Access for the Java™ 2 Platform

Steve Wilson, Jeff Kesselman
Java™ Platform Performance: Strategies and Tactics

The Jini™ Technology Series

Eric Freeman, Susanne Hupfer, Ken Arnold
JavaSpaces™ Principles, Patterns, and Practice

The Java™ Series, Enterprise Edition

Stephanie Bodoff, Dale Green, Kim Haase, Eric Jendrock
The J2EE™ Tutorial, Second Edition

Rick Cattell, Jim Inscore, Enterprise Partners
J2EE™ Technology in Practice: Building Business Applications with the Java™ 2 Platform, Enterprise Edition

Mark Hapner, Rich Burridge, Rahul Sharma, Joseph Fialli, Kim Haase
Java™ Message Service API Tutorial and Reference: Messaging for the J2EE™ Platform

Inderjeet Singh, Beth Stearns, Mark Johnson, Enterprise Team
Designing Enterprise Applications with the Java™ 2 Platform, Enterprise Edition

Vlada Matena, Sanjeev Krishnan, Linda DeMichiel, Beth Stearns
Applying Enterprise JavaBeans™, Second Edition: Component-Based Development for the J2EE™ Platform

Bill Shannon, Mark Hapner, Vlada Matena, James Davidson, Eduardo Pelegri-Llopart, Larry Cable, Enterprise Team
Java™ 2 Platform, Enterprise Edition: Platform and Component Specifications

Rahul Sharma, Beth Stearns, Tony Ng
J2EE™ Connector Architecture and Enterprise Application Integration

The J2EE™ Tutorial
Second Edition

Stephanie Bodoff
Eric Armstrong
Jennifer Ball
Debbie Bode Carson
Ian Evans
Dale Green
Kim Haase
Eric Jendrock

♦♦Addison-Wesley

Boston • San Francisco • New York • Toronto • Montreal
London • Munich • Paris • Madrid
Capetown • Sydney • Tokyo • Singapore • Mexico City

Many of the designations used by manufacturers and sellers to distinguish their products are claimed as trademarks. Where those designations appear in this book, and Addison-Wesley was aware of a trademark claim, the designations have been printed with initial capital letters or in all capitals.

The authors and publisher have taken care in the preparation of this book, but make no expressed or implied warranty of any kind and assume no responsibility for errors or omissions. No liability is assumed for incidental or consequential damages in connection with or arising out of the use of the information or programs contained herein.

The publisher offers discounts on this book when ordered in quantity for bulk purchases and special sales. For more information, please contact:

U.S. Corporate and Government Sales
(800) 382-3419
corpsales@pearsontechgroup.com

For sales outside of the U.S., please contact:

International Sales
(317) 581-3793
international@pearsontechgroup.com

Visit Addison-Wesley on the Web: www.awprofessional.com

Library of Congress Cataloging-in-Publication Data

The J2EE tutorial / Stephanie Bodoff ... [et al.].-- 2nd ed.
    p. cm.
    Includes bibliographical references and index.
    ISBN 0-321-24575-X (pbk. : alk. paper) *01 - 12 - 05*
  1. Java (Computer program language) 2. Business--Data processing. I. Bodoff, Stephanie.

    QA76.73.J38J32 2004
    005.2'762--dc22   2004005648

ISBN 0-321-24575-X
Text printed on recycled paper
2 3 4 5 6 7 8 9 10 11—CRW—0807060504
Second printing, September 2004

Contents

Chapter 27   Container-Managed Persistence Examples. 939

Foreword

When the first edition of *The J2EE™ Tutorial* was released, the Java™ 2 Platform, Enterprise Edition (J2EE) was the new kid on the block. Modeled after its forerunner, the Java 2 Platform, Standard Edition (J2SE™), the J2EE platform brought the benefits of "Write Once, Run Anywhere™" API compatibility to enterprise application servers. Now at version 1.4 and with widespread conformance in the application server marketplace, the J2EE platform has firmly established its position as the standard for enterprise application servers.

The J2EE™ Tutorial, Second Edition covers the J2EE 1.4 platform and more. If you have used the first edition of *The J2EE™ Tutorial*, you may notice that the second edition is triple the size. This reflects a major expansion in the J2EE platform and the availability of two upcoming J2EE technologies in the Sun Java System Application Server Platform Edition 8, the software on which the tutorial is based.

One of the most important additions to the J2EE 1.4 platform is substantial support for Web services with the JAX-RPC 1.1 API, which enables Web service endpoints based on servlets and enterprise beans. The platform also contains Web services support APIs for handling XML data streams directly (SAAJ) and for accessing Web services registries (JAXR). In addition, the J2EE 1.4 platform requires WS-I Basic Profile 1.0. This means that in addition to platform independence and complete Web services support, the J2EE 1.4 platform offers Web services interoperability.

The J2EE 1.4 platform contains major enhancements to the Java servlet and JavaServer Pages (JSP) technologies that are the foundation of the Web tier. The tutorial also showcases two exciting new technologies, not required by the J2EE 1.4 platform, that simplify the task of building J2EE application user interfaces: JavaServer Pages Standard Tag Library (JSTL) and JavaServer Faces. These new technologies are available in the Sun Java System Application Server. They will soon be featured in new developer tools and are strong candidates for inclusion in the next version of the J2EE platform.

Readers conversant with the core J2EE platform enterprise bean technology will notice major upgrades with the addition of the previously mentioned Web service endpoints, as well as a timer service, and enhancements to EJB QL and message-driven beans.

With all of these new features, I believe that you will find it well worth your time and energy to take on the J2EE 1.4 platform. You can increase the scope of the J2EE applications you develop, and your applications will run on the widest possible range of application server products.

To help you to learn all about the J2EE 1.4 platform, *The J2EE™ Tutorial, Second Edition* follows the familiar Java Series tutorial model of concise descriptions of the essential features of each technology with code examples that you can deploy and run on the Sun Java System Application Server. Read this tutorial and you will become part of the next wave of J2EE application developers.

Jeff Jackson
Vice President, J2EE Platform and Application Servers
Sun Microsystems
Santa Clara, CA
Thursday, June 3, 2004

About This Tutorial

THE *J2EE™ Tutorial, Second Edition* is a guide to developing enterprise applications for the Java 2 Platform, Enterprise Edition (J2EE) version 1.4. Here we cover all the things you need to know to make the best use of this tutorial.

Who Should Use This Tutorial

This tutorial is intended for programmers who are interested in developing and deploying J2EE 1.4 applications on the Sun Java System Application Server Platform Edition 8.

Prerequisites

Before proceeding with this tutorial you should have a good knowledge of the Java programming language. A good way to get to that point is to work through all the basic and some of the specialized trails in *The Java™ Tutorial*, Mary Campione et al. (Addison-Wesley, 2000). In particular, you should be familiar with relational database and security features described in the trails listed in Table 1.

Table 1 Prerequisite Trails in *The Java™ Tutorial*

Trail	URL
JDBC	`http://java.sun.com/docs/books/tutorial/jdbc`
Security	`http://java.sun.com/docs/books/tutorial/security1.2`

How to Read This Tutorial

The J2EE 1.4 platform is quite large, and this tutorial reflects this. However, you don't have to digest everything in it at once.

This tutorial opens with three introductory chapters, which you should read before proceeding to any specific technology area. Chapter 1 covers the J2EE 1.4 platform architecture and APIs along with the Sun Java System Application Server Platform Edition 8. Chapters 2 and 3 cover XML basics and getting started with Web applications.

When you have digested the basics, you can delve into one or more of the four main technology areas listed next. Because there are dependencies between some of the chapters, Figure 1 contains a roadmap for navigating through the tutorial.

- The Java XML chapters cover the technologies for developing applications that process XML documents and implement Web services components:
  - The Java API for XML Processing (JAXP)
  - The Java API for XML-based RPC (JAX-RPC)
  - SOAP with Attachments API for Java (SAAJ)
  - The Java API for XML Registries (JAXR)

- The Web-tier technology chapters cover the components used in developing the presentation layer of a J2EE or stand-alone Web application:
  - Java Servlet
  - JavaServer Pages (JSP)
  - JavaServer Pages Standard Tag Library (JSTL)
  - JavaServer Faces
  - Web application internationalization and localization

- The Enterprise JavaBeans (EJB) technology chapters cover the components used in developing the business logic of a J2EE application:
  - Session beans
  - Entity beans
  - Message-driven beans
  - Enterprise JavaBeans Query Language

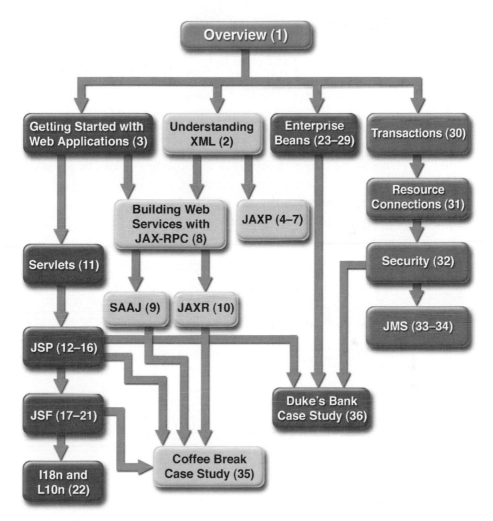

Figure 1 Roadmap to This Tutorial

- The platform services chapters cover the system services used by all the J2EE component technologies:
  - Transactions
  - Resource connections
  - Security
  - Java Message Service

After you have become familiar with some of the technology areas, you are ready to tackle the case studies, which tie together several of the technologies discussed in the tutorial. The Coffee Break Application (Chapter 35) describes an application that uses the Web application and Web services APIs. The Duke's Bank Application (Chapter 36) describes an application that employs Web application technologies and enterprise beans.

Finally, the appendixes contain auxiliary information helpful to the J2EE application developer along with a brief summary of the J2EE Connector architecture:

- Java Encoding Schemes (Appendix A)
- XML standards (Appendix B)
- HTTP Overview (Appendix C)
- J2EE Connector Architecture (Appendix D)

About the Examples

This section tells you everything you need to know to install, build, and run the examples.

Required Software

Tutorial Bundle

The tutorial example source is contained in the tutorial bundle, which is distributed on the accompanying CD-ROM.

After you have installed the tutorial bundle, the example source code is in the *<INSTALL>*/j2eetutorial14/examples/ directory, with subdirectories for each of the technologies discussed in the tutorial.

Application Server

The Sun Java System Application Server Platform Edition 8 is targeted as the build and runtime environment for the tutorial examples. To build, deploy, and run the examples, you need a copy of the Application Server and the Java 2 Software Development Kit, Standard Edition (J2SE SDK) 1.4.2_04 or higher.

The Application Server and J2SE SDK are contained in the J2EE 1.4 SDK, which is distributed on the CD-ROM accompanying the tutorial.

Application Server Installation Tips

In the Admin configuration pane of the Application Server installer,

- Select the Don't Prompt for Admin User Name radio button. This will save the user name and password so that you won't need to provide them when performing administrative operations with `asadmin` and `deploytool`. You will still have to provide the user name and password to log in to the Admin Console.

- Note the HTTP port at which the server is installed. This tutorial assumes that you are accepting the default port of 8080. If 8080 is in use during installation and the installer chooses another port, or if you decide to change it yourself, you will need to update the common build properties file (described in the next section) and the configuration files for some of the tutorial examples to reflect the correct port.

In the Installation Options pane, check the Add Bin Directory to PATH checkbox so that Application Server scripts (`asadmin`, `asant`, `deploytool`, and `wscompile`) override other installations.

Registry Server

You need a registry server to run the examples discussed in Chapters 10 and 35. Directions for obtaining and setting up a registry server are provided in those chapters.

Building the Examples

Most of the tutorial examples are distributed with a configuration file for `asant`, a portable build tool contained in the Application Server. This tool is an extension of the Ant tool developed by the Apache Software Foundation (`http://ant.apache.org`). The `asant` utility contains additional tasks that invoke the Application Server administration utility `asadmin`. Directions for building the examples are provided in each chapter.

Build properties and targets common to all the examples are specified in the files `<INSTALL>/j2eetutorial14/examples/common/build.properties` and

<INSTALL>/j2eetutorial14/examples/common/targets.xml. Build properties and targets common to a particular technology are specified in the files *<INSTALL>*/j2eetutorial14/examples/*tech*/common/build.properties and *<INSTALL>*/j2eetutorial14/examples/*tech*/common/targets.xml.

To run the asant scripts, you must set two common build properties as follows:

- Set the j2ee.home property in the file *<INSTALL>*/j2eetutorial14/ examples/common/build.properties to the location of your Application Server installation. The build process uses the j2ee.home property to include the libraries in *<J2EE_HOME>*/lib/ in the classpath. All examples that run on the Application Server include the J2EE library archive— *<J2EE_HOME>*/lib/j2ee.jar—in the build classpath. Some examples use additional libraries in *<J2EE_HOME>*/lib/ and *<J2EE_HOME>*/lib/ endorsed/; the required libraries are enumerated in the individual technology chapters. *<J2EE_HOME>* refers to the directory where you have installed the Application Server or the J2EE 1.4 SDK.

Note: On Windows, you must escape any backslashes in the j2ee.home property with another backslash or use forward slashes as a path separator. So, if your Application Server installation is C:\Sun\AppServer, you must set j2ee.home as follows:

j2ee.home = C:\\Sun\\AppServer

or

j2ee.home=C:/Sun/AppServer

- If you did not use port 8080 when you installed the Application Server, set the value of the domain.resources.port property in *<INSTALL>*/ j2eetutorial14/examples/common/build.properties to the correct port.

Tutorial Example Directory Structure

To facilitate iterative development and keep application source separate from compiled files, the source code for the tutorial examples is stored in the following structure under each application directory:

- `build.xml`: `asant` build file
- `src`: Java source of servlets and JavaBeans components; tag libraries
- `web`: JSP pages and HTML pages, tag files, and images

The `asant` build files (`build.xml`) distributed with the examples contain targets to create a `build` subdirectory and to copy and compile files into that directory.

Further Information

This tutorial includes the basic information that you need to deploy applications on and administer the Application Server.

For reference information on the tools distributed with the Application Server, see the man pages at `http://docs.sun.com/db/doc/817-6092`.

See the *Sun Java™ System Application Server Platform Edition 8 Developer's Guide* at `http://docs.sun.com/db/doc/817-6087` for information about developer features of the Application Server.

See the *Sun Java™ System Application Server Platform Edition 8 Administration Guide* at `http://docs.sun.com/db/doc/817-6088` for information about administering the Application Server.

Typographical Conventions

Table 2 lists the typographical conventions used in this tutorial.

Table 2 Typographical Conventions

Font Style	Uses
italic	Emphasis, titles, first occurrence of terms
`monospace`	URLs; code examples; file names; path names; tool names; application names; programming language keywords; tag, interface, class, method, and field names; properties
`italic monospace`	Variables in code, file paths, and URLs
`<italic monospace>`	User-selected file path components

Menu selections indicated with the right-arrow character →, for example, First→Second, should be interpreted as: select the First menu, then choose Second from the First submenu.

Acknowledgments

The J2EE tutorial team would like to thank the J2EE specification leads: Bill Shannon, Pierre Delisle, Mark Roth, Yutaka Yoshida, Farrukh Najmi, Phil Goodwin, Joseph Fialli, Kate Stout, and Ron Monzillo and the J2EE 1.4 SDK team members: Vivek Nagar, Tony Ng, Qingqing Ouyang, Ken Saks, Jean-Francois Arcand, Jan Luehe, Ryan Lubke, Kathy Walsh, Binod P G, Alejandro Murillo, and Manveen Kaur.

The chapters on custom tags and the Coffee Break and Duke's Bank applications use a template tag library that first appeared in *Designing Enterprise Applications with the J2EE™ Platform, Second Edition*, Inderjeet Singh et al., (Addison-Wesley, 2002).

The JavaServer Faces technology and JSP Documents chapters benefited greatly from the invaluable documentation reviews and example code contributions of these engineers: Ed Burns, Justyna Horwat, Roger Kitain, Jan Luehe, Craig McClanahan, Raj Premkumar, Mark Roth, and especially Jayashri Visvanathan.

The OrderApp example application described in the Container-Managed Persistence chapter was coded by Marina Vatkina with contributions from Markus Fuchs, Rochelle Raccah, and Deepa Singh. Ms. Vatkina's JDO/CMP team provided extensive feedback on the tutorial's discussion of CMP.

The security chapter writers are indebted to Raja Perumal, who was a key contributor both to the chapter and to the examples.

Monica Pawlan and Beth Stearns wrote the Overview and J2EE Connector chapters in the first edition of *The J2EE Tutorial* and much of that content has been carried forward to the current edition.

We are extremely grateful to the many internal and external reviewers who provided feedback on the tutorial. Their feedback helped improve the technical accuracy and presentation of the chapters and eliminate bugs from the examples.

We would like to thank our manager, Alan Sommerer, for his support and steadying influence.

We also thank Duarte Design, Inc., and Zana Vartanian for developing the illustrations in record time. Thanks are also due to our copy editor, Betsy Hardinger, for helping this multi-author project achieve a common style.

Finally, we would like to express our profound appreciation to Ann Sellers, Elizabeth Ryan, and the production team at Addison-Wesley for graciously seeing our large, complicated manuscript to publication.

Feedback

To send comments, broken link reports, errors, suggestions, and questions about this tutorial to the tutorial team, please use the feedback form at `http://java.sun.com/j2ee/1.4/docs/tutorial/information/sendusmail.html`.

Overview

TODAY, more and more developers want to write distributed transactional applications for the enterprise and thereby leverage the speed, security, and reliability of server-side technology. If you are already working in this area, you know that in the fast-moving and demanding world of e-commerce and information technology, enterprise applications must be designed, built, and produced for less money, with greater speed, and with fewer resources than ever before.

To reduce costs and fast-track application design and development, the Java™ 2 Platform, Enterprise Edition (J2EE™) provides a component-based approach to the design, development, assembly, and deployment of enterprise applications. The J2EE platform offers a multitiered distributed application model, reusable components, a unified security model, flexible transaction control, and Web services support through integrated data interchange on Extensible Markup Language (XML)-based open standards and protocols.

Not only can you deliver innovative business solutions to market faster than ever, but also your platform-independent J2EE component-based solutions are not tied to the products and application programming interfaces (APIs) of any one vendor. Vendors and customers enjoy the freedom to choose the products and components that best meet their business and technological requirements.

This tutorial uses examples to describe the features and functionalities available in the Sun Java System Application Server Platform Edition 8 for developing enterprise applications. Whether you are a new or an experienced developer, you should find the examples and accompanying text a valuable and accessible knowledge base for creating your own solutions.

If you are new to J2EE enterprise application development, this chapter is a good place to start. Here you will review development basics, learn about the J2EE architecture and APIs, become acquainted with important terms and concepts, and find out how to approach J2EE application programming, assembly, and deployment.

Distributed Multitiered Applications

The J2EE platform uses a distributed multitiered application model for enterprise applications. Application logic is divided into components according to function, and the various application components that make up a J2EE application are installed on different machines depending on the tier in the multitiered J2EE environment to which the application component belongs. Figure 1–1 shows two multitiered J2EE applications divided into the tiers described in the following list. The J2EE application parts shown in Figure 1–1 are presented in J2EE Components (page 3).

- Client-tier components run on the client machine.
- Web-tier components run on the J2EE server.
- Business-tier components run on the J2EE server.
- Enterprise information system (EIS)-tier software runs on the EIS server.

Although a J2EE application can consist of the three or four tiers shown in Figure 1–1, J2EE multitiered applications are generally considered to be three-tiered applications because they are distributed over three locations: client machines, the J2EE server machine, and the database or legacy machines at the back end. Three-tiered applications that run in this way extend the standard two-tiered client and server model by placing a multithreaded application server between the client application and back-end storage.

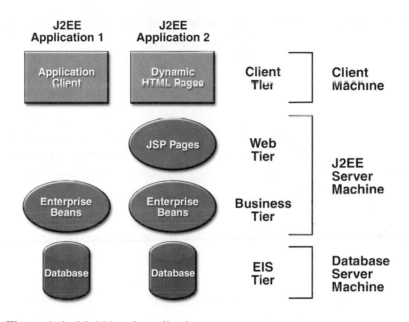

Figure 1–1   Multitiered Applications

J2EE Components

J2EE applications are made up of components. A *J2EE component* is a self-contained functional software unit that is assembled into a J2EE application with its related classes and files and that communicates with other components. The J2EE specification defines the following J2EE components:

- Application clients and applets are components that run on the client.
- Java Servlet and JavaServer Pages™ (JSP™) technology components are Web components that run on the server.
- Enterprise JavaBeans™ (EJB™) components (enterprise beans) are business components that run on the server.

J2EE components are written in the Java programming language and are compiled in the same way as any program in the language. The difference between J2EE components and "standard" Java classes is that J2EE components are assembled into a J2EE application, are verified to be well formed and in compliance with the J2EE specification, and are deployed to production, where they are run and managed by the J2EE server.

J2EE Clients

A J2EE client can be a Web client or an application client.

Web Clients

A *Web client* consists of two parts: (1) dynamic Web pages containing various types of markup language (HTML, XML, and so on), which are generated by Web components running in the Web tier, and (2) a Web browser, which renders the pages received from the server.

A Web client is sometimes called a *thin client*. Thin clients usually do not query databases, execute complex business rules, or connect to legacy applications. When you use a thin client, such heavyweight operations are off-loaded to enterprise beans executing on the J2EE server, where they can leverage the security, speed, services, and reliability of J2EE server-side technologies.

Applets

A Web page received from the Web tier can include an embedded applet. An *applet* is a small client application written in the Java programming language that executes in the Java virtual machine installed in the Web browser. However, client systems will likely need the Java Plug-in and possibly a security policy file in order for the applet to successfully execute in the Web browser.

Web components are the preferred API for creating a Web client program because no plug-ins or security policy files are needed on the client systems. Also, Web components enable cleaner and more modular application design because they provide a way to separate applications programming from Web page design. Personnel involved in Web page design thus do not need to understand Java programming language syntax to do their jobs.

Application Clients

An *application client* runs on a client machine and provides a way for users to handle tasks that require a richer user interface than can be provided by a markup language. It typically has a graphical user interface (GUI) created from the Swing or the Abstract Window Toolkit (AWT) API, but a command-line interface is certainly possible.

Application clients directly access enterprise beans running in the business tier. However, if application requirements warrant it, an application client can open an HTTP connection to establish communication with a servlet running in the Web tier.

The JavaBeans™ Component Architecture

The server and client tiers might also include components based on the Java-Beans component architecture (JavaBeans components) to manage the data flow between an application client or applet and components running on the J2EE server, or between server components and a database. JavaBeans components are not considered J2EE components by the J2EE specification.

JavaBeans components have properties and have get and set methods for accessing the properties. JavaBeans components used in this way are typically simple in design and implementation but should conform to the naming and design conventions outlined in the JavaBeans component architecture.

J2EE Server Communications

Figure 1–2 shows the various elements that can make up the client tier. The client communicates with the business tier running on the J2EE server either directly or, as in the case of a client running in a browser, by going through JSP pages or servlets running in the Web tier.

Your J2EE application uses a thin browser-based client or thick application client. In deciding which one to use, you should be aware of the trade-offs between keeping functionality on the client and close to the user (thick client) and off-loading as much functionality as possible to the server (thin client). The more functionality you off-load to the server, the easier it is to distribute, deploy, and manage the application; however, keeping more functionality on the client can make for a better perceived user experience.

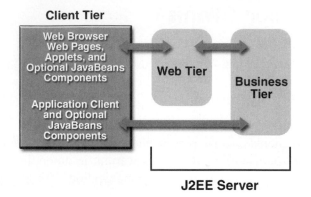

Figure 1–2 Server Communications

Web Components

J2EE Web components are either servlets or pages created using JSP technology (JSP pages). *Servlets* are Java programming language classes that dynamically process requests and construct responses. *JSP pages* are text-based documents that execute as servlets but allow a more natural approach to creating static content.

Static HTML pages and applets are bundled with Web components during application assembly but are not considered Web components by the J2EE specification. Server-side utility classes can also be bundled with Web components and, like HTML pages, are not considered Web components.

As shown in Figure 1–3, the Web tier, like the client tier, might include a Java-Beans component to manage the user input and send that input to enterprise beans running in the business tier for processing.

Business Components

Business code, which is logic that solves or meets the needs of a particular business domain such as banking, retail, or finance, is handled by enterprise beans running in the business tier. Figure 1–4 shows how an enterprise bean receives data from client programs, processes it (if necessary), and sends it to the enterprise information system tier for storage. An enterprise bean also retrieves data from storage, processes it (if necessary), and sends it back to the client program.

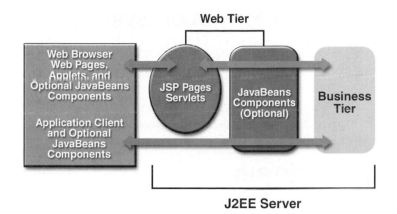

Figure 1–3 Web Tier and J2EE Applications

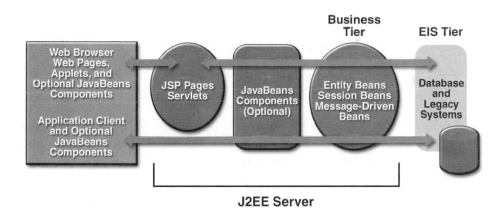

Figure 1–4 Business and EIS Tiers

There are three kinds of enterprise beans: session beans, entity beans, and message-driven beans. A *session bean* represents a transient conversation with a client. When the client finishes executing, the session bean and its data are gone. In contrast, an *entity bean* represents persistent data stored in one row of a database table. If the client terminates or if the server shuts down, the underlying services ensure that the entity bean data is saved. A *message-driven bean* combines features of a session bean and a Java Message Service (JMS) message listener, allowing a business component to receive JMS messages asynchronously.

Enterprise Information System Tier

The enterprise information system tier handles EIS software and includes enterprise infrastructure systems such as enterprise resource planning (ERP), mainframe transaction processing, database systems, and other legacy information systems. For example, J2EE application components might need access to enterprise information systems for database connectivity.

J2EE Containers

Normally, thin-client multitiered applications are hard to write because they involve many lines of intricate code to handle transaction and state management, multithreading, resource pooling, and other complex low-level details. The component-based and platform-independent J2EE architecture makes J2EE applications easy to write because business logic is organized into reusable components. In addition, the J2EE server provides underlying services in the form of a container for every component type. Because you do not have to develop these services yourself, you are free to concentrate on solving the business problem at hand.

Container Services

Containers are the interface between a component and the low-level platform-specific functionality that supports the component. Before a Web, enterprise bean, or application client component can be executed, it must be assembled into a J2EE module and deployed into its container.

The assembly process involves specifying container settings for each component in the J2EE application and for the J2EE application itself. Container settings customize the underlying support provided by the J2EE server, including services such as security, transaction management, Java Naming and Directory Interface™ (JNDI) lookups, and remote connectivity. Here are some of the highlights:

- The J2EE security model lets you configure a Web component or enterprise bean so that system resources are accessed only by authorized users.
- The J2EE transaction model lets you specify relationships among methods that make up a single transaction so that all methods in one transaction are treated as a single unit.
- JNDI lookup services provide a unified interface to multiple naming and directory services in the enterprise so that application components can access naming and directory services.

- The J2EE remote connectivity model manages low-level communications between clients and enterprise beans. After an enterprise bean is created, a client invokes methods on it as if it were in the same virtual machine.

Because the J2EE architecture provides configurable services, application components within the same J2EE application can behave differently based on where they are deployed. For example, an enterprise bean can have security settings that allow it a certain level of access to database data in one production environment and another level of database access in another production environment.

The container also manages nonconfigurable services such as enterprise bean and servlet life cycles, database connection resource pooling, data persistence, and access to the J2EE platform APIs described in section J2EE 1.4 Platform APIs (page 16). Although data persistence is a nonconfigurable service, the J2EE architecture lets you override container-managed persistence by including the appropriate code in your enterprise bean implementation when you want more control than the default container-managed persistence provides. For example, you might use bean-managed persistence to implement your own finder (search) methods or to create a customized database cache.

Container Types

The deployment process installs J2EE application components in the J2EE containers illustrated in Figure 1–5.

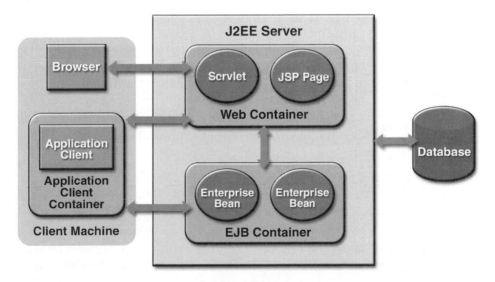

Figure 1–5 J2EE Server and Containers

J2EE server

The runtime portion of a J2EE product. A J2EE server provides EJB and Web containers.

Enterprise JavaBeans (EJB) container

Manages the execution of enterprise beans for J2EE applications. Enterprise beans and their container run on the J2EE server.

Web container

Manages the execution of JSP page and servlet components for J2EE applications. Web components and their container run on the J2EE server.

Application client container

Manages the execution of application client components. Application clients and their container run on the client.

Applet container

Manages the execution of applets. Consists of a Web browser and Java Plug-in running on the client together.

Web Services Support

Web services are Web-based enterprise applications that use open, XML-based standards and transport protocols to exchange data with calling clients. The J2EE platform provides the XML APIs and tools you need to quickly design, develop, test, and deploy Web services and clients that fully interoperate with other Web services and clients running on Java-based or non-Java-based platforms.

To write Web services and clients with the J2EE XML APIs, all you do is pass parameter data to the method calls and process the data returned; or for document-oriented Web services, you send documents containing the service data back and forth. No low-level programming is needed because the XML API implementations do the work of translating the application data to and from an XML-based data stream that is sent over the standardized XML-based transport protocols. These XML-based standards and protocols are introduced in the following sections.

The translation of data to a standardized XML-based data stream is what makes Web services and clients written with the J2EE XML APIs fully interoperable. This does not necessarily mean that the data being transported includes XML tags because the transported data can itself be plain text, XML data, or any kind of binary data such as audio, video, maps, program files, computer-aided design (CAD) documents and the like. The next section introduces XML and explains how parties doing business can use XML tags and schemas to exchange data in a meaningful way.

XML

XML is a cross-platform, extensible, text-based standard for representing data. When XML data is exchanged between parties, the parties are free to create their own tags to describe the data, set up schemas to specify which tags can be used in a particular kind of XML document, and use XML stylesheets to manage the display and handling of the data.

For example, a Web service can use XML and a schema to produce price lists, and companies that receive the price lists and schema can have their own stylesheets to handle the data in a way that best suits their needs. Here are examples:

- One company might put XML pricing information through a program to translate the XML to HTML so that it can post the price lists to its intranet.
- A partner company might put the XML pricing information through a tool to create a marketing presentation.
- Another company might read the XML pricing information into an application for processing.

SOAP Transport Protocol

Client requests and Web service responses are transmitted as Simple Object Access Protocol (SOAP) messages over HTTP to enable a completely interoperable exchange between clients and Web services, all running on different platforms and at various locations on the Internet. HTTP is a familiar request-and-response standard for sending messages over the Internet, and SOAP is an XML-based protocol that follows the HTTP request-and-response model.

The SOAP portion of a transported message handles the following:

- Defines an XML-based envelope to describe what is in the message and how to process the message
- Includes XML-based encoding rules to express instances of application-defined data types within the message
- Defines an XML-based convention for representing the request to the remote service and the resulting response

WSDL Standard Format

The Web Services Description Language (WSDL) is a standardized XML format for describing network services. The description includes the name of the service, the location of the service, and ways to communicate with the service. WSDL service descriptions can be stored in UDDI registries or published on the Web (or both). The J2EE platform provides a tool for generating the WSDL specification of a Web service that uses remote procedure calls to communicate with clients.

UDDI and ebXML Standard Formats

Other XML-based standards, such as Universal Description, Discovery and Integration (UDDI) and ebXML, make it possible for businesses to publish information on the Internet about their products and Web services, where the information can be readily and globally accessed by clients who want to do business.

Packaging Applications

A J2EE application is delivered in an Enterprise Archive (EAR) file, a standard Java Archive (JAR) file with an `.ear` extension. Using EAR files and modules makes it possible to assemble a number of different J2EE applications using some of the same components. No extra coding is needed; it is only a matter of assembling (or packaging) various J2EE modules into J2EE EAR files.

An EAR file (see Figure 1–6) contains J2EE modules and deployment descriptors. A *deployment descriptor* is an XML document with an `.xml` extension that describes the deployment settings of an application, a module, or a component. Because deployment descriptor information is declarative, it can be changed without the need to modify the source code. At runtime, the J2EE server reads the deployment descriptor and acts upon the application, module, or component accordingly.

There are two types of deployment descriptors: J2EE and runtime. A *J2EE deployment descriptor* is defined by a J2EE specification and can be used to configure deployment settings on any J2EE-compliant implementation. A *runtime deployment descriptor* is used to configure J2EE implementation-specific parameters. For example, the Sun Java System Application Server Platform Edition 8 runtime deployment descriptor contains information such as the context

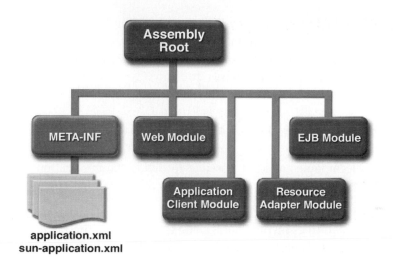

application.xml
sun-application.xml

Figure 1–6   EAR File Structure

root of a Web application, the mapping of portable names of an application's resources to the server's resources, and Application Server implementation-specific parameters, such as caching directives. The Application Server runtime deployment descriptors are named sun-*moduleType*.xml and are located in the same directory as the J2EE deployment descriptor.

A *J2EE module* consists of one or more J2EE components for the same container type and one component deployment descriptor of that type. An enterprise bean module deployment descriptor, for example, declares transaction attributes and security authorizations for an enterprise bean. A J2EE module without an application deployment descriptor can be deployed as a *stand-alone* module. The four types of J2EE modules are as follows:

- EJB modules, which contain class files for enterprise beans and an EJB deployment descriptor. EJB modules are packaged as JAR files with a .jar extension.

- Web modules, which contain servlet class files, JSP files, supporting class files, GIF and HTML files, and a Web application deployment descriptor. Web modules are packaged as JAR files with a .war (Web archive) extension.

- Application client modules, which contain class files and an application client deployment descriptor. Application client modules are packaged as JAR files with a .jar extension.

- Resource adapter modules, which contain all Java interfaces, classes, native libraries, and other documentation, along with the resource adapter deployment descriptor. Together, these implement the Connector architecture (see J2EE Connector Architecture, page 20) for a particular EIS. Resource adapter modules are packaged as JAR files with an `.rar` (resource adapter archive) extension.

Development Roles

Reusable modules make it possible to divide the application development and deployment process into distinct roles so that different people or companies can perform different parts of the process.

The first two roles involve purchasing and installing the J2EE product and tools. After software is purchased and installed, J2EE components can be developed by application component providers, assembled by application assemblers, and deployed by application deployers. In a large organization, each of these roles might be executed by different individuals or teams. This division of labor works because each of the earlier roles outputs a portable file that is the input for a subsequent role. For example, in the application component development phase, an enterprise bean software developer delivers EJB JAR files. In the application assembly role, another developer combines these EJB JAR files into a J2EE application and saves it in an EAR file. In the application deployment role, a system administrator at the customer site uses the EAR file to install the J2EE application into a J2EE server.

The different roles are not always executed by different people. If you work for a small company, for example, or if you are prototyping a sample application, you might perform the tasks in every phase.

J2EE Product Provider

The J2EE product provider is the company that designs and makes available for purchase the J2EE platform APIs, and other features defined in the J2EE specification. Product providers are typically operating system, database system, application server, or Web server vendors who implement the J2EE platform according to the Java 2 Platform, Enterprise Edition specification.

Tool Provider

The tool provider is the company or person who creates development, assembly, and packaging tools used by component providers, assemblers, and deployers.

Application Component Provider

The application component provider is the company or person who creates Web components, enterprise beans, applets, or application clients for use in J2EE applications.

Enterprise Bean Developer

An enterprise bean developer performs the following tasks to deliver an EJB JAR file that contains the enterprise bean(s):

- Writes and compiles the source code
- Specifics the deployment descriptor
- Packages the `.class` files and deployment descriptor into the EJB JAR file

Web Component Developer

A Web component developer performs the following tasks to deliver a WAR file containing the Web component(s):

- Writes and compiles servlet source code
- Writes JSP and HTML files
- Specifies the deployment descriptor
- Packages the `.class`, `.jsp`, and `.html` files and deployment descriptor into the WAR file

Application Client Developer

An application client developer performs the following tasks to deliver a JAR file containing the application client:

- Writes and compiles the source code
- Specifies the deployment descriptor for the client
- Packages the `.class` files and deployment descriptor into the JAR file

Application Assembler

The application assembler is the company or person who receives application modules from component providers and assembles them into a J2EE application EAR file. The assembler or deployer can edit the deployment descriptor directly or can use tools that correctly add XML tags according to interactive selections. A software developer performs the following tasks to deliver an EAR file containing the J2EE application:

- Assembles EJB JAR and WAR files created in the previous phases into a J2EE application (EAR) file
- Specifies the deployment descriptor for the J2EE application
- Verifies that the contents of the EAR file are well formed and comply with the J2EE specification

Application Deployer and Administrator

The application deployer and administrator is the company or person who configures and deploys the J2EE application, administers the computing and networking infrastructure where J2EE applications run, and oversees the runtime environment. Duties include such things as setting transaction controls and security attributes and specifying connections to databases.

During configuration, the deployer follows instructions supplied by the application component provider to resolve external dependencies, specify security settings, and assign transaction attributes. During installation, the deployer moves the application components to the server and generates the container-specific classes and interfaces.

A deployer or system administrator performs the following tasks to install and configure a J2EE application:

- Adds the J2EE application (EAR) file created in the preceding phase to the J2EE server
- Configures the J2EE application for the operational environment by modifying the deployment descriptor of the J2EE application
- Verifies that the contents of the EAR file are well formed and comply with the J2EE specification
- Deploys (installs) the J2EE application EAR file into the J2EE server

J2EE 1.4 Platform APIs

Figure 1–7 illustrates the availability of the J2EE 1.4 platform APIs in each J2EE container type. The following sections give a brief summary of the technologies

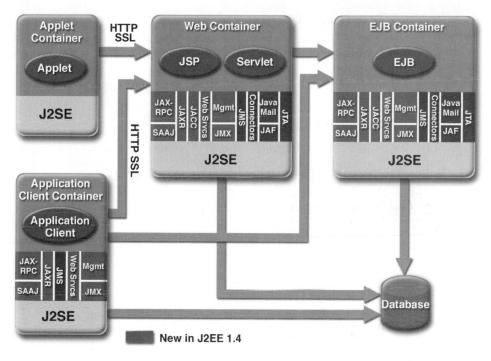

Figure 1–7 J2EE Platform APIs

required by the J2EE platform and the J2SE enterprise APIs (JDBC and JNDI) that would be used in J2EE applications.

Enterprise JavaBeans Technology

An Enterprise JavaBeans™ (EJB™) component, or *enterprise bean*, is a body of code having fields and methods to implement modules of business logic. You can think of an enterprise bean as a building block that can be used alone or with other enterprise beans to execute business logic on the J2EE server.

As mentioned earlier, there are three kinds of enterprise beans: session beans, entity beans, and message-driven beans. Enterprise beans often interact with databases. One of the benefits of entity beans is that you do not have to write any SQL code or use the JDBC™ API (see JDBC API, page 21) directly to perform database access operations; the EJB container handles this for you. However, if you override the default container-managed persistence for any reason, you will need to use the JDBC API. Also, if you choose to have a session bean access the database, you must use the JDBC API.

Java Servlet Technology

Java servlet technology lets you define HTTP-specific servlet classes. A servlet class extends the capabilities of servers that host applications that are accessed by way of a request-response programming model. Although servlets can respond to any type of request, they are commonly used to extend the applications hosted by Web servers.

JavaServer Pages Technology

JavaServer Pages™ (JSP™) technology lets you put snippets of servlet code directly into a text-based document. A JSP page is a text-based document that contains two types of text: static data (which can be expressed in any text-based format such as HTML, WML, and XML) and JSP elements, which determine how the page constructs dynamic content.

Java Message Service API

The Java Message Service (JMS) API is a messaging standard that allows J2EE application components to create, send, receive, and read messages. It enables distributed communication that is loosely coupled, reliable, and asynchronous.

Java Transaction API

The Java Transaction API (JTA) provides a standard interface for demarcating transactions. The J2EE architecture provides a default auto commit to handle transaction commits and rollbacks. An *auto commit* means that any other applications that are viewing data will see the updated data after each database read or write operation. However, if your application performs two separate database access operations that depend on each other, you will want to use the JTA API to demarcate where the entire transaction, including both operations, begins, rolls back, and commits.

JavaMail API

J2EE applications use the JavaMail™ API to send email notifications. The Java-Mail API has two parts: an application-level interface used by the application components to send mail, and a service provider interface. The J2EE platform includes JavaMail with a service provider that allows application components to send Internet mail.

JavaBeans Activation Framework

The JavaBeans Activation Framework (JAF) is included because JavaMail uses it. JAF provides standard services to determine the type of an arbitrary piece of data, encapsulate access to it, discover the operations available on it, and create the appropriate JavaBeans component to perform those operations.

Java API for XML Processing

The Java API for XML Processing (JAXP) supports the processing of XML documents using Document Object Model (DOM), Simple API for XML (SAX), and Extensible Stylesheet Language Transformations (XSLT). JAXP enables applications to parse and transform XML documents independent of a particular XML processing implementation.

JAXP also provides namespace support, which lets you work with schemas that might otherwise have naming conflicts. Designed to be flexible, JAXP lets you use any XML-compliant parser or XSL processor from within your application and supports the W3C schema. You can find information on the W3C schema at this URL: `http://www.w3.org/XML/Schema`.

Java API for XML-Based RPC

The Java API for XML-based RPC (JAX-RPC) uses the SOAP standard and HTTP, so client programs can make XML-based remote procedure calls (RPCs) over the Internet. JAX-RPC also supports WSDL, so you can import and export WSDL documents. With JAX-RPC and a WSDL, you can easily interoperate with clients and services running on Java-based or non-Java-based platforms such as .NET. For example, based on the WSDL document, a Visual Basic .NET client can be configured to use a Web service implemented in Java technology, or a Web service can be configured to recognize a Visual Basic .NET client.

JAX-RPC relies on the HTTP transport protocol. Taking that a step further, JAX-RPC lets you create service applications that combine HTTP with a Java technology version of the Secure Socket Layer (SSL) and Transport Layer Security

(TLS) protocols to establish basic or mutual authentication. SSL and TLS ensure message integrity by providing data encryption with client and server authentication capabilities.

Authentication is a measured way to verify whether a party is eligible and able to access certain information as a way to protect against the fraudulent use of a system or the fraudulent transmission of information. Information transported across the Internet is especially vulnerable to being intercepted and misused, so it's very important to configure a JAX-RPC Web service to protect data in transit.

SOAP with Attachments API for Java

The SOAP with Attachments API for Java (SAAJ) is a low-level API on which JAX-RPC depends. SAAJ enables the production and consumption of messages that conform to the SOAP 1.1 specification and SOAP with Attachments note. Most developers do not use the SAAJ API, instead using the higher-level JAX-RPC API.

Java API for XML Registries

The Java API for XML Registries (JAXR) lets you access business and general-purpose registries over the Web. JAXR supports the ebXML Registry and Repository standards and the emerging UDDI specifications. By using JAXR, developers can learn a single API and gain access to both of these important registry technologies.

Additionally, businesses can submit material to be shared and search for material that others have submitted. Standards groups have developed schemas for particular kinds of XML documents; two businesses might, for example, agree to use the schema for their industry's standard purchase order form. Because the schema is stored in a standard business registry, both parties can use JAXR to access it.

J2EE Connector Architecture

The J2EE Connector architecture is used by J2EE tools vendors and system integrators to create resource adapters that support access to enterprise information systems that can be plugged in to any J2EE product. A *resource adapter* is a software component that allows J2EE application components to access and interact with the underlying resource manager of the EIS. Because a resource adapter is specific to its resource manager, typically there is a different resource adapter for each type of database or enterprise information system.

The J2EE Connector architecture also provides a performance-oriented, secure, scalable, and message-based transactional integration of J2EE-based Web services with existing EISs that can be either synchronous or asynchronous. Existing applications and EISs integrated through the J2EE Connector architecture into the J2EE platform can be exposed as XML-based Web services by using JAX-RPC and J2EE component models. Thus JAX-RPC and the J2EE Connector architecture are complementary technologies for enterprise application integration (EAI) and end-to-end business integration.

JDBC API

The JDBC API lets you invoke SQL commands from Java programing language methods. You use the JDBC API in an enterprise bean when you override the default container-managed persistence or have a session bean access the database. With container-managed persistence, database access operations are handled by the container, and your enterprise bean implementation contains no JDBC code or SQL commands. You can also use the JDBC API from a servlet or a JSP page to access the database directly without going through an enterprise bean.

The JDBC API has two parts: an application-level interface used by the application components to access a database, and a service provider interface to attach a JDBC driver to the J2EE platform.

Java Naming and Directory Interface

The Java Naming and Directory Interface™ (JNDI) provides naming and directory functionality. It provides applications with methods for performing standard directory operations, such as associating attributes with objects and searching for objects using their attributes. Using JNDI, a J2EE application can store and retrieve any type of named Java object.

J2EE naming services provide application clients, enterprise beans, and Web components with access to a JNDI naming environment. A *naming environment* allows a component to be customized without the need to access or change the component's source code. A container implements the component's environment and provides it to the component as a JNDI *naming context*.

A J2EE component locates its environment naming context using JNDI interfaces. A component creates a `javax.naming.InitialContext` object and looks up the environment naming context in `InitialContext` under the name `java:comp/env`. A component's naming environment is stored directly in the environment naming context or in any of its direct or indirect subcontexts.

A J2EE component can access named system-provided and user-defined objects. The names of system-provided objects, such as JTA `UserTransaction` objects, are stored in the environment naming context, `java:comp/env`. The J2EE platform allows a component to name user-defined objects, such as enterprise beans, environment entries, JDBC `DataSource` objects, and message connections. An object should be named within a subcontext of the naming environment according to the type of the object. For example, enterprise beans are named within the subcontext `java:comp/env/ejb`, and JDBC `DataSource` references in the subcontext `java:comp/env/jdbc`.

Because JNDI is independent of any specific implementation, applications can use JNDI to access multiple naming and directory services, including existing naming and directory services such as LDAP, NDS, DNS, and NIS. This allows J2EE applications to coexist with legacy applications and systems. For more information on JNDI, see *The JNDI Tutorial*:

```
http://java.sun.com/products/jndi/tutorial/index.html
```

Java Authentication and Authorization Service

The Java Authentication and Authorization Service (JAAS) provides a way for a J2EE application to authenticate and authorize a specific user or group of users to run it.

JAAS is a Java programing language version of the standard Pluggable Authentication Module (PAM) framework, which extends the Java 2 Platform security architecture to support user-based authorization.

Simplified Systems Integration

The J2EE platform is a platform-independent, full systems integration solution that creates an open marketplace in which every vendor can sell to every customer. Such a marketplace encourages vendors to compete, not by trying to lock customers into their technologies but instead by trying to outdo each other in providing products and services that benefit customers, such as better performance, better tools, or better customer support.

The J2EE APIs enable systems and applications integration through the following:

- Unified application model across tiers with enterprise beans
- Simplified request-and-response mechanism with JSP pages and servlets
- Reliable security model with JAAS
- XML-based data interchange integration with JAXP, SAAJ, and JAX-RPC
- Simplified interoperability with the J2EE Connector architecture
- Easy database connectivity with the JDBC API
- Enterprise application integration with message-driven beans and JMS, JTA, and JNDI

You can learn more about using the J2EE platform to build integrated business systems by reading *J2EE Technology in Practice*, by Rick Cattell and Jim Inscore (Addison-Wesley, 2001):

```
http://java.sun.com/j2ee/inpractice/aboutthebook.html
```

Sun Java System Application Server Platform Edition 8

The Sun Java System Application Server Platform Edition 8 is a fully compliant implementation of the J2EE 1.4 platform. In addition to supporting all the APIs described in the previous sections, the Application Server includes a number of J2EE technologies and tools that are not part of the J2EE 1.4 platform but are provided as a convenience to the developer.

This section briefly summarizes the technologies and tools that make up the Application Server, and instructions for starting and stopping the Application Server, starting the Admin Console, starting deploytool, and starting and stopping the PointBase database server. Other chapters explain how to use the remaining tools.

Technologies

The Application Server includes two user interface technologies—JavaServer Pages Standard Tag Library and JavaServer™ Faces—that are built on and used in conjunction with the J2EE 1.4 platform technologies Java servlet and Java-Server Pages.

JavaServer Pages Standard Tag Library

The JavaServer Pages Standard Tag Library (JSTL) encapsulates core functionality common to many JSP applications. Instead of mixing tags from numerous vendors in your JSP applications, you employ a single, standard set of tags. This standardization allows you to deploy your applications on any JSP container that supports JSTL and makes it more likely that the implementation of the tags is optimized.

JSTL has iterator and conditional tags for handling flow control, tags for manipulating XML documents, internationalization tags, tags for accessing databases using SQL, and commonly used functions.

JavaServer Faces

JavaServer Faces technology is a user interface framework for building Web applications. The main components of JavaServer Faces technology are as follows:

- A GUI component framework.
- A flexible model for rendering components in different kinds of HTML or different markup languages and technologies. A Renderer object generates the markup to render the component and converts the data stored in a model object to types that can be represented in a view.
- A standard RenderKit for generating HTML/4.01 markup.

The following features support the GUI components:

- Input validation
- Event handling
- Data conversion between model objects and components
- Managed model object creation
- Page navigation configuration

All this functionality is available via standard Java APIs and XML-based configuration files.

Tools

The Application Server contains the tools listed in Table 1–1. Basic usage information for many of the tools appears throughout the tutorial. For detailed information, see the online help in the GUI tools and the man pages at `http://docs.sun.com/db/doc/817-6092` for the command-line tools.

Starting and Stopping the Application Server

To start and stop the Application Server, you use the `asadmin` utility. To start the Application Server, open a terminal window or command prompt and execute the following:

```
asadmin start-domain --verbose domain1
```

A *domain* is a set of one or more Application Server instances managed by one administration server. Associated with a domain are the following:

- The Application Server's port number. The default is 8080.
- The administration server's port number. The default is 4848.
- An administration user name and password.

You specify these values when you install the Application Server. The examples in this tutorial assume that you chose the default ports.

With no arguments, the `start-domain` command initiates the default domain, which is domain1. The `--verbose` flag causes all logging and debugging output to appear on the terminal window or command prompt (it will also go into the server log, which is located in `<J2EE_HOME>/domains/domain1/logs/server.log`).

Or, on Windows, you can choose

Programs→Sun Microsystems→J2EE 1.4 SDK→Start Default Server

Table 1–1 Application Server Tools

Component	Description
Admin Console	A Web-based GUI Application Server administration utility. Used to stop the Application Server and manage users, resources, and applications.
asadmin	A command-line Application Server administration utility. Used to start and stop the Application Server and manage users, resources, and applications.
asant	A portable command-line build tool that is an extension of the Ant tool developed by the Apache Software Foundation (see http://ant.apache.org/). asant contains additional tasks that interact with the Application Server administration utility.
appclient	A command-line tool that launches the application client container and invokes the client application packaged in the application client JAR file.
capture-schema	A command-line tool to extract schema information from a database, producing a schema file that the Application Server can use for container-managed persistence.
deploytool	A GUI tool to package applications, generate deployment descriptors, and deploy applications on the Application Server.
package-appclient	A command-line tool to package the application client container libraries and JAR files.
PointBase database	An evaluation copy of the PointBase database server.
verifier	A command-line tool to validate J2EE deployment descriptors.
wscompile	A command-line tool to generate stubs, ties, serializers, and WSDL files used in JAX-RPC clients and services.
wsdeploy	A command-line tool to generate implementation-specific, ready-to-deploy WAR files for Web service applications that use JAX-RPC.

After the server has completed its startup sequence, you will see the following output:

```
Domain domain1 started.
```

To stop the Application Server, open a terminal window or command prompt and execute

```
asadmin stop-domain domain1
```

Or, on Windows, choose

Programs→Sun Microsystems→J2EE 1.4 SDK→Stop Default Server

When the server has stopped you will see the following output:

```
Domain domain1 stopped.
```

Starting the Admin Console

To administer the Application Server and manage users, resources, and J2EE applications, you use the Admin Console tool. The Application Server must be running before you invoke the Admin Console. To start the Admin Console, open a browser at the following URL:

```
http://localhost:4848/asadmin/
```

On Windows, from the Start menu, choose

Programs→Sun Microsystems→J2EE 1.4 SDK→Admin Console

Starting the deploytool Utility

To package J2EE applications, specify deployment descriptor elements, and deploy applications on the Application Server, you use the `deploytool` utility. To start `deploytool`, open a terminal window or command prompt and execute

```
deploytool
```

On Windows, from the Start menu, choose

Programs→Sun Microsystems→J2EE 1.4 SDK→Deploytool

Starting and Stopping the PointBase Database Server

To start the PointBase database server, follow these steps.

1. In a terminal window, go to `<J2EE_HOME>/pointbase/tools/serveroption`.
2. Execute the `startserver` script.

On Windows, from the Start menu, choose

Programs→Sun Microsystems→J2EE 1.4 SDK→Start PointBase

To stop the PointBase server, follow these steps.

1. In a terminal window, go to `<J2EE_HOME>/pointbase/tools/serveroption`.
2. Execute the `stopserver` script.

On Windows, from the Start menu, choose

Programs→Sun Microsystems→J2EE 1.4 SDK→Stop PointBase

Debugging J2EE Applications

This section describes how to determine what is causing an error in your application deployment or execution.

Using the Server Log

One way to debug applications is to look at the server log in `<J2EE_HOME>/domains/domain1/logs/server.log`. The log contains output from the Application Server and your applications. You can log messages from any Java class in your application with `System.out.println` and the Java Logging APIs (documented at `http://java.sun.com/j2se/1.4.2/docs/guide/util/logging/index.html`) and from Web components with the `ServletContext.log` method.

If you start the application server with the `--verbose` flag, all logging and debugging output will appear on the terminal window or command prompt and the server log. If you start the application server in the background, debugging information is only available in the log. You can view the server log with a text editor or with the Admin Console log viewer. To use the log viewer:

1. Select the Application Server node.
2. Select the Logging tab.
3. Click the Open Log Viewer button. The log viewer will open and display the last 40 entries.

If you wish to display other entries:

1. Click the Modify Search button.
2. Specify any constraints on the entries you want to see.
3. Click the Search button at the bottom of the log viewer.

Using a Debugger

The Application Server supports the Java Platform Debugger Architecture (JPDA). With JPDA, you can configure the Application Server to communicate debugging information via a socket. In order to debug an application using a debugger:

1. Enable debugging in the Application Server using the Admin Console as follows:

   a. Select the Application Server node.

   b. Select the JVM Settings tab. The default debug options are set to:

   ```
   -Xdebug -Xrunjdwp:transport=dt_socket,server=y,
       suspend=n,address=1044
   ```

   As you can see, the default debugger socket port is 1044. You can change it to a port not in use by the Application Server or another service.

   c. Check the Enabled box of the Debug field.

   d. Click the Save button.

2. Stop the Application Server and then restart it.
3. Compile your Java source with the -g flag.
4. Package and deploy your application.
5. Start a debugger and connect to the debugger socket at the port you set when you enabled debugging.

2

Understanding XML

THIS chapter describes Extensible Markup Language (XML) and its related specifications. It also gives you practice in writing XML data so that you can become comfortably familiar with XML syntax.

Note: The XML files mentioned in this chapter can be found in *<INSTALL>/*
`j2eetutorial14/examples/xml/samples/`.

Introduction to XML

This section covers the basics of XML. The goal is to give you just enough information to get started so that you understand what XML is all about. (You'll learn more about XML in later sections of the tutorial.) We then outline the major features that make XML great for information storage and interchange, and give you a general idea of how XML can be used.

What Is XML?

XML is a text-based markup language that is fast becoming the standard for data interchange on the Web. As with HTML, you identify data using *tags* (identifiers enclosed in angle brackets: `<...>`). Collectively, the tags are known as markup.

But unlike HTML, XML tags *identify* the data rather than specify how to display it. Whereas an HTML tag says something like, "Display this data in bold font"

(...), an XML tag acts like a field name in your program. It puts a label on a piece of data that identifies it (for example, <message>...</message>).

Note: Because identifying the data gives you some sense of what it *means* (how to interpret it, what you should do with it), XML is sometimes described as a mechanism for specifying the *semantics* (meaning) of the data.

In the same way that you define the field names for a data structure, you are free to use any XML tags that make sense for a given application. Naturally, for multiple applications to use the same XML data, they must agree on the tag names they intend to use.

Here is an example of some XML data you might use for a messaging application:

```
<message>
   <to>you@yourAddress.com</to>
   <from>me@myAddress.com</from>
   <subject>XML Is Really Cool</subject>
   <text>
      How many ways is XML cool? Let me count the ways...
   </text>
</message>
```

Note: Throughout this tutorial, we use boldface text to highlight things we want to bring to your attention. XML does not require anything to be in bold!

The tags in this example identify the message as a whole, the destination and sender addresses, the subject, and the text of the message. As in HTML, the <to> tag has a matching end tag: </to>. The data between the tag and its matching end tag defines an element of the XML data. Note, too, that the content of the <to> tag is contained entirely within the scope of the <message>..</message> tag. It is this ability for one tag to contain others that lets XML represent hierarchical data structures.

Again, as with HTML, whitespace is essentially irrelevant, so you can format the data for readability and yet still process it easily with a program. Unlike HTML, however, in XML you can easily search a data set for messages containing, say, "cool" in the subject, because the XML tags identify the content of the data rather than specify its representation.

Tags and Attributes

Tags can also contain attributes—additional information included as part of the tag itself, within the tag's angle brackets. The following example shows an email message structure that uses attributes for the to, from, and subject fields:

```
<message to="you@yourAddress.com" from="me@myAddress.com"
    subject="XML Is Really Cool">
  <text>
    How many ways is XML cool? Let me count the ways...
  </text>
</message>
```

As in HTML, the attribute name is followed by an equal sign and the attribute value, and multiple attributes are separated by spaces. Unlike HTML, however, in XML commas between attributes are not ignored; if present, they generate an error.

Because you can design a data structure such as <message> equally well using either attributes or tags, it can take a considerable amount of thought to figure out which design is best for your purposes. Designing an XML Data Structure (page 74), includes ideas to help you decide when to use attributes and when to use tags.

Empty Tags

One big difference between XML and HTML is that an XML document is always constrained to be *well formed*. There are several rules that determine when a document is well formed, but one of the most important is that every tag has a closing tag. So, in XML, the </to> tag is not optional. The <to> element is never terminated by any tag other than </to>.

Note: Another important aspect of a well-formed document is that all tags are completely nested. So you can have <message>..<to>..</to>..</message>, but never <message>..<to>..</message>..</to>. A complete list of requirements is contained in the list of XML frequently asked questions (FAQ) at http://www.ucc.ie/xml/#FAQ-VALIDWF. (This FAQ is on the W3C "Recommended Reading" list at http://www.w3.org/XML/.)

Sometimes, though, it makes sense to have a tag that stands by itself. For example, you might want to add a tag that flags the message as important: <flag/>.

This kind of tag does not enclose any content, so it's known as an *empty* tag. You create an empty tag by ending it with /> instead of >. For example, the following message contains an empty flag tag:

```
<message to="you@yourAddress.com" from="me@myAddress.com"
    subject="XML Is Really Cool">
  <flag/>
  <text>
    How many ways is XML cool? Let me count the ways...
  </text>
</message>
```

Note: Using the empty tag saves you from having to code <flag></flag> in order to have a well-formed document. You can control which tags are allowed to be empty by creating a schema or a document type definition, or DTD (page 1346). If there is no DTD or schema associated with the document, then it can contain any kinds of tags you want, as long as the document is well formed.

Comments in XML Files

XML comments look just like HTML comments:

```
<message to="you@yourAddress.com" from="me@myAddress.com"
    subject="XML Is Really Cool">
  <!-- This is a comment -->
  <text>
    How many ways is XML cool? Let me count the ways...
  </text>
</message>
```

The XML Prolog

To complete this basic introduction to XML, note that an XML file always starts with a *prolog*. The minimal prolog contains a declaration that identifies the document as an XML document:

```
<?xml version="1.0"?>
```

The declaration may also contain additional information:

```
<?xml version="1.0" encoding="ISO-8859-1" standalone="yes"?>
```

The XML declaration is essentially the same as the HTML header, `<html>`, except that it uses `<?..?>` and it may contain the following attributes:

- `version`: Identifies the version of the XML markup language used in the data. This attribute is not optional.
- `encoding`: Identifies the character set used to encode the data. `ISO-8859-1` is `Latin-1`, the Western European and English language character set. (The default is 8-bit Unicode: `UTF-8`.)
- `standalone`: Tells whether or not this document references an external entity or an external data type specification. If there are no external references, then "yes" is appropriate.

The prolog can also contain definitions of *entities* (items that are inserted when you reference them from within the document) and specifications that tell which tags are valid in the document. Both declared in a document type definition (DTD, page 1346) that can be defined directly within the prolog, as well as with pointers to external specification files. But those are the subject of later tutorials. For more information on these and many other aspects of XML, see the Recommended Reading list on the W3C XML page at `http://www.w3.org/XML/`.

Note: The declaration is actually optional, but it's a good idea to include it whenever you create an XML file. The declaration should have the version number, at a minimum, and ideally the encoding as well. That standard simplifies things if the XML standard is extended in the future and if the data ever needs to be localized for different geographical regions.

Everything that comes after the XML prolog constitutes the document's *content*.

Processing Instructions

An XML file can also contain *processing instructions* that give commands or information to an application that is processing the XML data. Processing instructions have the following format:

```
<?target instructions?>
```

target is the name of the application that is expected to do the processing, and *instructions* is a string of characters that embodies the information or commands for the application to process.

Because the instructions are application-specific, an XML file can have multiple processing instructions that tell different applications to do similar things, although in different ways. The XML file for a slide show, for example, might have processing instructions that let the speaker specify a technical- or executive-level version of the presentation. If multiple presentation programs were used, the program might need multiple versions of the processing instructions (although it would be nicer if such applications recognized standard instructions).

Note: The target name "xml" (in any combination of upper- or lowercase letters) is reserved for XML standards. In one sense, the declaration is a processing instruction that fits that standard. (However, when you're working with the parser later, you'll see that the method for handling processing instructions never sees the declaration.)

Why Is XML Important?

There are a number of reasons for XML's surging acceptance. This section lists a few of the most prominent.

Plain Text

Because XML is not a binary format, you can create and edit files using anything from a standard text editor to a visual development environment. That makes it easy to debug your programs, and it makes XML useful for storing small amounts of data. At the other end of the spectrum, an XML front end to a database makes it possible to efficiently store large amounts of XML data as well. So XML provides scalability for anything from small configuration files to a company-wide data repository.

Data Identification

XML tells you what kind of data you have, not how to display it. Because the markup tags identify the information and break the data into parts, an email program can process it, a search program can look for messages sent to particular people, and an address book can extract the address information from the rest of the message. In short, because the different parts of the information have been identified, they can be used in different ways by different applications.

Stylability

When display is important, the stylesheet standard, XSL (page 1347), lets you dictate how to portray the data. For example, consider this XML:

```
<to>you@yourAddress.com</to>
```

The stylesheet for this data can say

1. Start a new line.
2. Display "To:" in bold, followed by a space
3. Display the destination data.

This set of instructions produces:

To: you@yourAddress

Of course, you could have done the same thing in HTML, but you wouldn't be able to process the data with search programs and address-extraction programs and the like. More importantly, because XML is inherently style-free, you can use a completely different stylesheet to produce output in Postscript, TEX, PDF, or some new format that hasn't even been invented. That flexibility amounts to what one author described as "future proofing" your information. The XML documents you author today can be used in future document-delivery systems that haven't even been imagined.

Inline Reusability

One of the nicer aspects of XML documents is that they can be composed from separate entities. You can do that with HTML, but only by linking to other documents. Unlike HTML, XML entities can be included "inline" in a document. The included sections look like a normal part of the document: you can search the whole document at one time or download it in one piece. That lets you modularize your documents without resorting to links. You can single-source a section so that an edit to it is reflected everywhere the section is used, and yet a document composed from such pieces looks for all the world like a one-piece document.

Linkability

Thanks to HTML, the ability to define links between documents is now regarded as a necessity. Appendix B discusses the link-specification initiative. This initiative lets you define two-way links, multiple-target links, expanding links (where clicking a link causes the targeted information to appear inline), and links between two existing documents that are defined in a third.

Easily Processed

As mentioned earlier, regular and consistent notation makes it easier to build a program to process XML data. For example, in HTML a `<dt>` tag can be delimited by `</dt>`, another `<dt>`, `<dd>`, or `</dl>`. That makes for some difficult programming. But in XML, the `<dt>` tag must always have a `</dt>` terminator, or it must be an empty tag such as `<dt/>`. That restriction is a critical part of the constraints that make an XML document well formed. (Otherwise, the XML parser won't be able to read the data.) And because XML is a vendor-neutral standard, you can choose among several XML parsers, any one of which takes the work out of processing XML data.

Hierarchical

Finally, XML documents benefit from their hierarchical structure. Hierarchical document structures are, in general, faster to access because you can drill down to the part you need, as if you were stepping through a table of contents. They are also easier to rearrange, because each piece is delimited. In a document, for example, you could move a heading to a new location and drag everything under it along with the heading, instead of having to page down to make a selection, cut, and then paste the selection into a new location.

How Can You Use XML?

There are several basic ways to use XML:

- Traditional data processing, where XML encodes the data for a program to process
- Document-driven programming, where XML documents are containers that build interfaces and applications from existing components

- Archiving—the foundation for document-driven programming—where the customized version of a component is saved (archived) so that it can be used later

- Binding, where the DTD or schema that defines an XML data structure is used to automatically generate a significant portion of the application that will eventually process that data

Traditional Data Processing

XML is fast becoming the data representation of choice for the Web. It's terrific when used in conjunction with network-centric Java platform programs that send and retrieve information. So a client-server application, for example, could transmit XML-encoded data back and forth between the client and the server.

In the future, XML is potentially the answer for data interchange in all sorts of transactions, as long as both sides agree on the markup to use. (For example, should an email program expect to see tags named <FIRST> and <LAST>, or <FIRSTNAME> and <LASTNAME>?) The need for common standards will generate a lot of industry-specific standardization efforts in the years ahead. In the meantime, mechanisms that let you "translate" the tags in an XML document will be important. Such mechanisms include projects such as the Resource Description Framework initiative (RDF, page 1351), which defines meta tags, and the Extensible Stylesheet Language specification (XSL, page 1347), which lets you translate XML tags into other XML tags.

Document-Driven Programming

The newest approach to using XML is to construct a document that describes what an application page should look like. The document, rather than simply being displayed, consists of references to user interface components and business-logic components that are "hooked together" to create an application on-the-fly.

Of course, it makes sense to use the Java platform for such components. To construct such applications, you can use JavaBeans components for interfaces and Enterprise JavaBeans components for the business logic. Although none of the efforts undertaken so far is ready for commercial use, much preliminary work has been done.

Note: The Java programming language is also excellent for writing XML-processing tools that are as portable as XML. Several visual XML editors have been written for the Java platform. For a listing of editors, see `http://www.xml.com/pub/pt/3`. For processing tools and other XML resources, see Robin Cover's SGML/XML Web page at `http://xml.coverpages.org/software.html`.

Binding

After you have defined the structure of XML data using either a DTD or one of the schema standards, a large part of the processing you need to do has already been defined. For example, if the schema says that the text data in a `<date>` element must follow one of the recognized date formats, then one aspect of the validation criteria for the data has been defined; it only remains to write the code. Although a DTD specification cannot go into the same level of detail, a DTD (like a schema) provides a grammar that tells which data structures can occur and in what sequences. That specification tells you how to write the high-level code that processes the data elements.

But when the data structure (and possibly format) is fully specified, the code you need to process it can just as easily be generated automatically. That process is known as *binding*—creating classes that recognize and process different data elements by processing the specification that defines those elements. As time goes on, you should find that you are using the data specification to generate significant chunks of code, and you can focus on the programming that is unique to your application.

Archiving

The Holy Grail of programming is the construction of reusable, modular components. Ideally, you'd like to take them off the shelf, customize them, and plug them together to construct an application, with a bare minimum of additional coding and additional compilation.

The basic mechanism for saving information is called *archiving*. You archive a component by writing it to an output stream in a form that you can reuse later. You can then read it and instantiate it using its saved parameters. (For example, if you saved a table component, its parameters might be the number of rows and columns to display.) Archived components can also be shuffled around the Web and used in a variety of ways.

When components are archived in binary form, however, there are some limitations on the kinds of changes you can make to the underlying classes if you want to retain compatibility with previously saved versions. If you could modify the archived version to reflect the change, that would solve the problem. But that's hard to do with a binary object. Such considerations have prompted a number of investigations into using XML for archiving. But if an object's state were archived in text form using XML, then anything and everything in it could be changed as easily as you can say, "Search and replace."

XML's text-based format could also make it easier to transfer objects between applications written in different languages. For all these reasons, there is a lot of interest in XML-based archiving.

Summary

XML is pretty simple and very flexible. It has many uses yet to be discovered, and we are only beginning to scratch the surface of its potential. It is the foundation for a great many standards yet to come, providing a common language that different computer systems can use to exchange data with one another. As each industry group comes up with standards for what it wants to say, computers will begin to link to each other in ways previously unimaginable.

Generating XML Data

This section takes you step by step through the process of constructing an XML document. Along the way, you'll gain experience with the XML components you'll typically use to create your data structures.

Writing a Simple XML File

You'll start by writing the kind of XML data you can use for a slide presentation. To become comfortable with the basic format of an XML file, you'll use your text editor to create the data. You'll use this file and extend it in later exercises.

Creating the File

Using a standard text editor, create a file called `slideSample.xml`.

Note: Here is a version of it that already exists: `slideSample01.xml`. (The browsable version is `slideSample01-xml.html`.) You can use this version to compare your work or just review it as you read this guide.

Writing the Declaration

Next, write the *declaration*, which identifies the file as an XML document. The declaration starts with the characters <?, which is also the standard XML identifier for a *processing instruction*. (You'll see processing instructions later in this tutorial.)

```
<?xml version='1.0' encoding='utf-8'?>
```

This line identifies the document as an XML document that conforms to version 1.0 of the XML specification and says that it uses the 8-bit Unicode character-encoding scheme. (For information on encoding schemes, see Appendix A.)

Because the document has not been specified as `standalone`, the parser assumes that it may contain references to other documents. To see how to specify a document as `standalone`, see The XML Prolog (page 34).

Adding a Comment

Comments are ignored by XML parsers. A program will never see them unless you activate special settings in the parser. To put a comment into the file, add the following highlighted text.

```
<?xml version='1.0' encoding='utf-8'?>

<!-- A SAMPLE set of slides -->
```

Defining the Root Element

After the declaration, every XML file defines exactly one element, known as the *root element*. Any other elements in the file are contained within that element.

Enter the following highlighted text to define the root element for this file, slideshow:

```
<?xml version='1.0' encoding='utf-8'?>

<!-- A SAMPLE set of slides -->

<slideshow>

</slideshow>
```

Note: XML element names are case-sensitive. The end tag must exactly match the start tag.

Adding Attributes to an Element

A slide presentation has a number of associated data items, none of which requires any structure. So it is natural to define these data items as attributes of the slideshow element. Add the following highlighted text to set up some attributes:

```
...
  <slideshow
    title="Sample Slide Show"
    date="Date of publication"
    author="Yours Truly"
    >
  </slideshow>
```

When you create a name for a tag or an attribute, you can use hyphens (-), underscores (_), colons (:), and periods (.) in addition to characters and numbers. Unlike HTML, values for XML attributes are always in quotation marks, and multiple attributes are never separated by commas.

Note: Colons should be used with care or avoided, because they are used when defining the namespace for an XML document.

Adding Nested Elements

XML allows for hierarchically structured data, which means that an element can contain other elements. Add the following highlighted text to define a slide element and a title element contained within it:

```
<slideshow
  ...
  >

  <!-- TITLE SLIDE -->
  <slide type="all">
    <title>Wake up to WonderWidgets!</title>
  </slide>

</slideshow>
```

Here you have also added a `type` attribute to the slide. The idea of this attribute is that you can earmark slides for a mostly technical or mostly executive audience using `type="tech"` or `type="exec"`, or identify them as suitable for both audiences using `type="all"`.

More importantly, this example illustrates the difference between things that are more usefully defined as elements (the `title` element) and things that are more suitable as attributes (the `type` attribute). The visibility heuristic is primarily at work here. The title is something the audience will see, so it is an element. The type, on the other hand, is something that never gets presented, so it is an attribute. Another way to think about that distinction is that an element is a container, like a bottle. The type is a characteristic of the *container* (tall or short, wide or narrow). The title is a characteristic of the *contents* (water, milk, or tea). These are not hard-and-fast rules, of course, but they can help when you design your own XML structures.

Adding HTML-Style Text

Because XML lets you define any tags you want, it makes sense to define a set of tags that look like HTML. In fact, the XHTML standard does exactly that. You'll see more about that toward the end of the SAX tutorial. For now, type the following highlighted text to define a slide with a couple of list item entries that use an HTML-style `<em>` tag for emphasis (usually rendered as italicized text):

```
...
<!-- TITLE SLIDE -->
<slide type="all">
   <title>Wake up to WonderWidgets!</title>
</slide>

<!-- OVERVIEW -->
<slide type="all">
   <title>Overview</title>
   <item>Why <em>WonderWidgets</em> are great</item>
   <item>Who <em>buys</em> WonderWidgets</item>
</slide>

</slideshow>
```

Note that defining a *title* element conflicts with the XHTML element that uses the same name. Later in this tutorial, we discuss the mechanism that produces the conflict (the DTD), along with possible solutions.

Adding an Empty Element

One major difference between HTML and XML is that all XML must be well formed, which means that every tag must have an ending tag or be an empty tag. By now, you're getting pretty comfortable with ending tags. Add the following highlighted text to define an empty list item element with no contents:

```
...
<!-- OVERVIEW -->
<slide type="all">
   <title>Overview</title>
   <item>Why <em>WonderWidgets</em> are great</item>
   <item/>
   <item>Who <em>buys</em> WonderWidgets</item>
</slide>

</slideshow>
```

Note that any element can be an empty element. All it takes is ending the tag with /> instead of >. You could do the same thing by entering <item></item>, which is equivalent.

Note: Another factor that makes an XML file well formed is proper nesting. So `<b><i>some_text</i></b>` is well formed, because the `<i>...</i>` sequence is completely nested within the `<b>..</b>` tag. This sequence, on the other hand, is not well formed: `<b><i>some_text</b></i>`.

The Finished Product

Here is the completed version of the XML file:

```xml
<?xml version='1.0' encoding='utf-8'?>

<!--  A SAMPLE set of slides  -->

<slideshow
   title="Sample Slide Show"
   date="Date of publication"
   author="Yours Truly"
   >

   <!-- TITLE SLIDE -->
   <slide type="all">
      <title>Wake up to WonderWidgets!</title>
   </slide>

   <!-- OVERVIEW -->
   <slide type="all">
      <title>Overview</title>
      <item>Why <em>WonderWidgets</em> are great</item>
      <item/>
      <item>Who <em>buys</em> WonderWidgets</item>
   </slide>
</slideshow>
```

Save a copy of this file as `slideSample01.xml` so that you can use it as the initial data structure when experimenting with XML programming operations.

Writing Processing Instructions

It sometimes makes sense to code application-specific processing instructions in the XML data. In this exercise, you'll add a processing instruction to your `slideSample.xml` file.

Note: The file you'll create in this section is `slideSample02.xml`. (The browsable version is `slideSample02-xml.html`.)

As you saw in Processing Instructions (page 35), the format for a processing instruction is `<?target data?>`, where *target* is the application that is expected to do the processing, and *data* is the instruction or information for it to process. Add the following highlighted text to add a processing instruction for a mythical slide presentation program that will query the user to find out which slides to display (technical, executive-level, or all):

```
<slideshow
   ...
   >

   <!-- PROCESSING INSTRUCTION -->
   <?my.presentation.Program QUERY="exec, tech, all"?>

   <!-- TITLE SLIDE -->
```

Notes:

- The data portion of the processing instruction can contain spaces or it can even be null. But there cannot be any space between the initial `<?` and the target identifier.
- The data begins after the first space.
- It makes sense to fully qualify the target with the complete Web-unique package prefix, to preclude any conflict with other programs that might process the same data.
- For readability, it seems like a good idea to include a colon (:) after the name of the application:

```
<?my.presentation.Program: QUERY="..."?>
```

The colon makes the target name into a kind of "label" that identifies the intended recipient of the instruction. However, even though the W3C spec allows a colon in a target name, some versions of Internet Explorer 5 (IE5) consider it an error. For this tutorial, then, we avoid using a colon in the target name.

Save a copy of this file as `slideSample02.xml` so that you can use it when experimenting with processing instructions.

Introducing an Error

The parser can generate three kinds of errors: a fatal error, an error, and a warning. In this exercise, you'll make a simple modification to the XML file to introduce a fatal error. Later you'll see how it's handled in the Echo app.

Note: The XML structure you'll create in this exercise is in `slideSampleBad1.xml`. (The browsable version is `slideSampleBad1-xml.html`.)

One easy way to introduce a fatal error is to remove the final / from the empty `item` element to create a tag that does not have a corresponding end tag. That constitutes a fatal error, because all XML documents must, by definition, be well formed. Do the following:

1. Copy `slideSample02.xml` to `slideSampleBad1.xml`.

2. Edit `slideSampleBad1.xml` and remove the character shown here:

```
...
<!-- OVERVIEW -->
   <slide type="all">
   <title>Overview</title>
   <item>Why <em>WonderWidgets</em> are great</item>
   <item/>
   <item>Who <em>buys</em> WonderWidgets</item>
</slide>
...
```

This change produces the following:

```
...
<item>Why <em>WonderWidgets</em> are great</item>
<item>
<item>Who <em>buys</em> WonderWidgets</item>
...
```

Now you have a file that you can use to generate an error in any parser, any time. (XML parsers are required to generate a fatal error for this file, because the lack of an end tag for the `<item>` element means that the XML structure is no longer well formed.)

Substituting and Inserting Text

In this section, you'll learn about

- Handling special characters (<, &, and so on)
- Handling text with XML-style syntax

Handling Special Characters

In XML, an entity is an XML structure (or plain text) that has a name. Referencing the entity by name causes it to be inserted into the document in place of the entity reference. To create an entity reference, the entity name is surrounded by an ampersand and a semicolon, like this:

```
&entityName;
```

Later, when you learn how to write a DTD, you'll see that you can define your own entities so that &yourEntityName; expands to all the text you defined for that entity. For now, though, we'll focus on the predefined entities and character references that don't require any special definitions.

Predefined Entities

An entity reference such as & contains a name (in this case, amp) between the start and end delimiters. The text it refers to (&) is substituted for the name, as with a macro in a programming language. Table 2–1 shows the predefined entities for special characters.

Table 2–1 Predefined Entitics

Character	Name	Reference
&	ampersand	&
<	less than	<
>	greater than	>
"	quote	"
'	apostrophe	'

Character References

A character reference such as “ contains a hash mark (#) followed by a number. The number is the Unicode value for a single character, such as 65 for the letter A, 147 for the left curly quote, or 148 for the right curly quote. In this case, the "name" of the entity is the hash mark followed by the digits that identify the character.

Note: XML expects values to be specified in decimal. However, the Unicode charts at `http://www.unicode.org/charts/` specify values in hexadecimal! So you'll need to do a conversion to get the right value to insert into your XML data set.

Using an Entity Reference in an XML Document

Suppose you want to insert a line like this in your XML document:

```
Market Size < predicted
```

The problem with putting that line into an XML file directly is that when the parser sees the left angle bracket (<), it starts looking for a tag name, which throws off the parse. To get around that problem, you put < in the file instead of <.

Note: The results of the next modifications are contained in `slideSample03.xml`.

Add the following highlighted text to your `slideSample.xml` file, and save a copy of it for future use as `slideSample03.xml`:

```
<!-- OVERVIEW -->
<slide type="all">
   <title>Overview</title>
   ...
</slide>

<slide type="exec">
   <title>Financial Forecast</title>
   <item>Market Size &lt; predicted</item>
   <item>Anticipated Penetration</item>
   <item>Expected Revenues</item>
   <item>Profit Margin</item>
</slide>

</slideshow>
```

When you use an XML parser to echo this data, you will see the desired output:

```
Market Size < predicted
```

You see an angle bracket (<) where you coded <, because the XML parser converts the reference into the entity it represents and passes that entity to the application.

Handling Text with XML-Style Syntax

When you are handling large blocks of XML or HTML that include many special characters, it is inconvenient to replace each of them with the appropriate entity reference. For those situations, you can use a CDATA section.

Note: The results of the next modifications are contained in slideSample04.xml.

A CDATA section works like <pre>...</pre> in HTML, only more so: all whitespace in a CDATA section is significant, and characters in it are not interpreted as XML. A CDATA section starts with <![CDATA[and ends with]]>.

Add the following highlighted text to your slideSample.xml file to define a CDATA section for a fictitious technical slide, and save a copy of the file as slideSample04.xml:

```
    ...
    <slide type="tech">
      <title>How it Works</title>
      <item>First we fozzle the frobmorten</item>
      <item>Then we framboze the staten</item>
      <item>Finally, we frenzle the fuznaten</item>
      <item><![CDATA[Diagram:
      frobmorten <-------------- fuznaten
         |                  <3>                ^
         | <1>                                 | <1> = fozzle
         V                                     | <2> = framboze
      staten-------------------------+ <3> = frenzle
               <2>
      ]]></item>
    </slide>
  </slideshow>
```

When you echo this file with an XML parser, you see the following output:

```
Diagram:
frobmorten <--------------- fuznaten
  |               <3>           ^
  | <1>                         | <1> = fozzle
  V                             | <2> = framboze
staten-------------------------+ <3> = frenzle
          <2>
```

The point here is that the text in the CDATA section arrives as it was written. Because the parser doesn't treat the angle brackets as XML, they don't generate the fatal errors they would otherwise cause. (If the angle brackets weren't in a CDATA section, the document would not be well formed.)

Creating a Document Type Definition

After the XML declaration, the document prolog can include a DTD, which lets you specify the kinds of tags that can be included in your XML document. In addition to telling a validating parser which tags are valid and in what arrangements, a DTD tells both validating and nonvalidating parsers where text is expected, which lets the parser determine whether the whitespace it sees is significant or *ignorable*.

Basic DTD Definitions

To begin learning about DTD definitions, let's start by telling the parser where text is expected and where any text (other than whitespace) would be an error. (Whitespace in such locations is ignorable.)

Note: The DTD defined in this section is contained in `slideshow1a.dtd`. (The browsable version is `slideshow1a-dtd.html`.)

Start by creating a file named `slideshow.dtd`. Enter an XML declaration and a comment to identify the file:

```
<?xml version='1.0' encoding='utf-8'?>

<!--
  DTD for a simple "slide show"
-->
```

Next, add the following highlighted text to specify that a slideshow element contains slide elements and nothing else:

```
<!-- DTD for a simple "slide show" -->

<!ELEMENT slideshow (slide+)>
```

As you can see, the DTD tag starts with <! followed by the tag name (ELEMENT). After the tag name comes the name of the element that is being defined (slideshow) and, in parentheses, one or more items that indicate the valid contents for that element. In this case, the notation says that a slideshow consists of one or more slide elements.

Without the plus sign, the definition would be saying that a slideshow consists of a single slide element. The qualifiers you can add to an element definition are listed in Table 2–2.

You can include multiple elements inside the parentheses in a comma-separated list and use a qualifier on each element to indicate how many instances of that element can occur. The comma-separated list tells which elements are valid and the order they can occur in.

You can also nest parentheses to group multiple items. For an example, after defining an image element (discussed shortly), you can specify ((image, title)+) to declare that every image element in a slide must be paired with a title element. Here, the plus sign applies to the image/title pair to indicate that one or more pairs of the specified items can occur.

Table 2–2 DTD Element Qualifiers

Qualifier	Name	Meaning
?	Question mark	Optional (zero or one)
*	Asterisk	Zero or more
+	Plus sign	One or more

Defining Text and Nested Elements

Now that you have told the parser something about where *not* to expect text, let's see how to tell it where text *can* occur. Add the following highlighted text to define the `slide`, `title`, `item`, and `list` elements:

```
<!ELEMENT slideshow (slide+)>
<!ELEMENT slide (title, item*)>
<!ELEMENT title (#PCDATA)>
<!ELEMENT item (#PCDATA | item)* >
```

The first line you added says that a slide consists of a `title` followed by zero or more `item` elements. Nothing new there. The next line says that a title consists entirely of *parsed character data* (PCDATA). That's known as "text" in most parts of the country, but in XML-speak it's called "parsed character data." (That distinguishes it from CDATA sections, which contain character data that is not parsed.) The # that precedes PCDATA indicates that what follows is a special word rather than an element name.

The last line introduces the vertical bar (|), which indicates an *or* condition. In this case, either PCDATA or an `item` can occur. The asterisk at the end says that either element can occur zero or more times in succession. The result of this specification is known as a *mixed-content model*, because any number of `item` elements can be interspersed with the text. Such models must always be defined with #PCDATA specified first, followed by some number of alternate items divided by vertical bars (|), and an asterisk (*) at the end.

Save a copy of this DTD as `slideSample1a.dtd` for use when you experiment with basic DTD processing.

Limitations of DTDs

It would be nice if we could specify that an `item` contains either text, or text followed by one or more list items. But that kind of specification turns out to be hard to achieve in a DTD. For example, you might be tempted to define an `item` this way:

```
<!ELEMENT item (#PCDATA | (#PCDATA, item+)) >
```

That would certainly be accurate, but as soon as the parser sees #PCDATA and the vertical bar, it requires the remaining definition to conform to the mixed-content model. This specification doesn't, so you can get an error that says Illegal mixed content model for 'item'. Found (..., where the hex character 28 is the angle bracket that ends the definition.

Trying to double-define the item element doesn't work either. Suppose you try a specification like this:

```
<!ELEMENT item (#PCDATA) >
<!ELEMENT item (#PCDATA, item+) >
```

This sequence produces a "duplicate definition" warning when the validating parser runs. The second definition is, in fact, ignored. So it seems that defining a mixed-content model (which allows item elements to be interspersed in text) is the best we can do.

In addition to the limitations of the mixed-content model we've mentioned, there is no way to further qualify the kind of text that can occur where PCDATA has been specified. Should it contain only numbers? Should it be in a date format, or possibly a monetary format? There is no way to specify such things in a DTD.

Finally, note that the DTD offers no sense of hierarchy. The definition of the title element applies equally to a slide title and to an item title. When we expand the DTD to allow HTML-style markup in addition to plain text, it would make sense to, for example, restrict the size of an item title compared with that of a slide title. But the only way to do that would be to give one of them a different name, such as item-title. The bottom line is that the lack of hierarchy in the DTD forces you to introduce a "hyphenation hierarchy" (or its equivalent) in your namespace. All these limitations are fundamental motivations behind the development of schema-specification standards.

Special Element Values in the DTD

Rather than specify a parenthesized list of elements, the element definition can use one of two special values: ANY or EMPTY. The ANY specification says that the element can contain any other defined element, or PCDATA. Such a specification is usually used for the root element of a general-purpose XML document such as you might create with a word processor. Textual elements can occur in any order in such a document, so specifying ANY makes sense.

The EMPTY specification says that the element contains no contents. So the DTD for email messages that let you flag the message with <flag/> might have a line like this in the DTD:

```
<!ELEMENT flag EMPTY>
```

Referencing the DTD

In this case, the DTD definition is in a separate file from the XML document. With this arrangement, you reference the DTD from the XML document, and that makes the DTD file part of the *external subset* of the full document type definition for the XML file. As you'll see later on, you can also include parts of the DTD within the document. Such definitions constitute the *local subset* of the DTD.

Note: The XML written in this section is contained in `slideSample05.xml`. (The browsable version is `slideSample05-xml.html`.)

To reference the DTD file you just created, add the following highlighted line to your `slideSample.xml` file, and save a copy of the file as `slideSample05.xml`:

```
<!--  A SAMPLE set of slides  -->

<!DOCTYPE slideshow SYSTEM "slideshow.dtd">

<slideshow>
```

Again, the DTD tag starts with `<!`. In this case, the tag name, `DOCTYPE`, says that the document is a `slideshow`, which means that the document consists of the `slideshow` element and everything within it:

```
<slideshow>
...
</slideshow>
```

This tag defines the `slideshow` element as the root element for the document. An XML document must have exactly one root element. This is where that element is specified. In other words, this tag identifies the document *content* as a `slideshow`.

The `DOCTYPE` tag occurs after the XML declaration and before the root element. The `SYSTEM` identifier specifies the location of the DTD file. Because it does not start with a prefix such as `http:/` or `file:/`, the path is relative to the location of the XML document. The parser is using that information to find the DTD file, just as your application would use it to find a file relative to the XML document. A `PUBLIC` identifier can also be used to specify the DTD file using a unique name, but the parser would have to be able to resolve it.

The DOCTYPE specification can also contain DTD definitions within the XML document, rather than refer to an external DTD file. Such definitions are contained in square brackets:

```
<!DOCTYPE slideshow SYSTEM "slideshow1.dtd" [
   ...local subset definitions here...
]>
```

You'll take advantage of that facility in a moment to define some entities that can be used in the document.

Documents and Data

Earlier, you learned that one reason you hear about XML *documents*, on the one hand, and XML *data*, on the other, is that XML handles both comfortably, depending on whether text is or is not allowed between elements in the structure.

In the sample file you have been working with, the slideshow element is an example of a *data element*: it contains only subelements with no intervening text. The item element, on the other hand, might be termed a *document element*, because it is defined to include both text and subelements.

As you work through this tutorial, you will see how to expand the definition of the title element to include HTML-style markup, which will turn it into a document element as well.

Defining Attributes and Entities in the DTD

The DTD you've defined so far is fine for use with a nonvalidating parser. It tells where text is expected and where it isn't, and that is all the nonvalidating parser pays attention to. But for use with the validating parser, the DTD must specify the valid attributes for the different elements. You'll do that in this section, and then you'll define one internal entity and one external entity that you can reference in your XML file.

Defining Attributes in the DTD

Let's start by defining the attributes for the elements in the slide presentation.

Note: The XML written in this section is contained in `slideshow1b.dtd`. (The browsable version is `slideshow1b-dtd.html`.)

Add the following highlighted text to define the attributes for the `slideshow` element:

```
<!ELEMENT slideshow (slide+)>
<!ATTLIST slideshow
    title   CDATA       #REQUIRED
    date    CDATA       #IMPLIED
    author  CDATA       "unknown"
>
<!ELEMENT slide (title, item*)>
```

The DTD tag `ATTLIST` begins the series of attribute definitions. The name that follows `ATTLIST` specifies the element for which the attributes are being defined. In this case, the element is the `slideshow` element. (Note again the lack of hierarchy in DTD specifications.)

Each attribute is defined by a series of three space-separated values. Commas and other separators are not allowed, so formatting the definitions as shown here is helpful for readability. The first element in each line is the name of the attribute: `title`, `date`, or `author`, in this case. The second element indicates the type of the data: `CDATA` is character data—unparsed data, again, in which a left angle bracket (<) will never be construed as part of an XML tag. Table 2–3 presents the valid choices for the attribute type.

When the attribute type consists of a parenthesized list of choices separated by vertical bars, the attribute must use one of the specified values. For an example, add the following highlighted text to the DTD:

```
<!ELEMENT slide (title, item*)>
<!ATTLIST slide
    type    (tech | exec | all) #IMPLIED
>
<!ELEMENT title (#PCDATA)>
<!ELEMENT item (#PCDATA | item)* >
```

This specification says that the `slide` element's `type` attribute must be given as `type="tech"`, `type="exec"`, or `type="all"`. No other values are acceptable. (DTD-aware XML editors can use such specifications to present a pop-up list of choices.)

Table 2–3 Attribute Types

Attribute Type	Specifies...
(value1 | value2 | ...)	A list of values separated by vertical bars
CDATA	Unparsed character data (a text string)
ID	A name that no other ID attribute shares
IDREF	A reference to an ID defined elsewhere in the document
IDREFS	A space-separated list containing one or more ID references
ENTITY	The name of an entity defined in the DTD
ENTITIES	A space-separated list of entities
NMTOKEN	A valid XML name composed of letters, numbers, hyphens, underscores, and colons
NMTOKENS	A space-separated list of names
NOTATION	The name of a DTD-specified notation, which describes a non-XML data format, such as those used for image files. (This is a rapidly obsolescing specification that is discussed in greater length toward the end of this section.)

The last entry in the attribute specification determines the attribute's default value, if any, and tells whether or not the attribute is required. Table 2–4 shows the possible choices.

Table 2–4 Attribute-Specification Parameters

Specification	Specifies...
#REQUIRED	The attribute value must be specified in the document.
#IMPLIED	The value need not be specified in the document. If it isn't, the application will have a default value it uses.
"*defaultValue*"	The default value to use if a value is not specified in the document.
#FIXED "*fixedValue*"	The value to use. If the document specifies any value at all, it must be the same.

Finally, save a copy of the DTD as `slideshow1b.dtd` for use when you experiment with attribute definitions.

Defining Entities in the DTD

So far, you've seen predefined entities such as `&amp;` and you've seen that an attribute can reference an entity. It's time now for you to learn how to define entities of your own.

Note: The XML you'll create here is contained in `slideSample06.xml`. (The browsable version is `slideSample06-xml.html`.)

Add the following highlighted text to the `DOCTYPE` tag in your XML file:

```
<!DOCTYPE slideshow SYSTEM "slideshow.dtd" [
  <!ENTITY product  "WonderWidget">
  <!ENTITY products "WonderWidgets">
]>
```

The `ENTITY` tag name says that you are defining an entity. Next comes the name of the entity and its definition. In this case, you are defining an entity named `product` that will take the place of the product name. Later when the product name changes (as it most certainly will), you need only change the name in one place, and all your slides will reflect the new value.

The last part is the substitution string that replaces the entity name whenever it is referenced in the XML document. The substitution string is defined in quotes, which are not included when the text is inserted into the document.

Just for good measure, we defined two versions—one singular and one plural—so that when the marketing mavens come up with "Wally" for a product name, you will be prepared to enter the plural as "Wallies" and have it substituted correctly.

Note: Truth be told, this is the kind of thing that really belongs in an external DTD so that all your documents can reference the new name when it changes. But, hey, this is only an example.

Now that you have the entities defined, the next step is to reference them in the slide show. Make the following highlighted changes:

```
<slideshow
  title="WonderWidget&product; Slide Show"
  ...

  <!-- TITLE SLIDE -->
  <slide type="all">
    <title>Wake up to WonderWidgets&products;!</title>
  </slide>

   <!-- OVERVIEW -->
  <slide type="all">
    <title>Overview</title>
    <item>Why <em>WonderWidgets&products;</em> are great</item>
    <item/>
    <item>Who <em>buys</em> WonderWidgets&products;</item>
  </slide>
```

Notice two points. Entities you define are referenced with the same syntax (&entityName;) that you use for predefined entities, and the entity can be referenced in an attribute value as well as in an element's contents.

When you echo this version of the file with an XML parser, here is the kind of thing you'll see:

```
Wake up to WonderWidgets!
```

Note that the product name has been substituted for the entity reference.

To finish, save a copy of the file as `slideSample06.xml`.

Additional Useful Entities

Here are several other examples for entity definitions that you might find useful when you write an XML document:

```
<!ENTITY ldquo  "&#147;"> <!-- Left Double Quote -->
<!ENTITY rdquo  "&#148;"> <!-- Right Double Quote -->
<!ENTITY trade  "&#153;"> <!-- Trademark Symbol (TM) -->
<!ENTITY rtrade "&#174;"> <!-- Registered Trademark (R) -->
<!ENTITY copyr  "&#169;"> <!-- Copyright Symbol -->
```

Referencing External Entities

You can also use the SYSTEM or PUBLIC identifier to name an entity that is defined in an external file. You'll do that now.

Note: The XML defined here is contained in slideSample07.xml and in copyright.xml. (The browsable versions are slideSample07-xml.html and copyright-xml.html.)

To reference an external entity, add the following highlighted text to the DOCTYPE statement in your XML file:

```
<!DOCTYPE slideshow SYSTEM "slideshow.dtd" [
  <!ENTITY product  "WonderWidget">
  <!ENTITY products "WonderWidgets">
  <!ENTITY copyright SYSTEM "copyright.xml">
]>
```

This definition references a copyright message contained in a file named copyright.xml. Create that file and put some interesting text in it, perhaps something like this:

```
<!--  A SAMPLE copyright  -->

This is the standard copyright message that our lawyers
make us put everywhere so we don't have to shell out a
million bucks every time someone spills hot coffee in their
lap...
```

Finally, add the following highlighted text to your slideSample.xml file to reference the external entity, and save a copy of the file as slideSample07.html:

```
<!-- TITLE SLIDE -->
  ...
</slide>

<!-- COPYRIGHT SLIDE -->
<slide type="all">
  <item>&copyright;</item>
</slide>
```

You could also use an external entity declaration to access a servlet that produces the current date using a definition something like this:

```
<!ENTITY currentDate SYSTEM
   "http://www.example.com/servlet/Today?fmt=dd-MMM-yyyy">
```

You would then reference that entity the same as any other entity:

```
Today's date is &currentDate;.
```

When you echo the latest version of the slide presentation with an XML parser, here is what you'll see:

```
...
<slide type="all">
   <item>
This is the standard copyright message that our lawyers
make us put everywhere so we don't have to shell out a
million bucks every time someone spills hot coffee in their
lap...
   </item>
</slide>
...
```

You'll notice that the newline that follows the comment in the file is echoed as a character, but that the comment itself is ignored. This newline is the reason that the copyright message appears to start on the next line after the `<item>` element instead of on the same line: the first character echoed is actually the newline that follows the comment.

Summarizing Entities

An entity that is referenced in the document content, whether internal or external, is termed a *general entity*. An entity that contains DTD specifications that are referenced from within the DTD is termed a *parameter entity*. (More on that later.)

An entity that contains XML (text and markup), and is therefore parsed, is known as a *parsed entity*. An entity that contains binary data (such as images) is known as an *unparsed entity*. (By its nature, it must be external.) In the next section, we discuss references to unparsed entities.

Referencing Binary Entities

This section discusses the options for referencing binary files such as image files and multimedia data files.

Using a MIME Data Type

There are two ways to reference an unparsed entity such as a binary image file. One is to use the DTD's NOTATION specification mechanism. However, that mechanism is a complex, unintuitive holdover that exists mostly for compatibility with SGML documents.

Note: SGML stands for Standard Generalized Markup Language. It was extremely powerful but *so* general that a program had to read the beginning of a document just to find out how to parse the remainder of it. Some very large document-management systems were built using it, but it was so large and complex that only the largest organizations managed to deal with it. XML, on the other hand, chose to remain small and simple—more like HTML than SGML—and, as a result, it has enjoyed rapid, widespread deployment. This story may well hold a moral for schema standards as well. Time will tell.

We will have occasion to discuss the subject in a bit more depth when we look at the DTDHandler API, but suffice it for now to say that the XML namespaces standard, in conjunction with the MIME data types defined for electronic messaging attachments, together provide a much more useful, understandable, and extensible mechanism for referencing unparsed external entities.

Note: The XML described here is in slideshow1b.dtd. (The browsable version is slideshow1b-dtd.html.) It shows how binary references can be made, assuming that the application that will process the XML data knows how to handle such references.

To set up the slide show to use image files, add the following highlighted text to your slideshow1b.dtd file:

```
<!ELEMENT slide (image?, title, item*)>
<!ATTLIST slide
    type   (tech | exec | all) #IMPLIED
>
<!ELEMENT title (#PCDATA)>
```

```
<!ELEMENT item (#PCDATA | item)* >
<!ELEMENT image EMPTY>
<!ATTLIST image
     alt     CDATA     #IMPLIED
     src     CDATA     #REQUIRED
     type    CDATA     "image/gif"
>
```

These modifications declare `image` as an optional element in a `slide`, define it as empty element, and define the attributes it requires. The `image` tag is patterned after the HTML 4.0 `img` tag, with the addition of an image type specifier, `type`. (The `img` tag is defined in the HTML 4.0 specification.)

The `image` tag's attributes are defined by the `ATTLIST` entry. The `alt` attribute, which defines alternative text to display in case the image can't be found, accepts character data (CDATA). It has an implied value, which means that it is optional and that the program processing the data knows enough to substitute something such as "Image not found." On the other hand, the `src` attribute, which names the image to display, is required.

The `type` attribute is intended for the specification of a MIME data type, as defined at `http://www.iana.org/assignments/media-types/`. It has a default value: `image/gif`.

Note: It is understood here that the character data (CDATA) used for the type attribute will be one of the MIME data types. The two most common formats are `image/gif` and `image/jpeg`. Given that fact, it might be nice to specify an attribute list here, using something like

```
type ("image/gif", "image/jpeg")
```

That won't work, however, because attribute lists are restricted to name tokens. The forward slash isn't part of the valid set of name-token characters, so this declaration fails. Also, creating an attribute list in the DTD would limit the valid MIME types to those defined today. Leaving it as CDATA leaves things more open-ended so that the declaration will continue to be valid as additional types are defined.

In the document, a reference to an image named "intro-pic" might look something like this:

```
<image src="image/intro-pic.gif", alt="Intro Pic",
  type="image/gif" />
```

The Alternative: Using Entity References

Using a MIME data type as an attribute of an element is a flexible and expandable mechanism. To create an external ENTITY reference using the notation mechanism, you need DTD NOTATION elements for JPEG and GIF data. Those can, of course, be obtained from a central repository. But then you need to define a different ENTITY element for each image you intend to reference! In other words, adding a new image to your document always requires both a new entity definition in the DTD and a reference to it in the document. Given the anticipated ubiquity of the HTML 4.0 specification, the newer standard is to use the MIME data types and a declaration such as image, which assumes that the application knows how to process such elements.

Defining Parameter Entities and Conditional Sections

Just as a general entity lets you reuse XML data in multiple places, a parameter entity lets you reuse parts of a DTD in multiple places. In this section you'll see how to define and use parameter entities. You'll also see how to use parameter entities with conditional sections in a DTD.

Creating and Referencing a Parameter Entity

Recall that the existing version of the slide presentation cannot be validated because the document uses <em> tags, and they are not part of the DTD. In general, we'd like to use a variety of HTML-style tags in the text of a slide, and not just one or two, so using an existing DTD for XHTML makes more sense than defining such tags ourselves. A parameter entity is intended for exactly that kind of purpose.

Note: The DTD specifications shown here are contained in slideshow2.dtd and xhtml.dtd. The XML file that references it is slideSample08.xml. (The browsable versions are slideshow2-dtd.html, xhtml-dtd.html, and slideSample08-xml.html.)

Open your DTD file for the slide presentation and add the following highlighted text to define a parameter entity that references an external DTD file:

```
<!ELEMENT slide (image?, title?, item*)>
<!ATTLIST slide
          ...
>

<!ENTITY % xhtml SYSTEM "xhtml.dtd">
%xhtml;

<!ELEMENT title ...
```

Here, you use an `<!ENTITY>` tag to define a parameter entity, just as for a general entity, but you use a somewhat different syntax. You include a percent sign (%) before the entity name when you define the entity, and you use the percent sign instead of an ampersand when you reference it.

Also, note that there are always two steps to using a parameter entity. The first is to define the entity name. The second is to reference the entity name, which actually does the work of including the external definitions in the current DTD. Because the uniform resource identifier (URI) for an external entity could contain slashes (/) or other characters that are not valid in an XML name, the definition step allows a valid XML name to be associated with an actual document. (This same technique is used in the definition of namespaces and anywhere else that XML constructs need to reference external documents.)

Notes:

- The DTD file referenced by this definition is `xhtml.dtd`. (The browsable version is `xhtml-dtd.html`.) You can either copy that file to your system or modify the `SYSTEM` identifier in the `<!ENTITY>` tag to point to the correct URL.
- This file is a small subset of the XHTML specification, loosely modeled after the Modularized XHTML draft, which aims at breaking up the DTD for XHTML into bite-sized chunks, which can then be combined to create different XHTML subsets for different purposes. When work on the modularized XHTML draft has been completed, this version of the DTD should be replaced with something better. For now, this version will suffice for our purposes.

The point of using an XHTML-based DTD is to gain access to an entity it defines that covers HTML-style tags like `<em>` and `<b>`. Looking through `xhtml.dtd` reveals the following entity, which does exactly what we want:

```
<!ENTITY % inline "#PCDATA|em|b|a|img|br">
```

This entity is a simpler version of those defined in the Modularized XHTML draft. It defines the HTML-style tags we are most likely to want to use—emphasis, bold, and break—plus a couple of others for images and anchors that we may or may not use in a slide presentation. To use the `inline` entity, make the following highlighted changes in your DTD file:

```
<!ELEMENT title (#PCDATA %inline;)*>
<!ELEMENT item (#PCDATA %inline; | item)* >
```

These changes replace the simple #PCDATA item with the `inline` entity. It is important to notice that #PCDATA is first in the `inline` entity and that `inline` is first wherever we use it. That sequence is required by XML's definition of a mixed-content model. To be in accord with that model, you also must add an asterisk at the end of the `title` definition.

Save the DTD as `slideshow2.dtd` for use when you experiment with parameter entities.

Note: The Modularized XHTML DTD defines both `inline` and `Inline` entities, and does so somewhat differently. Rather than specify #PCDATA|em|b|a|img|br, the definitions are more like (#PCDATA|em|b|a|img|br)*. Using one of those definitions, therefore, looks more like this:

```
<!ELEMENT title %Inline; >
```

Conditional Sections

Before we proceed with the next programming exercise, it is worth mentioning the use of parameter entities to control *conditional sections*. Although you cannot conditionalize the content of an XML document, you can define conditional sections in a DTD that becomes part of the DTD only if you specify `include`. If you specify `ignore`, on the other hand, then the conditional section is not included.

Suppose, for example, that you wanted to use slightly different versions of a DTD, depending on whether you were treating the document as an XML document or as a SGML document. You can do that with DTD definitions such as the following:

```
someExternal.dtd:
  <![ INCLUDE [
    ... XML-only definitions
  ]]>
  <![ IGNORE [
    ... SGML-only definitions
  ]]>
  ... common definitions
```

The conditional sections are introduced by `<![`, followed by the `INCLUDE` or `IGNORE` keyword and another `[`. After that comes the contents of the conditional section, followed by the terminator: `]]>`. In this case, the XML definitions are included, and the SGML definitions are excluded. That's fine for XML documents, but you can't use the DTD for SGML documents. You could change the keywords, of course, but that only reverses the problem.

The solution is to use references to parameter entities in place of the `INCLUDE` and `IGNORE` keywords:

```
someExternal.dtd:
  <![ %XML; [
    ... XML-only definitions
  ]]>
  <![ %SGML; [
    ... SGML-only definitions
  ]]>
  ... common definitions
```

Then each document that uses the DTD can set up the appropriate entity definitions:

```
<!DOCTYPE foo SYSTEM "someExternal.dtd" [
  <!ENTITY % XML  "INCLUDE" >
  <!ENTITY % SGML "IGNORE" >
]>
<foo>
  ...
</foo>
```

This procedure puts each document in control of the DTD. It also replaces the INCLUDE and IGNORE keywords with variable names that more accurately reflect the purpose of the conditional section, producing a more readable, self-documenting version of the DTD.

Resolving a Naming Conflict

The XML structures you have created thus far have actually encountered a small naming conflict. It seems that xhtml.dtd defines a title element that is entirely different from the title element defined in the slide-show DTD. Because there is no hierarchy in the DTD, these two definitions conflict.

Note: The Modularized XHTML DTD also defines a title element that is intended to be the document title, so we can't avoid the conflict by changing xhtml.dtd. The problem would only come back to haunt us later.

You can use XML namespaces to resolve the conflict. You'll take a look at that approach in the next section. Alternatively, you can use one of the more hierarchical schema proposals described in Schema Standards (page 1348). The simplest way to solve the problem for now is to rename the title element in slideshow.dtd.

Note: The XML shown here is contained in slideshow3.dtd and slideSample09.xml, which references copyright.xml and xhtml.dtd. (The browsable versions are slideshow3-dtd.html, slideSample09-xml.html, copyright-xml.html, and xhtml-dtd.html.)

To keep the two title elements separate, you'll create a *hyphenation hierarchy*. Make the following highlighted changes to change the name of the title element in slideshow.dtd to slide-title:

```
<!ELEMENT slide (image?, slide-title?, item*)>
<!ATTLIST slide
        type   (tech | exec | all) #IMPLIED
>

<!-- Defines the %inline; declaration -->
<!ENTITY % xhtml SYSTEM "xhtml.dtd">
%xhtml;

<!ELEMENT slide-title (%inline;)*>
```

Save this DTD as `slideshow3.dtd`.

The next step is to modify the XML file to use the new element name. To do that, make the following highlighted changes:

```
...
<slide type="all">
<slide-title>Wake up to ... </slide-title>
</slide>

...

<!-- OVERVIEW -->
<slide type="all">
<slide-title>Overview</slide-title>
<item>...
```

Save a copy of this file as `slideSample09.xml`.

Using Namespaces

As you saw earlier, one way or another it is necessary to resolve the conflict between the `title` element defined in `slideshow.dtd` and the one defined in `xhtml.dtd` when the same name is used for different purposes. In the preceding exercise, you hyphenated the name in order to put it into a different namespace. In this section, you'll see how to use the XML namespace standard to do the same thing without renaming the element.

The primary goal of the namespace specification is to let the document author tell the parser which DTD or schema to use when parsing a given element. The parser can then consult the appropriate DTD or schema for an element definition. Of course, it is also important to keep the parser from aborting when a "duplicate" definition is found and yet still generate an error if the document references an element such as `title` without *qualifying* it (identifying the DTD or schema to use for the definition).

Note: Namespaces apply to attributes as well as to elements. In this section, we consider only elements. For more information on attributes, consult the namespace specification at `http://www.w3.org/TR/REC-xml-names/`.

Defining a Namespace in a DTD

In a DTD, you define a namespace that an element belongs to by adding an attribute to the element's definition, where the attribute name is `xmlns` ("xml namespace"). For example, you can do that in `slideshow.dtd` by adding an entry such as the following in the `title` element's attribute-list definition:

```
<!ELEMENT title (%inline;)*>
<!ATTLIST title
   xmlns CDATA #FIXED "http://www.example.com/slideshow"
>
```

Declaring the attribute as `FIXED` has several important features:

- It prevents the document from specifying any nonmatching value for the `xmlns` attribute.

- The element defined in this DTD is made unique (because the parser understands the `xmlns` attribute), so it does not conflict with an element that has the same name in another DTD. That allows multiple DTDs to use the same element name without generating a parser error.

- When a document specifies the `xmlns` attribute for a tag, the document selects the element definition that has a matching attribute.

To be thorough, every element name in your DTD would get exactly the same attribute, with the same value. (Here, though, we're concerned only about the `title` element.) Note, too, that you are using a CDATA string to supply the URI. In this case, we've specified a URL. But you could also specify a universal resource name (URN), possibly by specifying a prefix such as `urn:` instead of `http:`. (URNs are currently being researched. They're not seeing a lot of action at the moment, but that could change in the future.)

Referencing a Namespace

When a document uses an element name that exists in only one of the DTDs or schemas it references, the name does not need to be qualified. But when an element name that has multiple definitions is used, some sort of qualification is a necessity.

Note: In fact, an element name is always qualified by its *default namespace*, as defined by the name of the DTD file it resides in. As long as there is only one definition for the name, the qualification is implicit.

You qualify a reference to an element name by specifying the `xmlns` attribute, as shown here:

```
<title xmlns="http://www.example.com/slideshow">
  Overview
</title>
```

The specified namespace applies to that element and to any elements contained within it.

Defining a Namespace Prefix

When you need only one namespace reference, it's not a big deal. But when you need to make the same reference several times, adding `xmlns` attributes becomes unwieldy. It also makes it harder to change the name of the namespace later.

The alternative is to define a *namespace prefix*, which is as simple as specifying `xmlns`, a colon (:), and the prefix name before the attribute value:

```
<SL:slideshow xmlns:SL='http:/www.example.com/slideshow'
  ...>
  ...
</SL:slideshow>
```

This definition sets up `SL` as a prefix that can be used to qualify the current element name and any element within it. Because the prefix can be used on any of the contained elements, it makes the most sense to define it on the XML document's root element, as shown here.

Note: The namespace URI can contain characters that are not valid in an XML name, so it cannot be used directly as a prefix. The prefix definition associates an XML name with the URI, and that allows the prefix name to be used instead. It also makes it easier to change references to the URI in the future.

When the prefix is used to qualify an element name, the end tag also includes the prefix, as highlighted here:

```
<SL:slideshow xmlns:SL='http:/www.example.com/slideshow'
   ...>
  ...
  <slide>
```

```
    <SL:title>Overview</SL:title>
    </slide>
    ...
</SL:slideshow>
```

Finally, note that multiple prefixes can be defined in the same element:

```
<SL:slideshow xmlns:SL='http:/www.example.com/slideshow'
    xmlns:xhtml='urn:...'>
    ...
</SL:slideshow>
```

With this kind of arrangement, all the prefix definitions are together in one place, and you can use them anywhere they are needed in the document. This example also suggests the use of a URN instead of a URL to define the xhtml prefix. That definition would conceivably allow the application to reference a local copy of the XHTML DTD or some mirrored version, with a potentially beneficial impact on performance.

Designing an XML Data Structure

This section covers some heuristics you can use when making XML design decisions.

Saving Yourself Some Work

Whenever possible, use an existing schema definition. It's usually a lot easier to ignore the things you don't need than to design your own from scratch. In addition, using a standard DTD makes data interchange possible, and may make it possible to use data-aware tools developed by others.

So if an industry standard exists, consider referencing that DTD by using an external parameter entity. One place to look for industry-standard DTDs is at the Web site created by the Organization for the Advancement of Structured Information Standards (OASIS). You can find a list of technical committees at http://www.oasis-open.org/ or check its repository of XML standards at http://www.XML.org.

Note: Many more good thoughts on the design of XML structures are at the OASIS page http://www.oasis-open.org/cover/elementsAndAttrs.html.

Attributes and Elements

One of the issues you will encounter frequently when designing an XML structure is whether to model a given data item as a subelement or as an attribute of an existing element. For example, you can model the title of a slide this way:

```
<slide>
  <title>This is the title</title>
</slide>
```

Or you can do it this way:

```
<slide title="This is the title">...</slide>
```

In some cases, the different characteristics of attributes and elements make it easy to choose. Let's consider those cases first and then move on to the cases where the choice is more ambiguous.

Forced Choices

Sometimes, the choice between an attribute and an element is forced on you by the nature of attributes and elements. Let's look at a few of those considerations:

- **The data contains substructures:** In this case, the data item must be modeled as an *element*. It can't be modeled as an attribute, because attributes take only simple strings. So if the title can contain emphasized text (The `<em>Best</em> Choice`) then the title must be an element.

- **The data contains multiple lines:** Here, it also makes sense to use an *element*. Attributes need to be simple, short strings or else they become unreadable, if not unusable.

- **Multiple occurrences are possible:** Whenever an item can occur multiple times, such as paragraphs in an article, it must be modeled as an *element*. The element that contains it can have only one attribute of a particular kind, but it can have many subelements of the same type.

- **The data changes frequently:** When the data will be frequently modified with an editor, it may make sense to model it as an *element*. Many XML-aware editors make it easy to modify element data, whereas attributes can be somewhat harder to get to.

- **The data is a small, simple string that rarely if ever changes:** This is data that can be modeled as an *attribute*. However, just because you *can* does not mean that you should. Check the Stylistic Choices section next, to be sure.

- **The data is confined to a small number of fixed choices:** If you are using a DTD, it really makes sense to use an *attribute*. A DTD can prevent an attribute from taking on any value that is not in the preapproved list, but it cannot similarly restrict an element. (With a schema, on the other hand, both attributes and elements can be restricted, so you could use either element or an attribute.)

Stylistic Choices

As often as not, the choices are not as cut-and-dried as those just shown. When the choice is not forced, you need a sense of "style" to guide your thinking. The question to answer, then, is what makes good XML style, and why.

Defining a sense of style for XML is, unfortunately, as nebulous a business as defining style when it comes to art or music. There are, however, a few ways to approach it. The goal of this section is to give you some useful thoughts on the subject of XML style.

One heuristic for thinking about XML elements and attributes uses the concept of *visibility*. If the data is intended to be shown—to be displayed to an end user—then it should be modeled as an element. On the other hand, if the information guides XML processing but is never seen by a user, then it may be better to model it as an attribute. For example, in order-entry data for shoes, shoe size would definitely be an element. On the other hand, a manufacturer's code number would be reasonably modeled as an attribute.

Another way of thinking about the visibility heuristic is to ask, who is the consumer and the provider of the information? The shoe size is entered by a human sales clerk, so it's an element. The manufacturer's code number for a given shoe model, on the other hand, may be wired into the application or stored in a database, so that would be an attribute. (If it were entered by the clerk, though, it should perhaps be an element.)

Perhaps the best way of thinking about elements and attributes is to think of an element as a *container*. To reason by analogy, the *contents* of the container (water or milk) correspond to XML data modeled as elements. Such data is essentially variable. On the other hand, the *characteristics* of the container (whether a blue or a white pitcher) can be modeled as attributes. That kind of information tends to be more immutable. Good XML style separates each container's contents from its characteristics in a consistent way.

To show these heuristics at work, in our slide-show example the `type` of the slide (executive or technical) is best modeled as an attribute. It is a characteristic of the slide that lets it be selected or rejected for a particular audience. The `title` of the slide, on the other hand, is part of its contents. The visibility heuristic is also satisfied here. When the slide is displayed, the `title` is shown but the `type` of the slide isn't. Finally, in this example, the consumer of the `title` information is the presentation audience, whereas the consumer of the `type` information is the presentation program.

Normalizing Data

In Saving Yourself Some Work (page 74), you saw that it is a good idea to define an external entity that you can reference in an XML document. Such an entity has all the advantages of a modularized routine: changing that one copy affects every document that references it. The process of eliminating redundancies is known as *normalizing*, and defining entities is one good way to normalize your data.

In an HTML file, the only way to achieve that kind of modularity is to use HTML links, but then the document is fragmented rather than whole. XML entities, on the other hand, suffer no such fragmentation. The entity reference acts like a macro: the entity's contents are expanded in place, producing a whole document rather than a fragmented one. And when the entity is defined in an external file, multiple documents can reference it.

The considerations for defining an entity reference, then, are pretty much the same as those you would apply to modularized program code:

- Whenever you find yourself writing the same thing more than once, think entity. That lets you write it in one place and reference it in multiple places.
- If the information is likely to change, especially if it is used in more than one place, definitely think in terms of defining an entity. An example is defining `productName` as an entity so that you can easily change the documents when the product name changes.
- If the entity will never be referenced anywhere except in the current file, define it in the local subset of the document's DTD, much as you would define a method or inner class in a program.
- If the entity will be referenced from multiple documents, define it as an external entity, in the same way that you would define any generally usable class as an external class.

External entities produce modular XML that is smaller, easier to update, and easier to maintain. They can also make the resulting document somewhat more difficult to visualize, much as a good object-oriented design can be easy to change, after you understand it, but harder to wrap your head around at first.

You can also go overboard with entities. At an extreme, you could make an entity reference for the word *the*. It wouldn't buy you much, but you could do it.

Note: The larger an entity is, the more likely it is that changing it will have the expected effect. For example, when you define an external entity that covers a whole section of a document, such as installation instructions, then any changes you make will likely work out fine wherever that section is used. But small inline substitutions can be more problematic. For example, if `productName` is defined as an entity and if the name changes to a different part of speech, the results can be unfortunate. Suppose the product name is something like HtmlEdit. That's a verb. So you write a sentence like, "You can HtmlEdit your file...", using the `productName` entity. That sentence works, because a verb fits in that context. But if the name is eventually changed to "HtmlEditor", the sentence becomes "You can HtmlEditor your file...", which clearly doesn't work. Still, even if such simple substitutions can sometimes get you into trouble, they also have the potential to save a lot of time. (One way to avoid the problem would be to set up entities named `productNoun`, `productVerb`, `productAdj`, and `productAdverb`.)

Normalizing DTDs

Just as you can normalize your XML document, you can also normalize your DTD declarations by factoring out common pieces and referencing them with a parameter entity. Factoring out the DTDs (also known as *modularizing*) gives the same advantages and disadvantages as normalized XML—easier to change, somewhat more difficult to follow.

You can also set up conditionalized DTDs. If the number and size of the conditional sections are small relative to the size of the DTD as a whole, conditionalizing can let you single-source the same DTD for multiple purposes. If the number of conditional sections gets large, though, the result can be a complex document that is difficult to edit.

Summary

Congratulations! You have now created a number of XML files that you can use for testing purposes. Table 2–5 describes the files you have constructed.

Table 2–5 Listing of Sample XML Files

File	Contents
slideSample01.xml	A basic file containing a few elements and attributes as well as comments.
slideSample02.xml	Includes a processing instruction.
SlideSampleBad1.xml	A file that is *not* well formed.
slideSample03.xml	Includes a simple entity reference (<).
slideSample04.xml	Contains a CDATA section.
slideSample05.xml	References either a simple external DTD for elements (slideshow1a.dtd) for use with a nonvalidating parser, or else a DTD that defines attributes (slideshow1b.dtd) for use with a validating parser.
slideSample06.xml	Defines two entities locally (product and products) and references slideshow1b.dtd.
slideSample07.xml	References an external entity defined locally (copy-right.xml) and references slideshow1b.dtd.
slideSample08.xml	References xhtml.dtd using a parameter entity in slideshow2.dtd, producing a naming conflict because title is declared in both.
slideSample09.xml	Changes the title element to slide-title so that it can reference xhtml.dtd using a parameter entity in slideshow3.dtd without conflict.

3

Getting Started with Web Applications

A Web application is a dynamic extension of a Web or application server. There are two types of Web applications:

- *Presentation-oriented*: A presentation-oriented Web application generates interactive Web pages containing various types of markup language (HTML, XML, and so on) and dynamic content in response to requests. Chapters 11 through 22 cover how to develop presentation-oriented Web applications.

- *Service-oriented*: A service-oriented Web application implements the endpoint of a Web service. Presentation-oriented applications are often clients of service-oriented Web applications. Chapters 8 and 9 cover how to develop service-oriented Web applications.

In the Java 2 platform, *Web components* provide the dynamic extension capabilities for a Web server. Web components are either Java servlets, JSP pages, or Web service endpoints. The interaction between a Web client and a Web application is illustrated in Figure 3–1. The client sends an HTTP request to the Web server. A Web server that implements Java Servlet and JavaServer Pages technology converts the request into an `HTTPServletRequest` object. This object is delivered to a Web component, which can interact with JavaBeans components

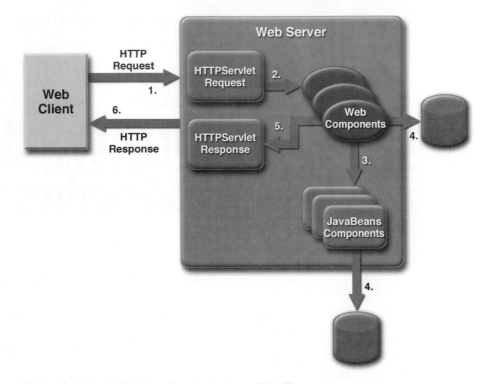

Figure 3–1   Java Web Application Request Handling

or a database to generate dynamic content. The Web component can then generate an HTTPServletResponse or it can pass the request to another Web component. Eventually a Web component generates a HTTPServletResponse object. The Web server converts this object to an HTTP response and returns it to the client.

Servlets are Java programming language classes that dynamically process requests and construct responses. *JSP pages* are text-based documents that execute as servlets but allow a more natural approach to creating static content. Although servlets and JSP pages can be used interchangeably, each has its own strengths. Servlets are best suited for service-oriented applications (Web service endpoints are implemented as servlets) and the control functions of a presentation-oriented application, such as dispatching requests and handling nontextual data. JSP pages are more appropriate for generating text-based markup such as HTML, Scalable Vector Graphics (SVG), Wireless Markup Language (WML), and XML.

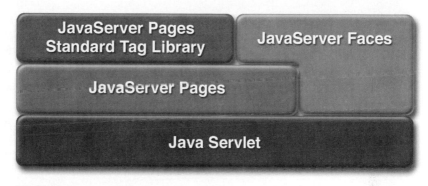

Figure 3–2 Java Web Application Technologies

Since the introduction of Java Servlet and JSP technology, additional Java technologies and frameworks for building interactive Web applications have been developed. These technologies and their relationships are illustrated in Figure 3–2.

Notice that Java Servlet technology is the foundation of all the Web application technologies, so you should familiarize yourself with the material in Chapter 11 even if you do not intend to write servlets. Each technology adds a level of abstraction that makes Web application prototyping and development faster and the Web applications themselves more maintainable, scalable, and robust.

Web components are supported by the services of a runtime platform called a *Web container*. A Web container provides services such as request dispatching, security, concurrency, and life-cycle management. It also gives Web components access to APIs such as naming, transactions, and email.

Certain aspects of Web application behavior can be configured when the application is installed, or *deployed*, to the Web container. The configuration information is maintained in a text file in XML format called a *Web application deployment descriptor* (DD). A DD must conform to the schema described in the Java Servlet Specification.

Most Web applications use the HTTP protocol, and support for HTTP is a major aspect of Web components. For a brief summary of HTTP protocol features see Appendix C.

This chapter gives a brief overview of the activities involved in developing Web applications. First we summarize the Web application life cycle. Then we describe how to package and deploy very simple Web applications on the Sun Java System Application Server Platform Edition 8. We move on to configuring

Web applications and discuss how to specify the most commonly used configuration parameters. We then introduce an example—Duke's Bookstore—that we use to illustrate all the J2EE Web-tier technologies and we describe how to set up the shared components of this example. Finally we discuss how to access databases from Web applications and set up the database resources needed to run Duke's Bookstore.

Web Application Life Cycle

A Web application consists of Web components, static resource files such as images, and helper classes and libraries. The Web container provides many supporting services that enhance the capabilities of Web components and make them easier to develop. However, because a Web application must take these services into account, the process for creating and running a Web application is different from that of traditional stand-alone Java classes. The process for creating, deploying, and executing a Web application can be summarized as follows:

1. Develop the Web component code.
2. Develop the Web application deployment descriptor.
3. Compile the Web application components and helper classes referenced by the components.
4. Optionally package the application into a deployable unit.
5. Deploy the application into a Web container.
6. Access a URL that references the Web application.

Developing Web component code is covered in the later chapters. Steps 2 through 4 are expanded on in the following sections and illustrated with a Hello, World-style presentation-oriented application. This application allows a user to enter a name into an HTML form (Figure 3–3) and then displays a greeting after the name is submitted (Figure 3–4).

The Hello application contains two Web components that generate the greeting and the response. This chapter discusses two versions of the application: a JSP version called `hello1`, in which the components are implemented by two JSP pages (`index.jsp` and `response.jsp`) and a servlet version called `hello2`, in which the components are implemented by two servlet classes (`GreetingServlet.java` and `ResponseServlet.java`). The two versions are used to illustrate

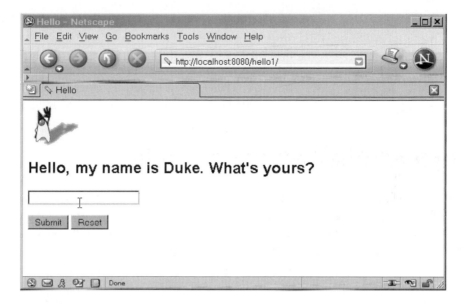

Figure 3–3   Greeting Form

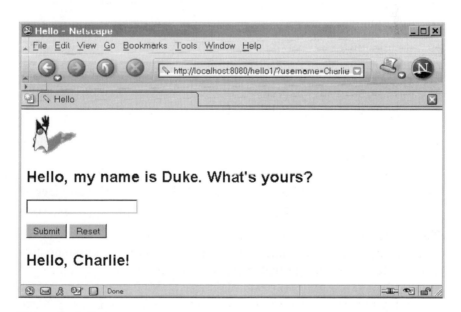

Figure 3–4   Response

tasks involved in packaging, deploying, configuring, and running an application that contains Web components. The section About the Examples (page xl) explains how to get the code for these examples. After you install the tutorial bundle, the source code for the examples is in `<INSTALL>`/j2eetutorial14/examples/web/hello1/ and `<INSTALL>`/j2eetutorial14/examples/web/hello2/.

Web Modules

In the J2EE architecture, Web components and static Web content files such as images are called *Web resources*. A *Web module* is the smallest deployable and usable unit of Web resources. A J2EE Web module corresponds to a *Web application* as defined in the Java Servlet Specification.

In addition to Web components and Web resources, a Web module can contain other files:

- Server-side utility classes (database beans, shopping carts, and so on). Often these classes conform to the JavaBeans component architecture.
- Client-side classes (applets and utility classes).

A Web module has a specific structure. The top-level directory of a Web module is the *document root* of the application. The document root is where JSP pages, *client-side* classes and archives, and static Web resources, such as images, are stored.

The document root contains a subdirectory named /WEB-INF/, which contains the following files and directories:

- web.xml: The Web application deployment descriptor
- Tag library descriptor files (see Tag Library Descriptors, page 589)
- classes: A directory that contains *server-side classes*: servlets, utility classes, and JavaBeans components
- tags: A directory that contains tag files, which are implementations of tag libraries (see Tag File Location, page 576)
- lib: A directory that contains JAR archives of libraries called by server-side classes

You can also create application-specific subdirectories (that is, package directories) in either the document root or the /WEB-INF/classes/ directory.

A Web module can be deployed as an unpacked file structure or can be packaged in a JAR file known as a Web archive (WAR) file. Because the contents and use of WAR files differ from those of JAR files, WAR file names use a .war extension. The Web module just described is portable; you can deploy it into any Web container that conforms to the Java Servlet specification.

To deploy a WAR on the Application Server, the file must also contain a runtime deployment descriptor. The runtime deployment descriptor is an XML file that contains information such as the context root of the Web application and the mapping of the portable names of an application's resources to the Application Server's resources. The Application Server Web application runtime DD is named sun-web.xml and is located in /WEB-INF/ along with the Web application DD. The structure of a Web module that can be deployed on the Application Server is shown in Figure 3–5.

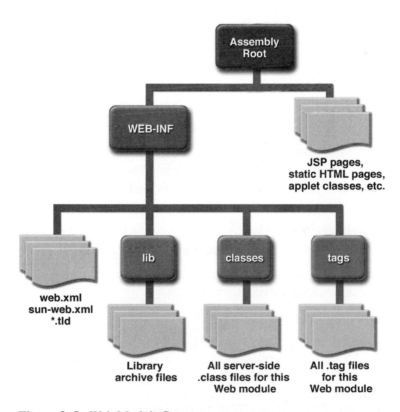

Figure 3–5 Web Module Structure

Packaging Web Modules

A Web module must be packaged into a WAR in certain deployment scenarios and whenever you want to distribute the Web module. You package a Web module into a WAR using the Application Server `deploytool` utility, by executing the `jar` command in a directory laid out in the format of a Web module, or by using the `asant war` task. This tutorial uses the first approach. To build and package the `hello1` application into a WAR named `hello1.war`, follow these steps:

1. In a terminal window, go to *<INSTALL>*/j2eetutorial14/examples/ web/hello1/.

2. Run `asant build`. This target will spawn any necessary compilations and will copy files to the *<INSTALL>*/j2eetutorial14/examples/web/ hello1/build/ directory.

3. Start `deploytool`.

4. Create a Web application called `hello1` by running the New Web Component wizard. Select File→New→Web Component.

5. In the New Web Component wizard:

   a. Select the Create New Stand-Alone WAR Module radio button.

   b. In the WAR Location field, enter *<INSTALL>*/j2eetutorial14/examples/web/hello1/hello1.war.

   c. In the WAR Name field, enter `hello1`.

   d. Click Edit Contents to add the content files.

   e. In the Edit Contents dialog box, navigate to *<INSTALL>*/ j2eetutorial14/examples/web/hello1/build/. Select duke.waving.gif, index.jsp, and response.jsp and click Add. Click OK.

   f. Click Next.

   g. Select the No Component radio button.

   h. Click Next.

   i. Click Finish.

6. Select File→Save.

A sample `hello1.war` is provided in *<INSTALL>*/j2eetutorial14/examples/ web/provided-wars/. To open this WAR with `deploytool`, follow these steps:

1. Select File→Open.

2. Navigate to the provided-wars directory.

3. Select the WAR.

4. Click Open Module.

Deploying Web Modules

You can deploy a Web module to the Application Server in several ways:

- By pointing the Application Server at an unpackaged Web module directory structure using `asadmin` or the Admin Console.
- By packaging the Web module and
  - Copying the WAR into the `<J2EE_HOME>`/domains/domain1/autodeploy/ directory.
  - Using the Admin Console, `asadmin`, or `deploytool` to deploy the WAR.

All these methods are described briefly in this chapter; however, throughout the tutorial, we use `deploytool` for packaging and deploying.

Setting the Context Root

A *context root* identifies a Web application in a J2EE server. You specify the context root when you deploy a Web module. A context root must start with a forward slash (/) and end with a string.

In a packaged Web module for deployment on the Application Server, the context root is stored in `sun-web.xml`. If you package the Web application with `deploytool`, then `sun-web.xml` is created automatically.

Deploying an Unpackaged Web Module

It is possible to deploy a Web module without packaging it into a WAR. The advantage of this approach is that you do not need to rebuild the package every time you update a file contained in the Web module. In addition, the Application Server automatically detects updates to JSP pages, so you don't even have to redeploy the Web module when they change.

However, to deploy an unpackaged Web module, you must create the Web module directory structure and provide the Web application deployment descriptor `web.xml`. Because this tutorial uses `deploytool` for generating deployment descriptors, it does not document how to develop descriptors from scratch. You can view the structure of deployment descriptors in two ways:

- In `deploytool`, select Tools→Descriptor Viewer→Descriptor Viewer to view `web.xml` and Tools→Descriptor Viewer→Application Server Descriptor to view `sun-web.xml`.
- Unpackage one of the WARs in `<INSTALL>`/j2eetutorial14/examples/web/provided-wars/ and extract the descriptors.

Since you explicitly specify the context root when you deploy an unpackaged Web module, usually it is not necessary to provide `sun-web.xml`.

Deploying with the Admin Console

1. Expand the Applications node.
2. Select the Web Applications node.
3. Click the Deploy button.
4. Select the No radio button next to Upload File.
5. Type the full path to the Web module directory in the File or Directory field. Although the GUI gives you the choice to browse to the directory, this option applies only to deploying a packaged WAR.
6. Click Next.
7. Type the application name.
8. Type the context root.
9. Select the Enabled box.
10. Click the OK button.

Deploying with asadmin

To deploy an unpackaged Web module with `asadmin`, open a terminal window or command prompt and execute

```
asadmin deploydir full-path-to-web-module-directory
```

The `build` task for the `hello1` application creates a `build` directory (including `web.xml`) in the structure of a Web module. To deploy `hello1` using `asadmin deploydir`, execute:

```
asadmin deploydir --contextroot /hello1
    <INSTALL>/j2eetutorial14/examples/web/hello1/build
```

After you deploy the `hello1` application, you can run the Web application by pointing a browser at

```
http://localhost:8080/hello1
```

You should see the greeting form depicted earlier in Figure 3–3.

A Web module is executed when a Web browser references a URL that contains the Web module's context root. Because no Web component appears in `http://localhost:8080/hello1/`, the Web container executes the default component, `index.jsp`. The section Mapping URLs to Web Components (page 96) describes how to specify Web components in a URL.

Deploying a Packaged Web Module

If you have deployed the `hello1` application, before proceeding with this section, undeploy the application by following one of the procedures described in Undeploying Web Modules (page 95).

Deploying with deploytool

To deploy the `hello1` Web module with `deploytool`:

1. Select the `hello1` WAR you created in Packaging Web Modules (page 88).
2. Select the General tab.
3. Type `/hello1` in the Context Root field.
4. Select File→Save.
5. Select Tools→Deploy.
6. Click OK.

You can use one of the following methods to deploy the WAR you packaged with `deploytool`, or one of the WARs contained in *<INSTALL>*/`j2eetutorial14/examples/web/provided-wars/`.

Deploying with the Admin Console

1. Expand the Applications node.
2. Select the Web Applications node.
3. Click the Deploy button.
4. Select the No radio button next to Upload File.

5. Type the full path to the WAR file (or click on Browse to find it), and then click the OK button.

6. Click Next.

7. Type the application name.

8. Type the context root.

9. Select the Enabled box.

10. Click the OK button.

Deploying with asadmin

To deploy a WAR with `asadmin`, open a terminal window or command prompt and execute

```
asadmin deploy full-path-to-war-file
```

Listing Deployed Web Modules

The Application Server provides three ways to view the deployed Web modules:

- `deploytool`
  a. Select localhost:4848 from the Servers list.
  b. View the Deployed Objects list in the General tab.

- Admin Console
  a. Open the URL `http://localhost:4848/asadmin` in a browser.
  b. Expand the nodes Applications→Web Applications.

- `asadmin`
  a. Execute

     ```
     asadmin list-components
     ```

Updating Web Modules

A typical iterative development cycle involves deploying a Web module and then making changes to the application components. To update a deployed Web module, you must do the following:

1. Recompile any modified classes.

2. If you have deployed a packaged Web module, update any modified components in the WAR.

3. Redeploy the module.

4. Reload the URL in the client.

Updating an Unpackaged Web Module

To update an unpackaged Web module using either of the methods discussed in Deploying an Unpackaged Web Module (page 89), reexecute the `deploydir` operation. If you have changed only JSP pages in the Web module directory, you do not have to redeploy; simply reload the URL in the client.

Updating a Packaged Web Module

This section describes how to update the `hello1` Web module that you packaged with `deploytool`.

First, change the greeting in the file `<INSTALL>/j2eetutorial14/examples/web/hello1/web/index.jsp` to

```
<h2>Hi, my name is Duke. What's yours?</h2>
```

Run `asant build` to copy the modified JSP page into the build directory. To update the Web module using `deploytool` follow these steps:

1. Select the `hello1` WAR.
2. Select Tools→Update Module Files. A popup dialog box will display the modified file. Click OK.
3. Select Tools→Deploy. A popup dialog box will query whether you want to redeploy. Click Yes.
4. Click OK.

To view the modified module, reload the URL in the browser.

You should see the screen in Figure 3–6 in the browser.

Dynamic Reloading

If dynamic reloading is enabled, you do not have to redeploy an application or module when you change its code or deployment descriptors. All you have to do is copy the changed JSP or class files into the deployment directory for the application or module. The deployment directory for a Web module named `context_root` is `<J2EE_HOME>/domains/domain1/applications/j2ee-modules/context_root`. The server checks for changes periodically and redeploys the application, automatically and dynamically, with the changes.

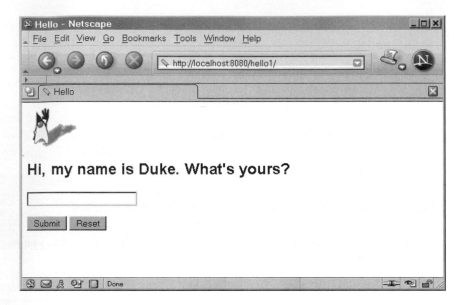

Figure 3–6   New Greeting

This capability is useful in a development environment, because it allows code changes to be tested quickly. Dynamic reloading is not recommended for a production environment, however, because it may degrade performance. In addition, whenever a reload is done, the sessions at that time become invalid and the client must restart the session.

To enable dynamic reloading, use the Admin Console:

1. Select the Applications node.
2. Check the Reload Enabled box to enable dynamic reloading.
3. Enter a number of seconds in the Reload Poll Interval field to set the interval at which applications and modules are checked for code changes and dynamically reloaded.
4. Click the Save button.

In addition, to load new servlet files or reload deployment descriptor changes, you must do the following:

1. Create an empty file named `.reload` at the root of the module:

   ```
   <J2EE_HOME>/domains/domain1/applications/j2ee-modules/
   context_root/.reload
   ```

2. Explicitly update the `.reload` file's time stamp each time you make these changes. On UNIX, execute

```
touch .reload
```

For JSP pages, changes are reloaded automatically at a frequency set in the Reload Pool Interval. To disable dynamic reloading of JSP pages, set the reload-interval property to –1.

Undeploying Web Modules

You can undeploy Web modules in three ways:

- `deploytool`
  a. Select localhost:4848 from the Servers list.
  b. Select the Web module in the Deployed Objects list of the General tab.
  c. Click the Undeploy button.

- Admin Console
  a. Open the URL `http://localhost:4848/asadmin` in a browser.
  b. Expand the Applications node.
  c. Select Web Applications.
  d. Click the checkbox next to the module you wish to undeploy.
  e. Click the Undeploy button.

- `asadmin`
  a. Execute
     ```
     asadmin undeploy context_root
     ```

Configuring Web Applications

Web applications are configured via elements contained in the Web application deployment descriptor. The `deploytool` utility generates the descriptor when you create a WAR and adds elements when you create Web components and associated classes. You can modify the elements via the inspectors associated with the WAR.

The following sections give a brief introduction to the Web application features you will usually want to configure. A number of security parameters can be specified; these are covered in Web-Tier Security (page 1092).

In the following sections, examples demonstrate procedures for configuring the Hello, World application. If Hello, World does not use a specific configuration feature, the section gives references to other examples that illustrate how to specify the deployment descriptor element and describes generic procedures for specifying the feature using deploytool. Extended examples that demonstrate how to use deploytool appear in later tutorial chapters.

Mapping URLs to Web Components

When a request is received by the Web container it must determine which Web component should handle the request. It does so by mapping the URL path contained in the request to a Web application and a Web component. A URL path contains the context root and an alias:

```
http://host:port/context_root/alias
```

Setting the Component Alias

The *alias* identifies the Web component that should handle a request. The alias path must start with a forward slash (/) and end with a string or a wildcard expression with an extension (for example, *.jsp). Since Web containers automatically map an alias that ends with *.jsp, you do not have to specify an alias for a JSP page unless you wish to refer to the page by a name other than its file name. To set up the mappings for the servlet version of the hello application with deploytool, first package it:

1. In a terminal window, go to *<INSTALL>*/j2eetutorial14/examples/web/hello2/.
2. Run asant build. This target will compile the servlets to the *<INSTALL>*/j2eetutorial14/examples/web/hello2/build/ directory.
3. Start deploytool.
4. Create a Web application called hello2 by running the New Web Component wizard. Select File→New→Web Component.
5. In the New Web Component wizard:
    a. Select the Create New Stand-Alone WAR Module radio button.
    b. In the WAR Location field, enter *<INSTALL>*/j2eetutorial14/examples/web/hello2/hello2.war.
    c. In the WAR Name field, enter hello2.
    d. In the Context Root field, enter /hello2.
    e. Click Edit Contents to add the content files.

f. In the Edit Contents dialog box, navigate to *<INSTALL>*/
   j2eetutorial14/examples/web/hello2/build/. Select duke.wav-
   ing.gif and the servlets package and click Add. Click OK.

g. Click Next

h. Select the Servlet radio button.

i. Click Next.

j. Select GreetingServlet from the Servlet Class combo box.

k. Click Finish.

6. Select File→New→Web Component.

a. Click the Add to Existing WAR Module radio button and select hello2
   from the combo box. Because the WAR contains all the servlet classes,
   you do not have to add any more content.

b. Click Next.

c. Select the Servlet radio button.

d. Click Next.

e. Select ResponseServlet from the Servlet Class combo box.

f. Click Finish.

Then, to set the aliases, follow these steps:

1. Select the GreetingServlet Web component.

2. Select the Aliases tab.

3. Click Add to add a new mapping.

4. Type /greeting in the aliases list.

5. Select the ResponseServlet Web component.

6. Click Add.

7. Type /response in the aliases list.

8. Select File→Save.

To run the application, first deploy the Web module, and then open the URL
http://localhost:8000/hello2/greeting in a browser.

Declaring Welcome Files

The *welcome files* mechanism allows you to specify a list of files that the Web
container will use for appending to a request for a URL (called a *valid partial
request*) that is not mapped to a Web component.

For example, suppose you define a welcome file `welcome.html`. When a client requests a URL such as *host:port/webapp/directory*, where *directory* is not mapped to a servlet or JSP page, the file *host:port/webapp/directory/*`welcome.html` is returned to the client.

If a Web container receives a valid partial request, the Web container examines the welcome file list and appends to the partial request each welcome file in the order specified and checks whether a static resource or servlet in the WAR is mapped to that request URL. The Web container then sends the request to the first resource in the WAR that matches.

If no welcome file is specified, the Application Server will use a file named `index.`*XXX*, where *XXX* can be `html` or `jsp`, as the default welcome file. If there is no welcome file and no file named `index.`*XXX*, the Application Server returns a directory listing.

To specify welcome files with `deploytool`, follow these steps:

1. Select the WAR.
2. Select the File Ref's tab in the WAR inspector.
3. Click Add File in the Welcome Files pane.
4. Select the welcome file from the drop-down list.

The example discussed in Encapsulating Reusable Content Using Tag Files (page 573) has a welcome file.

Setting Initialization Parameters

The Web components in a Web module share an object that represents their application context (see Accessing the Web Context, page 463). You can pass initialization parameters to the context or to a Web component.

To add a context parameter with `deploytool`, follow these steps:

1. Select the WAR.
2. Select the Context tab in the WAR inspector.
3. Click Add.

For a sample context parameter, see the example discussed in The Example JSP Pages (page 476).

To add a Web component initialization parameter with `deploytool`, follow these steps:

1. Select the Web component.
2. Select the Init. Parameters tab in the Web component inspector.
3. Click Add.

Mapping Errors to Error Screens

When an error occurs during execution of a Web application, you can have the application display a specific error screen according to the type of error. In particular, you can specify a mapping between the status code returned in an HTTP response or a Java programming language exception returned by any Web component (see Handling Errors, page 443) and any type of error screen. To set up error mappings with `deploytool`:

1. Select the WAR.
2. Select the File Ref's tab in the WAR inspector.
3. Click Add Error in the Error Mapping pane.
4. Enter the HTTP status code (see HTTP Responses, page 1356) or the fully qualified class name of an exception in the Error/Exception field.
5. Enter the name of a Web resource to be invoked when the status code or exception is returned. The name should have a leading forward slash (/).

Note: You can also define error screens for a JSP page contained in a WAR. If error screens are defined for both the WAR and a JSP page, the JSP page's error page takes precedence. See Handling Errors (page 485).

For a sample error page mapping, see the example discussed in The Example Servlets (page 436).

Declaring Resource References

If your Web component uses objects such as databases and enterprise beans, you must declare the references in the Web application deployment descriptor. For a sample resource reference, see Specifying a Web Application's Resource Reference (page 103). For a sample enterprise bean reference, see Specifying the Web Client's Enterprise Bean Reference (page 866).

Duke's Bookstore Examples

In Chapters 11 through 22 a common example—Duke's Bookstore—is used to illustrate the elements of Java Servlet technology, JavaServer Pages technology, the JSP Standard Tag Library, and JavaServer Faces technology. The example emulates a simple online shopping application. It provides a book catalog from which users can select books and add them to a shopping cart. Users can view and modify the shopping cart. When users are finished shopping, they can purchase the books in the cart.

The Duke's Bookstore examples share common classes and a database schema. These files are located in the directory `<INSTALL>/j2eetutorial14/examples/web/bookstore/`. The common classes are packaged into a JAR. To create the bookstore library JAR, follow these steps:

1. In a terminal window, go to `<INSTALL>/j2eetutorial14/examples/web/bookstore/`.
2. Run `asant build` to compile the bookstore files.
3. Run `asant package-bookstore` to create a library named `bookstore.jar` in `<INSTALL>/j2eetutorial14/examples/bookstore/dist/`.

The next section describes how to create the bookstore database tables and resources required to run the examples.

Accessing Databases from Web Applications

Data that is shared between Web components and is persistent between invocations of a Web application is usually maintained in a database. Web applications use the JDBC API to access relational databases. For information on this API, see

```
http://java.sun.com/docs/books/tutorial/jdbc
```

source that it represents. These properties include information such as the location of the database server, the name of the database, the network protocol to use to communicate with the server, and so on.

Web applications access a data source using a connection, and a DataSource object can be thought of as a factory for connections to the particular data source that the DataSource instance represents. In a basic DataSource implementation, a call to the getConnection method returns a connection object that is a physical connection to the data source. In the Application Server, a data source is referred to as a JDBC resource. See DataSource Objects and Connection Pools (page 1077) for further information about data sources in the Application Server.

If a DataSource object is registered with a JNDI naming service, an application can use the JNDI API to access that DataSource object, which can then be used to connect to the data source it represents.

To maintain the catalog of books, the Duke's Bookstore examples described in Chapters 11 through 22 use the PointBase evaluation database included with the Application Server. See the PointBase support site at

```
http://docs.sun.com/db/ApplicationServer8_04qZ
```

for detailed information about the PointBase database.

This section describes how to

- Populate the database with bookstore data
- Create a data source in the Application Server
- Specify a Web application's resource reference
- Map the resource reference to the data source defined in the Application Server

Populating the Example Database

To populate the database for the Duke's Bookstore examples, follow these steps:

1. Start the PointBase database server. For instructions, see Starting and Stopping the PointBase Database Server (page 28).
2. In a terminal window, go to `<INSTALL>/j2eetutorial14/examples/web/bookstore/`.

3. Run `asant create-db_common`. This task runs a PointBase commander tool command to read the file `books.sql` and execute the SQL commands contained in the file. The table named `books` is created for the user `pbpublic` in the `sun-appserv-samples` PointBase database.

4. At the end of the processing, you should see the following output:

```
...
[java] SQL> INSERT INTO books VALUES('207', 'Thrilled', 'Ben',
[java]  'The Green Project: Programming for Consumer Devices',
[java]  30.00, false, 1998, 'What a cool book', 20);
[java] 1 row(s) affected

[java] SQL> INSERT INTO books VALUES('208', 'Tru', 'Itzal',
[java]  'Duke: A Biography of the Java Evangelist',
[java]  45.00, true, 2001, 'What a cool book.', 20);
[java] 1 row(s) affected
```

You can check that the table exists with the PointBase console tool as follows:

1. In a terminal window, go to *<J2EE_HOME>*`/pointbase/tools/serveroption/`.

2. Execute `startconsole`.

3. In the Connect to Database dialog box:

   a. Enter `jdbc:pointbase:server://localhost/sun-appserv-samples` in the URL field.

   b. Enter `PBPUBLIC` in the password field.

4. Click OK.

5. Expand the SCHEMAS→PBPUBLIC→TABLES nodes. Notice that there is a table named BOOKS.

6. To see the contents of the `books` table:

   a. In the Enter SQL commands text area, enter `select * from books;`.

   b. Click the Execute button.

Creating a Data Source in the Application Server

Data sources in the Application Server implement connection pooling. To define the Duke's Bookstore data source, you use the installed PointBase connection pool named PointBasePool.

You create the data source using the Application Server Admin Console, following this procedure:

1. Expand the JDBC node.
2. Select the JDBC Resources node.
3. Click the New... button.
4. Type jdbc/BookDB in the JNDI Name field.
5. Choose PointBasePool for the Pool Name.
6. Click OK.

Specifying a Web Application's Resource Reference

To access a database from a Web application, you must declare a resource reference in the application's Web application deployment descriptor (see Declaring Resource References, page 99). The resource reference specifies a JNDI name, the type of the data resource, and the kind of authentication used when the resource is accessed. To specify a resource reference for a Duke's Bookstore example using deploytool, follow these steps:

1. Select the WAR (created in Chapters 11 through 22).
2. Select the Resource Ref's tab.
3. Click Add.
4. Type jdbc/BookDB in the Coded Name field.
5. Accept the default type javax.sql.DataSource.
6. Accept the default authorization Container.
7. Accept the default Sharable selected.

To create the connection to the database, the data access object database.BookDBAO looks up the JNDI name of the bookstore data source object:

```
public BookDBAO () throws Exception {
  try {
    Context initCtx = new InitialContext();
    Context envCtx = (Context)
      initCtx.lookup("java:comp/env");
    DataSource ds = (DataSource) envCtx.lookup("jdbc/BookDB");
    con =  ds.getConnection();
    System.out.println("Created connection to database.");
  } catch (Exception ex) {
```

```
    System.out.println("Couldn't create connection." +
    ex.getMessage());
    throw new
    Exception("Couldn't open connection to database: "
    + ex.getMessage());
}
```

Mapping the Resource Reference to a Data Source

Both the Web application resource reference and the data source defined in the Application Server have JNDI names. See JNDI Naming (page 1075) for a discussion of the benefits of using JNDI naming for resources.

To connect the resource reference to the data source, you must map the JNDI name of the former to the latter. This mapping is stored in the Web application runtime deployment descriptor. To create this mapping using `deploytool`, follow these steps:

1. Select localhost:4848 in the Servers list to retrieve the data sources defined in the Application Server.
2. Select the WAR in the Web WARs list.
3. Select the Resource Ref's tab.
4. Select the Resource Reference Name, `jdbc/BookDB`, defined in the previous section.
5. In the Sun-specific Settings frame, select `jdbc/BookDB` from the JNDI Name drop-down list.

Further Information

For more information about Web applications, refer to the following:

- Java Servlet specification:
  `http://java.sun.com/products/servlet/download.html#specs`
- The Java Servlet Web site:
  `http://java.sun.com/products/servlet`

4

Java API for XML Processing

THE Java API for XML Processing (JAXP) is for processing XML data using applications written in the Java programming language. JAXP leverages the parser standards Simple API for XML Parsing (SAX) and Document Object Model (DOM) so that you can choose to parse your data as a stream of events or to build an object representation of it. JAXP also supports the Extensible Stylesheet Language Transformations (XSLT) standard, giving you control over the presentation of the data and enabling you to convert the data to other XML documents or to other formats, such as HTML. JAXP also provides namespace support, allowing you to work with DTDs that might otherwise have naming conflicts.

Designed to be flexible, JAXP allows you to use any XML-compliant parser from within your application. It does this with what is called a *pluggability layer*, which lets you plug in an implementation of the SAX or DOM API. The pluggability layer also allows you to plug in an XSL processor, letting you control how your XML data is displayed.

The JAXP APIs

The main JAXP APIs are defined in the `javax.xml.parsers` package. That package contains vendor-neutral factory classes—SAXParserFactory, DocumentBuilderFactory, and TransformerFactory—which give you a SAXParser, a `DocumentBuilder`, and an XSLT transformer, respectively. `DocumentBuilder`, in turn, creates a DOM-compliant `Document` object.

The factory APIs let you plug in an XML implementation offered by another vendor without changing your source code. The implementation you get depends on the setting of the `javax.xml.parsers.SAXParserFactory`, `javax.xml.parsers.DocumentBuilderFactory`, and `javax.xml.transform.TransformerFactory` system properties, using `System.setProperties()` in the code, `<sysproperty key="..." value="..."/>` in an Ant build script, or `-DpropertyName="..."` on the command line. The default values (unless overridden at runtime on the command line or in the code) point to Sun's implementation.

Note: When you're using J2SE platform version 1.4, it is also necessary to use the endorsed standards mechanism, rather than the classpath, to make the implementation classes available to the application. This procedure is described in detail in Compiling and Running the Program (page 128).

Now let's look at how the various JAXP APIs work when you write an application.

An Overview of the Packages

The SAX and DOM APIs are defined by the XML-DEV group and by the W3C, respectively. The libraries that define those APIs are as follows:

- `javax.xml.parsers`: The JAXP APIs, which provide a common interface for different vendors' SAX and DOM parsers
- `org.w3c.dom`: Defines the `Document` class (a DOM) as well as classes for all the components of a DOM
- `org.xml.sax`: Defines the basic SAX APIs
- `javax.xml.transform`: Defines the XSLT APIs that let you transform XML into other forms

The Simple API for XML is the event-driven, serial-access mechanism that does element-by-element processing. The API for this level reads and writes XML to a data repository or the Web. For server-side and high-performance applications, you will want to fully understand this level. But for many applications, a minimal understanding will suffice.

The DOM API is generally an easier API to use. It provides a familiar tree structure of objects. You can use the DOM API to manipulate the hierarchy of application objects it encapsulates. The DOM API is ideal for interactive applications because the entire object model is present in memory, where it can be accessed and manipulated by the user.

On the other hand, constructing the DOM requires reading the entire XML structure and holding the object tree in memory, so it is much more CPU- and memory-intensive. For that reason, the SAX API tends to be preferred for server-side applications and data filters that do not require an in-memory representation of the data.

Finally, the XSLT APIs defined in `javax.xml.transform` let you write XML data to a file or convert it into other forms. And, as you'll see in the XSLT section of this tutorial, you can even use it in conjunction with the SAX APIs to convert legacy data to XML.

The Simple API for XML APIs

The basic outline of the SAX parsing APIs is shown in Figure 4–1. To start the process, an instance of the `SAXParserFactory` class is used to generate an instance of the parser.

The parser wraps a `SAXReader` object. When the parser's `parse()` method is invoked, the reader invokes one of several callback methods implemented in the application. Those methods are defined by the interfaces `ContentHandler`, `ErrorHandler`, `DTDHandler`, and `EntityResolver`.

Here is a summary of the key SAX APIs:

`SAXParserFactory`
> A `SAXParserFactory` object creates an instance of the parser determined by the system property, `javax.xml.parsers.SAXParserFactory`.

`SAXParser`
> The `SAXParser` interface defines several kinds of `parse()` methods. In general, you pass an XML data source and a `DefaultHandler` object to the parser, which processes the XML and invokes the appropriate methods in the handler object.

`SAXReader`
> The `SAXParser` wraps a `SAXReader`. Typically, you don't care about that, but every once in a while you need to get hold of it using `SAXParser`'s `getXML-Reader()` so that you can configure it. It is the `SAXReader` that carries on the conversation with the SAX event handlers you define.

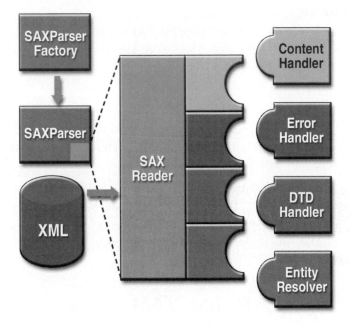

Figure 4–1   SAX APIs

DefaultHandler

> Not shown in the diagram, a DefaultHandler implements the ContentHandler, ErrorHandler, DTDHandler, and EntityResolver interfaces (with null methods), so you can override only the ones you're interested in.

ContentHandler

> Methods such as startDocument, endDocument, startElement, and endElement are invoked when an XML tag is recognized. This interface also defines the methods characters and processingInstruction, which are invoked when the parser encounters the text in an XML element or an inline processing instruction, respectively.

ErrorHandler

> Methods error, fatalError, and warning are invoked in response to various parsing errors. The default error handler throws an exception for fatal errors and ignores other errors (including validation errors). That's one reason you need to know something about the SAX parser, even if you are using the DOM. Sometimes, the application may be able to recover from a validation error. Other times, it may need to generate an exception. To ensure the correct handling, you'll need to supply your own error handler to the parser.

DTDHandler

> Defines methods you will generally never be called upon to use. Used when processing a DTD to recognize and act on declarations for an *unparsed entity*.

EntityResolver

> The resolveEntity method is invoked when the parser must identify data identified by a URI. In most cases, a URI is simply a URL, which specifies the location of a document, but in some cases the document may be identified by a URN—a *public identifier*, or name, that is unique in the Web space. The public identifier may be specified in addition to the URL. The Entity-Resolver can then use the public identifier instead of the URL to find the document—for example, to access a local copy of the document if one exists.

A typical application implements most of the ContentHandler methods, at a minimum. Because the default implementations of the interfaces ignore all inputs except for fatal errors, a robust implementation may also want to implement the ErrorHandler methods.

The SAX Packages

The SAX parser is defined in the packages listed in Table 4-1.

Table 4–1 SAX Packages

Package	Description
org.xml.sax	Defines the SAX interfaces. The name org.xml is the package prefix that was settled on by the group that defined the SAX API.
org.xml.sax.ext	Defines SAX extensions that are used for doing more sophisticated SAX processing—for example, to process a document type definition (DTD) or to see the detailed syntax for a file.
org.xml.sax.helpers	Contains helper classes that make it easier to use SAX—for example, by defining a default handler that has null methods for all the interfaces so that you only need to override the ones you actually want to implement.
javax.xml.parsers	Defines the SAXParserFactory class, which returns the SAX-Parser. Also defines exception classes for reporting errors.

The Document Object Model APIs

Figure 4–2 shows the DOM APIs in action.

You use the `javax.xml.parsers.DocumentBuilderFactory` class to get a `DocumentBuilder` instance, and you use that instance to produce a `Document` object that conforms to the DOM specification. The builder you get, in fact, is determined by the system property `javax.xml.parsers.DocumentBuilderFactory`, which selects the factory implementation that is used to produce the builder. (The platform's default value can be overridden from the command line.)

You can also use the `DocumentBuilder newDocument()` method to create an empty `Document` that implements the `org.w3c.dom.Document` interface. Alternatively, you can use one of the builder's parse methods to create a `Document` from existing XML data. The result is a DOM tree like that shown in Figure 4–2.

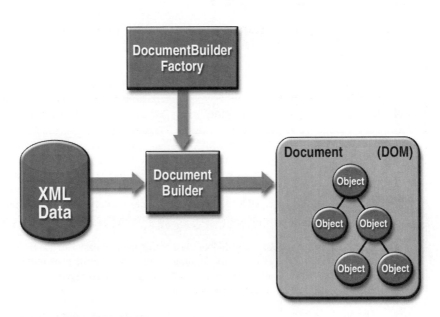

Figure 4–2   DOM APIs

> **Note:** Although they are called objects, the entries in the DOM tree are actually fairly low-level data structures. For example, consider this structure: `<color>blue</color>`. There is an *element node* for the `color` tag, and under that there is a *text node* that contains the data, `blue`! This issue will be explored at length in the DOM section of the tutorial, but developers who are expecting objects are usually surprised to find that invoking `getNodeValue()` on the element node returns nothing! For a truly object-oriented tree, see the JDOM API at `http://www.jdom.org`.

The DOM Packages

The Document Object Model implementation is defined in the packages listed in Table 4–2.

Table 4–2　DOM Packages

Package	Description
`org.w3c.dom`	Defines the DOM programming interfaces for XML (and, optionally, HTML) documents, as specified by the W3C.
`javax.xml.parsers`	Defines the `DocumentBuilderFactory` class and the `Document-Builder` class, which returns an object that implements the W3C `Document` interface. The factory that is used to create the builder is determined by the `javax.xml.parsers` system property, which can be set from the command line or overridden when invoking the `new Instance` method. This package also defines the `ParserConfigurationException` class for reporting errors.

The Extensible Stylesheet Language Transformations APIs

Figure 4–3 shows the XSLT APIs in action.

A `TransformerFactory` object is instantiated and used to create a `Transformer`. The source object is the input to the transformation process. A source object can be created from a SAX reader, from a DOM, or from an input stream.

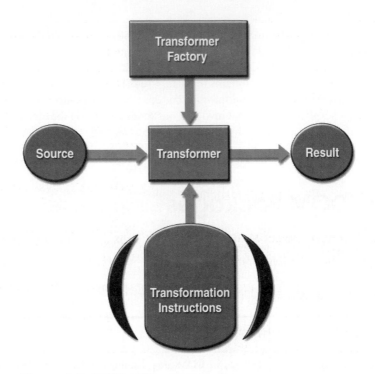

Figure 4–3   XSLT APIs

Similarly, the result object is the result of the transformation process. That object can be a SAX event handler, a DOM, or an output stream.

When the transformer is created, it can be created from a set of transformation instructions, in which case the specified transformations are carried out. If it is created without any specific instructions, then the transformer object simply copies the source to the result.

The XSLT Packages

The XSLT APIs are defined in the packages shown in Table 4–3.

Table 4–3 XSLT Packages

Package	Description
`javax.xml.transform`	Defines the `TransformerFactory` and `Transformer` classes, which you use to get an object capable of doing transformations. After creating a transformer object, you invoke its `transform()` method, providing it with an input (source) and output (result).
`javax.xml.transform.dom`	Classes to create input (source) and output (result) objects from a DOM.
`javax.xml.transform.sax`	Classes to create input (source) objects from a SAX parser and output (result) objects from a SAX event handler.
`javax.xml.transform.stream`	Classes to create input (source) objects and output (result) objects from an I/O stream.

Using the JAXP Libraries

In the Application Server, the JAXP libraries are distributed in the directory *<J2EE_HOME>*/lib/endorsed. To run the sample programs, you use the Java 2 platform's *endorsed standards* mechanism to access those libraries. For details, see Compiling and Running the Program (page 128).

Where Do You Go from Here?

At this point, you have enough information to begin picking your own way through the JAXP libraries. Your next step depends on what you want to accomplish. You might want to go to any of these chapters:

Chapter 5
   If the data structures have already been determined, and you are writing a server application or an XML filter that needs to do fast processing.

Chapter 6

If you need to build an object tree from XML data so you can manipulate it in an application, or convert an in-memory tree of objects to XML.

Chapter 7

If you need to transform XML tags into some other form, if you want to generate XML output, or (in combination with the SAX API) if you want to convert legacy data structures to XML.

5

Simple API for XML

In this chapter we focus on the Simple API for XML (SAX), an event-driven, serial-access mechanism for accessing XML documents. This protocol is frequently used by servlets and network-oriented programs that need to transmit and receive XML documents, because it's the fastest and least memory-intensive mechanism that is currently available for dealing with XML documents, other than StAX.

Note: In a nutshell, SAX is oriented towards *state independent* processing, where the handling of an element does not depend on the elements that came before. StAX, on the other hand, is oriented towards *state dependent* processing. For a more detailed comparison, see SAX and StAX in Basic Standards (page 1344) and When to Use SAX (page 116).

Setting up a program to use SAX requires a bit more work than setting up to use the Document Object Model (DOM). SAX is an event-driven model (you provide the callback methods, and the parser invokes them as it reads the XML data), and that makes it harder to visualize. Finally, you can't "back up" to an earlier part of the document, or rearrange it, any more than you can back up a serial data stream or rearrange characters you have read from that stream.

For those reasons, developers who are writing a user-oriented application that displays an XML document and possibly modifies it will want to use the DOM mechanism described in Chapter 6.

However, even if you plan to build DOM applications exclusively, there are several important reasons for familiarizing yourself with the SAX model:

- **Same Error Handling:** The same kinds of exceptions are generated by the SAX and DOM APIs, so the error handling code is virtually identical.

- **Handling Validation Errors:** By default, the specifications require that validation errors (which you'll learn more about in this part of the tutorial) are ignored. If you want to throw an exception in the event of a validation error (and you probably do), then you need to understand how SAX error handling works.

- **Converting Existing Data:** As you'll see in Chapter 6, there is a mechanism you can use to convert an existing data set to XML. However, taking advantage of that mechanism requires an understanding of the SAX model.

Note: The XML files used in this chapter can be found in `<INSTALL>/`
`j2eetutorial14/examples/xml/samples/`.
The programs and output listings can be found in `<INSTALL>/j2eetutorial14/`
`examples/jaxp/sax/samples/`.

When to Use SAX

It is helpful to understand the SAX event model when you want to convert existing data to XML. As you'll see in Generating XML from an Arbitrary Data Structure (page 264), the key to the conversion process is to modify an existing application to deliver SAX events as it reads the data.

SAX is fast and efficient, but its event model makes it most useful for such state-independent filtering. For example, a SAX parser calls one method in your application when an element tag is encountered and calls a different method when text is found. If the processing you're doing is state-independent (meaning that it does not depend on the elements that have come before), then SAX works fine.

On the other hand, for state-dependent processing, where the program needs to do one thing with the data under element A but something different with the data under element B, then a *pull parser* such as the Streaming API for XML (StAX) would be a better choice. With a pull parser, you get the next node, whatever it happens to be, at any point in the code that you ask for it. So it's easy to vary the way you process text (for example), because you can process it multiple places in the program. (For more detail, see Further Information, page 173.)

SAX requires much less memory than DOM, because SAX does not construct an internal representation (tree structure) of the XML data, as a DOM does. Instead, SAX simply sends data to the application as it is read; your application can then do whatever it wants to do with the data it sees.

Pull parsers and the SAX API both act like a serial I/O stream. You see the data as it streams in, but you can't go back to an earlier position or leap ahead to a different position. In general, such parsers work well when you simply want to read data and have the application act on it.

But when you need to modify an XML structure—especially when you need to modify it interactively—an in-memory structure makes more sense. DOM is one such model. However, although DOM provides many powerful capabilities for large-scale documents (like books and articles), it also requires a lot of complex coding. The details of that process are highlighted in When to Use DOM (page 176).

For simpler applications, that complexity may well be unnecessary. For faster development and simpler applications, one of the object-oriented XML-programming standards, such as JDOM and dom4j (page 1345), may make more sense.

Echoing an XML File with the SAX Parser

In real life, you will have little need to echo an XML file with a SAX parser. Usually, you'll want to process the data in some way in order to do something useful with it. (If you want to echo it, it's easier to build a DOM tree and use that for output.) But echoing an XML structure is a great way to see the SAX parser in action, and it can be useful for debugging.

In this exercise, you'll echo SAX parser events to `System.out`. Consider it the "Hello World" version of an XML-processing program. It shows you how to use the SAX parser to get at the data and then echoes it to show you what you have.

Note: The code discussed in this section is in `Echo01.java`. The file it operates on is `slideSample01.xml`, as described in Writing a Simple XML File (page 41). (The browsable version is `slideSample01-xml.html`.)

Creating the Skeleton

Start by creating a file named `Echo.java` and enter the skeleton for the application:

```
public class Echo
{
  public static void main(String argv[])
  {

  }

}
```

Because you'll run it standalone, you need a `main` method. And you need command-line arguments so that you can tell the application which file to echo.

Importing Classes

Next, add the `import` statements for the classes the application will use:

```
import java.io.*;
import org.xml.sax.*;
import org.xml.sax.helpers.DefaultHandler;
import javax.xml.parsers.SAXParserFactory;
import javax.xml.parsers.ParserConfigurationException;
import javax.xml.parsers.SAXParser;

public class Echo
{
   ...
```

The classes in `java.io`, of course, are needed to do output. The `org.xml.sax` package defines all the interfaces we use for the SAX parser. The `SAX-ParserFactory` class creates the instance we use. It throws a `ParserConfigu-rationException` if it cannot produce a parser that matches the specified configuration of options. (Later, you'll see more about the configuration options.) The `SAXParser` is what the factory returns for parsing, and the `DefaultHandler` defines the class that will handle the SAX events that the parser generates.

Setting Up for I/O

The first order of business is to process the command-line argument, get the name of the file to echo, and set up the output stream. Add the following highlighted text to take care of those tasks and do a bit of additional housekeeping:

```
public static void main(String argv[])

{
  if (argv.length != 1) {
    System.err.println("Usage: cmd filename");
    System.exit(1);
  }
  try {
    // Set up output stream
    out = new OutputStreamWriter(System.out, "UTF8");
  }
  catch (Throwable t) {
      t.printStackTrace();
  }
  System.exit(0);
}

static private Writer out;
```

When we create the output stream writer, we are selecting the UTF-8 character encoding. We could also have chosen US-ASCII or UTF-16, which the Java platform also supports. For more information on these character sets, see Java Encoding Schemes (page 1341).

Implementing the ContentHandler Interface

The most important interface for our current purposes is ContentHandler. This interface requires a number of methods that the SAX parser invokes in response to various parsing events. The major event-handling methods are: startDocument, endDocument, startElement, endElement, and characters.

The easiest way to implement this interface is to extend the `DefaultHandler` class, defined in the `org.xml.sax.helpers` package. That class provides do-nothing methods for all the `ContentHandler` events. Enter the following high-lighted code to extend that class:

```
public class Echo extends DefaultHandler
{
  ...
}
```

Note: `DefaultHandler` also defines do-nothing methods for the other major events, defined in the `DTDHandler`, `EntityResolver`, and `ErrorHandler` interfaces. You'll learn more about those methods as we go along.

Each of these methods is required by the interface to throw a `SAXException`. An exception thrown here is sent back to the parser, which sends it on to the code that invoked the parser. In the current program, this sequence means that it winds up back at the `Throwable` exception handler at the bottom of the `main` method.

When a start tag or end tag is encountered, the name of the tag is passed as a `String` to the `startElement` or the `endElement` method, as appropriate. When a start tag is encountered, any attributes it defines are also passed in an `Attributes` list. Characters found within the element are passed as an array of characters, along with the number of characters (`length`) and an offset into the array that points to the first character.

Setting up the Parser

Now (at last) you're ready to set up the parser. Add the following highlighted code to set it up and get it started:

```
public static void main(String argv[])
{
  if (argv.length != 1) {
    System.err.println("Usage: cmd filename");
    System.exit(1);
  }
```

```
    // Use an instance of ourselves as the SAX event handler
    DefaultHandler handler = new Echo();

    // Use the default (non-validating) parser
    SAXParserFactory factory = SAXParserFactory.newInstance();
    try {
        // Set up output stream
        out = new OutputStreamWriter(System.out, "UTF8");

        // Parse the input
        SAXParser saxParser = factory.newSAXParser();
        saxParser.parse( new File(argv[0]), handler );

    } catch (Throwable t) {
        t.printStackTrace();
    }
    System.exit(0);
}
```

With these lines of code, you create a SAXParserFactory instance, as determined by the setting of the javax.xml.parsers.SAXParserFactory system property. You then get a parser from the factory and give the parser an instance of this class to handle the parsing events, telling it which input file to process.

Note: The javax.xml.parsers.SAXParser class is a wrapper that defines a number of convenience methods. It wraps the (somewhat less friendly) org.xml.sax.Parser object. If needed, you can obtain that parser using the SAX-Parser's getParser() method.

For now, you are simply catching any exception that the parser might throw. You'll learn more about error processing in a later section of this chapter, Handling Errors with the Nonvalidating Parser (page 139).

Writing the Output

The ContentHandler methods throw SAXExceptions but not IOExceptions, which can occur while writing. The SAXException can wrap another exception, though, so it makes sense to do the output in a method that takes care of the exception-handling details. Add the following highlighted code to define an emit method that does that:

```
static private Writer out;

private void emit(String s)
throws SAXException
{
  try {
    out.write(s);
    out.flush();
  } catch (IOException e) {
    throw new SAXException("I/O error", e);
  }
}
...
```

When emit is called, any I/O error is wrapped in SAXException along with a message that identifies it. That exception is then thrown back to the SAX parser. You'll learn more about SAX exceptions later. For now, keep in mind that emit is a small method that handles the string output. (You'll see it called often in later code.)

Spacing the Output

Here is another bit of infrastructure we need before doing some real processing. Add the following highlighted code to define an nl() method that writes the kind of line-ending character used by the current system:

```
private void emit(String s)
  ...
}

private void nl()
throws SAXException
{
  String lineEnd = System.getProperty("line.separator");
  try {
    out.write(lineEnd);
  } catch (IOException e) {
    throw new SAXException("I/O error", e);
  }
}
```

Note: Although it seems like a bit of a nuisance, you will be invoking nl() many times in later code. Defining it now will simplify the code later on. It also provides a place to indent the output when we get to that section of the tutorial.

Handling Content Events

Finally, let's write some code that actually processes the ContentHandler events.

Document Events

Add the following highlighted code to handle the start-document and end-document events:

```
static private Writer out;

public void startDocument()
throws SAXException
{
  emit("<?xml version='1.0' encoding='UTF-8'?>");
  nl();
}

public void endDocument()
throws SAXException
{
  try {
    nl();
    out.flush();
  } catch (IOException e) {
    throw new SAXException("I/O error", e);
  }
}

private void echoText()
...
```

Here, you are echoing an XML declaration when the parser encounters the start of the document. Because you set up OutputStreamWriter using UTF-8 encoding, you include that specification as part of the declaration.

Note: However, the IO classes don't understand the hyphenated encoding names, so you specified UTF8 for the `OutputStreamWriter` rather than UTF-8.

At the end of the document, you simply put out a final newline and flush the output stream. Not much going on there.

Element Events

Now for the interesting stuff. Add the following highlighted code to process the start-element and end-element events:

```
public void startElement(String namespaceURI,
        String sName, // simple name
        String qName, // qualified name
        Attributes attrs)
throws SAXException
{
  String eName = sName; // element name
  if ("".equals(eName)) eName = qName; // not namespace-aware
  emit("<"+eName);
  if (attrs != null) {
     for (int i = 0; i < attrs.getLength(); i++) {
        String aName = attrs.getLocalName(i); // Attr name
        if ("".equals(aName)) aName = attrs.getQName(i);
        emit(" ");
        emit(aName+"=\""+attrs.getValue(i)+"\"");
     }
  }
  emit(">");
}

public void endElement(String namespaceURI,
        String sName, // simple name
        String qName  // qualified name
        )
throws SAXException
{
  String eName = sName; // element name
  if ("".equals(eName)) eName = qName; // not namespace-aware
  emit("</"+eName+">");
}

private void emit(String s)
...
```

With this code, you echo the element tags, including any attributes defined in the start tag. Note that when the `startElement()` method is invoked, if namespace processing is not enabled, then the simple name (*local name*) for elements and attributes could turn out to be the empty string. The code handles that case by using the qualified name whenever the simple name is the empty string.

Character Events

To finish handling the content events, you need to handle the characters that the parser delivers to your application.

Parsers are not required to return any particular number of characters at one time. A parser can return anything from a single character at a time up to several thousand and still be a standard-conforming implementation. So if your application needs to process the characters it sees, it is wise to accumulate the characters in a buffer and operate on them only when you are sure that all of them have been found.

Add the following highlighted line to define the text buffer:

```
public class Echo01 extends DefaultHandler
{
    StringBuffer textBuffer;

    public static void main(String argv[])
    {

...
```

Then add the following highlighted code to accumulate the characters the parser delivers in the buffer:

```
public void endElement(...)
throws SAXException
{
    ...
}

public void characters(char buf[], int offset, int len)
throws SAXException
{
    String s = new String(buf, offset, len);
    if (textBuffer == null) {
        textBuffer = new StringBuffer(s);
```

```
      } else {
         textBuffer.append(s);
      }
   }

   private void emit(String s)
   ...
```

Next, add the following highlighted method to send the contents of the buffer to the output stream.

```
   public void characters(char buf[], int offset, int len)
   throws SAXException
   {
      ...
   }

   private void echoText()
   throws SAXException
   {
      if (textBuffer == null) return;
      String s = ""+textBuffer;
      emit(s);
      textBuffer = null;
   }

   private void emit(String s)
   ...
```

When this method is called twice in a row (which will happen at times, as you'll see next), the buffer will be null. In that case, the method simply returns. When the buffer is not null, however, its contents are sent to the output stream.

Finally, add the following highlighted code to echo the contents of the buffer whenever an element starts or ends:

```
   public void startElement(...)
   throws SAXException
   {
      echoText();
      String eName = sName; // element name
      ...
   }
```

```
public void endElement(...)
throws SAXException
{
   echoText();
   String eName = sName; // element name
   ...
}
```

You're finished accumulating text when an element ends, of course. So you echo it at that point, and that action clears the buffer before the next element starts.

But you also want to echo the accumulated text when an element starts! That's necessary for document-style data, which can contain XML elements that are intermixed with text. For example, consider this document fragment:

```
<para>This paragraph contains <bold>important</bold> ideas.</
para>
```

The initial text, This paragraph contains, is terminated by the start of the <bold> element. The text important is terminated by the end tag, </bold>, and the final text, ideas., is terminated by the end tag, </para>.

Note: Most of the time, though, the accumulated text will be echoed when an endElement() event occurs. When a startElement() event occurs after that, the buffer will be empty. The first line in the echoText() method checks for that case, and simply returns.

Congratulations! At this point you have written a complete SAX parser application. The next step is to compile and run it.

Note: To be strictly accurate, the character handler should scan the buffer for ampersand characters (&); and left-angle bracket characters (<) and replace them with the strings & or <, as appropriate. You'll find out more about that kind of processing when we discuss entity references in Displaying Special Characters and CDATA (page 147).

Compiling and Running the Program

In the Application Server, the JAXP libraries are in the directory *<J2EE_HOME>*/ lib/endorsed. These are newer versions of the standard JAXP libraries that are part of the Java 2 platform.

The Application Server automatically uses the newer libraries when a program runs. So you don't have to be concerned with where they reside when you deploy an application. And because the JAXP APIs are identical in both versions, you don't need to be concerned at compile time either. So compiling the program you created is as simple as issuing this command:

```
javac Echo.java
```

But to run the program outside the server container, you must make sure that the java runtime finds the newer versions of the JAXP libraries. That situation can occur, for example, when you're unit-testing parts of your application outside of server, as well as here, when you're running the XML tutorial examples.

There are two ways to make sure that the program uses the latest version of the JAXP libraries:

- Copy the *<J2EE_HOME>*/lib/endorsed directory to *<J2EE_HOME>*jdk/ jre/lib/endorsed. You can then run the program with this command:

  <J2EE_HOME>/jdk/bin/java Echo slideSample.xml

  The libraries will then be found in the endorsed standards directory, *<J2EE_HOME>*/jdk/jre/lib/endorsed.

- Use the endorsed directories system property to specify the location of the libraries, by specifying this option on the java command line:

  -D"java.endorsed.dirs=*<J2EE_HOME>*/lib/endorsed"

Note: Because the JAXP *APIs* are already built into the Java 2 platform, they don't need to be specified at compile time. (In fact, the -D option is not even allowed at compile time, because endorsed standards are *required* to maintain consistent APIs.) However, when the JAXP factories instantiate an *implementation*, the endorsed directories mechanism is employed to make sure that the desired implementation is instantiated.

Checking the Output

Here is part of the program's output, showing some of its weird spacing:

```
...
<slideshow title="Sample Slide Show" date="Date of publication"
author="Yours Truly">


  <slide type="all">
    <title>Wake up to WonderWidgets!</title>
  </slide>
  ...
```

Note: The program's output is contained in `Echo01-01.txt`. (The browsable version is `Echo01-01.html`.)

When we look at this output, a number of questions arise. Where is the excess vertical whitespace coming from? And why are the elements indented properly, when the code isn't doing it? We'll answer those questions in a moment. First, though, there are a few points to note about the output:

- The comment defined at the top of the file

  ```
  <!-- A SAMPLE set of slides -->
  ```

  does not appear in the listing. Comments are ignored unless you implement a `LexicalHandler`. You'll see more on that subject later in this tutorial.

- Element attributes are listed all together on a single line. If your window isn't really wide, you won't see them all.

- The single-tag empty element you defined (`<item/>`) is treated exactly the same as a two-tag empty element (`<item></item>`). It is, for all intents and purposes, identical. (It's just easier to type and consumes less space.)

Identifying the Events

This version of the echo program might be useful for displaying an XML file, but it doesn't tell you much about what's going on in the parser. The next step is to modify the program so that you see where the spaces and vertical lines are coming from.

Note: The code discussed in this section is in `Echo02.java`. The output it produces is shown in `Echo02-01.txt`. (The browsable version is `Echo02-01.html`.)

Make the following highlighted changes to identify the events as they occur:

```java
public void startDocument()
throws SAXException
{
  nl();
  nl();
  emit("START DOCUMENT");
  nl();
  emit("<?xml version='1.0' encoding='UTF-8'?>");
  nl();
}

public void endDocument()
throws SAXException
{
  nl();
  emit("END DOCUMENT");
  try {
  ...
}

public void startElement(...)
throws SAXException
{
  echoText();
  nl();
  emit("ELEMENT: ");
  String eName = sName; // element name
  if ("".equals(eName)) eName = qName; // not namespac-aware
  emit("<"+eName);
  if (attrs != null) {
    for (int i = 0; i < attrs.getLength(); i++) {
      String aName = attrs.getLocalName(i); // Attr name
      if ("".equals(aName)) aName = attrs.getQName(i);
      emit(" ");
      emit(aName+"=\""+attrs.getValue(i)+"\"");
      nl();
      emit("   ATTR: ");
      emit(aName);
      emit("\t\"");
      emit(attrs.getValue(i));
      emit("\"");
```

```
        }
    }
    if (attrs.getLength() > 0) nl();
    emit(">");
}

public void endElement(...)
throws SAXException
{
    echoText();
    nl();
    emit("END_ELM: ");
    String eName = sName; // element name
    if ("".equals(eName)) eName = qName; // not namespace-aware
    emit("<"+eName+">");
}

...

private void echoText()
throws SAXException
{
    if (textBuffer == null) return;
    nl();
    emit("CHARS: |");
    String s = ""+textBuffer;
    emit(s);
    emit("|");
    textBuffer = null;
}
```

Compile and run this version of the program to produce a more informative output listing. The attributes are now shown one per line, and that is nice. But, more importantly, output lines such as the following show that both the indentation space and the newlines that separate the attributes come from the data that the parser passes to the characters() method.

```
    CHARS: |

|
```

Note: The XML specification requires all input line separators to be normalized to a single newline. The newline character is specified as in Java, C, and UNIX systems, but goes by the alias "linefeed" in Windows systems.

Compressing the Output

To make the output more readable, modify the program so that it outputs only characters whose values are something other than whitespace.

Note: The code discussed in this section is in Echo03.java.

Make the following changes to suppress output of characters that are all whitespace:

```
public void echoText()
throws SAXException
{
  nl();
  emit("CHARS: |");
  emit("CHARS:   ");
  String s = ""+textBuffer;
  if (!s.trim().equals("")) emit(s);
  emit("|");
}
```

Next, add the following highlighted code to echo each set of characters delivered by the parser:

```
public void characters(char buf[], int offset, int len)
throws SAXException
{
  if (textBuffer != null) {
    echoText();
    textBuffer = null;
  }
  String s = new String(buf, offset, len);
  ...
}
```

If you run the program now, you will see that you have also eliminated the indentation, because the indent space is part of the whitespace that precedes the start of an element. Add the following highlighted code to manage the indentation:

```
static private Writer out;

private String indentString = "    "; // Amount to indent
private int indentLevel = 0;

...
```

```
public void startElement(...)
throws SAXException
{
   indentLevel++;
   nl();
   emit("ELEMENT: ");
   ...
}

public void endElement(...)
throws SAXException
{
   nl();
   emit("END_ELM: ");
   emit("</"+sName+">");
   indentLevel--;
}
...
private void nl()
throws SAXException
{
   ...
   try {
      out.write(lineEnd);
      for (int i=0; i < indentLevel; i++)
         out.write(indentString);
   } catch (IOException e) {
   ...
}
```

This code sets up an indent string, keeps track of the current indent level, and outputs the indent string whenever the nl method is called. If you set the indent string to "", the output will not be indented. (Try it. You'll see why it's worth the work to add the indentation.)

You'll be happy to know that you have reached the end of the "mechanical" code in the Echo program. From this point on, you'll be doing things that give you more insight into how the parser works. The steps you've taken so far, though, have given you a lot of insight into how the parser sees the XML data it processes. You have also gained a helpful debugging tool that you can use to see what the parser sees.

Inspecting the Output

Here is part of the output from this version of the program:

```
ELEMENT: <slideshow
...
>
CHARS:
CHARS:
   ELEMENT: <slide
   ...
   END_ELM: </slide>
CHARS:
CHARS:
```

Note: The complete output is Echo03-01.txt. (The browsable version is Echo03-01.html.)

Note that the characters method is invoked twice in a row. Inspecting the source file slideSample01.xml shows that there is a comment before the first slide. The first call to characters comes before that comment. The second call comes after. (Later, you'll see how to be notified when the parser encounters a comment, although in most cases you won't need such notifications.)

Note, too, that the characters method is invoked after the first slide element, as well as before. When you are thinking in terms of hierarchically structured data, that seems odd. After all, you intended for the slideshow element to contain slide elements and not text. Later, you'll see how to restrict the slideshow element by using a DTD. When you do that, the characters method will no longer be invoked.

In the absence of a DTD, though, the parser must assume that any element it sees contains text such as that in the first item element of the overview slide:

```
<item>Why <em>WonderWidgets</em> are great</item>
```

Here, the hierarchical structure looks like this:

```
ELEMENT:   <item>
CHARS:     Why
  ELEMENT:   <em>
  CHARS.     WonderWidgets
  END_ELM:  </em>
CHARS:     are great
END_ELM:  </item>
```

Documents and Data

In this example, it's clear that there are characters intermixed with the hierarchical structure of the elements. The fact that text can surround elements (or be prevented from doing so with a DTD or schema) helps to explain why you sometimes hear talk about "XML data" and other times hear about "XML documents." XML comfortably handles both structured data and text documents that include markup. The only difference between the two is whether or not text is allowed between the elements.

Note: In a later section of this tutorial, you will work with the `ignorable-Whitespace` method in the `ContentHandler` interface. This method can be invoked only when a DTD is present. If a DTD specifies that `slideshow` does not contain text, then all the whitespace surrounding the `slide` elements is by definition ignorable. On the other hand, if `slideshow` can contain text (which must be assumed to be true in the absence of a DTD), then the parser must assume that spaces and lines it sees between the `slide` elements are significant parts of the document.

Adding Additional Event Handlers

In addition to `ignorableWhitespace`, there are two other `ContentHandler` methods that can find uses in even simple applications: `setDocumentLocator` and `processingInstruction`. In this section, you'll implement those two event handlers.

Identifying the Document's Location

A *locator* is an object that contains the information necessary to find a document. The `Locator` class encapsulates a system ID (URL) or a public identifier (URN) or both. You would need that information if you wanted to find something relative to the current document—in the same way, for example, that an HTML browser processes an `href="anotherFile"` attribute in an anchor tag. The browser uses the location of the current document to find `anotherFile`.

You could also use the locator to print good diagnostic messages. In addition to the document's location and public identifier, the locator contains methods that give the column and line number of the most recently processed event. The `set-DocumentLocator` method, however, is called only once: at the beginning of the parse. To get the current line or column number, you would save the locator when `setDocumentLocator` is invoked and then use it in the other event-handling methods.

Note: The code discussed in this section is in `Echo04.java`. Its output is in `Echo04-01.txt`. (The browsable version is `Echo04-01.html`.)

Start by removing the extra character-echoing code you added for the last example:

```
public void characters(char buf[], int offset, int len)
throws SAXException
{
   if (textBuffer != null) {
      echoText();
      textBuffer = null;
   }
   String s = new String(buf, offset, len);
   ...
}
```

Next, add the following highlighted method to the Echo program to get the document locator and use it to echo the document's system ID.

```
...
private String indentString = "    "; // Amount to indent
private int indentLevel = 0;
```

```
public void setDocumentLocator(Locator l)
{
  try {
    out.write("LOCATOR");
    out.write("SYS ID. " + l.getSystemId() );
    out.flush();
  } catch (IOException e) {
    // Ignore errors
  }
}

public void startDocument()
...
```

Notes:

- This method, in contrast to every other ContentHandler method, does not return a SAXException. So rather than use emit for output, this code writes directly to System.out. (This method is generally expected to simply save the Locator for later use rather than do the kind of processing that generates an exception, as here.)
- The spelling of these methods is Id, not ID. So you have getSystemId and getPublicId.

When you compile and run the program on slideSample01.xml, here is the significant part of the output:

```
LOCATOR
SYS ID: file:<path>/../samples/slideSample01.xml

START DOCUMENT
<?xml version='1.0' encoding='UTF-8'?>
...
```

Here, it is apparent that setDocumentLocator is called before startDocument. That can make a difference if you do any initialization in the event-handling code.

Handling Processing Instructions

It sometimes makes sense to code application-specific processing instructions in the XML data. In this exercise, you'll modify the Echo program to display a processing instruction contained in slideSample02.xml.

Note: The code discussed in this section is in `Echo05.java`. The file it operates on is `slideSample02.xml`, as described in Writing Processing Instructions (page 46). The output is in `Echo05-02.txt`. (The browsable versions are `slideSample02-xml.html` and `Echo05-02.html`.)

As you saw in Writing Processing Instructions (page 46), the format for a processing instruction is `<?target data?>`, where *target* is the application that is expected to do the processing, and *data* is the instruction or information for it to process. The sample file `slideSample02.xml` contains a processing instruction for a mythical slide presentation program that queries the user to find out which slides to display (technical, executive-level, or all):

```
<slideshow
  ...
  >

<!-- PROCESSING INSTRUCTION -->
<?my.presentation.Program QUERY="exec, tech, all"?>

<!-- TITLE SLIDE -->
```

To display that processing instruction, add the following highlighted code to the Echo app:

```
public void characters(char buf[], int offset, int len)
...
}

public void processingInstruction(String target, String data)
throws SAXException
{
  nl();
  emit("PROCESS: ");
  emit("<?"+target+" "+data+"?>");
}

private void echoText()
...
```

When your edits are complete, compile and run the program. The relevant part of the output should look like this:

```
ELEMENT: <slideshow
   ...
>
PROCESS. <?my.presentation.Program QUERY="exec, tech, all"?>
CHARS:
...
```

Summary

With the minor exception of ignorableWhitespace, you have used most of the ContentHandler methods that you need to handle the most commonly useful SAX events. You'll see ignorableWhitespace a little later. Next, though, you'll get deeper insight into how you handle errors in the SAX parsing process.

Handling Errors with the Nonvalidating Parser

The parser can generate three kinds of errors: a fatal error, an error, and a warning. In this exercise, you'll see how the parser handles a fatal error.

This version of the Echo program uses the nonvalidating parser. So it can't tell whether the XML document contains the right tags or whether those tags are in the right sequence. In other words, it can't tell you whether the document is valid. It can, however, tell whether or not the document is well formed.

In this section, you'll modify the slide-show file to generate various kinds of errors and see how the parser handles them. You'll also find out which error conditions are ignored by default, and you'll see how to handle them.

Note: The XML file used in this exercise is slideSampleBad1.xml, as described in Introducing an Error (page 48). The output is in Echo05-Bad1.txt. (The browsable versions are slideSampleBad1-xml.html and Echo05-Bad1.html.)

When you created `slideSampleBad1.xml`, you deliberately created an XML file that was not well formed. Run the Echo program on that file now. The output now gives you an error message that looks like this (after formatting for readability):

```
org.xml.sax.SAXParseException:
  The element type "item" must be terminated by the
  matching end-tag "</item>".
...
at org.apache.xerces.parsers.AbstractSAXParser...
...
at Echo.main(...)
```

Note: The foregoing message was generated by the JAXP 1.2 libraries. If you are using a different parser, the error message is likely to be somewhat different.

When a fatal error occurs, the parser cannot continue. So if the application does not generate an exception (which you'll see how to do a moment), then the default error-event handler generates one. The stack trace is generated by the `Throwable` exception handler in your `main` method:

```
    ...
} catch (Throwable t) {
    t.printStackTrace();
}
```

That stack trace is not very useful. Next, you'll see how to generate better diagnostics when an error occurs.

Handling a SAXParseException

When the error was encountered, the parser generated a `SAXParseException`—a subclass of `SAXException` that identifies the file and location where the error occurred.

Note: The code you'll create in this exercise is in `Echo06.java`. The output is in `Echo06-Bad1.txt`. (The browsable version is `Echo06-Bad1.html`.)

Add the following highlighted code to generate a better diagnostic message when the exception occurs:

```
...
} catch (SAXParseException spe) [
  // Error generated by the parser
  System.out.println("\n** Parsing error"
    + ", line " + spe.getLineNumber()
    + ", uri " + spe.getSystemId());
  System.out.println("   " + spe.getMessage() );

} catch (Throwable t) {
  t.printStackTrace();
}
```

Running this version of the program on `slideSampleBad1.xml` generates an error message that is a bit more helpful:

```
** Parsing error, line 22, uri file:<path>/slideSampleBad1.xml
   The element type "item" must be ...
```

Note: The text of the error message depends on the parser used. This message was generated using JAXP 1.2.

Note: Catching all throwables is not generally a great idea for production applications. We're doing it now so that we can build up to full error handling gradually. In addition, it acts as a catch-all for null pointer exceptions that can be thrown when the parser is passed a null value.

Handling a SAXException

A more general `SAXException` instance may sometimes be generated by the parser, but it more frequently occurs when an error originates in one of application's event-handling methods. For example, the signature of the `startDocument` method in the `ContentHandler` interface is defined as returning a `SAXException`:

```
public void startDocument() throws SAXException
```

All the `ContentHandler` methods (except for `setDocumentLocator`) have that signature declaration.

A `SAXException` can be constructed using a message, another exception, or both. So, for example, when `Echo.startDocument` outputs a string using the `emit` method, any I/O exception that occurs is wrapped in a `SAXException` and sent back to the parser:

```
private void emit(String s)
throws SAXException
{
  try {
    out.write(s);
    out.flush();
  } catch (IOException e) {
    throw new SAXException("I/O error", e);
  }
}
```

Note: If you saved the `Locator` object when `setDocumentLocator` was invoked, you could use it to generate a `SAXParseException`, identifying the document and location, instead of generating a `SAXException`.

When the parser delivers the exception back to the code that invoked the parser, it makes sense to use the original exception to generate the stack trace. Add the following highlighted code to do that:

```
  ...
} catch (SAXParseException err) {
  System.out.println("\n** Parsing error"
    + ", line " + err.getLineNumber()
    + ", uri " + err.getSystemId());
  System.out.println("   " + err.getMessage());

} catch (SAXException sxe) {
  // Error generated by this application
  // (or a parser-initialization error)
  Exception  x = sxe;
  if (sxe.getException() != null)
    x = sxe.getException();
  x.printStackTrace();

} catch (Throwable t) {
  t.printStackTrace();
}
```

This code tests to see whether the SAXException is wrapping another exception. If it is, it generates a stack trace originating where the exception occurred to make it easier to pinpoint the responsible code. If the exception contains only a message, the code prints the stack trace starting from the location where the exception was generated.

Improving the SAXParseException Handler

Because the SAXParseException can also wrap another exception, add the following highlighted code to use the contained exception for the stack trace:

```
    ...
} catch (SAXParseException err) {
    System.out.println("\n** Parsing error"
        + ", line " + err.getLineNumber()
        + ", uri " + err.getSystemId());
    System.out.println("   " + err.getMessage());

    // Use the contained exception, if any
    Exception  x = spe;
    if (spe.getException() != null)
        x = spe.getException();
    x.printStackTrace();

} catch (SAXException sxe) {
    // Error generated by this application
    // (or a parser-initialization error)
    Exceptionx = sxe;
    if (sxe.getException() != null)
        x = sxe.getException();
    x.printStackTrace();

} catch (Throwable t) {
    t.printStackTrace();
}
```

The program is now ready to handle any SAX parsing exceptions it sees. You've seen that the parser generates exceptions for fatal errors. But for nonfatal errors and warnings, exceptions are never generated by the default error handler, and no messages are displayed. In a moment, you'll learn more about errors and warnings and will find out how to supply an error handler to process them.

Handling a ParserConfigurationException

Recall that the SAXParserFactory class can throw an exception if it cannot create a parser. Such an error might occur if the factory cannot find the class needed to create the parser (class not found error), is not permitted to access it (illegal access exception), or cannot instantiate it (instantiation error).

Add the following highlighted code to handle such errors:

```
} catch (SAXException sxe) {
  Exceptionx = sxe;
  if (sxe.getException() != null)
    x = sxe.getException();
  x.printStackTrace();

} catch (ParserConfigurationException pce) {
  // Parser with specified options can't be built
  pce.printStackTrace();

} catch (Throwable t) {
  t.printStackTrace();
```

Admittedly, there are quite a few error handlers here. But at least now you know the kinds of exceptions that can occur.

Note: A javax.xml.parsers.FactoryConfigurationError can also be thrown if the factory class specified by the system property cannot be found or instantiated. That is a nontrappable error, because the program is not expected to be able to recover from it.

Handling an IOException

While we're at it, let's add a handler for IOExceptions:

```
} catch (ParserConfigurationException pce) {
  // Parser with specified options can't be built
  pce.printStackTrace();

} catch (IOException ioe) {
  // I/O error
  ioe.printStackTrace();
```

```
    }

  } catch (Throwable t) {
    ...
```

We'll leave the handler for Throwables to catch null pointer errors, but note that at this point it is doing the same thing as the IOFxception handler. Here, we're merely illustrating the kinds of exceptions that *can* occur, in case there are some that your application could recover from.

Handling NonFatal Errors

A *nonfatal* error occurs when an XML document fails a validity constraint. If the parser finds that the document is not valid, then an error event is generated. Such errors are generated by a validating parser, given a DTD or schema, when a document has an invalid tag, when a tag is found where it is not allowed, or (in the case of a schema) when the element contains invalid data.

You won't deal with validation issues until later in this tutorial. But because we're on the subject of error handling, you'll write the error-handling code now.

The most important principle to understand about nonfatal errors is that they are ignored by default. But if a validation error occurs in a document, you probably don't want to continue processing it. You probably want to treat such errors as fatal. In the code you write next, you'll set up the error handler to do just that.

Note: The code for the program you'll create in this exercise is in Echo07.java.

To take over error handling, you override the DefaultHandler methods that handle fatal errors, nonfatal errors, and warnings as part of the ErrorHandler interface. The SAX parser delivers a SAXParseException to each of these methods, so generating an exception when an error occurs is as simple as throwing it back.

Add the following highlighted code to override the handler for errors:

```
public void processingInstruction(String target, String data)
throws SAXException
{
  ...
}
```

```
// treat validation errors as fatal
public void error(SAXParseException e)
throws SAXParseException
{
   throw e;
}
```

Note: It can be instructive to examine the error-handling methods defined in `org.xml.sax.helpers.DefaultHandler`. You'll see that the `error()` and `warning()` methods do nothing, whereas `fatalError()` throws an exception. Of course, you could always override the `fatalError()` method to throw a different exception. But if your code *doesn't* throw an exception when a fatal error occurs, then the SAX parser will. The XML specification requires it.

Handling Warnings

Warnings, too, are ignored by default. Warnings are informative and can only be generated in the presence of a DTD or schema. For example, if an element is defined twice in a DTD, a warning is generated. It's not illegal, and it doesn't cause problems, but it's something you might like to know about because it might not have been intentional.

Add the following highlighted code to generate a message when a warning occurs:

```
// treat validation errors as fatal
public void error(SAXParseException e)
throws SAXParseException
{
   throw e;
}

// dump warnings too
public void warning(SAXParseException err)
throws SAXParseException
{
   System.out.println("** Warning"
      + ", line " + err.getLineNumber()
      + ", uri " + err.getSystemId());
   System.out.println("   " + err.getMessage());
}
```

Because there is no good way to generate a warning without a DTD or schema, you won't be seeing any just yet. But when one does occur, you're ready!

Displaying Special Characters and CDATA

The next thing we will do with the parser is to customize it a bit so that you can see how to get information it usually ignores. In this section, you'll learn how the parser handles

- Special characters (<, &, and so on)
- Text with XML-style syntax

Handling Special Characters

In XML, an entity is an XML structure (or plain text) that has a name. Referencing the entity by name causes it to be inserted into the document in place of the entity reference. To create an entity reference, you surround the entity name with an ampersand and a semicolon:

```
&entityName;
```

Earlier, you put an entity reference into your XML document by coding

```
Market Size &lt; predicted
```

Note: The file containing this XML is `slideSample03.xml`, as described in Using an Entity Reference in an XML Document (page 50). The results of processing it are shown in `Echo07-03.txt`. (The browsable versions are `slideSample03-xml.html` and `Echo07-03.html`.)

When you run the Echo program on `slideSample03.xml`, you see the following output:

```
ELEMENT:   <item>
CHARS:     Market Size < predicted
END_ELM:   </item>
```

The parser has converted the reference into the entity it represents and has passed the entity to the application.

Handling Text with XML-Style Syntax

When you are handling large blocks of XML or HTML that include many special characters, you use a CDATA section.

Note: The XML file used in this example is `slideSample04.xml`. The results of processing it are shown in `Echo07-04.txt`. (The browsable versions are `slideSample04-xml.html` and `Echo07-04.html`.)

A CDATA section works like `<pre>...</pre>` in HTML, only more so: all whitespace in a CDATA section is significant, and characters in it are not interpreted as XML. A CDATA section starts with `<![CDATA[` and ends with `]]>`. The file `slideSample04.xml` contains this CDATA section for a fictitious technical slide:

```
...
<slide type="tech">
  <title>How it Works</title>
  <item>First we fozzle the frobmorten</item>
  <item>Then we framboze the staten</item>
  <item>Finally, we frenzle the fuznaten</item>
  <item><![CDATA[Diagram:
    frobmorten <-------------- fuznaten
       |                  <3>           ^
       | <1>                            | <1> = fozzle
       V                                | <2> = framboze
    staten-----------------------+ <3> = frenzle
            <2>
  ]]></item>
</slide>
</slideshow>
```

When you run the Echo program on the new file, you see the following output:

```
ELEMENT: <item>
CHARS:   Diagram:
frobmorten <-------------- fuznaten
   |              <3>           ^
   | <1>                        | <1> = fozzle
   V                            | <2> = framboze
```

```
staten------------------------+ <3> = frenzle
        <2>

END_ELM: </item>
```

You can see here that the text in the CDATA section arrived as it was written. Because the parser didn't treat the angle brackets as XML, they didn't generate the fatal errors they would otherwise cause. (If the angle brackets weren't in a CDATA section, the document would not be well formed.)

Handling CDATA and Other Characters

The existence of CDATA makes the proper echoing of XML a bit tricky. If the text to be output is *not* in a CDATA section, then any angle brackets, ampersands, and other special characters in the text should be replaced with the appropriate entity reference. (Replacing left angle brackets and ampersands is most important, other characters will be interpreted properly without misleading the parser.)

But if the output text *is* in a CDATA section, then the substitutions should not occur, resulting in text like that in the earlier example. In a simple program such as our Echo application, it's not a big deal. But many XML-filtering applications will want to keep track of whether the text appears in a CDATA section, so that they can treat special characters properly. (Later, you will see how to use a Lex-icalHandler to find out whether or not you are processing a CDATA section.)

One other area to watch for is attributes. The text of an attribute value can also contain angle brackets and semicolons that need to be replaced by entity references. (Attribute text can never be in a CDATA section, though, so there is never any question about doing that substitution.)

Parsing with a DTD

After the XML declaration, the document prolog can include a DTD, reference an external DTD, or both. In this section, you'll see the effect of the DTD on the data that the parser delivers to your application.

DTD's Effect on the Nonvalidating Parser

In this section, you'll use the Echo program to see how the data appears to the SAX parser when the data file references a DTD.

Note: The XML file used in this section is `slideSample05.xml`, which references `slideshow1a.dtd`. The output is shown in `Echo07-05.txt`. (The browsable versions are `slideshow1a-dtd.html`, `slideSample05-xml.html`, and `Echo07-05.html`.)

Running the Echo program on your latest version of `slideSample.xml` shows that many of the superfluous calls to the `characters` method have now disappeared.

Before, you saw this:

```
   ...
>
PROCESS: ...
CHARS:
   ELEMENT:   <slide
     ATTR: ...
   >
        ELEMENT:   <title>
        CHARS:     Wake up to ...
        END_ELM:   </title>
   END_ELM:   </slide>
CHARS:
   ELEMENT:   <slide
     ATTR: ...
   >
   ...
```

Now you see this:

```
   ...
>
PROCESS: ...
   ELEMENT:   <slide
     ATTR: ...
   >
        ELEMENT:   <title>
        CHARS:     Wake up to ...
        END_ELM:   </title>
   END_ELM:   </slide>
   ELEMENT:   <slide
     ATTR: ...
   >
   ...
```

It is evident that the whitespace characters that were formerly being echoed around the `slide` elements are no longer being delivered by the parser, because the DTD declares that `slideshow` consists solely of `slide` elements:

```
<!ELEMENT slideshow (slide+)>
```

Tracking Ignorable Whitespace

Now that the DTD is present, the parser is no longer calling the `characters` method with whitespace that it knows to be irrelevant. From the standpoint of an application that is interested in processing only the XML data, that is great. The application is never bothered with whitespace that exists purely to make the XML file readable.

On the other hand, if you were writing an application that was filtering an XML data file and if you wanted to output an equally readable version of the file, then that whitespace would no longer be irrelevant: it would be essential. To get those characters, you add the `ignorableWhitespace` method to your application. You'll do that next.

Note: The code written in this section is contained in Echo08.java. The output is in Echo08-05.txt. (The browsable version is Echo08-05.html.)

To process the (generally) ignorable whitespace that the parser is seeing, add the following highlighted code to implement the `ignorableWhitespace` event handler in your version of the Echo program:

```
public void characters (char buf[], int offset, int len)
...
}

public void ignorableWhitespace char buf[], int offset, int Len)
throws SAXException
{
  nl();
  emit("IGNORABLE");
}

public void processingInstruction(String target, String data)
...
```

This code simply generates a message to let you know that ignorable whitespace was seen.

Note: Again, not all parsers are created equal. The SAX specification does not require that this method be invoked. The Java XML implementation does so whenever the DTD makes it possible.

When you run the Echo application now, your output looks like this:

```
ELEMENT: <slideshow
  ATTR: ...
>
IGNORABLE
IGNORABLE
PROCESS: ...
IGNORABLE
IGNORABLE
  ELEMENT: <slide
    ATTR: ...
  >
  IGNORABLE
    ELEMENT: <title>
    CHARS:   Wake up to ...
    END_ELM: </title>
  IGNORABLE
  END_ELM: </slide>
IGNORABLE
IGNORABLE
  ELEMENT: <slide
    ATTR: ...
  >
  ...
```

Here, it is apparent that the `ignorableWhitespace` is being invoked before and after comments and slide elements, whereas `characters` was being invoked before there was a DTD.

Cleanup

Now that you have seen ignorable whitespace echoed, remove that code from your version of the Echo program. You won't need it any more in the exercises that follow.

Note: That change has been made in `Echo09.java`.

Empty Elements, Revisited

Now that you understand how certain instances of whitespace can be ignorable, it is time revise the definition of an empty element. That definition can now be expanded to include

```
<foo>    </foo>
```

where there is whitespace between the tags and the DTD says that the whitespace is ignorable.

Echoing Entity References

When you wrote `slideSample06.xml`, you defined entities for the singular and plural versions of the product name in the DTD:

```
<!ENTITY product  "WonderWidget">
<!ENTITY products "WonderWidgets">
```

You referenced them in the XML this way:

```
<title>Wake up to &products;!</title>
```

Now it's time to see how they're echoed when you process them with the SAX parser.

Note: The XML used here is contained in `slideSample06.xml`, which references `slideshow1b.dtd`, as described in Defining Attributes and Entities in the DTD (page 57). The output is shown in `Echo09-06.txt`. (The browsable versions are `slideSample06-xml.html`, `slideshow1b-dtd.html`, and `Echo09-06.html`.)

When you run the Echo program on `slideSample06.xml`, here is the kind of thing you see:

```
ELEMENT:  <title>
CHARS:    Wake up to WonderWidgets!
END_ELM:  </title>
```

Note that the product name has been substituted for the entity reference.

Echoing the External Entity

In `slideSample07.xml`, you defined an external entity to reference a copyright file.

Note: The XML used here is contained in `slideSample07.xml` and in `copyright.xml`. The output is shown in `Echo09-07.txt`. (The browsable versions are `slideSample07-xml.html`, `copyright-xml.html`, and `Echo09-07.html`.)

When you run the Echo program on that version of the slide presentation, here is what you see:

```
...
END_ELM: </slide>
ELEMENT: <slide
   ATTR: type "all"
>
   ELEMENT: <item>
   CHARS:
This is the standard copyright message that our lawyers
make us put everywhere so we don't have to shell out a
million bucks every time someone spills hot coffee in their
lap...
   END_ELM: </item>
END_ELM: </slide>
...
```

Note that the newline that follows the comment in the file is echoed as a character, but the comment itself is ignored. That is why the copyright message appears to start on the next line after the CHARS: label instead of immediately after the label: the first character echoed is actually the newline that follows the comment.

Summarizing Entities

An entity that is referenced in the document content, whether internal or external, is termed a *general entity*. An entity that contains DTD specifications that are referenced from within the DTD is termed a *parameter entity*. (More on that later.)

An entity that contains XML (text and markup), and is therefore parsed, is known as a *parsed entity*. An entity that contains binary data (such as images) is known as an *unparsed entity*. (By its nature, it must be external.) We'll discuss references to unparsed entities later, in Using the DTDHandler and EntityResolver (page 171).

Choosing Your Parser Implementation

If no other factory class is specified, the default `SAXParserFactory` class is used. To use a parser from a different manufacturer, you can change the value of the environment variable that points to it. You can do that from the command line:

```
java -Djavax.xml.parsers.SAXParserFactory=yourFactoryHere ...
```

The factory name you specify must be a fully qualified class name (all package prefixes included). For more information, see the documentation in the `newInstance()` method of the `SAXParserFactory` class.

Using the Validating Parser

By now, you have done a lot of experimenting with the nonvalidating parser. It's time to have a look at the validating parser to find out what happens when you use it to parse the sample presentation.

You need to understand about two things about the validating parser at the outset:

- A schema or document type definition (DTD) is required.
- Because the schema or DTD is present, the `ignorableWhitespace` method is invoked whenever possible.

Configuring the Factory

The first step is to modify the Echo program so that it uses the validating parser instead of the nonvalidating parser.

Note: The code in this section is contained in `Echo10.java`.

To use the validating parser, make the following highlighted changes:

```
public static void main(String argv[])
{
  if (argv.length != 1) {
    ...
  }
  // Use the default (non-validating) parser
  // Use the validating parser
  SAXParserFactory factory = SAXParserFactory.newInstance();
  factory.setValidating(true);
  try {
    ...
```

Here, you configure the factory so that it will produce a validating parser when `newSAXParser` is invoked. To configure it to return a namespace-aware parser, you can also use `setNamespaceAware(true)`. Sun's implementation supports any combination of configuration options. (If a combination is not supported by a particular implementation, it is required to generate a factory configuration error.)

Validating with XML Schema

Although a full treatment of XML Schema is beyond the scope of this tutorial, this section shows you the steps you take to validate an XML document using an existing schema written in the XML Schema language. (To learn more about XML Schema, you can review the online tutorial, *XML Schema Part 0: Primer*, at `http://www.w3.org/TR/xmlschema-0/`. You can also examine the sample programs that are part of the JAXP download. They use a simple XML Schema definition to validate personnel data stored in an XML file.)

Note: There are multiple schema-definition languages, including RELAX NG, Schematron, and the W3C "XML Schema" standard. (Even a DTD qualifies as a "schema," although it is the only one that does not use XML syntax to describe schema constraints.) However, "XML Schema" presents us with a terminology challenge. Although the phrase "XML Schema schema" would be precise, we'll use the phrase "XML Schema definition" to avoid the appearance of redundancy.

To be notified of validation errors in an XML document, the parser factory must be configured to create a validating parser, as shown in the preceding section. In addition, the following must be true:

- The appropriate properties must be set on the SAX parser.
- The appropriate error handler must be set.
- The document must be associated with a schema.

Setting the SAX Parser Properties

It's helpful to start by defining the constants you'll use when setting the properties:

```
static final String JAXP_SCHEMA_LANGUAGE =
    "http://java.sun.com/xml/jaxp/properties/schemaLanguage";

static final String W3C_XML_SCHEMA =
    "http://www.w3.org/2001/XMLSchema";
```

Next, you configure the parser factory to generate a parser that is namespace-aware as well as validating:

```
...
SAXParserFactory factory = SAXParserFactory.newInstance();
factory.setNamespaceAware(true);
factory.setValidating(true);
```

You'll learn more about namespaces in Validating with XML Schema (page 237). For now, understand that schema validation is a namespace-oriented process. Because JAXP-compliant parsers are not namespace-aware by default, it is necessary to set the property for schema validation to work.

The last step is to configure the parser to tell it which schema language to use. Here, you use the constants you defined earlier to specify the W3C's XML Schema language:

```
saxParser.setProperty(JAXP_SCHEMA_LANGUAGE, W3C_XML_SCHEMA);
```

In the process, however, there is an extra error to handle. You'll take a look at that error next.

Setting Up the Appropriate Error Handling

In addition to the error handling you've already learned about, there is one error that can occur when you are configuring the parser for schema-based validation. If the parser is not 1.2-compliant and therefore does not support XML Schema, it can throw a SAXNotRecognizedException.

To handle that case, you wrap the setProperty() statement in a try/catch block, as shown in the code highlighted here:

```
...
SAXParser saxParser = factory.newSAXParser();
try {
   saxParser.setProperty(JAXP_SCHEMA_LANGUAGE, W3C_XML_SCHEMA);
}
catch (SAXNotRecognizedException x) {
   // Happens if the parser does not support JAXP 1.2
   ...
}
...
```

Associating a Document with a Schema

Now that the program is ready to validate the data using an XML Schema definition, it is only necessary to ensure that the XML document is associated with one. There are two ways to do that:

• By including a schema declaration in the XML document

• By specifying the schema to use in the application

Note: When the application specifies the schema to use, it overrides any schema declaration in the document.

To specify the schema definition in the document, you create XML such as this:

```
<documentRoot
   xmlns:xsi="http://www.w3.org/2001/XMLSchema-instance"
   xsi:noNamespaceSchemaLocation='YourSchemaDefinition.xsd'
>
   ...
```

The first attribute defines the XML namespace (xmlns) prefix, xsi, which stands for XML Schema instance. The second line specifies the schema to use for elements in the document that do *not* have a namespace prefix—that is, for the elements you typically define in any simple, uncomplicated XML document.

Note: You'll learn about namespaces in Validating with XML Schema (page 237). For now, think of these attributes as the "magic incantation" you use to validate a simple XML file that doesn't use them. After you've learned more about namespaces, you'll see how to use XML Schema to validate complex documents that use them. Those ideas are discussed in Validating with Multiple Namespaces (page 239).

You can also specify the schema file in the application:

```
static final String JAXP_SCHEMA_SOURCE =
    "http://java.sun.com/xml/jaxp/properties/schemaSource";

...
SAXParser saxParser = spf.newSAXParser();
...
saxParser.setProperty(JAXP_SCHEMA_SOURCE,
    new File(schemaSource));
```

Now that you know how to use an XML Schema definition, we'll turn to the kinds of errors you can see when the application is validating its incoming data. To do that, you'll use a document type definition (DTD) as you experiment with validation.

Experimenting with Validation Errors

To see what happens when the XML document does not specify a DTD, remove the DOCTYPE statement from the XML file and run the Echo program on it.

Note: The output shown here is contained in `Echo10-01.txt`. (The browsable version is `Echo10-01.html`.)

The result you see looks like this:

```
<?xml version='1.0' encoding='UTF-8'?>
** Parsing error, line 9, uri .../slideSample01.xml
   Document root element "slideshow", must match DOCTYPE root
"null"
```

Note: This message was generated by the JAXP 1.2 libraries. If you are using a different parser, the error message is likely to be somewhat different.

This message says that the root element of the document must match the element specified in the DOCTYPE declaration. That declaration specifies the document's DTD. Because you don't yet have one, it's value is null. In other words, the message is saying that you are trying to validate the document, but no DTD has been declared, because no DOCTYPE declaration is present.

So now you know that a DTD is a requirement for a valid document. That makes sense. What happens when you run the parser on your current version of the slide presentation, with the DTD specified?

Note: The output shown here is produced using slideSample07.xml, as described in Referencing Binary Entities (page 64). The output is contained in Echo10-07.txt. (The browsable version is Echo10-07.html.)

This time, the parser gives a different error message:

```
** Parsing error, line 29, uri file:...
The content of element type "slide" must match
"(image?,title,item*)"
```

This message says that the element found at line 29 (<item>) does not match the definition of the <slide> element in the DTD. The error occurs because the definition says that the slide element requires a title. That element is not optional, and the copyright slide does not have one. To fix the problem, add a question mark to make title an optional element:

```
<!ELEMENT slide (image?, title?, item*)>
```

Now what happens when you run the program?

Note: You could also remove the copyright slide, producing the same result shown next, as reflected in Echo10-06.txt. (The browsable version is Echo10-06.html.)

The answer is that everything runs fine until the parser runs into the <em> tag contained in the overview slide. Because that tag is not defined in the DTD, the attempt to validate the document fails. The output looks like this:

```
...
ELEMENT: <title>
CHARS:   Overview
END_ELM: </title>
ELEMENT: <item>
CHARS:   Why ** Parsing error, line 28, uri: ...
Element "em" must be declared.
org.xml.sax.SAXParseException: ...
...
```

The error message identifies the part of the DTD that caused validation to fail. In this case it is the line that defines an item element as (#PCDATA | item).

As an exercise, make a copy of the file and remove all occurrences of <em> from it. Can the file be validated now? (In the next section, you'll learn how to define parameter entries so that we can use XHTML in the elements we are defining as part of the slide presentation.)

Error Handling in the Validating Parser

It is important to recognize that the only reason an exception is thrown when the file fails validation is as a result of the error-handling code you entered in the early stages of this tutorial. That code is reproduced here:

```
public void error(SAXParseException e)
throws SAXParseException
{
   throw e;
}
```

If that exception is not thrown, the validation errors are simply ignored. Try commenting out the line that throws the exception. What happens when you run the parser now?

In general, a SAX parsing *error* is a validation error, although you have seen that it can also be generated if the file specifies a version of XML that the parser is not prepared to handle. Remember that your application will not generate a validation exception unless you supply an error handler such as the one here.

Parsing a Parameterized DTD

This section uses the Echo program to see what happens when you reference `xhtml.dtd` in `slideshow2.dtd`. It also covers the kinds of warnings that are generated by the SAX parser when a DTD is present.

Note: The XML file used here is `slideSample08.xml`, which references `slideshow2.dtd`. The output is contained in `Echo10-08.txt`. (The browsable versions are `slideSample08-xml.html`, `slideshow2-dtd.html`, and `Echo10-08.html`.)

When you try to echo the slide presentation, you will find that it now contains a new error. The relevant part of the output is shown here (formatted for readability):

```
<?xml version='1.0' encoding='UTF-8'?>
** Parsing error, line 22, uri: .../slideshow.dtd
Element type "title" must not be declared more than once.
```

Note: The foregoing message was generated by the JAXP 1.2 libraries. If you are using a different parser, the error message is likely to be somewhat different.

The problem is that `xhtml.dtd` defines a `title` element that is entirely different from the `title` element defined in the slideshow DTD. Because there is no hierarchy in the DTD, these two definitions conflict.

The `slideSample09.xml` version solves the problem by changing the name of the slide title. Run the Echo program on that version of the slide presentation. It should run to completion and display output like that shown in `Echo10-09`.

Congratulations! You have now read a fully validated XML document. The change in that version of the file has the effect of putting the DTD's `title` element into a `slideshow` "namespace" that you artificially constructed by hyphenating the name, so the `title` element in the "slideshow namespace" (slide-title, really) is no longer in conflict with the `title` element in `xhtml.dtd`.

Note: As mentioned in Using Namespaces (page 71), namespaces let you accomplish the same goal without having to rename any elements.

Next, we'll take a look at the kinds of warnings that the validating parser can produce when processing the DTD.

DTD Warnings

As mentioned earlier, warnings are generated only when the SAX parser is processing a DTD. Some warnings are generated only by the validating parser. The nonvalidating parser's main goal is to operate as rapidly as possible, but it too generates some warnings. (The explanations that follow tell which does what.)

The XML specification suggests that warnings should be generated as a result of the following:

- Providing additional declarations for entities, attributes, or notations. (Such declarations are ignored. Only the first is used. Also, note that duplicate definitions of *elements* always produce a fatal error when validating, as you saw earlier.)
- Referencing an undeclared element type. (A validity error occurs only if the undeclared type is actually used in the XML document. A warning results when the undeclared element is referenced in the DTD.)
- Declaring attributes for undeclared element types.

The Java XML SAX parser also emits warnings in other cases:

- No `<!DOCTYPE ...>` when validating.
- References to an undefined parameter entity when not validating. (When validating, an error results. Although nonvalidating parsers are not required to read parameter entities, the Java XML parser does so. Because it is not a requirement, the Java XML parser generates a warning, rather than an error.)
- Certain cases where the character-encoding declaration does not look right.

At this point, you have digested many XML concepts, including DTDs and external entities. You have also learned your way around the SAX parser. The remainder of this chapter covers advanced topics that you will need to understand only if you are writing SAX-based applications. If your primary goal is to write DOM-based applications, you can skip ahead to Chapter 6, Document Object Model (page 175).

Handling Lexical Events

You saw earlier that if you are writing text out as XML, you need to know whether you are in a CDATA section. If you are, then angle brackets (<) and ampersands (&) should be output unchanged. But if you're not in a CDATA section, they should be replaced by the predefined entities < and &. But how do you know whether you're processing a CDATA section?

Then again, if you are filtering XML in some way, you want to pass comments along. Normally the parser ignores comments. How can you get comments so that you can echo them?

Finally, there are the parsed entity definitions. If an XML-filtering app sees &myEntity; it needs to echo the same string, and not the text that is inserted in its place. How do you go about doing that?

This section answers those questions. It shows you how to use `org.xml.sax.ext.LexicalHandler` to identify comments, CDATA sections, and references to parsed entities.

Comments, CDATA tags, and references to parsed entities constitute *lexical* information—that is, information that concerns the text of the XML itself, rather than the XML's information content. Most applications, of course, are concerned only with the *content* of an XML document. Such applications will not use the `LexicalEventListener` API. But applications that output XML text will find it invaluable.

Note: Lexical event handling is an optional parser feature. Parser implementations are not required to support it. (The reference implementation does so.) This discussion assumes that your parser does so.

How the LexicalHandler Works

To be informed when the SAX parser sees lexical information, you configure the `XmlReader` that underlies the parser with a `LexicalHandler`. The `LexicalHandler` interface defines these event-handling methods:

`comment(String comment)`
    Passes comments to the application

startCDATA(), endCDATA()
>   Tells when a CDATA section is starting and ending, which tells your application what kind of characters to expect the next time `characters()` is called

startEntity(String name), endEntity(String name)
>   Gives the name of a parsed entity

startDTD(String name, String publicId, String systemTd), endDTD()
>   Tells when a DTD is being processed, and identifies it

Working with a LexicalHandler

In the remainder of this section, you'll convert the Echo app into a lexical handler and play with its features.

Note: The code shown in this section is in `Echo11.java`. The output is shown in `Echo11-09.txt`. (The browsable version is `Echo11-09.html`.)

To start, add the following highlighted code to implement the `LexicalHandler` interface and add the appropriate methods.

```
import org.xml.sax.*;
import org.xml.sax.helpers.DefaultHandler;
import org.xml.sax.ext.LexicalHandler;
...
public class Echo extends HandlerBase
   implements LexicalHandler
{
   public static void main(String argv[])
      {
         ...
         // Use an instance of ourselves as the SAX event handler
         DefaultHandler handler = new Echo();
         Echo handler = new Echo();
         ...
```

At this point, the Echo class extends one class and implements an additional interface. You have changed the class of the handler variable accordingly, so you can use the same instance as either a `DefaultHandler` or a `LexicalHandler`, as appropriate.

Next, add the following highlighted code to get the XMLReader that the parser delegates to, and configure it to send lexical events to your lexical handler:

```
public static void main(String argv[])
{
  ...
  try {
    ...
    // Parse the input
    SAXParser saxParser = factory.newSAXParser();
    XMLReader xmlReader = saxParser.getXMLReader();
    xmlReader.setProperty(
      "http://xml.org/sax/properties/lexical-handler",
      handler
      );
    saxParser.parse( new File(argv[0]), handler);
  } catch (SAXParseException spe) {
    ...
```

Here, you configure the XMLReader using the setProperty() method defined in the XMLReader class. The property name, defined as part of the SAX standard, is the URN, http://xml.org/sax/properties/lexical-handler.

Finally, add the following highlighted code to define the appropriate methods that implement the interface.

```
public void warning(SAXParseException err)
  ...
}

public void comment(char[] ch, int start, int length)
throws SAXException
{
}

public void startCDATA()
throws SAXException
{
}

pubic void endCDATA()
throws SAXException
{
}
```

```
public void startEntity(String name)
throws SAXException
{
}

public void endEntity(String name)
throws SAXException
{
}

public void startDTD(
  String name, String publicId, String systemId)
throws SAXException
{
}

public void endDTD()
throws SAXException
{
}

private void echoText()
  . . .
```

You have now turned the Echo class into a lexical handler. In the next section, you'll start experimenting with lexical events.

Echoing Comments

The next step is to do something with one of the new methods. Add the following highlighted code to echo comments in the XML file:

```
public void comment(char[] ch, int start, int length)
  throws SAXException
{
  String text = new String(ch, start, length);
  nl();
  emit("COMMENT: "+text);
}
```

When you compile the Echo program and run it on your XML file, the result looks something like this:

```
COMMENT:   A SAMPLE set of slides
COMMENT:   FOR WALLY / WALLIES
COMMENT:
  DTD for a simple "slide show".

COMMENT:  Defines the %inline; declaration
COMMENT:  ...
```

The line endings in the comments are passed as part of the comment string, again normalized to newlines. You can also see that comments in the DTD are echoed along with comments from the file. (That can pose problems when you want to echo only comments that are in the data file. To get around that problem, you can use the startDTD and endDTD methods.)

Echoing Other Lexical Information

To finish learning about lexical events, you'll exercise the remaining Lexical-Handler methods.

Note: The code shown in this section is in Echo12.java. The file it operates on is slideSample09.xml. The results of processing are in Echo12-09.txt. (The browsable versions are slideSample09-xml.html and Echo12-09.html.)

Make the following highlighted changes to remove the comment echo (you no longer need that) and echo the other events, along with any characters that have been accumulated when an event occurs:

```
public void comment(char[] ch, int start, int length)
throws SAXException
{
  String text = new String(ch, start, length);
  nl();
  emit("COMMENT: "+text);
}
```

```
public void startCDATA()
throws SAXException
{
   echoText();
   nl();
   emit("START CDATA SECTION");
}

public void endCDATA()
throws SAXException
{
   echoText();
   nl();
   emit("END CDATA SECTION");
}

public void startEntity(String name)
throws SAXException
{
   echoText();
   nl();
   emit("START ENTITY: "+name);
}

public void endEntity(String name)
throws SAXException
{
   echoText();
   nl();
   emit("END ENTITY: "+name);
}

public void startDTD(String name, String publicId, String
systemId)
throws SAXException
{
   nl();
   emit("START DTD: "+name
      +"           publicId=" + publicId
      +"           systemId=" + systemId);
}

public void endDTD()
throws SAXException
{
   nl();
   emit("END DTD");
}
```

Here is what you see when the DTD is processed:

```
START DTD: slideshow
        publicId=null
        systemId=slideshow3.dtd
START ENTITY: ...
...
END DTD
```

Note: To see events that occur while the DTD is being processed, use `org.xml.sax.ext.DeclHandler`.

Here is some of the additional output you see when the internally defined prod-ucts entity is processed with the latest version of the program:

```
START ENTITY: products
CHARS:    WonderWidgets
END ENTITY: products
```

And here is the additional output you see as a result of processing the external copyright entity:

```
START ENTITY: copyright
CHARS:
This is the standard copyright message that our lawyers
make us put everywhere so we don't have to shell out a
million bucks every time someone spills hot coffee in their
lap...

END ENTITY: copyright
```

Finally, you get output that shows when the CDATA section was processed:

```
START CDATA SECTION
CHARS:    Diagram:

frobmorten <--------------fuznaten
    |               <3>           ^
    | <1>                         |   <1> = fozzle
    V                             |   <2> = framboze
    staten--------------------+   <3> = frenzle
                <2>

END CDATA SECTION
```

In summary, the LexicalHandler gives you the event notifications you need to produce an accurate reflection of the original XML text.

Note: To accurately echo the input, you would modify the characters() method to echo the text it sees in the appropriate fashion, depending on whether or not the program was in CDATA mode.

Using the DTDHandler and EntityResolver

In this section, we discuss the two remaining SAX event handlers: DTDHandler and EntityResolver. The DTDHandler is invoked when the DTD encounters an unparsed entity or a notation declaration. The EntityResolver comes into play when a URN (public ID) must be resolved to a URL (system ID).

The DTDHandler API

In Choosing Your Parser Implementation (page 155) you saw a method for referencing a file that contains binary data, such as an image file, using MIME data types. That is the simplest, most extensible mechanism. For compatibility with older SGML-style data, though, it is also possible to define an unparsed entity.

The NDATA keyword defines an unparsed entity:

```
<!ENTITY myEntity SYSTEM "..URL.." NDATA gif>
```

The NDATA keyword says that the data in this entity is not parsable XML data but instead is data that uses some other notation. In this case, the notation is named gif. The DTD must then include a declaration for that notation, which would look something like this:

```
<!NOTATION gif SYSTEM "..URL..">
```

When the parser sees an unparsed entity or a notation declaration, it does nothing with the information except to pass it along to the application using the `DTDHandler` interface. That interface defines two methods:

notationDecl(String name, String publicId, String systemId)

unparsedEntityDecl(String name, String publicId,
    String systemId, String notationName)

The `notationDecl` method is passed the name of the notation and either the public or the system identifier, or both, depending on which is declared in the DTD. The `unparsedEntityDecl` method is passed the name of the entity, the appropriate identifiers, and the name of the notation it uses.

Note: The `DTDHandler` interface is implemented by the `DefaultHandler` class.

Notations can also be used in attribute declarations. For example, the following declaration requires notations for the GIF and PNG image-file formats:

```
<!ENTITY image EMPTY>
<!ATTLIST image
    ...
    type  NOTATION  (gif | png) "gif"
>
```

Here, the `type` is declared as being either `gif` or `png`. The default, if neither is specified, is `gif`.

Whether the notation reference is used to describe an unparsed entity or an attribute, it is up to the application to do the appropriate processing. The parser knows nothing at all about the semantics of the notations. It only passes on the declarations.

The EntityResolver API

The `EntityResolver` API lets you convert a public ID (URN) into a system ID (URL). Your application may need to do that, for example, to convert something like `href="urn:/someName"` into `"http://someURL"`.

The `EntityResolver` interface defines a single method:

resolveEntity(String publicId, String systemId)

This method returns an `InputSource` object, which can be used to access the entity's contents. Converting a URL into an `InputSource` is easy enough. But the URL that is passed as the system ID will be the location of the original document which is, as likely as not, somewhere out on the Web. To access a local copy, if there is one, you must maintain a catalog somewhere on the system that maps names (public IDs) into local URLs.

Further Information

For further information on the SAX standard, see

- The SAX standard page: `http://www.saxproject.org/`

For more information on the StAX pull parser, see:

- The Java Community Process page:
  `http://jcp.org/en/jsr/detail?id=173`.
- Elliot Rusty Harold's introduction at
  `http://www.xml.com/pub/a/2003/09/17/stax.html`.

For more information on schema-based validation mechanisms, see

- The W3C standard validation mechanism, XML Schema:
  `http://www.w3c.org/XML/Schema`
- RELAX NG's regular-expression-based validation mechanism:
  `http://www.oasis-open.org/committees/relax-ng/`
- Schematron's assertion-based validation mechanism:
  `http://www.ascc.net/xml/resource/schematron/schematron.html`

6

Document Object Model

IN Chapter 5, you wrote an XML file that contains slides for a presentation. You then used the SAX API to echo the XML to your display.

In this chapter, you'll use the Document Object Model (DOM) to build a small application called SlideShow. You'll start by constructing and inspecting a DOM. Then see how to write a DOM as an XML structure, display it in a GUI, and manipulate the tree structure.

A DOM is a garden-variety tree structure, where each node contains one of the components from an XML structure. The two most common types of nodes are *element nodes* and *text nodes*. Using DOM functions lets you create nodes, remove nodes, change their contents, and traverse the node hierarchy.

In this chapter, you'll parse an existing XML file to construct a DOM, display and inspect the DOM hierarchy, convert the DOM into a display-friendly JTree, and explore the syntax of namespaces. You'll also create a DOM from scratch, and see how to use some of the implementation-specific features in Sun's JAXP implementation to convert an existing data set to XML.

First though, we'll make sure that DOM is the most appropriate choice for your application.

Note: The examples in this chapter can be found in `<INSTALL>/j2eetutorial14/`
`examples/jaxp/dom/samples/`.

When to Use DOM

The Document Object Model standard is, above all, designed for *documents* (for example, articles and books). In addition, the JAXP 1.2 implementation supports XML Schema, something that may be an important consideration for any given application.

On the other hand, if you are dealing with simple *data* structures and if XML Schema isn't a big part of your plans, then you may find that one of the more object-oriented standards, such as JDOM and dom4j (page 1345), is better suited for your purpose.

From the start, DOM was intended to be language-neutral. Because it was designed for use with languages such as C and Perl, DOM does not take advantage of Java's object-oriented features. That fact, in addition to the distinction between documents and data, also helps to account for the ways in which processing a DOM differs from processing a JDOM or dom4j structure.

In this section, we'll examine the differences between the models underlying those standards to help you choose the one that is most appropriate for your application.

Documents Versus Data

The major point of departure between the document model used in DOM and the data model used in JDOM or dom4j lies in

- The kind of node that exists in the hierarchy
- The capacity for mixed content

It is the difference in what constitutes a "node" in the data hierarchy that primarily accounts for the differences in programming with these two models. However, the capacity for mixed content, more than anything else, accounts for the difference in how the standards define a node. So we start by examining DOM's mixed-content model.

Mixed-Content Model

Recall from the discussion of Documents and Data (page 135) that text and elements can be freely intermixed in a DOM hierarchy. That kind of structure is dubbed *mixed content* in the DOM model.

Mixed content occurs frequently in documents. For example, suppose you wanted to represent this structure:

```
<sentence>This is an <bold>important</bold> idea.</sentence>
```

The hierarchy of DOM nodes would look something like this, where each line represents one node:

```
ELEMENT: sentence
  + TEXT: This is an
  + ELEMENT: bold
      + TEXT: important
  + TEXT: idea.
```

Note that the sentence element contains text, followed by a subelement, followed by additional text. It is the intermixing of text and elements that defines the mixed-content model.

Kinds of Nodes

To provide the capacity for mixed content, DOM nodes are inherently very simple. In the foregoing example, the "content" of the first element (its *value*) simply identifies the kind of node it is.

First-time users of a DOM are usually thrown by this fact. After navigating to the `<sentence>` node, they ask for the node's content and expect to get something useful. Instead, all they can find is the name of the element, `sentence`.

Note: The DOM Node API defines `nodeValue()`, `nodeType()`, and `nodeName()` methods. For the first element node, `nodeName()` returns `sentence`, while `nodeValue()` returns null. For the first text node, `nodeName()` returns `#text`, and `nodeValue()` returns `This is an`. The important point is that the *value* of an element is not the same as its *content*.

Instead, obtaining the content you care about when processing a DOM means inspecting the list of subelements the node contains, ignoring those you aren't interested in and processing the ones you do care about.

In our example, what does it mean if you ask for the "text" of the sentence? Any of the following could be reasonable, depending on your application:

- This is an
- This is an idea.
- This is an important idea.
- This is an <bold>important</bold> idea.

A Simpler Model

With DOM, you are free to create the semantics you need. However, you are also required to do the processing necessary to implement those semantics. Standards such as JDOM and dom4j, on the other hand, make it easier to do simple things, because each node in the hierarchy is an object.

Although JDOM and dom4j make allowances for elements having mixed content, they are not primarily designed for such situations. Instead, they are targeted for applications where the XML structure contains data.

As described in Documents and Data (page 135), the elements in a data structure typically contain either text or other elements, but not both. For example, here is some XML that represents a simple address book:

```
<addressbook>
  <entry>
    <name>Fred</name>
    <email>fred@home</email>
  </entry>
    ...
</addressbook>
```

Note: For very simple XML data structures like this one, you could also use the regular-expression package (`java.util.regex`) built into version 1.4 of the Java platform.

In JDOM and dom4j, after you navigate to an element that contains text, you invoke a method such as `text()` to get its content. When processing a DOM, though, you must inspect the list of subelements to "put together" the text of the node, as you saw earlier—even if that list contains only one item (a TEXT node).

So for simple data structures such as the address book, you can save yourself a bit of work by using JDOM or dom4j. It may make sense to use one of those models even when the data is technically "mixed" but there is always one (and only one) segment of text for a given node.

Here is an example of that kind of structure, which would also be easily processed in JDOM or dom4j:

```
<addressbook>
  <entry>Fred
    <email>fred@home</email>
  </entry>
    ...
</addressbook>
```

Here, each entry has a bit of identifying text, followed by other elements. With this structure, the program could navigate to an entry, invoke text() to find out whom it belongs to, and process the <email> subelement if it is at the correct node.

Increasing the Complexity

But for you to get a full understanding of the kind of processing you need to do when searching or manipulating a DOM, it is important to know the kinds of nodes that a DOM can conceivably contain.

Here is an example that tries to bring the point home. It is a representation of this data:

```
<sentence>
  The &projectName; <![CDATA[<i>project</i>]]> is
  <?editor: red><bold>important</bold><?editor: normal>.
</sentence>
```

This sentence contains an *entity reference*—a pointer to an entity that is defined elsewhere. In this case, the entity contains the name of the project. The example also contains a CDATA section (uninterpreted data, like <pre> data in HTML) as well as *processing instructions* (<?...?>), which in this case tell the editor which color to use when rendering the text.

Here is the DOM structure for that data. It's fairly representative of the kind of structure that a robust application should be prepared to handle:

```
+ ELEMENT: sentence
  + TEXT: The
  + ENTITY REF: projectName
    + COMMENT: The latest name we're using
    + TEXT: Eagle
  + CDATA: <i>project</i>
  + TEXT: is
  + PI: editor: red
  + ELEMENT: bold
    + TEXT: important
  + PI: editor: normal
```

This example depicts the kinds of nodes that may occur in a DOM. Although your application may be able to ignore most of them most of the time, a truly robust implementation needs to recognize and deal with each of them.

Similarly, the process of navigating to a node involves processing subelements—ignoring the ones you don't care about and inspecting the ones you do care about—until you find the node you are interested in.

A program that works on fixed, internally generated data can afford to make simplifying assumptions: that processing instructions, comments, CDATA nodes, and entity references will not exist in the data structure. But truly robust applications that work on a variety of data—especially data coming from the outside world—must be prepared to deal with all possible XML entities.

(A "simple" application will work only as long as the input data contains the simplified XML structures it expects. But there are no validation mechanisms to ensure that more complex structures will not exist. After all, XML was specifically designed to allow them.)

To be more robust, a DOM application must do these things:

1. When searching for an element:
   a. Ignore comments, attributes, and processing instructions.
   b. Allow for the possibility that subelements do not occur in the expected order.
   c. Skip over TEXT nodes that contain ignorable whitespace, if not validating.

2. When extracting text for a node:

   a. Extract text from CDATA nodes as well as text nodes.

   b. Ignore comments, attributes, and processing instructions when gathering the text.

   c. If an entity reference node or another element node is encountered, recurse (that is, apply the text-extraction procedure to all subnodes).

Note: The JAXP 1.2 parser does not insert entity reference nodes into the DOM. Instead, it inserts a TEXT node containing the contents of the reference. The JAXP 1.1 parser which is built into the 1.4 platform, on the other hand, does insert entity reference nodes. So a robust implementation that is parser-independent needs to be prepared to handle entity reference nodes.

Of course, many applications won't have to worry about such things, because the kind of data they see will be strictly controlled. But if the data can come from a variety of external sources, then the application will probably need to take these possibilities into account.

The code you need to carry out these functions is given near the end of the DOM tutorial in Searching for Nodes (page 234) and Obtaining Node Content (page 235). Right now, the goal is simply to determine whether DOM is suitable for your application.

Choosing Your Model

As you can see, when you are using DOM, even a simple operation such as getting the text from a node can take a bit of programming. So if your programs handle simple data structures, then JDOM, dom4j, or even the 1.4 regular-expression package (`java.util.regex`) may be more appropriate for your needs.

For full-fledged documents and complex applications, on the other hand, DOM gives you a lot of flexibility. And if you need to use XML Schema, then again DOM is the way to go—for now, at least.

If you process both documents *and* data in the applications you develop, then DOM may still be your best choice. After all, after you have written the code to examine and process a DOM structure, it is fairly easy to customize it for a specific purpose. So choosing to do everything in DOM means that you'll only have to deal with one set of APIs, rather than two.

In addition, the DOM standard *is* a codified standard for an in-memory document model. It's powerful and robust, and it has many implementations. That is a significant decision-making factor for many large installations, particularly for large-scale applications that need to minimize costs resulting from API changes.

Finally, even though the text in an address book may not permit bold, italics, colors, and font sizes today, someday you may want to handle these things. Because DOM will handle virtually anything you throw at it, choosing DOM makes it easier to futureproof your application.

Reading XML Data into a DOM

In this section, you'll construct a Document Object Model by reading in an existing XML file. In the following sections, you'll see how to display the XML in a Swing tree component and practice manipulating the DOM.

Note: In Chapter 7, you'll see how to write out a DOM as an XML file. (You'll also see how to convert an existing data file into XML with relative ease.)

Creating the Program

The Document Object Model provides APIs that let you create, modify, delete, and rearrange nodes. So it is relatively easy to create a DOM, as you'll see later in Creating and Manipulating a DOM (page 228).

Before you try to create a DOM, however, it is helpful to understand how a DOM is structured. This series of exercises will make DOM internals visible by displaying them in a Swing `JTree`.

Create the Skeleton

Now let's build a simple program to read an XML document into a DOM and then write it back out again.

Note: The code discussed in this section is in `DomEcho01.java`. The file it operates on is `slideSample01.xml`. (The browsable version is `slideSample01-xml.html`.)

Start with the normal basic logic for an app, and check to make sure that an argument has been supplied on the command line:

```
public class DomEcho {
  public static void main(String argv[])
  {
    if (argv.length != 1) {
      System.err.println(
          "Usage: java DomEcho filename");
      System.exit(1);
    }
  }// main
}// DomEcho
```

Import the Required Classes

In this section, all the classes are individually named so you that can see where each class comes from when you want to reference the API documentation. In your own applications, you may well want to replace the import statements shown here with the shorter form, such as javax.xml.parsers.*

Add these lines to import the JAXP APIs you'll use:

```
import javax.xml.parsers.DocumentBuilder;
import javax.xml.parsers.DocumentBuilderFactory;
import javax.xml.parsers.FactoryConfigurationError;
import javax.xml.parsers.ParserConfigurationException;
```

Add these lines for the exceptions that can be thrown when the XML document is parsed:

```
import org.xml.sax.SAXException;
import org.xml.sax.SAXParseException;
```

Add these lines to read the sample XML file and identify errors:

```
import java.io.File;
import java.io.IOException;
```

Finally, import the W3C definition for a DOM and DOM exceptions:

```
import org.w3c.dom.Document;
import org.w3c.dom.DOMException;
```

Note: A `DOMException` is thrown only when traversing or manipulating a DOM. Errors that occur during parsing are reported using a different mechanism that is covered later.

Declare the DOM

The `org.w3c.dom.Document` class is the W3C name for a DOM. Whether you parse an XML document or create one, a `Document` instance will result. You'll want to reference that object from another method later, so define it as a global object here:

```
public class DomEcho
{
    static Document document;

    public static void main(String argv[])
    {
```

It needs to be `static` because you'll generate its contents from the `main` method in a few minutes.

Handle Errors

Next, put in the error-handling logic. This logic is basically the same as the code you saw in Handling Errors with the Nonvalidating Parser (page 139) in Chapter 5, so we don't go into it in detail here. The major point is that a JAXP-conformant document builder is required to report SAX exceptions when it has trouble parsing the XML document. The DOM parser does not have to actually use a SAX parser internally, but because the SAX standard is already there, it makes sense to use it for reporting errors. As a result, the error-handling code for DOM applications is very similar to that for SAX applications:

```
public static void main(String argv[])
{
    if (argv.length != 1) {
        ...
    }

    try {

    } catch (SAXParseException spe) {
    // Error generated by the parser
```

```
        System.out.println("\n** Parsing error"
           + ", line " + spe.getLineNumber()
           + ", uri " + spe.getSystemId());
        System.out.println("   " + spe.getMessage() );

        // Use the contained exception, if any
        Exception  x = spe;
        if (spe.getException() != null)
           x = spe.getException();
        x.printStackTrace();

     } catch (SAXException sxe) {
        // Error generated during parsing
        Exception  x = sxe;
        if (sxe.getException() != null)
           x = sxe.getException();
        x.printStackTrace();

      } catch (ParserConfigurationException pce) {
        // Parser with specified options can't be built
        pce.printStackTrace();

      } catch (IOException ioe) {
        // I/O error
        ioe.printStackTrace();
      }

   }// main
```

Instantiate the Factory

Next, add the following highlighted code to obtain an instance of a factory that can give us a document builder:

```
   public static void main(String argv[])
   {
      if (argv.length != 1) {
         ...
      }
      DocumentBuilderFactory factory =
         DocumentBuilderFactory.newInstance();
      try {
```

Get a Parser and Parse the File

Now, add the following highlighted code to get an instance of a builder, and use it to parse the specified file:

```
try {
  DocumentBuilder builder = factory.newDocumentBuilder();
  document = builder.parse( new File(argv[0]) );
} catch (SAXParseException spe) {
```

Note: By now, you should be getting the idea that every JAXP application starts in pretty much the same way. You're right! Save this version of the file as a template. You'll use it later on as the basis for XSLT transformation application.

Run the Program

Throughout most of the DOM tutorial, you'll use the sample slide shows you saw in the Chapter 5. In particular, you'll use slideSample01.xml, a simple XML file with nothing much in it, and slideSample10.xml, a more complex example that includes a DTD, processing instructions, entity references, and a CDATA section.

For instructions on how to compile and run your program, see Compiling and Running the Program (page 128) from Chapter 5. Substitute DomEcho for Echo as the name of the program, and you're ready to roll.

For now, just run the program on slideSample01.xml. If it runs without error, you have successfully parsed an XML document and constructed a DOM. Congratulations!

Note: You'll have to take my word for it, for the moment, because at this point you don't have any way to display the results. But that feature is coming shortly...

Additional Information

Now that you have successfully read in a DOM, there are one or two more things you need to know in order to use DocumentBuilder effectively. You need to know about:

- Configuring the factory
- Handling validation errors

Configuring the Factory

By default, the factory returns a nonvalidating parser that knows nothing about namespaces. To get a validating parser, or one that understands namespaces (or both), you configure the factory to set either or both of those options using the following highlighted commands:

```
public static void main(String argv[])
{
   if (argv.length != 1) {
      ...
   }
   DocumentBuilderFactory factory =
      DocumentBuilderFactory.newInstance();
   factory.setValidating(true);
   factory.setNamespaceAware(true);
   try {
      ...
```

Note: JAXP-conformant parsers are not required to support all combinations of those options, even though the reference parser does. If you specify an invalid combination of options, the factory generates a `ParserConfigurationException` when you attempt to obtain a parser instance.

You'll learn more about how to use namespaces in Validating with XML Schema (page 237). To complete this section, though, you'll want to learn something about handling validation errors.

Handling Validation Errors

Remember when you were wading through the SAX tutorial in Chapter 5, and all you really wanted to do was construct a DOM? Well, now that information begins to pay off.

Recall that the default response to a validation error, as dictated by the SAX standard, is to do nothing. The JAXP standard requires throwing SAX exceptions, so you use exactly the same error-handling mechanisms as you use for a SAX application. In particular, you use the `DocumentBuilder`'s `setErrorHandler` method to supply it with an object that implements the SAX `ErrorHandler` interface.

Note: `DocumentBuilder` also has a `setEntityResolver` method you can use.

The following code uses an anonymous inner class to define that `ErrorHandler`. The highlighted code makes sure that validation errors generate an exception.

```
builder.setErrorHandler(
    new org.xml.sax.ErrorHandler() {
        // ignore fatal errors (an exception is guaranted)
        public void fatalError(SAXParseException exception)
        throws SAXException {
        }
        // treat validation errors as fatal
        public void error(SAXParseException e)
        throws SAXParseException
        {
            throw e;
        }

         // dump warnings too
        public void warning(SAXParseException err)
        throws SAXParseException
        {
            System.out.println("** Warning"
                + ", line " + err.getLineNumber()
                + ", uri " + err.getSystemId());
            System.out.println("    " + err.getMessage());
        }
    }
);
```

This code uses an anonymous inner class to generate an instance of an object that implements the `ErrorHandler` interface. It's "anonymous" because it has no class name. You can think of it as an "ErrorHandler" instance, although technically it's a no-name instance that implements the specified interface. The code is substantially the same as that described in Handling Errors with the Nonvalidating Parser (page 139). For a more complete background on validation issues, refer to Using the Validating Parser (page 155).

Looking Ahead

In the next section, you'll display the DOM structure in a `JTree` and begin to explore its structure. For example, you'll see what entity references and `CDATA` sections look like in the DOM. And perhaps most importantly, you'll see how text nodes (which contain the actual data) reside *under* element nodes in a DOM.

Displaying a DOM Hierarchy

To create or manipulate a DOM, it helps to have a clear idea of how the nodes in a DOM are structured. In this section of the tutorial, you'll expose the internal structure of a DOM.

At this point you need a way to expose the nodes in a DOM so that you can see what it contains. To do that, you'll convert a DOM into a JTreeModel and display the full DOM in a JTree. It takes a bit of work, but the end result will be a diagnostic tool you can use in the future, as well as something you can use to learn about DOM structure now.

Note: In this section, we build a Swing GUI that can display a DOM. The code is in DomEcho02.java. If you have no interest in the Swing details, you can skip ahead to Examining the Structure of a DOM (page 205) and copy DomEcho02.java to proceed from there. (But be sure to look at Table 6–1, Node Types, page 196.)

Convert DomEcho to a GUI App

Because the DOM is a tree and because the Swing JTree component is all about displaying trees, it makes sense to stuff the DOM into a JTree so that you can look at it. The first step is to hack up the DomEcho program so that it becomes a GUI application.

Add Import Statements

Start by importing the GUI components you'll need to set up the application and display a JTree:

```
// GUI components and layouts
import javax.swing.JFrame;
import javax.swing.JPanel;
import javax.swing.JScrollPane;
import javax.swing.JTree;
```

Later, you'll tailor the DOM display to generate a user-friendly version of the JTree display. When the user selects an element in that tree, you'll display sub-elements in an adjacent editor pane. So while you're doing the setup work here, import the components you need to set up a divided view (JSplitPane) and to display the text of the subelements (JEditorPane):

```
import javax.swing.JSplitPane;
import javax.swing.JEditorPane;
```

Next, add a few support classes you'll need to get this thing off the ground:

```
// GUI support classes
import java.awt.BorderLayout;
import java.awt.Dimension;
import java.awt.Toolkit;
import java.awt.event.WindowEvent;
import java.awt.event.WindowAdapter;
```

And, import some classes to make a fancy border:

```
// For creating borders
import javax.swing.border.EmptyBorder;
import javax.swing.border.BevelBorder;
import javax.swing.border.CompoundBorder;
```

(These are optional. You can skip them and the code that depends on them if you want to simplify things.)

Create the GUI Framework

The next step is to convert the application into a GUI application. To do that, you make the static main method create an instance of the class, which will have become a GUI pane.

Start by converting the class into a GUI pane by extending the Swing JPanel class:

```
public class DomEcho02 extends JPanel
{
    // Global value so it can be ref'd by the tree adapter
    static Document document;
    ...
```

While you're there, define a few constants you'll use to control window sizes:

```
public class DomEcho02 extends JPanel
{
    // Global value so it can be ref'd by the tree adapter
    static Document document;
```

```
static final int windowHeight = 460;
static final int leftWidth = 300;
static final int rightWidth = 340;
static final int windowWidth = leftWidth + rightWidth;
```

Now, In the main method, invoke a method that will create the outer frame that the GUI pane will sit in:

```
public static void main(String argv[])
{
   ...
   DocumentBuilderFactory factory ...
   try {
      DocumentBuilder builder = factory.newDocumentBuilder();
      document = builder.parse( new File(argv[0]) );
      makeFrame();

   } catch (SAXParseException spe) {
      ...
```

Next, you'll define the makeFrame method itself. It contains the standard code to create a frame, handle the exit condition gracefully, give it an instance of the main panel, size it, locate it on the screen, and make it visible:

```
   ...
} // main

public static void makeFrame()
{
   // Set up a GUI framework
   JFrame frame = new JFrame("DOM Echo");
   frame.addWindowListener(new WindowAdapter() {
      public void windowClosing(WindowEvent e)
         {System.exit(0);}
   });

   // Set up the tree, the views, and display it all
   final DomEcho02 echoPanel = new DomEcho02();
   frame.getContentPane().add("Center", echoPanel );
   frame.pack();
   Dimension screenSize =
      Toolkit.getDefaultToolkit().getScreenSize();
   int w = windowWidth + 10;
   int h = windowHeight + 10;
   frame.setLocation(screenSize.width/3 - w/2,
            screenSize.height/2 - h/2);
   frame.setSize(w, h);
   frame.setVisible(true)
} // makeFrame
```

Add the Display Components

The only thing left in the effort to convert the program to a GUI application is to create the class constructor and make it create the panel's contents. Here is the constructor:

```
public class DomEcho02 extends JPanel
{
   ...
   static final int windowWidth = leftWidth + rightWidth;

   public DomEcho02()
   {
   } // Constructor
```

Here, you use the border classes you imported earlier to make a regal border (optional):

```
public DomEcho02()
{
   // Make a nice border
   EmptyBorder eb = new EmptyBorder(5,5,5,5);
   BevelBorder bb = new BevelBorder(BevelBorder.LOWERED);
   CompoundBorder cb = new CompoundBorder(eb,bb);
   this.setBorder(new CompoundBorder(cb,eb));

} // Constructor
```

Next, create an empty tree and put it into a JScrollPane so that users can see its contents as it gets large:

```
public DomEcho02(
{
   ...

   // Set up the tree
   JTree tree = new JTree();

   // Build left-side view
   JScrollPane treeView = new JScrollPane(tree);
   treeView.setPreferredSize(
      new Dimension( leftWidth, windowHeight ));

} // Constructor
```

Now create a noneditable `JEditPane` that will eventually hold the contents pointed to by selected `JTree` nodes:

```
public DomEcho02(
{
   ....

   // Build right-side view
   JEditorPane htmlPane = new JEditorPane("text/html","");
   htmlPane.setEditable(false);
   JScrollPane htmlView = new JScrollPane(htmlPane);
   htmlView.setPreferredSize(
      new Dimension( rightWidth, windowHeight ));

} // Constructor
```

With the left-side `JTree` and the right-side `JEditorPane` constructed, create a `JSplitPane` to hold them:

```
public DomEcho02()
{
   ....

   // Build split-pane view
   JSplitPane splitPane =
      new JSplitPane(JSplitPane.HORIZONTAL_SPLIT,
            treeView, htmlView );
   splitPane.setContinuousLayout( true );
   splitPane.setDividerLocation( leftWidth );
   splitPane.setPreferredSize(
      new Dimension( windowWidth + 10, windowHeight+10 ));

} // Constructor
```

With this code, you set up the `JSplitPane` with a vertical divider. That produces a horizontal split between the tree and the editor pane. (It's really more of a horizontal layout.) You also set the location of the divider so that the tree gets the width it prefers, with the remainder of the window width allocated to the editor pane.

Finally, specify the layout for the panel and add the split pane:

```
public DomEcho02()
{
   ...
```

```
        // Add GUI components
        this.setLayout(new BorderLayout());
        this.add("Center", splitPane );

    } // Constructor
```

Congratulations! The program is now a GUI application. You can run it now to see what the general layout will look like on the screen. For reference, here is the completed constructor:

```
    public DomEcho02()
    {
        // Make a nice border
        EmptyBorder eb = new EmptyBorder(5,5,5,5);
        BevelBorder bb = new BevelBorder(BevelBorder.LOWERED);
        CompoundBorder CB = new CompoundBorder(eb,bb);
        this.setBorder(new CompoundBorder(CB,eb));

        // Set up the tree
        JTree tree = new JTree();

        // Build left-side view
        JScrollPane treeView = new JScrollPane(tree);
        treeView.setPreferredSize(
            new Dimension( leftWidth, windowHeight ));

        // Build right-side view
        JEditorPane htmlPane = new JEditorPane("text/html","");
        htmlPane.setEditable(false);
        JScrollPane htmlView = new JScrollPane(htmlPane);
        htmlView.setPreferredSize(
            new Dimension( rightWidth, windowHeight ));

        // Build split-pane view
        JSplitPane splitPane =
            new JSplitPane(JSplitPane.HORIZONTAL_SPLIT,
                    treeView, htmlView )
        splitPane.setContinuousLayout( true );
        splitPane.setDividerLocation( leftWidth );
        splitPane.setPreferredSize(
            new Dimension( windowWidth + 10, windowHeight+10 ));

        // Add GUI components
        this.setLayout(new BorderLayout());
        this.add("Center", splitPane );

    } // Constructor
```

Create Adapters to Display the DOM in a JTree

Now that you have a GUI framework to display a JTree in, the next step is to get the JTree to display the DOM. But a JTree wants to display a TreeModel. A DOM is a tree, but it's not a TreeModel. So you'll create an adapter class that makes the DOM look like a TreeModel to a JTree.

Now, when the TreeModel passes nodes to the JTree, JTree uses the toString function of those nodes to get the text to display in the tree. The value returned by the standard toString function isn't very pretty, so you'll wrap the DOM nodes in an AdapterNode that returns the text we want. What the TreeModel gives to the JTree, then, will in fact be AdapterNode objects that wrap DOM nodes.

Note: The classes that follow are defined as inner classes. If you are coding for the 1.1 platform, you will need to define these classes as external classes.

Define the AdapterNode Class

Start by importing the tree, event, and utility classes you'll need to make this work:

```
// For creating a TreeModel
import javax.swing.tree.*;
import javax.swing.event.*;
import java.util.*;

public class DomEcho extends JPanel
{
```

Moving back down to the end of the program, define a set of strings for the node element types:

```
        . . .
} // makeFrame

// An array of names for DOM node types
// (Array indexes = nodeType() values.)
static final String[] typeName = {
  "none",
  "Element",
```

```
            "Attr",
            "Text",
            "CDATA",
            "EntityRef",
            "Entity",
            "ProcInstr",
            "Comment",
            "Document",
            "DocType",
            "DocFragment",
            "Notation",
        };
```

} // DomEcho

These are the strings that will be displayed in the JTree. The specification of these node types can be found in the DOM Level 2 Core Specification at http://www.w3.org/TR/2000/REC-DOM-Level-2-Core-20001113, under the specification for Node. Table 6–1 is adapted from that specification.

Table 6–1   Node Types

Node	nodeName()	nodeValue()	Attributes	nodeType()
Attr	Name of attribute	Value of attribute	null	2
CDATASection	#cdata-section	Content of the CDATA section	null	4
Comment	#comment	Content of the comment	null	8
Document	#document	null	null	9
DocumentFragment	#document-fragment	null	null	11
DocumentType	Document type name	null	null	10
Element	Tag name	null	Named-NodeMap	1
Entity	Entity name	null	null	6

Table 6–1 Node Types *(Continued)*

Node	nodeName()	nodeValue()	Attributes	nodeType()
EntityReference	Name of entity referenced	null	null	5
Notation	Notation name	null	null	12
ProcessingInstruction	Target	Entire content excluding the target	null	7
Text	#text	Content of the text node	null	3

Note: Print this table and keep it handy! You need it when working with the DOM, because all these types are intermixed in a DOM tree. So your code is forever asking, "Is this the kind of node I'm interested in?"

Next, define the `AdapterNode` wrapper for DOM nodes as an inner class:

```
static final String[] typeName = {
   ...
};

public class AdapterNode
{
   org.w3c.dom.Node domNode;

   // Construct an Adapter node from a DOM node
   public AdapterNode(org.w3c.dom.Node node) {
      domNode = node;
   }

   // Return a string that identifies this node
   //    in the tree
   public String toString() {
      String s = typeName[domNode.getNodeType()];
      String nodeName = domNode.getNodeName();
```

```
      if (! nodeName.startsWith("#")) {
         s += ": " + nodeName;
      }
      if (domNode.getNodeValue() != null) {
         if (s.startsWith("ProcInstr"))
             s += ", ";
         else
             s += ": ";

         // Trim the value to get rid of NL's
         //    at the front
         String t = domNode.getNodeValue().trim();
         int x = t.indexOf("\n");
         if (x >= 0) t = t.substring(0, x);
         s += t;
      }
      return s;
   }

   } // AdapterNode

   } // DomEcho
```

This class declares a variable to hold the DOM node and requires it to be specified as a constructor argument. It then defines the toString operation, which returns the node type from the String array, and then adds more information from the node to further identify it.

As you can see in Table 6–1, every node has a type, a name, and a value, which may or may not be empty. Where the node name starts with #, that field duplicates the node type, so there is no point in including it. That explains the lines that read

```
if (! nodeName.startsWith("#")) {
   s += ": " + nodeName;
}
```

The remainder of the toString method deserves a couple of notes. For example these lines merely provide a little syntactic sugar:

```
if (s.startsWith("ProcInstr"))
   s += ", ";
else
   s += ": ";
```

The `type` field for processing instructions ends with a colon (:) anyway, so those lines keep the code from doubling the colon.

The other interesting lines are

```
String t = domNode.getNodeValue().trim();
int x = t.indexOf("\n");
if (x >= 0) t = t.substring(0, x);
s += t;
```

These lines trim the value field down to the first newline (linefeed) character in the field. If you omit these lines, you will see some funny characters (square boxes, typically) in the JTree.

Note: Recall that XML stipulates that all line endings are normalized to newlines, regardless of the system the data comes from. That makes programming quite a bit simpler.

Wrapping a DomNode and returning the desired string are the AdapterNode's major functions. But because the TreeModel adapter must answer questions such as "How many children does this node have?" and must satisfy commands such as "Give me this node's Nth child," it will be helpful to define a few additional utility methods. (The adapter can always access the DOM node and get that information for itself, but this way things are more encapsulated.)

Next, add the following highlighted code to return the index of a specified child, the child that corresponds to a given index, and the count of child nodes:

```
public class AdapterNode
{
  ...
  public String toString() {
    ...
  }

  public int index(AdapterNode child) {
    //System.err.println("Looking for index of " + child);
    int count = childCount();
    for (int i=0; i<count; i++) {
      AdapterNode n = this.child(i);
      if (child == n) return i;
    }
    return -1; // Should never get here.
  }
```

```
    public AdapterNode child(int searchIndex) {
      //Note: JTree index is zero-based.
      org.w3c.dom.Node node =
        domNode.getChildNodes().item(searchIndex);
      return new AdapterNode(node);
    }

    public int childCount() {
      return domNode.getChildNodes().getLength();
    }

  } // AdapterNode

} // DomEcho
```

Note: During development, it was only after I started writing the TreeModel adapter that I realized these were needed and went back to add them. In a moment, you'll see why.

Define the TreeModel Adapter

Now, at last, you are ready to write the TreeModel adapter. One of the really nice things about the JTree model is the ease with which you can convert an existing tree for display. One reason for that is the clear separation between the display-able view, which JTree uses, and the modifiable view, which the application uses. For more on that separation, see "Understanding the TreeModel" at http:/ /java.sun.com/products/jfc/tsc/articles/jtree/index.html. For now, the important point is that to satisfy the TreeModel interface we need only (a) provide methods to access and report on children and (b) register the appropriate JTree listener so that it knows to update its view when the underlying model changes.

Add the following highlighted code to create the TreeModel adapter and specify the child-processing methods:

```
    ...
  } // AdapterNode

  // This adapter converts the current Document (a DOM) into
  // a JTree model.
  public class DomToTreeModelAdapter implements
  javax.swing.tree.TreeModel
  {
```

```java
// Basic TreeModel operations
public Object  getRoot() {
   //System.err.println("Returning root: " +document);
   return new AdapterNode(document);
}

public boolean isLeaf(Object aNode) {
   // Determines whether the icon shows up to the left.
   // Return true for any node with no children
   AdapterNode node = (AdapterNode) aNode;
   if (node.childCount() > 0) return false;
   return true;
}

public int     getChildCount(Object parent)
   AdapterNode node = (AdapterNode) parent;
   return node.childCount();
}

public Object  getChild(Object parent, int index) {
   AdapterNode node = (AdapterNode) parent;
   return node.child(index);
}

public int     getIndexOfChild(Object parent, Object child) {
   AdapterNode node = (AdapterNode) parent;
   return node.index((AdapterNode) child);
}

public void valueForPathChanged(
        TreePath path, Object newValue)
{
   // Null. We won't be making changes in the GUI
   // If we did, we would ensure the new value was
   // really new and then fire a TreeNodesChanged event.
}

} // DomToTreeModelAdapter

} // DomEcho
```

In this code, the getRoot method returns the root node of the DOM, wrapped as an AdapterNode object. From this point on, all nodes returned by the adapter will be AdapterNodes that wrap DOM nodes. By the same token, whenever the JTree asks for the child of a given parent, the number of children that parent has, and so on, the JTree will pass us an AdapterNode. We know that, because we control every node the JTree sees, starting with the root node.

JTree uses the `isLeaf` method to determine whether or not to display a clickable expand/contract icon to the left of the node, so that method returns true only if the node has children. In this method, we see the cast from the generic object JTree sends us to the `AdapterNode` object we know it must be. *We* know it is sending us an adapter object, but the interface, to be general, defines objects, so we must do the casts.

The next three methods return the number of children for a given node, the child that lives at a given index, and the index of a given child, respectively. That's all straightforward.

The last method is invoked when the user changes a value stored in the JTree. In this app, we won't support that. But if we did, the application would have to make the change to the underlying model and then inform any listeners that a change has occurred. (The JTree might not be the only listener. In many applications, it isn't.)

To inform listeners that a change has occurred, you'll need the ability to register them. That brings us to the last two methods required to implement the Tree-Model interface. Add the following highlighted code to define them:

```
public class DomToTreeModelAdapter ...
{
   ...
   public void valueForPathChanged(
      TreePath path, Object newValue)
   {
      ...
   }
   private Vector listenerList = new Vector();
   public void addTreeModelListener(
      TreeModelListener listener ) {
      if ( listener != null
      && ! listenerList.contains(listener) ) {
         listenerList.addElement( listener );
      }
   }

   public void removeTreeModelListener(
      TreeModelListener listener )
   {
      if ( listener != null ) {
         listenerList.removeElement( listener );
      }
   }

} // DomToTreeModelAdapter
```

Because this application won't be making changes to the tree, these methods will go unused for now. However, they'll be there in the future when you need them.

Note: This example uses Vector so that it will work with 1.1 applications. If coding for 1.2 or later, though, I'd use the excellent collections framework instead:
```
private LinkedList listenerList = new LinkedList();
```

The operations on the List are then add and remove. To iterate over the list, as in the following operations, you would use

```
Iterator it = listenerList.iterator();
while ( it.hasNext() ) {
   TreeModelListener listener = (TreeModelListener) it.next();
      ...
}
```

Here, too, are some optional methods you won't use in this application. At this point, though, you have constructed a reasonable template for a TreeModel adapter. In the interest of completeness, you might want to add the following highlighted code. You can then invoke them whenever you need to notify JTree listeners of a change:

```
public void removeTreeModelListener(
   TreeModelListener listener)
{
   ...
}

public void fireTreeNodesChanged( TreeModelEvent e ) {
   Enumeration listeners = listenerList.elements();
   while ( listeners.hasMoreElements() ) {
      TreeModelListener listener =
         (TreeModelListener) listeners.nextElement();
      listener.treeNodesChanged( e );
   }
}

public void fireTreeNodesInserted( TreeModelEvent e ) {
   Enumeration listeners = listenerList.elements();
   while ( listeners.hasMoreElements() ) {
      TreeModelListener listener =
         (TreeModelListener) listeners.nextElement();
      listener.treeNodesInserted( e );
   }
}
```

```java
public void fireTreeNodesRemoved( TreeModelEvent e ) {
   Enumeration listeners = listenerList.elements();
   while ( listeners.hasMoreElements() ) {
      TreeModelListener listener =
         (TreeModelListener) listeners.nextElement();
      listener.treeNodesRemoved( e );
   }
}

public void fireTreeStructureChanged( TreeModelEvent e ) {
   Enumeration listeners = listenerList.elements();
   while ( listeners.hasMoreElements() ) {
      TreeModelListener listener =
         (TreeModelListener) listeners.nextElement();
      listener.treeStructureChanged( e );
   }
}

} // DomToTreeModelAdapter
```

Note: These methods are taken from the TreeModelSupport class described in "Understanding the TreeModel." That architecture was produced by Tom Santos and Steve Wilson and is a lot more elegant than the quick hack going on here. It seemed worthwhile to put them here, though, so that they would be immediately at hand when and if they're needed.

Finishing Up

At this point, you are basically finished constructing the GUI. All you need to do is to jump back to the constructor and add the code to construct an adapter and deliver it to the JTree as the TreeModel:

```java
// Set up the tree
JTree tree = new JTree(new DomToTreeModelAdapter());
```

You can now compile and run the code on an XML file. In the next section, you will do that, as well as explore the DOM structures that result.

Examining the Structure of a DOM

In this section, you'll use the GUIfied DomEcho application created in the preceding section to visually examine a DOM. You'll see what nodes make up the DOM and how they are arranged. With the understanding you acquire, you'll be well prepared to construct and modify Document Object Model structures in the future.

Displaying a Simple Tree

We'll start by displaying a simple file so that you get an idea of basic DOM structure. Then we'll look at the structure that results when you include some advanced XML elements.

Note: The code used to create the figures in this section is in `DomEcho02.java`. The file displayed is `slideSample01.xml`. (The browsable version is `slideSample01-xml.html`.)

Figure 6–1 shows the tree you see when you run the DomEcho program on the first XML file you created, `slideSample01.xml`.

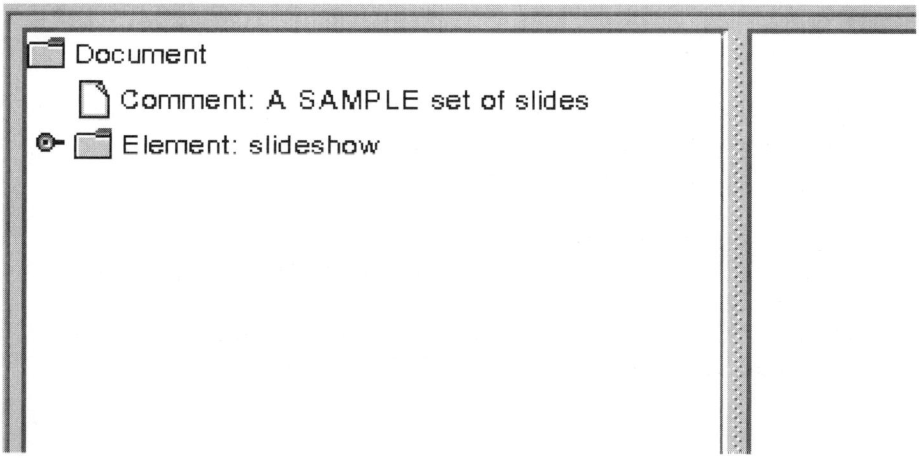

Figure 6–1 Document, Comment, and Element Nodes Displayed

Recall that the first bit of text displayed for each node is the element `type`. After that comes the element `name`, if any, and then the element `value`. This view shows three element types: `Document`, `Comment`, and `Element`. There is only one node of `Document` type for the whole tree, the root node. The `Comment` node displays the `value` attribute, and the `Element` node displays the element `name`, `slideshow`.

Compare Figure 6–1 with the code in the `AdapterNode`'s `toString` method to see whether the name or the value is being displayed for a particular node. If you need to make it more clear, modify the program to indicate which property is being displayed (for example, with N: *name*, V: *value*).

Expanding the `slideshow` element brings up the display shown in Figure 6–2.

Here, you can see the `Text` nodes and `Comment` nodes, which are interspersed between `slide` elements. The empty `Text` nodes exist because there is no DTD to tell the parser that no text exists. (Generally, the vast majority of nodes in a DOM tree will be `Element` and `Text` nodes.)

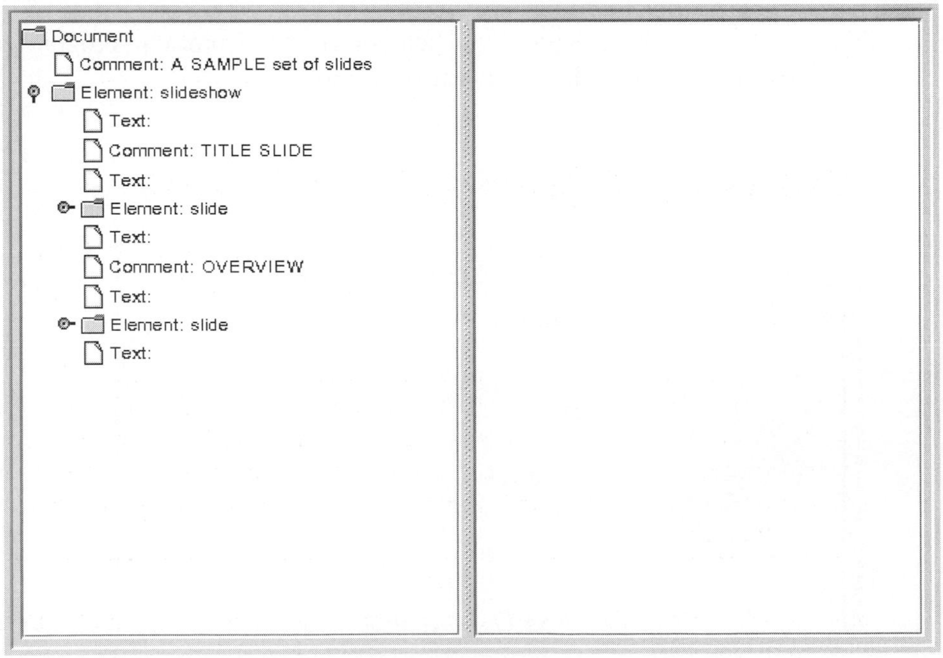

Figure 6–2   Element Node Expanded, No Attribute Nodes Showing

---

Note: Important! Text nodes exist *under* element nodes in a DOM, and data is *always* stored in text nodes. Perhaps the most common error in DOM processing is to navigate to an element node and expect it to contain the data that is stored in that element. Not so! Even the simplest element node has a text node under it that contains the data. For example, given `<size>12</size>`, there is an element node (`size`), *and a text node under it* that contains the actual data (`12`).

Notably absent from this picture are the `Attribute` nodes. An inspection of the table in `org.w3c.dom.Node` shows that there is indeed an `Attribute` node type. But they are not included as children in the DOM hierarchy. They are instead obtained via the `Node` interface `getAttributes` method.

Note: The display of the text nodes is the reason for including the following lines in the `AdapterNode`'s `toString` method. If you remove them, you'll see the funny characters (typically square blocks) that are generated by the newline characters that are in the text.

```
String t = domNode.getNodeValue().trim();
int x = t.indexOf("\n");
if (x >= 0) t = t.substring(0, x);
s += t;
```

Displaying a More Complex Tree

Here, you'll display the example XML file you created at the end of Chapter 5 to see what entity references, processing instructions, and CDATA sections look like in the DOM.

Note: The file displayed in this section is `slideSample10.xml`. The `slideSample10.xml` file references `slideshow3.dtd`, which, in turn, references `copyright.xml` and a (very simplistic) `xhtml.dtd`. (The browsable versions are `slideSample10-xml.html`, `slideshow3-dtd.html`, `copyright-xml.html`, and `xhtml-dtd.html`.)

Figure 6–3 shows the result of running the DomEcho application on `slideSample10.xml`, which includes a DOCTYPE entry that identifies the document's DTD.

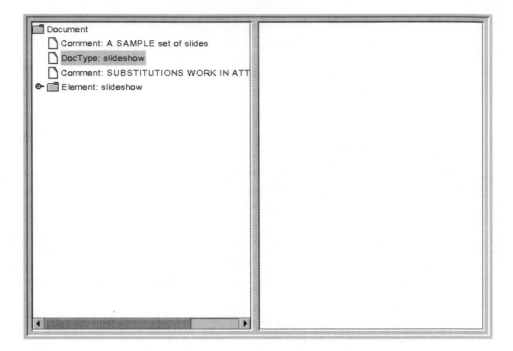

Figure 6–3 DocType Node Displayed

The DocType interface is actually an extension of w3c.org.dom.Node. It defines a getEntities method, which you use to obtain Entity nodes—the nodes that define entities such as the product entity, which has the value WonderWidgets. Like Attribute nodes, Entity nodes do not appear as children of DOM nodes.

When you expand the slideshow node, you get the display shown in Figure 6–4.

Here, the processing instruction node is highlighted, showing that those nodes do appear in the tree. The name property contains the target specification, which identifies the application that the instruction is directed to. The value property contains the text of the instruction.

Note that empty text nodes are also shown here, even though the DTD specifies that a slideshow can contain slide elements only, never text. Logically, then, you might think that these nodes would not appear. (When this file was run

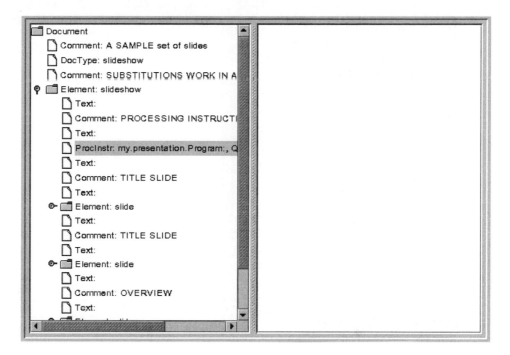

Figure 6–4 Processing Instruction Node Displayed

through the SAX parser, those elements generated `ignorableWhitespace` events rather than `character` events.)

Moving down to the second `slide` element and opening the `item` element under it brings up the display shown in Figure 6–5.

Here, you can see that a text node containing the copyright text (rather than the entity reference that points to it) was inserted into the DOM.

For most applications, the insertion of the text is exactly what you want. In that way, when you're looking for the text under a node, you don't have to worry about any entity references it might contain. For other applications, though, you may need the ability to reconstruct the original XML. For example, an editor application would need to save the result of user modifications without throwing away entity references in the process.

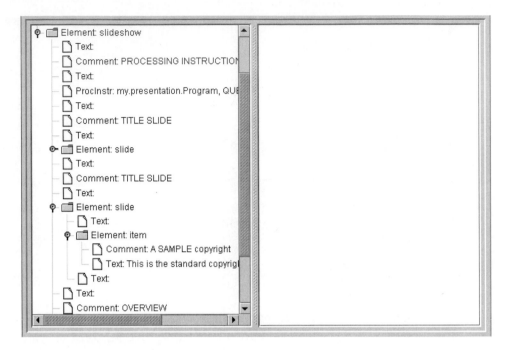

Figure 6–5 JAXP 1.2 DOM: Item Text Returned from an Entity Reference

Various `DocumentBuilderFactory` APIs give you control over the kind of DOM structure that is created. For example, add the following highlighted line to produce the DOM structure shown in Figure 6–6.

```
public static void main(String argv[])
{
  ...
  DocumentBuilderFactory factory =
  DocumentBuilderFactory.newInstance();
  factory.setExpandEntityReferences(false);
  ...
```

Here, the entity reference node is highlighted. Note that the entity reference contains multiple nodes under it. This example shows only comment and text nodes, but the entity could conceivably contain other element nodes.

Moving down to the last `item` element under the last `slide` brings up the display shown in Figure 6–7.

Here, the `CDATA` node is highlighted. Note that there are no nodes under it. Because a `CDATA` section is entirely uninterpreted, all its contents are contained in the node's `value` property.

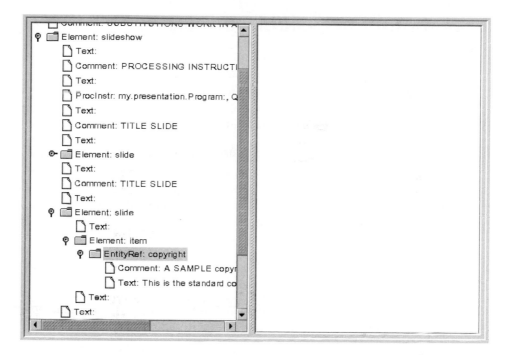

Figure 6–6 JAXP 1.1 in 1.4 Platform: Entity Reference Node Displayed

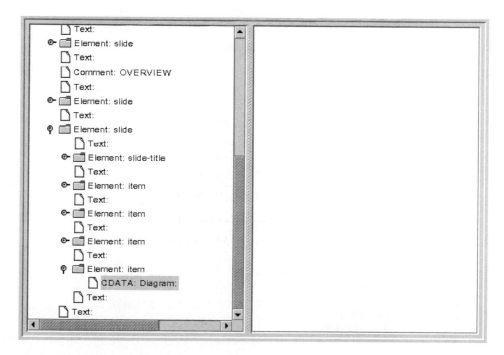

Figure 6–7 CDATA Node Displayed

Summary of Lexical Controls

Lexical information is the information you need to reconstruct the original syntax of an XML document. As discussed earlier, preserving lexical information is important in editing applications, where you want to save a document that is an accurate reflection of the original—complete with comments, entity references, and any CDATA sections it may have included at the outset.

Most applications, however, are concerned only with the content of the XML structures. They can afford to ignore comments, and they don't care whether data was coded in a CDATA section or as plain text, or whether it included an entity reference. For such applications, a minimum of lexical information is desirable, because it simplifies the number and kind of DOM nodes that the application must be prepared to examine.

The following DocumentBuilderFactory methods give you control over the lexical information you see in the DOM:

- setCoalescing(): To convert CDATA nodes to Text nodes and append to an adjacent Text node (if any)
- setExpandEntityReferences(): To expand entity reference nodes
- setIgnoringComments(): To ignore comments
- setIgnoringElementContentWhitespace(): To ignore whitespace that is not a significant part of element content

The default values for all these properties is false, which preserves all the lexical information necessary to reconstruct the incoming document in its original form. Setting them to true lets you construct the simplest possible DOM so that the application can focus on the data's semantic content without having to worry about lexical syntax details. Table 6–2 summarizes the effects of the settings.

Table 6–2 Configuring DocumentBuilderFactory

API	Preserve Lexical Info	Focus on Content
setCoalescing()	false	true
setExpandEntityReferences()	false	true
setIgnoringComments()	false	true
setIgnoringElement ContentWhitespace()	false	true

Finishing Up

At this point, you have seen most of the nodes you will ever encounter in a DOM tree. There are one or two more that we'll mention in the next section, but you now know what you need to know to create or modify a DOM structure.

Constructing a User-Friendly JTree from a DOM

Now that you know what a DOM looks like internally, you'll be better prepared to modify a DOM or construct one from scratch. Before we go on to that, though, this section presents some modifications to the JTreeModel that let you produce a more user-friendly version of the JTree suitable for use in a GUI.

Note: In this section, we modify the Swing GUI to improve the display, culminating in DomEcho04.java. If you have no interest in the Swing details, you can skip ahead to Creating and Manipulating a DOM (page 228) and use DomEcho04.java to proceed from there.

Compressing the Tree View

Displaying the DOM in tree form is all very well for experimenting and for learning how a DOM works. But it's not the kind of friendly display that most users want to see in a JTree. However, it turns out that very few modifications are needed to turn the TreeModel adapter into something that presents a user-friendly display. In this section, you'll make those modifications.

Note: The code discussed in this section is in DomEcho03.java. The file the program operates on is slideSample01.xml. (The browsable version is slideSample01-xml.html.)

Make the Operation Selectable

When you modify the adapter, you're going to *compress* the view of the DOM, eliminating all but the nodes you really want to display. Start by defining a boolean variable that controls whether you want the compressed or the uncompressed view of the DOM:

```
public class DomEcho extends JPanel
{
   static Document document;
   boolean compress = true;
   static final int windowHeight = 460;
   ...
```

Identify Tree Nodes

The next step is to identify the nodes you want to show up in the tree. To do that, add the following highlighted code:

```
...
import org.w3c.dom.Document;
import org.w3c.dom.DOMException;
import org.w3c.dom.Node;

public class DomEcho extends JPanel
{
   ...

   public static void makeFrame() {
      ...
   }

   // An array of names for DOM node type
   static final String[] typeName = {
      ...
   };

   static final int ELEMENT_TYPE = Node.ELEMENT_NODE;

   // The list of elements to display in the tree
   static String[] treeElementNames = {
      "slideshow",
      "slide",
      "title",         // For slide show #1
      "slide-title",   // For slide show #10
      "item",
   };
```

```
boolean treeElement(String elementName) {
   for (int i=0; i<treeElementNames.length; i++) {
      if ( elementName.equals(treeElementNames[i]) )
         return true;
   }
   return false;
}
```

This code sets up a constant you can use to identify the ELEMENT node type, declares the names of the elements you want in the tree, and creates a method that tells whether or not a given element name is a tree element. Because slideSample01.xml has title elements and because slideSample10.xml has slide-title elements, you set up the contents of this array so that it will work with either data file.

Note: The mechanism you are creating here depends on the fact that *structure* nodes like slideshow and slide never contain text, whereas text usually does appear in *content* nodes like item. Although those "content" nodes may contain subelements in slideShow10.xml, the DTD constrains those subelements to be XHTML nodes. Because they are XHTML nodes (an XML version of HTML that is constrained to be well formed), the entire substructure under an item node can be combined into a single string and displayed in the htmlPane that makes up the other half of the application window. In the second part of this section, you'll do that concatenation, displaying the text and XHTML as content in the htmlPane.

Although you could simply reference the node types defined in the class org.w3c.dom.Node, defining the ELEMENT_TYPE constant keeps the code a little more readable. Each node in the DOM has a name, a type, and (potentially) a list of subnodes. The functions that return these values are getNodeName(), getNodeType, and getChildNodes(). Defining our own constants will let us write code like this:

```
Node node = nodeList.item(i);
int type = node.getNodeType();
if (type == ELEMENT_TYPE) {
   ....
```

As a stylistic choice, the extra constants help us keep the reader (and ourselves!) clear about what we're doing. Here, it is fairly clear when we are dealing with a node object, and when we are dealing with a type constant. Otherwise, it would be tempting to code something like if (node == ELEMENT_NODE), which of course would not work at all.

Control Node Visibility

The next step is to modify the AdapterNode's childCount function so that it counts only tree element nodes—nodes that are designated as displayable in the JTree. Make the following highlighted modifications to do that:

```
public class DomEcho extends JPanel
{
   ...
   public class AdapterNode
   {
      ...
      public AdapterNode child(int searchIndex) {
         ...
      }
      public int childCount() {
         if (!compress) {
            // Indent this
            return domNode.getChildNodes().getLength();
         }
         int count = 0;
         for (int i=0;
            i<domNode.getChildNodes().getLength(); i++)
         {
            org.w3c.dom.Node node =
               domNode.getChildNodes().item(i);
            if (node.getNodeType() == ELEMENT_TYPE
            &&  treeElement( node.getNodeName() ))
            {
               ++count;
            }
         }
         return count;
      }
   } // AdapterNode
```

The only tricky part about this code is checking to make sure that the node is an element node before comparing the node. The DocType node makes that necessary, because it has the same name (slideshow) as the slideshow element.

Control Child Access

Finally, you need to modify the AdapterNode's child function to return the Nth item from the list of displayable nodes, rather than the Nth item from all nodes in the list. Add the following highlighted code to do that:

```
public class DomEcho extends JPanel
{
   ...
   public class AdapterNode
   {
      ...
      public int index(AdapterNode child) {
         ...
      }
      public AdapterNode child(int searchIndex) {
      //Note: JTree index is zero-based.
      org.w3c.dom.Node node =
         domNode.getChildNodes()Item(searchIndex);
      if (compress) {
         // Return Nth displayable node
         int elementNodeIndex = 0;
         for (int i=0;
            i<domNode.getChildNodes().getLength(); i++)
         {
            node = domNode.getChildNodes()Item(i);
            if (node.getNodeType() == ELEMENT_TYPE
            && treeElement( node.getNodeName() )
            && elementNodeIndex++ == searchIndex) {
               break;
            }
         }
      }
      return new AdapterNode(node);
   } // child
} // AdapterNode
```

There's nothing special going on here. It's a slightly modified version of the same logic you used when returning the child count.

Check the Results

When you compile and run this version of the application on slideSample01.xml and then expand the nodes in the tree, you see the results shown in Figure 6–8. The only nodes remaining in the tree are the high-level "structure" nodes.

Extra Credit

The way the application stands now, the information that tells the application how to compress the tree for display is hardcoded. Here are some ways you can consider extending the app:

- *Use a command-line argument*: Whether you compress or don't compress the tree could be determined by a command-line argument rather than being a hardcoded Boolean variable. On the other hand, the list of elements that goes into the tree is still hardcoded, so maybe that option doesn't make much sense, unless...

- *Read the treeElement list from a file*: If you read the list of elements to include in the tree from an external file, that would make the whole application command-driven. That would be good. But wouldn't it be really

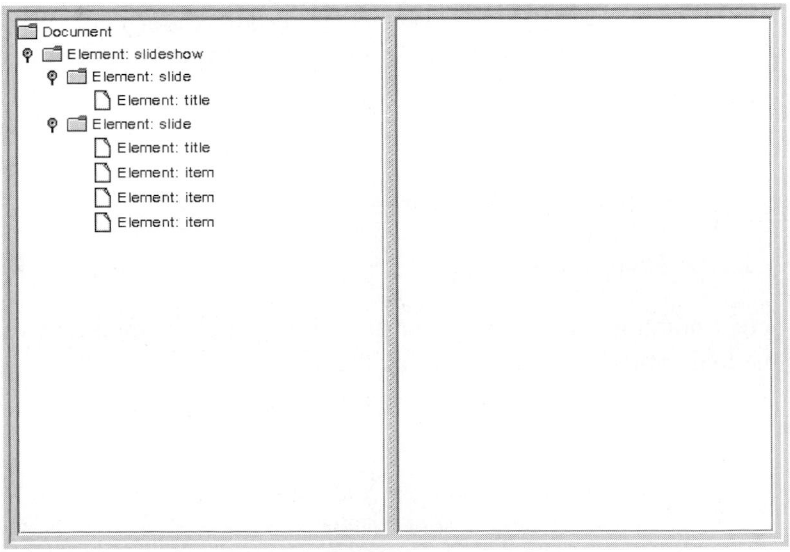

Figure 6–8   Tree View with a Collapsed Hierarchy

nice to derive that information from the DTD or schema instead? So you might want to consider...

- *Automatically build the list*: Watch out, though! As things stand right now, there are no standard DTD parsers! If you use a DTD, then, you'll need to write your parser to make sense out of its somewhat arcane syntax. You'll probably have better luck if you use a schema instead of a DTD. The nice thing about schemas is that they use XML syntax, so you can use an XML parser to read the schema in the same way you use it to read any other XML file.

As you analyze the schema, note that the JTree-displayable *structure* nodes are those that have no text, whereas the *content* nodes may contain text and, optionally, XHTML subnodes. That distinction works for this example and will likely work for a large body of real world applications. It's easy to construct cases that will create a problem, though, so you'll have to be on the lookout for schema/DTD specifications that embed non-XHTML elements in text-capable nodes, and take the appropriate action.

Acting on Tree Selections

Now that the tree is being displayed properly, the next step is to concatenate the subtrees under selected nodes to display them in the htmlPane. While you're at it, you'll use the concatenated text to put node-identifying information back in the JTree.

Note: The code discussed in this section is in DomEcho04.java.

Identify Node Types

When you concatenate the subnodes under an element, the processing you do depends on the type of node. So the first thing to do is to define constants for the remaining node types. Add the following highlighted code:

```
public class DomEcho extends JPanel
{
   ...
   // An array of names for DOM node types
   static final String[] typeName = {
      ...
   };
```

```
static final int ELEMENT_TYPE =    1;
static final int ATTR_TYPE =Node.ATTRIBUTE_NODE;
static final int TEXT_TYPE =Node.TEXT_NODE;
static final int CDATA_TYPE = Node.CDATA_SECTION_NODE;
static final int ENTITYREF_TYPE =
              Node.ENTITY_REFERENCE_NODE;
static final int ENTITY_TYPE =Node.ENTITY_NODE;
static final int PROCINSTR_TYPE =
              Node.PROCESSING_INSTRUCTION_NODE;
static final int COMMENT_TYPE = Node.COMMENT_NODE;
static final int DOCUMENT_TYPE =Node.DOCUMENT_NODE;
static final int DOCTYPE_TYPE =Node.DOCUMENT_TYPE_NODE;
static final int DOCFRAG_TYPE =Node.DOCUMENT_FRAGMENT_NODE;
static final int NOTATION_TYPE =Node.NOTATION_NODE;
```

Concatenate Subnodes to Define Element Content

Next, you define the method that concatenates the text and subnodes for an element and returns it as the element's content. To define the content method, you'll add the following big chunk of highlighted code, but this is the last big chunk of code in the DOM tutorial.

```
public class DomEcho extends JPanel
{
  ...
  public class AdapterNode
  {
    ...
    public String toString() {
    ...
    }
    public String content() {
      String s = "";
      org.w3c.dom.NodeList nodeList =
        domNode.getChildNodes();
      for (int i=0; i<nodeList.getLength(); i++) {
        org.w3c.dom.Node node = nodeList.item(i);
        int type = node.getNodeType();
        AdapterNode adpNode = new AdapterNode(node);
        if (type == ELEMENT_TYPE) {
          if ( treeElement(node.getNodeName()) )
            continue;
          s += "<" + node.getNodeName() + ">";
          s += adpNode.content();
          s += "</" + node.getNodeName() + ">";
```

```
        } else if (type == TEXT_TYPE) {
            s += node.getNodeValue();
        } else if (type == ENTITYREF_TYPE) {
            // The content is in the TEXT node under it
            s += adpNode.content();
        } else if (type == CDATA_TYPE) {
            StringBuffer sb = new StringBuffer(
              node.getNodeValue() );
            for (int j=0; j<sb.length(); j++) {
                if (sb.charAt(j) == '<') {
                    sb.setCharAt(j, '&');
                    sb.insert(j+1, "lt;");
                    j += 3;
                } else if (sb.charAt(j) == '&') {
                    sb.setCharAt(j, '&');
                    sb.insert(j+1, "amp;");
                    j += 4;
                }
            }
            s += "<pre>" + sb + "</pre>";
        }
    }
    return s;
}
...
} // AdapterNode
```

Note: This code collapses `EntityRef` nodes, as inserted by the JAXP 1.1 parser that is included in the Java 1.4 platform. With JAXP 1.2, that portion of the code is not necessary because entity references are converted to text nodes by the parser. Other parsers may insert such nodes, however, so including this code futureproofs your application, should you use a different parser in the future.

Although this code is not the most efficient that anyone ever wrote, it works and will do fine for our purposes. In this code, you are recognizing and dealing with the following data types:

Element

For elements with names such as the XHTML em node, you return the node's content sandwiched between the appropriate <em> and </em> tags. However, when processing the content for the slideshow element, for example, you don't include tags for the slide elements it contains, so when returning a node's content, you skip any subelements that are themselves displayed in the tree.

Text

No surprise here. For a text node, you simply return the node's `value`.

Entity Reference

Unlike `CDATA` nodes, entity references can contain multiple subelements. So the strategy here is to return the concatenation of those subelements.

CDATA

As with a text node, you return the node's `value`. However, because the text in this case may contain angle brackets and ampersands, you need to convert them to a form that displays properly in an HTML pane. Unlike the XML CDATA tag, the HTML `<pre>` tag does not prevent the parsing of character-format tags, break tags, and the like. So you must convert left angle brackets (`<`) and ampersands (`&`) to get them to display properly.

On the other hand, there are quite a few node types you are *not* processing with the preceding code. It's worth a moment to examine them and understand why:

Attribute

These nodes do not appear in the DOM but are obtained by invoking `getAttributes` on element nodes.

Entity

These nodes also do not appear in the DOM. They are obtained by invoking `getEntities` on `DocType` nodes.

Processing Instruction

These nodes don't contain displayable data.

Comment

Ditto. Nothing you want to display here.

Document

This is the root node for the DOM. There's no data to display for that.

DocType

The `DocType` node contains the DTD specification, with or without external pointers. It appears only under the root node and has no data to display in the tree.

Document Fragment

This node is equivalent to a document node. It's a root node that the DOM specification intends for holding intermediate results during operations such as cut-and-paste. As with a document node, there's no data to display.

Notation

We're just ignoring this one. These nodes are used to include binary data in the DOM. As discussed earlier in Choosing Your Parser Implementation (page 155) and Using the DTDHandler and EntityResolver (page 171), the MIME types (in conjunction with namespaces) make a better mechanism for that.

Display the Content in the JTree

With the content concatenation out of the way, only a few small programming steps remain. The first is to modify `toString` so that it uses the first line of the node's content for identifying information. Add the following highlighted code:

```
public class DomEcho extends JPanel
{
  ...
  public class AdapterNode
  {
    ...
    public String toString() {
      ...
      if (! nodeName.startsWith("#")) {
        s += ": " + nodeName;
      }
      if (compress) {
        String t = content().trim();
        int x = t.indexOf("\n");
        if (x >= 0) t = t.substring(0, x);
        s += " " + t;
        return s;
      }
      if (domNode.getNodeValue() != null) {
        ...
      }
      return s;
    }
}
```

Wire the JTree to the JEditorPane

Returning now to the app's constructor, create a tree selection listener and use it to wire the JTree to the JEditorPane:

```
public class DomEcho extends JPanel
{
  ...
  public DomEcho()
  {
    ...
```

```
        // Build right-side view
        JEditorPane htmlPane = new JEditorPane("text/html","");
        htmlPane.setEditable(false);
        JScrollPane htmlView = new JScrollPane(htmlPane);
        htmlView.setPreferredSize(
           new Dimension( rightWidth, windowHeight ));

           tree.addTreeSelectionListener(
              new TreeSelectionListener() {
                 public void valueChanged(TreeSelectionEvent e)
                 {
                   TreePath p = e.getNewLeadSelectionPath();
                   if (p != null) {
                    AdapterNode adpNode =
                       (AdapterNode)
                          p.getLastPathComponent();
                    htmlPane.setText(adpNode.content());
                   }
                 }
              }
           );
```

Now, when a JTree node is selected, its contents are delivered to the htmlPane.

Note: The TreeSelectionListener in this example is created using an anonymous inner-class adapter. If you are programming for the 1.1 version of the platform, you'll need to define an external class for this purpose.

If you compile this version of the app, you'll discover immediately that the html-Pane needs to be specified as final to be referenced in an inner class, so add the following highlighted keyword:

```
public DomEcho04()
{
   ...
   // Build right-side view
   final JEditorPane htmlPane = new
      JEditorPane("text/html","");
   htmlPane.setEditable(false);
   JScrollPane htmlView = new JScrollPane(htmlPane);
   htmlView.setPreferredSize(
      new Dimension( rightWidth, windowHeight ));
```

Run the App

When you compile the application and run it on slideSample10.xml (the browsable version is slideSample10-xml.html), you get a display like that shown in Figure 6–9. Expanding the hierarchy shows that the JTree now includes identifying text for a node whenever possible.

Selecting an item that includes XHTML subelements produces a display like that shown in Figure 6–10.

Selecting a node that contains an entity reference causes the entity text to be included, as shown in Figure 6–11.

Finally, selecting a node that includes a CDATA section produces results like those shown in Figure 6–12.

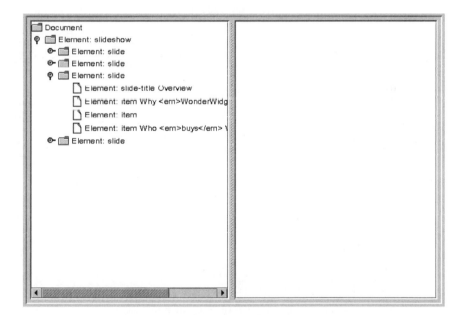

Figure 6–9   Collapsed Hierarchy Showing Text in Nodes

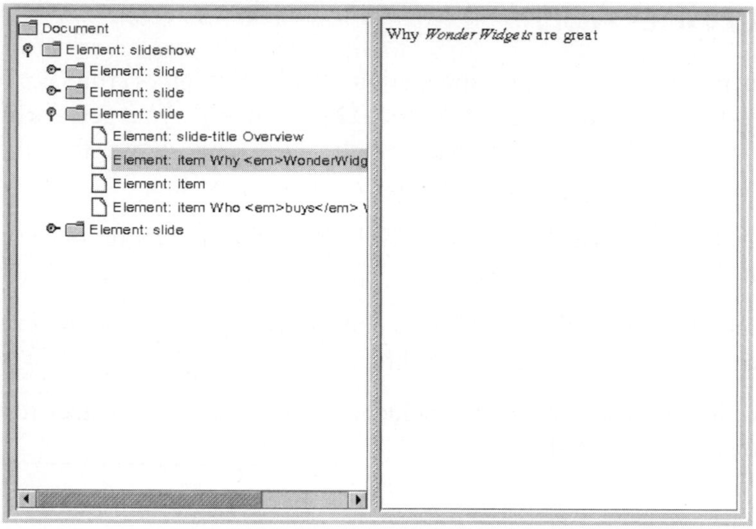

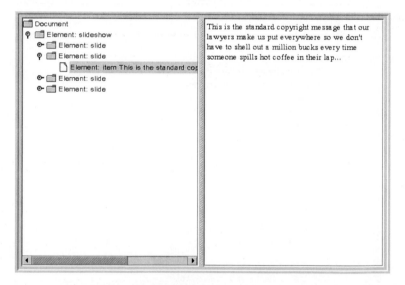

Figure 6–10 Node with `<em>` Tag Selected

Figure 6–11 Node with Entity Reference Selected

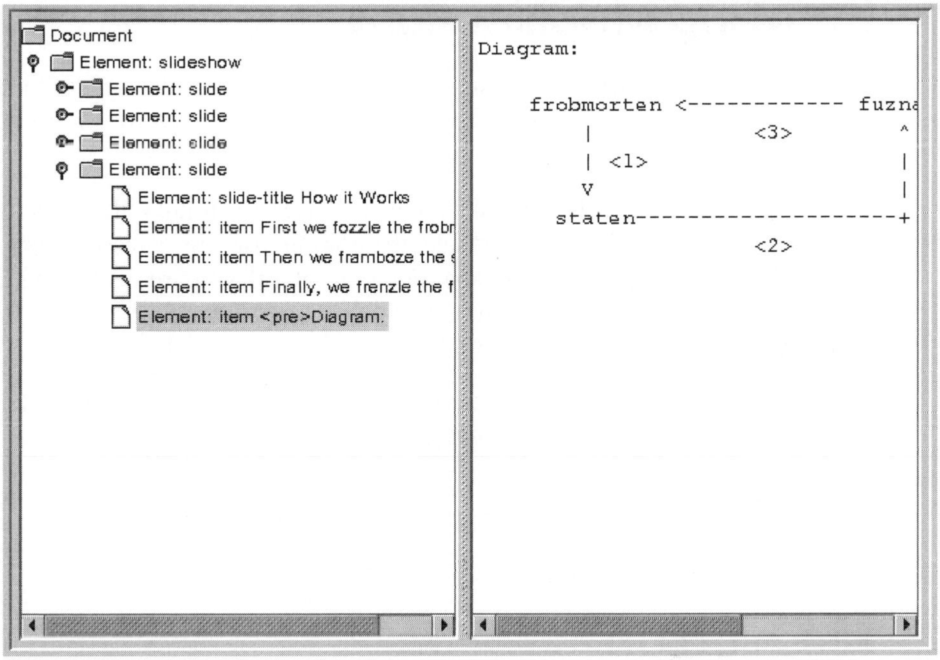

```
Document
  Element: slideshow
    Element: slide
    Element: slide
    Element: slide
    Element: slide
        Element: slide-title How it Works
        Element: item First we fozzle the frobr
        Element: item Then we framboze the
        Element: item Finally, we frenzle the f
        Element: item <pre>Diagram:
```

```
Diagram:

    frobmorten <----------- fuzna
       |                <3>       ^
       | <1>                      |
       v                          |
    staten--------------------+
                    <2>
```

Figure 6–12   Node with CDATA Component Selected

Extra Credit

Now that you have the application working, here are some ways you might think about extending it in the future:

- *Use title text to identify slides:* Special-case the slide element so that the contents of the title node are used as the identifying text. When selected, convert the title node's contents to a centered H1 tag, and ignore the title element when constructing the tree.

- *Convert item elements to lists:* Remove item elements from the JTree and convert them to HTML lists using <ul>, <li>, and </ul> tags, including them in the slide's content when the slide is selected.

Handling Modifications

A full discussion of the mechanisms for modifying the `JTree`'s underlying data model is beyond the scope of this tutorial. However, a few words on the subject are in order.

Most importantly, note that if you allow the user to modify the structure by manipulating the `JTree`, you must take the compression into account when you figure out where to apply the change. For example, if you are displaying text in the tree and the user modifies that, the changes would have to be applied to text subelements and perhaps would require a rearrangement of the XHTML subtree.

When you make those changes, you'll need to understand more about the interactions between a `JTree`, its `TreeModel`, and an underlying data model. That subject is covered in depth in the Swing Connection article, "Understanding the TreeModel" at `http://java.sun.com/products/jfc/tsc/articles/jtree/index.html`.

Finishing Up

You now understand what there is to know about the structure of a DOM, and you know how to adapt a DOM to create a user-friendly display in a `JTree`. It has taken quite a bit of coding, but in return you have obtained valuable tools for exposing a DOM's structure and a template for GUI applications. In the next section, you'll make a couple of minor modifications to the code that turn the application into a vehicle for experimentation, and then you'll experiment with building and manipulating a DOM.

Creating and Manipulating a DOM

By now, you understand the structure of the nodes that make up a DOM. Creating a DOM is easy. This section of the DOM tutorial is going to take much less work than anything you've seen up to now. All the foregoing work, however, has generated the basic understanding that will make this section a piece of cake.

Obtaining a DOM from the Factory

In this version of the application, you'll still create a document builder factory, but this time you'll tell it to create a new DOM instead of parsing an existing

XML document. You'll keep all the existing functionality intact, however, and add the new functionality in such a way that you can flick a switch to get back the parsing behavior.

Note: The code discussed in this section is in `DomEcho05.java`.

Modify the Code

Start by turning off the compression feature. As you work with the DOM in this section, you'll want to see all the nodes:

```
public class DomEcho05  extends JPanel
{
  ...
  boolean compress = true;
  boolean compress = false;
```

Next, you create a `buildDom` method that creates the document object. The easiest way is to create the method and then copy the DOM-construction section from the `main` method to create the `buildDom`. The modifications shown next show you the changes needed to make that code suitable for the `buildDom` method.

```
public class DomEcho05  extends JPanel
{
  ...
  public static void makeFrame() {
    ...
  }
  public static void buildDom()
  {
    DocumentBuilderFactory factory =
      DocumentBuilderFactory.newInstance();
    try {
      DocumentBuilder builder =
        factory.newDocumentBuilder();
      document = builder.parse( new File(argv[0]) );
      document = builder.newDocument();
    } catch (SAXException sxe) {
      ...
    } catch (ParserConfigurationException pce) {
      // Parser with specified options can't be built
      pce.printStackTrace();
```

```
        } catch (IOException ioe) {
          ...
        }
    }
```

In this code, you replace the line that does the parsing with one that creates a DOM. Then, because the code is no longer parsing an existing file, you remove exceptions that are no longer thrown: SAXException and IOException.

And because you will be working with Element objects, add the statement to import that class at the top of the program:

```
import org.w3c.dom.Document;
import org.w3c.dom.DOMException;
import org.w3c.dom.Element;
```

Create Element and Text Nodes

Now, for your first experiment, add the Document operations to create a root node and several children:

```
public class DomEcho05  extends JPanel
{
  ...
  public static void buildDom()
  {
    DocumentBuilderFactory factory =
      DocumentBuilderFactory.newInstance();
    try {
      DocumentBuilder builder =
         factory.newDocumentBuilder();
      document = builder.newDocument();
      // Create from whole cloth
      Element root =
        (Element)
          document.createElement("rootElement");
      document.appendChild(root);
      root.appendChild(
        document.createTextNode("Some") );
      root.appendChild(
        document.createTextNode(" ")     );
```

```
        root.appendChild(
            document.createTextNode("text") );
    } catch (ParserConfigurationException pce) {
        // Parser with specified options can't be built
        pce.printStackTrace();
    }
}
```

Finally, modify the argument-list checking code at the top of the main method so that you invoke buildDom and makeFrame instead of generating an error:

```
public class DomEcho05  extends JPanel
{
    ...
    public static void main(String argv[])
    {
        if (argv.length != 1) {
            System.err.println("...");
            System.exit(1);
            buildDom();
            makeFrame();
            return;
        }
```

That's all there is to it! Now if you supply an argument the specified file is parsed, and if you don't, the experimental code that builds a DOM is executed.

Run the App

Compile and run the program with no arguments, producing the result shown in Figure 6–13.

Normalizing the DOM

In this experiment, you'll manipulate the DOM you created by normalizing it after it has been constructed.

Note: The code discussed in this section is in DomEcho06.java.

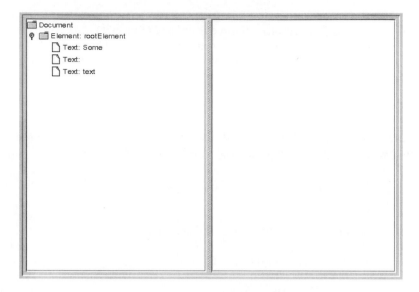

Figure 6–13 Element Node and Text Nodes Created

Add the following highlighted code to normalize the DOM:

```
public static void buildDom()
{
  DocumentBuilderFactory factory =
    DocumentBuilderFactory.newInstance();
  try {
    ...
    root.appendChild( document.createTextNode("Some") );
    root.appendChild( document.createTextNode(" ")    );
    root.appendChild( document.createTextNode("text") );
    document.getDocumentElement().normalize();

  } catch (ParserConfigurationException pce) {
      ...
```

In this code, `getDocumentElement` returns the document's root node, and the `normalize` operation manipulates the tree under it.

When you compile and run the application now, the result looks like Figure 6–14.

Here, you can see that the adjacent text nodes have been combined into a single node. The normalize operation is one that you typically use after making modifications to a DOM, to ensure that the resulting DOM is as compact as possible.

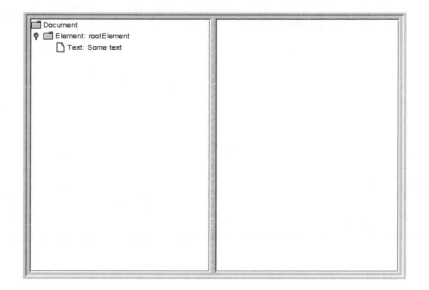

Figure 6–14 Text Nodes Merged after Normalization

Note: Now that you have this program to experiment with, see what happens to other combinations of CDATA, entity references, and text nodes when you normalize the tree.

Other Operations

To complete this section, we'll take a quick look at some of the other operations you might want to apply to a DOM:

- Traversing nodes
- Searching for nodes
- Obtaining node content
- Creating attributes
- Removing and changing nodes
- Inserting nodes

Traversing Nodes

The `org.w3c.dom.Node` interface defines a number of methods you can use to traverse nodes, including `getFirstChild`, `getLastChild`, `getNextSibling`, `getPreviousSibling`, and `getParentNode`. Those operations are sufficient to get from anywhere in the tree to any other location in the tree.

Searching for Nodes

When you are searching for a node with a particular name, there is a bit more to take into account. Although it is tempting to get the first child and inspect it to see whether it is the right one, the search must account for the fact that the first child in the sublist could be a comment or a processing instruction. If the XML data hasn't been validated, it could even be a text node containing ignorable whitespace.

In essence, you need to look through the list of child nodes, ignoring the ones that are of no concern and examining the ones you care about. Here is an example of the kind of routine you need to write when searching for nodes in a DOM hierarchy. It is presented here in its entirety (complete with comments) so that you can use it as a template in your applications.

```java
/**
 * Find the named subnode in a node's sublist.
 * <li>Ignores comments and processing instructions.
 * <li>Ignores TEXT nodes (likely to exist and contain
 *    ignorable whitespace, if not validating.
 * <li>Ignores CDATA nodes and EntityRef nodes.
 * <li>Examines element nodes to find one with
 *    the specified name.
 * </ul>
 * @param name  the tag name for the element to find
 * @param node  the element node to start searching from
 * @return the Node found
 */
public Node findSubNode(String name, Node node) {
    if (node.getNodeType() != Node.ELEMENT_NODE) {
        System.err.println(
            "Error: Search node not of element type");
        System.exit(22);
    }

    if (! node.hasChildNodes()) return null;
```

```
        NodeList list = node.getChildNodes();
        for (int i=0; i < list.getLength(); i++) {
           Node subnode = list.item(i);
           if (subnode.getNodeType() == Node.ELEMENT_NODE) {
              if (subnode.getNodeName().equals(name)) return subnode;
           }
        }
        return null;
     }
```

For a deeper explanation of this code, see Increasing the Complexity (page 179) in When to Use DOM (page 176).

Note, too, that you can use APIs described in Summary of Lexical Controls (page 212) to modify the kind of DOM the parser constructs. The nice thing about this code, though, is that it will work for almost any DOM.

Obtaining Node Content

When you want to get the text that a node contains, you again need to look through the list of child nodes, ignoring entries that are of no concern and accumulating the text you find in TEXT nodes, CDATA nodes, and EntityRef nodes.

Here is an example of the kind of routine you can use for that process:

```
   /**
    * Return the text that a node contains. This routine:<ul>
    * <li>Ignores comments and processing instructions.
    * <li>Concatenates TEXT nodes, CDATA nodes, and the results of
    *      recursively processing EntityRef nodes.
    * <li>Ignores any element nodes in the sublist.
    *      (Other possible options are to recurse into element
    *      sublists or throw an exception.)
    * </ul>
    * @param   node   a  DOM node
    * @return   a String representing its contents
    */
   public String getText(Node node) {
      StringBuffer result = new StringBuffer();
      if (! node.hasChildNodes()) return "";

      NodeList list = node.getChildNodes();
      for (int i=0; i < list.getLength(); i++) {
         Node subnode = list.item(i);
```

```
        if (subnode.getNodeType() == Node.TEXT_NODE) {
           result.append(subnode.getNodeValue());
        }
        else if (subnode.getNodeType() ==
              Node.CDATA_SECTION_NODE)
        {
           result.append(subnode.getNodeValue());
        }
        else if (subnode.getNodeType() ==
              Node.ENTITY_REFERENCE_NODE)
        {
           // Recurse into the subtree for text
           // (and ignore comments)
           result.append(getText(subnode));
        }
     }
     return result.toString();
}
```

For a deeper explanation of this code, see Increasing the Complexity (page 179) in When to Use DOM (page 176).

Again, you can simplify this code by using the APIs described in Summary of Lexical Controls (page 212) to modify the kind of DOM the parser constructs. But the nice thing about this code is that it will work for almost any DOM.

Creating Attributes

The `org.w3c.dom.Element` interface, which extends Node, defines a `setAttribute` operation, which adds an attribute to that node. (A better name from the Java platform standpoint would have been `addAttribute`. The attribute is not a property of the class, and a new object is created.)

You can also use the `Document`'s `createAttribute` operation to create an instance of `Attribute` and then use the `setAttributeNode` method to add it.

Removing and Changing Nodes

To remove a node, you use its parent `Node`'s `removeChild` method. To change it, you can use either the parent node's `replaceChild` operation or the node's `setNodeValue` operation.

Inserting Nodes

The important thing to remember when creating new nodes is that when you create an element node, the only data you specify is a name. In effect, that node gives you a hook to hang things on. You hang an item on the hook by adding to its list of child nodes. For example, you might add a text node, a CDATA node, or an attribute node. As you build, keep in mind the structure you examined in the exercises you've seen in this tutorial. Remember: Each node in the hierarchy is extremely simple, containing only one data element.

Finishing Up

Congratulations! You've learned how a DOM is structured and how to manipulate it. And you now have a DomEcho application that you can use to display a DOM's structure, condense it to GUI-compatible dimensions, and experiment with to see how various operations affect the structure. Have fun with it!

Validating with XML Schema

You're now ready to take a deeper look at the process of XML Schema validation. Although a full treatment of XML Schema is beyond the scope of this tutorial, this section shows you the steps you take to validate an XML document using an XML Schema definition. (To learn more about XML Schema, you can review the online tutorial, *XML Schema Part 0: Primer*, at http://www.w3.org/ TR/xmlschema-0/. You can also examine the sample programs that are part of the JAXP download. They use a simple XML Schema definition to validate personnel data stored in an XML file.)

At the end of this section, you'll also learn how to use an XML Schema definition to validate a document that contains elements from multiple namespaces.

Overview of the Validation Process

To be notified of validation errors in an XML document, the following must be true:

- The factory must configured, and the appropriate error handler set.
- The document must be associated with at least one schema, and possibly more.

Configuring the DocumentBuilder Factory

It's helpful to start by defining the constants you'll use when configuring the factory. (These are the same constants you define when using XML Schema for SAX parsing.)

```
static final String JAXP_SCHEMA_LANGUAGE =
    "http://java.sun.com/xml/jaxp/properties/schemaLanguage";

static final String W3C_XML_SCHEMA =
    "http://www.w3.org/2001/XMLSchema";
```

Next, you configure `DocumentBuilderFactory` to generate a namespace-aware, validating parser that uses XML Schema:

```
...
   DocumentBuilderFactory factory =
        DocumentBuilderFactory.newInstance()
   factory.setNamespaceAware(true);
   factory.setValidating(true);
try {
   factory.setAttribute(JAXP_SCHEMA_LANGUAGE, W3C_XML_SCHEMA);
}
catch (IllegalArgumentException x) {
   // Happens if the parser does not support JAXP 1.2
   ...
}
```

Because JAXP-compliant parsers are not namespace-aware by default, it is necessary to set the property for schema validation to work. You also set a factory attribute to specify the parser language to use. (For SAX parsing, on the other hand, you set a property on the parser generated by the factory.)

Associating a Document with a Schema

Now that the program is ready to validate with an XML Schema definition, it is necessary only to ensure that the XML document is associated with (at least) one. There are two ways to do that:

- With a schema declaration in the XML document
- By specifying the schema(s) to use in the application

Note: When the application specifies the schema(s) to use, it overrides any schema declarations in the document.

To specify the schema definition in the document, you create XML like this:

```
<documentRoot
    xmlns:xsi="http://www.w3.org/2001/XMLSchema-instance"
    xsi:noNamespaceSchemaLocation='YourSchemaDefinition.xsd'
>
    ...
```

The first attribute defines the XML namespace (xmlns) prefix, xsi, which stands for "XML Schema instance." The second line specifies the schema to use for elements in the document that do *not* have a namespace prefix—that is, for the elements you typically define in any simple, uncomplicated XML document. (You'll see how to deal with multiple namespaces in the next section.)

You can also specify the schema file in the application:

```
static final String schemaSource = "YourSchemaDefinition.xsd";
static final String JAXP_SCHEMA_SOURCE =
    "http://java.sun.com/xml/jaxp/properties/schemaSource";
...
DocumentBuilderFactory factory =
    DocumentBuilderFactory.newInstance()
...
factory.setAttribute(JAXP_SCHEMA_SOURCE,
    new File(schemaSource));
```

Here, too, there are mechanisms at your disposal that will let you specify multiple schemas. We'll take a look at those next.

Validating with Multiple Namespaces

Namespaces let you combine elements that serve different purposes in the same document without having to worry about overlapping names.

Note: The material discussed in this section also applies to validating when using the SAX parser. You're seeing it here, because at this point you've learned enough about namespaces for the discussion to make sense.

To contrive an example, consider an XML data set that keeps track of personnel data. The data set may include information from the W2 tax form as well as information from the employee's hiring form, with both elements named <form> in their respective schemas.

If a prefix is defined for the `tax` namespace, and another prefix defined for the `hiring` namespace, then the personnel data could include segments like this:

```
<employee id="...">
  <name>....</name>
  <tax:form>
     ...w2 tax form data...
  </tax:form>
  <hiring:form>
     ...employment history, etc....
  </hiring:form>
</employee>
```

The contents of the `tax:form` element would obviously be different from the contents of the `hiring:form` and would have to be validated differently.

Note, too, that in this example there is a default namespace that the unqualified element names `employee` and `name` belong to. For the document to be properly validated, the schema for that namespace must be declared, as well as the schemas for the `tax` and `hiring` namespaces.

Note: The default" namespace is actually a *specific* namespace. It is defined as the "namespace that has no name." So you can't simply use one namespace as your default this week, and another namespace as the default later. This "unnamed namespace" (or "null namespace") is like the number zero. It doesn't have any value to speak of (no name), but it is still precisely defined. So a namespace that does have a name can never be used as the default namespace.

When parsed, each element in the data set will be validated against the appropriate schema, as long as those schemas have been declared. Again, the schemas can be declared either as part of the XML data set or in the program. (It is also possible to mix the declarations. In general, though, it is a good idea to keep all the declarations together in one place.)

Declaring the Schemas in the XML Data Set

To declare the schemas to use for the preceding example in the data set, the XML code would look something like this:

```
<documentRoot
    xmlns:xsi="http://www.w3.org/2001/XMLSchema-instance"
    xsi:noNamespaceSchemaLocation="employeeDatabase.xsd"
    xsi:schemaLocation=
        "http://www.irs.gov/ fullpath/w2TaxForm.xsd
         http://www.ourcompany.com/ relpath/hiringForm.xsd"
    xmlns:tax="http://www.irs.gov/"
    xmlns:hiring="http://www.ourcompany.com/"
>
    ...
```

The `noNamespaceSchemaLocation` declaration is something you've seen before, as are the last two entries, which define the namespace prefixes `tax` and `hiring`. What's new is the entry in the middle, which defines the locations of the schemas to use for each namespace referenced in the document.

The `xsi:schemaLocation` declaration consists of entry pairs, where the first entry in each pair is a fully qualified URI that specifies the namespace, and the second entry contains a full path or a relative path to the schema definition. (In general, fully qualified paths are recommended. In that way, only one copy of the schema will tend to exist.)

Note that you cannot use the namespace prefixes when defining the schema locations. The `xsi:schemaLocation` declaration understands only namespace names and not prefixes.

Declaring the Schemas in the Application

To declare the equivalent schemas in the application, the code would look something like this:

```
static final String employeeSchema = "employeeDatabase.xsd";
static final String taxSchema = "w2TaxForm.xsd";
static final String hiringSchema = "hiringForm.xsd";

static final String[] schemas = {
    employeeSchema,
    taxSchema,
    hiringSchema,
    };
```

```
static final String JAXP_SCHEMA_SOURCE =
    "http://java.sun.com/xml/jaxp/properties/schemaSource";

...
DocumentBuilderFactory factory =
    DocumentBuilderFactory.newInstance()
...
factory.setAttribute(JAXP_SCHEMA_SOURCE, schemas);
```

Here, the array of strings that points to the schema definitions (.xsd files) is passed as the argument to the factory.setAttribute method. Note the differences from when you were declaring the schemas to use as part of the XML data set:

- There is no special declaration for the default (unnamed) schema.
- You don't specify the namespace name. Instead, you only give pointers to the .xsd files.

To make the namespace assignments, the parser reads the .xsd files, and finds in them the name of the *target namespace* they apply to. Because the files are specified with URIs, the parser can use an EntityResolver (if one has been defined) to find a local copy of the schema.

If the schema definition does not define a target namespace, then it applies to the default (unnamed, or null) namespace. So, in our example, you would expect to see these target namespace declarations in the schemas:

- employeeDatabase.xsd: none
- w2TaxForm.xsd: http://www.irs.gov/
- hiringForm.xsd: http://www.ourcompany.com

At this point, you have seen two possible values for the schema source property when invoking the factory.setAttribute() method: a File object in factory.setAttribute(JAXP_SCHEMA_SOURCE, new File(schemaSource)) and an array of strings in factory.setAttribute(JAXP_SCHEMA_SOURCE, schemas). Here is a complete list of the possible values for that argument:

- A string that points to the URI of the schema
- An InputStream with the contents of the schema
- A SAX InputSource
- A File
- An array of Objects, each of which is one of the types defined here

---

Note: An array of Objects can be used only when the schema language (like `http://java.sun.com/xml/jaxp/properties/schemaLanguage`) has the ability to assemble a schema at runtime. Also, when an array of Objects is passed it is illegal to have two schemas that share the same namespace.

Further Information

For further information on the `TreeModel`, see

- "Understanding the TreeModel": `http://java.sun.com/products/jfc/tsc/articles/jtree/index.html`

For further information on the W3C Document Object Model (DOM), see

- The DOM standard page: `http://www.w3.org/DOM/`

For more information on schema-based validation mechanisms, see

- The W3C standard validation mechanism, XML Schema: `http://www.w3.org/XML/Schema`
- RELAX NG's regular-expression based validation mechanism: `http://www.oasis-open.org/committees/relax-ng/`
- Schematron's assertion-based validation mechanism: `http://www.ascc.net/xml/resource/schematron/schematron.html`

7

Extensible Stylesheet Language Transformations

THE Extensible Stylesheet Language Transformations (XSLT) standard defines mechanisms for addressing XML data (XPath) and for specifying transformations on the data in order to convert it into other forms. JAXP includes an interpreting implementation of XSLT called Xalan ("ZAY-lahn").

Note: The term Xalan doesn't appear to be stand for anything. It is said to be the name of a rare musical instrument, but the only instrument that comes close is the *Xalam* ("zah-LAHM"), an early precursor to the banjo.

In this chapter, you'll learn how to use Xalan. You'll write out a Document Object Model as an XML file, and you'll see how to generate a DOM from an arbitrary data file in order to convert it to XML. Finally, you'll convert XML data into a different form, unlocking the mysteries of the XPath addressing mechanism along the way.

Note: The examples in this chapter can be found in `<INSTALL>`/j2eetutorial14/examples/jaxp/xslt/samples/.

Introducing XSL, XSLT and XPath

The Extensible Stylesheet Language (XSL) has three major subcomponents:

XSL-FO

> The Formatting Objects standard. By far the largest subcomponent, this standard gives mechanisms for describing font sizes, page layouts, and other aspects of object rendering. This subcomponent is *not* covered by JAXP, nor is it included in this tutorial.

XSLT

> This is the transformation language, which lets you define a transformation from XML into some other format. For example, you might use XSLT to produce HTML or a different XML structure. You could even use it to produce plain text or to put the information in some other document format. (And as you'll see in Generating XML from an Arbitrary Data Structure [page 264], a clever application can press it into service to manipulate non-XML data as well.)

XPath

> At bottom, XSLT is a language that lets you specify what sorts of things to do when a particular element is encountered. But to write a program for different parts of an XML data structure, you need to specify the part of the structure you are talking about at any given time. XPath is that specification language. It is an addressing mechanism that lets you specify a path to an element so that, for example, `<article><title>` can be distinguished from `<person><title>`. In that way, you can describe different kinds of translations for the different `<title>` elements.

The remainder of this section describes the packages that make up the JAXP Transformation APIs.

The JAXP Transformation Packages

Here is a description of the packages that make up the JAXP Transformation APIs:

`javax.xml.transform`

> This package defines the factory class you use to get a `Transformer` object. You then configure the transformer with input (source) and output (result)

objects, and invoke its `transform()` method to make the transformation happen. The source and result objects are created using classes from one of the other three packages.

`javax.xml.transform.dom`
> Defines the `DOMSource` and `DOMResult` classes, which let you use a DOM as an input to or output from a transformation.

`javax.xml.transform.sax`
> Defines the `SAXSource` and `SAXResult` classes, which let you use a SAX event generator as input to a transformation, or deliver SAX events as output to a SAX event processor.

`javax.xml.transform.stream`
> Defines the `StreamSource` and `StreamResult` classes, which let you use an I/O stream as an input to or output from a transformation.

How XPath Works

The XPath specification is the foundation for a variety of specifications, including XSLT and linking/addressing specifications such as XPointer. So an understanding of XPath is fundamental to a lot of advanced XML usage. This section provides a thorough introduction to XPath in the context of XSLT so that you can refer to it as needed.

Note: In this tutorial, you won't actually use XPath until later, in the section, Transforming XML Data with XSLT (page 278). So, if you like, you can skip this section and go on ahead to the next section, Writing Out a DOM as an XML File (page 257). (When you get to the end of that section, there will be a note that refers you back here so that you don't forget!)

XPath Expressions

In general, an XPath expression specifies a *pattern* that selects a set of XML nodes. XSLT templates then use those patterns when applying transformations. (XPointer, on the other hand, adds mechanisms for defining a *point* or a *range* so that XPath expressions can be used for addressing.)

The nodes in an XPath expression refer to more than just elements. They also refer to text and attributes, among other things. In fact, the XPath specification defines an abstract document model that defines seven kinds of nodes:

- Root
- Element
- Text
- Attribute
- Comment
- Processing instruction
- Namespace

Note: The root element of the XML data is modeled by an *element* node. The XPath root node contains the document's root element as well as other information relating to the document.

The XSLT/XPath Data Model

Like the Document Object Model, the XSLT/XPath data model consists of a tree containing a variety of nodes. Under any given element node, there are text nodes, attribute nodes, element nodes, comment nodes, and processing instruction nodes.

In this abstract model, syntactic distinctions disappear, and you are left with a normalized view of the data. In a text node, for example, it makes no difference whether the text was defined in a CDATA section or whether it included entity references. The text node will consist of normalized data, as it exists after all parsing is complete. So the text will contain a < character, whether or not an entity reference such as < or a CDATA section was used to include it. (Similarly, the text will contain an & character, whether it was delivered using & or it was in a CDATA section.)

In this section, we'll deal mostly with element nodes and text nodes. For the other addressing mechanisms, see the XPath specification.

Templates and Contexts

An XSLT *template* is a set of formatting instructions that apply to the nodes selected by an XPath expression. In a stylesheet, an XSLT template would look something like this:

```
<xsl:template match="//LIST">
    ...
</xsl:template>
```

The expression //LIST selects the set of LIST nodes from the input stream. Additional instructions within the template tell the system what to do with them.

The set of nodes selected by such an expression defines the *context* in which other expressions in the template are evaluated. That context can be considered as the whole set—for example, when determining the number of the nodes it contains.

The context can also be considered as a single member of the set, as each member is processed one by one. For example, inside the LIST-processing template, the expression @type refers to the type attribute of the current LIST node. (Similarly, the expression @* refers to all the attributes for the current LIST element.)

Basic XPath Addressing

An XML document is a tree-structured (hierarchical) collection of nodes. As with a hierarchical directory structure, it is useful to specify a *path* that points to a particular node in the hierarchy (hence the name of the specification: XPath). In fact, much of the notation of directory paths is carried over intact:

- The forward slash (/) is used as a path separator.
- An absolute path from the root of the document starts with a /.
- A relative path from a given location starts with anything else.
- A double period (. .) indicates the parent of the current node.
- A single period (.) indicates the current node.

For example, In an Extensible HTML (XHTML) document (an XML document that looks like HTML but is *well formed* according to XML rules), the path /h1/ h2/ would indicate an h2 element under an h1. (Recall that in XML, element names are case-sensitive, so this kind of specification works much better in XHTML than it would in plain HTML, because HTML is case-insensitive.)

In a pattern-matching specification such as XPath, the specification /h1/h2 selects *all* h2 elements that lie under an h1 element. To select a specific h2 element, you use square brackets [] for indexing (like those used for arrays). The path /h1[4]/h2[5] would therefore select the fifth h2 element under the fourth h1 element.

Note: In XHTML, all element names are in lowercase. That is a fairly common convention for XML documents. However, uppercase names are easier to read in a tutorial like this one. So for the remainder of the XSLT tutorial, all XML element names will be in uppercase. (Attribute names, on the other hand, will remain in lowercase.)

A name specified in an XPath expression refers to an element. For example, h1 in /h1/h2 refers to an h1 element. To refer to an attribute, you prefix the attribute name with an @ sign. For example, @type refers to the type attribute of an element. Assuming that you have an XML document with LIST elements, for example, the expression LIST/@type selects the type attribute of the LIST element.

Note: Because the expression does not begin with /, the reference specifies a list node relative to the current context—whatever position in the document that happens to be.

Basic XPath Expressions

The full range of XPath expressions takes advantage of the wildcards, operators, and functions that XPath defines. You'll learn more about those shortly. Here, we look at a couple of the most common XPath expressions simply to introduce them.

The expression @type="unordered" specifies an attribute named type whose value is unordered. As you know, an expression such as LIST/@type specifies the type attribute of a LIST element.

You can combine those two notations to get something interesting! In XPath, the square-bracket notation ([]) normally associated with indexing is extended to specify *selection criteria*. So the expression LIST[@type="unordered"] selects all LIST elements whose type value is unordered.

Similar expressions exist for elements. Each element has an associated *string-value*, which is formed by concatenating all the text segments that lie under the element. (A more detailed explanation of how that process works is coming up in String-Value of an Element, page 253.)

Suppose you model what's going on in your organization using an XML structure that consists of PROJECT elements and ACTIVITY elements that have a text string with the project name, multiple PERSON elements to list the people involved and, optionally, a STATUS element that records the project status. Here are other examples that use the extended square-bracket notation:

- /PROJECT[.="MyProject"]: Selects a PROJECT named "MyProject"
- /PROJECT[STATUS]: Selects all projects that have a STATUS child element
- /PROJECT[STATUS="Critical"]: Selects all projects that have a STATUS child element with the string-value Critical

Combining Index Addresses

The XPath specification defines quite a few addressing mechanisms, and they can be combined in many different ways. As a result, XPath delivers a lot of expressive power for a relatively simple specification. This section illustrates other interesting combinations:

- LIST[@type="ordered"][3]: Selects all LIST elements of type ordered, and returns the third
- LIST[3][@type="ordered"]: Selects the third LIST element, but only if it is of type ordered

---

Note: Many more combinations of address operators are listed in section 2.5 of the XPath specification. This is arguably the most useful section of the spec for defining an XSLT transform.

Wildcards

By definition, an unqualified XPath expression selects a set of XML nodes that matches that specified pattern. For example, /HEAD matches all top-level HEAD entries, whereas /HEAD[1] matches only the first. Table 7–1 lists the wildcards that can be used in XPath expressions to broaden the scope of the pattern matching.

Table 7–1   XPath Wildcards

Wildcard	Meaning
*	Matches any element node (not attributes or text)
node()	Matches any node of any kind: element node, text node, attribute node, processing instruction node, namespace node, or comment node
@*	Matches any attribute node

In the project database example, `/*/PERSON[.="Fred"]` matches any `PROJECT` or `ACTIVITY` element that names Fred.

Extended-Path Addressing

So far, all the patterns you've seen have specified an exact number of levels in the hierarchy. For example, `/HEAD` specifies any `HEAD` element at the first level in the hierarchy, whereas `/*/*` specifies any element at the second level in the hierarchy. To specify an indeterminate level in the hierarchy, use a double forward slash (`//`). For example, the XPath expression `//PARA` selects all `paragraph` elements in a document, wherever they may be found.

The `//` pattern can also be used within a path. So the expression `/HEAD/LIST//PARA` indicates all paragraph elements in a subtree that begins from `/HEAD/LIST`.

XPath Data Types and Operators

XPath expressions yield either a set of nodes, a string, a Boolean (a true/false value), or a number. Table 7–2 lists the operators that can be used in an Xpath expression.

Expressions can be grouped in parentheses, so you don't have to worry about operator precedence.

Note: *Operator precedence* is a term that answers the question, "If you specify `a + b * c`, does that mean `(a+b) * c` or `a + (b*c)`?" (The operator precedence is roughly the same as that shown in the table.)

Table 7–2 XPath Operators

Operator	Meaning
|	Alternative. For example, PARA|LIST selects all PARA and LIST elements.
or, and	Returns the or/and of two Boolean values.
=, !=	Equal or not equal, for Booleans, strings, and numbers.
<, >, <=, >=	Less than, greater than, less than or equal to, greater than or equal to, for numbers.
+, -, *, div, mod	Add, subtract, multiply, floating-point divide, and modulus (remainder) operations (e.g., 6 mod 4 = 2)

String-Value of an Element

The string-value of an element is the concatenation of all descendent text nodes, no matter how deep. Consider this mixed-content XML data:

```
<PARA>This paragraph contains a <B>bold</B> word</PARA>
```

The string-value of the <PARA> element is This paragraph contains a bold word. In particular, note that <B> is a child of <PARA> and that the text bold is a child of <B>. The point is that all the text in all children of a node joins in the concatenation to form the string-value.

Also, it is worth understanding that the text in the abstract data model defined by XPath is fully normalized. So whether the XML structure contains the entity reference < or < in a CDATA section, the element's string-value will contain the < character. Therefore, when generating HTML or XML with an XSLT stylesheet, you must convert occurrences of < to < or enclose them in a CDATA section. Similarly, occurrences of & must be converted to &.

XPath Functions

This section ends with an overview of the XPath functions. You can use XPath functions to select a collection of nodes in the same way that you would use an element specification such as those you have already seen. Other functions

return a string, a number, or a Boolean value. For example, the expression /
PROJECT/text() gets the string-value of PROJECT nodes.

Many functions depend on the current context. In the preceding example, the
context for each invocation of the text() function is the PROJECT node that is
currently selected.

There are many XPath functions—too many to describe in detail here. This section provides a brief listing that shows the available XPath functions, along with
a summary of what they do.

Note: Skim the list of functions to get an idea of what's there. For more information,
see section 4 of the XPath specification.

Node-Set Functions

Many XPath expressions select a set of nodes. In essence, they return a *node-set*.
One function does that, too.

- id(...): Returns the node with the specified ID.

(Elements have an ID only when the document has a DTD, which specifies
which attribute has the ID type.)

Positional Functions

These functions return positionally based numeric values.

- last(): Returns the index of the last element. For example, /
  HEAD[last()] selects the last HEAD element.
- position(): Returns the index position. For example, /HEAD[position()
  <= 5] selects the first five HEAD elements.
- count(...): Returns the count of elements. For example, /
  HEAD[count(HEAD)=0] selects all HEAD elements that have no subheads.

String Functions

These functions operate on or return strings.

- concat(*string*, *string*, ...): Concatenates the string values.
- starts-with(*string1*, *string2*): Returns true if *string1* starts with *string2*.
- contains(*string1*, *string2*): Returns true if *string1* contains *string2*.
- substring-before(*string1*, *string2*): Returns the start of *string1* before *string2* occurs in it.
- substring-after(*string1*, *string2*): Returns the remainder of *string1* after *string2* occurs in it.
- substring(*string*, *idx*): Returns the substring from the index position to the end, where the index of the first char = 1.
- substring(*string*, *idx*, *len*): Returns the substring of the specified length from the index position.
- string-length(): Returns the size of the context node's string-value; the *context node* is the currently selected node—the node that was selected by an XPath expression in which a function such as string-length() is applied.
- string-length(*string*): Returns the size of the specified string.
- normalize-space(): Returns the normalized string-value of the current node (no leading or trailing whitespace, and sequences of whitespace characters converted to a single space).
- normalize-space(*string*): Returns the normalized string-value of the specified string.
- translate(*string1*, *string2*, *string3*): Converts *string1*, replacing occurrences of characters in *string2* with the corresponding character from *string3*.

Note: XPath defines three ways to get the text of an element: text(), string(object), and the string-value implied by an element name in an expression like this: /PROJECT[PERSON="Fred"].

Boolean Functions

These functions operate on or return Boolean values.

- `not(...)`: Negates the specified Boolean value.
- `true()`: Returns true.
- `false()`: Returns false.
- `lang(string)`: Returns true if the language of the context node (specified by `xml:Lang` attributes) is the same as (or a sublanguage of) the specified language; for example, `Lang("en")` is true for `<PARA_xml:Lang="en">...</PARA>`.

Numeric Functions

These functions operate on or return numeric values.

- `sum(...)`: Returns the sum of the numeric value of each node in the specified node-set.
- `floor(N)`: Returns the largest integer that is not greater than *N*.
- `ceiling(N)`: Returns the smallest integer that is not less than *N*.
- `round(N)`: Returns the integer that is closest to *N*.

Conversion Functions

These functions convert one data type to another.

- `string(...)`: Returns the string value of a number, Boolean, or node-set.
- `boolean(...)`: Returns a Boolean value for a number, string, or node-set (a non-zero number, a nonempty node-set, and a nonempty string are all true).
- `number(...)`: Returns the numeric value of a Boolean, string, or node-set (true is 1, false is 0, a string containing a number becomes that number, the string-value of a node-set is converted to a number).

Namespace Functions

These functions let you determine the namespace characteristics of a node.

- `local-name()`: Returns the name of the current node, minus the namespace prefix.
- `local-name(...)`: Returns the name of the first node in the specified node set, minus the namespace prefix.
- `namespace-uri()`: Returns the namespace URI from the current node.
- `namespace-uri(...)`: Returns the namespace URI from the first node in the specified node-set.
- `name()`: Returns the expanded name (URI plus local name) of the current node.
- `name(...)`: Returns the expanded name (URI plus local name) of the first node in the specified node-set.

Summary

XPath operators, functions, wildcards, and node-addressing mechanisms can be combined in wide variety of ways. The introduction you've had so far should give you a good head start at specifying the pattern you need for any particular purpose.

Writing Out a DOM as an XML File

After you have constructed a DOM—either by parsing an XML file or building it programmatically—you frequently want to save it as XML. This section shows you how to do that using the Xalan transform package.

Using that package, you'll create a transformer object to wire a `DOMSource` to a `StreamResult`. You'll then invoke the transformer's `transform()` method to write out the DOM as XML data.

Reading the XML

The first step is to create a DOM in memory by parsing an XML file. By now, you should be getting comfortable with the process.

Note: The code discussed in this section is in `TransformationApp01.java`.

The following code provides a basic template to start from. (It should be familiar. It's basically the same code you wrote at the start of Chapter 6. If you saved it then, that version should be essentially equivalent to what you see here.)

```java
import javax.xml.parsers.DocumentBuilder;
import javax.xml.parsers.DocumentBuilderFactory;
import javax.xml.parsers.FactoryConfigurationError;
import javax.xml.parsers.ParserConfigurationException;

import org.xml.sax.SAXException;
import org.xml.sax.SAXParseException;

import org.w3c.dom.Document;
import org.w3c.dom.DOMException;

import java.io.*;

public class TransformationApp
{
   static Document document;

   public static void main(String argv[])
   {
      if (argv.length != 1) {
         System.err.println (
            "Usage: java TransformationApp filename");
         System.exit (1);
      }

      DocumentBuilderFactory factory =
         DocumentBuilderFactory.newInstance();
      //factory.setNamespaceAware(true);
      //factory.setValidating(true);

      try {
         File f = new File(argv[0]);
```

```
        DocumentBuilder builder =
            factory.newDocumentBuilder();
        document = builder.parse(f);

    } catch (SAXParseException spe) {
        // Error generated by the parser
        System.out.println("\n** Parsing error"
            + ", line " + spe.getLineNumber()
            + ", uri " + spe.getSystemId());
        System.out.println("   " + spe.getMessage() );

        // Use the contained exception, if any
        Exception x = spe;
        if (spe.getException() != null)
            x = spe.getException();
        x.printStackTrace();

    } catch (SAXException sxe) {
        // Error generated by this application
        // (or a parser-initialization error)
        Exception x = sxe;
        if (sxe.getException() != null)
            x = sxe.getException();
        x.printStackTrace();

    } catch (ParserConfigurationException pce) {
        // Parser with specified options can't be built
        pce.printStackTrace();

    } catch (IOException ioe) {
        // I/O error
        ioe.printStackTrace();
    }
  } // main
}
```

Creating a Transformer

The next step is to create a transformer you can use to transmit the XML to `System.out`.

Note: The code discussed in this section is in `TransformationApp02.java`. The file it runs on is `slideSample01.xml`. The output is in `TransformationLog02.txt`. (The browsable versions are `slideSample01-xml.html` and `TransformationLog02.html`.)

Start by adding the following highlighted import statements:

```
import javax.xml.transform.Transformer;
import javax.xml.transform.TransformerFactory;
import javax.xml.transform.TransformerException;
import javax.xml.transform.TransformerConfigurationException;

import javax.xml.transform.dom.DOMSource;

import javax.xml.transform.stream.StreamResult;

import java.io.*;
```

Here, you add a series of classes that should now be forming a standard pattern: an entity (`Transformer`), the factory to create it (`TransformerFactory`), and the exceptions that can be generated by each. Because a transformation always has a *source* and a *result*, you then import the classes necessary to use a DOM as a source (`DOMSource`) and an output stream for the result (`StreamResult`).

Next, add the code to carry out the transformation:

```
try {
  File f = new File(argv[0]);
  DocumentBuilder builder = factory.newDocumentBuilder();
  document = builder.parse(f);

  // Use a Transformer for output
  TransformerFactory tFactory =
    TransformerFactory.newInstance();
  Transformer transformer = tFactory.newTransformer();

  DOMSource source = new DOMSource(document);
  StreamResult result = new StreamResult(System.out);
  transformer.transform(source, result);
```

Here, you create a transformer object, use the DOM to construct a source object, and use `System.out` to construct a result object. You then tell the transformer to operate on the source object and output to the result object.

In this case, the "transformer" isn't actually changing anything. In XSLT terminology, you are using the *identity transform*, which means that the "transformation" generates a copy of the source, unchanged.

Note: You can specify a variety of output properties for transformer objects, as defined in the W3C specification at http://www.w3.org/TR/xslt#output. For example, to get indented output, you can invoke

```
transformer.setOutputProperty(OutputKeys.INDENT, "yes");
```

Finally, add the following highlighted code to catch the new errors that can be generated:

```
} catch (TransformerConfigurationException tce) {
    // Error generated by the parser
    System.out.println ("* Transformer Factory error");
    System.out.println("  " + tce.getMessage() );

     // Use the contained exception, if any
    Throwable x = tce;
    if (tce.getException() != null)
       x = tce.getException();
    x.printStackTrace();

} catch (TransformerException te) {
    // Error generated by the parser
    System.out.println ("* Transformation error");
    System.out.println("  " + te.getMessage() );

    // Use the contained exception, if any
    Throwable x = te;
    if (te.getException() != null)
       x = te.getException();
    x.printStackTrace();

} catch (SAXParseException spe) {
    ...
```

Notes:

- `TransformerExceptions` are thrown by the transformer object.
- `TransformerConfigurationExceptions` are thrown by the factory.
- To preserve the XML document's DOCTYPE setting, it is also necessary to add the following code:

```
import javax.xml.transform.OutputKeys;
...
if (document.getDoctype() != null){
```

```
String systemValue = (new
    File(document.getDoctype().getSystemId())).getName();
transformer.setOutputProperty(
  OutputKeys.DOCTYPE_SYSTEM, systemValue
);
}
```

Writing the XML

For instructions on how to compile and run the program, see Compiling and Running the Program (page 128) from the SAX tutorial, Chapter 5. (If you're working along, substitute TransformationApp for Echo as the name of the program. If you are compiling the sample code, use TransformationApp02.) When you run the program on slideSample01.xml, this is the output you see:

```
<?xml version="1.0" encoding="UTF-8"?>
<!-- A SAMPLE set of slides -->
<slideshow author="Yours Truly" date="Date of publication"
title="Sample Slide Show">

  <!-- TITLE SLIDE -->
  <slide type="all">
    <title>Wake up to WonderWidgets!</title>
  </slide>

  <!-- OVERVIEW -->
  <slide type="all">
    <title>Overview</title>
    <item>Why <em>WonderWidgets</em> are great</item>
    <item/>
    <item>Who <em>buys</em> WonderWidgets</item>
  </slide>

</slideshow>
```

Note: The order of the attributes may vary, depending on which parser you are using.

To find out more about configuring the factory and handling validation errors, see Reading XML Data into a DOM (page 182), and Additional Information (page 186).

Writing Out a Subtree of the DOM

It is also possible to operate on a subtree of a DOM. In this section, you'll experiment with that option.

Note: The code discussed in this section is in `TransformationApp03.java`. The output is in `TransformationLog03.txt`. (The browsable version is `TransformationLog03.html`.)

The only difference in the process is that now you will create a `DOMSource` using a node in the DOM, rather than the entire DOM. The first step is to import the classes you need to get the node you want. Add the following highlighted code to do that:

```
import org.w3c.dom.Document;
import org.w3c.dom.DOMException;
import org.w3c.dom.Node;
import org.w3c.dom.NodeList;
```

The next step is to find a good node for the experiment. Add the following highlighted code to select the first `<slide>` element:

```
try {
   File f = new File(argv[0]);
   DocumentBuilder builder = factory.newDocumentBuilder();
   document = builder.parse(f);

   // Get the first <slide> element in the DOM
   NodeList list = document.getElementsByTagName("slide");
   Node node = list.item(0);
```

Then make the following changes to construct a source object that consists of the subtree rooted at that node:

```
DOMSource source = new DOMSource(document);
DOMSource source = new DOMSource(node);
StreamResult result = new StreamResult(System.out);
transformer.transform(source, result);
```

Now run the app. Your output should look like this:

```
<?xml version="1.0" encoding="UTF-8"?>
<slide type="all">
    <title>Wake up to WonderWidgets!</title>
  </slide>
```

Cleaning Up

Because it will be easiest to do now, make the following changes to back out the additions you made in this section. (`TransformationApp04.java` contains these changes.)

```
Import org.w3c.dom.DOMException;
import org.w3c.dom.Node;
import org.w3c.dom.NodeList;
...
  try {
    ...
    // Get the first <slide> element in the DOM
    NodeList list = document.getElementsByTagName("slide");
    Node node = list.item(0);
    ...
    DOMSource source = new DOMSource(node);
    StreamResult result = new StreamResult(System.out);
    transformer.transform(source, result);
```

Summary

At this point, you've seen how to use a transformer to write out a DOM and how to use a subtree of a DOM as the source object in a transformation. In the next section, you'll see how to use a transformer to create XML from any data structure you are capable of parsing.

Generating XML from an Arbitrary Data Structure

In this section, you'll use XSLT to convert an *arbitrary data structure* to XML.

Here is an outline of the process:

1. You'll modify an existing program that reads the data, to make it generate SAX events. (Whether that program is a real parser or simply a data filter of some kind is irrelevant for the moment.)

2. You'll then use the SAX "parser" to construct a SAXSource for the transformation.

3. You'll use the same StreamResult object you created in the last exercise so that you can see the results. (But note that you could just as easily create a DOMResult object to create a DOM in memory.)

4. You'll wire the source to the result using the transformer object to make the conversion.

For starters, you need a data set you want to convert and a program capable of reading the data. In the next two sections, you'll create a simple data file and a program that reads it.

Creating a Simple File

We'll start by creating a data set for an address book. You can duplicate the process, if you like, or simply use the data stored in PersonalAddress-Book.ldif.

The file shown here was produced by creating a new address book in Netscape Messenger, giving it some dummy data (one address card), and then exporting it in LDIF format.

Note: LDIF stands for LDAP Data Interchange Format. LDAP, in turn, stands for Lightweight Directory Access Protocol. I prefer to think of LDIF as the "Line Delimited Interchange Format" because that is pretty much what it is.

Figure 7–1 shows the address book entry that was created.

Exporting the address book produces a file like the one shown next. The parts of the file that we care about are shown in bold.

```
dn: cn=Fred Flintstone,mail=fred@barneys.house
modifytimestamp: 20010409210816Z
cn: Fred Flintstone
xmozillanickname: Fred
mail: Fred@barneys.house
```

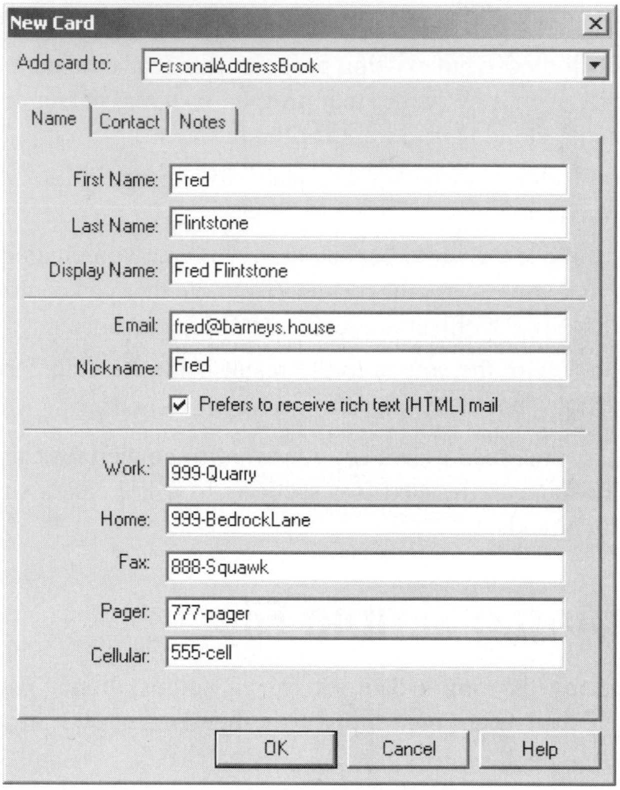

Figure 7–1 Address Book Entry

```
xmozillausehtmlmail: TRUE
givenname: Fred
sn: Flintstone
telephonenumber: 999-Quarry
homephone: 999-BedrockLane
facsimiletelephonenumber: 888-Squawk
pagerphone: 777-pager
cellphone: 555-cell
xmozillaanyphone: 999-Quarry
objectclass: top
objectclass: person
```

Note that each line of the file contains a variable name, a colon, and a space followed by a value for the variable. The sn variable contains the person's surname (last name) and the variable cn contains the DisplayName field from the address book entry.

Creating a Simple Parser

The next step is to create a program that parses the data.

Note: The code discussed in this section is in `AddressBookReader01.java`. The output is in `AddressBookReaderLog01.txt`.

The text for the program is shown next. It's an absurdly simple program that doesn't even loop for multiple entries because, after all, it's only a demo!

```java
import java.io.*;

public class AddressBookReader
{

  public static void main(String argv[])
  {
    // Check the arguments
    if (argv.length != 1) {
      System.err.println (
         "Usage: java AddressBookReader filename");
      System.exit (1);
    }
    String filename = argv[0];
    File f = new File(filename);
    AddressBookReader01 reader = new AddressBookReader01();
    reader.parse(f);
  }

  /** Parse the input */
  public void parse(File f)
  {
    try {
      // Get an efficient reader for the file
      FileReader r = new FileReader(f);
      BufferedReader br = new BufferedReader(r);

       // Read the file and display its contents.
      String line = br.readLine();
      while (null != (line = br.readLine())) {
        if (line.startsWith("xmozillanickname: "))
          break;
      }
      output("nickname", "xmozillanickname", line);
      line = br.readLine();
```

```
            output("email",     "mail",                 line);
            line = br.readLine();
            output("html",      "xmozillausehtmlmail", line);
            line = br.readLine();
            output("firstname","givenname",            line);
            line = br.readLine();
            output("lastname", "sn",                    line);
            line = br.readLine();
            output("work",      "telephonenumber",  line);
            line = br.readLine();
            output("home",      "homephone",            line);
            line = br.readLine();
            output("fax",       "facsimiletelephonenumber",
               line);
            line = br.readLine();
            output("pager",     "pagerphone",          line);
            line = br.readLine();
            output("cell",      "cellphone",            line);

        }
        catch (Exception e) {
           e.printStackTrace();
        }
   }

   void output(String name, String prefix, String line)
   {
      int startIndex = prefix.length() + 2;
         // 2=length of ": "
      String text = line.substring(startIndex);
      System.out.println(name + ": " + text);
   }
}
```

This program contains three methods:

main

The main method gets the name of the file from the command line, creates an instance of the parser, and sets it to work parsing the file. This method will be going away when we convert the program into a SAX parser. (That's one reason for putting the parsing code into a separate method.)

parse

This method operates on the File object sent to it by the main routine. As you can see, it's about as simple as it can get. The only nod to efficiency is the use of a BufferedReader, which can become important when you start operating on large files.

output

The `output` method contains the logic for the structure of a line. It takes three arguments. The first argument gives the method a name to display, so we can output `html` as a variable name, instead of `xmozillausehtmlmail`. The second argument gives the variable name stored in the file (`xmozil-lausehtmlmail`). The third argument gives the line containing the data. The routine then strips off the variable name from the start of the line and outputs the desired name, plus the data.

Running this program on `PersonalAddressBook.ldif` produces this output:

```
nickname: Fred
email: Fred@barneys.house
html: TRUE
firstname: Fred
lastname: Flintstone
work: 999-Quarry
home: 999-BedrockLane
fax: 888-Squawk
pager: 777-pager
cell: 555-cell
```

I think we can all agree that this is a bit more readable.

Modifying the Parser to Generate SAX Events

The next step is to modify the parser to generate SAX events so that you can use it as the basis for a `SAXSource` object in an XSLT `transform`.

Note: The code discussed in this section is in `AddressBookReader02.java`.

Start by importing the additional classes you'll need:

```
import java.io.*;

import org.xml.sax.*;
import org.xml.sax.helpers.AttributesImpl;
```

Next, modify the application so that it extends `XmlReader`. That change converts the application into a parser that generates the appropriate SAX events.

```
public class AddressBookReader
   implements XMLReader
{
```

Now remove the `main` method. You won't need it any more.

```
public static void main(String argv[])
{
  // Check the arguments
  if (argv.length != 1) {
     System.err.println ("Usage: Java AddressBookReader
filename");
     System.exit (1);
  }
  String filename = argv[0];
  File f = new File(filename);
  AddressBookReader02 reader = new AddressBookReader02();
  reader.parse(f);
}
```

Add some global variables that will come in handy in a few minutes:

```
public class AddressBookReader
   implements XMLReader
{

  ContentHandler handler;

  // We're not doing namespaces, and we have no
  // attributes on our elements.
  String nsu = "";   // NamespaceURI
  Attributes atts = new AttributesImpl();
  String rootElement = "addressbook";

  String indent = "\n        "; // for readability!
```

The SAX `ContentHandler` is the object that will get the SAX events generated by the parser. To make the application into an `XmlReader`, you'll define a `set-ContentHandler` method. The `handler` variable will hold a reference to the object that is sent when `setContentHandler` is invoked.

And when the parser generates SAX *element* events, it will need to supply namespace and attribute information. Because this is a simple application, you're defining null values for both of those.

You're also defining a root element for the data structure (addressbook) and setting up an indent string to improve the readability of the output.

Next, modify the parse method so that it takes an InputSource (rather than a File) as an argument and account for the exceptions it can generate:

```
public void parse(File f)InputSource input)
throws IOException, SAXException
```

Now make the following changes to get the reader encapsulated by the Input-Source object:

```
try {
   // Get an efficient reader for the file
   FileReader r = new FileReader(f);
   java.io.Reader r = input.getCharacterStream();
   BufferedReader Br = new BufferedReader(r);
```

Note: In the next section, you'll create the input source object and what you put in it will, in fact, be a buffered reader. But the AddressBookReader could be used by someone else, somewhere down the line. This step makes sure that the processing will be efficient, regardless of the reader you are given.

The next step is to modify the parse method to generate SAX events for the start of the document and the root element. Add the following highlighted code to do that:

```
/** Parse the input */
public void parse(InputSource input)
...
{
   try {
      ...
      // Read the file and display its contents.
      String line = br.readLine();
      while (null != (line = br.readLine())) {
         if (line.startsWith("xmozillanickname: ")) break;
      }

      if (handler==null) {
         throw new SAXException("No content handler");
      }

      handler.startDocument();
      handler.startElement(nsu, rootElement,
```

```
        rootElement, atts);

    output("nickname", "xmozillanickname", line);
    ...
    output("cell",      "cellphone",       line);

    handler.ignorableWhitespace("\n".toCharArray(),
            0, // start index
            1  // length
            );
    handler.endElement(nsu, rootElement, rootElement);
    handler.endDocument();
}
catch (Exception e) {
...
```

Here, you check to make sure that the parser is properly configured with a
ContentHandler. (For this app, we don't care about anything else.) You then
generate the events for the start of the document and the root element, and you
finish by sending the end event for the root element and the end event for the
document.

A couple of items are noteworthy at this point:

- We haven't bothered to send the setDocumentLocator event, because that
  is optional. Were it important, that event would be sent immediately before
  the startDocument event.

- We've generated an ignorableWhitespace event before the end of the
  root element. This, too, is optional, but it drastically improves the readability of the output, as you'll see in a few moments. (In this case, the
  whitespace consists of a single newline, which is sent in the same way that
  characters are sent to the characters method: as a character array, a starting index, and a length.)

Now that SAX events are being generated for the document and the root element, the next step is to modify the output method to generate the appropriate
element events for each data item. Make the following changes to do that:

```
void output(String name, String prefix, String line)
throws SAXException
{
    int startIndex = prefix.length() + 2; // 2=length of ": "
    String text = line.substring(startIndex);
    System.out.println(name + ": " + text);
```

```
    int textLength = line.length() - startIndex;
    handler.ignorableWhitespace(indent.toCharArray(),
                    0, // start index
                    indent.length()
                    );
    handler.startElement(nsu, name, name /*"qName"*/, atts);
    handler.characters(line.toCharArray(),
            startIndex,
            textLength);
    handler.endElement(nsu, name, name);
}
```

Because the ContentHandler methods can send SAXExceptions back to the parser, the parser must be prepared to deal with them. In this case, we don't expect any, so we'll simply allow the application to fail if any occur.

You then calculate the length of the data, again generating some ignorable whitespace for readability. In this case, there is only one level of data, so we can use a fixed-indent string. (If the data were more structured, we would have to calculate how much space to indent, depending on the nesting of the data.)

Note: The indent string makes no difference to the data but will make the output a lot easier to read. When everything is working, try generating the result without that string! All the elements will wind up concatenated end to end:
`<addressbook><nickname>Fred</nickname><email>...`

Next, add the method that configures the parser with the ContentHandler that is to receive the events it generates:

```
void output(String name, String prefix, String line)
  throws SAXException
{
  ...
}

/** Allow an application to register a content event handler. */
public void setContentHandler(ContentHandler handler) {
  this.handler = handler;
}

/** Return the current content handler. */
public ContentHandler getContentHandler() {
  return this.handler;
}
```

Several other methods must be implemented in order to satisfy the `XmlReader` interface. For the purpose of this exercise, we'll generate null methods for all of them. For a production application, though, you may want to consider implementing the error handler methods to produce a more robust app. For now, add the following highlighted code to generate null methods for them:

```
/** Allow an application to register an error event handler. */
public void setErrorHandler(ErrorHandler handler)
{ }

/** Return the current error handler. */
public ErrorHandler getErrorHandler()
{ return null; }
```

Then add the following highlighted code to generate null methods for the remainder of the `XmlReader` interface. (Most of them are of value to a real SAX parser but have little bearing on a data-conversion application like this one.)

```
/** Parse an XML document from a system identifier (URI). */
public void parse(String systemId)
throws IOException, SAXException
{ }

 /** Return the current DTD handler. */
public DTDHandler getDTDHandler()
{ return null; }

/** Return the current entity resolver. */
public EntityResolver getEntityResolver()
{ return null; }

/** Allow an application to register an entity resolver. */
public void setEntityResolver(EntityResolver resolver)
{ }

/** Allow an application to register a DTD event handler. */
public void setDTDHandler(DTDHandler handler)
{ }

/** Look up the value of a property. */
public Object getProperty(String name)
{ return null; }

/** Set the value of a property. */
public void setProperty(String name, Object value)
{ }
```

```
/** Set the state of a feature. */
public void setFeature(String name, boolean value)
{ }

/** Look up the value of a feature. */
public boolean getFeature(String name)
{ return false; }
```

Congratulations! You now have a parser you can use to generate SAX events. In the next section, you'll use it to construct a SAX source object that will let you transform the data into XML.

Using the Parser as a SAXSource

Given a SAX parser to use as an event source, you can (easily!) construct a transformer to produce a result. In this section, you'll modify the `Transformer-App` you've been working with to produce a stream output result, although you could just as easily produce a DOM result.

Note: The code discussed in this section is in `TransformationApp04.java`. The results of running it are in `TransformationLog04.txt`.

Make sure that you put the `AddressBookReader` aside and open the `TransformationApp`. The work you do in this section affects the `TransformationApp`! (They look similar, so it's easy to start working on the wrong one.)

Start by making the following changes to import the classes you'll need to construct a `SAXSource` object. (You won't need the DOM classes at this point, so they are discarded here, although leaving them in doesn't do any harm.)

```
import org.xml.sax.SAXException;
import org.xml.sax.SAXParseException;
import org.xml.sax.ContentHandler;
import org.xml.sax.InputSource;
import org.w3c.dom.Document;
import org.w3c.dom.DOMException;
...
import javax.xml.transform.dom.DOMSource;
import javax.xml.transform.sax.SAXSource;
import javax.xml.transform.stream.StreamResult;
```

Next, remove a few other holdovers from our DOM-processing days, and add the code to create an instance of the AddressBookReader:

```
public class TransformationApp
{
  // Global value so it can be ref'd by the tree-adapter
  static Document document;

   public static void main(String argv[])
  {
    ...
    DocumentBuilderFactory factory =
      DocumentBuilderFactory.newInstance();
    //factory.setNamespaceAware(true);
    //factory.setValidating(true);

    // Create the sax "parser".
    AddressBookReader saxReader = new AddressBookReader();

    try {
      File f = new File(argv[0]);
      DocumentBuilder builder =
        factory.newDocumentBuilder();
      document = builder.parse(f);
```

Guess what—you're almost finished. Just a couple of steps to go. Add the following highlighted code to construct a SAXSource object:

```
// Use a Transformer for output
...
Transformer transformer = tFactory.newTransformer();

// Use the parser as a SAX source for input
FileReader fr = new FileReader(f);
BufferedReader br = new BufferedReader(fr);
InputSource inputSource = new InputSource(br);
SAXSource source = new SAXSource(saxReader, inputSource);

StreamResult result = new StreamResult(System.out);
transformer.transform(source, result);
```

Here, you construct a buffered reader (as mentioned earlier) and encapsulate it in an input source object. You then create a SAXSource object, passing it the reader and the InputSource object, and pass that to the transformer.

When the application runs, the transformer configures itself as the ContentHandler for the SAX parser (the AddressBookReader) and tells the parser to operate on the inputSource object. Events generated by the parser then go to the transformer, which does the appropriate thing and passes the data on to the result object.

Finally, remove the exceptions you no longer need to worry about, because the TransformationApp no longer generates them:

```
catch (SAXParseException spe) {
   // Error generated by the parser
   System.out.println("\n** Parsing error"
      + ", line " + spe.getLineNumber()
      + ", uri " + spe.getSystemId());
   System.out.println("   " + spe.getMessage() );

   // Use the contained exception, if any
   Exception  x = spe;
   if (spe.getException() != null)
      x = spe.getException();
   x.printStackTrace();

} catch (SAXException sxe) {
   // Error generated by this application
   // (or a parser-initialization error)
   Exception  x = sxe;
   if (sxe.getException() != null)
      x = sxe.getException();
   x.printStackTrace();

} catch (ParserConfigurationException pce) {
   // Parser with specified options can't be built
   pce.printStackTrace();

} catch (IOException ioe) {
   ...
```

You're finished! You have now created a transformer that uses a SAXSource as input and produces a StreamResult as output.

Doing the Conversion

Now run the application on the address book file. Your output should look like this:

```
<?xml version="1.0" encoding="UTF-8"?>
<addressbook>
  <nickname>Fred</nickname>
  <email>fred@barneys.house</email>
  <html>TRUE</html>
  <firstname>Fred</firstname>
  <lastname>Flintstone</lastname>
  <work>999-Quarry</work>
  <home>999-BedrockLane</home>
  <fax>888-Squawk</fax>
  <pager>777-pager</pager>
  <cell>555-cell</cell>
</addressbook>
```

You have now successfully converted an existing data structure to XML. And it wasn't even very hard. Congratulations!

Transforming XML Data with XSLT

The Extensible Stylesheet Language Transformations (XSLT) APIs can be used for many purposes. For example, with a sufficiently intelligent stylesheet, you could generate PDF or PostScript output from the XML data. But generally, XSLT is used to generate formatted HTML output, or to create an alternative XML representation of the data.

In this section, you'll use an XSLT transform to translate XML input data to HTML output.

Note: The XSLT specification is large and complex, so this tutorial can only scratch the surface. It will give you enough background to get started so that you can undertake simple XSLT processing tasks. It should also give you a head start when you investigate XSLT further. For a more thorough grounding, consult a good reference manual, such as Michael Kay's *XSLT: Programmer's Reference* (Wrox, 2001).

Defining a Simple <article> Document Type

We'll start by defining a very simple document type that can be used for writing articles. Our <article> documents will contain these structure tags:

- <TITLE>: The title of the article
- <SECT>: A section, consisting of a *heading* and a *body*
- <PARA>: A paragraph
- <LIST>: A list
- <ITEM>: An entry in a list
- <NOTE>: An aside, that is offset from the main text

The slightly unusual aspect of this structure is that we won't create a separate element tag for a section heading. Such elements are commonly created to distinguish the heading text (and any tags it contains) from the body of the section (that is, any structure elements underneath the heading).

Instead, we'll allow the heading to merge seamlessly into the body of a section. That arrangement adds some complexity to the stylesheet, but it will give us a chance to explore XSLT's template-selection mechanisms. It also matches our intuitive expectations about document structure, where the text of a heading is followed directly by structure elements, an arrangement that can simplify outline-oriented editing.

Note: This kind of structure is not easily validated, because XML's mixed-content model allows text anywhere in a section, whereas we want to confine text and inline elements so that they appear only before the first structure element in the body of the section. The assertion-based validator (Schematron, page 1350) can do it, but most other schema mechanisms can't. So we'll dispense with defining a DTD for the document type.

In this structure, sections can be nested. The depth of the nesting will determine what kind of HTML formatting to use for the section heading (for example, h1 or h2). Using a plain SECT tag (instead of numbered sections) is also useful with outline-oriented editing, because it lets you move sections around at will without having to worry about changing the numbering for any of the affected sections.

For lists, we'll use a `type` attribute to specify whether the list entries are unordered (bulleted), `alpha` (enumerated with lowercase letters), `ALPHA` (enumerated with uppercase letters), or `numbered`.

We'll also allow for some inline tags that change the appearance of the text:

- `<B>`: Bold
- `<I>`: Italics
- `<U>`: Underline
- `<DEF>`: Definition
- `<LINK>`: Link to a URL

Note: An *inline* tag does not generate a line break, so a style change caused by an inline tag does not affect the flow of text on the page (although it will affect the appearance of that text). A *structure* tag, on the other hand, demarcates a new segment of text, so at a minimum it always generates a line break in addition to other format changes.

The `<DEF>` tag will be used for terms that are defined in the text. Such terms will be displayed in italics, the way they ordinarily are in a document. But using a special tag in the XML will allow an index program to find such definitions and add them to an index, along with keywords in headings. In the preceding *Note*, for example, the definitions of inline tags and structure tags could have been marked with `<DEF>` tags for future indexing.

Finally, the `LINK` tag serves two purposes. First, it will let us create a link to a URL without having to put the URL in twice; so we can code `<link>http//...</link>` instead of `<a href="http//...">http//...</a>`. Of course, we'll also want to allow a form that looks like `<link target="...">...name...</link>`. That leads to the second reason for the `<link>` tag. It will give us an opportunity to play with conditional expressions in XSLT.

Note: Although the article structure is exceedingly simple (consisting of only 11 tags), it raises enough interesting problems to give us a good view of XSLT's basic capabilities. But we'll still leave large areas of the specification untouched. In What Else Can XSLT Do? (page 301), we'll point out the major features we skipped.

Creating a Test Document

Here, you'll create a simple test document using nested <SECT> elements, a few <PARA> elements, a <NOTE> element, a <LINK>, and a <LIST type="unordered">. The idea is to create a document with one of everything so that we can explore the more interesting translation mechanisms.

Note: The sample data described here is contained in `article1.xml`. (The browsable version is `article1-xml.html`.)

To make the test document, create a file called `article.xml` and enter the following XML data.

```
<?xml version="1.0"?>
<ARTICLE>
  <TITLE>A Sample Article</TITLE>
  <SECT>The First Major Section
    <PARA>This section will introduce a subsection.</PARA>
    <SECT>The Subsection Heading
      <PARA>This is the text of the subsection.
      </PARA>
    </SECT>
  </SECT>
</ARTICLE>
```

Note that in the XML file, the subsection is totally contained within the major section. (In HTML, on the other hand, headings do not *contain* the body of a section.) The result is an outline structure that is harder to edit in plain-text form, like this, but is much easier to edit with an outline-oriented editor.

Someday, given a tree-oriented XML editor that understands inline tags such as <B> and <I>, it should be possible to edit an article of this kind in outline form, without requiring a complicated stylesheet. (Such an editor would allow the writer to focus on the structure of the article, leaving layout until much later in the process.) In such an editor, the article fragment would look something like this:

```
<ARTICLE>
  <TITLE>A Sample Article
  <SECT>The First Major Section
    <PARA>This section will introduce a subsection.
    <SECT>The Subheading
      <PARA>This is the text of the subsection. Note that ...
```

Note: At the moment, tree-structured editors exist, but they treat inline tags such as <B> and <I> in the same way that they treat structure tags, and that can make the "outline" a bit difficult to read.

Writing an XSLT Transform

Now it's time to begin writing an XSLT transform that will convert the XML article and render it in HTML.

Note: The transform described in this section is contained in `article1a.xsl`. (The browsable version is `article1a-xsl.html`.)

Start by creating a normal XML document:

```
<?xml version="1.0" encoding="ISO-8859-1"?>
```

Then add the following highlighted lines to create an XSL stylesheet:

```
<?xml version="1.0" encoding="ISO-8859-1"?>
<xsl:stylesheet
  xmlns:xsl="http://www.w3.org/1999/XSL/Transform"
  version="1.0"
  >

</xsl:stylesheet>
```

Now set it up to produce HTML-compatible output:

```
<xsl:stylesheet
  ...
  >
  <xsl:output method="html"/>

    ...

</xsl:stylesheet>
```

We'll get into the detailed reasons for that entry later in this section. For now, note that if you want to output anything other than well-formed XML, then you'll need an <xsl:output> tag like the one shown, specifying either text or html. (The default value is xml.)

> **Note:** When you specify XML output, you can add the `indent` attribute to produce nicely indented XML output. The specification looks like this:
> ```
> <xsl:output method="xml" indent="yes"/>.
> ```

Processing the Basic Structure Elements

You'll start filling in the stylesheet by processing the elements that go into creating a table of contents: the root element, the title element, and headings. You'll also process the PARA element defined in the test document.

> **Note:** If on first reading you skipped the section that discusses the XPath addressing mechanisms, How XPath Works (page 247), now is a good time to go back and review that section.

Begin by adding the main instruction that processes the root element:

```
<xsl:template match="/">
   <html><body>
      <xsl:apply-templates/>
   </body></html>
</xsl:template>

</xsl:stylesheet>
```

The new XSL commands are shown in bold. (Note that they are defined in the xsl namespace.) The instruction `<xsl:apply-templates>` processes the children of the current node. In this case, the current node is the root node.

Despite its simplicity, this example illustrates a number of important ideas, so it's worth understanding thoroughly. The first concept is that a stylesheet contains a number of *templates*, defined with the `<xsl:template>` tag. Each template contains a `match` attribute, which uses the XPath addressing mechanisms described in How XPath Works (page 247) to select the elements that the template will be applied to.

Within the template, tags that do not start with the xsl: namespace prefix are simply copied. The newlines and whitespace that follow them are also copied, and that helps to make the resulting output readable.

Note: When a newline is not present, whitespace is generally ignored. To include whitespace in the output in such cases, or to include other text, you can use the `<xsl:text>` tag. Basically, an XSLT stylesheet expects to process tags. So everything it sees needs to be either an `<xsl:...>` tag, some other tag, or whitespace.

In this case, the non-XSL tags are HTML tags. So when the root tag is matched, XSLT outputs the HTML start tags, processes any templates that apply to children of the root, and then outputs the HTML end tags.

Process the <TITLE> Element

Next, add a template to process the article title:

```
<xsl:template match="/ARTICLE/TITLE">
   <h1 align="center"> <xsl:apply-templates/> </h1>
</xsl:template>

</xsl:stylesheet>
```

In this case, you specify a complete path to the TITLE element and output some HTML to make the text of the title into a large, centered heading. In this case, the `apply-templates` tag ensures that if the title contains any inline tags such as italics, links, or underlining, they also will be processed.

More importantly, the `apply-templates` instruction causes the *text* of the title to be processed. Like the DOM data model, the XSLT data model is based on the concept of *text nodes* contained in *element nodes* (which, in turn, can be contained in other element nodes, and so on). That hierarchical structure constitutes the source tree. There is also a result tree, which contains the output.

XSLT works by transforming the source tree into the result tree. To visualize the result of XSLT operations, it is helpful to understand the structure of those trees, and their contents. (For more on this subject, see The XSLT/XPath Data Model, page 248.)

Process Headings

To continue processing the basic structure elements, add a template to process the top-level headings:

```
<xsl:template match="/ARTICLE/SECT">
  <h2> <xsl:apply-templates
    select="text()|B|I|U|DEF|LINK"/> </h2>
  <xsl:apply-templates select="SECT|PARA|LIST|NOTE"/>
</xsl:template>

</xsl:stylesheet>
```

Here, you specify the path to the topmost SECT elements. But this time, you apply templates in two stages using the `select` attribute. For the first stage, you select text nodes, as well as inline tags such as bold and italics, using the XPath `text()` function. (The vertical pipe (|) is used to match multiple items: text *or* a bold tag *or* an italics tag, etc.) In the second stage, you select the other structure elements contained in the file, for sections, paragraphs, lists, and notes.

Using the `select` attribute lets you put the text and inline elements between the `<h2>...</h2>` tags, while making sure that all the structure tags in the section are processed afterward. In other words, you make sure that the nesting of the headings in the XML document is *not* reflected in the HTML formatting, a distinction that is important for HTML output.

In general, using the `select` clause lets you apply all templates to a subset of the information available in the current context. As another example, this template selects all attributes of the current node:

```
<xsl:apply-templates select="@*"/></attributes>
```

Next, add the virtually identical template to process subheadings that are nested one level deeper:

```
<xsl:template match="/ARTICLE/SECT/SECT">
  <h3> <xsl:apply-templates
    select="text()|B|I|U|DEF|LINK"/> </h3>
  <xsl:apply-templates select="SECT|PARA|LIST|NOTE"/>
</xsl:template>

</xsl:stylesheet>
```

Generate a Runtime Message

You could add templates for deeper headings, too, but at some point you must stop, if only because HTML goes down only to five levels. For this example, you'll stop at two levels of section headings. But if the XML input happens to contain a third level, you'll want to deliver an error message to the user. This section shows you how to do that.

Note: We *could* continue processing SECT elements that are further down, by selecting them with the expression /SECT/SECT//SECT. The // selects any SECT elements, at any depth, as defined by the XPath addressing mechanism. But instead we'll take the opportunity to play with messaging.

Add the following template to generate an error when a section is encountered that is nested too deep:

```
<xsl:template match="/ARTICLE/SECT/SECT/SECT">
  <xsl:message terminate="yes">
    Error: Sections can only be nested 2 deep.
  </xsl:message>
</xsl:template>

</xsl:stylesheet>
```

The terminate="yes" clause causes the transformation process to stop after the message is generated. Without it, processing could still go on, with everything in that section being ignored.

As an additional exercise, you could expand the stylesheet to handle sections nested up to four sections deep, generating <h2>...<h5> tags. Generate an error on any section nested five levels deep.

Finally, finish the stylesheet by adding a template to process the PARA tag:

```
<xsl:template match="PARA">
  <p><xsl:apply-templates/></p>
</xsl:template>

</xsl:stylesheet>
```

Writing the Basic Program

Now you'll modify the program that uses XSLT to echo an XML file unchanged, changing it so that it uses your stylesheet.

Note: The code shown in this section is contained in `Stylizer.java`. The result is `stylizer1a.html`. (The browser-displayable version of the HTML source is `stylizer1a-src.html`.)

Start by copying `TransformationApp02`, which parses an XML file and writes to `System.out`. Save it as `Stylizer.java`.

Next, modify occurrences of the class name and the usage section of the program:

```
public class ~~TransformationApp~~Stylizer
{
   if (argv.length != ~~1~~ 2) {
      System.err.println (
         ~~"Usage: java TransformationApp filename");~~
         "Usage: java Stylizer stylesheet xmlfile");
      System.exit (1);
   }
   ...
```

Then modify the program to use the stylesheet when creating the `Transformer` object.

```
   ...
import javax.xml.transform.dom.DOMSource;
import javax.xml.transform.stream.StreamSource;
import javax.xml.transform.stream.StreamResult;
   ...

public class Stylizer
{
   ...
   public static void main (String argv[])
   {
      ...
      try {
         File f = new File(argv[0]);
         File stylesheet = new File(argv[0]);
         File datafile  = new File(argv[1]);
```

```
DocumentBuilder builder =
    factory.newDocumentBuilder();
document = builder.parse(f datafile);
...
StreamSource stylesource =
    new StreamSource(stylesheet);
Transformer transformer =
    Factory.newTransformer(stylesource);
...
```

This code uses the file to create a StreamSource object and then passes the source object to the factory class to get the transformer.

Note: You can simplify the code somewhat by eliminating the DOMSource class. Instead of creating a DOMSource object for the XML file, create a StreamSource object for it, as well as for the stylesheet.

Now compile and run the program using article1a.xsl to transform article1.xml. The results should look like this:

```
<html>
<body>

<h1 align="center">A Sample Article</h1>

<h2>The First Major Section

    </h2>
<p>This section will introduce a subsection.</p>
<h3>The Subsection Heading

        </h3>
<p>This is the text of the subsection.

        </p>

</body>
</html>
```

At this point, there is quite a bit of excess whitespace in the output. In the next section, you'll see how to eliminate most of it.

Trimming the Whitespace

Recall that when you look at the structure of a DOM, there are many text nodes that contain nothing but ignorable whitespace. Most of the excess whitespace in the output comes from these nodes. Fortunately, XSL gives you a way to eliminate them. (For more about the node structure, see The XSLT/XPath Data Model, page 248.)

Note: The stylesheet described here is `article1b.xsl`. The result is `stylizer1b.html`. (The browser-displayable versions are `article1b-xsl.html` and `stylizer1b-src.html`.)

To remove some of the excess whitespace, add the following highlighted line to the stylesheet.

```
<xsl:stylesheet ...
   >
   <xsl:output method="html"/>
   <xsl:strip-space elements="SECT"/>
   ...
```

This instruction tells XSL to remove any text nodes under SECT elements that contain nothing but whitespace. Nodes that contain text other than whitespace will not be affected, nor will other kinds of nodes.

Now, when you run the program the result looks like this:

```
<html>
<body>

<h1 align="center">A Sample Article</h1>

<h2>The First Major Section
   </h2>
<p>This section will introduce a subsection.</p>
<h3>The Subsection Heading
      </h3>
<p>This is the text of the subsection.
      </p>

</body>
</html>
```

That's quite an improvement. There are still newline characters and whitespace after the headings, but those come from the way the XML is written:

```
<SECT>The First Major Section
____<PARA>This section will introduce a subsection.</PARA>
^^^^
```

Here, you can see that the section heading ends with a newline and indentation space, before the PARA entry starts. That's not a big worry, because the browsers that will process the HTML compress and ignore the excess space routinely. But there is still one more formatting tool at our disposal.

Note: The stylesheet described here is `article1c.xsl`. The result is `stylizer1c.html`. (The browser-displayable versions are `article1c-xsl.html` and `stylizer1c-src.html`.)

To get rid of that last little bit of whitespace, add this template to the stylesheet:

```
<xsl:template match="text()">
  <xsl:value-of select="normalize-space()"/>
</xsl:template>

</xsl:stylesheet>
```

The output now looks like this:

```
<html>
<body>
<h1 align="center">A Sample Article</h1>
<h2>The First Major Section</h2>
<p>This section will introduce a subsection.</p>
<h3>The Subsection Heading</h3>
<p>This is the text of the subsection.</p>
</body>
</html>
```

That is quite a bit better. Of course, it would be nicer if it were indented, but that turns out to be somewhat harder than expected. Here are some possible avenues of attack, along with the difficulties:

Indent option

Unfortunately, the `indent="yes"` option that can be applied to XML output is not available for HTML output. Even if that option were available, it wouldn't help, because HTML elements are rarely nested! Although HTML source is frequently indented to show the *implied* structure, the HTML tags themselves are not nested in a way that creates a *real* structure.

Indent variables

The `<xsl:text>` function lets you add any text you want, including whitespace. So it could conceivably be used to output indentation space. The problem is to vary the *amount* of indentation space. XSLT variables seem like a good idea, but they don't work here. The reason is that when you assign a value to a variable in a template, the value is known only *within* that template (statically, at compile time). Even if the variable is defined globally, the assigned value is not stored in a way that lets it be dynamically known by other templates at runtime. When `<apply-templates/>` invokes other templates, those templates are unaware of any variable settings made elsewhere.

Parameterized templates

Using a *parameterized template* is another way to modify a template's behavior. But determining the amount of indentation space to pass as the parameter remains the crux of the problem.

At the moment, then, there does not appear to be any good way to control the indentation of HTML formatted output. That would be inconvenient if you needed to display or edit the HTML as plain text. But it's not a problem if you do your editing on the XML form, using the HTML version only for display in a browser. (When you view `stylizer1c.html`, for example, you see the results you expect.)

Processing the Remaining Structure Elements

In this section, you'll process the `LIST` and `NOTE` elements, which add more structure to an article.

Note: The sample document described in this section is `article2.xml`, and the stylesheet used to manipulate it is `article2.xsl`. The result is `stylizer2.html`. (The browser-displayable versions are `article2-xml.html`, `article2-xsl.html`, and `stylizer2-src.html`.)

Start by adding some test data to the sample document:

```xml
<?xml version="1.0"?>
<ARTICLE>
  <TITLE>A Sample Article</TITLE>
  <SECT>The First Major Section
    ...
  </SECT>
  <SECT>The Second Major Section
    <PARA>This section adds a LIST and a NOTE.
    <PARA>Here is the LIST:
      <LIST type="ordered">
        <ITEM>Pears</ITEM>
        <ITEM>Grapes</ITEM>
      </LIST>
    </PARA>
    <PARA>And here is the NOTE:
      <NOTE>Don't forget to go to the hardware store
        on your way to the grocery!
      </NOTE>
    </PARA>
  </SECT>
</ARTICLE>
```

Note: Although the list and note in the XML file are contained in their respective paragraphs, it really makes no difference whether they are contained or not; the generated HTML will be the same either way. But having them contained will make them easier to deal with in an outline-oriented editor.

Modify <PARA> Handling

Next, modify the PARA template to account for the fact that we are now allowing some of the structure elements to be embedded with a paragraph:

```xml
<xsl:template match="PARA">
  <p><xsl:apply-templates/></p>
  <p> <xsl:apply-templates select="text()|B|I|U|DEF|LINK"/>
    </p>
  <xsl:apply-templates select="PARA|LIST|NOTE"/>
</xsl:template>
```

This modification uses the same technique you used for section headings. The only difference is that SECT elements are not expected within a paragraph. (However, a paragraph could easily exist inside another paragraph—for example, as quoted material.)

Process <LIST> and <ITEM> Elements

Now you're ready to add a template to process LIST elements:

```
<xsl:template match="LIST">
  <xsl:if test="@type='ordered'">
    <ol>
    <xsl:apply-templates/>
    </ol>
  </xsl:if>
  <xsl:if test="@type='unordered'">
    <ul>
    <xsl:apply-templates/>
    </ul>
  </xsl:if>
</xsl:template>

</xsl:stylesheet>
```

The <xsl:if> tag uses the test="" attribute to specify a Boolean condition. In this case, the value of the type attribute is tested, and the list that is generated changes depending on whether the value is ordered or unordered.

Note two important things in this example:

- There is no else clause, nor is there a return or exit statement, so it takes two <xsl:if> tags to cover the two options. (Or the <xsl:choose> tag could have been used, which provides case-statement functionality.)
- Single quotes are required around the attribute values. Otherwise, the XSLT processor attempts to interpret the word ordered as an XPath function instead of as a string.

Now finish LIST processing by handling ITEM elements:

```
<xsl:template match="ITEM">
  <li><xsl:apply-templates/>
  </li>
</xsl:template>

</xsl:stylesheet>
```

Ordering Templates in a Stylesheet

By now, you should have the idea that templates are independent of one another, so it doesn't generally matter where they occur in a file. So from this point on, we'll show only the template you need to add. (For the sake of comparison, they're always added at the end of the example stylesheet.)

Order *does* make a difference when two templates can apply to the same node. In that case, the one that is defined *last* is the one that is found and processed. For example, to change the ordering of an indented list to use lowercase alphabetics, you could specify a template pattern that looks like this: //LIST//LIST. In that template, you would use the HTML option to generate an alphabetic enumeration, instead of a numeric one.

But such an element could also be identified by the pattern //LIST. To make sure that the proper processing is done, the template that specifies //LIST would have to appear *before* the template that specifies //LIST//LIST.

Process <NOTE> Elements

The last remaining structure element is the NOTE element. Add the following template to handle that.

```
<xsl:template match="NOTE">
    <blockquote><b>Note:</b><br/>
  <xsl:apply-templates/>
  </p></blockquote>
</xsl:template>

</xsl:stylesheet>
```

This code brings up an interesting issue that results from the inclusion of the <br/> tag. For the file to be well-formed XML, the tag must be specified in the stylesheet as <br/>, but that tag is not recognized by many browsers. And although most browsers recognize the sequence
</br>, they all treat it like a paragraph break instead of a single line break.

In other words, the transformation *must* generate a <br> tag, but the stylesheet must specify <br/>. That brings us to the major reason for that special output tag we added early in the stylesheet:

```
<xsl:stylesheet ... >
  <xsl:output method="html"/>
  ...
</xsl:stylesheet>
```

That output specification converts empty tags such as <br/> to their HTML form, <br>, on output. That conversion is important, because most browsers do not recognize the empty tags. Here is a list of the affected tags:

```
area       frame    isindex
base       hr       link
basefont   img      meta
br         input    param
col
```

To summarize, by default XSLT produces well-formed XML on output. And because an XSL stylesheet is well-formed XML to start with, you cannot easily put a tag such as <br> in the middle of it. The <xsl:output method="html"/> tag solves the problem so that you can code <br/> in the stylesheet but get <br> in the output.

The other major reason for specifying <xsl:output method="html"/> is that, as with the specification <xsl:output method="text"/>, generated text is *not* escaped. For example, if the stylesheet includes the < entity reference, it will appear as the < character in the generated text. When XML is generated, on the other hand, the < entity reference in the stylesheet would be unchanged, so it would appear as < in the generated text.

Note: If you actually want < to be generated as part of the HTML output, you'll need to encode it as &lt;. That sequence becomes < on output, because only the & is converted to an & character.

Run the Program

Here is the HTML that is generated for the second section when you run the program now:

```
...
<h2>The Second Major Section</h2>
<p>This section adds a LIST and a NOTE.</p>
<p>Here is the LIST:</p>
<ol>
<li>Pears</li>
<li>Grapes</li>
</ol>
<p>And here is the NOTE:</p>
<blockquote>
<b>Note:</b>
<br>Don't forget to go to the hardware store on your way to the
grocery!
</blockquote>
```

Process Inline (Content) Elements

The only remaining tags in the ARTICLE type are the *inline* tags—the ones that don't create a line break in the output, but instead are integrated into the stream of text they are part of.

Inline elements are different from structure elements in that inline elements are part of the *content* of a tag. If you think of an element as a node in a document tree, then each node has both *content* and *structure*. The *content* is composed of the text and inline tags it contains. The *structure* consists of the other elements (structure elements) under the tag.

Note: The sample document described in this section is article3.xml, and the stylesheet used to manipulate it is article3.xsl. The result is stylizer3.html. (The browser-displayable versions are article3-xml.html, article3-xsl.html, and stylizer3-src.html.)

Start by adding one more bit of test data to the sample document:

```
<?xml version="1.0"?>
<ARTICLE>
  <TITLE>A Sample Article</TITLE>
  <SECT>The First Major Section
```

```
   . . .
   </SECT>
   <SECT>The Second Major Section
      . . .
   </SECT>
   <SECT>The <I>Third</I> Major Section
      <PARA>In addition to the inline tag in the heading,
         this section defines the term <DEF>inline</DEF>,
         which literally means "no line break". It also
         adds a simple link to the main page for the Java
         platform (<LINK>http://java.sun.com</LINK>),
         as well as a link to the
         <LINK target="http://java.sun.com/xml">XML</LINK>
         page.
      </PARA>
   </SECT>
</ARTICLE>
```

Now process the inline <DEF> elements in paragraphs, renaming them to HTML italics tags:

```
<xsl:template match="DEF">
  <i> <xsl:apply-templates/> </i>
</xsl:template>
```

Next, comment out the text-node normalization. It has served its purpose, and now you're to the point that you need to preserve important spaces:

```
<!--
  <xsl:template match="text()">
    <xsl:value-of select="normalize-space()"/>
  </xsl:template>
-->
```

This modification keeps us from losing spaces before tags such as <I> and <DEF>. (Try the program without this modification to see the result.)

Now process basic inline HTML elements such as <B>, <I>, and <U> for bold, italics, and underlining.

```
<xsl:template match="B|I|U">
  <xsl:element name="{name()}">
    <xsl:apply-templates/>
  </xsl:element>
</xsl:template>
```

The `<xsl:element>` tag lets you compute the element you want to generate. Here, you generate the appropriate inline tag using the name of the current element. In particular, note the use of curly braces (`{}`) in the `name=".."` expression. Those curly braces cause the text inside the quotes to be processed as an XPath expression instead of being interpreted as a literal string. Here, they cause the XPath `name()` function to return the name of the current node.

Curly braces are recognized anywhere that an *attribute value template* can occur. (Attribute value templates are defined in section 7.6.2 of the XSLT specification, and they appear several places in the template definitions.). In such expressions, curly braces can also be used to refer to the value of an attribute, `{@foo}`, or to the content of an element `{foo}`.

Note: You can also generate attributes using `<xsl:attribute>`. For more information, see section 7.1.3 of the XSLT Specification.

The last remaining element is the `LINK` tag. The easiest way to process that tag will be to set up a *named template* that we can drive with a parameter:

```
<xsl:template name="htmLink">
  <xsl:param name="dest" select="UNDEFINED"/>
  <xsl:element name="a">
    <xsl:attribute name="href">
      <xsl:value-of select="$dest"/>
    </xsl:attribute>
    <xsl:apply-templates/>
  </xsl:element>
</xsl:template>
```

The major difference in this template is that, instead of specifying a `match` clause, you give the template a name using the `name=""` clause. So this template gets executed only when you invoke it.

Within the template, you also specify a parameter named `dest` using the `<xsl:param>` tag. For a bit of error checking, you use the `select` clause to give that parameter a default value of UNDEFINED. To reference the variable in the `<xsl:value-of>` tag, you specify `$dest`.

Note: Recall that an entry in quotes is interpreted as an expression unless it is further enclosed in single quotes. That's why the single quotes were needed earlier in `"@type='ordered'"`—to make sure that `ordered` was interpreted as a string.

The <xsl:element> tag generates an element. Previously, you have been able to simply specify the element we want by coding something like <html>. But here you are dynamically generating the content of the HTML anchor (<a>) in the body of the <xsl:element> tag. And you are dynamically generating the href attribute of the anchor using the <xsl:attribute> tag.

The last important part of the template is the <apply-templates> tag, which inserts the text from the text node under the LINK element. Without it, there would be no text in the generated HTML link.

Next, add the template for the LINK tag, and call the named template from within it:

```
<xsl:template match="LINK">
  <xsl:if test="@target">
    <!--Target attribute specified.-->
    <xsl:call-template name="htmLink">
      <xsl:with-param name="dest" select="@target"/>
    </xsl:call-template>
  </xsl:if>
</xsl:template>

<xsl:template name="htmLink">
  ...
```

The test="@target" clause returns true if the target attribute exists in the LINK tag. So this <xsl-if> tag generates HTML links when the text of the link and the target defined for it are different.

The <xsl:call-template> tag invokes the named template, whereas <xsl:with-param> specifies a parameter using the name clause and specifies its value using the select clause.

As the very last step in the stylesheet construction process, add the <xsl-if> tag to process LINK tags that do not have a target attribute.

```
<xsl:template match="LINK">
  <xsl:if test="@target">
    ...
  </xsl:if>

  <xsl:if test="not(@target)">
    <xsl:call-template name="htmLink">
      <xsl:with-param name="dest">
        <xsl:apply-templates/>
      </xsl:with-param>
    </xsl:call-template>
  </xsl:if>
</xsl:template>
```

The not(...) clause inverts the previous test (remember, there is no else clause). So this part of the template is interpreted when the target attribute is not specified. This time, the parameter value comes not from a select clause, but from the *contents* of the <xsl:with-param> element.

Note: Just to make it explicit: Parameters and variables (which are discussed in a few moments in What Else Can XSLT Do? (page 301) can have their value specified *either* by a select clause, which lets you use XPath expressions, *or* by the content of the element, which lets you use XSLT tags.

In this case, the content of the parameter is generated by the <xsl:apply-templates/> tag, which inserts the contents of the text node under the LINK element.

Run the Program

When you run the program now, the results should look something like this:

```
...
<h2>The <I>Third</I> Major Section
    </h2>
<p>In addition to the inline tag in the heading, this section
    defines the term <i>inline</i>, which literally means
    "no line break". It also adds a simple link to the
    main page for the Java platform (<a href="http://java.
    sun.com">http://java.sun.com</a>),
    as well as a link to the
    <a href="http://java.sun.com/xml">XML</a> page.
</p>
```

Good work! You have now converted a rather complex XML file to HTML. (As simple as it appears at first, it certainly provides a lot of opportunity for exploration.)

Printing the HTML

You have now converted an XML file to HTML. One day, someone will produce an HTML-aware printing engine that you'll be able to find and use through the Java Printing Service API. At that point, you'll have ability to print an arbitrary XML file by generating HTML. All you'll have to do is to set up a stylesheet and use your browser.

What Else Can XSLT Do?

As lengthy as this section has been, it has only scratched the surface of XSLT's capabilities. Many additional possibilities await you in the XSLT specification. Here are a few things to look for:

import (section 2.6.2) and include (section 2.6.1)
> Use these statements to modularize and combine XSLT stylesheets. The include statement simply inserts any definitions from the included file. The import statement lets you override definitions in the imported file with definitions in your own stylesheet.

for-each loops (section 8)
> Loop over a collection of items and process each one in turn.

choose (case statement) for conditional processing (section 9.2)
> Branch to one of multiple processing paths depending on an input value.

Generating numbers (section 7.7)
> Dynamically generate numbered sections, numbered elements, and numeric literals. XSLT provides three numbering modes:

> * *Single:* Numbers items under a single heading, like an ordered list in HTML.

> * *Multiple:* Produces multilevel numbering such as "A.1.3."

> * *Any:* Consecutively numbers items wherever they appear, as with footnotes in a chapter.

Formatting numbers (section 12.3)
> Control enumeration formatting so that you get numerics (format="1"), uppercase alphabetics (format="A"), lowercase alphabetics (format="a"), or compound numbers, like "A.1," as well as numbers and currency amounts suited for a specific international locale.

Sorting output (section 10)
> Produce output in a desired sorting order.

Mode-based templates (section 5.7)
> Process an element multiple times, each time in a different "mode." You add a mode attribute to templates and then specify <apply-templates mode="..."> to apply only the templates with a matching mode. Combine with the <apply-templates select="..."> attribute to apply mode-based processing to a subset of the input data.

Variables (section 11)
> Variables are something like method parameters, in that they let you control a template's behavior. But they are not as valuable as you might think. The

value of a variable is known only within the scope of the current template or
`<xsl:if>` tag (for example) in which it is defined. You can't pass a value
from one template to another, or even from an enclosed part of a template to
another part of the same template.

These statements are true even for a "global" variable. You can change its
value in a template, but the change applies only to that template. And when
the expression used to define the global variable is evaluated, that evaluation
takes place in the context of the structure's root node. In other words, global
variables are essentially runtime constants. Those constants can be useful for
changing the behavior of a template, especially when coupled with `include`
and `import` statements. But variables are not a general-purpose data-man-
agement mechanism.

The Trouble with Variables

It is tempting to create a single template and set a variable for the destination of
the link, rather than go to the trouble of setting up a parameterized template and
calling it two different ways. The idea is to set the variable to a default value
(say, the text of the `LINK` tag) and then, if the `target` attribute exists, set the destination variable to the value of the `target` attribute.

That would be a good idea—if it worked. But again, the issue is that variables
are known only in the scope within which they are defined. So when you code an
`<xsl:if>` tag to change the value of the variable, the value is known only within
the context of the `<xsl:if>` tag. Once `</xsl:if>` is encountered, any change to
the variable's setting is lost.

A similarly tempting idea is the possibility of replacing the
`text()|B|I|U|DEF|LINK` specification with a variable (`$inline`). But because
the value of the variable is determined by where it is defined, the value of a global `inline` variable consists of text nodes, `<B>` nodes, and so on, that happen to
exist at the root level. In other words, the value of such a variable, in this case, is
null.

Transforming from the Command Line with Xalan

To run a transform from the command line, you initiate a Xalan `Process` using the following command:

```
java org.apache.xalan.xslt.Process
   -IN article3.xml -XSL article3.xsl
```

Note: Remember to use the endorsed directories mechanism to access the Xalan libraries, as described in Compiling and Running the Program (page 128).

With this command, the output goes to `System.out`. The `-OUT` option can also be used to output to a file.

The `Process` command also allows for a variety of other options. For details, see `http://xml.apache.org/xalan-j/commandline.html`.

Concatenating Transformations with a Filter Chain

It is sometimes useful to create a *filter chain*: a concatenation of XSLT transformations in which the output of one transformation becomes the input of the next. This section shows you how to do that.

Writing the Program

Start by writing a program to do the filtering. This example shows the full source code, but to make things easier you can use one of the programs you've been working on as a basis.

Note: The code described here is contained in `FilterChain.java`.

The sample program includes the import statements that identify the package locations for each class:

```java
import javax.xml.parsers.FactoryConfigurationError;
import javax.xml.parsers.ParserConfigurationException;
import javax.xml.parsers.SAXParser;
import javax.xml.parsers.SAXParserFactory;

import org.xml.sax.SAXException;
import org.xml.sax.SAXParseException;
import org.xml.sax.InputSource;
import org.xml.sax.XMLReader;
import org.xml.sax.XMLFilter;

import javax.xml.transform.Transformer;
import javax.xml.transform.TransformerException;
import javax.xml.transform.TransformerFactory;
import javax.xml.transform.TransformerConfigurationException;

import javax.xml.transform.sax.SAXTransformerFactory;
import javax.xml.transform.sax.SAXSource;
import javax.xml.transform.sax.SAXResult;

import javax.xml.transform.stream.StreamSource;
import javax.xml.transform.stream.StreamResult;

import java.io.*;
```

The program also includes the standard error handlers you're used to. They're listed here, all gathered together in one place:

```java
}
catch (TransformerConfigurationException tce) {
   // Error generated by the parser
   System.out.println ("* Transformer Factory error");
   System.out.println("   " + tce.getMessage() );

   // Use the contained exception, if any
   Throwable x = tce;
   if (tce.getException() != null)
      x = tce.getException();
   x.printStackTrace();
}
catch (TransformerException te) {
   // Error generated by the parser
   System.out.println ("* Transformation error");
   System.out.println("   " + te.getMessage() );
```

```
        // Use the contained exception, if any
        Throwable x = te;
        if (te.getException() != null)
          x = te.getException();
        x.printStackTrace();
    }
    catch (SAXException sxe) {
        // Error generated by this application
        // (or a parser-initialization error)
        Exception  x = sxe;
        if (sxe.getException() != null)
          x = sxe.getException();
        x.printStackTrace();
    }
    catch (ParserConfigurationException pce) {
        // Parser with specified options can't be built
        pce.printStackTrace();
    }
    catch (IOException ioe) {
        // I/O error
        ioe.printStackTrace();
    }
```

Between the import statements and the error handling, the core of the program consists of the following code.

```
public static void main (String argv[])
{
    if (argv.length != 3) {
        System.err.println (
          "Usage: java FilterChain style1 style2 xmlfile");
        System.exit (1);
    }

    try {
        // Read the arguments
        File stylesheet1 = new File(argv[0]);
        File stylesheet2 = new File(argv[1]);
        File datafile = new File(argv[2]);

        // Set up the input stream
        BufferedInputStream bis = new
          BufferedInputStream(newFileInputStream(datafile));
        InputSource input = new InputSource(bis);

        // Set up to read the input file (see Note #1)
        SAXParserFactory spf = SAXParserFactory.newInstance();
        spf.setNamespaceAware(true);
```

```
SAXParser parser = spf.newSAXParser();
XMLReader reader = parser.getXMLReader();

// Create the filters (see Note #2)
SAXTransformerFactory stf =
   (SAXTransformerFactory)
      TransformerFactory.newInstance();
XMLFilter filter1 = stf.newXMLFilter(
   new StreamSource(stylesheet1));
XMLFilter filter2 = stf.newXMLFilter(
   new StreamSource(stylesheet2));

// Wire the output of the reader to filter1 (see Note #3)
// and the output of filter1 to filter2
filter1.setParent(reader);
filter2.setParent(filter1);

// Set up the output stream
StreamResult result = new StreamResult(System.out);

// Set up the transformer to process the SAX events
// generated by the last filter in the chain
Transformer transformer = stf.newTransformer();
SAXSource transformSource = new SAXSource(
   filter2, input);
transformer.transform(transformSource, result);
} catch (...) {
...
```

Notes:

1. The Xalan transformation engine currently requires a namespace-aware SAX parser.

2. This weird bit of code is explained by the fact that SAXTransformerFactory extends TransformerFactory, adding methods to obtain filter objects. The newInstance() method is a static method (defined in TransformerFactory), which (naturally enough) returns a TransformerFactory object. In reality, though, it returns a SAXTransformerFactory. So to get at the extra methods defined by SAXTransformerFactory, the return value must be cast to the actual type.

3. An XMLFilter object is both a SAX reader and a SAX content handler. As a SAX reader, it generates SAX events to whatever object has registered to receive them. As a content handler, it consumes SAX events generated by its "parent" object—which is, of necessity, a SAX reader as well. (Calling

the event generator a "parent" must make sense when looking at the internal architecture. From an external perspective, the name doesn't appear to be particularly fitting.) The fact that filters both generate and consume SAX events allows them to be chained together.

Understanding How the Filter Chain Works

The code listed earlier shows you how to set up the transformation. Figure 7–2 should help you understand what's happening when it executes.

When you create the transformer, you pass it a SAXSource object, which encapsulates a reader (in this case, filter2) and an input stream. You also pass it a pointer to the result stream, where it directs its output. Figure 7–2 shows what happens when you invoke transform() on the transformer. Here is an explanation of the steps:

1. The transformer sets up an internal object as the content handler for filter2 and tells it to parse the input source.

2. filter2, in turn, sets itself up as the content handler for filter1 and tells *it* to parse the input source.

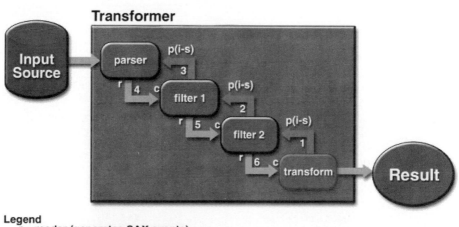

Legend
r = reader (generates SAX events)
c = content handler (consumes SAX events)
p(i-s) = parse(inputSource) instruction

Figure 7–2   Operation of Chained Filters

3. `filter1`, in turn, tells the `parser` object to parse the input source.

4. The `parser` does so, generating SAX events, which it passes to `filter1`.

5. `filter1`, acting in its capacity as a content handler, processes the events and does its transformations. Then, acting in its capacity as a SAX reader (`XMLReader`), it sends SAX events to `filter2`.

6. `filter2` does the same, sending its events to the transformer's content handler, which generates the output stream.

Testing the Program

To try out the program, you'll create an XML file based on a tiny fraction of the XML `DocBook` format, and convert it to the `ARTICLE` format defined here. Then you'll apply the `ARTICLE` stylesheet to generate an HTML version. (The DocBook specification is large and complex. For other simplified formats, see Further Information, page 311.)

Note: This example processes `small-docbook-article.xml` using `docbookToArticle.xsl` and `article1c.xsl`. The result is `filterout.html`. (The browser-displayable versions are `small-docbook-article-xml.html`, `docbookToArticle-xsl.html`, `article1c-xsl.html`, and `filterout-src.html`.)

Start by creating a small article that uses a minute subset of the XML `DocBook` format:

```
<?xml version="1.0"?>
<Article>
  <ArtHeader>
    <Title>Title of my (Docbook) article</Title>
  </ArtHeader>
  <Sect1>
    <Title>Title of Section 1.</Title>
    <Para>This is a paragraph.</Para>
  </Sect1>
</Article>
```

Next, create a stylesheet to convert it into the ARTICLE format:

```
<xsl:stylesheet
  xmlns:xsl="http://www.w3.org/1999/XSL/Transform"
  version="1.0"
  >
  <xsl:output method="xml"/> (see Note 1)

  <xsl:template match="/">
    <ARTICLE>
      <xsl:apply-templates/>
    </ARTICLE>
  </xsl:template>

  <!-- Lower level titles strip element tag --> (see Note 2)

  <!-- Top-level title -->
  <xsl:template match="/Article/ArtHeader/Title"> (see Note 3)
    <TITLE> <xsl:apply-templates/> </TITLE>
  </xsl:template>

  <xsl:template match="//Sect1"> (see Note 4)
    <SECT><xsl:apply-templates/></SECT>
  </xsl:template>

  <xsl:template match="Para">
    <PARA><xsl:apply-templates/></PARA> (see Note 5)
  </xsl:template>

</xsl:stylesheet>
```

Notes:

1. This time, the stylesheet is generating XML output.
2. The template that follows (for the top-level title element) matches only the main title. For section titles, the TITLE tag gets stripped. (Because no template conversion governs those title elements, they are ignored. The text nodes they contain, however, are still echoed as a result of XSLT's built-in template rules—so only the tag is ignored, not the text.)
3. The title from the DocBook article header becomes the ARTICLE title.
4. Numbered section tags are converted to plain SECT tags.
5. This template carries out a case conversion, so Para becomes PARA.

Although it hasn't been mentioned explicitly, XSLT defines a number of built-in (default) template rules. The complete set is listed in section 5.8 of the specification. Mainly, these rules provide for the automatic copying of text and attribute nodes and for skipping comments and processing instructions. They also dictate that inner elements are processed, even when their containing tags don't have templates. That is why the text node in the section title is processed, even though the section title is not covered by any template.

Now run the `FilterChain` program, passing it the stylesheet (`docbookToArticle.xsl`), the ARTICLE stylesheet (`article1c.xsl`), and the small DocBook file (`small-docbook-article.xml`), in that order. The result should like this:

```
<html>
<body>
<h1 align="center">Title of my (Docbook) article</h1>
<h2>Title of Section 1.</h2>
<p>This is a paragraph.</p>
</body>
</html>
```

Note: This output was generated using JAXP 1.0. However, with some later versions of JAXP, the first filter in the chain does not translate any of the tags in the input file. If you have one of those versions, the output you see will consist of concatenated plain text in the HTML output, like this: "`Title of my (Docbook) article Title of Section 1. This is a paragraph.`"

Further Information

For more information on XSL stylesheets, XSLT, and transformation engines, see

- A great introduction to XSLT that starts with a simple HTML page and uses XSLT to customize it, one step at a time: `http://www.xfront.com/rescuing-xslt.html`

- Extensible Stylesheet Language (XSL): `http://www.w3.org/Style/XSL/`

- The XML Path Language: `http://www.w3.org/TR/xpath`

- The Xalan transformation engine: `http://xml.apache.org/xalan-j/`

- Output properties that can be programmatically specified on transformer objects: `http://www.w3.org/TR/xslt#output`.

- `DocBookLite`, a smaller, more lightweight version of `DocBook` used for O'Reilly's books and supported by several editors: `http://www.docbook.org/wiki/moin.cgi/DocBookLite`.

- `Simplified DocBook`, intended for articles: `http://www.docbook.org/specs/wd-docbook-simple-1.1b1.html`

- Using Xalan from the command line: `http://xml.apache.org/xalan-j/commandline.html`

8

**Building Web Services
with JAX-RPC**

J AX-RPC stands for Java API for XML-based RPC. JAX-RPC is a technology for building Web services and clients that use *remote procedure calls* (RPC) and XML. Often used in a distributed client-server model, an RPC mechanism enables clients to execute procedures on other systems.

In JAX-RPC, a remote procedure call is represented by an XML-based protocol such as SOAP. The SOAP specification defines the envelope structure, encoding rules, and conventions for representing remote procedure calls and responses. These calls and responses are transmitted as SOAP messages (XML files) over HTTP.

Although SOAP messages are complex, the JAX-RPC API hides this complexity from the application developer. On the server side, the developer specifies the remote procedures by defining methods in an interface written in the Java programming language. The developer also codes one or more classes that implement those methods. Client programs are also easy to code. A client creates a proxy (a local object representing the service) and then simply invokes methods on the proxy. With JAX-RPC, the developer does not generate or parse SOAP messages. It is the JAX-RPC runtime system that converts the API calls and responses to and from SOAP messages.

With JAX-RPC, clients and Web services have a big advantage: the platform independence of the Java programming language. In addition, JAX-RPC is not restrictive: a JAX-RPC client can access a Web service that is not running on the

Java platform, and vice versa. This flexibility is possible because JAX-RPC uses technologies defined by the World Wide Web Consortium (W3C): HTTP, SOAP, and the Web Service Description Language (WSDL). WSDL specifies an XML format for describing a service as a set of endpoints operating on messages.

Setting the Port

Several files in the JAX-RPC examples depend on the port that you specified when you installed the Application Server. The tutorial examples assume that the server runs on the default port, 8080. If you have changed the port, you must update the port number in the following files before building and running the JAX-RPC examples:

- *<INSTALL>*/j2eetutorial14/examples/jaxrpc/staticstub/ config-wsdl.xml
- *<INSTALL>*/j2eetutorial14/examples/jaxrpc/ dynamicproxy/config-wsdl.xml
- *<INSTALL>*/j2eetutorial14/examples/jaxrpc/appclient/ config-wsdl.xml
- *<INSTALL>*/j2eetutorial14/examples/jaxrpc/webclient/ config-wsdl.xml
- *<INSTALL>*/j2eetutorial14/examples/jaxrpc/ webclient/web/response.jsp
- *<INSTALL>*/j2eetutorial14/examples/security/ basicauthclient/SecureHello.wsdl
- *<INSTALL>*/j2eetutorial14/examples/security/ mutualauthclient/SecureHello.wsdl

Creating a Simple Web Service and Client with JAX-RPC

This section shows how to build and deploy a simple Web service and client. A later section, Web Service Clients (page 326), provides examples of additional JAX-RPC clients that access the service. The source code for the service is in *<INSTALL>*/j2eetutorial14/examples/jaxrpc/helloservice/ and the client is in *<INSTALL>*/j2eetutorial14/examples/jaxrpc/staticstub/.

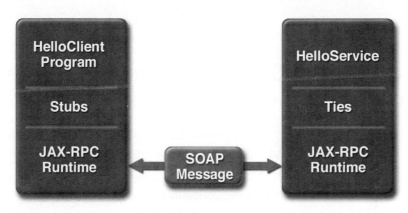

Figure 8–1 Communication Between a JAX-RPC Web Service and a
Client

Figure 8–1 illustrates how JAX-RPC technology manages communication
between a Web service and client.

The starting point for developing a JAX-RPC Web service is the service endpoint
interface. A *service endpoint interface* (SEI) is a Java interface that declares the
methods that a client can invoke on the service.

You use the SEI, the wscompile tool, and two configuration files to generate
the WSDL specification of the Web service and the stubs that connect a Web
service client to the JAX-RPC runtime. For reference documentation on
wscompile, see the Application Server man pages at http://docs.sun.com/
db/doc/817-6092.

Together, the wscompile tool, the deploytool utility, and the Application Server
provide the Application Server's implementation of JAX-RPC.

These are the basic steps for creating the Web service and client:

1. Code the SEI and implementation class and interface configuration file.
2. Compile the SEI and implementation class.
3. Use wscompile to generate the files required to deploy the service.
4. Use deploytool to package the files into a WAR file.
5. Deploy the WAR file. The tie classes (which are used to communicate with
   clients) are generated by the Application Server during deployment.
6. Code the client class and WSDL configuration file.
7. Use wscompile to generate and compile the stub files.
8. Compile the client class.
9. Run the client.

The sections that follow cover these steps in greater detail.

Coding the Service Endpoint Interface and Implementation Class

In this example, the service endpoint interface declares a single method named sayHello. This method returns a string that is the concatenation of the string Hello with the method parameter.

A service endpoint interface must conform to a few rules:

- It extends the java.rmi.Remote interface.
- It must not have constant declarations, such as public final static.
- The methods must throw the java.rmi.RemoteException or one of its subclasses. (The methods may also throw service-specific exceptions.)
- Method parameters and return types must be supported JAX-RPC types (see Types Supported by JAX-RPC, page 324).

In this example, the service endpoint interface is named HelloIF:

```
package helloservice;

import java.rmi.Remote;
import java.rmi.RemoteException;

public interface HelloIF extends Remote {
    public String sayHello(String s) throws RemoteException;
}
```

In addition to the interface, you'll need the class that implements the interface. In this example, the implementation class is called HelloImpl:

```
package helloservice;

public class HelloImpl implements HelloIF {

    public String message ="Hello";

    public String sayHello(String s) {
        return message + s;
    }
}
```

Building the Service

To build `MyHelloService`, in a terminal window go to the *<INSTALL>*/
`j2eetutorial14/examples/jaxrpc/helloservice/` directory and type the
following:

```
asant build
```

The `build` task command executes these `asant` subtasks:

- `compile-service`
- `generate-wsdl`

The compile-service Task

This `asant` task compiles `HelloIF.java` and `HelloImpl.java`, writing the class
files to the `build` subdirectory.

The generate-wsdl Task

The `generate-wsdl` task runs `wscompile`, which creates the WSDL and mapping files. The WSDL file describes the Web service and is used to generate the
client stubs in Static Stub Client (page 321). The mapping file contains information that correlates the mapping between the Java interfaces and the WSDL definition. It is meant to be portable so that any J2EE-compliant deployment tool
can use this information, along with the WSDL file and the Java interfaces, to
generate stubs and ties for the deployed Web services.

The files created in this example are `MyHelloService.wsdl` and `mapping.xml`.
The `generate-wsdl` task runs `wscompile` with the following arguments:

```
wscompile -define -mapping build/mapping.xml -d build -nd build
    -classpath build config-interface.xml
```

The `-classpath` flag instructs `wscompile` to read the SEI in the `build` directory,
and the `-define` flag instructs `wscompile` to create WSDL and mapping files.
The `-mapping` flag specifies the mapping file name. The `-d` and `-nd` flags tell the
tool to write class and WSDL files to the `build` subdirectory.

The `wscompile` tool reads an interface configuration file that specifies information about the SEI. In this example, the configuration file is named `config-interface.xml` and contains the following:

```
<?xml version="1.0" encoding="UTF-8"?>
<configuration
  xmlns="http://java.sun.com/xml/ns/jax-rpc/ri/config">
  <service
      name="MyHelloService"
      targetNamespace="urn:Foo"
      typeNamespace="urn:Foo"
      packageName="helloservice">
      <interface name="helloservice.HelloIF"/>
  </service>
</configuration>
```

This configuration file tells `wscompile` to create a WSDL file named `MyHello Service.wsdl` with the following information:

- The service name is `MyHelloService`.
- The WSDL target and type namespace is `urn:Foo`. The choice for what to use for the namespaces is up to you. The role of the namespaces is similar to the use of Java package names—to distinguish names that might otherwise conflict. For example, a company can decide that all its Java code should be in the package `com.wombat.*`. Similarly, it can also decide to use the namespace `http://wombat.com`.
- The SEI is `helloservice.HelloIF`.

The `packageName` attribute instructs `wscompile` to put the service classes into the `helloservice` package.

Packaging the Service

Behind the scenes, a JAX-RPC Web service is implemented as a servlet. Because a servlet is a Web component, you run the New Web Component wizard of the `deploytool` utility to package the service. During this process the wizard performs the following tasks:

- Creates the Web application deployment descriptor
- Creates a WAR file
- Adds the deployment descriptor and service files to the WAR file

To start the New Web Component wizard, select File→New→Web Component. The wizard displays the following dialog boxes.

1. Introduction dialog box

    a. Read the explanatory text for an overview of the wizard's features.

    b. Click Next.

2. WAR File dialog box

    a. Select the button labeled Create New Stand-Alone WAR Module.

    b. In the WAR Location field, click Browse and navigate to *<INSTALL>*/ j2eetutorial14/examples/jaxrpc/helloservice/.

    c. In the File Name field, enter MyHelloService.

    d. Click Create Module File.

    e. Click Edit Contents.

    f. In the tree under Available Files, locate the *<INSTALL>*/j2eetutorial14/ examples/jaxrpc/helloservice/ directory.

    g. Select the build subdirectory.

    h. Click Add.

    i. Click OK.

    j. Click Next.

3. Choose Component Type dialog box

    a. Select the Web Services Endpoint button.

    b. Click Next.

4. Choose Service dialog box

    a. In the WSDL File combo box, select WEB-INF/wsdl/MyHelloService.wsdl.

    b. In the Mapping File combo box, select build/mapping.xml.

    c. Click Next.

5. Component General Properties dialog box

    a. In the Service Endpoint Implementation combo box, select helloservice.HelloImpl.

    b. Click Next.

6. Web Service Endpoint dialog box

    a. In the Service Endpoint Interface combo box, select helloservice.HelloIF.

   b. In the Namespace combo box, select `urn:Foo`.

   c. In the Local Part combo box, select `HelloIFPort`.

   d. The `deploytool` utility will enter a default Endpoint Address URI `HelloImpl` in this dialog. This endpoint address *must* be updated in the next section.

   e. Click Next.

   f. Click Finish.

Specifying the Endpoint Address

To access `MyHelloService`, the tutorial clients will specify this service endpoint address URI:

```
http://localhost:8080/hello-jaxrpc/hello
```

The `/hello-jaxrpc` string is the context root of the servlet that implements `MyHelloService`. The `/hello` string is the servlet alias. To specify the endpoint address, you set the context root and alias as follows:

1. In `deploytool`, select `MyHelloService` in the tree.
2. Select the General tab.
3. In the Context Root field, enter `/hello-jaxrpc`.
4. In the tree, select `HelloImpl`.
5. Select the Aliases tab.
6. In the Component Aliases table, add `/hello`.
7. In the Endpoint tab, select `hello` for the Endpoint Address in the Sun-specific Settings frame.
8. Select File→Save.

Deploying the Service

In `deploytool`, perform these steps:

1. In the tree, select `MyHelloService`.
2. Select Tools→Deploy.

You can view the WSDL file of the deployed service by requesting the URL `http://localhost:8080/hello-jaxrpc/hello?WSDL` in a Web browser. Now you are ready to create a client that accesses this service.

Static Stub Client

`HelloClient` is a stand-alone program that calls the `sayHello` method of the `MyHelloService`. It makes this call through a *stub*, a local object that acts as a proxy for the remote service. Because the stub is created by `wscompile` at development time (as opposed to runtime), it is usually called a *static stub*.

Coding the Static Stub Client

Before it can invoke the remote methods on the stub, the client performs these steps:

1. Creates a `Stub` object:

    ```
    (Stub)(new MyHelloService_Impl().getHelloIFPort())
    ```

    The code in this method is implementation-specific because it relies on a `MyHelloService_Impl` object, which is not defined in the specifications. The `MyHelloService_Impl` class will be generated by `wscompile` in the following section.

2. Sets the endpoint address that the stub uses to access the service:

    ```
    stub._setProperty
    (javax.xml.rpc.Stub.ENDPOINT_ADDRESS_PROPERTY, args[0]);
    ```

    At runtime, the endpoint address is passed to `HelloClient` in `args[0]` as a command-line parameter, which `asant` gets from the `endpoint.address` property in the `build.properties` file. This address must match the one you set for the service in Specifying the Endpoint Address (page 320).

3. Casts `stub` to the service endpoint interface, `HelloIF`:

    ```
    HelloIF hello = (HelloIF)stub;
    ```

Here is the full source code listing for the `HelloClient.java` file, which is located in the directory *<INSTALL>*/j2eetutorial14/examples/jaxrpc/staticstub/src/:

```
package staticstub;

import javax.xml.rpc.Stub;

public class HelloClient {

    private String endpointAddress;

    public static void main(String[] args) {

        System.out.println("Endpoint address = " + args[0]);
        try {
            Stub stub = createProxy();
            stub._setProperty
                (javax.xml.rpc.Stub.ENDPOINT_ADDRESS_PROPERTY,
                 args[0]);
            HelloIF hello = (HelloIF)stub;
            System.out.println(hello.sayHello("Duke!"));
        } catch (Exception ex) {
            ex.printStackTrace();
        }
    }

    private static Stub createProxy() {
       // Note: MyHelloService_Impl is implementation-specific.
       return
       (Stub) (new MyHelloService_Impl().getHelloIFPort());
    }
}
```

Building and Running the Static Stub Client

To build and package the client, go to the *<INSTALL>*/j2eetutorial14/examples/jaxrpc/staticstub/ directory and type the following:

```
asant build
```

The `build` task invokes three asant subtasks:

- `generate-stubs`
- `compile-client`
- `package-client`

The `generate-stubs` task runs the `wscompile` tool with the following arguments:

```
wscompile -gen:client -d build -classpath build config-wsdl.xml
```

This `wscompile` command reads the `MyHelloService.wsdl` file that was generated in Building the Service (page 317). The command generates files based on the information in the WSDL file and the command-line flags.

The `-gen:client` flag instructs `wscompile` to generate the stubs, other runtime files such as serializers, and value types. The `-d` flag tells the tool to write the generated output to the `build/staticstub` subdirectory.

The `wscompile` tool reads a WSDL configuration file that specifies the location of the WSDL file. In this example, the configuration file is named `config-wsdl.xml`, and it contains the following:

```
<configuration
  xmlns="http://java.sun.com/xml/ns/jax-rpc/ri/config">
  <wsdl location="http://localhost:8080/hello-jaxrpc/
hello?WSDL" packageName="staticstub"/>
</configuration>
```

The `packageName` attribute specifies the Java package for the generated stubs. Notice that the location of the WSDL file is specified as a URL. This causes the `wscompile` command to request the WSDL file from the Web service, and this means that the Web service must be correctly deployed and running in order for the command to succeed. If the Web service is not running or if the port at which the service is deployed is different from the port in the configuration file, the command will fail.

The `compile-client` task compiles `src/HelloClient.java` and writes the class file to the `build` subdirectory.

The `package-client` task packages the files created by the `generate-stubs` and `compile-client` tasks into the `dist/client.jar` file. Except for the `HelloClient.class`, all the files in `client.jar` were created by `wscompile`. Note that `wscompile` generated the `HelloIF.class` based on the information it read from the `MyHelloService.wsdl` file.

To run the client, type the following:

```
asant run
```

This task invokes the Web service client, passing the string Duke for the Web service method parameter. When you run this task, you should get the following output:

```
Hello Duke!
```

Types Supported by JAX-RPC

Behind the scenes, JAX-RPC maps types of the Java programming language to XML/WSDL definitions. For example, JAX-RPC maps the java.lang.String class to the xsd:string XML data type. Application developers don't need to know the details of these mappings, but they should be aware that not every class in the Java 2 Platform, Standard Edition (J2SE) can be used as a method parameter or return type in JAX-RPC.

J2SE SDK Classes

JAX-RPC supports the following J2SE SDK classes:

```
java.lang.Boolean
java.lang.Byte
java.lang.Double
java.lang.Float
java.lang.Integer
java.lang.Long
java.lang.Short
java.lang.String

java.math.BigDecimal
java.math.BigInteger

java.net.URI

java.util.Calendar
java.util.Date
```

Primitives

JAX-RPC supports the following primitive types of the Java programming language:

```
boolean
byte
double
float
int
long
short
```

Arrays

JAX-RPC also supports arrays that have members of supported JAX-RPC types. Examples of supported arrays are `int[]` and `String[]`. Multidimensional arrays, such as `BigDecimal[][]`, are also supported.

Value Types

A *value type* is a class whose state can be passed between a client and a remote service as a method parameter or return value. For example, in an application for a university library, a client might call a remote procedure with a value type parameter named `Book`, a class that contains the fields `Title`, `Author`, and `Publisher`.

To be supported by JAX-RPC, a value type must conform to the following rules:

- It must have a public default constructor.
- It must not implement (either directly or indirectly) the `java.rmi.Remote` interface.
- Its fields must be supported JAX-RPC types.

The value type can contain public, private, or protected fields. The field of a value type must meet these requirements:

- A public field cannot be final or transient.
- A nonpublic field must have corresponding getter and setter methods.

JavaBeans Components

JAX-RPC also supports JavaBeans components, which must conform to the same set of rules as application classes. In addition, a JavaBeans component must have a getter and a setter method for each bean property. The type of the bean property must be a supported JAX-RPC type. For an example of using a JavaBeans component in a Web service, see JAX-RPC Coffee Supplier Service (page 1257).

Web Service Clients

This section shows how to create and run these types of clients:

- Dynamic proxy
- Dynamic invocation interface (DII)
- Application client

When you run these client examples, they will access the `MyHelloService` that you deployed in Creating a Simple Web Service and Client with JAX-RPC (page 314).

Dynamic Proxy Client

This example resides in the `<INSTALL>/j2eetutorial14/examples/jaxrpc/dynamicproxy/` directory.

The client in the preceding section uses a static stub for the proxy. In contrast, the client example in this section calls a remote procedure through a *dynamic proxy*, a class that is created during runtime. Although the source code for the static stub client relies on an implementation-specific class, the code for the dynamic proxy client does not have this limitation.

Coding the Dynamic Proxy Client

The `DynamicProxyHello` program constructs the dynamic proxy as follows:

1. Creates a `Service` object named `helloService`:

```
Service helloService =
    serviceFactory.createService(helloWsdlUrl,
    new QName(nameSpaceUri, serviceName));
```

A `Service` object is a factory for proxies. To create the `Service` object (`helloService`), the program calls the `createService` method on another type of factory, a `ServiceFactory` object.

The `createService` method has two parameters: the URL of the WSDL file and a `QName` object. At runtime, the client gets information about the service by looking up its WSDL. In this example, the URL of the WSDL file points to the WSDL that was deployed with `MyHelloService`:

```
http://localhost:8080/hello-jaxrpc/hello?WSDL
```

A `QName` object is a tuple that represents an XML qualified name. The tuple is composed of a namespace URI and the local part of the qualified name. In the `QName` parameter of the `createService` invocation, the local part is the service name, `MyHelloService`.

2. The program creates a proxy (`myProxy`) with a type of the service endpoint interface (`HelloIF`):

```
dynamicproxy.HelloIF myProxy =
    (dynamicproxy.HelloIF)helloService.getPort(
    new QName(nameSpaceUri, portName),
    dynamicproxy.HelloIF.class);
```

The `helloService` object is a factory for dynamic proxies. To create `myProxy`, the program calls the `getPort` method of `helloService`. This method has two parameters: a `QName` object that specifies the port name and a `java.lang.Class` object for the service endpoint interface (`HelloIF`). The `HelloIF` class is generated by `wscompile`. The port name (`HelloIFPort`) is specified by the WSDL file.

Here is the listing for the `HelloClient.java` file, located in the *<INSTALL>*/j2eetutorial14/examples/jaxrpc/dynamicproxy/src/ directory:

```
package dynamicproxy;

import java.net.URL;
import javax.xml.rpc.Service;
import javax.xml.rpc.JAXRPCException;
import javax.xml.namespace.QName;
import javax.xml.rpc.ServiceFactory;
import dynamicproxy.HelloIF;

public class HelloClient {

    public static void main(String[] args) {
        try {
```

```
            String UrlString = args[0] + "?WSDL";
            String nameSpaceUri = "urn:Foo";
            String serviceName = "MyHelloService";
            String portName = "HelloIFPort";

            System.out.println("UrlString = " + UrlString);
            URL helloWsdlUrl = new URL(UrlString);

            ServiceFactory serviceFactory =
                ServiceFactory.newInstance();

            Service helloService =
                serviceFactory.createService(helloWsdlUrl,
                new QName(nameSpaceUri, serviceName));

            dynamicproxy.HelloIF myProxy =
                (dynamicproxy.HelloIF)
                helloService.getPort(
                new QName(nameSpaceUri, portName),
                dynamicproxy.HelloIF.class);

            System.out.println(myProxy.sayHello("Buzz"));

        } catch (Exception ex) {
            ex.printStackTrace();
        }
    }
}
```

Building and Running the Dynamic Proxy Client

Before performing the steps in this section, you must first create and deploy MyHelloService as described in Creating a Simple Web Service and Client with JAX-RPC (page 314).

To build and package the client, go to the <INSTALL>/j2eetutorial14/exam-ples/jaxrpc/dynamicproxy/ directory and type the following:

```
asant build
```

The preceding command runs these tasks:

- generate-interface
- compile-client
- package-dynamic

The `generate-interface` task runs `wscompile` with the `-import` option. The `wscompile` command reads the `MyHelloService.wsdl` file and generates the service endpoint interface class (`HelloIF.class`). Although this `wscompile` invocation also creates stubs, the dynamic proxy client does not use these stubs, which are required only by static stub clients.

The `compile-client` task compiles the `src/HelloClient.java` file.

The `package-dynamic` task creates the `dist/client.jar` file, which contains `HelloIF.class` and `HelloClient.class`.

To run the client, type the following:

```
asant run
```

The client should display the following line:

```
Hello Buzz
```

Dynamic Invocation Interface Client

This example resides in the `<INSTALL>/j2eetutorial14/examples/jaxrpc/dii/` directory.

With the dynamic invocation interface (DII), a client can call a remote procedure even if the signature of the remote procedure or the name of the service is unknown until runtime. In contrast to a static stub or dynamic proxy client, a DII client does not require runtime classes generated by `wscompile`. However, as you'll see in the following section, the source code for a DII client is more complicated than the code for the other two types of clients.

This example is for advanced users who are familiar with WSDL documents. (See Further Information, page 337.)

Coding the DII Client

The `DIIHello` program performs these steps:

1. Creates a `Service` object:
   ```
   Service service =
       factory.createService(new QName(qnameService));
   ```

   To get a `Service` object, the program invokes the `createService` method of a `ServiceFactory` object. The parameter of the `createService` method is a QName object that represents the name of the service, MyHel-loService. The WSDL file specifies this name as follows:

```
<service name="MyHelloService">
```

2. From the Service object, creates a Call object:

```
QName port = new QName(qnamePort);
Call call = service.createCall(port);
```

A Call object supports the dynamic invocation of the remote procedures of a service. To get a Call object, the program invokes the Service object's createCall method. The parameter of createCall is a QName object that represents the service endpoint interface, MyHelloService-RPC. In the WSDL file, the name of this interface is designated by the portType element:

```
<portType name="HelloIF">
```

3. Sets the service endpoint address on the Call object:

```
call.setTargetEndpointAddress(endpoint);
```

In the WSDL file, this address is specified by the <soap:address> element.

4. Sets these properties on the Call object:

```
SOAPACTION_USE_PROPERTY
SOAPACTION_URI_PROPERTY
ENCODING_STYLE_PROPERTY
```

To learn more about these properties, refer to the SOAP and WSDL documents listed in Further Information (page 337).

5. Specifies the method's return type, name, and parameter:

```
QName QNAME_TYPE_STRING = new QName(NS_XSD, "string");
call.setReturnType(QNAME_TYPE_STRING);

call.setOperationName(new QName(BODY_NAMESPACE_VALUE,
    "sayHello"));

call.addParameter("String_1", QNAME_TYPE_STRING,
    ParameterMode.IN);
```

To specify the return type, the program invokes the setReturnType method on the Call object. The parameter of setReturnType is a QName object that represents an XML string type.

The program designates the method name by invoking the setOpera-tionName method with a QName object that represents sayHello.

To indicate the method parameter, the program invokes the addParameter method on the `Call` object. The `addParameter` method has three arguments: a `String` for the parameter name (`String_1`), a QName object for the XML type, and a `ParameterMode` object to indicate the passing mode of the parameter (`IN`).

6. Invokes the remote method on the `Call` object:

```
String[] params = { "Murphy" };
String result = (String)call.invoke(params);
```

The program assigns the parameter value (`Murphy`) to a `String` array (`params`) and then executes the `invoke` method with the `String` array as an argument.

Here is the listing for the `HelloClient.java` file, located in the *<INSTALL>/* `j2eetutorial14/examples/jaxrpc/dii/src/` directory:

```
package dii;

import javax.xml.rpc.Call;
import javax.xml.rpc.Service;
import javax.xml.rpc.JAXRPCException;
import javax.xml.namespace.QName;
import javax.xml.rpc.ServiceFactory;
import javax.xml.rpc.ParameterMode;

public class HelloClient {

    private static String qnameService = "MyHelloService";
    private static String qnamePort = "HelloIF";

    private static String BODY_NAMESPACE_VALUE =
        "urn:Foo";
    private static String ENCODING_STYLE_PROPERTY =
        "javax.xml.rpc.encodingstyle.namespace.uri";
    private static String NS_XSD =
        "http://www.w3.org/2001/XMLSchema";
    private static String URI_ENCODING =
        "http://schemas.xmlsoap.org/soap/encoding/";

    public static void main(String[] args) {

        System.out.println("Endpoint address = " + args[0]);

        try {
            ServiceFactory factory =
                ServiceFactory.newInstance();
```

```
                Service service =
                    factory.createService(
                    new QName(qnameService));

                QName port = new QName(qnamePort);

                Call call = service.createCall(port);
                call.setTargetEndpointAddress(args[0]);

                call.setProperty(Call.SOAPACTION_USE_PROPERTY,
                    new Boolean(true));
                call.setProperty(Call.SOAPACTION_URI_PROPERTY
                    "");
                call.setProperty(ENCODING_STYLE_PROPERTY,
                    URI_ENCODING);
                QName QNAME_TYPE_STRING =
                        new QName(NS_XSD, "string");
                call.setReturnType(QNAME_TYPE_STRING);

                call.setOperationName(
                    new QName(BODY_NAMESPACE_VALUE,"sayHello"));
                call.addParameter("String_1", QNAME_TYPE_STRING,
                    ParameterMode.IN);
                String[] params = { "Murph!" };

                String result = (String)call.invoke(params);
                System.out.println(result);

            } catch (Exception ex) {
                ex.printStackTrace();
            }
        }
    }
```

Building and Running the DII Client

Before performing the steps in this section, you must first create and deploy
MyHelloService as described in Creating a Simple Web Service and Client with
JAX-RPC (page 314).

To build and package the client, go to the *<INSTALL>*/j2eetutorial14/exam-
ples/jaxrpc/dii/ directory and type the following:

```
    asant build
```

This build task compiles HelloClient and packages it into the dist/ client.jar file. Unlike the previous client examples, the DII client does not require files generated by wscompile.

To run the client, type this command:

```
asant run
```

The client should display this line:

```
Hello Murph!
```

Application Client

Unlike the stand-alone clients in the preceding sections, the client in this section is an application client. Because it's a J2EE component, an application client can locate a local Web service by invoking the JNDI lookup method.

J2EE Application HelloClient Listing

Here is the listing for the HelloClient.java file, located in the *<INSTALL>*/ j2eetutorial14/examples/jaxrpc/appclient/src/ directory:

```
package appclient;

import javax.xml.rpc.Stub;
import javax.naming.*;

public class HelloClient {

    private String endpointAddress;

    public static void main(String[] args) {

        System.out.println("Endpoint address = " + args[0]);

        try {
            Context ic = new InitialContext();
            MyHelloService myHelloService = (MyHelloService)
             ic.lookup("java:comp/env/service/MyJAXRPCHello");
            appclient.HelloIF helloPort =
                myHelloService.getHelloIFPort();
            ((Stub)helloPort)._setProperty
                (Stub.ENDPOINT_ADDRESS_PROPERTY,args[0]);
```

```
                System.out.println(helloPort.sayHello("Jake!"));
                System.exit(0);

            } catch (Exception ex) {
                ex.printStackTrace();
                System.exit(1);
            }
        }
    }
```

Building the Application Client

Before performing the steps in this section, you must first create and deploy MyHelloService as described in Creating a Simple Web Service and Client with JAX-RPC (page 314).

To build the client, go to the *<INSTALL>*/j2eetutorial14/examples/jaxrpc/ appclient/ directory and type the following:

```
asant build
```

As with the static stub client, the preceding command compiles HelloClient.java and runs wscompile by invoking the generate-stubs target.

Packaging the Application Client

Packaging this client is a two-step process:

1. Create an EAR file for a J2EE application.
2. Create a JAR file for the application client and add it to the EAR file.

To create the EAR file, follow these steps:

1. In deploytool, select File→New→Application.
2. Click Browse.
3. In the file chooser, navigate to *<INSTALL>*/j2eetutorial14/examples/ jaxrpc/appclient.
4. In the File Name field, enter HelloServiceApp.
5. Click New Application.
6. Click OK.

To start the New Application Client wizard, select File→New→Application Client. The wizard displays the following dialog boxes.

1. Introduction dialog box

   a. Read the explanatory text for an overview of the wizard's features.

   b. Click Next.

2. JAR File Contents dialog box

   a. Select the button labeled Create New AppClient Module in Application.

   b. In the combo box below this button, select HelloServiceApp.

   c. In the AppClient Display Name field, enter HelloClient.

   d. Click Edit Contents.

   e. In the tree under Available Files, locate the <INSTALL>/j2eetutorial14/examples/jaxrpc/appclient directory.

   f. Select the build directory.

   g. Click Add.

   h. Click OK.

   i. Click Next.

3. General dialog box

   a. In the Main Class combo box, select appclient.HelloClient.

   b. Click Next.

   c. Click Finish.

Specifying the Web Reference

When it invokes the lookup method, the HelloClient refers to the Web service as follows:

```
MyHelloService myHelloService = (MyHelloService)
ic.lookup("java:comp/env/service/MyJAXRPCHello");
```

You specify this reference as follows.

1. In the tree, select HelloClient.

2. Select the Web Service Refs tab.

3. Click Add.

4. In the Coded Name field, enter `service/MyJAXRPCHello`.

5. In the Service Interface combo box, select `appclient.MyHelloService`.

6. In the WSDL File combo box, select `META-INF/wsdl/MyHelloSer-vice.wsdl`.

7. In the Namespace field, enter `urn:Foo`.

8. In the Local Part field, enter `MyHelloService`.

9. In the Mapping File combo box, select `mapping.xml`.

10. Click OK.

Deploying and Running the Application Client

To deploy the application client, follow these steps:

1. Select the `HelloServiceApp` application.

2. Select Tools→Deploy.

3. In the Deploy Module dialog box select the checkbox labeled Return Client JAR.

4. In the field below the checkbox, enter this directory:

   `<INSTALL>/j2eetutorial14/examples/jaxrpc/appclient`

5. Click OK.

To run the client follow these steps:

1. In a terminal window, go to the `<INSTALL>/j2eetutorial14/examples/jaxrpc/appclient/` directory.

2. Type the following on a single line:

   ```
   appclient -client HelloServiceAppClient.jar
   http://localhost:8080/hello-jaxrpc/hello
   ```

The client should display this line:

```
Hello Jake!
```

More JAX-RPC Clients

Other chapters in this book also have JAX-RPC client examples:

• Chapter 16 shows how a JSP page can be a static stub client that accesses a remote Web service. See The Example JSP Pages (page 618).

- Chapter 32 includes a static stub client that demonstrates basic authentication. See Example: Basic Authentication with JAX-RPC (page 1126).

- Chapter 32 includes a static stub client that demonstrates mutual authentication. See Example: Client-Certificate Authentication over HTTP/SSL with JAX-RPC (page 1133).

Web Services Interoperability and JAX-RPC

JAX-RPC 1.1 supports the Web Services Interoperability (WS-I) Basic Profile Version 1.0, Working Group Approval Draft. The WS-I Basic Profile is a document that clarifies the SOAP 1.1 and WSDL 1.1 specifications in order to promote SOAP interoperability. For links related to WS-I, see Further Information (page 337).

To support WS-I, JAX-RPC has the following features:

- When run with the -f:wsi option, wscompile verifies that a WSDL is WS-I-compliant or generates classes needed by JAX-RPC services and clients that are WS-I-compliant.

- The JAX-RPC runtime supports doc/literal and rpc/literal encodings for services, static stubs, dynamic proxies, and DII.

Further Information

For more information about JAX-RPC and related technologies, refer to the following:

- Java API for XML-based RPC 1.1 specification
  `http://java.sun.com/xml/downloads/jaxrpc.html`
- JAX-RPC home
  `http://java.sun.com/xml/jaxrpc/`
- Simple Object Access Protocol (SOAP) 1.1 W3C Note
  `http://www.w3.org/TR/SOAP/`
- Web Services Description Language (WSDL) 1.1 W3C Note
  `http://www.w3.org/TR/wsdl`
- WS-I Basic Profile 1.0
  `http://www.ws-i.org`

9

SOAP with
Attachments API
for Java

SOAP with Attachments API for Java (SAAJ) is used mainly for the SOAP
messaging that goes on behind the scenes in JAX-RPC and JAXR implementations. Secondarily, it is an API that developers can use when they choose to write
SOAP messaging applications directly rather than use JAX-RPC. The SAAJ API
allows you to do XML messaging from the Java platform: By simply making
method calls using the SAAJ API, you can read and write SOAP-based XML
messages, and you can optionally send and receive such messages over the Internet (some implementations may not support sending and receiving). This chapter
will help you learn how to use the SAAJ API.

The SAAJ API conforms to the Simple Object Access Protocol (SOAP) 1.1
specification and the SOAP with Attachments specification. The SAAJ 1.2 specification defines the `javax.xml.soap` package, which contains the API for creating and populating a SOAP message. This package has all the API necessary for
sending request-response messages. (Request-response messages are explained
in SOAPConnection Objects, page 344.)

> **Note:** The `javax.xml.messaging` package, defined in the Java API for XML Messaging (JAXM) 1.1 specification, is not part of the J2EE 1.4 platform and is not discussed in this chapter. The JAXM API is available as a separate download from `http://java.sun.com/xml/jaxm/`.

This chapter starts with an overview of messages and connections, giving some of the conceptual background behind the SAAJ API to help you understand why certain things are done the way they are. Next, the tutorial shows you how to use the basic SAAJ API, giving examples and explanations of the commonly used features. The code examples in the last part of the tutorial show you how to build an application. The case study in Chapter 35 includes SAAJ code for both sending and consuming a SOAP message.

Overview of SAAJ

This section presents a high-level view of how SAAJ messaging works and explains concepts in general terms. Its goal is to give you some terminology and a framework for the explanations and code examples that are presented in the tutorial section.

The overview looks at SAAJ from two perspectives: messages and connections.

Messages

SAAJ messages follow SOAP standards, which prescribe the format for messages and also specify some things that are required, optional, or not allowed. With the SAAJ API, you can create XML messages that conform to the SOAP 1.1 and WS-I Basic Profile 1.0 specifications simply by making Java API calls.

The Structure of an XML Document

> **Note:** For more information on XML documents, see Chapters 2 and 4.

An XML document has a hierarchical structure made up of elements, subelements, subsubelements, and so on. You will notice that many of the SAAJ classes and interfaces represent XML elements in a SOAP message and have the word *element* or *SOAP* (or both) in their names.

An element is also referred to as a *node*. Accordingly, the SAAJ API has the interface Node, which is the base class for all the classes and interfaces that represent XML elements in a SOAP message. There are also methods such as SOAPElement.addTextNode, Node.detachNode, and Node.getValue, which you will see how to use in the tutorial section.

What Is in a Message?

The two main types of SOAP messages are those that have attachments and those that do not.

Messages with No Attachments

The following outline shows the very high-level structure of a SOAP message with no attachments. Except for the SOAP header, all the parts listed are required to be in every SOAP message.

I. SOAP message

    A. SOAP part

        1. SOAP envelope

            a. SOAP header (optional)

            b. SOAP body

The SAAJ API provides the SOAPMessage class to represent a SOAP message, the SOAPPart class to represent the SOAP part, the SOAPEnvelope interface to represent the SOAP envelope, and so on. Figure 9–1 illustrates the structure of a SOAP message with no attachments.

> **Note:** Many SAAJ API interfaces extend DOM interfaces. In a SAAJ message, the SOAPPart class is also a DOM document. See SAAJ and DOM (page 344) for details.

When you create a new SOAPMessage object, it will automatically have the parts that are required to be in a SOAP message. In other words, a new SOAPMessage object has a SOAPPart object that contains a SOAPEnvelope object. The SOAPEnvelope object in turn automatically contains an empty SOAPHeader object followed by an empty SOAPBody object. If you do not need the SOAPHeader object, which is optional, you can delete it. The rationale for having it automatically

Figure 9–1 SOAPMessage Object with No Attachments

included is that more often than not you will need it, so it is more convenient to have it provided.

The SOAPHeader object can include one or more headers that contain metadata about the message (for example, information about the sending and receiving parties). The SOAPBody object, which always follows the SOAPHeader object if there is one, contains the message content. If there is a SOAPFault object (see Using SOAP Faults, page 366), it must be in the SOAPBody object.

Messages with Attachments

A SOAP message may include one or more attachment parts in addition to the SOAP part. The SOAP part must contain only XML content; as a result, if any of the content of a message is not in XML format, it must occur in an attachment part. So if, for example, you want your message to contain a binary file, your message must have an attachment part for it. Note that an attachment part can contain any kind of content, so it can contain data in XML format as well. Figure 9–2 shows the high-level structure of a SOAP message that has two attachments.

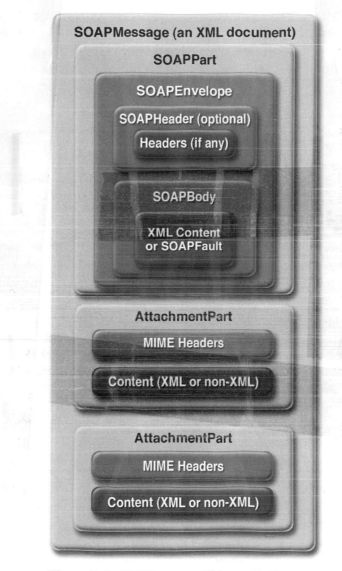

Figure 9–2   SOAPMessage Object with Two
AttachmentPart Objects

The SAAJ API provides the AttachmentPart class to represent an attachment part of a SOAP message. A SOAPMessage object automatically has a SOAPPart object and its required subelements, but because AttachmentPart objects are optional, you must create and add them yourself. The tutorial section walks you through creating and populating messages with and without attachment parts.

If a SOAPMessage object has one or more attachments, each AttachmentPart object must have a MIME header to indicate the type of data it contains. It may also have additional MIME headers to identify it or to give its location. These headers are optional but can be useful when there are multiple attachments. When a SOAPMessage object has one or more AttachmentPart objects, its SOAPPart object may or may not contain message content.

SAAJ and DOM

In SAAJ 1.2, the SAAJ APIs extend their counterparts in the org.w3c.dom package:

- The Node interface extends the org.w3c.dom.Node interface.
- The SOAPElement interface extends both the Node interface and the org.w3c.dom.Element interface.
- The SOAPPart class implements the org.w3c.dom.Document interface.
- The Text interface extends the org.w3c.dom.Text interface.

Moreover, the SOAPPart of a SOAPMessage is also a DOM Level 2 Document and can be manipulated as such by applications, tools, and libraries that use DOM. See Chapter 6 for details about DOM. For details on how to use DOM documents with the SAAJ API, see Adding Content to the SOAPPart Object (page 356) and Adding a Document to the SOAP Body (page 357).

Connections

All SOAP messages are sent and received over a connection. With the SAAJ API, the connection is represented by a SOAPConnection object, which goes from the sender directly to its destination. This kind of connection is called a *point-to-point* connection because it goes from one endpoint to another endpoint. Messages sent using the SAAJ API are called *request-response messages*. They are sent over a SOAPConnection object with the call method, which sends a message (a request) and then blocks until it receives the reply (a response).

SOAPConnection Objects

The following code fragment creates the SOAPConnection object connection and then, after creating and populating the message, uses connection to send the message. As stated previously, all messages sent over a SOAPConnection object are sent with the `call` method, which both sends the message and blocks until it receives the response. Thus, the return value for the `call` method is the `SOAPMessage` object that is the response to the message that was sent. The `request` parameter is the message being sent; `endpoint` represents where it is being sent.

```
SOAPConnectionFactory factory =
  SOAPConnectionFactory.newInstance();
SOAPConnection connection = factory.createConnection();

. . .// create a request message and give it content

java.net.URL endpoint =
  new URL("http://fabulous.com/gizmo/order");
SOAPMessage response = connection.call(request, endpoint);
```

Note that the second argument to the `call` method, which identifies where the message is being sent, can be a `String` object or a `URL` object. Thus, the last two lines of code from the preceding example could also have been the following:

```
String endpoint = "http://fabulous.com/gizmo/order";
SOAPMessage response = connection.call(request, endpoint);
```

A Web service implemented for request-response messaging must return a response to any message it receives. The response is a `SOAPMessage` object, just as the request is a `SOAPMessage` object. When the request message is an update, the response is an acknowledgment that the update was received. Such an acknowledgment implies that the update was successful. Some messages may not require any response at all. The service that gets such a message is still required to send back a response because one is needed to unblock the `call` method. In this case, the response is not related to the content of the message; it is simply a message to unblock the `call` method.

Now that you have some background on SOAP messages and SOAP connections, in the next section you will see how to use the SAAJ API.

Tutorial

This tutorial walks you through how to use the SAAJ API. First, it covers the basics of creating and sending a simple SOAP message. Then you will learn more details about adding content to messages, including how to create SOAP faults and attributes. Finally, you will learn how to send a message and retrieve the content of the response. After going through this tutorial, you will know how to perform the following tasks:

- Creating and sending a simple message
- Adding content to the header
- Adding content to the `SOAPPart` object
- Adding a document to the SOAP body
- Manipulating message content using SAAJ or DOM APIs
- Adding attachments
- Adding attributes
- Using SOAP faults

In the section Code Examples (page 371), you will see the code fragments from earlier parts of the tutorial in runnable applications, which you can test yourself. To see how the SAAJ API can be used in server code, see the SAAJ part of the Coffeebreak case study (SAAJ Coffee Supplier Service, page 1265), which shows an example of both the client and the server code for a Web service application.

A SAAJ client can send request-response messages to Web services that are implemented to do request-response messaging. This section demonstrates how you can do this.

Creating and Sending a Simple Message

This section covers the basics of creating and sending a simple message and retrieving the content of the response. It includes the following topics:

- Creating a message
- Parts of a message
- Accessing elements of a message
- Adding content to the body
- Getting a `SOAPConnection` object
- Sending a message
- Getting the content of a message

Creating a Message

The first step is to create a message using a `MessageFactory` object. The SAAJ API provides a default implementation of the `MessageFactory` class, thus making it easy to get an instance. The following code fragment illustrates getting an instance of the default message factory and then using it to create a message.

```
MessageFactory factory = MessageFactory.newInstance();
SOAPMessage message = factory.createMessage();
```

As is true of the `newInstance` method for `SOAPConnectionFactory`, the `newInstance` method for `MessageFactory` is static, so you invoke it by calling `MessageFactory.newInstance`.

Parts of a Message

A `SOAPMessage` object is required to have certain elements, and, as stated previously, the SAAJ API simplifies things for you by returning a new `SOAPMessage` object that already contains these elements. So `message`, which was created in the preceding line of code, automatically has the following:

I. A `SOAPPart` object that contains

    A. A `SOAPEnvelope` object that contains

        1. An empty `SOAPHeader` object

        2. An empty `SOAPBody` object

The `SOAPHeader` object is optional and can be deleted if it is not needed. However, if there is one, it must precede the `SOAPBody` object. The `SOAPBody` object can hold either the content of the message or a *fault* message that contains status information or details about a problem with the message. The section Using SOAP Faults (page 366) walks you through how to use `SOAPFault` objects.

Accessing Elements of a Message

The next step in creating a message is to access its parts so that content can be added. There are two ways to do this. The `SOAPMessage` object `message`, created in the preceding code fragment, is the place to start.

The first way to access the parts of the message is to work your way through the structure of the message. The message contains a SOAPPart object, so you use the getSOAPPart method of message to retrieve it:

```
SOAPPart soapPart = message.getSOAPPart();
```

Next you can use the getEnvelope method of soapPart to retrieve the SOAPEnvelope object that it contains.

```
SOAPEnvelope envelope = soapPart.getEnvelope();
```

You can now use the getHeader and getBody methods of envelope to retrieve its empty SOAPHeader and SOAPBody objects.

```
SOAPHeader header = envelope.getHeader();
SOAPBody body = envelope.getBody();
```

The second way to access the parts of the message is to retrieve the message header and body directly, without retrieving the SOAPPart or SOAPEnvelope. To do so, use the getSOAPHeader and getSOAPBody methods of SOAPMessage:

```
SOAPHeader header = message.getSOAPHeader();
SOAPBody body = message.getSOAPBody();
```

This example of a SAAJ client does not use a SOAP header, so you can delete it. (You will see more about headers later.) Because all SOAPElement objects, including SOAPHeader objects, are derived from the Node interface, you use the method Node.detachNode to delete header.

```
header.detachNode();
```

Adding Content to the Body

The SOAPBody object contains either content or a fault. To add content to the body, you normally create one or more SOAPBodyElement objects to hold the content. You can also add subelements to the SOAPBodyElement objects by using the addChildElement method. For each element or child element, you add content by using the addTextNode method.

When you create any new element, you also need to create an associated Name object so that it is uniquely identified. One way to create Name objects is by using SOAPEnvelope methods, so you can use the envelope variable from the earlier code fragment to create the Name object for your new element. Another way to create Name objects is to use SOAPFactory methods, which are useful if you do not have access to the SOAPEnvelope.

Note: The SOAPFactory class also lets you create XML elements when you are not creating an entire message or do not have access to a complete SOAPMessage object. For example, JAX-RPC implementations often work with XML fragments rather than complete SOAPMessage objects. Consequently, they do not have access to a SOAPEnvelope object, and this makes using a SOAPFactory object to create Name objects very useful. In addition to a method for creating Name objects, the SOAPFactory class provides methods for creating Detail objects and SOAP fragments. You will find an explanation of Detail objects in Overview of SOAP Faults (page 366) and Creating and Populating a SOAPFault Object (page 368).

Name objects associated with SOAPBodyElement or SOAPHeaderElement objects must be fully qualified; that is, they must be created with a local name, a prefix for the namespace being used, and a URI for the namespace. Specifying a namespace for an element makes clear which one is meant if more than one element has the same local name.

The following code fragment retrieves the SOAPBody object body from message, uses a SOAPFactory to create a Name object for the element to be added, and adds a new SOAPBodyElement object to body.

```
SOAPBody body = message.getSOAPBody();
SOAPFactory soapFactory = SOAPFactory.newInstance();
Name bodyName = soapFactory.createName("GetLastTradePrice",
    "m", "http://wombat.ztrade.com");
SOAPBodyElement bodyElement = body.addBodyElement(bodyName);
```

At this point, body contains a SOAPBodyElement object identified by the Name object bodyName, but there is still no content in bodyElement. Assuming that you want to get a quote for the stock of Sun Microsystems, Inc., you need to create a child element for the symbol using the addChildElement method. Then you need to give it the stock symbol using the addTextNode method. The Name object for the new SOAPElement object symbol is initialized with only a local name because child elements inherit the prefix and URI from the parent element.

```
Name name = soapFactory.createName("symbol");
SOAPElement symbol = bodyElement.addChildElement(name);
symbol.addTextNode("SUNW");
```

You might recall that the headers and content in a `SOAPPart` object must be in XML format. The SAAJ API takes care of this for you, building the appropriate XML constructs automatically when you call methods such as `addBody-Element`, `addChildElement`, and `addTextNode`. Note that you can call the method `addTextNode` only on an element such as `bodyElement` or any child elements that are added to it. You cannot call `addTextNode` on a `SOAPHeader` or `SOAPBody` object because they contain elements and not text.

The content that you have just added to your `SOAPBody` object will look like the following when it is sent over the wire:

```
<SOAP-ENV:Envelope
 xmlns:SOAP-ENV="http://schemas.xmlsoap.org/soap/envelope/">
  <SOAP-ENV:Body>
    <m:GetLastTradePrice xmlns:m="http://wombat.ztrade.com">
      <symbol>SUNW</symbol>
    </m:GetLastTradePrice>
  </SOAP-ENV:Body>
</SOAP-ENV:Envelope>
```

Let's examine this XML excerpt line by line to see how it relates to your SAAJ code. Note that an XML parser does not care about indentations, but they are generally used to indicate element levels and thereby make it easier for a human reader to understand.

Here is the SAAJ code:

```
SOAPMessage message = messageFactory.createMessage();
SOAPHeader header = message.getSOAPHeader();
SOAPBody body = message.getSOAPBody();
```

Here is the XML it produces:

```
<SOAP-ENV:Envelope
 xmlns:SOAP-ENV="http://schemas.xmlsoap.org/soap/envelope/">
  <SOAP-ENV:Header/>
  <SOAP-ENV:Body>
    . . .
  </SOAP-ENV:Body>
</SOAP-ENV:Envelope>
```

The outermost element in this XML example is the SOAP envelope element, indicated by `SOAP-ENV:Envelope`. Note that `Envelope` is the name of the element, and `SOAP-ENV` is the namespace prefix. The interface `SOAPEnvelope` represents a SOAP envelope.

The first line signals the beginning of the SOAP envelope element, and the last line signals the end of it; everything in between is part of the SOAP envelope. The second line is an example of an attribute for the SOAP envelope element. Because a SOAP envelope element always contains this attribute with this value, a `SOAPMessage` object comes with it automatically included. `xmlns` stands for "XML namespace," and its value is the URI of the namespace associated with `Envelope`.

The next line is an empty SOAP header. We could remove it by calling `header.detachNode` after the `getSOAPHeader` call.

The next two lines mark the beginning and end of the SOAP body, represented in SAAJ by a `SOAPBody` object. The next step is to add content to the body.

Here is the SAAJ code:

```
Name bodyName = soapFactory.createName("GetLastTradePrice",
    "m", "http://wombat.ztrade.com");
SOAPBodyElement bodyElement = body.addBodyElement(bodyName);
```

Here is the XML it produces:

```
<m:GetLastTradePrice
 xmlns:m="http://wombat.ztrade.com">
 . . . .
</m:GetLastTradePrice>
```

These lines are what the `SOAPBodyElement bodyElement` in your code represents. `GetLastTradePrice` is its local name, `m` is its namespace prefix, and `http://wombat.ztrade.com` is its namespace URI.

Here is the SAAJ code:

```
Name name = soapFactory.createName("symbol");
SOAPElement symbol = bodyElement.addChildElement(name);
symbol.addTextNode("SUNW");
```

Here is the XML it produces:

```
<symbol>SUNW</symbol>
```

The `String` "SUNW" is the text node for the element `<symbol>`. This `String` object is the message content that your recipient, the stock quote service, receives.

The following example shows how to add multiple SOAPElement objects and add text to each of them. The code first creates the SOAPBodyElement object purchaseLineItems, which has a fully qualified name associated with it. That is, the Name object for it has a local name, a namespace prefix, and a namespace URI. As you saw earlier, a SOAPBodyElement object is required to have a fully qualified name, but child elements added to it, such as SOAPElement objects, can have Name objects with only the local name.

```
SOAPBody body = message.getSOAPBody();
Name bodyName = soapFactory.createName("PurchaseLineItems",
   "PO", "http://sonata.fruitsgalore.com");
SOAPBodyElement purchaseLineItems =
   body.addBodyElement(bodyName);

Name childName = soapFactory.createName("Order");
SOAPElement order =
   purchaseLineItems.addChildElement(childName);

childName = soapFactory.createName("Product");
SOAPElement product = order.addChildElement(childName);
product.addTextNode("Apple");

childName = soapFactory.createName("Price");
SOAPElement price = order.addChildElement(childName);
price.addTextNode("1.56");

childName = soapFactory.createName("Order");
SOAPElement order2 =
   purchaseLineItems.addChildElement(childName);

childName = soapFactory.createName("Product");
SOAPElement product2 = order2.addChildElement(childName);
product2.addTextNode("Peach");

childName = soapFactory.createName("Price");
SOAPElement price2 = order2.addChildElement(childName);
price2.addTextNode("1.48");
```

The SAAJ code in the preceding example produces the following XML in the SOAP body:

```
<PO:PurchaseLineItems
 xmlns:PO="http://sonata.fruitsgalore.com">
  <Order>
    <Product>Apple</Product>
    <Price>1.56</Price>
  </Order>
```

```
    <Order>
      <Product>Peach</Product>
      <Price>1.48</Price>
    </Order>
</PO:PurchaseLineItems>
```

Getting a SOAPConnection Object

The SAAJ API is focused primarily on reading and writing messages. After you have written a message, you can send it using various mechanisms (such as JMS or JAXM). The SAAJ API does, however, provide a simple mechanism for request-response messaging.

To send a message, a SAAJ client can use a `SOAPConnection` object. A `SOAP-Connection` object is a point-to-point connection, meaning that it goes directly from the sender to the destination (usually a URL) that the sender specifies.

The first step is to obtain a `SOAPConnectionFactory` object that you can use to create your connection. The SAAJ API makes this easy by providing the `SOAP-ConnectionFactory` class with a default implementation. You can get an instance of this implementation using the following line of code.

```
SOAPConnectionFactory soapConnectionFactory =
    SOAPConnectionFactory.newInstance();
```

Now you can use `soapConnectionFactory` to create a `SOAPConnection` object.

```
SOAPConnection connection =
    soapConnectionFactory.createConnection();
```

You will use `connection` to send the message that you created.

Sending a Message

A SAAJ client calls the `SOAPConnection` method `call` on a `SOAPConnection` object to send a message. The `call` method takes two arguments: the message being sent and the destination to which the message should go. This message is going to the stock quote service indicated by the URL object `endpoint`.

```
java.net.URL endpoint = new URL(
    "http://wombat.ztrade.com/quotes");

SOAPMessage response = connection.call(message, endpoint);
```

The content of the message you sent is the stock symbol SUNW; the SOAP-Message object `response` should contain the last stock price for Sun Microsystems, which you will retrieve in the next section.

A connection uses a fair amount of resources, so it is a good idea to close a connection as soon as you are finished using it.

```
connection.close();
```

Getting the Content of a Message

The initial steps for retrieving a message's content are the same as those for giving content to a message: Either you use the Message object to get the SOAPBody object, or you access the SOAPBody object through the SOAPPart and SOAPEnvelope objects.

Then you access the SOAPBody object's SOAPBodyElement object, because that is the element to which content was added in the example. (In a later section you will see how to add content directly to the SOAPPart object, in which case you would not need to access the SOAPBodyElement object to add content or to retrieve it.)

To get the content, which was added with the method SOAPElement.addText-Node, you call the method Node.getValue. Note that getValue returns the value of the immediate child of the element that calls the method. Therefore, in the following code fragment, the getValue method is called on bodyElement, the element on which the addTextNode method was called.

To access bodyElement, you call the getChildElements method on soapBody. Passing bodyName to getChildElements returns a java.util.Iterator object that contains all the child elements identified by the Name object bodyName. You already know that there is only one, so calling the next method on it will return the SOAPBodyElement you want. Note that the Iterator.next method returns a Java Object, so you need to cast the Object it returns to a SOAPBodyElement object before assigning it to the variable bodyElement.

```
SOAPBody soapBody = response.getSOAPBody();
java.util.Iterator iterator =
  soapBody.getChildElements(bodyName);
SOAPBodyElement bodyElement =
  (SOAPBodyElement)iterator.next();
String lastPrice = bodyElement.getValue();
System.out.print("The last price for SUNW is ");
System.out.println(lastPrice);
```

If more than one element had the name bodyName, you would have to use a while loop using the Iterator.hasNext method to make sure that you got all of them.

```
while (iterator.hasNext()) {
    SOAPBodyElement bodyElement =
        (SOAPBodyElement)iterator.next();
    String lastPrice = bodyElement.getValue();
    System.out.print("The last price for SUNW is ");
    System.out.println(lastPrice);
}
```

At this point, you have seen how to send a very basic request-response message and get the content from the response. The next sections provide more detail on adding content to messages.

Adding Content to the Header

To add content to the header, you create a SOAPHeaderElement object. As with all new elements, it must have an associated Name object, which you can create using the message's SOAPEnvelope object or a SOAPFactory object.

For example, suppose you want to add a conformance claim header to the message to state that your message conforms to the WS-I Basic Profile. The following code fragment retrieves the SOAPHeader object from message and adds a new SOAPHeaderElement object to it. This SOAPHeaderElement object contains the correct qualified name and attribute for a WS-I conformance claim header.

```
SOAPHeader header = message.getSOAPHeader();
Name headerName = soapFactory.createName("Claim",
    "wsi", "http://ws-i.org/schemas/conformanceClaim/");
SOAPHeaderElement headerElement =
    header.addHeaderElement(headerName);
headerElement.addAttribute(soapFactory.createName(
    "conformsTo"), "http://ws-i.org/profiles/basic1.0/");
```

At this point, header contains the SOAPHeaderElement object headerElement identified by the Name object headerName. Note that the addHeaderElement method both creates headerElement and adds it to header.

A conformance claim header has no content. This code produces the following XML header:

```
<SOAP-ENV:Header>
  <wsi:Claim conformsTo="http://ws-i.org/profiles/basic1.0/"
    xmlns:wsi="http://ws-i.org/schemas/conformanceClaim/"/>
</SOAP-ENV:Header>
```

For more information about creating SOAP messages that conform to WS-I, see the Messaging section of the WS-I Basic Profile.

For a different kind of header, you might want to add content to `headerElement`. The following line of code uses the method `addTextNode` to do this.

```
headerElement.addTextNode("order");
```

Now you have the `SOAPHeader` object `header` that contains a `SOAPHeaderElement` object whose content is `"order"`.

Adding Content to the SOAPPart Object

If the content you want to send is in a file, SAAJ provides an easy way to add it directly to the `SOAPPart` object. This means that you do not access the `SOAPBody` object and build the XML content yourself, as you did in the preceding section.

To add a file directly to the `SOAPPart` object, you use a `javax.xml.transform.Source` object from JAXP (the Java API for XML Processing). There are three types of `Source` objects: `SAXSource`, `DOMSource`, and `StreamSource`. A `StreamSource` object holds an XML document in text form. `SAXSource` and `DOMSource` objects hold content along with the instructions for transforming the content into an XML document.

The following code fragment uses the JAXP API to build a `DOMSource` object that is passed to the `SOAPPart.setContent` method. The first three lines of code get a `DocumentBuilderFactory` object and use it to create the `DocumentBuilder` object `builder`. Because SOAP messages use namespaces, you should set the NamespaceAware property for the factory to true. Then builder parses the content file to produce a Document object.

```
DocumentBuilderFactory dbFactory =
    DocumentBuilderFactory.newInstance();
dbFactory.setNamespaceAware(true);
DocumentBuilder builder = dbFactory.newDocumentBuilder();
Document document =
    builder.parse("file:///music/order/soap.xml");
DOMSource domSource = new DOMSource(document);
```

The following two lines of code access the SOAPPart object (using the SOAPMessage object message) and set the new Document object as its content. The SOAPPart.setContent method not only sets content for the SOAPBody object but also sets the appropriate header for the SOAPHeader object.

```
SOAPPart soapPart = message.getSOAPPart();
soapPart.setContent(domSource);
```

The XML file you use to set the content of the SOAPPart object must include Envelope and Body elements:

```
<SOAP-ENV:Envelope
xmlns="http://schemas.xmlsoap.org/soap/envelope/">
  <SOAP-ENV:Body>
  ...
  </SOAP-ENV:Body>
</SOAP-ENV:Envelope>
```

You will see other ways to add content to a message in the sections Adding a Document to the SOAP Body (page 357) and Adding Attachments (page 358).

Adding a Document to the SOAP Body

In addition to setting the content of the entire SOAP message to that of a DOMSource object, you can add a DOM document directly to the body of the message. This capability means that you do not have to create a javax.xml.transform.Source object. After you parse the document, you can add it directly to the message body:

```
SOAPBody body = message.getSOAPBody();
SOAPBodyElement docElement = body.addDocument(document);
```

Manipulating Message Content Using SAAJ or DOM APIs

Because SAAJ nodes and elements implement the DOM Node and Element interfaces, you have many options for adding or changing message content:

- Use only DOM APIs.
- Use only SAAJ APIs.
- Use SAAJ APIs and then switch to using DOM APIs.
- Use DOM APIs and then switch to using SAAJ APIs.

The first three of these cause no problems. After you have created a message, whether or not you have imported its content from another document, you can start adding or changing nodes using either SAAJ or DOM APIs.

But if you use DOM APIs and then switch to using SAAJ APIs to manipulate the document, any references to objects within the tree that were obtained using DOM APIs are no longer valid. If you must use SAAJ APIs after using DOM APIs, you should set all your DOM typed references to null, because they can become invalid. For more information about the exact cases in which references become invalid, see the SAAJ API documentation.

The basic rule is that you can continue manipulating the message content using SAAJ APIs as long as you want to, but after you start manipulating it using DOM, you should no longer use SAAJ APIs.

Adding Attachments

An AttachmentPart object can contain any type of content, including XML. And because the SOAP part can contain only XML content, you must use an AttachmentPart object for any content that is not in XML format.

Creating an AttachmentPart Object and Adding Content

The SOAPMessage object creates an AttachmentPart object, and the message also must add the attachment to itself after content has been added. The SOAP-Message class has three methods for creating an AttachmentPart object.

The first method creates an attachment with no content. In this case, an `AttachmentPart` method is used later to add content to the attachment.

```
AttachmentPart attachment = message.createAttachmentPart();
```

You add content to `attachment` by using the `AttachmentPart` method `setContent`. This method takes two parameters: a Java `Object` for the content, and a `String` object for the MIME content type that is used to encode the object. Content in the `SOAPBody` part of a message automatically has a `Content-Type` header with the value `"text/xml"` because the content must be in XML. In contrast, the type of content in an `AttachmentPart` object must be specified because it can be any type.

Each `AttachmentPart` object has one or more MIME headers associated with it. When you specify a type to the `setContent` method, that type is used for the header `Content-Type`. Note that `Content-Type` is the only header that is required. You may set other optional headers, such as `Content-Id` and `Content-Location`. For convenience, SAAJ provides `get` and `set` methods for the headers `Content-Type`, `Content-Id`, and `Content-Location`. These headers can be helpful in accessing a particular attachment when a message has multiple attachments. For example, to access the attachments that have particular headers, you can call the `SOAPMessage` method `getAttachments` and pass it a `MIMEHeaders` object containing the MIME headers you are interested in.

The following code fragment shows one of the ways to use the method `setContent`. The Java `Object` in the first parameter can be a `String`, a stream, a `javax.xml.transform.Source` object, or a `javax.activation.DataHandler` object. The Java `Object` being added in the following code fragment is a `String`, which is plain text, so the second argument must be `"text/plain"`. The code also sets a content identifier, which can be used to identify this `AttachmentPart` object. After you have added content to `attachment`, you must add it to the `SOAPMessage` object, something that is done in the last line.

```
String stringContent = "Update address for Sunny Skies " +
    "Inc., to 10 Upbeat Street, Pleasant Grove, CA 95439";

attachment.setContent(stringContent, "text/plain");
attachment.setContentId("update_address");

message.addAttachmentPart(attachment);
```

The `attachment` variable now represents an `AttachmentPart` object that contains the string `stringContent` and has a header that contains the string `"text/plain"`. It also has a `Content-Id` header with `"update_address"` as its value. And `attachment` is now part of `message`.

The other two `SOAPMessage.createAttachment` methods create an `AttachmentPart` object complete with content. One is very similar to the `AttachmentPart.setContent` method in that it takes the same parameters and does essentially the same thing. It takes a Java `Object` containing the content and a `String` giving the content type. As with `AttachmentPart.setContent`, the `Object` can be a `String`, a stream, a `javax.xml.transform.Source` object, or a `javax.activation.DataHandler` object.

The other method for creating an `AttachmentPart` object with content takes a `DataHandler` object, which is part of the JavaBeans Activation Framework (JAF). Using a `DataHandler` object is fairly straightforward. First, you create a `java.net.URL` object for the file you want to add as content. Then you create a `DataHandler` object initialized with the URL object:

```
URL url = new URL("http://greatproducts.com/gizmos/img.jpg");
DataHandler dataHandler = new DataHandler(url);
AttachmentPart attachment =
  message.createAttachmentPart(dataHandler);
attachment.setContentId("attached_image");

message.addAttachmentPart(attachment);
```

You might note two things about this code fragment. First, it sets a header for `Content-ID` using the method `setContentId`. This method takes a `String` that can be whatever you like to identify the attachment. Second, unlike the other methods for setting content, this one does not take a `String` for `Content-Type`. This method takes care of setting the `Content-Type` header for you, something that is possible because one of the things a `DataHandler` object does is to determine the data type of the file it contains.

Accessing an AttachmentPart Object

If you receive a message with attachments or want to change an attachment to a message you are building, you need to access the attachment. The `SOAPMessage` class provides two versions of the `getAttachments` method for retrieving its `AttachmentPart` objects. When it is given no argument, the method `SOAPMessage.getAttachments` returns a `java.util.Iterator` object over all the

`AttachmentPart` objects in a message. When `getAttachments` is given a `Mime-Headers` object, which is a list of MIME headers, `getAttachments` returns an iterator over the `AttachmentPart` objects that have a header that matches one of the headers in the list. The following code uses the `getAttachments` method that takes no arguments and thus retrieves all the `AttachmentPart` objects in the `SOAPMessage` object `message`. Then it prints the content ID, the content type, and the content of each `AttachmentPart` object.

```
java.util.Iterator iterator = message.getAttachments();
while (iterator.hasNext()) {
  AttachmentPart attachment =
    (AttachmentPart)iterator.next();
  String id = attachment.getContentId();
  String type = attachment.getContentType();
  System.out.print("Attachment " + id +
    " has content type " + type);
  if (type == "text/plain") {
    Object content = attachment.getContent();
    System.out.println("Attachment " +
      "contains:\n" + content);
  }
}
```

Adding Attributes

An XML element can have one or more attributes that give information about that element. An attribute consists of a name for the attribute followed immediately by an equal sign (=) and its value.

The `SOAPElement` interface provides methods for adding an attribute, for getting the value of an attribute, and for removing an attribute. For example, in the following code fragment, the attribute named `id` is added to the `SOAPElement` object `person`. Because `person` is a `SOAPElement` object rather than a `SOAPBodyElement` object or `SOAPHeaderElement` object, it is legal for its `Name` object to contain only a local name.

```
Name attributeName = envelope.createName("id");
person.addAttribute(attributeName, "Person7");
```

These lines of code will generate the first line in the following XML fragment.

```
<person id="Person7">
  ...
</person>
```

The following line of code retrieves the value of the attribute whose name is id.

```
String attributeValue =
    person.getAttributeValue(attributeName);
```

If you had added two or more attributes to person, the preceding line of code would have returned only the value for the attribute named id. If you wanted to retrieve the values for all the attributes for person, you would use the method getAllAttributes, which returns an iterator over all the values. The following lines of code retrieve and print each value on a separate line until there are no more attribute values. Note that the Iterator.next method returns a Java Object, which is cast to a Name object so that it can be assigned to the Name object attributeName. (The examples in DOMExample.java and DOMSrcExample.java (page 381) use code similar to this.)

```
Iterator iterator = person.getAllAttributes();
while (iterator.hasNext()){
  Name attributeName = (Name) iterator.next();
  System.out.println("Attribute name is " +
    attributeName.getQualifiedName());
  System.out.println("Attribute value is " +
    element.getAttributeValue(attributeName));
}
```

The following line of code removes the attribute named id from person. The variable successful will be true if the attribute was removed successfully.

```
boolean successful = person.removeAttribute(attributeName);
```

In this section you have seen how to add, retrieve, and remove attributes. This information is general in that it applies to any element. The next section discusses attributes that can be added only to header elements.

Header Attributes

Attributes that appear in a SOAPHeaderElement object determine how a recipient processes a message. You can think of header attributes as offering a way to extend a message, giving information about such things as authentication, transaction management, payment, and so on. A header attribute refines the meaning of the header, whereas the header refines the meaning of the message contained in the SOAP body.

The SOAP 1.1 specification defines two attributes that can appear only in SOAP-HeaderElement objects: actor and mustUnderstand. The next two sections discuss these attributes.

See HeaderExample.java (page 380) for an example that uses the code shown in this section.

The Actor Attribute

The actor attribute is optional, but if it is used, it must appear in a SOAPHeader-Element object. Its purpose is to indicate the recipient of a header element. The default actor is the message's ultimate recipient; that is, if no actor attribute is supplied, the message goes directly to the ultimate recipient.

An *actor* is an application that can both receive SOAP messages and forward them to the next actor. The ability to specify one or more actors as intermediate recipients makes it possible to route a message to multiple recipients and to supply header information that applies specifically to each of the recipients.

For example, suppose that a message is an incoming purchase order. Its SOAP-Header object might have SOAPHeaderElement objects with actor attributes that route the message to applications that function as the order desk, the shipping desk, the confirmation desk, and the billing department. Each of these applications will take the appropriate action, remove the SOAPHeaderElement objects relevant to it, and send the message on to the next actor.

Note: Although the SAAJ API provides the API for adding these attributes, it does not supply the API for processing them. For example, the actor attribute requires that there be an implementation such as a messaging provider service to route the message from one actor to the next.

An actor is identified by its URI. For example, the following line of code, in which orderHeader is a SOAPHeaderElement object, sets the actor to the given URI.

```
orderHeader.setActor("http://gizmos.com/orders");
```

Additional actors can be set in their own SOAPHeaderElement objects. The following code fragment first uses the SOAPMessage object message to get its SOAPHeader object header. Then header creates four SOAPHeaderElement objects, each of which sets its actor attribute.

```
SOAPHeader header = message.getSOAPHeader();
SOAPFactory soapFactory = SOAPFactory.newInstance();

String nameSpace = "ns";
String nameSpaceURI = "http://gizmos.com/NSURI";

Name order = soapFactory.createName("orderDesk",
   nameSpace, nameSpaceURI);
SOAPHeaderElement orderHeader =
   header.addHeaderElement(order);
orderHeader.setActor("http://gizmos.com/orders");

Name shipping =
   soapFactory.createName("shippingDesk",
      nameSpace, nameSpaceURI);
SOAPHeaderElement shippingHeader =
   header.addHeaderElement(shipping);
shippingHeader.setActor("http://gizmos.com/shipping");

Name confirmation =
   soapFactory.createName("confirmationDesk",
      nameSpace, nameSpaceURI);
SOAPHeaderElement confirmationHeader =
   header.addHeaderElement(confirmation);
confirmationHeader.setActor(
   "http://gizmos.com/confirmations");

Name billing = soapFactory.createName("billingDesk",
   nameSpace, nameSpaceURI);
SOAPHeaderElement billingHeader =
   header.addHeaderElement(billing);
billingHeader.setActor("http://gizmos.com/billing");
```

The SOAPHeader interface provides two methods that return a java.util.Iterator object over all the SOAPHeaderElement objects that have an actor that matches the specified actor. The first method, examineHeaderElements, returns an iterator over all the elements that have the specified actor.

```
java.util.Iterator headerElements =
   header.examineHeaderElements("http://gizmos.com/orders");
```

The second method, `extractHeaderElements`, not only returns an iterator over all the `SOAPHeaderElement` objects that have the specified actor attribute but also detaches them from the `SOAPHeader` object. So, for example, after the order desk application did its work, it would call `extractHeaderElements` to remove all the `SOAPHeaderElement` objects that applied to it.

```
java.util.Iterator headerElements =
    header.extractHeaderElements("http://gizmos.com/orders");
```

Each `SOAPHeaderElement` object can have only one actor attribute, but the same actor can be an attribute for multiple `SOAPHeaderElement` objects.

Two additional `SOAPHeader` methods—`examineAllHeaderElements` and `extractAllHeaderElements`—allow you to examine or extract all the header elements, whether or not they have an actor attribute. For example, you could use the following code to display the values of all the header elements:

```
Iterator allHeaders =
    header.examineAllHeaderElements();
while (allHeaders.hasNext()) {
    SOAPHeaderElement headerElement =
        (SOAPHeaderElement)allHeaders.next();
    Name headerName =
        headerElement.getElementName();
    System.out.println("\nHeader name is " +
        headerName.getQualifiedName());
    System.out.println("Actor is " +
        headerElement.getActor());
}
```

The mustUnderstand Attribute

The other attribute that must be added only to a `SOAPHeaderElement` object is `mustUnderstand`. This attribute says whether or not the recipient (indicated by the `actor` attribute) is required to process a header entry. When the value of the `mustUnderstand` attribute is `true`, the actor must understand the semantics of the header entry and must process it correctly to those semantics. If the value is `false`, processing the header entry is optional. A `SOAPHeaderElement` object with no `mustUnderstand` attribute is equivalent to one with a `mustUnderstand` attribute whose value is `false`.

The `mustUnderstand` attribute is used to call attention to the fact that the semantics in an element are different from the semantics in its parent or peer elements. This allows for robust evolution, ensuring that a change in semantics will not be silently ignored by those who may not fully understand it.

If the actor for a header that has a `mustUnderstand` attribute set to `true` cannot process the header, it must send a SOAP fault back to the sender. (See Using SOAP Faults, page 366.) The actor must not change state or cause any side effects, so that, to an outside observer, it appears that the fault was sent before any header processing was done.

The following code fragment creates a `SOAPHeader` object with a `SOAPHeader-Element` object that has a `mustUnderstand` attribute.

```
SOAPHeader header = message.getSOAPHeader();

Name name = soapFactory.createName("Transaction", "t",
    "http://gizmos.com/orders");

SOAPHeaderElement transaction = header.addHeaderElement(name);
transaction.setMustUnderstand(true);
transaction.addTextNode("5");
```

This code produces the following XML:

```
<SOAP-ENV:Header>
  <t:Transaction
      xmlns:t="http://gizmos.com/orders"
      SOAP-ENV:mustUnderstand="1">
    5
  </t:Transaction>
</SOAP-ENV:Header>
```

You can use the `getMustUnderstand` method to retrieve the value of the `must-Understand` attribute. For example, you could add the following to the code fragment at the end of the preceding section:

```
System.out.println("mustUnderstand is " +
    headerElement.getMustUnderstand());
```

Using SOAP Faults

In this section, you will see how to use the API for creating and accessing a SOAP fault element in an XML message.

Overview of SOAP Faults

If you send a message that was not successful for some reason, you may get back a response containing a SOAP fault element, which gives you status information, error information, or both. There can be only one SOAP fault element in a message, and it must be an entry in the SOAP body. Furthermore, if there is a SOAP fault element in the SOAP body, there can be no other elements in the SOAP body. This means that when you add a SOAP fault element, you have effectively completed the construction of the SOAP body.

A SOAPFault object, the representation of a SOAP fault element in the SAAJ API, is similar to an Exception object in that it conveys information about a problem. However, a SOAPFault object is quite different in that it is an element in a message's SOAPBody object rather than part of the try/catch mechanism used for Exception objects. Also, as part of the SOAPBody object, which provides a simple means for sending mandatory information intended for the ultimate recipient, a SOAPFault object only reports status or error information. It does not halt the execution of an application, as an Exception object can.

If you are a client using the SAAJ API and are sending point-to-point messages, the recipient of your message may add a SOAPFault object to the response to alert you to a problem. For example, if you sent an order with an incomplete address for where to send the order, the service receiving the order might put a SOAPFault object in the return message telling you that part of the address was missing.

Another example of who might send a SOAP fault is an intermediate recipient, or actor. As stated in the section Adding Attributes (page 361), an actor that cannot process a header that has a mustUnderstand attribute with a value of true must return a SOAP fault to the sender.

A SOAPFault object contains the following elements:

- A *fault code*: Always required. The fault code must be a fully qualified name: it must contain a prefix followed by a local name. The SOAP 1.1 specification defines a set of fault code local name values in section 4.4.1, which a developer can extend to cover other problems. The default fault code local names defined in the specification relate to the SAAJ API as follows:
  - VersionMismatch: The namespace for a SOAPEnvelope object was invalid.
  - MustUnderstand: An immediate child element of a SOAPHeader object had its mustUnderstand attribute set to true, and the processing party did not understand the element or did not obey it.
  - Client: The SOAPMessage object was not formed correctly or did not contain the information needed to succeed.
  - Server: The SOAPMessage object could not be processed because of a processing error, not because of a problem with the message itself.

- A *fault string*: Always required. A human-readable explanation of the fault.
- A *fault actor*: Required if the SOAPHeader object contains one or more actor attributes; optional if no actors are specified, meaning that the only actor is the ultimate destination. The fault actor, which is specified as a URI, identifies who caused the fault. For an explanation of what an actor is, see The Actor Attribute, page 363.
- A *Detail object*: Required if the fault is an error related to the SOAPBody object. If, for example, the fault code is Client, indicating that the message could not be processed because of a problem in the SOAPBody object, the SOAPFault object must contain a Detail object that gives details about the problem. If a SOAPFault object does not contain a Detail object, it can be assumed that the SOAPBody object was processed successfully.

Creating and Populating a SOAPFault Object

You have seen how to add content to a SOAPBody object; this section walks you through adding a SOAPFault object to a SOAPBody object and then adding its constituent parts.

As with adding content, the first step is to access the SOAPBody object.

```
SOAPBody body = message.getSOAPBody();
```

With the SOAPBody object body in hand, you can use it to create a SOAPFault object. The following line of code creates a SOAPFault object and adds it to body.

```
SOAPFault fault = body.addFault();
```

The SOAPFault interface provides convenience methods that create an element, add the new element to the SOAPFault object, and add a text node, all in one operation. For example, in the following lines of code, the method setFault-Code creates a faultcode element, adds it to fault, and adds a Text node with the value "SOAP-ENV:Server" by specifying a default prefix and the namespace URI for a SOAP envelope.

```
Name faultName =
  soapFactory.createName("Server",
    "", SOAPConstants.URI_NS_SOAP_ENVELOPE);
fault.setFaultCode(faultName);
fault.setFaultActor("http://gizmos.com/orders");
fault.setFaultString("Server not responding");
```

The SOAPFault object fault, created in the preceding lines of code, indicates that the cause of the problem is an unavailable server and that the actor at http:// /gizmos.com/orders is having the problem. If the message were being routed only to its ultimate destination, there would have been no need to set a fault actor. Also note that fault does not have a Detail object because it does not relate to the SOAPBody object.

The following code fragment creates a SOAPFault object that includes a Detail object. Note that a SOAPFault object can have only one Detail object, which is simply a container for DetailEntry objects, but the Detail object can have multiple DetailEntry objects. The Detail object in the following lines of code has two DetailEntry objects added to it.

```
SOAPFault fault = body.addFault();

Name faultName = soapFactory.createName("Client",
   "", SOAPConstants.URI_NS_SOAP_ENVELOPE);
fault.setFaultCode(faultName);
fault.setFaultString("Message does not have necessary info");

Detail detail = fault.addDetail();

Name entryName = soapFactory.createName("order",
   "PO", "http://gizmos.com/orders/");
DetailEntry entry = detail.addDetailEntry(entryName);
entry.addTextNode("Quantity element does not have a value");

Name entryName2 = soapFactory.createName("confirmation",
   "PO", "http://gizmos.com/confirm");
DetailEntry entry2 = detail.addDetailEntry(entryName2);
entry2.addTextNode("Incomplete address: no zip code");
```

See SOAPFaultTest.java (page 387) for an example that uses code like that shown in this section.

Retrieving Fault Information

Just as the SOAPFault interface provides convenience methods for adding information, it also provides convenience methods for retrieving that information. The following code fragment shows what you might write to retrieve fault information from a message you received. In the code fragment, newMessage is the SOAPMessage object that has been sent to you. Because a SOAPFault object must be part of the SOAPBody object, the first step is to access the SOAPBody object. Then the code tests to see whether the SOAPBody object contains a SOAPFault object. If it does, the code retrieves the SOAPFault object and uses it to retrieve its contents. The convenience methods getFaultCode, getFaultString, and getFaultActor make retrieving the values very easy.

```
SOAPBody body = newMessage.getSOAPBody();
if ( body.hasFault() ) {
  SOAPFault newFault = body.getFault();
  Name code = newFault.getFaultCodeAsName();
  String string = newFault.getFaultString();
  String actor = newFault.getFaultActor();
```

Next the code prints the values it has just retrieved. Not all messages are required to have a fault actor, so the code tests to see whether there is one. Testing whether the variable actor is null works because the method getFaultActor returns null if a fault actor has not been set.

```
System.out.println("SOAP fault contains: ");
System.out.println("  Fault code = " +
   code.getQualifiedName());
System.out.println("  Fault string = " + string);

if ( actor != null ) {
   System.out.println("  Fault actor = " + actor);
}
```

The final task is to retrieve the Detail object and get its DetailEntry objects. The code uses the SOAPFault object newFault to retrieve the Detail object newDetail, and then it uses newDetail to call the method getDetailEntries. This method returns the java.util.Iterator object entries, which contains all the DetailEntry objects in newDetail. Not all SOAPFault objects are required to have a Detail object, so the code tests to see whether newDetail is null. If it is not, the code prints the values of the DetailEntry objects as long as there are any.

```
Detail newDetail = newFault.getDetail();
if ( newDetail != null) {
    Iterator entries = newDetail.getDetailEntries();
    while ( entries.hasNext() ) {
        DetailEntry newEntry =
            (DetailEntry)entries.next();
        String value = newEntry.getValue();
        System.out.println("  Detail entry = " + value);
    }
}
```

In summary, you have seen how to add a SOAPFault object and its contents to a message as well as how to retrieve the contents. A SOAPFault object, which is optional, is added to the SOAPBody object to convey status or error information. It must always have a fault code and a String explanation of the fault. A SOAP-Fault object must indicate the actor that is the source of the fault only when there are multiple actors; otherwise, it is optional. Similarly, the SOAPFault object must contain a Detail object with one or more DetailEntry objects only when the contents of the SOAPBody object could not be processed successfully.

See SOAPFaultTest.java (page 387) for an example that uses code like that shown in this section.

Code Examples

The first part of this tutorial uses code fragments to walk you through the fundamentals of using the SAAJ API. In this section, you will use some of those code fragments to create applications. First, you will see the program Request.java. Then you will see how to run the programs MyUddiPing.java, HeaderExample.java, DOMExample.java, DOMSrcExample.java, Attachments.java, and SOAPFaultTest.java.

You do not have to start the Sun Java System Application Server Platform Edition 8 in order to run these examples.

Request.java

The class Request.java puts together the code fragments used in the section Tutorial (page 345) and adds what is needed to make it a complete example of a client sending a request-response message. In addition to putting all the code together, it adds import statements, a main method, and a try/catch block with exception handling.

```
import javax.xml.soap.*;
import java.util.*;
import java.net.URL;

public class Request {
  public static void main(String[] args){
    try {
      SOAPConnectionFactory soapConnectionFactory =
        SOAPConnectionFactory.newInstance();
```

```
SOAPConnection connection =
    soapConnectionFactory.createConnection();
SOAPFactory soapFactory =
    SOAPFactory.newInstance();

MessageFactory factory =
    MessageFactory.newInstance();
SOAPMessage message = factory.createMessage();

SOAPHeader header = message.getSOAPHeader();
SOAPBody body = message.getSOAPBody();
header.detachNode();

Name bodyName = soapFactory.createName(
    "GetLastTradePrice", "m",
    "http://wombats.ztrade.com");
SOAPBodyElement bodyElement =
    body.addBodyElement(bodyName);

Name name = soapFactory.createName("symbol");
SOAPElement symbol =
    bodyElement.addChildElement(name);
symbol.addTextNode("SUNW");

URL endpoint = new URL
    ("http://wombat.ztrade.com/quotes");
SOAPMessage response =
    connection.call(message, endpoint);

connection.close();

SOAPBody soapBody = response.getSOAPBody();

Iterator iterator =
    soapBody.getChildElements(bodyName);
bodyElement = (SOAPBodyElement)iterator.next();
String lastPrice = bodyElement.getValue();

System.out.print("The last price for SUNW is ");
System.out.println(lastPrice);

    } catch (Exception ex) {
      ex.printStackTrace();
    }
  }
}
```

For `Request.java` to be runnable, the second argument supplied to the `call` method would have to be a valid existing URI, and this is not true in this case. However, the application in the next section is one that you can run.

MyUddiPing.java

The program `MyUddiPing.java` is another example of a SAAJ client application. It sends a request to a Universal Description, Discovery and Integration (UDDI) service and gets back the response. A UDDI service is a business registry and repository from which you can get information about businesses that have registered themselves with the registry service. For this example, the MyUddiPing application is not actually accessing a UDDI service registry but rather a test (demo) version. Because of this, the number of businesses you can get information about is limited. Nevertheless, MyUddiPing demonstrates a request being sent and a response being received.

Setting Up

The MyUddiPing example is in the following directory:

```
<INSTALL>/j2eetutorial14/examples/saaj/myuddiping/
```

Note: `<INSTALL>` is the directory where you installed the tutorial bundle.

In the `myuddiping` directory, you will find two files and the `src` directory. The `src` directory contains one source file, `MyUddiPing.java`.

The file `uddi.properties` contains the URL of the destination (a UDDI test registry) and the proxy host and proxy port of the sender. By default, the destination is the IBM test registry; the Microsoft test registry is commented out.

If you access the Internet from behind a firewall, edit the `uddi.properties` file to supply the correct proxy host and proxy port. If you are not sure what the values for these are, consult your system administrator or another person with that information. The typical value of the proxy port is 8080. You can also edit the file to specify another registry.

The file `build.xml` is the `asant` build file for this example. It includes the file `<INSTALL>/j2eetutorial14/examples/saaj/common/targets.xml`, which contains a set of targets common to all the SAAJ examples.

The prepare target creates a directory named build. To invoke the prepare target, you type the following at the command line:

```
asant prepare
```

The target named build compiles the source file MyUddiPing.java and puts the resulting .class file in the build directory. So to do these tasks, you type the following at the command line:

```
asant build
```

Examining MyUddiPing

We will go through the file MyUddiPing.java a few lines at a time, concentrating on the last section. This is the part of the application that accesses only the content you want from the XML message returned by the UDDI registry.

The first few lines of code import the packages used in the application.

```
import javax.xml.soap.*;
import java.net.*;
import java.util.*;
import java.io.*;
```

The next few lines begin the definition of the class MyUddiPing, which starts with the definition of its main method. The first thing it does is to check to see whether two arguments were supplied. If they were not, it prints a usage message and exits. The usage message mentions only one argument; the other is supplied by the build.xml target.

```
public class MyUddiPing {
    public static void main(String[] args) {
        try {
            if (args.length != 2) {
                System.err.println("Usage: asant run " +
                    "-Dbusiness-name=<name>");
                System.exit(1);
            }
```

The following lines create a java.util.Properties object that contains the system properties and the properties from the file uddi.properties, which is in the myuddiping directory.

```
            Properties myprops = new Properties();
            myprops.load(new FileInputStream(args[0]));
```

```
Properties props = System.getProperties();

Enumeration enum = myprops.propertyNames();
while (enum.hasMoreElements()) {
    String s = (String)enum.nextElement();
    props.setProperty(s, myprops.getProperty(s));
}
```

The next four lines create a SOAPMessage object. First, the code gets an instance of SOAPConnectionFactory and uses it to create a connection. Then it gets an instance of MessageFactory and uses it to create a message.

```
SOAPConnectionFactory soapConnectionFactory =
    SOAPConnectionFactory.newInstance();
SOAPConnection connection =
    soapConnectionFactory.createConnection();
MessageFactory messageFactory =
    MessageFactory.newInstance();

SOAPMessage message =
    messageFactory.createMessage();
```

The next lines of code retrieve the SOAPHeader and SOAPBody objects from the message and remove the header.

```
SOAPHeader header = message.getSOAPHeader();
SOAPBody body = message.getSOAPBody();
header.detachNode();
```

The following lines of code create the UDDI find_business message. The first line gets a SOAPFactory instance that we will use to create names. The next line adds the SOAPBodyElement with a fully qualified name, including the required namespace for a UDDI version 2 message. The next lines add two attributes to the new element: the required attribute generic, with the UDDI version number 2.0, and the optional attribute maxRows, with the value 100. Then the code adds a child element that has the Name object name and adds text to the element by using the method addTextNode. The added text is the business name you will supply at the command line when you run the application.

```
SOAPFactory soapFactory =
    SOAPFactory.newInstance();
SOAPBodyElement findBusiness =
    body.addBodyElement(soapFactory.createName(
        "find_business", "",
        "urn:uddi-org:api_v2"));
```

```
findBusiness.addAttribute(soapFactory.createName(
    "generic"), "2.0");
findBusiness.addAttribute(soapFactory.createName(
    "maxRows"), "100");
SOAPElement businessName =
    findBusiness.addChildElement(
        soapFactory.createName("name"));
businessName.addTextNode(args[1]);
```

The next line of code saves the changes that have been made to the message. This method will be called automatically when the message is sent, but it does not hurt to call it explicitly.

```
message.saveChanges();
```

The following lines display the message that will be sent:

```
System.out.println("\n--- Request Message ---\n");
message.writeTo(System.out);
```

The next line of code creates the `java.net.URL` object that represents the destination for this message. It gets the value of the property named URL from the system property file.

```
URL endpoint = new URL(
    System.getProperties().getProperty("URL"));
```

Next, the message `message` is sent to the destination that `endpoint` represents, which is the UDDI test registry. The `call` method will block until it gets a SOAP-Message object back, at which point it returns the reply.

```
SOAPMessage reply =
    connection.call(message, endpoint);
```

In the next lines of code, the first line prints a line giving the URL of the sender (the test registry), and the others display the returned message.

```
System.out.println("\n\nReceived reply from: " +
    endpoint);
System.out.println("\n---- Reply Message ----\n");
reply.writeTo(System.out);
```

The returned message is the complete SOAP message, an XML document, as it looks when it comes over the wire. It is a `businessList` that follows the format specified in `http://uddi.org/pubs/DataStructure-V2.03-Published-20020719.htm#_Toc25130802`.

As interesting as it is to see the XML that is actually transmitted, the XML document format does not make it easy to see the text that is the message's content. To remedy this, the last part of `MyUddiPing.java` contains code that prints only the text content of the response, making it much easier to see the information you want.

Because the content is in the `SOAPBody` object, the first step is to access it, as shown in the following line of code.

```
SOAPBody replyBody = reply.getSOAPBody();
```

Next, the code displays a message describing the content:

```
System.out.println("\n\nContent extracted from " +
    "the reply message:\n");
```

To display the content of the message, the code uses the known format of the reply message. First, it gets all the reply body's child elements named `businessList`:

```
Iterator businessListIterator =
    replyBody.getChildElements(
        soapFactory.createName("businessList",
            "", "urn:uddi-org:api_v2"));
```

The method `getChildElements` returns the elements in the form of a `java.util.Iterator` object. You access the child elements by calling the method `next` on the `Iterator` object. An immediate child of a `SOAPBody` object is a `SOAPBodyElement` object.

We know that the reply can contain only one `businessList` element, so the code then retrieves this one element by calling the iterator's `next` method. Note that the method `Iterator.next` returns an `Object`, which must be cast to the specific kind of object you are retrieving. Thus, the result of calling `businessListIterator.next` is cast to a `SOAPBodyElement` object:

```
SOAPBodyElement businessList =
    (SOAPBodyElement)businessListIterator.next();
```

The next element in the hierarchy is a single `businessInfos` element, so the code retrieves this element in the same way it retrieved the `businessList`. Children of SOAPBodyElement objects and all child elements from this point forward are SOAPElement objects.

```
Iterator businessInfosIterator =
    businessList.getChildElements(
        soapFactory.createName("businessInfos",
            "", "urn:uddi-org:api_v2"));

SOAPElement businessInfos =
    (SOAPElement)businessInfosIterator.next();
```

The `businessInfos` element contains zero or more `businessInfo` elements. If the query returned no businesses, the code prints a message saying that none were found. If the query returned businesses, however, the code extracts the name and optional description by retrieving the child elements that have those names. The method `Iterator.hasNext` can be used in a `while` loop because it returns `true` as long as the next call to the method `next` will return a child element. Accordingly, the loop ends when there are no more child elements to retrieve.

```
Iterator businessInfoIterator =
    businessInfos.getChildElements(
        soapFactory.createName("businessInfo",
            "", "urn:uddi-org:api_v2"));

if (! businessInfoIterator.hasNext()) {
    System.out.println("No businesses found " +
        "matching the name '" + args[1] +
        "'.");
} else {
    while (businessInfoIterator.hasNext()) {
        SOAPElement businessInfo = (SOAPElement)
            businessInfoIterator.next();
        // Extract name and description from the
        // businessInfo
        Iterator nameIterator =
            businessInfo.getChildElements(
                soapFactory.createName("name",
                    "", "urn:uddi-org:api_v2"));
        while (nameIterator.hasNext()) {
            businessName =
                (SOAPElement)nameIterator.next();
            System.out.println("Company name: " +
                businessName.getValue());
```

```
        }
        Iterator descriptionIterator =
           businessInfo.getChildElements(
              soapFactory.createName(
                 "description", "",
                 "urn:uddi-org:api_v2"));
        while (descriptionIterator.hasNext()) {
           SOAPElement businessDescription =
              (SOAPElement)
              descriptionIterator.next();
           System.out.println("Description: " +
              businessDescription.getValue());
        }
        System.out.println("");
     }
```

Running MyUddiPing

Make sure you have edited the uddi.properties file and compiled MyUddiPing.java as described in Setting Up (page 373).

With the code compiled, you are ready to run MyUddiPing. The run target takes two arguments, but you need to supply only one of them. The first argument is the file uddi.properties, which is supplied by a property set in build.xml. The other argument is the name of the business for which you want to get a description, and you need to supply this argument on the command line. Note that any property set on the command line overrides any value set for that property in the build.xml file.

Use the following command to run the example:

```
asant run -Dbusiness-name=food
```

Output similar to the following will appear after the full XML message:

```
Content extracted from the reply message:

Company name: Food
Description: Test Food

Company name: Food Manufacturing

Company name: foodCompanyA
Description: It is a food company sells biscuit
```

If you want to run MyUddiPing again, you may want to start over by deleting the build directory and the .class file it contains. You can do this by typing the following at the command line:

```
asant clean
```

HeaderExample.java

The example HeaderExample.java, based on the code fragments in the section Adding Attributes (page 361), creates a message that has several headers. It then retrieves the contents of the headers and prints them. You will find the code for HeaderExample in the following directory:

```
<INSTALL>/j2eetutorial14/examples/saaj/headers/src/
```

Running HeaderExample

To run HeaderExample, you use the file build.xml that is in the directory *<INSTALL>*/j2eetutorial14/examples/saaj/headers/.

To run HeaderExample, use the following command:

```
asant run
```

This command executes the prepare, build, and run targets in the build.xml and targets.xml files.

When you run HeaderExample, you will see output similar to the following:

```
----- Request Message ----

<SOAP-ENV:Envelope
xmlns:SOAP-ENV="http://schemas.xmlsoap.org/soap/envelope/">
<SOAP-ENV:Header>
<ns:orderDesk SOAP-ENV:actor="http://gizmos.com/orders"
xmlns:ns="http://gizmos.com/NSURI"/>
<ns:shippingDesk SOAP-ENV:actor="http://gizmos.com/shipping"
xmlns:ns="http://gizmos.com/NSURI"/>
<ns:confirmationDesk
SOAP-ENV:actor="http://gizmos.com/confirmations"
xmlns:ns="http://gizmos.com/NSURI"/>
<ns:billingDesk SOAP-ENV:actor="http://gizmos.com/billing"
xmlns:ns="http://gizmos.com/NSURI"/>
```

```
<t:Transaction SOAP-ENV:mustUnderstand="1" xmlns:t="http://
gizmos.com/orders">5</t:Transaction>
</SOAP-ENV:Header><SOAP-ENV:Body/></SOAP-ENV:Envelope>
Header name is ns:orderDesk
Actor is http://gizmos.com/orders
mustUnderstand is false

Header name is ns:shippingDesk
Actor is http://gizmos.com/shipping
mustUnderstand is false

Header name is ns:confirmationDesk
Actor is http://gizmos.com/confirmations
mustUnderstand is false

Header name is ns:billingDesk
Actor is http://gizmos.com/billing
mustUnderstand is false

Header name is t:Transaction
Actor is null
mustUnderstand is true
```

DOMExample.java and DOMSrcExample.java

The examples `DOMExample.java` and `DOMSrcExample.java` show how to add a DOM document to a message and then traverse its contents. They show two ways to do this:

- `DOMExample.java` creates a DOM document and adds it to the body of a message.
- `DOMSrcExample.java` creates the document, uses it to create a `DOMSource` object, and then sets the `DOMSource` object as the content of the message's SOAP part.

You will find the code for DOMExample and DOMSrcExample in the following directory:

<INSTALL>/j2eetutorial14/examples/saaj/dom/src/

Examining DOMExample

DOMExample first creates a DOM document by parsing an XML document, almost exactly like the JAXP example DomEcho01.java in the directory *<INSTALL>*/j2eetutorial14/examples/jaxp/dom/samples/. The file it parses is one that you specify on the command line.

```
static Document document;
...
  DocumentBuilderFactory factory =
    DocumentBuilderFactory.newInstance();
  factory.setNamespaceAware(true);
  try {
    DocumentBuilder builder =
      factory.newDocumentBuilder();
    document = builder.parse( new File(args[0]) );
    ...
```

Next, the example creates a SOAP message in the usual way. Then it adds the document to the message body:

```
SOAPBodyElement docElement = body.addDocument(document);
```

This example does not change the content of the message. Instead, it displays the message content and then uses a recursive method, getContents, to traverse the element tree using SAAJ APIs and display the message contents in a readable form.

```
public void getContents(Iterator iterator, String indent) {

  while (iterator.hasNext()) {
    Node node = (Node) iterator.next();
    SOAPElement element = null
    Text text = null;
    if (node instanceof SOAPElement) {
      element = (SOAPElement)node;
      Name name = element.getElementName();
      System.out.println(indent + "Name is " +
        name.getQualifiedName());
      Iterator attrs = element.getAllAttributes();
      while (attrs.hasNext()){
        Name attrName = (Name)attrs.next();
        System.out.println(indent +
          " Attribute name is " +
```

```
                     attrName.getQualifiedName());
                 System.out.println(indent +
                     " Attribute value is " +
                     element.getAttributeValue(attrName));
             }
             Iterator iter2 = element.getChildElements();
             getContents(iter2, indent + " ");
         } else {
             text = (Text) node;
             String content = text.getValue();
             System.out.println(indent +
                 "Content is: " + content);
         }
     }
 }
```

Examining DOMSrcExample

DOMSrcExample differs from DOMExample in only a few ways. First, after it parses the document, DOMSrcExample uses the document to create a DOM-Source object. This code is the same as that of DOMExample except for the last line:

```
static DOMSource domSource;
...
try {
   DocumentBuilder builder =
      factory.newDocumentBuilder();
   document = builder.parse( new File(args[0]) );
   domSource = new DOMSource(document);
   ...
```

Then, after DOMSrcExample creates the message, it does not get the header and body and add the document to the body, as DOMExample does. Instead, DOM-SrcExample gets the SOAP part and sets the DOMSource object as its content:

```
// Create a message
SOAPMessage message =
  messageFactory.createMessage();

// Get the SOAP part and set its content to domSource
SOAPPart soapPart = message.getSOAPPart();
soapPart.setContent(domSource);
```

The example then uses the `getContents` method to obtain the contents of both the header (if it exists) and the body of the message.

The most important difference between these two examples is the kind of document you can use to create the message. Because DOMExample adds the document to the body of the SOAP message, you can use any valid XML file to create the document. But because DOMSrcExample makes the document the entire content of the message, the document must already be in the form of a valid SOAP message, and not just any XML document.

Running DOMExample and DOMSrcExample

To run DOMExample and DOMSrcExample, you use the file `build.xml` that is in the directory `<INSTALL>/j2eetutorial14/examples/saaj/dom/`. This directory also contains several sample XML files you can use:

- `domsrc1.xml`, an example that has a SOAP header (the contents of the `HeaderExample` output) and the body of a UDDI query
- `domsrc2.xml`, an example of a reply to a UDDI query (specifically, some sample output from the MyUddiPing example), but with spaces added for readability
- `uddimsg.xml`, similar to `domsrc2.xml` except that it is only the body of the message and contains no spaces
- `slide.xml`, similar to the `slideSample01.xml` file in `<INSTALL>/j2eetutorial14/examples/jaxp/dom/samples/`

To run DOMExample, use a command like the following:

```
asant run-dom -Dxml-file=uddimsg.xml
```

After running DOMExample, you will see output something like the following:

```
Running DOMExample.
Name is businessList
Attribute name is generic
Attribute value is 2.0
Attribute name is operator
Attribute value is www.ibm.com/services/uddi
Attribute name is truncated
Attribute value is false
Attribute name is xmlns
Attribute value is urn:uddi-org:api_v2
...
```

To run DOMSrcExample, use a command like the following:

```
asant run-domsrc -Dxml-file=domsrc2.xml
```

When you run DOMSrcExample, you will see output that begins like the following:

```
run-domsrc:
   Running DOMSrcExample.
   Body contents:
   Content is:

   Name is businessList
    Attribute name is generic
    Attribute value is 2.0
    Attribute name is operator
    Attribute value is www.ibm.com/services/uddi
    Attribute name is truncated
    Attribute value is false
    Attribute name is xmlns
    Attribute value is urn:uddi-org:api_v2
    ...
```

If you run DOMSrcExample with the file uddimsg.xml or slide.xml, you will see runtime errors.

Attachments.java

The example Attachments.java, based on the code fragments in the sections Creating an AttachmentPart Object and Adding Content (page 358) and Accessing an AttachmentPart Object (page 360), creates a message that has a text attachment and an image attachment. It then retrieves the contents of the attachments and prints the contents of the text attachment. You will find the code for Attachments in the following directory:

```
<INSTALL>/j2eetutorial14/examples/saaj/attachments/src/
```

Attachments first creates a message in the usual way. It then creates an AttachmentPart for the text attachment:

```
AttachmentPart attachment1 = message.createAttachmentPart();
```

After it reads input from a file into a string named `stringContent`, it sets the content of the attachment to the value of the string and the type to `text/plain` and also sets a content ID.

```
attachment1.setContent(stringContent, "text/plain");
attachment1.setContentId("attached_text");
```

It then adds the attachment to the message:

```
message.addAttachmentPart(attachment1);
```

The example uses a `javax.activation.DataHandler` object to hold a reference to the graphic that constitutes the second attachment. It creates this attachment using the form of the `createAttachmentPart` method that takes a `DataHandler` argument.

```
// Create attachment part for image
URL url = new URL("file:///../xml-pic.jpg");
DataHandler dataHandler = new DataHandler(url);
AttachmentPart attachment2 =
  message.createAttachmentPart(dataHandler);
attachment2.setContentId("attached_image");

message.addAttachmentPart(attachment2);
```

The example then retrieves the attachments from the message. It displays the `contentId` and `contentType` attributes of each attachment and the contents of the text attachment.

Running Attachments

To run Attachments, you use the file `build.xml` that is in the directory `<INSTALL>/j2eetutorial14/examples/saaj/attachments/`.

To run Attachments, use the following command:

```
asant run -Dfile=path_name
```

Specify any text file as the *path_name* argument. The `attachments` directory contains a file named `addr.txt` that you can use:

```
asant run -Dfile=addr.txt
```

When you run Attachments using this command line, you will see output like the following:

```
Running Attachments.
Attachment attached_text has content type text/plain
Attachment contains:
Update address for Sunny Skies, Inc., to
10 Upbeat Street
Pleasant Grove, CA 95439

Attachment attached_image has content type image/jpeg
```

SOAPFaultTest.java

The example SOAPFaultTest.java, based on the code fragments in the sections Creating and Populating a SOAPFault Object (page 368) and Retrieving Fault Information (page 369), creates a message that has a SOAPFault object. It then retrieves the contents of the SOAPFault object and prints them. You will find the code for SOAPFaultTest in the following directory:

```
<INSTALL>/j2eetutorial14/examples/saaj/fault/src/
```

Running SOAPFaultTest

To run SOAPFaultTest, you use the file build.xml that is in the directory *<INSTALL>*/j2eetutorial14/examples/saaj/fault/.

To run SOAPFaultTest, use the following command:

```
asant run
```

When you run SOAPFaultTest, you will see output like the following (line breaks have been inserted in the message for readability):

```
Here is what the XML message looks like:

<SOAP-ENV:Envelope
xmlns:SOAP-ENV="http://schemas.xmlsoap.org/soap/envelope/">
<SOAP-ENV:Header/><SOAP-ENV:Body>
<SOAP-ENV:Fault><faultcode>SOAP-ENV:Client</faultcode>
<faultstring>Message does not have necessary info</faultstring>
<faultactor>http://gizmos.com/order</faultactor>
<detail>
```

```
<PO:order xmlns:PO="http://gizmos.com/orders/">
Quantity element does not have a value</PO:order>
<PO:confirmation xmlns:PO="http://gizmos.com/confirm">
Incomplete address: no zip code</PO:confirmation>
</detail></SOAP-ENV:Fault>
</SOAP-ENV:Body></SOAP-ENV:Envelope>

SOAP fault contains:
    Fault code = SOAP-ENV:Client
    Local name = Client
    Namespace prefix = SOAP-ENV, bound to
http://schemas.xmlsoap.org/soap/envelope/
    Fault string = Message does not have necessary info
    Fault actor = http://gizmos.com/order
    Detail entry = Quantity element does not have a value
    Detail entry = Incomplete address: no zip code
```

Further Information

For more information about SAAJ, SOAP, and WS-I, see the following:

- SAAJ 1.2 specification, available from

  `http://java.sun.com/xml/downloads/saaj.html`

- SAAJ Web site:

  `http://java.sun.com/xml/saaj/`

- WS-I Basic Profile:

  `http://www.ws-i.org/Profiles/Basic/2003-08/`
  `BasicProfile-1.0a.html`

- JAXM Web site:

  `http://java.sun.com/xml/jaxm/`

10

Java API for XML Registries

THE Java API for XML Registries (JAXR) provides a uniform and standard Java API for accessing various kinds of XML registries.

After providing a brief overview of JAXR, this chapter describes how to imple ment a JAXR client to publish an organization and its Web services to a registry and to query a registry to find organizations and services. Finally, it explains how to run the examples provided with this tutorial and offers links to more information on JAXR.

Overview of JAXR

This section provides a brief overview of JAXR. It covers the following topics:

- What is a registry?
- What is JAXR?
- JAXR architecture

What Is a Registry?

An XML *registry* is an infrastructure that enables the building, deployment, and discovery of Web services. It is a neutral third party that facilitates dynamic and loosely coupled business-to-business (B2B) interactions. A registry is available to organizations as a shared resource, often in the form of a Web-based service.

Currently there are a variety of specifications for XML registries. These include

- The ebXML Registry and Repository standard, which is sponsored by the Organization for the Advancement of Structured Information Standards (OASIS) and the United Nations Centre for the Facilitation of Procedures and Practices in Administration, Commerce and Transport (U.N./CEFACT)
- The Universal Description, Discovery, and Integration (UDDI) project, which is being developed by a vendor consortium

A *registry provider* is an implementation of a business registry that conforms to a specification for XML registries.

What Is JAXR?

JAXR enables Java software programmers to use a single, easy-to-use abstraction API to access a variety of XML registries. A unified JAXR information model describes content and metadata within XML registries.

JAXR gives developers the ability to write registry client programs that are portable across various target registries. JAXR also enables value-added capabilities beyond those of the underlying registries.

The current version of the JAXR specification includes detailed bindings between the JAXR information model and both the ebXML Registry and the UDDI version 2 specifications. You can find the latest version of the specification at

```
http://java.sun.com/xml/downloads/jaxr.html
```

At this release of the J2EE platform, JAXR implements the level 0 capability profile defined by the JAXR specification. This level allows access to both UDDI and ebXML registries at a basic level. At this release, JAXR supports access only to UDDI version 2 registries.

Currently several public UDDI version 2 registries exist.

The Java Web Services Developer Pack (Java WSDP) Registry Server provides a UDDI version 2 registry that you can use to test your JAXR applications in a private environment. You can download the Java WSDP from http://

`java.sun.com/webservices/downloads/`. The Registry Server includes a database based on the native XML database Xindice, which is part of the Apache XML project. This database provides the repository for registry data. The Registry Server does not support messages defined in the UDDI Version 2.0 Replication Specification.

To use the Java WSDP Registry Server, follow these steps:

1. Stop the Application Server.
2. Start the Java WSDP install program.
3. Choose the Custom install option.
4. When the install program requests that you choose which features to install, deselect everything except the Java WSDP Registry Server.
5. Select the Sun Java System Application Server Platform Edition 8 for the Web container. The Registry Server and its backing repository Xindice are installed into the Application Server as Web applications.
6. Start the Application Server.
7. Confirm that the Registry Server and Xindice Web applications are running using the Admin Console or `deploytool`.

Several ebXML registries are under development, and one is available at the Center for E-Commerce Infrastructure Development (CECID), Department of Computer Science Information Systems, The University of Hong Kong (HKU). For information, see `http://www.cecid.hku.hk/Release/PR09APR2002.html`.

A JAXR provider for ebXML registries is available in open source at `http://ebxmlrr.sourceforge.net/jaxr`.

JAXR Architecture

The high-level architecture of JAXR consists of the following parts:

- A *JAXR client*: This is a client program that uses the JAXR API to access a business registry via a JAXR provider.
- A *JAXR provider*: This is an implementation of the JAXR API that provides access to a specific registry provider or to a class of registry providers that are based on a common specification.

A JAXR provider implements two main packages:

- `javax.xml.registry`, which consists of the API interfaces and classes that define the registry access interface.
- `javax.xml.registry.infomodel`, which consists of interfaces that define the information model for JAXR. These interfaces define the types of objects that reside in a registry and how they relate to each other. The basic interface in this package is the `RegistryObject` interface. Its subinterfaces include `Organization`, `Service`, and `ServiceBinding`.

The most basic interfaces in the `javax.xml.registry` package are

- `Connection`. The `Connection` interface represents a client session with a registry provider. The client must create a connection with the JAXR provider in order to use a registry.
- `RegistryService`. The client obtains a `RegistryService` object from its connection. The `RegistryService` object in turn enables the client to obtain the interfaces it uses to access the registry.

The primary interfaces, also part of the `javax.xml.registry` package, are

- `BusinessQueryManager`, which allows the client to search a registry for information in accordance with the `javax.xml.registry.infomodel` interfaces. An optional interface, `DeclarativeQueryManager`, allows the client to use SQL syntax for queries. (The implementation of JAXR in the Application Server does not implement `DeclarativeQueryManager`.)
- `BusinessLifeCycleManager`, which allows the client to modify the information in a registry by either saving it (updating it) or deleting it.

When an error occurs, JAXR API methods throw a `JAXRException` or one of its subclasses.

Many methods in the JAXR API use a `Collection` object as an argument or a returned value. Using a `Collection` object allows operations on several registry objects at a time.

Figure 10–1 illustrates the architecture of JAXR. In the Application Server, a JAXR client uses the capability level 0 interfaces of the JAXR API to access the JAXR provider. The JAXR provider in turn accesses a registry. The Application Server supplies a JAXR provider for UDDI registries.

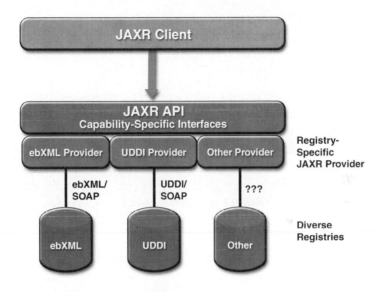

Figure 10–1 JAXR Architecture

Implementing a JAXR Client

This section describes the basic steps to follow in order to implement a JAXR client that can perform queries and updates to a UDDI registry. A JAXR client is a client program that can access registries using the JAXR API. This section covers the following topics:

- Establishing a connection
- Querying a registry
- Managing registry data
- Using taxonomies in JAXR clients

This tutorial does not describe how to implement a JAXR provider. A JAXR provider provides an implementation of the JAXR specification that allows access to an existing registry provider, such as a UDDI or ebXML registry. The implementation of JAXR in the Application Server itself is an example of a JAXR provider.

The Application Server provides JAXR in the form of a resource adapter using the J2EE Connector architecture. The resource adapter is in the directory *<J2EE_HOME>*/lib/install/applications/jaxr-ra. (*<J2EE_HOME>* is the directory where the Application Server is installed.)

This tutorial includes several client examples, which are described in Running the Client Examples (page 417), and a J2EE application example, described in Using JAXR Clients in J2EE Applications (page 425). The examples are in the directory *<INSTALL>*/j2eetutorial14/examples/jaxr/. (*<INSTALL>* is the directory where you installed the tutorial bundle.) Each example directory has a build.xml file (which refers to a targets.xml file) and a build.properties file in the directory *<INSTALL>*/j2eetutorial14/examples/jaxr/common/.

Establishing a Connection

The first task a JAXR client must complete is to establish a connection to a registry. Establishing a connection involves the following tasks:

- Preliminaries: Getting access to a registry
- Creating or looking up a connection factory
- Creating a connection
- Setting connection properties
- Obtaining and using a RegistryService object

Preliminaries: Getting Access to a Registry

Any user of a JAXR client can perform queries on a registry. To add data to the registry or to update registry data, however, a user must obtain permission from the registry to access it. To register with one of the public UDDI version 2 registries, go to one of the following Web sites and follow the instructions:

- http://test.uddi.microsoft.com/ (Microsoft)
- http://uddi.ibm.com/testregistry/registry.html (IBM)
- http://udditest.sap.com/ (SAP)

These UDDI version 2 registries are intended for testing purposes. When you register, you will obtain a user name and password. You will specify this user name and password for some of the JAXR client example programs.

You do not have to register with the Java WSDP Registry Server in order to add or update data. You can use the default user name and password: `testuser` and `testuser`.

Note: The JAXR API has been tested with the Microsoft and IBM registries and with the Java WSDP Registry Server, but not with the SAP registry.

Creating or Looking Up a Connection Factory

A client creates a connection from a connection factory. A JAXR provider can supply one or more preconfigured connection factories. Clients can obtain these factories by looking them up using the Java Naming and Directory Interface (JNDI) API.

At this release of the Application Server, JAXR supplies a connection factory through the JAXR RA, but you need to create a connector resource whose JNDI name is `eis/JAXR` to access this connection factory from a J2EE application. To look up this connection factory in a J2EE component, use code like the following:

```
import javax.xml.registry.*;
import javax.naming.*;
...
  Context context = new InitialContext();
  ConnectionFactory connFactory = (ConnectionFactory)
    context.lookup("java:comp/env/eis/JAXR");
```

Later in this chapter you will learn how to create this connector resource.

To use JAXR in a stand-alone client program, you must create an instance of the abstract class `ConnectionFactory`:

```
import javax.xml.registry.*;
...
ConnectionFactory connFactory =
  ConnectionFactory.newInstance();
```

Creating a Connection

To create a connection, a client first creates a set of properties that specify the URL or URLs of the registry or registries being accessed. For example, the following code provides the URLs of the query service and publishing service for the IBM test registry. (There should be no line break in the strings.)

```
Properties props = new Properties();
props.setProperty("javax.xml.registry.queryManagerURL",
    "http://uddi.ibm.com/testregistry/inquiryapi");
props.setProperty("javax.xml.registry.lifeCycleManagerURL",
    "https://uddi.ibm.com/testregistry/publishapi");
```

With the Application Server implementation of JAXR, if the client is accessing a registry that is outside a firewall, it must also specify proxy host and port information for the network on which it is running. For queries it may need to specify only the HTTP proxy host and port; for updates it must specify the HTTPS proxy host and port.

```
props.setProperty("com.sun.xml.registry.http.proxyHost",
    "myhost.mydomain");
props.setProperty("com.sun.xml.registry.http.proxyPort",
    "8080");
props.setProperty("com.sun.xml.registry.https.proxyHost",
    "myhost.mydomain");
props.setProperty("com.sun.xml.registry.https.proxyPort",
    "8080");
```

The client then sets the properties for the connection factory and creates the connection:

```
connFactory.setProperties(props);
Connection connection = connFactory.createConnection();
```

The makeConnection method in the sample programs shows the steps used to create a JAXR connection.

Setting Connection Properties

The implementation of JAXR in the Application Server allows you to set a number of properties on a JAXR connection. Some of these are standard properties defined in the JAXR specification. Other properties are specific to the implementation of JAXR in the Application Server. Tables 10–1 and 10–2 list and describe these properties.

Table 10–1 Standard JAXR Connection Properties

Property Name and Description	Data Type	Default Value
`javax.xml.registry.queryManagerURL` Specifies the URL of the query manager service within the target registry provider.	String	None
`javax.xml.registry.lifeCycleManagerURL` Specifies the URL of the life-cycle manager service within the target registry provider (for registry updates).	String	Same as the specified `queryManagerURL` value
`javax.xml.registry.semanticEquivalences` Specifies semantic equivalents of concepts as one or more tuples of the ID values of two equivalent concepts separated by a comma. The tuples are separated by vertical bars: `id1,id2|id3,id4`.	String	None
`javax.xml.registry.security.authenticationMethod` Provides a hint to the JAXR provider on the authentication method to be used for authenticating with the registry provider.	String	None; `UDDI_GET_AUTHTOKEN` is the only supported value
`javax.xml.registry.uddi.maxRows` The maximum number of rows to be returned by find operations. Specific to UDDI providers.	Integer	None
`javax.xml.registry.postalAddressScheme` The ID of a `ClassificationScheme` to be used as the default postal address scheme. See Specifying Postal Addresses (page 414) for an example.	String	None

Table 10–2 Implementation-Specific JAXR Connection Properties

Property Name and Description	Data Type	Default Value
`com.sun.xml.registry.http.proxyHost` Specifies the HTTP proxy host to be used for accessing external registries.	String	None
`com.sun.xml.registry.http.proxyPort` Specifies the HTTP proxy port to be used for accessing external registries; usually 8080.	String	None
`com.sun.xml.registry.https.proxyHost` Specifies the HTTPS proxy host to be used for accessing external registries.	String	Same as HTTP proxy host value
`com.sun.xml.registry.https.proxyPort` Specifies the HTTPS proxy port to be used for accessing external registries; usually 8080.	String	Same as HTTP proxy port value
`com.sun.xml.registry.http.proxyUserName` Specifies the user name for the proxy host for HTTP proxy authentication, if one is required.	String	None
`com.sun.xml.registry.http.proxyPassword` Specifies the password for the proxy host for HTTP proxy authentication, if one is required.	String	None
`com.sun.xml.registry.useCache` Tells the JAXR implementation to look for registry objects in the cache first and then to look in the registry if not found.	Boolean, passed in as String	True
`com.sun.xml.registry.userTaxonomyFile-names` For details on setting this property, see Defining a Taxonomy (page 412).	String	None

You set these properties in a JAXR client program. Here is an example:

```
Properties props = new Properties();
props.setProperty("javax.xml.registry.queryManagerURL",
  "http://uddi.ibm.com/testregistry/inquiryapi");
props.setProperty("javax.xml.registry.lifeCycleManagerURL",
  "https://uddi.ibm.com/testregistry/publishapi");
...
ConnectionFactory factory = ConnectionFactory.newInstance();
factory.setProperties(props);
connection = factory.createConnection();
```

Obtaining and Using a RegistryService Object

After creating the connection, the client uses the connection to obtain a RegistryService object and then the interface or interfaces it will use:

```
RegistryService rs = connection.getRegistryService();
BusinessQueryManager bqm = rs.getBusinessQueryManager();
BusinessLifeCycleManager blcm =
  rs.getBusinessLifeCycleManager();
```

Typically, a client obtains both a BusinessQueryManager object and a BusinessLifeCycleManager object from the RegistryService object. If it is using the registry for simple queries only, it may need to obtain only a BusinessQueryManager object.

Querying a Registry

The simplest way for a client to use a registry is to query it for information about the organizations that have submitted data to it. The BusinessQueryManager interface supports a number of find methods that allow clients to search for data using the JAXR information model. Many of these methods return a BulkResponse (a collection of objects) that meets a set of criteria specified in the method arguments. The most useful of these methods are as follows:

- findOrganizations, which returns a list of organizations that meet the specified criteria—often a name pattern or a classification within a classification scheme
- findServices, which returns a set of services offered by a specified organization
- findServiceBindings, which returns the *service bindings* (information about how to access the service) that are supported by a specified service

The JAXRQuery program illustrates how to query a registry by organization name and display the data returned. The JAXRQueryByNAICSClassification and JAXRQueryByWSDLClassification programs illustrate how to query a registry using classifications. All JAXR providers support at least the following taxonomies for classifications:

- The North American Industry Classification System (NAICS). See http://www.census.gov/epcd/www/naics.html for details.
- The Universal Standard Products and Services Classification (UNSPSC). See http://www.eccma.org/unspsc/ for details.
- The ISO 3166 country codes classification system maintained by the International Organization for Standardization (ISO). See http://www.iso.org/iso/en/prods-services/iso3166ma/index.html for details.

The following sections describe how to perform some common queries:

- Finding organizations by name
- Finding organizations by classification
- Finding services and service bindings

Finding Organizations by Name

To search for organizations by name, you normally use a combination of find qualifiers (which affect sorting and pattern matching) and name patterns (which specify the strings to be searched). The findOrganizations method takes a collection of findQualifier objects as its first argument and takes a collection of namePattern objects as its second argument. The following fragment shows how to find all the organizations in the registry whose names begin with a specified string, qString, and sort them in alphabetical order.

```
// Define find qualifiers and name patterns
Collection findQualifiers = new ArrayList();
findQualifiers.add(FindQualifier.SORT_BY_NAME_DESC);
Collection namePatterns = new ArrayList();
namePatterns.add(qString);

// Find using the name
BulkResponse response =
  bqm.findOrganizations(findQualifiers,
      namePatterns, null, null, null, null);
Collection orgs = response.getCollection();
```

A client can use percent signs (%) to specify that the query string can occur anywhere within the organization name. For example, the following code fragment performs a case-sensitive search for organizations whose names contain qString:

```
Collection findQualifiers = new ArrayList();
findQualifiers.add(FindQualifier.CASE_SENSITIVE_MATCH);
Collection namePatterns = new ArrayList();
namePatterns.add("%" + qString + "%");

// Find orgs with name containing qString
BulkResponse response =
  bqm.findOrganizations(findQualifiers, namePatterns, null,
    null, null, null);
Collection orgs = response.getCollection();
```

Finding Organizations by Classification

To find organizations by classification, you establish the classification within a particular classification scheme and then specify the classification as an argument to the findOrganizations method.

The following code fragment finds all organizations that correspond to a particular classification within the NAICS taxonomy. (You can find the NAICS codes at http://www.census.gov/epcd/naics/naicscod.txt.)

```
ClassificationScheme cScheme =
  bqm.findClassificationSchemeByName(null,
    "ntis-gov:naics");
Classification classification =
  blcm.createClassification(cScheme,
    "Snack and Nonalcoholic Beverage Bars", "722213");
Collection classifications = new ArrayList();
classifications.add(classification);
// make JAXR request
BulkResponse response = bqm.findOrganizations(null,
  null, classifications, null, null, null);
Collection orgs = response.getCollection();
```

You can also use classifications to find organizations that offer services based on technical specifications that take the form of WSDL (Web Services Description Language) documents. In JAXR, a *concept* is used as a proxy to hold the information about a specification. The steps are a little more complicated than in the preceding example, because the client must first find the specification concepts and then find the organizations that use those concepts.

The following code fragment finds all the WSDL specification instances used within a given registry. You can see that the code is similar to the NAICS query code except that it ends with a call to findConcepts instead of findOrganizations.

```
String schemeName = "uddi-org:types";
ClassificationScheme uddiOrgTypes =
  bqm.findClassificationSchemeByName(null, schemeName);

/*
 * Create a classification, specifying the scheme
 *  and the taxonomy name and value defined for WSDL
 *  documents by the UDDI specification.
 */
Classification wsdlSpecClassification =
blcm.createClassification(uddiOrgTypes,
  "wsdlSpec", "wsdlSpec");

Collection classifications = new ArrayList();
classifications.add(wsdlSpecClassification);

// Find concepts
BulkResponse br = bqm.findConcepts(null, null,
  classifications, null, null);
```

To narrow the search, you could use other arguments of the findConcepts method (search qualifiers, names, external identifiers, or external links).

The next step is to go through the concepts, find the WSDL documents they correspond to, and display the organizations that use each document:

```
// Display information about the concepts found
Collection specConcepts = br.getCollection();
Iterator iter = specConcepts.iterator();
if (!iter.hasNext()) {
  System.out.println("No WSDL specification concepts found");
} else {
  while (iter.hasNext()) {
    Concept concept = (Concept) iter.next();

    String name = getName(concept);

    Collection links = concept.getExternalLinks();
    System.out.println("\nSpecification Concept:\n\tName: " +
      name + "\n\tKey: " +
      concept.getKey().getId() +
      "\n\tDescription: " +
      getDescription(concept));
```

```
        if (links.size() > 0) {
          ExternalLink link =
              (ExternalLink) links.iterator().next();
          System.out.println("\tURL of WSDL document: '" +
              link.getExternalURI() + "'");
        }

        // Find organizations that use this concept
        Collection specConcepts1 = new ArrayList();
        specConcepts1.add(concept);
        br = bqm.findOrganizations(null, null, null,
            specConcepts1, null, null);

        // Display information about organizations
        ...
    }
```

If you find an organization that offers a service you wish to use, you can invoke the service using the JAX-RPC API.

Finding Services and Service Bindings

After a client has located an organization, it can find that organization's services and the service bindings associated with those services.

```
    Iterator orgIter = orgs.iterator();
    while (orgIter.hasNext()) {
      Organization org = (Organization) orgIter.next();
      Collection services = org.getServices();
      Iterator svcIter = services.iterator();
      while (svcIter.hasNext()) {
        Service svc = (Service) svcIter.next();
        Collection serviceBindings =
            svc.getServiceBindings();
        Iterator sbIter = serviceBindings.iterator();
        while (sbIter.hasNext()) {
          ServiceBinding sb =
              (ServiceBinding) sbIter.next();
        }
      }
    }
```

Managing Registry Data

If a client has authorization to do so, it can submit data to a registry, modify it, and remove it. It uses the `BusinessLifeCycleManager` interface to perform these tasks.

Registries usually allow a client to modify or remove data only if the data is being modified or removed by the same user who first submitted the data.

Managing registry data involves the following tasks:

- Getting authorization from the registry
- Creating an organization
- Adding classifications
- Adding services and service bindings to an organization
- Publishing an organization
- Publishing a specification concept
- Removing data from the registry

Getting Authorization from the Registry

Before it can submit data, the client must send its user name and password to the registry in a set of *credentials*. The following code fragment shows how to do this.

```
String username = "myUserName";
String password = "myPassword";

// Get authorization from the registry
PasswordAuthentication passwdAuth =
  new PasswordAuthentication(username,
    password.toCharArray());

Set creds = new HashSet();
creds.add(passwdAuth);
connection.setCredentials(creds);
```

Creating an Organization

The client creates the organization and populates it with data before publishing it.

An `Organization` object is one of the more complex data items in the JAXR API. It normally includes the following:

- A `Name` object.

- A `Description` object.

- A `Key` object, representing the ID by which the organization is known to the registry. This key is created by the registry, not by the user, and is returned after the organization is submitted to the registry.

- A `PrimaryContact` object, which is a `User` object that refers to an authorized user of the registry. A `User` object normally includes a `PersonName` object and collections of `TelephoneNumber`, `EmailAddress`, and `Postal-Address` objects.

- A collection of `Classification` objects.

- `Service` objects and their associated `ServiceBinding` objects.

For example, the following code fragment creates an organization and specifies its name, description, and primary contact. When a client creates an organization to be published to a UDDI registry, it does not include a key; the registry returns the new key when it accepts the newly created organization. The `blcm` object in the following code fragment is the `BusinessLifeCycleManager` object returned in Obtaining and Using a RegistryService Object (page 399). An `InternationalString` object is used for string values that may need to be localized.

```
// Create organization name and description
Organization org =
  blcm.createOrganization("The Coffee Break");
InternationalString s =
  blcm.createInternationalString("Purveyor of " +
    "the finest coffees. Established 1914");
org.setDescription(s);

// Create primary contact, set name
User primaryContact = blcm.createUser();
PersonName pName = blcm.createPersonName("Jane Doe");
primaryContact.setPersonName(pName);

// Set primary contact phone number
TelephoneNumber tNum = blcm.createTelephoneNumber();
tNum.setNumber("(800) 555-1212");
Collection phoneNums = new ArrayList();
phoneNums.add(tNum);
primaryContact.setTelephoneNumbers(phoneNums);
```

```
// Set primary contact email address
EmailAddress emailAddress =
    blcm.createEmailAddress("jane.doe@TheCoffeeBreak.com");
Collection emailAddresses = new ArrayList();
emailAddresses.add(emailAddress);
primaryContact.setEmailAddresses(emailAddresses);

// Set primary contact for organization
org.setPrimaryContact(primaryContact);
```

Adding Classifications

Organizations commonly belong to one or more classifications based on one or
more classification schemes (taxonomies). To establish a classification for an
organization using a taxonomy, the client first locates the taxonomy it wants to
use. It uses the `BusinessQueryManager` to find the taxonomy. The
`findClassificationSchemeByName` method takes a set of `FindQualifier`
objects as its first argument, but this argument can be null.

```
// Set classification scheme to NAICS
ClassificationScheme cScheme =
    bqm.findClassificationSchemeByName(null, "ntis-gov:naics");
```

The client then creates a classification using the classification scheme and a concept (a taxonomy element) within the classification scheme. For example, the
following code sets up a classification for the organization within the NAICS
taxonomy. The second and third arguments of the `createClassification`
method are the name and the value of the concept.

```
// Create and add classification
Classification classification =
    blcm.createClassification(cScheme,
        "Snack and Nonalcoholic Beverage Bars", "722213");
Collection classifications = new ArrayList();
classifications.add(classification);
org.addClassifications(classifications);
```

Services also use classifications, so you can use similar code to add a classification to a `Service` object.

Adding Services and Service Bindings to an Organization

Most organizations add themselves to a registry in order to offer services, so the JAXR API has facilities to add services and service bindings to an organization.

Like an Organization object, a Service object has a name, a description, and a unique key that is generated by the registry when the service is registered. It may also have classifications associated with it.

A service also commonly has *service bindings*, which provide information about how to access the service. A ServiceBinding object normally has a description, an access URI, and a specification link, which provides the linkage between a service binding and a technical specification that describes how to use the service by using the service binding.

The following code fragment shows how to create a collection of services, add service bindings to a service, and then add the services to the organization. It specifies an access URI but not a specification link. Because the access URI is not real and because JAXR by default checks for the validity of any published URI, the binding sets its validateURI property to false.

```
// Create services and service
Collection services = new ArrayList();
Service service = blcm.createService("My Service Name");
InternationalString is =
    blcm.createInternationalString("My Service Description");
service.setDescription(is);

// Create service bindings
Collection serviceBindings = new ArrayList();
ServiceBinding binding = blcm.createServiceBinding();
is = blcm.createInternationalString("My Service Binding " +
    "Description");
binding.setDescription(is);
// allow us to publish a fictitious URI without an error
binding.setValidateURI(false);
binding.setAccessURI("http://TheCoffeeBreak.com:8080/sb/");
serviceBindings.add(binding);

// Add service bindings to service
service.addServiceBindings(serviceBindings);

// Add service to services, then add services to organization
services.add(service);
org.addServices(services);
```

Publishing an Organization

The primary method a client uses to add or modify organization data is the saveOrganizations method, which creates one or more new organizations in a registry if they did not exist previously. If one of the organizations exists but some of the data have changed, the saveOrganizations method updates and replaces the data.

After a client populates an organization with the information it wants to make public, it saves the organization. The registry returns the key in its response, and the client retrieves it.

```
// Add organization and submit to registry
// Retrieve key if successful
Collection orgs = new ArrayList();
orgs.add(org);
BulkResponse response = blcm.saveOrganizations(orgs);
Collection exceptions = response.getException();
if (exceptions == null) {
  System.out.println("Organization saved");

  Collection keys = response.getCollection();
  Iterator keyIter = keys.iterator();
  if (keyIter.hasNext()) {
    javax.xml.registry.infomodel.Key orgKey =
      (javax.xml.registry.infomodel.Key) keyIter.next();
    String id = orgKey.getId();
    System.out.println("Organization key is " + id);
  }
}
```

Publishing a Specification Concept

A service binding can have a technical specification that describes how to access the service. An example of such a specification is a WSDL document. To publish the location of a service's specification (if the specification is a WSDL document), you create a Concept object and then add the URL of the WSDL document to the Concept object as an ExternalLink object. The following code fragment shows how to create a concept for the WSDL document associated with the simple Web service example in Creating a Simple Web Service and Client with JAX-RPC (page 314). First, you call the createConcept method to create a concept named HelloConcept. After setting the description of the concept, you create an external link to the URL of the Hello service's WSDL document, and then add the external link to the concept.

```
Concept specConcept =
  blcm.createConcept(null, "HelloConcept", "");
InternationalString s =
  blcm.createInternationalString(
    "Concept for Hello Service");
specConcept.setDescription(s);
ExternalLink wsdlLink =
  blcm.createExternalLink(
    "http://localhost:8080/hello-jaxrpc/hello?WSDL",
    "Hello WSDL document");
specConcept.addExternalLink(wsdlLink);
```

Next, you classify the Concept object as a WSDL document. To do this for a UDDI registry, you search the registry for the well-known classification scheme uddi-org:types. (The UDDI term for a classification scheme is *tModel*.) Then you create a classification using the name and value wsdlSpec. Finally, you add the classification to the concept.

```
String schemeName = "uddi-org:types";
ClassificationScheme uddiOrgTypes =
  bqm.findClassificationSchemeByName(null, schemeName);

Classification wsdlSpecClassification =
    blcm.createClassification(uddiOrgTypes,
    "wsdlSpec", "wsdlSpec");
specConcept.addClassification(wsdlSpecClassification);
```

Finally, you save the concept using the saveConcepts method, similarly to the way you save an organization:

```
Collection concepts = new ArrayList();
concepts.add(specConcept);
BulkResponse concResponse = blcm.saveConcepts(concepts);
```

After you have published the concept, you normally add the concept for the WSDL document to a service binding. To do this, you can retrieve the key for the concept from the response returned by the saveConcepts method; you use a code sequence very similar to that of finding the key for a saved organization.

```
String conceptKeyId = null;
Collection concExceptions = concResponse.getExceptions();
javax.xml.registry.infomodel.Key concKey = null;
if (concExceptions == null) {
  System.out.println("WSDL Specification Concept saved");
```

```
Collection keys = concResponse.getCollection();
Iterator keyIter = keys.iterator();
if (keyIter.hasNext()) {
   concKey =
      (javax.xml.registry.infomodel.Key) keyIter.next();
   conceptKeyId = concKey.getId();
   System.out.println("Concept key is " + conceptKeyId);
}
}
```

Then you can call the getRegistryObject method to retrieve the concept from the registry:

```
Concept specConcept =
   (Concept) bqm.getRegistryObject(conceptKeyId,
      LifeCycleManager.CONCEPT);
```

Next, you create a SpecificationLink object for the service binding and set the concept as the value of its SpecificationObject:

```
SpecificationLink specLink =
   blcm.createSpecificationLink();
specLink.setSpecificationObject(specConcept);
binding.addSpecificationLink(specLink);
```

Now when you publish the organization with its service and service bindings, you have also published a link to the WSDL document. Now the organization can be found via queries such as those described in Finding Organizations by Classification (page 401).

If the concept was published by someone else and you don't have access to the key, you can find it using its name and classification. The code looks very similar to the code used to search for a WSDL document in Finding Organizations by Classification (page 401), except that you also create a collection of name patterns and include that in your search. Here is an example:

```
// Define name pattern
Collection namePatterns = new ArrayList();
namePatterns.add("HelloConcept");

BulkResponse br = bqm.findConcepts(null, namePatterns,
   classifications, null, null);
```

Removing Data from the Registry

A registry allows you to remove from it any data that you have submitted to it. You use the key returned by the registry as an argument to one of the Business-LifeCycleManager delete methods: deleteOrganizations, deleteServices, deleteServiceBindings, deleteConcepts, and others.

The JAXRDelete sample program deletes the organization created by the JAXR-Publish program. It deletes the organization that corresponds to a specified key string and then displays the key again so that the user can confirm that it has deleted the correct one.

```
String id = key.getId();
System.out.println("Deleting organization with id " + id);
Collection keys = new ArrayList();
keys.add(key);
BulkResponse response = blcm.deleteOrganizations(keys);
Collection exceptions = response.getException();
if (exceptions == null) {
  System.out.println("Organization deleted");
  Collection retKeys = response.getCollection();
  Iterator keyIter = retKeys.iterator();
  javax.xml.registry.infomodel.Key orgKey = null;
  if (keyIter.hasNext()) {
    orgKey =
      (javax.xml.registry.infomodel.Key) keyIter.next();
    id = orgKey.getId();
    System.out.println("Organization key was " + id);
  }
}
```

A client can use a similar mechanism to delete concepts, services, and service bindings.

Using Taxonomies in JAXR Clients

In the JAXR API, a taxonomy is represented by a ClassificationScheme object. This section describes how to use the implementation of JAXR in the Application Server

- To define your own taxonomies
- To specify postal addresses for an organization

Defining a Taxonomy

The JAXR specification requires that a JAXR provider be able to add user-defined taxonomies for use by JAXR clients. The mechanisms clients use to add and administer these taxonomies are implementation-specific.

The implementation of JAXR in the Application Server uses a simple file-based approach to provide taxonomies to the JAXR client. These files are read at runtime, when the JAXR provider starts up.

The taxonomy structure for the Application Server is defined by the JAXR Predefined Concepts DTD, which is declared both in the file jaxrconcepts.dtd and, in XML schema form, in the file jaxrconcepts.xsd. The file jaxrconcepts.xml contains the taxonomies for the implementation of JAXR in the Application Server. All these files are contained in the *<J2EE_HOME>*/lib/jaxr-impl.jar file. This JAR file also includes files that define the well-known taxonomies used by the implementation of JAXR in the Application Server: naics.xml, iso3166.xml, and unspsc.xml.

The entries in the jaxrconcepts.xml file look like this:

```
<PredefinedConcepts>
<JAXRClassificationScheme id="schId" name="schName">
<JAXRConcept id="schId/conCode" name="conName"
parent="parentId" code="conCode"></JAXRConcept>
...
</JAXRClassificationScheme>
</PredefinedConcepts>
```

The taxonomy structure is a containment-based structure. The element PredefinedConcepts is the root of the structure and must be present. The JAXRClassificationScheme element is the parent of the structure, and the JAXRConcept elements are children and grandchildren. A JAXRConcept element may have children, but it is not required to do so.

In all element definitions, attribute order and case are significant.

To add a user-defined taxonomy, follow these steps.

1. Publish the JAXRClassificationScheme element for the taxonomy as a ClassificationScheme object in the registry that you will be accessing. For example, you can publish the ClassificationScheme object to the Java WSDP Registry Server. To publish a ClassificationScheme object, you must set its name. You also give the scheme a classification within a known classification scheme such as uddi-org:types. In the following

code fragment, the name is the first argument of the LifeCycle-Manager.createClassificationScheme method call.

```
ClassificationScheme cScheme =
   blcm.createClassificationScheme("MyScheme",
      "A Classification Scheme");
ClassificationScheme uddiOrgTypes =
   bqm.findClassificationSchemeByName(null,
      "uddi-org:types");
if (uddiOrgTypes != null) {
   Classification classification =
      blcm.createClassification(uddiOrgTypes,
         "postalAddress", "postalAddress" );
   postalScheme.addClassification(classification);
   ExternalLink externalLink =
      blcm.createExternalLink(
         "http://www.mycom.com/myscheme.html",
         "My Scheme");
   postalScheme.addExternalLink(externalLink);
   Collection schemes = new ArrayList();
   schemes.add(cScheme);
   BulkResponse br =
      blcm.saveClassificationSchemes(schemes);
}
```

The BulkResponse object returned by the saveClassificationSchemes method contains the key for the classification scheme, which you need to retrieve:

```
if (br.getStatus() == JAXRResponse.STATUS_SUCCESS) {
   System.out.println("Saved ClassificationScheme");
   Collection schemeKeys = br.getCollection();
   Iterator keysIter = schemeKeys.iterator();
   while (keysIter.hasNext()) {
      javax.xml.registry.infomodel.Key key =
         (javax.xml.registry.infomodel.Key)
            keysIter.next();
      System.out.println("The postalScheme key is " +
         key.getId());
      System.out.println("Use this key as the scheme" +
         " uuid in the taxonomy file");
   }
}
```

2. In an XML file, define a taxonomy structure that is compliant with the JAXR Predefined Concepts DTD. Enter the ClassificationScheme element in your taxonomy XML file by specifying the returned key ID value as the id attribute and the name as the name attribute. For the foregoing

code fragment, for example, the opening tag for the `JAXRClassifica-tionScheme` element looks something like this (all on one line):

```
<JAXRClassificationScheme
id="uuid:nnnnnnnn-nnnn-nnnn-nnnn-nnnnnnnnnnnn"
name="MyScheme">
```

The `ClassificationScheme id` must be a universally unique identifier (UUID).

3. Enter each `JAXRConcept` element in your taxonomy XML file by specifying the following four attributes, in this order:

   a. `id` is the `JAXRClassificationScheme id` value, followed by a / separator, followed by the code of the `JAXRConcept` element.

   b. `name` is the name of the `JAXRConcept` element.

   c. `parent` is the immediate parent `id` (either the `ClassificationScheme id` or that of the parent `JAXRConcept`).

   d. `code` is the `JAXRConcept` element code value.

   The first `JAXRConcept` element in the `naics.xml` file looks like this (all on one line):

```
<JAXRConcept
id="uuid:C0B9FE13-179F-413D-8A5B-5004DB8E5BB2/11"
name="Agriculture, Forestry, Fishing and Hunting"
parent="uuid:C0B9FE13-179F-413D-8A5B-5004DB8E5BB2"
code="11"></JAXRConcept>
```

4. To add the user-defined taxonomy structure to the JAXR provider, specify the connection property `com.sun.xml.registry.userTaxonomyFile-names` in your client program. You set the property as follows:

```
props.setProperty
("com.sun.xml.registry.userTaxonomyFilenames",
   "c:\mydir\xxx.xml|c:\mydir\xxx2.xml");
```

Use the vertical bar (|) as a separator if you specify more than one file name.

Specifying Postal Addresses

The JAXR specification defines a postal address as a structured interface with attributes for street, city, country, and so on. The UDDI specification, on the other hand, defines a postal address as a free-form collection of address lines, each of which can also be assigned a meaning. To map the JAXR `Postal-Address` format to a known UDDI address format, you specify the UDDI format as a ClassificationScheme object and then specify the semantic equivalences between the concepts in the UDDI format classification scheme and the comments in the JAXR PostalAddress classification scheme. The JAXR Postal-Address classification scheme is provided by the implementation of JAXR in the Application Server.

In the JAXR API, a PostalAddress object has the fields streetNumber, street, city, state, postalCode, and country. In the implementation of JAXR in the Application Server, these are predefined concepts in the jaxrconcepts.xml file, within the ClassificationScheme named PostalAddressAttributes.

To specify the mapping between the JAXR postal address format and another format, you set two connection properties:

- The javax.xml.registry.postalAddressScheme property, which specifies a postal address classification scheme for the connection
- The javax.xml.registry.semanticEquivalences property, which specifies the semantic equivalences between the JAXR format and the other format

For example, suppose you want to use a scheme named MyPostalAddress-Scheme, which you published to a registry with the UUID uuid:f7922839-f1f7-9228-c97d-ce0b4594736c.

```
<JAXRClassificationScheme id="uuid:f7922839-f1f7-9228-c97d-
ce0b4594736c" name="MyPostalAddressScheme">
```

First, you specify the postal address scheme using the id value from the JAXR-ClassificationScheme element (the UUID). Case does not matter:

```
props.setProperty("javax.xml.registry.postalAddressScheme",
    "uuid:f7922839-f1f7-9228-c97d-ce0b4594736c");
```

Next, you specify the mapping from the id of each JAXRConcept element in the default JAXR postal address scheme to the id of its counterpart in the scheme you published:

```
props.setProperty("javax.xml.registry.semanticEquivalences",
    "urn:uuid:PostalAddressAttributes/StreetNumber," +
    "uuid:f7922839-f1f7-9228-c97d-ce0b4594736c/
StreetAddressNumber|" +
    "urn:uuid:PostalAddressAttributes/Street," +
    "urn:uuid:f7922839-f1f7-9228-c97d-ce0b4594736c/
StreetAddress|" +
    "urn:uuid:PostalAddressAttributes/City," +
```

```
"urn:uuid:f7922839-f1f7-9228-c97d-ce0b4594736c/City|" +
"urn:uuid:PostalAddressAttributes/State," +
"urn:uuid:f7922839-f1f7-9228-c97d-ce0b4594736c/State|" +
"urn:uuid:PostalAddressAttributes/PostalCode," +
"urn:uuid:f7922839-f1f7-9228-c97d-ce0b4594736c/ZipCode|" +
"urn:uuid:PostalAddressAttributes/Country," +
"urn:uuid:f7922839-f1f7-9228-c97d-ce0b4594736c/Country");
```

After you create the connection using these properties, you can create a postal address and assign it to the primary contact of the organization before you publish the organization:

```
String streetNumber = "99";
String street = "Imaginary Ave. Suite 33";
String city = "Imaginary City";
String state = "NY";
String country = "USA";
String postalCode = "00000";
String type = "";
PostalAddress postAddr =
  blcm.createPostalAddress(streetNumber, street, city, state,
     country, postalCode, type);
Collection postalAddresses = new ArrayList();
postalAddresses.add(postAddr);
primaryContact.setPostalAddresses(postalAddresses);
```

If the postal address scheme and semantic equivalences for the query are the same as those specified for the publication, a JAXR query can then retrieve the postal address using `PostalAddress` methods. To retrieve postal addresses when you do not know what postal address scheme was used to publish them, you can retrieve them as a collection of `Slot` objects. The `JAXRQueryPostal.java` sample program shows how to do this.

In general, you can create a user-defined postal address taxonomy for any `PostalAddress` tModels that use the well-known categorization in the `uddi-org:types` taxonomy, which has the tModel UUID `uuid:c1acf26d-9672-4404-9d70-39b756e62ab4` with a value of `postalAddress`. You can retrieve the tModel `overviewDoc`, which points to the technical detail for the specification of the scheme, where the taxonomy structure definition can be found. (The JAXR equivalent of an `overviewDoc` is an `ExternalLink`.)

Running the Client Examples

The simple client programs provided with this tutorial can be run from the command line. You can modify them to suit your needs. They allow you to specify the IBM registry, the Microsoft registry, or the Java WSDP Registry Server for queries and updates; you can specify any other UDDI version 2 registry.

The client examples, in the `<INSTALL>/j2eetutorial14/examples/jaxr/simple/src/` directory, are as follows:

- `JAXRQuery.java` shows how to search a registry for organizations.
- `JAXRQueryByNAICSClassification.java` shows how to search a registry using a common classification scheme.
- `JAXRQueryByWSDLClassification.java` shows how to search a registry for Web services that describe themselves by means of a WSDL document.
- `JAXRPublish.java` shows how to publish an organization to a registry.
- `JAXRDelete.java` shows how to remove an organization from a registry.
- `JAXRSaveClassificationScheme.java` shows how to publish a classification scheme (specifically, a postal address scheme) to a registry.
- `JAXRPublishPostal.java` shows how to publish an organization with a postal address for its primary contact.
- `JAXRQueryPostal.java` shows how to retrieve postal address data from an organization.
- `JAXRDeleteScheme.java` shows how to delete a classification scheme from a registry.
- `JAXRPublishConcept.java` shows how to publish a concept for a WSDL document.
- `JAXRPublishHelloOrg.java` shows how to publish an organization with a service binding that refers to a WSDL document.
- `JAXRDeleteConcept.java` shows how to delete a concept.
- `JAXRGetMyObjects.java` lists all the objects that you own in a registry.

The `<INSTALL>/j2eetutorial14/examples/jaxr/simple/` directory also contains the following:

- A `build.xml` file for the examples
- A `JAXRExamples.properties` file, in the `src` subdirectory, that supplies string values used by the sample programs
- A file called `postalconcepts.xml` that serves as the taxonomy file for the postal address examples

You do not have to have the Application Server running in order to run these client examples. You do need to have it running in order to run `JAXRPublishConcept.java` and `JAXRPublishHelloOrg.java`.

Before You Compile the Examples

Before you compile the examples, edit the file `<INSTALL>`/j2eetutorial14/ examples/jaxr/simple/src/JAXRExamples.properties as follows.

1. Edit the following lines to specify the registry you wish to access. For both the `queryURL` and the `publishURL` assignments, comment out all but the registry you wish to access. The default is the Java WSDP Registry Server.

   ```
   ## Uncomment one pair of query and publish URLs.
   ## IBM:
   #query.url=http://uddi.ibm.com/testregistry/inquiryapi
   #publish.url=https://uddi.ibm.com/testregistry/publishapi
   ## Microsoft:
   #query.url=http://test.uddi.microsoft.com/inquire
   #publish.url=https://test.uddi.microsoft.com/publish
   ## Registry Server:
   query.url=http://localhost:8080/RegistryServer/
   publish.url=http://localhost:8080/RegistryServer/
   ```

   If you are using the Java WSDP Registry Server and if it is running on a system other than your own, specify the fully qualified host name instead of `localhost`. Do not use `https:` for the `publishURL`. If you specified a nondefault HTTP port when you installed the Application Server, change `8080` to the correct value for your system.

   The IBM and Microsoft registries both contain a considerable amount of data that you can perform queries on. Moreover, you do not have to register if you are only going to perform queries.

   We have not included the URLs of the SAP registry; feel free to add them.

   If you want to publish to any of the public registries, the registration process for obtaining access to them is not difficult (see Preliminaries: Getting Access to a Registry, page 394). Each of them, however, allows you to have only one organization registered at a time. If you publish an organization to one of them, you must delete it before you can publish another. Because the organization that the `JAXRPublish` example publishes is fictitious, you will want to delete it immediately anyway.

Be aware also that because the public registries are test registries, they do not always behave reliably.

The Java WSDP Registry Server gives you more freedom to experiment with JAXR. You can publish as many organizations, concepts, and classification schemes to it as you wish. However, this registry comes with an empty database, so you must publish data to it yourself before you can perform queries on the data.

2. To use a public registry, edit the following lines to specify the user name and password you obtained when you registered with the registry. Do not change the lines if you will use the Registry Server.

```
## To use a public registry, edit user name and password.
## To use the Registry Server, use testuser/testuser.
registry.username=testuser
registry.password=testuser
```

3. If you will be using a public registry, edit the following lines, which contain empty strings for the proxy hosts, to specify your own proxy settings. The proxy host is the system on your network through which you access the Internet; you usually specify it in your Internet browser settings. You can leave this value empty to use the Java WSDP Registry Server.

```
## HTTP and HTTPS proxy host and port;
##    ignored by Registry Server
http.proxyHost=
http.proxyPort=8080
https.proxyHost=
https.proxyPort=8080
```

The proxy ports have the value 8080, which is the usual one; change this string if your proxy uses a different port.

For a public registry, your entries usually follow this pattern:

```
http.proxyHost=proxyhost.mydomain
http.proxyPort=8080
https.proxyHost=proxyhost.mydomain
https.proxyPort=8080
```

4. If you are running the Application Server on a system other than your own or if it is using a nondefault HTTP port, change the following lines:

```
link.uri=http://localhost:8080/hello-jaxrpc/hello?WSDL
...
wsdlorg.svcbnd.uri=http://localhost:8080/hello-jaxrpc/hello
```

Specify the fully qualified host name instead of localhost, or change 8080 to the correct value for your system.

5. Feel free to change any of the organization data in the remainder of the file. This data is used by the publishing and postal address examples. If you will be using a public registry, try to make the organization names unusual so that queries will return relatively few results.

You can edit the `src/JAXRExamples.properties` file at any time. The `asant` targets that run the client examples will use the latest version of the file.

Compiling the Examples

To compile the programs, go to the `<INSTALL>/j2eetutorial14/examples/jaxr/simple/` directory. A `build.xml` file allows you to use the following command to compile all the examples:

```
asant compile
```

The `asant` tool creates a subdirectory called `build`.

The runtime classpath setting in the `build.xml` file lists several JAR files in the Application Server lib directory. If you will run the examples with the Java WSDP Registry Server, edit this class path (named `jaxr.classpath`) to contain only one include line:

```
<include name = "*.jar"/>
```

Running the Examples

If you are running the examples with the Java WSDP Registry Server, start the Application Server as described in Starting and Stopping the Application Server (page 25).

The Registry Server is a Web application that is loaded when the Application Server starts.

You do not need to start the Application Server in order to run the examples against public registries.

Running the JAXRPublish Example

To run the `JAXRPublish` program, use the `run-publish` target with no command-line arguments:

```
asant run-publish
```

The program output displays the string value of the key of the new organization, which is named The Coffee Break.

After you run the `JAXRPublish` program but before you run `JAXRDelete`, you can run `JAXRQuery` to look up the organization you published.

Running the JAXRQuery Example

To run the `JAXRQuery` example, use the `asant` target `run-query`. Specify a `query-string` argument on the command line to search the registry for organizations whose names contain that string. For example, the following command line searches for organizations whose names contain the string "coff" (searching is not case-sensitive):

```
asant -Dquery-string=coff run-query
```

Running the JAXRQueryByNAICSClassification Example

After you run the `JAXRPublish` program, you can also run the `JAXRQueryByNAICSClassification` example, which looks for organizations that use the Snack and Nonalcoholic Beverage Bars classification, the same one used for the organization created by `JAXRPublish`. To do so, use the `asant` target `run-query-naics`:

```
asant run-query-naics
```

Running the JAXRDelete Example

To run the `JAXRDelete` program, specify the key string displayed by the `JAXRPublish` program as input to the `run-delete` target:

```
asant -Dkey-string=keyString run-delete
```

Publishing a Classification Scheme

To publish organizations with postal addresses to public registries, you must first publish a classification scheme for the postal address.

To run the `JAXRSaveClassificationScheme` program, use the target `run-save-scheme`:

```
asant run-save-scheme
```

The program returns a UUID string, which you will use in the next section.

You do not have to run this program if you are using the Java WSDP Registry Server, because it does not validate these objects.

The public registries allow you to own more than one classification scheme at a time (the limit is usually a total of about 10 classification schemes and concepts put together).

Running the Postal Address Examples

Before you run the postal address examples, open the file `src/postalconcepts.xml` in an editor. Wherever you see the string `uuid-from-save`, replace it with the UUID string returned by the `run-save-scheme` target (including the `uuid:` prefix). For the Java WSDP Registry Server, you can use any string that is formatted as a UUID.

For a given registry, you only need to publish the classification scheme and edit `postalconcepts.xml` once. After you perform those two steps, you can run the `JAXRPublishPostal` and `JAXRQueryPostal` programs multiple times.

1. Run the `JAXRPublishPostal` program. Specify the string you entered in the `postalconcepts.xml` file, including the `uuid:` prefix, as input to the `run-publish-postal` target:

   ```
   asant -Duuid-string=uuidstring run-publish-postal
   ```

   The *uuidstring* would look something like this (case is not significant):

   ```
   uuid:938d9ccd-a74a-4c7e-864a-e6e2c6822519
   ```

   The program output displays the string value of the key of the new organization.

2. Run the `JAXRQueryPostal` program. The `run-query-postal` target specifies the `postalconcepts.xml` file in a `<sysproperty>` tag.

   As input to the `run-query-postal` target, specify both a `query-string` argument and a `uuid-string` argument on the command line to search the registry for the organization published by the `run-publish-postal` target:

```
asant -Dquery-string=coffee
-Duuid-string=uuidstring run-query-postal
```

The postal address for the primary contact will appear correctly with the JAXR `PostalAddress` methods. Any postal addresses found that use other postal address schemes will appear as `Slot` lines.

3. If you are using a public registry, make sure to follow the instructions in Running the JAXRDelete Example (page 421) to delete the organization you published.

Deleting a Classification Scheme

To delete the classification scheme you published after you have finished using it, run the `JAXRDeleteScheme` program using the `run-delete-scheme` target:

```
asant -Duuid-string=uuidstring run-delete-scheme
```

For the public UDDI registries, deleting a classification scheme removes it from the registry logically but not physically. The classification scheme will still be visible if, for example, you call the method `QueryManager.getRegisteredObjects`. However, you can no longer use the classification scheme. Therefore, you may prefer not to delete the classification scheme from the registry, in case you want to use it again. The public registries normally allow you to own up to 10 of these objects.

Publishing a Concept for a WSDL Document

To publish the location of the WSDL document for the JAX-RPC `Hello` service, first deploy the service as described in Creating a Simple Web Service and Client with JAX-RPC (page 314).

Then run the `JAXRPublishConcept` program using the `run-publish-concept` target:

```
asant run-publish-concept
```

The program output displays the UUID string of the new specification concept, which is named HelloConcept. You will use this string in the next section.

After you run the `JAXRPublishConcept` program, you can run `JAXRPublish-HelloOrg` to publish an organization that uses this concept.

Publishing an Organization with a WSDL Document in Its Service Binding

To run the `JAXRPublishHelloOrg` example, use the `asant` target `run-publish-hello-org`. Specify the string returned from `JAXRPublishConcept` (including the `uuid:` prefix) as input to this target:

```
asant -Duuid-string=uuidstring run-publish-hello-org
```

The *uuidstring* would look something like this (case is not significant):

```
UUID:A499E230-5296-11D8-B936-000629DC0A53
```

The program output displays the string value of the key of the new organization, which is named Hello Organization.

After you publish the organization, run the `JAXRQueryByWSDLClassification` example to search for it. To delete it, run `JAXRDelete`.

Running the JAXRQueryByWSDLClassification Example

To run the `JAXRQueryByWSDLClassification` example, use the `asant` target `run-query-wsdl`. Specify a `query-string` argument on the command line to search the registry for specification concepts whose names contain that string. For example, the following command line searches for concepts whose names contain the string "`helloconcept`" (searching is not case-sensitive):

```
asant -Dquery-string=helloconcept run-query-wsdl
```

This example finds the concept and organization you published. A common string such as "`hello`" returns many results from the public registries and is likely to run for several minutes.

Deleting a Concept

To run the `JAXRDeleteConcept` program, specify the UUID string displayed by the `JAXRPublishConcept` program as input to the `run-delete-concept` target:

```
asant -Duuid-string=uuidString run-delete-concept
```

Deleting a concept from a public UDDI registry is similar to deleting a classification scheme: The concept is removed logically but not physically. Do not delete the concept until after you have deleted any organizations that refer to it.

Getting a List of Your Registry Objects

To get a list of the objects you own in the registry—organizations, classification schemes, and concepts—run the `JAXRGetMyObjects` program by using the `run-get-objects` target:

```
asant run-get-objects
```

If you run this program with the Java WSDP Registry Server, it returns all the standard UDDI taxonomies provided with the Registry Server and not just the objects you have created.

Other Targets

To remove the `build` directory and class files, use the command

```
asant clean
```

To obtain a syntax reminder for the targets, use the command

```
asant -projecthelp
```

Using JAXR Clients in J2EE Applications

You can create J2EE applications that use JAXR clients to access registries. This section explains how to write, compile, package, deploy, and run a J2EE application that uses JAXR to publish an organization to a registry and then query the registry for that organization. The application in this section uses two components: an application client and a stateless session bean.

The section covers the following topics:

- Coding the application client: `MyAppClient.java`
- Coding the `PubQuery` session bean
- Compiling the source files
- Importing certificates
- Starting the Application Server
- Creating JAXR resources
- Creating and packaging the application
- Deploying the application
- Running the application client

You will find the source files for this section in the directory `<INSTALL>/`
`j2eetutorial14/examples/jaxr/clientsession`. Path names in this section
are relative to this directory.

The following directory contains a built version of this application:

> `<INSTALL>/j2eetutorial14/examples/jaxr/provided-ears`

If you run into difficulty at any time, you can open the EAR file in `deploytool`
and compare that file to your own version.

Coding the Application Client: MyAppClient.java

The application client class, `src/MyAppClient.java`, obtains a handle to the
`PubQuery` enterprise bean's remote home interface, using the JNDI API naming
context `java:comp/env`. The program then creates an instance of the bean and
calls the bean's two business methods: `executePublish` and `executeQuery`.

Before you compile the application, edit the `PubQueryBeanExamples.proper-`
`ties` file in the same way you edited the `JAXRExamples.properties` file to run
the simple examples.

1. If you are using the Java WSDP Registry Server, specify the correct host
   and port values for the `queryManagerURL` and `lifeCycleManagerURL`
   entries. To use another registry, comment out the property that specifies the
   Registry Server, and remove the comment from the other registry.

2. If you are using a public registry, change the values for the regis-try.username and registry.password properties to specify the user name and password you obtained when you registered with the registry. Change the values for the http.proxyHost and https.proxyHost entries so that they specify the system on your network through which you access the Internet.

Coding the PubQuery Session Bean

The PubQuery bean is a stateless session bean that has one create method and two business methods. The bean uses remote interfaces rather than local interfaces because it is accessed from the application client.

The remote home interface source file is src/PubQueryHome.java.

The remote interface, src/PubQueryRemote.java, declares two business methods: executePublish and executeQuery. The bean class, src/PubQuery-Bean.java, implements the executePublish and executeQuery methods and their helper methods getName, getDescription, and getKey. These methods are very similar to the methods of the same name in the simple examples JAXR-Query.java and JAXRPublish.java. The executePublish method uses information in the file PubQueryBeanExample.properties to create an organization named The Coffee Enterprise Bean Break. The executeQuery method uses the organization name, specified in the application client code, to locate this organization.

The bean class also implements the required methods ejbCreate, setSession-Context, ejbRemove, ejbActivate, and ejbPassivate.

The ejbCreate method of the bean class allocates resources—in this case, by looking up the ConnectionFactory and creating the Connection.

The ejbRemove method must deallocate the resources that were allocated by the ejbCreate method. In this case, the ejbRemove method closes the Connection.

Compiling the Source Files

To compile the application source files, go to the directory <INSTALL>/ j2eetutorial14/examples/jaxr/clientsession. Use the following command:

```
asant compile
```

The `compile` target places the properties file and the class files in the `build` directory.

Importing Certificates

If you will be using the Java WSDP Registry Server, skip this section.

In order to run the `ClientSessionApp` application against the Microsoft or IBM registry, you need to import certificates from your version of the Java 2, Standard Edition Software Development Kit (J2SE SDK) into the Application Server. The simple client programs use the J2SE SDK certificates, but the Application Server does not have these certificates, so running a J2EE application that uses JAXR against an external registry requires special steps.

1. Verify the alias names of the Certificate Authorities (CA) you want to migrate by running the following command:

   ```
   keytool -list -v -keystore J2SE_SDK_truststore_file
   ```

   The default location for *J2SE_SDK_truststore_file* is *<JAVA_HOME>*/`jre/lib/security/cacerts`.

   To access the Microsoft registry, you need the CA with the alias name `verisignclass3ca`. To access the IBM registry, you need the CA with the alias name `verisignserverca`.

2. Export the CA with the desired alias name from the J2SE SDK truststore to a file in the current directory:

   ```
   keytool -export -alias alias_name -keystore
   J2SE_SDK_truststore_file -file export_CA_file
   ```

   When you are asked for a password, type `changeit`.

   For example, you could type the following (all on one line) to export the Microsoft CA:

   ```
   keytool -export -alias verisignclass3ca -keystore
   C:\j2sdk1.4.2_04\jre\lib\security\cacerts -file ca_for_ms
   ```

3. Import the *export_CA_file* into the Application Server truststore:

   ```
   keytool -import -alias alias_name -storepass changeit
   -keystore <INSTALL>/domains/domain1/config/cacerts.jks
   -file export_CA_file
   ```

   When you are asked, "Trust this certificate?", type `yes`.

For example, you could type the following (all on one line) to import the CA you just exported:

```
keytool -import -alias verisignclass3ca -storepass changeit
-keystore
C:\Sun\AppServer\domains\domain1\config\cacerts.jks
-file ca_for_ms
```

4. If the Application Server is running, stop and restart it.

Starting the Application Server

To run this example, you need to start the Application Server. Follow the instructions in Starting and Stopping the Application Server (page 25).

Creating JAXR Resources

To use JAXR in a J2EE application that uses the Application Server, you need to access the JAXR resource adapter (see Implementing a JAXR Client, page 393) through a connector connection pool and a connector resource. You can create these resources in the Admin Console.

If you have not done so, start the Admin Console as described in Starting the Admin Console (page 27).

To create the connector connection pool, perform the following steps:

1. Expand the Connectors node, and then click Connector Connection Pools.
2. Click New.
3. On the Create Connector Connection Pool page:
   a. Type jaxr-pool in the Name field.
   b. Choose jaxr-ra from the Resource Adapter combo box.
   c. Click Next.
4. On the next page, choose javax.xml.registry.ConnectionFactory (the only choice) from the Connection Definition combo box, and click Next.
5. On the next page, click Finish.

To create the connector resource, perform the following steps:

1. Under the Connectors node, click Connector Resources.
2. Click New. The Create Connector Resource page appears.
3. In the JNDI Name field, type `eis/JAXR`.
4. Choose `jaxr-pool` from the Pool Name combo box.
5. Click OK.

If you are in a hurry, you can create these objects using the following `asant` target in the `build.xml` file for this example:

```
asant create-resource
```

Creating and Packaging the Application

Creating and packaging this application involve four steps:

1. Starting `deploytool` and creating the application
2. Packaging the session bean
3. Packaging the application client
4. Checking the JNDI names

Starting deploytool and Creating the Application

1. Start `deploytool`. On Windows systems, choose Start→Programs→Sun Microsystems→J2EE 1.4 SDK→Deploytool. On UNIX systems, use the `deploytool` command.
2. Choose File→New→Application.
3. Click Browse (next to the Application File Name field), and use the file chooser to locate the directory `clientsession`.
4. In the File Name field, type `ClientSessionApp`.
5. Click New Application.
6. Click OK.

Packaging the Session Bean

1. Choose File→New→Enterprise Bean to start the Enterprise Bean wizard. Then click Next.

2. In the EJB JAR General Settings screen:

   a. Select Create New JAR Module in Application, and make sure that the application is `ClientSessionApp`.

   b. In the JAR Name field, type `PubQueryJAR`.

   c. Click Edit Contents.

   d. In the dialog box, locate the `clientsession/build` directory. Select `PubQueryBean.class`, `PubQueryHome.class`, `PubQueryRemote.class`, and `PubQueryBeanExample.properties` from the Available Files tree area. Click Add, and then OK.

3. In the Bean General Settings screen:

   a. From the Enterprise Bean Class menu, choose `PubQueryBean`.

   b. Verify that the Enterprise Bean Name is `PubQueryBean` and that the Enterprise Bean Type is Stateless Session.

   c. In the Remote Interfaces area, choose `PubQueryHome` from the Remote Home Interface menu, and choose `PubQueryRemote` from the Remote Interface menu.

After you finish the wizard, perform the following steps:

1. Click the `PubQueryBean` node, and then click the Transactions tab. In the inspector pane, select the Container-Managed radio button.

2. Click the `PubQueryBean` node, and then click the Resource Ref's tab. In the inspector pane:

   a. Click Add.

   b. In the Coded Name field, type `eis/JAXR`.

   c. From the Type menu, choose `javax.xml.registry.ConnectionFactory`.

   d. In the Deployment Settings area, type `eis/JAXR` in the JNDI name field, and type `j2ee` in both the User Name and the Password fields.

Packaging the Application Client

1. Choose File→New→Application Client to start the Application Client Wizard. Then click Next.

2. In the JAR File Contents screen:

   a. Make sure that Create New AppClient Module in Application is selected and that the application is `ClientSessionApp`.

   b. In the AppClient Name field, type `MyAppClient`.

   c. Click Edit Contents.

   d. In the dialog box, locate the `clientsession/build` directory. Select `MyAppClient.class` from the Available Files tree area. Click Add, and then OK.

3. In the General screen, select `MyAppClient` in the Main Class combo box.

After you finish the wizard, click the EJB Ref's tab, and then click Add in the inspector pane. In the dialog box, follow these steps:

1. Type `ejb/remote/PubQuery` in the Coded Name field.

2. Choose Session from the EJB Type menu.

3. Choose Remote from the Interfaces menu.

4. Type `PubQueryHome` in the Home Interface field.

5. Type `PubQueryRemote` in the Local/Remote Interface field.

6. In the Target EJB area, select JNDI Name and type `PubQueryBean` in the field. The session bean uses remote interfaces, so the client accesses the bean through the JNDI name rather than the bean name.

Checking the JNDI Names

Select the application, click Sun-specific Settings on the General page, and verify that the JNDI names for the application components are correct. They should appear as shown in Tables 10–3 and 10–4.

Table 10–3 Application Pane for `ClientSessionApp`

Component Type	Component	JNDI Name
EJB	PubQueryBean	PubQueryBean

Table 10–4 References Pane for `ClientSessionApp`

Ref. Type	Referenced By	Reference Name	JNDI Name
EJB Ref	`MyAppClient`	`ejb/remote/PubQuery`	`PubQueryBean`
Resource	`PubQueryBean`	`eis/JAXR`	`eis/JAXR`

Deploying the Application

1. Save the application.
2. Choose Tools→Deploy.
3. In the dialog box, type your administrative user name and password (if they are not already filled in), and click OK.
4. In the Application Client Stub Directory area, select the Return Client Jar checkbox, and make sure that the directory is `clientsession`.
5. Click OK.
6. In the Distribute Module dialog box, click Close when the process completes. You will find a file named `ClientSessionAppClient.jar` in the specified directory.

Running the Application Client

To run the client, use the following command:

```
appclient -client ClientSessionAppClient.jar
```

The program output in the terminal window looks like this:

```
Looking up EJB reference
Looked up home
Narrowed home
Got the EJB
See server log for bean output
```

In the server log, you will find the output from the `executePublish` and `executeQuery` methods, wrapped in logging information.

After you run the example using a public registry, use the `run-delete` target in the `simple` directory to delete the organization that was published.

Further Information

For more information about JAXR, registries, and Web services, see the following:

- Java Specification Request (JSR) 93: JAXR 1.0:
  `http://jcp.org/jsr/detail/093.jsp`
- JAXR home page:
  `http://java.sun.com/xml/jaxr/`
- Universal Description, Discovery and Integration (UDDI) project:
  `http://www.uddi.org/`
- ebXML:
  `http://www.ebxml.org/`
- Open Source JAXR Provider for ebXML Registries:
  `http://ebxmlrr.sourceforge.net/jaxr/`
- Java 2 Platform, Enterprise Edition:
  `http://java.sun.com/j2ee/`
- Java Technology and XML:
  `http://java.sun.com/xml/`
- Java Technology and Web Services:
  `http://java.sun.com/webservices/`

11

Java Servlet Technology

As soon as the Web began to be used for delivering services, service providers recognized the need for dynamic content. Applets, one of the earliest attempts toward this goal, focused on using the client platform to deliver dynamic user experiences. At the same time, developers also investigated using the server platform for this purpose. Initially, Common Gateway Interface (CGI) scripts were the main technology used to generate dynamic content. Although widely used, CGI scripting technology has a number of shortcomings, including platform dependence and lack of scalability. To address these limitations, Java servlet technology was created as a portable way to provide dynamic, user-oriented content.

What Is a Servlet?

A *servlet* is a Java programming language class that is used to extend the capabilities of servers that host applications access via a request-response programming model. Although servlets can respond to any type of request, they are commonly used to extend the applications hosted by Web servers. For such applications, Java Servlet technology defines HTTP-specific servlet classes.

The `javax.servlet` and `javax.servlet.http` packages provide interfaces and classes for writing servlets. All servlets must implement the `Servlet` interface, which defines life-cycle methods. When implementing a generic service, you can use or extend the GenericServlet class provided with the Java Servlet API. The HttpServlet class provides methods, such as doGet and doPost, for handling HTTP-specific services.

This chapter focuses on writing servlets that generate responses to HTTP requests. Some knowledge of the HTTP protocol is assumed; if you are unfamiliar with this protocol, you can get a brief introduction to HTTP in Appendix C.

The Example Servlets

This chapter uses the Duke's Bookstore application to illustrate the tasks involved in programming servlets. Table 11–1 lists the servlets that handle each bookstore function. Each programming task is illustrated by one or more servlets. For example, BookDetailsServlet illustrates how to handle HTTP GET requests, BookDetailsServlet and CatalogServlet show how to construct responses, and CatalogServlet illustrates how to track session information.

Table 11–1   Duke's Bookstore Example Servlets

Function	Servlet
Enter the bookstore	BookStoreServlet
Create the bookstore banner	BannerServlet
Browse the bookstore catalog	CatalogServlet
Put a book in a shopping cart	CatalogServlet, BookDetailsServlet
Get detailed information on a specific book	BookDetailsServlet
Display the shopping cart	ShowCartServlet
Remove one or more books from the shopping cart	ShowCartServlet
Buy the books in the shopping cart	CashierServlet
Send an acknowledgment of the purchase	ReceiptServlet

The data for the bookstore application is maintained in a database and accessed through the database access class `database.BookDBAO`. The `database` package also contains the class `BookDetails`, which represents a book. The shopping cart and shopping cart items are represented by the classes `cart.ShoppingCart` and `cart.ShoppingCartItem`, respectively.

The source code for the bookstore application is located in the `<INSTALL>/ j2eetutorial14/examples/web/bookstore1/` directory, which is created when you unzip the tutorial bundle (see Building the Examples, page xli). A sample `bookstore1.war` is provided in `<INSTALL>/j2eetutorial14/examples/ web/provided-wars/`. To build, package, deploy, and run the example using `deploytool`, follow these steps:

1. Build and package the bookstore common files as described in Duke's Bookstore Examples (page 100).

2. In a terminal window, go to `<INSTALL>/j2eetutorial14/examples/ web/bookstore1/`.

3. Run `asant build`. This target will spawn any necessary compilations and copy files to the `<INSTALL>/j2eetutorial14/examples/web/bookstore1/ build/` directory.

4. Start the Application Server.

5. Perform all the operations described in Accessing Databases from Web Applications (page 100).

6. Start `deploytool`.

7. Create a Web application called `bookstore1` by running the New Web Component wizard. Select File→New →Web Component.

8. In the New Web Component wizard:

    a. Select the Create New Stand-Alone WAR Module radio button.

    b. In the WAR Location field, enter `<INSTALL>/j2eetutorial14/ examples/web/bookstore1/bookstore1.war`.

    c. In the WAR Name field, enter `bookstore1`.

    d. In the Context Root field, enter `/bookstore1`.

    e. Click Edit Contents.

    f. In the Edit Archive Contents dialog box, navigate to `<INSTALL>/ j2eetutorial14/examples/web/bookstore1/build/`. Select error-page.html, duke.books.gif, and the `servlets`, `database`, `filters`, `listeners`, and `util` packages. Click Add.

g. Add the shared bookstore library. Navigate to *<INSTALL>/* `j2eetutorial14/examples/web/bookstore/dist/`. Select `book-` `store.jar` and click Add.

h. Click OK.

i. Click Next.

j. Select the Servlet radio button.

k. Click Next.

l. Select `BannerServlet` from the Servlet Class combo box.

m. Click Finish.

9. Add the rest of the Web components listed in Table 11–2. For each servlet:

a. Select File→New→Web Component.

b. Click the Add to Existing WAR Module radio button. Because the WAR contains all the servlet classes, you do not have to add any more content.

c. Click Next.

d. Select the Servlet radio button.

e. Click Next.

f. Select the servlet from the Servlet Class combo box.

g. Click Finish.

Table 11–2 Duke's Bookstore Web Components

Web Component Name	Servlet Class	Alias
BannerServlet	BannerServlet	/banner
BookStoreServlet	BookStoreServlet	/bookstore
CatalogServlet	CatalogServlet	/bookcatalog
BookDetailsServlet	BookDetailsServlet	/bookdetails
ShowCartServlet	ShowCartServlet	/bookshowcart
CashierServlet	CashierServlet	/bookcashier
ReceiptServlet	ReceiptServlet	/bookreceipt

10. Set the alias for each Web component.

    a. Select the component.

    b. Select the Aliases tab.

    c. Click the Add button.

    d. Enter the alias.

11. Add the listener class `listeners.ContextListener` (described in Handling Servlet Life-Cycle Events, page 441).

    a. Select the Event Listeners tab.

    b. Click Add.

    c. Select the `listeners.ContextListener` class from the drop-down field in the Event Listener Classes pane.

12. Add an error page (described in Handling Errors, page 443).

    a. Select the File Ref's tab.

    b. In the Error Mapping pane, click Add Error.

    c. Enter `exception.BookNotFoundException` in the Error/Exception field.

    d. Enter `/errorpage.html` in the Resource to be Called field.

    e. Repeat for `exception.BooksNotFoundException` and `javax.servlet.UnavailableException`.

13. Add the filters `filters.HitCounterFilter` and `filters.OrderFilter` (described in Filtering Requests and Responses, page 454).

    a. Select the Filter Mapping tab.

    b. Click Edit Filter List.

    c. Click Add Filter.

    d. Select `filters.HitCounterFilter` from the Filter Class column. `deploytool` will automatically enter `HitCounterFilter` in the Display Name column.

    e. Click Add Filter.

    f. Select `filters.OrderFilter` from the Filter Class column. `deploytool` will automatically enter `OrderFilter` in the Display Name column.

    g. Click OK.

    h. Click Add.

    i. Select `HitCounterFilter` from the Filter Name drop-down menu.

    j. Select the Filter this Servlet radio button in the Filter target frame.

    k. Select the `BookStoreServlet` from the Servlet Name drop-down menu.

    l. Click OK.

    m. Repeat for `OrderFilter`. Select `ReceiptServlet` from the Servlet Name drop-down menu.

14. Add a resource reference for the database.

    a. Select the Resource Ref's tab.

    b. Click Add.

    c. Enter `jdbc/BookDB` in the Coded Name field.

    d. Accept the default type `javax.sql.DataSource`.

    e. Accept the default authorization `Container`.

    f. Accept the default selected `Shareable`.

    g. Enter `jdbc/BookDB` in the JNDI name field of the Sun-specific Settings frame.

15. Select File→Save.

16. Deploy the application.

    a. Select Tools→Deploy.

    b. In the Connection Settings frame, enter the user name and password you specified when you installed the Application Server.

    c. Click OK.

17. To run the application, open the bookstore URL `http://localhost:8080/bookstore1/bookstore`.

Troubleshooting

The Duke's Bookstore database access object returns the following exceptions:

- `BookNotFoundException`: Returned if a book can't be located in the bookstore database. This will occur if you haven't loaded the bookstore database with data by running `asant create-db_common` or if the database server hasn't been started or it has crashed.

- `BooksNotFoundException`: Returned if the bookstore data can't be retrieved. This will occur if you haven't loaded the bookstore database with data or if the database server hasn't been started or it has crashed.

- UnavailableException: Returned if a servlet can't retrieve the Web context attribute representing the bookstore. This will occur if the database server hasn't been started.

Because we have specified an error page, you will see the message

```
The application is unavailable. Please try later.
```

If you don't specify an error page, the Web container generates a default page containing the message

```
A Servlet Exception Has Occurred
```

and a stack trace that can help you diagnose the cause of the exception. If you use `errorpage.html`, you will have to look in the server log to determine the cause of the exception.

Servlet Life Cycle

The life cycle of a servlet is controlled by the container in which the servlet has been deployed. When a request is mapped to a servlet, the container performs the following steps.

1. If an instance of the servlet does not exist, the Web container
   a. Loads the servlet class.
   b. Creates an instance of the servlet class.
   c. Initializes the servlet instance by calling the `init` method. Initialization is covered in Initializing a Servlet (page 447).
2. Invokes the `service` method, passing request and response objects. Service methods are discussed in Writing Service Methods (page 448).

If the container needs to remove the servlet, it finalizes the servlet by calling the servlet's `destroy` method. Finalization is discussed in Finalizing a Servlet (page 467).

Handling Servlet Life-Cycle Events

You can monitor and react to events in a servlet's life cycle by defining listener objects whose methods get invoked when life-cycle events occur. To use these listener objects you must define and specify the listener class.

Defining the Listener Class

You define a listener class as an implementation of a listener interface. Table 11–3 lists the events that can be monitored and the corresponding interface that must be implemented. When a listener method is invoked, it is passed an event that contains information appropriate to the event. For example, the methods in the `HttpSessionListener` interface are passed an `HttpSessionEvent`, which contains an `HttpSession`.

The `listeners.ContextListener` class creates and removes the database access and counter objects used in the Duke's Bookstore application. The methods retrieve the Web context object from `ServletContextEvent` and then store (and remove) the objects as servlet context attributes.

Table 11–3 Servlet Life-Cycle Events

Object	Event	Listener Interface and Event Class
Web context (see Accessing the Web Context, page 463)	Initialization and destruction	`javax.servlet.ServletContextListener` and `ServletContextEvent`
	Attribute added, removed, or replaced	`javax.servlet.ServletContextAttributeListener` and `ServletContextAttributeEvent`
Session (See Maintaining Client State, page 464)	Creation, invalidation, activation, passivation, and timeout	`javax.servlet.http.HttpSessionListener`, `javax.servlet.http.HttpSessionActivationListener`, and `HttpSessionEvent`
	Attribute added, removed, or replaced	`javax.servlet.http.HttpSessionAttributeListener` and `HttpSessionBindingEvent`
Request	A servlet request has started being processed by Web components	`javax.servlet.ServletRequestListener` and `ServletRequestEvent`
	Attribute added, removed, or replaced	`javax.servlet.ServletRequestAttributeListener` and `ServletRequestAttributeEvent`

```
import database.BookDBAO;
import javax.servlet.*;
import util.Counter;

public final class ContextListener
   implements ServletContextListener {
   private ServletContext context = null;
   public void contextInitialized(ServletContextEvent event) {
      context = event.getServletContext();
      try {
         BookDBAO bookDB = new BookDBAO();
         context.setAttribute("bookDB", bookDB);
      } catch (Exception ex) {
         System.out.println(
            "Couldn't create database: " + ex.getMessage());
      }
      Counter counter = new Counter();
      context.setAttribute("hitCounter", counter);
      counter = new Counter();
      context.setAttribute("orderCounter", counter);
   }

   public void contextDestroyed(ServletContextEvent event) {
      context = event.getServletContext();
      BookDBAO bookDB = context.getAttribute("bookDB");
      bookDB.remove();
      context.removeAttribute("bookDB");
      context.removeAttribute("hitCounter");
      context.removeAttribute("orderCounter");
   }
}
```

Specifying Event Listener Classes

You specify an event listener class in the Event Listener tab of the WAR inspector. Review step 11. in The Example Servlets (page 436) for the deploytool procedure for specifying the ContextListener listener class.

Handling Errors

Any number of exceptions can occur when a servlet is executed. When an exception occurs, the Web container will generate a default page containing the message

```
A Servlet Exception Has Occurred
```

But you can also specify that the container should return a specific error page for a given exception. Review step 12. in The Example Servlets (page 436) for `deploytool` procedures for mapping the exceptions `exception.BookNotFound`, `exception.BooksNotFound`, and `exception.OrderException` returned by the Duke's Bookstore application to `errorpage.html`.

Sharing Information

Web components, like most objects, usually work with other objects to accomplish their tasks. There are several ways they can do this. They can use private helper objects (for example, JavaBeans components), they can share objects that are attributes of a public scope, they can use a database, and they can invoke other Web resources. The Java servlet technology mechanisms that allow a Web component to invoke other Web resources are described in Invoking Other Web Resources (page 460).

Using Scope Objects

Collaborating Web components share information via objects that are maintained as attributes of four scope objects. You access these attributes using the `[get|set]Attribute` methods of the class representing the scope. Table 11–4 lists the scope objects.

Table 11–4   Scope Objects

Scope Object	Class	Accessible From
Web context	`javax.servlet.` `ServletContext`	Web components within a Web context. See Accessing the Web Context (page 463).
Session	`javax.servlet.` `http.HttpSession`	Web components handling a request that belongs to the session. See Maintaining Client State (page 464).
Request	subtype of `javax.servlet.` `ServletRequest`	Web components handling the request.
Page	`javax.servlet.` `jsp.JspContext`	The JSP page that creates the object. See Using Implicit Objects (page 488).

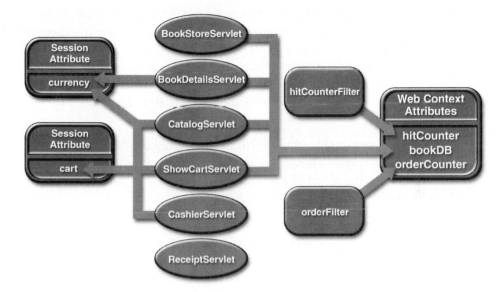

Figure 11–1 Duke's Bookstore Scoped Attributes

Figure 11–1 shows the scoped attributes maintained by the Duke's Bookstore application.

Controlling Concurrent Access to Shared Resources

In a multithreaded server, it is possible for shared resources to be accessed concurrently. In addition to scope object attributes, shared resources include in-memory data (such as instance or class variables) and external objects such as files, database connections, and network connections. Concurrent access can arise in several situations:

- Multiple Web components accessing objects stored in the Web context.
- Multiple Web components accessing objects stored in a session.
- Multiple threads within a Web component accessing instance variables. A Web container will typically create a thread to handle each request. If you want to ensure that a servlet instance handles only one request at a time, a servlet can implement the SingleThreadModel interface. If a servlet implements this interface, you are guaranteed that no two threads will execute concurrently in the servlet's service method. A Web container can

implement this guarantee by synchronizing access to a single instance of the servlet, or by maintaining a pool of Web component instances and dispatching each new request to a free instance. This interface does not prevent synchronization problems that result from Web components accessing shared resources such as static class variables or external objects. In addition, the Servlet 2.4 specification deprecates the `SingleThreadModel` interface.

When resources can be accessed concurrently, they can be used in an inconsistent fashion. To prevent this, you must control the access using the synchronization techniques described in the Threads lesson in *The Java Tutorial*, by Mary Campione et al. (Addison-Wesley, 2000).

In the preceding section we show five scoped attributes shared by more than one servlet: bookDB, `cart`, `currency`, `hitCounter`, and `orderCounter`. The bookDB attribute is discussed in the next section. The cart, currency, and counters can be set and read by multiple multithreaded servlets. To prevent these objects from being used inconsistently, access is controlled by synchronized methods. For example, here is the `util.Counter` class:

```
public class Counter {
   private int counter;
   public Counter() {
      counter = 0;
   }
   public synchronized int getCounter() {
      return counter;
   }
   public synchronized int setCounter(int c) {
      counter = c;
      return counter;
   }
   public synchronized int incCounter() {
      return(++counter);
   }
}
```

Accessing Databases

Data that is shared between Web components and is persistent between invocations of a Web application is usually maintained by a database. Web components use the JDBC API to access relational databases. The data for the bookstore application is maintained in a database and is accessed through the database access class `database.BookDBAO`. For example, `ReceiptServlet` invokes the

BookDBAO.buyBooks method to update the book inventory when a user makes a purchase. The buyBooks method invokes buyBook for each book contained in the shopping cart. To ensure that the order is processed in its entirety, the calls to buyBook are wrapped in a single JDBC transaction. The use of the shared database connection is synchronized via the [get|release]Connection methods.

```java
public void buyBooks(ShoppingCart cart) throws OrderException {
    Collection items = cart.getItems();
    Iterator i = items.iterator();
    try {
        getConnection();
        con.setAutoCommit(false);
        while (i.hasNext()) {
            ShoppingCartItem sci = (ShoppingCartItem)i.next();
            BookDetails bd = (BookDetails)sci.getItem();
            String id = bd.getBookId();
            int quantity = sci.getQuantity();
            buyBook(id, quantity);
        }
        con.commit();
        con.setAutoCommit(true);
        releaseConnection();
    } catch (Exception ex) {
        try {
        con.rollback();
        releaseConnection();
        throw new OrderException("Transaction failed: " +
            ex.getMessage());
        } catch (SQLException sqx) {
            releaseConnection();
            throw new OrderException("Rollback failed: " +
                sqx.getMessage());
        }
    }
}
```

Initializing a Servlet

After the Web container loads and instantiates the servlet class and before it delivers requests from clients, the Web container initializes the servlet. To customize this process to allow the servlet to read persistent configuration data, initialize resources, and perform any other one-time activities, you override the init method of the Servlet interface. A servlet that cannot complete its initialization process should throw UnavailableException.

All the servlets that access the bookstore database (BookStoreServlet, Cata-logServlet, BookDetailsServlet, and ShowCartServlet) initialize a variable in their init method that points to the database access object created by the Web context listener:

```
public class CatalogServlet extends HttpServlet {
  private BookDBAO bookDB;
  public void init() throws ServletException {
    bookDB = (BookDBAO)getServletContext().
      getAttribute("bookDB");
    if (bookDB == null) throw new
      UnavailableException("Couldn't get database.");
  }
}
```

Writing Service Methods

The service provided by a servlet is implemented in the service method of a GenericServlet, in the do*Method* methods (where *Method* can take the value Get, Delete, Options, Post, Put, or Trace) of an HttpServlet object, or in any other protocol-specific methods defined by a class that implements the Servlet interface. In the rest of this chapter, the term *service method* is used for any method in a servlet class that provides a service to a client.

The general pattern for a service method is to extract information from the request, access external resources, and then populate the response based on that information.

For HTTP servlets, the correct procedure for populating the response is to first retrieve an output stream from the response, then fill in the response headers, and finally write any body content to the output stream. Response headers must always be set before the response has been committed. Any attempt to set or add headers after the response has been committed will be ignored by the Web container. The next two sections describe how to get information from requests and generate responses.

Getting Information from Requests

A request contains data passed between a client and the servlet. All requests implement the `ServletRequest` interface. This interface defines methods for accessing the following information:

- Parameters, which are typically used to convey information between clients and servlets
- Object-valued attributes, which are typically used to pass information between the servlet container and a servlet or between collaborating servlets
- Information about the protocol used to communicate the request and about the client and server involved in the request
- Information relevant to localization

For example, in `CatalogServlet` the identifier of the book that a customer wishes to purchase is included as a parameter to the request. The following code fragment illustrates how to use the `getParameter` method to extract the identifier:

```
String bookId = request.getParameter("Add");
if (bookId != null) {
   BookDetails book = bookDB.getBookDetails(bookId);
```

You can also retrieve an input stream from the request and manually parse the data. To read character data, use the `BufferedReader` object returned by the request's `getReader` method. To read binary data, use the `ServletInputStream` returned by `getInputStream`.

HTTP servlets are passed an HTTP request object, `HttpServletRequest`, which contains the request URL, HTTP headers, query string, and so on.

An HTTP request URL contains the following parts:

```
http://[host]:[port][request path]?[query string]
```

The request path is further composed of the following elements:

- *Context path*: A concatenation of a forward slash (/) with the context root of the servlet's Web application.
- *Servlet path*: The path section that corresponds to the component alias that activated this request. This path starts with a forward slash (/).
- *Path info*: The part of the request path that is not part of the context path or the servlet path.

If the context path is /catalog and for the aliases listed in Table 11–5, Table 11–6 gives some examples of how the URL will be parsed.

Query strings are composed of a set of parameters and values. Individual parameters are retrieved from a request by using the getParameter method. There are two ways to generate query strings:

- A query string can explicitly appear in a Web page. For example, an HTML page generated by the CatalogServlet could contain the link <a href="/bookstore1/catalog?Add=101">Add To Cart</a>. CatalogServlet extracts the parameter named Add as follows:

      String bookId = request.getParameter("Add");

- A query string is appended to a URL when a form with a GET HTTP method is submitted. In the Duke's Bookstore application, CashierServlet generates a form, then a user name input to the form is appended to the URL that maps to ReceiptServlet, and finally ReceiptServlet extracts the user name using the getParameter method.

Table 11–5 Aliases

Pattern	Servlet
/lawn/*	LawnServlet
/*.jsp	JSPServlet

Table 11–6 Request Path Elements

Request Path	Servlet Path	Path Info
/catalog/lawn/index.html	/lawn	/index.html
/catalog/help/feedback.jsp	/help/feedback.jsp	null

Constructing Responses

A response contains data passed between a server and the client. All responses implement the `ServletResponse` interface. This interface defines methods that allow you to:

- Retrieve an output stream to use to send data to the client. To send character data, use the `PrintWriter` returned by the response's `getWriter` method. To send binary data in a MIME body response, use the `ServletOutputStream` returned by `getOutputStream`. To mix binary and text data, for example—to create a multipart response—use a `ServletOutputStream` and manage the character sections manually.

- Indicate the content type (for example, `text/html`) being returned by the response with the `setContentType(String)` method. This method must be called before the response is committed. A registry of content type names is kept by the Internet Assigned Numbers Authority (IANA) at:

  `http://www.iana.org/assignments/media-types/`

- Indicate whether to buffer output with the `setBufferSize(int)` method. By default, any content written to the output stream is immediately sent to the client. Buffering allows content to be written before anything is actually sent back to the client, thus providing the servlet with more time to set appropriate status codes and headers or forward to another Web resource. The method must be called before any content is written or before the response is committed.

- Set localization information such as locale and character encoding. See Chapter 22 for details.

HTTP response objects, `HttpServletResponse`, have fields representing HTTP headers such as the following:

- Status codes, which are used to indicate the reason a request is not satisfied or that a request has been redirected.

- Cookies, which are used to store application-specific information at the client. Sometimes cookies are used to maintain an identifier for tracking a user's session (see Session Tracking, page 466).

In Duke's Bookstore, `BookDetailsServlet` generates an HTML page that displays information about a book that the servlet retrieves from a database. The servlet first sets response headers: the content type of the response and the buffer size. The servlet buffers the page content because the database access can generate an exception that would cause forwarding to an error page. By buffering the response, the servlet prevents the client from seeing a concatenation of part of a Duke's Bookstore page with the error page should an error occur. The doGet method then retrieves a PrintWriter from the response.

To fill in the response, the servlet first dispatches the request to BannerServlet, which generates a common banner for all the servlets in the application. This process is discussed in Including Other Resources in the Response (page 461). Then the servlet retrieves the book identifier from a request parameter and uses the identifier to retrieve information about the book from the bookstore database. Finally, the servlet generates HTML markup that describes the book information and then commits the response to the client by calling the close method on the PrintWriter.

```java
public class BookDetailsServlet extends HttpServlet {
    public void doGet (HttpServletRequest request,
        HttpServletResponse response)
        throws ServletException, IOException {
    // set headers before accessing the Writer
    response.setContentType("text/html");
    response.setBufferSize(8192);
    PrintWriter out = response.getWriter();

    // then write the response
    out.println("<html>" +
      "<head><title>+
      messages.getString("TitleBookDescription")
      +</title></head>");

    // Get the dispatcher; it gets the banner to the user
    RequestDispatcher dispatcher =
      getServletContext().
      getRequestDispatcher("/banner");
    if (dispatcher != null)
      dispatcher.include(request, response);

    // Get the identifier of the book to display
    String bookId = request.getParameter("bookId");
    if (bookId != null) {
      // and the information about the book
      try {
        BookDetails bd =
          bookDB.getBookDetails(bookId);
        ...
```

```
        // Print the information obtained
        out.println("<h2>" + bd.getTitle() + "</h2>" +
        ...
    } catch (BookNotFoundException ex) {
        response.resetBuffer();
        throw new ServletException(ex);
    }
}
out.println("</body></html>");
out.close();
}
}
```

BookDetailsServlet generates a page that looks like Figure 11–2.

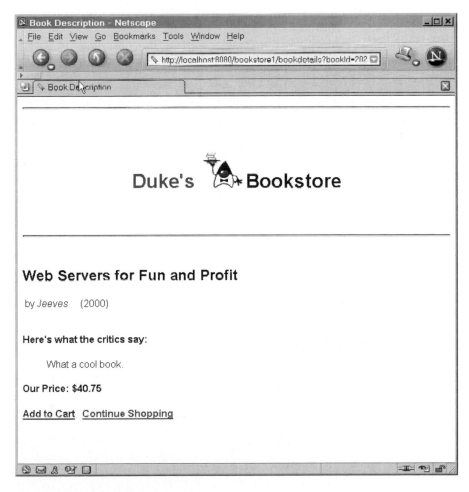

Figure 11–2 Book Details

Filtering Requests and Responses

A *filter* is an object that can transform the header and content (or both) of a request or response. Filters differ from Web components in that filters usually do not themselves create a response. Instead, a filter provides functionality that can be "attached" to any kind of Web resource. Consequently, a filter should not have any dependencies on a Web resource for which it is acting as a filter; this way it can be composed with more than one type of Web resource. The main tasks that a filter can perform are as follows:

- Query the request and act accordingly.
- Block the request-and-response pair from passing any further.
- Modify the request headers and data. You do this by providing a customized version of the request.
- Modify the response headers and data. You do this by providing a customized version of the response.
- Interact with external resources.

Applications of filters include authentication, logging, image conversion, data compression, encryption, tokenizing streams, XML transformations, and so on.

You can configure a Web resource to be filtered by a chain of zero, one, or more filters in a specific order. This chain is specified when the Web application containing the component is deployed and is instantiated when a Web container loads the component.

In summary, the tasks involved in using filters are

- Programming the filter
- Programming customized requests and responses
- Specifying the filter chain for each Web resource

Programming Filters

The filtering API is defined by the `Filter`, `FilterChain`, and `FilterConfig` interfaces in the `javax.servlet` package. You define a filter by implementing the `Filter` interface. The most important method in this interface is `doFilter`, which is passed request, response, and filter chain objects. This method can perform the following actions:

- Examine the request headers.
- Customize the request object if the filter wishes to modify request headers or data.
- Customize the response object if the filter wishes to modify response headers or data.
- Invoke the next entity in the filter chain. If the current filter is the last filter in the chain that ends with the target Web component or static resource, the next entity is the resource at the end of the chain; otherwise, it is the next filter that was configured in the WAR. The filter invokes the next entity by calling the doFilter method on the chain object (passing in the request and response it was called with, or the wrapped versions it may have created). Alternatively, it can choose to block the request by not making the call to invoke the next entity. In the latter case, the filter is responsible for filling out the response.
- Examine response headers after it has invoked the next filter in the chain.
- Throw an exception to indicate an error in processing.

In addition to doFilter, you must implement the init and destroy methods. The init method is called by the container when the filter is instantiated. If you wish to pass initialization parameters to the filter, you retrieve them from the FilterConfig object passed to init.

The Duke's Bookstore application uses the filters HitCounterFilter and OrderFilter to increment and log the value of counters when the entry and receipt servlets are accessed.

In the doFilter method, both filters retrieve the servlet context from the filter configuration object so that they can access the counters stored as context attributes. After the filters have completed application-specific processing, they invoke doFilter on the filter chain object passed into the original doFilter method. The elided code is discussed in the next section.

```
public final class HitCounterFilter implements Filter {
   private FilterConfig filterConfig = null;

   public void init(FilterConfig filterConfig)
      throws ServletException {
      this.filterConfig = filterConfig;
   }
```

```
public void destroy() {
   this.filterConfig = null;
}
public void doFilter(ServletRequest request,
   ServletResponse response, FilterChain chain)
   throws IOException, ServletException {
   if (filterConfig == null)
      return;
   StringWriter sw = new StringWriter();
   PrintWriter writer = new PrintWriter(sw);
   Counter counter = (Counter)filterConfig.
      getServletContext().
      getAttribute("hitCounter");
   writer.println();
   writer.println("===============");
   writer.println("The number of hits is: " +
      counter.incCounter());
   writer.println("===============");
   // Log the resulting string
   writer.flush();
   System.out.println(sw.getBuffer().toString());
   ...
   chain.doFilter(request, wrapper);
   ...
   }
}
```

Programming Customized Requests and Responses

There are many ways for a filter to modify a request or response. For example, a filter can add an attribute to the request or can insert data in the response. In the Duke's Bookstore example, HitCounterFilter inserts the value of the counter into the response.

A filter that modifies a response must usually capture the response before it is returned to the client. To do this, you pass a stand-in stream to the servlet that generates the response. The stand-in stream prevents the servlet from closing the original response stream when it completes and allows the filter to modify the servlet's response.

To pass this stand-in stream to the servlet, the filter creates a response wrapper that overrides the getWriter or getOutputStream method to return this stand-in stream. The wrapper is passed to the doFilter method of the filter chain. Wrapper methods default to calling through to the wrapped request or response object.

This approach follows the well-known Wrapper or Decorator pattern described in *Design Patterns, Elements of Reusable Object-Oriented Software*, by Erich Gamma et al. (Addison-Wesley, 1995). The following sections describe how the hit counter filter described earlier and other types of filters use wrappers.

To override request methods, you wrap the request in an object that extends ServletRequestWrapper or HttpServletRequestWrapper. To override response methods, you wrap the response in an object that extends Servlet-ResponseWrapper or HttpServletResponseWrapper.

HitCounterFilter wraps the response in a CharResponseWrapper. The wrapped response is passed to the next object in the filter chain, which is Book-StoreServlet. Then BookStoreServlet writes its response into the stream created by CharResponseWrapper. When chain.doFilter returns, HitCounter-Filter retrieves the servlet's response from PrintWriter and writes it to a buffer. The filter inserts the value of the counter into the buffer, resets the content length header of the response, and then writes the contents of the buffer to the response stream.

```
PrintWriter out = response.getWriter();
CharResponseWrapper wrapper = new CharResponseWrapper(
   (HttpServletResponse)response);
chain.doFilter(request, wrapper);
CharArrayWriter caw = new CharArrayWriter();
caw.write(wrapper.toString().substring(0,
   wrapper.toString().indexOf("</body>")-1));
caw.write("<p>\n<center>" +
   messages.getString("Visitor") + "<font color='red'>" +
   counter.getCounter() + "</font></center>");
caw.write("\n</body></html>");
response.setContentLength(caw.toString().getBytes().length);
out.write(caw.toString());
out.close();

public class CharResponseWrapper extends
   HttpServletResponseWrapper {
   private CharArrayWriter output;
   public String toString() {
      return output.toString();
   }
   public CharResponseWrapper(HttpServletResponse response){
      super(response);
      output = new CharArrayWriter();
   }
   public PrintWriter getWriter(){
      return new PrintWriter(output);
   }
}
```

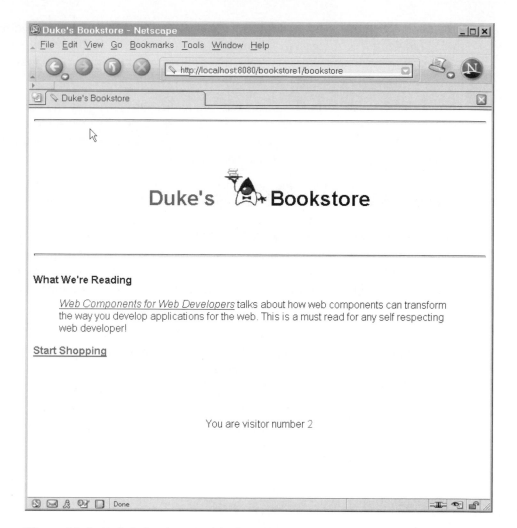

Figure 11–3   Duke's Bookstore with Hit Counter

Figure 11–3 shows the entry page for Duke's Bookstore with the hit counter.

Specifying Filter Mappings

A Web container uses filter mappings to decide how to apply filters to Web resources. A filter mapping matches a filter to a Web component by name, or to Web resources by URL pattern. The filters are invoked in the order in which filter mappings appear in the filter mapping list of a WAR. You specify a filter mapping list for a WAR by using `deploytool` or by coding the list directly in the Web application deployment descriptor as follows:

1. Declare the filter. This element creates a name for the filter and declares the filter's implementation class and initialization parameters.

2. Map the filter to a Web resource by name or by URL pattern.

3. Constrain how the filter will be applied to requests by choosing one of the enumerated dispatcher options:

   - REQUEST: Only when the request comes directly from the client

   - FORWARD: Only when the request has been forwarded to a component (see Transferring Control to Another Web Component, page 462)

   - INCLUDE: Only when the request is being processed by a component that has been included (see Including Other Resources in the Response, page 461)

   - ERROR: Only when the request is being processed with the error page mechanism (see Handling Errors, page 443)

   You can direct the filter to be applied to any combination of the preceding situations by including multiple `dispatcher` elements. If no elements are specified, the default option is REQUEST.

If you want to log every request to a Web application, you map the hit counter filter to the URL pattern `/*`. Step 13. in The Example Servlets (page 436) shows how to create and map the filters for the Duke's Bookstore application. Table 11–7 summarizes the filter definition and mapping list for the Duke's Bookstore application. The filters are matched by servlet name, and each filter chain contains only one filter.

You can map a filter to one or more Web resources and you can map more than one filter to a Web resource. This is illustrated in Figure 11–4, where filter F1 is mapped to servlets S1, S2, and S3, filter F2 is mapped to servlet S2, and filter F3 is mapped to servlets S1 and S2.

Table 11–7 Duke's Bookstore Filter Definition and Mapping List

Filter	Class	Servlet
HitCounterFilter	filters.HitCounterFilter	BookStoreServlet
OrderFilter	filters.OrderFilter	ReceiptServlet

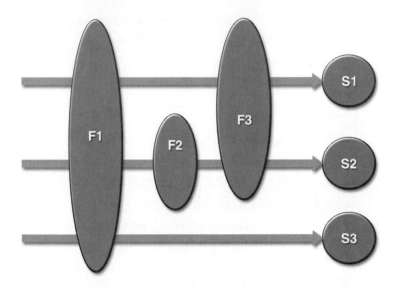

Figure 11–4   Filter-to-Servlet Mapping

Recall that a filter chain is one of the objects passed to the doFilter method of a filter. This chain is formed indirectly via filter mappings. The order of the filters in the chain is the same as the order in which filter mappings appear in the Web application deployment descriptor.

When a filter is mapped to servlet S1, the Web container invokes the doFilter method of F1. The doFilter method of each filter in S1's filter chain is invoked by the preceding filter in the chain via the chain.doFilter method. Because S1's filter chain contains filters F1 and F3, F1's call to chain.doFilter invokes the doFilter method of filter F3. When F3's doFilter method completes, control returns to F1's doFilter method.

Invoking Other Web Resources

Web components can invoke other Web resources in two ways: indirectly and directly. A Web component indirectly invokes another Web resource when it embeds a URL that points to another Web component in content returned to a client. In the Duke's Bookstore application, most Web components contain embedded URLs that point to other Web components. For example, ShowCart-Servlet indirectly invokes the CatalogServlet through the embedded URL /bookstore1/catalog.

A Web component can also directly invoke another resource while it is executing. There are two possibilities: The Web component can include the content of another resource, or it can forward a request to another resource.

To invoke a resource available on the server that is running a Web component, you must first obtain a `RequestDispatcher` object using the `getRequestDispatcher("URL")` method.

You can get a `RequestDispatcher` object from either a request or the Web context; however, the two methods have slightly different behavior. The method takes the path to the requested resource as an argument. A request can take a relative path (that is, one that does not begin with a /), but the Web context requires an absolute path. If the resource is not available or if the server has not implemented a `RequestDispatcher` object for that type of resource, `getRequestDispatcher` will return null. Your servlet should be prepared to deal with this condition.

Including Other Resources in the Response

It is often useful to include another Web resource—for example, banner content or copyright information—in the response returned from a Web component. To include another resource, invoke the `include` method of a `RequestDispatcher` object:

```
include(request, response);
```

If the resource is static, the `include` method enables programmatic server-side includes. If the resource is a Web component, the effect of the method is to send the request to the included Web component, execute the Web component, and then include the result of the execution in the response from the containing servlet. An included Web component has access to the request object, but it is limited in what it can do with the response object:

- It can write to the body of the response and commit a response.
- It cannot set headers or call any method (for example, `setCookie`) that affects the headers of the response.

The banner for the Duke's Bookstore application is generated by `BannerServlet`. Note that both `doGet` and `doPost` are implemented because `BannerServlet` can be dispatched from either method in a calling servlet.

```
public class BannerServlet extends HttpServlet {
  public void doGet (HttpServletRequest request,
    HttpServletResponse response)
    throws ServletException, IOException {
      output(request, response);
  }
  public void doPost (HttpServletRequest request,
    HttpServletResponse response)
    throws ServletException, IOException {
      output(request, response);
  }
}

private void output(HttpServletRequest request,
    HttpServletResponse response)
    throws ServletException, IOException {
    PrintWriter out = response.getWriter();
    out.println("<body bgcolor=\"#ffffff\">" +
    "<center>" + "<hr> <br>  " + "<h1>" +
    "<font size=\"+3\" color=\"#CC0066\">Duke's </font>" +
    <img src=\"" + request.getContextPath() +
    "/duke.books.gif\">" +
    "<font size=\"+3\" color=\"black\">Bookstore</font>" +
    "</h1>" + "</center>" + "<br>   <hr> <br> ");
  }
}
```

Each servlet in the Duke's Bookstore application includes the result from `Ban-nerServlet` using the following code:

```
RequestDispatcher dispatcher =
  getServletContext().getRequestDispatcher("/banner");
if (dispatcher != null)
  dispatcher.include(request, response);
}
```

Transferring Control to Another Web Component

In some applications, you might want to have one Web component do prelimi-nary processing of a request and have another component generate the response. For example, you might want to partially process a request and then transfer to another component depending on the nature of the request.

To transfer control to another Web component, you invoke the `forward` method of a `RequestDispatcher`. When a request is forwarded, the request URL is set to the path of the forwarded page. The original URI and its constituent parts are saved as request attributes javax.servlet.forward.[request_uri|context-path|servlet_path|path_info|query_string]. The Dispatcher servlet, used by a version of the Duke's Bookstore application described in The Example JSP Pages (page 564), saves the path information from the original URL, retrieves a RequestDispatcher from the request, and then forwards to the JSP page template.jsp.

```
public class Dispatcher extends HttpServlet {
   public void doGet(HttpServletRequest request,
      HttpServletResponse response) {
      RequestDispatcher dispatcher = request.
         getRequestDispatcher("/template.jsp");
      if (dispatcher != null)
         dispatcher.forward(request, response);
   }
   public void doPost(HttpServletRequest request,
   ...
}
```

The forward method should be used to give another resource responsibility for replying to the user. If you have already accessed a ServletOutputStream or PrintWriter object within the servlet, you cannot use this method; doing so throws an IllegalStateException.

Accessing the Web Context

The context in which Web components execute is an object that implements the ServletContext interface. You retrieve the Web context using the getServlet-Context method. The Web context provides methods for accessing:

- Initialization parameters
- Resources associated with the Web context
- Object-valued attributes
- Logging capabilities

The Web context is used by the Duke's Bookstore filters filters.HitCounter-Filter and OrderFilter, which are discussed in Filtering Requests and Responses (page 454). Each filter stores a counter as a context attribute. Recall from Controlling Concurrent Access to Shared Resources (page 445) that the counter's access methods are synchronized to prevent incompatible operations by servlets that are running concurrently. A filter retrieves the counter object using the context's getAttribute method. The incremented value of the counter is recorded in the log.

```
public final class HitCounterFilter implements Filter {
    private FilterConfig filterConfig = null;
    public void doFilter(ServletRequest request,
        ServletResponse response, FilterChain chain)
        throws IOException, ServletException {
        ...
        StringWriter sw = new StringWriter();
        PrintWriter writer = new PrintWriter(sw);
        ServletContext context = filterConfig.
            getServletContext();
        Counter counter = (Counter)context.
            getAttribute("hitCounter");
        ...
        writer.println("The number of hits is: " +
            counter.incCounter());
        ...
        System.out.println(sw.getBuffer().toString());
        ...
    }
}
```

Maintaining Client State

Many applications require that a series of requests from a client be associated with one another. For example, the Duke's Bookstore application saves the state of a user's shopping cart across requests. Web-based applications are responsible for maintaining such state, called a *session*, because HTTP is stateless. To support applications that need to maintain state, Java servlet technology provides an API for managing sessions and allows several mechanisms for implementing sessions.

Accessing a Session

Sessions are represented by an HttpSession object. You access a session by calling the getSession method of a request object. This method returns the current session associated with this request, or, if the request does not have a session, it creates one.

Associating Objects with a Session

You can associate object-valued attributes with a session by name. Such attributes are accessible by any Web component that belongs to the same Web context *and* is handling a request that is part of the same session.

The Duke's Bookstore application stores a customer's shopping cart as a session attribute. This allows the shopping cart to be saved between requests and also allows cooperating servlets to access the cart. `CatalogServlet` adds items to the cart; `ShowCartServlet` displays, deletes items from, and clears the cart; and `CashierServlet` retrieves the total cost of the books in the cart.

```
public class CashierServlet extends HttpServlet {
   public void doGet (HttpServletRequest request,
      HttpServletResponse response)
      throws ServletException, IOException {

      // Get the user's session and shopping cart
      HttpSession session = request.getSession();
      ShoppingCart cart =
         (ShoppingCart)session.
            getAttribute("cart");
      ...
      // Determine the total price of the user's books
      double total = cart.getTotal();
```

Notifying Objects That Are Associated with a Session

Recall that your application can notify Web context and session listener objects of servlet life-cycle events (Handling Servlet Life-Cycle Events, page 441). You can also notify objects of certain events related to their association with a session such as the following:

- When the object is added to or removed from a session. To receive this notification, your object must implement the `javax.http.HttpSession-BindingListener` interface.

- When the session to which the object is attached will be passivated or activated. A session will be passivated or activated when it is moved between virtual machines or saved to and restored from persistent storage. To receive this notification, your object must implement the `javax.http.HttpSessionActivationListener` interface.

Session Management

Because there is no way for an HTTP client to signal that it no longer needs a session, each session has an associated timeout so that its resources can be reclaimed. The timeout period can be accessed by using a session's [get|set]MaxInactiveInterval methods. You can also set the timeout period using deploytool:

1. Select the WAR.
2. Select the General tab.
3. Click the Advanced Setting button.
4. Enter the timeout period in the Session Timeout field.

To ensure that an active session is not timed out, you should periodically access the session via service methods because this resets the session's time-to-live counter.

When a particular client interaction is finished, you use the session's invalidate method to invalidate a session on the server side and remove any session data. The bookstore application's ReceiptServlet is the last servlet to access a client's session, so it has the responsibility to invalidate the session:

```
public class ReceiptServlet extends HttpServlet {
   public void doPost(HttpServletRequest request,
            HttpServletResponse response)
            throws ServletException, IOException {
      // Get the user's session and shopping cart
      HttpSession session = request.getSession();
      // Payment received -- invalidate the session
      session.invalidate();
      ...
```

Session Tracking

A Web container can use several methods to associate a session with a user, all of which involve passing an identifier between the client and the server. The identifier can be maintained on the client as a cookie, or the Web component can include the identifier in every URL that is returned to the client.

If your application uses session objects, you must ensure that session tracking is enabled by having the application rewrite URLs whenever the client turns off cookies. You do this by calling the response's encodeURL(URL) method on all

URLs returned by a servlet. This method includes the session ID in the URL only if cookies are disabled; otherwise, it returns the URL unchanged.

The doGet method of ShowCartServlet encodes the three URLs at the bottom of the shopping cart display page as follows:

```
out.println("<p>   <p><strong><a href=\"" +
    response.encodeURL(request.getContextPath() +
        "/bookcatalog") +
        "\">" + messages.getString("ContinueShopping") +
        "</a>      " +
        "<a href=\"" +
    response.encodeURL(request.getContextPath() +
        "/bookcashier") +
        "\">" + messages.getString("Checkout") +
        "</a>      " +
        "<a href=\"" +
    response.encodeURL(request.getContextPath() +
        "/bookshowcart?Clear=clear") +
        "\">" + messages.getString("ClearCart") +
        "</a></strong>");
```

If cookies are turned off, the session is encoded in the Check Out URL as follows:

```
http://localhost:8080/bookstore1/cashier;
    jsessionid=c0o7fszeb1
```

If cookies are turned on, the URL is simply

```
http://localhost:8080/bookstore1/cashier
```

Finalizing a Servlet

When a servlet container determines that a servlet should be removed from service (for example, when a container wants to reclaim memory resources or when it is being shut down), the container calls the destroy method of the Servlet interface. In this method, you release any resources the servlet is using and save any persistent state. The following destroy method releases the database object created in the init method described in Initializing a Servlet (page 447):

```
public void destroy() {
    bookDB = null;
}
```

All of a servlet's service methods should be complete when a servlet is removed. The server tries to ensure this by calling the `destroy` method only after all service requests have returned or after a server-specific grace period, whichever comes first. If your servlet has operations that take a long time to run (that is, operations that may run longer than the server's grace period), the operations could still be running when `destroy` is called. You must make sure that any threads still handling client requests complete; the remainder of this section describes how to do the following:

- Keep track of how many threads are currently running the `service` method
- Provide a clean shutdown by having the `destroy` method notify long-running threads of the shutdown and wait for them to complete
- Have the long-running methods poll periodically to check for shutdown and, if necessary, stop working, clean up, and return

Tracking Service Requests

To track service requests, include in your servlet class a field that counts the number of service methods that are running. The field should have synchronized access methods to increment, decrement, and return its value.

```
public class ShutdownExample extends HttpServlet {
    private int serviceCounter = 0;
    ...
    // Access methods for serviceCounter
    protected synchronized void enteringServiceMethod() {
        serviceCounter++;
    }
    protected synchronized void leavingServiceMethod() {
        serviceCounter--;
    }
    protected synchronized int numServices() {
        return serviceCounter;
    }
}
```

The `service` method should increment the service counter each time the method is entered and should decrement the counter each time the method returns. This is one of the few times that your `HttpServlet` subclass should override the `service` method. The new method should call `super.service` to preserve the functionality of the original `service` method:

```
protected void service(HttpServletRequest req,
            HttpServletResponse resp)
            throws ServletException,IOException {
```

```
      enteringServiceMethod();
      try {
         super.service(req, resp);
      } finally {
         leavingServiceMethod();
      }
   }
}
```

Notifying Methods to Shut Down

To ensure a clean shutdown, your `destroy` method should not release any shared resources until all the service requests have completed. One part of doing this is to check the service counter. Another part is to notify the long-running methods that it is time to shut down. For this notification, another field is required. The field should have the usual access methods:

```
public class ShutdownExample extends HttpServlet {
   private boolean shuttingDown;
   ...
   //Access methods for shuttingDown
   protected synchronized void setShuttingDown(boolean flag) {
      shuttingDown = flag;
   }
   protected synchronized boolean isShuttingDown() {
      return shuttingDown;
   }
}
```

Here is an example of the `destroy` method using these fields to provide a clean shutdown:

```
public void destroy() {
   /* Check to see whether there are still service methods /*
   /* running, and if there are, tell them to stop. */
   if (numServices() > 0) {
      setShuttingDown(true);
   }

   /* Wait for the service methods to stop. */
   while(numServices() > 0) {
      try {
         Thread.sleep(interval);
      } catch (InterruptedException e) {
      }
   }
}
```

Creating Polite Long-Running Methods

The final step in providing a clean shutdown is to make any long-running methods behave politely. Methods that might run for a long time should check the value of the field that notifies them of shutdowns and should interrupt their work, if necessary.

```
public void doPost(...) {
  ...
  for(i = 0; ((i < lotsOfStuffToDo) &&
     !isShuttingDown()); i++) {
    try {
      partOfLongRunningOperation(i);
    } catch (InterruptedException e) {
      ...
    }
  }
}
```

Further Information

For further information on Java Servlet technology, see

- Java Servlet 2.4 specification:
  `http://java.sun.com/products/servlet/download.html#specs`
- The Java Servlet Web site:
  `http://java.sun.com/products/servlet`

12

JavaServer Pages Technology

J AVASERVER Pages (JSP) technology allows you to easily create Web content that has both static and dynamic components. JSP technology makes available all the dynamic capabilities of Java Servlet technology but provides a more natural approach to creating static content. The main features of JSP technology are as follows:

- A language for developing JSP pages, which are text-based documents that describe how to process a request and construct a response
- An expression language for accessing server-side objects
- Mechanisms for defining extensions to the JSP language

JSP technology also contains an API that is used by developers of Web containers, but this API is not covered in this tutorial.

What Is a JSP Page?

A *JSP page* is a text document that contains two types of text: static data, which can be expressed in any text-based format (such as HTML, SVG, WML, and XML), and JSP elements, which construct dynamic content.

The recommended file extension for the source file of a JSP page is `.jsp`. The page can be composed of a top file that includes other files that contain either a complete JSP page or a fragment of a JSP page. The recommended extension for the source file of a fragment of a JSP page is `.jspf`.

The JSP elements in a JSP page can be expressed in two syntaxes—standard and XML—though any given file can use only one syntax. A JSP page in XML syntax is an XML document and can be manipulated by tools and APIs for XML documents. This chapter and Chapters 14 through 16 document only the standard syntax. The XML syntax is covered in Chapter 13. A syntax card and reference that summarizes both syntaxes is available at

```
http://java.sun.com/products/jsp/docs.html#syntax
```

Example

The Web page in Figure 12–1 is a form that allows you to select a locale and displays the date in a manner appropriate to the locale.

The source code for this example is in the `<INSTALL>`/j2eetutorial14/ examples/web/date/ directory. The JSP page, index.jsp, used to create the form appears in a moment; it is a typical mixture of static HTML markup and JSP elements. If you have developed Web pages, you are probably familiar with the HTML document structure statements (`<head>`, `<body>`, and so on) and the HTML statements that create a form (`<form>`) and a menu (`<select>`).

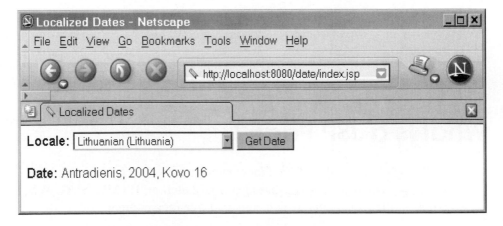

Figure 12–1 Localized Date Form

The lines in bold in the example code contain the following types of JSP constructs:

- A page directive (**<%@page ... %>**) sets the content type returned by the page.

- Tag library directives (**<%@taglib ... %>**) import custom tag libraries.

- **jsp:useBean** creates an object containing a collection of locales and initializes an identifier that points to that object.

- JSP expression language expressions (**${ }**) retrieve the value of object properties. The values are used to set custom tag attribute values and create dynamic content.

- Custom tags set a variable (**c:set**), iterate over a collection of locale names (**c:forEach**), and conditionally insert HTML text into the response (**c:if**, **c:choose**, **c:when**, **c:otherwise**).

- **jsp:setProperty** sets the value of an object property.

- A function (**f:equals**) tests the equality of an attribute and the current item of a collection. (Note: A built-in == operator is usually used to test equality).

Here is the JSP page:

```
<%@ page contentType="text/html; charset=UTF-8" %>
<%@ taglib uri="http://java.sun.com/jsp/jstl/core"
    prefix="c" %>
<%@ taglib uri="/functions" prefix="f" %>
<html>
<head><title>Localized Dates</title></head>
<body bgcolor="white">
<jsp:useBean id="locales" scope="application"
  class="mypkg.MyLocales"/>

<form name="localeForm" action="index.jsp" method="post">
<c:set var="selectedLocaleString" value="${param.locale}" />
<c:set var="selectedFlag"
  value="${!empty selectedLocaleString}" />
<b>Locale:</b>
<select name=locale>
<c:forEach var="localeString" items="${locales.localeNames}" >
<c:choose>
  <c:when test="${selectedFlag}">
```

```
    <c:choose>
      <c:when
          test="${f:equals(selectedLocaleString,
            localeString)}" >
          <option selected>${localeString}</option>
      </c:when>
      <c:otherwise>
          <option>${localeString}</option>
      </c:otherwise>
    </c:choose>
  </c:when>
  <c:otherwise>
      <option>${localeString}</option>
  </c:otherwise>
</c:choose>
</c:forEach>
</select>
<input type="submit" name="Submit" value="Get Date">
</form>

<c:if test="${selectedFlag}" >
  <jsp:setProperty name="locales"
    property="selectedLocaleString"
    value="${selectedLocaleString}" />
  <jsp:useBean id="date" class="mypkg.MyDate"/>
  <jsp:setProperty name="date" property="locale"
    value="${locales.selectedLocale}"/>
  <b>Date: </b>${date.date}
</c:if>
</body>
</html>
```

A sample date.war is provided in *<INSTALL>*/j2eetutorial14/examples/ web/provided-wars/. To build, package, deploy, and execute this example:

1. In a terminal window, go to *<INSTALL>*/j2eetutorial14/examples/ web/date/.

2. Run asant build. This target will spawn any necessary compilations and copy files to the *<INSTALL>*/j2eetutorial14/examples/web/date/ build/ directory.

3. Start the Application Server.

4. Start `deploytool`.

5. Create a Web application called `date` by running the New Web Component wizard. Select File→New→Web Component.

6. In the New Web Component wizard:

   a. Select the Create New Stand-Alone WAR Module radio button.

   b. In the WAR Location field, enter `<INSTALL>/docs/tutorial/examples/web/date/date.war`.

   c. In the WAR Name field, enter `date`.

   d. In the Context Root field, enter `/date`.

   e. Click Edit Contents.

   f. In the Edit Contents dialog box, navigate to `<INSTALL>/j2eetutorial14/examples/web/date/build/`. Select `index.jsp`, `functions.tld`, and the `mypkg` directory and click Add, then click OK.

   g. Click Next.

   h. Select the No Component radio button.

   i. Click Next.

   j. Click Finish.

7. Select File→Save.

8. Deploy the application.

   a. Select Tools→Deploy.

   b. In the Connection Settings frame, enter the user name and password you specified when you installed the Application Server.

   c. Click OK.

   d. A pop-up dialog box will display the results of the deployment. Click Close.

9. Set the character encoding in your browser to UTF-8.

10. Open the URL `http://localhost:8080/date` in a browser.

You will see a combo box whose entries are locales. Select a locale and click Get Date. You will see the date expressed in a manner appropriate for that locale.

The Example JSP Pages

To illustrate JSP technology, this chapter rewrites each servlet in the Duke's Bookstore application introduced in The Example Servlets (page 436) as a JSP page (see Table 12–1).

The data for the bookstore application is still maintained in a database and is accessed through `database.BookDBAO`. However, the JSP pages access `BookDBAO` through the JavaBeans component `database.BookDB`. This class allows the JSP pages to use JSP elements designed to work with JavaBeans components (see JavaBeans Component Design Conventions, page 497).

The implementation of the database bean follows. The bean has two instance variables: the current book and the data access object.

Table 12–1   Duke's Bookstore Example JSP Pages

Function	JSP Pages
Enter the bookstore.	`bookstore.jsp`
Create the bookstore banner.	`banner.jsp`
Browse the books offered for sale.	`bookcatalog.jsp`
Add a book to the shopping cart.	`bookcatalog.jsp` and `bookdetails.jsp`
Get detailed information on a specific book.	`bookdetails.jsp`
Display the shopping cart.	`bookshowcart.jsp`
Remove one or more books from the shopping cart.	`bookshowcart.jsp`
Buy the books in the shopping cart.	`bookcashier.jsp`
Receive an acknowledgment for the purchase.	`bookreceipt.jsp`

```
package database;
public class BookDB {
  private String bookId = "0";
  private BookDBAO database = null;

  public BookDB () throws Exception {
  }
  public void setBookId(String bookId) {
    this.bookId = bookId;
  }
  public void setDatabase(BookDAO database) {
    this.database = database;
  }
  public BookDetails getBookDetails()
    throws Exception {
    return (BookDetails)database.getBookDetails(bookId);
  }
  ...
}
```

This version of the Duke's Bookstore application is organized along the Model-View-Controller (MVC) architecture. The MVC architecture is a widely used architectural approach for interactive applications that distributes functionality among application objects so as to minimize the degree of coupling between the objects. To achieve this, it divides applications into three layers: model, view, and controller. Each layer handles specific tasks and has responsibilities to the other layers:

- The *model* represents business data, along with business logic or operations that govern access and modification of this business data. The model notifies views when it changes and lets the view query the model about its state. It also lets the controller access application functionality encapsulated by the model. In the Duke's Bookstore application, the shopping cart and database access object contain the business logic for the application.

- The *view* renders the contents of a model. It gets data from the model and specifies how that data should be presented. It updates data presentation when the model changes. A view also forwards user input to a controller. The Duke's Bookstore JSP pages format the data stored in the session-scoped shopping cart and the page-scoped database bean.

- The *controller* defines application behavior. It dispatches user requests and selects views for presentation. It interprets user inputs and maps them into actions to be performed by the model. In a Web application, user inputs are

HTTP GET and POST requests. A controller selects the next view to display based on the user interactions and the outcome of the model operations. In the Duke's Bookstore application, the Dispatcher servlet is the controller. It examines the request URL, creates and initializes a session-scoped JavaBeans component—the shopping cart—and dispatches requests to view JSP pages.

Note: When employed in a Web application, the MVC architecture is often referred to as a Model-2 architecture. The bookstore example discussed in Chapter 11, which intermixes presentation and business logic, follows what is known as a Model-1 architecture. The Model-2 architecture is the recommended approach to designing Web applications.

In addition, this version of the application uses several custom tags from the JavaServer Pages Standard Tag Library (JSTL), described in Chapter 14:

- c:if, c:choose, c:when, and c:otherwise for flow control
- c:set for setting scoped variables
- c:url for encoding URLs
- fmt:message, fmt:formatNumber, and fmt:formatDate for providing locale-sensitive messages, numbers, and dates

Custom tags are the preferred mechanism for performing a wide variety of dynamic processing tasks, including accessing databases, using enterprise services such as email and directories, and implementing flow control. In earlier versions of JSP technology, such tasks were performed with JavaBeans components in conjunction with scripting elements (discussed in Chapter 16). Although still available in JSP 2.0 technology, scripting elements tend to make JSP pages more difficult to maintain because they mix presentation and logic, something that is discouraged in page design. Custom tags are introduced in Using Custom Tags (page 502) and described in detail in Chapter 15.

Finally, this version of the example contains an applet to generate a dynamic digital clock in the banner. See Including an Applet (page 508) for a description of the JSP element that generates HTML for downloading the applet.

The source code for the application is located in the <INSTALL>/ j2eetutorial14/examples/web/bookstore2/ directory (see Building the Examples, page xli). A sample bookstore2.war is provided in <INSTALL>/

j2eetutorial14/examples/web/provided-wars/. To build, package, deploy, and run the example, follow these steps:

1. Build and package the bookstore common files as described in Duke's Bookstore Examples (page 100).

2. In a terminal window, go to `<INSTALL>`/j2eetutorial14/examples/web/bookstore2/.

3. Run `asant build`. This target will spawn any necessary compilations and will copy files to the `<INSTALL>`/j2eetutorial14/examples/web/bookstore2/build/ directory.

4. Start the Application Server.

5. Perform all the operations described in Accessing Databases from Web Applications (page 100).

6. Start `deploytool`.

7. Create a Web application called `bookstore2` by running the New Web Component wizard. Select File→New→Web Component.

8. In the New Web Component wizard:

   a. Select the Create New Stand-Alone WAR Module radio button.

   b. Click Browse.

   c. In the WAR Location field, enter `<INSTALL>`/j2eetutorial14/examples/web/bookstore2/bookstore2.war.

   d. In the WAR Name field, enter bookstore2.

   e. In the Context Root field, enter /bookstore2.

   f. Click Edit Contents.

   g. In the Edit Contents dialog box, navigate to `<INSTALL>`/j2eetutorial14/examples/web/bookstore2/build/. Select the JSP pages bookstore.jsp, bookdetails.jsp, bookcatalog.jsp, bookshowcart.jsp, bookcashier.jsp, bookordererror.jsp, bookreceipt.jsp, duke.books.gif, and the clock, dispatcher, database, listeners, and template directories and click Add.

   h. Move /WEB-INF/classes/clock/ to the root directory of the WAR. By default, deploytool packages all classes in /WEB-INF/classes/. Because clock/DigitalClock.class is a client-side class, it must be packaged in the root directory. To do this, simply drag the clock directory from /WEB-INF/classes/ to the root directory in the pane labeled Contents of bookstore2.

i. Add the shared bookstore library. Navigate to *<INSTALL>*/ `j2eetutorial14/examples/web/bookstore/dist/`. Select `book-store.jar`, and click Add.

j. Click OK.

k. Click Next.

l. Select the Servlet radio button.

m. Click Next.

n. Select `dispatcher.Dispatcher` from the Servlet class combo box.

o. Click Finish.

9. Add the listener class `listeners.ContextListener` (described in Handling Servlet Life-Cycle Events, page 441).

a. Select the Event Listeners tab.

b. Click Add.

c. Select the `listeners.ContextListener` class from drop-down field in the Event Listener Classes pane.

10. Add the aliases.

a. Select the `Dispatcher` Web component.

b. Select the Aliases tab.

c. Click Add and then type `/bookstore` in the `Aliases` field. Repeat to add the aliases `/bookcatalog`, `/bookdetails`, `/bookshowcart`, `/bookcashier`, `/bookordererror`, and `/bookreceipt`.

11. Add the context parameter that specifies the JSTL resource bundle base name.

a. Select the Web module.

b. Select the Context tab.

c. Click Add.

d. Enter `javax.servlet.jsp.jstl.fmt.localizationContext` in the Coded Parameter field.

e. Enter `messages.BookstoreMessages` in the Value field.

12. Set the prelude and coda for all JSP pages.

a. Select the JSP Properties tab.

b. Click the Add button next to the Name list.

    c. Enter `bookstore2`.

    d. Click the Add button next to the URL Pattern list.

    e. Enter `*.jsp`.

    f. Click the Edit button next to the Include Preludes list.

    g. Click Add.

    h. Enter `/template/prelude.jspf`.

    i. Click OK.

    j. Click the Edit button next to the Include Codas list.

    k. Click Add.

    l. Enter `/template/coda.jspf`.

    m. Click OK.

13. Add a resource reference for the database.

    a. Select the Resource Ref's tab.

    b. Click Add.

    c. Enter `jdbc/BookDB` in the Coded Name field.

    d. Accept the default type `javax.sql.DataSource`.

    e. Accept the default authorization `Container`.

    f. Accept the default selected `Shareable`.

    g. Enter `jdbc/BookDB` in the JNDI name field of the Sun-specific Settings frame.

14. Select File→Save.

15. Deploy the application.

    a. Select Tools→Deploy.

    b. Click OK.

16. Open the bookstore URL `http://localhost:8080/bookstore2/book-store`. Click on the Start Shopping link and you will see the screen in Figure 12–2.

See Troubleshooting (page 440) for help with diagnosing common problems related to the database server. If the messages in your pages appear as strings of the form ??? *Key* ???, the likely cause is that you have not provided the correct resource bundle base name as a context parameter.

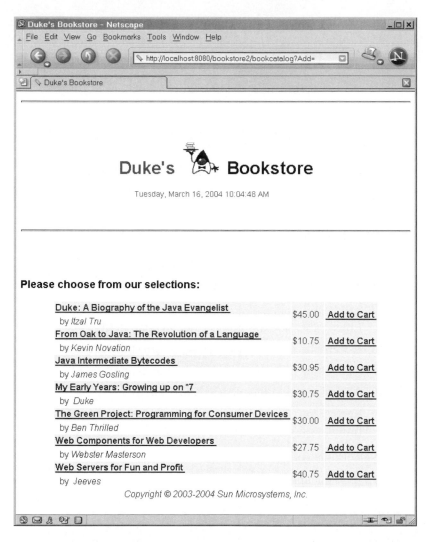

Figure 12–2 Book Catalog

The Life Cycle of a JSP Page

A JSP page services requests as a servlet. Thus, the life cycle and many of the capabilities of JSP pages (in particular the dynamic aspects) are determined by Java Servlet technology. You will notice that many sections in this chapter refer to classes and methods described in Chapter 11.

When a request is mapped to a JSP page, the Web container first checks whether the JSP page's servlet is older than the JSP page. If the servlet is older, the Web container translates the JSP page into a servlet class and compiles the class. During development, one of the advantages of JSP pages over servlets is that the build process is performed automatically.

Translation and Compilation

During the translation phase each type of data in a JSP page is treated differently. Static data is transformed into code that will emit the data into the response stream. JSP elements are treated as follows:

- Directives are used to control how the Web container translates and executes the JSP page.
- Scripting elements are inserted into the JSP page's servlet class. See Chapter 16 for details.
- Expression language expressions are passed as parameters to calls to the JSP expression evaluator.
- `jsp:[set|get]Property` elements are converted into method calls to JavaBeans components.
- `jsp:[include|forward]` elements are converted into invocations of the Java Servlet API.
- The `jsp:plugin` element is converted into browser-specific markup for activating an applet.
- Custom tags are converted into calls to the tag handler that implements the custom tag.

If you would like the Sun Java System Application Server Platform Edition 8 to keep the generated servlets for a Web module in `deploytool`, perform these steps:

1. Select the WAR.
2. Select the General tab.
3. Click the Sun-specific Settings button.
4. Select the Servlet/JSP Settings option from the View combo box.
5. Click the Add button in the JSP Configuration frame.
6. Select keepgenerated from the Name column.
7. Select true from the Value column.
8. Click Close.

In the Application Server, the source for the servlet created from a JSP page named *pageName* is in this file:

```
<J2EE_HOME>/domains/domain1/generated/
   jsp/WAR_NAME/pageName_jsp.java
```

For example, the source for the index page (named `index.jsp`) for the `date` localization example discussed at the beginning of the chapter would be named

```
<J2EE_HOME>/domains/domain1/generated/
   jsp/date/index_jsp.java
```

Both the translation and the compilation phases can yield errors that are observed only when the page is requested for the first time. If an error is encountered during either phase, the server will return `JasperException` and a message that includes the name of the JSP page and the line where the error occurred.

After the page has been translated and compiled, the JSP page's servlet (for the most part) follows the servlet life cycle described in Servlet Life Cycle (page 441):

1. If an instance of the JSP page's servlet does not exist, the container

   a. Loads the JSP page's servlet class

   b. Instantiates an instance of the servlet class

   c. Initializes the servlet instance by calling the `jspInit` method

2. The container invokes the `_jspService` method, passing request and response objects.

If the container needs to remove the JSP page's servlet, it calls the `jspDestroy` method.

Execution

You can control various JSP page execution parameters by using `page` directives. The directives that pertain to buffering output and handling errors are discussed here. Other directives are covered in the context of specific page-authoring tasks throughout the chapter.

Buffering

When a JSP page is executed, output written to the response object is automatically buffered. You can set the size of the buffer using the following page directive:

```
<%@ page buffer="none|xxxkb" %>
```

A larger buffer allows more content to be written before anything is actually sent back to the client, thus providing the JSP page with more time to set appropriate status codes and headers or to forward to another Web resource. A smaller buffer decreases server memory load and allows the client to start receiving data more quickly.

Handling Errors

Any number of exceptions can arise when a JSP page is executed. To specify that the Web container should forward control to an error page if an exception occurs, include the following `page` directive at the beginning of your JSP page:

```
<%@ page errorPage="file_name" %>
```

The Duke's Bookstore application page `prelude.jspf` contains the directive

```
<%@ page errorPage="errorpage.jsp"%>
```

The following page directive at the beginning of `errorpage.jsp` indicates that it is serving as an error page

```
<%@ page isErrorPage="true" %>
```

This directive makes an object of type `javax.servlet.jsp.ErrorData` available to the error page so that you can retrieve, interpret, and possibly display information about the cause of the exception in the error page. You access the error data object in an expression language (see Expression Language, page 489) expression via the page context. Thus, `${pageContext.errorData.status-Code}` is used to retrieve the status code, and `${pageContext.error-Data.throwable}` retrieves the exception. If the exception is generated during the evaluation of an EL expression, you can retrieve the root cause of the exception using this expression:

```
${pageContext.errorData.throwable.rootCause}
```

For example, the error page for Duke's Bookstore is as follows:

```
<%@ page isErrorPage="true" %>
<%@ taglib uri="http://java.sun.com/jsp/jstl/core"
  prefix="c" %>
<%@ taglib uri="http://java.sun.com/jsp/jstl/fmt"
  prefix="fmt" %>
<html>
<head>
<title><fmt:message key="ServerError"/></title>
</head>
<body bgcolor="white">
<h3>
<fmt:message key="ServerError"/>
</h3>
<p>
${pageContext.errorData.throwable}
<c:choose>
  <c:when test="${!empty
    pageContext.errorData.throwable.cause}">
    : ${pageContext.errorData.throwable.cause}
  </c:when>
  <c:when test="${!empty
    pageContext.errorData.throwable.rootCause}">
    : ${pageContext.errorData.throwable.rootCause}
  </c:when>
</c:choose>
</body>
</html>
```

Note: You can also define error pages for the WAR that contains a JSP page. If error pages are defined for both the WAR and a JSP page, the JSP page's error page takes precedence.

Creating Static Content

You create static content in a JSP page simply by writing it as if you were creating a page that consisted only of that content. Static content can be expressed in any text-based format, such as HTML, Wireless Markup Language (WML), and XML. The default format is HTML. If you want to use a format other than HTML, at the beginning of your JSP page you include a page directive with the contentType attribute set to the content type. The purpose of the contentType directive is to allow the browser to correctly interpret the resulting content. So if you wanted a page to contain data expressed in WML, you would include the following directive:

```
<%@ page contentType="text/vnd.wap.wml"%>
```

A registry of content type names is kept by the IANA at

```
http://www.iana.org/assignments/media-types/
```

Response and Page Encoding

You also use the contentType attribute to specify the encoding of the response. For example, the date application specifies that the page should be encoded using UTF-8, an encoding that supports almost all locales, using the following page directive:

```
<%@ page contentType="text/html; charset=UTF-8" %>
```

If the response encoding weren't set, the localized dates would not be rendered correctly.

To set the source encoding of the page itself, you would use the following page directive.

```
<%@ page pageEncoding="UTF-8" %>
```

You can also set the page encoding of a set of JSP pages. The value of the page encoding varies depending on the configuration specified in the JSP configuration section of the Web application deployment descriptor (see Declaring Page Encodings, page 512).

Creating Dynamic Content

You create dynamic content by accessing Java programming language object properties.

Using Objects within JSP Pages

You can access a variety of objects, including enterprise beans and JavaBeans components, within a JSP page. JSP technology automatically makes some objects available, and you can also create and access application-specific objects.

Using Implicit Objects

Implicit objects are created by the Web container and contain information related to a particular request, page, session, or application. Many of the objects are defined by the Java servlet technology underlying JSP technology and are discussed at length in Chapter 11. The section Implicit Objects (page 492) explains how you access implicit objects using the JSP expression language.

Using Application-Specific Objects

When possible, application behavior should be encapsulated in objects so that page designers can focus on presentation issues. Objects can be created by developers who are proficient in the Java programming language and in accessing databases and other services. The main way to create and use application-specific objects within a JSP page is to use JSP standard tags (discussed in JavaBeans Components, page 497) to create JavaBeans components and set their properties, and EL expressions to access their properties. You can also access JavaBeans components and other objects in scripting elements, which are described in Chapter 16.

Using Shared Objects

The conditions affecting concurrent access to shared objects (described in Controlling Concurrent Access to Shared Resources, page 445) apply to objects accessed from JSP pages that run as multithreaded servlets. You can use the following page directive to indicate how a Web container should dispatch multiple client requests

```
<%@ page isThreadSafe="true|false" %>
```

When the isThreadSafe attribute is set to true, the Web container can choose to dispatch multiple concurrent client requests to the JSP page. This is the *default* setting. If using true, you must ensure that you properly synchronize access to any shared objects defined at the page level. This includes objects created within declarations, JavaBeans components with page scope, and attributes of the page context object (see Implicit Objects, page 492).

If isThreadSafe is set to false, requests are dispatched one at a time in the order they were received, and access to page-level objects does not have to be controlled. However, you still must ensure that access is properly synchronized to attributes of the application or session scope objects and to JavaBeans components with application or session scope. Furthermore, it is not recommended to set isThreadSafe to false: The JSP page's generated servlet will implement the javax.servlet.SingleThreadModel interface, and because the Servlet 2.4 specification deprecates SingleThreadModel, the generated servlet will contain deprecated code.

Expression Language

A primary feature of JSP technology version 2.0 is its support for an expression language (EL). An expression language makes it possible to easily access application data stored in JavaBeans components. For example, the JSP expression language allows a page author to access a bean using simple syntax such as ${name} for a simple variable or ${name.foo.bar} for a nested property.

The test attribute of the following conditional tag is supplied with an EL expression that compares the number of items in the session-scoped bean named cart with 0:

```
<c:if test="${sessionScope.cart.numberOfItems > 0}">
    ...
</c:if>
```

The JSP expression evaluator is responsible for handling EL expressions, which are enclosed by the ${ } characters and can include literals. Here's an example:

```
<c:if test="${bean1.a < 3}" >
    ...
</c:if>
```

Any value that does not begin with ${ is treated as a literal and is parsed to the expected type using the PropertyEditor for the type:

```
<c:if test="true" >
...
</c:if>
```

Literal values that contain the ${ characters must be escaped as follows:

```
<mytags:example attr1="an expression is ${'${'}true}" />
```

Deactivating Expression Evaluation

Because the pattern that identifies EL expressions—${ }—was not reserved in the JSP specifications before JSP 2.0, there may be applications where such a pattern is intended to pass through verbatim. To prevent the pattern from being evaluated, you can deactivate EL evaluation.

To deactivate the evaluation of EL expressions, you specify the isELIgnored attribute of the page directive:

```
<%@ page isELIgnored ="true|false" %>
```

The valid values of this attribute are true and false. If it is true, EL expressions are ignored when they appear in static text or tag attributes. If it is false, EL expressions are evaluated by the container.

The default value varies depending on the version of the Web application deployment descriptor. The default mode for JSP pages delivered using a Servlet 2.3 or earlier descriptor is to ignore EL expressions; this provides backward compatibility. The default mode for JSP pages delivered with a Servlet 2.4 descriptor is to evaluate EL expressions; this automatically provides the default that most applications want. You can also deactivate EL expression evaluation for a group of JSP pages (see Deactivating EL Expression Evaluation, page 511).

Using Expressions

EL expressions can be used:

- In static text
- In any standard or custom tag attribute that can accept an expression

The value of an expression in static text is computed and inserted into the current output. If the static text appears in a tag body, note that an expression *will not* be evaluated if the body is declared to be tagdependent (see body-content Attribute, page 579).

There are three ways to set a tag attribute value:

- With a single expression construct:

```
<some:tag value="${expr}"/>
```

  The expression is evaluated and the result is coerced to the attribute's expected type.

- With one or more expressions separated or surrounded by text:

```
<some:tag value="some${expr}${expr}text${expr}"/>
```

  The expressions are evaluated from left to right. Each expression is coerced to a `String` and then concatenated with any intervening text. The resulting `String` is then coerced to the attribute's expected type.

- With text only:

```
<some:tag value="sometext"/>
```

  In this case, the attribute's `String` value is coerced to the attribute's expected type.

Expressions used to set attribute values are evaluated in the context of an expected type. If the result of the expression evaluation does not match the expected type exactly, a type conversion will be performed. For example, the expression `${1.2E4 + 1.4}` provided as the value of an attribute of type `float` will result in the following conversion:

```
Float.valueOf("1.2E4 + 1.4").floatValue()
```

See section JSP2.8 of the JSP 2.0 specification for the complete type conversion rules.

Variables

The Web container evaluates a variable that appears in an expression by looking up its value according to the behavior of `PageContext.findAttribute(String)`. For example, when evaluating the expression `${product}`, the container will look for `product` in the page, request, session, and application scopes and will return its value. If `product` is not found, `null` is returned. A variable that matches one of the implicit objects described in Implicit Objects (page 492) will return that implicit object instead of the variable's value.

Properties of variables are accessed using the `.` operator and can be nested arbitrarily.

The JSP expression language unifies the treatment of the `.` and `[]` operators. `expr-a.expr-b` is equivalent to `a["expr-b"]`; that is, the expression `expr-b` is used to construct a literal whose value is the identifier, and then the `[]` operator is used with that value.

To evaluate `expr-a[expr-b]`, evaluate `expr-a` into `value-a` and evaluate `expr-b` into `value-b`. If either `value-a` or `value-b` is null, return `null`.

- If `value-a` is a `Map`, return `value-a.get(value-b)`. If `!value-a.containsKey(value-b)`, then return `null`.
- If `value-a` is a `List` or array, coerce `value-b` to `int` and return `value-a.get(value-b)` or `Array.get(value-a, value-b)`, as appropriate. If the coercion couldn't be performed, an error is returned. If the `get` call returns an `IndexOutOfBoundsException`, `null` is returned. If the `get` call returns another exception, an error is returned.
- If `value-a` is a JavaBeans object, coerce `value-b` to `String`. If `value-b` is a readable property of `value-a`, then return the result of a `get` call. If the `get` method throws an exception, an error is returned.

Implicit Objects

The JSP expression language defines a set of implicit objects:

- `pageContext`: The context for the JSP page. Provides access to various objects including:
  - `servletContext`: The context for the JSP page's servlet and any Web components contained in the same application. See Accessing the Web Context (page 463).
  - `session`: The session object for the client. See Maintaining Client State (page 464).
  - `request`: The request triggering the execution of the JSP page. See Getting Information from Requests (page 449).
  - `response`: The response returned by the JSP page. See Constructing Responses (page 451).

In addition, several implicit objects are available that allow easy access to the following objects:

- `param`: Maps a request parameter name to a single value
- `paramValues`: Maps a request parameter name to an array of values
- `header`: Maps a request header name to a single value

- headerValues: Maps a request header name to an array of values
- cookie: Maps a cookie name to a single cookie
- initParam: Maps a context initialization parameter name to a single value

Finally, there are objects that allow access to the various scoped variables described in Using Scope Objects (page 444).

- pageScope: Maps page-scoped variable names to their values
- requestScope: Maps request-scoped variable names to their values
- sessionScope: Maps session-scoped variable names to their values
- applicationScope: Maps application-scoped variable names to their values

When an expression references one of these objects by name, the appropriate object is returned instead of the corresponding attribute. For example, ${pageContext} returns the PageContext object, even if there is an existing pageContext attribute containing some other value.

Literals

The JSP expression language defines the following literals:

- Boolean: true and false
- Integer: as in Java
- Floating point: as in Java
- String: with single and double quotes; " is escaped as \", ' is escaped as \', and \ is escaped as \\.
- Null: null

Operators

In addition to the . and [] operators discussed in Variables (page 491), the JSP expression language provides the following operators:

- Arithmetic: +, - (binary), *, / and div, % and mod, - (unary)
- Logical: and, &&, or, ||, not, !
- Relational: ==, eq, !=, ne, <, lt, >, gt, <=, ge, >=, le. Comparisons can be made against other values, or against boolean, string, integer, or floating point literals.

- Empty: The `empty` operator is a prefix operation that can be used to determine whether a value is `null` or empty.
- Conditional: `A ? B : C`. Evaluate `B` or `C`, depending on the result of the evaluation of `A`.

The precedence of operators highest to lowest, left to right is as follows:

- `[] .`
- `()` - Used to change the precedence of operators.
- `-` (unary) `not ! empty`
- `* / div % mod`
- `+ -` (binary)
- `< > <= >= lt gt le ge`
- `== != eq ne`
- `&& and`
- `|| or`
- `? :`

Reserved Words

The following words are reserved for the JSP expression language and should not be used as identifiers.

```
and   eq   gt   true    instanceof
or    ne   le   false   empty
not   lt   ge   null    div    mod
```

Note that many of these words are not in the language now, but they may be in the future, so you should avoid using them.

Examples

Table 12–2 contains example EL expressions and the result of evaluating them.

Table 12–2 Example Expressions

EL Expression	Result
`${1 > (4/2)]`	false
`${4.0 >= 3}`	true
`${100.0 == 100}`	true
`${(10*10) ne 100}`	false
`${'a' < 'b'}`	true
`${'hip' gt 'hit'}`	false
`${4 > 3}`	true
`${1.2E4 + 1.4}`	12001.4
`${3 div 4}`	0.75
`${10 mod 4}`	2
`${!empty param.Add}`	True if the request parameter named Add is null or an empty string
`${pageContext.request.contextPath}`	The context path
`${sessionScope.cart.numberOfItems}`	The value of the numberOfItems property of the session-scoped attribute named cart
`${param['mycom.productId']}`	The value of the request parameter named mycom.productId
`${header["host"]}`	The host
`${departments[deptName]}`	The value of the entry named deptName in the departments map
`${requestScope['javax.servlet.forward.servlet_path']}`	The value of the request-scoped attribute named javax.servlet.forward.servlet_path

Functions

The JSP expression language allows you to define a function that can be invoked in an expression. Functions are defined using the same mechanisms as custom tags (See Using Custom Tags, page 502 and Chapter 15).

Using Functions

Functions can appear in static text and tag attribute values.

To use a function in a JSP page, you use a `taglib` directive to import the tag library containing the function. Then you preface the function invocation with the prefix declared in the directive.

For example, the date example page `index.jsp` imports the `/functions` library and invokes the function `equals` in an expression:

```
<%@ taglib prefix="f" uri="/functions"%>
...
    <c:when
        test="${f:equals(selectedLocaleString,
            localeString)}" >
```

Defining Functions

To define a function you program it as a public static method in a public class. The `mypkg.MyLocales` class in the `date` example defines a function that tests the equality of two `Strings` as follows:

```
package mypkg;
public class MyLocales {

    ...
    public static boolean equals( String l1, String l2 ) {
        return l1.equals(l2);
    }
}
```

Then you map the function name as used in the EL expression to the defining class and function signature in a TLD. The following `functions.tld` file in the date example maps the `equals` function to the class containing the implementation of the function `equals` and the signature of the function:

```
<function>
  <name>equals</name>
  <function-class>mypkg.MyLocales</function-class>
  <function-signature>boolean equals( java.lang.String,
    java.lang.String )</function-signature>
</function>
```

A tag library can have only one `function` element that has any given `name` element.

JavaBeans Components

JavaBeans components are Java classes that can be easily reused and composed together into applications. Any Java class that follows certain design conventions is a JavaBeans component.

JavaServer Pages technology directly supports using JavaBeans components with standard JSP language elements. You can easily create and initialize beans and get and set the values of their properties.

JavaBeans Component Design Conventions

JavaBeans component design conventions govern the properties of the class and govern the public methods that give access to the properties.

A JavaBeans component property can be

- Read/write, read-only, or write-only
- Simple, which means it contains a single value, or indexed, which means it represents an array of values

A property does not have to be implemented by an instance variable. It must simply be accessible using public methods that conform to the following conventions:

- For each readable property, the bean must have a method of the form

    ```
    PropertyClass getProperty() { ... }
    ```

- For each writable property, the bean must have a method of the form

    ```
    setProperty(PropertyClass pc) { ... }
    ```

In addition to the property methods, a JavaBeans component must define a constructor that takes no parameters.

The Duke's Bookstore application JSP pages bookstore.jsp, bookdetails.jsp, catalog.jsp, and showcart.jsp use the database.BookDB and database.BookDetails JavaBeans components. BookDB provides a JavaBeans component front end to the access object database.BookDBAO. The JSP pages showcart.jsp and cashier.jsp access the bean cart.ShoppingCart, which represents a user's shopping cart.

The BookDB bean has two writable properties, bookId and database, and three readable properties: bookDetails, numberOfBooks, and books. These latter properties do not correspond to any instance variables but rather are a function of the bookId and database properties.

```
package database;
public class BookDB {
private String bookId = "0";
private BookDBAO database = null;
  public BookDB () {
  }
  public void setBookId(String bookId) {
  this.bookId = bookId;
  }
  public void setDatabase(BookDBAO database) {
  this.database = database;
  }
  public BookDetails getBookDetails() throws
     BookNotFoundException {
     return (BookDetails)database.getBookDetails(bookId);
  }
  public List getBooks() throws BooksNotFoundException {
     return database.getBooks();
  }
  public void buyBooks(ShoppingCart cart)
     throws OrderException {
     database.buyBooks(cart);
  }
  public int getNumberOfBooks() throws BooksNotFoundException {
     return database.getNumberOfBooks();
  }
 }
}
```

Creating and Using a JavaBeans Component

To declare that your JSP page will use a JavaBeans component, you use a jsp:useBean element. There are two forms:

```
<jsp:useBean id="beanName"
  class="fully_qualified_classname" scope="scope"/>
```

and

```
<jsp:useBean id="beanName"
  class="fully_qualified_classname" scope="scope">
  <jsp:setProperty .../>
</jsp:useBean>
```

The second form is used when you want to include jsp:setProperty statements, described in the next section, for initializing bean properties.

The jsp:useBean element declares that the page will use a bean that is stored within and is accessible from the specified scope, which can be application, session, request, or page. If no such bean exists, the statement creates the bean and stores it as an attribute of the scope object (see Using Scope Objects, page 444). The value of the id attribute determines the *name* of the bean in the scope and the *identifier* used to reference the bean in EL expressions, other JSP elements, and scripting expressions (see Chapter 16). The value supplied for the class attribute must be a fully qualified class name. Note that beans cannot be in the unnamed package. Thus the format of the value must be *package_name.class_name*.

The following element creates an instance of mypkg.myLocales if none exists, stores it as an attribute of the application scope, and makes the bean available throughout the application by the identifier locales:

```
<jsp:useBean id="locales" scope="application"
  class="mypkg.MyLocales"/>
```

Setting JavaBeans Component Properties

The standard way to set JavaBeans component properties in a JSP page is by using the `jsp:setProperty` element. The syntax of the `jsp:setProperty` element depends on the source of the property value. Table 12–3 summarizes the various ways to set a property of a JavaBeans component using the `jsp:setProperty` element.

A property set from a constant string or request parameter must have one of the types listed in Table 12–4. Because constants and request parameters are strings, the Web container automatically converts the value to the property's type; the conversion applied is shown in the table.

Table 12–3 Valid Bean Property Assignments from String Values

Value Source	Element Syntax
String constant	`<jsp:setProperty name="beanName"` `    property="propName" value="string constant"/>`
Request parameter	`<jsp:setProperty name="beanName"` `    property="propName" param="paramName"/>`

Request parameter name that matches bean property	`<jsp:setProperty name="beanName"`
	`    property="propName"/>`
	
	`<jsp:setProperty name="beanName"`
	`    property="*"/>`

Expression	`<jsp:setProperty name="beanName"`
	`    property="propName" value="expression"/>`
	
	`<jsp:setProperty name="beanName"`
	`    property="propName" >`
	`<jsp:attribute name="value">`
	`expression`
	`</jsp:attribute>`
	`</jsp:setProperty>`

	1. *beanName* must be the same as that specified for the `id` attribute in a `useBean` element. 2. There must be a *setPropName* method in the JavaBeans component. 3. *paramName* must be a request parameter name.

Table 12–4 Valid Property Value Assignments from String Values

Property Type	Conversion on String Value
Bean property	Uses `setAsText(string-literal)`
`boolean` or `Boolean`	As indicated in `java.lang.Boolean.valueOf(String)`
`byte` or `Byte`	As indicated in `java.lang.Byte.valueOf(String)`
`char` or `Character`	As indicated in `java.lang.String.charAt(0)`
`double` or `Double`	As indicated in `java.lang.Double.valueOf(String)`
`int` or `Integer`	As indicated in `java.lang.Integer.valueOf(String)`
`float` or `Float`	As indicated in `java.lang.Float.valueOf(String)`
`long` or `Long`	As indicated in `java.lang.Long.valueOf(String)`
`short` or `Short`	As indicated in `java.lang.Short.valueOf(String)`
`Object`	new `String(string-literal)`

`String` values can be used to assign values to a property that has a `PropertyEditor` class. When that is the case, the `setAsText(String)` method is used. A conversion failure arises if the method throws an `IllegalArgumentException`.

The value assigned to an indexed property must be an array, and the rules just described apply to the elements.

You use an expression to set the value of a property whose type is a compound Java programming language type. The type returned from an expression must match or be castable to the type of the property.

The Duke's Bookstore application demonstrates how to use the `setProperty` element to set the current book from a request parameter in the database bean in `bookstore2/web/bookdetails.jsp`:

```
<c:set var="bid" value="${param.bookId}"/>
<jsp:setProperty name="bookDB" property="bookId"
  value="${bid}" />
```

The following fragment from the page `bookstore2/web/bookshowcart.jsp` illustrates how to initialize a `BookDB` bean with a `database` object. Because the initialization is nested in a `useBean` element, it is executed only when the bean is created.

```
<jsp:useBean id="bookDB" class="database.BookDB" scope="page">
  <jsp:setProperty name="bookDB" property="database"
    value="${bookDBAO}" />
</jsp:useBean>
```

Retrieving JavaBeans Component Properties

The main way to retrieve JavaBeans component properties is by using the JSP EL expressions. Thus, to retrieve a book title, the Duke's Bookstore application uses the following expression:

```
${bookDB.bookDetails.title}
```

Another way to retrieve component properties is to use the `jsp:getProperty` element. This element converts the value of the property into a `String` and inserts the value into the response stream:

```
<jsp:getProperty name="beanName" property="propName"/>
```

Note that *beanName* must be the same as that specified for the `id` attribute in a `useBean` element, and there must be a get*PropName* method in the JavaBeans component. Although the preferred approach to getting properties is to use an EL expression, the `getProperty` element is available if you need to disable expression evaluation.

Using Custom Tags

Custom tags are user-defined JSP language elements that encapsulate recurring tasks. Custom tags are distributed in a *tag library*, which defines a set of related custom tags and contains the objects that implement the tags.

Custom tags have the syntax

```
<prefix:tag attr1="value" ... attrN="value" />
```

or

```
<prefix:tag attr1="value" ... attrN="value" >
  body
</prefix:tag>
```

where `prefix` distinguishes tags for a library, `tag` is the tag identifier, and `attr1` ... `attrN` are attributes that modify the behavior of the tag.

To use a custom tag in a JSP page, you must

- Declare the tag library containing the tag
- Make the tag library implementation available to the Web application

See Chapter 15 for detailed information on the different types of tags and how to implement tags.

Declaring Tag Libraries

To declare that a JSP page will use tags defined in a tag library, you include a `taglib` directive in the page before any custom tag from that tag library is used. If you forget to include the `taglib` directive for a tag library in a JSP page, the JSP compiler will treat any invocation of a custom tag from that library as static data and will simply insert the text of the custom tag call into the response.

```
<%@ taglib prefix="tt" [tagdir=/WEB-INF/tags/dir | uri=URI ] %>
```

The `prefix` attribute defines the prefix that distinguishes tags defined by a given tag library from those provided by other tag libraries.

If the tag library is defined with tag files (see Encapsulating Reusable Content Using Tag Files, page 573), you supply the `tagdir` attribute to identify the location of the files. The value of the attribute must start with `/WEB-INF/tags/`. A translation error will occur if the value points to a directory that doesn't exist or if it is used in conjunction with the `uri` attribute.

The `uri` attribute refers to a URI that uniquely identifies the tag library descriptor (TLD), a document that describes the tag library (see Tag Library Descriptors, page 589).

Tag library descriptor file names must have the extension `.tld`. TLD files are stored in the `WEB-INF` directory or subdirectory of the WAR file or in the `META-INF/` directory or subdirectory of a tag library packaged in a JAR. You can reference a TLD directly or indirectly.

The following `taglib` directive directly references a TLD file name:

```
<%@ taglib prefix="tlt" uri="/WEB-INF/iterator.tld"%>
```

This `taglib` directive uses a short logical name to indirectly reference the TLD:

```
<%@ taglib prefix="tlt" uri="/tlt"%>
```

The `iterator` example defines and uses a simple iteration tag. The JSP pages use a logical name to reference the TLD. A sample `iterator.war` is provided in `<INSTALL>/j2eetutorial14/examples/web/provided-wars/`. To build and package the example, follow these steps:

1. In a terminal window, go to `<INSTALL>/j2eetutorial14/examples/web/iterator/`.
2. Run `asant build`. This target will spawn any necessary compilations and will copy files to the `<INSTALL>/j2eetutorial14/examples/web/iterator/build/` directory.
3. Start `deploytool`.
4. Create a Web application called `iterator` by running the New Web Component wizard. Select File→New→Web Component.
5. In the New Web Component wizard:
   a. Select the Create New Stand-Alone WAR Module radio button.
   b. Click Browse.
   c. In the WAR Location field, enter `<INSTALL>/docs/tutorial/examples/web/iterator/iterator.war`.
   d. In the WAR Name field, enter `iterator`.
   e. In the Context Root field, enter `/iterator`.
   f. Click Edit Contents.
   g. In the Edit Contents dialog box, navigate to `<INSTALL>/docs/tutorial/examples/web/iterator/build/`. Select the `index.jsp` and `list.jsp` JSP pages and `iterator.tld` and click Add. Notice that `iterator.tld` is put into `/WEB-INF/`.
   h. Click Next.
   i. Select the No Component radio button.
   j. Click Next.
   k. Click Finish.

You map a logical name to an absolute location in the Web application deployment descriptor. For the `iterator` example, map the logical name `/tlt` to the absolute location `/WEB-INF/iterator.tld` using deploytool by following these steps:

1. Select the File Ref's tab.
2. Click the Add Tag Library button in the JSP Tag Libraries tab.
3. Enter the relative URI `/tlt` in the Coded Reference field.
4. Enter the absolute location `/WEB-INF/iterator.tld` in the Tag Library field.

You can also reference a TLD in a `taglib` directive by using an absolute URI. For example, the absolute URIs for the JSTL library are as follows:

- *Core*: `http://java.sun.com/jsp/jstl/core`
- *XML*: `http://java.sun.com/jsp/jstl/xml`
- *Internationalization*: `http://java.sun.com/jsp/jstl/fmt`
- *SQL*: `http://java.sun.com/jsp/jstl/sql`
- *Functions*: `http://java.sun.com/jsp/jstl/functions`

When you reference a tag library with an absolute URI that exactly matches the URI declared in the `taglib` element of the TLD (see Tag Library Descriptors, page 589), you do not have to add the `taglib` element to `web.xml`; the JSP container automatically locates the TLD inside the JSTL library implementation.

Including the Tag Library Implementation

In addition to declaring the tag library, you also must make the tag library implementation available to the Web application. There are several ways to do this. Tag library implementations can be included in a WAR in an unpacked format: Tag files are packaged in the `/WEB-INF/tag/` directory, and tag handler classes are packaged in the `/WEB-INF/classes/` directory of the WAR. Tag libraries already packaged into a JAR file are included in the `/WEB-INF/lib/` directory of the WAR. Finally, an application server can load a tag library into all the Web applications running on the server. For example, in the Application Server, the JSTL TLDs and libraries are distributed in the archive `appserv-jstl.jar` in `<J2EE_HOME>/lib/`. This library is automatically loaded into the classpath of all Web applications running on the Application Server so you don't need to add it to your Web application.

To package the `iterator` tag library implementation in the `/WEB-INF/classes/` directory and deploy the `iterator` example with `deploytool`, follow these steps:

1. Select the General tab.
2. Click Edit Contents.
3. Add the iterator tag library classes.
   a. In the Edit Contents dialog box, navigate to `<INSTALL>/docs/tutorial/examples/web/iterator/build/`.
   b. Select the `iterator` and `myorg` packages and click Add. Notice that the tag library implementation classes are packaged into `/WEB-INF/classes/`.
4. Click OK.
5. Select File→Save.
6. Start the Application Server.
7. Deploy the application.
   a. Select Tools→Deploy.
   b. Click OK.

To run the `iterator` application, open the URL `http://localhost:8080/iterator` in a browser.

Reusing Content in JSP Pages

There are many mechanisms for reusing JSP content in a JSP page. Three mechanisms that can be categorized as direct reuse—the `include` directive, preludes and codas, and the `jsp:include` element—are discussed here. An indirect method of content reuse occurs when a tag file is used to define a custom tag that is used by many Web applications. Tag files are discussed in the section Encapsulating Reusable Content Using Tag Files (page 573) in Chapter 15.

The `include` directive is processed when the JSP page is *translated* into a servlet class. The effect of the directive is to insert the text contained in another file— either static content or another JSP page—into the including JSP page. You would probably use the `include` directive to include banner content, copyright information, or any chunk of content that you might want to reuse in another page. The syntax for the `include` directive is as follows:

```
<%@ include file="filename" %>
```

For example, all the Duke's Bookstore application pages could include the file `banner.jspf`, which contains the banner content, by using the following directive:

```
<%@ include file="banner.jspf" %>
```

Another way to do a static include is to use the prelude and coda mechanisms described in Defining Implicit Includes (page 512). This is the approach used by the Duke's Bookstore application.

Because you must put an `include` directive in each file that reuses the resource referenced by the directive, this approach has its limitations. Preludes and codas can be applied only to the beginnings and ends of pages. For a more flexible approach to building pages out of content chunks, see A Template Tag Library (page 610).

The `jsp:include` element is processed when a JSP page is *executed*. The `include` action allows you to include either a static or a dynamic resource in a JSP file. The results of including static and dynamic resources are quite different. If the resource is static, its content is inserted into the calling JSP file. If the resource is dynamic, the request is sent to the included resource, the included page is executed, and then the result is included in the response from the calling JSP page. The syntax for the `jsp:include` element is

```
<jsp:include page="includedPage" />
```

The `hello1` application discussed in Packaging Web Modules (page 88) uses the following statement to include the page that generates the response:

```
<jsp:include page="response.jsp"/>
```

Transferring Control to Another Web Component

The mechanism for transferring control to another Web component from a JSP page uses the functionality provided by the Java Servlet API as described in Transferring Control to Another Web Component (page 462). You access this functionality from a JSP page by using the `jsp:forward` element:

```
<jsp:forward page="/main.jsp" />
```

Note that if any data has already been returned to a client, the `jsp:forward` element will fail with an `IllegalStateException`.

jsp:param Element

When an `include` or `forward` element is invoked, the original request object is provided to the target page. If you wish to provide additional data to that page, you can append parameters to the request object by using the `jsp:param` element:

```
<jsp:include page="..." >
  <jsp:param name="param1" value="value1"/>
</jsp:include>
```

When `jsp:include` or `jsp:forward` is executed, the included page or forwarded page will see the original request object, with the original parameters augmented with the new parameters and new values taking precedence over existing values when applicable. For example, if the request has a parameter A=foo and a parameter A=bar is specified for forward, the forwarded request will have A=bar,foo. Note that the new parameter has precedence.

The scope of the new parameters is the `jsp:include` or `jsp:forward` call; that is, in the case of an `jsp:include` the new parameters (and values) will not apply after the include.

Including an Applet

You can include an applet or a JavaBeans component in a JSP page by using the `jsp:plugin` element. This element generates HTML that contains the appropriate client-browser-dependent construct (`<object>` or `<embed>`) that will result in the download of the Java Plug-in software (if required) and the client-side component and in the subsequent execution of any client-side component. The syntax for the `jsp:plugin` element is as follows:

```
<jsp:plugin
  type="bean|applet"
  code="objectCode"
  codebase="objectCodebase"
  { align="alignment" }
  { archive="archiveList" }
  { height="height" }
  { hspace="hspace" }
  { jreversion="jreversion" }
  { name="componentName" }
  { vspace="vspace" }
  { width="width" }
```

```
    { nspluginurl="url" }
    { iepluginurl="url" } >
    { <jsp:params>
        { <jsp:param name="paramName" value= paramValue" /> }+
    </jsp:params> }
    { <jsp:fallback> arbitrary_text </jsp:fallback> }
</jsp:plugin>
```

The `jsp:plugin` tag is replaced by either an `<object>` or an `<embed>` tag as appropriate for the requesting client. The attributes of the `jsp:plugin` tag provide configuration data for the presentation of the element as well as the version of the plug-in required. The `nspluginurl` and `iepluginurl` attributes override the default URL where the plug-in can be downloaded.

The `jsp:params` element specifies parameters to the applet or JavaBeans component. The `jsp:fallback` element indicates the content to be used by the client browser if the plug-in cannot be started (either because `<object>` or `<embed>` is not supported by the client or because of some other problem).

If the plug-in can start but the applet or JavaBeans component cannot be found or started, a plug-in-specific message will be presented to the user, most likely a pop-up window reporting a `ClassNotFoundException`.

The Duke's Bookstore page `/template/prelude.jspf` creates the banner that displays a dynamic digital clock generated by `DigitalClock` (see Figure 12–3).

Here is the `jsp:plugin` element that is used to download the applet:

```
<jsp:plugin
    type="applet"
    code="DigitalClock.class"
    codebase="/bookstore2"
    jreversion="1.4"
    align="center" height="25" width="300"
    nspluginurl="http://java.sun.com/j2se/1.4.2/download.html"
    iepluginurl="http://java.sun.com/j2se/1.4.2/download.html" >
    <jsp:params>
        <jsp:param name="language"
            value="${pageContext.request.locale.language}" />
        <jsp:param name="country"
            value="${pageContext.request.locale.country}" />
        <jsp:param name="bgcolor" value="FFFFFF" />
        <jsp:param name="fgcolor" value="CC0066" />
    </jsp:params>
    <jsp:fallback>
        <p>Unable to start plugin.</p>
    </jsp:fallback>
</jsp:plugin>
```

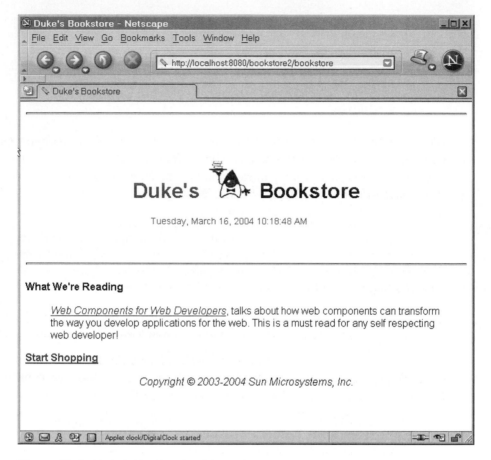

Figure 12–3 Duke's Bookstore with Applet

Setting Properties for Groups of JSP Pages

It is possible to specify certain properties for a group of JSP pages:

- Expression language evaluation
- Treatment of scripting elements (see Disabling Scripting, page 620)
- Page encoding
- Automatic prelude and coda includes

A JSP property group is defined by naming the group and specifying one or more URL patterns; all the properties in the group apply to the resources that match any of the URL patterns. If a resource matches URL patterns in more than one group, the pattern that is most specific applies. To define a property group using deploytool, follow these steps:

1. Select the WAR.
2. Select the JSP Properties tab.
3. Click the Add button next to the Name list.
4. Enter the name of the property group.
5. Click the Add button next to the URL Pattern list.
6. Enter the URL pattern (a regular expression, such as *.jsp).

The following sections discuss the properties and explain how they are interpreted for various combinations of group properties, individual page directives, and Web application deployment descriptor versions.

Deactivating EL Expression Evaluation

Each JSP page has a default mode for EL expression evaluation. The default value varies depending on the version of the Web application deployment descriptor. The default mode for JSP pages delivered using a Servlet 2.3 or earlier descriptor is to ignore EL expressions; this provides backward compatibility. The default mode for JSP pages delivered with a Servlet 2.4 descriptor is to evaluate EL expressions; this automatically provides the default that most applications want. For tag files (see Encapsulating Reusable Content Using Tag Files, page 573), the default is to always evaluate expressions.

You can override the default mode through the isELIgnored attribute of the page directive in JSP pages and through the isELIgnored attribute of the tag directive in tag files. You can also explicitly change the default mode by setting the value of the EL Evaluation Ignored checkbox in the JSP Properties tab. Table 12–5 summarizes the EL evaluation settings for JSP pages and their meanings.

Table 12–6 summarizes the EL evaluation settings for tag files and their meanings.

Table 12–5 EL Evaluation Settings for JSP Pages

JSP Configuration	Page Directive `isELIgnored`	EL Encountered
Unspecified	Unspecified	Evaluated if 2.4 `web.xml` Ignored if <= 2.3 `web.xml`
`false`	Unspecified	Evaluated
`true`	Unspecified	Ignored
Overridden by page directive	`false`	Evaluated
Overridden by page directive	`true`	Ignored

Table 12–6 EL Evaluation Settings for Tag Files

Tag Directive `isELIgnored`	EL Encountered
Unspecified	Evaluated
`false`	Evaluated
`true`	Ignored

Declaring Page Encodings

You set the page encoding of a group of JSP pages by selecting a page encoding from the Page Encoding drop-down list. Valid values are the same as those of the `pageEncoding` attribute of the `page` directive. A translation-time error results if you define the page encoding of a JSP page with one value in the JSP configuration element and then give it a different value in a `pageEncoding` directive.

Defining Implicit Includes

You can implicitly include preludes and codas for a group of JSP pages by adding items to the Include Preludes and Codas lists. Their values are context-relative paths that must correspond to elements in the Web application. When the elements are present, the given paths are automatically included (as in an include directive) at the beginning and end, respectively, of each JSP page in the property group. When there is more than one include or coda element in a group, they are included in the order they appear. When more than one JSP property group applies to a JSP page, the corresponding elements will be processed in the same order as they appear in the JSP configuration section.

For example, the Duke's Bookstore application uses the files `/template/prelude.jspf` and `/template/coda.jspf` to include the banner and other boilerplate in each screen. To add these files to the Duke's Bookstore property group using `deploytool`, follow these steps:

1. Define a property group with name `bookstore2` and URL pattern `*.jsp`.
2. Click the Edit button next to the Include Preludes list.
3. Click Add.
4. Enter `/template/prelude.jspf`.
5. Click OK.
6. Click the Edit button next to the Include Codas list.
7. Click Add.
8. Enter `/template/coda.jspf`.
9. Click OK.

Preludes and codas can put the included code only at the beginning and end of each file. For a more flexible approach to building pages out of content chunks, see A Template Tag Library (page 610).

Further Information

For further information on JavaServer Pages technology, see the following:

* JavaServer Pages 2.0 specification:
  `http://java.sun.com/products/jsp/download.html#specs`
* The JavaServer Pages Web site:
  `http://java.sun.com/products/jsp`

13

JavaServer Pages Documents

A *JSP document* is a JSP page written in XML syntax as opposed to the standard syntax described in Chapter 12. Because it is written in XML syntax, a JSP document is also an XML document and therefore gives you all the benefits offered by the XML standard:

- You can author a JSP document using one of the many XML-aware tools on the market, enabling you to ensure that your JSP document is well-formed XML.

- You can validate the JSP document against a document type definition (DTD).

- You can nest and scope namespaces within a JSP document.

- You can use a JSP document for data interchange between Web applications and as part of a compile-time XML pipeline.

In addition to these benefits, the XML syntax gives the JSP page author less complexity and more flexibility. For example, a page author can use any XML document as a JSP document. Also, elements in XML syntax can be used in JSP pages written in standard syntax, allowing a gradual transition from JSP pages to JSP documents.

This chapter gives you details on the benefits of JSP documents and uses a simple example to show you how easy it is to create a JSP document.

You can also write tag files in XML syntax. This chapter covers only JSP documents. Writing tag files in XML syntax will be addressed in a future release of the tutorial.

The Example JSP Document

This chapter uses the Duke's Bookstore and books applications to demonstrate how to write JSP pages in XML syntax. The JSP pages of the bookstore5 application use the JSTL XML tags (see XML Tag Library, page 550) to manipulate the book data from an XML stream. The books application contains the JSP document books.jspx, which accesses the book data from the database and converts it into the XML stream. The bookstore5 application accesses this XML stream to get the book data.

These applications show how easy it is to generate XML data and stream it between Web applications. The books application can be considered the application hosted by the book warehouse's server. The bookstore5 application can be considered the application hosted by the book retailer's server. In this way, the customer of the bookstore Web site sees the list of books currently available, according to the warehouse's database.

The source for the Duke's Bookstore application is located in the *<INSTALL>*/ j2eetutorial14/examples/web/bookstore5/ directory, which is created when you unzip the tutorial bundle (see About the Examples, page xl). Sample bookstore5.war and books.war files are provided in *<INSTALL>*/ j2eetutorial14/examples/web/provided-wars/.

To build, package, deploy, and run the applications, follow these steps:

1. Build and package the bookstore common files as described in Duke's Bookstore Examples (page 100).
2. In a terminal window, go to *<INSTALL>*/j2eetutorial14/examples/ web/bookstore5/.
3. Run asant build. This target will spawn any necessary compilations and copy files to the *<INSTALL>*/j2eetutorial14/examples/web/ bookstore5/build/ directory.
4. Start the Application Server.
5. Perform all the operations described in Accessing Databases from Web Applications (page 100).
6. Start deploytool.

7. Create a Web application called bookstore5 by running the New Web Application Wizard. Select File→New→Web Component.

8. In the New Web Component wizard:

   a. In the WAR File screen, select the Create New Stand-Alone WAR Module radio button.

   b. Click Browse and in the file chooser, navigate to *<INSTALL>*/ j2eetutorial14/examples/web/bookstore5/.

   c. In the File Name field, enter bookstore5.

   d. Click Create Module File.

   e. In the WAR Name field, enter bookstore5.

   f. In the Context Root field, enter /bookstore5.

   g. Click Edit Contents.

   h. In the Edit Contents dialog box, navigate to *<INSTALL>*/ j2eetutorial14/examples/web/bookstore5/build/. Select the JSP pages bookcashier.jsp, bookcatalog.jsp, bookdetails.jsp, bookreceipt.jsp, bookshowcart.jsp, bookstore.jsp, and parse-books.jsp along with the template directory and click Add. Keep the Edit Contents dialog open.

   i. Add the shared bookstore library. Navigate to *<INSTALL>*/ j2eetutorial14/examples/build/web/bookstore/dist/. Select bookstore.jar.

   j. Click Add.

   k. Click OK.

   l. Click Next.

   m. Select the JSP Page radio button.

   n. Click Next.

   o. Select /bookstore.jsp from the JSP Filename combo box.

   p. Click Finish.

9. Add each of the Web components listed in Table 13–1. For each component do the following:

   a. Select File→New→Web Component.

   b. In the WAR File screen, click the Add to Existing WAR Module radio button. The WAR file contains all the JSP pages, so you do not have to add any more content.

   c. Click Next.

    d. Select the JSP Page radio button.

    e. Click Next.

    f. Select the page from the JSP Filename combo box.

    g. Click Finish.

    h. From the tree, select the Web component you added.

    i. Select the Aliases tab.

    j. Click Add. Enter the alias as shown in Table 13–1.

10. Add the context parameter that specifies the JSTL resource bundle base name.

    a. Select the `bookstore5` WAR file from the tree.

    b. Select the Context tab.

    c. Click Add.

    d. Enter `javax.servlet.jsp.jstl.fmt.localizationContext` in the Coded Parameter field.

    e. Enter `messages.BookstoreMessages` for the Value field.

11. Add the context parameter that identifies the context path to the XML stream.

    a. On the Context tab, again click Add.

    b. Enter `booksURL` for the Coded Parameter.

    c. Enter `http://localhost:8080/books/books.jspx` in the Value field.

Table 13–1 Duke's Bookstore Web Components

Web Component Name	JSP Page	Component Alias
bookcashier	bookcashier.jsp	/bookcashier
bookcatalog	bookcatalog.jsp	/bookcatalog
bookdetails	bookdetails.jsp	/bookdetails
bookreceipt	bookreceipt.jsp	/bookreceipt
bookshowcart	bookshowcart.jsp	/bookshowcart
bookstore	bookstore.jsp	/bookstore

12. Set the prelude and coda for all JSP pages.
    a. Select the JSP Properties tab.
    b. Click the Add button next to the Name list.
    c. Enter `bookstore5`.
    d. Click the Add URL button next to the URL Pattern list.
    e. Enter `*.jsp`.
    f. Click the Edit Preludes button next to the Include Preludes list.
    g. Click Add.
    h. Enter `/template/prelude.jspf`.
    i. Click OK.
    j. Click the Edit Codas button next to the Include Codas list.
    k. Click Add.
    l. Enter `/template/coda.jspf`.
    m. Click OK.

13. Select File→Save.

14. Deploy the application.
    a. Select Tools→Deploy.
    b. Click OK.
    c. A pop-up dialog box will display the results of the deployment. Click Close.

15. Create a Web application called `books` by running the New Web Component wizard. Select File→New→Web Component.

16. In the New Web Component wizard:
    a. In the WAR File screen, select the Create New Stand-Alone WAR Module radio button.
    b. Click Browse and in the file chooser, navigate to `<INSTALL>/j2eetutorial14/examples/web/bookstore5/`.
    c. In the File Name field, enter `books`.
    d. Click Create Module File.
    e. In the WAR Display Name field, enter `books`.
    f. In the Context Root field, enter `/books`.
    g. Click Edit Contents.

    h. In the Edit Contents dialog box, navigate to `<INSTALL>/`
        `j2eetutorial14/examples/web/bookstore5/build/`. Select the
        JSP document `books.jspx` and the `database`, `listeners`, and `tem-`
        `plate` directories and click Add.

    i. Add the shared bookstore library. Navigate to `<INSTALL>/`
        `j2eetutorial14/examples/build/web/bookstore/dist/`. Select
        `bookstore.jar` and click Add. Click OK.

    j. Click Next.

    k. Select the JSP Page radio button.

    l. Click Next.

    m. Select /`books.jspx` from the JSP Filename combo box.

    n. Click Finish.

17. Identify `books.jspx` as an XML document.

    a. Select the JSP Properties tab.

    b. Click the Add button next to the Name list.

    c. Enter `books`.

    d. Click the Add URL button next to the URL Pattern list.

    e. Enter `*.jspx`.

    f. Select the Is XML Document checkbox.

18. Add the listener class `listeners.ContextListener` (described in Han-
    dling Servlet Life-Cycle Events, page 441).

    a. Select the Event Listeners tab.

    b. Click Add.

    c. Select the `listeners.ContextListener` class from the drop-down
        field in the Event Listener Classes pane.

19. Add a resource reference for the database.

    a. Select the Resource Ref's tab.

    b. Click Add.

    c. Enter `jdbc/BookDB` in the Coded Name field.

    d. Accept the default type `javax.sql.DataSource`.

    e. Accept the default authorization `Container`.

    f. Accept the default selected `Shareable`.

    g. Enter `jdbc/BookDB` in the JNDI name field of the Sun-specific Settings
        for jdbc/BookDB frame.

20. Select File→Save.

21. Deploy the application.

   a. Select the books WAR file from the tree.

   b. Select Tools→Deploy.

   c. Click OK.

   d. A pop-up dialog box will display the results of the deployment. Click Close.

22. Open the bookstore URL `http://localhost:8080/bookstore5/book-store`.

Creating a JSP Document

A JSP document is an XML document and therefore must comply with the XML standard. Fundamentally, this means that a JSP document must be well formed, meaning that each start tag must have a corresponding end tag and that the document must have only one root element. In addition, JSP elements included in the JSP document must comply with the XML syntax.

Much of the standard JSP syntax is already XML-compliant, including all the standard actions. Those elements that are not compliant are summarized in Table 13–2 along with the equivalent elements in XML syntax. As you can see, JSP

Table 13–2 Standard Syntax Versus XML Syntax

Syntax Elements	Standard Syntax	XML Syntax
Comments	`<%-- .. --%>`	`<!-- .. -->`
Declarations	`<%! ..%>`	`<jsp:declaration> .. </jsp:declaration>`
Directives	`<%@ include .. %>`	`<jsp:directive.include .. />`
	`<%@ page .. %>`	`<jsp:directive.page .. />`
	`<%@ taglib .. %>`	`xmlns:prefix="tag library URL"`
Expressions	`<%= ..%>`	`<jsp:expression> .. </jsp:expression>`
Scriptlets	`<% ..%>`	`<jsp:scriptlet> .. </jsp:scriptlet>`

documents are not much different from JSP pages. If you know standard JSP syntax, you will find it easy to convert your current JSP pages to XML syntax and to create new JSP documents.

To illustrate how simple it is to transition from standard syntax to XML syntax, let's convert a simple JSP page to a JSP document. The standard syntax version is as follows:

```
<%@ taglib uri="http://java.sun.com/jsp/jstl/core"
  prefix="c" %>
<%@ taglib uri="http://java.sun.com/jsp/jstl/functions"
  prefix="fn" %>
<html>
  <head><title>Hello</title></head>
  <body bgcolor="white">
    <img src="duke.waving.gif">
    <h2>My name is Duke. What is yours?</h2>
    <form method="get">
      <input type="text" name="username" size="25">
      <p></p>
      <input type="submit" value="Submit">
      <input type="reset" value="Reset">
    </form>
    <jsp:useBean id="userNameBean" class="hello.UserNameBean"
        scope="request"/>
    <jsp:setProperty name="userNameBean" property="name"
        value="${param.username}" />
    <c:if test="${fn:length(userNameBean.name) > 0}" >
      <%@include file="response.jsp" %>
    </c:if>
  </body>
</html>
```

Here is the same page in XML syntax:

```
<html
  xmlns:c="http://java.sun.com/jsp/jstl/core"
  xmlns:fn="http://java.sun.com/jsp/jstl/functions"
>
  <head><title>Hello</title></head>
  <body bgcolor="white" />
  <img src="duke.waving.gif" />
  <h2>My name is Duke. What is yours?</h2>
  <form method="get">
    <input type="text" name="username" size="25" />
    <p></p>
    <input type="submit" value="Submit" />
```

```
      <input type="reset" value="Reset" />
   </form>
   <jsp:useBean id="userNameBean" class="hello.UserNameBean"
      scope="request"/>
   <jsp:setProperty name="userNameBean" property="name"
      value="${param.username}" />
   <c:if test="${fn:length(userNameBean.name) gt 0}" >
      <jsp:directive.include="response.jsp" />
   </c:if>
   </body>
</html>
```

As you can see, a number of constructs that are legal in standard syntax have been changed to comply with XML syntax:

- The `taglib` directives have been removed. Tag libraries are now declared using XML namespaces, as shown in the `html` element.

- The `img` and `input` tags did not have matching end tags and have been made XML-compliant by the addition of a / to the start tag.

- The > symbol in the EL expression has been replaced with `gt`.

- The `include` directive has been changed to the XML-compliant `jsp:directive.include` tag.

With only these few small changes, when you save the file with a `.jspx` extension, this page is a JSP document.

Using the example described in The Example JSP Document (page 516), the rest of this chapter gives you more details on how to transition from standard syntax to XML syntax. It explains how to use XML namespaces to declare tag libraries, include directives, and create static and dynamic content in your JSP documents. It also describes `jsp:root` and `jsp:output`, two elements that are used exclusively in JSP documents.

Declaring Tag Libraries

This section explains how to use XML namespaces to declare tag libraries.

In standard syntax, the `taglib` directive declares tag libraries used in a JSP page. Here is an example of a `taglib` directive:

```
<%@ taglib uri="http://java.sun.com/jsp/jstl/core"
   prefix="c" %>
```

This syntax is not allowed in JSP documents. To declare a tag library in a JSP document, you use the `xmlns` attribute, which is used to declare namespaces according to the XML standard:

```
...
xmlns:c="http://java.sun.com/jsp/jstl/core"
...
```

The value that identifies the location of the tag library can take three forms:

- A plain URI that is a unique identifier for the tag library. The container tries to match it against any `<taglib-uri>` elements in the application's `web.xml` file or the `<uri>` element of tag library descriptors (TLDs) in JAR files in `WEB-INF/lib` or TLDs under `WEB-INF`.
- A URN of the form `urn:jsptld:path`.
- A URN of the form `urn:jsptagdir:path`.

The URN of the form `urn:jsptld:path` points to one tag library packaged with the application:

```
xmlns:u="urn:jsptld:/WEB-INF/tlds/my.tld"
```

The URN of the form `urn:jsptagdir:path` must start with `/WEB-INF/tags/` and identifies tag extensions (implemented as tag files) installed in the `WEB-INF/tags/` directory or a subdirectory of it:

```
xmlns:u="urn:jsptagdir:/WEB-INF/tags/mytaglibs/"
```

You can include the `xmlns` attribute in any element in your JSP document, just as you can in an XML document. This capability has many advantages:

- It follows the XML standard, making it easier to use any XML document as a JSP document.
- It allows you to scope prefixes to an element and override them.
- It allows you to use `xmlns` to declare other namespaces and not just tag libraries.

The `books.jspx` page declares the tag libraries it uses with the `xmlns` attributes in the root element, `books`:

```
<books
  xmlns:jsp="http://java.sun.com/JSP/Page"
  xmlns:c="http://java.sun.com/jsp/jstl/core"
>
```

In this way, all elements within the books element have access to these tag libraries.

As an alternative, you can scope the namespaces:

```
<books>
...
  <jsp:useBean xmlns:jsp="http://java.sun.com/JSP/Page"
               id="bookDB"
               class="database.BookDB"
               scope="page">
    <jsp:setProperty name="bookDB"
               property="database" value="${bookDBAO}" />
  </jsp:useBean>
  <c:forEach xmlns:c="http://java.sun.com/jsp/jstl/core"
             var="book" begin="0" items="${bookDB.books}">
             ...
  </c:forEach>
</books>
```

In this way, the tag library referenced by the jsp prefix is available only to the jsp:useBean element and its subelements. Similarly, the tag library referenced by the c prefix is only available to the c:forEach element.

Scoping the namespaces also allows you to override the prefix. For example, in another part of the page, you could bind the c prefix to a different namespace or tag library. In contrast, the jsp prefix must always be bound to the JSP namespace: http://java.sun.com/JSP/Page.

Including Directives in a JSP Document

Directives are elements that relay messages to the JSP container and affect how it compiles the JSP page. The directives themselves do not appear in the XML output.

There are three directives: include, page, and taglib. The taglib directive is covered in the preceding section.

The jsp:directive.page element defines a number of page-dependent properties and communicates these to the JSP container. This element must be a child of the root element. Its syntax is

```
<jsp:directive.page page_directive_attr_list />
```

The `page_directive_attr_list` is the same list of attributes that the `<@ page ...>` directive has. These are described in Chapter 12. All the attributes are optional. Except for the `import` and `pageEncoding` attributes, there can be only one instance of each attribute in an element, but an element can contain more than one attribute.

An example of a page directive is one that tells the JSP container to load an error page when it throws an exception. You can add this error page directive to the `books.jspx` page:

```
<books xmlns:jsp="http://java.sun.com/JSP/Page">
  <jsp:directive.page errorPage="errorpage.jsp" />
  ...
</books>
```

If there is an error when you try to execute the page (perhaps when you want to see the XML output of `books.jspx`), the error page is accessed.

The `jsp:directive.include` element is used to insert the text contained in another file—either static content or another JSP page—into the including JSP document. You can place this element anywhere in a document. Its syntax is:

```
<jsp:directive.include file="relativeURLspec" />
```

The XML view of a JSP document does not contain `jsp:directive.include` elements; rather the included file is expanded in place. This is done to simplify validation.

Suppose that you want to use an `include` directive to add a JSP document containing magazine data inside the JSP document containing the books data. To do this, you can add the following `include` directive to `books.jspx`, assuming that `magazines.jspx` generates the magazine XML data.

```
<jsp:root version="2.0" >
  <books ...>
  ...
  </books>
  <jsp:directive.include file="magazine.jspx" />
</jsp:root>
```

Note that `jsp:root` is required because otherwise `books.jspx` would have two root elements: `<books>` and `<magazines>`. The output generated from `books.jspx` will be a sequence of XML documents: one with `<books>` and the other with `<magazines>` as its root element.

The output of this example will not be well-formed XML because of the two root elements, so the client might refuse to process it. However, it is still a legal JSP document.

In addition to including JSP documents in JSP documents, you can also include JSP pages written in standard syntax in JSP documents, and you can include JSP documents in JSP pages written in standard syntax. The container detects the page you are including and parses it as either a standard syntax JSP page or a JSP document and then places it into the XML view for validation.

Creating Static and Dynamic Content

This section explains how to represent static text and dynamic content in a JSP document. You can represent static text in a JSP document using uninterpreted XML tags or the `jsp:text` element. The `jsp:text` element passes its content through to the output.

If you use `jsp:text`, all whitespace is preserved. For example, consider this example using XML tags:

```
<books>
  <book>
    Web Servers for Fun and Profit
  </book>
</books>
```

The output generated from this XML has all whitespace removed:

```
<books><book>
    Web Servers for Fun and Profit
</book></books>
```

If you wrap the example XML with a `<jsp:text>` tag, all whitespace is preserved. The whitespace characters are #x20, #x9, #xD, and #xA.

You can also use `jsp:text` to output static data that is not well formed. The `${counter}` expression in the following example would be illegal in a JSP document if it were not wrapped in a `jsp:text` tag.

```
<c:forEach var="counter" begin="1" end="${3}">
  <jsp:text>${counter}</jsp:text>
</c:forEach>
```

This example will output

```
123
```

The `jsp:text` tag must not contain any other elements. Therefore, if you need to nest a tag inside `jsp:text`, you must wrap the tag inside CDATA.

You also need to use CDATA if you need to output some elements that are not well-formed. The following example requires CDATA wrappers around the `blockquote` start and end tags because the `blockquote` element is not well formed. This is because the `blockquote` element overlaps with other elements in the example.

```
<c:forEach var="i" begin="1" end="${x}">
  <![CDATA[<blockquote>]]>
</c:forEach>
...
<c:forEach var="i" begin="1" end="${x}">
  <![CDATA[</blockquote>]]>
</c:forEach>
```

Just like JSP pages, JSP documents can generate dynamic content using expressions language (EL) expressions, scripting elements, standard actions, and custom tags. The `books.jspx` document uses EL expressions and custom tags to generate the XML book data.

As shown in this snippet from `books.jspx`, the `c:forEach` JSTL tag iterates through the list of books and generates the XML data stream. The EL expressions access the JavaBeans component, which in turn retrieves the data from the database:

```
<c:forEach var="book" begin="0" items="${bookDB.books}">
  <book id="${book.bookId}" >
    <surname>${book.surname}</surname>
    <firstname>${book.firstName}</firstname>
    <title>${book.title}</title>
    <price>${book.price}</price>
    <year>${book.year}</year>
    <description>${book.description}</description>
    <inventory>${book.inventory}</inventory>
  </book>
</c:forEach>
```

Table 13–3 EL Operators and JSP Document-Compliant Alternative Notation

EL Operator	JSP Document Notation
<	lt
>	gt
<=	le
>=	ge
!=	ne

When using the expression language in your JSP documents, you must substitute alternative notation for some of the operators so that they will not be interpreted as XML markup. Table 13–3 enumerates the more common operators and their alternative syntax in JSP documents.

You can also use EL expressions with `jsp:element` to generate tags dynamically rather than hardcode them. This example could be used to generate an HTML header tag with a `lang` attribute:

```
<jsp:element name="${content.headerName}"
    xmlns:jsp="http://java.sun.com/JSP/Page">
  <jsp:attribute name="lang">${content.lang}</jsp:attribute>
  <jsp:body>${content.body}</jsp:body>
</jsp:element>
```

The `name` attribute identifies the generated tag's name. The `jsp:attribute` tag generates the `lang` attribute. The body of the `jsp:attribute` tag identifies the value of the `lang` attribute. The `jsp:body` tag generates the body of the tag. The output of this example `jsp:element` could be

```
<h1 lang="fr">Heading in French</h1>
```

As shown in Table 13–2, scripting elements (described in Chapter 16) are represented as XML elements when they appear in a JSP document. The only exception is a scriptlet expression used to specify a request-time attribute value. Instead of using <%=expr %>, a JSP document uses %= expr % to represent a request-time attribute value.

The three scripting elements are declarations, scriptlets, and expressions.

A `jsp:declaration` element declares a scripting language construct that is available to other scripting elements. A `jsp:declaration` element has no attributes and its body is the declaration itself. Its syntax is

```
<jsp:declaration> declaration goes here </jsp:declaration>
```

A `jsp:scriptlet` element contains a Java program fragment called a scriptlet. This element has no attributes, and its body is the program fragment that constitutes the scriptlet. Its syntax is

```
<jsp:scriptlet> code fragment goes here </jsp:scriptlet>
```

The `jsp:expression` element inserts the value of a scripting language expression, converted into a string, into the data stream returned to the client. A `jsp:expression` element has no attributes and its body is the expression. Its syntax is

```
<jsp:expression> expression goes here </jsp:expression>
```

Using the jsp:root Element

The `jsp:root` element represents the root element of a JSP document. A `jsp:root` element is not required for JSP documents. You can specify your own root element, enabling you to use any XML document as a JSP document. The root element of the `books.jspx` example JSP document is `books`.

Although the `jsp:root` element is not required, it is still useful in these cases:

- When you want to identify the document as a JSP document to the JSP container without having to add any configuration attributes to the deployment descriptor or name the document with a `.jspx` extension
- When you want to generate—from a single JSP document—more than one XML document or XML content mixed with non-XML content

The `version` attribute is the only required attribute of the `jsp:root` element. It specifies the JSP specification version that the JSP document is using.

The `jsp:root` element can also include `xmlns` attributes for specifying tag libraries used by the other elements in the page.

The `books.jspx` page does not need a `jsp:root` element and therefore doesn't include one. However, suppose that you want to generate two XML documents from `books.jspx`: one that lists books and another that lists magazines (assuming magazines are in the database). This example is similar to the one in the section Including Directives in a JSP Document (page 525). To do this, you can use this `jsp:root` element:

```
<jsp:root
    xmlns:jsp="http://java.sun.com/JSP/Page" version="2.0" >
    <books>...</books>
    <magazines>...</magazines>
</jsp:root>
```

Notice in this example that `jsp:root` defines the JSP namespace because both the books and the magazines elements use the elements defined in this namespace.

Using the jsp:output Element

The `jsp:output` element specifies the XML declaration or the document type declaration in the request output of the JSP document. For more information on the XML declaration, see The XML Prolog (page 34). For more information on the document type declaration, see Referencing the DTD (page 56).

The XML declaration and document type declaration that are declared by the `jsp:output` element are not interpreted by the JSP container. Instead, the container simply directs them to the request output.

To illustrate this, here is an example of specifying a document type declaration with `jsp:output`:

```
<jsp:output doctype-root-element="books"
            doctype-system="books.dtd" />
```

The resulting output is:

```
<!DOCTYPE books SYSTEM "books.dtd" >
```

Specifying the document type declaration in the `jsp:output` element will not cause the JSP container to validate the JSP document against the `books.dtd`.

If you want the JSP document to be validated against the DTD, you must manually include the document type declaration within the JSP document, just as you would with any XML document.

Table 13-4 `jsp:output` Attributes

Attribute	What It Specifies
`omit-xml-declaration`	A value of `true` or `yes` omits the XML declaration. A value of `false` or `no` generates an XML declaration.
`doctype-root-element`	Indicates the root element of the XML document in the DOC-TYPE. Can be specified only if `doctype-system` is specified.
`doctype-system`	Specifies that a DOCTYPE is generated in output and gives the SYSTEM literal.
`doctype-public`	Specifies the value for the Public ID of the generated DOC-TYPE. Can be specified only if `doctype-system` is specified.

Table 13-4 shows all the `jsp:output` attributes. They are all optional, but some attributes depend on other attributes occurring in the same `jsp:output` element, as shown in the table. The rest of this section explains more about using `jsp:output` to generate an XML declaration and a document type declaration.

Generating XML Declarations

Here is an example of an XML declaration:

```
<?xml version="1.0" encoding="UTF-8" ?>
```

This declaration is the default XML declaration. It means that if the JSP container is generating an XML declaration, this is what the JSP container will include in the output of your JSP document.

Neither a JSP document nor its request output is required to have an XML declaration. In fact, if the JSP document is not producing XML output then it shouldn't have an XML declaration.

The JSP container will *not* include the XML declaration in the output when either of the following is true:

- You set the `omit-xml-declaration` attribute of the `jsp:output` element to either `true` or `yes`.
- You have a `jsp:root` element in your JSP document, and you do not specify `omit-xml-declaration="false"` in `jsp:output`.

The JSP container will include the XML declaration in the output when either of the following is true:

- You set the `omit-xml-declaration` attribute of the `jsp:output` element to either `false` or `no`.
- You do not have a `jsp:root` action in your JSP document, and you do not specify the `omit-xml-declaration` attribute in `jsp:output`.

The `books.jspx` JSP document does not include a `jsp:root` action nor a `jsp:output`. Therefore, the default XML declaration is generated in the output.

Generating a Document Type Declaration

A document type declaration (DTD) defines the structural rules for the XML document in which the document type declaration occurs. XML documents are not required to have a DTD associated with them. In fact, the `books` example does not include one.

This section shows you how to use the `jsp:output` element to add a document type declaration to the XML output of `books.jspx`. It also shows you how to enter the document type declaration manually into `books.jspx` so that the JSP container will interpret it and validate the document against the DTD.

As shown in Table 13–4, the `jsp:output` element has three attributes that you use to generate the document type declaration:

- `doctype-root-element`: Indicates the root element of the XML document
- `doctype-system`: Indicates the URI reference to the DTD
- `doctype-public`: A more flexible way to reference the DTD. This identifier gives more information about the DTD without giving a specific location. A public identifier resolves to the same actual document on any system even though the location of that document on each system may vary. See the XML 1.0 specification for more information.

The rules for using the attributes are as follows:

- The doctype attributes can appear in any order
- The `doctype-root` attribute must be specified if the `doctype-system` attribute is specified
- The `doctype-public` attribute must not be specified unless `doctype-system` is specified

This syntax notation summarizes these rules:

```
<jsp:output (omit-xml-declaration="yes"|"no"|"true"|"false")
    {doctypeDecl} />

doctypeDecl:=(doctype-root-element="rootElement"
        doctype-public="PublicLiteral"
    doctype-system="SystemLiteral")
    | (doctype-root-element="rootElement"
    doctype-system="SystemLiteral")
```

Suppose that you want to reference a DTD, called books.DTD, from the output of the books.jspx page. The DTD would look like this:

```
<!ELEMENT books (book+) >
<!ELEMENT book (surname, firstname, title, price, year,
                description, inventory) >
<!ATTLIST book id CDATA #REQUIRED >
<!ELEMENT surname (#PCDATA) >
<!ELEMENT firstname (#PCDATA) >
<!ELEMENT title (#PCDATA) >
<!ELEMENT price (#PCDATA) >
<!ELEMENT year (#PCDATA) >
<!ELEMENT description (#PCDATA) >
<!ELEMENT inventory (#PCDATA) >
```

To add a document type declaration that references the DTD to the XML request output generated from books.jspx, include this jsp:output element in books.jspx:

```
<jsp:output doctype-root-element="books"
        doctype-system="books.DTD" />
```

With this jsp:output action, the JSP container generates this document type declaration in the request output:

```
<!DOCTYPE books SYSTEM "books.DTD" />
```

The jsp:output need not be located before the root element of the document. The JSP container will automatically place the resulting document type declaration before the start of the output of the JSP document.

Note that the JSP container will not interpret anything provided by jsp:output. This means that the JSP container will not validate the XML document against the DTD. It only generates the document type declaration in the XML request output. To see the XML output, run http://localhost:8080/books/ books.jspx in your browser after you have updated books.WAR with books.DTD and the jsp:output element. When using some browsers, you might need to view the source of the page to actually see the output.

Directing the document type declaration to output without interpreting it is useful in situations when another system receiving the output expects to see it. For example, two companies that do business via a Web service might use a standard DTD, against which any XML content exchanged between the companies is validated by the consumer of the content. The document type declaration tells the consumer what DTD to use to validate the XML data that it receives.

For the JSP container to validate books.jspx against book.DTD, you must manually include the document type declaration in the books.jspx file rather than use jsp:output. However, you must add definitions for all tags in your DTD, including definitions for standard elements and custom tags, such as jsp:use-Bean and c:forEach. You also must ensure that the DTD is located in the *<J2EE_HOME>*/domains/domain1/config/ directory so that the JSP container will validate the JSP document against the DTD.

Identifying the JSP Document to the Container

A JSP document must be identified as such to the Web container so that the container interprets it as an XML document. There are three ways to do this:

- In your application's web.xml file, set the is-xml element of the jsp-property-group element to true. Step 17. in The Example JSP Document (page 516) explains how to do this if you are using deploytool to build the application WAR file.

- Use a Java Servlet Specification version 2.4 web.xml file and give your JSP document the .jspx extension.

- Include a jsp:root element in your JSP document. This method is backward-compatible with JSP 1.2.

14

JavaServer Pages Standard Tag Library

$\mathbf{T}$HE JavaServer Pages Standard Tag Library (JSTL) encapsulates core functionality common to many JSP applications. Instead of mixing tags from numerous vendors in your JSP applications, JSTL allows you to employ a single, standard set of tags. This standardization allows you to deploy your applications on any JSP container supporting JSTL and makes it more likely that the implementation of the tags is optimized.

JSTL has tags such as iterators and conditionals for handling flow control, tags for manipulating XML documents, internationalization tags, tags for accessing databases using SQL, and commonly used functions.

This chapter demonstrates JSTL through excerpts from the JSP version of the Duke's Bookstore application discussed in the earlier chapters. It assumes that you are familiar with the material in the Using Custom Tags (page 502) section of Chapter 12.

This chapter does not cover every JSTL tag, only the most commonly used ones. Please refer to the reference pages at `http://java.sun.com/products/jsp/jstl/1.1/docs/tlddocs/index.html` for a complete list of the JSTL tags and their attributes.

The Example JSP Pages

This chapter illustrates JSTL using excerpts from the JSP version of the Duke's Bookstore application discussed in Chapter 12. Here, they are rewritten to replace the JavaBeans component database access object with direct calls to the database via the JSTL SQL tags. For most applications, it is better to encapsulate calls to a database in a bean. JSTL includes SQL tags for situations where a new application is being prototyped and the overhead of creating a bean may not be warranted.

The source for the Duke's Bookstore application is located in the *<INSTALL>*/ j2eetutorial14/examples/web/bookstore4/ directory created when you unzip the tutorial bundle (see About the Examples, page xl). A sample bookstore4.war is provided in *<INSTALL>*/j2eetutorial14/examples/web/ provided-wars/. To build, package, deploy, and run the example, follow these steps:

1. Build and package the bookstore common files as described in Duke's Bookstore Examples (page 100).

2. In a terminal window, go to *<INSTALL>*/j2eetutorial14/examples/ web/bookstore4/.

3. Run asant build. This target will copy files to the *<INSTALL>*/ j2eetutorial14/examples/web/bookstore4/build/ directory.

4. Start the Application Server.

5. Perform all the operations described in Accessing Databases from Web Applications, page 100.

6. Start deploytool.

7. Create a Web application called bookstore4 by running the New Web Component wizard. Select File→New→Web Component.

8. In the New Web Component wizard:

   a. Select the Create New Stand-Alone WAR Module radio button.

   b. In the WAR Location field, enter *<INSTALL>*/j2eetutorial14/exam-ples/web/bookstore4/bookstore4.war.

   c. In the WAR Name field, enter bookstore4.

   d. In the Context Root field, enter /bookstore4.

   e. Click Edit Contents.

   f. In the Edit Contents dialog box, navigate to *<INSTALL>*/ j2eetutorial14/examples/web/bookstore4/build/. Select the

JSP pages `bookstore.jsp`, `bookdetails.jsp`, `bookcatalog.jsp`, `bookshowcart.jsp`, `bookcashier.jsp`, and `bookreceipt.jsp` and the `template` directory and click Add.

g. Add the shared bookstore library. Navigate to `<INSTALL>/j2eetutorial14/examples/web/bookstore/dist/`. Select `bookstore.jar` and click Add.

h. Click OK.

i. Click Next.

j. Select the JSP Page radio button.

k. Click Next.

l. Select `bookstore.jsp` from the JSP Filename combo box.

m. Click Next.

n. Click Add. Enter the alias `/bookstore`.

o. Click Finish.

9. Add each of the Web components listed in Table 14–1. For each component:

a. Select File→New→Web Component.

b. Click the Add to Existing WAR Module radio button. Because the WAR contains all the JSP pages, you do not have to add any more content.

c. Click Next.

d. Select the JSP Page radio button and the Component Aliases checkbox.

e. Click Next.

f. Select the page from the JSP Filename combo box.

g. Click Finish.

Table 14–1 Duke's Bookstore Web Components

Web Component Name	JSP Page	Alias
bookcatalog	bookcatalog.jsp	/bookcatalog
bookdetails	bookdetails.jsp	/bookdetails
bookshowcart	bookshowcart.jsp	/bookshowcart
bookcashier	bookcashier.jsp	/bookcashier
bookreceipt	bookreceipt.jsp	/bookreceipt

10. Set the alias for each Web component.

    a. Select the component.

    b. Select the Aliases tab.

    c. Click the Add button.

    d. Enter the alias.

11. Add the context parameter that specifies the JSTL resource bundle base name.

    a. Select the Web module.

    b. Select the Context tab.

    c. Click Add.

    d. Enter `javax.servlet.jsp.jstl.fmt.localizationContext` in the Coded Parameter field.

    e. Enter `messages.BookstoreMessages` in the Value field.

12. Set the prelude and coda for all JSP pages.

    a. Select the JSP Properties tab.

    b. Click the Add button next to the Name list.

    c. Enter `bookstore4`.

    d. Click the Add button next to the URL Pattern list.

    e. Enter `*.jsp`.

    f. Click the Edit button next to the Include Preludes list.

    g. Click Add.

    h. Enter `/template/prelude.jspf`.

    i. Click OK.

    j. Click the Edit button next to the Include Codas list.

    k. Click Add.

    l. Enter `/template/coda.jspf`.

    m. Click OK.

13. Add a resource reference for the database.

    a. Select the Resource Ref's tab.

    b. Click Add.

    c. Enter `jdbc/BookDB` in the Coded Name field.

    d. Accept the default type `javax.sql.DataSource`.

    e. Accept the default authorization `Container`.

      f. Accept the default selected `Shareable`.

      g. Enter `jdbc/BookDB` in the JNDI name field of the Sun-specific Settings frame.

14. Select File→Save.

15. Deploy the application.

      a. Select Tools→Deploy.

      b. Click OK.

16. Open the bookstore URL `http://localhost:8080/bookstore4/book-store`.

See Troubleshooting (page 440) for help with diagnosing common problems.

Using JSTL

JSTL includes a wide variety of tags that fit into discrete functional areas. To reflect this, as well as to give each area its own namespace, JSTL is exposed as multiple tag libraries. The URIs for the libraries are as follows:

- *Core*: `http://java.sun.com/jsp/jstl/core`
- *XML*: `http://java.sun.com/jsp/jstl/xml`
- *Internationalization*: `http://java.sun.com/jsp/jstl/fmt`
- *SQL*: `http://java.sun.com/jsp/jstl/sql`
- *Functions*: `http://java.sun.com/jsp/jstl/functions`

Table 14–2 summarizes these functional areas along with the prefixes used in this tutorial.

Thus, the tutorial references the JSTL core tags in JSP pages by using the following `taglib` directive:

```
<%@ taglib uri="http://java.sun.com/jsp/jstl/core"
    prefix="c" %>
```

In addition to declaring the tag libraries, tutorial examples access the JSTL API and implementation. In the Sun Java System Application Server Platform Edition 8, the JSTL TLDs and libraries are distributed in the archive *<J2EE_HOME>*`/lib/appserv-jstl.jar`. This library is automatically loaded into the classpath of all Web applications running on the Application Server, so you don't need to add it to your Web application.

Table 14–2   JSTL Tags

Area	Subfunction	Prefix
Core	Variable support	c
	Flow control	
	URL management	
	Miscellaneous	
XML	Core	x
	Flow control	
	Transformation	
I18n	Locale	fmt
	Message formatting	
	Number and date formatting	
Database	SQL	sql
Functions	Collection length	fn
	String manipulation	

Tag Collaboration

Tags usually collaborate with their environment in implicit and explicit ways. *Implicit* collaboration is done via a well-defined interface that allows nested tags to work seamlessly with the ancestor tag that exposes that interface. The JSTL conditional tags employ this mode of collaboration.

Explicit collaboration happens when a tag exposes information to its environment. JSTL tags expose information as JSP EL variables; the convention followed by JSTL is to use the name var for any tag attribute that exports information about the tag. For example, the forEach tag exposes the current item of the shopping cart it is iterating over in the following way:

```
<c:forEach var="item" items="${sessionScope.cart.items}">
   ...
</c:forEach>
```

In situations where a tag exposes more than one piece of information, the name var is used for the primary piece of information being exported, and an appropriate name is selected for any other secondary piece of information exposed. For example, iteration status information is exported by the forEach tag via the attribute status.

When you want to use an EL variable exposed by a JSTL tag in an expression in the page's scripting language (see Chapter 16), you use the standard JSP element jsp:useBean to declare a scripting variable.

For example, bookshowcart.jsp removes a book from a shopping cart using a scriptlet. The ID of the book to be removed is passed as a request parameter. The value of the request parameter is first exposed as an EL variable (to be used later by the JSTL sql:query tag) and then is declared as a scripting variable and passed to the cart.remove method:

```
<c:set var="bookId" value="${param.Remove}"/>
<jsp:useBean id="bookId" type="java.lang.String" />
<% cart.remove(bookId); %>
<sql:query var="books"
  dataSource="${applicationScope.bookDS}">
  select * from PUBLIC.books where id = ?
  <sql:param value="${bookId}" />
</sql:query>
```

Core Tag Library

Table 14–3 summarizes the core tags, which include those related to variables and flow control, as well as a generic way to access URL-based resources whose content can then be included or processed within the JSP page.

Variable Support Tags

The set tag sets the value of an EL variable or the property of an EL variable in any of the JSP scopes (page, request, session, or application). If the variable does not already exist, it is created.

Table 14–3 Core Tags

Area	Function	Tags	Prefix
Core	Variable support	remove set	c
	Flow control	choose when otherwise forEach forTokens if	
	URL management	import param redirect param url param	
	Miscellaneous	catch out	

The JSP EL variable or property can be set either from the attribute value:

```
<c:set var="foo" scope="session" value="..."/>
```

or from the body of the tag:

```
<c:set var="foo">
  ...
</c:set>
```

For example, the following sets an EL variable named bookID with the value of the request parameter named Remove:

```
<c:set var="bookId" value="${param.Remove}"/>
```

To remove an EL variable, you use the remove tag. When the bookstore JSP page bookreceipt.jsp is invoked, the shopping session is finished, so the cart session attribute is removed as follows:

```
<c:remove var="cart" scope="session"/>
```

Flow Control Tags

To execute flow control logic, a page author must generally resort to using script-lets. For example, the following scriptlet is used to iterate through a shopping cart:

```
<%
   Iterator i = cart.getItems().iterator();
   while (i.hasNext()) {
      ShoppingCartItem item =
         (ShoppingCartItem)i.next();
      ...
%>
      <tr>
      <td align="right" bgcolor="#ffffff">
      ${item.quantity}
      </td>
      ...
<%
   }
%>
```

Flow control tags eliminate the need for scriptlets. The next two sections have examples that demonstrate the conditional and iterator tags.

Conditional Tags

The if tag allows the conditional execution of its body according to the value of the test attribute. The following example from bookcatalog.jsp tests whether the request parameter Add is empty. If the test evaluates to true, the page queries the database for the book record identified by the request parameter and adds the book to the shopping cart:

```
<c:if test="${!empty param.Add}">
  <c:set var="bid" value="${param.Add}"/>
  <jsp:useBean id="bid"  type="java.lang.String" />
   <sql:query var="books"
     dataSource="${applicationScope.bookDS}">
     select * from PUBLIC.books where id = ?
     <sql:param value="${bid}" />
  </sql:query>
  <c:forEach var="bookRow" begin="0" items="${books.rows}">
     <jsp:useBean id="bookRow" type="java.util.Map" />
```

```
    <jsp:useBean id="addedBook"
      class="database.BookDetails" scope="page" />
  ...
  <% cart.add(bid, addedBook); %>
...
</c:if>
```

The choose tag performs conditional block execution by the embedded when subtags. It renders the body of the first when tag whose test condition evaluates to true. If none of the test conditions of nested when tags evaluates to true, then the body of an otherwise tag is evaluated, if present.

For example, the following sample code shows how to render text based on a customer's membership category.

```
<c:choose>
  <c:when test="${customer.category == 'trial'}" >
    ...
  </c:when>
  <c:when test="${customer.category == 'member'}" >
    ...
  </c:when>
    <c:when test="${customer.category == 'preferred'}" >
    ...
  </c:when>
  <c:otherwise>
    ...
  </c:otherwise>
</c:choose>
```

The choose, when, and otherwise tags can be used to construct an if-then-else statement as follows:

```
<c:choose>
  <c:when test="${count == 0}" >
    No records matched your selection.
  </c:when>
  <c:otherwise>
    ${count} records matched your selection.
  </c:otherwise>
</c:choose>
```

Iterator Tags

The forEach tag allows you to iterate over a collection of objects. You specify the collection via the items attribute, and the current item is available through a variable named by the var attribute.

A large number of collection types are supported by forEach, including all implementations of java.util.Collection and java.util.Map. If the items attribute is of type java.util.Map, then the current item will be of type java.util.Map.Entry, which has the following properties:

- key: The key under which the item is stored in the underlying Map
- value: The value that corresponds to the key

Arrays of objects as well as arrays of primitive types (for example, int) are also supported. For arrays of primitive types, the current item for the iteration is automatically wrapped with its standard wrapper class (for example, Integer for int, Float for float, and so on).

Implementations of java.util.Iterator and java.util.Enumeration are supported, but they must be used with caution. Iterator and Enumeration objects are not resettable, so they should not be used within more than one iteration tag. Finally, java.lang.String objects can be iterated over if the string contains a list of comma-separated values (for example: Monday,Tuesday,Wednesday,Thursday,Friday).

Here's the shopping cart iteration from the preceding section, now with the forEach tag:

```
<c:forEach var="item" items="${sessionScope.cart.items}">
  ...
  <tr>
    <td align="right" bgcolor="#ffffff">
    ${item.quantity}
  </td>
  ...
</c:forEach>
```

The forTokens tag is used to iterate over a collection of tokens separated by a delimiter.

URL Tags

The `jsp:include` element provides for the inclusion of static and dynamic resources in the same context as the current page. However, `jsp:include` cannot access resources that reside outside the Web application, and it causes unnecessary buffering when the resource included is used by another element.

In the following example, the `transform` element uses the content of the included resource as the input of its transformation. The `jsp:include` element reads the content of the response and writes it to the body content of the enclosing transform element, which then rereads exactly the same content. It would be more efficient if the `transform` element could access the input source directly and thereby avoid the buffering involved in the body content of the transform tag.

```
<acme:transform>
  <jsp:include page="/exec/employeesList"/>
<acme:transform/>
```

The `import` tag is therefore the simple, generic way to access URL-based resources, whose content can then be included and/or processed within the JSP page. For example, in XML Tag Library (page 550), `import` is used to read in the XML document containing book information and assign the content to the scoped variable `xml`:

```
<c:import url="/books.xml" var="xml" />
<x:parse doc="${xml}" var="booklist"
  scope="application" />
```

The `param` tag, analogous to the `jsp:param` tag (see jsp:param Element, page 508), can be used with `import` to specify request parameters.

In Session Tracking (page 466) we discuss how an application must rewrite URLs to enable session tracking whenever the client turns off cookies. You can use the `url` tag to rewrite URLs returned from a JSP page. The tag includes the session ID in the URL only if cookies are disabled; otherwise, it returns the URL unchanged. Note that this feature requires that the URL be *relative*. The `url` tag takes `param` subtags to include parameters in the returned URL. For example, `bookcatalog.jsp` rewrites the URL used to add a book to the shopping cart as follows:

```
<c:url var="url" value="/catalog" >
  <c:param name="Add" value="${bookId}" />
</c:url>
<p><strong><a href="${url}">
```

The `redirect` tag sends an HTTP redirect to the client. The `redirect` tag takes `param` subtags for including parameters in the returned URL.

Miscellaneous Tags

The `catch` tag provides a complement to the JSP error page mechanism. It allows page authors to recover gracefully from error conditions that they can control. Actions that are of central importance to a page should *not* be encapsulated in a `catch`; in this way their exceptions will propagate instead to an error page. Actions with secondary importance to the page should be wrapped in a `catch` so that they never cause the error page mechanism to be invoked.

The exception thrown is stored in the variable identified by `var`, which always has page scope. If no exception occurred, the scoped variable identified by `var` is removed if it existed. If `var` is missing, the exception is simply caught and not saved.

The `out` tag evaluates an expression and outputs the result of the evaluation to the current `JspWriter` object. The syntax and attributes are as follows:

```
<c:out value="value" [escapeXml="{true|false}"]
    [default="defaultValue"] />
```

If the result of the evaluation is a `java.io.Reader` object, then data is first read from the `Reader` object and then written into the current `JspWriter` object. The special processing associated with `Reader` objects improves performance when a large amount of data must be read and then written to the response.

If `escapeXml` is true, the character conversions listed in Table 14–4 are applied.

Table 14–4   Character Conversions

Character	Character Entity Code
<	<
>	>
&	&
'	'
"	"

XML Tag Library

The JSTL XML tag set is listed in Table 14–5.

A key aspect of dealing with XML documents is to be able to easily access their content. XPath (see How XPath Works, page 247), a W3C recommendation since 1999, provides an easy notation for specifying and selecting parts of an XML document. In the JSTL XML tags, XPath expressions specified using the `select` attribute are used to select portions of XML data streams. Note that XPath is used as a *local* expression language only for the `select` attribute. This means that values specified for `select` attributes are evaluated using the XPath expression language but that values for all other attributes are evaluated using the rules associated with the JSP 2.0 expression language.

In addition to the standard XPath syntax, the JSTL XPath engine supports the following scopes to access Web application data within an XPath expression:

- `$foo`
- `$param:`
- `$header:`
- `$cookie:`
- `$initParam:`
- `$pageScope:`
- `$requestScope:`
- `$sessionScope:`
- `$applicationScope:`

Table 14–5 XML Tags

Area	Function	Tags	Prefix
XML	Core	out parse set	x
	Flow control	choose when otherwise forEach if	
	Transformation	transform param	

Table 14–6 Example XPath Expressions

XPath Expression	Result
`$sessionScope:profile`	The session-scoped EL variable named `profile`
`$initParam:mycom.productId`	The `String` value of the `mycom.productId` context parameter

These scopes are defined in exactly the same way as their counterparts in the JSP expression language discussed in Implicit Objects (page 492). Table 14–6 shows some examples of using the scopes.

The XML tags are illustrated in another version (`bookstore5`) of the Duke's Bookstore application. This version replaces the database with an XML representation of the bookstore database, which is retrieved from another Web application. The directions for building and deploying this version of the application are in The Example JSP Document (page 516). A sample `bookstore5.war` is provided in `<INSTALL>/j2eetutorial14/examples/web/provided-wars/`.

Core Tags

The core XML tags provide basic functionality to easily parse and access XML data.

The `parse` tag parses an XML document and saves the resulting object in the EL variable specified by attribute `var`. In `bookstore5`, the XML document is parsed and saved to a context attribute in `parsebooks.jsp`, which is included by all JSP pages that need access to the document:

```
<c:if test="${applicationScope:booklist == null}" >
  <c:import url="${initParam.booksURL}" var="xml" />
  <x:parse doc="${xml}" var="booklist" scope="application" />
</c:if>
```

The `set` and `out` tags parallel the behavior described in Variable Support Tags (page 543) and Miscellaneous Tags (page 549) for the XPath local expression language. The `set` tag evaluates an XPath expression and sets the result into a JSP EL variable specified by attribute `var`. The `out` tag evaluates an XPath expression on the current context node and outputs the result of the evaluation to the current `JspWriter` object.

The JSP page bookdetails.jsp selects a book element whose id attribute matches the request parameter bookId and sets the abook attribute. The out tag then selects the book's title element and outputs the result.

```
<x:set var="abook"
  select="$applicationScope.booklist/
    books/book[@id=$param:bookId]" />
<h2><x:out select="$abook/title"/></h2>
```

As you have just seen, x:set stores an internal XML representation of a *node* retrieved using an XPath expression; it doesn't convert the selected node into a String and store it. Thus, x:set is primarily useful for storing parts of documents for later retrieval.

If you want to store a String, you must use x:out within c:set. The x:out tag converts the node to a String, and c:set then stores the String as an EL variable. For example, bookdetails.jsp stores an EL variable containing a book price, which is later provided as the value of a fmt tag, as follows:

```
<c:set var="price">
  <x:out select="$abook/price"/>
</c:set>
<h4><fmt:message key="ItemPrice"/>:
  <fmt:formatNumber value="${price}" type="currency"/>
```

The other option, which is more direct but requires that the user have more knowledge of XPath, is to coerce the node to a String manually by using XPath's string function.

```
<x:set var="price" select="string($abook/price)"/>
```

Flow Control Tags

The XML flow control tags parallel the behavior described in Flow Control Tags (page 545) for XML data streams.

The JSP page bookcatalog.jsp uses the forEach tag to display all the books contained in booklist as follows:

```
<x:forEach var="book"
  select="$applicationScope:booklist/books/*">
  <tr>
    <c:set var="bookId">
      <x:out select="$book/@id"/>
    </c:set>=
    <td bgcolor="#ffffaa">
      <c:url var="url"
      value="/bookdetails" >
        <c:param name="bookId" value="${bookId}" />
        <c:param name="Clear" value="0" />
      </c:url>
      <a href="${url}">
      <strong><x:out select="$book/title"/> 
      </strong></a></td>
    <td bgcolor="#ffffaa" rowspan=2>
      <c:set var="price">
        <x:out select="$book/price"/>
      </c:set>
      <fmt:formatNumber value="${price}" type="currency"/>
       
    </td>
    <td bgcolor="#ffffaa" rowspan=2>
    <c:url var="url" value="/catalog" >
      <c:param name="Add" value="${bookId}" />
    </c:url>
    <p><strong><a href="${url}"> 
      <fmt:message key="CartAdd"/> </a>
    </td>
  </tr>
  <tr>
    <td bgcolor="#ffffff">
      <fmt:message key="By"/> <em>
      <x:out select="$book/firstname"/> 
      <x:out select="$book/surname"/></em></td></tr>
</x:forEach>
```

Transformation Tags

The transform tag applies a transformation, specified by an XSLT stylesheet set by the attribute xslt, to an XML document, specified by the attribute doc. If the doc attribute is not specified, the input XML document is read from the tag's body content.

The `param` subtag can be used along with `transform` to set transformation parameters. The attributes `name` and `value` are used to specify the parameter. The `value` attribute is optional. If it is not specified, the value is retrieved from the tag's body.

Internationalization Tag Library

Chapter 22 covers how to design Web applications so that they conform to the language and formatting conventions of client locales. This section describes tags that support the internationalization of JSP pages.

JSTL defines tags for setting the locale for a page, creating locale-sensitive messages, and formatting and parsing data elements such as numbers, currencies, dates, and times in a locale-sensitive or customized manner. Table 14–7 lists the tags.

JSTL i18n tags use a localization context to localize their data. A *localization context* contains a locale and a resource bundle instance. To specify the localization context at deployment time, you define the context parameter `javax.servlet.jsp.jstl.fmt.localizationContext`, whose value can be a `javax.servlet.jsp.jstl.fmt.LocalizationContext` or a `String`. A `String` context parameter is interpreted as a resource bundle base name. For the Duke's

Table 14–7 Internationalization Tags

Area	Function	Tags	Prefix
I18n	Setting Locale	`setLocale` `requestEncoding`	fmt

	Messaging	`bundle`
		`message`
		`  param`
		`setBundle`	

	Number and Date Formatting	`formatNumber`
		`formatDate`
		`parseDate`
		`parseNumber`
		`setTimeZone`
		`timeZone`	

Bookstore application, the context parameter is the `String messages.Book-storeMessages`. When a request is received, JSTL automatically sets the locale based on the value retrieved from the request header and chooses the correct resource bundle using the base name specified in the context parameter.

Setting the Locale

The `setLocale` tag is used to override the client-specified locale for a page. The `requestEncoding` tag is used to set the request's character encoding, in order to be able to correctly decode request parameter values whose encoding is different from `ISO-8859-1`.

Messaging Tags

By default, the capability to sense the browser locale setting is enabled in JSTL. This means that the client determines (via its browser setting) which locale to use, and allows page authors to cater to the language preferences of their clients.

The setBundle and bundle Tags

You can set the resource bundle at runtime with the JSTL `fmt:setBundle` and `fmt:bundle` tags. `fmt:setBundle` is used to set the localization context in a variable or configuration variable for a specified scope. `fmt:bundle` is used to set the resource bundle for a given tag body.

The message Tag

The `message` tag is used to output localized strings. The following tag from `bookcatalog.jsp` is used to output a string inviting customers to choose a book from the catalog.

```
<h3><fmt:message key="Choose"/></h3>
```

The `param` subtag provides a single argument (for parametric replacement) to the compound message or pattern in its parent `message` tag. One `param` tag must be specified for each variable in the compound message or pattern. Parametric replacement takes place in the order of the `param` tags.

Formatting Tags

JSTL provides a set of tags for parsing and formatting locale-sensitive numbers and dates.

The `formatNumber` tag is used to output localized numbers. The following tag from `bookshowcart.jsp` is used to display a localized price for a book.

```
<fmt:formatNumber value="${book.price}" type="currency"/>
```

Note that because the price is maintained in the database in dollars, the localization is somewhat simplistic, because the `formatNumber` tag is unaware of exchange rates. The tag formats currencies but does not convert them.

Analogous tags for formatting dates (`formatDate`) and for parsing numbers and dates (`parseNumber`, `parseDate`) are also available. The `timeZone` tag establishes the time zone (specified via the `value` attribute) to be used by any nested `formatDate` tags.

In `bookreceipt.jsp`, a "pretend" ship date is created and then formatted with the `formatDate` tag:

```
<jsp:useBean id="now" class="java.util.Date" />
<jsp:setProperty name="now" property="time"
  value="${now.time + 432000000}" />
<fmt:message key="ShipDate"/>
<fmt:formatDate value="${now}" type="date"
  dateStyle="full"/>.
```

SQL Tag Library

The JSTL SQL tags for accessing databases listed in Table 14–8 are designed for quick prototyping and simple applications. For production applications, database operations are normally encapsulated in JavaBeans components.

The `setDataSource` tag allows you to set data source information for the database. You can provide a JNDI name or `DriverManager` parameters to set the data source information. All of the Duke's Bookstore pages that have more than one SQL tag use the following statement to set the data source:

```
<sql:setDataSource dataSource="jdbc/BookDB" />
```

Table 14–8 SQL Tags

Area	Function	Tags	Prefix
Database		setDataSource	sql

	SQL	query
		  dateParam
		  param
		transaction
		update
		  dateParam
		  param	

The query tag performs an SQL query that returns a result set. For parameterized SQL queries, you use a nested param tag inside the query tag.

In bookcatalog.jsp, the value of the Add request parameter determines which book information should be retrieved from the database. This parameter is saved as the attribute name bid and is passed to the param tag.

```
<c:set var="bid" value="${param.Add}"/>
<sql:query var="books" >
  select * from PUBLIC.books where id = ?
  <sql:param value="${bid}" />
</sql:query>
```

The update tag is used to update a database row. The transaction tag is used to perform a series of SQL statements atomically.

The JSP page bookreceipt.jsp page uses both tags to update the database inventory for each purchase. Because a shopping cart can contain more than one book, the transaction tag is used to wrap multiple queries and updates. First, the page establishes that there is sufficient inventory; then the updates are performed.

```
<c:set var="sufficientInventory" value="true" />
<sql:transaction>
  <c:forEach var="item" items="${sessionScope.cart.items}">
    <c:set var="book" value="${item.item}" />
    <c:set var="bookId" value="${book.bookId}" />
```

```
<sql:query var="books"
   sql="select * from PUBLIC.books where id = ?" >
   <sql:param value="${bookId}" />
</sql:query>
<jsp:useBean id="inventory"
   class="database.BookInventory" />
<c:forEach var="bookRow" begin="0"
   items="${books.rowsByIndex}">
   <jsp:useBean id="bookRow"  type="java.lang.Object[]" />
   <jsp:setProperty name="inventory" property="quantity"
      value="${bookRow[7]}" />

   <c:if test="${item.quantity > inventory.quantity}">
      <c:set var="sufficientInventory" value="false" />
      <h3><font color="red" size="+2">
      <fmt:message key="OrderError"/>
      There is insufficient inventory for
      <i>${bookRow[3]}</i>.</font></h3>
   </c:if>
</c:forEach>
</c:forEach>

<c:if test="${sufficientInventory == 'true'}" />
   <c:forEach var="item" items="${sessionScope.cart.items}">
      <c:set var="book" value="${item.item}" />
      <c:set var="bookId" value="${book.bookId}" />

      <sql:query var="books"
         sql="select * from PUBLIC.books where id = ?" >
         <sql:param value="${bookId}" />
      </sql:query>

      <c:forEach var="bookRow" begin="0"
         items="${books.rows}">
         <sql:update var="books" sql="update PUBLIC.books set
            inventory = inventory - ? where id = ?" >
            <sql:param value="${item.quantity}" />
            <sql:param value="${bookId}" />
         </sql:update>
      </c:forEach>
   </c:forEach>
   <h3><fmt:message key="ThankYou"/>
      ${param.cardname}.</h3><br>
</c:if>
</sql:transaction>
```

query Tag Result Interface

The `Result` interface is used to retrieve information from objects returned from a query tag.

```
public interface Result
    public String[] getColumnNames();
    public int getRowCount()
    public Map[] getRows();
    public Object[][] getRowsByIndex();
    public boolean isLimitedByMaxRows();
```

For complete information about this interface, see the API documentation for the JSTL packages.

The `var` attribute set by a query tag is of type `Result`. The `getRows` method returns an array of maps that can be supplied to the `items` attribute of a `forEach` tag. The JSTL expression language converts the syntax `${result.rows}` to a call to `result.getRows`. The expression `${books.rows}` in the following example returns an array of maps.

When you provide an array of maps to the `forEach` tag, the `var` attribute set by the tag is of type `Map`. To retrieve information from a row, use the `get("colname")` method to get a column value. The JSP expression language converts the syntax `${map.colname}` to a call to `map.get("colname")`. For example, the expression `${book.title}` returns the value of the title entry of a book map.

The Duke's Bookstore page `bookdetails.jsp` retrieves the column values from the book map as follows.

```
<c:forEach var="book" begin="0" items="${books.rows}">
  <h2>${book.title}</h2>
   <fmt:message key="By"/> <em>${book.firstname}
  ${book.surname}</em>  
  (${book.year})<br>   <br>
  <h4><fmt:message key="Critics"/></h4>
  <blockquote>${book.description}</blockquote>
  <h4><fmt:message key="ItemPrice"/>:
  <fmt:formatNumber value="${book.price}" type="currency"/>
  </h4>
</c:forEach>
```

The following excerpt from `bookcatalog.jsp` uses the `Row` interface to retrieve values from the columns of a book row using scripting language expressions. First, the book row that matches a request parameter (`bid`) is retrieved from the database. Because the `bid` and `bookRow` objects are later used by tags that use scripting language expressions to set attribute values and by a scriptlet that adds a book to the shopping cart, both objects are declared as scripting variables using the `jsp:useBean` tag. The page creates a bean that describes the book, and scripting language expressions are used to set the book properties from book row column values. Then the book is added to the shopping cart.

You might want to compare this version of `bookcatalog.jsp` to the versions in JavaServer Pages Technology (page 471) and Custom Tags in JSP Pages (page 563) that use a book database JavaBeans component.

```
<sql:query var="books"
  dataSource="${applicationScope.bookDS}">
  select * from PUBLIC.books where id = ?
  <sql:param value="${bid}" />
</sql:query>
<c:forEach var="bookRow" begin="0"
      items="${books.rowsByIndex}">
  <jsp:useBean id="bid"  type="java.lang.String" />
  <jsp:useBean id="bookRow" type="java.lang.Object[]" />
  <jsp:useBean id="addedBook" class="database.BookDetails"
    scope="page" >
    <jsp:setProperty name="addedBook"  property="bookId"
      value="${bookRow[0]}" />
    <jsp:setProperty name="addedBook"  property="surname"
      value="${bookRow[1]}" />
    <jsp:setProperty name="addedBook"  property="firstName"
      value="${bookRow[2]}" />
    <jsp:setProperty name="addedBook"  property="title"
      value="${bookRow[3]}" />
    <jsp:setProperty name="addedBook"  property="price"
      value="${bookRow[4])}" />
    <jsp:setProperty name="addedBook"  property="year"
      value="${bookRow[6]}" />
    <jsp:setProperty name="addedBook"
      property="description"
      value="${bookRow[7]}" />
    <jsp:setProperty name="addedBook"  property="inventory"
      value="${bookRow[8]}" />
  </jsp:useBean>
  <% cart.add(bid, addedBook); %>
  ...
</c:forEach>
```

Functions

Table 14–9 lists the JSTL functions.

Although the `java.util.Collection` interface defines a `size` method, it does not conform to the JavaBeans component design pattern for properties and so cannot be accessed via the JSP expression language. The `length` function can be applied to any collection supported by the `c:forEach` and returns the length of the collection. When applied to a `String`, it returns the number of characters in the string.

For example, the `index.jsp` page of the `hello1` application introduced in Chapter 3 uses the `fn:length` function and the `c:if` tag to determine whether to include a response page:

```
<%@ taglib uri="http://java.sun.com/jsp/jstl/core"
  prefix="c" %>
<%@ taglib uri="http://java.sun.com/jsp/jstl/functions"
  prefix="fn" %>
<html>
<head><title>Hello</title></head>
...
<input type="text" name="username" size="25">
<p></p>
<input type="submit" value="Submit">
<input type="reset" value="Reset">
</form>

<c:if test="${fn:length(param.username) > 0}" >
  <%@include file="response.jsp" %>
</c:if>
</body>
</html>
```

The rest of the JSTL functions are concerned with string manipulation:

- `toUpperCase`, `toLowerCase`: Changes the capitalization of a string
- `substring`, `substringBefore`, `substringAfter`: Gets a subset of a string
- `trim`: Trims whitespace from a string
- `replace`: Replaces characters in a string
- `indexOf`, `startsWith`, `endsWith`, `contains`, `containsIgnoreCase`: Checks whether a string contains another string
- `split`: Splits a string into an array
- `join`: Joins a collection into a string
- `escapeXml`: Escapes XML characters in a string

Table 14–9 Functions

Area	Function	Tags	Prefix
Functions	Collection length	`length`	

	String manipulation	`toUpperCase, toLowerCase`
		`substring, substringAfter,`
		`substringBefore`
		`trim`
		`replace`
		`indexOf, startsWith, endsWith,`
		`contains, containsIgnoreCase`
		`split, join`
		`escapeXml`
			`fn`

Further Information

For further information on JSTL, see the following:

- The tag reference documentation:

  `http://java.sun.com/products/jsp/jstl/1.1/docs/tlddocs/`
  `index.html`

- The API reference documentation:

  `http://java.sun.com/products/jsp/jstl/1.1/docs/api/`
  `index.html`

- The JSTL 1.1 specification:

  `http://java.sun.com/products/jsp/jstl/downloads/`
  `index.html#specs`

- The JSTL Web site:

  `http://java.sun.com/products/jsp/jstl`

15

Custom Tags in JSP Pages

THE standard JSP tags simplify JSP page development and maintenance. JSP technology also provides a mechanism for encapsulating other types of dynamic functionality in *custom tags*, which are extensions to the JSP language. Some examples of tasks that can be performed by custom tags include operating on implicit objects, processing forms, accessing databases and other enterprise services such as email and directories, and implementing flow control. Custom tags increase productivity because they can be reused in more than one application.

Custom tags are distributed in a *tag library*, which defines a set of related custom tags and contains the objects that implement the tags. The object that implements a custom tag is called a *tag handler*. JSP technology defines two types of tag handlers: simple and classic. *Simple* tag handlers can be used only for tags that do not use scripting elements in attribute values or the tag body. *Classic* tag handlers must be used if scripting elements are required. Simple tag handlers are covered in this chapter, and classic tag handlers are discussed in Chapter 16.

You can write simple tag handlers using the JSP language or using the Java language. A *tag file* is a source file containing a reusable fragment of JSP code that is translated into a simple tag handler by the Web container. Tag files can be used to develop custom tags that are presentation-centric or that can take advantage of existing tag libraries, or by page authors who do not know Java. When the flexibility of the Java programming language is needed to define the tag, JSP technology provides a simple API for developing a tag handler in the Java programming language.

This chapter assumes that you are familiar with the material in Chapter 12, especially the section Using Custom Tags (page 502). For more information about tag libraries and for pointers to some freely available libraries, see

```
http://java.sun.com/products/jsp/taglibraries/index.jsp
```

What Is a Custom Tag?

A custom tag is a user-defined JSP language element. When a JSP page containing a custom tag is translated into a servlet, the tag is converted to operations on a tag handler. The Web container then invokes those operations when the JSP page's servlet is executed.

Custom tags have a rich set of features. They can

- Be customized via attributes passed from the calling page.
- Pass variables back to the calling page.
- Access all the objects available to JSP pages.
- Communicate with each other. You can create and initialize a JavaBeans component, create a public EL variable that refers to that bean in one tag, and then use the bean in another tag.
- Be nested within one another and communicate via private variables.

The Example JSP Pages

This chapter describes the tasks involved in defining simple tags. We illustrate the tasks using excerpts from the JSP version of the Duke's Bookstore application discussed in The Example JSP Pages (page 476), rewritten here to take advantage of several custom tags:

- A catalog tag for rendering the book catalog
- A shipDate tag for rendering the ship date of an order
- A template library for ensuring a common look and feel among all screens and composing screens out of content chunks

The last section in the chapter, Examples (page 608), describes several tags in detail: a simple iteration tag and the set of tags in the `tutorial-template` tag library.

The `tutorial-template` tag library defines a set of tags for creating an application template. The template is a JSP page that has placeholders for the parts that need to change with each screen. Each of these placeholders is referred to as a *parameter* of the template. For example, a simple template might include a title parameter for the top of the generated screen and a body parameter to refer to a JSP page for the custom content of the screen. The template is created using a set of nested tags—`definition`, `screen`, and `parameter`—that are used to build a table of screen definitions for Duke's Bookstore. An `insert` tag is used to insert parameters from the table into the screen.

Figure 15–1 shows the flow of a request through the following Duke's Bookstore Web components:

- `template.jsp`, which determines the structure of each screen. It uses the `insert` tag to compose a screen from subcomponents.

- `screendefinitions.jsp`, which defines the subcomponents used by each screen. All screens have the same banner but different title and body content (specified by the JSP Pages column in Table 12–1).

- `Dispatcher`, a servlet, which processes requests and forwards to `template.jsp`.

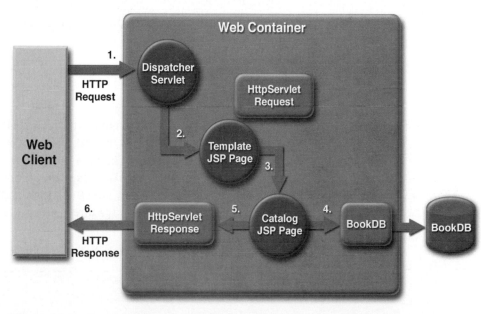

Figure 15–1 Request Flow through Duke's Bookstore Components

The source code for the Duke's Bookstore application is located in the `<INSTALL>/j2eetutorial14/examples/web/bookstore3/` directory created when you unzip the tutorial bundle (see About the Examples, page xl). A sample `bookstore3.war` is provided in `<INSTALL>/j2eetutorial14/examples/web/provided-wars/`. To build, package, deploy, and run the example, follow these steps:

1. Build and package the bookstore common files as described in Duke's Bookstore Examples (page 100).

2. In a terminal window, go to `<INSTALL>/j2eetutorial14/examples/bookstore3/`.

3. Run `asant build`. This target will spawn any necessary compilations and will copy files to the `<INSTALL>/j2eetutorial14/examples/web/bookstore3/build/` directory.

4. Start the Application Server.

5. Perform all the operations described in Accessing Databases from Web Applications, page 100.

6. Start `deploytool`.

7. Create a Web application called `bookstore3`. Select File→New→Web Component.

8. In the New Web Component wizard:

   a. Select the Create New Stand-Alone WAR Module radio button.

   b. In the WAR Location field, enter `<INSTALL>/j2eetutorial14/examples/web/bookstore3/bookstore3.war`.

   c. In the WAR Name field, enter `bookstore3`.

   d. In the Context Root field, enter `/bookstore3`.

   e. Click Edit Contents.

   f. In the Edit Contents dialog box, navigate to `<INSTALL>/j2eetutorial14/examples/web/bookstore3/build/`. Select the JSP pages `bookstore.jsp`, `bookdetails.jsp`, `bookcatalog.jsp`, `bookshowcart.jsp`, `bookcashier.jsp`, `bookreceipt.jsp`, and `bookordererror.jsp`, the tag files `catalog.tag` and `shipDate.tag` and the `dispatcher`, `database`, `listeners`, and `template` directories and click Add. Click OK.

g. Add the shared bookstore library. Navigate to *<INSTALL>*/ `j2eetutorial14/examples/web/bookstore/dist/`. Select `bookstore.jar`, and click Add.

h. Click Next.

i. Select the Servlet radio button.

j. Click Next.

k. Select `dispatcher.Dispatcher` from the Servlet class combo box.

l. Click Finish.

9. Add the listener class `listeners.ContextListener` (described in Handling Servlet Life-Cycle Events, page 441).

a. Select the Event Listeners tab.

b. Click Add.

c. Select the `listeners.ContextListener` class from drop-down field in the Event Listener Classes pane.

10. Add the aliases.

a. Select `Dispatcher`.

b. Select the Aliases tab.

c. Click Add and then type `/bookstore` in the Aliases field. Repeat to add the aliases `/bookcatalog`, `/bookdetails`, `/bookshowcart`, `/bookcashier`, `/bookordererror`, and `/bookreceipt`.

11. Add the context parameter that specifies the JSTL resource bundle basename.

a. Select the Web module.

b. Select the Context tab.

c. Click Add.

d. Enter `javax.servlet.jsp.jstl.fmt.localizationContext` in the Coded Parameter field.

e. Enter `messages.BookstoreMessages` in the Value field.

12. Set the prelude for all JSP pages.

a. Select the JSP Properties tab.

b. Click the Add button next to the Name list.

      c. Enter `bookstore3`.

      d. Click the Add button next to the URL Pattern list.

      e. Enter `*.jsp`.

      f. Click the Edit button next to the Include Preludes list.

      g. Click Add.

      h. Enter `/template/prelude.jspf`.

      i. Click OK.

13. Add a resource reference for the database.

      a. Select the Resource Ref's tab.

      b. Click Add.

      c. Enter `jdbc/BookDB` in the Coded Name field.

      d. Accept the default type `javax.sql.DataSource`.

      e. Accept the default authorization `Container`.

      f. Accept the default selected `Shareable`.

      g. Enter `jdbc/BookDB` in the JNDI name field of the Sun-specific Settings frame.

14. Deploy the application.

      a. Select Tools→Deploy.

      b. Click OK.

      c. A pop-up dialog box will display the results of the deployment. Click Close.

15. Open the bookstore URL:
`http://localhost:8080/bookstore3/bookstore`.

See Troubleshooting (page 440) for help with diagnosing common problems.

Types of Tags

Simple tags are invoked using XML syntax. They have a start tag and an end tag, and possibly a body:

```
<tt:tag>
  body
</tt:tag>
```

A custom tag with no body is expressed as follows:

```
<tt:tag /> or <tt:tag></tt:tag>
```

Tags with Attributes

A simple tag can have attributes. Attributes customize the behavior of a custom tag just as parameters customize the behavior of a method. There are three types of attributes:

- Simple attributes
- Fragment attributes
- Dynamic attributes

Simple Attributes

Simple attributes are evaluated by the container before being passed to the tag handler. Simple attributes are listed in the start tag and have the syntax `attr="value"`. You can set a simple attribute value from a `String` constant, or an expression language (EL), or by using a `jsp:attribute` element (see jsp:attribute Element, page 571). The conversion process between the constants and expressions and attribute types follows the rules described for JavaBeans component properties in Setting JavaBeans Component Properties (page 500).

The Duke's Bookstore page `bookcatalog.jsp` calls the `catalog` tag, which has two attributes. The first attribute, a reference to a book database object, is set by an EL expression. The second attribute, which sets the color of the rows in a table that represents the bookstore catalog, is set with a `String` constant.

```
<sc:catalog bookDB ="${bookDB}" color="#cccccc">
```

Fragment Attributes

A *JSP fragment* is a portion of JSP code passed to a tag handler that can be invoked as many times as needed. You can think of a fragment as a template that is used by a tag handler to produce customized content. Thus, unlike a simple attribute which is evaluated by the container, a fragment attribute is evaluated by a tag handler during tag invocation.

To declare a fragment attribute, you use the `fragment` attribute of the `attribute` directive (see Declaring Tag Attributes in Tag Files, page 579) or use the `fragment` subelement of the `attribute` TLD element (see Declaring Tag Attributes for Tag Handlers, page 595). You define the value of a fragment attribute by using a `jsp:attribute` element. When used to specify a fragment attribute, the body of the `jsp:attribute` element can contain only static text and standard and custom tags; it *cannot* contain scripting elements (see Chapter 16).

JSP fragments can be parametrized via expression language variables in the JSP code that composes the fragment. The EL variables are set by the tag handler, thus allowing the handler to customize the fragment each time it is invoked (see Declaring Tag Variables in Tag Files, page 579, and Declaring Tag Variables for Tag Handlers, page 596).

The `catalog` tag discussed earlier accepts two fragments: `normalPrice`, which is displayed for a product that's full price, and `onSale`, which is displayed for a product that's on sale.

```
<sc:catalog bookDB ="${bookDB}" color="#cccccc">
  <jsp:attribute name="normalPrice">
    <fmt:formatNumber value="${price}" type="currency"/>
  </jsp:attribute>
  <jsp:attribute name="onSale">
    <strike><fmt:formatNumber value="${price}"
      type="currency"/></strike><br/>
    <font color="red"><fmt:formatNumber value="${salePrice}"
      type="currency"/></font>
  </jsp:attribute>
</sc:catalog>
```

The tag executes the `normalPrice` fragment, using the values for the `price` EL variable, if the product is full price. If the product is on sale, the tag executes the `onSale` fragment using the `price` and `salePrice` variables.

Dynamic Attributes

A *dynamic attribute* is an attribute that is not specified in the definition of the tag. Dynamic attributes are used primarily by tags whose attributes are treated in a uniform manner but whose names are not necessarily known at development time.

For example, this tag accepts an arbitrary number of attributes whose values are colors and outputs a bulleted list of the attributes colored according to the values:

```
<colored:colored color1="red" color2="yellow" color3="blue"/>
```

You can also set the value of dynamic attributes using an EL expression or using the jsp:attribute element.

jsp:attribute Element

The jsp:attribute element allows you to define the value of a tag attribute in the *body* of an XML element instead of in the value of an XML attribute.

For example, the Duke's Bookstore template page screendefinitions.jsp uses jsp:attribute to use the output of fmt:message to set the value of the value attribute of tt:parameter:

```
...
<tt:screen id="/bookcatalog">
  <tt:parameter name="title" direct="true">
    <jsp:attribute name="value" >
      <fmt:message key="TitleBookCatalog"/>
    </jsp:attribute>
  </tt:parameter>
  <tt:parameter name="banner" value="/template/banner.jsp"
    direct="false"/>
  <tt:parameter name="body" value="/bookcatalog.jsp"
    direct="false"/>
</tt:screen>
...
```

jsp:attribute accepts a name attribute and a trim attribute. The name attribute identifies which tag attribute is being specified. The optional trim attribute determines whether or not whitespace appearing at the beginning and end of the element body should be discarded. By default, the leading and trailing whitespace is discarded. The whitespace is trimmed when the JSP page is translated. If a body contains a custom tag that produces leading or trailing whitespace, that whitespace is preserved regardless of the value of the trim attribute.

An empty body is equivalent to specifying "" as the value of the attribute.

The body of `jsp:attribute` is restricted according to the type of attribute being specified:

- For simple attributes that accept an EL expression, the body can be any JSP content.
- For simple attributes that do not accept an EL expression, the body can contain only static text.
- For fragment attributes, the body must not contain any scripting elements (see Chapter 16).

Tags with Bodies

A simple tag can contain custom and core tags, HTML text, and tag-dependent body content between the start tag and the end tag.

In the following example, the Duke's Bookstore application page bookshow-cart.jsp uses the JSTL `c:if` tag to print the body if the request contains a parameter named `Clear`:

```
<c:if test="${param.Clear}">
  <font color="#ff0000" size="+2"><strong>
  You just cleared your shopping cart!
  </strong><br> <br></font>
</c:if>
```

jsp:body Element

You can also explicitly specify the body of a simple tag by using the `jsp:body` element. If one or more attributes are specified with the `jsp:attribute` element, then `jsp:body` is the only way to specify the body of the tag. If one or more `jsp:attribute` elements appear in the body of a tag invocation but you don't include a `jsp:body` element, the tag has an empty body.

Tags That Define Variables

A simple tag can define an EL variable that can be used within the calling page. In the following example, the `iterator` tag sets the value of the EL variable `departmentName` as it iterates through a collection of department names.

```
<tlt:iterator var="departmentName" type="java.lang.String"
    group="${myorg.departmentNames}">
  <tr>
    <td><a href="list.jsp?deptName=${departmentName}">
      ${departmentName}</a></td>
  </tr>
</tlt:iterator>
```

Communication between Tags

Custom tags communicate with each other through shared objects. There are two types of shared objects: public and private.

In the following example, the c:set tag creates a public EL variable called aVariable, which is then reused by anotherTag.

```
<c:set var="aVariable" value="aValue" />
<tt:anotherTag attr1="${aVariable}" />
```

Nested tags can share private objects. In the next example, an object created by outerTag is available to innerTag. The inner tag retrieves its parent tag and then retrieves an object from the parent. Because the object is not named, the potential for naming conflicts is reduced.

```
<tt:outerTag>
  <tt:innerTag />
</tt:outerTag>
```

The Duke's Bookstore page template.jsp uses a set of cooperating tags that share public and private objects to define the screens of the application. These tags are described in A Template Tag Library (page 610).

Encapsulating Reusable Content Using Tag Files

A tag file is a source file that contains a fragment of JSP code that is reusable as a custom tag. Tag files allow you to create custom tags using JSP syntax. Just as a JSP page gets translated into a servlet class and then compiled, a tag file gets translated into a tag handler and then compiled.

The recommended file extension for a tag file is `.tag`. As is the case with JSP files, the tag can be composed of a top file that includes other files that contain either a complete tag or a fragment of a tag file. Just as the recommended extension for a fragment of a JSP file is `.jspf`, the recommended extension for a fragment of a tag file is `.tagf`.

The following version of the Hello, World application introduced in Chapter 3 uses a tag to generate the response. The `response` tag, which accepts two attributes—a greeting string and a name—is encapsulated in `response.tag`:

```
<%@ attribute name="greeting" required="true" %>
<%@ attribute name="name" required="true" %>
<h2><font color="black">${greeting}, ${name}!</font></h2>
```

The highlighted line in the `greeting.jsp` page invokes the `response` tag if the length of the `username` request parameter is greater than 0:

```
<%@ taglib tagdir="/WEB-INF/tags" prefix="h" %>
<%@ taglib uri="http://java.sun.com/jsp/jstl/core"
   prefix="c" %>
<%@ taglib uri="http://java.sun.com/jsp/jstl/functions"
   prefix="fn" %>
<html>
<head><title>Hello</title></head>
<body bgcolor="white">
<img src="duke.waving.gif">
<c:set var="greeting" value="Hello" />
<h2>${greeting}, my name is Duke. What's yours?</h2>
<form method="get">
<input type="text" name="username" size="25">
<p></p>
<input type="submit" value="Submit">
<input type="reset" value="Reset">
</form>

<c:if test="${fn:length(param.username) > 0}" >
  <h:response greeting="${greeting}"
     name="${param.username}"/>
</c:if>
</body>
</html>
```

A sample `hello3.war` is provided in `<INSTALL>`/j2eetutorial14/examples/
web/provided-wars/. To build, package, deploy, and run the `hello3` application, follow these steps:

1. In a terminal window, go to `<INSTALL>`/j2eetutorial14/examples/
   web/hello3/.

2. Run `asant build`. This target will spawn any necessary compilations and
   copy files to the `<INSTALL>`/j2eetutorial14/examples/web/hello3/
   build/ directory.

3. Start the Application Server.

4. Start `deploytool`.

5. Create a Web application called `hello3` by running the New Web Component wizard. Select File→New→Web Component.

6. In the New Web Component wizard:

   a. Select the Create New Stand-Alone WAR Module radio button.

   b. In the WAR Location field, enter `<INSTALL>`/j2eetutorial14/examples/web/hello3/hello3.war.

   c. In the WAR Name field enter `hello3`.

   d. In the Context Root field, enter /hello3.

   e. Click Edit Contents.

   f. In the Edit Contents dialog, navigate to `<INSTALL>`/j2eetutorial14/
      examples/web/hello3/build/. Select duke.waving.gif, greeting.jsp, and `response.tag` and click Add. Click OK.

   g. Click Next.

   h. Select the No Component radio button.

   i. Click Next.

   j. Click Finish.

7. Set `greeting.jsp` to be a welcome file (see Declaring Welcome
   Files, page 97).

   a. Select the File Ref's tab.

   b. Click Add to add a welcome file.

   c. Select `greeting.jsp` from the drop-down list.

8. Select File→Save.

9. Deploy the application.

   a. Select Tools→Deploy.

   b. In the Connection Settings frame, enter the user name and password you specified when you installed the Application Server.

   c. Click OK.

   d. A pop-up dialog box will display the results of the deployment. Click Close.

10. Open your browser to `http://localhost:8080/hello3`

Tag File Location

Tag files can be placed in one of two locations: in the `/WEB-INF/tags/` directory or subdirectory of a Web application or in a JAR file (see Packaged Tag Files, page 593) in the `/WEB-INF/lib/` directory of a Web application. Packaged tag files require a tag library descriptor (see Tag Library Descriptors, page 589), an XML document that contains information about a library as a whole and about each tag contained in the library. Tag files that appear in any other location are not considered tag extensions and are ignored by the Web container.

Tag File Directives

Directives are used to control aspects of tag file translation to a tag handler, and to specify aspects of the tag, attributes of the tag, and variables exposed by the tag. Table 15–1 lists the directives that you can use in tag files.

Declaring Tags

The `tag` directive is similar to the JSP page's `page` directive but applies to tag files. Some of the elements in the `tag` directive appear in the `tag` element of a TLD (see Declaring Tag Handlers, page 594). Table 15–2 lists the `tag` directive attributes.

Table 15–1 Tag File Directives

Directive	Description
`taglib`	Identical to `taglib` directive (see Declaring Tag Libraries, page 503) for JSP pages.
`include`	Identical to `include` directive (see Reusing Content in JSP Pages, page 506) for JSP pages. Note that if the included file contains syntax unsuitable for tag files, a translation error will occur.
`tag`	Similar to the `page` directive in a JSP page, but applies to tag files instead of JSP pages. As with the `page` directive, a translation unit can contain more than one instance of the `tag` directive. All the attributes apply to the complete translation unit. However, there can be only one occurrence of any attribute or value defined by this directive in a given translation unit. With the exception of the `import` attribute, multiple attribute or value (re)definitions result in a translation error. Also used for declaring custom tag properties such as display name. See Declaring Tags (page 576).
`attribute`	Declares an attribute of the custom tag defined in the tag file. See Declaring Tag Attributes in Tag Files (page 579).
`variable`	Declares an EL variable exposed by the tag to the calling page. See Declaring Tag Variables in Tag Files (page 579).

Table 15–2 `tag` Directive Attributes

Attribute	Description
`display-name`	(optional) A short name that is intended to be displayed by tools. Defaults to the name of the tag file without the extension `.tag`.
`body-content`	(optional) Provides information on the content of the body of the tag. Can be either `empty`, `tagdependent`, or `scriptless`. A translation error will result if JSP or any other value is used. Defaults to `scriptless`. See body-content Attribute (page 579).

Continues

Table 15–2 `tag` Directive Attributes *(Continued)*

Attribute	Description
`dynamic-attributes`	(optional) Indicates whether this tag supports additional attributes with dynamic names. The value identifies a scoped attribute in which to place a `Map` containing the names and values of the dynamic attributes passed during invocation of the tag. A translation error results if the value of the `dynamic-attributes` of a `tag` directive is equal to the value of a `name-given` of a `variable` directive or the value of a `name` attribute of an `attribute` directive.
`small-icon`	(optional) Relative path, from the tag source file, of an image file containing a small icon that can be used by tools. Defaults to no small icon.
`large-icon`	(optional) Relative path, from the tag source file, of an image file containing a large icon that can be used by tools. Defaults to no large icon.
`description`	(optional) Defines an arbitrary string that describes this tag. Defaults to no description.
`example`	(optional) Defines an arbitrary string that presents an informal description of an example of a use of this action. Defaults to no example.
`language`	(optional) Carries the same syntax and semantics of the `language` attribute of the `page` directive.
`import`	(optional) Carries the same syntax and semantics of the `import` attribute of the `page` directive.
`pageEncoding`	(optional) Carries the same syntax and semantics of the `pageEncoding` attribute in the `page` directive.
`isELIgnored`	(optional) Carries the same syntax and semantics of the `isELIgnored` attribute of the `page` directive.

body-content Attribute

You specify the type of a tag's body content using the `body-content` attribute:

```
bodycontent="empty | scriptless | tagdependent"
```

You must declare the body content of tags that do not accept a body as `empty`. For tags that have a body there are two options. Body content containing custom and standard tags and HTML text is specified as `scriptless`. All other types of body content—for example, SQL statements passed to the `query` tag—is specified as `tagdependent`. If no attribute is specified, the default is `scriptless`.

Declaring Tag Attributes in Tag Files

To declare the attributes of a custom tag defined in a tag file, you use the `attribute` directive. A TLD has an analogous `attribute` element (see Declaring Tag Attributes for Tag Handlers, page 595). Table 15–3 lists the `attribute` directive attributes.

Declaring Tag Variables in Tag Files

Tag attributes are used to customize tag behavior much as parameters are used to customize the behavior of object methods. In fact, using tag attributes and EL variables, it is possible to emulate various types of parameters—`IN`, `OUT`, and nested.

To emulate `IN` parameters, use tag attributes. A tag attribute is communicated between the calling page and the tag file when the tag is invoked. No further communication occurs between the calling page and the tag file.

To emulate `OUT` or nested parameters, use EL variables. The variable is not initialized by the calling page but instead is set by the tag file. Each type of parameter is synchronized with the calling page at various points according to the scope of the variable. See Variable Synchronization (page 580) for details.

To declare an EL variable exposed by a tag file, you use the `variable` directive. A TLD has an analogous `variable` element (see Declaring Tag Variables for Tag Handlers, page 596). Table 15–4 lists the `variable` directive attributes.

Table 15–3 `attribute` Directive Attributes

Attribute	Description
`description`	(optional) Description of the attribute. Defaults to no description.
`name`	The unique name of the attribute being declared. A translation error results if more than one `attribute` directive appears in the same translation unit with the same `name`. A translation error results if the value of a `name` attribute of an `attribute` directive is equal to the value of the `dynamic-attributes` attribute of a `tag` directive or the value of a `name-given` attribute of a `variable` directive.
`required`	(optional) Whether this attribute is required (`true`) or optional (`false`). Defaults to `false`.
`rtexprvalue`	(optional) Whether the attribute's value can be dynamically calculated at runtime by an expression. Defaults to `true`.
`type`	(optional) The runtime type of the attribute's value. Defaults to `java.lang.String`.
`fragment`	(optional) Whether this attribute is a fragment to be evaluated by the tag handler (`true`) or a normal attribute to be evaluated by the container before being passed to the tag handler. If this attribute is `true`: You do not specify the `rtexprvalue` attribute. The container fixes the `rtexprvalue` attribute at `true`. You do not specify the `type` attribute. The container fixes the `type` attribute at `javax.servlet.jsp.tagext.JspFragment`. Defaults to `false`.

Variable Synchronization

The Web container handles the synchronization of variables between a tag file and a calling page. Table 15–5 summarizes when and how each object is synchronized according to the object's scope.

Table 15–4 `variable` Directive Attributes

Attribute	Description
`description`	(optional) An optional description of this variable. Defaults to no description.
`name-given` | `name-from-attribute`	Defines an EL variable to be used in the page invoking this tag. Either `name-given` or `name-from-attribute` must be specified. If `name-given` is specified, the value is the name of the variable. If `name-from-attribute` is specified, the value is the name of an attribute whose (translation-time) value at the start of the tag invocation will give the name of the variable. Translation errors arise in the following circumstances: 1. Specifying neither `name-given` nor `name-from-attribute`. 2. If two `variable` directives have the same `name-given`. 3. If the value of a `name-given` attribute of a `variable` directive is equal to the value of a name attribute of an `attribute` directive or the value of a `dynamic-attributes` attribute of a `tag` directive.
`alias`	Defines a variable, local to the tag file, to hold the value of the EL variable. The container will synchronize this value with the variable whose name is given in `name-from-attribute`. Required when `name-from-attribute` is specified. A translation error results if used without `name-from-attribute`. A translation error results if the value of `alias` is the same as the value of a `name` attribute of an `attribute` directive or the `name-given` attribute of a `variable` directive.
`variable-class`	(optional) The name of the class of the variable. The default is `java.lang.String`.
`declare`	(optional) Whether or not the variable is declared. `True` is the default.
`scope`	(optional) The scope of the variable. Can be either `AT_BEGIN`, `AT_END`, or `NESTED`. Defaults to `NESTED`.

Table 15–5 Variable Synchronization Behavior

Tag File Location	AT_BEGIN	NESTED	AT_END
Beginning	Not sync.	Save	Not sync.
Before any fragment invocation via `jsp:invoke` or `jsp:doBody` (see Evaluating Fragments Passed to Tag Files, page 584)	Tag→page	Tag→page	Not sync.
End	Tag→page	Restore	Tag→page

If `name-given` is used to specify the variable name, then the name of the variable in the calling page and the name of the variable in the tag file are the same and are equal to the value of `name-given`.

The `name-from-attribute` and `alias` attributes of the `variable` directive can be used to customize the name of the variable in the calling page while another name is used in the tag file. When using these attributes, you set the name of the variable in the calling page from the value of `name-from-attribute` at the time the tag was called. The name of the corresponding variable in the tag file is the value of `alias`.

Synchronization Examples

The following examples illustrate how variable synchronization works between a tag file and its calling page. All the example JSP pages and tag files reference the JSTL core tag library with the prefix c. The JSP pages reference a tag file located in /WEB-INF/tags with the prefix my.

AT_BEGIN Scope

In this example, the AT_BEGIN scope is used to pass the value of the variable named x to the tag's body and at the end of the tag invocation.

```
<%-- callingpage.jsp --%>
<c:set var="x" value="1"/>
${x} <%-- (x == 1) --%>
<my:example>
   ${x} <%-- (x == 2) --%>
</my:example>
${x} <%-- (x == 4) --%>
```

```
<%-- example.tag --%>
<%@ variable name-given="x" scope="AT_BEGIN" %>
${x} <%-- (x == null) --%>
<c:set var="x" value="2"/>
<jsp:doBody/>
${x} <%-- (x == 2) --%>
<c:set var="x" value="4"/>
```

NESTED Scope

In this example, the NESTED scope is used to make a variable named x available only to the tag's body. The tag sets the variable to 2, and this value is passed to the calling page before the body is invoked. Because the scope is NESTED and because the calling page also had a variable named x, its original value, 1, is restored when the tag completes.

```
<%-- callingpage.jsp --%>
<c:set var="x" value="1"/>
${x} <%-- (x == 1) --%>
<my:example>
   ${x} <%-- (x == 2) --%>
</my:example>
${x} <%-- (x == 1) --%>


<%-- example.tag --%>
<%@ variable name-given="x" scope-"NESTED" %>
${x} <%-- (x == null) --%>
<c:set var="x" value="2"/>
<jsp:doBody/>
${x} <%-- (x == 2) --%>
<c:set var="x" value="4"/>
```

AT_END Scope

In this example, the AT_END scope is used to return a value to the page. The body of the tag is not affected.

```
<%-- callingpage.jsp --%>
<c:set var="x" value="1"/>
${x} <%-- (x == 1) --%>
<my:example>
   ${x} <%-- (x == 1) --%>
</my:example>
${x} <%-- (x == 4) --%>
```

```
<%-- example.tag --%>
<%@ variable name-given="x" scope="AT_END" %>
${x} <%-- (x == null) --%>
<c:set var="x" value="2"/>
<jsp:doBody/>
${x} <%-- (x == 2) --%>
<c:set var="x" value="4"/>
```

AT_BEGIN and name-from-attribute

In this example the AT_BEGIN scope is used to pass an EL variable to the tag's body and make to it available to the calling page at the end of the tag invocation. The name of the variable is specified via the value of the attribute var. The variable is referenced by a local name, result, in the tag file.

```
<%-- callingpage.jsp --%>
<c:set var="x" value="1"/>
${x} <%-- (x == 1) --%>
<my:example var="x">
   ${x} <%-- (x == 2) --%>
   ${result} <%-- (result == null) --%>
   <c:set var="result" value="invisible"/>
</my:example>
${x} <%-- (x == 4) --%>
${result} <%-- (result == 'invisible') --%>

<%-- example.tag --%>
<%@ attribute name="var" required="true" rtexprvalue="false"%>
<%@ variable alias="result" name-from-attribute="var"
   scope="AT_BEGIN" %>
${x} <%-- (x == null) --%>
${result} <%-- (result == null) --%>
<c:set var="x" value="ignored"/>
<c:set var="result" value="2"/>
<jsp:doBody/>
${x} <%-- (x == 'ignored') --%>
${result} <%-- (result == 2) --%>
<c:set var="result" value="4"/>
```

Evaluating Fragments Passed to Tag Files

When a tag file is executed, the Web container passes it two types of fragments: fragment attributes and the tag body. Recall from the discussion of fragment attributes that fragments are evaluated by the tag handler as opposed to the Web container. Within a tag file, you use the jsp:invoke element to evaluate a fragment attribute and use the jsp:doBody element to evaluate a tag file body.

The result of evaluating either type of fragment is sent to the response or is stored in an EL variable for later manipulation. To store the result of evaluating a fragment to an EL variable, you specify the var or varReader attribute. If var is specified, the container stores the result in an EL variable of type String with the name specified by var. If varReader is specified, the container stores the result in an EL variable of type java.io.Reader, with the name specified by varReader. The Reader object can then be passed to a custom tag for further processing. A translation error occurs if both var and varReader are specified.

An optional scope attribute indicates the scope of the resulting variable. The possible values are page (default), request, session, or application. A translation error occurs if you use this attribute without specifying the var or varReader attribute.

Examples

Simple Attribute Example

The Duke's Bookstore shipDate tag, defined in shipDate.tag, is a custom tag that has a simple attribute. The tag generates the date of a book order according to the type of shipping requested.

```
<%@ taglib prefix="sc" tagdir="/WEB-INF/tags" %>
<h3><fmt:message key="ThankYou"/> ${param.cardname}.</h3><br>
<fmt:message key="With"/>
<em><fmt:message key="${param.shipping}"/></em>,
<fmt:message key="ShipDateLC"/>
<sc:shipDate shipping="${param.shipping}" />
```

The tag determines the number of days until shipment from the shipping attribute passed to it by the page bookreceipt.jsp. From the number of days, the tag computes the ship date. It then formats the ship date.

```
<%@ attribute name="shipping" required="true" %>

<jsp:useBean id="now" class="java.util.Date" />
<jsp:useBean id="shipDate" class="java.util.Date" />
<c:choose>
  <c:when test="${shipping == 'QuickShip'}">
    <c:set var="days" value="2" />
  </c:when>
```

```
    <c:when test="${shipping == 'NormalShip'}">
      <c:set var="days" value="5" />
    </c:when>
    <c:when test="${shipping == 'SaverShip'}">
      <c:set var="days" value="7" />
    </c:when>
  </c:choose>
  <jsp:setProperty name="shipDate" property="time"
    value="${now.time + 86400000 * days}" />
  <fmt:formatDate value="${shipDate}" type="date"
    dateStyle="full"/>.<br><br>
```

Simple and Fragment Attribute and Variable Example

The Duke's Bookstore `catalog` tag, defined in `catalog.tag`, is a custom tag with simple and fragment attributes and variables. The tag renders the catalog of a book database as an HTML table. The tag file declares that it sets variables named `price` and `salePrice` via `variable` directives. The fragment `normalPrice` uses the variable `price`, and the fragment `onSale` uses the variables `price` and `salePrice`. Before the tag invokes the fragment attributes using the `jsp:invoke` element, the Web container passes values for the variables back to the calling page.

```
<%@ attribute name="bookDB" required="true"
  type="database.BookDB" %>
<%@ attribute name="color" required="true" %>
<%@ attribute name="normalPrice" fragment="true" %>
<%@ attribute name="onSale" fragment="true" %>

<%@ variable name-given="price" %>
<%@ variable name-given="salePrice" %>

<center>
<table>
<c:forEach var="book" begin="0" items="${bookDB.books}">
  <tr>
  <c:set var="bookId" value="${book.bookId}" />
  <td bgcolor="${color}">
    <c:url var="url" value="/bookdetails" >
      <c:param name="bookId" value="${bookId}" />
    </c:url>
```

```
    <a href="${url}"><
        strong>${book.title} </strong></a></td>
    <td bgcolor="${color}" rowspan=2>
    <c:set var="salePrice" value="${book.price * .85}" />
    <c:set var="price" value="${book.price}" />
    <c:choose>
        <c:when test="${book.onSale}" >
            <jsp:invoke fragment="onSale" />
        </c:when>
        <c:otherwise>
            <jsp:invoke fragment="normalPrice"/>
        </c:otherwise>
    </c:choose>

     </td>


    ...
</table>
</center>
```

The page `bookcatalog.jsp` invokes the `catalog` tag that has the simple attributes bookDB, which contains catalog data, and color, which customizes the coloring of the table rows. The formatting of the book price is determined by two fragment attributes—normalPrice and onSale—that are conditionally invoked by the tag according to data retrieved from the book database.

```
<sc:catalog bookDB ="${bookDB}" color="#cccccc">
    <jsp:attribute name="normalPrice">
        <fmt:formatNumber value="${price}" type="currency"/>
    </jsp:attribute>
    <jsp:attribute name="onSale">
        <strike>
        <fmt:formatNumber value="${price}" type="currency"/>
        </strike><br/>
        <font color="red">
        <fmt:formatNumber value="${salePrice}" type="currency"/>
        </font>
    </jsp:attribute>
</sc:catalog>
```

The screen produced by `bookcatalog.jsp` is shown in Figure 15–2. You can compare it to the version in Figure 12–2.

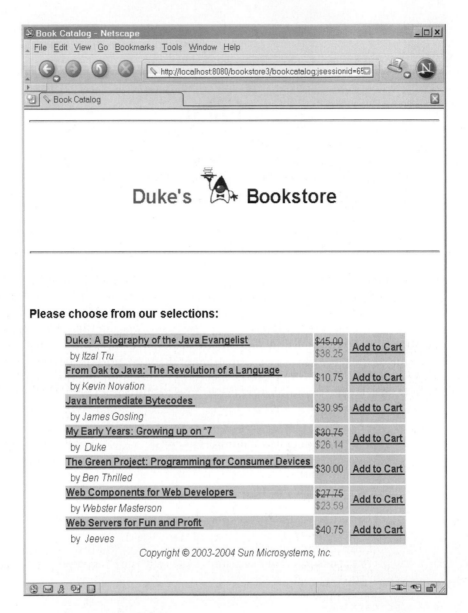

Figure 15–2   Book Catalog

Dynamic Attribute Example

The following code implements the tag discussed in Dynamic Attributes (page 570). An arbitrary number of attributes whose values are colors are stored in a

Map named by the dynamic-attributes attribute of the tag directive. The JSTL forEach tag is used to iterate through the Map and the attribute keys and colored attribute values are printed in a bulleted list.

```
<%@ tag dynamic-attributes="colorMap"%>
<ul>
<c:forEach var="color" begin="0" items="${colorMap}">
  <li>${color.key} =
      <font color="${color.value}">${color.value}</font><li>
</c:forEach>
</ul>
```

Tag Library Descriptors

If you want to redistribute your tag files or implement your custom tags with tag handlers written in Java, you must declare the tags in a tag library descriptor (TLD). A *tag library descriptor* is an XML document that contains information about a library as a whole and about each tag contained in the library. TLDs are used by a Web container to validate the tags and by JSP page development tools.

Tag library descriptor file names must have the extension .tld and must be packaged in the /WEB-INF/ directory or subdirectory of the WAR file or in the /META-INF/ directory or subdirectory of a tag library packaged in a JAR. If a tag is implemented as a tag file and is packaged in /WEB-INF/tags/ or a subdirectory, a TLD will be generated automatically by the Web container, though you can provide one if you wish.

A TLD must begin with a root taglib element that specifies the schema and required JSP version:

```
<taglib xmlns="http://java.sun.com/xml/ns/j2ee"
   xmlns:xsi="http://www.w3.org/2001/XMLSchema-instance"
   xsi:schemaLocation="http://java.sun.com/xml/ns/j2ee/web-
jsptaglibrary_2_0.xsd"
   version="2.0">
```

Table 15–6 lists the subelements of the taglib element.

Table 15–6 `taglib` Subelements

Element	Description
`description`	(optional) A string describing the use of the tag library.
`display-name`	(optional) Name intended to be displayed by tools.
`icon`	(optional) Icon that can be used by tools.
`tlib-version`	The tag library's version.
`short-name`	(optional) Name that can be used by a JSP page-authoring tool to create names with a mnemonic value.
`uri`	A URI that uniquely identifies the tag library.
`validator`	See validator Element (page 590).
`listener`	See listener Element (page 591).
`tag-file	tag`	Declares the tag files or tags defined in the tag library. See Declaring Tag Files (page 591) and Declaring Tag Handlers (page 594). A tag library is considered invalid if a `tag-file` element has a `name` subelement with the same content as a `name` subelement in a `tag` element.
`function`	Zero or more EL functions (see Functions, page 496) defined in the tag library.
`tag-extension`	(optional) Extensions that provide extra information about the tag library for tools.

Top-Level Tag Library Descriptor Elements

This section describes some top-level TLD elements. Subsequent sections describe how to declare tags defined in tag files, how to declare tags defined in tag handlers, and how to declare tag attributes and variables.

validator Element

This element defines an optional tag library validator that can be used to validate the conformance of any JSP page importing this tag library to its requirements. Table 15–7 lists the subelements of the `validator` element.

Table 15–7 `validator` Subelements

Element	Description
`validator-class`	The class implementing `javax.servlet.jsp.tagext.TagLibraryValidator`
`init-param`	(optional) Initialization parameters

listener Element

A tag library can specify some classes that are event listeners (see Handling Servlet Life-Cycle Events, page 441). The listeners are listed in the TLD as `listener` elements, and the Web container will instantiate the listener classes and register them in a way analogous to that of listeners defined at the WAR level. Unlike WAR-level listeners, the order in which the tag library listeners are registered is undefined. The only subelement of the `listener` element is the `listener-class` element, which must contain the fully qualified name of the listener class.

Declaring Tag Files

Although not required for tag files, providing a TLD allows you to share the tag across more than one tag library and lets you import the tag library using a URI instead of the `tagdir` attribute.

tag-file TLD Element

A tag file is declared in the TLD using a `tag-file` element. Its subelements are listed in Table 15–8.

Unpackaged Tag Files

Tag files placed in a subdirectory of `/WEB-INF/tags/` do not require a TLD file and don't have to be packaged. Thus, to create reusable JSP code, you simply create a new tag file and place the code inside it.

Table 15–8 `tag-file` Subelements

Element	Description
`description`	(optional) A description of the tag.
`display-name`	(optional) Name intended to be displayed by tools.
`icon`	(optional) Icon that can be used by tools.
`name`	The unique tag name.
`path`	Where to find the tag file implementing this tag, relative to the root of the Web application or the root of the JAR file for a tag library packaged in a JAR. This must begin with `/WEB-INF/tags/` if the tag file resides in the WAR, or `/META-INF/tags/` if the tag file resides in a JAR.
`example`	(optional) Informal description of an example use of the tag.
`tag-extension`	(optional) Extensions that provide extra information about the tag for tools.

The Web container generates an implicit tag library for each directory under and including `/WEB-INF/tags/`. There are no special relationships between subdirectories; they are allowed simply for organizational purposes. For example, the following Web application contains three tag libraries:

```
/WEB-INF/tags/
/WEB-INF/tags/a.tag
/WEB-INF/tags/b.tag
/WEB-INF/tags/foo/
/WEB-INF/tags/foo/c.tag
/WEB-INF/tags/bar/baz/
/WEB-INF/tags/bar/baz/d.tag
```

The implicit TLD for each library has the following values:

- `tlib-version` for the tag library. Defaults to 1.0.
- `short-name` is derived from the directory name. If the directory is `/WEB-INF/tags/`, the short name is simply `tags`. Otherwise, the full directory path (relative to the Web application) is taken, minus the `/WEB-INF/tags/` prefix. Then all `/` characters are replaced with -(hyphen), which yields the short name. Note that short names are not guaranteed to be unique.

- A `tag-file` element is considered to exist for each tag file, with the following subelements:
  - The `name` for each is the filename of the tag file, without the `.tag` extension.
  - The `path` for each is the path of the tag file, relative to the root of the Web application.

So, for the example, the implicit TLD for the `/WEB-INF/tags/bar/baz/` directory would be as follows:

```
<taglib>
   <tlib-version>1.0</tlib-version>
   <short-name>bar-baz</short-name>
   <tag-file>
      <name>d</name>
      <path>/WEB-INF/tags/bar/baz/d.tag</path>
   </tag-file>
</taglib>
```

Despite the existence of an implicit tag library, a TLD in the Web application can still create additional tags from the same tag files. To accomplish this, you add a `tag-file` element with a `path` that points to the tag file.

Packaged Tag Files

Tag files can be packaged in the `/META-INF/tags/` directory in a JAR file installed in the `/WEB-INF/lib/` directory of the Web application. Tags placed here are typically part of a reusable library of tags that can be used easily in any Web application.

Tag files bundled in a JAR require a tag library descriptor. Tag files that appear in a JAR but are not defined in a TLD are ignored by the Web container.

When used in a JAR file, the `path` subelement of the `tag-file` element specifies the full path of the tag file from the root of the JAR. Therefore, it must always begin with `/META-INF/tags/`.

Tag files can also be compiled into Java classes and bundled as a tag library. This is useful when you wish to distribute a binary version of the tag library without the original source. If you choose this form of packaging, you must use a tool that produces portable JSP code that uses only standard APIs.

Declaring Tag Handlers

When tags are implemented with tag handlers written in Java, each tag in the library must be declared in the TLD with a `tag` element. The `tag` element contains the tag name, the class of its tag handler, information on the tag's attributes, and information on the variables created by the tag (see Tags That Define Variables, page 572).

Each attribute declaration contains an indication of whether the attribute is required, whether its value can be determined by request-time expressions, the type of the attribute, and whether the attribute is a fragment. Variable information can be given directly in the TLD or through a tag extra info class. Table 15–9 lists the subelements of the `tag` element.

Table 15–9 `tag` Subelements

Element	Description
description	(optional) A description of the tag.
display-name	(optional) Name intended to be displayed by tools.
icon	(optional) Icon that can be used by tools.
name	The unique tag name.
tag-class	The fully qualified name of the tag handler class.
tei-class	(optional) Subclass of `javax.servlet.jsp.tagext.TagExtraInfo`. See Declaring Tag Variables for Tag Handlers (page 596).
body-content	The body content type. See body-content Element (page 595).
variable	(optional) Declares an EL variable exposed by the tag to the calling page. See Declaring Tag Variables for Tag Handlers (page 596).
attribute	Declares an attribute of the custom tag. See Declaring Tag Attributes for Tag Handlers (page 595).
dynamic-attributes	Whether the tag supports additional attributes with dynamic names. Defaults to `false`. If true, the tag handler class must implement the `javax.servlet.jsp.tagext.DynamicAttributes` interface.
example	(optional) Informal description of an example use of the tag.
tag-extension	(optional) Extensions that provide extra information about the tag for tools.

body-content Element

You specify the type of body that is valid for a tag by using the `body-content` element. This element is used by the Web container to validate that a tag invocation has the correct body syntax and is used by page-composition tools to assist the page author in providing a valid tag body. There are three possible values:

- `tagdependent`: The body of the tag is interpreted by the tag implementation itself, and is most likely in a different language, for example, embedded SQL statements.
- `empty`: The body must be empty.
- `scriptless`: The body accepts only static text, EL expressions, and custom tags. No scripting elements are allowed.

Declaring Tag Attributes for Tag Handlers

For each tag attribute, you must specify whether the attribute is required, whether the value can be determined by an expression, the type of the attribute in an `attribute` element (optional), and whether the attribute is a fragment. If the `rtexprvalue` element is `true` or `yes`, then the `type` element defines the return type expected from any expression specified as the value of the attribute. For static values, the type is always `java.lang.String`. An attribute is specified in a TLD in an `attribute` element. Table 15–10 lists the subelements of the `attribute` element.

If a tag attribute is not required, a tag handler should provide a default value.

The `tag` element for a tag that outputs its body if a test evaluates to `true` declares that the `test` attribute is required and that its value can be set by a runtime expression.

```
<tag>
  <name>present</name>
      <tag-class>condpkg.IfSimpleTag</tag-class>
  <body-content>scriptless</body-content>
  ...
  <attribute>
    <name>test</name>
    <required>true</required>
    <rtexprvalue>true</rtexprvalue>
  </attribute>
  ...
</tag>
```

Table 15–10 `attribute` Subelements

Element	Description
description	(optional) A description of the attribute.
name	The unique name of the attribute being declared. A translation error results if more than one `attribute` element appears in the same tag with the same `name`.
required	(optional) Whether the attribute is required. The default is `false`.
rtexprvalue	(optional) Whether the attribute's value can be dynamically calculated at runtime by an EL expression. The default is `false`.
type	(optional) The runtime type of the attribute's value. Defaults to `java.lang.String` if not specified.
fragment	(optional) Whether this attribute is a fragment to be evaluated by the tag handler (`true`) or a normal attribute to be evaluated by the container before being passed to the tag handler. If this attribute is `true`: You do not specify the `rtexprvalue` attribute. The container fixes the `rtexprvalue` attribute at `true`. You do not specify the `type` attribute. The container fixes the `type` attribute at `javax.servlet.jsp.tagext.JspFragment`. Defaults to `false`.

Declaring Tag Variables for Tag Handlers

The example described in Tags That Define Variables (page 572) defines an EL variable `departmentName`:

```
<tlt:iterator var="departmentName" type="java.lang.String"
    group="${myorg.departmentNames}">
  <tr>
    <td><a href="list.jsp?deptName=${departmentName}">
      ${departmentName}</a></td>
  </tr>
</tlt:iterator>
```

When the JSP page containing this tag is translated, the Web container generates code to synchronize the variable with the object referenced by the variable. To generate the code, the Web container requires certain information about the variable:

- Variable name
- Variable class
- Whether the variable refers to a new or an existing object
- The availability of the variable

There are two ways to provide this information: by specifying the `variable` TLD subelement or by defining a tag extra info class and including the `tei-class` element in the TLD (see TagExtraInfo Class, page 604). Using the `variable` element is simpler but less dynamic. With the `variable` element, the only aspect of the variable that you can specify at runtime is its name (via the `name-from-attribute` element). If you provide this information in a tag extra info class, you can also specify the type of the variable at runtime.

Table 15–11 lists the subelements of the `variable` element.

Table 15–11 `variable` Subelements

Element	Description
`description`	(optional) A description of the variable.
`name-given` | `name-from-attribute`	Defines an EL variable to be used in the page invoking this tag. Either `name-given` or `name-from-attribute` must be specified. If `name-given` is specified, the value is the name of the variable. If `name-from-attribute` is specified, the value is the name of an attribute whose (translation-time) value at the start of the tag invocation will give the name of the variable. Translation errors arise in the following circumstances: 1. Specifying neither `name-given` nor `name-from-attribute`. 2. If two `variable` elements have the same `name-given`.
`variable-class`	(optional) The fully qualified name of the class of the object. `java.lang.String` is the default.
`declare`	(optional) Whether or not the object is declared. `True` is the default. A translation error results if both `declare` and `fragment` are specified.
`scope`	(optional) The scope of the variable defined. Can be either `AT_BEGIN`, `AT_END`, or `NESTED` (see Table 15–12). Defaults to `NESTED`.

Table 15–12   Variable Availability

Value	Availability
NESTED	Between the start tag and the end tag.
AT_BEGIN	From the start tag until the scope of any enclosing tag. If there's no enclosing tag, then to the end of the page.
AT_END	After the end tag until the scope of any enclosing tag. If there's no enclosing tag, then to the end of the page.

Table 15–12 summarizes a variable's availability according to its declared scope.

You can define the following `variable` element for the `tlt:iterator` tag:

```
<tag>
  <variable>
    <name-given>var</name-given>
    <variable-class>java.lang.String</variable-class>
    <declare>true</declare>
    <scope>NESTED</scope>
  </variable>
</tag>
```

Programming Simple Tag Handlers

The classes and interfaces used to implement simple tag handlers are contained in the `javax.servlet.jsp.tagext` package. Simple tag handlers implement the `SimpleTag` interface. Interfaces can be used to take an existing Java object and make it a tag handler. For most newly created handlers, you would use the `SimpleTagSupport` classes as a base class.

The heart of a simple tag handler is a single method—doTag—which gets invoked when the end element of the tag is encountered. Note that the default implementation of the doTag method of `SimpleTagSupport` does nothing.

A tag handler has access to an API that allows it to communicate with the JSP page. The entry point to the API is the JSP context object (`javax.servlet.jsp.JspContext`). The `JspContext` object provides access to implicit objects. `PageContext` extends `JspContext` with servlet-specific behavior. Through these objects, a tag handler can retrieve all the other implicit objects (request, session, and application) that are accessible from a JSP page. If the tag is nested, a tag handler also has access to the handler (called the *parent*) that is associated with the enclosing tag.

Including Tag Handlers in Web Applications

Tag handlers can be made available to a Web application in two basic ways. The classes implementing the tag handlers can be stored in an unpacked form in the WEB-INF/classes/ subdirectory of the Web application. Alternatively, if the library is distributed as a JAR, it is stored in the WEB-INF/lib/ directory of the Web application.

How Is a Simple Tag Handler Invoked?

The SimpleTag interface defines the basic protocol between a simple tag handler and a JSP page's servlet. The JSP page's servlet invokes the setJspContext, setParent, and attribute setting methods before calling doStartTag.

```
ATag t = new ATag();
t.setJSPContext(...);
t.setParent(...);
t.setAttribute1(value1);
t.setAttribute2(value2);
...
t.setJspBody(new JspFragment(...))
t.doTag();
```

The following sections describe the methods that you need to develop for each type of tag introduced in Types of Tags (page 568).

Tag Handlers for Basic Tags

The handler for a basic tag without a body must implement the doTag method of the SimpleTag interface. The doTag method is invoked when the end element of the tag is encountered.

The basic tag discussed in the first section, <tt:basic />, would be implemented by the following tag handler:

```
public HelloWorldSimpleTag extends SimpleTagSupport {
    public void doTag() throws JspException, IOException {
        getJspContext().getOut().write("Hello, world.");
    }
}
```

Tag Handlers for Tags with Attributes

Defining Attributes in a Tag Handler

For each tag attribute, you must define a set method in the tag handler that conforms to the JavaBeans architecture conventions. For example, consider the tag handler for the JSTL `c:if` tag:

```
<c:if test="${Clear}">
```

This tag handler contains the following method:

```
public void setTest(boolean test) {
  this.test = test;
}
```

Attribute Validation

The documentation for a tag library should describe valid values for tag attributes. When a JSP page is translated, a Web container will enforce any constraints contained in the TLD element for each attribute.

The attributes passed to a tag can also be validated at translation time using the `validate` method of a class derived from `TagExtraInfo`. This class is also used to provide information about variables defined by the tag (see TagExtraInfo Class, page 604).

The `validate` method is passed the attribute information in a `TagData` object, which contains attribute-value tuples for each of the tag's attributes. Because the validation occurs at translation time, the value of an attribute that is computed at request time will be set to `TagData.REQUEST_TIME_VALUE`.

The tag `<tt:twa attr1="value1"/>` has the following TLD attribute element:

```
<attribute>
  <name>attr1</name>
  <required>true</required>
  <rtexprvalue>true</rtexprvalue>
</attribute>
```

This declaration indicates that the value of attr1 can be determined at runtime.

The following validate method checks whether the value of attr1 is a valid Boolean value. Note that because the value of attr1 can be computed at runtime, validate must check whether the tag user has chosen to provide a runtime value.

```
public class TwaTEI extends TagExtraInfo {
   public ValidationMessage[] validate(TagData data) {
      Object o = data.getAttribute("attr1");
      if (o != null && o != TagData.REQUEST_TIME_VALUE) {
         if (((String)o).toLowerCase().equals("true") ||
            ((String)o).toLowerCase().equals("false") )
            return null;
         else
            return new ValidationMessage(data.getId(),
               "Invalid boolean value.");
      }
      else
         return null;
   }
}
```

Setting Dynamic Attributes

Simple tag handlers that support dynamic attributes must declare that they do so in the tag element of the TLD (see Declaring Tag Handlers, page 594). In addition, your tag handler must implement the setDynamicAttribute method of the DynamicAttributes interface. For each attribute specified in the tag invocation that does not have a corresponding attribute element in the TLD, the Web container calls setDynamicAttribute, passing in the namespace of the attribute (or null if in the default namespace), the name of the attribute, and the value of the attribute. You must implement the setDynamicAttribute method to remember the names and values of the dynamic attributes so that they can be used later when doTag is executed. If the setDynamicAttribute method throws an exception, the doTag method is not invoked for the tag, and the exception must be treated in the same manner as if it came from an attribute setter method.

The following implementation of `setDynamicAttribute` saves the attribute names and values in lists. Then, in the `doTag` method, the names and values are echoed to the response in an HTML list.

```
private ArrayList keys = new ArrayList();
private ArrayList values = new ArrayList();

public void setDynamicAttribute(String uri,
   String localName, Object value ) throws JspException {
   keys.add( localName );
   values.add( value );
}

public void doTag() throws JspException, IOException {
   JspWriter out = getJspContext().getOut();
   for( int i = 0; i < keys.size(); i++ ) {
      String key = (String)keys.get( i );
      Object value = values.get( i );
      out.println( "<li>" + key + " = " + value + "</li>" );
   }
}
```

Tag Handlers for Tags with Bodies

A simple tag handler for a tag with a body is implemented differently depending on whether or not the tag handler needs to manipulate the body. A tag handler manipulates the body when it reads or modifies the contents of the body.

Tag Handler Does Not Manipulate the Body

If a tag handler needs simply to evaluate the body, it gets the body using the `getJspBody` method of `SimpleTag` and then evaluates the body using the `invoke` method.

The following tag handler accepts a `test` parameter and evaluates the body of the tag if the test evaluates to `true`. The body of the tag is encapsulated in a JSP fragment. If the test is `true`, the handler retrieves the fragment using the `getJspBody` method. The `invoke` method directs all output to a supplied writer or, if the writer is `null`, to the `JspWriter` returned by the `getOut` method of the `JspContext` associated with the tag handler.

```
public class IfSimpleTag extends SimpleTagSupport {
  private boolean test;
  public void setTest(boolean test) {
    this.test = test;
  }
  public void doTag() throws JspException, IOException {
    if(test){
      getJspBody().invoke(null);
    }
  }
}
```

Tag Handler Manipulates the Body

If the tag handler needs to manipulate the body, the tag handler must capture the body in a `StringWriter`. The `invoke` method directs all output to a supplied writer. Then the modified body is written to the `JspWriter` returned by the `getOut` method of the `JspContext`. Thus, a tag that converts its body to upper-case could be written as follows:

```
public class SimpleWriter extends SimpleTagSupport {
  public void doTag() throws JspException, IOException {
    StringWriter sw = new StringWriter();
    jspBody.invoke(sw);
    jspContext().
      getOut().println(sw.toString().toUpperCase());
  }
}
```

Tag Handlers for Tags That Define Variables

Similar communication mechanisms exist for communication between JSP page and tag handlers as for JSP pages and tag files.

To emulate IN parameters, use tag attributes. A tag attribute is communicated between the calling page and the tag handler when the tag is invoked. No further communication occurs between the calling page and the tag handler.

To emulate OUT or nested parameters, use variables with availability AT_BEGIN, AT_END, or NESTED. The variable is not initialized by the calling page but instead is set by the tag handler.

For `AT_BEGIN` availability, the variable is available in the calling page from the start tag until the scope of any enclosing tag. If there's no enclosing tag, then the variable is available to the end of the page. For `AT_END` availability, the variable is available in the calling page after the end tag until the scope of any enclosing tag. If there's no enclosing tag, then the variable is available to the end of the page. For nested parameters, the variable is available in the calling page between the start tag and the end tag.

When you develop a tag handler you are responsible for creating and setting the object referenced by the variable into a context that is accessible from the page. You do this by using the `JspContext().setAttribute(name, value)` or `Jsp-Context.setAttribute(name, value, scope)` method. You retrieve the page context using the `getJspContext` method of `SimpleTag`.

Typically, an attribute passed to the custom tag specifies the name of the variable and the value of the variable is dependent on another attribute. For example, the `iterator` tag introduced in Chapter 12 retrieves the name of the variable from the `var` attribute and determines the value of the variable from a computation performed on the `group` attribute.

```
public void doTag() throws JspException, IOException {
  if (iterator == null)
    return;
  while (iterator.hasNext()) {
    getJspContext().setAttribute(var, iterator.next());
    getJspBody().invoke(null);
  }
}
public void setVar(String var) {
  this.var = var;
}
public void setGroup(Collection group) {
  this.group = group;
  if(group.size() > 0)
    iterator = group.iterator();
}
```

The scope that a variable can have is summarized in Table 15–13. The scope constrains the accessibility and lifetime of the object.

TagExtraInfo Class

In Declaring Tag Variables for Tag Handlers (page 596) we discussed how to provide information about tag variables in the tag library descriptor. Here we describe another approach: defining a tag extra info class. You define a tag extra

Table 15–13 Scope of Objects

Name	Accessible From	Lifetime
page	Current page	Until the response has been sent back to the user or the request is passed to a new page
request	Current page and any included or forwarded pages	Until the response has been sent back to the user
session	Current request and any subsequent request from the same browser (subject to session lifetime)	The life of the user's session
application	Current and any future request in the same Web application	The life of the application

info class by extending the class javax.servlet.jsp.tagext.TagExtraInfo. A TagExtraInfo must implement the getVariableInfo method to return an array of VariableInfo objects containing the following information:

- Variable name
- Variable class
- Whether the variable refers to a new object
- The availability of the variable

The Web container passes a parameter of type javax.servlet.jsp.tagext.TagData to the getVariableInfo method, which contains attribute-value tuples for each of the tag's attributes. These attributes can be used to provide the VariableInfo object with an EL variable's name and class.

The following example demonstrates how to provide information about the variable created by the iterator tag in a tag extra info class. Because the name (var) and class (type) of the variable are passed in as tag attributes, they can be retrieved using the data.getAttributeString method and can be used to fill in the VariableInfo constructor. To allow the variable var to be used only within the tag body, you set the scope of the object to NESTED.

```
package iterator;
public class IteratorTEI extends TagExtraInfo {
  public VariableInfo[] getVariableInfo(TagData data) {
    String type = data.getAttributeString("type");
```

```
    if (type == null)
      type = "java.lang.Object";
    return new VariableInfo[] {
      new VariableInfo(data.getAttributeString("var"),
      type,
      true,
      VariableInfo.NESTED)
    };
  }
}
```

The fully qualified name of the tag extra info class defined for an EL variable must be declared in the TLD in the `tei-class` subelement of the `tag` element. Thus, the `tei-class` element for `IteratorTei` would be as follows:

```
<tei-class>
  iterator.IteratorTEI
</tei-class>
```

Cooperating Tags

Tags cooperate by sharing objects. JSP technology supports two styles of object sharing.

The first style requires that a shared object be named and stored in the page context (one of the implicit objects accessible to JSP pages as well as tag handlers). To access objects created and named by another tag, a tag handler uses the `pageContext.getAttribute(name, scope)` method.

In the second style of object sharing, an object created by the enclosing tag handler of a group of nested tags is available to all inner tag handlers. This form of object sharing has the advantage that it uses a private namespace for the objects, thus reducing the potential for naming conflicts.

To access an object created by an enclosing tag, a tag handler must first obtain its enclosing tag by using the static method `SimpleTagSupport.findAncestorWithClass(from, class)` or the `SimpleTagSupport.getParent` method. The former method should be used when a specific nesting of tag handlers cannot be guaranteed. After the ancestor has been retrieved, a tag handler can access any statically or dynamically created objects. Statically created objects are members of the parent. Private objects can also be created dynamically. Such privately named objects would have to be managed by the tag handler; one approach would be to use a Map to store name-object pairs.

The following example illustrates a tag handler that supports both the named approach and the private object approach to sharing objects. In the example, the handler for a query tag checks whether an attribute named connectionId has been set. If the connectionId attribute has been set, the handler retrieves the connection object from the page context. Otherwise, the tag handler first retrieves the tag handler for the enclosing tag and then retrieves the connection object from that handler.

```
public class QueryTag extends SimpleTagSupport {
    public int doTag() throws JspException {
        String cid = getConnectionId();
        Connection connection;
        if (cid != null) {
        // there is a connection id, use it
            connection =(Connection)pageContext.
                getAttribute(cid);
        } else {
            ConnectionTag ancestorTag =
                (ConnectionTag)findAncestorWithClass(this,
                    ConnectionTag.class);
            if (ancestorTag == null) {
                throw new JspTagException("A query without
                    a connection attribute must be nested
                    within a connection tag.");
            }
            connection = ancestorTag.getConnection();
            ...
        }
    }
}
```

The query tag implemented by this tag handler can be used in either of the following ways:

```
<tt:connection cid="con01" ... >
   ...
</tt:connection>
<tt:query id="balances" connectionId="con01">
   SELECT account, balance FROM acct_table
      where customer_number = ?
   <tt:param value="${requestScope.custNumber}" />
</tt:query>

<tt:connection ... >
   <tt:query cid="balances">
      SELECT account, balance FROM acct_table
```

```
      where customer_number = ?
      <tt:param value="${requestScope.custNumber}" />
   </tt:query>
</tt:connection>
```

The TLD for the tag handler uses the following declaration to indicate that the `connectionId` attribute is optional:

```
<tag>
   ...
   <attribute>
      <name>connectionId</name>
      <required>false</required>
   </attribute>
</tag>
```

Examples

The simple tags described in this section demonstrate solutions to two recurring problems in developing JSP applications: minimizing the amount of Java programming in JSP pages and ensuring a common look and feel across applications. In doing so, they illustrate many of the styles of tags discussed in the first part of the chapter.

An Iteration Tag

Constructing page content that is dependent on dynamically generated data often requires the use of flow control scripting statements. By moving the flow control logic to tag handlers, flow control tags reduce the amount of scripting needed in JSP pages. Iteration is a very common flow control function and is easily handled by a custom tag.

The discussion on using tag libraries in Chapter 12 introduced a tag library containing an `iterator` tag. The tag retrieves objects from a collection stored in a JavaBeans component and assigns them to an EL variable. The body of the tag retrieves information from the variable. As long as elements remain in the collection, the `iterator` tag causes the body to be reevaluated. The tag in this example is simplified to make it easy to demonstrate how to program a custom tag. Web applications requiring such functionality should use the JSTL `forEach` tag, which is discussed in Iterator Tags (page 547).

JSP Page

The `index.jsp` page invokes the `iterator` tag to iterate through a collection of department names. Each item in the collection is assigned to the `department-Name` variable.

```
<%@ taglib uri="/tlt" prefix="tlt" %>
<html>
  <head>
  <title>Departments</title>
  </head>
  <body bgcolor="white">
  <jsp:useBean id="myorg" class="myorg.Organization"/>
  <table border=2 cellspacing=3 cellpadding=3>
    <tr>
      <td><b>Departments</b></td>
    </tr>
  <tlt:iterator var="departmentName" type="java.lang.String"
      group="${myorg.departmentNames}">
    <tr>
      <td><a href="list.jsp?deptName=${departmentName}">
        ${departmentName}</a></td>
    </tr>
  </tlt:iterator>
  </table>
  </body>
</html>
```

Tag Handler

The collection is set in the tag handler via the `group` attribute. The tag handler retrieves an element from the group and passes the element back to the page in the EL variable whose name is determined by the `var` attribute. The variable is accessed in the calling page using the JSP expression language. After the variable is set, the tag body is evaluated with the `invoke` method.

```
public void doTag() throws JspException, IOException {
  if (iterator == null)
    return;
  while (iterator.hasNext()) {
    getJspContext().setAttribute(var, iterator.next());
    getJspBody().invoke(null);
  }
}
public void setVar(String var) {
  this.var = var;
}
```

```
public void setGroup(Collection group) {
  this.group = group;
  if(group.size() > 0)
     iterator = group.iterator();
}
```

A Template Tag Library

A template provides a way to separate the common elements that are part of each screen from the elements that change with each screen of an application. Putting all the common elements together into one file makes it easier to maintain and enforce a consistent look and feel in all the screens. It also makes development of individual screens easier because the designer can focus on portions of a screen that are specific to that screen while the template takes care of the common portions.

The template is a JSP page that has placeholders for the parts that need to change with each screen. Each of these placeholders is referred to as a *parameter* of the template. For example, a simple template might include a title parameter for the top of the generated screen and a body parameter to refer to a JSP page for the custom content of the screen.

The template uses a set of nested tags—`definition`, `screen`, and `parameter`—to define a table of screen definitions and uses an `insert` tag to insert parameters from a screen definition into a specific application screen.

JSP Pages

The template for the Duke's Bookstore example, `template.jsp`, is shown next. This page includes a JSP page that creates the screen definition and then uses the `insert` tag to insert parameters from the definition into the application screen.

```
<%@ taglib uri="/tutorial-template" prefix="tt" %>
<%@ page errorPage="/template/errorinclude.jsp" %>
<%@ include file="/template/screendefinitions.jsp" %>
<html>
<head>
<title>
<tt:insert definition="bookstore" parameter="title"/>
</title>
</head>
<body  bgcolor="#FFFFFF">
  <tt:insert definition="bookstore" parameter="banner"/>
<tt:insert definition="bookstore" parameter="body"/>
```

```
<center><em>Copyright &copy; 2002 Sun Microsystems, Inc. </
em></center>
</body>
</html>
```

The `screendefinitions.jsp` page creates a screen definition specified by the request attribute `javax.servlet.forward.servlet_path`:

```
<tt:definition name="bookstore"
screen="${requestScope
  ['javax.servlet.forward.servlet_path']}">
  <tt:screen id="/bookstore">
  <tt:parameter name="title" value="Duke's Bookstore"
    direct="true"/>
  <tt:parameter name="banner" value="/template/banner.jsp"
    direct="false"/>
  <tt:parameter name="body" value="/bookstore.jsp"
    direct="false"/>
  </tt:screen>
  <tt:screen id="/bookcatalog">
  <tt:parameter name="title" direct="true">
      <jsp:attribute name="value" >
        <fmt:message key="TitleBookCatalog"/>
      </jsp:attribute>
    </tt:parameter>
    <tt:parameter name="banner" value="/template/banner.jsp"
    direct="false"/>
    <tt:parameter name="body" value="/bookcatalog.jsp"
    direct="false"/>
  </tt:screen>
  ...
</tt:definition>
```

The template is instantiated by the `Dispatcher` servlet. `Dispatcher` first gets the requested screen. `Dispatcher` performs business logic and updates model objects based on the requested screen. For example, if the requested screen is `/bookcatalog`, `Dispatcher` determines whether a book is being added to the cart based on the value of the Add request parameter. It sets the price of the book if it's on sale, and then adds the book to the cart. Finally, the servlet dispatches the request to `template.jsp`:

```
public class Dispatcher extends HttpServlet {
  public void doGet(HttpServletRequest request,
    HttpServletResponse response) {
    String bookId = null;
    BookDetails book = null;
```

```
String clear = null;
BookDBAO bookDBAO =
   (BookDBAO)getServletContext().
      getAttribute("bookDBAO");
HttpSession session = request.getSession();
String selectedScreen = request.getServletPath();
ShoppingCart cart = (ShoppingCart)session.
   getAttribute("cart");
if (cart == null) {
   cart = new ShoppingCart();
   session.setAttribute("cart", cart);
}
if (selectedScreen.equals("/bookcatalog")) {
   bookId = request.getParameter("Add");
   if (!bookId.equals("")) {
      try {
         book = bookDBAO.getBookDetails(bookId);
         if ( book.getOnSale() ) {
            double sale = book.getPrice() * .85;
            Float salePrice = new Float(sale);
            book.setPrice(salePrice.floatValue());
         }
         cart.add(bookId, book);
      } catch (BookNotFoundException ex) {
         // not possible
      }
   }
} else if (selectedScreen.equals("/bookshowcart")) {
   bookId =request.getParameter("Remove");
   if (bookId != null) {
      cart.remove(bookId);
   }
   clear = request.getParameter("Clear");
   if (clear != null && clear.equals("clear")) {
      cart.clear();
   }
} else if (selectedScreen.equals("/bookreceipt")) {
// Update the inventory
   try {
      bookDBAO.buyBooks(cart);
   } catch (OrderException ex) {
      request.setAttribute("selectedScreen",
         "/bookOrderError");
   }
}
try {
```

```
                request.
                    getRequestDispatcher(
                    "/template/template.jsp").
                    forward(request, response);
            } catch(Exception ex) {
                ex.printStackTrace();
            }
        }

        public void doPost(HttpServletRequest request,
            HttpServletResponse response) {
            request.setAttribute("selectedScreen",
                request.getServletPath());
            try {
                request.
                    getRequestDispatcher(
                    "/template/template.jsp").
                    forward(request, response);
            } catch(Exception ex) {
                ex.printStackTrace();
            }
        }
    }
```

Tag Handlers

The template tag library contains four tag handlers—DefinitionTag, ScreenTag, ParameterTag, and InsertTag—that demonstrate the use of cooperating tags. DefinitionTag, ScreenTag, and ParameterTag constitute a set of nested tag handlers that share private objects. DefinitionTag creates a public object named bookstore that is used by InsertTag.

In doTag, DefinitionTag creates a private object named screens that contains a hash table of screen definitions. A screen definition consists of a screen identifier and a set of parameters associated with the screen. These parameters are loaded when the body of the definition tag, which contains nested screen and parameter tags, is invoked. DefinitionTag creates a public object of class Definition, selects a screen definition from the screens object based on the URL passed in the request, and uses this screen definition to initialize a public Definition object.

```
    public int doTag() {
        try {
            screens = new HashMap();
            getJspBody().invoke(null);
            Definition definition = new Definition();
```

```
      PageContext context = (PageContext)getJspContext();
      ArrayList params = (ArrayList) screens.get(screenId);
      Iterator ir = null;
      if (params != null) {
         ir = params.iterator();
         while (ir.hasNext())
            definition.setParam((Parameter)ir.next());
      // put the definition in the page context
      context.setAttribute(definitionName, definition,
         context.APPLICATION_SCOPE);
      }
   }
```

The table of screen definitions is filled in by `ScreenTag` and `ParameterTag` from text provided as attributes to these tags. Table 15–14 shows the contents of the screen definitions hash table for the Duke's Bookstore application.

If the URL passed in the request is /bookstore, the `Definition` object contains the items from the first row of Table 15–14 (see Table 15–15).

Table 15–14   Screen Definitions

Screen ID	Title	Banner	Body
/bookstore	Duke's Bookstore	/banner.jsp	/bookstore.jsp
/bookcatalog	Book Catalog	/banner.jsp	/bookcatalog.jsp
/bookdetails	Book Description	/banner.jsp	/bookdetails.jsp
/bookshowcart	Shopping Cart	/banner.jsp	/bookshowcart.jsp
/bookcashier	Cashier	/banner.jsp	/bookcashier.jsp
/bookreceipt	Receipt	/banner.jsp	/bookreceipt.jsp

Table 15–15   Definition Object Contents for URL /bookstore

Title	Banner	Body
Duke's Bookstore	/banner.jsp	/bookstore.jsp

Table 15–16 Parameters for the URL /bookstore

Parameter Name	Parameter Value	isDirect
title	Duke's Bookstore	true
banner	/banner.jsp	false
body	/bookstore.jsp	false

The parameters for the URL /bookstore are shown in Table 15–16. The parameters specify that the value of the title parameter, Duke's Bookstore, should be inserted directly into the output stream, but the values of banner and body should be included dynamically.

InsertTag inserts parameters of the screen definition into the response. The doTag method retrieves the definition object from the page context and then inserts the parameter value. If the parameter is direct, it is directly inserted into the response; otherwise, the request is sent to the parameter, and the response is dynamically included into the overall response.

```
public void doTag() throws JspTagException {
    Definition definition = null;
    Parameter parameter = null;
    boolean directInclude = false;
    PageContext context = (PageContext)getJspContext();

    // get the definition from the page context
    definition = (Definition)context.getAttribute(
        definitionName, context.APPLICATION_SCOPE);
    // get the parameter
    if (parameterName != null && definition != null)
        parameter = (Parameter)
            definition.getParam(parameterName);

    if (parameter != null)
        directInclude = parameter.isDirect();
```

```
    try {
      // if parameter is direct, print to out
      if (directInclude && parameter  != null)
        context.getOut().print(parameter.getValue());
      // if parameter is indirect,
          include results of dispatching to page
      else {
        if ((parameter != null) &&
          (parameter.getValue() !=  null))
        context.include(parameter.getValue());
      }
    } catch (Exception ex) {
        throw new JspTagException(ex.getMessage());
    }
  }
```

16

Scripting in JSP Pages

JSP scripting elements allow you to use Java programming language statements in your JSP pages. Scripting elements are typically used to create and access objects, define methods, and manage the flow of control. Many tasks that require the use of scripts can be eliminated by using custom tag libraries, in particular the JSP Standard Tag Library. Because one of the goals of JSP technology is to separate static data from the code needed to dynamically generate content, very sparing use of JSP scripting is recommended. Nevertheless, there may be some circumstances that require its use.

There are three ways to create and use objects in scripting elements:

- Instance and class variables of the JSP page's servlet class are created in *declarations* and accessed in *scriptlets* and *expressions*.
- Local variables of the JSP page's servlet class are created and used in *scriptlets* and *expressions*.
- Attributes of scope objects (see Using Scope Objects, page 444) are created and used in *scriptlets* and *expressions*.

This chapter briefly describes the syntax and usage of JSP scripting elements.

The Example JSP Pages

This chapter illustrates JSP scripting elements using `webclient`, a version of the `hello1` example introduced in Chapter 3 that accesses a Web service. To build, package, deploy, and run the `webclient` example, follow these steps:

1. Build and deploy the JAX-RPC Web service `MyHelloService` described in Creating a Simple Web Service and Client with JAX-RPC (page 314).

2. In a terminal window, go to *<INSTALL>*/j2eetutorial14/examples/ jaxrpc/webclient/.

3. Run `asant build`. This target will spawn any necessary compilations and will copy files to the *<INSTALL>*/j2eetutorial14/examples/jaxrpc/ webclient/build/ directory.

4. Start the Application Server.

5. Start `deploytool`.

6. Create a Web application called `webclient` by running the New Web Component wizard. Select File→New→Web Component.

7. In the New Web Component wizard:

    a. Select the Create New Stand-Alone WAR Module radio button.

    b. Click Browse and in the file chooser, navigate to *<INSTALL>*/ j2eetutorial14/examples/jaxrpc/webclient/.

    c. In the File Name field, enter `webclient`.

    d. Click Choose Module File.

    e. In the WAR Display Name field, enter `webclient`.

    f. In the Context Root field, enter `/webclient`.

    g. Click Edit Contents.

    h. In the Edit Contents dialog box, navigate to *<INSTALL>*/j2eetutorial14/ examples/jaxrpc/webclient/build/. Select duke.waving.gif, greet- ing.jsp, response.jsp, and the webclient directory, and click Add.

    i. Click OK.

    j. Click Next.

    k. Select the JSP Page radio button.

    l. Click Next.

    m. Select `greeting.jsp` from the JSP Filename combo box.

    n. Click Finish.

8. Add an alias to the `greeting` Web component.

    a. Select the `greeting` Web component.

    b. Select the Aliases tab.

    c. Click Add to add a new mapping.

    d. Type `/greeting` in the Aliases list.

9. Select File→Save.

10. Deploy the WAR.

11. Open your browser to `http://localhost:8080/webclient/greeting`

Note: The example assumes that the Application Server runs on the default port, 8080. If you have changed the port, you must update the port number in the file `<INSTALL>/j2eetutorial14/examples/jaxrpc/webclient/response.jsp` before building and running the example.

Using Scripting

JSP technology allows a container to support any scripting language that can call Java objects. If you wish to use a scripting language other than the default, `java`, you must specify it in the `language` attribute of the `page` directive at the beginning of a JSP page:

```
<%@ page language="scripting language" %>
```

Because scripting elements are converted to programming language statements in the JSP page's servlet class, you must import any classes and packages used by a JSP page. If the page language is `java`, you import a class or package with the `import` attribute of the `page` directive:

```
<%@ page import="fully_qualified_classname, packagename.*" %>
```

The `webclient` JSP page `response.jsp` uses the following `page` directive to import the classes needed to access the JAX-RPC stub class and the Web service client classes:

```
<%@ page import="javax.xml.rpc.Stub,webclient.*" %>
```

Disabling Scripting

By default, scripting in JSP pages is valid. Because scripting can make pages difficult to maintain, some JSP page authors or page authoring groups may want to follow a methodology in which scripting elements are not allowed.

You can disable scripting for a group of JSP pages by using `deploytool` and setting the value of the Scripting Invalid checkbox in the JSP Properties tab of a WAR. For information on how to define a group of JSP pages, see Setting Properties for Groups of JSP Pages (page 510). When scripting is invalid, it means that scriptlets, scripting expressions, and declarations will produce a translation error if present in any of the pages in the group. Table 16–1 summarizes the scripting settings and their meanings.

Table 16–1   Scripting Settings

JSP Configuration	Scripting Encountered
Unspecified	Valid
`false`	Valid
`true`	Translation error

Declarations

A *JSP declaration* is used to declare variables and methods in a page's scripting language. The syntax for a declaration is as follows:

```
<%! scripting language declaration %>
```

When the scripting language is the Java programming language, variables and methods in JSP declarations become declarations in the JSP page's servlet class.

Initializing and Finalizing a JSP Page

You can customize the initialization process to allow the JSP page to read persistent configuration data, initialize resources, and perform any other one-time activities; to do so, you override the `jspInit` method of the `JspPage` interface.

You release resources using the `jspDestroy` method. The methods are defined using JSP declarations.

For example, an older version of the Duke's Bookstore application retrieved the object that accesses the bookstore database from the context and stored a reference to the object in the variable bookDBAO in the `jspInit` method. The variable definition and the initialization and finalization methods `jspInit` and `jspDestroy` were defined in a declaration:

```
<%!
private BookDBAO bookDBAO;
public void jspInit() {
bookDBAO =
   (BookDBAO)getServletContext().getAttribute("bookDB");
   if (bookDBAO == null)
      System.out.println("Couldn't get database.");
}
%>
```

When the JSP page was removed from service, the `jspDestroy` method released the BookDBAO variable.

```
<%!
public void jspDestroy() {
   bookDBAO = null;
}
%>
```

Scriptlets

A *JSP scriptlet* is used to contain any code fragment that is valid for the scripting language used in a page. The syntax for a scriptlet is as follows:

```
<%
   scripting language statements
%>
```

When the scripting language is set to `java`, a scriptlet is transformed into a Java programming language statement fragment and is inserted into the service method of the JSP page's servlet. A programming language variable created within a scriptlet is accessible from anywhere within the JSP page.

In the Web service version of the `hello1` application, `greeting.jsp` contains a scriptlet to retrieve the request parameter named `username` and test whether it is empty. If the `if` statement evaluates to `true`, the response page is included. Because the `if` statement opens a block, the HTML markup would be followed by a scriptlet that closes the block.

```
<%
   String username = request.getParameter("username");
   if ( username != null && username.length() > 0 ) {
%>
   <%@include file="response.jsp" %>
<%
   }
%>
```

Expressions

A *JSP expression* is used to insert the value of a scripting language expression, converted into a string, into the data stream returned to the client. When the scripting language is the Java programming language, an expression is transformed into a statement that converts the value of the expression into a `String` object and inserts it into the implicit `out` object.

The syntax for an expression is as follows:

```
<%= scripting language expression %>
```

Note that a semicolon is not allowed within a JSP expression, even if the same expression has a semicolon when you use it within a scriptlet.

In the Web service version of the `hello1` application, `response.jsp` contains the following scriptlet, which creates a JAX-RPC stub, sets the endpoint on the stub, and then invokes the `sayHello` method on the stub, passing the user name retrieved from a request parameter:

```
<%
    String resp = null;
    try {
      Stub stub = (Stub)(new
        MyHelloService_Impl().getHelloIFPort());
      stub._setProperty(
        javax.xml.rpc.Stub.ENDPOINT_ADDRESS_PROPERTY,
        "http://localhost:8080/hello-jaxrpc/hello");
      HelloIF hello = (HelloIF)stub;
      resp =
        hello.sayHello(request.getParameter("username"));
```

```
        } catch (Exception ex) {
            resp = ex.toString();
        }
    %>
```

A scripting expression is then used to insert the value of resp into the output stream:

```
<h2><font color="black"><%= resp %>!</font></h2>
```

Programming Tags That Accept Scripting Elements

Tags that accept scripting elements in attribute values or in the body cannot be programmed as simple tags; they must be implemented as classic tags. The following sections describe the TLD elements and JSP tag extension API specific to classic tag handlers. All other TLD elements are the same as for simple tags.

TLD Elements

You specify the character of a classic tag's body content using the body-content element:

```
<body-content>empty | JSP | tagdependent</body-content>
```

You must declare the body content of tags that do not have a body as empty. For tags that have a body, there are two options. Body content containing custom and core tags, scripting elements, and HTML text is categorized as JSP. All other types of body content—for example, SQL statements passed to the query tag—are labeled tagdependent.

Tag Handlers

The classes and interfaces used to implement classic tag handlers are contained in the javax.servlet.jsp.tagext package. Classic tag handlers implement either the Tag, the IterationTag, or the BodyTag interface. Interfaces can be used to take an existing Java object and make it a tag handler. For newly created classic tag handlers, you can use the TagSupport and BodyTagSupport classes as base classes. These classes and interfaces are contained in the `javax.servlet.jsp.tagext` package.

Tag handler methods defined by the `Tag` and `BodyTag` interfaces are called by the JSP page's servlet at various points during the evaluation of the tag. When the start element of a custom tag is encountered, the JSP page's servlet calls methods to initialize the appropriate handler and then invokes the handler's `doStartTag` method. When the end element of a custom tag is encountered, the handler's `doEndTag` method is invoked for all but simple tags. Additional methods are invoked in between when a tag handler needs to manipulate the body of the tag. For further information, see Tags with Bodies (page 626). To provide a tag handler implementation, you must implement the methods, summarized in Table 16–2, that are invoked at various stages of processing the tag.

A tag handler has access to an API that allows it to communicate with the JSP page. The entry points to the API are two objects: the JSP context (`javax.servlet.jsp.JspContext`) for simple tag handlers and the page context (`javax.servlet.jsp.PageContext`) for classic tag handlers. `JspContext` provides access to implicit objects. `PageContext` extends `JspContext` with HTTP-specific behavior. A tag handler can retrieve all the other implicit objects (request, session, and application) that are accessible from a JSP page through these objects. In addition, implicit objects can have named attributes associated with them. Such attributes are accessed using `[set|get]Attribute` methods.

If the tag is nested, a tag handler also has access to the handler (called the *parent*) associated with the enclosing tag.

Table 16–2   Tag Handler Methods

Tag Type	Interface	Methods
Basic	`Tag`	`doStartTag, doEndTag`
Attributes	`Tag`	`doStartTag, doEndTag,` `setAttribute1,...,N, release`
Body	`Tag`	`doStartTag, doEndTag, release`
Body, iterative evaluation	`IterationTag`	`doStartTag, doAfterBody, doEndTag,` `release`
Body, manipulation	`BodyTag`	`doStartTag, doEndTag, release, doInit-` `Body, doAfterBody`

How Is a Classic Tag Handler Invoked?

The `Tag` interface defines the basic protocol between a tag handler and a JSP page's servlet. It defines the life cycle and the methods to be invoked when the start and end tags are encountered.

The JSP page's servlet invokes the `setPageContext`, `setParent`, and attribute-setting methods before calling `doStartTag`. The JSP page's servlet also guarantees that `release` will be invoked on the tag handler before the end of the page.

Here is a typical tag handler method invocation sequence:

```
ATag t = new ATag();
t.setPageContext(...);
t.setParent(...);
t.setAttribute1(value1);
t.setAttribute2(value2);
t.doStartTag();
t.doEndTag();
t.release();
```

The `BodyTag` interface extends `Tag` by defining additional methods that let a tag handler access its body. The interface provides three new methods:

- `setBodyContent`: Creates body content and adds to the tag handler
- `doInitBody`: Called before evaluation of the tag body
- `doAfterBody`: Called after evaluation of the tag body

A typical invocation sequence is as follows:

```
t.doStartTag();
out = pageContext.pushBody();
t.setBodyContent(out);
// perform any initialization needed after body content is set
t.doInitBody();
t.doAfterBody();
// while doAfterBody returns EVAL_BODY_AGAIN we
// iterate body evaluation
...
t.doAfterBody();
t.doEndTag();
out = pageContext.popBody();
t.release();
```

Tags with Bodies

A tag handler for a tag with a body is implemented differently depending on whether or not the tag handler needs to manipulate the body. A tag handler manipulates the body when it reads or modifies the contents of the body.

Tag Handler Does Not Manipulate the Body

If the tag handler does not need to manipulate the body, the tag handler should implement the `Tag` interface. If the tag handler implements the `Tag` interface and the body of the tag needs to be evaluated, the `doStartTag` method must return `EVAL_BODY_INCLUDE`; otherwise it should return `SKIP_BODY`.

If a tag handler needs to iteratively evaluate the body, it should implement the `IterationTag` interface. The tag handler should return `EVAL_BODY_AGAIN` from the `doAfterBody` method if it determines that the body needs to be evaluated again.

Tag Handler Manipulates the Body

If the tag handler needs to manipulate the body, the tag handler must implement `BodyTag` (or must be derived from `BodyTagSupport`).

When a tag handler implements the `BodyTag` interface, it must implement the `doInitBody` and the `doAfterBody` methods. These methods manipulate body content passed to the tag handler by the JSP page's servlet.

A `BodyContent` object supports several methods to read and write its contents. A tag handler can use the body content's `getString` or `getReader` method to extract information from the body, and the `writeOut(out)` method to write the body contents to an `out` stream. The writer supplied to the `writeOut` method is obtained using the tag handler's `getPreviousOut` method. This method is used to ensure that a tag handler's results are available to an enclosing tag handler.

If the body of the tag needs to be evaluated, the `doStartTag` method must return `EVAL_BODY_BUFFERED`; otherwise, it should return `SKIP_BODY`.

doInitBody Method

The `doInitBody` method is called after the body content is set but before it is evaluated. You generally use this method to perform any initialization that depends on the body content.

doAfterBody Method

The doAfterBody method is called *after* the body content is evaluated. doAfterBody must return an indication of whether to continue evaluating the body. Thus, if the body should be evaluated again, as would be the case if you were implementing an iteration tag, doAfterBody should return EVAL_BODY_AGAIN; otherwise, doAfterBody should return SKIP_BODY.

The following example reads the content of the body (which contains an SQL query) and passes it to an object that executes the query. Because the body does not need to be reevaluated, doAfterBody returns SKIP_BODY.

```
public class QueryTag extends BodyTagSupport {
   public int doAfterBody() throws JspTagException {
      BodyContent bc = getBodyContent();
      // get the bc as string
      String query = bc.getString();
      // clean up
      bc.clearBody();
      try {
         Statement stmt = connection.createStatement();
         result = stmt.executeQuery(query);
      } catch (SQLException e) {
         throw new JspTagException("QueryTag: " +
            e.getMessage());
      }
      return SKIP_BODY;
   }
}
```

release Method

A tag handler should reset its state and release any private resources in the release method.

Cooperating Tags

Tags cooperate by sharing objects. JSP technology supports two styles of object sharing.

The first style requires that a shared object be named and stored in the page context (one of the implicit objects accessible to JSP pages as well as tag handlers). To access objects created and named by another tag, a tag handler uses the pageContext.getAttribute(name, scope) method.

In the second style of object sharing, an object created by the enclosing tag handler of a group of nested tags is available to all inner tag handlers. This form of object sharing has the advantage that it uses a private namespace for the objects, thus reducing the potential for naming conflicts.

To access an object created by an enclosing tag, a tag handler must first obtain its enclosing tag using the static method `TagSupport.findAncestorWith-Class(from, class)` or the `TagSupport.getParent` method. The former method should be used when a specific nesting of tag handlers cannot be guaranteed. After the ancestor has been retrieved, a tag handler can access any statically or dynamically created objects. Statically created objects are members of the parent. Private objects can also be created dynamically. Such objects can be stored in a tag handler using the `setValue` method and can be retrieved using the `getValue` method.

The following example illustrates a tag handler that supports both the named approach and the private object approach to sharing objects. In the example, the handler for a query tag checks whether an attribute named `connectionId` has been set. If the `connection` attribute has been set, the handler retrieves the connection object from the page context. Otherwise, the tag handler first retrieves the tag handler for the enclosing tag and then retrieves the connection object from that handler.

```
public class QueryTag extends BodyTagSupport {
  public int doStartTag() throws JspException {
    String cid = getConnectionId();
    Connection connection;
    if (cid != null) {
    // there is a connection id, use it
      connection =(Connection)pageContext.
        getAttribute(cid);
    } else {
      ConnectionTag ancestorTag =
        (ConnectionTag)findAncestorWithClass(this,
          ConnectionTag.class);
      if (ancestorTag == null) {
        throw new JspTagException("A query without
          a connection attribute must be nested
          within a connection tag.");
      }
      connection = ancestorTag.getConnection();
      ...
    }
  }
}
```

The query tag implemented by this tag handler can be used in either of the following ways:

```
<tt:connection cid="con01" ... >
  ...
</tt:connection>
<tt:query id="balances" connectionId="con01">
  SELECT account, balance FROM acct_table
    where customer_number = ?
  <tt:param value="${requestScope.custNumber}" />
</tt:query>

<tt:connection ... >
  <tt:query cid="balances">
    SELECT account, balance FROM acct_table
    where customer_number = ?
    <tt:param value="${requestScope.custNumber}" />
  </tt:query>
</tt:connection>
```

The TLD for the tag handler uses the following declaration to indicate that the `connectionId` attribute is optional:

```
<tag>
  ...
  <attribute>
    <name>connectionId</name>
    <required>false</required>
  </attribute>
</tag>
```

Tags That Define Variables

The mechanisms for defining variables in classic tags are similar to those described in Chapter 15. You must declare the variable in a `variable` element of the TLD or in a tag extra info class. You use `PageContext().set-Attribute(name, value)` or `PageContext.setAttribute(name, value, scope)` methods in the tag handler to create or update an association between a name that is accessible in the page context and the object that is the value of the variable. For classic tag handlers, Table 16–3 illustrates how the availability of a variable affects when you may want to set or update the variable's value.

A variable defined by a custom tag can also be accessed in a scripting expression. For example, the Web service described in the preceding section can be

Table 16–3 Variable Availability

Value	Availability	In Methods
NESTED	Between the start tag and the end tag	doStartTag, doInitBody, and doAfterBody
AT_BEGIN	From the start tag until the end of the page	doStartTag, doInitBody, doAfterBody, and doEndTag
AT_END	After the end tag until the end of the page	doEndTag

encapsulated in a custom tag that returns the response in a variable named by the var attribute, and then var can be accessed in a scripting expression as follows:

```
<ws:hello var="response"
    name="<%=request.getParameter("username")%>" />
<h2><font color="black"><%= response %>!</font></h2>
```

Remember that in situations where scripting is not allowed (in a tag body where the body-content is declared as scriptless and in a page where scripting is specified to be invalid), you wouldn't be able to access the variable in a scriptlet or an expression. Instead, you would have to use the JSP expression language to access the variable.

17

JavaServer Faces Technology

JAVASERVER Faces technology is a server-side user interface component framework for Java technology-based Web applications.

The main components of JavaServer Faces technology are as follows:

- An API for representing UI components and managing their state; handling events, server-side validation, and data conversion; defining page navigation; supporting internationalization and accessibility; and providing extensibility for all these features

- Two JavaServer Pages (JSP) custom tag libraries for expressing UI components within a JSP page and for wiring components to server-side objects

The well-defined programming model and tag libraries significantly ease the burden of building and maintaining Web applications with server-side UIs. With minimal effort, you can

- Wire client-generated events to server-side application code

- Bind UI components on a page to server-side data

- Construct a UI with reusable and extensible components

- Save and restore UI state beyond the life of server requests

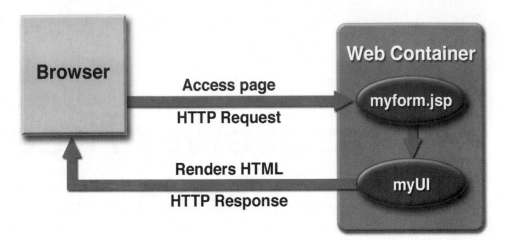

Figure 17–1 The UI Runs on the Server

As shown in Figure 17–1, the user interface you create with JavaServer Faces technology (represented by myUI in the graphic) runs on the server and renders back to the client.

The JSP page, myform.jsp, is a *JavaServer Faces page*, which is a JSP page that includes JavaServer Faces tags. It expresses the user interface components by using custom tags defined by JavaServer Faces technology. The UI for the Web application (represented by myUI in the figure) manages the objects referenced by the JSP page. These objects include

- The UI component objects that map to the tags on the JSP page
- The event listeners, validators, and converters that are registered on the components
- The objects that encapsulate the data and application-specific functionality of the components

This chapter gives an overview of JavaServer Faces technology. After going over some of the primary benefits of using JavaServer Faces technology and explaining what a JavaServer Faces application is, it lists the various application development roles that users of this technology fall into. It then describes a simple application and specifies which part of the application the developers of each role work on. The chapter then moves on to summarizing each of the main features of JavaServer Faces technology and how the various pieces of an application that uses these features fit together. Finally, this chapter uses a page from a simple application to summarize the life cycle of a JavaServer Faces page.

JavaServer Faces Technology Benefits

One of the greatest advantages of JavaServer Faces technology is that it offers a clean separation between behavior and presentation. Web applications built using JSP technology achieve this separation in part. However, a JSP application cannot map HTTP requests to component-specific event handling nor manage UI elements as stateful objects on the server, as a JavaServer Faces application can. JavaServer Faces technology allows you to build Web applications that implement the finer-grained separation of behavior and presentation that is traditionally offered by client-side UI architectures.

The separation of logic from presentation also allows each member of a Web application development team to focus on his or her piece of the development process, and it provides a simple programming model to link the pieces. For example, page authors with no programming expertise can use JavaServer Faces technology UI component tags to link to server-side objects from within a Web page without writing any scripts.

Another important goal of JavaServer Faces technology is to leverage familiar UI-component and Web-tier concepts without limiting you to a particular scripting technology or markup language. Although JavaServer Faces technology includes a JSP custom tag library for representing components on a JSP page, the JavaServer Faces technology APIs are layered directly on top of the Servlet API, as shown in Figure 3–2. This layering of APIs enables several important application use cases, such as using another presentation technology instead of JSP pages, creating your own custom components directly from the component classes, and generating output for various client devices.

Most importantly, JavaServer Faces technology provides a rich architecture for managing component state, processing component data, validating user input, and handling events.

What Is a JavaServer Faces Application?

For the most part, JavaServer Faces applications are just like any other Java Web application. They run in a servlet container, and they typically contain the following:

- JavaBeans components containing application-specific functionality and data
- Event listeners
- Pages, such as JSP pages
- Server-side helper classes, such as database access beans

In addition to these items, a JavaServer Faces application also has

- A custom tag library for rendering UI components on a page
- A custom tag library for representing event handlers, validators, and other actions
- UI components represented as stateful objects on the server
- *Backing bean*s, which define properties and functions for UI components
- Validators, converters, event listeners, and event handlers
- An application configuration resource file for configuring application resources

A typical JavaServer Faces application that is using JSP pages for rendering HTML must include a custom tag library that defines the tags representing UI components. It must also have a custom tag library for representing other core actions, such as validators and event handlers. Both of these tag libraries are provided by the JavaServer Faces implementation.

The component tag library eliminates the need to hardcode UI components in HTML or another markup language, resulting in completely reusable UI components. The core tag library makes it easy to register events, validators, and other actions on the components.

This chapter provides more detail on each of these features.

Framework Roles

Because of the division of labor enabled by the JavaServer Faces technology design, JavaServer Faces application development and maintenance can proceed quickly and easily. In many teams, individual developers play more than one of these roles; however, it is still useful to consider JavaServer Faces technology from a variety of perspectives based on primary responsibility. The members of a typical development team are as follows:

- *Page authors*, who use a markup language, such as HTML, to author pages for Web applications and usually have experience with graphic design. When using the JavaServer Faces technology framework, page authors are the primary users of the custom tag libraries included with JavaServer Faces technology.
- *Application developers*, who program the objects, the event handlers, and the validators. Application developers can also provide the extra helper classes.

- *Component writers*, who have user interface programming experience and prefer to create custom UI components using a programming language. These people can create their own components directly from the UI component classes, or they can extend the standard components provided by JavaServer Faces technology.
- *Application architects*, who design Web applications, ensure their scalability, define page navigation, configure beans, and register objects with the application.
- *Tools vendors*, who provide tools (such as the Sun Java Studio Creator application development tool) that leverage JavaServer Faces technology to make building server-side user interfaces even easier.

The primary users of JavaServer Faces technology are page authors, application developers, and application architects. The next section walks through a simple application, explaining which piece of the application is developed by the page author, application developer, and application architect.

Chapter 20 covers the responsibilities of a component writer.

A Simple JavaServer Faces Application

This section describes the process of developing a simple JavaServer Faces application. You'll see what features a typical JavaServer Faces application contains and what part each role has in developing the application.

Steps in the Development Process

Developing a simple JavaServer Faces application usually requires these tasks:

- Create the pages using the UI component and core tags.
- Define page navigation in the application configuration resource file.
- Develop the backing beans.
- Add managed bean declarations to the application configuration resource file.

These tasks can be done simultaneously or in any order. However, the people performing the tasks will need to communicate during the development process. For example, the page author needs to know the names of the objects in order to access them from the page.

Hi. My name is Duke. I'm thinking of a number from 0 to 10. Can you guess it?

Figure 17–2   The greeting.jsp Page of the guessNumber Application

The example used in this section is the guessNumber application, located in the *<INSTALL>*/j2eetutorial14/examples/web/ directory. It asks you to guess a number between 0 and 10, inclusive. The second page tells you whether you guessed correctly. The example also checks the validity of your input. The system log prints Duke's number. Figure 17–2 shows what the first page looks like.

The source for the guessNumber application is located in the *<INSTALL>*/ j2eetutorial14/examples/web/guessNumber/ directory created when you unzip the tutorial bundle (see About the Examples, page xl). A sample guess-Number.war is provided in *<INSTALL>*/j2eetutorial14/examples/web/pro-vided-wars/.

To package, deploy, and execute this example, follow these steps:

1. Go to *<INSTALL>*/j2eetutorial14/examples/web/guessNumber/.
2. Run asant build.
3. Start the Sun Java System Application Server Platform Edition 8.
4. Start deploytool.
5. Create a Web application called guessNumber by running the New Web Component wizard. Select File→New→Web Component.
6. In the New Web Component wizard:
   a. Select the Create New Stand-Alone WAR Module radio button.
   b. In the WAR Location field, enter *<INSTALL>*/j2eetutorial14/ examples/web/guessNumber/guessNumber.war.

    c. In the WAR Name field, enter `guessNumber`.

    d. In the Context Root field, enter `/guessNumber`.

    e. Click Edit Contents.

    f. In the Edit Contents dialog box, navigate to `<INSTALL>/`
`j2eetutorial14/examples/web/guessNumber/build/`. Select the
`greeting.jsp`, `index.jsp`, and `response.jsp` JSP pages, the
`wave.med.gif` file, the `guessNumber` package, and `faces-`
`config.xml`, which is located in the `WEB-INF` directory. Click Add.

    g. In the Contents of guessNumber pane, drag the `faces-config.xml`
file from the root level to the `WEB-INF` directory.

    h. While in the Edit Contents dialog box, navigate to `<J2EE_HOME>/`
`lib/` and select the `jsf-api.jar`. Click Add, and then click OK.

    i. Click Next.

    j. Select the Servlet radio button.

    k. Click Next.

    l. Select `javax.faces.webapp.FacesServlet` from the Servlet Class
combo box.

    m. In the Startup Load Sequence Position combo box, enter 1.

    n. Click Finish.

7. In the Web Component tabbed panes:

    a. Select the `FacesServlet` Web component that is contained in the
`guessNumber` Web application from the tree.

    b. Select the Aliases tab.

    c. Click Add, and enter `/guess/*` in the Aliases field.

    d. Select the `guessNumber` Web component from the tree.

8. Select File→Save.

9. Deploy the application.

10. Select Tools→Deploy.

11. In the Connection Settings frame, enter the user name and password you
specified when you installed the Application Server.

12. Click OK.

13. A pop-up dialog box will display the results of the deployment. Click
Close.

14. Open the URL `http://localhost:8080/guessNumber` in a browser.

Creating the Pages

Creating the pages is the page author's responsibility. This task involves laying out UI components on the pages, mapping the components to beans, and adding other core tags.

Here is the `greeting.jsp` page, the first page of the `guessNumber` application:

```
<HTML>
  <HEAD> <title>Hello</title> </HEAD>
  <%@ taglib uri="http://java.sun.com/jsf/html" prefix="h" %>
  <%@ taglib uri="http://java.sun.com/jsf/core" prefix="f" %>
  <body bgcolor="white">
  <f:view>
    <h:form id="helloForm" >
      <h2>Hi. My name is Duke.  I'm thinking of a number from
      <h:outputText value="#{UserNumberBean.minimum}"/> to
      <h:outputText value="#{UserNumberBean.maximum}"/>.
      Can you guess it?</h2>
      <h:graphicImage id="waveImg" url="/wave.med.gif" />
      <h:inputText id="userNo"
        value="#{UserNumberBean.userNumber}">
        <f:validateLongRange minimum="0" maximum="10" />
      </h:inputText>
      <h:commandButton id="submit" action="success"
        value="Submit" /> <p>
      <h:message style="color: red;
        font-family: 'New Century Schoolbook', serif;
        font-style: oblique;
        text-decoration: overline"
        id="errors1"
        for="userNo"/>
    </h:form>
  </f:view>
</HTML>
```

This page demonstrates a few important features that you will use in most of your JavaServer Faces applications. These features are described in the following subsections.

User Interface Component Model (page 644) includes a table that lists all the component tags included with JavaServer Faces technology. Using the HTML Component Tags (page 680) discusses the tags in more detail.

The form Tag

The form tag represents an input form that allows the user to input some data and submit it to the server, usually by clicking a button. All UI component tags that represent editable components (such as text fields and menus) must be nested inside the form tag. In the case of the greeting.jsp page, some of the tags contained in the form are inputText, commandButton, and message.

The inputText Tag

The inputText tag represents a text field component. In the guessNumber example, this text field takes an integer. The instance of this tag included in greeting.jsp has two attributes: id and value.

The id attribute corresponds to the ID of the component object represented by this tag. If you don't include an id attribute, the JavaServer Faces implementation will generate one for you. See Using the HTML Component Tags (page 680) for more information. In this case, the inputText tag requires an id attribute because the message tag needs to refer to the userNo component.

The value attribute binds the userNo component value to the bean property UserNumberBean.userNumber, which holds the data entered into the text field. A page author can also bind a component instance to a property using the tag's binding attribute.

See Backing Bean Management (page 656) for more information on creating beans, binding to bean properties, referencing bean methods, and configuring beans.

See The UIInput and UIOutput Components (page 690) for more information on the inputText tag.

The commandButton Tag

The commandButton tag represents the button used to submit the data entered in the text field. The action attribute specifies an outcome that helps the navigation mechanism decide which page to open next. Defining Page Navigation (page 640) discusses this further. See The UICommand Component (page 684) for more information on the commandButton tag.

The message Tag

The message tag displays an error message if the data entered in the field does not comply with the rules specified by the LongRangeValidator implementation. The error message displays wherever you place the message tag on the page. The style attribute allows you to specify the formatting style for the message text. The for attribute refers to the component whose value failed validation, in this case the userNo component represented by the inputText tag in the greeting.jsp page. Note that the tag representing the component whose value is validated must include an id attribute so that the for attribute of the message tag can refer to it. See The UIMessage and UIMessages Components (page 698) for more information on the message tag.

The validateLongRange Tag

The LongRangeValidator instance registered on the userNo component checks whether the component's local data is within a certain range, defined by the validateLongRange tag's minimum and maximum attributes, which are set to the literal values 0 and 10, respectively. These attributes can instead get the values from the minimum and maximum properties of UserNumberBean using the value binding expressions #{UserNumberBean.minimum} and #{UserNumberBean.maximum}. See Backing Bean Management (page 656) for details on value-binding expressions. For more information on the standard validators included with JavaServer Faces technology, see Using the Standard Validators (page 712).

Defining Page Navigation

Defining page navigation involves determining which page to go to after the user clicks a button or a hyperlink. Navigation for the application is defined in the application configuration resource file using a powerful rule-based system. Here are the navigation rules defined for the guessNumber example:

```
<navigation-rule>
  <from-view-id>/greeting.jsp</from-view-id>
  <navigation-case>
    <from-outcome>success</from-outcome>
    <to-view-id>/response.jsp</to-view-id>
  </navigation-case>
</navigation-rule>
```

```
<navigation-rule>
  <from-view-id>/response.jsp</from-view-id>
  <navigation-case>
     <from-outcome>success</from-outcome>
     <to-view-id>/greeting.jsp</to-view-id>
  </navigation-case>
</navigation-rule>
```

Each `navigation-rule` element defines how to get from one page (specified in the `from-view-id` element) to the other pages of the application. The `navigation-rule` elements can contain any number of `navigation-case` elements, each of which defines the page to open next (defined by `to-view-id`) based on a logical outcome (defined by `from-outcome`).

The outcome can be defined by the `action` attribute of the `UICommand` component that submits the form, as it is in the `guessNumber` example:

```
<h:commandButton id="submit" action="success"
  value="Submit" />
```

The outcome can also come from the return value of an *action method* in a backing bean. This method performs some processing to determine the outcome. For example, the method can check whether the password the user entered on the page matches the one on file. If it does, the method might return `success`; otherwise, it might return `failure`. An outcome of `failure` might result in the logon page being reloaded. An outcome of `success` might cause the page displaying the user's credit card activity to open. If you want the outcome to be returned by a method on a bean, you must refer to the method using a method-binding expression, using the `action` attribute, as shown by this example:

```
<h:commandButton id="submit"
  action="#{userNumberBean.getOrderStatus}" value="Submit" />
```

To learn more about how navigation works and how to define navigation rules, see Navigation Model (page 654) and Configuring Navigation Rules (page 805). For information on referencing an action method, see Referencing a Method That Performs Navigation (page 720). For information on writing an action method, see Writing a Method to Handle Navigation (page 755).

Developing the Beans

Developing beans is one responsibility of the application developer. The page author and the application developer—if they are two different people—will need to work in tandem to make sure that the component tags refer to the proper UI component properties, to ensure that the properties have the acceptable types, and to take care of other such details.

A typical JavaServer Faces application couples a backing bean with each page in the application. The backing bean defines properties and methods that are associated with the UI components used on the page. Each backing bean property is bound to either a component instance or its value.

A backing bean can also define a set of methods that perform functions for the component, such as validating the component's data, handling events that the component fires, and performing processing associated with navigation when the component is activated.

The page author binds a component's value to a bean property using the component tag's `value` attribute to refer to the property. Similarly, the page author binds a component instance to a bean property by referring to the property using the component tag's `binding` attribute.

Here is the `UserNumberBean` backing bean property that maps to the data for the `userNo` component:

```
Integer userNumber = null;
...
public void setUserNumber(Integer user_number) {
  userNumber = user_number;
}
public Integer getUserNumber() {
  return userNumber;
}
public String getResponse() {
  if(userNumber != null &&
    userNumber.compareTo(randomInt) == 0) {
      return "Yay! You got it!";
  } else {
    return "Sorry, "+userNumber+" is incorrect.";
  }
}
```

As you can see, this bean property is just like any other bean property: It has a set of accessor methods and a private data field. This means that you can reference beans you've already written from your JavaServer Faces pages.

A property can be any of the basic primitive and numeric types or any Java object type for which an appropriate converter is available. JavaServer Faces technology automatically converts the data to the type specified by the bean property. See Writing Component Properties (page 730) for information on which types are accepted by which component tags.

You can also use a converter to convert the component's value to a type not supported by the component's data. See Creating a Custom Converter (page 744) for more information on applying a converter to a component.

In addition to binding components and their values to backing bean properties using component tag attributes, the page author can refer to a backing bean method from a component tag. See Backing Bean Management (page 656) for more information on referencing methods from a component tag.

Adding Managed Bean Declarations

After developing the backing beans to be used in the application, you need to configure them in the application configuration resource file so that the Java-Server Faces implementation can automatically create new instances of the beans whenever they are needed.

The task of adding managed bean declarations to the application configuration resource file is the application architect's responsibility. Here is a managed bean declaration for UserNumberBean:

```
<managed-bean>
  <managed-bean-name>UserNumberBean</managed-bean-name>
  <managed-bean-class>
    guessNumber.UserNumberBean
  </managed-bean-class>
  <managed-bean-scope>session</managed-bean-scope>
  <managed-property>
    <property-name>minimum</property-name>
    <property-class>long</property-class>
    <value>0</value>
  </managed-property>
```

```
<managed-property>
  <property-name>maximum</property-name>
  <property-class>long</property-class>
  <value>10</value>
</managed-property>
</managed-bean>
```

One `outputText` tag on the `greeting.jsp` page binds its component's value to the `minimum` property of `UserNumberBean`. The other `outputText` tag binds its component's value to the `maximum` property of `UserNumberBean`:

```
<h:outputText value="#{UserNumberBean.minimum}"/>
<h:outputText value="#{UserNumberBean.maximum}"/>
```

As shown in the tags, the part of the expression before the . matches the name defined by the `managed-bean-name` element. The part of the expression after the . matches the name defined by the `property-name` element corresponding to the same `managed-bean` declaration.

Notice that the `managed-property` elements configure the `minimum` and `maximum` properties with values. These values are set when the bean is initialized, which happens when it is first referenced from a page.

Also notice that the application configuration resource file does not configure the `userNumber` property. Any property that does not have a corresponding `managed-property` element will be initialized to whatever the constructor of the bean class has the instance variable set to.

The JavaServer Faces implementation processes this file on application startup time. When the `UserNumberBean` is first referenced from the page, the JavaServer Faces implementation initializes it and stores it in session scope if no instance exists. The bean is then available for all pages in the application. For more information, see Backing Bean Management (page 656).

User Interface Component Model

JavaServer Faces UI components are configurable, reusable elements that compose the user interfaces of JavaServer Faces applications. A component can be simple, such as a button, or compound, such as a table, which can be composed of multiple components.

JavaServer Faces technology provides a rich, flexible component architecture that includes the following:

- A set of `UIComponent` classes for specifying the state and behavior of UI components
- A rendering model that defines how to render the components in various ways
- An event and listener model that defines how to handle component events
- A conversion model that defines how to register data converters onto a component
- A validation model that defines how to register validators onto a component

This section briefly describes each of these pieces of the component architecture.

User Interface Component Classes

JavaServer Faces technology provides a set of UI component classes and associated behavioral interfaces that specify all the UI component functionality, such as holding component state, maintaining a reference to objects, and driving event handling and rendering for a set of standard components.

The component classes are completely extensible, allowing component writers to create their own custom components. See Chapter 20 for an example of a custom image map component.

All JavaServer Faces UI component classes extend `UIComponentBase`, which defines the default state and behavior of a UI component. The following set of UI component classes are included with JavaServer Faces technology:

- `UIColumn`: Represents a single column of data in a `UIData` component.
- `UICommand`: Represents a control that fires actions when activated.
- `UIData`: Represents a data binding to a collection of data represented by a `DataModel` instance.
- `UIForm`: Encapsulates a group of controls that submit data to the application. This component is analogous to the `form` tag in HTML.
- `UIGraphic`: Displays an image.
- `UIInput`: Takes data input from a user. This class is a subclass of `UIOutput`.

- `UIMessage`: Displays a localized message.
- `UIMessages`: Displays a set of localized messages.
- `UIOutput`: Displays data output on a page.
- `UIPanel`: Manages the layout of its child components.
- `UIParameter`: Represents substitution parameters.
- `UISelectBoolean`: Allows a user to set a `boolean` value on a control by selecting or deselecting it. This class is a subclass of `UIInput`.
- `UISelectItem`: Represents a single item in a set of items.
- `UISelectItems`: Represents an entire set of items.
- `UISelectMany`: Allows a user to select multiple items from a group of items. This class is a subclass of `UIInput`.
- `UISelectOne`: Allows a user to select one item from a group of items. This class is a subclass of `UIInput`.
- `UIViewRoot`: Represents the root of the component tree.

In addition to extending `UIComponentBase`, the component classes also implement one or more *behavioral interfaces*, each of which defines certain behavior for a set of components whose classes implement the interface.

These behavioral interfaces are as follows:

- `ActionSource`: Indicates that the component can fire an action event.
- `EditableValueHolder`: Extends `ValueHolder` and specifies additional features for editable components, such as validation and emitting value-change events.
- `NamingContainer`: Mandates that each component rooted at this component have a unique ID.
- `StateHolder`: Denotes that a component has state that must be saved between requests.
- `ValueHolder`: Indicates that the component maintains a local value as well as the option of accessing data in the model tier.

`UICommand` implements `ActionSource` and `StateHolder`. `UIOutput` and component classes that extend `UIOutput` implement `StateHolder` and `ValueHolder`. `UIInput` and component classes that extend `UIInput` implement `EditableValueHolder`, `StateHolder`, and `ValueHolder`. `UIComponentBase` implements `StateHolder`. See the JavaServer Faces Technology 1.0 API Specification (http://java.sun.com/j2ee/javaserverfaces/1.0/docs/api/ index.html) for more information on these interfaces.

Only component writers will need to use the component classes and behavioral interfaces directly. Page authors and application developers will use a standard UI component by including a tag that represents it on a JSP page. Most of the components can be rendered in different ways on a page. For example, a UICommand component can be rendered as a button or a hyperlink.

The next section explains how the rendering model works and how page authors choose how to render the components by selecting the appropriate tags.

Component Rendering Model

The JavaServer Faces component architecture is designed such that the functionality of the components is defined by the component classes, whereas the component rendering can be defined by a separate renderer. This design has several benefits, including these two:

- Component writers can define the behavior of a component once but create multiple renderers, each of which defines a different way to render the component to the same client or to different clients.
- Page authors and application developers can change the appearance of a component on the page by selecting the tag that represents the appropriate combination of component and renderer.

A *render kit* defines how component classes map to component tags that are appropriate for a particular client. The JavaServer Faces implementation includes a standard HTML render kit for rendering to an HTML client.

For every UI component that a render kit supports, the render kit defines a set of Renderer objects. Each Renderer defines a different way to render the particular component to the output defined by the render kit. For example, a UISelectOne component has three different renderers. One of them renders the component as a set of radio buttons. Another renders the component as a combo box. The third one renders the component as a list box.

Each JSP custom tag defined in the standard HTML render kit is composed of the component functionality (defined in the UIComponent class) and the rendering attributes (defined by the Renderer). For example, the two tags in Table 17–1 represent a UICommand component rendered in two different ways.

The command part of the tags shown in Table 17–1 corresponds to the UICommand class, specifying the functionality, which is to fire an action. The button and hyperlink parts of the tags each correspond to a separate Renderer, which defines how the component appears on the page.

Table 17–1　UICommand Tags

Tag	Rendered As
`commandButton`	Login
`commandLink`	<u>hyperlink</u>

The JavaServer Faces implementation provides a custom tag library for rendering components in HTML. It supports all the component tags listed in Table 17–2. To learn how to use the tags in an example, see Using the HTML Component Tags (page 680).

Table 17–2　The UI Component Tags

Tag	Functions	Rendered As	Appearance
`column`	Represents a column of data in a `UIData` component.	A column of data in an HTML table	A column in a table
`commandButton`	Submits a form to the application.	An HTML `<input type=type>` element, where the `type` value can be `submit`, `reset`, or `image`	A button
`commandLink`	Links to another page or location on a page.	An HTML `<a href>` element	A hyperlink
`dataTable`	Represents a data wrapper.	An HTML `<table>` element	A table that can be updated dynamically

Table 17–2 The UI Component Tags *(Continued)*

Tag	Functions	Rendered As	Appearance
form	Represents an input form. The inner tags of the form receive the data that will be submitted with the form.	An HTML <form> element	No appearance
graphicImage	Displays an image.	An HTML <img> element	An image
inputHidden	Allows a page author to include a hidden variable in a page.	An HTML <input type=hidden> element	No appearance
inputSecret	Allows a user to input a string without the actual string appearing in the field.	An HTML <input type=password> element	A text field, which displays a row of characters instead of the actual string entered
inputText	Allows a user to input a string.	An HTML <input type=text> element	A text field
inputTextarea	Allows a user to enter a multiline string.	An HTML <textarea> element	A multirow text field
message	Displays a localized message.	An HTML <span> tag if styles are used	A text string
messages	Displays localized messages.	A set of HTML <span> tags if styles are used	A text string
outputLabel	Displays a nested component as a label for a specified input field.	An HTML <label> element	Plain text
outputLink	Links to another page or location on a page without generating an ActionEvent.	An HTML <a> element	A hyperlink

Continues

Table 17–2 The UI Component Tags *(Continued)*

Tag	Functions	Rendered As	Appearance
`outputFormat`	Displays a localized message.	Plain text	Plain text
`outputText`	Displays a line of text.	Plain text	Plain text
`panelGrid`	Displays a table.	An HTML `<table>` element with `<tr>` and `<td>` elements	A table
`panelGroup`	Groups a set of components under one parent.		A row in a table
`selectBoolean Checkbox`	Allows a user to change the value of a Boolean choice.	An HTML `<input type=checkbox>` element.	A checkbox
`selectItem`	Represents one item in a list of items in a `UISelectOne` component.	An HTML `<option>` element	No appearance
`selectItems`	Represents a list of items in a `UISelectOne` component.	A list of HTML `<option>` elements	No appearance
`selectMany Checkbox`	Displays a set of checkboxes from which the user can select multiple values.	A set of HTML `<input>` elements of type `checkbox`	A set of checkboxes
`selectMany Listbox`	Allows a user to select multiple items from a set of items, all displayed at once.	An HTML `<select>` element	A list box
`selectManyMenu`	Allows a user to select multiple items from a set of items.	An HTML `<select>` element	A scrollable combo box

Table 17–2 The UI Component Tags *(Continued)*

Tag	Functions	Rendered As	Appearance
selectOne Listbox	Allows a user to select one item from a set of items, all displayed at once.	An HTML <select> element	A list box
selectOneMenu	Allows a user to select one item from a set of items.	An HTML <select> element	A scrollable combo box
selectOneRadio	Allows a user to select one item from a set of items.	An HTML <input type=radio> element	A set of radio buttons

Conversion Model

A JavaServer Faces application can optionally associate a component with server-side object data. This object is a JavaBeans component, such as a backing bean. An application gets and sets the object data for a component by calling the appropriate object properties for that component.

When a component is bound to an object, the application has two views of the component's data:

- The model view, in which data is represented as data types, such as int or long.
- The presentation view, in which data is represented in a manner that can be read or modified by the user. For example, a java.util.Date might be represented as a text string in the format mm/dd/yy or as a set of three text strings.

The JavaServer Faces implementation automatically converts component data between these two views when the bean property associated with the component is of one of the types supported by the component's data. For example, if a UISelectBoolean component is associated with a bean property of type java.lang.Boolean, the JavaServer Faces implementation will automatically convert the component's data from String to Boolean. In addition, some component data must be bound to properties of a particular type. For example, a UISelectBoolean component must be bound to a property of type boolean or java.lang.Boolean.

Sometimes you might want to convert a component's data to a type other than a standard type, or you might want to convert the format of the data. To facilitate this, JavaServer Faces technology allows you to register a `Converter` implementation on `UIOutput` components and components whose classes subclass `UIOutput`. If you register the `Converter` implementation on a component, the `Converter` implementation converts the component's data between the two views.

You can either use the standard converters supplied with the JavaServer Faces implementation or create your own custom converter.

To create and use a custom converter in your application, three things must happen:

- The application developer must implement the `Converter` class. See Creating a Custom Converter (page 744).
- The application architect must register the `Converter` with the application. See Registering a Custom Converter (page 804).
- The page author must refer to the `Converter` from the tag of the component whose data must be converted. See Using a Custom Converter (page 724).

Event and Listener Model

The JavaServer Faces event and listener model is similar to the JavaBeans event model in that it has strongly typed event classes and listener interfaces. Like the JavaBeans event model, JavaServer Faces technology defines `Listener` and `Event` classes that an application can use to handle events generated by UI components.

An `Event` object identifies the component that generated the event and stores information about the event. To be notified of an event, an application must provide an implementation of the `Listener` class and must register it on the component that generates the event. When the user activates a component, such as by clicking a button, an event is fired. This causes the JavaServer Faces implementation to invoke the listener method that processes the event.

JavaServer Faces technology supports three kinds of events: value-change events, action events, and data-model events.

An *action event* occurs when the user activates a component that implements `ActionSource`. These components include buttons and hyperlinks.

A *value-change* event occurs when the user changes the value of a component represented by UIInput or one of its subclasses. An example is selecting a checkbox, an action that results in the component's value changing to true. The component types that generate these types of events are the UIInput, UISelectOne, UISelectMany, and UISelectBoolean components. Value-change events are fired only if no validation errors were detected.

Depending on the value of the immediate property (see The immediate Attribute, page 681) of the component emitting the event, action events can be processed during the invoke application phase or the apply request values phase, and value-change events can be processed during the process validations phase or the apply request values phase.

A *data-model event* occurs when a new row of a UIData component is selected. The discussion of data-model events is an advanced topic. It is not covered in this tutorial but may be discussed in future versions of this tutorial.

There are two ways to cause your application to react to action events or value-change events emitted by a standard component:

- Implement an event listener class to handle the event and register the listener on the component by nesting either a valueChangeListener tag or an actionListener tag inside the component tag.

- Implement a method of a backing bean to handle the event and refer to the method with a method-binding expression from the appropriate attribute of the component's tag.

See Implementing an Event Listener (page 747) for information on how to implement an event listener. See Registering Listeners on Components (page 710) for information on how to register the listener on a component.

See Writing a Method to Handle an Action Event (page 757) and Writing a Method to Handle a Value-Change Event (page 758) for information on how to implement backing bean methods that handle these events.

See Referencing a Backing Bean Method (page 719) for information on how to refer to the backing bean method from the component tag.

When emitting events from custom components, you must implement the appropriate Event class and manually queue the event on the component in addition to implementing an event listener class or a backing bean method that handles the event. Handling Events for Custom Components (page 788) explains how to do this.

Validation Model

JavaServer Faces technology supports a mechanism for validating the local data of editable components (such as text fields). This validation occurs before the corresponding model data is updated to match the local value.

Like the conversion model, the validation model defines a set of standard classes for performing common data validation checks. The JavaServer Faces core tag library also defines a set of tags that correspond to the standard `Validator` implementations. See Table 18–7 for a list of all the standard validation classes and corresponding tags.

Most of the tags have a set of attributes for configuring the validator's properties, such as the minimum and maximum allowable values for the component's data. The page author registers the validator on a component by nesting the validator's tag within the component's tag.

The validation model also allows you to create your own custom validator and corresponding tag to perform custom validation. The validation model provides two ways to implement custom validation:

- Implement a `Validator` interface that performs the validation. See Implementing the Validator Interface (page 751) for more information.
- Implement a backing bean method that performs the validation. See Writing a Method to Perform Validation (page 757) for more information.

If you are implementing a `Validator` interface, you must also:

- Register the `Validator` implementation with the application. See Registering a Custom Validator (page 803) for more information.
- Create a custom tag or use a `validator` tag to register the validator on the component. See Creating a Custom Tag (page 753) for more information.

If you are implementing a backing bean method to perform validation, you also must reference the validator from the component tag's `validator` attribute. See Referencing a Method That Performs Validation (page 722) for more information.

Navigation Model

Virtually all Web applications are made up of a set of pages. One of the primary concerns of a Web application developer is to manage the navigation between these pages. The JavaServer Faces navigation model makes it easy to define page navigation and to handle any additional processing needed to choose the sequence in which pages are loaded.

As defined by JavaServer Faces technology, *navigation* is a set of rules for choosing the next page to be displayed after a button or hyperlink is clicked. These rules are defined by the application architect in the application configuration resource file (see Application Configuration Resource File, page 792) using a small set of XML elements.

To handle navigation in the simplest application, you simply

- Define the rules in the application configuration resource file.
- Refer to an outcome `String` from the button or hyperlink component's `action` attribute. This outcome `String` is used by the JavaServer Faces implementation to select the navigation rule.

In more complicated applications, you also must provide one or more action methods, which perform some processing to determine what page should be displayed next. The component that triggers navigation references this method. The rest of this section describes what happens when that component is activated.

When a button or hyperlink is clicked, the component associated with it generates an action event. This event is handled by the default `ActionListener` instance, which calls the action method referenced by the component that triggered the event.

This action method is located in a backing bean and is provided by the application developer. It performs some processing and returns a logical outcome `String`, which describes the result of the processing. The listener passes the logical outcome and a reference to the action method that produced the outcome to the default `NavigationHandler`. The `NavigationHandler` selects the page to display next by matching the outcome or the action method reference against the navigation rules in the application configuration resource file.

Each navigation rule defines how to navigate from one particular page to any number of other pages in the application. Each navigation case within the navigation rule defines a target page and either a logical outcome, a reference to an action method, or both. Here is an example navigation rule from the `guessNumber` application described in Defining Page Navigation (page 640):

```
<navigation-rule>
  <from-view-id>/greeting.jsp</from-view-id>
  <navigation-case>
     <from-outcome>success</from-outcome>
     <to-view-id>/response.jsp</to-view-id>
  </navigation-case>
</navigation-rule>
```

This rule states that when the button or hyperlink component on `greeting.jsp` is activated, the application will navigate from the `greeting.jsp` page to the `response.jsp` page if the outcome referenced by the button or hyperlink component's tag is `success`.

The `NavigationHandler` selects the navigation rule that matches the page currently displayed. It then matches the outcome or the action method reference it received from the default `ActionListener` with those defined by the navigation cases. It first tries to match both the method reference and the outcome against the same navigation case. If that fails, it will attempt to match the outcome. Finally, it will attempt to match the action method reference if the previous two attempts failed.

When the `NavigationHandler` achieves a match, the render response phase begins. During this phase, the page selected by the `NavigationHandler` will be rendered.

For more information on how to define navigation rules, see Configuring Navigation Rules (page 805).

For more information on how to implement action methods to handle navigation, see Writing a Method to Handle an Action Event (page 757).

For more information on how to reference outcomes or action methods from component tags, see Referencing a Method That Performs Navigation (page 720).

Backing Bean Management

Another critical function of Web applications is proper management of resources. This includes separating the definition of UI component objects from objects that perform application-specific processing and hold data. It also includes storing and managing these object instances in the proper scope.

A typical JavaServer Faces application includes one or more backing beans, which are JavaBeans components (see JavaBeans Components, page 497) associated with UI components used in a page. A backing bean defines UI component properties, each of which is bound to either a component's value or a component instance. A backing bean can also define methods that perform functions associated with a component, including validation, event handling, and navigation processing.

To bind UI component values and instances to backing bean properties or to reference backing bean methods from UI component tags, page authors use the JavaServer Faces expression language (EL) syntax. This syntax uses the delimiters #{}. A JavaServer Faces expression can be a value-binding expression (for binding UI components or their values to external data sources) or a method-binding expression (for referencing backing bean methods). It can also accept mixed literals and the evaluation syntax and operators of the JSP 2.0 expression language (see Expression Language, page 489).

To illustrate a value-binding expression and a method-binding expression, let's suppose that the `userNo` tag of the `guessNumber` application referenced a method that performed the validation of user input rather than using `LongRangeValidator`:

```
<h:inputText id="userNo"
  value="#{UserNumberBean.userNumber}"
  validator="#{UserNumberBean.validate}" />
```

This tag binds the `userNo` component's value to the `UserNumberBean.userNumber` backing bean property. It also refers to the `UserNumberBean.validate` method, which performs validation of the component's local value, which is whatever the user enters into the field corresponding to this tag.

The property bound to the component's value must be of a type supported by the component. For example, the `userNumber` property returns an `Integer`, which is one of the types that a `UIInput` component supports, as shown in Developing the Beans (page 642).

In addition to the `validator` attribute, tags representing a `UIInput` can also use a `valueChangeListener` attribute to refer to a method that responds to `ValueChangeEvents`, which a `UIInput` component can fire.

A tag representing a component that implements `ActionSource` can refer to backing bean methods using `actionListener` and `action` attributes. The `actionListener` attribute refers to a method that handles an action event. The `action` attribute refers to a method that performs some processing associated with navigation and returns a logical outcome, which the navigation system uses to determine which page to display next.

A tag can also bind a component instance to a backing bean property. It does this by referencing the property from the `binding` attribute:

```
<inputText binding="#{UserNumberBean.userNoComponent}" />
```

The property referenced from the `binding` attribute must accept and return the same component type as the component instance to which it's bound. Here is an example property that can be bound to the component represented by the preceding example `inputText` tag:

```
UIInput userNoComponent = null;
...
public void setUserNoComponent(UIInput userNoComponent) {
    this.userNoComponent = userNoComponent;
}
public UIInput getUserNoComponent() {
    return userNoComponent;
}
```

When a component instance is bound to a backing bean property, the property holds the component's local value. Conversely, when a component's value is bound to a backing bean property, the property holds its model value, which is updated with the local value during the update model values phase of the life cycle.

Binding a component instance to a bean property has these advantages:

- The backing bean can programmatically modify component attributes.
- The backing bean can instantiate components rather than let the page author do so.

Binding a component's value to a bean property has these advantages:

- The page author has more control over the component attributes.
- The backing bean has no dependencies on the JavaServer Faces API (such as the UI component classes), allowing for greater separation of the presentation layer from the model layer.
- The JavaServer Faces implementation can perform conversions on the data based on the type of the bean property without the developer needing to apply a converter.

In most situations, you will bind a component's value rather than its instance to a bean property. You'll need to use a component binding only when you need to change one of the component's attributes dynamically. For example, if a component has validation errors, the property that it's bound to can add an asterisk next to the component when the page is rendered again to display the errors.

Backing beans are created and stored with the application using the managed bean creation facility, which is configured in the application configuration resource file, as shown in Adding Managed Bean Declarations (page 643). When the application starts up, it processes this file, making the beans available to the application and instantiating them when the component tags reference them.

In addition to referencing bean properties using `value` and `binding` attributes, you can reference bean properties (as well as methods and resource bundles) from a custom component attribute by creating a `ValueBinding` instance for it. See Creating the Component Tag Handler (page 772) and Enabling Value-Binding of Component Properties (page 783) for more information on enabling your component's attributes to support value binding.

For more information on configuring beans using the managed bean creation Facility, see Configuring Beans (page 793).

For more information on writing the beans and their properties, see Writing Component Properties (page 730).

For more information on binding component instances or data to properties, see Binding Component Values and Instances to External Data Sources (page 714).

For information on referencing backing bean methods from component tags, see Referencing a Backing Bean Method (page 719).

How the Pieces Fit Together

Previous sections of this chapter introduce you to the various parts of the application: the JSP pages, the backing beans, the listeners, the UI components, and so on. This section shows how these pieces fit together in a real application.

Chapters 17-21 of this tutorial use the Duke's Bookstore application (see The Example JavaServer Faces Application, page 672) to explain basic concepts of creating JavaServer Faces applications.

The example emulates a simple online shopping application. It provides a book catalog from which users can select books and add them to a shopping cart.

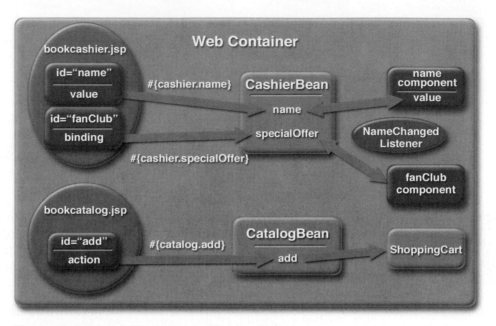

Figure 17–3 Duke's Bookstore Application Objects

Users can view and modify the shopping cart. When users are finished shopping, they can purchase the books in the cart.

Figure 17–3 shows how three components from two different pages of the Duke's Bookstore application are wired to back-end objects and how these objects are connected to each other on the server side. These pages and objects are shown in Table 17–3.

The bookcashier.jsp page represents a form into which customers enter their personal information. The tag that represents the name component on the book-cashier.jsp page renders a text field. When a user enters a value in the field, the name component fires a value-change event, which is processed after the user submits the form. The NameChanged value-change listener handles this event. The tag representing the name component on the page binds the component's value to the name property of the CashierBean using the value-binding expression #{cashier.name} from its value attribute.

The bookcashier.jsp page also includes a selectBooleanCheckbox tag that renders the fanClub component. This tag binds the fanClub component instance to the specialOffer property of CashierBean using the value-binding expression #{cashier.specialOffer} from its binding attribute. When the customer clicks the Submit button on the page, the submit method of CashierBean

Table 17–3 JSP Pages and Objects of Duke's Bookstore

JSP Page or Server-side Object	Description
`bookcashier.jsp`	A form that allows customers to fill out their information, including their name, when ordering books from the Web site.
`bookcatalog.jsp`	Displays a table containing all the books from the database and allows the user to add a book to the shopping cart.
`CashierBean`	The backing bean for the `bookcashier.jsp` page.
`CatalogBean`	The backing bean for the `bookcatalog.jsp` page.
name component	A component represented by the `name` tag on the `bookcashier.jsp` page.
`fanClub` component	A component represented by the `fanClub` tag on the `bookcashier.jsp` page.
`NameChanged` value change listener	Handles the event of users entering their name in the `name` text field rendered by the `name` tag on `bookcashier.jsp`.
`ShoppingCart`	Holds the data for all the books that the user has added to the shopping cart.

checks if the customer has ordered more than $100 (or 100 euros) worth of books. If he or she has, the `fanClub` component and its label are rendered. This component allows the customer to choose to become a member in the Duke fan club as a reward for ordering more than $100 (or 100 euros) worth of books.

The `fanClub` component's tag binds the component rather than its value to a backing bean property because `CashierBean` must have access to the `rendered` property of the `fanClub` component so that it can dynamically set the property to `true`. Because the component rather than the component value is bound to the backing bean property, the backing bean can manipulate the component properties more readily. Binding a Component Instance to a Bean Property (page 718) provides more information on component binding.

The `bookcatalog.jsp` page represents a form in which all the books in the database are displayed in a table. The `UIData` component generates this table, which contains a row for each book. See The UIData Component (page 686) for information on how the `UIData` component works. Each row also includes a button called Add to Cart, which the customer clicks to add the book to the cart. The `commandButton` tag that renders each Add to Cart button references the `add` method of `CatalogBean` using the method-binding expression `#{catalog.add}` from its `action` attribute.

When one of the Add to Cart buttons on the `bookcatalog.jsp` page is clicked, the `add` method of `CatalogBean` is invoked. This method updates the shopping cart.

The `ShoppingCart` object is a model object, whose purpose is to handle application data, including retrieving data from the database.

The Life Cycle of a JavaServer Faces Page

The life cycle of a JavaServer Faces page is similar to that of a JSP page: The client makes an HTTP request for the page, and the server responds with the page translated to HTML. However, because of the extra features that JavaServer Faces technology offers, the life cycle provides some additional services to process a page.

This section details the life cycle for the benefit of developers who need to know information such as when validations, conversions, and events are usually handled and what they can do to change how and when they are handled. Page authors don't necessarily need to know the details of the life cycle.

A JavaServer Faces page is represented by a tree of UI components, called a *view*. When a client makes a request for the page, the life cycle starts. During the life cycle, the JavaServer Faces implementation must build the view while considering state saved from a previous submission of the page. When the client submits a page, the JavaServer Faces implementation must perform several tasks, such as validating the data input of components in the view and converting input data to types specified on the server side. The JavaServer Faces implementation performs all these tasks as a series of steps in the life cycle.

Which steps in the life cycle are executed depends on whether or not the request originated from a JavaServer Faces application and whether or not the response is generated with the rendering phase of the JavaServer Faces life cycle. This section first explains the various life cycle scenarios. It then explains each of these life cycle phases using the `guessNumber` example.

Request Processing Life Cycle Scenarios

A JavaServer Faces application supports two kinds of responses and two kinds of requests:

- Faces response: A servlet response that was created by the execution of the Render Response Phase (page 668) of the request processing life cycle.

- Non-Faces response: A servlet response that was not created by the execution of the render response phase. An example is a JSP page that does not incorporate JavaServer Faces components.

- Faces request: A servlet request that was sent from a previously generated Faces response. An example is a form submit from a JavaServer Faces user interface component, where the request URI identifies the JavaServer Faces component tree to use for processing the request.

- Non-Faces request: A servlet request that was sent to an application component, such as a servlet or JSP page, rather than directed to a JavaServer Faces component tree.

These different requests and responses result in three possible life cycle scenarios that can exist for a JavaServer Faces application:

Scenario 1: Non-Faces Request Generates Faces Response

An example of this scenario occurs when clicking a hyperlink on an HTML page opens a JavaServer Faces page. To render a Faces response from a Non-Faces request, an application must provide a mapping to `FacesServlet`, which accepts incoming requests and passes them to the life cycle implementation for processing. Identifying the Servlet for Life Cycle Processing (page 812) describes how to provide a mapping to the `FacesServlet`. When generating a Faces response, the application must create a new view, store it in the `FacesContext`, acquire object references needed by the view, and call `FacesContext.renderResponse`, which forces immediate rendering of the view by skipping to the Render Response Phase (page 668).

Scenario 2: Faces Request Generates Non-Faces Response

Sometimes a JavaServer Faces application might need to redirect to a different Web application resource or might need to generate a response that does not contain any JavaServer Faces components. In these situations, the developer must skip the rendering phase (Render Response Phase, page 668) by calling `FacesContext.responseComplete`. The `FacesContext` contains all the information associated with a particular Faces request. This method can be invoked during the Apply Request Values Phase (page 666), Process Validations Phase (page 666), or the Update Model Values Phase (page 667).

Scenario 3: Faces Request Generates Faces Response

This is the most common scenario for the life cycle of a JavaServer Faces application. It is also the scenario represented by the standard request processing life cycle described in the next section. This scenario involves JavaServer Faces components submitting a request to a JavaServer Faces application utilizing the `FacesServlet`. Because the request has been handled by the JavaServer Faces implementation, no additional steps are required by the application to generate the response. All listeners, validators and converters will automatically be invoked during the appropriate phase of the standard life cycle, which the next section describes.

Standard Request Processing Life Cycle

The standard request processing life cycle represents scenario 3, described in the preceding section. Most users of JavaServer Faces technology don't need to concern themselves with the request processing life cycle. Indeed, JavaServer Faces technology is sophisticated enough to perform the processing of a page so that developers don't need to deal with complex rendering issues, such as state changes on individual components. For example, if the selection of a component such as a checkbox affects the appearance of another component on the page, JavaServer Faces technology will handle this event properly and will not allow the page to be rendered without reflecting this change.

Figure 17–4 illustrates the steps in the JavaServer Faces request-response life cycle.

The life cycle handles both kinds of requests: *initial requests* and *postbacks*. When a user makes an initial request for a page, he or she is requesting the page for the first time. When a user executes a postback, he or she submits the form contained on a page that was previously loaded into the browser as a result of executing an initial request. When the life cycle handles an initial request, it only executes the restore view and render response phases because there is no user input or actions to process. Conversely, when the life cycle handles a postback, it executes all of the phases.

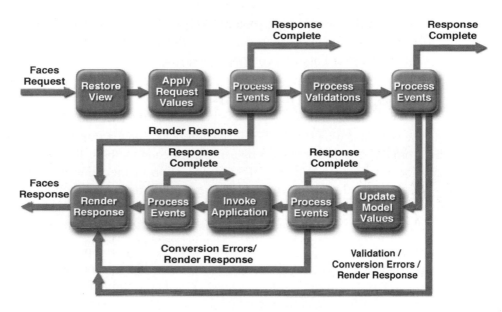

Figure 17–4 JavaServer Faces Standard Request-Response Life Cycle

Restore View Phase

When a request for a JavaServer Faces page is made, such as when a link or a button is clicked, the JavaServer Faces implementation begins the restore view phase.

During this phase, the JavaServer Faces implementation builds the view of the page, wires event handlers and validators, and saves the view in the FacesContext instance. The FacesContext instance contains all the information needed to process a single request. All the application's component tags, event handlers, converters, and validators have access to the FacesContext instance.

If the request for the page is an initial request, the JavaServer Faces implementation creates an empty view during this phase and the life cycle advances to the render response phase. The empty view will be populated when the page is processed during a postback.

If the request for the page is a postback, a view corresponding to this page already exists. During this phase, the JavaServer Faces implementation restores the view by using the state information saved on the client or the server.

The view for the `greeting.jsp` page of the `guessNumber` example would have the `UIView` component at the root of the tree, with `helloForm` as its child and the rest of the JavaServer Faces UI components as children of `helloForm`.

Apply Request Values Phase

After the component tree is restored, each component in the tree extracts its new value from the request parameters by using its `decode` method. The value is then stored locally on the component. If the conversion of the value fails, an error message associated with the component is generated and queued on `FacesContext`. This message will be displayed during the render response phase, along with any validation errors resulting from the process validations phase.

In the case of the `userNo` component on the `greeting.jsp` page, the value is whatever the user entered in the field. Because the object property bound to the component has an `Integer` type, the JavaServer Faces implementation converts the value from a `String` to an `Integer`.

If any `decode` methods or event listeners called `renderResponse` on the current `FacesContext` instance, the JavaServer Faces implementation skips to the render response phase.

If events have been queued during this phase, the JavaServer Faces implementation broadcasts the events to interested listeners.

If some components on the page have their `immediate` attributes (see The immediate Attribute, page 681) set to `true`, then the validation, conversion, and events associated with these components will be processed during this phase.

At this point, if the application needs to redirect to a different Web application resource or generate a response that does not contain any JavaServer Faces components, it can call `FacesContext.responseComplete`.

At the end of this phrase, the components are set to their new values, and messages and events have been queued.

Process Validations Phase

During this phase, the JavaServer Faces implementation processes all validators registered on the components in the tree. It examines the component attributes that specify the rules for the validation and compares these rules to the local value stored for the component.

If the local value is invalid, the JavaServer Faces implementation adds an error message to the `FacesContext` instance, and the life cycle advances directly to the render response phase so that the page is rendered again with the error messages displayed. If there were conversion errors from the apply request values phase, the messages for these errors are also displayed.

If any validate methods or event listeners called `renderResponse` on the current `FacesContext` instance, the JavaServer Faces implementation skips to the render response phase.

At this point, if the application needs to redirect to a different Web application resource or generate a response that does not contain any JavaServer Faces components, it can call `FacesContext.responseComplete`.

If events have been queued during this phase, the JavaServer Faces implementation broadcasts them to interested listeners.

In the `greeting.jsp` page, the JavaServer Faces implementation processes the standard validator registered on the `userNo inputText` tag. It verifies that the data the user entered in the text field is an integer in the range 0 to 10. If the data is invalid or if conversion errors occurred during the apply request values phase, processing jumps to the render response phase, during which the `greeting.jsp` page is rendered again, with the validation and conversion error messages displayed in the component associated with the `message` tag.

Update Model Values Phase

After the JavaServer Faces implementation determines that the data is valid, it can walk the component tree and set the corresponding server-side object properties to the components' local values. The JavaServer Faces implementation will update only the bean properties pointed at by an input component's value attribute. If the local data cannot be converted to the types specified by the bean properties, the life cycle advances directly to the render response phase so that the page is rerendered with errors displayed. This is similar to what happens with validation errors.

If any `updateModels` methods or any listeners called `renderResponse` on the current `FacesContext` instance, the JavaServer Faces implementation skips to the render response phase.

At this point, if the application needs to redirect to a different Web application resource or generate a response that does not contain any JavaServer Faces components, it can call `FacesContext.responseComplete`.

If events have been queued during this phase, the JavaServer Faces implementation broadcasts them to interested listeners.

At this stage, the `userNumber` property of the `UserNumberBean` is set to the local value of the `userNo` component.

Invoke Application Phase

During this phase, the JavaServer Faces implementation handles any application-level events, such as submitting a form or linking to another page.

At this point, if the application needs to redirect to a different Web application resource or generate a response that does not contain any JavaServer Faces components, it can call `FacesContext.responseComplete`.

If the view being processed was reconstructed from state information from a previous request and if a component has fired an event, these events are broadcast to interested listeners.

The `greeting.jsp` page from the `guessNumber` example has one application-level event associated with the `UICommand` component. When processing this event, a default `ActionListener` implementation retrieves the outcome, `success`, from the component's `action` attribute. The listener passes the outcome to the default `NavigationHandler`. The `NavigationHandler` matches the outcome to the proper navigation rule defined in the application's application configuration resource file to determine which page needs to be displayed next. See Configuring Navigation Rules (page 805) for more information on managing page navigation. The JavaServer Faces implementation then sets the response view to that of the new page. Finally, the JavaServer Faces implementation transfers control to the render response phase.

Render Response Phase

During this phase, the JavaServer Faces implementation delegates authority for rendering the page to the JSP container if the application is using JSP pages. If this is an initial request, the components represented on the page will be added to the component tree as the JSP container executes the page. If this is not an initial request, the components are already added to the tree so they needn't be added again. In either case, the components will render themselves as the JSP container traverses the tags in the page.

If the request is a postback and errors were encountered during the apply request values phase, process validations phase, or update model values phase, the original page is rendered during this phase. If the pages contain `message` or `messages` tags, any queued eror messages are displayed on the page.

After the content of the view is rendered, the state of the response is saved so that subsequent requests can access it and it is available to the restore view phase.

In the case of the `guessNumber` example, if a request for the `greeting.jsp` page is an initial request, the view represnting this page is built and saved in `Faces-Context` during the restore view phase and then rendered during this phase. If a request for the page is a postback (such as when the user enters some invalid data and clicks Submit), the tree is rebuilt during the restore view phase and continues through the request processing life cycle phases.

Further Information

For further information on the technologies discussed in this tutorial see the following Web sites:

- The JavaServer Faces 1.0 TLD documentation:

  `http://java.sun.com/j2ee/javaserverfaces/1.0/docs/tlddocs/index.html`

- The JavaServer Faces 1.0 standard RenderKit documentation:

  `http://java.sun.com/j2ee/javaserverfaces/1.0/docs/render-kitdocs/index.html`

- The JavaServer Faces 1.0 API Specification:

  `http://java.sun.com/j2ee/javaserverfaces/1.0/docs/api/index.html`

- The JavaServer Faces 1.0 Specification:

  `http://java.sun.com/j2ee/javaserverfaces/download.html`

- The JavaServer Faces Web site:

  `http://java.sun.com/j2ee/javaserverfaces`

18

Using JavaServer Faces Technology in JSP Pages

T HE page author's responsibility is to design the pages of a JavaServer Faces application. This includes laying out the components on the page and wiring them to backing beans, validators, converters, and other back-end objects associated with the page. This chapter uses the Duke's Bookstore application and the Coffee Break application (see Chapter 35) to describe how page authors use the JavaServer Faces tags to

- Lay out standard UI components on a page
- Reference localized messages
- Register converters, validators, and listeners on components
- Bind components and their values to back-end objects
- Reference backing bean methods that perform navigation processing, handle events, and perform validation

This chapter also describes how to include custom objects created by application developers and component writers on a JSP page.

The Example JavaServer Faces Application

The JavaServer Faces technology chapters of this tutorial primarily use a rewritten version of the Duke's Bookstore example to illustrate the basic concepts of JavaServer Faces technology. This version of the Duke's Bookstore example includes several JavaServer Faces technology features:

- The JavaServer Faces implementation provides `FacesServlet`, whose instances accept incoming requests and pass them to the implementation for processing. Therefore, the application does not need to include a servlet (such as the `Dispatcher` servlet) that processes request parameters and dispatches to application logic, as do the other versions of Duke's Bookstore.

- A custom image map component that allows you to select the locale for the application.

- Navigation configured in a centralized application configuration resource file. This eliminates the need to calculate URLs, as other versions of the Duke's Bookstore application must do.

- Backing beans associated with the pages. These beans hold the component data and perform other processing associated with the components. This processing includes handling the event generated when a user clicks a button or hyperlink.

- Tables that display the books from the database and the shopping cart are rendered with the `dataTable` tag, which is used to dynamically render data in a table. The `dataTable` tag on `bookshowcart.jsp` also includes input components.

- A custom validator and a custom converter are registered on the credit card field of the `bookcashier.jsp` page.

- A value-change listener is registered on the Name field of `bookcashier.jsp`. This listener saves the name in a parameter so that `bookreceipt.jsp` can access it.

This version of Duke's Bookstore includes the same pages listed in Table 12–1. It also includes the `chooselocale.jsp` page, which displays the custom image map that allows you to select the locale of the application. This page is displayed first and advances directly to the `bookstore.jsp` page after the locale is selected.

The packages of the Duke's Bookstore application are:

- `backing`: Includes the backing bean classes
- `components`: Includes the custom UI component classes
- `converters`: Includes the custom converter class
- `listeners`: Includes the event handler and event listener classes
- `model`: Includes a model bean class
- `renderers`: Includes the custom renderers
- `resources`: Includes custom error messages for the custom converter and validator
- `taglib`: Includes custom tag handler classes
- `util`: Includes a message factory class
- `validators`: Includes a custom validator class

Chapter 19 describes how to program backing beans, custom converters and validators, and event listeners. Chapter 20 describes how to program event handlers, custom components, renderers, and tag handlers.

The source code for the application is located in the *<INSTALL>*/j2ee-tutorial14/examples/web/bookstore6/ directory. A sample `bookstore6.war` is provided in *<INSTALL>*/j2eetutorial14/examples/web/provided-wars/. To build, package, deploy, and run the example, follow these steps:

1. Build and package the `bookstore` common files as described in Duke's Bookstore Examples (page 100).
2. Go to *<INSTALL>*/j2eetutorial14/examples/web/bookstore6/ and run `asant build`.
3. Start the Sun Java System Application Server Platform Edition 8.
4. Perform all the operations described in Accessing Databases from Web Applications, page 100.
5. Start `deploytool`.
6. Create a Web application called `bookstore6` by running the New Web Component Wizard. Select File→New→Web Component.
7. In the New Web Component wizard:
   a. Select the Create New Stand-Alone WAR Module radio button.
   b. In the WAR Location field, enter *<INSTALL>*/j2eetutorial14/examples/web/bookstore6.war.
   c. In the WAR Name field, enter bookstore6.

    d. In the Context Root field, enter /bookstore6.

    e. Click Edit Contents.

    f. In the Edit Contents dialog box, navigate to *<INSTALL>*/j2ee-tutorial14/examples/web/bookstore6/build/. Select everything in the build directory and click Add.

    g. In the Contents tree, drag the resources package to the WEB-INF/classes directory.

    h. In the Contents tree, drag faces-config.xml to the WEB-INF directory.

    i. In the Edit Contents dialog box, navigate to <INSTALL>/j2eetutorial14/examples/web/bookstore/dist/. Select bookstore.jar and click Add.

    j. In the Edit Contents dialog box, navigate to *<J2EE_HOME>*/lib/ and select the jsf-api.jar. Click Add, and then Click OK.

    k. Click Next.

    l. Select the Servlet radio button.

    m. Click Next.

    n. Select javax.faces.webapp.FacesServlet from the Servlet Class combo box.

    o. In the Startup Load Sequence Position combo box, enter 1.

    p. Click Finish.

8. Provide a mapping for the FacesServlet Web component.

    a. Select the FacesServlet Web component that is contained in the bookstore6 Web application from the tree.

    b. Select the Aliases tab.

    c. Click Add and enter *.faces in the Aliases field.

9. Specify where state is saved.

    a. Select the bookstore6 WAR from the tree.

    b. Select the Context tabbed pane and click Add.

    c. Enter javax.faces.STATE_SAVING_METHOD in the Coded Parameter field.

    d. Enter client in the Value field.

10. Set preludes and codas for all JSP pages.

    a. Select the JSP Properties tab.

    b. Click Add.

    c. Enter bookstore6 in the Name field.

d. Click Add URL.

e. Enter `*.jsp` in the URL Patterns field.

f. Click Edit Preludes.

g. Click Add.

h. Enter `/template/prelude.jspf`.

i. Click OK.

j. Click Edit Codas.

k. Click Add.

l. Enter `/template/coda.jspf`.

m. Click OK.

11. Add the listener class `listeners.ContextListener` (described in Handling Servlet Life-Cycle Events, page 441).

a. Select the Event Listeners tab.

b. Click Add.

c. Select the `listeners.ContextListener` class from the drop-down menu in the Event Listener Classes pane.

12. Add a resource reference for the database.

a. Select the Resource Ref's tab.

b. Click Add.

c. Enter `jdbc/BookDB` in the Coded Name field.

d. Accept the default type `javax.sql.DataSource`.

e. Accept the default authorization `Container`.

f. Accept the default selected `Shareable`.

g. Enter `jdbc/BookDB` in the JNDI Name field of the Sun-specific Settings frame.

13. Select File→Save.

14. Deploy the application.

15. Select Tools→Deploy.

16. In the Connection Settings frame, enter the user name and password you specified when you installed the Application Server.

17. Click OK.

18. A pop-up dialog box will display the results of the deployment. Click Close.

19. Open the URL `http://localhost:8080/bookstore6` in a browser.

Setting Up a Page

To use the JavaServer Faces UI components in your JSP page, you need to give the page access to the two tag libraries: the JavaServer Faces standard HTML render kit tag library and the JavaServer Faces core tag library. The JavaServer Faces standard HTML render kit tag library defines tags that represent common HTML user interface components. The JavaServer Faces core tag library defines tags that perform core actions and are independent of a particular render kit.

Using these tag libraries is similar to using any other custom tag library. This chapter assumes that you are familiar with the basics of using custom tags in JSP pages (see Using Custom Tags, page 502).

As is the case with any tag library, each JavaServer Faces tag library must have a TLD that describes it. The `html_basic` TLD describes the The JavaServer Faces standard HTML render kit tag library. The `jsf_core` TLD describes the Java-Server Faces core tag library.

Please refer to the TLD documentation at `http://java.sun.com/j2ee/javaserverfaces/1.0/docs/tlddocs/index.html` for a complete list of the JavaServer Faces tags and their attributes.

Your application needs access to these TLDs in order for your pages to use them. The Application Server includes these TLDs in `jsf-impl.jar`, located in *<J2EE_HOME>*/`lib`.

To use any of the JavaServer Faces tags, you need to include these `taglib` directives at the top of each page containing the tags defined by these tag libraries:

```
<%@ taglib uri="http://java.sun.com/jsf/html" prefix="h" %>
<%@ taglib uri="http://java.sun.com/jsf/core" prefix="f" %>
```

The `uri` attribute value uniquely identifies the TLD. The `prefix` attribute value is used to distinguish tags belonging to the tag library. You can use other prefixes rather than the h or f prefixes. However, you must use the prefix you have chosen when including the tag in the page. For example, the `form` tag must be referenced in the page via the h prefix because the preceding tag library directive uses the h prefix to distinguish the tags defined in `html_basic.tld`:

```
<h:form ...>
```

A page containing JavaServer Faces tags is represented by a tree of components. At the root of the tree is the `UIViewRoot` component. The `view` tag represents this component on the page. Thus, all component tags on the page must be enclosed in the `view` tag, which is defined in the `jsf_core` TLD:

```
<f:view>
    ... other JavaServer Faces tags and possibly other content ...
</f:view>
```

You can enclose other content, including HTML and other JSP tags, within the `view` tag, but all JavaServer Faces tags must be enclosed within the `view` tag.

The `view` tag has an optional `locale` attribute. If this attribute is present, its value overrides the `Locale` stored in the `UIViewRoot` component. This value is specified as a `String` and must be of this form:

```
:language:[{-,_}:country:[{-,_}:variant]
```

The `:language:`, `:country:`, and `:variant:` parts of the expression are as specified in `java.util.Locale`.

A typical JSP page includes a form, which is submitted when a button or hyperlink on the page is clicked. For the data of other components on the page to be submitted with the form, the tags representing the components must be nested inside the `form` tag. See The UIForm Component (page 683) for more details on using the `form` tag.

If you want to include a page containing JavaServer Faces tags within another JSP page (which could also contain JavaServer Faces tags), you must enclose the entire nested page in a `subview` tag. You can add the `subview` tag on the parent page and nest a `jsp:include` inside it to include the page:

```
<f:subview id="myNestedPage">
  <jsp:include page="theNestedPage.jsp"/>
<f:subview>
```

You can also include the `subview` tag inside the nested page, but it must enclose all the JavaServer Faces tags on the nested page.

In summary, a typical JSP page that uses JavaServer Faces tags will look somewhat like this:

```
<%@ taglib uri="http://java.sun.com/jsf/html" prefix="h" %>
<%@ taglib uri="http://java.sun.com/jsf/core" prefix="f" %>

<f:view>
```

```
<h:form>
    other JavaServer Faces tags and core tags,
    including one or more button or hyperlink components for
    submitting the form
</h:form>
</f:view>
```

The sections Using the Core Tags (page 678) and Using the HTML Component Tags (page 680) describe how to use the core tags from the JavaServer Faces core tag library and the component tags from the JavaServer Faces standard HTML render kit tag library.

Using the Core Tags

The tags included in the JavaServer Faces core tag library are used to perform core actions that are independent of a particular render kit. These tags are listed in Table 18–1.

Table 18–1 The `jsf_core` Tags

Tag Categories	Tags	Functions
Event-handling tags	`actionListener`	Registers an action listener on a parent component
	`valueChangeListener`	Registers a value-change listener on a parent component
Attribute configuration tag	`attribute`	Adds configurable attributes to a parent component
Data conversion tags	`converter`	Registers an arbitrary converter on the parent component
	`convertDateTime`	Registers a `DateTime` converter instance on the parent component
	`convertNumber`	Registers a `Number` converter instance on the parent component
Facet tag	`facet`	Signifies a nested component that has a special relationship to its enclosing tag

Table 18–1 The `jsf_core` Tags *(Continued)*

Tag Categories	Tags	Functions
Localization tag	loadBundle	Specifies a ResourceBundle that is exposed as a Map
Parameter substitution tag	param	Substitutes parameters into a Message-Format instance and adds query string name-value pairs to a URL
Tags for representing items in a list	selectItem	Represents one item in a list of items in a UISelectOne or UISelectMany component
	selectItems	Represents a set of items in a UISelectOne or UISelectMany component
Container tag	subview	Contains all JavaServer Faces tags in a page that is included in another JSP page containing JavaServer Faces tags
Validator tags	validateDoubleRange	Registers a DoubleRangeValidator on a component
	validateLength	Registers a LengthValidator on a component
	validateLongRange	Registers a LongRangeValidator on a component
	validator	Registers a custom validator on a component
Output tag	verbatim	Generates a UIOutput component that gets its content from the body of this tag
Container for form tags	view	Encloses all JavaServer Faces tags on the page

These tags are used in conjunction with component tags and are therefore explained in other sections of this tutorial. Table 18–2 lists the sections that explain how to use specific `jsf_core` tags.

Table 18–2 Where the `jsf_core` Tags Are Explained

Tags	Where Explained
Event-handling tags	Registering Listeners on Components (page 710)
Data conversion tags	Using the Standard Converters (page 705)
`facet`	The UIData Component (page 686) and The UIPanel Component (page 694)
`loadBundle`	Using Localized Messages (page 703)
`param`	Using the outputFormat Tag (page 693) and
`selectItem` and `selectItems`	The UISelectItem, UISelectItems, and UISelectItem-Group Components (page 700)
`subview`	Setting Up a Page (page 676)
`verbatim`	Using the outputLink Tag (page 692)
`view`	Setting Up a Page (page 676)
Validator tags	Using the Standard Validators (page 712) and Creating a Custom Validator (page 750)

Using the HTML Component Tags

The tags defined by the JavaServer Faces standard HTML render kit tag library represent HTML form controls and other basic HTML elements. These controls display data or accept data from the user. This data is collected as part of a form and is submitted to the server, usually when the user clicks a button. This section explains how to use each of the component tags shown in Table 17–2, and is organized according to the `UIComponent` classes from which the tags are derived.

The next section explains the more important tag attributes that are common to most component tags. Please refer to the TLD documentation at `http://java.sun.com/j2ee/javaserverfaces/1.0/docs/tlddocs/index.html` for a complete list of tags and their attributes.

For each of the components discussed in the following sections, Writing Component Properties (page 730) explains how to write a bean property bound to a particular UI component or its value.

UI Component Tag Attributes

In general, most of the component tags support these attributes:

- `id`: Uniquely identifies the component
- `immediate`: If set to `true`, indicates that any events, validation, and conversion associated with the component should happen in the apply request values phase rather than a later phase.
- `rendered`: Specifies a condition in which the component should be rendered. If the condition is not satisfied, the component is not rendered.
- `style`: Specifies a Cascading Style Sheet (CSS) style for the tag.
- `styleClass`: Specifies a CSS stylesheet class that contains definitions of the styles.
- `value`: Identifies an external data source and binds the component's value to it.
- `binding`: Identifies a bean property and binds the component instance to it.

All of the UI component tag attributes (except `id` and `var`) are value-binding-enabled, which means that they accept JavaServer Faces EL expressions. These expressions allow you to use mixed literals and JSP 2.0 expression language syntax and operators. See Expression Language (page 489) for more information about the JSP 2.0 expression language.

The id Attribute

The `id` attribute is not required for a component tag except in these situations:

- Another component or a server-side class must refer to the component.
- The component tag is impacted by a JSTL conditional or iterator tag (for more information, see Flow Control Tags, page 545).

If you don't include an `id` attribute, the JavaServer Faces implementation automatically generates a component ID.

The immediate Attribute

`UIInput` components and command components (those that implement `Action-Source`, such as buttons and hyperlinks) can set the `immediate` attribute to `true` to force events, validations, and conversions to be processed during the apply request values phase of the life cycle. Page authors need to carefully consider how the combination of an input component's `immediate` value and a command component's `immediate` value determines what happens when the command component is activated.

Assume that you have a page with a button and a field for entering the quantity of a book in a shopping cart. If both the button's and the field's `immediate` attributes are set to `true`, the new value of the field will be available for any processing associated with the event that is generated when the button is clicked. The event associated with the button and the event, validation, and conversion associated with the field are all handled during the apply request values phase.

If the button's `immediate` attribute is set to `true` but the field's `immediate` attribute is set to `false`, the event associated with the button is processed without updating the field's local value to the model layer. This is because any events, conversion, or validation associated with the field occurs during its usual phases of the life cycle, which come after the apply request values phase.

The `bookshowcart.jsp` page of the Duke's Bookstore application has examples of components using the `immediate` attribute to control which component's data is updated when certain buttons are clicked. The `quantity` field for each book has its `immediate` attribute set to `false`. (The `quantity` fields are generated by the `UIData` component. See The UIData Component, page 686, for more information.) The `immediate` attribute of the Continue Shopping hyperlink is set to `true`. The `immediate` attribute of the Update Quantities hyperlink is set to `false`.

If you click the Continue Shopping hyperlink, none of the changes entered into the quantity input fields will be processed. If you click the Update Quantities hyperlink, the values in the quantity fields will be updated in the shopping cart.

The rendered Attribute

A component tag uses a Boolean JavaServer Faces (EL) expression, along with the `rendered` attribute, to determine whether or not the component will be rendered. For example, the `check` `commandLink` component on the `bookcatalog.jsp` page is not rendered if the cart contains no items:

```
<h:commandLink id="check"
  ...
  rendered="#{cart.numberOfItems > 0}">
  <h:outputText
    value="#{bundle.CartCheck}"/>
</h:commandLink>
```

The style and styleClass Attributes

The `style` and `styleClass` attributes allow you to specify Cascading Style Sheets (CSS) styles for the rendered output of your component tags. The UIMessage and UIMessages Components (page 698) describes an example of using the `style` attribute to specify styles directly in the attribute. A component tag can instead refer to a CSS stylesheet class. The `dataTable` tag on the `bookcatalog.jsp` page of the Duke's Bookstore application references the style class `list-background`:

```
<h:dataTable id="books"
    ...
    styleClass="list-background"
    value="#{bookDBAO.books}"
    var="book">
```

The stylesheet that defines this class is `stylesheet.css`, which is included in the application. For more information on defining styles, please see the Cascading Style Sheets Specification at `http://www.w3.org/Style/CSS/`.

The value and binding Attributes

A tag representing a component defined by `UIOutput` or a subclass of `UIOutput` uses `value` and `binding` attributes to bind its component's value or instance to an external data source. Binding Component Values and Instances to External Data Sources (page 714) explains how to use these attributes.

The UIForm Component

A `UIForm` component represents an input form that has child components representing data that is either presented to the user or submitted with the form. The `form` tag encloses all the controls that display or collect data from the user. Here is an example:

```
<h:form>
... other JavaServer Faces tags and other content...
</h:form>
```

The `form` tag can also include HTML markup to lay out the controls on the page. The `form` tag itself does not perform any layout; its purpose is to collect data and to declare attributes that can be used by other components in the form. A page can include multiple form tags, but only the values from the form that the user submits will be included in the postback.

The UIColumn Component

The UIColumn component represents a column of data in a UIData component. While the UIData component is iterating over the rows of data, it processes the UIColumn component for each row. UIColumn has no renderer associated with it and is represented on the page with a column tag. Here is an example column tag from the bookshowcart.jsp page of the Duke's Bookstore example:

```
<h:dataTable id="items"
  ...
  value="#{cart.items}"
  var="item">
  ...
  <h:column>
    <f:facet name="header">
      <h:outputText value="#{bundle.ItemQuantity}"/>
    </f:facet>
    <h:inputText
      ...
      value="#{item.quantity}">
      <f:validateLongRange minimum="1"/>
    </h:inputText>
  </h:column>
  ...
</h:dataTable>
```

The UIData component in this example iterates through the list of books (cart.items) in the shopping cart and displays their titles, authors, and prices. The column tag shown in the example renders the column that displays text fields that allow customers to change the quantity of each book in the shopping cart. Each time UIData iterates through the list of books, it renders one cell in each column.

The UICommand Component

The UICommand component performs an action when it is activated. The most common example of such a component is the button. This release supports Button and Link as UICommand component renderers.

In addition to the tag attributes listed in Using the HTML Component Tags (page 680), the `commandButton` and `commandLink` tags can use these attributes:

- `action`, which is either a logical outcome `String` or a method-binding expression that points to a bean method that returns a logical outcome `String`. In either case, the logical outcome `String` is used by the default `NavigationHandler` instance to determine what page to access when the `UICommand` component is activated.

- `actionListener`, which is a method-binding expression that points to a bean method that processes an action event fired by the `UICommand` component.

See Referencing a Method That Performs Navigation (page 720) for more information on using the `action` attribute.

See Referencing a Method That Handles an Action Event (page 721) for details on using the `actionListener` attribute.

Using the commandButton Tag

The `bookcashier.jsp` page of the Duke's Bookstore application includes a `commandButton` tag. When a user clicks the button, the data from the current page is processed, and the next page is opened. Here is the `commandButton` tag from `bookcashier.jsp`:

```
<h:commandButton value="#{bundle.Submit}"
  action="#{cashier.submit}"/>
```

Clicking the button will cause the `submit` method of `CashierBean` to be invoked because the `action` attribute references the `submit` method of the `CashierBean` backing bean. The `submit` method performs some processing and returns a logical outcome. This is passed to the default `NavigationHandler`, which matches the outcome against a set of navigation rules defined in the application configuration resource file.

The `value` attribute of the preceding example `commandButton` tag references the localized message for the button's label. The `bundle` part of the expression refers to the `ResourceBundle` that contains a set of localized messages. The `Submit` part of the expression is the key that corresponds to the message that is displayed on the button. For more information on referencing localized messages, see Using Localized Messages (page 703). See Referencing a Method That Performs Navigation (page 720) for information on how to use the `action` attribute.

Using the commandLink Tag

The commandLink tag represents an HTML hyperlink and is rendered as an HTML `<a>` element. The commandLink tag is used to submit an action event to the application. See Implementing Action Listeners (page 749) for more information on action events.

A commandLink tag must include a nested outputText tag, which represents the text the user clicks to generate the event. The following tag is from the choose-locale.jsp page from the Duke's Bookstore application.

```
<h:commandLink id="NAmerica" action="bookstore"
  actionListener="#{localeBean.chooseLocaleFromLink}">
  <h:outputText value="#{bundle.English}" />
</h:commandLink>
```

This tag will render the following HTML:

```
<a id="_id3:NAmerica" href="#"
  onclick="document.forms['_id3']['_id3:NAmerica'].
  value='_id3:NAmerica';
  document.forms['_id3'].submit();
  return false;">English</a>
```

Note: Notice that the commandLink tag will render JavaScript. If you use this tag, make sure your browser is JavaScript-enabled.

The UIData Component

The UIData component supports data binding to a collection of data objects. It does the work of iterating over each record in the data source. The standard Table renderer displays the data as an HTML table. The UIColumn component represents a column of data within the table. Here is a portion of the dataTable tag used by the bookshowcart.jsp page of the Duke's Bookstore example:

```
<h:dataTable id="items"
  columnClasses="list-column-center, list-column-left,
    list-column-right, list-column-center"
  footerClass="list-footer"
  headerClass="list-header"
  rowClasses="list-row-even, list-row-odd"
  styleClass="list-background"
  value="#{cart.items}"
  var="item">
```

```
<h:column >
  <f:facet name="header">
    <h:outputText value="#{bundle.ItemQuantity}" />
  </f:facet>
  <h:inputText id="quantity" size="4"
    value="#{item.quantity}" /> ...
  </h:inputText> ...
</h:column>
<h:column>
  <f:facet name="header">
    <h:outputText value="#{bundle.ItemTitle}"/>
  </f:facet>
  <h:commandLink action="#{showcart.details}">
    <h:outputText value="#{item.item.title}"/>
  </h:commandLink>
</h:column>
...
<f:facet name="footer"
  <h:panelGroup>
    <h:outputText value="#{bundle.Subtotal}"/>
    <h:outputText value="#{cart.total}" />
      <f:convertNumber type="currency" />
    </h:outputText>
  </h:panelGroup>
</f:facet>
</h:dataTable>
```

Figure 18–1 shows a data grid that this dataTable tag can display.

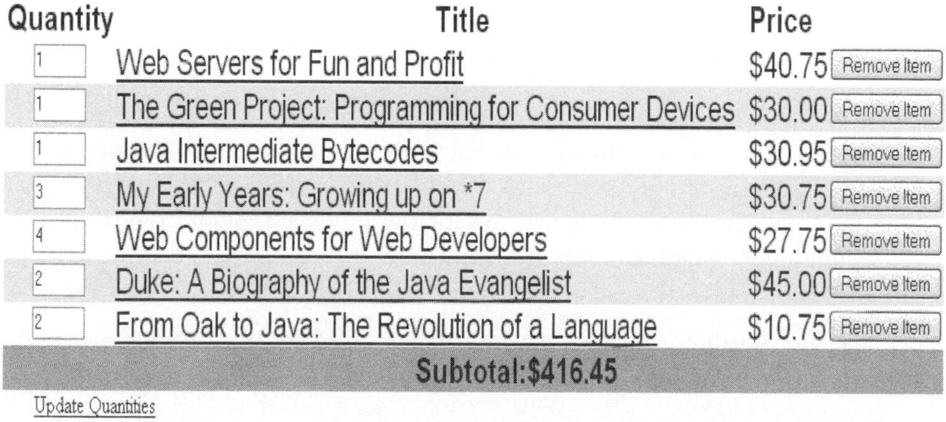

Quantity	Title	Price	
1	Web Servers for Fun and Profit	$40.75	Remove Item
1	The Green Project: Programming for Consumer Devices	$30.00	Remove Item
1	Java Intermediate Bytecodes	$30.95	Remove Item
3	My Early Years: Growing up on *7	$30.75	Remove Item
4	Web Components for Web Developers	$27.75	Remove Item
2	Duke: A Biography of the Java Evangelist	$45.00	Remove Item
2	From Oak to Java: The Revolution of a Language	$10.75	Remove Item
	Subtotal:$416.45		

Update Quantities

Figure 18–1 Table on the bookshowcart.jsp Page

The example `dataTable` tag displays the books in the shopping cart as well as the number of each book in the shopping cart, the prices, and a set of buttons, which the user can click to remove books from the shopping cart.

The `facet` tag inside the first `column` tag renders a header for that column. The other column tags also contain `facet` tags. Facets can have only one child, and so a `panelGroup` tag is needed if you want to group more than one component within a `facet`. Because the facet tag representing the footer includes more than one tag, the `panelGroup` is needed to group those tags.

A `facet` tag is usually used to represent headers and footers. In general, a *facet* is used to represent a component that is independent of the parent-child relationship of the page's component tree. In the case of a data grid, header and footer data is not repeated like the other rows in the table, and therefore, the elements representing headers and footers are not updated as are the other components in the tree.

This example is a classic use case for a `UIData` component because the number of books might not be known to the application developer or the page author at the time the application is developed. The `UIData` component can dynamically adjust the number of rows of the table to accommodate the underlying data.

The `value` attribute of a `dataTable` tag references the data to be included in the table. This data can take the form of

- A list of beans
- An array of beans
- A single bean
- A `javax.faces.model.DataModel`
- A `java.sql.ResultSet`
- A `javax.servlet.jsp.jstl.sql.ResultSet`
- A `javax.sql.RowSet`

All data sources for `UIData` components have a `DataModel` wrapper. Unless you explicitly construct a `DataModel` wrapper, the JavaServer Faces implementation will create one around data of any of the other acceptable types. See Writing Component Properties (page 730) for more information on how to write properties for use with a `UIData` component.

The `var` attribute specifies a name that is used by the components within the `dataTable` tag as an alias to the data referenced in the `value` attribute of `dataTable`.

In the `dataTable` tag from the `bookshowcart.jsp` page, the `value` attribute points to a list of books. The `var` attribute points to a single book in that list. As the `UIData` component iterates through the list, each reference to `item` points to the current book in the list.

The `UIData` component also has the ability to display only a subset of the underlying data. This is not shown in the preceding example. To display a subset of the data, you use the optional `first` and `rows` attributes.

The `first` attribute specifies the first row to be displayed. The `rows` attribute specifies the number of rows—starting with the first row—to be displayed. By default, both `first` and `rows` are set to zero, and this causes all the rows of the underlying data to display. For example, if you wanted to display records 2 through 10 of the underlying data, you would set `first` to 2 and `rows` to 9. When you display a subset of the data in your pages, you might want to consider including a link or button that causes subsequent rows to display when clicked.

The `dataTable` tag also has a set of optional attributes for adding styles to the table:

- `columnClasses`: Defines styles for all the columns
- `footerClass`: Defines styles for the footer
- `headerClass`: Defines styles for the header
- `rowClasses`: Defines styles for the rows
- `styleClass`: Defines styles for the entire table

Each of these attributes can specify more than one style. If `columnClasses` or `rowClasses` specifies more than one style, the styles are applied to the columns or rows in the order that the styles are listed in the attribute. For example, if `columnClasses` specifies styles `list-column-center` and `list-column-right` and if there are two columns in the table, the first column will have style `list-column-center`, and the second column will have style `list-column-right`.

If the `style` attribute specifies more styles than there are columns or rows, the remaining styles will be assigned to columns or rows starting from the first column or row. Similarly, if the `style` attribute specifies fewer styles than there are columns or rows, the remaining columns or rows will be assigned styles starting from the first style.

The UIGraphic Component

The `UIGraphic` component displays an image. The Duke's Bookstore application uses a `graphicImage` tag to display the map image on the `chooselocale.jsp` page:

```
<h:graphicImage id="mapImage" url="/template/world.jpg"
    alt="#{bundle.chooseLocale}" usemap="#worldMap" />
```

The `url` attribute specifies the path to the image. It also corresponds to the local value of the `UIGraphic` component so that the URL can be retrieved, possibly from a backing bean. The URL of the example tag begins with a /, which adds the relative context path of the Web application to the beginning of the path to the image.

The `alt` attribute specifies the alternative text displayed when the user mouses over the image. In this example, the `alt` attribute refers to a localized message. See Performing Localization (page 741) for details on how to localize your JavaServer Faces application.

The `usemap` attribute refers to the image map defined by the custom component, `MapComponent`, which is on the same page. See Chapter 20 for more information on the image map.

The UIInput and UIOutput Components

The `UIInput` component displays a value to the user and allows the user to modify this data. The most common example is a text field. The `UIOutput` component displays data that cannot be modified. The most common example is a label.

The `UIInput` and `UIOutput` components can each be rendered in four ways. Table 18–3 lists the renderers of `UIInput` and `UIOutput`. Recall from Component Rendering Model (page 647) that the tags are composed of the component and the renderer. For example, the `inputText` tag refers to a `UIInput` component that is rendered with the `Text` renderer.

The `UIInput` component supports the following tag attributes in addition to the tag attributes described at the beginning of Using the HTML Component Tags (page 680). The `UIOutput` component supports the first of the following tag attributes in addition to those listed in Using the HTML Component Tags (page 680).

- `converter`: Identifies a converter that will be used to convert the component's local data. See Using the Standard Converters (page 705) for more information on how to use this attribute.

- validator: Identifies a method-binding expression pointing to a backing bean method that performs validation on the component's data. See Referencing a Method That Performs Validation (page 722) for an example of using the validator tag.

- valueChangeListener: Identifies a method-binding expression pointing to a backing bean method that handles the event of entering a value in this component. See Referencing a Method That Handles a Value-Change Event (page 722) for an example of using valueChangeListener.

The rest of this section explains how to use selected tags listed in Table 18–3. The other tags are written in a similar way.

Using the outputText and inputText Tags

The Text renderer can render both UIInput and UIOutput components. The inputText tag displays and accepts a single line string. The outputText tag displays a single-line string. This section shows you how to use the inputText tag. The outputText tag is written in a similar way.

Table 18–3 UIInput and UIOutput Renderers

Component	Renderer	Tag	Function
UIInput	Hidden	inputHidden	Allows a page author to include a hidden variable in a page
	Secret	inputSecret	Accepts one line of text with no spaces and displays it as a set of asterisks as it is typed
	Text	inputText	Accepts a text string of one line
	TextArea	inputTextarea	Accepts multiple lines of text
UIOutput	Label	outputLabel	Displays a nested component as a label for a specified input field
	Link	outputLink	Displays an <a href> tag that links to another page without generating an action event
	OutputMessage	outputFormat	Displays a localized message
	Text	outputText	Displays a text string of one line

Here is an example of an `inputText` tag from the `bookcashier.jsp` page:

```
<h:inputText id="name" size="50"
  value="#{cashier.name}"
  required="true">
  <f:valueChangeListener type="listeners.NameChanged" />
</h:inputText>
```

The `value` attribute refers to the `name` property of `CashierBean`. This property holds the data for the `name` component. After the user submits the form, the value of the `name` property in `CashierBean` will be set to the text entered in the field corresponding to this tag.

The `required` attribute causes the page to reload with errors displayed if the user does not enter a value in the `name` text field. See Requiring a Value (page 713) for more information on requiring input for a component.

Using the outputLabel Tag

The `outputLabel` tag is used to attach a label to a specified input field for accessibility purposes. The `bookcashier.jsp` page uses an `outputLabel` tag to render the label of a checkbox:

```
<h:selectBooleanCheckbox
  id="fanClub"
  rendered="false"
  binding="#{cashier.specialOffer}" />
<h:outputLabel for="fanClub"
  rendered="false"
  binding="#{cashier.specialOfferText}"  >
  <h:outputText id="fanClubLabel"
    value="#{bundle.DukeFanClub}" />
</h:outputLabel>
```

The `for` attribute of the `outputLabel` tag maps to the `id` of the input field to which the label is attached. The `outputText` tag nested inside the `outputLabel` tag represents the actual label component. The `value` attribute on the `outputText` tag indicates the text that is displayed next to the input field.

Using the outputLink Tag

The `outputLink` tag is used to render a hyperlink that, when clicked, loads another page but does not generate an action event. You should use this tag instead of the commandLink tag if you always want the URL—specified by the outputLink tag's value attribute—to open and do not have to perform any processing when the user clicks on the link. The Duke's Bookstore application does not utilize this tag, but here is an example of it:

```
<h:outputLink value="javadocs">
  <f:verbatim>Documentation for this demo</f:verbatim>
</h:outputLink>
```

As shown in this example, the outputLink tag requires a nested verbatim tag, which identifies the text the user clicks to get to the next page.

You can use the verbatim tag on its own when you want to simply output some text on the page.

Using the outputFormat Tag

The outputFormat tag allows a page author to display concatenated messages as a MessageFormat pattern, as described in the API documentation for java.text.MessageFormat (see http://java.sun.com/j2se/1.4.2/docs/api/java/text/MessageFormat.html). Here is an example of an outputFormat tag from the bookshowcart.jsp page of the Duke's Bookstore application:

```
<h:outputFormat value="#{bundle.CartItemCount}">
  <f:param value="#{cart.numberOfItems}"/>
</h:outputFormat>
```

The value attribute specifies the MessageFormat pattern. The param tag specifies the substitution parameters for the message.

In the example outputFormat tag, the value for the parameter maps to the number of items in the shopping cart. When the message is displayed on the page, the number of items in the cart replaces the {0} in the message corresponding to the CartItemCount key in the bundle resource bundle:

```
Your shopping cart contains " + "{0,choice,0#no items|1#one
item|1< {0} items
```

This message represents three possibilities:

- Your shopping cart contains no items.
- Your shopping cart contains one item.
- Your shopping cart contains {0} items.

The value of the parameter replaces the {0} from the message in the sentence in the third bullet. This is an example of a value-binding-enabled tag attribute accepting a complex JSP 2.0 EL expression.

An `outputFormat` tag can include more than one `param` tag for those messages that have more than one parameter that must be concatenated into the message. If you have more than one parameter for one message, make sure that you put the `param` tags in the proper order so that the data is inserted in the correct place in the message.

A page author can also hardcode the data to be substituted in the message by using a literal value with the `value` attribute on the `param` tag.

Using the inputSecret Tag

The `inputSecret` tag renders an `<input type="password">` HTML tag. When the user types a string into this field, a row of asterisks is displayed instead of the text the user types. The Duke's Bookstore application does not include this tag, but here is an example of one:

```
<h:inputSecret redisplay="false"
  value="#{LoginBean.password}" />
```

In this example, the `redisplay` attribute is set to `false`. This will prevent the password from being displayed in a query string or in the source file of the resulting HTML page.

The UIPanel Component

The `UIPanel` component is used as a layout container for its children. When you use the renderers from the HTML render kit, `UIPanel` is rendered as an HTML table. This component differs from `UIData` in that `UIData` can dynamically add or delete rows to accommodate the underlying data source, whereas `UIPanel` must have the number of rows predetermined. Table 18–4 lists all the renderers and tags corresponding to the `UIPanel` component.

The `panelGrid` tag is used to represent an entire table. The `panelGroup` tag is used to represent rows in a table. Other UI component tags are used to represent individual cells in the rows.

Table 18–4 `UIPanel` Renderers and Tags

Renderer	Tag	Renderer Attributes	Function
Grid	panelGrid	columnClasses, columns, footerClass, headerClass, panel-Class, rowClasses	Displays a table
Group	panelGroup		Groups a set of components under one parent

The `panelGrid` tag has a set of attributes that specify CSS stylesheet classes: `columnClasses`, `footerClass`, `headerClass`, `panelClass`, and `rowClasses`. These stylesheet attributes are not required. It also has a `columns` attribute. The `columns` attribute is required if you want your table to have more than one column because the `columns` attribute tells the renderer how to group the data in the table.

If a `headerClass` is specified, the `panelGrid` must have a header as its first child. Similarly, if a `footerClass` is specified, the `panelGrid` must have a footer as its last child.

The Duke's Bookstore application includes three `panelGrid` tags on the book-cashier.jsp page. Here is a portion of one of them:

```
<h:panelGrid columns="3" headerClass="list-header"
  rowClasses="list-row-even, list-row-odd"
  styleClass="list-background"
  title="#{bundle.Checkout}">
  <f:facet name="header">
    <h:outputText value="#{bundle.Checkout}"/>
  </f:facet>
  <h:outputText value="#{bundle.Name}" />
  <h:inputText id="name" size="50"
    value="#{cashier.name}"
    required="true">
    <f:valueChangeListener
      type="listeners.NameChanged" />
  </h:inputText>
  <h:message styleClass="validationMessage" for="name"/>
  <h:outputText value="#{bundle.CCNumber}"/>
```

```
    <h:inputText id="ccno" size="19"
      converter="CreditCardConverter" required="true">
      <bookstore:formatValidator
        formatPatterns="9999999999999999|
          9999 9999 9999 9999|9999-9999-9999-9999"/>
    </h:inputText>
    <h:message styleClass="validationMessage"  for="ccno"/>
    ...
  </h:panelGrid>
```

This `panelGrid` tag is rendered to a table that contains controls for the customer of the bookstore to input personal information. This `panelGrid` uses stylesheet classes to format the table. The CSS classes are defined in the `stylesheet.css` file in the *<INSTALL>*/j2eetutorial14/examples/web/bookstore6/web/ directory. The `list-header` definition is

```
.list-header {
  background-color: #ffffff;
  color: #000000;
  text-align: center;
}
```

Because the `panelGrid` tag specifies a `headerClass`, the `panelGrid` must contain a header. The example `panelGrid` tag uses a `facet` tag for the header. Facets can have only one child, and so a `panelGroup` tag is needed if you want to group more than one component within a `facet`. Because the example `panelGrid` tag has only one cell of data, a `panelGroup` tag is not needed.

A `panelGroup` tag can also be used to encapsulate a nested tree of components so that the tree of components appears as a single component to the parent component.

The data represented by the nested component tags is grouped into rows according to the value of the `columns` attribute of the `panelGrid` tag. The `columns` attribute in the example is set to "3", and therefore the table will have three columns. In which column each component is displayed is determined by the order that the component is listed on the page modulo 3. So if a component is the fifth one in the list of components, that component will be in the 5 modulo 3 column, or column 2.

The UISelectBoolean Component

The `UISelectBoolean` class defines components that have a `boolean` value. The `selectBooleanCheckbox` tag is the only tag that JavaServer Faces technology provides for representing `boolean` state. The Duke's Bookstore application includes a `selectBooleanCheckbox` tag on the `bookcashier.jsp` page:

```
<h:selectBooleanCheckbox
    id="fanClub"
    rendered="false"
    binding="#{cashier.specialOffer}" />
<h:outputLabel
    for="fanClub"
    rendered="false"
    binding="#{cashier.specialOfferText}">
    <h:outputText
        id="fanClubLabel"
        value="#{bundle.DukeFanClub}" />
</h:outputLabel>
```

This example tag displays a checkbox to allow users to indicate whether they want to join the Duke Fan Club. The label for the checkbox is rendered by the `outputLabel` tag. The actual text is represented by the nested `outputText` tag. Binding a Component Instance to a Bean Property (page 718) discusses this example in more detail.

The UISelectMany Component

The `UISelectMany` class defines a component that allows the user to select zero or more values from a set of values. This component can be rendered as a set of checkboxes, a list box, or a menu. This section explains the `selectManyCheckbox` tag. The `selectManyListbox` tag and `selectManyMenu` tag are written in a similar way.

A list box differs from a menu in that it displays a subset of items in a box, whereas a menu displays only one item at a time until you select the menu. The `size` attribute of the `selectManyListbox` tag determines the number of items displayed at one time. The list box includes a scrollbar for scrolling through any remaining items in the list.

Using the selectManyCheckbox Tag

The `selectManyCheckbox` tag renders a set of checkboxes, with each checkbox representing one value that can be selected. Duke's Bookstore uses a `select-ManyCheckbox` tag on the `bookcashier.jsp` page to allow the user to subscribe to one or more newsletters:

```
<h:selectManyCheckbox
   id="newsletters"
   layout="pageDirection"
   value="#{cashier.newsletters}">
   <f:selectItems
      value="#{newsletters}"/>
</h:selectManyCheckbox>
```

The `value` attribute of the `selectManyCheckbox` tag identifies the `CashierBean` backing bean property, `newsletters`, for the current set of newsletters. This property holds the values of the currently selected items from the set of checkboxes.

The `layout` attribute indicates how the set of checkboxes are arranged on the page. Because layout is set to `pageDirection`, the checkboxes are arranged vertically. The default is `lineDirection`, which aligns the checkboxes horizontally.

The `selectManyCheckbox` tag must also contain a tag or set of tags representing the set of checkboxes. To represent a set of items, you use the `selectItems` tag. To represent each item individually, you use a `selectItem` tag for each item. The UISelectItem, UISelectItems, and UISelectItemGroup Components (page 700) explains these two tags in more detail.

The UIMessage and UIMessages Components

The `UIMessage` and `UIMessages` components are used to display error messages. Here is an example `message` tag from the `guessNumber` application, discussed in Steps in the Development Process (page 635):

```
<h:inputText id="userNo" value="#{UserNumberBean.userNumber}"
   <f:validateLongRange minimum="0" maximum="10" />
...
<h:message
```

```
style="color: red;
font-family: 'New Century Schoolbook', serif;
font-style: oblique;
text-decoration: overline" id="errors1" for="userNo"/>
```

The `for` attribute refers to the ID of the component that generated the error message. The `message` tag will display the error message wherever it appears on the page.

The `style` attribute allows you to specify the style of the text of the message. In the example in this section, the text will be red, New Century Schoolbook, serif font family, and oblique style, and a line will appear over the text.

If you use the `messages` tag instead of the `message` tag, all error messages will display.

The UISelectOne Component

A `UISelectOne` component allows the user to select one value from a set of values. This component can be rendered as a list box, a set of radio buttons, or a menu. This section explains the `selectOneMenu` tag. The `selectOneRadio` and `selectOneListbox` tags are written in a similar way. The `selectOneListbox` tag is similar to the `selectOneMenu` tag except that `selectOneListbox` defines a `size` attribute that determines how many of the items are displayed at once.

Using the selectOneMenu Tag

The `selectOneMenu` tag represents a component that contains a list of items, from which a user can choose one item. The menu is also commonly known as a drop-down list or a combo box. The following code example shows the `select-OneMenu` tag from the `bookcashier.jsp` page of the Duke's Bookstore application. This tag allows the user to select a shipping method:

```
<h:selectOneMenu    id="shippingOption"
   required="true"
   value="#{cashier.shippingOption}">
   <f:selectItem
      itemValue="2"
      itemLabel="#{bundle.QuickShip}"/>
   <f:selectItem
      itemValue="5"
      itemLabel="#{bundle.NormalShip}"/>
```

```
    <f:selectItem
        itemValue="7"
        itemLabel="#{bundle.SaverShip}"/>
</h:selectOneMenu>
```

The `value` attribute of the `selectOneMenu` tag maps to the property that holds the currently selected item's value.

Like the `selectOneRadio` tag, the `selectOneMenu` tag must contain either a `selectItems` tag or a set of `selectItem` tags for representing the items in the list. The next section explains these two tags.

The UISelectItem, UISelectItems, and UISelectItemGroup Components

`UISelectItem` and `UISelectItems` represent components that can be nested inside a `UISelectOne` or a `UISelectMany` component. `UISelectItem` is associated with a `SelectItem` instance, which contains the value, label, and description of a single item in the `UISelectOne` or `UISelectMany` component.

The `UISelectItems` instance represents either of the following:

- A set of `SelectItem` instances, containing the values, labels, and descriptions of the entire list of items
- A set of `SelectItemGroup` instances, each of which represents a set of `SelectItem` instances

Figure 18–2 shows an example of a list box constructed with a `SelectItems` component representing two `SelectItemGroup` instances, each of which represents two categories of beans. Each category is an array of `SelectItem` instances.

The `selectItem` tag represents a `UISelectItem` component. The `selectItems` tag represents a `UISelectItems` component. You can use either a set of `selectItem` tags or a single `selectItems` tag within your `selectOne` or `selectMany` tag.

The advantages of using the `selectItems` tag are as follows:

- You can represent the items using different data structures, including `Array`, `Map`, and `Collection`. The data structure is composed of `SelectItem` instances or `SelectItemGroup` instances.

Figure 18–2   An Example List Box Created Using
SelectItemGroup Instances

- You can concatenate different lists together into a single UISelectMany or UISelectOne component and group the lists within the component, as shown in Figure 18–2.
- You can dynamically generate values at runtime.

The advantages of using selectItem are as follows:

- The page author can define the items in the list from the page.
- You have less code to write in the bean for the selectItem properties.

For more information on writing component properties for the UISelectItems components, see Writing Component Properties (page 730). The rest of this section shows you how to use the selectItems and selectItem tags.

Using the selectItems Tag

Here is the selectManyCheckbox tag from the section The UISelectMany Component (page 697):

```
<h:selectManyCheckbox
   id="newsletters"
   layout="pageDirection"
   value="#{cashier.newsletters}">
   <f:selectItems
      value="#{newsletters}"/>
</h:selectManyCheckbox>
```

The value attribute of the selectItems tag is bound to the newsletters managed bean, which is configured in the application configuration resource file. The newsletters managed bean is configured as a list:

```
<managed-bean>
   <managed-bean-name>newsletters</managed-bean-name>
   <managed-bean-class>
      java.util.ArrayList</managed-bean-class>
   <managed-bean-scope>application</managed-bean-scope>
   <list-entries>
      <value-class>javax.faces.model.SelectItem</value-class>
      <value>#{newsletter0}</value>
      <value>#{newsletter1}</value>
      <value>#{newsletter2}</value>
      <value>#{newsletter3}</value>
   </list-entries>
</managed-bean>
<managed-bean>
<managed-bean-name>newsletter0</managed-bean-name>
<managed-bean-class>
   javax.faces.model.SelectItem</managed-bean-class>
<managed-bean-scope>none</managed-bean-scope>
<managed-property>
   <property-name>label</property-name>
   <value>Duke's Quarterly</value>
</managed-property>
<managed-property>
   <property-name>value</property-name>
   <value>200</value>
</managed-property>
</managed-bean>
...
```

As shown in the managed-bean element, the UISelectItems component is a collection of SelectItem instances. See Initializing Array and List Properties (page 799) for more information on configuring collections as beans.

You can also create the list corresponding to a UISelectMany or UISelectOne component programmatically in the backing bean. See Writing Component Properties (page 730) for information on how to write a backing bean property corresponding to a UISelectMany or UISelectOne component.

The arguments to the `SelectItem` constructor are:

- An `Object` representing the value of the item
- A `String` representing the label that displays in the `UISelectMany` component on the page
- A `String` representing the description of the item

UISelectItems Properties (page 737) describes in more detail how to write a backing bean property for a `UISelectItems` component.

Using the selectItem Tag

The `selectItem` tag represents a single item in a list of items. Here is the example from Using the selectOneMenu Tag (page 699):

```
<h:selectOneMenu
   id="shippingOption" required="true"
   value="#{cashier.shippingOption}">
   <f:selectItem
      itemValue="2"
      itemLabel="#{bundle.QuickShip}"/>
   <f:selectItem
      itemValue="5"
      itemLabel="#{bundle.NormalShip}"/>
   <f:selectItem
      itemValue="7"
      itemLabel="#{bundle.SaverShip}"/>
</h:selectOneMenu>
```

The `itemValue` attribute represents the default value of the `SelectItem` instance. The `itemLabel` attribute represents the `String` that appears in the drop-down menu component on the page.

The `itemValue` and `itemLabel` attributes are value-binding-enabled, meaning that they can use value-binding expressions to refer to values in external objects. They can also define literal values, as shown in the example `selectOneMenu` tag.

Using Localized Messages

All data and messages in the Duke's Bookstore application have been completely localized for Spanish, French, German, and American English. Performing

Localization (page 741) explains how to produce the localized messages as well as how to localize dynamic data and messages.

The image map on the first page allows you to select your preferred locale. See Chapter 20 for information on how the image map custom component was created.

This section explains how to use localized static data and messages for JavaServer Faces applications. If you are not familiar with the basics of localizing Web applications, see Chapter 22. Localized static data can be included in a page by using the loadBundle tag, defined in jsf_core.tld. Follow these steps:

1. Reference a ResourceBundle from the page.
2. Reference the localized message located within the bundle.

A ResourceBundle contains a set of localized messages. For more information about resource bundles, see

```
http://java.sun.com/docs/books/tutorial/i18n/index.html
```

After the application developer has produced a ResourceBundle, the application architect puts it in the same directory as the application classes. Much of the data for the Duke's Bookstore application is stored in a ResourceBundle called BookstoreMessages.

Referencing a ResourceBundle from a Page

For a page with JavaServer Faces tags to use the localized messages contained in a ResourceBundle, the page must reference the ResourceBundle using a loadBundle tag.

The loadBundle tag from bookstore.jsp is

```
<f:loadBundle var="bundle"
  basename="messages.BookstoreMessages" />
```

The basename attribute value refers to the ResourceBundle, located in the messages package of the bookstore application. Make sure that the basename attribute specifies the fully qualified class name of the file.

The var attribute is an alias to the ResourceBundle. This alias can be used by other tags in the page in order to access the localized messages.

Referencing a Localized Message

To reference a localized message from a ResourceBundle, you use a value-binding expression from an attribute of the component tag that will display the localized data. You can reference the message from any component tag attribute that is value-binding-enabled.

The value-binding expression has the notation "var.message", in which var matches the var attribute of the loadBundle tag, and message matches the key of the message contained in the ResourceBundle referred to by the var attribute. Here is an example from bookstore.jsp:

```
<h:outputText value="#{bundle.Talk}"/>
```

Notice that bundle matches the var attribute from the loadBundle tag and that Talk matches the key in the ResourceBundle.

Another example is the graphicImage tag from chooseLocale.jsp:

```
<h:graphicImage id="mapImage" url="/template/world.jpg"
    alt="#{bundle.ChooseLocale}"
    usemap="#worldMap" />
```

The alt attribute is value-binding-enabled, and this means that it can use value-binding expressions. In this case, the alt attribute refers to localized text, which will be included in the alternative text of the image rendered by this tag.

See Creating the Component Tag Handler (page 772) and Enabling Value-Binding of Component Properties (page 783) for information on how to enable value binding on your custom component's attributes.

Using the Standard Converters

The JavaServer Faces implementation provides a set of Converter implementations that you can use to convert component data. For more information on the conceptual details of the conversion model, see Conversion Model (page 651).

The standard `Converter` implementations, located in the `javax.faces.convert` package, are as follows:

- `BigDecimalConverter`
- `BigIntegerConverter`
- `BooleanConverter`
- `ByteConverter`
- `CharacterConverter`
- `DateTimeConverter`
- `DoubleConverter`
- `FloatConverter`
- `IntegerConverter`
- `LongConverter`
- `NumberConverter`
- `ShortConverter`

Two of these standard converters (`DateTimeConverter` and `NumberConverter`) have their own tags, which allow you to configure the format of the component data by configuring the tag attributes. Using DateTimeConverter (page 707) discusses using `DateTimeConverter`. Using NumberConverter (page 709) discusses using `NumberConverter`.

You can use the other standard converters in one of three ways:

- You can make sure that the component that uses the converter has its value bound to a backing bean property of the same type as the converter.
- You can refer to the converter by class or by its ID using the component tag's `converter` attribute. The ID is defined in the application configuration resource file (see Application Configuration Resource File, page 792).
- You can refer to the converter by its ID using the `converterId` attribute of the `converter` tag.

The latter two will convert the component's local value. The first method will convert the model value of the component. For example, if you want a component's data to be converted to an `Integer`, you can bind the component to a property similar to this:

```
Integer age = 0;
public Integer getAge(){ return age;}
public void setAge(Integer age) {this.age = age;}
```

Alternatively, if the component is not bound to a bean property, you can use the converter attribute on the component tag:

```
<h:inputText
  converter="javax.faces.convert.IntegerConverter" />
```

The data corresponding to this tag will be converted to a java.lang.Integer. Notice that the Integer type is already a supported type of the NumberConverter. If you don't need to specify any formatting instructions using the convertNumber tag attributes, and if one of the other converters will suffice, you can simply reference that converter using the component tag's converter attribute.

Finally, you can nest a converter tag within the component tag and refer to the converter's ID via the converter tag's converterId attribute. If the tag is referring to a custom converter, the value of converterID must match the ID in the application configuration resource file. Here is an example:

```
<h:inputText value="#{LoginBean.Age}" />
  <f:converter converterId="Integer" />
</h:inputText>
```

Using DateTimeConverter

You can convert a component's data to a java.util.Date by nesting the convertDateTime tag inside the component tag. The convertDateTime tag has several attributes that allow you to specify the format and type of the data. Table 18–5 lists the attributes.

Here is a simple example of a convertDateTime tag from the bookreceipt.jsp page:

```
<h:outputText value="#{cashier.shipDate}">
  <f:convertDateTime dateStyle="full" />
</h:outputText>
```

Here is an example of a date and time that this tag can display:

```
Saturday, Feb 22, 2003
```

You can also display the same date and time using this tag:

```
<h:outputText value="#{cashier.shipDate}">
  <f:convertDateTime
    pattern="EEEEEEEE, MMM dd, yyyy" />
</h:outputText>
```

Table 18–5 convertDateTime Tag Attributes

Attribute	Type	Description
dateStyle	String	Defines the format, as specified by java.text.DateFormat, of a date or the date part of a date string. Applied only if type is date (or both) and pattern is not defined. Valid values: default, short, medium, long, and full. If no value is specified, default is used.
locale	String or Locale	Locale whose predefined styles for dates and times are used during formatting or parsing. If not specified, the Locale returned by FacesContext.getLocale will be used.
pattern	String	Custom formatting pattern that determines how the date/time string should be formatted and parsed. If this attribute is specified, dateStyle, timeStyle, and type attributes are ignored.
timeStyle	String	Defines the format, as specified by java.text.DateFormat, of a time or the time part of a date string. Applied only if type is time and pattern is not defined. Valid values: default, short, medium, long, and full. If no value is specified, default is used.
timeZone	String or TimeZone	Time zone in which to interpret any time information in the date string.
type	String	Specifies whether the string value will contain a date, a time, or both. Valid values are date, time, or both. If no value is specified, date is used.

If you want to display the example date in Spanish, you can use the locale attribute:

```
<h:inputText value="#{cashier.shipDate}">
  <f:convertDateTime dateStyle="full"
    locale="Locale.SPAIN"
    timeStyle="long" type="both" />
</h:inputText>
```

This tag would display

```
Sabado, Feb 22, 2003
```

Please refer to the Customizing Formats lesson of the Java Tutorial at `http://java.sun.com/docs/books/tutorial/i18n/format/simpleDateFormat.html` for more information on how to format the output using the `pattern` attribute of the `convertDateTime` tag.

Using NumberConverter

You can convert a component's data to a `java.lang.Number` by nesting the `convertNumber` tag inside the component tag. The `convertNumber` tag has several attributes that allow you to specify the format and type of the data. Table 18–6 lists the attributes.

Table 18–6   `convertNumber` Attributes

Attribute	Type	Description
currencyCode	String	ISO4217 currency code, used only when formatting currencies.
currencySymbol	String	Currency symbol, applied only when formatting currencies.
groupingUsed	boolean	Specifies whether formatted output contains grouping separators.
integerOnly	boolean	Specifies whether only the integer part of the value will be parsed.
maxFractionDigits	int	Maximum number of digits formatted in the fractional part of the output.
maxIntegerDigits	int	Maximum number of digits formatted in the integer part of the output.
minFractionDigits	int	Minimum number of digits formatted in the fractional part of the output.
minIntegerDigits	int	Minimum number of digits formatted in the integer part of the output.

Continues

Table 18–6 convertNumber Attributes *(Continued)*

Attribute	Type	Description
locale	String or Locale	Locale whose number styles are used to format or parse data.
pattern	String	Custom formatting pattern that determines how the number string is formatted and parsed.
type	String	Specifies whether the string value is parsed and formatted as a number, currency, or percentage. If not specified, number is used.

The bookcashier.jsp page of Duke's Bookstore uses a convertNumber tag to display the total prices of the books in the shopping cart:

```
<h:outputText value="#{cart.total}" >
  <f:convertNumber type="currency"
</h:outputText>
```

Here is an example of a number this tag can display

```
$934
```

This number can also be displayed using this tag:

```
<h:outputText id="cartTotal"
  value="#{cart.Total}" >
  <f:convertNumber pattern="$####" />
</h:outputText>
```

Please refer to the Customizing Formats lesson of the Java Tutorial at http://java.sun.com/docs/books/tutorial/i18n/format/decimalFormat.html for more information on how to format the output using the pattern attribute of the convertNumber tag.

Registering Listeners on Components

A page author can register a listener implementation class on a component by nesting either a valuechangeListener tag or an actionListener tag within the component's tag on the page.

An application developer can instead implement these listeners as backing bean methods. To reference these methods, a page author uses the component tag's valueChangeListener and actionListener attributes, as described in Referencing a Method That Handles an Action Event (page 721) and Referencing a Method That Handles a Value-Change Event (page 722).

The Duke's Bookstore application includes a value-change listener implementation class but does not use an action listener implementation class. This section explains how to register the NameChanged Value-Change listener and a hypothetical LocaleChange action listener implementation on components. Implementing Value-Change Listeners (page 748) explains how to implement NameChanged. Implementing Action Listeners (page 749) explains how to implement the hypothetical LocaleChange.

Registering a Value-Change Listener on a Component

A page author can register a ValueChangeListener implementation on a UIInput component or a component represented by one of the subclasses of UIInput by nesting a valueChangeListener tag within the component's tag on the page. Here is the tag corresponding to the name component from the book-cashier.jsp page:

```
<h:inputText  id="name" size="50" value="#{cashier.name}"
   required="true">
   <f:valueChangeListener type="listeners.NameChanged" />
</h:inputText>
```

The type attribute of the valueChangeListener tag specifies the fully qualified class name of the ValueChangeListener implementation.

After this component tag is processed and local values have been validated, its corresponding component instance will queue the ValueChangeEvent associated with the specified ValueChangeListener to the component.

Registering an Action Listener on a Component

A page author can register an ActionListener implementation on a UICommand component by nesting an actionListener tag within the component's tag on the page. Duke's Bookstore does not use any `ActionListener` implementations. Here is one of the `commandLink` tags on the `chooselocale.jsp` page, changed to reference an `ActionListener` implementation rather than a backing bean method:

```
<h:commandLink id="NAmerica" action="bookstore">
    <f:actionListener type="listeners.LocaleChange" />
</h:commandLink>
```

The `type` attribute of the `actionListener` tag specifies the fully qualified class name of the `ActionListener` implementation.

When this tag's component is activated, the component's `decode` method (or its associated `Renderer`) automatically queues the `ActionEvent` implementation associated with the specified `ActionListener` implementation to the component.

Using the Standard Validators

JavaServer Faces technology provides a set of standard classes and associated tags that page authors and application developers can use to validate a component's data. Table 18–7 lists all the standard validator classes and the tags that allow you to use the validators from the page.

Table 18–7 The Validator Classes

Validator Class	Tag	Function
DoubleRangeValidator	validateDoubleRange	Checks whether the local value of a component is within a certain range. The value must be floating-point or convertible to floating-point.
LengthValidator	validateLength	Checks whether the length of a component's local value is within a certain range. The value must be a `java.lang.String`.
LongRangeValidator	validateLongRange	Checks whether the local value of a component is within a certain range. The value must be any numeric type or String that can be converted to a `long`.

All these validator classes implement the `Validator` interface. Component writers and application developers can also implement this interface to define their own set of constraints for a component's value.

To use the standard `Validator` implementations, simply nest the standard validator tag of your choice inside a tag that represents a component of type `UIInput` (or a subclass of `UIInput`) and provide any necessary constraints using the validator tag's attributes. The attributes of all the standard validator tags are value-binding enabled, which means that they can accept value-binding expressions as well as literal values. Validation can be performed only on `UIInput` components or components whose classes extend `UIInput` because these components accept values that can be validated.

This section shows you how to use the standard `Validator` implementations. See The UIMessage and UIMessages Components (page 698) for information on how to display validation error messages on the page.

Requiring a Value

The `name inputText` tag on the `bookcashier.jsp` page has a `required` attribute, which is set to `true`. Because of this, the JavaServer Faces implementation checks whether the value of the component is `null` or is an empty `String`.

If your component must have a non-`null` value or a `String` value at least one character in length, you should add a `required` attribute to your component tag and set it to `true`. If your tag does have a `required` attribute that is set to `true` and the value is `null` or a zero-length string, no other validators registered on the tag are called. If your tag does not have a `required` attribute set to `true`, other validators registered on the tag are called, but those validators must handle the possibility of a `null` or zero-length string.

Here is the `name inputText` tag:

```
<h:inputText id="name" size="50"
  value="#{cashier.name}" required="true">
  ...
</h:inputText>
```

Using the LongRangeValidator

The Duke's Bookstore application uses a `validateLongRange` tag on the quantity input field of the `bookshowcart.jsp` page:

```
<h:inputText id="quantity" size="4"
  value="#{item.quantity}" >
  <f:validateLongRange minimum="1"/>
</h:inputText>
<h:message for="quantity"/>
```

This tag requires that the user enter a number that is at least 1. The `size` attribute specifies that the number can have no more than four digits. The `validateLongRange` tag also has a `maximum` attribute, with which you can set a maximum value of the input.

Binding Component Values and Instances to External Data Sources

As explained in Backing Bean Management (page 656), a component tag can wire its component's data to a back-end data object by doing one of the following:

- Binding its component's value to a bean property or other external data source
- Binding its component's instance to a bean property

A component tag's `value` attribute uses a value-binding expression to bind a component's value to an external data source, such as a bean property. A component tag's `binding` attribute uses a value-binding expression to bind a component instance to a bean property.

When referencing the property using the component tag's `value` attribute, you need to use the proper syntax. For example, suppose a backing bean called `MyBean` has this `int` property:

```
int currentOption = null;
int getCurrentOption(){...}
void setCurrentOption(int option){...}
```

The `value` attribute that references this property must have this value-binding expression:

```
"#{MyBean.currentOption}"
```

Table 18–8 Example Value-Binding Expressions

Value	Expression
A Boolean	`cart.numberOfItems > 0`
A property initialized from a context `init` parameter	`initParam.quantity`
A bean property	`CashierBean.name`
Value in an array	`books[3]`
Value in a collection	`books["fiction"]`
Property of an object in an array of objects	`books[3].price`

In addition to binding a component's value to a bean property, the `value` attribute can specify a literal value or can map the component's data to any primitive (such as `int`), structure (such as an array), or collection (such as a list), independent of a JavaBeans component. Table 18–8 lists some example value-binding expressions that you can use with the `value` attribute.

The next two sections explain in more detail how to use the `value` attribute to bind a component's value to a bean property or other external data sources and how to use the `binding` attribute to bind a component instance to a bean property

Binding a Component Value to a Property

To bind a component's value to a bean property, you specify the name of the bean and the property using the `value` attribute. As explained in Backing Bean Management (page 656), the value-binding expression of the component tag's `value` attribute must match the corresponding managed bean declaration in the application configuration resource file.

This means that the name of the bean in the value-binding expression must match the `managed-bean-name` element of the managed bean declaration up to the first . in the expression. Similarly, the part of the value-binding expression after the . must match the name specified in the corresponding `property-name` element in the application configuration resource file.

For example, consider this managed bean configuration, which configures the `ImageArea` bean corresponding to the North America part of the image map on the `chooselocale.jsp` page of the Duke's Bookstore application:

```
<managed-bean>
  <managed-bean-name> NA </managed-bean-name>
  <managed-bean-class> model.ImageArea </managed-bean-class>
  <managed-bean-scope> application </managed-bean-scope>
  <managed-property>
     <property-name>shape</property-name>
     <value>poly</value>
  </managed-property>
  <managed-property>
     <property-name>alt</property-name>
     <value>NAmerica</value>
  </managed-property>
  ...
</managed-bean>
```

This example configures a bean called `NA`, which has several properties, one of which is called `shape`.

Although the `area` tags on the `chooselocale.jsp` page do not bind to an `ImageArea` property (they bind to the bean itself), to do this, you refer to the property using a value-binding expression from the `value` attribute of the component's tag:

```
<h:outputText value="#{NA.shape}" />
```

Much of the time you will not include definitions for a managed bean's properties when configuring it. You need to define a property and its value only when you want the property to be initialized with a value when the bean is initialized.

If a component tag's `value` attribute must refer to a property that is not initialized in the `managed-bean` configuration, the part of the value-binding expression after the . must match the property name as it is defined in the backing bean.

See Application Configuration Resource File (page 792) for information on how to configure beans in the application configuration resource file.

Writing Component Properties (page 730) explains in more detail how to write the backing bean properties for each of the component types.

Binding a Component Value to an Implicit Object

One external data source that a `value` attribute can refer to is an implicit object.

The `bookreceipt.jsp` page of the Duke's Bookstore application includes a reference to an implicit object from a parameter substitution tag:

```
<h:outputFormat  title="thanks" value="#{bundle.ThankYouParm}">
  <f:param value="#{sessionScope.name}"/>
</h:outputFormat>
```

This tag gets the name of the customer from the session scope and inserts it into the parameterized message at the key ThankYouParm from the resource bundle. For example, if the name of the customer is Gwen Canigetit, this tag will render:

```
Thank you, Gwen Canigetit, for purchasing your books from us.
```

The name tag on the `bookcashier.jsp` page has the NameChanged listener implementation registered on it. This listener saves the customer's name in the session scope when the `bookcashier.jsp` page is submitted. See Implementing Value-Change Listeners (page 748) for more information on how this listener works. See Registering a Value-Change Listener on a Component (page 711) to learn how the listener is registered on the tag.

Retrieving values from other implicit objects is done in a similar way to the example shown in this section. Table 18–9 lists the implicit objects that a value attribute can refer to. All of the implicit objects except for the scope objects are read-only and therefore should not be used as a value for a UIInput component.

Table 18–9 Implicit Objects

Implicit Object	What It Is
applicationScope	A Map of the application scope attribute values, keyed by attribute name
cookie	A Map of the cookie values for the current request, keyed by cookie name
facesContext	The FacesContext instance for the current request

Continues

Table 18–9   Implicit Objects *(Continued)*

Implicit Object	What It Is
header	A Map of HTTP header values for the current request, keyed by header name
headerValues	A Map of String arrays containing all the header values for HTTP headers in the current request, keyed by header name
initParam	A Map of the context initialization parameters for this Web application
param	A Map of the request parameters for this request, keyed by parameter name
paramValues	A Map of String arrays containing all the parameter values for request parameters in the current request, keyed by parameter name
requestScope	A Map of the request attributes for this request, keyed by attribute name
sessionScope	A Map of the session attributes for this request, keyed by attribute name
view	The root UIComponent in the current component tree stored in the FacesRequest for this request

Binding a Component Instance to a Bean Property

A component instance can be bound to a bean property using a value-binding expression with the binding attribute of the component's tag. You usually bind a component instance rather than its value to a bean property if the bean must dynamically change the component's attributes.

Here are two tags from the bookcashier.jsp page that bind components to bean properties:

```
<h:selectBooleanCheckbox
  id="fanClub"
  rendered="false"
  binding="#{cashier.specialOffer}" />
<h:outputLabel for="fanClub"
  rendered="false"
  binding="#{cashier.specialOfferText}"  >
```

```
    <h:outputText id="fanClubLabel"
      value="#{bundle.DukeFanClub}"
    />
  </h:outputLabel>
```

The `selectBooleanCheckbox` tag renders a checkbox and binds the `fanClub` `UISelectBoolean` component to the `specialOffer` property of `CashierBean`. The `outputLabel` tag binds the component representing the checkbox's label to the `specialOfferText` property of `CashierBean`. If the application's locale is English, the `outputLabel` tag renders:

```
  I'd like to join the Duke Fan Club, free with my purchase of
  over $100
```

The `rendered` attributes of both tags are set to `false`, which prevents the checkbox and its label from being rendered. If the customer orders more than $100 (or 100 euros) worth of books and clicks the `Submit` button, the `submit` method of `CashierBean` sets both components' `rendered` properties to `true`, causing the checkbox and its label to be rendered.

These tags use component bindings rather than value bindings because the backing bean must dynamically set the values of the components' `rendered` properties.

If the tags were to use value bindings instead of component bindings, the backing bean would not have direct access to the components, and would therefore require additional code to access the components from the `FacesContext` instance to change the components' `rendered` properties.

Writing Properties Bound to Component Instances (page 739) explains how to write the bean properties bound to the example components and also discusses how the `submit` method sets the `rendered` properties of the components.

Referencing a Backing Bean Method

A component tag has a set of attributes for referencing backing bean methods that can perform certain functions for the component associated with the tag. These attributes are summarized in Table 18–10.

Only components that implement `ActionSource` can use the `action` and `actionListener` attributes. Only `UIInput` components or components that extend `UIInput` can use the `validator` or `valueChangeListener` attributes.

Table 18–10 Component Tag Attributes that Reference Backing Bean Methods

Attribute	Function
`action`	Refers to a backing bean method that performs navigation processing for the component and returns a logical outcome `String`
`actionListener`	Refers to a backing bean method that handles action events
`validator`	Refers to a backing bean method that performs validation on the component's value
`valueChangeListener`	Refers to a backing bean method that handles value-change events

The component tag refers to a backing bean method using a method-binding expression as a value of one of the attributes. The following four sections give examples of how to use the four different attributes.

Referencing a Method That Performs Navigation

If your page includes a component (such as a button or hyperlink) that causes the application to navigate to another page when the component is activated, the tag corresponding to this component must include an `action` attribute. This attribute does one of the following:

- Specifies a logical outcome `String` that tells the application which page to access next
- References a backing bean method that performs some processing and returns a logical outcome `String`

The `bookcashier.jsp` page of the Duke's Bookstore application has a `command-Button` tag that refers to a backing bean method that calculates the shipping date. If the customer has ordered more than $100 (or 100 euros) worth of books, this method also sets the `rendered` properties of some of the components to `true` and returns `null`; otherwise it returns `receipt`, which causes the `bookreceipt.jsp` page to display. Here is the `commandButton` tag from the `bookcashier.jsp` page:

```
<h:commandButton
  value="#{bundle.Submit}"
  action="#{cashier.submit}" />
```

The `action` attribute uses a method-binding expression to refer to the `submit` method of `CashierBean`. This method will process the event fired by the component corresponding to this tag.

Writing a Method to Handle Navigation (page 755) describes how to implement the `submit` method of `CashierBean`.

The application architect must configure a navigation rule that determines which page to access given the current page and the logical outcome, which is either returned from the backing bean method or specified in the tag. See Configuring Navigation Rules (page 805) for information on how to define navigation rules in the application configuration resource file.

Referencing a Method That Handles an Action Event

If a component on your page generates an action event, and if that event is handled by a backing bean method, you refer to the method by using the component's `actionListener` attribute.

The `chooselocale.jsp` page of the Duke's Bookstore application includes some components that generate action events. One of them is the `NAmerica` component:

```
<h:commandLink id="NAmerica" action="bookstore"
  actionListener="#{localeBean.chooseLocaleFromLink}">
```

The `actionListener` attribute of this component tag references the `chooseLocaleFromLink` method using a method-binding expression. The `chooseLocaleFromLink` method handles the event of a user clicking on the hyperlink rendered by this component.

The `actionListener` attribute can be used only with the tags of components that implement `ActionSource`. These include `UICommand` components.

Writing a Method to Handle an Action Event (page 757) describes how to implement a method that handles an action event.

Referencing a Method That Performs Validation

If the input of one of the components on your page is validated by a backing bean method, you refer to the method from the component's tag using the `validator` attribute.

The Coffee Break application includes a method that performs validation of the `email` input component on the `checkoutForm.jsp` page. Here is the tag corresponding to this component:

```
<h:inputText id="email" value="#{checkoutFormBean.email}"
   size="25" maxlength="125"
   validator="#{checkoutFormBean.validateEmail}"/>
```

This tag references the `validateEmail` method described in Writing a Method to Perform Validation (page 757) using a method-binding expression.

The `validator` attribute can be used only with `UIInput` components or those components whose classes extend `UIInput`.

Writing a Method to Perform Validation (page 757) describes how to implement a method that performs validation.

Referencing a Method That Handles a Value-Change Event

If you want a component on your page to generate a value-change event and you want that event to be handled by a backing bean method, you refer to the method using the component's `valueChangeListener` attribute.

The `name` component on the `bookcashier.jsp` page of the Duke's Bookstore application references a `ValueChangeListener` implementation that handles the event of a user entering a name in the `name` input field:

```
<h:inputText
   id="name"
   size="50"
   value="#{cashier.name}"
   required="true">
   <f:valueChangeListener type="listeners.NameChanged" />
</h:inputText>
```

For illustration, Writing a Method to Handle a Value-Change Event (page 758) describes how to implement this listener with a backing bean method instead of a listener implementation class. To refer to this backing bean method, the tag uses the `valueChangeListener` attribute:

```
<h:inputText
  id="name"
  size="50"
  value="#{cashier.name}"
  required="true"
  valueChangeListener="#{cashier.processValueChangeEvent}" />
</h:inputText>
```

The `valueChangeListener` attribute of this component tag references the `processValueChange` method of `CashierBean` using a method-binding expression. The `processValueChange` method handles the event of a user entering his name in the input field rendered by this component.

The `valueChangeListener` attribute can be used only with the tags of `UIInput` components and components whose classes extend `UIInput`.

Writing a Method to Handle a Value-Change Event (page 758) describes how to implement a method that handles a `ValueChangeEvent`.

Using Custom Objects

As a page author, you might need to use custom converters, validators, or components packaged with the application on your JSP pages.

A custom converter is applied to a component either by using the component tag's `converter` attribute or by nesting a `converter` tag inside the component's tag.

A custom validator is applied to a component by nesting either a `validator` tag or the validator's custom tag inside the component's tag.

To use a custom component, you use the custom tag associated with the component.

As explained in Setting Up a Page (page 676), you must ensure that the TLD that defines the custom tags is packaged in the application. TLD files are stored in the `WEB-INF` directory or subdirectory of the WAR file or in the `META-INF/` directory or subdirectory of a tag library packaged in a JAR.

Next, you include a `taglib` declaration so that the page has access to the tags. All custom objects for the Duke's Bookstore application are defined in bookstore.tld. Here is the `taglib` declaration that you would include on your page so that you can use the tags from this TLD:

```
<%@ taglib uri="/WEB-INF/bookstore.tld" prefix="bookstore" %>
```

When including the custom tag in the page, you can consult the TLD to determine which attributes the tag supports and how they are used.

The next three sections describe how to use the custom converter, validator, and UI components included in the Duke's Bookstore application.

Using a Custom Converter

To apply the data conversion performed by a custom converter to a particular component's value, you must either set the `converter` attribute of the component's tag to the `Converter` implementation's identifier or set the nested `converter` tag's `converterId` attribute to the `Converter` implementation's identifier. The application architect provides this identifier when registering the `Converter` with the application, as explained in Registering a Custom Converter (page 804). Creating a Custom Converter (page 744) explains how a custom converter is implemented.

The identifier for the `CreditCardConverter` is `creditCardConverter`. The `CreditCardConverter` is registered on the `ccno` component, as shown in this tag from the `bookcashier.jsp` page:

```
<h:inputText id="ccno"
    size="19"
    converter="CreditCardConverter"
    required="true">
    ...
</h:inputText>
```

By setting the `converter` attribute of a component's tag to the converter's identifier, you cause that component's local value to be automatically converted according to the rules specified in the `Converter` implementation.

A page author can use the same custom converter with any similar component by simply supplying the `Converter` implementation's identifier to the `converter` attribute of the component's tag or to the `convertId` attribute of the nested converter tag.

Using a Custom Validator

To use a custom validator in a JSP page, you must nest the validator's custom tag inside the tag of the component whose value you want to be validated by the custom validator.

Here is the `formatValidator` tag from the `ccno` field on the `bookcashier.jsp` page of the Duke's Bookstore application:

```
<h:inputText id="ccno" size="19"
  ...
  required="true">
  <bookstore:formatValidator
    formatPatterns="9999999999999999|9999 9999 9999 9999|
    9999-9999-9999-9999" />
</h:inputText>
<h:message styleClass="validationMessage"  for="ccno"/>
```

This tag validates the input of the `ccno` field against the patterns defined by the page author in the `formatPatterns` attribute.

You can use the same custom validator for any similar component by simply nesting the custom validator tag within the component tag.

Creating a Custom Validator (page 750) describes how to create the custom validator and its custom tag.

If the application developer who created the custom validator prefers to configure the attributes in the `Validator` implementation rather than allow the page author to configure the attributes from the page, the developer will not create a custom tag for use with the validator.

Instead, the page author must follow these steps:

1. Nest the `validator` tag inside the tag of the component whose data needs to be validated.
2. Set the `validator` tag's `validatorId` attribute to the ID of the validator that is defined in the application configuration resource file. Registering a Custom Validator (page 803) explains how to configure the validator in the application configuration resource file.

The following tag registers a hypothetical validator on a component using a `validator` tag and referencing the ID of the validator:

```
<h:inputText id="name" value="#{CustomerBean.name}"
      size="10" ... >
  <f:validator validatorId="customValidator" />
  ...
</h:inputText>
```

Using a Custom Component

Using a custom component on a page is similar to using a custom validator, except that custom validator tags must be nested inside component tags. In order to use the custom component in the page, you need to declare the tag library that defines the custom tag that renders the custom component. This is explained in Using Custom Objects (page 723).

The Duke's Bookstore application includes a custom image map component on the `chooselocale.jsp` page. This component allows you to select the locale for the application by clicking on a region of the image map:

```
...
<h:graphicImage id="mapImage" url="/template/world.jpg"
  alt="#{bundle.chooseLocale}"
  usemap="#worldMap" />
  <bookstore:map id="worldMap" current="NAmericas"
    immediate="true"
    action="bookstore"
    actionListener="#{localeBean.chooseLocaleFromMap}">
    <bookstore:area id="NAmerica" value="#{NA}"
      onmouseover="/template/world_namer.jpg"
      onmouseout="/template/world.jpg"
      targetImage="mapImage" />
    ...
    <bookstore:area id="France" value="#{fraA}"
      onmouseover="/template/world_france.jpg"
      onmouseout="/template/world.jpg"
      targetImage="mapImage" />
</bookstore:map>
```

The `graphicImage` tag associates an image (`world.jpg`) with an image map that is referenced in the `usemap` attribute value.

The custom map tag that represents the custom component, MapComponent, specifies the image map, and contains a set of custom area tags. Each area tag represents a custom AreaComponent and specifies a region of the image map.

On the page, the onmouseover and onmouseout attributes define the image that is displayed when the user performs the actions described by the attributes. The page author defines what these images are. The custom renderer also renders an onclick attribute.

In the rendered HTML page, the onmouseover, onmouseout, and onclick attributes define which JavaScript code is executed when these events occur. When the user moves the mouse over a region, the onmouseover function associated with the region displays the map with that region highlighted. When the user moves the mouse out of a region, the onmouseout function redisplays the original image. When the user clicks a region, the onclick function sets the value of a hidden input tag to the ID of the selected area and submits the page.

When the custom renderer renders these attributes in HTML, it also renders the JavaScript code. The custom renderer also renders the entire onclick attribute rather than let the page author set it.

The custom renderer that renders the map tag also renders a hidden input component that holds the current area. The server-side objects retrieve the value of the hidden input field and set the locale in the FacesContext instance according to which region was selected.

Chapter 20 describes the custom tags in more detail and also explains how to create the custom image map components, renderers, and tags.

19

Developing with
JavaServer Faces
Technology

$\mathbf{C}$HAPTER 18 shows how the page author can bind components to back-end objects by using the component tags and core tags on the JSP page. The application developer's responsibility is to program the back-end objects of a JavaServer Faces application. These objects include backing beans, converters, event handlers, and validators. This chapter uses the Duke's Bookstore application (see The Example JavaServer Faces Application, page 672) to explain all of the application developer's responsibilities, including

- Programming properties and methods of a backing bean
- Localizing an application
- Creating custom converters and validators
- Implementing event listeners
- Writing backing bean methods to perform navigation processing and validation and handle events

Writing Component Properties

As explained in Backing Bean Management (page 656), there are two kinds of backing bean properties: those that are bound to a component's value and those that are bound to a component instance. These properties follow JavaBeans component conventions (see JavaBeans Components, page 497).

The component tag binds the component's value to a property using its `value` attribute. The component tag binds the component instance to a property using its `binding` attribute. Using the attributes to bind components and their values to properties is discussed in Binding Component Values and Instances to External Data Sources (page 714).

To bind a component's value to a backing bean property, the type of the property must match the type of the component's value to which it is bound. For example, if a backing bean property is bound to a `UISelectBoolean` component's value, the property should accept and return a `boolean` value or a `Boolean` wrapper `Object` instance.

To bind a component instance, the property must match the component type. For example, if a backing bean property is bound to a `UISelectBoolean` instance, the property should accept and return `UISelectBoolean`.

The rest of this section explains how to write properties that can be bound to component values and component instances for the component objects described in Using the HTML Component Tags (page 680).

Writing Properties Bound to Component Values

To write a backing bean property bound to a component's value, you must know the types that the component's value can be so that you can make the property match the type of the component's value.

Table 19–1 lists all the component classes described in Using the HTML Component Tags (page 680) and the acceptable types of their values.

When page authors bind components to properties using the `value` attributes of the component tags, they need to ensure that the corresponding properties match the types of the components' values.

Table 19–1 Acceptable Types of Component Values

Component	Acceptable Types of Component Values
`UIInput, UIOutput, UISelectItem, UISelectOne`	Any of the basic primitive and numeric types or any Java programming language object type for which an appropriate `Converter` implementation is available.
`UIData`	array of beans, `List` of beans, single bean, `java.sql.ResultSet`, `javax.servlet.jsp.jstl.sql.Result`, `javax.sql.RowSet`.
`UISelectBoolean`	`boolean` or `Boolean`.
`UISelectItems`	`java.lang.String, Collection, Array, Map`.
`UISelectMany`	`array` or `List`. Elements of the `array` or `List` can be any of the standard types.

UIInput and UIOutput Properties

The following tag binds the name component to the name property of Cashier-Bean.

```
<h:inputText id="name" size="50"
  value="#{cashier.name}"
  required="true">
  <f:valueChangeListener type="listeners.NameChanged" />
</h:inputText>
```

Here is the bean property bound to the name component:

```
protected String name = null;
public void setName(String name) {
  this.name = name;
}
public String getName() {
  return this.name;
}
```

As Using the Standard Converters (page 705) describes, to convert the value of a UIInput or UIOutput component, you can either apply a converter or create the bean property bound to the component with the desired type. Here is the example tag explained in Using DateTimeConverter (page 707) that displays the date books will be shipped:

```
<h:outputText value="#{cashier.shipDate}">
  <f:convertDateTime dateStyle="full" />
</h:outputText>
```

The application developer must ensure that the property bound to the component represented by this tag has a type of `java.util.Date`. Here is the `shipDate` property in `CashierBean`:

```
protected Date shipDate;
public Date getShipDate() {
  return this.shipDate;
}
public void setShipDate(Date shipDate) {
  this.shipDate = shipDate;
}
```

See Binding Component Values and Instances to External Data Sources (page 714) for more information on applying a `Converter` implementation.

UIData Properties

`UIData` components must be bound to one of the types listed in Table 19–1. The `UIData` component from the `bookshowcart.jsp` page of the Duke's Bookstore example is discussed in the section The UIData Component (page 686). Here is part of the start tag of `dataTable` from that section:

```
<h:dataTable  id="items"
  ...
  value="#{cart.items}"
  var="item" >
```

The value-binding expression points to the `items` property of the `ShoppingCart` bean. The `ShoppingCart` bean maintains a map of `ShoppingCartItem` beans.

The getItems method from ShoppingCart populates a List with Shopping-
CartItem instances that are saved in the items map from when the customer
adds books to the cart:

```
public synchronized List getItems() {
  List results = new ArrayList();
  Iterator items = this.items.values().iterator();
  while (items.hasNext()) {
    results.add(items.next());
  }
  return (results);
}
```

All the components contained in the UIData component are bound to the properties of the ShoppingCart bean that is bound to the entire UIData component. For
example, here is the outputText tag that displays the book title in the table:

```
<h:commandLink action="#{showcart.details}">
  <h:outputText value="#{item.item.title}"/>
</h:commandLink>
```

The book title is actually a hyperlink to the bookdetails.jsp page. The outputText tag uses the value-binding expression #{item.item.title} to bind its
UIOutput component to the title property of the BookDetails bean. The first
item in the expression is the ShoppingCartItem instance that the dataTable tag
is referencing while rendering the current row. The second item in the expression refers to the item property of ShoppingCartItem, which returns a BookDetails bean. The title part of the expression refers to the title property of
BookDetails. The value of the UIOutput component corresponding to this tag is
bound to the title property of the BookDetails bean:

```
private String title = null;

public String getTitle() {
  return this.title;
}
public void setTitle(String title) {
  this.title=title;
}
```

UISelectBoolean Properties

Properties that hold the `UISelectBoolean` component's data must be of `boolean` or `Boolean` type. The example `selectBooleanCheckbox` tag from the section The UISelectBoolean Component (page 697) binds a component to a property. Here is an example that binds a component value to a property:

```
<h:selectBooleanCheckbox title="#{bundle.receiveEmails}"
  value="#{custFormBean.receiveEmails}" >
</h:selectBooleanCheckbox>
<h:outputText value="#{bundle.receiveEmails}">
```

Here is an example property that can be bound to the component represented by the example tag:

```
protected boolean receiveEmails = false;
  ...
public void setReceiveEmails(boolean receiveEmails) {
   this.receiveEmails = receiveEmails;
}
public boolean getReceiveEmails() {
   return receiveEmails;
}
```

UISelectMany Properties

Because a `UISelectMany` component allows a user to select one or more items from a list of items, this component must map to a bean property of type `List` or `array`. This bean property represents the set of currently selected items from the list of available items.

Here is the example `selectManyCheckbox` tag from Using the selectMany-Checkbox Tag (page 698):

```
<h:selectManyCheckbox
  id="newsletters"
  layout="pageDirection"
  value="#{cashier.newsletters}">
  <f:selectItems value="#{newsletters}"/>
</h:selectManyCheckbox>
```

Here is a bean property that maps to the value of this selectManyCheckbox example:

```
protected String newsletters[] = new String[0];

public void setNewsletters(String newsletters[]) {
  this.newsletters = newsletters;
}
public String[] getNewsletters() {
  return this.newsletters;
}
```

As explained in the section The UISelectMany Component (page 697), the UISelectItem and UISelectItems components are used to represent all the values in a UISelectMany component. See UISelectItem Properties (page 736) and UISelectItems Properties (page 737) for information on how to write the bean properties for the UISelectItem and UISelectItems components.

UISelectOne Properties

UISelectOne properties accept the same types as UIInput and UIOutput properties. This is because a UISelectOne component represents the single selected item from a set of items. This item can be any of the primitive types and anything else for which you can apply a converter.

Here is the example selectOneMenu tag from Using the selectOneMenu Tag (page 699):

```
<h:selectOneMenu    id="shippingOption"
  required="true"
  value="#{cashier.shippingOption}">
  <f:selectItem
    itemValue="2"
    itemLabel="#{bundle.QuickShip}"/>
  <f:selectItem
    itemValue="5"
    itemLabel="#{bundle.NormalShip}"/>
  <f:selectItem
    itemValue="7"
    itemLabel="#{bundle.SaverShip}"/>
</h:selectOneMenu>
```

Here is the property corresponding to this tag:

```
protected String shippingOption = "2";

public void setShippingOption(String shippingOption) {
   this.shippingOption = shippingOption;
}
public String getShippingOption() {
   return this.shippingOption;
}
```

Note that `shippingOption` represents the currently selected item from the list of items in the `UISelectOne` component.

As explained in the section The UISelectOne Component (page 699), the `UISelectItem` and `UISelectItems` components are used to represent all the values in a `UISelectOne` component. See UISelectItem Properties (page 736) and UISelectItems Properties (page 737) for information on how to write the backing bean properties for the `UISelectItem` and `UISelectItems` components.

UISelectItem Properties

A `UISelectItem` component represents one value in a set of values in a `UISelectMany` or `UISelectOne` component. The backing bean property that a `UISelectItem` component is bound to must be of type `SelectItem`. A `SelectItem` object is composed of an `Object` representing the value, along with two `Strings` representing the label and description of the `SelectItem` object.

The Duke's Bookstore application does not use any `UISelectItem` components whose values are bound to backing beans. The example `selectOneMenu` tag from Using the selectOneMenu Tag (page 699) contains `selectItem` tags that set the values of the list of items in the page. Here is an example bean property that can set the values for this list in the bean:

```
SelectItem itemOne = null;

SelectItem getItemOne(){
   return itemOne
}

void setItemOne(SelectItem item) {
   itemOne = item;
}
```

UISelectItems Properties

UISelectItems components are children of UISelectMany and UISelectOne components. Each UISelectItems component is composed of either a set of SelectItem instances or a set of SelectItemGroup instances. As described in Using the selectItems Tag (page 701), a SelectItemGroup is composed of a set of SelectItem instance. This section describes how to write the properties for selectItems tags containing SelectItem instances and for selectItems tags containing SelectItemGroup instance.

Properties for SelectItems Composed of SelectItem Instances

Using the selectItems Tag (page 701) describes how the newsletters list of the Duke's Bookstore application is populated using the application configuration resource file. You can also populate the SelectItems with SelectItem instances programmatically in the backing bean. This section explains how to do this.

In your backing bean, you create a list that is bound to the SelectItem component. Then you define a set of SelectItem objects, set their values, and populate the list with the SelectItem objects. Here is an example code snippet that shows how to create a SelectItems property:

```
import javax.faces.component.SelectItem;
...
protected ArrayList options = null;
protected SelectItem newsletter0 =
  new SelectItem("200", "Duke's Quarterly", "");
...
//in constructor, populate the list...
options.add(newsletter0);
options.add(newsletter1);
options.add(newsletter2);
...
public SelectItem getNewsLetter0(){
  return newsletter0;
}

void setNewsLetter0()(SelectItem firstNL){
  newsletter0 = firstNL;
}
// Other SelectItem properties
```

```
public Collection[] getOptions(){
  return options;
}
public void setOptions(Collection[] options)]{
  this.options = new ArrayList(options);
}
```

The code first initializes `options` as a list. Each newsletter property is defined with values. Then, each newsletter `SelectItem` is added to the list. Finally, the code includes the obligatory `setOptions` and `getOptions` accessor methods.

Properties for SelectItems Composed of SelectItemGroup Instances

The preceding section explains how to write the bean property for a `SelectItems` component composed of `SelectItem` instances. This section explains how to change the example property from the preceding section so that the `SelectItems` is composed of `SelectItemGroup` instances.

Let's separate the newsletters into two groups: One group includes Duke's newsletters, and the other group includes the *Innovator's Almanac* and *Random Ramblings* newsletters.

In your backing bean, you need a list that contains two `SelectItemGroup` instances. Each `SelectItemGroup` instance contains two `SelectItem` instances, each representing a newsletter:

```
import javax.faces.model.SelectItemGroup;
...
private ArrayList optionsGroup = null;

optionsGroup = new ArrayList(2);

private static final SelectItem options1[] = {
  new SelectItem("200", "Duke's Quarterly", "");
  new SelectItem("202",
      "Duke's Diet and Exercise Journal", "");
};
private static final SelectItem options2[] = {
  new SelectItem("201", "Innovator's Almanac", "");
  new SelectItem("203", "Random Ramblings", "");
};

SelectItemGroup group1 =
  new SelectItemGroup("Duke's", null, true, options1);
```

```
SelectItemGroup group2 =
  new SelectItemGroup("General Interest", null, true,
    options2);

optionsGroup.add(group1);
optionsGroup.add(group2);
...
public Collection getOptionsGroup() {
  return optionsGroup;
}
public void setOptionsGroup(Collection newGroupOptions) {
  optionsGroup = new ArrayList(newGroupOptions);
}
```

The code first initializes optionsGroup as a list. The optionsGroup list contains two SelectItemGroup objects. Each object is initialized with the label of the group appearing in the list or menu; a value; a Boolean indicating whether or not the label is disabled; and an array containing two SelectItem instances. Then each SelectItemGroup is added to the list. Finally, the code includes the setOptionsGroup and getOptionsGroup accessor methods so that the tag can access the values. The selectItems tag references the optionsGroup property to get the SelectItemGroup objects for populating the list or menu on the page.

Writing Properties Bound to Component Instances

A property bound to a component instance returns and accepts a component instance rather than a component value. Here are the tags described in Binding a Component Instance to a Bean Property (page 718) that bind components to backing bean properties:

```
<h:selectBooleanCheckbox
  id="fanClub"
  rendered="false"
  binding="#{cashier.specialOffer}" />
<h:outputLabel for="fanClub"
  rendered="false"
  binding="#{cashier.specialOfferText}"  >
  <h:outputText id="fanClubLabel"
    value="#{bundle.DukeFanClub}" />
</h:outputLabel>
```

As Binding a Component Instance to a Bean Property (page 718) explains, the `selectBooleanCheckbox` tag renders a checkbox and binds the `fanClub UISelectBoolean` component to the `specialOffer` property of `CashierBean`. The `outputLabel` tag binds the `fanClubLabel` component (which represents the checkbox's label) to the `specialOfferText` property of `CashierBean`. If the user orders more than $100 (or 100 euros) worth of books and clicks the Submit button, the `submit` method of `CashierBean` sets both components' `rendered` properties to `true`, causing the checkbox and label to display when the page is rerendered.

Because the components corresponding to the example tags are bound to the backing bean properties, these properties must match the components' types. This means that the `specialOfferText` property must be of `UIOutput` type, and the `specialOffer` property must be of `UISelectBoolean` type:

```
UIOutput specialOfferText = null;

public UIOutput getSpecialOfferText() {
   return this.specialOfferText;
}
public void setSpecialOfferText(UIOutput specialOfferText) {
   this.specialOfferText = specialOfferText;
}

UISelectBoolean specialOffer = null;

public UISelectBoolean getSpecialOffer() {
   return this.specialOffer;
}
public void setSpecialOffer(UISelectBoolean specialOffer) {
   this.specialOffer = specialOffer;
}
```

See Backing Bean Management (page 656) for more general information on component binding.

See Referencing a Method That Performs Navigation (page 720) for information on how to reference a backing bean method that performs navigation when a button is clicked.

See Writing a Method to Handle Navigation (page 755) for more information on writing backing bean methods that handle navigation.

Performing Localization

As mentioned in Using Localized Messages (page 703), data and messages in the Duke's Bookstore application have been localized for French, German, Spanish, and American English.

This section explains how to produce the localized messages as well as how to localize dynamic data and messages.

Using Localized Messages (page 703) describes how page authors access localized data from the page using the `loadBundle` tag.

If you are not familiar with the basics of localizing Web applications, see Chapter 22.

Creating a Resource Bundle

A `ResourceBundle` contains a set of localized messages. To learn how to create a `ResourceBundle`, see

```
http://java.sun.com/docs/books/tutorial/i18n/index.html
```

After you create the `ResourceBundle`, put it in the same directory as your classes. Much of the data for the Duke's Bookstore application is stored in a `ResourceBundle` called `BookstoreMessages`, located in *<INSTALL>*/j2ee-tutorial14/examples/web/bookstore/src/messages/.

Localizing Dynamic Data

The Duke's Bookstore application has some data that is set dynamically in backing beans. Because of this, the beans must load the localized data themselves; the data can't be loaded from the page.

The `message` method in `AbstractBean` is a general-purpose method that looks up localized messages used in the backing beans:

```
protected void message(String clientId, String key) {
    // Look up the requested message text
    String text = null;
```

```
    try {
      ResourceBundle bundle =
        ResourceBundle.getBundle("messages.BookstoreMessages",
          context().getViewRoot().getLocale());
      text = bundle.getString(key);
    } catch (Exception e) {
      text = "???" + key + "???";
    }
    // Construct and add a FacesMessage containing it
    context().addMessage(clientId, new FacesMessage(text));
  }
```

This method gets the current locale from the `UIViewRoot` instance of the current request and loads the localized data for the messages using the `getBundle` method, passing in the path to the `ResourceBundle` and the current locale.

The other backing beans call this method by using the key to the message that they are trying to retrieve from the resource bundle. Here is a call to the `message` method from `ShowCartBean`:

```
message(null, "Quantities Updated");
```

Localizing Messages

The JavaServer Faces API provides two ways to create messages from a `ResourceBundle`:

- You can register the `ResourceBundle` with the application configuration resource file and use a message factory pattern to examine the `ResouceBundle` and to generate localized `FacesMessage` instances, which represent single localized messages. The message factory pattern is required to access messages that are registered with the `Application` instance. Instead of writing your own message factory pattern, you can use the one included with the Duke's Bookstore application. It is called `MessageFactory` and is located in *<INSTALL>*/j2eetutorial14/examples/web/bookstore6/src/util/.

- You can use the `FacesMessage` class to get the localized string directly from the `ResourceBundle`.

Registering Messages (page 802) includes an example of registering a `ResourceBundle` in the application configuration resource file.

Creating a Message with a Message Factory

To use a message factory to create a message, follow these steps:

1. Register the `ResourceBundle` with the application. This is explained in Registering Messages (page 802).

2. Create a message factory implementation. You can simply copy the `MessageFactory` class included with the Duke's Bookstore application to your application.

3. Access a message from your application by calling the `getMessage(Faces-Context, String, Object)` method of the `MessageFactory` class method. The `MessageFactory` class uses `FacesContext` to access the `Application` instance on which the messages are registered. The `String` argument is the key that corresponds to the message in the `ResourceBundle`. The `Object` instance typically contains the substitution parameters that are embedded in the message. For example, the custom validator described in Implementing the Validator Interface (page 751) will substitute the format pattern for the {0} in this error message:

```
Input must match one of the following patterns {0}
```

Implementing the Validator Interface (page 751) gives an example of accessing messages.

Using FacesMessage to Create a Message

Instead of registering messages in the application configuration resource file, you can access the `ResourceBundle` directly from the code. The `validateEmail` method from the Coffee Break example does this:

```
...
String message = "";
...
message = CoffeeBreakBean.loadErrorMessage(context,
  CoffeeBreakBean.CB_RESOURCE_BUNDLE_NAME,
    "EMailError");
context.addMessage(toValidate.getClientId(context),
  new FacesMessage(message));
...
```

These lines also call the `loadErrorMessage` to get the message from the `ResourceBundle`. Here is the `loadErrorMessage` method from `CoffeeBreak-Bean`:

```
public static String loadErrorMessage(FacesContext context,
    String basename, String key) {
    if ( bundle == null ) {
        try {
            bundle = ResourceBundle.getBundle(basename,
                context.getViewRoot().getLocale());
        } catch (Exception e) {
            return null;
        }
    }
    return bundle.getString(key);
}
```

Creating a Custom Converter

As explained in Conversion Model (page 651), if the standard converters included with JavaServer Faces technology don't perform the data conversion that you need, you can easily create a custom converter to perform this specialized conversion.

All custom converters must implement the `Converter` interface. This implementation, at a minimum, must define how to convert data both ways between the two views of the data described in Conversion Model (page 651).

This section explains how to implement the `Converter` interface to perform a custom data conversion. To make this implementation available to the application, the application architect registers it with the application, as explained in Registering a Custom Converter (page 804). To use the implementation, the page author must register it on a component, as explained in Using a Custom Converter (page 724).

The Duke's Bookstore application uses a custom `Converter` implementation, called `CreditCardConverter`, to convert the data entered in the Credit Card Number field on the `bookcashier.jsp` page. It strips blanks and hyphens from the text string and formats it so that a blank space separates every four characters.

To define how the data is converted from the presentation view to the model view, the Converter implementation must implement the getAsObject(Faces-Context, UIComponent, String) method from the Converter interface. Here is the implementation of this method from CreditCardConverter:

```
public Object getAsObject(FacesContext context,
    UIComponent component, String newValue)
      throws ConverterException {

String convertedValue = null;
if ( newValue == null ) {
   return newValue;
}
// Since this is only a String to String conversion,
// this conversion does not throw ConverterException.

convertedValue = newValue.trim();
if ( ((convertedValue.indexOf("-")) != -1) ||
   ((convertedValue.indexOf(" ")) != -1)) {
   char[] input = convertedValue.toCharArray();
   StringBuffer buffer = new StringBuffer(50);
   for ( int i = 0; i < input.length; ++i ) {
      if ( input[i] == '-' || input[i] == ' ' ) {
         continue;
      } else {
         buffer.append(input[i]);
      }
   }
   convertedValue = buffer.toString();
}
   return convertedValue;
}
```

During the apply request values phase, when the components' decode methods are processed, the JavaServer Faces implementation looks up the component's local value in the request and calls the getAsObject method. When calling this method, the JavaServer Faces implementation passes in the current FacesContext instance, the component whose data needs conversion, and the local value as a String. The method then writes the local value to a character array, trims the hyphens and blanks, adds the rest of the characters to a String, and returns the String.

To define how the data is converted from the model view to the presentation view, the Converter implementation must implement the getAsString(FacesContext, UIComponent, Object) method from the Converter interface. Here is the implementation of this method from CreditCardConverter:

```
public String getAsString(FacesContext context,
   UIComponent component, Object value)
   throws ConverterException {

   String inputVal = null;
   if ( value == null ) {
      return null;
   }
   // value must be of the type that can be cast to a String.
   try {
      inputVal = (String)value;
   } catch (ClassCastException ce) {
      FacesMessage errMsg = MessageFactory.getMessage(
      CONVERSION_ERROR_MESSAGE_ID,
      (new Object[] { value, inputVal }));
      throw new ConverterException(errMsg.getSummary());
   }
   // insert spaces after every four characters for better
   // readability if it doesn't already exist.
   char[] input = inputVal.toCharArray();
   StringBuffer buffer = new StringBuffer(50);
   for ( int i = 0; i < input.length; ++i ) {
      if ( (i % 4) == 0 && i != 0) {
         if (input[i] != ' ' || input[i] != '-'){
            buffer.append(" ");
            // if there are any "-"'s convert them to blanks.
         } else if (input[i] == '-') {
            buffer.append(" ");
         }
      }
      buffer.append(input[i]);
   }
   String convertedValue = buffer.toString();
   return convertedValue;
}
```

During the render response phase, in which the components' encode methods are called, the JavaServer Faces implementation calls the getAsString method in order to generate the appropriate output. When the JavaServer Faces implementation calls this method, it passes in the current FacesContext, the UIComponent whose value needs to be converted, and the bean value to be converted. Because this converter does a String-to-String conversion, this method can cast the bean value to a String.

If the value cannot be converted to a `String`, the method throws an exception, passing the error message from the `ResourceBundle`, which is registered with the application. Registering Messages (page 802) explains how to register the error messages with the application. Performing Localization (page 741) explains more about working with localized messages.

If the value can be converted to a `String`, the method reads the `String` to a character array and loops through the array, adding a space after every four characters.

Implementing an Event Listener

As explained in Event and Listener Model (page 652), JavaServer Faces technology supports action events and value-change events.

Action events occur when the user activates a component that implements `ActionSource`. These events are represented by the `javax.faces.event.Action-Event` class.

Value-change events occur when the user changes the value of a `UIInput` component or a component whose class extends `UIInput`. These events are represented by the `javax.faces.event.ValueChangeEvent` class.

One way to handle these events is to implement the appropriate listener classes. Listener classes that handle the action events in an application must implement `javax.faces.event.ActionListener`. Similarly, listeners that handle the value-change events must implement `javax.faces.event.ValueChangeListener`.

This section explains how to implement the two listener classes.

If you need to handle events generated by custom components, you must implement an event handler and manually queue the event on the component as well as implement an event listener. See Handling Events for Custom Components (page 788) for more information.

Note: You need not create an `ActionListener` implementation to handle an event that results solely in navigating to a page and does not perform any other application-specific processing. See Writing a Method to Handle Navigation (page 755) for information on how to manage page navigation.

Implementing Value-Change Listeners

A `ValueChangeListener` implementation must include a `processValue-Change(ValueChangeEvent)` method. This method processes the specified `ValueChangeEvent` instance and is invoked by the JavaServer Faces implementation when the value-change event occurs. The `ValueChangeEvent` instance stores the old and the new values of the component that fired the event.

The `NameChanged` listener implementation is registered on the `name UIInput` component on the `bookcashier.jsp` page. This listener stores into session scope the name the user entered in the text field corresponding to the `name` component. When the `bookreceipt.jsp` page is loaded, it displays the first name inside the message:

    "Thank you, {0} for purchasing your books from us."

Here is part of the `NameChanged` listener implementation:

```
...
public class NameChanged extends Object implements
  ValueChangeListener {

   public void processValueChange(ValueChangeEvent event)
     throws AbortProcessingException {

     if (null != event.getNewValue()) {
        FacesContext.getCurrentInstance().
         getExternalContext().getSessionMap().
           put("name", event.getNewValue());
     }
   }
}
```

When the user enters the name in the text field, a value-change event is generated, and the `processValueChange(ValueChangeEvent)` method of the `NameChanged` listener implementation is invoked. This method first gets the ID of the component that fired the event from the `ValueChangeEvent` object. Next, it puts the value, along with an attribute name, into the session map of the `FacesContext` instance.

Registering a Value-Change Listener on a Component (page 711) explains how to register this listener onto a component.

Implementing Action Listeners

An `ActionListener` implementation must include a `processAction(Action-Event)` method. The `processAction(ActionEvent)` method processes the specified action event. The JavaServer Faces implementation invokes the `processAction(ActionEvent)` method when the action event occurs.

The Duke's Bookstore application does not use any `ActionListener` implementations. Instead, it uses method-binding expressions from `actionListener` attributes to refer to backing bean methods that handle events. This section explains how to turn one of these methods into an `ActionListener` implementation.

The `chooselocale.jsp` page allows the user to select a locale for the application by clicking on one of a set of hyperlinks. When the user clicks one of the hyperlinks, an action event is generated, and the `chooseLocaleFromLink(ActionEvent)` method of `LocaleBean` is invoked. Instead of implementing a bean method to handle this event, you can create a listener implementation to handle it. To do this, you do the following:

- Move the `chooseLocaleFromLink(ActionEvent)` method to a class that implements `ActionListener`
- Rename the method to `processAction(ActionEvent)`

The listener implementation would look something like this:

```
...
public class LocaleChangeListener extends Object implements
   ActionListener {

   private Map locales = null;

   public LocaleChangeListener() {
      locales = new HashMap();
      locales.put("NAmerica", new Locale("en", "US"));
      locales.put("SAmerica", new Locale("es", "MX"));
      locales.put("Germany", new Locale("de", "DE"));
      locales.put("France", new Locale("fr", "FR"));
   }

   public void processAction(ActionEvent event)
      throws AbortProcessingException {
```

```
            String current = event.getComponent().getId();
            FacesContext context = FacesContext.getCurrentInstance();
            context.getViewRoot().setLocale((Locale)
            locales.get(current));
    }
}
```

Registering an Action Listener on a Component (page 711) explains how to register this listener onto a component.

Creating a Custom Validator

If the standard validators don't perform the validation checking you need, you can easily create a custom validator to validate user input. As explained in Validation Model (page 654), there are two ways to implement validation code:

- Implement a backing bean method that performs the validation.
- Provide an implementation of the `Validator` interface to perform the validation.

Writing a Method to Perform Validation (page 757) explains how to implement a backing bean method to perform validation. The rest of this section explains how to implement the `Validator` interface.

If you choose to implement the `Validator` interface and you want to allow the page author to configure the validator's attributes from the page, you also must create a custom tag for registering the validator on a component.

If you prefer to configure the attributes in the implementation, you can forgo creating a custom tag and instead let the page author register the validator on a component using a `validator` tag. This tag simply refers to the `Validator` implementation, which handles the configuration of the validator's attributes. See Using a Custom Validator (page 725) for information on how the page author uses a custom validator in the page.

Usually, you will want to display an error message when data fails validation. You need to store these error messages in a `ResourceBundle`. For more information on creating a `ResourceBundle`, see Creating a Resource Bundle (page 741).

When validation fails, you can queue the error messages onto the `FacesContext` programmatically. Alternatively, you can have the application architect register the error messages using the application configuration resource file. Registering Messages (page 802) explains how to register error messages with the application.

The Duke's Bookstore application uses a general-purpose custom validator (called `FormatValidator`) that validates input data against a format pattern that is specified in the custom validator tag. This validator is used with the Credit Card Number field on the `bookcashier.jsp` page. Here is the custom validator tag:

```
<bookstore:formatValidator
  formatPatterns="9999999999999999|9999 9999 9999 9999|
    9999-9999-9999-9999"/>
```

According to this validator, the data entered in the field must be either:

- A 16-digit number with no spaces
- A 16-digit number with a space between every four digits
- A 16-digit number with hyphens between every four digits

The rest of this section describes how this validator is implemented and how to create a custom tag so that the page author can register the validator on a component.

Implementing the Validator Interface

A `Validator` implementation must contain a constructor, a set of accessor methods for any attributes on the tag, and a `validate` method, which overrides the `validate` method of the `Validator` interface.

The `FormatValidator` class also defines accessor methods for setting the attribute `formatPatterns`, which specifies the acceptable format patterns for input into the fields. In addition, the class overrides the `validate` method of the `Validator` interface. This method validates the input and also accesses the custom error messages to be displayed when the `String` is invalid.

The `validate` method performs the actual validation of the data. It takes the `FacesContext` instance, the component whose data needs to be validated, and the value that needs to be validated. A validator can validate only data of a `UIInput` component or a component that extends `UIInput`.

Here is the `validate` method from `FormatValidator`:

```
public void validate(FacesContext context, UIComponent
component, Object toValidate) {

  boolean valid = false;
```

```
    String value = null;
    if ((context == null) || (component == null)) {
        throw new NullPointerException();
    }
    if (!(component instanceof UIInput)) {
        return;
    }
    if ( null == formatPatternsList || null == toValidate) {
        return;
    }
    value = toValidate.toString();
    //validate the value against the list of valid patterns.
    Iterator patternIt = formatPatternsList.iterator();
    while (patternIt.hasNext()) {
        valid = isFormatValid(
            ((String)patternIt.next()), value);
        if (valid) {
            break;
        }
    }
    if ( !valid ) {
        FacesMessage errMsg =
            MessageFactory.getMessage(context,
                FORMAT_INVALID_MESSAGE_ID,
                    (new Object[] {formatPatterns}));
            throw new ValidatorException(errMsg);
    }
}
```

This method gets the local value of the component and converts it to a `String`. It then iterates over the `formatPatternsList` list, which is the list of acceptable patterns as specified in the `formatPatterns` attribute of the custom validator tag.

While iterating over the list, this method checks the pattern of the component's local value against the patterns in the list. If the pattern of the local value does not match any pattern in the list, this method generates an error message. It then passes the message to the constructor of `ValidatorException`. Eventually the message is queued onto the `FacesContext` instance so that the message is displayed on the page during the render response phase.

The error messages are retrieved from the `Application` instance by `Message-Factory`. An application that creates its own custom messages must provide a class, such as `MessageFactory`, that retrieves the messages from the `Application` instance. When creating your own application, you can simply copy the `MessageFactory` class from the Duke's Bookstore application to your application.

The getMessage(FacesContext, String, Object) method of MessageFac-tory takes a FacesContext, a static String that represents the key into the Properties file, and the format pattern as an Object. The key corresponds to the static message ID in the FormatValidator class:

```
public static final String FORMAT_INVALID_MESSAGE_ID =
    "FormatInvalid";
}
```

When the error message is displayed, the format pattern will be substituted for the {0} in the error message, which, in English, is

```
Input must match one of the following patterns {0}
```

Creating a Custom Tag

If you implemented a Validator interface rather than implementing a backing bean method that performs the validation, you need to do one of the following:

- Allow the page author to specify the Validator implementation to use with the validator tag. In this case, the Validator implementation must define its own properties. Using a Custom Validator (page 725) explains how to use the validator tag.

- Create a custom tag that provides attributes for configuring the properties of the validator from the page. Because the Validator implementation from the preceding section does not define its attributes, the application developer must create a custom tag so that the page author can define the format patterns in the tag.

To create a custom tag, you need to do two things:

- Write a tag handler to create and register the Validator implementation on the component.
- Write a TLD to define the tag and its attributes.

Using a Custom Validator (page 725) explains how to use the custom validator tag on the page.

Writing the Tag Handler

The tag handler associated with a custom validator tag must extend the ValidatorTag class. This class is the base class for all custom tag handlers that create `Validator` instances and register them on UI components. The `FormatValidatorTag` is the class that registers the `FormatValidator` instance.

The `FormatValidatorTag` tag handler class does the following:

- Sets the ID of the `Validator` by calling `super.setValidatorId("FormatValidator")`.
- Provides a set of accessor methods for each attribute defined on the tag.
- Implements the `createValidator` method of the `ValidatorTag` class. This method creates an instance of the validator and sets the range of values accepted by the validator.

Here is the `createValidator` method from `FormatValidatorTag`:

```
protected Validator createValidator() throws JspException {
   FormatValidator result = null;
   result = (FormatValidator) super.createValidator();
   result.setFormatPatterns(formatPatterns);
   return result;
}
```

This method first calls `super.createValidator` to get a new `Validator` and casts it to `FormatValidator`.

Next, the tag handler sets the `Validator` instance's attribute values to those supplied as the values of the `formatPatterns` tag attribute. The handler gets the attribute values from the page via the accessor methods that correspond to the attributes.

Writing the Tag Library Descriptor

To define a tag, you declare it in a tag library descriptor (TLD), which is an XML document that describes a tag library. A TLD contains information about a library and each tag contained in it. See Tag Library Descriptors (page 589) for more information about TLDs.

The custom validator tag is defined in `bookstore.tld`, located in *<INSTALL>/* `j2eetutorial14/examples/web/bookstore6/web/` directory. It contains a tag definition for `formatValidator`:

```
<tag>
   <name>formatValidator</name>
   ...
   <tag-class>taglib.FormatValidatorTag</tag-class>
```

```
<attribute>
   <name>formatPatterns</name>
   <required>true</required>
   <rtexprvalue>false</rtexprvalue>
   <type>String</type>
</attribute>
</tag>
```

The name element defines the name of the tag as it must be used in the page. The tag-class element defines the tag handler class. The attribute elements define each of the tag's attributes.

Writing Backing Bean Methods

Methods of a backing bean perform application-specific functions for components on the page. These functions include performing validation on the component's value, handling action events, handling value-change events, and performing processing associated with navigation.

By using a backing bean to perform these functions, you eliminate the need to implement the Validator interface to handle the validation or the Listener interface to handle events. Also, by using a backing bean instead of a Validator implementation to perform validation, you eliminate the need to create a custom tag for the Validator implementation. Creating a Custom Validator (page 750) describes implementing a custom validator. Implementing an Event Listener (page 747) describes implementing a listener class.

In general, it's good practice to include these methods in the same backing bean that defines the properties for the components referencing these methods. The reason is that the methods might need to access the component's data to determine how to handle the event or to perform the validation associated with the component.

This section describes the requirements for writing the backing bean methods.

Writing a Method to Handle Navigation

A backing bean method that handles navigation processing—called an action method—must be a public method that takes no parameters and returns a String, which is the logical outcome string that the navigation system uses to determine what page to display next. This method is referenced using the component tag's action attribute.

The following action method in CashierBean is invoked when a user clicks the Submit button on the bookcashier.jsp page. If the user has ordered more than $100 (or 100 euros) worth of books, this method sets the rendered properties of the fanClub and specialOffer components to true. This causes them to be displayed on the page the next time the page is rendered.

After setting the components' rendered properties to true, this method returns the logical outcome null. This causes the JavaServer Faces implementation to rerender the bookcashier.jsp page without creating a new view of the page. If this method were to return purchase (which is the logical outcome to use to advance to bookcashier.jsp, as defined by the application configuration resource file), the bookcashier.jsp page would rerender without retaining the customer's input. In this case, we want to rerender the page without clearing the data.

If the user does not purchase more than $100 (or 100 euros) worth of books or the thankYou component has already been rendered, the method returns receipt.

The default NavigationHandler provided by the JavaServer Faces implementation matches the logical outcome, as well as the starting page (bookcashier.jsp) against the navigation rules in the application configuration resource file to determine which page to access next. In this case, the JavaServer Faces implementation loads the bookreceipt.jsp page after this method returns.

```
public String submit() {
    ...
    if(cart().getTotal() > 100.00 &&
       specialOffer.isRendered() != true)
    {
        specialOfferText.setRendered(true);
        specialOffer.setRendered(true);
        return null;
    } else if (specialOffer.isRendered() == true &&
        thankYou.isRendered() != true){
        thankYou.setRendered(true);
        return null;
    } else {
        clear();
        return ("receipt");
    }
}
```

How the Pieces Fit Together (page 659) provides more detail on this example. Referencing a Method That Performs Navigation (page 720) explains how a component tag references this method. Binding a Component Instance to a Bean Property (page 718) discusses how the page author can bind these components to bean properties. Writing Properties Bound to Component Instances (page 739) discusses how to write the bean properties to which the components arc bound. Configuring Navigation Rules (page 805) provides more information on configuring navigation rules.

Writing a Method to Handle an Action Event

A backing bean method that handles an action event must be a public method that accepts an action event and returns void. This method is referenced using the component tag's actionListener attribute. Only components that implement ActionSource can refer to this method.

The following backing bean method from LocaleBean of the Duke's Bookstore application processes the event of a user clicking one of the hyperlinks on the chooselocale.jsp page:

```
public void chooseLocaleFromLink(ActionEvent event) {
    String current = event.getComponent().getId();
    FacesContext context = FacesContext.getCurrentInstance();
    context.getViewRoot().setLocale((Locale)
        locales.get(current));
}
```

This method gets the component that generated the event from the event object. Then it gets the component's ID. The ID indicates a region of the world. The method matches the ID against a HashMap object that contains the locales available for the application. Finally, it sets the locale using the selected value from the HashMap object.

Referencing a Method That Handles an Action Event (page 721) explains how a component tag references this method.

Writing a Method to Perform Validation

Rather than implement the Validator interface to perform validation for a component, you can include a method in a backing bean to take care of validating input for the component.

A backing bean method that performs validation must accept a FacesContext context, the component whose data must be validated, and the data to be validated, just as the validate method of the Validator interface does. A component refers to this method via its validator attribute. Only values of UIInput components or values of components that extend UIInput can be validated.

Here is the backing bean method of CheckoutFormBean from the Coffee Break example:

```
public void validateEmail(FacesContext context,
    UIComponent toValidate, Object value) {

    String message = "";
    String email = (String) value;
    if (email.indexOf('@') == -1) {
      ((UIInput)toValidate).setValid(false);
      message = CoffeeBreakBean.loadErrorMessage(context,
        CoffeeBreakBean.CB_RESOURCE_BUNDLE_NAME,
        "EMailError");
      context.addMessage(toValidate.getClientId(context),
        new FacesMessage(message));
    }
}
```

The validateEmail method first gets the local value of the component. It then checks whether the @ character is contained in the value. If it isn't, the method sets the component's valid property to false. The method then loads the error message and queues it onto FacesContext, associating the message with the component ID.

See Referencing a Method That Performs Validation (page 722) for information on how a component tag references this method.

Writing a Method to Handle a Value-Change Event

A backing bean that handles a value-change event must be a public method that accepts a ValueChangeEvent object and returns void. This method is referenced using the component's valueChangeListener attribute.

The Duke's Bookstore application does not have any backing bean methods that handle value-change events. It does have a `ValueChangeListener` implementation, as explained in the Implementing Value-Change Listeners (page 748) section.

For illustration, this section explains how to write a backing bean method that can replace the `ValueChangeListener` implementation.

As explained in Registering a Value-Change Listener on a Component (page 711), the `name` component of the `bookcashier.jsp` page has a `ValueChangeListener` instance registered on it. This `ValueChangeListener` instance handles the event of entering a value in the field corresponding to the component. When the user enters a value, a value-change event is generated, and the `processValueChange(ValueChangeEvent)` method of the `ValueChangeListener` class is invoked.

Instead of implementing `ValueChangeListener`, you can write a backing bean method to handle this event. To do this, you move the `processValueChange(ValueChangeEvent)` method from the `ValueChangeListener` class, called `NameChanged`, to your backing bean.

Here is the backing bean method that processes the event of entering a value in the `name` field on the `bookcashier.jsp` page:

```
public void processValueChange(ValueChangeEvent event)
    throws AbortProcessingException {
    if (null != event.getNewValue()) {
      FacesContext.getCurrentInstance().
        getExternalContext().getSessionMap().
          put("name", event.getNewValue());
    }
}
```

The page author can make this method handle the `ValueChangeEvent` object emitted by a `UIInput` component by referencing this method from the component tag's `valueChangeListener` attribute. See Referencing a Method That Handles a Value-Change Event (page 722) for more information.

20

Creating Custom UI Components

JAVASERVER Faces technology offers a rich set of standard, reusable UI components that enable page authors and application developers to quickly and easily construct UIs for Web applications. But often an application requires a component that has additional functionality or requires a completely new component. JavaServer Faces technology allows a component writer to extend the standard components to enhance their functionality or create custom components.

In addition to extending the functionality of standard components, a component writer might want to give a page author the ability to change the appearance of the component on the page. Or the component writer might want to render a component to a different client. Enabled by the flexible JavaServer Faces architecture, a component writer can separate the definition of the component behavior from its appearance by delegating the rendering of the component to a separate renderer. In this way, a component writer can define the behavior of a custom component once but create multiple renderers, each of which defines a different way to render the component.

As well as providing a means to create custom components and renderers easily, the JavaServer Faces design also makes it easy to reference them from the page through JSP custom tag library technology.

This chapter uses the image map custom component from the Duke's Bookstore application (see The Example JavaServer Faces Application, page 672) to explain how a component writer can create simple custom components, custom renderers, and associated custom tags, and take care of all the other details associated with using the components and renderers in an application.

Determining Whether You Need a Custom Component or Renderer

The JavaServer Faces implementation supports a rich set of components and associated renderers, which are enough for most simple applications. This section helps you decide whether you need a custom component or custom renderer or instead can use a standard component and renderer.

When to Use a Custom Component

A component class defines the state and behavior of a UI component. This behavior includes converting the value of a component to the appropriate markup, queuing events on components, performing validation, and other functionality.

You need to create a custom component in these situations:

- You need to add new behavior to a standard component, such as generating an additional type of event.

- You need to aggregate components to create a new component that has its own unique behavior. The new component must be a custom component. One example is a date chooser component consisting of three drop-down lists.

- You need a component that is supported by an HTML client but is not currently implemented by JavaServer Faces technology. The current release does not contain standard components for complex HTML components, such as frames; however, because of the extensibility of the component architecture, you can use JavaServer Faces technology to create components like these.

- You need to render to a non-HTML client that requires extra components not supported by HTML. Eventually, the standard HTML render kit will provide support for all standard HTML components. However, if you are rendering to a different client, such as a phone, you might need to create custom components to represent the controls uniquely supported by the client. For example, some component architectures for wireless clients include support for tickers and progress bars, which are not available on an

HTML client. In this case, you might also need a custom renderer along with the component; or you might need only a custom renderer.

You do not need to create a custom component in these cases:

- You simply need to manipulate data on the component or add application-specific functionality to it. In this situation, you should create a backing bean for this purpose and bind it to the standard component rather than create a custom component. See Backing Bean Management (page 656) for more information on backing beans.

- You need to convert a component's data to a type not supported by its renderer. See Using the Standard Converters (page 705) for more information about converting a component's data.

- You need to perform validation on the component data. Standard validators and custom validators can be added to a component by using the validator tags from the page. See Using the Standard Validators (page 712) and Creating a Custom Validator (page 750) for more information about validating a component's data.

- You need to register event listeners on components. You can either register event listeners on components using the valueChangeListener and actionListener tags, or you can point at an event-processing method on a backing bean using the component's actionListener or valueChangeListener attribute. See Implementing an Event Listener (page 747) and Writing Backing Bean Methods (page 755) for more information.

When to Use a Custom Renderer

If you are creating a custom component, you need to ensure, among other things, that your component class performs these operations:

- *Decoding*: Converting the incoming request parameters to the local value of the component

- *Encoding*: Converting the current local value of the component into the corresponding markup that represents it in the response

The JavaServer Faces specification supports two programming models for handling encoding and decoding:

- *Direct implementation*: The component class itself implements the decoding and encoding.

- *Delegated implementation*: The component class delegates the implementation of encoding and decoding to a separate renderer.

By delegating the operations to the renderer, you have the option of associating your custom component with different renderers so that you can represent the component in different ways on the page. If you don't plan to render a particular component in different ways, it's simpler to let the component class handle the rendering.

If you aren't sure whether you will need the flexibility offered by separate renderers but you want to use the simpler direct-implementation approach, you can actually use both models. Your component class can include some default rendering code, but it can delegate rendering to a renderer if there is one.

Component, Renderer, and Tag Combinations

When you create a custom component, you will usually create a custom renderer to go with it. You will also need a custom tag to associate the component with the renderer and to reference the component from the page.

In rare situations, however, you might use a custom renderer with a standard component rather than a custom component. Or you might use a custom tag without a renderer or a component. This section gives examples of these situations and summarizes what's required for a custom component, renderer, and tag.

You would use a custom renderer without a custom component if you wanted to add some client-side validation on a standard component. You would implement the validation code with a client-side scripting language, such as JavaScript, and then render the JavaScript with the custom renderer. In this situation, you need a custom tag to go with the renderer so that its tag handler can register the renderer on the standard component.

Custom components as well as custom renderers need custom tags associated with them. However, you can have a custom tag without a custom renderer or custom component. For example, suppose that you need to create a custom validator that requires extra attributes on the validator tag. In this case, the custom tag corresponds to a custom validator and not to a custom component or custom renderer. In any case, you still need to associate the custom tag with a server-side object.

Table 20–1 summarizes what you must or can associate with a custom component, custom renderer, or custom tag.

Table 20–1 Requirements for Custom Components, Custom Renderers, and Custom Tags

Custom Item	Must Have	Can Have
Custom component	Custom tag	Custom renderer or standard renderer
Custom renderer	Custom tag	Custom component or standard component
Custom JavaServer Faces tag	Some server-side object, like a component, a custom renderer, or custom validator	Custom component or standard component associated with a custom renderer

Understanding the Image Map Example

Duke's Bookstore includes a custom image map component on the `chooselocale.jsp` page. This image map displays a map of the world. When the user clicks on one of a particular set of regions in the map, the application sets the locale on the `UIViewRoot` component of the current `FacesContext` to the language spoken in the selected region. The hotspots of the map are the United States, Spanish-speaking Central and South America, France, and Germany.

Why Use JavaServer Faces Technology to Implement an Image Map?

JavaServer Faces technology is an ideal framework to use for implementing this kind of image map because it can perform the work that must be done on the server without requiring you to create a server-side image map.

In general, client-side image maps are preferred over server-side image maps for several reasons. One reason is that the client-side image map allows the browser to provide immediate feedback when a user positions the mouse over a hotspot. Another reason is that client-side image maps perform better because they don't require round-trips to the server. However, in some situations, your image map might need to access the server to retrieve data or to change the appearance of nonform controls, tasks that a client-side image map cannot do.

Because the image map custom component uses JavaServer Faces technology, it has the best of both styles of image maps: It can handle the parts of the application that need to be performed on the server, while allowing the other parts of the application to be performed on the client side.

Understanding the Rendered HTML

Here is an abbreviated version of the form part of the HTML page that the application needs to render:

```
<form id="_id0" method="post"
  action="/bookstore6/chooselocale.faces" ... >
  ...
  <img id="_id0:mapImage" src="/bookstore6/template/world.jpg"
    alt="Choose Your Preferred Locale from the Map"
    usemap="#worldMap" />
  <map name="worldMap">
    <area alt="NAmerica"
      coords="53,109,1,110,2,167,,..."
      shape="poly"
      onmouseout=
        "document.forms[0]['_id0:mapImage'].src=
          '/bookstore6/template/world.jpg'"
      onmouseover=
        "document.forms[0]['_id0:mapImage'].src=
          '/bookstore6/template/world_namer.jpg'"
      onclick=
        "document.forms[0]['worldMap_current'].
          value=
            'NAmerica';document.forms[0].submit()"
    />
    <input type="hidden" name="worldMap_current">
  </map>
  ...
</form>
```

The img tag associates an image (world.jpg) with the image map referenced in the usemap attribute value.

The map tag specifies the image map and contains a set of area tags.

Each area tag specifies a region of the image map. The onmouseover, onmouseout, and onclick attributes define which JavaScript code is executed when these events occur. When the user moves the mouse over a region, the onmouseover function associated with the region displays the map with that region highlighted. When the user moves the mouse out of a region, the onmouseout function redisplays the original image. If the user clicks on a region, the onclick function sets the value of the input tag to the ID of the selected area and submits the page.

The input tag represents a hidden control that stores the value of the currently selected area between client-server exchanges so that the server-side component classes can retrieve the value.

The server-side objects retrieve the value of worldMap_current and set the locale in FacesContext according to the region that was selected.

Understanding the JSP Page

Here is an abbreviated form of the JSP page that the image map component will use to generate the HTML page shown in the preceding section:

```
<f:view>
<f:loadBundle basename="messages.BookstoreMessages"
  var="bundle"/>
  <h:form>
    ...
    <h:graphicImage id="mapImage" url="/template/world.jpg"
      alt="#{bundle.ChooseLocale}"
      usemap="#worldMap" />
    <bookstore:map id="worldMap" current="NAmericas"
      immediate="true" action="bookstore"
      actionListener="#{localeBean.chooseLocaleFromMap}">
      <bookstore:area id="NAmerica" value="#{NA}"
        onmouseover="/template/world_namer.jpg"
        onmouseout="/template/world.jpg"
        targetImage="mapImage" />
      <bookstore:area id="SAmerica" value="#{SA}"
        onmouseover="/template/world_samer.jpg"
        onmouseout="/template/world.jpg"
        targetImage="mapImage" />
      <bookstore:area id="Germany" value="#{gerA}"
        onmouseover="/template/world_germany.jpg"
        onmouseout="/template/world.jpg"
        targetImage="mapImage" />
```

```
        <bookstore:area id="France" value="#{fraA}"
            onmouseover="/template/world_france.jpg"
            onmouseout="/template/world.jpg"
            targetImage="mapImage" />
        </bookstore:map>
      ...
    </h:form>
  </f:view>
```

The `alt` attribute of `graphicImage` maps to the localized string `"Choose Your Locale from the Map."`

The `actionListener` attribute of the `map` tag points at a method in `LocaleBean` that accepts an action event. This method changes the locale according to the area selected from the image map. The way this event is handled is explained more in Handling Events for Custom Components (page 788).

The `action` attribute specifies a logical outcome `String`, which is matched against the navigation rules in the application configuration resource file. For more information on navigation, see the section Configuring Navigation Rules (page 805).

The `immediate` attribute of the `map` tag is set to `true`, which indicates that the default `ActionListener` implementation should execute during the apply request values phase of the request-processing life cycle, instead of waiting for the invoke application phase. Because the request resulting from clicking the map does not require any validation, data conversion, or server-side object updates, it makes sense to skip directly to the invoke application phase.

The `current` attribute of the `map` tag is set to the default area, which is `NAmerica`.

Notice that the `area` tags do not contain any of the JavaScript, coordinate, or shape data that is displayed on the HTML page. The JavaScript is generated by the `AreaRenderer` class. The `onmouseover` and `onmouseout` attribute values indicate the image to be loaded when these events occur. How the JavaScript is generated is explained more in Performing Encoding (page 780).

The coordinate, shape, and alternate text data are obtained through the `value` attribute, whose value refers to an attribute in application scope. The value of this attribute is a bean, which stores the coordinate, shape, and alt data. How these beans are stored in the application scope is explained more in the next section.

Configuring Model Data

In a JavaServer Faces application, data such as the coordinates of a hotspot of an image map is retrieved from the `value` attribute via a bean. However, the shape and coordinates of a hotspot should be defined together because the coordinates are interpreted differently depending on what shape the hotspot is. Because a component's value can be bound only to one property, the `value` attribute cannot refer to both the shape and the coordinates.

To solve this problem, the application encapsulates all of this information in a set of `ImageArea` objects. These objects are initialized into application scope by the managed bean creation facility (see Backing Bean Management (page 656)). Here is part of the managed bean declaration for the `ImageArea` bean corresponding to the South America hotspot:

```
<managed-bean>
    ...
    <managed-bean-name>SA</managed-bean-name>
    <managed-bean-class>
        components.model.ImageArea
    </managed-bean-class>
    <managed-bean-scope>application</managed-bean-scope>
    <managed-property>
        <property-name>shape</property-name>
        <value>poly</value>
    </managed-property>
    <managed-property>
        <property-name>alt</property-name>
        <value>SAmerica</value>
    </managed-property>
    <managed-property>
        <property-name>coords</property-name>
        <value>89,217,95,100...</value>
    </managed-property>
</managed-bean>
```

For more information on initializing managed beans with the managed bean creation facility, see the section Application Configuration Resource File (page 792).

The `value` attributes of the `area` tags refer to the beans in the application scope, as shown in this `area` tag from `chooselocale.jsp`:

```
<bookstore:area id="NAmerica"
    value="#{NA}"
    onmouseover="/template/world_namer.jpg"
    onmouseout="/template/world.jpg" />
```

To reference the ImageArea model object bean values from the component class, you implement a getValue method in the component class. This method calls super.getValue. The superclass of AreaComponent, UIOutput, has a getValue method that does the work of finding the ImageArea object associated with AreaComponent. The AreaRenderer class, which needs to render the alt, shape, and coords values from the ImageArea object, calls the getValue method of AreaComponent to retrieve the ImageArea object.

```
ImageArea iarea = (ImageArea) area.getValue();
```

ImageArea is only a simple bean, so you can access the shape, coordinates, and alternative values by calling the appropriate accessor methods of ImageArea. Creating the Renderer Class (page 786) explains how to do this in the AreaRenderer class.

Summary of the Application Classes

Table 20–2 summarizes all the classes needed to implement the image map component.

Table 20–2 Image Map Classes

Class	Function
AreaSelectedEvent	The ActionEvent indicating that an AreaComponent from the MapComponent has been selected.
AreaTag	The tag handler that implements the area custom tag.
MapTag	The tag handler that implements the map custom tag.
AreaComponent	The class that defines AreaComponent, which corresponds to the area custom tag.
MapComponent	The class that defines MapComponent, which corresponds to the map custom tag.
AreaRenderer	This Renderer performs the delegated rendering for AreaComponent.
ImageArea	The bean that stores the shape and coordinates of the hotspots.
LocaleBean	The backing bean for the chooselocale.jsp page.

AreaSelectedEvent and AreaSelectedListener are located in *<INSTALL>*/ j2eetutorial14/examples/web/bookstore6/src/listeners. AreaTag and MapTag are located in *<INSTALL>*/j2eetutorial14/examples/web/ bookstore6/src/taglib/. AreaComponent and MapComponent are located in *<INSTALL>*/j2eetutorial14/examples/web/bookstore6/src/components/. AreaRenderer is located in *<INSTALL>*/j2eetutorial14/examples/web/ bookstore6/src/renderers/. ImageArea is located in *<INSTALL>*/ j2eetutorial14/examples/web/bookstore6/src/model/. LocaleBean is located in *<INSTALL>*/j2eetutorial14/examples/web/bookstore6/src/ backing/.

Steps for Creating a Custom Component

Before we describe how the image map works, it helps to summarize the basic steps for creating a custom component. You can apply the following steps while developing your own custom component.

1. Write a tag handler class that extends javax.faces.web-app.UIComponentTag. In this class, you need a getRendererType method, which returns the type of your custom renderer if you are using one (explained in step 4); a getComponentType method, which returns the type of the custom component; and a setProperties method, in which you set all the new attributes of your component

2. Create a tag library descriptor (TLD) that defines the custom tag.

3. Create a custom component class

4. Include the rendering code in the component class or delegate it to a renderer (explained in step 7).

5. If your component generates events, queue the event on the component.

6. Save and restore the component state.

7. Delegate rendering to a renderer if your component does not handle the rendering.

   a. Create a custom renderer class by extending javax.faces.ren-der.Renderer.

   b. Register the renderer to a render kit.

   c. Identify the renderer type in the component tag handler.

8. Register the component.

9. Create an event handler if your component generates events.

The application architect does the work of registering the custom component and the renderer. See Registering a Custom Converter (page 804) and Registering a Custom Renderer with a Render Kit (page 808) for more information. Using a Custom Component (page 726) explains how to use a custom component on a page.

Creating the Component Tag Handler

If you've created your own JSP custom tags before, creating a component tag and tag handler should be easy for you.

In JavaServer Faces applications, the tag handler class associated with a component drives the render response phase of the JavaServer Faces life cycle. For more information on the JavaServer Faces life cycle, see The Life Cycle of a JavaServer Faces Page (page 662).

The first thing that the tag handler does is to retrieve the type of the component associated with the tag. Next, it sets the component's attributes to the values given in the page. Finally, it returns the type of the renderer (if there is one) to the JavaServer Faces implementation so that the component's encoding can be performed when the tag is processed.

The image map custom component includes two tag handlers: AreaTag and MapTag. To see how the operations on a JavaServer Faces tag handler are implemented, let's take a look at MapTag:

```
public class MapTag extends UIComponentTag {
  private String current = null;
  public void setCurrent(String current) {
    this.current = current;
  }
  private String actionListener = null;
  public void setActionListener(String actionListener) {
    this.actionListener = actionListener;
  }
  private String action = null;
  public void setAction(String action) {
    this.action = action;
  }
  private String immediate = null;
```

```java
public void setImmediate(String immediate) {
   this.immediate = immediate;
}
private String styleClass = null;
public void setStyleClass(String styleClass) {
   this.styleClass = styleClass;
}
public String getComponentType() {
   return ("DemoMap");
}
public String getRendererType() {
   return ("DemoMap");
}
public void release() {
   super.release();
   current = null;
   styleClass = null;
   actionListener = null;
   action = null;
   immediate = null;
}
protected void setProperties(UIComponent component) {
   super.setProperties(component);
   MapComponent map = (MapComponent) component;
   if (styleClass != null) {
      if (isValueReference(styleClass)) {
         ValueBinding vb =
            FacesContext.getCurrentInstance().
               getApplication().
                  createValueBinding(styleClass);
         map.setValueBinding("styleClass", vb);
      } else {
         map.getAttributes().put("styleClass", styleClass);
      }
   }
   if(actionListener != null) {
      if(isValueReference(actionListener)) {
         Class args[] = {ActionEvent.class};
         MethodBinding mb =
            FacesContext.getCurrentInstance().
               getApplication().
                  createMethodBinding(actionListener, args);
         map.setActionListener(mb);
      } else {
         Object params[] = {actionListener};
         throw new javax.faces.FacesException();
      }
   }
}
```

```
        if (action != null) {
          if (isValueReference(action)) {
            MethodBinding vb = FacesContext.
              getCurrentInstance().getApplication().
                createMethodBinding(action, null);
            map.setAction(vb);
          } else {
            map.setAction(
              Util.createConstantMethodBinding(action));
          }
        }
        if (immediate != null) {
          if (isValueReference(immediate)) {
            ValueBinding vb = FacesContext.
              getCurrentInstance().getApplication().
                createValueBinding(immediate);
            map.setValueBinding("immediate", vb);
          } else {
            boolean _immediate =
              new Boolean(immediate).booleanValue();
            map.setImmediate(_immediate);
          }
        }
      }
    }
```

The first thing to notice is that MapTag extends UIComponentTag, which supports jsp.tagext.Tag functionality as well as JavaServer Faces-specific functionality. UIComponentTag is the base class for all JavaServer Faces tags that correspond to a component. Tags that need to process their tag bodies should instead subclass UIComponentBodyTag.

As explained earlier, the first thing MapTag does is to retrieve the type of the component. It uses the getComponentType operation:

```
    public String getComponentType() {
        return ("DemoMap");
    }
```

Next, the tag handler sets the component's attribute values to those supplied as tag attributes in the page. The MapTag handler gets the attribute values from the page via JavaBeans properties that correspond to the attributes. MapComponent has several attributes. Here is the property that is used to access the value of immediate:

```
    private String immediate = null;
    public void setImmediate(String immediate) {
        this.immediate = immediate;
    }
```

To pass the value of the tag attributes to `MapComponent`, the tag handler implements the `setProperties` method.

Some tag attributes can refer to literal values or use value-binding expressions, which point to values typically stored in a bean. It is recommended that you enable your component attributes to accept value-binding expressions because this is what a page author expects.

If you do make your tag attributes accept value-binding expressions, and if you are updating a property of the underlying component, then the component property must also be enabled for value-binding expressions. See Enabling Value-Binding of Component Properties (page 783) for more information. In addition, an attribute that accepts a value-binding expression must be of type `String`. This is why `immediate` is of type `String`, as shown in the code snippet.

For each `MapComponent` attribute that accepts a JavaServer Faces EL expression, the `setProperties` method must get either a `MethodBinding` or a `ValueBinding` for it from the `Application` instance. A `ValueBinding` object is used to evaluate value-binding expressions that refer to backing bean properties. A `MethodBinding` object is used to evaluate method-binding expressions that refer to backing bean methods.

For example, the value of the `actionListener` attribute must be a method-binding expression that points to a method on a backing bean that takes an `Action-Event` object as its argument. The `setProperties` method of `MapTag` creates a `MethodBinding` for the `actionListener` attribute, passing in the signature that this method must have, and it sets the `MethodBinding` object as the value of the `actionListener` attribute of `MapComponent`.

The `action` attribute can take a literal `String` or a method-binding expression that points to a backing bean method that takes no parameters and returns a literal `String`. To handle the case of the literal `String`, the `setProperties` method creates a special constant method binding around the literal `String` in order to satisfy the requirement that the argument to the `action` attribute of `Map-Component` be a `MethodBinding` instance. To handle the method-binding expression, `setProperties` creates the `MethodBinding` object as it does for the `actionListener` attribute.

`MapComponent`'s `immediate` attribute value is a value-binding expression. This expression points to a backing bean property. Therefore, `setProperties` must obtain a `ValueBinding` instance for it. After obtaining the `ValueBinding` instance, the `setProperties` method sets the value of the property on `MapComponent` by calling `MapComponent`'s `setValueBinding` method, passing in the `ValueBinding` obtained from the `Application` instance and the name of the attribute.

The following piece of `setProperties` sets the `immediate` property of MapComponent:

```
...
if (immediate != null) {
  if (isValueReference(immediate)) {
    ValueBinding vb = FacesContext.
      getCurrentInstance().getApplication().
        createValueBinding(immediate);
    map.setValueBinding("immediate", vb);
  } else {
    boolean _immediate =
      new Boolean(immediate).booleanValue();
    map.setImmediate(_immediate);
  }
}
```

Finally, the tag handler provides a renderer type—if there is a renderer associated with the component—to the JavaServer Faces implementation. It does this using the `getRendererType` method:

```
public String getRendererType() {return "DemoMap";}
```

The renderer type that is returned is the name under which the renderer is registered with the application. See Delegating Rendering to a Renderer (page 786) for more information. If your component does not have a renderer associated with it, `getRendererType` should return `null`.

It's recommended practice that all tag handlers implement a `release` method, which releases resources allocated during the execution of the tag handler. The release method of `MapTag` is as follows:

```
public void release() {
  super.release();
  current = null;
  styleClass = null;
  actionListener = null;
  immediate = null;
  action = null;
}
```

This method first calls the `UIComponentTag.release` method to release resources associated with `UIComponentTag`. Next, the method sets all attribute values to `null`.

Defining the Custom Component Tag in a Tag Library Descriptor

To define a tag, you declare it in a TLD. The Web container uses the TLD to validate the tag. The set of tags that are part of the HTML render kit are defined in the html_basic TLD.

The custom tags area and map are defined in bookstore.tld. The bookstore.tld file defines tags for all the custom components and the custom validator tag described in Creating a Custom Tag (page 753).

All tag definitions must be nested inside the taglib element in the TLD. Each tag is defined by a tag element. Here is part of the tag definition of the map tag:

```
<tag>
    <name>map</name>
    <tag-class>taglib.MapTag</tag-class>
    <attribute>
        <name>binding</name>
        <required>false</required>
        <rtexprvalue>false</rtexprvalue>
        <type>String</type>
    </attribute>
    <attribute>
        <name>current</name>
        <required>false</required>
        <rtexprvalue>false</rtexprvalue>
        <type>String</type>
    </attribute>
    <attribute>
        <name>id</name>
        <required>false</required>
        <rtexprvalue>false</rtexprvalue>
        <type>String</type>
    </attribute>
    ...
</tag>
```

At a minimum, each tag must have a name (the name of the tag) and a tag-class (the tag handler) attribute. For more information on defining tags in a TLD, please consult the Tag Library Descriptors (page 589) section of this tutorial.

Creating Custom Component Classes

As explained in When to Use a Custom Component (page 762), a component class defines the state and behavior of a UI component. The state information includes the component's type, identifier, and local value. The behavior defined by the component class includes the following:

- Decoding (converting the request parameter to the component's local value)
- Encoding (converting the local value into the corresponding markup)
- Saving the state of the component
- Updating the bean value with the local value
- Processing validation on the local value
- Queuing events

The UIComponentBase class defines the default behavior of a component class. All the classes representing the standard components extend from UIComponentBase. These classes add their own behavior definitions, as your custom component class will do.

Your custom component class must either extend UIComponentBase directly or extend a class representing one of the standard components. These classes are located in the javax.faces.component package and their names begin with UI.

If your custom component serves the same purpose as a standard component, you should extend that standard component rather than directly extend UIComponentBase. For example, suppose you want to create an editable menu component. It makes sense to have this component extend UISelectOne rather than UIComponentBase because you can reuse the behavior already defined in UISelectOne. The only new functionality you need to define is to make the menu editable.

Whether you decide to have your component extend UIComponentBase or a standard component, you might also want your component to implement one or more of these behavioral interfaces:

- ActionSource: Indicates that the component can fire an ActionEvent
- EditableValueHolder: Extends ValueHolder and specifies additional features for editable components, such as validation and emitting value-change events
- NamingContainer: Mandates that each component rooted at this component have a unique ID

- `StateHolder`: Denotes that a component has a state that must be saved between requests
- `ValueHolder`: Indicates that the component maintains a local value as well as the option of accessing data in the model tier

If your component extends `UICommand`, it automatically implements `Action-Source` and `StateHolder`. If your component extends `UIOutput` or one of the component classes that extend `UIOutput`, it automatically implements `State-Holder` and `ValueHolder`. If your component extends `UIInput`, it automatically implements `EditableValueHolder`, `StateHolder`, and `ValueHolder`. If your component extends `UIComponentBase`, it automatically implements only `State-Holder`. See the JavaServer Faces API Javadoc to find out what the other component classes implement.

If you want your component that extends `UIInput` to fire action events, your component must implement `ActionSource`.

`AreaComponent` and `MapComponent` are the two custom component classes. The `MapComponent` class extends `UICommand` and therefore implements `Action-Source`, which means it can fire action events when a user clicks on the map.

The `MapComponent` class represents the component corresponding to the map tag:

```
<bookstore:map id="worldMap" current="NAmericas"
  immediate="true"
  action="bookstore"
  actionListener="#{localeBean.chooseLocaleFromMap}">
```

The `AreaComponent` class represents the component corresponding to the area tag:

```
<bookstore:area id="NAmerica" value="#{NA}"
  onmouseover="/template/world_namer.jpg"
  onmouseout="/template/world.jpg"
  targetImage="mapImage" />
```

`MapComponent` has one or more `AreaComponent` instances as children. Its behavior consists of the following:

- Retrieving the value of the currently selected area
- Defining the properties corresponding to the component's values
- Generating an event when the user clicks on the image map
- Queuing the event
- Saving its state
- Rendering the map tag and the input tag

The rendering of the map and input tags is performed by MapRenderer, but Map-Component delegates this rendering to MapRenderer.

AreaComponent is bound to a bean that stores the shape and coordinates of the region of the image map. You'll see how all this data is accessed through the value expression in Creating the Renderer Class (page 786). The behavior of AreaComponent consists of the following:

- Retrieving the shape and coordinate data from the bean
- Setting the value of the hidden tag to the id of this component
- Rendering the area tag, including the JavaScript for the onmouseover, onmouseout, and onclick functions

Although these tasks are actually performed by AreaRenderer, AreaComponent must delegate the tasks to AreaRenderer. See Delegating Rendering to a Renderer (page 786) for more information.

The rest of this section details how MapRenderer performs encoding and decoding, how it defines properties for the component's local values, and how it saves the state of MapComponent. Handling Events for Custom Components (page 788) details how MapComponent handles events.

Since both custom components delegate their rendering, they both override the getFamily method to return the identifier of a component family, which is used with the renderer type to select the renderer for the component. The component family that getFamily returns must match that defined in the application configuration resource file. Registering a Custom Component (page 810) and Registering a Custom Renderer with a Render Kit (page 808) explain how to define the component family in the application configuration resource file.

Performing Encoding

During the render response phase, the JavaServer Faces implementation processes the encoding methods of all components and their associated renderers in the view. The encoding methods convert the current local value of the component into the corresponding markup that represents it in the response.

The UIComponentBase class defines a set of methods for rendering markup: encodeBegin, encodeChildren, and encodeEnd. If the component has child components, you might need to use more than one of these methods to render the component; otherwise, all rendering should be done in encodeEnd.

Because MapComponent is a parent component of AreaComponent, the area tags must be rendered after the beginning map tag and before the ending map tag. To accomplish this, the MapRenderer class renders the beginning map tag in encodeBegin and the rest of the map tag in encodeEnd.

The JavaServer Faces implementation automatically invokes the encodeEnd method of AreaComponent's renderer after it invokes MapRenderer's encodeBegin method and before it invokes MapRenderer's encodeEnd method. If a component needs to perform the rendering for its children, it does this in the encodeChildren method.

Here are the encodeBegin and encodeEnd methods of MapRenderer:

```
public void encodeBegin(FacesContext context,
  UIComponent component) throws IOException {
  if ((context == null)|| (component == null)){
    throw new NullPointerException();
  }
  MapComponent map=(MapComponent) component;
  ResponseWriter writer = context.getResponseWriter();
  writer.startElement("map", map);
  writer.writeAttribute("name", map.getId(),"id");
}

public void encodeEnd(FacesContext context) throws IOException
{
  if ((context == null) || (component == null)){
    throw new NullPointerException();
  }
  MapComponent map = (MapComponent) component;
  ResponseWriter writer = context.getResponseWriter();
  writer.startElement("input", map);
  writer.writeAttribute("type", "hidden", null);
  writer.writeAttribute("name",
    getName(context,map), "clientId");(
  writer.endElement("input");
  writer.endElement("map");
}
```

Notice that encodeBegin renders only the beginning map tag. The encodeEnd method renders the input tag and the ending map tag.

The encoding methods accept a UIComponent argument and a FacesContext argument. The FacesContext instance contains all the information associated with the current request. The UIComponent argument is the component that needs to be rendered. The renderer must be told what component it is rendering. So you must pass the component to the encoding methods of the renderer.

The rest of the method renders the markup to the `ResponseWriter` object, which writes out the markup to the current response. This basically involves passing the HTML tag names and attribute names to the `ResponseWriter` object as strings, retrieving the values of the component attributes, and passing these values to the `ResponseWriter` object.

The `startElement` method takes a `String` (the name of the tag) and the component to which the tag corresponds (in this case, `map`). (Passing this information to the `ResponseWriter` object helps design-time tools know which portions of the generated markup are related to which components.)

After calling `startElement`, you can call `writeAttribute` to render the tag's attributes. The `writeAttribute` method takes the name of the attribute, its value, and the name of a property or attribute of the containing component corresponding to the attribute. The last parameter can be `null`, and it won't be rendered.

The `name` attribute value of the `map` tag is retrieved using the `getId` method of `UIComponent`, which returns the component's unique identifier. The `name` attribute value of the input tag is retrieved using the `getName(FacesContext, UIComponent)` method of `MapRenderer`.

If you want your component to perform its own rendering but delegate to a renderer if there is one, include the following lines in the encoding method to check whether there is a renderer associated with this component.

```
if (getRendererType() != null) {
    super.encodeEnd(context);
    return;
}
```

If there is a renderer available, this method invokes the superclass's `encodeEnd` method, which does the work of finding the renderer. The `MapComponent` class delegates all rendering to `MapRenderer`, so it does not need to check for available renderers.

In some custom component classes that extend standard components, you might need to implement other methods in addition to `encodeEnd`. For example, if you need to retrieve the component's value from the request parameters—to, for example, update a bean's values—you must also implement the `decode` method.

Performing Decoding

During the apply request values phase, the JavaServer Faces implementation processes the decode methods of all components in the tree. The decode method extracts a component's local value from incoming request parameters and converts the value to a type that is acceptable to the component class.

A custom component class or its renderer must implement the decode method only if it must retrieve the local value or if it needs to queue events. The MapRenderer instance retrieves the local value of the hidden input field and sets the current attribute to this value by using its decode method. The setCurrent method of MapComponent queues the event by calling queueEvent, passing in the AreaSelectedEvent instance generated by MapComponent.

Here is the decode method of MapRenderer:

```
public void decode(FacesContext context, UIComponent component)
{
  if ((context == null) || (component == null)) {
    throw new NullPointerException();
  }
  MapComponent map = (MapComponent) component;
  String key = getName(context, map);
  String value = (String)context.getExternalContext().
    getRequestParameterMap().get(key);
  if (value != null)
    map.setCurrent(value);
  }
}
```

The decode method first gets the name of the hidden input field by calling get-Name(FacesContext, UIComponent). It then uses that name as the key to the request parameter map to retrieve the current value of the input field. This value represents the currently selected area. Finally, it sets the value of the MapComponent class's current attribute to the value of the input field.

Enabling Value-Binding of Component Properties

Creating the Component Tag Handler (page 772) describes how MapTag sets the component's values when processing the tag. For those component attributes that take value-binding expressions that point to a backing bean property, MapTag uses a ValueBinding instance to evaluate the expression.

To get the value of a component attribute that accepts a value-binding expression pointing to a backing bean property, the component class must get the Value-Binding instance associated with the attribute. Because MapComponent extends UICommand, the UICommand class already does the work of getting the Value-Binding instance associated with each of the attributes that it supports. However, if you have a custom component class that extends UIComponentBase, you will need to get the ValueBinding object associated with those attributes that are value-binding enabled. For example, if MapComponent extended UIComponent-Base instead of UICommand, it would need to include a method that gets the ValueBinding instance for the immediate attribute:

```
public boolean isImmediate() {
   if (this.immediateSet) {
       return (this.immediate);
   }
   ValueBinding vb = getValueBinding("immediate");
   if (vb != null) {
      Boolean value = (Boolean) vb.getValue(getFacesContext());
      return (value.booleanValue());
   } else {
       return (this.immediate);
   }
}
```

The properties corresponding to the component attribute that accepts a method-binding expression pointing to a backing bean method must accept and return a MethodBinding object. For example, if MapComponent extended UIComponent-Base instead of UICommand, it would need to provide an action property that returns and accepts a MethodBinding object:

```
public MethodBinding getAction() {
   return (this.action);
}
public void setAction(MethodBinding action) {
   this.action = action;
}
```

Saving and Restoring State

Because component classes implement `StateHolder`, they must implement the `saveState(FacesContext)` and `restoreState(FacesContext, Object)` methods to help the JavaServer Faces implementation save and restore the state of components across multiple requests.

To save a set of values, you must implement the `saveState(FacesContext)` method. This method is called during the render response phase, during which the state of the response is saved for processing on subsequent requests. Here is the method from `MapComponent`:

```
public Object saveState(FacesContext context) {
    Object values[] = new Object[2];
    values[0] = super.saveState(context);
    values[1] = current;
    return (values);
}
```

This method initializes an array, which will hold the saved state. It next saves all of the state associated with `MapComponent`.

A component that implements `StateHolder` must also provide an implementation for `restoreState(FacesContext, Object)`, which restores the state of the component to that saved with the `saveState(FacesContext)` method. The `restoreState(FacesContext, Object)` method is called during the restore view phase, during which the JavaServer Faces implementation checks whether there is any state that was saved during the last render response phase and needs to be restored in preparation for the next postback. Here is the `restoreState(FacesContext, Object)` method from `MapComponent`:

```
public void restoreState(FacesContext context, Object state) {
    Object values[] = (Object[]) state;
    super.restoreState(context, values[0]);
    current = (String) values[1];
}
```

This method takes a `FacesContext` instance and an `Object` instance, representing the array that is holding the state for the component. This method sets the component's properties to the values saved in the `Object` array.

When you implement these methods in your component class, be sure to specify in the deployment descriptor where you want the state to be saved: either client or server. If state is saved on the client, the state of the entire view is rendered to a hidden field on the page.

To specify where state is saved for a particular Web application, you need to launch `deploytool`, select the Web application from the tree, and set its `javax.faces.STATE-SAVING-METHOD` context parameter to either client or server. See Specifying Where State Is Saved (page 815) for more information on specifying where state is saved using `deploytool`.

Delegating Rendering to a Renderer

Both `MapComponent` and `AreaComponent` delegate all of their rendering to a separate renderer. The section Performing Encoding (page 780) explains how `MapRenderer` performs the encoding for `MapComponent`. This section explains in detail the process of delegating rendering to a renderer using `AreaRenderer`, which performs the rendering for `AreaComponent`.

To delegate rendering, you perform these tasks:

- Create the `Renderer` class
- Register the renderer with a render kit (explained in Registering a Custom Renderer with a Render Kit, page 808)
- Identify the renderer type in the component's tag handler

Creating the Renderer Class

When delegating rendering to a renderer, you can delegate all encoding and decoding to the renderer, or you can choose to do part of it in the component class. The `AreaComponent` class delegates encoding to the `AreaRenderer` class.

To perform the rendering for `AreaComponent`, `AreaRenderer` must implement an `encodeEnd` method. The `encodeEnd` method of `AreaRenderer` retrieves the shape, coordinates, and alternative text values stored in the `ImageArea` bean that is bound to `AreaComponent`. Suppose that the `area` tag currently being rendered has a `value` attribute value of "fraA." The following line from `encodeEnd` gets the value of the attribute "fraA" from the `FacesContext` instance.

```
ImageArea ia = (ImageArea)area.getValue();
```

The attribute value is the `ImageArea` bean instance, which contains the shape, coordinates, and alt values associated with the `fraA AreaComponent` instance. *Configuring Model Data* (page 769) describes how the application stores these values.

After retrieving the `ImageArea` object, it renders the values for `shape`, `coords`, and `alt` by simply calling the associated accessor methods and passing the returned values to the `ResponseWriter` object, as shown by these lines of code, which write out the shape and coordinates:

```
writer.startElement("area", area);
writer.writeAttribute("alt", iarea.getAlt(), "alt");
writer.writeAttribute("coords", iarea.getCoords(), "coords");
writer.writeAttribute("shape", iarea.getShape(), "shape");
```

The `encodeEnd` method also renders the JavaScript for the `onmouseout`, `onmouseover`, and `onclick` attributes. The page author need only provide the path to the images that are to be loaded during an `onmouseover` or `onmouseout` action:

```
<d:area id="France" value="#{fraA}"
   onmouseover="/template/world_france.jpg"
   onmouseout="/template/world.jpg" targetImage="mapImage" />
```

The `AreaRenderer` class takes care of generating the JavaScript for these actions, as shown in the following code from `encodeEnd`. The JavaScript that `AreaRenderer` generates for the `onclick` action sets the value of the hidden field to the value of the current area's component ID and submits the page.

```
sb = new StringBuffer("document.forms[0]['").
   append(targetImageId).append("'].src='");
sb.append(getURI(context,
   (String) area.getAttributes().get("onmouseout")));
sb.append("'");
writer.writeAttribute("onmouseout", sb.toString(),
   "onmouseout");
sb = new StringBuffer("document.forms[0]['").
   append(targetImageId).append("'].src='");
sb.append(getURI(context,
   (String) area.getAttributes().get("onmouseover")));
sb.append("'");
writer.writeAttribute("onmouseover", sb.toString(),
   "onmouseover");
sb = new StringBuffer("document.forms[0]['");
sb.append(getName(context, area));
```

```
sb.append("'].value='");
sb.append(iarea.getAlt());
sb.append("'; document.forms[0].submit()");
writer.writeAttribute("onclick", sb.toString(), "value");
writer.endElement("area");
```

By submitting the page, this code causes the JavaServer Faces life cycle to return back to the restore view phase. This phase saves any state information—including the value of the hidden field—so that a new request component tree is constructed. This value is retrieved by the decode method of the MapComponent class. This decode method is called by the JavaServer Faces implementation during the apply request values phase, which follows the restore view phase.

In addition to the encodeEnd method, AreaRenderer contains an empty constructor. This is used to create an instance of AreaRenderer so that it can be added to the render kit.

Note that AreaRenderer extends BaseRenderer, which in turn extends Renderer. It contains definitions of the Renderer class methods so that you don't have to include them in your renderer class.

Identifying the Renderer Type

During the render response phase, the JavaServer Faces implementation calls the getRendererType method of the component's tag to determine which renderer to invoke, if there is one.

The getRendererType method of the AreaTag class must return the type associated with AreaRenderer. Recall that you identified this type when you registered AreaRenderer with the render kit. Here is the getRendererType method from the AreaTag class:

```
public String getRendererType() { return ("DemoArea");}
```

Handling Events for Custom Components

As explained in Implementing an Event Listener (page 747), events are automatically queued on standard components that fire events. A custom component, on the other hand, must manually queue events from its decode method if it fires events.

Performing Decoding (page 783) explains how to queue an event on MapComponent using its decode method. This section explains how to write the class representing the event of clicking on the map and how to write the method that processes this event.

As explained in Understanding the JSP Page (page 767), the actionListener attribute of the map tag points to the chooseLocaleFromMap method of the bean LocaleBean. This method processes the event of clicking the image map. Here is the chooseLocaleFromMap method of LocaleBean:

```
public void chooseLocaleFromMap(ActionEvent actionEvent) {
   AreaSelectedEvent event = (AreaSelectedEvent) actionEvent;
   String current = event.getMapComponent().getCurrent();
   FacesContext context = FacesContext.getCurrentInstance();
   context.getViewRoot().setLocale((Locale)
      locales.get(current));
}
```

When the JavaServer Faces implementation calls this method, it passes in an ActionEvent object that represents the event generated by clicking on the image map. Next, it casts it to an AreaSelectedEvent object. Then this method gets the MapComponent associated with the event. It then gets the value of the Map-Component's current attribute, which indicates the currently selected area. The method then uses the value of the current property to get the Locale object from a HashMap object, which is constructed elsewhere in the LocaleBean class. Finally the method sets the locale of the FacesContext instance to the Locale obtained from the HashMap object.

In addition to the method that processes the event, you need the event class itself. This class is very simple to write: You have it extend ActionEvent and provide a constructor that takes the component on which the event is queued and a method that returns the component. Here is the AreaSelectedEvent class used with the image map:

```
public class AreaSelectedEvent extends ActionEvent {
   ...
   public AreaSelectedEvent(MapComponent map) {
      super(map);
   }
   public MapComponent getMapComponent() {
      return ((MapComponent) getComponent());
   }
}
```

As explained in the section Creating Custom Component Classes (page 778), in order for `MapComponent` to fire events in the first place, it must implement `ActionSource`. Because `MapComponent` extends `UICommand`, it also implements `ActionSource`.

21

Configuring JavaServer Faces Applications

THE responsibilities of the application architect include the following:

- Registering back-end objects with the application so that all parts of the application have access to them.
- Configuring backing beans and model beans so that they are instantiated with the proper values when a page makes reference to them.
- Defining navigation rules for each of the pages in the application so that the application has a smooth page flow.
- Packaging the application to include all the pages, objects, and other files so that the application can be deployed on any compliant container.

This chapter explains how to perform all the responsibilities of the application architect.

Application Configuration Resource File

JavaServer Faces technology provides a portable configuration format (as an XML document) for configuring resources. An application architect creates one or more files, called *application configuration resource files*, that use this format to register and configure objects and to define navigation rules. An application configuration resource file is usually called `faces-config.xml`.

The application configuration resource file must be valid against the DTD located at `http://java.sun.com/dtd/web-facesconfig_1_0.dtd`. In addition, each file must include the following, in this order:

- The XML version number:
  `<?xml version="1.0"?>`
- This `DOCTYPE` declaration:
  ```
  <!DOCTYPE faces-config PUBLIC
  "-//Sun Microsystems, Inc.//DTD JavaServer Faces Config 1.0//
  EN"
  "http://java.sun.com/dtd/web-facesconfig_1_0.dtd">
  ```
- A `faces-config` tag enclosing all the other declarations:
  ```
  <faces-config>
  ...
  </faces-config>
  ```

You can have more than one application configuration resource file. The Java-Server Faces implementation finds the file or files by looking for the following:

- A resource named `/META-INF/faces-config.xml` in any of the JAR files in the Web application's `/WEB-INF/lib/` directory and in parent class loaders. If a resource with this name exists, it is loaded as a configuration resource. This method is practical for a packaged library containing some components and renderers.
- A context initialization parameter, `javax.faces.application.CONFIG_FILES`, that specifies one or more (comma-delimited) paths to multiple configuration files for your Web application. This method will most likely be used for enterprise-scale applications that delegate to separate groups the responsibility for maintaining the file for each portion of a big application.
- A resource named `faces-config.xml` in the `/WEB-INF/` directory of your application. This is the way most simple applications will make their configuration files available.

To access resources registered with the application, an application developer uses an instance of the `Application` class, which is automatically created for each application. The `Application` instance acts as a centralized factory for resources that are defined in the XML file.

When an application starts up, the JavaServer Faces implementation creates a single instance of the `Application` class and configures it with the information you configure in the application configuration resource file.

Configuring Beans

To instantiate backing beans used in a JavaServer Faces application and store them in scope, you use the managed bean creation facility. This facility is configured in the application configuration resource file using `managed-bean` XML elements to define each bean. This file is processed at application startup time. When a page references a bean, the JavaServer Faces implementation initializes it according to its configuration in the application configuration resource file.

With the managed bean creation facility, you can

- Create beans in one centralized file that is available to the entire application, rather than conditionally instantiate beans throughout the application.
- Customize the bean's properties without any additional code.
- When a managed bean is created, customize the bean's property values directly from within the configuration file.
- Using `value` elements, set the property of one managed bean to be the result of evaluating another value-binding expression.

This section shows you how to initialize backing beans using the managed bean creation facility. Writing Component Properties (page 730) explains how to write backing bean properties. Writing Backing Bean Methods (page 755) explains how to write backing bean methods. Binding Component Values and Instances to External Data Sources (page 714) explains how to reference a managed bean from the component tags.

Using the managed-bean Element

You create a backing bean using a `managed-bean` element, which represents an instance of a bean class that must exist in the application. At runtime, the JavaServer Faces implementation processes the `managed-bean` element. If a page references the bean, the JavaServer Faces implementation instantiates the bean as specified by the element configuration if no instance exists.

Here is an example managed bean configuration from the Duke's Bookstore application:

```
<managed-bean>
  <managed-bean-name> NA </managed-bean-name>
    <managed-bean-class>
      model.ImageArea
    </managed-bean-class>
    <managed-bean-scope> application </managed-bean-scope>
    <managed-property>
      <property-name>shape</property-name>
      <value>poly</value>
    </managed-property>
    ...
  </managed-bean-name>
</managed-bean>
```

The `managed-bean-name` element defines the key under which the bean will be stored in a scope. For a component to map to this bean, the component tag's `value` attribute must match the `managed-bean-name` up to the first period. For example, this `value` expression maps to the `shape` property of `ImageArea`:

```
value="#{NA.shape}"
```

The part before the . matches the `managed-bean-name` of `ImageArea`. Using the HTML Component Tags (page 680) has more examples of using `value` to bind components to bean properties.

The `managed-bean-class` element defines the fully qualified name of the Java-Beans component class used to instantiate the bean. It is the application developer's responsibility to ensure that the class complies with the configuration of the bean in the application configuration resource file. For example, the property definitions must match those configured for the bean.

The `managed-bean-scope` element defines the scope in which the bean will be stored. The four acceptable scopes are `none`, `request`, `session`, or `application`. If you define the bean with a `none` scope, the bean is instantiated anew each time it is referenced, and so it does not get saved in any scope. One reason to use a scope of `none` is that a managed bean references another managed bean. The second bean should be in `none` scope if it is supposed to be created only when it is referenced. See Initializing Managed Bean Properties (page 799) for an example of initializing a managed bean property.

The managed-bean element can contain zero or more managed-property elements, each corresponding to a property defined in the bean class. These elements are used to initialize the values of the bean properties. If you don't want a particular property initialized with a value when the bean is instantiated, do not include a managed-property definition for it in your application configuration resource file.

If a managed-bean element does not contain other managed-bean elements, it can contain one map-entries element or list-entries element. The map-entries element configures a set of beans that are instances of Map. The list-entries element configures a set of beans that are instances of List.

To map to a property defined by a managed-property element, you must ensure that the part of a component tag's value expression after the . matches the managed-property element's property-name element. In the earlier example, the shape property is initialized with the value poly. The next section explains in more detail how to use the managed-property element.

Initializing Properties using the managed-property Element

A managed-property element must contain a property-name element, which must match the name of the corresponding property in the bean. A managed-property element must also contain one of a set of elements (listed in Table 21–1) that defines the value of the property. This value must be of the same type as that defined for the property in the corresponding bean. Which element you use to define the value depends on the type of the property defined in the bean. Table 21–1 lists all the elements used to initialize a value.

Table 21–1   Subelements of managed-property Elements that Define Property Values

Element	Value that it Defines
list-entries	Defines the values in a list
map-entries	Defines the values of a map
null-value	Explicitly sets the property to null
value	Defines a single value, such as a String or int, or a JavaServer Faces EL expression

Using the managed-bean Element (page 793) includes an example of initializing `String` properties using the `value` subelement. You also use the `value` subelement to initialize primitive and other reference types. The rest of this section describes how to use the `value` subelement and other subelements to initialize properties of type `java.util.Map`, `array`, and `Collection`, as well as initialization parameters.

Referencing an Initialization Parameter

Another powerful feature of the managed bean creation facility is the ability to reference implicit objects from a managed bean property.

Suppose that you have a page that accepts data from a customer, including the customer's address. Suppose also that most of your customers live in a particular area code. You can make the area code component render this area code by saving it in an implicit object and referencing it when the page is rendered.

You can save the area code as an initial default value in the context `initParam` implicit object by adding a context parameter to your Web application and setting its value using `deploytool`. For example, to set a context parameter called `defaultAreaCode` to `650`, launch `deploytool`, open the Web application, select the Web application from the tree, select the Context tab, add a new context parameter, and enter `defaultAreaCode` in the Coded Parameter field, and `650` in the Value field.

Next, you write a `managed-bean` declaration that configures a property that references the parameter:

```
<managed-bean>
  <managed-bean-name>customer</managed-bean-name>
    <managed-bean-class>CustomerBean</managed-bean-class>
    <managed-bean-scope>request</managed-bean-scope>
    <managed-property>
       <property-name>areaCode</property-name>
          <value> #{initParam.defaultAreaCode}</value>
       </managed-property>
       ...
</managed-bean>
```

To access the area code at the time the page is rendered, refer to the property from the `area` component tag's `value` attribute:

```
<h:inputText id=area value="#{customer.areaCode}"
```

Retrieving values from other implicit objects is done in a similar way. See Table 18–9 for a list of implicit objects.

Initializing Map Properties

The `map-entries` element is used to initialize the values of a bean property with a type of `java.util.Map` if the `map-entries` element is used within a `managed-property` element. Here is the definition of `map-entries` from the `web-facesconfig_1_0.dtd`, located at `http://java.sun.com/dtd/web-facesconfig_1_0.dtd` that defines the application configuration resource file:

```
<!ELEMENT map-entries (key-class?, value-class?, map-entry*) >
```

As this definition shows, a `map-entries` element contains an optional `key-class` element, an optional `value-class` element, and zero or more `map-entry` elements.

Here is the definition of `map-entry` from the DTD:

```
<!ELEMENT map-entry (key, (null-value|value )) >
```

According to this definition, each of the `map-entry` elements must contain a `key` element and either a `null-value` or `value` element. Here is an example that uses the `map-entries` element:

```
<managed-bean>
  ...
  <managed-property>
    <property-name>prices</property-name>
    <map-entries>
      <map-entry>
        <key>My Early Years: Growing Up on *7</key>
        <value>30.75</value>
      </map-entry>
      <map-entry>
        <key>Web Servers for Fun and Profit</key>
        <value>40.75</value>
      </map-entry>
    </map-entries>
  </managed-property>
</managed-bean>
```

The map that is created from this `map-entries` tag contains two entries. By default, all the keys and values are converted to `java.lang.String`. If you want to specify a different type for the keys in the map, embed the `key-class` element just inside the `map-entries` element:

```
<map-entries>
  <key-class>java.math.BigDecimal</key-class>
  ...
</map-entries>
```

This declaration will convert all the keys into `java.math.BigDecimal`. Of course, you must make sure that the keys can be converted to the type that you specify. The key from the example in this section cannot be converted to a `java.math.BigDecimal` because it is a `String`.

If you also want to specify a different type for all the values in the map, include the `value-class` element after the `key-class` element:

```
<map-entries>
  <key-class>int</key-class>
  <value-class>java.math.BigDecimal</value-class>
  ...
</map-entries>
```

Note that this tag sets only the type of all the `value` subelements.

The first `map-entry` in the preceding example includes a `value` subelement. The `value` subelement defines a single value, which will be converted to the type specified in the bean.

The second `map-entry` defines a `value` element, which references a property on another bean. Referencing another bean from within a bean property is useful for building a system from fine-grained objects. For example, a request-scoped form-handling object might have a pointer to an application-scoped database mapping object. Together the two can perform a form-handling task. Note that including a reference to another bean will initialize the bean if it does not already exist.

Instead of using a `map-entries` element, it is also possible to assign the entire map using a `value` element that specifies a map-typed expression.

Initializing Array and List Properties

The `values` element is used to initialize the values of an `array` or `List` property. Each individual value of the array or `List` is initialized using a `value` or `null-value` element. Here is an example:

```
<managed-bean>
   ...
   <managed-property>
      <property-name>books</property-name>
      <values>
         <value-type>java.lang.String</value-type>
         <value>Web Servers for Fun and Profit</value>
         <value>#{myBooks.bookId[3]}</value>
         <null-value/>
      </values>
   </managed-property>
</managed-bean>
```

This example initializes an `array` or a `List`. The type of the corresponding property in the bean determines which data structure is created. The `values` element defines the list of values in the `array` or `List`. The `value` element specifies a single value in the `array` or `List` and can reference a property in another bean. The `null-value` element will cause the `setBooks` method to be called with an argument of `null`. A `null` property cannot be specified for a property whose data type is a Java primitive, such as `int` or `boolean`.

Initializing Managed Bean Properties

Sometimes you might want to create a bean that also references other managed beans so that you can construct a graph or a tree of beans. For example, suppose that you want to create a bean representing a customer's information, including the mailing address and street address, each of which is also a bean. The following `managed-bean` declarations create a `CustomerBean` instance that has two `AddressBean` properties: one representing the mailing address, and the other representing the street address. This declaration results in a tree of beans with `CustomerBean` as its root and the two `AddressBean` objects as children.

```
<managed-bean>
   <managed-bean-name>customer</managed-bean-name>
   <managed-bean-class>
      com.mycompany.mybeans.CustomerBean
   </managed-bean-class>
```

```
    <managed-bean-scope> request </managed-bean-scope>
    <managed-property>
       <property-name>mailingAddress</property-name>
       <value> #{addressBean}</value>
    </managed-property>
    <managed-property>
       <property-name>streetAddress</property-name>
       <value> #{addressBean}</value>
    </managed-property>
    <managed-property>
       <property-name>customerType</property-name>
       <value>New</value>
    </managed-property>
  </managed-bean>
  <managed-bean>
    <managed-bean-name>addressBean</managed-bean-name>
    <managed-bean-class>
       com.mycompany.mybeans.AddressBean
    </managed-bean-class>
    <managed-bean-scope> none </managed-bean-scope>
    <managed-property>
       <property-name>street</property-name>
       <null-value/>
    <managed-property>
    ...
  </managed-bean>
```

The first `CustomerBean` declaration (with the `managed-bean-name` of `customer`) creates a `CustomerBean` in request scope. This bean has two properties: `mailingAddress` and `streetAddress`. These properties use the `value` element to reference a bean named `addressBean`.

The second managed bean declaration defines an `AddressBean` but does not create it because its `managed-bean-scope` element defines a scope of `none`. Recall that a scope of `none` means that the bean is created only when something else references it. Because both the `mailingAddress` and the `streetAddress` properties reference `addressBean` using the `value` element, two instances of `AddressBean` are created when `CustomerBean` is created.

When you create an object that points to other objects, do not try to point to an object with a shorter life span because it might be impossible to recover that scope's resources when it goes away. A session-scoped object, for example, cannot point to a request-scoped object. And objects with `none` scope have no effective life span managed by the framework, so they can point only to other `none` scoped objects. Table 21–2 outlines all of the allowed connections.

Table 21–2 Allowable Connections Between Scoped Objects

An Object of This Scope	May Point to an Object of This Scope
none	none
application	none, application
session	none, application, session
request	none, application, session, request

Initializing Maps and Lists

In addition to configuring `Map` and `List` properties, you can also configure a `Map` and a `List` directly so that you can reference them from a tag rather than referencing a property that wraps a `Map` or a `List`.

The Duke's Bookstore application configures a `List` to initialize the list of free newsletters, from which users can choose a set of newsletters to subscribe to on the `bookcashier.jsp` page:

```
<managed-bean>
  ...
<managed-bean-name>newsletters</managed-bean-name>
  <managed-bean-class>
     java.util.ArrayList
  </managed-bean-class>
  <managed-bean-scope>application</managed-bean-scope>
  <list-entries>
     <value-class>javax.faces.model.SelectItem</value-class>
     <value>#{newsletter0}</value>
     <value>#{newsletter1}</value>
     <value>#{newsletter2}</value>
     <value>#{newsletter3}</value>
  </list-entries>
</managed-bean>
<managed-bean>
  <managed-bean-name>newsletter0</managed-bean-name>
  <managed-bean-class>
     javax.faces.model.SelectItem
  </managed-bean-class>
  <managed-bean-scope>none</managed-bean-scope>
```

```
    <managed-property>
        <property-name>label</property-name>
        <value>Duke's Quarterly</value>
    </managed-property>
    <managed-property>
        <property-name>value</property-name>
        <value>200</value>
    </managed-property>
</managed-bean>
...
```

This configuration initializes a List called newsletters. This list is composed
of SelectItem instances, which are also managed beans. See The UISelectItem,
UISelectItems, and UISelectItemGroup Components (page 700) for more information on SelectItem. Note that, unlike the example in Initializing Map Properties (page 797), the newsletters list is not a property on a managed bean. (It is
not wrapped with a managed-property element.) Instead, the list is the managed
bean.

Registering Messages

If you create custom messages, you must make them available at application
startup time. You do this in one of two ways: by queuing the message onto the
FacesContext instance programmatically (as described in Performing Localization, page 741) or by registering the messages with your application using the
application configuration resource file.

Here is the part of the file that registers the messages for the Duke's Bookstore
application:

```
<application>
    <message-bundle>
        resources.ApplicationMessages
    </message-bundle>
    <locale-config>
        <default-locale>en</default-locale>
        <supported-locale>es</supported-locale>
    </locale-config>
</application>
```

This set of elements will cause your Application instance to be populated
with the messages contained in the specified ResourceBundle, which is
resources.ApplicationMessages.

The `message-bundle` element represents a set of localized messages. It must contain the fully qualified path to the `ResourceBundle` containing the localized messages—in this case, `resources.ApplicationMessages`.

The `locale-config` element lists the default locale and the other supported locales. The `locale-config` element enables the system to find the correct locale based on the browser's language settings. Duke's Bookstore manually sets the locale and so it overrides these settings. Therefore, it's not necessary to use `locale-config` to specify the default or supported locales in Duke's Bookstore.

The `supported-locale` and `default-locale` tags accept the lowercase, two-character codes as defined by ISO-639 (see `http://www.ics.uci.edu/pub/ietf/http/related/iso639.txt`). Make sure that your `ResourceBundle` actually contains the messages for the locales that you specify with these tags.

To access the localized message, the application developer merely references the key of the message from the resource bundle. See Performing Localization (page 741) for more information.

Registering a Custom Validator

If the application developer provides an implementation of the `Validator` interface to perform the validation, you must register this custom validator in the application configuration resource file by using the `validator` XML element:

```
<validator>
  ...
  <validator-id>FormatValidator</validator-id>
  <validator-class>
    validators.FormatValidator
  </validator-class>
  <attribute>
    ...
    <attribute-name>formatPatterns</attribute-name>
    <attribute-class>java.lang.String</attribute-class>
  </attribute>
</validator>
```

The `validator-id` and `validator-class` elements are required subelements. The `validator-id` element represents the identifier under which the `Validator` class should be registered. This ID is used by the tag class corresponding to the custom `validator` tag.

The `validator-class` element represents the fully qualified class name of the `Validator` class.

The `attribute` element identifies an attribute associated with the `Validator` implementation. It has required `attribute-name` and `attribute-class` subelements. The `attribute-name` element refers to the name of the attribute as it appears in the `validator` tag. The `attribute-class` element identifies the Java type of the value associated with the attribute.

Creating a Custom Validator (page 750) explains how to implement the `Validator` interface.

Using a Custom Validator (page 725) explains how to reference the validator from the page.

Registering a Custom Converter

As is the case with a custom validator, if the application developer creates a custom converter, you must register it with the application. Here is the converter configuration for `CreditCardConverter` from the Duke's Bookstore application:

```
<converter>
  <description>
    Converter for credit card numbers
    that normalizes the input to a standard
    format
  </description>
  <converter-id>creditcard</converter-id>
  <converter-class>
    converters.CreditCardConverter
  </converter-class>
</converter>
```

The `converter` element represents a `Converter` implementation and contains required `converter-id` and `converter-class` elements.

The `converter-id` element identifies an ID that is used by the `converter` attribute of a UI component tag to apply the converter to the component's data. Using a Custom Converter (page 724) includes an example of referencing the custom converter from a component tag.

The `converter-class` element identifies the `Converter` implementation.

Creating a Custom Converter (page 744) explains how to create a custom converter.

Configuring Navigation Rules

As explained in Navigation Model (page 654), navigation is a set of rules for choosing the next page to be displayed after a button or hyperlink component is clicked. Navigation rules are defined in the application configuration resource file.

Each navigation rule specifies how to navigate from one page to a set of other pages. The JavaServer Faces implementation chooses the proper navigation rule according to which page is currently displayed.

After the proper navigation rule is selected, the choice of which page to access next from the current page depends on the action method that was invoked when the component was clicked and the logical outcome that is referenced by the component's tag or was returned from the action method.

The outcome can be anything the developer chooses, but Table 21–3 lists some outcomes commonly used in Web applications.

Usually, the action method performs some processing on the form data of the current page. For example, the method might check whether the user name and password entered in the form match the user name and password on file. If they match, the method returns the outcome `success`. Otherwise, it returns the outcome `failure`. As this example demonstrates, both the method used to process the action and the outcome returned are necessary to determine the proper page to access.

Table 21–3 Common Outcome Strings

Outcome	What It Means
`success`	Everything worked. Go on to the next page.
`failure`	Something is wrong. Go on to an error page.
`logon`	The user needs to log on first. Go on to the logon page.
`no results`	The search did not find anything. Go to the search page again.

Here is a navigation rule that could be used with the example just described:

```
<navigation-rule>
  <from-view-id>/logon.jsp</from-view-id>
  <navigation-case>
    <from-action>#{LogonForm.logon}</from-action>
    <from-outcome>success</from-outcome>
    <to-view-id>/storefront.jsp</to-view-id>
  </navigation-case>
  <navigation-case>
    <from-action>#{LogonForm.logon}</from-action>
    <from-outcome>failure</from-outcome>
    <to-view-id>/logon.jsp</to-view-id>
  </navigation-case>
</navigation-rule>
```

This navigation rule defines the possible ways to navigate from logon.jsp. Each navigation-case element defines one possible navigation path from logon.jsp. The first navigation-case says that if LogonForm.logon returns an outcome of success, then storefront.jsp will be accessed. The second navigation-case says that logon.jsp will be rerendered if LogonForm.logon returns failure.

An application's navigation configuration consists of a set of navigation rules. Each rule is defined by the navigation-rule element in the faces-config.xml file.

The navigation rules of the Duke's Bookstore application are very simple. Here are two complex navigation rules that could be used with the Duke's Bookstore application:

```
<navigation-rule>
  <from-view-id>/catalog.jsp</from-view-id>
  <navigation-case>
    <from-outcome>success</from-outcome>
    <to-view-id>/bookcashier.jsp</to-view-id>
  </navigation-case>
  <navigation-case>
    <from-outcome>out of stock</from-outcome>
    <from-action>
       #{catalog.buy}
    </from-action>
    <to-view-id>/outofstock.jsp</to-view-id>
  </navigation-case>
```

```
  <navigation-case>
    <from-outcome>error</from-outcome>
    <to-view-id>/error.jsp</to-view-id>
  </navigation-case>
</navigation-rule>
```

The first navigation rule in this example says that the application will navigate from `catalog.jsp` to

- `bookcashier.jsp` if the item ordered is in stock
- `outofstock.jsp` if the item is out of stock

The second navigation rule says that the application will navigate from any page to `error.jsp` if the application encountered an error.

Each `navigation-rule` element corresponds to one component tree identifier defined by the optional `from-view-id` element. This means that each rule defines all the possible ways to navigate from one particular page in the application. If there is no `from-view-id` element, the navigation rules defined in the `navigation-rule` element apply to all the pages in the application. The `from-view-id` element also allows wildcard matching patterns. For example, this `from-view-id` element says that the navigation rule applies to all the pages in the books directory:

```
<from-view-id>/books/*</from-view-id>
```

As shown in the example navigation rule, a `navigation-rule` element can contain zero or more `navigation-case` elements. The `navigation-case` element defines a set of matching criteria. When these criteria are satisfied, the application will navigate to the page defined by the `to-view-id` element contained in the same `navigation-case` element.

The navigation criteria are defined by optional `from-outcome` and `from-action` elements. The `from-outcome` element defines a logical outcome, such as `success`. The `from-action` element uses a method-binding expression to refer to an action method that returns a `String`, which is the logical outcome. The method performs some logic to determine the outcome and returns the outcome.

The `navigation-case` elements are checked against the outcome and the method-binding expression in this order:

- Cases specifying both a `from-outcome` value and a `from-action` value. Both of these elements can be used if the action method returns different outcomes depending on the result of the processing it performs.
- Cases specifying only a `from-outcome` value. The `from-outcome` element must match either the outcome defined by the `action` attribute of the `UICommand` component or the outcome returned by the method referred to by the `UICommand` component.
- Cases specifying only a `from-action` value. This value must match the `action` expression specified by the component tag.

When any of these cases is matched, the component tree defined by the `to-view-id` element will be selected for rendering.

Referencing a Method That Performs Navigation (page 720) explains how to use a component tag's `action` attribute to point to an action method. Writing a Method to Handle Navigation (page 755) explains how to write an action method.

Registering a Custom Renderer with a Render Kit

For every UI component that a render kit supports, the render kit defines a set of `Renderer` objects that can render the component in different ways to the client supported by the render kit. For example, the standard `UISelectOne` component class defines a component that allows a user to select one item from a group of items. This component can be rendered using the `Listbox` renderer, the `Menu` renderer, or the `Radio` renderer. Each renderer produces a different appearance for the component. The `Listbox` renderer renders a menu that can display an entire set of values. The `Menu` renderer renders a subset of all possible values. The `Radio` renderer renders a set of radio buttons.

When the application developer creates a custom renderer, as described in Delegating Rendering to a Renderer (page 786), you must register it using the appropriate render kit. Because the image map application implements an HTML image map, `AreaRenderer` (as well as `MapRenderer`) should be registered using the HTML render kit.

You register the renderer using the `render-kit` element of the application configuration resource file. Here is the configuration of `AreaRenderer` from the Duke's Bookstore application:

```
<render-kit>
  <renderer>
     <component-family>Area</component-family>
     <renderer-type>DemoArea</renderer-type>
     <renderer-class>
        renders.AreaRenderer
     </renderer-class>
     <attribute>
        <attribute-name>onmouseout</attribute-name>
        <attribute-class>java.lang.String</attribute-class>
     </attribute>
     <attribute>
        <attribute-name>onmouseover</attribute-name>
        <attribute-class>java.lang.String</attribute-class>
     </attribute>
     <attribute>
        <attribute-name>styleClass</attribute-name>
        <attribute-class>java.lang.String</attribute-class>
     </attribute>
  </renderer>
  ...
```

The `render-kit` element represents a `RenderKit` implementation. If no `render-kit-id` is specified, the default HTML render kit is assumed. The renderer element represents a `Renderer` implementation. By nesting the `renderer` element inside the `render-kit` element, you are registering the renderer with the `RenderKit` associated with the `render-kit` element.

The `renderer-type` will be used by the tag handler, as explained in the next section. The `renderer-class` is the fully qualified class name of the `Renderer`.

The `component-family` and `render-type` elements are used by a component to find renderers that can render it. The `component-family` identifier must match that returned by the component class's `getFamily` method. The `renderertype` identifier must match that returned by the `getRendererType` method of the tag handler class. The `attribute` element doesn't affect the runtime execution of your application. Instead, it provides information to tools about the attributes the `Renderer` supports.

Registering a Custom Component

If the component writer creates any custom components, you must register them using the application configuration resource file. Here is the `component` element from the application configuration resource file that registers `AreaComponent`:

```
<component>
   <component-type>DemoArea</component-type>
   <component-class>
      components.AreaComponent
   </component-class>
   <property>
      <property-name>alt</property-name>
      <property-class>java.lang.String</property-class>
   </property>
   <property>
      <property-name>coords</property-name>
      <property-class>java.lang.String</property-class>
   </property>
   <property>
      <property-name>shape</property-name>
      <property-class>java.lang.String</property-class>
   </property>

   <component-extension>
      <component-family>Area</component-family>
      <renderer-type>DemoArea</renderer-type>
   </component-extension>

</component>
```

The `component-type` element indicates the name under which the component should be registered. Other objects referring to this component use this name. The `component-class` element indicates the component's fully qualified class name. The `property` elements specify the component properties and their types.

The `component-extension` element identifies a set of components and a renderer that can render these components. The `component-family` identifier must match that returned by the components' `getFamily` methods. The `renderer-type` identifier must match that returned by the tag handler's `getRendererType` method. This feature allows a component to be rendered by multiple renderers and allows a renderer to render multiple components.

Basic Requirements of a JavaServer Faces Application

In addition to configuring your application, you must satisfy other requirements of JavaServer Faces applications, including properly packaging all the necessary files and providing a deployment descriptor file. This section describes how to perform these administrative tasks.

JavaServer Faces applications must be compliant with the Servlet specification, version 2.3 (or later), and the JavaServer Pages specification, version 1.2 (or later). All applications compliant with these specifications are packaged in a WAR file, which must conform to specific requirements in order to execute across different containers. At a minimum, a WAR file for a JavaServer Faces application must contain the following:

- A Web application deployment descriptor, called web.xml, to configure resources required by a Web application
- A specific set of JAR files containing essential classes
- A set of application classes, JavaServer Faces pages, and other required resources, such as image files
- An application configuration resource file, which configures application resources

The WAR file typically has this directory structure:

```
index.html
JSP pages
WEB-INF/
    web.xml
    faces-config.xml
    tag library descriptors (optional)
    classes/
        class files
        Properties files
    lib/
        JAR files
```

The web.xml file (or deployment descriptor), the set of JAR files, and the set of application files must be contained in the WEB-INF directory of the WAR file. Usually, you will want to use the asant build tool to compile the classes. You will use deploytool to package the necessary files into the WAR and deploy the WAR file.

The `asant` tool and `deploytool` are included in the Sun Java System Application Server Platform Edition 8. You configure how the `asant` build tool builds your WAR file via a `build.xml` file. Each example in the tutorial has its own build file, to which you can refer when creating your own build file.

Configuring an Application Using deploytool

Web applications are configured via elements contained in the Web application deployment descriptor. The `deploytool` utility generates the descriptor when you create a WAR and adds elements when you create Web components and associated classes. You can modify the elements via the inspectors associated with the WAR.

The deployment descriptor for a JavaServer Faces application must specify certain configurations, which include the following:

- The servlet used to process JavaServer Faces requests
- The servlet mapping for the processing servlet
- The path to the configuration resource file if it is not located in a default location

The deployment descriptor can also specify other, optional configurations, including:

- Specifying where component state is saved
- Restricting access to pages containing JavaServer Faces tags
- Turning on XML validation
- Verifying custom objects

This section gives more details on these configurations and explains how to configure them in `deploytool`.

Identifying the Servlet for Life Cycle Processing

One requirement of a JavaServer Faces application is that all requests to the application that reference previously saved JavaServer Faces components must go through `FacesServlet`. The `FacesServlet` instance manages the request processing life cycle for Web applications and initializes the resources required by Java-Server Faces technology. To comply with this requirement, follow these steps.

1. While using the Edit Contents dialog box from the Web Component wizard, add the `jsf-api.jar` file from `<J2EE_HOME>`/lib/ to your WAR file. This JAR file is needed so that you have access to the `FacesServlet` instance when configuring your application with `deploytool`.

2. In the Choose Component Type dialog box of the Web Component wizard, select the Servlet radio button and click Next.

3. Select `FacesServlet` from the Servlet Class combo box.

4. In the Startup Load Sequence Position combo box, enter 1, indicating that the `FacesServlet` should be loaded when the application starts. Click Finish.

5. Select the `FacesServlet` Web component from the tree.

6. Select the Aliases tab and click Add.

7. Enter a path in the Aliases field. This path will be the path to `FacesServlet`. Users of the application will include this path in the URL when they access the application. For the `guessNumber` application, the path is `/guess/*`.

Before a JavaServer Faces application can launch the first JSP page, the Web container must invoke the `FacesServlet` instance in order for the application life cycle process to start. The application life cycle is described in the section The Life Cycle of a JavaServer Faces Page (page 662).

To make sure that the `FacesServlet` instance is invoked, you provide a mapping to it using the Aliases tab, as described in steps 5 through 7 above.

The mapping to `FacesServlet` described in the foregoing steps uses a prefix mapping to identify a JSP page as having JavaServer Faces content. Because of this, the URL to the first JSP page of the application must include the mapping. There are two ways to accomplish this:

- The page author can include an HTML page in the application that has the URL to the first JSP page. This URL must include the path to `FacesServlet`, as shown by this tag, which uses the mapping defined in the `guessNumber` application:

```
<a href="guess/greeting.jsp">
```

- Users of the application can include the path to FacesServlet in the URL to the first page when they enter it in their browser, as shown by this URL that accesses the guessNumber application:

```
http://localhost:8080/guessNumber/guess/greeting.jsp
```

The second method allows users to start the application from the first JSP page, rather than start it from an HTML page. However, the second method requires users to identify the first JSP page. When you use the first method, users need only enter

```
http://localhost:8080/guessNumber
```

You could define an extension mapping, such as *.faces, instead of the prefix mapping /guess/*. If a request comes to the server for a JSP page with a .faces extension, the container will send the request to FacesServlet, which will expect a corresponding JSP page of the same name to exist containing the content. For example, if the request URL is http://localhost/bookstore6/bookstore.faces, the FacesServlet will map it to the bookstore.jsp page.

Specifying a Path to an Application Configuration Resource File

As explained in Application Configuration Resource File (page 792), an application can have multiple application configuration resource files. If these files are not located in the directories that the implementation searches by default or the files are not named faces-config.xml, you need to specify paths to these files. To specify paths to the files using deploytool follow these steps:

1. Select the WAR from the tree.
2. Select the Context tabbed pane and click Add.
3. Enter javax.faces.application.CONFIG_FILES in the Coded Parameter field.
4. Enter the path to your application configuration resource file in the Value field. For example, the path to the guessNumber application's application configuration resource file is /WEB-INF/faces-config.xml
5. Repeat steps 2 through 4 for each application configuration resource file that your application contains.

Specifying Where State Is Saved

When implementing the state-holder methods (described in Saving and Restoring State, page 785), you specify in your deployment descriptor where you want the state to be saved, either client or server. You do this by setting a context parameter with `deploytool`.

1. While running `deploytool`, select the Web application from the tree.
2. Select the Context tabbed pane and click Add.
3. Enter `javax.faces.STATE_SAVING_METHOD` in the Coded Parameter field.
4. Enter either `client` or `server` in the Value field, depending on whether you want state saved on the client or the server.

If state is saved on the client, the state of the entire view is rendered to a hidden field on the page. The JavaServer Faces implementation saves the state on the client by default. Duke's Bookstore saves its state in the client.

Restricting Access to JavaServer Faces Components

In addition to identifying the `FacesServlet` instance and providing a mapping to it, you should also ensure that all applications use `FacesServlet` to process JavaServer Faces components. You do this by setting a security constraint.

1. Select your WAR file from the tree.
2. Select the Security tabbed pane.
3. Click Add Constraints and enter `Restricts Access to JSP Pages` in the Security Constraints field.
4. Click Add Collections and enter `Restricts Access to JSP Pages` in the Web Resource Collections field.
5. Click Edit Collections.
6. In the Edit Collections of Web Resource Collections dialog box, click Add URL Pattern and enter the path to a JSP page to which you want to restrict access, such as `/response.jsp`.
7. Continue to click Add URL Pattern again, and enter paths to all the JSP pages in your application and click OK.

Turning On Validation of XML Files

Your application contains one or more application configuration resource files written in XML. You can force the JavaServer Faces implementation to validate the XML of these files by setting the `validateXML` flag to `true`:

1. Select your WAR file from the tree.
2. Select the Context tabbed pane and click Add.
3. Enter `com.sun.faces.validateXml` in the Coded Parameter field.
4. Enter `true` in the Value field. The default value is `false`.

Verifying Custom Objects

If your application includes custom objects, such as components, converters, validators, and renderers, you can verify when the application starts that they can be created. To do this, you set the `verifyObjects` flag to `true`:

1. Select your WAR file from the tree.
2. Select the Context tabbed pane and click Add.
3. Enter `com.sun.faces.verifyObjects` in the Coded Parameter field.
4. Enter `true` in the Value field. The default value is `false`.

Normally, this flag should be set to `false` during development because it takes extra time to check the objects.

Including the Required JAR Files

JavaServer Faces applications require several JAR files to run properly. These JAR files are as follows:

- `jsf-api.jar` (contains the `javax.faces.*` API classes)
- `jsf-impl.jar` (contains the implementation classes of the JavaServer Faces implementation)
- `jstl.jar` (required to use JSTL tags and referenced by JavaServer Faces implementation classes)
- `standard.jar` (required to use JSTL tags and referenced by JavaServer Faces reference implementation classes)
- `commons-beanutils.jar` (utilities for defining and accessing JavaBeans component properties)

- commons-digester.jar (for processing XML documents)
- commons-collections.jar (extensions of the Java 2 SDK Collections Framework)
- commons-logging.jar (a general-purpose, flexible logging facility to allow developers to instrument their code with logging statements)

The jsf-api.jar and the jsf-impl.jar files are located in *<J2EE_HOME>*/lib/. The jstl.jar file is bundled in appserv-jstl.jar. The other JAR files are bundled in the appserv-rt.jar, also located in *<J2EE_HOME>*/lib/.

When packaging and deploying your JavaServer Faces application with deploytool, you do not need to package any of the JAR files, except the jsf-api.jar file, with your application. The jsf-api.jar file must be packaged with your application so that you have access to the FacesServlet instance and can configure the mapping for it.

Including the Classes, Pages, and Other Resources

When packaging Web applications using deploytool, you'll notice that deploytool automatically packages many of your Web application files in the appropriate directories in the WAR file. All JSP pages are placed at the top level of the WAR file. The TLD files and the web.xml that deploytool creates are packaged in the WEB-INF directory. All packages are stored in the WEB-TNF/ classes directory. However, deploytool does not copy faces-config.xml to the WEB-INF directory as it should. Therefore, when packaging your Web applications, you need to drag faces-config.xml to the WEB-INF directory.

22

Internationalizing and Localizing Web Applications

Internationalization is the process of preparing an application to support more than one language and data format. *Localization* is the process of adapting an internationalized application to support a specific region or locale. Examples of locale-dependent information include messages and user interface labels, character sets and encoding, and date and currency formats. Although all client user interfaces should be internationalized and localized, it is particularly important for Web applications because of the global nature of the Web.

Java Platform Localization Classes

In the Java 2 platform, `java.util.Locale` represents a specific geographical, political, or cultural region. The string representation of a locale consists of the international standard two-character abbreviation for language and country and an optional variant, all separated by underscore (_) characters. Examples of locale strings include `fr` (French), `de_CH` (Swiss German), and `en_US_POSIX` (English on a POSIX-compliant platform).

Locale-sensitive data is stored in a `java.util.ResourceBundle`. A resource bundle contains key-value pairs, where the keys uniquely identify a locale-specific object in the bundle. A resource bundle can be backed by a text file (properties resource bundle) or a class (list resource bundle) containing the pairs. You construct a resource bundle instance by appending a locale string representation to a base name.

For more details on internationalization and localization in the Java 2 platform, see `http://java.sun.com/docs/books/tutorial/i18n/index.html`.

In the Web technology chapters, the Duke's Bookstore applications contain resource bundles with the base name `messages.BookstoreMessages` for the locales `en_US`, `fr_FR`, `de_DE`, and `es_MX`.

Providing Localized Messages and Labels

Messages and labels should be tailored according to the conventions of a user's language and region. There are two approaches to providing localized messages and labels in a Web application:

- Provide a version of the JSP page in each of the target locales and have a controller servlet dispatch the request to the appropriate page depending on the requested locale. This approach is useful if large amounts of data on a page or an entire Web application need to be internationalized.
- Isolate any locale-sensitive data on a page into resource bundles, and access the data so that the corresponding translated message is fetched automatically and inserted into the page. Thus, instead of creating strings directly in your code, you create a resource bundle that contains translations and read the translations from that bundle using the corresponding key.

The Duke's Bookstore applications follow the second approach. Here are a few lines from the default resource bundle `messages.BookstoreMessages.java`:

```
{"TitleCashier", "Cashier"},
{"TitleBookDescription", "Book Description"},
{"Visitor", "You are visitor number "},
{"What", "What We're Reading"},
```

```
{"Talk", " talks about how Web components can transform the way
you develop applications for the Web. This is a must read for
any self respecting Web developer!"},
{"Start", "Start Shopping"},
```

Establishing the Locale

To get the correct strings for a given user, a Web application either retrieves the locale (set by a browser language preference) from the request using the `getLocale` method, or allows the user to explicitly select the locale.

The JSTL versions of Duke's Bookstore automatically retrieve the locale from the request and store it in a localization context (see Internationalization Tag Library, page 554). It is also possible for a component to set the locale explicitly via the `fmt:setLocale` tag.

The JavaServer Faces version of Duke's Bookstore allows the user to select the locale explicitly. The user selection triggers a method that stores the locale in the `FacesContext` object. The locale is then used in resource bundle selection and is available for localizing dynamic data and messages (see Localizing Dynamic Data, page 741):

```
<h:commandLink id="NAmerica" action="storeFront"
  actionListener="#{localeBean.chooseLocaleFromLink}">
  <h:outputText value="#{bundle.english}" />
</h:commandLink>

public void chooseLocaleFromLink(ActionEvent event) {
  String current = event.getComponent().getId();
  FacesContext context = FacesContext.getCurrentInstance();
  context.getViewRoot().setLocale((Locale)
     locales.get(current));
}
```

Setting the Resource Bundle

After the locale is set, the controller of a Web application typically retrieves the resource bundle for that locale and saves it as a session attribute (see Associating Objects with a Session, page 465) for use by other components:

```
messages = ResourceBundle.
  getBundle("messages.BookstoreMessages", locale);
session.setAttribute("messages", messages);
```

The resource bundle base name for the JSTL versions of Duke's Bookstore is set at deployment time through a context parameter. When a session is initiated, the resource bundle for the user's locale is stored in the localization context. It is also possible to override the resource bundle at runtime for a given scope using the `fmt:setBundle` tag and for a tag body using the `fmt:bundle` tag.

In the JavaServer Faces version of Duke's Bookstore, the JSP pages set the resource bundle using the `f:loadBundle` tag. This tag loads the correct resource bundle according to the locale stored in `FacesContext`.

```
<f:loadBundle basename="messages.BookstoreMessages"
  var="bundle"/>
```

For information on this tag, see Referencing a ResourceBundle from a Page (page 704).

Retrieving Localized Messages

A Web component written in the Java programming language retrieves the resource bundle from the session:

```
ResourceBundle messages =
  (ResourceBundle)session.getAttribute("messages");
```

Then it looks up the string associated with the key `Talk` as follows:

```
messages.getString("Talk");
```

The JSP versions of the Duke's Bookstore application uses the `fmt:message` tag to provide localized strings for messages, HTML link text, button labels, and error messages:

```
<fmt:message key="Talk"/>
```

For information on the JSTL messaging tags, see Messaging Tags (page 555).

The JavaServer Faces version of Duke's Bookstore retrieves messages from the `bundle` variable (created in the preceding section) by using the following tag:

```
<h:outputText value="#{bundle.Talk}"/>
```

For information on creating localized messages in JavaServer Faces, see Referencing a Localized Message (page 705).

Date and Number Formatting

Java programs use the `DateFormat.getDateInstance(int, locale)` to parse and format dates in a locale-sensitive manner. Java programs use the `Number-Format.get`*XXX*`Instance(locale)` method, where *XXX* can be `Currency`, `Number`, or `Percent`, to parse and format numerical values in a locale-sensitive manner. The servlet version of Duke's Bookstore uses the currency version of this method to format book prices.

JSTL applications use the `fmt:formatDate` and `fmt:parseDate` tags to handle localized dates and use the `fmt:formatNumber` and `fmt:parseNumber` tags to handle localized numbers, including currency values. For information on the JSTL formatting tags, see Formatting Tags (page 556). The JSTL version of Duke's bookstore uses the `fmt:formatNumber` tag to format book prices and the `fmt:formatDate` tag to format the ship date for an order:

```
<fmt:formatDate value="${shipDate}" type="date"
  dateStyle="full"/>.
```

The JavaServer Faces version of Duke's Bookstore uses date/time and number converters to format dates and numbers in a locale-sensitive manner. For example, the same shipping date is converted in the JavaServer Faces version as follows:

```
<h:outputText value="#{cashier.shipDate}">
  <f:convertDateTime dateStyle="full"/>
</h:outputText>
```

For information on JavaServer Faces converters, see Using the Standard Converters (page 705).

Character Sets and Encodings

Character Sets

A *character set* is a set of textual and graphic symbols, each of which is mapped to a set of nonnegative integers.

The first character set used in computing was US-ASCII. It is limited in that it can represent only American English. US-ASCII contains upper- and lowercase Latin alphabets, numerals, punctuation, a set of control codes, and a few miscellaneous symbols.

Unicode defines a standardized, universal character set that can be extended to accommodate additions. When the Java program source file encoding doesn't support Unicode, you can represent Unicode characters as escape sequences by using the notation \u*XXXX*, where *XXXX* is the character's 16-bit representation in hexadecimal. For example, the Spanish version of the Duke's Bookstore message file uses Unicode for non-ASCII characters:

```
{"TitleCashier", "Cajero"},
{"TitleBookDescription", "Descripci" + "\u00f3" + "n del
Libro"},
{"Visitor", "Es visitanten" + "\u00fa" + "mero "},
{"What", "Qu" + "\u00e9" + " libros leemos"},
{"Talk", " describe como componentes de software de web pueden
transformar la manera en que desrrollamos aplicaciones para el
web. Este libro es obligatorio para cualquier programador de
respeto!"},
{"Start", "Empezar a Comprar"},
```

Character Encoding

A *character encoding* maps a character set to units of a specific width and defines byte serialization and ordering rules. Many character sets have more than one encoding. For example, Java programs can represent Japanese character sets using the EUC-JP or Shift-JIS encodings, among others. Each encoding has rules for representing and serializing a character set.

The ISO 8859 series defines 13 character encodings that can represent texts in dozens of languages. Each ISO 8859 character encoding can have up to 256 characters. ISO 8859-1 (Latin-1) comprises the ASCII character set, characters with diacritics (accents, diaereses, cedillas, circumflexes, and so on), and additional symbols.

UTF-8 (Unicode Transformation Format, 8-bit form) is a variable-width character encoding that encodes 16-bit Unicode characters as one to four bytes. A byte in UTF-8 is equivalent to 7-bit ASCII if its high-order bit is zero; otherwise, the character comprises a variable number of bytes.

UTF-8 is compatible with the majority of existing Web content and provides access to the Unicode character set. Current versions of browsers and email clients support UTF-8. In addition, many new Web standards specify UTF-8 as their character encoding. For example, UTF-8 is one of the two required encodings for XML documents (the other is UTF-16).

See Appendix A for more information on character encodings in the Java 2 platform.

Web components usually use `PrintWriter` to produce responses; `PrintWriter` automatically encodes using ISO 8859-1. Servlets can also output binary data using `OutputStream` classes, which perform no encoding. An application that uses a character set that cannot use the default encoding must explicitly set a different encoding.

For Web components, three encodings must be considered:

- Request
- Page (JSP pages)
- Response

Request Encoding

The *request encoding* is the character encoding in which parameters in an incoming request are interpreted. Currently, many browsers do not send a request encoding qualifier with the `Content-Type` header. In such cases, a Web container will use the default encoding—ISO-8859-1—to parse request data.

If the client hasn't set character encoding and the request data is encoded with a different encoding from the default, the data won't be interpreted correctly. To remedy this situation, you can use the `ServletRequest.setCharacterEncoding(String enc)` method to override the character encoding supplied by the container. To control the request encoding from JSP pages, you can use the JSTL `fmt:requestEncoding` tag. You must call the method or tag before parsing any request parameters or reading any input from the request. Calling the method or tag once data has been read will not affect the encoding.

Page Encoding

For JSP pages, the *page encoding* is the character encoding in which the file is encoded.

For JSP pages in standard syntax, the page encoding is determined from the following sources:

- The page encoding value of a JSP property group (see Setting Properties for Groups of JSP Pages, page 510) whose URL pattern matches the page.
- The `pageEncoding` attribute of the `page` directive of the page. It is a translation-time error to name different encodings in the `pageEncoding` attribute of the page directive of a JSP page and in a JSP property group.
- The `CHARSET` value of the `contentType` attribute of the `page` directive.

If none of these is provided, ISO-8859-1 is used as the default page encoding.

For JSP pages in XML syntax (JSP documents), the page encoding is determined as described in section 4.3.3 and appendix F.1 of the XML specification.

The `pageEncoding` and `contentType` attributes determine the page character encoding of only the file that physically contains the `page` directive. A Web container raises a translation-time error if an unsupported page encoding is specified.

Response Encoding

The *response encoding* is the character encoding of the textual response generated by a Web component. The response encoding must be set appropriately so that the characters are rendered correctly for a given locale. A Web container sets an initial response encoding for a JSP page from the following sources:

- The `CHARSET` value of the `contentType` attribute of the `page` directive
- The encoding specified by the `pageEncoding` attribute of the `page` directive
- The page encoding value of a JSP property group whose URL pattern matches the page

If none of these is provided, ISO-8859-1 is used as the default response encoding.

The `setCharacterEncoding`, `setContentType`, and `setLocale` methods can be called repeatedly to change the character encoding. Calls made after the servlet response's `getWriter` method has been called or after the response is committed have no effect on the character encoding. Data is sent to the response stream on buffer flushes (for buffered pages) or on encountering the first content on unbuffered pages.

Calls to `setContentType` set the character encoding only if the given content type string provides a value for the `charset` attribute. Calls to `setLocale` set the character encoding only if neither `setCharacterEncoding` nor `setContentType` has set the character encoding before. To control the response encoding from JSP pages, you can use the JSTL `fmt.setLocale` tag.

To obtain the character encoding for a locale, the `setLocale` method checks the locale encoding mapping for the Web application. For example, to map Japanese to the Japanese-specific encoding `Shift_JIS`, follow these steps:

1. Select the WAR.
2. Click the Advanced Settings button.
3. In the Locale Character Encoding table, click the Add button.
4. Enter `ja` in the Extension column.
5. Enter `Shift_JIS` in the Character Encoding column.

If a mapping is not set for the Web application, `setLocale` uses a Sun Java System Application Server Platform Edition 8 mapping.

The first application in Chapter 12 allows a user to choose an English string representation of a locale from all the locales available to the Java 2 platform and then outputs a date localized for that locale. To ensure that the characters in the date can be rendered correctly for a wide variety of character sets, the JSP page that generates the date sets the response encoding to UTF-8 by using the following directive:

```
<%@ page contentType="text/html; charset=UTF-8" %>
```

Further Information

For a detailed discussion on internationalizing Web applications, see the Java BluePrints for the Enterprise:

```
http://java.sun.com/blueprints/enterprise
```

23

Enterprise Beans

Enterprise beans are the J2EE components that implement Enterprise Java-Beans (EJB) technology. Enterprise beans run in the EJB container, a runtime environment within the Application Server Platform Edition 8 (see Figure 1–5, page 9). Although transparent to the application developer, the EJB container provides system-level services such as transactions and security to its enterprise beans. These services enable you to quickly build and deploy enterprise beans, which form the core of transactional J2EE applications.

What Is an Enterprise Bean?

Written in the Java programming language, an *enterprise bean* is a server-side component that encapsulates the business logic of an application. The business logic is the code that fulfills the purpose of the application. In an inventory control application, for example, the enterprise beans might implement the business logic in methods called checkInventoryLevel and orderProduct. By invoking these methods, remote clients can access the inventory services provided by the application.

Benefits of Enterprise Beans

For several reasons, enterprise beans simplify the development of large, distributed applications. First, because the EJB container provides system-level services to enterprise beans, the bean developer can concentrate on solving business problems. The EJB container—and not the bean developer—is responsible for system-level services such as transaction management and security authorization.

Second, because the beans—and not the clients—contain the application's business logic, the client developer can focus on the presentation of the client. The client developer does not have to code the routines that implement business rules or access databases. As a result, the clients are thinner, a benefit that is particularly important for clients that run on small devices.

Third, because enterprise beans are portable components, the application assembler can build new applications from existing beans. These applications can run on any compliant J2EE server provided that they use the standard APIs.

When to Use Enterprise Beans

You should consider using enterprise beans if your application has any of the following requirements:

- The application must be scalable. To accommodate a growing number of users, you may need to distribute an application's components across multiple machines. Not only can the enterprise beans of an application run on different machines, but also their location will remain transparent to the clients.

- Transactions must ensure data integrity. Enterprise beans support transactions, the mechanisms that manage the concurrent access of shared objects.

- The application will have a variety of clients. With only a few lines of code, remote clients can easily locate enterprise beans. These clients can be thin, various, and numerous.

Types of Enterprise Beans

Table 23–1 summarizes the three types of enterprise beans. The following sections discuss each type in more detail.

Table 23–1   Enterprise Bean Types

Enterprise Bean Type	Purpose
Session	Performs a task for a client; implements a Web service
Entity	Represents a business entity object that exists in persistent storage
Message-Driven	Acts as a listener for the Java Message Service API, processing messages asynchronously

What Is a Session Bean?

A *session bean* represents a single client inside the Application Server. To access an application that is deployed on the server, the client invokes the session bean's methods. The session bean performs work for its client, shielding the client from complexity by executing business tasks inside the server.

As its name suggests, a session bean is similar to an interactive session. A session bean is not shared; it can have only one client, in the same way that an interactive session can have only one user. Like an interactive session, a session bean is not persistent. (That is, its data is not saved to a database.) When the client terminates, its session bean appears to terminate and is no longer associated with the client.

For code samples, see Chapter 25.

State Management Modes

There are two types of session beans: stateless and stateful.

Stateless Session Beans

A *stateless* session bean does not maintain a conversational state for the client. When a client invokes the method of a stateless bean, the bean's instance variables may contain a state, but only for the duration of the invocation. When the method is finished, the state is no longer retained. Except during method invocation, all instances of a stateless bean are equivalent, allowing the EJB container to assign an instance to any client.

Because stateless session beans can support multiple clients, they can offer better scalability for applications that require large numbers of clients. Typically, an application requires fewer stateless session beans than stateful session beans to support the same number of clients.

At times, the EJB container may write a stateful session bean to secondary storage. However, stateless session beans are never written to secondary storage. Therefore, stateless beans may offer better performance than stateful beans.

A stateless session bean can implement a Web service, but other types of enterprise beans cannot.

Stateful Session Beans

The state of an object consists of the values of its instance variables. In a *stateful* session bean, the instance variables represent the state of a unique client-bean session. Because the client interacts ("talks") with its bean, this state is often called the *conversational state*.

The state is retained for the duration of the client-bean session. If the client removes the bean or terminates, the session ends and the state disappears. This transient nature of the state is not a problem, however, because when the conversation between the client and the bean ends there is no need to retain the state.

When to Use Session Beans

In general, you should use a session bean if the following circumstances hold:

- At any given time, only one client has access to the bean instance.
- The state of the bean is not persistent, existing only for a short period (perhaps a few hours).
- The bean implements a Web service.

Stateful session beans are appropriate if any of the following conditions are true:

- The bean's state represents the interaction between the bean and a specific client.
- The bean needs to hold information about the client across method invocations.
- The bean mediates between the client and the other components of the application, presenting a simplified view to the client.

- Behind the scenes, the bean manages the work flow of several enterprise beans. For an example, see the `AccountControllerBean` session bean in Chapter 36.

To improve performance, you might choose a stateless session bean if it has any of these traits:

- The bean's state has no data for a specific client.
- In a single method invocation, the bean performs a generic task for all clients. For example, you might use a stateless session bean to send an email that confirms an online order.
- The bean fetches from a database a set of read-only data that is often used by clients. Such a bean, for example, could retrieve the table rows that represent the products that are on sale this month.

What Is an Entity Bean?

An *entity bean* represents a business object in a persistent storage mechanism. Some examples of business objects are customers, orders, and products. In the Application Server, the persistent storage mechanism is a relational database. Typically, each entity bean has an underlying table in a relational database, and each instance of the bean corresponds to a row in that table. For code examples of entity beans, please refer to Chapters 26 and 27.

What Makes Entity Beans Different from Session Beans?

Entity beans differ from session beans in several ways. Entity beans are persistent, allow shared access, have primary keys, and can participate in relationships with other entity beans.

Persistence

Because the state of an entity bean is saved in a storage mechanism, it is persistent. *Persistence* means that the entity bean's state exists beyond the lifetime of the application or the Application Server process. If you've worked with databases, you're familiar with persistent data. The data in a database is persistent because it still exists even after you shut down the database server or the applications it services.

There are two types of persistence for entity beans: bean-managed and container-managed. With *bean-managed* persistence, the entity bean code that you write contains the calls that access the database. If your bean has *container-managed* persistence, the EJB container automatically generates the necessary database access calls. The code that you write for the entity bean does not include these calls. For additional information, see the section Container-Managed Persistence (page 835).

Shared Access

Entity beans can be shared by multiple clients. Because the clients might want to change the same data, it's important that entity beans work within transactions. Typically, the EJB container provides transaction management. In this case, you specify the transaction attributes in the bean's deployment descriptor. You do not have to code the transaction boundaries in the bean; the container marks the boundaries for you. See Chapter 30 for more information.

Primary Key

Each entity bean has a unique object identifier. A customer entity bean, for example, might be identified by a customer number. The unique identifier, or *primary key*, enables the client to locate a particular entity bean. For more information, see the section Primary Keys for Bean-Managed Persistence (page 933).

Relationships

Like a table in a relational database, an entity bean may be related to other entity beans. For example, in a college enrollment application, `StudentBean` and `CourseBean` would be related because students enroll in classes.

You implement relationships differently for entity beans with bean-managed persistence than those with container-managed persistence. With bean-managed persistence, the code that you write implements the relationships. But with container-managed persistence, the EJB container takes care of the relationships for you. For this reason, relationships in entity beans with container-managed persistence are often referred to as *container-managed relationships*.

Container-Managed Persistence

The term container-managed persistence means that the EJB container handles all database access required by the entity bean. The bean's code contains no database access (SQL) calls. As a result, the bean's code is not tied to a specific persistent storage mechanism (database). Because of this flexibility, even if you redeploy the same entity bean on different J2EE servers that use different databases, you won't need to modify or recompile the bean's code. In short, your entity beans are more portable if you use container-managed persistence than if they use bean-managed persistence.

To generate the data access calls, the container needs information that you provide in the entity bean's abstract schema.

Abstract Schema

Part of an entity bean's deployment descriptor, the *abstract schema* defines the bean's persistent fields and relationships. The term *abstract* distinguishes this schema from the physical schema of the underlying data store. In a relational database, for example, the physical schema is made up of structures such as tables and columns.

You specify the name of an abstract schema in the deployment descriptor. This name is referenced by queries written in the Enterprise JavaBeans Query Language (EJB QL). For an entity bean with container-managed persistence, you must define an EJB QL query for every finder method (except `findByPrimaryKey`). The EJB QL query determines the query that is executed by the EJB container when the finder method is invoked. To learn more about EJB QL, see Chapter 29.

You'll probably find it helpful to sketch the abstract schema before writing any code. Figure 23–1 represents a simple abstract schema that describes the relationships between three entity beans. These relationships are discussed further in the sections that follow.

Persistent Fields

The persistent fields of an entity bean are stored in the underlying data store. Collectively, these fields constitute the state of the bean. At runtime, the EJB container automatically synchronizes this state with the database. During deployment, the container typically maps the entity bean to a database table and maps the persistent fields to the table's columns.

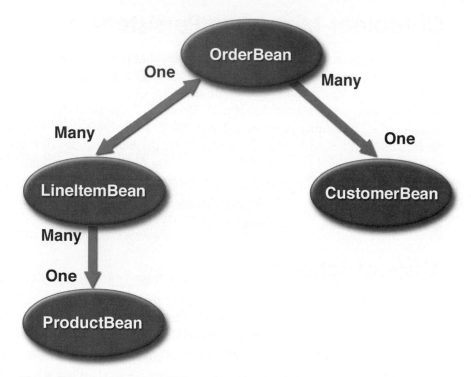

Figure 23–1   A High-Level View of an Abstract Schema

A `CustomerBean` entity bean, for example, might have persistent fields such as `firstName`, `lastName`, `phone`, and `emailAddress`. In container-managed persistence, these fields are virtual. You declare them in the abstract schema, but you do not code them as instance variables in the entity bean class. Instead, the persistent fields are identified in the code by access methods (getters and setters).

Relationship Fields

A *relationship field* is like a foreign key in a database table: it identifies a related bean. Like a persistent field, a relationship field is virtual and is defined in the enterprise bean class via access methods. But unlike a persistent field, a relationship field does not represent the bean's state. Relationship fields are discussed further in Direction in Container-Managed Relationships (page 837).

Multiplicity in Container-Managed Relationships

There are four types of multiplicities: one to one, one to many, many to one, and many-to-many.

One-to-one: Each entity bean instance is related to a single instance of another entity bean. For example, to model a physical warehouse in which each storage bin contains a single widget, `StorageBinBean` and `WidgetBean` would have a one-to-one relationship.

One-to-many: An entity bean instance can be related to multiple instances of the other entity bean. A sales order, for example, can have multiple line items. In the order application, `OrderBean` would have a one-to-many relationship with `LineItemBean`.

Many-to-one: Multiple instances of an entity bean can be related to a single instance of the other entity bean. This multiplicity is the opposite of a one-to-many relationship. In the example just mentioned, from the perspective of `LineItemBean`, the relationship to `OrderBean` is many-to-one.

Many-to-many: The entity bean instances can be related to multiple instances of each other. For example, in college each course has many students, and every student may take several courses. Therefore, in an enrollment application, `CourseBean` and `StudentBean` would have a many-to-many relationship.

Direction in Container-Managed Relationships

The direction of a relationship can be either bidirectional or unidirectional. In a *bidirectional* relationship, each entity bean has a relationship field that refers to the other bean. Through the relationship field, an entity bean's code can access its related object. If an entity bean has a relative field, then we often say that it "knows" about its related object. For example, if `OrderBean` knows what `LineItemBean` instances it has and if `LineItemBean` knows what `OrderBean` it belongs to, then they have a bidirectional relationship.

In a *unidirectional* relationship, only one entity bean has a relationship field that refers to the other. For example, `LineItemBean` would have a relationship field that identifies `ProductBean`, but `ProductBean` would not have a relationship field for `LineItemBean`. In other words, `LineItemBean` knows about `Product-Bean`, but `ProductBean` doesn't know which `LineItemBean` instances refer to it.

EJB QL queries often navigate across relationships. The direction of a relationship determines whether a query can navigate from one bean to another. For example, a query can navigate from `LineItemBean` to `ProductBean` but cannot navigate in the opposite direction. For `OrderBean` and `LineItemBean`, a query could navigate in both directions, because these two beans have a bidirectional relationship.

When to Use Entity Beans

You should probably use an entity bean under the following conditions:

- The bean represents a business entity and not a procedure. For example, `CreditCardBean` would be an entity bean, but `CreditCardVerifierBean` would be a session bean.
- The bean's state must be persistent. If the bean instance terminates or if the Application Server is shut down, the bean's state still exists in persistent storage (a database).

What Is a Message-Driven Bean?

A *message-driven bean* is an enterprise bean that allows J2EE applications to process messages asynchronously. It normally acts as a JMS message listener, which is similar to an event listener except that it receives JMS messages instead of events. The messages can be sent by any J2EE component—an application client, another enterprise bean, or a Web component—or by a JMS application or system that does not use J2EE technology. Message-driven beans can process either JMS messages or other kinds of messages.

For a simple code sample, see Chapter 28. For more information about using message-driven beans, see Using the JMS API in a J2EE Application (page 1212) and Chapter 34.

What Makes Message-Driven Beans Different from Session and Entity Beans?

The most visible difference between message-driven beans and session and entity beans is that clients do not access message-driven beans through interfaces. Interfaces are described in the section Defining Client Access with Interfaces (page 840). Unlike a session or entity bean, a message-driven bean has only a bean class.

In several respects, a message-driven bean resembles a stateless session bean.

- A message-driven bean's instances retain no data or conversational state for a specific client.
- All instances of a message-driven bean are equivalent, allowing the EJB container to assign a message to any message-driven bean instance. The container can pool these instances to allow streams of messages to be processed concurrently.
- A single message-driven bean can process messages from multiple clients.

The instance variables of the message-driven bean instance can contain some state across the handling of client messages—for example, a JMS API connection, an open database connection, or an object reference to an enterprise bean object.

Client components do not locate message-driven beans and invoke methods directly on them. Instead, a client accesses a message-driven bean through JMS by sending messages to the message destination for which the message-driven bean class is the `MessageListener`. You assign a message-driven bean's destination during deployment by using Application Server resources.

Message-driven beans have the following characteristics:

- They execute upon receipt of a single client message.
- They are invoked asynchronously.
- They are relatively short-lived.
- They do not represent directly shared data in the database, but they can access and update this data.
- They can be transaction-aware.
- They are stateless.

When a message arrives, the container calls the message-driven bean's `onMessage` method to process the message. The `onMessage` method normally casts the message to one of the five JMS message types and handles it in accordance with the application's business logic. The `onMessage` method can call helper methods, or it can invoke a session or entity bean to process the information in the message or to store it in a database.

A message can be delivered to a message-driven bean within a transaction context, so all operations within the `onMessage` method are part of a single transaction. If message processing is rolled back, the message will be redelivered. For more information, see Chapter 28.

When to Use Message-Driven Beans

Session beans and entity beans allow you to send JMS messages and to receive them synchronously, but not asynchronously. To avoid tying up server resources, you may prefer not to use blocking synchronous receives in a server-side component. To receive messages asynchronously, use a message-driven bean.

Defining Client Access with Interfaces

The material in this section applies only to session and entity beans and not to message-driven beans. Because they have a different programming model, message-driven beans do not have interfaces that define client access.

A client can access a session or an entity bean only through the methods defined in the bean's interfaces. These interfaces define the client's view of a bean. All other aspects of the bean—method implementations, deployment descriptor settings, abstract schemas, and database access calls—are hidden from the client.

Well-designed interfaces simplify the development and maintenance of J2EE applications. Not only do clean interfaces shield the clients from any complexities in the EJB tier, but they also allow the beans to change internally without affecting the clients. For example, even if you change your entity beans from bean-managed to container-managed persistence, you won't have to alter the client code. But if you were to change the method definitions in the interfaces, then you might have to modify the client code as well. Therefore, to isolate your clients from possible changes in the beans, it is important that you design the interfaces carefully.

When you design a J2EE application, one of the first decisions you make is the type of client access allowed by the enterprise beans: remote, local, or Web service.

Remote Clients

A remote client of an enterprise bean has the following traits:

- It can run on a different machine and a different Java virtual machine (JVM) than the enterprise bean it accesses. (It is not required to run on a different JVM.)
- It can be a Web component, an application client, or another enterprise bean.
- To a remote client, the location of the enterprise bean is transparent.

To create an enterprise bean that has remote access, you must code a remote inter-face and a home interface. The *remote interface* defines the business methods that are specific to the bean. For example, the remote interface of a bean named BankAccountBean might have business methods named deposit and credit. The *home interface* defines the bean's life-cycle methods: create and remove. For entity beans, the home interface also defines finder methods and home meth-ods. *Finder methods* are used to locate entity beans. *Home methods* are business methods that are invoked on all instances of an entity bean class. Figure 23–2 shows how the interfaces control the client's view of an enterprise bean.

Local Clients

A local client has these characteristics:

- It must run in the same JVM as the enterprise bean it accesses.
- It can be a Web component or another enterprise bean.
- To the local client, the location of the enterprise bean it accesses is not transparent.
- It is often an entity bean that has a container-managed relationship with another entity bean.

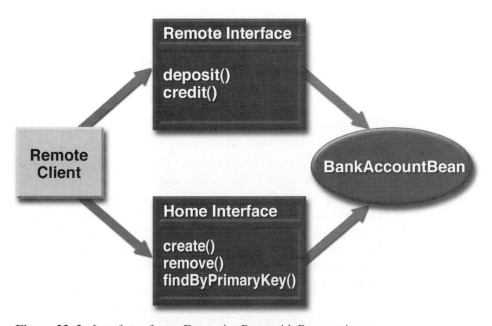

Figure 23–2 Interfaces for an Enterprise Bean with Remote Access

To build an enterprise bean that allows local access, you must code the local interface and the local home interface. The *local interface* defines the bean's business methods, and the *local home* interface defines its life-cycle and finder methods.

Local Interfaces and Container-Managed Relationships

If an entity bean is the target of a container-managed relationship, then it must have local interfaces. The direction of the relationship determines whether or not a bean is the target. In Figure 23–1, for example, ProductBean is the target of a unidirectional relationship with LineItemBean. Because LineItemBean accesses ProductBean locally, ProductBean must have the local interfaces. LineItemBean also needs local interfaces, not because of its relationship with ProductBean, but because it is the target of a relationship with OrderBean. And because the relationship between LineItemBean and OrderBean is bidirectional, both beans must have local interfaces.

Because they require local access, entity beans that participate in a container-managed relationship must reside in the same EJB JAR file. The primary benefit of this locality is increased performance: local calls are usually faster than remote calls.

Deciding on Remote or Local Access

Whether to allow local or remote access depends on the following factors.

- *Container-managed relationships*: If an entity bean is the target of a container-managed relationship, it must use local access.

- *Tight or loose coupling of related beans*: Tightly coupled beans depend on one another. For example, a completed sales order must have one or more line items, which cannot exist without the order to which they belong. The OrderBean and LineItemBean entity beans that model this relationship are tightly coupled. Tightly coupled beans are good candidates for local access. Because they fit together as a logical unit, they probably call each other often and would benefit from the increased performance that is possible with local access.

- *Type of client*: If an enterprise bean is accessed by application clients, then it should allow remote access. In a production environment, these clients almost always run on different machines than the Application Server does. If an enterprise bean's clients are Web components or other enterprise beans, then the type of access depends on how you want to distribute your components.

- *Component distribution*: J2EE applications are scalable because their server-side components can be distributed across multiple machines. In a distributed application, for example, the Web components may run on a different server than do the enterprise beans they access. In this distributed scenario, the enterprise beans should allow remote access.

- *Performance*: Because of factors such as network latency, remote calls may be slower than local calls. On the other hand, if you distribute components among different servers, you might improve the application's overall performance. Both of these statements are generalizations; actual performance can vary in different operational environments. Nevertheless, you should keep in mind how your application design might affect performance.

If you aren't sure which type of access an enterprise bean should have, then choose remote access. This decision gives you more flexibility. In the future you can distribute your components to accommodate growing demands on your application.

Although it is uncommon, it is possible for an enterprise bean to allow both remote and local access. Such a bean would require both remote and local interfaces.

Web Service Clients

A Web service client can access a J2EE application in two ways. First, the client can access a Web service created with JAX-RPC. (For more information on JAX-RPC, see Chapter 8, Building Web Services with JAX-RPC, page 313.) Second, a Web service client can invoke the business methods of a stateless session bean. Other types of enterprise beans cannot be accessed by Web service clients.

Provided that it uses the correct protocols (SOAP, HTTP, WSDL), any Web service client can access a stateless session bean, whether or not the client is written in the Java programming language. The client doesn't even "know" what technology implements the service—stateless session bean, JAX-RPC, or some other technology. In addition, enterprise beans and Web components can be clients of Web services. This flexibility enables you to integrate J2EE applications with Web services.

A Web service client accesses a stateless session bean through the bean's Web service endpoint interface. Like a remote interface, a *Web service endpoint interface* defines the business methods of the bean. In contrast to a remote interface, a Web service endpoint interface is not accompanied by a home interface, which defines the bean's life-cycle methods. The only methods of the bean that may be invoked by a Web service client are the business methods that are defined in the Web service endpoint interface.

For a code sample, see A Web Service Example: HelloServiceBean (page 884).

Method Parameters and Access

The type of access affects the parameters of the bean methods that are called by clients. The following topics apply not only to method parameters but also to method return values.

Isolation

The parameters of remote calls are more isolated than those of local calls. With remote calls, the client and bean operate on different copies of a parameter object. If the client changes the value of the object, the value of the copy in the bean does not change. This layer of isolation can help protect the bean if the client accidentally modifies the data.

In a local call, both the client and the bean can modify the same parameter object. In general, you should not rely on this side effect of local calls. Perhaps someday you will want to distribute your components, replacing the local calls with remote ones.

As with remote clients, Web service clients operate on different copies of parameters than does the bean that implements the Web service.

Granularity of Accessed Data

Because remote calls are likely to be slower than local calls, the parameters in remote methods should be relatively coarse-grained. A coarse-grained object contains more data than a fine-grained one, so fewer access calls are required.

For the same reason, the parameters of the methods called by Web service clients should also be coarse-grained.

For example, suppose that a `CustomerBean` entity bean is accessed remotely. This bean would have a single getter method that returns a `CustomerDetails` object, which encapsulates all of the customer's information. But if `Customer-Bean` is to be accessed locally, it could have a getter method for each instance variable: `getFirstName`, `getLastName`, `getPhoneNumber`, and so forth. Because local calls are fast, the multiple calls to these finer-grained getter methods would not significantly degrade performance.

The Contents of an Enterprise Bean

To develop an enterprise bean, you must provide the following files:

- *Deployment descriptor*: An XML file that specifies information about the bean such as its persistence type and transaction attributes. The `deploy-tool` utility creates the deployment descriptor when you step through the New Enterprise Bean wizard.

- *Enterprise bean class*: Implements the methods defined in the following interfaces.

- *Interfaces*: The remote and home interfaces are required for remote access. For local access, the local and local home interfaces are required. For access by Web service clients, the Web service endpoint interface is required. See the section Defining Client Access with Interfaces (page 840). (Please note that these interfaces are not used by message-driven beans.)

- *Helper classes*: Other classes needed by the enterprise bean class, such as exception and utility classes.

You package the files in the preceding list into an EJB JAR file (Figure 23–3), the module that stores the enterprise bean. An EJB JAR file is portable and can be used for different applications. To assemble a J2EE application, you package one or more modules—such as EJB JAR files—into an EAR file, the archive file that holds the application. When you deploy the EAR file that contains the bean's EJB JAR file, you also deploy the enterprise bean onto the Application Server. You can also deploy an EJB JAR that is not contained in an EAR file.

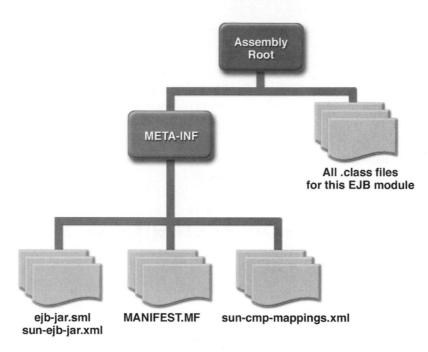

Figure 23–3 Structure of an Enterprise Bean JAR

Naming Conventions for Enterprise Beans

Because enterprise beans are composed of multiple parts, it's useful to follow a naming convention for your applications. Table 23–2 summarizes the conventions for the example beans in this tutorial.

Table 23–2 Naming Conventions for Enterprise Beans

Item	Syntax	Example
Enterprise bean name (DD[a])	*<name>*Bean	AccountBean
EJB JAR display name (DD)	*<name>*JAR	AccountJAR
Enterprise bean class	*<name>*Bean	AccountBean

Table 23–2 Naming Conventions for Enterprise Beans *(Continued)*

Item	Syntax	Example
Home interface	*\<name>*Home	AccountHome
Remote interface	*\<name>*	Account
Local home interface	*\<name>*LocalHome	AccountLocalHome
Local interface	*\<name>*Local	AccountLocal
Abstract schema (DD)	*\<name>*	Account

a. *DD* means that the item is an element in the bean's deployment descriptor.

The Life Cycles of Enterprise Beans

An enterprise bean goes through various stages during its lifetime, or life cycle. Each type of enterprise bean—session, entity, or message-driven—has a different life cycle.

The descriptions that follow refer to methods that are explained along with the code examples in the next two chapters. If you are new to enterprise beans, you should skip this section and try out the code examples first.

The Life Cycle of a Stateful Session Bean

Figure 23–4 illustrates the stages that a session bean passes through during its lifetime. The client initiates the life cycle by invoking the `create` method. The EJB container instantiates the bean and then invokes the `setSessionContext` and `ejbCreate` methods in the session bean. The bean is now ready to have its business methods invoked.

While in the ready stage, the EJB container may decide to deactivate, or *passivate*, the bean by moving it from memory to secondary storage. (Typically, the EJB container uses a least-recently used algorithm to select a bean for passivation.) The EJB container invokes the bean's `ejbPassivate` method immediately before passivating it. If a client invokes a business method on the bean while it is in the passive stage, the EJB container activates the bean, calls the bean's `ejbActivate` method, and then moves it to the ready stage.

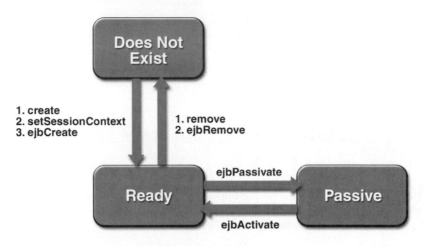

Figure 23–4 Life Cycle of a Stateful Session Bean

At the end of the life cycle, the client invokes the `remove` method, and the EJB container calls the bean's `ejbRemove` method. The bean's instance is ready for garbage collection.

Your code controls the invocation of only two life-cycle methods: the `create` and `remove` methods in the client. All other methods in Figure 23–4 are invoked by the EJB container. The `ejbCreate` method, for example, is inside the bean class, allowing you to perform certain operations right after the bean is instantiated. For example, you might wish to connect to a database in the `ejbCreate` method. See Chapter 31 for more information.

The Life Cycle of a Stateless Session Bean

Because a stateless session bean is never passivated, its life cycle has only two stages: nonexistent and ready for the invocation of business methods. Figure 23–5 illustrates the stages of a stateless session bean.

The Life Cycle of an Entity Bean

Figure 23–6 shows the stages that an entity bean passes through during its lifetime. After the EJB container creates the instance, it calls the `setEntityContext` method of the entity bean class. The `setEntityContext` method passes the entity context to the bean.

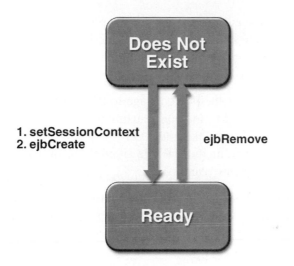

Figure 23–5   Life Cycle of a Stateless Session Bean

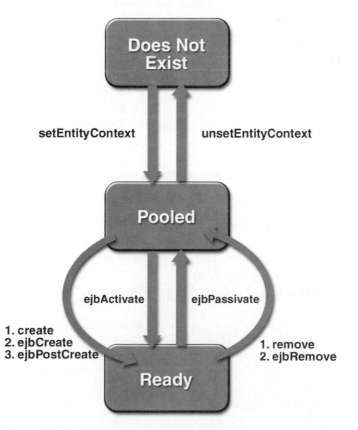

Figure 23–6   Life Cycle of an Entity Bean

After instantiation, the entity bean moves to a pool of available instances. While in the pooled stage, the instance is not associated with any particular EJB object identity. All instances in the pool are identical. The EJB container assigns an identity to an instance when moving it to the ready stage.

There are two paths from the pooled stage to the ready stage. On the first path, the client invokes the `create` method, causing the EJB container to call the `ejbCreate` and `ejbPostCreate` methods. On the second path, the EJB container invokes the `ejbActivate` method. While an entity bean is in the ready stage, its business methods can be invoked.

There are also two paths from the ready stage to the pooled stage. First, a client can invoke the `remove` method, which causes the EJB container to call the `ejbRemove` method. Second, the EJB container can invoke the `ejbPassivate` method.

At the end of the life cycle, the EJB container removes the instance from the pool and invokes the `unsetEntityContext` method.

In the pooled state, an instance is not associated with any particular EJB object identity. With bean-managed persistence, when the EJB container moves an instance from the pooled state to the ready state, it does not automatically set the primary key. Therefore, the `ejbCreate` and `ejbActivate` methods must assign a value to the primary key. If the primary key is incorrect, the `ejbLoad` and `ejbStore` methods cannot synchronize the instance variables with the database. In the section The SavingsAccountBean Example (page 903), the `ejbCreate` method assigns the primary key from one of the input parameters. The `ejbActivate` method sets the primary key (`id`) as follows:

```
id = (String)context.getPrimaryKey();
```

In the pooled state, the values of the instance variables are not needed. You can make these instance variables eligible for garbage collection by setting them to `null` in the `ejbPassivate` method.

The Life Cycle of a Message-Driven Bean

Figure 23–7 illustrates the stages in the life cycle of a message-driven bean.

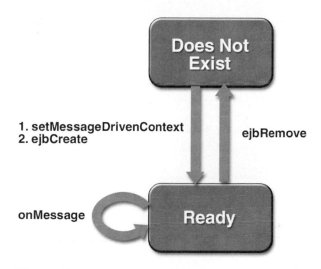

Figure 23–7 Life Cycle of a Message-Driven Bean

The EJB container usually creates a pool of message-driven bean instances. For each instance, the EJB container instantiates the bean and performs these tasks:

1. It calls the `setMessageDrivenContext` method to pass the context object to the instance.
2. It calls the instance's `ejbCreate` method.

Like a stateless session bean, a message-driven bean is never passivated, and it has only two states: nonexistent and ready to receive messages.

At the end of the life cycle, the container calls the `ejbRemove` method. The bean's instance is then ready for garbage collection.

Further Information

For further information on Enterprise JavaBeans technology, see the following:

- Enterprise JavaBeans 2.1 specification:
  `http://java.sun.com/products/ejb/docs.html`
- The Enterprise JavaBeans Web site:
  `http://java.sun.com/products/ejb`

Getting Started with Enterprise Beans

THIS chapter shows how to develop, deploy, and run a simple J2EE application named `ConverterApp`. The purpose of `ConverterApp` is to calculate currency conversions between yen and eurodollars. `ConverterApp` consists of an enterprise bean, which performs the calculations, and two types of clients: an application client and a Web client.

Here's an overview of the steps you'll follow in this chapter:

1. Create the J2EE application: `ConverterApp`.
2. Create the enterprise bean: `ConverterBean`.
3. Create the application client: `ConverterClient`.
4. Create the Web client in `ConverterWAR`.
5. Deploy `ConverterApp` onto the server.
6. From a terminal window, run `ConverterClient`.
7. Using a browser, run the Web client.

Before proceeding, make sure that you've done the following:

- Read Chapter 1.
- Become familiar with enterprise beans (see Chapter 23).
- Started the server (see Starting and Stopping the Application Server, page 25).
- Launched `deploytool` (see Starting the deploytool Utility, page 27).

Creating the J2EE Application

In this section, you'll create a J2EE application named `ConverterApp`, storing it in the file `ConverterApp.ear`.

1. In `deploytool`, select File→New→Application.
2. Click Browse.
3. In the file chooser, navigate to this directory:

   `<INSTALL>`/j2eetutorial14/examples/ejb/converter/
4. In the File Name field, enter `ConverterApp.ear`.
5. Click New Application.
6. Click OK.
7. Verify that the `ConverterApp.ear` file resides in the directory specified in step 3.

At this point, the application contains no J2EE components and cannot be deployed. In the sections that follow, when you run the `deploytool` wizards to create the components, `deploytool` will add the components to the `Converter-App.ear` file.

Creating the Enterprise Bean

The enterprise bean in our example is a stateless session bean called `Converter-Bean`. The source code for `ConverterBean` is in the `<INSTALL>`/j2eetutorial14/examples/ejb/converter/src/ directory.

Creating `ConverterBean` requires these steps:

1. Coding the bean's interfaces and class (the source code is provided)
2. Compiling the source code with `asant`
3. With `deploytool`, packaging the bean into an EJB JAR file and inserting the EJB JAR file into the application's `ConverterApp.ear` file

Coding the Enterprise Bean

The enterprise bean in this example needs the following code:

- Remote interface
- Home interface
- Enterprise bean class

Coding the Remote Interface

A *remote interface* defines the business methods that a client can call. The business methods are implemented in the enterprise bean code. The source code for the Converter remote interface follows.

```
import javax.ejb.EJBObject;
import java.rmi.RemoteException;
import java.math.*;

public interface Converter extends EJBObject {
    public BigDecimal dollarToYen(BigDecimal dollars)
        throws RemoteException;
    public BigDecimal yenToEuro(BigDecimal yen)
        throws RemoteException;
}
```

Coding the Home Interface

A *home interface* defines the methods that allow a client to create, find, or remove an enterprise bean. The ConverterHome interface contains a single create method, which returns an object of the remote interface type. Here is the source code for the ConverterHome interface:

```
import java.rmi.RemoteException;
import javax.ejb.CreateException;
import javax.ejb.EJBHome;

public interface ConverterHome extends EJBHome {
    Converter create() throws RemoteException, CreateException;
}
```

Coding the Enterprise Bean Class

The enterprise bean class for this example is called ConverterBean. This class implements the two business methods (dollarToYen and yenToEuro) that the Converter remote interface defines. The source code for the ConverterBean class follows.

```
import java.rmi.RemoteException;
import javax.ejb.SessionBean;
import javax.ejb.SessionContext;
import java.math.*;
```

```
public class ConverterBean implements SessionBean {

    BigDecimal yenRate = new BigDecimal("121.6000");
    BigDecimal euroRate = new BigDecimal("0.0077");

    public BigDecimal dollarToYen(BigDecimal dollars) {
        BigDecimal result = dollars.multiply(yenRate);
        return result.setScale(2,BigDecimal.ROUND_UP);
    }

     public BigDecimal yenToEuro(BigDecimal yen) {
         BigDecimal result = yen.multiply(euroRate);
         return result.setScale(2,BigDecimal.ROUND_UP);
     }

    public ConverterBean() {}
    public void ejbCreate() {}
    public void ejbRemove() {}
    public void ejbActivate() {}
    public void ejbPassivate() {}
    public void setSessionContext(SessionContext sc) {}
}
```

Compiling the Source Files

Now you are ready to compile the remote interface (`Converter.java`), the home interface (`ConverterHome.java`), and the enterprise bean class (`Converter-Bean.java`).

1. In a terminal window, go to this directory:

   `<INSTALL>/j2eetutorial14/examples/ejb/converter/`

2. Type the following command:

   `asant build`

This command compiles the source files for the enterprise bean and the application client, placing the class files in the `converter/build` subdirectory (not the `src` directory). The Web client in this example requires no compilation. For more information about `asant`, see Building the Examples (page xli).

Note: When compiling the code, the preceding `asant` task includes the `j2ee.jar` file in the classpath. This file resides in the `lib` directory of your Application Server Platform Edition 8 installation. If you plan to use other tools to compile the source code for J2EE components, make sure that the classpath includes the `j2ee.jar` file.

Packaging the Enterprise Bean

To package an enterprise bean, you run the Edit Enterprise Bean wizard of the `deploytool` utility. During this process, the wizard performs the following tasks:

- Creates the bean's deployment descriptor
- Packages the deployment descriptor and the bean's classes in an EJB JAR file
- Inserts the EJB JAR file into the `ConverterApp.ear` file

To start the Edit Enterprise Bean wizard, select File→New→Enterprise Bean. The wizard displays the following dialog boxes.

1. Introduction dialog box
   a. Read the explanatory text for an overview of the wizard's features.
   b. Click Next.

2. EJB JAR dialog box
   a. Select the button labeled Create New JAR Module in Application.
   b. In the combo box below this button, select `ConverterApp`.
   c. In the JAR Display Name field, enter `ConverterJAR`.
   d. Click Edit Contents.
   e. In the tree under Available Files, locate the `build/converter` subdirectory. (If the target directory is many levels down in the tree, you can simplify the tree view by entering all or part of the directory's path name in the Starting Directory field.)
   f. In the Available Files tree select these classes: `Converter.class`, `ConverterBean.class`, and `ConverterHome.class`. (You can also drag and drop these class files to the Contents text area.)
   g. Click Add.
   h. Click OK.
   i. Click Next.

3. General dialog box
   a. Under Bean Type, select the Stateless Session.
   b. In the Enterprise Bean Class combo box, select `converter.ConverterBean`.
   c. In the Enterprise Bean Name field, enter `ConverterBean`.

d. In the Remote Home Interface combo box, select `converter.Converter-Home`.

e. In the Remote Interface combo box, select `converter.Converter`.

f. Click Next.

4. In the Expose as Web Service Endpoint dialog box, select No and click Next.

5. Click Finish.

Creating the Application Client

An application client is a program written in the Java programming language. At runtime, the client program executes in a different virtual machine than the Application Server. For detailed information on the `appclient` command-line tool, see the man page at `http://java.sun.com/j2ee/1.4/docs/relnotes/cliref/index.html`.

The application client in this example requires two JAR files. The first JAR file is for the J2EE component of the client. This JAR file contains the client's deployment descriptor and class files; it is created when you run the New Application Client wizard. Defined by the *J2EE Specification*, this JAR file is portable across all compliant application servers.

The second JAR file contains stub classes that are required by the client program at runtime. These stub classes enable the client to access the enterprise beans that are running in the Application Server. The JAR file for the stubs is created by `deploytool` when you deploy the application. Because this JAR file is not covered by the J2EE specification, it is implementation-specific, intended only for the Application Server.

The application client source code is in the `ConverterClient.java` file, which is in this directory:

    <INSTALL>/j2eetutorial14/examples/ejb/converter/src/

You compiled this code along with the enterprise bean code in the section Compiling the Source Files (page 856).

Coding the Application Client

The `ConverterClient.java` source code illustrates the basic tasks performed by the client of an enterprise bean:

- Locating the home interface
- Creating an enterprise bean instance
- Invoking a business method

Locating the Home Interface

The `ConverterHome` interface defines life-cycle methods such as `create` and `remove`. Before the `ConverterClient` can invoke the `create` method, it must locate and instantiate an object whose type is `ConverterHome`. This is a four-step process.

1. Create an initial naming context.

   ```
   Context initial = new InitialContext();
   ```

   The `Context` interface is part of the Java Naming and Directory Interface (JNDI). A *naming context* is a set of name-to-object bindings. A name that is bound within a context is the *JNDI name* of the object.

   An `InitialContext` object, which implements the `Context` interface, provides the starting point for the resolution of names. All naming operations are relative to a context.

2. Obtain the environment naming context of the application client.

   ```
   Context myEnv = (Context)initial.lookup("java:comp/env");
   ```

   The `java:comp/env` name is bound to the environment naming context of the `ConverterClient` component.

3. Retrieve the object bound to the name `ejb/SimpleConverter`.

   ```
   Object objref = myEnv.lookup("ejb/SimpleConverter");
   ```

   The `ejb/SimpleConverter` name is bound to an *enterprise bean reference*, a logical name for the home of an enterprise bean. In this case, the `ejb/SimpleConverter` name refers to the `ConverterHome` object. The names of enterprise beans should reside in the `java:comp/env/ejb` subcontext.

4. Narrow the reference to a `ConverterHome` object.

```
ConverterHome home =
    (ConverterHome) PortableRemoteObject.narrow(objref,
    ConverterHome.class);
```

Creating an Enterprise Bean Instance

To create the bean instance, the client invokes the `create` method on the `ConverterHome` object. The `create` method returns an object whose type is `Converter`. The remote `Converter` interface defines the business methods of the bean that the client can call. When the client invokes the `create` method, the EJB container instantiates the bean and then invokes the `ConverterBean.ejbCreate` method. The client invokes the `create` method as follows:

```
Converter currencyConverter = home.create();
```

Invoking a Business Method

Calling a business method is easy: you simply invoke the method on the `Converter` object. The EJB container will invoke the corresponding method on the `ConverterBean` instance that is running on the server. The client invokes the `dollarToYen` business method in the following lines of code.

```
BigDecimal param = new BigDecimal ("100.00");
BigDecimal amount = currencyConverter.dollarToYen(param);
```

ConverterClient Source Code

The full source code for the `ConverterClient` program follows.

```
import javax.naming.Context;
import javax.naming.InitialContext;
import javax.rmi.PortableRemoteObject;
import java.math.BigDecimal;

public class ConverterClient {

    public static void main(String[] args) {
```

```
    try {
      Context myEnv =
        (Context)initial.lookup("java:comp/env");
      Object objref = myEnv.lookup("ejb/SimpleConverter");

      ConverterHome home =
        (ConverterHome)PortableRemoteObject.narrow(objref,
                              ConverterHome.class);

      Converter currencyConverter = home.create();

      BigDecimal param = new BigDecimal ("100.00");
      BigDecimal amount =
        currencyConverter.dollarToYen(param);
      System.out.println(amount);
      amount = currencyConverter.yenToEuro(param);
      System.out.println(amount);

      System.exit(0);

    } catch (Exception ex) {
      System.err.println("Caught an unexpected exception!");
      ex.printStackTrace();
    }
  }
}
```

Compiling the Application Client

The application client files are compiled at the same time as the enterprise bean files, as described in Compiling the Source Files (page 856).

Packaging the Application Client

To package an application client component, you run the New Application Client wizard of deploytool. During this process the wizard performs the following tasks.

- Creates the application client's deployment descriptor
- Puts the deployment descriptor and client files into a JAR file
- Adds the JAR file to the application's ConverterApp.ear file

To start the New Application Client wizard, select File→New→Application Client. The wizard displays the following dialog boxes.

1. Introduction dialog box
   a. Read the explanatory text for an overview of the wizard's features.
   b. Click Next.

2. JAR File Contents dialog box
   a. Select the button labeled Create New AppClient Module in Application.
   b. In the combo box below this button, select `ConverterApp`.
   c. In the AppClient Display Name field, enter `ConverterClient`.
   d. Click Edit Contents.
   e. In the tree under Available Files, locate this directory:

   `<INSTALL>/j2eetutorial14/examples/ejb/converter/build/`

   f. Select the `ConverterClient.class` file.
   g. Click Add.
   h. Click OK.
   i. Click Next.

3. General dialog box
   a. In the Main Class combo box, select `ConverterClient`.
   b. Click Next.
   c. Click Finish.

Specifying the Application Client's Enterprise Bean Reference

When it invokes the `lookup` method, the `ConverterClient` refers to the home of an enterprise bean:

```
Object objref = myEnv.lookup("ejb/SimpleConverter");
```

You specify this reference in `deploytool` as follows.

1. In the tree, select `ConverterClient`.
2. Select the EJB Ref's tab.

3. Click Add.

4. In the Coded Name field, enter `ejb/SimpleConverter`.

5. In the EJB Type field, select Session.

6. In the Interfaces field, select Remote.

7. In the Home Interface field enter, `converter.ConverterHome`.

8. In the Local/Remote Interface field, enter `converter.Converter`.

9. In the JNDI Name field, select `ConverterBean`.

10. Click OK.

Creating the Web Client

The Web client is contained in the JSP page `<INSTALL>/j2eetutorial14/examples/ejb/converter/web/index.jsp`. A JSP page is a text-based document that contains JSP elements, which construct dynamic content, and static template data, which can be expressed in any text-based format such as HTML, WML, and XML.

Coding the Web Client

The statements (in bold in the following code) for locating the home interface, creating an enterprise bean instance, and invoking a business method are nearly identical to those of the application client. The parameter of the `lookup` method is the only difference; the motivation for using a different name is discussed in Mapping the Enterprise Bean References (page 866).

The classes needed by the client are declared using a JSP page directive (enclosed within the `<%@ %>` characters). Because locating the home interface and creating the enterprise bean are performed only once, this code appears in a JSP declaration (enclosed within the `<%! %>` characters) that contains the initialization method, `jspInit`, of the JSP page. The declaration is followed by standard HTML markup for creating a form that contains an input field. A scriptlet (enclosed within the `<% %>` characters) retrieves a parameter from the request and converts it to a `BigDecimal` object. Finally, JSP expressions (enclosed within the `<%= %>` characters) invoke the enterprise bean's business methods and insert the result into the stream of data returned to the client.

```
<%@ page import="Converter,ConverterHome,javax.ejb.*,
javax.naming.*, javax.rmi.PortableRemoteObject,
java.rmi.RemoteException" %>
<%!
  private Converter converter = null;
  public void jspInit() {
    try {
      InitialContext ic = new InitialContext();
      Object objRef = ic.lookup("
        java:comp/env/ejb/TheConverter");
      ConverterHome home =
      (ConverterHome)PortableRemoteObject.narrow(
      objRef, ConverterHome.class);
      converter = home.create();
    } catch (RemoteException ex) {
      ...
    }
  }
  ...
%>
<html>
<head>
   <title>Converter</title>
</head>

<body bgcolor="white">
<h1><center>Converter</center></h1>
<hr>
<p>Enter an amount to convert:</p>
<form method="get">
<input type="text" name="amount" size="25">
<br>
<p>
<input type="submit" value="Submit">
<input type="reset" value="Reset">
</form>
<%
  String amount = request.getParameter("amount");
  if ( amount != null && amount.length() > 0 ) {
    BigDecimal d = new BigDecimal (amount);
%>
  <p><%= amount %> dollars are
    <%= converter.dollarToYen(d) %>  Yen.
  <p><%= amount %> Yen are
    <%= converter.yenToEuro(d) %>  Euro.
<%
  }
%>
</body>
</html>
```

Compiling the Web Client

The Application Server automatically compiles Web clients that are JSP pages. If the Web client were a servlet, you would have to compile it.

Packaging the Web Client

To package a Web client, you run the New Web Component wizard of the `deploytool` utility. During this process the wizard performs the following tasks.

- Creates the Web application deployment descriptor
- Adds the component files to a WAR file
- Adds the WAR file to the application's `ConverterApp.ear` file

To start the New Web Component wizard, select File→New→Web Component. The wizard displays the following dialog boxes.

1. Introduction dialog box
   a. Read the explanatory text for an overview of the wizard's features.
   b. Click Next.

2. WAR File dialog box
   a. Select the button labeled Create New WAR Module in Application.
   b. In the combo box below this button, select `ConverterApp`.
   c. In the WAR Name field, enter `ConverterWAR`.
   d. Click Edit Contents.
   e. In the tree under Available Files, locate this directory:

   `<INSTALL>/j2eetutorial14/examples/ejb/converter/web/`

   f. Select `index.jsp`.
   g. Click Add.
   h. Click OK.
   i. Click Next.

3. Choose Component Type dialog box
   a. Select the JSP Page button.
   b. Click Next.

4. Component General Properties dialog box
   a. In the JSP Filename combo box, select `index.jsp`.
   b. Click Finish.

Specifying the Web Client's Enterprise Bean Reference

When it invokes the `lookup` method, the Web client refers to the home of an enterprise bean:

```
Object objRef = ic.lookup("java:comp/env/ejb/TheConverter");
```

You specify this reference as follows:

1. In the tree, select `ConverterWAR`.
2. Select the EJB Ref's tab.
3. Click Add.
4. In the Coded Name field, enter `ejb/TheConverter`.
5. In the EJB Type field, select Session.
6. In the Interfaces field, select Remote.
7. In the Home Interface field, enter `converter.ConverterHome`.
8. In the Local/Remote Interface field, enter `converter.Converter`.
9. In the JNDI Name field, select `ConverterBean`.
10. Click OK.

Mapping the Enterprise Bean References

Although the application client and the Web client access the same enterprise bean, their code refers to the bean's home by different names. The application client refers to the bean's home as `ejb/SimpleConverter`, but the Web client refers to it as `ejb/TheConverter`. These references are in the parameters of the `lookup` calls. For the `lookup` method to retrieve the home object, you must map the references in the code to the enterprise bean's JNDI name. Although this mapping adds a level of indirection, it decouples the clients from the beans, making it easier to assemble applications from J2EE components.

To map the enterprise bean references in the clients to the JNDI name of the bean, follow these steps.

1. In the tree, select `ConverterApp`.
2. Click the Sun-specific Settings button.

3. Select the JNDI Names in the View field.

4. In the Application table, note that the JNDI name for the enterprise bean is `ConverterBean`.

5. In the References table, enter `ConverterBean` in the JNDI Name column for each row.

Figure 24–1 shows what the JNDI Names tab should look like after you've performed the preceding steps.

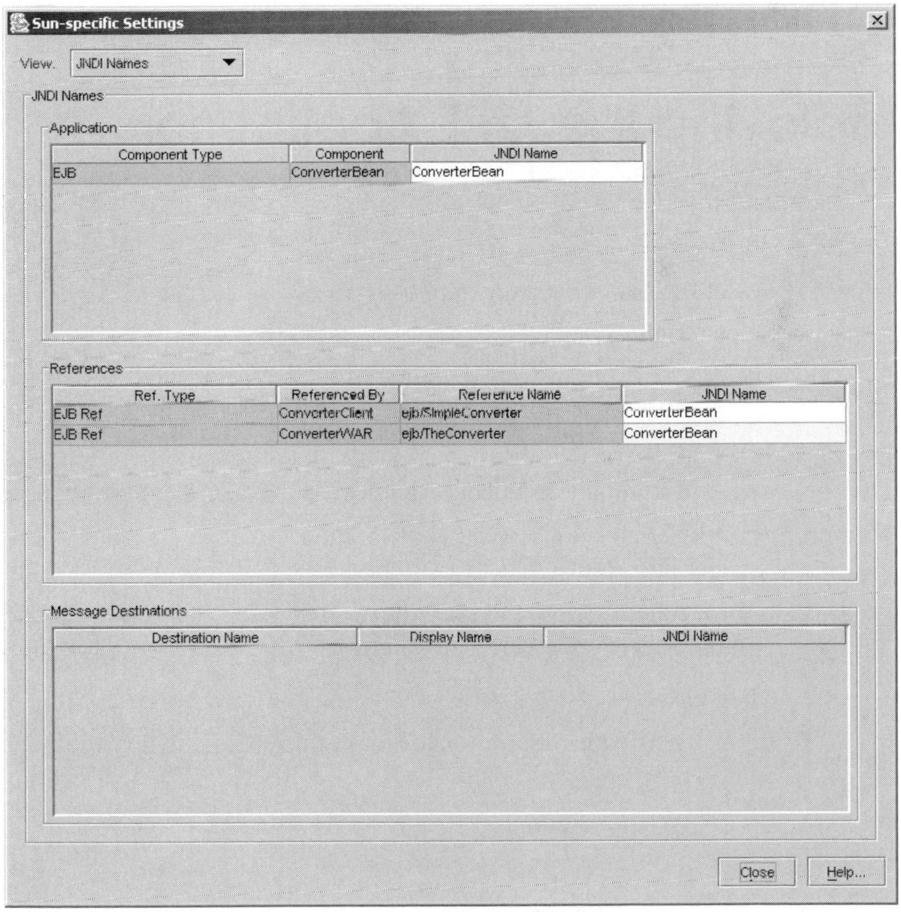

Figure 24–1 ConverterApp JNDI Names

Specifying the Web Client's Context Root

The context root identifies the Web application. To set the context root, follow these steps:

1. In the tree, select `ConverterApp`.
2. Select the Web Context tab.
3. In the Context Root field, enter `/converter`.

For more information, see Setting the Context Root (page 89).

Deploying the J2EE Application

Now that the J2EE application contains the components, it is ready for deployment.

1. Select the `ConverterApp` application.
2. Select Tools→Deploy.
3. Under Connection Settings, enter the user name and password for the Application Server.
4. Tell `deploytool` to create a JAR file that contains the client stubs. (For more information on client JAR files, see the description under Creating the Application Client, page 858.)
   a. Select the Return Client JAR checkbox.
   b. In the field below the checkbox, enter `<INSTALL>/j2eetutorial14/examples/ejb/converter`.
5. Click OK.
6. In the Distribute Module dialog box, click Close when the deployment completes.

7. Verify the deployment.

   a. In the tree, expand the Servers node and select the host that is running the Application Server.

   b. In the Deployed Objects table, make sure that the `ConverterApp` is listed and its status is Running.

8. Verify that a stub client JAR named `ConverterAppClient.jar` resides in `<INSTALL>/j2eetutorial14/examples/ejb/converter`.

Running the Application Client

To run the application client, perform the following steps.

1. In a terminal window, go to this directory:

   `<INSTALL>/j2eetutorial14/examples/ejb/converter/`

2. Type the following command:

   `appclient -client ConverterAppClient.jar`

3. In the terminal window, the client displays these lines:

   ```
   . . .
   12160.00
   0.77
   . . .
   ```

Running the Web Client

To run the Web client, point your browser at the following URL. Replace *<host>* with the name of the host running the Application Server. If your browser is running on the same host as the Application Server, you can replace *<host>* with `localhost`.

   `http://<host>:8080/converter`

After entering `100` in the input field and clicking Submit, you should see the screen shown in Figure 24–2.

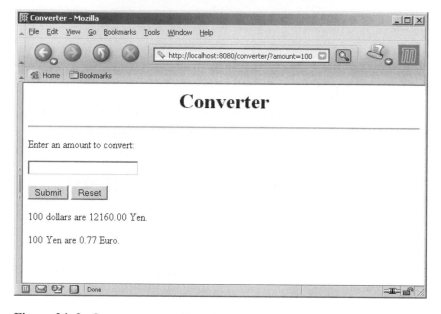

Figure 24–2 ConverterApp Web Client

Modifying the J2EE Application

The Application Server and deploytool support iterative development. Whenever you make a change to a J2EE application, you must redeploy the application.

Modifying a Class File

To modify a class file in an enterprise bean, you change the source code, recompile it, and redeploy the application. For example, if you want to change the exchange rate in the dollarToYen business method of the ConverterBean class, you would follow these steps.

1. Edit ConverterBean.java.
2. Recompile ConverterBean.java.
   a. In a terminal window, go to the <INSTALL>/j2eetutorial14/examples/ejb/converter/ subdirectory.
   b. Type asant build.

3. In `deploytool`, select Tools→Update Module Files.

4. The Update Files dialog box appears. If the modified files are listed at the top of the dialog, click OK and go to step 6. If the files are listed at the bottom, they have not been found. Select one of those files and click Edit Search Paths.

5. In the Edit Search Paths dialog box, specify the directories where the Update Files dialog will search for modified files.

   a. In the Search Root field, enter the fully qualified name of the directory from which the search will start.

   b. In the Path Directory list, add a row for each directory that you want searched. Unless fully qualified, these directory names are relative to the Search Root field.

   c. Click OK.

6. Select Tools→Deploy. Make sure that the checkbox labeled Save Object Before Deploying is checked. If you do not want to deploy at this time, select Tools→Save to save the search paths specified in step 5.

To modify the contents of a WAR file, you follow the preceding steps. The Update Files operation checks to see whether any files have changed, including HTML files and JSP pages. If you change the `index.jsp` file of `ConverterApp`, be sure to type `asant`. This task copies the `index.jsp` file from the web directory to the `build` directory.

Adding a File

To add a file to the EJB JAR or WAR of the application, perform these steps.

1. In `deploytool`, select the JAR or WAR in the tree.

2. Select the General tab.

3. Click Edit Contents.

4. In the tree of the Available Files field, locate the file and click Add.

5. Click OK.

6. From the main toolbar, select Tools→Update Module Files.

7. Select Tools→Deploy.

Modifying a Deployment Setting

To modify a deployment setting of ConverterApp, you edit the appropriate field in a tabbed pane and redeploy the application. For example, to change a JNDI name from ATypo to ConverterBean, you would follow these steps.

1. In deploytool, select ConverterApp in the tree.
2. Select the JNDI Names tab.
3. In the JNDI Name field, enter MyConverter.
4. From the main toolbar, select File→Save.
5. Select Tools→Update Module Files.
6. Select Tools→Deploy.

25

Session Bean Examples

SESSION beans are powerful because they extend the reach of your clients into remote servers yet are easy to build. In Chapter 24, you built a stateless session bean named `ConverterBean`. This chapter examines the source code of three more session beans:

- `CartBean`: a stateful session bean that is accessed by a remote client
- `HelloServiceBean`: a stateless session bean that implements a Web service
- `TimerSessionBean`: a stateless session bean that sets a timer

The CartBean Example

The `CartBean` session bean represents a shopping cart in an online bookstore. The bean's client can add a book to the cart, remove a book, or retrieve the cart's contents. To construct `CartBean`, you need the following code:

- Session bean class (`CartBean`)
- Home interface (`CartHome`)
- Remote interface (`Cart`)

All session beans require a session bean class. All enterprise beans that permit remote access must have a home and a remote interface. To meet the needs of a

873

specific application, an enterprise bean may also need some helper classes. The CartBean session bean uses two helper classes (BookException and IdVerifier) which are discussed in the section Helper Classes (page 880).

The source code for this example is in the <INSTALL>/j2eetutorial14/ examples/ejb/cart/ directory.

Session Bean Class

The session bean class for this example is called CartBean. Like any session bean, the CartBean class must meet these requirements:

- It implements the SessionBean interface.
- The class is defined as public.
- The class cannot be defined as abstract or final.
- It implements one or more ejbCreate methods.
- It implements the business methods.
- It contains a public constructor with no parameters.
- It must not define the finalize method.

The source code for the CartBean class follows.

```
import java.util.*;
import javax.ejb.*;

public class CartBean implements SessionBean {

    String customerName;
    String customerId;
    Vector contents;

    public void ejbCreate(String person)
      throws CreateException {

        if (person == null) {
            throw new CreateException("Null person not allowed.");
        }
        else {
            customerName = person;
        }

        customerId = "0";
        contents = new Vector();
    }
```

```java
public void ejbCreate(String person, String id)
    throws CreateException {

  if (person == null) {
    throw new CreateException("Null person not allowed.");
  }
  else {
    customerName = person;
  }

  IdVerifier idChecker = new IdVerifier();
  if (idChecker.validate(id)) {
    customerId = id;
  }
  else {
    throw new CreateException("Invalid id: "+ id);
  }

  contents = new Vector();
}

public void addBook(String title) {
  contents.addElement(title);
}

public void removeBook(String title) throws BookException {

  boolean result = contents.removeElement(title);
  if (result == false) {
    throw new BookException(title + "not in cart.");
  }
}

public Vector getContents() {
  return contents;
}

public CartBean() {}
public void ejbRemove() {}
public void ejbActivate() {}
public void ejbPassivate() {}
public void setSessionContext(SessionContext sc) {}

}
```

The SessionBean Interface

The `SessionBean` interface extends the `EnterpriseBean` interface, which in turn extends the `Serializable` interface. The `SessionBean` interface declares the `ejbRemove`, `ejbActivate`, `ejbPassivate`, and `setSessionContext` methods. The `CartBean` class doesn't use these methods, but it must implement them because they're declared in the `SessionBean` interface. Consequently, these methods are empty in the `CartBean` class. Later sections explain when you might use these methods.

The ejbCreate Methods

Because an enterprise bean runs inside an EJB container, a client cannot directly instantiate the bean. Only the EJB container can instantiate an enterprise bean. During instantiation, the example program performs the following steps.

1. The client invokes a `create` method on the home object:

```
Cart shoppingCart = home.create("Duke DeEarl","123");
```

2. The EJB container instantiates the enterprise bean.

3. The EJB container invokes the appropriate `ejbCreate` method in Cart-Bean:

```
public void ejbCreate(String person, String id)
    throws CreateException {

    if (person == null) {
        throw new CreateException("Null person not allowed.");
    }
    else {
        customerName = person;
    }

    IdVerifier idChecker = new IdVerifier();
    if (idChecker.validate(id)) {
        customerId = id;
    }
    else {
        throw new CreateException("Invalid id: "+ id);
    }

    contents = new Vector();
}
```

Typically, an `ejbCreate` method initializes the state of the enterprise bean. The preceding `ejbCreate` method, for example, initializes the `customerName` and `customerId` variables by using the arguments passed by the `create` method.

An enterprise bean must have one or more `ejbCreate` methods. The signatures of the methods must meet the following requirements:

- The access control modifier must be `public`.
- The return type must be `void`.
- If the bean allows remote access, the arguments must be legal types for the Java Remote Method Invocation (Java RMI) API.
- The modifier cannot be `static` or `final`.

The `throws` clause can include the `javax.ejb.CreateException` and other exceptions that are specific to your application. The `ejbCreate` method usually throws a `CreateException` if an input parameter is invalid.

Business Methods

The primary purpose of a session bean is to run business tasks for the client. The client invokes business methods on the remote object reference that is returned by the `create` method. From the client's perspective, the business methods appear to run locally, but they actually run remotely in the session bean. The following code snippet shows how the `CartClient` program invokes the business methods:

```
Cart shoppingCart = home.create("Duke DeEarl", "123");
...
shoppingCart.addBook("The Martian Chronicles");
shoppingCart.removeBook("Alice In Wonderland");
bookList = shoppingCart.getContents();
```

The `CartBean` class implements the business methods in the following code:

```
public void addBook(String title) {
    contents.addElement(title);
}

public void removeBook(String title) throws BookException {
    boolean result = contents.removeElement(title);
    if (result == false) {
        throw new BookException(title + "not in cart.");
    }
}

public Vector getContents() {
    return contents;
}
```

The signature of a business method must conform to these rules:

- The method name must not conflict with one defined by the EJB architecture. For example, you cannot call a business method ejbCreate or ejbActivate.
- The access control modifier must be public.
- If the bean allows remote access, the arguments and return types must be legal types for the Java RMI API.
- The modifier must not be static or final.

The throws clause can include exceptions that you define for your application. The removeBook method, for example, throws the BookException if the book is not in the cart.

To indicate a system-level problem, such as the inability to connect to a database, a business method should throw the javax.ejb.EJBException. When a business method throws an EJBException, the container wraps it in a RemoteException, which is caught by the client. The container will not wrap application exceptions such as BookException. Because EJBException is a subclass of RuntimeException, you do not need to include it in the throws clause of the business method.

Home Interface

A home interface extends the javax.ejb.EJBHome interface. For a session bean, the purpose of the home interface is to define the create methods that a remote client can invoke. The CartClient program, for example, invokes this create method:

```
Cart shoppingCart = home.create("Duke DeEarl", "123");
```

Every create method in the home interface corresponds to an ejbCreate method in the bean class. The signatures of the ejbCreate methods in the CartBean class follow:

```
public void ejbCreate(String person) throws CreateException
...
public void ejbCreate(String person, String id)
    throws CreateException
```

Compare the ejbCreate signatures with those of the create methods in the CartHome interface:

```
import java.io.Serializable;
import java.rmi.RemoteException;
import javax.ejb.CreateException;
import javax.ejb.EJBHome;

public interface CartHome extends EJBHome {
   Cart create(String person) throws
               RemoteException, CreateException;
   Cart create(String person, String id) throws
               RemoteException, CreateException;
}
```

The signatures of the ejbCreate and create methods are similar, but they differ in important ways. The rules for defining the signatures of the create methods of a home interface follow.

- The number and types of arguments in a create method must match those of its corresponding ejbCreate method.
- The arguments and return type of the create method must be valid RMI types.
- A create method returns the remote interface type of the enterprise bean. (But an ejbCreate method returns void.)
- The throws clause of the create method must include the java.rmi.RemoteException and the javax.ejb.CreateException.

Remote Interface

The remote interface, which extends javax.ejb.EJBObject, defines the business methods that a remote client can invoke. Here is the source code for the Cart remote interface:

```
import java.util.*;
import javax.ejb.EJBObject;
import java.rmi.RemoteException;

public interface Cart extends EJBObject {

    public void addBook(String title) throws RemoteException;
```

```
    public void removeBook(String title) throws
                BookException, RemoteException;
    public Vector getContents() throws RemoteException;
}
```

The method definitions in a remote interface must follow these rules:

- Each method in the remote interface must match a method implemented in the enterprise bean class.
- The signatures of the methods in the remote interface must be identical to the signatures of the corresponding methods in the enterprise bean class.
- The arguments and return values must be valid RMI types.
- The `throws` clause must include the `java.rmi.RemoteException`.

Helper Classes

The `CartBean` session bean has two helper classes: `BookException` and `IdVerifier`. The `BookException` is thrown by the `removeBook` method, and the `IdVerifier` validates the `customerId` in one of the `ejbCreate` methods. Helper classes must reside in the EJB JAR file that contains the enterprise bean class.

Building the CartBean Example

Now you are ready to compile the remote interface (`Cart.java`), the home interface (`CartHome.java`), the enterprise bean class (`CartBean.java`), the client class (`CartClient.java`), and the helper classes (`BookException.java` and `IdVerifier.java`).

1. In a terminal window, go to this directory:

   `<INSTALL>/j2eetutorial14/examples/ejb/cart/`

2. Type the following command:

   `asant build`

Creating the Application

In this section, you'll create a J2EE application named `CartApp`, storing it in the file `CartApp.ear`.

1. In `deploytool`, select File→New→Application.

2. Click Browse.

3. In the file chooser, navigate to *<INSTALL>*`/j2eetutorial14/examples/ejb/cart/`.

4. In the File Name field, enter `CartApp`.

5. Click New Application.

6. Click OK.

7. Verify that the `CartApp.ear` file resides in *<INSTALL>*`/j2eetutorial14/examples/ejb/cart/`.

Packaging the Enterprise Bean

1. In `deploytool`, select File→New→Enterprise Bean.

2. In the EJB JAR screen:

    a. Select Create New JAR Module in Application.

    b. In the Create New JAR Module in Application field, select `CartApp`.

    c. In the JAR Name field, enter `CartJAR`.

    d. Click Choose Module File.

    e. Click Edit Contents.

    f. Locate the *<INSTALL>*`/j2eetutorial14/examples/ejb/cart/build/` directory.

    g. Select `BookException.class`, `Cart.class`, `CartBean.class`, `CartHome.class`, and `IdVerifier.class`.

    h. Click Add.

    i. Click OK.

    j. Click Next.

3. In the General screen:

    a. In the Enterprise Bean Class field, select `CartBean`.

    b. In the Enterprise Bean Name field, enter `CartBean`.

    c. In the Enterprise Bean Type field, select `Stateful Session`.

    d. In the Remote Home Interface field, select `CartHome`.

    e. In the Remote Interface field, select `Cart`.

    f. Click Next.

4. Click Finish.

Packaging the Application Client

To package an application client component, you run the New Application Client wizard of `deploytool`. During this process the wizard performs the following tasks.

- Creates the application client's deployment descriptor
- Puts the deployment descriptor and client files into a JAR file
- Adds the JAR file to the application's `CartApp.ear` file

To start the New Application Client wizard, select File→New→Application Client. The wizard displays the following dialog boxes.

1. Introduction dialog box
   a. Read the explanatory text for an overview of the wizard's features.
   b. Click Next.

2. JAR File Contents dialog box
   a. Select the button labeled Create New AppClient Module in Application.
   b. In the combo box below this button, select `CartApp`.
   c. In the AppClient Display Name field, enter `CartClient`.
   d. Click Edit Contents.
   e. In the tree under Available Files, locate the `<INSTALL>`/`j2ee-tutorial14/examples/ejb/cart/build` directory.
   f. Select `CartClient.class`.
   g. Click Add.
   h. Click OK.
   i. Click Next.

3. General dialog box

   a. In the Main Class combo box, select `CartClient`.
   b. Click Next.
   c. Click Finish.

Specifying the Application Client's Enterprise Bean Reference

When it invokes the `lookup` method, the `CartClient` refers to the home of an enterprise bean:

```
Object objref =
    initial.lookup("java:comp/env/ejb/SimpleCart");
```

You specify this reference as follows:

1. In the tree, select `CartClient`.
2. Select the EJB Ref's tab.
3. Click Add.
4. In the Coded Name field, enter `ejb/SimpleCart`.
5. In the EJB Type field, select Session.
6. In the Interfaces field, select Remote.
7. In the Home Interface field, enter `CartHome`.
8. In the Local/Remote Interface field, enter `Cart`.
9. In the JNDI Name field, select `CartBean`.
10. Click OK.

Deploying the Enterprise Application

Now that the J2EE application contains the components, it is ready for deployment.

1. Select `CartApp`.
2. Select Tools→Deploy.
3. Under Connection Settings, enter the user name and password for the Application Server Platform Edition 8.
4. Under Application Client Stub Directory, check Return Client Jar.
5. In the field below the checkbox enter `<INSTALL>/j2eetutorial14/examples/ejb/cart/`.
6. Click OK.
7. In the Distribute Module dialog box, click Close when the deployment completes.

8. Verify the deployment.

   a. In the tree, expand the Servers node and select the host that is running the Application Server.

   b. In the Deployed Objects table, make sure that `CartApp` is listed and that its status is `Running`.

   c. Verify that `CartAppClient.jar` is in `<INSTALL>`/j2eetutorial14/ examples/ejb/cart/.

Running the Application Client

To run the application client, perform the following steps.

1. In a terminal window, go to the `<INSTALL>`/j2eetutorial14/ examples/ejb/cart/ directory.

2. Type the following command:

   ```
   appclient -client CartAppClient.jar
   ```

3. In the terminal window, the client displays these lines:

   ```
   The Martian Chronicles
   2001 A Space Odyssey
   The Left Hand of Darkness
   Caught a BookException: Alice in Wonderland not in cart.
   ```

A Web Service Example: HelloServiceBean

This example demonstrates a simple Web service that generates a response based on information received from the client. `HelloServiceBean` is a stateless session bean that implements a single method, `sayHello`. This method matches the `sayHello` method invoked by the clients described in Static Stub Client (page 321). Later in this section, you'll test the `HelloServiceBean` by running one of these JAX-RPC clients.

Web Service Endpoint Interface

`HelloService` is the bean's Web service endpoint interface. It provides the client's view of the Web service, hiding the stateless session bean from the client. A Web service endpoint interface must conform to the rules of a JAX-RPC service definition interface. For a summary of these rules, see Coding the Service Endpoint Interface and Implementation Class (page 316). Here is the source code for the `HelloService` interface:

```
package helloservice;
import java.rmi.RemoteException;
import java.rmi.Remote;

public interface HelloService extends Remote {

    public String sayHello(String name) throws RemoteException;
}
```

Stateless Session Bean Implementation Class

The `HelloServiceBean` class implements the `sayHello` method defined by the `HelloService` interface. The interface decouples the implementation class from the type of client access. For example, if you added remote and home interfaces to `HelloServiceBean`, the methods of the `HelloServiceBean` class could also be accessed by remote clients. No changes to the `HelloServiceBean` class would be necessary. The source code for the `HelloServiceBean` class follows:

```
package helloservice;
import java.rmi.RemoteException;
import javax.ejb.SessionBean;
import javax.ejb.SessionContext;

public class HelloServiceBean implements SessionBean {

    public String sayHello(String name) {

        return "Hello "+ name + " from HelloServiceBean";
    }

    public HelloServiceBean() {}
    public void ejbCreate() {}
    public void ejbRemove() {}
    public void ejbActivate() {}
    public void ejbPassivate() {}
    public void setSessionContext(SessionContext sc) {}
}
```

Building HelloServiceBean

In a terminal window, go to the *<INSTALL>*/j2eetutorial14/examples/ejb/helloservice/ directory. To build HelloServiceBean, type the following command:

```
asant build-service
```

This command performs the following tasks:

- Compiles the bean's source code files
- Creates the MyHelloService.wsdl file by running the following wscompile command:

  ```
  wscompile -define -d build/output -nd build -classpath build
  -mapping build/mapping.xml config-interface.xml
  ```

The wscompile tool writes the MyHelloService.wsdl file to the *<INSTALL>*/j2eetutorial14/examples/ejb/helloservice/build/ subdirectory. For more information about the wscompile tool, see Chapter 8.

Use deploytool to package and deploy this example.

Creating the Application

In this section, you'll create a J2EE application named HelloService, storing it in the file HelloService.ear.

1. In deploytool, select File→New→Application.
2. Click Browse.
3. In the file chooser, navigate to *<INSTALL>*/j2eetutorial14/examples/ejb/helloservice/.
4. In the File Name field, enter HelloServiceApp.
5. Click New Application.
6. Click OK.
7. Verify that the HelloServiceApp.ear file resides in *<INSTALL>*/j2eetutorial14/examples/ejb/helloservice/.

Packaging the Enterprise Bean

Start the Edit Enterprise Bean wizard by selecting File→New→Enterprise Bean.
The wizard displays the following dialog boxes.

1. Introduction dialog box
   a. Read the explanatory text for an overview of the wizard's features.
   b. Click Next.

2. EJB JAR dialog box
   a. Select the button labeled Create New JAR Module in Application.
   b. In the combo box below this button, select `HelloService`.
   c. In the JAR Display Name field, enter `HelloServiceJAR`.
   d. Click Edit Contents.
   e. In the tree under Available Files, locate the `<INSTALL>/j2ee-tutorial14/examples/ejb/helloservice/build/` directory.
   f. In the Available Files tree select the `helloservice` directory and `mapping.xml` and `MyHelloService.wsdl`.
   g. Click Add.
   h. Click OK.
   i. Click Next.

3. General dialog box
   a. In the Enterprise Bean Class combo box, select `helloservice.HelloServiceBean`.
   b. Under Enterprise Bean Type, select Stateless Session.
   c. In the Enterprise Bean Name field, enter `HelloServiceBean`.
   d. Click Next.

4. In the Configuration Options dialog box, click Next. The wizard will automatically select the Yes button for Expose Bean as Web Service Endpoint.

5. In the Choose Service dialog box:
   a. Select `META-INF/wsdl/MyHelloService.wsdl` in the WSDL File combo box.
   b. Select `mapping.xml` from the Mapping File combo box.
   c. Make sure that `MyHelloService` is in the Service Name and Service Display Name edit boxes.

6. In the Web Service Endpoint dialog box:

   a. Select `helloservice.HelloIF` in the Service Endpoint Interface combo box.

   b. In the WSDL Port section, set the Namespace to `urn:Foo`, and the Local Part to `HelloIFPort`.

   c. In the Sun-specific Settings section, set the Endpoint Address to `hello-ejb/hello`.

   d. Click Next.

7. Click Finish.

8. Select File→Save.

Deploying the Enterprise Application

Now that the J2EE application contains the enterprise bean, it is ready for deployment.

1. Select the `HelloService` application.

2. Select Tools→Deploy.

3. Under Connection Settings, enter the user name and password for the Application Server.

4. Click OK.

5. In the Distribute Module dialog box, click Close when the deployment completes.

6. Verify the deployment.

   a. In the tree, expand the Servers node and select the host that is running the Application Server.

   b. In the Deployed Objects table, make sure that `HelloService` is listed and that its status is `Running`.

Building the Web Service Client

In the next section, to test the Web service implemented by `HelloServiceBean`, you will run the JAX-RPC client described in Chapter 8.

To verify that `HelloServiceBean` has been deployed, click on the target application server in the Servers tree in `deploytool`. In the Deployed Objects tree you should see `HelloServiceApp`.

To build the static stub client, perform these steps:

1. In a terminal go to the *<INSTALL>*/j2eetutorial14/examples/jaxrpc/ helloservice/ directory and type

   `asant build`

2. In a terminal go to the *<INSTALL>*/j2eetutorial14/examples/jaxrpc/ staticstub/ directory.

3. Open `config-wsdl.xml` in a text editor and change the line that reads

   `<wsdl location="http://localhost:8080/hello-jaxrpc/hello?WSDL"`

   to

   `<wsdl location="http://localhost:8080/hello-ejb/hello?WSDL"`

4. Type

   `asant build`

5. Edit the `build.properties` file and change the `endpoint.address` property to

   `http://localhost:8080/hello-ejb/hello`

For details about creating the JAX-RPC service and client, see these sections: Creating a Simple Web Service and Client with JAX-RPC (page 314) and Static Stub Client (page 321).

Running the Web Service Client

To run the client, go to the *<INSTALL>*/j2eetutorial14/examples/jaxrpc/ staticstub/ directory and enter

   `asant run`

The client should display the following line:

   `Hello Duke! (from HelloServiceBean)`

Other Enterprise Bean Features

The topics that follow apply to session beans and entity beans.

Accessing Environment Entries

Stored in an enterprise bean's deployment descriptor, an *environment entry* is a name-value pair that allows you to customize the bean's business logic without changing its source code. An enterprise bean that calculates discounts, for example, might have an environment entry named Discount Percent. Before deploying the bean's application, you could run a development tool to assign Discount Percent a value of 0.05 in the bean's deployment descriptor. When you run the application, the bean fetches the 0.05 value from its environment.

In the following code example, the applyDiscount method uses environment entries to calculate a discount based on the purchase amount. First, the method locates the environment naming context by invoking lookup using the java:comp/env parameter. Then it calls lookup on the environment to get the values for the Discount Level and Discount Percent names. For example, if you assign a value of 0.05 to the Discount Percent entry, the code will assign 0.05 to the discountPercent variable. The applyDiscount method, which follows, is in the CheckerBean class. The source code for this example is in *<INSTALL>*/j2eetutorial14/examples/ejb/checker.

```
public double applyDiscount(double amount) {

    try {

        double discount;

        Context initial = new InitialContext();
          Context environment =
            (Context)initial.lookup("java:comp/env");

        Double discountLevel =
          (Double)environment.lookup("Discount Level");
            Double discountPercent =
              (Double)environment.lookup("Discount Percent");

        if (amount >= discountLevel.doubleValue()) {
          discount = discountPercent.doubleValue();
        }
        else {
          discount = 0.00;
        }

        return amount * (1.00 - discount);

    } catch (NamingException ex) {
```

```
        throw new EJBException("NamingException: "+
            ex.getMessage());
    }
}
```

Comparing Enterprise Beans

A client can determine whether two stateful session beans are identical by invoking the isIdentical method:

```
bookCart = home.create("Bill Shakespeare");
videoCart = home.create("Lefty Lee");
...
if (bookCart.isIdentical(bookCart)) {
    // true ... }
if (bookCart.isIdentical(videoCart)) {
    // false ... }
```

Because stateless session beans have the same object identity, the isIdentical method always returns true when used to compare them.

To determine whether two entity beans are identical, the client can invoke the isIdentical method, or it can fetch and compare the beans's primary keys:

```
String key1 = (String)accta.getPrimaryKey();
String key2 = (String)acctb.getPrimaryKey();

if (key1.compareTo(key2) == 0)
    System.out.println("equal");
```

Passing an Enterprise Bean's Object Reference

Suppose that your enterprise bean needs to pass a reference to itself to another bean. You might want to pass the reference, for example, so that the second bean can call the first bean's methods. You can't pass the this reference because it points to the bean's instance, which is running in the EJB container. Only the container can directly invoke methods on the bean's instance. Clients access the instance indirectly by invoking methods on the object whose type is the bean's remote interface. It is the reference to this object (the bean's remote reference) that the first bean would pass to the second bean.

A session bean obtains its remote reference by calling the `getEJBObject` method of the `SessionContext` interface. An entity bean would call the `getEJ-BObject` method of the `EntityContext` interface. These interfaces provide beans with access to the instance contexts maintained by the EJB container. Typically, the bean saves the context in the `setSessionContext` method. The following code fragment shows how a session bean might use these methods.

```
public class WagonBean implements SessionBean {

    SessionContext context;
    ...
    public void setSessionContext(SessionContext sc) {
        this.context = sc;
    }
    ...
    public void passItOn(Basket basket) {
    ...
        basket.copyItems(context.getEJBObject());
    }
```

Using the Timer Service

Applications that model business work flows often rely on timed notifications. The timer service of the enterprise bean container enables you to schedule timed notifications for all types of enterprise beans except for stateful session beans. You can schedule a timed notification to occur at a specific time, after a duration of time, or at timed intervals. For example, you could set timers to go off at 10:30 AM on May 23, in 30 days, or every 12 hours.

When a timer expires (goes off), the container calls the `ejbTimeout` method of the bean's implementation class. The `ejbTimeout` method contains the business logic that handles the timed event. Because `ejbTimeout` is defined by the `javax.ejb.TimedObject` interface, the bean class must implement `TimedObject`.

There are four interfaces in the `javax.ejb` package that are related to timers:

- `TimedObject`
- `Timer`
- `TimerHandle`
- `TimerService`

Creating Timers

To create a timer, the bean invokes one of the `createTimer` methods of the `TimerService` interface. (For details on the method signatures, see the `Timer-Service` API documentation.) When the bean invokes `createTimer`, the timer service begins to count down the timer duration.

The bean described in The TimerSessionBean Example (page 895) creates a timer as follows:

```
TimerService timerService = context.getTimerService();
Timer timer = timerService.createTimer(intervalDuration,
    "created timer");
```

In the `TimerSessionBean` example, `createTimer` is invoked in a business method, which is called by a client. An entity bean can also create a timer in a business method. If you want to create a timer for each instance of an entity bean, you can code the `createTimer` call in the bean's `ejbCreate` method.

Timers are persistent. If the server is shut down (or even crashes), timers are saved and will become active again when the server is restarted. If a timer expires while the server is down, the container will call `ejbTimeout` when the server is restarted.

A timer for an entity bean is associated with the bean's identity—that is, with a particular instance of the bean. If an entity bean sets a timer in `ejbCreate`, for example, each bean instance will have its own timer. In contrast, stateless session and message-driven beans do not have unique timers for each instance.

The `Date` and `long` parameters of the `createTimer` methods represent time with the resolution of milliseconds. However, because the timer service is not intended for real-time applications, a callback to `ejbTimeout` might not occur with millisecond precision. The timer service is for business applications, which typically measure time in hours, days, or longer durations.

Canceling and Saving Timers

Timers can be canceled by the following events:

- When a single-event timer expires, the EJB container calls `ejbTimeout` and then cancels the timer.
- When an entity bean instance is removed, the container cancels the timers associated with the instance.
- When the bean invokes the `cancel` method of the `Timer` interface, the container cancels the timer.

If a method is invoked on a canceled timer, the container throws the `javax.ejb.NoSuchObjectLocalException`.

To save a `Timer` object for future reference, invoke its `getHandle` method and store the `TimerHandle` object in a database. (A `TimerHandle` object is serializable.) To reinstantiate the `Timer` object, retrieve the handle from the database and invoke `getTimer` on the handle. A `TimerHandle` object cannot be passed as an argument of a method defined in a remote or Web service interface. In other words, remote clients and Web service clients cannot access a bean's `TimerHandle` object. Local clients, however, do not have this restriction.

Getting Timer Information

In addition to defining the `cancel` and `getHandle` methods, the `Timer` interface defines methods for obtaining information about timers:

```
public long getTimeRemaining();
public java.util.Date getNextTimeout();
public java.io.Serializable getInfo();
```

The `getInfo` method returns the object that was the last parameter of the `createTimer` invocation. For example, in the `createTimer` code snippet of the preceding section, this information parameter is a `String` object with the value `created timer`.

To retrieve all of a bean's active timers, call the `getTimers` method of the `TimerService` interface. The `getTimers` method returns a collection of `Timer` objects.

Transactions and Timers

An enterprise bean usually creates a timer within a transaction. If this transaction is rolled back, the timer creation is also rolled back. Similarly, if a bean cancels a timer within a transaction that gets rolled back, the timer cancellation is rolled back. In this case, the timer's duration is reset as if the cancellation had never occurred.

In beans that use container-managed transactions, the `ejbTimeout` method usually has the `RequiresNew` transaction attribute to preserve transaction integrity. With this attribute, the EJB container begins the new transaction before calling `ejbTimeout`. If the transaction is rolled back, the container will try to call `ejbTimeout` at least one more time.

The TimerSessionBean Example

The source code for this example is in the *<INSTALL>*/j2eetutorial14/examples/ejb/timersession/src/ directory.

TimerSessionBean is a stateless session bean that shows how to set a timer. The implementation class for TimerSessionBean is called TimerSessionBean. In the source code listing of TimerSessionBean that follows, note the myCreateTimer and ejbTimeout methods. Because it's a business method, myCreateTimer is defined in the bean's remote interface (TimerSession) and can be invoked by the client. In this example, the client invokes myCreateTimer with an interval duration of 30,000 milliseconds. The myCreateTimer method fetches a TimerService object from the bean's SessionContext. Then it creates a new timer by invoking the createTimer method of TimerService. Now that the timer is set, the EJB container will invoke the ejbTimer method of TimerSessionBean when the timer expires—in about 30 seconds. Here's the source code for the TimerSessionBean class:

```
import javax.ejb.*;

public class TimerSessionBean implements SessionBean,
    TimedObject {

    private SessionContext context;

    public TimerHandle myCreateTimer(long intervalDuration) {

        System.out.println
            ("TimerSessionBean: start createTimer ");
        TimerService timerService =
            context.getTimerService();
        Timer timer =
            timerService.createTimer(intervalDuration,
            "created timer");
    }

    public void ejbTimeout(Timer timer) {

        System.out.println("TimerSessionBean: ejbTimeout ");
    }

    public void setSessionContext(SessionContext sc) {
        System.out.println("TimerSessionBean:
            setSessionContext");
        context = sc;
    }
```

```
public void ejbCreate() {
    System.out.println("TimerSessionBean: ejbCreate");
}

public TimerSessionBean() {}
public void ejbRemove() {}
public void ejbActivate() {}
public void ejbPassivate() {}

}
```

Building TimerSessionBean

In a terminal window, go to the *<INSTALL>*/j2eetutorial14/examples/ejb/
timersession/ directory. To build TimerSessionBean, type the following
command:

```
asant build
```

Use deploytool to package and deploy this example.

Creating the Application

In this section, you'll create a J2EE application named TimerSessionApp, storing it in the file TimerSessionApp.ear.

1. In deploytool, select File→New→Application.
2. Click Browse.
3. In the file chooser, navigate to *<INSTALL>*/j2eetutorial14/examples/
   ejb/timersession/.
4. In the File Name field, enter TimerSessionApp.ear.
5. Click New Application.
6. Click OK.
7. Verify that the TimerSessonApp.ear file resides in *<INSTALL>*/
   j2eetutorial14/examples/ejb/timersession/.

Packaging the Enterprise Bean

Start the Edit Enterprise Bean wizard by selecting File→New→Enterprise Java-Bean. The wizard displays the following dialog boxes.

1. In the Introduction dialog box:
   a. Read the explanatory text for an overview of the wizard's features.
   b. Click Next.

2. In the EJB JAR dialog box:
   a. Select the button labeled Create New JAR Module in Application.
   b. In the combo box below this button, select `TimerSessionApp`.
   c. In the JAR Display Name field, enter `TimerSessionJAR`.
   d. Click Edit Contents.
   e. In the tree under Available Files, locate the `<INSTALL>/j2ee-tutorial14/examples/ejb/timersession/build/` directory.
   f. Select these classes: `TimerSession.class`, `TimerSessionBean.class`, and `TimerSessionHome.class`.
   g. Click Add.
   h. Click OK.
   i. Click Next.

3. In the General dialog box:
   a. In the Enterprise Bean Class combo box, select `TimerSessionBean`.
   b. In the Enterprise Bean Name field, enter `TimerSessionBean`.
   c. Under Bean Type, select Stateless Session.
   d. In the Remote Interfaces section, select `TimerSessionHome` for the Remote Home Interface, and `TimerSession` for the Remote Interface.
   e. Click Next.

4. In the Expose as Web Service Endpoint dialog box:
   a. Select No for Expose Bean as Web Service Endpoint.
   b. Click Next.

5. Click Finish.

Compiling the Application Client

The application client files are compiled at the same time as the enterprise bean files.

Packaging the Application Client

To package an application client component, you run the New Application Client wizard of `deploytool`. During this process the wizard performs the following tasks.

- Creates the application client's deployment descriptor
- Puts the deployment descriptor and client files into a JAR file
- Adds the JAR file to the application's `TimerSessionApp.ear` file

To start the New Application Client wizard, select File→New→Application Client. The wizard displays the following dialog boxes.

1. Introduction dialog box
   a. Read the explanatory text for an overview of the wizard's features.
   b. Click Next.

2. JAR File Contents dialog box
   a. Select the button labeled Create New AppClient Module in Application.
   b. In the combo box below this button, select `TimerSessionApp`.
   c. In the AppClient Display Name field, enter `TimerSessionClient`.
   d. Click Edit Contents.
   e. In the tree under Available Files, locate the `<INSTALL>/`
      `j2eetutorial14/examples/ejb/timersession/build` directory.
   f. Select the `TimerSessionClient.class` file.
   g. Click Add.
   h. Click OK.
   i. Click Next.

3. General dialog box
   a. In the Main Class combo box, select `TimerSessionClient`.
   b. Click Next.
   c. Click Finish.

Specifying the Application Client's Enterprise Bean Reference

When it invokes the lookup method, the TimerSessionClient refers to the home of an enterprise bean:

```
Object objref =
    initial.lookup("java:comp/env/ejb/SimpleTimerSession");
```

You specify this reference as follows.

1. In the tree, select TimerSessionClient.
2. Select the EJB Ref's tab.
3. Click Add.
4. In the Coded Name field, enter ejb/SimpleTimerSession.
5. In the EJB Type field, select Session.
6. In the Interfaces field, select Remote.
7. In the Home Interface field, enter TimerSessionHome.
8. In the Local/Remote Interface field, enter TimerSession.
9. In the JNDI Name field, select TimerSessionBean.
10. Click OK.

Deploying the Enterprise Application

Now that the J2EE application contains the components, it is ready for deployment.

1. Select TimerSessionApp.
2. Select Tools→Deploy.
3. Under Connection Settings, enter the user name and password for the Application Server.
4. Under Application Client Stub Directory, check Return Client Jar.
5. In the field below the checkbox, enter <INSTALL>/j2eetutorial14/ examples/ejb/timersession/.
6. Click OK.
7. In the Distribute Module dialog box, click Close when the deployment completes.

8. Verify the deployment.

   a. In the tree, expand the Servers node and select the host that is running the Application Server.

   b. In the Deployed Objects table, make sure that `TimerSessionApp` is listed and that its status is `Running`.

   c. Verify that `TimerSessionAppClient.jar` is in `<INSTALL>/j2ee-tutorial14/examples/ejb/timersession/`.

Running the Application Client

To run the application client, perform the following steps.

1. In a terminal window, go to the `<INSTALL>/j2eetutorial14/examples/ejb/timersession/` directory.

2. Type the following command:

   ```
   appclient -client TimerSessionAppClient.jar
   ```

3. In the terminal window, the client displays these lines:

   ```
   Creating a timer with an interval duration of 30000 ms.
   ```

The output from the timer is sent to the `server.log` file located in the `<J2EE_HOME>/domains/domain1/server/logs/` directory.

View the output in the Admin Console:

1. Open the Admin Console by opening a Web browser window to `http://localhost:4848/asadmin/admingui`

2. Click the Logging tab.

3. Click Open Log Viewer.

4. At the top of the page, you'll see these four lines in the Message column:

   ```
   ejbTimeout
   start createTimer
   ejbCreate
   setSessionContext
   ```

Alternatively, you can look at the log file directly. After about 30 seconds, open `server.log` in a text editor and you will see the following lines:

```
TimerSessionBean: setSessionContext
TimerSessionBean: ejbCreate
TimerSessionBean: start createTimer
TimerSessionBean: ejbTimeout
```

Handling Exceptions

The exceptions thrown by enterprise beans fall into two categories: system and application.

A *system exception* indicates a problem with the services that support an application. Examples of these problems include the following: a database connection cannot be obtained, an SQL insert fails because the database is full, or a lookup method cannot find the desired object. If your enterprise bean encounters a system-level problem, it should throw a `javax.ejb.EJBException`. The container will wrap the `EJBException` in a `RemoteException`, which it passes back to the client. Because the `EJBException` is a subclass of the `RuntimeException`, you do not have to specify it in the `throws` clause of the method declaration. If a system exception is thrown, the EJB container might destroy the bean instance. Therefore, a system exception cannot be handled by the bean's client program; it requires intervention by a system administrator.

An *application exception* signals an error in the business logic of an enterprise bean. There are two types of application exceptions: customized and predefined. A customized exception is one that you've coded yourself, such as the `InsufficientBalanceException` thrown by the `debit` business method of the `SavingsAccountBean` example. The `javax.ejb` package includes several predefined exceptions that are designed to handle common problems. For example, an `ejbCreate` method should throw a `CreateException` to indicate an invalid input parameter. When an enterprise bean throws an application exception, the container does not wrap it in another exception. The client should be able to handle any application exception it receives.

If a system exception occurs within a transaction, the EJB container rolls back the transaction. However, if an application exception is thrown within a transaction, the container does not roll back the transaction.

Table 25–1 summarizes the exceptions of the `javax.ejb` package. All of these exceptions are application exceptions, except for the `NoSuchEntityException` and the `EJBException`, which are system exceptions.

Table 25–1 Exceptions

Method Name	Exception It Throws	Reason for Throwing
`ejbCreate`	`CreateException`	An input parameter is invalid.
`ejbFindByPrimaryKey` (and other finder methods that return a single object)	`ObjectNotFoundException` (subclass of `FinderException`)	The database row for the requested entity bean cannot be found.
`ejbRemove`	`RemoveException`	The entity bean's row cannot be deleted from the database.
`ejbLoad`	`NoSuchEntityException`	The database row to be loaded into the entity bean cannot be found.
`ejbStore`	`NoSuchEntityException`	The database row to be updated cannot be found.
(all methods)	`EJBException`	A system problem has been encountered.

Bean-Managed Persistence Examples

$\mathbf{D}$ATA is at the heart of most business applications. In J2EE applications, entity beans represent the business objects that are stored in a database. For entity beans with bean-managed persistence, you must write the code for the database access calls. Although writing this code is an additional responsibility, you will have more control over how the entity bean accesses a database.

This chapter discusses the coding techniques for entity beans with bean-managed persistence. For conceptual information on entity beans, please see What Is an Entity Bean? (page 833).

The SavingsAccountBean Example

The entity bean illustrated in this section represents a simple bank account. The state of SavingsAccountBean is stored in the savingsaccount table of a relational database. The savingsaccount table is created by the following SQL statement:

```
CREATE TABLE savingsaccount
  (id VARCHAR(3)
  CONSTRAINT pk_savingsaccount PRIMARY KEY,
  firstname VARCHAR(24),
  lastname  VARCHAR(24),
  balance   NUMERIC(10,2));
```

The SavingsAccountBean example requires the following code:

- Entity bean class (SavingsAccountBean)
- Home interface (SavingsAccountHome)
- Remote interface (SavingsAccount)

This example also uses the following classes:

- A utility class named InsufficientBalanceException
- A client class called SavingsAccountClient

The source code for this example is in this directory:

`<INSTALL>/j2eetutorial14/ejb/savingsaccount/src/`

Entity Bean Class

The sample entity bean class is called SavingsAccountBean. As you look through its code, note that it meets the requirements of any entity bean that uses bean-managed persistence. First, it implements the following:

- EntityBean interface
- Zero or more ejbCreate and ejbPostCreate methods
- Finder methods
- Business methods
- Home methods

In addition, an entity bean class with bean-managed persistence has these requirements:

- The class is defined as public.
- The class cannot be defined as abstract or final.
- It contains an empty constructor.
- It does not implement the finalize method.

The EntityBean Interface

The EntityBean interface extends the EnterpriseBean interface, which extends the Serializable interface. The EntityBean interface declares a number of methods, such as ejbActivate and ejbLoad, which you must implement in your entity bean class. These methods are discussed in later sections.

The ejbCreate Method

When the client invokes a `create` method, the EJB container invokes the corresponding `ejbCreate` method. Typically, an `ejbCreate` method in an entity bean performs the following tasks:

- Inserts the entity state into the database
- Initializes the instance variables
- Returns the primary key

The `ejbCreate` method of `SavingsAccountBean` inserts the entity state into the database by invoking the private `insertRow` method, which issues the SQL `INSERT` statement. Here is the source code for the `ejbCreate` method:

```
public String ejbCreate(String id, String firstName,
    String lastName, BigDecimal balance)
    throws CreateException {

    if (balance.signum() == -1)  {
        throw new CreateException
            ("A negative initial balance is not allowed.");
    }

    try {
        insertRow(id, firstName, lastName, balance);
    } catch (Exception ex) {
        throw new EJBException("ejbCreate: " +
            ex.getMessage());
    }

    this.id = id;
    this.firstName = firstName;
    this.lastName = lastName;
    this.balance = balance;

    return id;
}
```

Although the `SavingsAccountBean` class has only one `ejbCreate` method, an enterprise bean can contain multiple `ejbCreate` methods. For an example, see the `CartBean.java` source code in this directory:

<INSTALL>/j2eetutorial14/examples/ejb/cart/src/

When you write an `ejbCreate` method for an entity bean, be sure to follow these rules:

- The access control modifier must be `public`.
- The return type must be the primary key.
- The arguments must be legal types for the Java RMI API.
- The method modifier cannot be `final` or `static`.

The `throws` clause can include the `javax.ejb.CreateException` and exceptions that are specific to your application. An `ejbCreate` method usually throws a `CreateException` if an input parameter is invalid. If an `ejbCreate` method cannot create an entity because another entity with the same primary key already exists, it should throw a `javax.ejb.DuplicateKeyException` (a subclass of `CreateException`). If a client receives a `CreateException` or a `DuplicateKeyException`, it should assume that the entity was not created.

The state of an entity bean can be directly inserted into the database by an application that is unknown to the Sun Java System Application Server Platform Edition 8. For example, an SQL script might insert a row into the `savingsaccount` table. Although the entity bean for this row was not created by an `ejbCreate` method, the bean can be located by a client program.

The ejbPostCreate Method

For each `ejbCreate` method, you must write an `ejbPostCreate` method in the entity bean class. The EJB container invokes `ejbPostCreate` immediately after it calls `ejbCreate`. Unlike the `ejbCreate` method, the `ejbPostCreate` method can invoke the `getPrimaryKey` and `getEJBObject` methods of the `EntityContext` interface. For more information on the `getEJBObject` method, see the section Passing an Enterprise Bean's Object Reference (page 891). Often, your `ejbPostCreate` methods will be empty.

The signature of an `ejbPostCreate` method must meet the following requirements:

- The number and types of arguments must match a corresponding `ejbCreate` method.
- The access control modifier must be `public`.
- The method modifier cannot be `final` or `static`.
- The return type must be `void`.

The `throws` clause can include the `javax.ejb.CreateException` and exceptions that are specific to your application.

The ejbRemove Method

A client deletes an entity bean by invoking the remove method. This invocation causes the EJB container to call the ejbRemove method, which deletes the entity state from the database. In the SavingsAccountBean class, the ejbRemove method invokes a private method named deleteRow, which issues an SQL DELETE statement. The ejbRemove method is short:

```
public void ejbRemove() {
    try {
        deleteRow(id);
    catch (Exception ex) {
        throw new EJBException("ejbRemove: " +
        ex.getMessage());
        }
    }
}
```

If the ejbRemove method encounters a system problem, it should throw the javax.ejb.EJBException. If it encounters an application error, it should throw a javax.ejb.RemoveException. For a comparison of system and application exceptions, see the section deploytool Tips for Entity Beans with Bean-Managed Persistence (page 937).

An entity bean can also be removed directly by a database deletion. For example, if an SQL script deletes a row that contains an entity bean state, then that entity bean is removed.

The ejbLoad and ejbStore Methods

If the EJB container needs to synchronize the instance variables of an entity bean with the corresponding values stored in a database, it invokes the ejbLoad and ejbStore methods. The ejbLoad method refreshes the instance variables from the database, and the ejbStore method writes the variables to the database. The client cannot call ejbLoad and ejbStore.

If a business method is associated with a transaction, the container invokes ejbLoad before the business method executes. Immediately after the business method executes, the container calls ejbStore. Because the container invokes ejbLoad and ejbStore, you do not have to refresh and store the instance variables in your business methods. The SavingsAccountBean class relies on the container to synchronize the instance variables with the database. Therefore, the business methods of SavingsAccountBean should be associated with transactions.

If the ejbLoad and ejbStore methods cannot locate an entity in the underlying database, they should throw the javax.ejb.NoSuchEntityException. This exception is a subclass of EJBException. Because EJBException is a subclass of RuntimeException, you do not have to include it in the throws clause. When NoSuchEntityException is thrown, the EJB container wraps it in a RemoteException before returning it to the client.

In the SavingsAccountBean class, ejbLoad invokes the loadRow method, which issues an SQL SELECT statement and assigns the retrieved data to the instance variables. The ejbStore method calls the storeRow method, which stores the instance variables in the database using an SQL UPDATE statement. Here is the code for the ejbLoad and ejbStore methods:

```
public void ejbLoad() {

  try {
    loadRow();
  } catch (Exception ex) {
    throw new EJBException("ejbLoad: " +
      ex.getMessage());
  }
}

public void ejbStore() {

  try {
    storeRow();
  } catch (Exception ex) {
    throw new EJBException("ejbStore: " +
      ex.getMessage());
  }
}
```

The Finder Methods

The finder methods allow clients to locate entity beans. The SavingsAccount-Client program locates entity beans using three finder methods:

```
SavingsAccount jones = home.findByPrimaryKey("836");
...
Collection c = home.findByLastName("Smith");
...
Collection c = home.findInRange(20.00, 99.00);
```

For every finder method available to a client, the entity bean class must implement a corresponding method that begins with the prefix `ejbFind`. The SavingsAccountBean class, for example, implements the `ejbFindByLastName` method as follows:

```
public Collection ejbFindByLastName(String lastName)
  throws FinderException {

  Collection result;

  try {
     result = selectByLastName(lastName);
  } catch (Exception ex) {
     throw new EJBException("ejbFindByLastName " +
        ex.getMessage());
  }
  return result;
}
```

The finder methods that are specific to your application, such as `ejbFindByLastName` and `ejbFindInRange`, are optional, but the `ejbFindByPrimaryKey` method is required. As its name implies, the `ejbFindByPrimaryKey` method accepts as an argument the primary key, which it uses to locate an entity bean. In the SavingsAccountBean class, the primary key is the `id` variable. Here is the code for the `ejbFindByPrimaryKey` method:

```
public String ejbFindByPrimaryKey(String primaryKey)
  throws FinderException {

  boolean result;

  try {
     result = selectByPrimaryKey(primaryKey);
  } catch (Exception ex) {
     throw new EJBException("ejbFindByPrimaryKey: " +
        ex.getMessage());
  }

  if (result) {
     return primaryKey;
  }
  else {
     throw new ObjectNotFoundException
        ("Row for id " + primaryKey + " not found.");
  }
}
```

The `ejbFindByPrimaryKey` method may look strange to you, because it uses a primary key for both the method argument and the return value. However, remember that the client does not call `ejbFindByPrimaryKey` directly. It is the EJB container that calls the `ejbFindByPrimaryKey` method. The client invokes the `findByPrimaryKey` method, which is defined in the home interface.

The following list summarizes the rules for the finder methods that you implement in an entity bean class with bean-managed persistence:

- The `ejbFindByPrimaryKey` method must be implemented.
- A finder method name must start with the prefix `ejbFind`.
- The access control modifier must be `public`.
- The method modifier cannot be `final` or `static`.
- The arguments and return type must be legal types for the Java RMI API. (This requirement applies only to methods defined in a remote—and not a local—home interface.)
- The return type must be the primary key or a collection of primary keys.

The `throws` clause can include the `javax.ejb.FinderException` and exceptions that are specific to your application. If a finder method returns a single primary key and the requested entity does not exist, the method should throw the `javax.ejb.ObjectNotFoundException` (a subclass of `FinderException`). If a finder method returns a collection of primary keys and it does not find any objects, it should return an empty collection.

The Business Methods

The business methods contain the business logic that you want to encapsulate within the entity bean. Usually, the business methods do not access the database, and this allows you to separate the business logic from the database access code. The `SavingsAccountBean` class contains the following business methods:

```
public void debit(BigDecimal amount)
    throws InsufficientBalanceException {

    if (balance.compareTo(amount) == -1) {
        throw new InsufficientBalanceException();
    }
    balance = balance.subtract(amount);
}

public void credit(BigDecimal amount) {
```

```
        balance = balance.add(amount);
    }

    public String getFirstName() {

        return firstName;
    }

    public String getLastName() {

        return lastName;
    }

    public BigDecimal getBalance() {

        return balance;
    }
```

The SavingsAccountClient program invokes the business methods as follows:

```
BigDecimal zeroAmount = new BigDecimal("0.00");
SavingsAccount duke = home.create("123", "Duke", "Earl",
    zeroAmount);
...
duke.credit(new BigDecimal("88.50"));
duke.debit(new BigDecimal("20.25"));
BigDecimal balance = duke.getBalance();
```

The requirements for the signature of a business method are the same for session beans and entity beans:

- The method name must not conflict with a method name defined by the EJB architecture. For example, you cannot call a business method ejb-Create or ejbActivate.

- The access control modifier must be public.

- The method modifier cannot be final or static.

- The arguments and return types must be legal types for the Java RMI API. This requirement applies only to methods defined in a remote—and not a local—home interface.

The throws clause can include the exceptions that you define for your application. The debit method, for example, throws the InsufficientBalanceException. To indicate a system-level problem, a business method should throw the javax.ejb.EJBException.

The Home Methods

A home method contains the business logic that applies to all entity beans of a particular class. In contrast, the logic in a business method applies to a single entity bean, an instance with a unique identity. During a home method invocation, the instance has neither a unique identity nor a state that represents a business object. Consequently, a home method must not access the bean's persistence state (instance variables). (For container-managed persistence, a home method also must not access relationships.)

Typically, a home method locates a collection of bean instances and invokes business methods as it iterates through the collection. This approach is taken by the ejbHomeChargeForLowBalance method of the SavingsAccountBean class. The ejbHomeChargeForLowBalance method applies a service charge to all savings accounts that have balances less than a specified amount. The method locates these accounts by invoking the findInRange method. As it iterates through the collection of SavingsAccount instances, the ejbHomeChargeForLowBalance method checks the balance and invokes the debit business method. Here is the source code of the ejbHomeChargeForLowBalance method:

```
public void ejbHomeChargeForLowBalance(
    BigDecimal minimumBalance, BigDecimal charge)
    throws InsufficientBalanceException {

    try {
        SavingsAccountHome home =
        (SavingsAccountHome)context.getEJBHome();
        Collection c = home.findInRange(new BigDecimal("0.00"),
            minimumBalance.subtract(new BigDecimal("0.01")));

        Iterator i = c.iterator();

        while (i.hasNext()) {
            SavingsAccount account = (SavingsAccount)i.next();
            if (account.getBalance().compareTo(charge) == 1) {
                account.debit(charge);
            }
        }

    } catch (Exception ex) {
        throw new EJBException("ejbHomeChargeForLowBalance: "
            + ex.getMessage());
    }
}
```

The home interface defines a corresponding method named `chargeForLowBalance` (see Home Method Definitions, page 915). Because the interface provides the client view, the `SavingsAccountClient` program invokes the home method as follows:

```
SavingsAccountHome home;
...
home.chargeForLowBalance(new BigDecimal("10.00"),
    new BigDecimal("1.00"));
```

In the entity bean class, the implementation of a home method must adhere to these rules:

- A home method name must start with the prefix `ejbHome`.
- The access control modifier must be `public`.
- The method modifier cannot be `static`.

The `throws` clause can include exceptions that are specific to your application; it must not throw the `java.rmi.RemoteException`.

Database Calls

Table 26–1 summarizes the database access calls in the `SavingsAccountBean` class. The business methods of the `SavingsAccountBean` class are absent from the preceding table because they do not access the database. Instead, these business methods update the instance variables, which are written to the database when the EJB container calls `ejbStore`. Another developer might have chosen to access the database in the business methods of the `SavingsAccountBean` class. This choice is one of those design decisions that depend on the specific needs of your application.

Before accessing a database, you must connect to it. For more information, see Chapter 31.

Table 26–1　SQL Statements in SavingsAccountBean

Method	SQL Statement
ejbCreate	INSERT
ejbFindByPrimaryKey	SELECT
ejbFindByLastName	SELECT
ejbFindInRange	SELECT
ejbLoad	SELECT
ejbRemove	DELETE
ejbStore	UPDATE

Home Interface

The home interface defines the create, finder, and home methods. The Savings-AccountHome interface follows:

```
import java.util.Collection;
import java.math.BigDecimal;
import java.rmi.RemoteException;
import javax.ejb.*;

public interface SavingsAccountHome extends EJBHome {

    public SavingsAccount create(String id, String firstName,
        String lastName, BigDecimal balance)
        throws RemoteException, CreateException;

    public SavingsAccount findByPrimaryKey(String id)
        throws FinderException, RemoteException;

    public Collection findByLastName(String lastName)
        throws FinderException, RemoteException;

    public Collection findInRange(BigDecimal low,
        BigDecimal high)
        throws FinderException, RemoteException;

    public void chargeForLowBalance(BigDecimal minimumBalance,
        BigDecimal charge)
        throws InsufficientBalanceException, RemoteException;
}
```

create Method Definitions

Each create method in the home interface must conform to the following requirements:

- It must have the same number and types of arguments as its matching ejbCreate method in the enterprise bean class.
- It must return the remote interface type of the enterprise bean.
- The throws clause must include the exceptions specified by the throws clause of the corresponding ejbCreate and ejbPostCreate methods.
- The throws clause must include the javax.ejb.CreateException.
- If the method is defined in a remote—and not a local—home interface, then the throws clause must include the java.rmi.RemoteException.

Finder Method Definitions

Every finder method in the home interface corresponds to a finder method in the entity bean class. The name of a finder method in the home interface begins with find, whereas the corresponding name in the entity bean class begins with ejbFind. For example, the SavingsAccountHome class defines the findByLast-Name method, and the SavingsAccountBean class implements the ejbFindByLastName method. The rules for defining the signatures of the finder methods of a home interface follow.

- The number and types of arguments must match those of the corresponding method in the entity bean class.
- The return type must be the entity bean's remote interface type or a collection of those types.
- The exceptions in the throws clause must include those of the corresponding method in the entity bean class.
- The throws clause must contain the javax.ejb.FinderException.
- If the method is defined in a remote—and not a local—home interface, then the throws clause must include the java.rmi.RemoteException.

Home Method Definitions

Each home method definition in the home interface corresponds to a method in the entity bean class. In the home interface, the method name is arbitrary, provided that it does not begin with create or find. In the bean class, the matching method name begins with ejbHome. For example, in the SavingsAccountBean class the name is ejbHomeChargeForLowBalance, but in the SavingsAccount-Home interface the name is chargeForLowBalance.

The home method signature must follow the same rules specified for finder methods in the preceding section (except that a home method does not throw a FinderException).

Remote Interface

The remote interface extends javax.ejb.EJBObject and defines the business methods that a remote client can invoke. Here is the SavingsAccount remote interface:

```
import javax.ejb.EJBObject;
import java.rmi.RemoteException;
import java.math.BigDecimal;

public interface SavingsAccount extends EJBObject {

    public void debit(BigDecimal amount)
        throws InsufficientBalanceException, RemoteException;

    public void credit(BigDecimal amount)
        throws RemoteException;

    public String getFirstName()
        throws RemoteException;

    public String getLastName()
        throws RemoteException;

    public BigDecimal getBalance()
        throws RemoteException;
}
```

The requirements for the method definitions in a remote interface are the same for session beans and entity beans:

- Each method in the remote interface must match a method in the enterprise bean class.
- The signatures of the methods in the remote interface must be identical to the signatures of the corresponding methods in the enterprise bean class.

- The arguments and return values must be valid RMI types.
- The `throws` clause must include `java.rmi.RemoteException`.

A local interface has the same requirements, with the following exceptions:

- The arguments and return values are not required to be valid RMI types.
- The `throws` clause does not include `java.rmi.RemoteException`.

Running the SavingsAccountBean Example

Before you run this example, you must define the data source, create the database, and deploy the `SavingsAccountApp.ear` file.

Defining the Data Source

Follow the instructions in Creating a Data Source (page 1079). This data source is a factory for database connections. For more information, see DataSource Objects and Connection Pools (page 1077).

Creating the Database Table

The instructions that follow explain how to use the `SavingsAccountBean` example with PointBase, the database software that is included in the Application Server bundle.

1. Start the PointBase server. For instructions, see Starting and Stopping the PointBase Database Server (page 28).
2. Create the `savingsaccount` database table by running the `create.sql` script.

   a. In a terminal window, go to this directory:

      `<INSTALL>/j2eetutorial14/examples/ejb/savingsaccount/`

   b. Type the following command, which runs the `create.sql` script:

      `asant create-db_common`

Deploying the Application

1. In `deploytool`, open the `SavingsAccountApp.ear` file, which resides in this directory:

   `<INSTALL>/j2eetutorial14/examples/ejb/provided-ears/`

2. Deploy the `SavingsAccountApp` application.

3. In the Deploy Module dialog box, do the following:

   a. Select the Return Client JAR checkbox.

   b. In the field below the checkbox, enter the following:

      `<INSTALL>/j2eetutorial14/examples/ejb/savingsaccount`

For detailed instructions, see Deploying the J2EE Application (page 868).

Running the Client

To run the `SavingsAccountClient` program, do the following:

1. In a terminal window, go to this directory:

   `<INSTALL>/j2eetutorial14/examples/ejb/savingsaccount/`

2. Type the following command on a single line:

   `appclient -client SavingsAccountAppClient.jar`

3. The client should display the following lines:

   ```
   balance = 68.25
   balance = 32.55
   456: 44.77
   730: 19.54
   268: 100.07
   836: 32.55
   456: 44.77
   4
   7
   ```

To modify this example, see the instructions in Modifying the J2EE Application (page 870).

Mapping Table Relationships for Bean-Managed Persistence

In a relational database, tables can be related by common columns. The relationships between the tables affect the design of their corresponding entity beans. The entity beans discussed in this section are backed up by tables with the following types of relationships:

- One-to-one
- One-to-many
- Many-to-many

One-to-One Relationships

In a one-to-one relationship, each row in a table is related to a single row in another table. For example, in a warehouse application, a `storagebin` table might have a one-to-one relationship with a `widget` table. This application would model a physical warehouse in which each storage bin contains one type of widget and each widget resides in one storage bin.

Figure 26–1 illustrates the `storagebin` and `widget` tables. Because the `storagebinid` uniquely identifies a row in the `storagebin` table, it is that table's primary key. The `widgetid` is the primary key of the `widget` table. The two tables are related because the `widgetid` is also a column in the `storagebin` table. By referring to the primary key of the `widget` table, the `widgetid` in the `storagebin` table identifies which widget resides in a particular storage bin in the warehouse. Because the `widgetid` of the `storagebin` table refers to the primary key of another table, it is called a *foreign key*. (The figures in this chapter denote a primary key with PK and a foreign key with FK.)

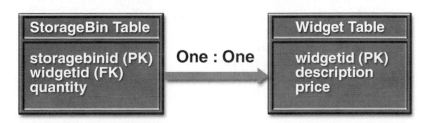

Figure 26–1 One-to-One Table Relationship

A dependent (child) table includes a foreign key that matches the primary key of the referenced (parent) table. The values of the foreign keys in the storagebin (child) table depend on the primary keys in the widget (parent) table. For example, if the storagebin table has a row with a widgetid of 344, then the widget table should also have a row whose widgetid is 344.

When designing a database application, you can choose to enforce the dependency between the parent and child tables. There are two ways to enforce such a dependency: by defining a referential constraint in the database or by performing checks in the application code. The storagebin table has a referential constraint named fk_widgetid:

```
CREATE TABLE storagebin
   (storagebinid VARCHAR(3)
    CONSTRAINT pk_storagebin PRIMARY KEY,
    widgetid VARCHAR(3),
    quantity INTEGER,
    CONSTRAINT fk_widgetid
    FOREIGN KEY (widgetid)
     REFERENCES widget(widgetid));
```

The source code for the following example is in this directory:

```
<INSTALL>/j2eetutorial14/examples/ejb/storagebin/src/
```

The StorageBinBean and WidgetBean classes illustrate the one-to-one relationship of the storagebin and widget tables. The StorageBinBean class contains variables for each column in the storagebin table, including the foreign key, widgetId:

```
private String storageBinId;
private String widgetId;
private int quantity;
```

The ejbFindByWidgetId method of the StorageBinBean class returns the storageBinId that matches a given widgetId:

```
public String ejbFindByWidgetId(String widgetId)
   throws FinderException {

   String storageBinId;
```

```
   try {
      storageBinId = selectByWidgetId(widgetId);
   } catch (Exception ex) {
         throw new EJBException("ejbFindByWidgetId: " +
            ex.getMessage());
   }

   if (storageBinId == null) {
      throw new ObjectNotFoundException
         ("Row for widgetId " + widgetId + " not found.");
   }
   else {
      return storageBinId;
   }
}
```

The ejbFindByWidgetId method locates the widgetId by querying the database in the selectByWidgetId method:

```
private String selectByWidgetId(String widgetId)
   throws SQLException {

   String storageBinId;

   makeConnection();
   String selectStatement =
         "select storagebinid " +
         "from storagebin where widgetid = ? ";
   PreparedStatement prepStmt =
         con.prepareStatement(selectStatement);
   prepStmt.setString(1, widgetId);

   ResultSet rs = prepStmt.executeQuery();

   if (rs.next()) {
      storageBinId = rs.getString(1);
   }
   else {
      storageBinId = null;
   }

   prepStmt.close();
   releaseConnection();
   return storageBinId;
}
```

To find out in which storage bin a widget resides, the StorageBinClient program calls the findByWidgetId method:

```
String widgetId = "777";
StorageBin storageBin =
    storageBinHome.findByWidgetId(widgetId);
String storageBinId = (String)storageBin.getPrimaryKey();
int quantity = storageBin.getQuantity();
```

Running the StorageBinBean Example

1. Create the storagebin database table.
    a. In a terminal window, go to this directory:
        `<INSTALL>/j2eetutorial14/examples/ejb/storagebin/`
    b. Type this command:

        `asant create-db_common`

2. In deploytool, deploy the StorageBinApp.ear file, which is in this directory:

    `<INSTALL>/j2eetutorial14/examples/ejb/provided-ears/`

3. Run the client.

    a. In a terminal window, go to this directory:

        `<INSTALL>/j2eetutorial14/examples/ejb/storagebin/`

    b. Type the following command on a single line:

        `appclient -client StorageBinAppClient.jar`

    c. The client should display the following:

```
. . .
777 388 500 1.0 Duct Tape
. . .
```

One-to-Many Relationships

If the primary key in a parent table matches multiple foreign keys in a child table, then the relationship is one-to-many. This relationship is common in database applications. For example, an application for a sports league might access a team table and a player table. Each team has multiple players, and each player belongs to a single team. Every row in the child table (`player`) has a foreign key identifying the player's team. This foreign key matches the `team` table's primary key.

The sections that follow describe how you might implement one-to-many relationships in entity beans. When designing such entity beans, you must decide whether both tables are represented by entity beans, or only one.

A Helper Class for the Child Table

Not every database table needs to be mapped to an entity bean. If a database table doesn't represent a business entity, or if it stores information that is contained in another entity, then you should use a helper class to represent the table. In an online shopping application, for example, each order submitted by a customer can have multiple line items. The application stores the information in the database tables shown by Figure 26–2.

Not only does a line item belong to an order, but it also does not exist without the order. Therefore, the `lineitems` table should be represented with a helper class and not with an entity bean. Using a helper class in this case is not required, but doing so might improve performance because a helper class uses fewer system resources than does an entity bean.

The source code for the following example is in this directory:

```
<INSTALL>/j2eetutorial14/examples/ejb/order/src/
```

The `LineItem` and `OrderBean` classes show how to implement a one-to-many relationship using a helper class (`LineItem`). The instance variables in the `LineItem` class correspond to the columns in the `lineitems` table. The `itemNo`

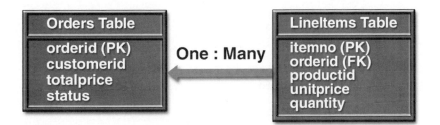

Figure 26–2   One-to-Many Relationship: Order and Line Items

variable matches the primary key for the lineitems table, and the orderId variable represents the table's foreign key. Here is the source code for the LineItem
class:

```
public class LineItem implements java.io.Serializable {

    String productId;
    int quantity;
    double unitPrice;
    int itemNo;
    String orderId;


    public LineItem(String productId, int quantity,
      double unitPrice, int itemNo, String orderId) {

       this.productId = productId;
       this.quantity = quantity;
       this.unitPrice = unitPrice;
       this.itemNo = itemNo;
       this.orderId = orderId;
    }

    public String getProductId() {
       return productId;
    }

    public int getQuantity() {
       return quantity;
    }

    public double getUnitPrice() {
       return unitPrice;
    }

    public int getItemNo() {
       return itemNo;
    }

    public String getOrderId() {
       return orderId;
    }
}
```

The OrderBean class contains an ArrayList variable named lineItems. Each
element in the lineItems variable is a LineItem object. The lineItems variable is passed to the OrderBean class in the ejbCreate method. For every

LineItem object in the lineItems variable, the ejbCreate method inserts a row into the lineitems table. It also inserts a single row into the orders table. The code for the ejbCreate method follows:

```
public String ejbCreate(String orderId, String customerId,
    String status, double totalPrice, ArrayList lineItems)
    throws CreateException {

    try {
        insertOrder(orderId, customerId, status, totalPrice);
        for (int i = 0; i < lineItems.size(); i++) {
            LineItem item = (LineItem)lineItems.get(i);
            insertItem(item);
        }
    } catch (Exception ex) {
        throw new EJBException("ejbCreate: " +
            ex.getMessage());
    }

    this.orderId = orderId;
    this.customerId = customerId;
    this.status = status;
    this.totalPrice = totalPrice;
    this.lineItems - lineItems ;

    return orderId;
}
```

The OrderClient program creates and loads an ArrayList of LineItem objects. The program passes this ArrayList to the entity bean when it invokes the create method:

```
ArrayList lineItems = new ArrayList();
lineItems.add(new LineItem("p23", 13, 12.00, 1, "123"));
lineItems.add(new LineItem("p67", 47, 89.00, 2, "123"));
lineItems.add(new LineItem("p11", 28, 41.00, 3, "123"));
...
Order duke = home.create("123", "c44", "open",
    totalItems(lineItems), lineItems);
```

Other methods in the OrderBean class also access both database tables. The ejbRemove method, for example, not only deletes a row from the orders table but also deletes all corresponding rows in the lineitems table. The ejbLoad and ejbStore methods synchronize the state of an OrderBean instance, including the lineItems ArrayList, with the orders and lineitems tables.

The ejbFindByProductId method enables clients to locate all orders that have a particular product. This method queries the lineitems table for all rows with a specific productId. The method returns a Collection of Order objects. The OrderClient program iterates through the Collection and prints the primary key of each order:

```
Collection c = home.findByProductId("p67");
Iterator i=c.iterator();
while (i.hasNext()) {
   Order order = (Order)i.next();
   String id = (String)order.getPrimaryKey();
   System.out.println(id);
}
```

Running the OrderBean Example

1. Create the order database table.
   a. In a terminal window, go to this directory:
      <INSTALL>/j2eetutorial14/examples/ejb/order/
   b. Type this command:

      asant create-db_common
2. In deploytool, deploy the OrderBean.ear file, which is in this directory:
   <INSTALL>/j2eetutorial14/examples/ejb/provided-ears/
3. Run the client.

   a. In a terminal window, go to this directory:
      <INSTALL>/j2eetutorial14/examples/ejb/order/
   b. Type the following command on a single line:
      appclient -client OrderBeanClient.jar
   c. The client should display the following lines:

      ```
      . . .
      123 1 p23 12.0
      123 2 p67 89.0
      123 3 p11 41.0

      123
      456
      ```

An Entity Bean for the Child Table

You should consider building an entity bean for a child table under the following conditions:

- The information in the child table is not dependent on the parent table.
- The business entity of the child table could exist without that of the parent table.
- The child table might be accessed by another application that does not access the parent table.

These conditions exist in the following scenario. Suppose that each sales representative in a company has multiple customers and that each customer has only one sales representative. The company tracks its sales force using a database application. In the database, each row in the salesrep table (parent) matches multiple rows in the customer table (child). Figure 26–3 illustrates this relationship.

The SalesRepBean and CustomerBean entity bean classes implement the one-to-many relationship of the sales and customer tables.

The source code for this example is in this directory:

```
<INSTALL>/j2eetutorial14/examples/ejb/salesrep/src/
```

The SalesRepBean class contains a variable named customerIds, which is an ArrayList of String elements. These String elements identify which customers belong to the sales representative. Because the customerIds variable reflects this relationship, the SalesRepBean class must keep the variable up-to-date.

The SalesRepBean class instantiates the customerIds variable in the setEntityContext method and not in ejbCreate. The container invokes setEntityContext only once—when it creates the bean instance—thereby ensuring that

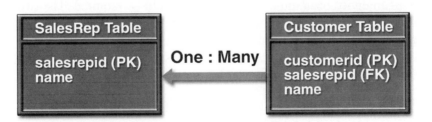

Figure 26–3 One-to-Many Relationship: Sales Representative and Customers

customerIds is instantiated only once. Because the same bean instance can assume different identities during its life cycle, instantiating `customerIds` in `ejbCreate` might cause multiple and unnecessary instantiations. Therefore, the `SalesRepBean` class instantiates the `customerIds` variable in `setEntity-Context`:

```
public void setEntityContext(EntityContext context) {

    this.context = context;
    customerIds = new ArrayList();

    try {
      Context initial = new InitialContext();
      Object objref =
        initial.lookup("java:comp/env/ejb/Customer");

      customerHome =
        (CustomerHome)PortableRemoteObject.narrow(objref,
          CustomerHome.class);
    } catch (Exception ex) {
      throw new EJBException("setEntityContext: " +
        ex.getMessage());
    }
}
```

Invoked by the `ejbLoad` method, `loadCustomerIds` is a private method that refreshes the `customerIds` variable. There are two approaches to coding a method such as `loadCustomerIds`: fetch the identifiers from the `customer` database table, or get them from the `CustomerBean` entity bean. Fetching the identifiers from the database might be faster, but it exposes the code in the `SalesRepBean` class to the `CustomerBean` bean's underlying database table. In the future, if you were to change the `CustomerBean` bean's table (or move the bean to a different Application Server), you might need to change the `SalesRep-Bean` code. But if the `SalesRepBean` class gets the identifiers from the `CustomerBean` entity bean, no coding changes would be required. The two approaches present a trade-off: performance versus flexibility. The `SalesRepBean` example opts for flexibility, loading the `customerIds` variable by calling the `find-BySalesRep` and `getPrimaryKey` methods of `CustomerBean`. Here is the code for the `loadCustomerIds` method:

```
private void loadCustomerIds() {

    customerIds.clear();
```

```
    try {
        Collection c = customerHome.findBySalesRep(salesRepId);
        Iterator i=c.iterator();

        while (i.hasNext()) {
            Customer customer = (Customer)i.next();
            String id = (String)customer.getPrimaryKey();
            customerIds.add(id);
        }

    } catch (Exception ex) {
        throw new EJBException("Exception in loadCustomerIds: " +
            ex.getMessage());
    }
}
```

If a customer's sales representative changes, the client program updates the database by calling the setSalesRepId method of the CustomerBean class. The next time a business method of the SalesRepBean class is called, the ejbLoad method invokes loadCustomerIds, which refreshes the customerIds variable. (To ensure that ejbLoad is invoked before each business method, set the transaction attributes of the business methods to Required.) For example, the Sales-RepClient program changes the salesRepId for a customer named Mary Jackson as follows:

```
Customer mary = customerHome.findByPrimaryKey("987");
mary.setSalesRepId("543");
```

The salesRepId value 543 identifies a sales representative named Janice Martin. To list all of Janice's customers, the SalesRepClient program invokes the getCustomerIds method, iterates through the ArrayList of identifiers, and locates each CustomerBean entity bean by calling its findByPrimaryKey method:

```
SalesRep janice = salesHome.findByPrimaryKey("543");
ArrayList a = janice.getCustomerIds();
i = a.iterator();

while (i.hasNext()) {
    String customerId = (String)i.next();
    Customer customer =
customerHome.findByPrimaryKey(customerId);
    String name = customer.getName();
    System.out.println(customerId + ": " + name);
}
```

Running the SalesRepBean Example

1. Create the `salesrep` database table.

    a. In a terminal window, go to this directory:

        `<INSTALL>`/j2eetutorial14/examples/ejb/salesrep/

    b. Type this command:

        asant create-db_common

2. In `deploytool`, deploy the `SalesRepApp.ear` file, which is in this directory:

    `<INSTALL>`/j2eetutorial14/examples/ejb/provided-ears/

3. Run the client.

    a. In a terminal window, go to this directory:

        `<INSTALL>`/j2eetutorial14/examples/ejb/salesrep/

    b. Type the following command on a single line:

        appclient -client SalesRepAppClient.jar

    c. The client should display the following lines:

```
. . .
customerId = 221
customerId = 388
customerId = 456
customerId = 844

987: Mary Jackson
221: Alice Smith
388: Bill Williamson
456: Joe Smith
844: Buzz Murphy
. . .
```

Many-to-Many Relationships

In a many-to-many relationship, each entity can be related to multiple occurrences of the other entity. For example, a college course has many students and each student may take several courses. In a database, this relationship is represented by a cross-reference table containing the foreign keys. In Figure 26–4, the cross-reference table is the `enrollment` table. These tables are accessed by the `StudentBean`, `CourseBean`, and `EnrollerBean` classes.

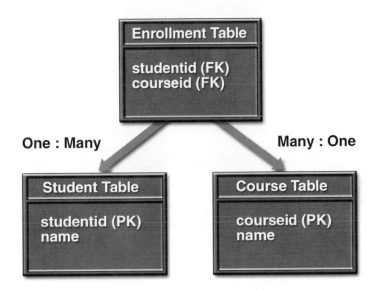

Figure 26–4 Many-to-Many Relationship: Students and Courses

The source code for this example is in this directory:

```
<INSTALL>/j2eetutorial14/examples/ejb/enroller/src/
```

The StudentBean and CourseBean classes are complementary. Each class contains an ArrayList of foreign keys. The StudentBean class contains an ArrayList named courseIds, which identifies the courses the student is enrolled in. Similarly, the CourseBean class contains an ArrayList named studentIds.

The ejbLoad method of the StudentBean class adds elements to the courseIds ArrayList by calling loadCourseIds, a private method. The loadCourseIds method gets the course identifiers from the EnrollerBean session bean. The source code for the loadCourseIds method follows:

```
private void loadCourseIds() {

    courseIds.clear();

    try {
        Enroller enroller = enrollerHome.create();
        ArrayList a = enroller.getCourseIds(studentId);
        courseIds.addAll(a);
```

```
    } catch (Exception ex) {
        throw new EJBException("Exception in loadCourseIds: " +
            ex.getMessage());
    }
}
```

Invoked by the `loadCourseIds` method, the `getCourseIds` method of the `EnrollerBean` class queries the `enrollment` table:

```
select courseid from enrollment
where studentid = ?
```

Only the `EnrollerBean` class accesses the `enrollment` table. Therefore, the `EnrollerBean` class manages the student-course relationship represented in the `enrollment` table. If a student enrolls in a course, for example, the client calls the `enroll` business method, which inserts a row:

```
insert into enrollment
values (studentid, courseid)
```

If a student drops a course, the `unEnroll` method deletes a row:

```
delete from enrollment
where studentid = ? and courseid = ?
```

And if a student leaves the school, the `deleteStudent` method deletes all rows in the table for that student:

```
delete from enrollment
where student = ?
```

The `EnrollerBean` class does not delete the matching row from the `student` table. That action is performed by the `ejbRemove` method of the `StudentBean` class. To ensure that both deletes are executed as a single operation, you must ensure that they belong to the same transaction. See Chapter 30 for more information.

Running the EnrollerBean Example

1. Create the `enroller` database table.
   a. In a terminal window, go to this directory:

      `<INSTALL>/j2eetutorial14/examples/ejb/enroller/`

   b. Type this command:

```
asant create-db_common
```

2. In `deploytool`, deploy the `EnrollerApp.ear` file, which is in this directory:

```
<INSTALL>/j2eetutorial14/examples/ejb/provided-ears/
```

3. Run the client.

   a. In a terminal window, go to this directory:

```
<INSTALL>/j2eetutorial14/examples/ejb/enroller/
```

   b. Type the following command on a single line:

```
appclient -client EnrollerAppClient.jar
```

   c. The client should display the following lines:

```
. . .
Denise Smith:
220 Power J2EE Programming
333 XML Made Easy
777 An Introduction to Java Programming

An Introduction to Java Programming:
823 Denise Smith
456 Joe Smith
388 Elizabeth Willis
. . .
```

Primary Keys for Bean-Managed Persistence

You specify the primary key class in the entity bean's deployment descriptor. In most cases, your primary key class will be a `String`, an `Integer`, or some other class that belongs to the J2SE or J2EE standard libraries. For some entity beans, you will need to define your own primary key class. For example, if the bean has a composite primary key (that is, one composed of multiple fields), then you must create a primary key class.

The Primary Key Class

The following primary key class is a composite key; the `productId` and `vendorId` fields together uniquely identify an entity bean.

```java
public class ItemKey implements java.io.Serializable {

    public String productId;
    public String vendorId;

    public ItemKey() { };

    public ItemKey(String productId, String vendorId) {

      this.productId = productId;
      this.vendorId = vendorId;
    }

    public String getProductId() {

       return productId;
    }

    public String getVendorId() {

       return vendorId;
    }

    public boolean equals(Object other) {

       if (other instanceof ItemKey) {
          return (productId.equals(((ItemKey)other).productId)
                 && vendorId.equals(((ItemKey)other).vendorId));
       }
       return false;
    }

    public int hashCode() {

       return productId.concat(vendorId).hashCode();
    }
}
```

For bean-managed persistence, a primary key class must meet these requirements:

- The access control modifier of the class must be public.
- All fields must be declared as public.
- The class must have a public default constructor.
- The class must implement the hashCode() and equals(Object other) methods.
- The class must be serializable.

Primary Keys in the Entity Bean Class

With bean-managed persistence, the ejbCreate method assigns the input parameters to instance variables and then returns the primary key class:

```
public ItemKey ejbCreate(String productId, String vendorId,
    String description) throws CreateException {

    if (productId == null || vendorId == null) {
        throw new CreateException(
                "The productId and vendorId are required.");
    }

    this.productId = productId;
    this.vendorId = vendorId;
    this.description = description;

    return new ItemKey(productId, vendorId);
}
```

The ejbFindByPrimaryKey verifies the existence of the database row for the given primary key:

```
public ItemKey ejbFindByPrimaryKey(ItemKey primaryKey)
    throws FinderException {

    try {
        if (selectByPrimaryKey(primaryKey))
            return primaryKey;
    ...
}
```

```
private boolean selectByPrimaryKey(ItemKey primaryKey)
   throws SQLException {

   String selectStatement =
         "select productid " +
         "from item where productid = ? and vendorid = ?";
   PreparedStatement prepStmt =
         con.prepareStatement(selectStatement);
   prepStmt.setString(1, primaryKey.getProductId());
   prepStmt.setString(2, primaryKey.getVendorId());
   ResultSet rs = prepStmt.executeQuery();
   boolean result = rs.next();
   prepStmt.close();
   return result;
}
```

Getting the Primary Key

A client can fetch the primary key of an entity bean by invoking the `get-PrimaryKey` method of the `EJBObject` class:

```
SavingsAccount account;
...
String id = (String)account.getPrimaryKey();
```

The entity bean retrieves its own primary key by calling the `getPrimaryKey` method of the `EntityContext` class:

```
EntityContext context;
...
String id = (String) context.getPrimaryKey();
```

deploytool Tips for Entity Beans with Bean-Managed Persistence

Chapter 25 gives step-by-step instructions for creating and packaging a session bean. To build an entity bean, you follow the same procedures, but with the following exceptions.

1. In the New Enterprise Bean wizard, specify the bean's type and persistent management.

   a. In the General dialog box, select the Entity radio button.

   b. In the Entity Settings dialog box, select Bean-Managed Persistence.

2. In the Resource Ref's tab, specify the resource factories referenced by the bean. These settings enable the bean to connect to the database. For more information on resource references, see Database Connections (page 1078).

3. Before you deploy the bean, verify that the JNDI names are correct.

   a. Select the application from the tree.

   b. Click the Sun-specific Settings button.

   c. Select JNDI Names in the View combo-box.

27

Container-Managed Persistence Examples

AN entity bean with container-managed persistence (CMP) offers important advantages to the bean developer. First, the EJB container handles all database storage and retrieval calls. Second, the container manages the relationships between the entity beans. Because of these services, you don't have to code the database access calls in the entity bean. Instead, you specify settings in the bean's deployment descriptor. Not only does this approach save you time, but it also makes the bean portable across various database servers.

This chapter focuses on the source code and deployment settings for an example called `RosterApp`, an application that features entity beans with container-managed persistence. If you are unfamiliar with the terms and concepts mentioned in this chapter, please consult the section Container-Managed Persistence (page 835).

Overview of the RosterApp Application

The `RosterApp` application maintains the team rosters for players in sports leagues. The application has five components. The `RosterAppClient` component is an application client that accesses the `RosterBean` session bean through the bean's remote interfaces. `RosterBean` accesses three entity beans—`Player-Bean`, `TeamBean`, and `LeagueBean`—through their local interfaces.

The entity beans use container-managed persistence and relationships. The `TeamBean` and `PlayerBean` entity beans have a bidirectional, many-to-many relationship. In a bidirectional relationship, each bean has a relationship field whose value identifies the related bean instance. The multiplicity of the `TeamBean`–`PlayerBean` relationship is many-to-many: Players who participate in more than one sport belong to multiple teams, and each team has multiple players. The `LeagueBean` and `TeamBean` entity beans also have a bidirectional relationship, but the multiplicity is one-to-many: A league has many teams, but a team can belong to only one league.

Figure 27–1 shows the components and relationships of the `RosterApp` application. The dotted lines represent the access gained through invocations of the JNDI `lookup` method. The solid lines represent the container-managed relationships.

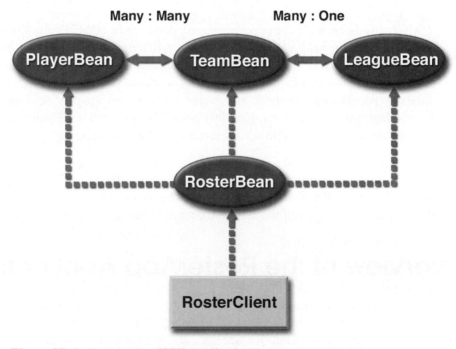

Figure 27–1   `RosterApp` J2EE Application

The PlayerBean Code

The `PlayerBean` entity bean represents a player in a sports league. Like any local entity bean with container-managed persistence, `PlayerBean` needs the following code:

- Entity bean class (`PlayerBean`)
- Local home interface (`LocalPlayerHome`)
- Local interface (`LocalPlayer`)

The source code for this example is in the `<INSTALL>`/j2eetutorial14/examples/ejb/cmproster directory.

Entity Bean Class

The code of the entity bean class must meet the container-managed persistence syntax requirements. First, the class must be defined as `public` and `abstract`. Second, the class must implement the following:

- The `EntityBean` interface
- Zero or more `ejbCreate` and `ejbPostCreate` methods
- The `get` and `set` access methods, defined as `abstract`, for the persistent and relationship fields
- Any select methods, defining them as `abstract`
- The home methods
- The business methods

The entity bean class must not implement these methods:

- The finder methods
- The `finalize` method

Differences between Container-Managed and Bean-Managed Code

Because it contains no calls to access the database, an entity bean with container-managed persistence requires a lot less code than one with bean-managed persistence. For example, the `PlayerBean.java` source file discussed in this

Table 27–1 Coding Differences between Persistent Types

Difference	Container-Managed	Bean-Managed
Class definition	Abstract	Not abstract
Database access calls	Handled by container	Coded by developers
Persistent state	Represented by virtual persistent fields	Coded as instance variables
Access methods for persistent and relationship fields	Required	None
`findByPrimaryKey` method	Handled by container	Coded by developers
Customized finder methods	Handled by container, but the developer must define the EJB QL queries	Coded by developers
Select methods	Handled by container	None
Return value of `ejbCreate`	`null`	Must be the primary key

chapter is much smaller than the `SavingsAccountBean.java` code documented in Chapter 26. Table 27–1 compares the code of the two types of entity beans.

Note that for both types of persistence, the rules for implementing business and home methods are the same. See the sections The Business Methods (page 910) and The Home Methods (page 912) in Chapter 26.

Access Methods

An entity bean with container-managed persistence has persistent and relationship fields. These fields are virtual, so you do not code them in the class as instance variables. Instead, you specify them in the bean's deployment descriptor. To permit access to the fields, you define abstract `get` and `set` methods in the entity bean class.

Access Methods for Persistent Fields

The EJB container automatically performs the database storage and retrieval of the bean's persistent fields. The deployment descriptor of `PlayerBean` specifies the following persistent fields:

- `playerId` (primary key)
- `name`
- `position`
- `salary`

The `PlayerBean` class defines the access methods for the persistent fields as follows:

```
public abstract String getPlayerId();
public abstract void setPlayerId(String id);

public abstract String getName();
public abstract void setName(String name);

public abstract String getPosition();
public abstract void setPosition(String position);

public abstract double getSalary();
public abstract void setSalary(double salary);
```

The name of an access method begins with `get` or `set`, followed by the capitalized name of the persistent or relationship field. For example, the accessor methods for the `salary` field are `getSalary` and `setSalary`. This naming convention is similar to that of JavaBeans components.

Access Methods for Relationship Fields

In the `RosterApp` application, a player can belong to multiple teams, so a `PlayerBean` instance may be related to many `TeamBean` instances. To specify this relationship, the deployment descriptor of `PlayerBean` defines a relationship field named `teams`. In the `PlayerBean` class, the access methods for the `teams` relationship field are as follows:

```
public abstract Collection getTeams();
public abstract void setTeams(Collection teams);
```

Finder and Select Methods

Finder and select methods use EJB QL queries to return objects and state information of entity beans using container-managed persistence.

A select method is similar to a finder method in the following ways:

- A select method can return a local or remote interface (or a collection of interfaces).
- A select method queries a database.
- The deployment descriptor specifies an EJB QL query for a select method.
- The entity bean class does not implement the select method.

However, a select method differs significantly from a finder method:

- A select method can return a persistent field (or a collection thereof) of a related entity bean. A finder method can return only a local or remote interface (or a collection of interfaces).
- Because it is not exposed in any of the local or remote interfaces, a select method cannot be invoked by a client. It can be invoked only by the methods implemented within the entity bean class. A select method is usually invoked by either a business or a home method.
- A select method is defined in the entity bean class. For bean-managed persistence, a finder method is defined in the entity bean class, but for container-managed persistence it is not.

The `PlayerBean` class defines these select methods:

```
public abstract Collection ejbSelectLeagues(LocalPlayer player)
    throws FinderException;
public abstract Collection ejbSelectSports(LocalPlayer player)
    throws FinderException;
```

The signature for a select method must follow these rules:

- The prefix of the method name must be `ejbSelect`.
- The access control modifier must be `public`.
- The method must be declared as `abstract`.
- The `throws` clause must include the `javax.ejb.FinderException`.

Business Methods

Because clients cannot invoke select methods, the PlayerBean class wraps them in the getLeagues and getSports business methods:

```
public Collection getLeagues() throws FinderException {

  LocalPlayer player =
    (team.LocalPlayer)context.getEJBLocalObject();
  return ejbSelectLeagues(player);
}

public Collection getSports() throws FinderException {

  LocalPlayer player =
    (team.LocalPlayer)context.getEJBLocalObject();
  return ejbSelectSports(player);
}
```

Entity Bean Methods

Because the container handles persistence, the life-cycle methods in the Player-Bean class are nearly empty.

The ejbCreate method initializes the bean instance by assigning the input arguments to the persistent fields. At the end of the transaction that contains the create call, the container inserts a row into the database. Here is the source code for the ejbCreate method:

```
public String ejbCreate (String id, String name,
    String position, double salary) throws CreateException {

    setPlayerId(id);
    setName(name);
    setPosition(position);
    setSalary(salary);
    return null;
}
```

The ejbPostCreate method returns void, and it has the same input parameters as the ejbCreate method. If you want to set a relationship field to initialize the bean instance, you should do so in the ejbPostCreate method. You cannot set a relationship field in the ejbCreate method.

Except for a debug statement, the `ejbRemove` method in the `PlayerBean` class is empty. The container invokes `ejbRemove` before removing the entity object.

The container automatically synchronizes the state of the entity bean with the database. After the container loads the bean's state from the database, it invokes the `ejbLoad` method. In like manner, before storing the state in the database, the container invokes the `ejbStore` method.

Local Home Interface

The local home interface defines the `create`, finder, and home methods that can be invoked by local clients.

The syntax rules for a `create` method follow:

- The name must begin with `create`.
- It must have the same number and types of arguments as its matching `ejbCreate` method in the entity bean class.
- It must return the local interface type of the entity bean.
- The `throws` clause must include the exceptions specified by the `throws` clause of the corresponding `ejbCreate` method.
- The `throws` clause must contain the `javax.ejb.CreateException`.

These rules apply for a finder method:

- The name must begin with `find`.
- The return type must be the entity bean's local interface type or a collection of those types.
- The `throws` clause must contain the `javax.ejb.FinderException`.
- The `findByPrimaryKey` method must be defined.

An excerpt of the `LocalPlayerHome` interface follows.

```
package team;

import java.util.*;
import javax.ejb.*;

public interface LocalPlayerHome extends EJBLocalHome {

    public LocalPlayer create (String id, String name,
        String position, double salary)
        throws CreateException;
```

```
    public LocalPlayer findByPrimaryKey (String id)
        throws FinderException;

    public Collection findByPosition(String position)
        throws FinderException;
      ...
    public Collection findByLeague(LocalLeague league)
        throws FinderException;
      ...
}
```

Local Interface

This interface defines the business and access methods that a local client can invoke. The PlayerBean class implements two business methods: getLeagues and getSports. It also defines several get and set access methods for the persistent and relationship fields. The set methods are hidden from the bean's clients because they are not defined in the LocalPlayer interface. However, the get methods are exposed to the clients by the interface:

```
    package team;

    import java.util.*;
    import javax.ejb.*;

    public interface LocalPlayer extends EJBLocalObject {

        public String getPlayerId();
        public String getName();
        public String getPosition();
        public double getSalary();
        public Collection getTeams();

        public Collection getLeagues() throws FinderException;
        public Collection getSports() throws FinderException;
    }
```

Method Invocations in RosterApp

To show how the various components interact, this section describes the sequence of method invocations that occur for particular functions. The source code for the components is in the *<INSTALL>*/j2eetutorial14/examples/ejb/ cmproster directory.

Creating a Player

1. RosterClient

The `RosterClient` invokes the `createPlayer` business method of the `Roster-Bean` session bean to create a new player. In the following line of code, the type of the `myRoster` object is `Roster`, the remote interface of `RosterBean`. The argument of the `createPlayer` method is a `PlayerDetails` object, which encapsulates information about a particular player.

```
myRoster.createPlayer(new PlayerDetails("P1", "Phil Jones",
    "goalkeeper", 100.00));
```

2. RosterBean

The `createPlayer` method of the `RosterBean` session bean creates a new instance of the `PlayerBean` entity bean. Because the access of `PlayerBean` is local, the `create` method is defined in the local home interface, `LocalPlayer-Home`. The type of the `playerHome` object is `LocalPlayerHome`. Here is the source code for the `createPlayer` method:

```
public void createPlayer(PlayerDetails details) {

try {
  LocalPlayer player = playerHome.create(details.getId(),
      details.getName(), details.getPosition(),
        details.getSalary());
} catch (Exception ex) {
    throw new EJBException(ex.getMessage());
  }
}
```

3. PlayerBean

The `ejbCreate` method assigns the input arguments to the bean's persistent fields by calling the `set` access methods. At the end of the transaction that contains the `create` call, the container saves the persistent fields in the database by issuing an SQL `INSERT` statement. The code for the `ejbCreate` method follows.

```
public String ejbCreate (String id, String name,
    String position, double salary) throws CreateException {

    setPlayerId(id);
    setName(name);
```

```
      setPosition(position);
      setSalary(salary);
      return null;
   }
```

Adding a Player to a Team

1. RosterClient

The `RosterClient` calls the `addPlayer` business method of the `RosterBean` session bean to add player P1 to team T1. The P1 and T1 parameters are the primary keys of the `PlayerBean` and `TeamBean` instances, respectively.

```
      myRoster.addPlayer("P1", "T1");
```

2. RosterBean

The `addPlayer` method performs two steps. First, it calls `findByPrimaryKey` to locate the `PlayerBean` and `TeamBean` instances. Second, it invokes the `addPlayer` business method of the `TeamBean` entity bean. Here is the source code for the `addPlayer` method of the `RosterBean` session bean:

```
   public void addPlayer(String playerId, String teamId) {

      try {
         LocalTeam team = teamHome.findByPrimaryKey(teamId);
         LocalPlayer player =
            playerHome.findByPrimaryKey(playerId);
         team.addPlayer(player);
      } catch (Exception ex) {
         throw new EJBException(ex.getMessage());
      }
   }
```

3. TeamBean

The `TeamBean` entity bean has a relationship field named `players`, a `Collection` that represents the players that belong to the team. The access methods for the `players` relationship field are as follows:

```
   public abstract Collection getPlayers();
   public abstract void setPlayers(Collection players);
```

The addPlayer method of TeamBean invokes the getPlayers access method to fetch the Collection of related LocalPlayer objects. Next, the addPlayer method invokes the add method of the Collection interface. Here is the source code for the addPlayer method:

```
public void addPlayer(LocalPlayer player) {
   try {
      Collection players = getPlayers();
      players.add(player);
   } catch (Exception ex) {
      throw new EJBException(ex.getMessage());
   }
}
```

Removing a Player

1. RosterClient

To remove player P4, the client would invoke the removePlayer method of the RosterBean session bean:

```
myRoster.removePlayer("P4");
```

2. RosterBean

The removePlayer method locates the PlayerBean instance by calling findBy-PrimaryKey and then invokes the remove method on the instance. This invocation signals the container to delete the row in the database that corresponds to the PlayerBean instance. The container also removes the item for this instance from the players relationship field in the TeamBean entity bean. By this removal, the container automatically updates the TeamBean-PlayerBean relationship. Here is the removePlayer method of the RosterBean session bean:

```
public void removePlayer(String playerId) {
   try {
      LocalPlayer player =
         playerHome.findByPrimaryKey(playerId);
      player.remove();
   } catch (Exception ex) {
      throw new EJBException(ex.getMessage());
   }
}
```

Dropping a Player from a Team

1. RosterClient

To drop player P2 from team T1, the client would call the dropPlayer method of the RosterBean session bean:

```
myRoster.dropPlayer("P2", "T1");
```

2. RosterBean

The dropPlayer method retrieves the PlayerBean and TeamBean instances by calling their findByPrimaryKey methods. Next, it invokes the dropPlayer business method of the TeamBean entity bean. The dropPlayer method of the RosterBean session bean follows:

```
public void dropPlayer(String playerId, String teamId) {

    try {
        LocalPlayer player =
            playerHome.findByPrimaryKey(playerId);
        LocalTeam team = teamHome.findByPrimaryKey(teamId);
        team.dropPlayer(player);
    } catch (Exception ex) {
        throw new EJBException(ex.getMessage());
    }
}
```

3. TeamBean

The dropPlayer method updates the TeamBean-PlayerBean relationship. First, the method retrieves the Collection of LocalPlayer objects that correspond to the players relationship field. Next, it drops the target player by calling the remove method of the Collection interface. Here is the dropPlayer method of the TeamBean entity bean:

```
public void dropPlayer(LocalPlayer player) {

    try {
        Collection players = getPlayers();
        players.remove(player);
    } catch (Exception ex) {
        throw new EJBException(ex.getMessage());
    }
}
```

Getting the Players of a Team

1. RosterClient

The client can fetch a team's players by calling the `getPlayersOfTeam` method of the `RosterBean` session bean. This method returns an `ArrayList` of `Player-Details` objects. A `PlayerDetail` object contains four variables—`playerId`, `name`, `position`, and `salary`—which are copies of the `PlayerBean` persistent fields. The `RosterClient` calls the `getPlayersOfTeam` method as follows:

```
playerList = myRoster.getPlayersOfTeam("T2");
```

2. RosterBean

The `getPlayersOfTeam` method of the `RosterBean` session bean locates the `LocalTeam` object of the target team by invoking the `findByPrimaryKey` method. Next, the `getPlayersOfTeam` method calls the `getPlayers` method of the `TeamBean` entity bean. Here is the source code for the `getPlayersOfTeam` method:

```
public ArrayList getPlayersOfTeam(String teamId) {

   Collection players = null;

   try {
      LocalTeam team = teamHome.findByPrimaryKey(teamId);
      players = team.getPlayers();
   } catch (Exception ex) {
      throw new EJBException(ex.getMessage());
   }

   return copyPlayersToDetails(players);
}
```

The `getPlayersOfTeam` method returns the `ArrayList` of `PlayerDetails` objects that is generated by the `copyPlayersToDetails` method:

```
private ArrayList copyPlayersToDetails(Collection players) {

   ArrayList detailsList = new ArrayList();
   Iterator i = players.iterator();
```

```
    while (i.hasNext()) {
        LocalPlayer player = (LocalPlayer) i.next();
        PlayerDetails details =
            new PlayerDetails(player.getPlayerId(),
                player.getName(), player.getPosition(),
                player.getSalary());
            detailsList.add(details);
    }

    return detailsList;
}
```

3. TeamBean

The getPlayers method of the TeamBean entity bean is an access method of the players relationship field:

```
public abstract Collection getPlayers();
```

This method is exposed to local clients because it is defined in the local interface, LocalTeam:

```
public Collection getPlayers();
```

When invoked by a local client, a get access method returns a reference to the relationship field. If the local client alters the object returned by a get access method, it also alters the value of the relationship field inside the entity bean. For example, a local client of the TeamBean entity bean could drop a player from a team as follows:

```
LocalTeam team = teamHome.findByPrimaryKey(teamId);
Collection players = team.getPlayers();
players.remove(player);
```

If you want to prevent a local client from modifying a relationship field in this manner, you should take the approach described in the next section.

Getting a Copy of a Team's Players

In contrast to the methods discussed in the preceding section, the methods in this section demonstrate the following techniques:

- Filtering the information passed back to the remote client
- Preventing the local client from directly modifying a relationship field

1. RosterClient

If you wanted to hide the salary of a player from a remote client, you would require the client to call the `getPlayersOfTeamCopy` method of the `RosterBean` session bean. Like the `getPlayersOfTeam` method, the `getPlayersOfTeamCopy` method returns an `ArrayList` of `PlayerDetails` objects. However, the objects returned by `getPlayersOfTeamCopy` are different: their `salary` variables have been set to zero. The `RosterClient` calls the `getPlayersOfTeamCopy` method as follows:

```
playerList = myRoster.getPlayersOfTeamCopy("T5");
```

2. RosterBean

Unlike the `getPlayersOfTeam` method, the `getPlayersOfTeamCopy` method does not invoke the `getPlayers` access method that is exposed in the `LocalTeam` interface. Instead, the `getPlayersOfTeamCopy` method retrieves a copy of the player information by invoking the `getCopyOfPlayers` business method that is defined in the `LocalTeam` interface. As a result, the `getPlayersOfTeamCopy` method cannot modify the `players` relationship field of `TeamBean`. Here is the source code for the `getPlayersOfTeamCopy` method of `RosterBean`:

```
public ArrayList getPlayersOfTeamCopy(String teamId) {

   ArrayList playersList = null;

   try {
      LocalTeam team = teamHome.findByPrimaryKey(teamId);
      playersList = team.getCopyOfPlayers();
   } catch (Exception ex) {
      throw new EJBException(ex.getMessage());
   }

   return playersList;
}
```

3. TeamBean

The `getCopyOfPlayers` method of `TeamBean` returns an `ArrayList` of `Player-Details` objects. To create this `ArrayList`, the method iterates through the `Collection` of related `LocalPlayer` objects and copies information to the variables of the `PlayerDetails` objects. The method copies the values of `PlayerBean` persistent fields—except for the `salary` field, which it sets to zero. As a result, a player's salary is hidden from a client that invokes the `getPlayersOfTeamCopy` method. The source code for the `getCopyOfPlayers` method of `TeamBean` follows.

```
public ArrayList getCopyOfPlayers() {

   ArrayList playerList = new ArrayList();
   Collection players = getPlayers();

   Iterator i = players.iterator();
   while (i.hasNext()) {
      LocalPlayer player = (LocalPlayer) i.next();
      PlayerDetails details =
         new PlayerDetails(player.getPlayerId(),
            player.getName(), player.getPosition(), 0.00);
      playerList.add(details);
   }

   return playerList;
}
```

Finding the Players by Position

1. RosterClient

The client starts the procedure by invoking the `getPlayersByPosition` method of the `RosterBean` session bean:

```
playerList = myRoster.getPlayersByPosition("defender");
```

2. RosterBean

The `getPlayersByPosition` method retrieves the `players` list by invoking the `findByPosition` method of the `PlayerBean` entity bean:

```
public ArrayList getPlayersByPosition(String position) {

   Collection players = null;
```

```
    try {
       players = playerHome.findByPosition(position);
    } catch (Exception ex) {
       throw new EJBException(ex.getMessage());
    }

    return copyPlayersToDetails(players);
}
```

3. PlayerBean

The LocalPlayerHome interface defines the findByPosition method:

```
public Collection findByPosition(String position)
   throws FinderException;
```

Because the PlayerBean entity bean uses container-managed persistence, the entity bean class (PlayerBean) does not implement its finder methods. To specify the queries associated with the finder methods, EJB QL queries must be defined in the bean's deployment descriptor. For example, the findByPosition method has this EJB QL query:

```
SELECT DISTINCT OBJECT(p) FROM Player p
WHERE p.position = ?1
```

At runtime, when the container invokes the findByPosition method, it will execute the corresponding SQL SELECT statement.

For details about EJB QL, please refer to Chapter 29. To learn how to view and edit an EJB QL query in deploytool, see the section Finder/Select Methods Dialog Box (PlayerBean) (page 978).

Getting the Sports of a Player

1. RosterClient

The client invokes the getSportsOfPlayer method of the RosterBean session bean:

```
sportList = myRoster.getSportsOfPlayer("P28");
```

2. RosterBean

The getSportsOfPlayer method returns an ArrayList of String objects that represent the sports of the specified player. It constructs the ArrayList from a Collection returned by the getSports business method of the PlayerBean entity bean. Here is the source code for the getSportsOfPlayer method of the RosterBean session bean:

```
public ArrayList getSportsOfPlayer(String playerId) {

    ArrayList sportsList = new ArrayList();
    Collection sports = null;

    try {
      LocalPlayer player =
        playerHome.findByPrimaryKey(playerId);
      sports = player.getSports();
    } catch (Exception ex) {
      throw new EJBException(ex.getMessage());
    }

    Iterator i = sports.iterator();
    while (i.hasNext()) {
      String sport = (String) i.next();
      sportsList.add(sport);
    }
    return sportsList;
}
```

3. PlayerBean

The getSports method is a wrapper for the ejbSelectSports method. Because the parameter of the ejbSelectSports method is of type LocalPlayer, the getSports method passes along a reference to the entity bean instance. The PlayerBean class implements the getSports method as follows:

```
public Collection getSports() throws FinderException {

    LocalPlayer player =
      (team.LocalPlayer)context.getEJBLocalObject();
    return ejbSelectSports(player);
}
```

The `PlayerBean` class defines the `ejbSelectSports` method:

```
public abstract Collection ejbSelectSports(LocalPlayer player)
    throws FinderException;
```

The bean's deployment descriptor specifies the following EJB QL query for the `ejbSelectSports` method:

```
SELECT DISTINCT t.league.sport
FROM Player p, IN (p.teams) AS t
WHERE p = ?1
```

Because `PlayerBean` uses container-managed persistence, when the `ejbSelectSports` method is invoked, the EJB container will execute its corresponding SQL SELECT statement.

Building and Running the RosterApp Example

Now that you understand the structure of the `RosterApp` example EAR file, you will assemble the enterprise application and the application client and then run the example. This section gives detailed instructions on how to build and run the `RosterApp` example, which is located at `<INSTALL>`/j2eetutorial14/examples/ejb/cmproster/.

Creating the Database Tables

The `RosterApp` application uses the database tables shown in Figure 27–2.

The instructions that follow explain how to use the `RosterApp` example with PointBase, the database software that is included in the Application Server bundle.

1. Start the PointBase server. For instructions, see Starting and Stopping the PointBase Database Server (page 28).
2. Create the database tables by running the `create.sql` script.

   a. In a terminal window, go to this directory:

      `<INSTALL>`/j2eetutorial14/examples/ejb/cmproster/

   b. Type the following command, which runs the `create.sql` script:

      ```
      asant create-db_common
      ```

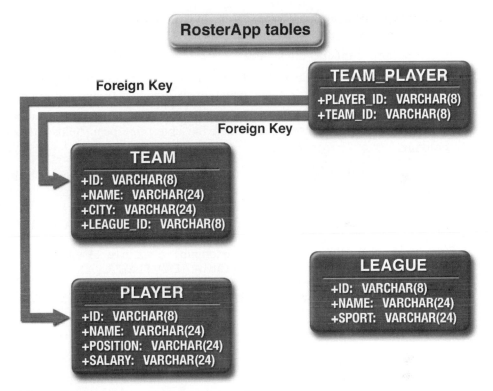

Figure 27–2 Database Tables in RosterApp

Creating the Data Source

You must create the jdbc/ejbTutorialDB data source. For instructions on creating this resource in the Admin Console, see Creating a Data Source (page 1079).

Capturing the Table Schema

You will now create a database schema file, which will allow you to map fields from the enterprise beans to columns in the database tables created earlier.

1. Make sure that the PointBase server is running.
2. In a terminal window, go to

   `<INSTALL>/j2eetutorial14/examples/ejb/cmproster/`

3. Type the following command to create the database schema file, named `cmproster.dbschema`, in the `./build/` directory:

```
asant capture-db-schema
```

The `capture-db-schema` task calls the `capture-schema` utility to output an XML file, `cmproster.dbschema`, which represents the structure of the database tables you created in Creating the Database Tables. The `cmproster.dbschema` file will be used to automatically map the enterprise bean fields to database columns.

The command that's called when you run the `capture-db-schema` task is as follows:

```
capture-schema -dburl jdbc:pointbase:server://localhost:9092/
sun-appserv-samples
-username pbpublic -password pbpublic -table LEAGUE
-table PLAYER -table TEAM -table TEAM_PLAYER
-schemaname PBPUBLIC
-driver com.pointbase.jdbc.jdbcUniversalDriver
-out build/cmproster.dbschema
```

Building the Enterprise Beans

You will now build the enterprise beans.

1. In a terminal window, go to this directory:

   <INSTALL>/j2eetutorial14/examples/ejb/cmproster/

2. Type the following command:

   ```
   asant build
   ```

Creating the Enterprise Application

Create a new application in `deploytool` called `RosterApp`.

1. In `deploytool` select File→New→Application.
2. In the Application File Name field, click Browse.
3. Navigate to *<INSTALL>*/j2eetutorial14/examples/ejb/cmproster/.
4. In the File Name field enter `RosterApp`.
5. Click New Application.
6. Click OK.

Packaging the Enterprise Beans

You will now package the four enterprise beans: RosterBean, LeagueBean, PlayerBean, and TeamBean. Note that RosterBean, a stateful session bean, will be packaged in RosterJAR. The others (LeagueBean, PlayerBean, and Team-Bean) are entity beans using container-managed persistence, and will be packaged in TeamJAR.

Packaging RosterBean

RosterBean is a stateful session bean that accesses the data in the entity beans. Clients will access and manipulate that data through RosterBean.

1. Create a new enterprise bean in RosterApp by selecting File→New→ Enterprise Bean.
2. In the EJB JAR screen:
    a. Select Create New JAR Module in Application.
    b. Enter RosterJAR under JAR Name.
    c. Click Edit Contents.
    d. Navigate to *<INSTALL>*/j2eetutorial14/examples/ejb/cmproster/build/.
    e. Select the roster and util directories.
    f. Click Add.
    g. Click OK.
    h. Click Next.
3. In the General screen:
    a. Select roster.RosterBean under Enterprise Bean Class.
    b. Enter RosterBean under Enterprise Bean Name.
    c. Select Stateful Session under Enterprise Bean Type.
    d. Select roster.RosterHome under Remote Home Interface.
    e. Select roster.Roster under Remote Interface.
    f. Select Next.
4. Click Finish.

Packaging LeagueBean, PlayerBean, and TeamBean

To package `LeagueBean`, `PlayerBean`, and `TeamBean`, follow these steps:

1. Create a new enterprise bean in `RosterApp` by selecting File→New→Enterprise Bean.

2. In the EJB JAR screen:

   a. Select Create New JAR Module in Application.

   b. Enter `TeamJAR` under JAR Name.

   c. Click Edit Contents.

   d. Navigate to `<INSTALL>/j2eetutorial14/examples/ejb/cmproster/build/`.

   e. Select the `team` and `util` directories, and the `cmproster.dbschema` file.

   f. Click Add.

   g. Click OK.

   h. Click Next.

3. In the General screen:

   a. Select `team.LeagueBean` under Enterprise Bean Class.

   b. Enter `LeagueBean` under Enterprise Bean Name.

   c. Select `team.LocalLeagueHome` under Local Home Interface.

   d. Select `team.LocalLeague` under Local Interface.

   e. Click Next.

Note: Be sure to enter the correct name in the Enterprise Bean Name field for `LeagueBean`, `PlayerBean`, and `TeamBean` to allow the automatic mapping of persistent fields and relationships.

---

4. In the Entity Settings screen:

   a. In the Persistence Management Type field, select Container-Managed Persistence (2.0).

   b. In the Fields To Be Persisted frame, check `name`, `leagueId`, and `sport`.

   c. In the Abstract Schema Name field, enter `League`.

    d. In the Primary Key Class field, choose Select an Existing Field.

    e. Select `leagueId [java.lang.String]`.

    f. Click Next.

  5. Click Finish.

Now we'll add `PlayerBean` to `TeamJAR`.

  1. Create a new enterprise bean in `TeamJAR` by selecting File→New→Enterprise Bean.

  2. In the EJB JAR screen:

    a. Select Add To Existing JAR Module.

    b. Select `TeamJAR (RosterApp)` under Add To Existing JAR Module.

    c. Click Next.

  3. In the General screen:

    a. Select `team.PlayerBean` under Enterprise Bean Class.

    b. Enter `PlayerBean` under Enterprise Bean Name.

    c. Select `team.LocalPlayerHome` under Local Home Interface.

    d. Select `team.LocalPlayer` under Local Interface.

    e. Click Next.

  4. In the Entity Settings screen:

    a. In the Persistence Management Type field, select Container-Managed Persistence (2.0).

    b. In the Fields To Be Persisted frame, check `name`, `position`, `playerId`, and `salary`.

    c. In the Abstract Schema Name field, enter `Player`.

    d. In the Primary Key Class field choose Select an Existing Field.

    e. Select `playerId [java.lang.String]`.

    f. Click Next.

  5. Click Finish.

Now we'll add `TeamBean` to `TeamJAR`.

  1. Create a new enterprise bean in `TeamJAR` by selecting File→New→Enterprise Bean.

2. In the EJB JAR screen:

   a. Select Add To Existing JAR Module.

   b. Select `TeamJAR (RosterApp)` under Add To Existing JAR Module.

   c. Click Next.

3. In the General screen:

   a. Select `team.TeamBean` under Enterprise Bean Class.

   b. Enter `TeamBean` under Enterprise Bean Name.

   c. Select `team.LocalTeamHome` under Local Home Interface.

   d. Select `team.LocalTeam` under Local Interface.

   e. Click Next.

4. In the Entity Settings screen:

   a. In the Persistence Management Type field, select Container-Managed Persistence (2.0).

   b. In the Fields To Be Persisted frame, check `name`, `teamId`, and `city`.

   c. In the Abstract Schema Name field, enter `Team`.

   d. In the Primary Key Class field, choose Select an Existing Field.

   e. Select `teamId [java.lang.String]`.

   f. Click Next.

5. Click Finish.

Adding EJB QL Queries to PlayerBean

`PlayerBean` contains finder and selector methods that use EJB QL queries. These steps will add the appropriate EJB QL queries to the methods. See Chapter 29 for more details.

1. Select `PlayerBean` in the tree in `deploytool`.

2. Select the Entity tabbed pane.

3. Click Find/Select Queries.

4. In Select Local Finders:

   a. For the `findAll` method, enter

```
select object(p) from Player p
```

b. For the `findByCity` method, enter

```
select distinct object(p) from Player p,
in (p.teams) as t
where t.city = ?1
```

c. For the `findByHigherSalary` method, enter

```
select distinct object(p1)
from Player p1, Player p2
where p1.salary > p2.salary and
p2.name = ?1
```

d. For the `findByLeague` method, enter

```
select distinct object(p) from Player p,
in (p.teams) as t
where t.league = ?1
```

e. For the `findByPosition` method, enter

```
select distinct object(p) from Player p
where p.position = ?1
```

f. For the `findByPositionAndName` method, enter

```
select distinct object(p) from Player p
where p.position = ?1 and p.name = ?2
```

g. For the `findBySalaryRange` method, enter

```
select distinct object(p) from Player p
where p.salary between ?1 and ?2
```

h. For the `findBySport` method, enter

```
select distinct object(p) from Player p,
in (p.teams) as t
where t.league.sport = ?1
```

i. For the `findByTest` method, enter

```
select distinct object(p) from Player p
where p.name = ?1
```

j. For the `findNotOnTeam` method, enter

```
select object(p) from Player p
where p.teams is empty
```

5. In Show Select Methods:

   a. For the `ejbSelectLeagues` method, enter

   ```
   select distinct t.league
   from Player p, in (p.teams) as t
   where p = ?1
   ```

   b. For the `ejbSelectSports` method, enter

   ```
   select distinct t.league.sport
   from Player p, in (p.teams) as t
   where p = ?1
   ```

   c. Under Return EJBs of Type, select None for `ejbSelectSports`.

6. Click OK.

7. Select File→Save.

Establishing Relationships between Enterprise Beans

`TeamJAR` has the relationships shown in Figure 27–3.

To create the container-managed relationships between the enterprise beans, do the following:

1. Select `TeamJAR` in the tree in `deploytool`.

2. Select the Relationships tabbed pane.

3. Click Add.

4. In the Add Relationship dialog box:

   a. In the Multiplicity field, select `Many to Many (*:*)`.

   b. In the Enterprise Bean A section:

      1. In the Enterprise Bean Name field, select `TeamBean`.

      2. In the Field Referencing Bean B field, select `players`.

      3. In the Field Type field, select `java.util.Collection`.

   c. In the Enterprise Bean B section:

      1. In the Enterprise Bean Name field, select `PlayerBean`.

      2. In the Field Referencing Bean A field, select `teams`.

      3. In the Field Type field, select `java.util.Collection`.

   d. Click OK.

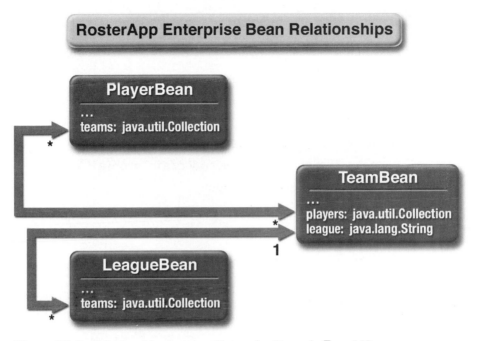

Figure 27-3 Relationships between Enterprise Beans in TeamJAR

5. Click Add.

6. In the Add Relationship dialog box:

   a. In the Multiplicity field, select One to Many (1:*).

   b. In the Enterprise Bean A section:

   1. In the Enterprise Bean Name field, select LeagueBean.

   2. In the Field Referencing Bean B field, select teams.

   3. In the Field Type field, select java.util.Collection.

   c. In the Enterprise Bean B section:

   1. In the Enterprise Bean Name field, select TeamBean.

   2. In the Field Referencing Bean A field, select league.

   3. Check Delete When Bean A Is Deleted.

   d. Click OK.

Creating the Field and Relationship Mappings

To set the container-managed fields and relationships, do the following:

1. Select `TeamJAR` from the tree in `deploytool`.
2. Select the General tabbed pane.
3. Click Sun-specific Settings.
4. In the Sun-specific Settings dialog box:
   a. In the JNDI Name field, enter `jdbc/ejbTutorialDB`.
   b. Click Create Database Mappings.
5. In the Create Database Mappings dialog box:
   a. Select Map to Tables in Database Schema File.
   b. Select `cmproster.dbschema` under Database Schema Files in Module.
   c. Click OK.
6. Confirm that all the fields and relationships have been mapped.
7. Click Close.

Setting RosterBean's Transaction Attributes

1. Select `RosterBean` in `deploytool`'s tree.
2. Click the Transactions tabbed pane.
3. In the Transaction Management field, click Container-Managed.

Setting the Enterprise Bean References

First, you'll set the enterprise bean reference for `ejb/SimpleLeague`.

1. Select `RosterBean` in `deploytool`'s tree.
2. Click the EJB Ref's tabbed pane.
3. Click Add.
4. In the Add Enterprise Bean Reference dialog box:
   a. In the Coded Name field, enter `ejb/SimpleLeague`.
   b. In the EJB Type field, select `Entity`.

c. In the Interfaces field, select `Local`.

d. In the Home Interface field, enter `team.LocalLeagueHome`.

e. In the Local/Remote Interface field, enter `team.LocalLeague`.

f. Under Target EJB, select `ejb-jar-icl.jar#LeagueBean` in the Enterprise Bean Name drop-down list.

g. Click OK.

Next, you'll set the enterprise bean reference for `ejb/SimplePlayer`.

1. Click Add.

2. In the Add Enterprise Bean Reference dialog box:

    a. In the Coded Name field, enter `ejb/SimplePlayer`.

    b. In the EJB Type field, select `Entity`.

    c. In the Interfaces field, select `Local`.

    d. In the Home Interface field, enter `team.LocalPlayerHome`.

    e. In the Local/Remote Interface field, enter `team.LocalPlayer`.

    f. Under Target EJB, select `ejb-jar-icl.jar#PlayerBean` in the Enterprise Bean Name drop-down list.

    g. Click OK.

Finally, you'll set the enterprise bean reference for `ejb/SimpleTeam`.

1. Click Add.

2. In the Add Enterprise Bean Reference dialog box:

    a. In the Coded Name field, enter `ejb/SimpleTeam`.

    b. In the EJB Type field, select `Entity`.

    c. In the Interfaces field, select `Local`.

    d. In the Home Interface field, enter `team.LocalTeamHome`.

    e. In the Local/Remote Interface field, enter `team.LocalTeam`.

    f. Under Target EJB, select `ejb-jar-icl.jar#TeamBean` in the Enterprise Bean Name drop-down list.

    g. Click OK.

3. Select File→Save.

Packaging the Enterprise Application Client

To package the application client, do the following:

1. Create a new application client in `RosterApp` by selecting File→New→ Application Client.

2. In the JAR File Contents screen:

   a. Select `RosterApp` under Create New AppClient Module in Application.

   b. Enter `RosterClient` under AppClient Name.

   c. Click Edit Contents.

   d. Navigate to `<INSTALL>`/j2eetutorial14/examples/ejb/cmproster/build/.

   e. Select the `client` directory.

   f. Click Add.

   g. Click OK.

   h. Click Next.

3. In the General screen:

   a. Select `client.RosterClient` under Main Class.

   b. Select (`Use container-managed authentication`) under Callback Handler Class.

   c. Click Next.

4. Click Finish.

Setting the Enterprise Bean Reference

You must map the coded JNDI name in the client to the `RosterBean` stateful session bean. To do this, follow these steps:

1. Select RosterClient in `deploytool`'s tree.

2. Select the EJB Ref's tabbed pane.

3. Click Add.

4. In the Add Enterprise Bean Reference dialog box:

   a. In the Coded Name field enter `ejb/SimpleRoster`.

   b. In the EJB Type field, select `Session`.

c. In the Interfaces field, select `Remote`.

d. In the Home Interface field, enter `roster.RosterHome`.

e. In the Local/Remote Interface field, enter `roster.Roster`.

f. Under Target EJB, select JNDI Name.

g. Select `RosterBean` under JNDI Name.

h. Click OK.

5. Select File→Save.

Deploying the Enterprise Application

You can now deploy the enterprise application by following these steps:

1. Select Tools→Deploy.

2. In the Deploy Module `RosterApp` dialog box, enter the user name and password.

3. Under Application Client Stub Directory, check Return Client Jar.

4. Confirm that the path in the field below the checkbox is `<INSTALL>/j2eetutorial14/examples/ejb/cmproster/`. If it isn't, click Browse and navigate to `<INSTALL>/j2eetutorial14/examples/ejb/cmproster/build/`.

5. Click OK.

6. Confirm that the application deployed and started correctly and that the client stub JAR was created at `<INSTALL>/j2eetutorial14/examples/ejb/cmproster/build/`.

7. Click Close.

Running the Client Application

To run the client, follow these steps:

1. In a terminal, go to `<INSTALL>/j2eetutorial14/examples/ejb/cmproster/`.

2. Type the following command:

```
appclient -client RosterAppClient.jar
```

3. In the terminal window, the client displays the following output:

```
P7 Rebecca Struthers midfielder 777.0
P6 Ian Carlyle goalkeeper 555.0
P9 Jan Wesley defender 100.0
P10 Terry Smithson midfielder 100.0
P8 Anne Anderson forward 65.0

T2 Gophers Manteca
T5 Crows Orland
T1 Honey Bees Visalia

P2 Alice Smith defender 505.0
P5 Barney Bold defender 100.0
P25 Frank Fletcher defender 399.0
P9 Jan Wesley defender 100.0
P22 Janice Walker defender 857.0

L1 Mountain Soccer
L2 Valley Basketball
```

Note: Re-create the database tables using the `create-db_common` task before re-running the client.

A Guided Tour of the RosterApp Settings

This section introduces you to the settings of the deployment descriptors for entity beans with container-managed persistence and relationships. As this tour guides you through the `deploytool` screens, it discusses the highlights of the tabs and dialog boxes that appear.

To begin our tour, please run `deploytool` and open the `RosterApp.ear` file, which is in the `<INSTALL>`/j2eetutorial14/examples/ejb/provided-ears/ directory.

RosterApp

To view the deployment settings for the application, select the `RosterApp` node in the tree view.

General Tab (RosterApp)

The Contents field displays the files contained in the RosterApp.ear file, including the two EJB JAR files (ejb-jar-ic.jar and ejb-jar-ic1.jar) and the application client JAR file (app-client-ic.jar). See Figure 27–4.

JNDI Names Tab (RosterApp)

The Application table lists the JNDI names for the enterprise beans in the RosterApp application.

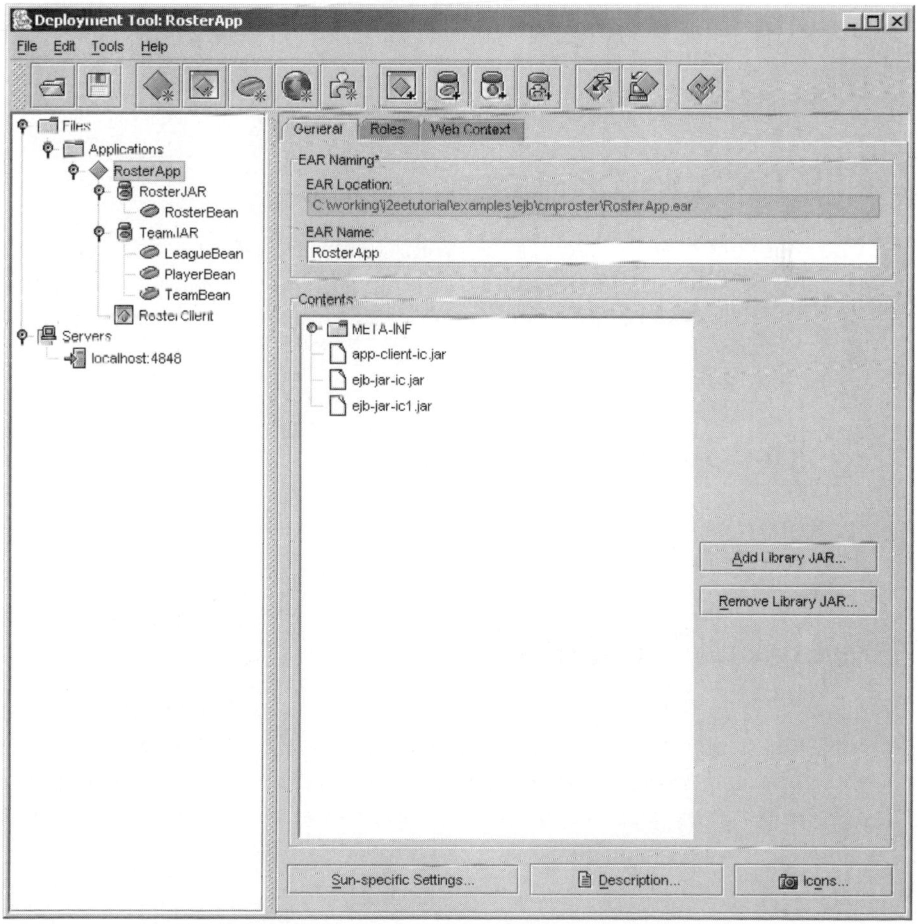

Figure 27–4 General Tab of RosterApp

The References table has one entry. The EJB Ref entry maps the coded name (ejb/SimpleRoster) in the RosterClient to the JNDI name of the RosterBean session bean.

RosterClient

To view this client, expand the RosterApp node by clicking its adjacent key icon in the tree view. Next, select RosterClient.

JAR File Tab (RosterClient)

The Contents field shows the files contained by the app-client-ic.jar file: two XML files (the deployment descriptors) and the class files (RosterClient.class, Debug.class, LeagueDetails.class, PlayerDetails.class, and TeamDetails.class).

EJB Ref's Tab (RosterClient)

The RosterClient accesses a single bean, the RosterBean session bean. Because this access is remote, the value in the Interfaces column is Remote and the value for the Local/Remote Interface column is the bean's remote interface (roster.Roster).

RosterJAR

In the tree view, select RosterJAR. This JAR file contains the RosterBean session bean.

General Tab (RosterJAR)

The Contents field lists three packages of class files. The roster package contains the class files required for RosterBean: the session bean class, remote interface, and home interface. The team package includes the local interfaces for the entity beans accessed by the RosterBean session bean. The util package holds the utility classes for this application.

RosterBean

In the tree view, expand the `RosterJAR` node and select `RosterBean`.

General Tab (RosterBean)

This tab shows that `RosterBean` is a stateful session bean with remote access. Because it allows no local access, the Local Interfaces fields are empty.

EJB Ref's Tab (RosterBean)

The `RosterBean` session bean accesses three entity beans: `PlayerBean`, `TeamBean`, and `LeagueBean`. Because this access is local, the entries in the Interfaces columns are defined as Local. The Home Interface column lists the local home interfaces of the entity beans. The Local/Remote Interfaces column displays the local interfaces of the entity beans.

To view the runtime deployment settings, select a row in the table. For example, when you select the row with the Coded Name of `ejb/SimpleLeague`, the `LeagueBean` name appears in the Enterprise Bean Name field. If a component references a local entity bean, then you must enter the name of the referenced bean in the Enterprise Bean Name field.

TeamJAR

In the tree view, select the `TeamJAR` node. This JAR file contains the three related entity beans: `LeagueBean`, `TeamBean`, and `PlayerBean`.

General Tab (TeamJAR)

The Contents field shows two packages of class files: `team` and `util`. The `team` package has the entity bean classes, local interfaces, and local home interfaces for all three entity beans. The `util` package contains utility classes. It also shows the database schema file that is used to map the enterprise bean's fields to the database.

Relationships Tab (TeamJAR)

On this tab (Figure 27–5) you define the relationships between entity beans that use container-managed persistence.

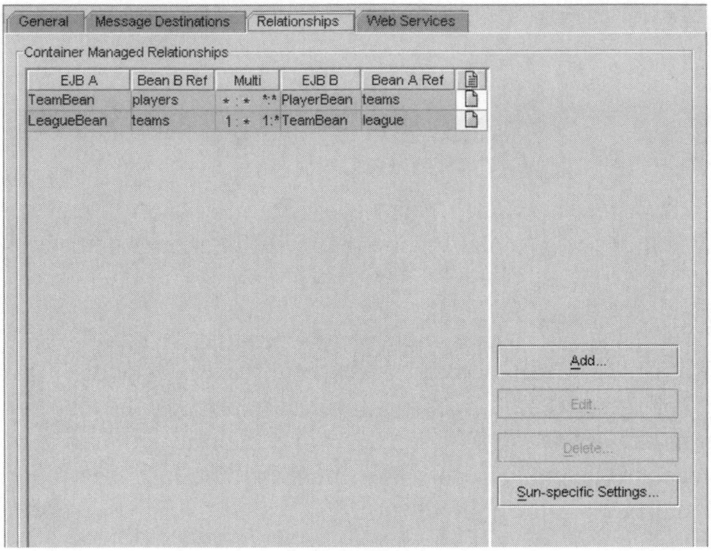

Figure 27–5   Relationships Tab of `TeamJAR`

The Container Managed Relationships table summarizes two relationships: `TeamBean-PlayerBean` and `LeagueBean-TeamBean`. In the `TeamBean-Player-Bean` relationship, `TeamBean` is designated as EJB A and `PlayerBean` as EJB B. (This designation is arbitrary. We could have assigned `PlayerBean` to EJB A, and assigned `TeamBean` to EJB B.)

Edit Relationship Dialog Box (TeamJAR)

To view the Edit Relationship dialog box (Figure 27–6), on the Relationships tab select a row and click Edit. For example, to view the `TeamBean-PlayerBean` relationship, select the row in which the EJB A value is `Team` and then click Edit.

TeamBean-PlayerBean Relationship

The Multiplicity combo box offers four choices. For this relationship, the Many To Many choice should be selected because a team has many players and a player can belong to more than one team.

The information in the Enterprise Bean A box defines the `TeamBean` side of the relationship. The Field Referencing Bean B combo box displays the relationship field (`players`) in `TeamBean`. This field corresponds to the relationship access methods in the `TeamBean.java` source code:

```
public abstract Collection getPlayers();
public abstract void setPlayers(Collection players);
```

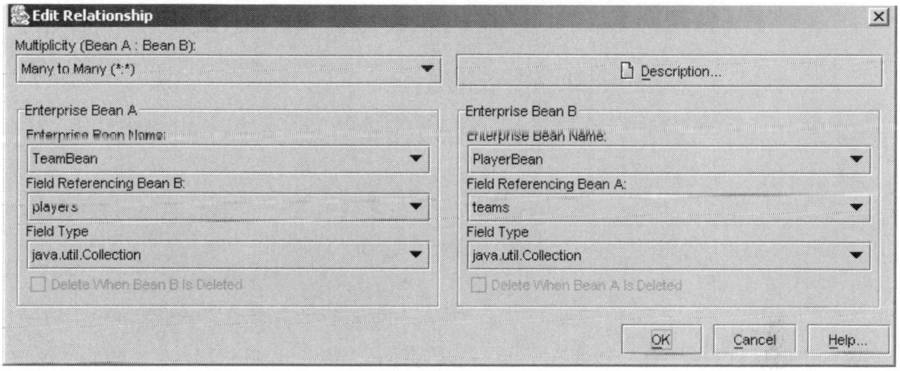

Figure 27–6 Edit Relationship Dialog Box of TeamJAR

The selection of the Field Type combo box is `java.util.Collection`, which matches the `players` type in the access methods. The `players` type is a multi-valued object (`Collection`) because on the `TeamBean` side of the relationship the multiplicity is many.

The `TeamBean`–`PlayerBean` relationship is bidirectional: each bean has a relationship field that identifies the related bean. If this relationship were unidirectional, then one of the beans would not have a relationship field identifying the other bean. For the bean without the relationship field, the value of the Field Referencing combo box would be <none>.

LeagueBean-TeamBean Relationship

In the Edit Relationship dialog box, the Multiplicity choice should be One To Many. This choice indicates that a single league has multiple teams.

For `LeagueBean`, the relationship field is `teams`, and for `TeamBean` it is `league`. Because `TeamBean` is on the multiple side of the relationship, the `teams` field is a `Collection`. In contrast, because `LeagueBean` is on the single side of the relationship, the `league` field is a single-valued object, a `LocalLeague`. The `Team-Bean.java` code defines the league relationship field with these access methods:

```
public abstract LocalLeague getLeague();
public abstract void setLeague(LocalLeague league);
```

For `TeamBean` (Enterprise Bean B), the Delete When Bean A Is Deleted checkbox is selected. Because of this selection, when a `LeagueBean` instance is deleted the related `TeamBean` instances are automatically deleted. This type of deletion, in which one deletion triggers another, is called a *cascade delete*. For League-Bean, the corresponding checkbox is disabled: If you delete a team, you don't want to automatically delete the league, because there may be other teams in that league. In general, if a bean is on the multiple side of a relationship, the other bean cannot be automatically deleted.

PlayerBean

In the tree view, expand the TeamJAR node and select the PlayerBean entity bean.

General Tab (PlayerBean)

This tab shows the enterprise bean class and interfaces. Because the PlayerBean entity bean uses container-managed persistence, it has local interfaces. It does not have remote interfaces because it does not allow remote access.

Entity Tab (PlayerBean)

The field at the top of the tabbed page defines the bean's persistence type (Figure 27–7). For PlayerBean, this type is Container-Managed Persistence, version 2.0. (Because version 1.1 did not support relationships, it is not recommended. These version numbers identify a particular release of the Enterprise JavaBeans specification, not the Application Server software.)

The Fields To Be Persisted box lists the persistent and relationship fields defined by the access methods in the PlayerBean.java code. The checkboxes for the persistent fields must be selected, but those for the relationship fields must not be selected. The PlayerBean entity bean has one relationship field: teams.

The abstract schema name is Player, a name that represents the relationships and persistent fields of the PlayerBean entity bean. This abstract name is referenced in the PlayerBean EJB QL queries. For more information on EJB QL, see Chapter 29.

Finder/Select Methods Dialog Box (PlayerBean)

To open this dialog box, click Finder/Select Methods on the Entity tab. This dialog box (Figure 27–8) enables you to view and edit the EJB QL queries for a bean's finder and select methods. For example, to list the finder methods defined in the LocalPlayerHome interface, select the Local Finders radio button. When you select the finder method, its EJB QL query appears in an editable text field.

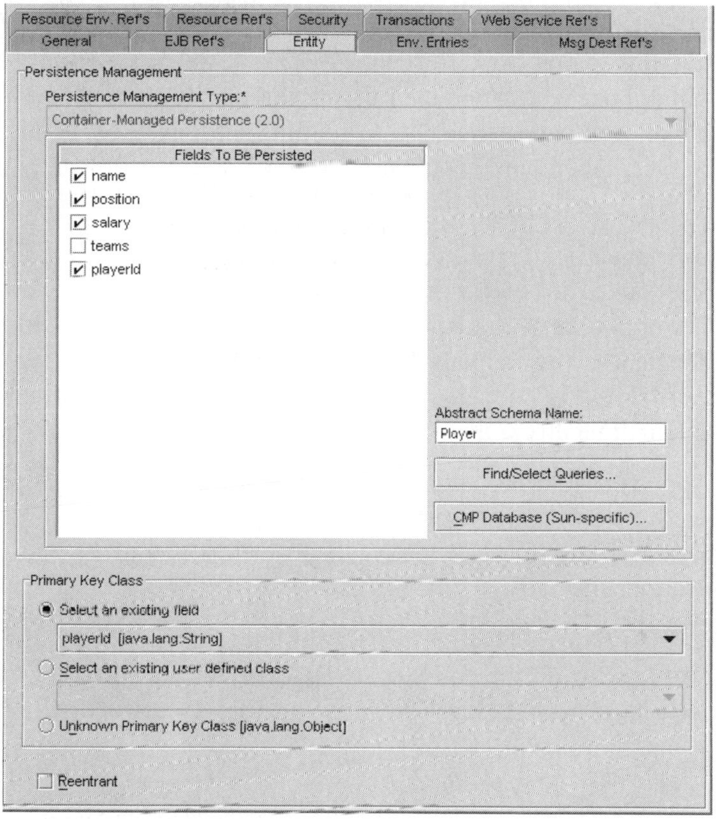

Figure 27–7   Entity Tab of PlayerBean

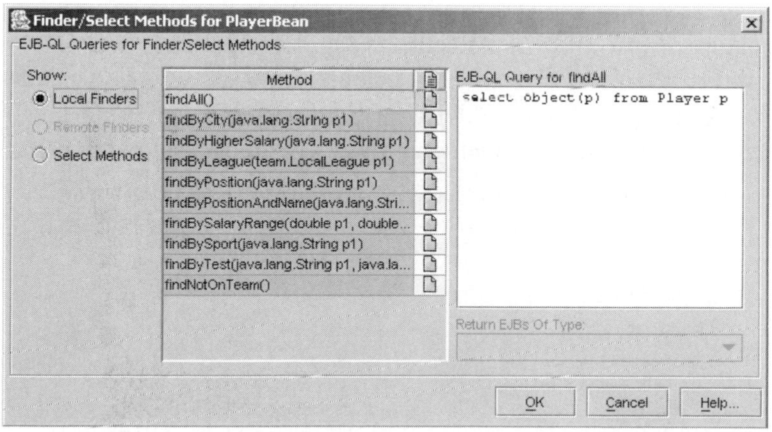

Figure 27–8   Finder/Select Methods Dialog Box of PlayerBean

Sun-Specific CMP Settings Dialog Box (PlayerBean)

To view this dialog box, click Sun-specific CMP Settings in the Entity tab. In this dialog box, you define the runtime settings of an entity bean that uses container-managed persistence. These runtime settings are specific to the Application Server; other implementations of the J2EE platform may take a different approach.

In the Application Server, the bean's persistent fields are stored in a relational database table. In the checkboxes of the Database Table box, you specify whether or not the server automatically creates or drops the table. If you want to save the data in your table between deployments, then make sure that the Delete Table checkbox is not selected. Otherwise, every time you undeploy the bean, the table will be deleted.

The Application Server accesses the database by issuing SQL calls. In an entity bean with container-managed persistence, you do not code these calls. The container creates the SQL calls automatically when you access the persistent fields and relationships.

In the Persistent Field Mapping section (see Figure 27–9), the mappings and relationships for all the entity beans in `TeamJAR` are listed. For example, to see the mappings and relationships for `PlayerBean`, select it from the Enterprise Bean field.

Primary Keys for Container-Managed Persistence

Sometimes you must implement the class and package it along with the entity bean. For example, if your entity bean requires a composite primary key (which is made up of multiple fields) or if a primary key field is a Java programming language primitive type, then you must provide a customized primary key class.

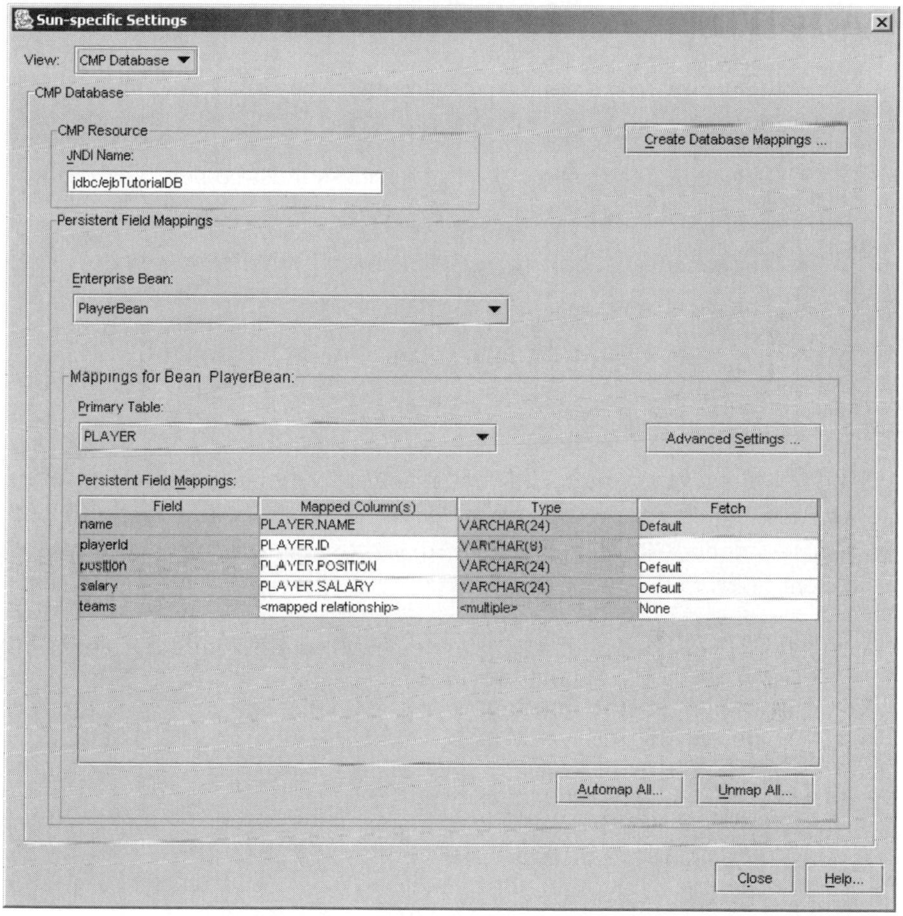

Figure 27–9 CMP Settings for PlayerBean

The Primary Key Class

For container-managed persistence, a primary key class must meet the following requirements:

- The access control modifier of the class must be `public`.
- All fields must be declared as `public`.
- The fields must be a subset of the bean's persistent fields.
- The class must have a public default constructor.
- The class must implement the `hashCode()` and `equals(Object other)` methods.
- The class must be serializable.

In the following example, the `PurchaseOrderKey` class implements a composite key for the `PurchaseOrderBean` entity bean. The key is composed of two fields—`productModel` and `vendorId`—whose names must match two of the persistent fields in the entity bean class.

```
public class PurchaseOrderKey implements java.io.Serializable {

    public String productModel;
    public String vendorId;

    public PurchaseOrderKey() { };

    public boolean equals(Object other) {

        if (other instanceof PurchaseOrderKey) {
            return (productModel.equals(
                ((PurchaseOrderKey)other).productModel) &&
                vendorId.equals(
                ((PurchaseOrderKey)other).vendorId));
        }
        return false;
    }

    public int hashCode() {

        return productModel.concat(vendorId).hashCode();
    }
}
```

Primary Keys in the Entity Bean Class

In the `PurchaseOrderBean` class, the following access methods define the persistent fields (`vendorId` and `productModel`) that make up the primary key:

```
public abstract String getVendorId();
public abstract void setVendorId(String id);

public abstract String getProductModel();
public abstract void setProductModel(String name);
```

The next code sample shows the `ejbCreate` method of the `PurchaseOrderBean` class. The return type of the `ejbCreate` method is the primary key, but the return value is `null`. Although it is not required, the `null` return value is recommended for container-managed persistence. This approach saves overhead because the bean does not have to instantiate the primary key class for the return value.

```
public PurchaseOrderKey ejbCreate (String vendorId,
    String productModel, String productName)
    throws CreateException {

    setVendorId(vendorId);
    setProductModel(productModel);
    setProductName(productName);

    return null;
}
```

Generating Primary Key Values

For some entity beans, the value of a primary key has a meaning for the business entity. For example, in an entity bean that represents a player on a sports team, the primary key might be the player's driver's license number. But for other beans, the key's value is arbitrary, provided that it's unique. With container-managed persistence, these key values can be generated automatically by the EJB container. To take advantage of this feature, an entity bean must meet these requirements:

- In the deployment descriptor, the primary key class must be defined as a `java.lang.Object`. The primary key field is not specified.
- In the home interface, the argument of the `findByPrimaryKey` method must be a `java.lang.Object`.
- In the entity bean class, the return type of the `ejbCreate` method must be a `java.lang.Object`.

In these entity beans, the primary key values are in an internal field that only the EJB container can access. You cannot associate the primary key with a persistent field or any other instance variable. However, you can fetch the bean's primary key by invoking the `getPrimaryKey` method on the bean reference, and you can locate the bean by invoking its `findByPrimaryKey` method.

Advanced CMP Topics: The OrderApp Example

The `OrderApp` application is an advanced CMP example. It contains entity beans that have self-referential relationships, one-to-one relationships, unidirectional relationships, unknown primary keys, primitive primary key types, and composite primary keys.

Structure of OrderApp

`OrderApp` is a simple inventory and ordering application for maintaining a catalog of parts and placing an itemized order of those parts. It has entity beans that represent parts, vendors, orders, and line items. These entity beans are accessed using a stateful session bean that holds the business logic of the application. A simple command-line client adds data to the entity beans, manipulates the data, and displays data from the catalog.

The information contained in an order can be divided into different elements. What is the order number? What parts are included in the order? What parts make up that part? Who makes the part? What are the specifications for the part? Are there any schematics for the part? `OrderApp` is a simplified version of an ordering system that has all these elements.

This example assumes that you have successfully built, assembled, and deployed the `RosterApp` example application and that you are familiar with assembling entity beans in `deploytool`.

`OrderApp` consists of three modules: `DataRegistryJAR`, an enterprise bean JAR file containing the entity beans, the support classes, and the database schema file; `RequestJAR`, an enterprise bean JAR containing a stateful session bean that accesses the data in the entity beans; and `OrderAppClient`, the application client that populates the entity beans with data and manipulates the data, displaying the results in a terminal. Figure 27–10 shows `OrderApp`'s database tables.

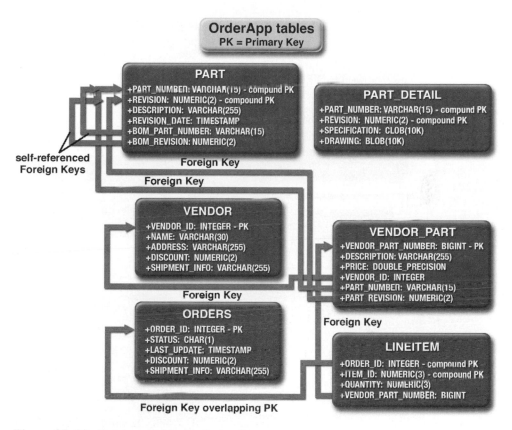

Figure 27–10 Database Tables in OrderApp

Bean Relationships in OrderApp

The RosterApp example application shows how to set up one-to-many and many-to-many relationships between entity beans. OrderApp demonstrates two additional types of entity bean relationships (see Figure 27–11): one-to-one and self-referential relationships.

Self-Referential Relationships

A *self-referential* relationship is a relationship between container-managed relationship fields (CMR) in the same entity bean. PartBean has a CMR field bomPart that has a one-to-many relationship with the CMR field parts, which is

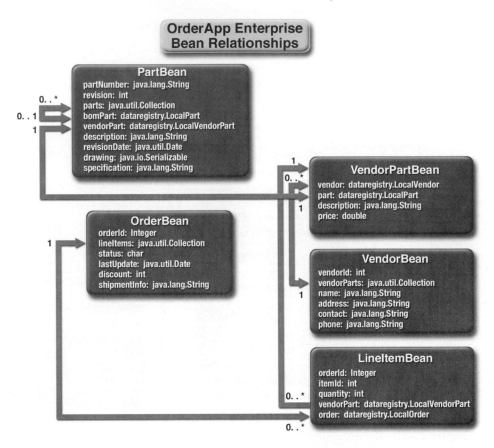

Figure 27–11   Relationships between Entity Beans in OrderApp

also in PartBean. That is, a part can be made up of many parts, and each of those parts has exactly one bill-of-material part.

The primary key for PartBean is a compound primary key, a combination of the partNumber and revision fields. It is mapped to the PART_NUMBER and REVISION columns in the PART table.

One-to-One Relationships

PartBean has a CMR field, vendorPart, that has a one-to-one relationship with VendorPartBean's CMR field part. That is, each part has exactly one vendor part, and vice versa.

One-to-Many Relationship Mapped to Overlapping Primary and Foreign Keys

OrderBean has a CMR field, lineItems, that has a one-to-many relationship with LineItemBean's CMR field order. That is, each order has one or more line items.

LineItemBean uses a compound primary key that is made up of the orderId and itemId fields. This compound primary key maps to the ORDER_ID and ITEM_ID columns in the LINEITEM database table. ORDER_ID is a foreign key to the ORDER_ID column in the ORDERS table. This means that the ORDER_ID column is mapped twice: once as a primary key field, orderId, and again as a relationship field, order.

Unidirectional Relationships

LineItemBean has a CMR field, vendorPart, that has a unidirectional many-to-one relationship with VendorPartBean. That is, there is no CMR field in the target entity bean in this relationship.

Primary Keys In OrderApp's Entity Beans

The OrderApp example uses more complicated primary keys than does RosterApp.

Unknown Primary Keys

In OrderApp, VendorPartBean uses an unknown primary key. That is, the enterprise bean does not specify primary key fields and uses java.lang.Object as the primary key class. See The Primary Key Class (page 982) for more information on primary keys.

Primitive Type Primary Keys

VendorBean uses a primary key that is a Java programming language primitive type, an int. To use a primitive type as the primary key, you must create a wrapper class. VendorKey is the wrapper class for VendorBean.

The wrapper primary key class has the same requirements as described in The Primary Key Class (page 982). This is the VendorKey wrapper class:

```java
package dataregistry;
public final class VendorKey implements java.io.Serializable {

    public int vendorId;

    public boolean equals(Object otherOb) {

        if (this == otherOb) {
            return true;
        }
        if (!(otherOb instanceof VendorKey)) {
            return false;
        }
        VendorKey other = (VendorKey) otherOb;
        return (vendorId == other.vendorId);
    }
    public int hashCode() {
        return vendorId;
    }
    public String toString() {
        return "" + vendorId;
    }
}
```

Compound Primary Keys

A compound primary key is made up of multiple fields and follows the requirements described in The Primary Key Class (page 982). To use a compound primary key, you must create a wrapper class.

In OrderApp, two entity beans use compound primary keys: PartBean and LineItemBean.

PartBean uses the PartKey wrapper class. PartBean's primary key is a combination of the part number and the revision number. PartKey encapsulates this primary key.

LineItemBean uses the LineItemKey class. LineItemBean's primary key is a combination of the order number and the item number. LineItemKey encapsulates this primary key. This is the LineItemKey compound primary key wrapper class:

```
package dataregistry;

public final class LineItemKey implements
        java.io.Serializable {

   public Integer orderId;
   public int itemId;

   public boolean equals(Object otherOb) {
      if (this == otherOb) {
         return true;
      }
      if (!(otherOb instanceof LineItemKey)) {
         return false;
      }
      LineItemKey other = (LineItemKey) otherOb;
      return ((orderId==null?other.orderId==null:orderId.equals
         (other.orderId)) && (itemId == other.itemId));
   }

   public int hashCode() {
      return ((orderId==null?0:orderId.hashCode())
         ^ ((int) itemId));
   }

   public String toString() {
      return "" + orderId + "-" + itemId;
   }
}
```

Entity Bean Mapped to More Than One Database Table

PartBean's fields map to more than one database table: PART and PART_DETAIL. The PART_DETAIL table holds the specification and schematics for the part. When you set up the container-managed fields and relationships in deploytool, you will add PART_DETAIL as a secondary table for PartBean.

Finder and Selector Methods

VendorBean has two finder methods: findByPartialName and findByOrder. The findByPartialName method searches through the vendor list for matches to a partial name. findByOrder finds all vendors for a particular order.

LineItemBean has one finder method, findAll, which finds all line items.

OrderBean has one selector method, ejbSelectAll, which returns all orders.

VendorPartBean has two selector methods. ejbSelectAvgPrice returns the average price of all parts from a vendor. ejbSelectTotalPricePerVendor returns the price of all the parts from a particular vendor.

Selector methods cannot be accessed outside a bean instance because the selector methods are not defined in the bean interface. If you are using a selector method to return data to a caller, the selector method must be called from a home or business method. In OrderApp, the LocalVendorPartHome.getAvgPrice method returns the result of the ejbSelectAvgPrice method in VendorPart-Bean.

The return type of a selector query is usually defined by the return type of the ejbSelect methods. You must specify the return type as Remote if the method returns a remote interface or a java.util.Collection of remote interfaces. If the return type is a local interface or a java.util.Collection of local interfaces, set the return type to Local. If the return type is neither a local nor a remote interface, nor a collection of local or remote interfaces, do not set the return type (in deploytool, set the return type to None). The OrderBean.ejbSelectAll method returns a collection of local interfaces. VendorPartBean.ejbSelectAvgPrice and VendorPartBean.ejbSelectTotalPricePerVendor return a Double, so the return type is set to None.

Using Home Methods

Home methods are defined in the home interface of a bean and correspond to methods named ejbHome<*METHOD*> in the bean class. For example, a method getValue, defined in the LocalExampleHome interface, corresponds to the ejbHomeGetValue method implemented in ExampleBean. The ejbHome<*METHOD*> methods are implemented by the bean developer.

OrderApp uses three home methods: LocalOrderHome.adjustDiscount, LocalVendorPartHome.getAvgPrice, and LocalVendorPartHome.getTotalPricePerVendor. Home methods operate on all instances of a bean rather than on any particular bean instance. That is, home methods cannot access the container-managed fields and relationships of a bean instance on which the method is called.

For example, `LocalOrderHome.adjustDiscount` is used to increase or decrease the discount on all orders.

Cascade Deletes in OrderApp

Entity beans that use container-managed relationships often have dependencies on the existence of the other bean in the relationship. For example, a line item is part of an order, and if the order is deleted, then the line item should also be deleted. This is called a cascade delete relationship.

In `OrderApp`, there are two cascade delete dependencies in the bean relationships. If the `OrderBean` to which a `LineItemBean` is related is deleted, then the `LineItemBean` should also be deleted. If the `VendorBean` to which a `VendorPartBean` is related is deleted, then the `VendorPartBean` should also be deleted.

BLOB and CLOB Database Types in OrderApp

The `PART_DETAIL` table in the database has a column, `DRAWING`, of type `BLOB`. `BLOB` stands for binary large objects, which are used for storing binary data such as an image. The `DRAWING` column is mapped to the container-managed field `PartBean.drawing` of type `java.io.Serializable`.

`PART_DETAIL` also has a column, `SPECIFICATION`, of type `CLOB`. `CLOB` stands for character large objects, which are used to store string data too large to be stored in a `VARCHAR` column. `SPECIFICATION` is mapped to the container-managed field `PartBean.specification` of type `java.lang.String`.

Note: You cannot use a `BLOB` or `CLOB` column in the `WHERE` clause of a finder or selector EJB QL query.

Building and Running the OrderApp Example

This section assumes that you are familiar with how to package entity beans in `deploytool` as described in Building and Running the RosterApp Example (page 958), have started the PointBase server, and have created the JDBC resource.

Create the Database Tables

To create the database tables, do the following:

1. In a terminal, navigate to
   `<INSTALL>/j2eetutorial14/examples/ejb/cmporder/`
2. Enter the following command:
   `asant create-db_common`

Capture the Database Schema

To capture the database schema, do the following:

1. In a terminal, navigate to
   `<INSTALL>/j2eetutorial14/examples/ejb/cmporder/`
2. Enter the following command:
   `asant capture-db-schema`

Build the Application

To build the application components of `OrderApp`, do the following:

1. Navigate to
   `<INSTALL>/j2eetutorial14/examples/ejb/cmporder/`
2. Enter the following command:
   `asant build`

Package the Application

You will now package the enterprise beans, support classes, database schema, and client class in `deploytool`. This section assumes that you are familiar with how to package these application modules in `deploytool`.

Create the Application Modules

1. Create a new application in `deploytool` named `OrderApp` in
   `<INSTALL>/j2eetutorial14/examples/ejb/cmporder/`

2. Create an enterprise bean JAR named `RequestJAR` that contains the files in
   `<INSTALL>/j2eetutorial14/examples/ejb/cmporder/build/request/`

3. Set up a stateful session bean, `RequestBean`, in `RequestJAR` with a remote home interface of `request.RequestHome` and a remote interface of `request.Request`.

4. Create an enterprise bean JAR named `DataRegistryJAR` that contains the files in
   `<INSTALL>/j2eetutorial14/examples/ejb/cmporder/build/dataregistry`

   And the database schema file:

   `<INSTALL>/j2eetutorial14/examples/ejb/cmporder/build/cmporder.dbschema`

5. Set up the entity beans (`LineItemBean`, `OrderBean`, `PartBean`, `VendorBean`, and `VendorPartBean`) according to Table 27–2 through Table 27–6.

Table 27–2 Settings for `LineItemBean`

Setting	Value
Local Home Interface	`dataregistry.LocalLineItemHome`
Local Interface	`dataregistry.LocalLineItem`
Persistent Fields	`orderId, itemId, quantity`
Abstract Schema Name	`LineItem`
Primary Key Class	User-defined class `dataregistry.LineItemKey`

Table 27–3   Settings for `OrderBean`

Setting	Value
Local Home Interface	`dataregistry.LocalOrderHome`
Local Interface	`dataregistry.LocalOrder`
Persistent Fields	`status, orderId, discount, lastUpdate, ship-mentInfo`
Abstract Schema Name	`Order`
Primary Key Class	Existing field `orderId`

Table 27–4   Settings for `PartBean`

Setting	Value
Local Home Interface	`dataregistry.LocalPartHome`
Local Interface	`dataregistry.LocalPart`
Persistent Fields	`description, partNumber, revision, revisionDate, drawing, specification`
Abstract Schema Name	`Part`
Primary Key Class	User-defined class `dataregistry.PartKey`

Table 27–5   Settings for `VendorBean`

Setting	Value
Local Home Interface	`dataregistry.LocalVendorHome`
Local Interface	`dataregistry.LocalVendor`
Persistent Fields	`address, name, vendorId, contact, phone`
Abstract Schema Name	`Vendor`
Primary Key Class	User-defined class `dataregistry.VendorKey`

Table 27–6 Settings for `VendorPartBean`

Setting	Value
Local Home Interface	`dataregistry.LocalVendorPartHome`
Local Interface	`dataregistry.LocalVendorPart`
Persistent Fields	`description, price`
Abstract Schema Name	`VendorPart`
Primary Key Class	Unknown Primary Key Class

Configure the Entity Bean Relationships

Now we'll configure the relationships of the entity beans and map the fields and relationships to the database tables.

1. Set up the bean relationships according to Table 27–7:

Table 27–7 `OrderApp` Bean Relationships

Multi-plicity	Bean A	Field Referencing Bean B and Field Type	Delete When Bean B Is Deleted?	Bean B	Field Referencing Bean A and Field Type	Delete When Bean A Is Deleted?
*:1	PartBean	`bomPart`		PartBean	`parts, java.util. Collection`	
1:*	OrderBean	`lineItems, java.util. Collection`		Line ItemBean	`order`	Yes
*:1	Vendor PartBean	`vendor`	Yes	Vendor Bean	`vendor- Parts, java.util. Collection`	
1:1	Vendor PartBean	`part`		PartBean	`vendorPart`	
*:1	Line ItemBean	`vendorPart`		Vendor PartBean	`<none>`	

2. Set the JNDI Name of the CMP Resource to `jdbc/ejbTutorialDB`.

3. Create the database mappings using the `cmporder.dbschema` file in the Sun-specific Settings dialog box, CMP Database view.

4. Manually map `OrderBean` to the `ORDERS` database table in the Sun-specific Settings dialog box, CMP Database view:

   a. Select `OrderBean` in the Enterprise Bean field under Persistent Field Mappings.

   b. Select `ORDERS` in the Primary Table drop-down. `ORDER` is a reserved keyword in SQL, so the table name is `ORDERS`.

5. Map `PartBean` to the `PART` and `PART_DETAIL` database tables:

   a. Select `PartBean` in the Enterprise Bean field under Persistent Field Mappings.

   b. Click Advanced Settings under Mappings for Bean `PartBean`.

   c. Click Add.

   d. In the Secondary Table field, select `PART_DETAIL`.

   e. Select `PART_NUMBER` in the Primary Table Column.

   f. Select `PART_NUMBER` in the Secondary Table Column.

   g. Click Add Pair.

   h. Select `REVISION` in the Primary Table Column.

   i. Select `REVISION` in the Secondary Table Column.

   j. Click OK.

   k. Click OK.

6. Click Automap All to automatically map the fields and relationships to the database tables. Repeat this step for all the entity beans until all the relationships and fields are mapped.

7. Click Close.

Add the Finder and Selector Queries

Add the finder and selector queries to the entity beans as listed in Table 27–8 and Table 27–9:

Note: The queries are included in the `cmporderQueries.txt` file, located in `<INSTALL>/j2eetutorial14/examples/ejb/cmporder/` to make it easier to enter the queries.

Table 27–8 Finder Queries in `OrderApp`

Enterprise Bean	Method	EJB QL Query

VendorBean	findByOrder	`SELECT DISTINCT`
		`l.vendorPart.vendor`
		`FROM Order o, IN(o.lineItems) AS l`
		`WHERE o.orderId = ?1 ORDER BY`
		`l.vendorPart.vendor.name`

VendorBean	findByPartialName	`SELECT OBJECT(v) FROM Vendor v` `WHERE LOCATE(?1, v.name) > 0`
LineItemBean	findAll	`SELECT OBJECT(l)` `FROM LineItem l`

Table 27–9 Selector Queries in `OrderApp`

Enterprise Bean	Method	EJB QL Query	Return EJB Type
OrderBean	ejbSelectAll	`SELECT OBJECT(o)` `FROM Order o`	Local
Vendor-PartBean	ejbSelectAvgPrice	`SELECT AVG(vp.price)` `FROM VendorPart vp`	None

Vendor-PartBean	ejbSelectTotal PricePerVendor	`SELECT SUM(vp.price)`
		`FROM VendorPart vp`
		`WHERE vp.vendor.vendorId = ?1`
			None

Set the Transaction Attributes

The transactions for all our enterprise beans (`RequestBean`, `LineItemBean`, `OrderBean`, `PartBean`, `VendorBean`, and `VendorPartBean`) must be managed by the container.

1. Select the enterprise bean in `deploytool`.
2. Select the Transactions tab.
3. Select Container-Managed under Transaction Management. All transaction attributes for the bean's methods will automatically be set to `Required`.

Set RequestBean's Enterprise Bean References

RequestBean accesses the local entity beans contained in DataRegistryJAR. You must set the references to the entity beans in RequestBean.

1. Select RequestBean in RequestJAR.
2. Click the EJB Ref's tab.
3. Enter the references according to Table 27–10. All the references are to local entity beans.

Package the Application Client

Now we'll add the application client to the EAR.

1. Create a new application client in OrderApp named OrderAppClient.
2. Add the contents of the following directory:

   <INSTALL>/j2eetutorial14/examples/ejb/cmporder/build/client/
3. Set the main class of the client to client.Client.

Table 27–10   Enterprise Bean References in RequestBean

Coded Name	Home Interface	Local Interface	Target Enterprise Bean Name
ejb/SimpleLineItem	dataregistry. LocalLineItem-Home	dataregistry. LocalLineItem	LineItemBean
ejb/SimpleVendorPart	dataregistry. LocalVendor-PartHome	dataregistry. LocalVendorPart	VendorPart-Bean
ejb/SimpleOrder	dataregistry. LocalOrderHome	dataregistry. LocalOrder	OrderBean
ejb/SimplePart	dataregistry. LocalPartHome	dataregistry. LocalPart	PartBean
ejb/SimpleVendor	dataregistry. LocalVendorHome	dataregistry. LocalVendor	VendorBean

4. Set the enterprise bean reference for the client:

    a. Set the Coded Name to `ejb/Request`.

    b. Set the EJB Type to `Session`.

    c. Set the Interfaces to `Remote`.

    d. Set the Home Interface to `request.RequestHome`.

    e. Set the Remote Interface to `request.Request`.

    f. Enter `RequestBean` in the JNDI Name field under Target EJB.

    g. Click OK.

Deploy the Enterprise Application

`OrderApp` is now ready to be deployed:

1. Select File→Save.

2. Select `OrderApp` in `deploytool`.

3. Select Tools→Deploy.

4. Check Return Client Jar in the Deploy Module dialog box.

Run the Client Application

The client application accesses the `RequestBean` session bean, which in turn manipulates data in `OrderApp`'s entity beans.

Note: This example will perform poorly compared with a well-designed CMP application. `OrderApp` is designed primarily for instructional purposes, and does not follow the best practices recommendations as outlined in the book *Designing Enterprise Applications with the J2EE™ Platform, Second Edition*, Inderjeet Singh et al., (Addison-Wesley, 2002).

To run the client, follow these steps:

1. In a terminal, go to

    `<INSTALL>/j2eetutorial14/examples/ejb/cmporder/`

2. Enter the following command:

    `appclient -client OrderAppClient.jar`

3. You will see the following output in the terminal:

```
Cost of Bill of Material for PN SDFG-ERTY-BN Rev: 7:
$241.86
Cost of Order 1111:   $664.68
Cost of Order 4312:   $2,011.44

Adding 5% discount
Cost of Order 1111:   $627.75
Cost of Order 4312:   $1,910.87

Removing 7% discount
Cost of Order 1111:   $679.45
Cost of Order 4312:   $2,011.44

Average price of all parts: :  $117.55

Total price of parts for Vendor 100: :  $501.06

Ordered list of vendors for order 1111
200 Gadget, Inc. Mrs. Smith
100 WidgetCorp Mr. Jones

Found 6 line items

Removing Order
Found 3 line items

Found 1 out of 2 vendors with 'I' in the name:
Gadget, Inc.
```

Note: Re-create the database tables using the `create-db_common` task before re-running the client.

---

deploytool Tips for Entity Beans with Container-Managed Persistence

Chapter 24 covers the basic steps for building and packaging enterprise beans. This section highlights the tasks in `deploytool` that are needed for entity beans with container-managed persistence. The examples referenced in this section are from A Guided Tour of the RosterApp Settings (page 972).

Selecting the Persistent Fields and Abstract Schema Name

In the Entity tab of the enterprise bean, enter the field information and the abstract schema name.

1. In the Fields To Be Persisted list, select the fields that will be saved in the database. The names of the persistent fields are determined by the access methods defined in the entity bean code. Be sure not to select container-managed relationship fields.

2. Enter values in the Primary Key Class and Primary Key Field Name fields. The primary key uniquely identifies the entity bean.

3. In the Abstract Schema Name field, enter a name that represents the entity bean. This name will be referenced in the EJB QL queries.

An example is shown in the section Entity Tab (PlayerBean) (page 978).

Defining EJB QL Queries for Finder and Select Methods

You specify these settings in the Finder/Select Methods dialog box.

1. To open the Finder/Select Methods dialog box, go to the Entity tab and click Finder/Select Methods.

2. To display a set of finder or select methods, click one of the radio buttons under the Show label.

3. To specify an EJB QL query, choose the name of the finder or select a method from the Method list, and then enter the query in the field labeled EJB QL Query.

An example is shown in the section Finder/Select Methods Dialog Box (Player-Bean) (page 978).

Defining Relationships

The Relationships tab enables you to define relationships between entity beans that reside in the same EJB JAR file.

1. Before you create a relationship between two entity beans, you must first create both beans using the New Enterprise Bean wizard.
2. To display the Relationships tab, select the EJB JAR in the tree view and then select the Relationships tab.
3. To add or edit a relationship, go to the Relationships tab and click the appropriate button.
4. The Add (or Edit) Relationship dialog box appears. (The Add Relationship and Edit Relationship dialog boxes are identical.)

An example is shown in the section Edit Relationship Dialog Box (TeamJAR) (page 976).

Creating the Database Tables at Deploy Time in deploytool

The `RosterApp` example uses a database schema file to map database tables to enterprise bean fields. Alternatively, you can have the container create the database tables at deploy time by setting some options in `deploytool`.

1. Select `TeamJAR` in the tree in `deploytool`.
2. Select the Relationships tabbed pane.
3. Click Sun-specific Settings.
4. Click Create Database Mappings.
5. Select Automatically Generate Necessary Tables.
6. Click OK.

When you deploy `RosterApp`, the tables will be created and named according to the values in the Persistent Field Mappings table.

28

A Message-Driven Bean Example

Because message-driven beans are based on the Java Message Service (JMS) technology, to understand the example in this chapter you should be familiar with basic JMS concepts such as queues and messages. To learn about these concepts, see Chapter 33.

This chapter describes the source code of a simple message-driven bean example. Before proceeding, you should read the basic conceptual information in the section What Is a Message-Driven Bean? (page 838) as well as Using Message-Driven Beans (page 1214) in Chapter 33.

Example Application Overview

The `SimpleMessageApp` application has the following components:

- `SimpleMessageClient`: An application client that sends several messages to a queue
- `SimpleMessageEJB`: A message-driven bean that asynchronously receives and processes the messages that are sent to the queue

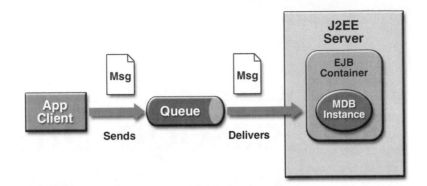

Figure 28–1   The `SimpleMessageApp` Application

Figure 28–1 illustrates the structure of this application. The application client sends messages to the queue, which was created administratively using the Admin Console. The JMS provider (in this case, the Application Server) delivers the messages to the instances of the message-driven bean, which then processes the messages.

The source code for this application is in the *<INSTALL>*/j2eetutorial14/ examples/ejb/simplemessage directory.

The Application Client

The `SimpleMessageClient` sends messages to the queue that the `Simple-MessageBean` listens to. The client starts by locating the connection factory and queue:

```
connectionFactory =
    (ConnectionFactory) jndiContext.lookup
    ("java:comp/env/jms/MyConnectionFactory");
destination =
    (Queue) jndiContext.lookup("java:comp/env/jms/QueueName");
```

Next, the client creates the queue connection, session, and sender:

```
connection = connectionFactory.createConnection();
session = connection.createSession(false,
    Session.AUTO_ACKNOWLEDGE);
messageProducer = session.createProducer(destination);
```

Finally, the client sends several messages to the queue:

```
message = session.createTextMessage();

for (int i = 0; i < NUM_MSGS; i++) {
    message.setText("This is message " + (i + 1));
    System.out.println("Sending message: " +
        message.getText());
    messageProducer.send(message);
}
```

The Message-Driven Bean Class

The code for the `SimpleMessageBean` class illustrates the requirements of a message-driven bean class:

- It must implement the `MessageDrivenBean` and `MessageListener` interfaces.
- The class must be defined as `public`.
- The class cannot be defined as `abstract` or `final`.
- It must implement one `onMessage` method.
- It must implement one `ejbCreate` method and one `ejbRemove` method.
- It must contain a public constructor with no arguments.
- It must not define the `finalize` method.

Unlike session and entity beans, message-driven beans do not have the remote or local interfaces that define client access. Client components do not locate message-driven beans and invoke methods on them. Although message-driven beans do not have business methods, they may contain helper methods that are invoked internally by the `onMessage` method.

The onMessage Method

When the queue receives a message, the EJB container invokes the `onMessage` method of the message-driven bean.

The `onMessage` method is called by the bean's container when a message has arrived for the bean to service. This method contains the business logic that handles the processing of the message. It is the message-driven bean's responsibility to parse the message and perform the necessary business logic.

The onMessage method has a single argument: the incoming message.

The message-driven bean class defines one onMessage method, whose signature must follow these rules:

- The method must be declared as public and must not be declared as final or static.
- The return type must be void.
- The method must have a single argument of type javax.jms.Message.
- The throws clause must not define any application exceptions.
- The onMessage method must be invoked in the scope of a transaction that is determined by the transaction attribute specified in the deployment descriptor.

In the SimpleMessageBean class, the onMessage method casts the incoming message to a TextMessage and displays the text:

```
public void onMessage(Message inMessage) {
    TextMessage msg = null;

    try {
        if (inMessage instanceof TextMessage) {
            msg = (TextMessage) inMessage;
            logger.info
                ("MESSAGE BEAN: Message received: " +
                msg.getText());
        } else {
            logger.warning
                ("Message of wrong type: " +
                inMessage.getClass().getName());
        }
    } catch (JMSException e) {
        e.printStackTrace();
        mdc.setRollbackOnly();
    } catch (Throwable te) {
        te.printStackTrace();
    }
}
```

The ejbCreate and ejbRemove Methods

The signatures of these methods have the following requirements:

- The access control modifier must be `public`.
- The return type must be `void`.
- The modifier cannot be `static` or `final`.
- The `throws` clause must not define any application exceptions.
- The method has no arguments.

In the `SimpleMessageBean` class, the `ejbCreate` and `ejbRemove` methods are empty.

Deploying and Running SimpleMessageApp

To deploy and run this example, go to the `<INSTALL>`/`j2eetutorial14/examples/ejb/simplemessage` directory.

Creating the Administered Objects

This example requires the following:

- A JMS connection factory resource
- A JMS destination resource
- A physical destination to which the destination resource refers

If you have run the simple JMS examples in Chapter 33 and have not deleted the resources, you already have these resources and do not need to perform these steps.

To start the Admin Console, follow the instructions in Starting the Admin Console (page 27).

To create the connection factory, perform the following steps:

1. In the tree component, expand the Java Message Service node.

2. Select the Connection Factories node.

3. On the JMS Connection Factories page, click New. The Create JMS Connection Factory page appears.

4. In the JNDI Name field, type `jms/QueueConnectionFactory`.

5. Choose `javax.jms.QueueConnectionFactory` from the Type combo box.

6. Select the Enabled checkbox.

7. Click OK.

To create the physical destination, perform the following steps:

1. In the tree component, select the Physical Destinations node.

2. On the Physical Destinations page, click New. The Create Physical Destination page appears.

3. In the Physical Destination Name field, type `PhysicalQueue`.

4. Choose `queue` from the Type combo box.

5. Click OK.

To create the destination resource and link it to the physical destination, perform the following steps:

1. In the tree component, expand Destination Resources.

2. On the JMS Destination Resources page, click New. The Create JMS Destination Resource page appears.

3. In the JNDI Name field, type `jms/Queue`.

4. Choose `javax.jms.Queue` from the Type combo box.

5. Select the Enabled checkbox.

6. Under Additional Properties, click Add.

7. Type `Name` in the Name field.

8. Type `PhysicalQueue` in the Value field.

9. Click OK.

Deploying the Application

1. In `deploytool`, open the `SimpleMessageApp.ear` file, which resides in this directory:

   `<INSTALL>/j2eetutorial14/examples/ejb/provided-ears/`

2. Deploy the `SimpleMessageApp` application.

3. In the Deploy Module dialog box:

   a. Select the Return Client JAR checkbox.

   b. In the field below the checkbox, enter the following:

   `<INSTALL>/j2eetutorial14/examples/ejb/simplemessage`

Running the Client

After you deploy the application, you run the client as follows:

1. In the directory `<INSTALL>/j2eetutorial14/examples/ejb/simple-message`, type the following command on a single line:

   `appclient -client SimpleMessageAppClient.jar`

2. The client displays these lines:

   ```
   Sending message: This is message 1
   Sending message: This is message 2
   Sending message: This is message 3
   ```

   To see if the bean received the messages, check
   `<install_dir>/domains/domain1/logs/server.log`.

3. In the server log file, the following lines should be displayed, wrapped in logging information:

   ```
   MESSAGE BEAN: Message received: This is message 1
   MESSAGE BEAN: Message received: This is message 2
   MESSAGE BEAN: Message received: This is message 3
   ```

Undeploy the application after you finish running the client.

Removing the Administered Objects

After you run the example, you can use the Admin Console to delete the connection factory and queue. These resources are needed for the JMS examples in Chapters 33 and 34, however, so if you plan to run those examples, do not delete the resources.

deploytool Tips for Message-Driven Beans

Chapter 24 covers the basic steps for building and packaging enterprise beans. This section describes the tasks in `deploytool` that are necessary for message-driven beans. To view this example in `deploytool`, expand the `SimpleMessageApp` node in the tree view, and then expand the `MDBJAR` node and select `SimpleMessageBean`.

Specifying the Bean's Type

You specify the type when you create the bean using the New Enterprise Bean wizard.

1. To start the wizard, select File→New→Enterprise Bean.
2. In the General dialog box of the wizard, choose the enterprise bean class of the bean, and accept the bean class name (the default) as the display name. The Enterprise Bean Type appears as Message-Driven by default.

Setting the Message-Driven Bean's Characteristics

You can specify these settings in two places:

- The Message-Driven Bean Settings dialog box of the New Enterprise Bean wizard
- The Message-Driven tab of the bean

These settings are as follows:

1. For the Messaging Service, accept the default, JMS.
2. For the Destination Type, choose either `javax.jms.Queue` or `javax.jms.Topic`. A queue uses the point-to-point messaging domain and can have at most one consumer. A topic uses the publish/subscribe messaging domain; it can have zero, one, or many consumers. For this example, you would select `javax.jms.Queue`.
3. For the Target Destination Name, type the name of the physical destination that you created administratively. For an example, see the section Creating the Administered Objects (page 1007). The destination is either a `queue` or

a `topic` object; it represents the source of incoming messages and the target of outgoing messages. For this example, you would type `Physical-Queue`.

4. If your bean will be a durable subscriber to a topic, select the Durable Subscription checkbox and enter a subscription name. If the bean uses a message selector, enter the value in the Message Selector text area. For an example that uses these features, see A J2EE Application That Uses the JMS API with a Session Bean (page 1222). You normally leave the Acknowledgement Mode set to Auto-Acknowledge.

   For information on durable subscriptions, see Creating Durable Subscriptions (page 1200). For information on message selectors, see Message Selectors (page 1169). For information on message acknowledgment, see Controlling Message Acknowledgment (page 1193).

5. In the Connection Factory JNDI Name (Sun-specific) field, type the JNDI name of the connection factory the bean will use. For this example, you would type `jms/QueueConnectionFactory`.

Use the tabbed panes as follows:

1. In the Transactions tab of the bean:
   a. Select the Container-Managed radio button.
   b. Verify that the `onMessage` method has the `Required` attribute.

2. In the Message Destinations tab of the bean JAR file:
   a. Click Add.
   b. Type the physical destination name (for this example, `PhysicalQueue`) in the Destination Name field, and press Enter.
   c. Type the JNDI name of the destination resource (for this example, `jms/Queue`) in the JNDI Name field.

deploytool Tips for Components That Send Messages

You set resource references and message destination references for any component that sends messages: a client, a session or entity bean, or even another message-driven bean. For examples, see Chapter 34. In this application, the client is the sending component. To view this example in `deploytool`, expand the `SimpleMessageApp` node, and then select `SimpleMessageClient` from the tree view.

Setting the Resource References

You use the Resource Ref's tabbed pane to specify the connection factory references for the component.

1. In the tree view, select the component node.
2. Select the Resource Ref's tab.
3. Click Add.
4. In the Coded Name field, enter the name that matches the parameter of the `lookup` method in the component code. For example, because the `lookup` parameter is `java:comp/env/jms/MyConnectionFactory`, the coded name should be `jms/MyConnectionFactory`.
5. In the Type field, select the connection factory class that matches the destination type. The destination class in the code is `javax.jms.ConnectionFactory`, so select that class.
6. In the Authentication field, in most cases you will select Container. You would select Application if your code explicitly logged on to the messaging service.
7. In the Sharable field, make sure that the checkbox is selected. This choice allows the container to optimize connections.
8. In the Sun-specific Settings area, enter the name of the connection factory (in this case, `jms/QueueConnectionFactory`) in the JNDI Name field. Enter `j2ee` in both the User Name and the Password fields.

Setting the Message Destination References

For any new application, you use the Msg Dest Ref's tab to specify the destination of messages. The Resource Env Ref's tab provides similar information, but it is available primarily for backward compatibility.

1. Select the Msg Dest Ref's tab.
2. Click Add.

3. In the Coded Name field of the dialog box that appears, type a name that matches the parameter of the `lookup` call that locates the queue or topic. In this example, the `lookup` parameter is `java:comp/env/jms/Queue-Name`, so the coded name is `jms/QueueName`.

4. In the Destination Type combo box, choose the class that matches the destination type (in this case, `javax.jms.Queue`).

5. From the Usage combo box, choose either Produces or ConsumesProduces, depending on whether this component sends messages or both sends and receives messages. For this example, choose Produces.

6. In the Destination Name field, type the name of the physical destination you created (in this case, `PhysicalQueue`).

Setting the Message Destinations

When you use the Msg Dest Ref's tab, you also use the Message Destinations tab of the component JAR file to link the destination to its JNDI name.

1. Select the Message Destinations tab.

2. Click Add.

3. In the Destination Name field, type the name of the destination (in this case, `PhysicalQueue`) and press Return. The name also appears in the Display Name field. The names of the components that consume and produce messages for the destination appear in the Producers and Consumers areas.

4. In the JNDI Name field, type the name of the JMS resource you created (in this case, `jms/Queue`).

Specifying the JNDI Names

The JNDI name for a message-driven bean is the name of the destination resource.

1. In the tree view, select the application's node.

2. Click Sun-specific Settings on the General screen.

3. On the JNDI Names screen, enter the appropriate names. For example, the `SimpleMessageApp` discussed in this chapter uses the JNDI names shown in Table 28–1.

Table 28–1   JNDI Names for the `SimpleMessageApp` Application

Component or Reference Name	JNDI Name
SimpleMessageBean	jms/Queue
jms/MyConnectionFactory	jms/QueueConnectionFactory

29

Enterprise JavaBeans
Query Language

$\mathbf{T}$HE Enterprise JavaBeans Query Language (EJB QL) defines the queries for the finder and select methods of an entity bean that uses container-managed persistence. A subset of SQL92, EJB QL has extensions that allow navigation over the relationships defined in an entity bean's abstract schema. The scope of an EJB QL query spans the abstract schemas of related entity beans that are packaged in the same EJB JAR file.

You define EJB QL queries in the deployment descriptor of the entity bean. Typically, a tool will translate these queries into the target language of the underlying data store. Because of this translation, entity beans with container-managed persistence are portable; their code is not tied to a specific type of data store.

This chapter relies on the material presented in earlier chapters. For conceptual information, see the section Container-Managed Persistence (page 835). For code examples, see Chapter 27.

Terminology

The following list defines some of the terms referred to in this chapter.

- *Abstract schema*: The part of an entity bean's deployment descriptor that defines the bean's persistent fields and relationships.

- *Abstract schema name*: A logical name that is referenced in EJB QL queries. You specify an abstract schema name for each entity bean that uses container-managed persistence.

- *Abstract schema type*: All EJB QL expressions evaluate to a type. If the expression is an abstract schema name, by default its type is the local interface of the entity bean for which the abstract schema name is defined.

- *Backus-Naur Form (BNF)*: A notation that describes the syntax of high-level languages. The syntax diagrams in this chapter are in BNF notation.

- *Navigation*: The traversal of relationships in an EJB QL expression. The navigation operator is a period.

- *Path expression*: An expression that navigates to a related entity bean.

- *Persistent field*: A virtual field of an entity bean with container-managed persistence; it is stored in a database.

- *Relationship field*: A virtual field of an entity bean with container-managed persistence; it identifies a related entity bean.

Simplified Syntax

This section briefly describes the syntax of EJB QL so that you can quickly move on to the next section, Example Queries. When you are ready to learn about the syntax in more detail, see the section Full Syntax (page 1022).

An EJB QL query has four clauses: SELECT, FROM, WHERE, and ORDER BY. The SELECT and FROM clauses are required, but the WHERE and ORDER BY clauses are optional. Here is the high-level BNF syntax of an EJB QL query:

```
EJB QL ::= select_clause from_clause [where_clause][orderby_
clause]
```

The SELECT clause defines the types of the objects or values returned by the query. A return type is either a local interface, a remote interface, or a persistent field.

The FROM clause defines the scope of the query by declaring one or more identification variables, which can be referenced in the SELECT and WHERE clauses. An identification variable represents one of the following elements:

- The abstract schema name of an entity bean
- A member of a collection that is the multiple side of a one-to-many relationship

The WHERE clause is a conditional expression that restricts the objects or values retrieved by the query. Although it is optional, most queries have a WHERE clause.

The ORDER BY clause sorts the objects or values returned by the query into a specified order.

Example Queries

The following queries are from the PlayerBean entity bean of the RosterApp J2EE application, which is documented in Chapter 27. To see the relationships between the beans of the RosterApp, see Figure 27–3, page 967.

Simple Finder Queries

If you are unfamiliar with EJB QL, these simple queries are a good place to start.

Example 1

```
SELECT OBJECT(p)
FROM Player p
```

Data retrieved: All players.

Finder method: findall()

Description: The FROM clause declares an identification variable named p, omitting the optional keyword AS. If the AS keyword were included, the clause would be written as follows:

```
FROM Player AS p
```

The Player element is the abstract schema name of the PlayerBean entity bean. Because the bean defines the findall method in the LocalPlayerHome interface, the objects returned by the query have the LocalPlayer type.

See also: Identification Variables (page 1028)

Example 2

```
SELECT DISTINCT OBJECT(p)
FROM Player p
WHERE p.position = ?1
```

Data retrieved: The players with the position specified by the finder method's parameter.

Finder method: `findByPosition(String position)`

Description: In a SELECT clause, the OBJECT keyword must precede a stand-alone identification variable such as p. (A stand-alone identification variable is not part of a path expression.) The DISTINCT keyword eliminates duplicate values.

The WHERE clause restricts the players retrieved by checking their position, a persistent field of the PlayerBean entity bean. The ?1 element denotes the input parameter of the findByPosition method.

See also: Input Parameters (page 1033), DISTINCT and OBJECT Keywords (page 1042)

Example 3

```
SELECT DISTINCT OBJECT(p)
FROM Player p
WHERE p.position = ?1 AND p.name = ?2
```

Data retrieved: The players having the specified positions and names.

Finder method: `findByPositionAndName(String position, String name)`

Description: The position and name elements are persistent fields of the PlayerBean entity bean. The WHERE clause compares the values of these fields with the parameters of the findByPositionAndName method. EJB QL denotes an input parameter using a question mark followed by an integer. The first input parameter is ?1, the second is ?2, and so forth.

Finder Queries That Navigate to Related Beans

In EJB QL, an expression can traverse (or navigate) to related beans. These expressions are the primary difference between EJB QL and SQL. EJB QL navigates to related beans, whereas SQL joins tables.

Example 4

```
SELECT DISTINCT OBJECT(p)
FROM Player p, IN (p.teams) AS t
WHERE t.city = ?1
```

Data retrieved: The players whose teams belong to the specified city.

Finder method: findByCity(String city)

Description: The FROM clause declares two identification variables: p and t. The p variable represents the PlayerBean entity bean, and the t variable represents the related TeamBean beans. The declaration for t references the previously declared p variable. The IN keyword signifies that teams is a collection of related beans. The p.teams expression navigates from a PlayerBean bean to its related TeamBean beans. The period in the p.teams expression is the navigation operator.

In the WHERE clause, the period preceding the persistent variable city is a delimiter, not a navigation operator. Strictly speaking, expressions can navigate to relationship fields (related beans), but not to persistent fields. To access a persistent field, an expression uses the period as a delimiter.

Expressions cannot navigate beyond (or further qualify) relationship fields that are collections. In the syntax of an expression, a collection-valued field is a terminal symbol. Because the teams field is a collection, the WHERE clause cannot specify p.teams.city—an illegal expression.

See also: Path Expressions (page 1030)

Example 5

```
SELECT DISTINCT OBJECT(p)
FROM Player p, IN (p.teams) AS t
WHERE t.league = ?1
```

Data retrieved: The players that belong to the specified league.

Finder method: `findByLeague(LocalLeague league)`

Description: The expressions in this query navigate over two relationships. The `p.teams` expression navigates the `PlayerBean-TeamBean` relationship, and the `t.league` expression navigates the `TeamBean-LeagueBean` relationship.

In the other examples, the input parameters are `String` objects, but in this example the parameter is an object whose type is a `LocalLeague` interface. This type matches the `league` relationship field in the comparison expression of the `WHERE` clause.

Example 6

```
SELECT DISTINCT OBJECT(p)
FROM Player p, IN (p.teams) AS t
WHERE t.league.sport = ?1
```

Data retrieved: The players who participate in the specified sport.

Finder method: `findBySport(String sport)`

Description: The `sport` persistent field belongs to the `LeagueBean` bean. To reach the `sport` field, the query must first navigate from the `PlayerBean` bean to the `TeamBean` bean (`p.teams`) and then from the `TeamBean` bean to the `League-Bean` bean (`t.league`). Because the `league` relationship field is not a collection, it can be followed by the `sport` persistent field.

Finder Queries with Other Conditional Expressions

Every `WHERE` clause must specify a conditional expression, of which there are several kinds. In the previous examples, the conditional expressions are comparison expressions that test for equality. The following examples demonstrate some of the other kinds of conditional expressions. For descriptions of all conditional expressions, see the section WHERE Clause (page 1032).

Example 7

```
SELECT OBJECT(p)
FROM Player p
WHERE p.teams IS EMPTY
```

Data retrieved: All players who do not belong to a team.

Finder method: `findNotOnTeam()`

Description: The `teams` relationship field of the `PlayerBean` bean is a collection. If a player does not belong to a team, then the `teams` collection is empty and the conditional expression is `TRUE`.

See also: Empty Collection Comparison Expressions (page 1037)

Example 8

```
SELECT DISTINCT OBJECT(p)
FROM Player p
WHERE p.salary BETWEEN ?1 AND ?2
```

Data retrieved: The players whose salaries fall within the range of the specified salaries.

Finder method: `findBySalaryRange(double low, double high)`

Description: This `BETWEEN` expression has three arithmetic expressions: a persistent field (`p.salary`) and the two input parameters (`?1` and `?2`). The following expression is equivalent to the `BETWEEN` expression:

```
p.salary >= ?1 AND p.salary <= ?2
```

See also: BETWEEN Expressions (page 1035)

Example 9

```
SELECT DISTINCT OBJECT(p1)
FROM Player p1, Player p2
WHERE p1.salary > p2.salary AND p2.name = ?1
```

Data retrieved: All players whose salaries are higher than the salary of the player with the specified name.

Finder method: `findByHigherSalary(String name)`

Description: The `FROM` clause declares two identification variables (p1 and p2) of the same type (`Player`). Two identification variables are needed because the `WHERE` clause compares the salary of one player (p2) with that of the other players (p1).

See also: Identification Variables (page 1028)

Select Queries

The queries in this section are for select methods. Unlike finder methods, a select method can return persistent fields or other entity beans.

Example 10

```
SELECT DISTINCT t.league
FROM Player p, IN (p.teams) AS t
WHERE p = ?1
```

Data retrieved: The leagues to which the specified player belongs.

Select method: `ejbSelectLeagues(LocalPlayer player)`

Description: The return type of this query is the abstract schema type of the `LeagueBean` entity bean. This abstract schema type maps to the `LocalLeague-Home` interface. Because the expression `t.league` is not a stand-alone identification variable, the `OBJECT` keyword is omitted.

See also: SELECT Clause (page 1040)

Example 11

```
SELECT DISTINCT t.league.sport
FROM Player p, IN (p.teams) AS t
WHERE p = ?1
```

Data retrieved: The sports that the specified player participates in.

Select method: `ejbSelectSports(LocalPlayer player)`

Description: This query returns a `String` named `sport`, which is a persistent field of the `LeagueBean` entity bean.

Full Syntax

This section discusses the EJB QL syntax, as defined in the Enterprise Java-Beans specification. Much of the following material paraphrases or directly quotes the specification.

BNF Symbols

Table 29–1 describes the BNF symbols used in this chapter.

Table 29–1 BNF Symbol Summary

Symbol	Description
::=	The element to the left of the symbol is defined by the constructs on the right.
*	The preceding construct may occur zero or more times.
{...}	The constructs within the curly braces are grouped together.
[...]	The constructs within the square brackets are optional.
		An exclusive OR.
BOLDFACE	A keyword (although capitalized in the BNF diagram, keywords are not case-sensitive).
Whitespace	A whitespace character can be a space, a horizontal tab, or a linefeed.

BNF Grammar of EJB QL

Here is the entire BNF diagram for EJB QL:

```
EJB QL ::= select_clause from_clause [where_clause] [orderby_
clause]

from_clause ::=FROM identification_variable_declaration
    [, identification_variable_declaration]*

identification_variable_declaration ::= collection_member_
declaration |
    range_variable_declaration

collection_member_declaration ::= IN ( collection_valued_path_
expression) [AS ] identifier

range_variable_declaration ::=
    abstract_schema_name [AS ] identifier
```

```
cmp_path_expression ::=
    {identification_variable |
     single_valued_cmr_path_expression}.cmp_field

single_valued_cmr_path_expression ::=
    identification_variable.[single_valued_cmr_field.]*
      single_valued_cmr_field

single_valued_path_expression ::=
    cmp_path_expression | single_valued_cmr_path_expression

collection_valued_path_expression ::=
    identification_variable.[single_valued_cmr_field.]
    *collection_valued_cmr_field

select_clause ::= SELECT [DISTINCT ] {select_expression
    |OBJECT( identification_variable) }

select_expression ::= single_valued_path_expression |
aggregate_select_expression

aggregate_select_expression ::=
    {AVG |MAX |MIN |SUM |COUNT }( [DISTINCT ]
      cmp_path_expression) |
    COUNT ( [DISTINCT ] identification_variable |
      single_valued_cmr_path_expression)

where_clause ::= WHERE conditional_expression

conditional_expression ::= conditional_term |
    conditional_expression OR conditional_term

conditional_term ::= conditional_factor |
    conditional_term AND conditional_factor

conditional_factor ::= [NOT ] conditional_primary

conditional_primary ::= simple_cond_expression |
    (conditional_expression)

simple_cond_expression ::=
    comparison_expression | between_expression |
    like_expression | in_expression |
    null_comparison_expression |
    empty_collection_comparison_expression |
    collection_member_expression
```

```
between_expression ::=
    arithmetic_expression [NOT ]BETWEEN
    arithmetic_expression AND arithmetic_expression

in_expression ::=
    cmp_path_expression [NOT ] IN
    ( {literal | input_parameter}
    [, { literal | input_parameter} ]*)

like_expression ::=
    cmp_path_expression [NOT ] LIKE
    pattern_value [ESCAPE escape_character]

null_comparison_expression ::=
    {single_valued_path_expression |
    input_parameter}IS [NOT ] NULL

empty_collection_comparison_expression ::=
    collection_valued_path_expression IS [NOT] EMPTY

collection_member_expression ::=
    {single_valued_cmr_path_expression |
     identification_variable | input_parameter}
    [NOT ] MEMBER [OF ] collection_valued_path_expression

comparison_expression ::=
    string_value comparison_operator string_expression |
    boolean_value {= |<> } boolean_expression} |
    datetime_value comparison_operator datetime_expression |
    entity_bean_value {= |<> } entity_bean_expression |
    arithmetic_value comparison_operator arithmetic_expression

arithmetic_value ::= cmp_path_expression |
    functions_returning_numerics

comparison_operator ::=
    = |> |>= |< |<= |<>

arithmetic_expression ::= arithmetic_term |
    arithmetic_expression {+ |- } arithmetic_term

arithmetic_term ::= arithmetic_factor |
    arithmetic_term {* |/ } arithmetic_factor

arithmetic_factor ::= [{+ |- }] arithmetic_primary
```

```
arithmetic_primary ::= cmp_path_expression | literal |
    (arithmetic_expression) | input_parameter |
    functions_returning_numerics

string_value ::= cmp_path_expression |
    functions_returning_strings

string_expression ::= string_primary | input_parameter

string_primary ::= cmp_path_expression | literal |
    (string_expression) | functions_returning_strings

datetime_value ::= cmp_path_expression

datetime_expression ::= datetime_value | input_parameter

boolean_value ::= cmp_path_expression

boolean_expression ::= cmp_path_expression | literal |
    input_parameter

entity_bean_value ::= single_valued_cmr_path_expression |
    identification_variable

entity_bean_expression ::= entity_bean_value | input_parameter

functions_returning_strings ::=
    CONCAT( string_expression, string_expression) |
    SUBSTRING( string_expression, arithmetic_expression,
    arithmetic_expression)


functions_returning_numerics ::=
    LENGTH( string_expression) |
    LOCATE( string_expression, string_expression
    [, arithmetic_expression]) |
    ABS( arithmetic_expression) |
    SQRT( arithmetic_expression) |
    MOD( arithmetic_expression, arithmetic_expression)

orderby_clause ::= ORDER BY orderby_item [, orderby_item]*

orderby_item ::= cmp_path_expression [ASC |DESC ]
```

FROM Clause

The FROM clause defines the domain of the query by declaring identification variables. Here is the syntax of the FROM clause:

```
from_clause ::= FROM identification_variable_declaration
    [, identification_variable_declaration]*


identification_variable_declaration ::=
    collection_member_declaration |
    range_variable_declaration

collection_member_declaration ::=
    IN (collection_valued_path_expression) [AS] identifier

range_variable_declaration ::=
    abstract_schema_name [AS] identifier
```

Identifiers

An identifier is a sequence of one or more characters. The first character must be a valid first character (letter, $, _) in an identifier of the Java programming language (hereafter in this chapter called simply "Java"). Each subsequent character in the sequence must be a valid nonfirst character (letter, digit, $, _) in a Java identifier. (For details, see the J2SE API documentation of the isJavaIdentifierStart and isJavaIdentifierPart methods of the Character class.) The question mark (?) is a reserved character in EJB QL and cannot be used in an identifier. Unlike a Java variable, an EJB QL identifier is not case-sensitive.

An identifier cannot be the same as an EJB QL keyword:

AND	FALSE	NULL
AS	FROM	OBJECT
ASC	IN	OF
AVG	IS	OR
BETWEEN	LIKE	ORDER
BY	MAX	SELECT
COUNT	MEMBER	SUM
DESC	MIN	TRUE
DISTINCT	MOD	UNKNOWN
EMPTY	NOT	WHERE

EJB QL keywords are also reserved words in SQL. In the future, the list of EJB QL keywords may expand to include other reserved SQL words. The Enterprise JavaBeans specification recommends that you not use other reserved SQL words for EJB QL identifiers.

Identification Variables

An *identification variable* is an identifier declared in the FROM clause. Although the SELECT and WHERE clauses can reference identification variables, they cannot declare them. All identification variables must be declared in the FROM clause.

Because an identification variable is an identifier, it has the same naming conventions and restrictions as an identifier. For example, an identification variable is not case-sensitive, and it cannot be the same as an EJB QL keyword. (See the preceding section for more naming rules.) Also, within a given EJB JAR file, an identifier name must not match the name of any entity bean or abstract schema.

The FROM clause can contain multiple declarations, separated by commas. A declaration can reference another identification variable that has been previously declared (to the left). In the following FROM clause, the variable t references the previously declared variable p:

```
FROM Player p, IN (p.teams) AS t
```

Even if an identification variable is not used in the WHERE clause, its declaration can affect the results of the query. For an example, compare the next two queries. The following query returns all players, whether or not they belong to a team:

```
SELECT OBJECT(p)
FROM Player p
```

In contrast, because the next query declares the t identification variable, it fetches all players that belong to a team:

```
SELECT OBJECT(p)
FROM Player p, IN (p.teams) AS t
```

The following query returns the same results as the preceding query, but the WHERE clause makes it easier to read:

```
SELECT OBJECT(p)
FROM Player p
WHERE p.teams IS NOT EMPTY
```

An identification variable always designates a reference to a single value whose type is that of the expression used in the declaration. There are two kinds of declarations: range variable and collection member.

Range Variable Declarations

To declare an identification variable as an abstract schema type, you specify a range variable declaration. In other words, an identification variable can range over the abstract schema type of an entity bean. In the following example, an identification variable named p represents the abstract schema named Player:

```
FROM Player p
```

A range variable declaration can include the optional AS operator:

```
FROM Player AS p
```

In most cases, to obtain objects a query uses path expressions to navigate through the relationships. But for those objects that cannot be obtained by navigation, you can use a range variable declaration to designate a starting point (or *root*).

If the query compares multiple values of the same abstract schema type, then the FROM clause must declare multiple identification variables for the abstract schema:

```
FROM Player p1, Player p2
```

For a sample of such a query, see Example 9 (page 1021).

Collection Member Declarations

In a one-to-many relationship, the multiple side consists of a collection of entity beans. An identification variable can represent a member of this collection. To access a collection member, the path expression in the variable's declaration navigates through the relationships in the abstract schema. (For more information on path expressions, see the following section.) Because a path expression can be based on another path expression, the navigation can traverse several relationships. See Example 6 (page 1020).

A collection member declaration must include the IN operator, but it can omit the optional AS operator.

In the following example, the entity bean represented by the abstract schema named Player has a relationship field called teams. The identification variable called t represents a single member of the teams collection.

```
FROM Player p, IN (p.teams) AS t
```

Path Expressions

Path expressions are important constructs in the syntax of EJB QL, for several reasons. First, they define navigation paths through the relationships in the abstract schema. These path definitions affect both the scope and the results of a query. Second, they can appear in any of the three main clauses of an EJB QL query (SELECT, WHERE, FROM). Finally, although much of EJB QL is a subset of SQL, path expressions are extensions not found in SQL.

Syntax

Here is the syntax for path expressions:

```
cmp_path_expression ::=
    {identification_variable |
     single_valued_cmr_path_expression}.cmp_field

single_valued_cmr_path_expression ::=
    identification_variable.[single_valued_cmr_field.]*
    single_valued_cmr_field

single_valued_path_expression ::=
    cmp_path_expression | single_valued_cmr_path_expression

collection_valued_path_expression ::=
    identification_variable.[single_valued_cmr_field.]
    *collection_valued_cmr_field
```

In the preceding diagram, the cmp_field element represents a persistent field, and the cmr_field element designates a relationship field. The term single_valued qualifies the relationship field as the single side of a one-to-one or one-to-many relationship; the term collection_valued designates it as the multiple (collection) side of a relationship. The single_valued_cmr_path_expression is the abstract schema type of the related entity bean.

The period (.) in a path expression serves two functions. If a period precedes a persistent field, it is a delimiter between the field and the identification variable. If a period precedes a relationship field, it is a navigation operator.

Examples

In the following query, the WHERE clause contains a cmp_path_expression. The p is an identification variable, and salary is a persistent field of Player.

```
SELECT DISTINCT OBJECT(p)
FROM Player p
WHERE p.salary BETWEEN ?1 AND ?2
```

The WHERE clause of the next example also contains a cmp_path_expression. The t is an identification variable, league is a single-valued relationship field, and sport is a persistent field of league.

```
SELECT DISTINCT OBJECT(p)
FROM Player p, IN (p.teams) AS t
WHERE t.league.sport = ?1
```

In the next query, the WHERE clause contains a collection_valued_path_ expression. The p is an identification variable, and teams designates a collection-valued relationship field.

```
SELECT DISTINCT OBJECT(p)
FROM Player p
WHERE p.teams IS EMPTY
```

Expression Types

The type of an expression is the type of the object represented by the ending element, which can be one of the following:

- Persistent field
- Single-valued relationship field
- Collection-valued relationship field

For example, the type of the expression p.salary is double because the terminating persistent field (salary) is a double.

In the expression p.teams, the terminating element is a collection-valued relationship field (teams). This expression's type is a collection of the abstract schema type named Team. Because Team is the abstract schema name for the TeamBean entity bean, this type maps to the bean's local interface, LocalTeam. For more information on the type mapping of abstract schemas, see the section Return Types (page 1040).

Navigation

A path expression enables the query to navigate to related entity beans. The terminating elements of an expression determine whether navigation is allowed. If an expression contains a single-valued relationship field, the navigation can continue to an object that is related to the field. However, an expression cannot navigate beyond a persistent field or a collection-valued relationship field. For example, the expression `p.teams.league.sport` is illegal, because `teams` is a collection-valued relationship field. To reach the `sport` field, the FROM clause could define an identification variable named `t` for the `teams` field:

```
FROM Player AS p, IN (p.teams) t
WHERE t.league.sport = 'soccer'
```

WHERE Clause

The WHERE clause specifies a conditional expression that limits the values returned by the query. The query returns all corresponding values in the data store for which the conditional expression is TRUE. Although usually specified, the WHERE clause is optional. If the WHERE clause is omitted, then the query returns all values. The high-level syntax for the WHERE clause follows:

```
where_clause ::= WHERE conditional_expression
```

Literals

There are three kinds of literals: string, numeric, and Boolean.

String Literals

A string literal is enclosed in single quotes:

```
'Duke'
```

If a string literal contains a single quote, you indicate the quote by using two single quotes:

```
'Duke''s'
```

Like a Java String, a string literal in EJB QL uses the Unicode character encoding.

Numeric Literals

There are two types of numeric literals: exact and approximate.

An exact numeric literal is a numeric value without a decimal point, such as 65, –233, and +12. Using the Java integer syntax, exact numeric literals support numbers in the range of a Java long.

An approximate numeric literal is a numeric value in scientific notation, such as 57., –85.7, and +2.1. Using the syntax of the Java floating-point literal, approximate numeric literals support numbers in the range of a Java double.

Boolean Literals

A Boolean literal is either TRUE or FALSE. These keywords are not case-sensitive.

Input Parameters

An input parameter is designated by a question mark (?) followed by an integer. For example, the first input parameter is ?1, the second is ?2, and so forth.

The following rules apply to input parameters:

- They can be used only in a WHERE clause.
- Their use is restricted to a single-valued path expression within a conditional expression.
- They must be numbered, starting with the integer 1.
- The number of input parameters in the WHERE clause must not exceed the number of input parameters in the corresponding finder or select method.
- The type of an input parameter in the WHERE clause must match the type of the corresponding argument in the finder or select method.

Conditional Expressions

A WHERE clause consists of a conditional expression, which is evaluated from left to right within a precedence level. You can change the order of evaluation by using parentheses.

Here is the syntax of a conditional expression:

```
conditional_expression ::= conditional_term |
    conditional_expression OR conditional_term

conditional_term ::= conditional_factor |
    conditional_term AND conditional_factor

conditional_factor ::= [NOT ] conditional_primary

conditional_primary ::= simple_cond_expression |
    (conditional_expression)

simple_cond_expression ::=
    comparison_expression | between_expression |
    like_expression | in_expression |
    null_comparison_expression |
    empty_collection_comparison_expression |
    collection_member_expression
```

Operators and Their Precedence

Table 29–2 lists the EJB QL operators in order of decreasing precedence.

Table 29–2   EJB QL Operator Precedence

Type	Precedence Order
Navigation	. (a period)
Arithmetic	+ - (unary) * / (multiplication and division) + - (addition and subtraction)
Comparison	= > >= < <= <> (not equal)
Logical	NOT AND OR

BETWEEN Expressions

A BETWEEN expression determines whether an arithmetic expression falls within a range of values. The syntax of the BETWEEN expression follows:

```
between_expression ::=
   arithmetic_expression [NOT] BETWEEN
   arithmetic_expression AND arithmetic_expression
```

These two expressions are equivalent:

```
p.age BETWEEN 15 AND 19
p.age >= 15 AND p.age <= 19
```

The following two expressions are also equivalent:

```
p.age NOT BETWEEN 15 AND 19
p.age < 15 OR p.age > 19
```

If an arithmetic expression has a NULL value, then the value of the BETWEEN expression is unknown.

IN Expressions

An IN expression determines whether or not a string belongs to a set of string literals. Here is the syntax of the IN expression:

```
in_expression ::=
    cmp_path_expression [NOT ] IN
    ( {literal | input_parameter}
    [, { literal | input_parameter} ]*)
```

The path expression must have a string or numeric value. If the path expression has a NULL value, then the value of the IN expression is unknown.

In the following example, if the country is UK the expression is TRUE. If the country is Peru it is FALSE.

```
o.country IN ('UK', 'US', 'France')
```

LIKE Expressions

A LIKE expression determines whether a wildcard pattern matches a string. Here is the syntax:

```
like_expression ::=
    cmp_path_expression [NOT ] LIKE
    pattern_value [ESCAPE escape_character]
```

The path expression must have a string or numeric value. If this value is NULL, then the value of the LIKE expression is unknown. The pattern value is a string literal that can contain wildcard characters. The underscore (_) wildcard character represents any single character. The percent (%) wildcard character represents zero or more characters. The ESCAPE clause specifies an escape character for the wildcard characters in the pattern value. Table 29–3 shows some sample LIKE expressions.

NULL Comparison Expressions

A NULL comparison expression tests whether a single-valued path expression or an input parameter has a NULL value. Usually, the NULL comparison expression is used to test whether or not a single-valued relationship has been set. Here is the syntax of a NULL comparison expression:

```
null_comparison_expression ::=
    {single_valued_path_expression |

 input_parameter}IS [NOT ] NULL
```

Table 29–3 LIKE Expression Examples

Expression	TRUE	FALSE
address.phone LIKE '12%3'	'123' '12993'	'1234'
asentence.word LIKE 'l_se'	'lose'	'loose'
aword.underscored LIKE '_%' ESCAPE '\'	'_foo'	'bar'
address.phone NOT LIKE '12%3'	'1234'	'123' '12993'

Empty Collection Comparison Expressions

An empty collection comparison expression tests whether a collection-valued path expression has no elements. In other words, it tests whether or not a collection-valued relationship has been set. Here is the syntax:

```
empty_collection_comparison_expression ::=
    collection_valued_path_expression IS [NOT] EMPTY
```

If the collection-valued path expression is NULL, then the empty collection comparison expression has a NULL value.

Collection Member Expressions

The collection member expression determines whether a value is a member of a collection. The value and the collection members must have the same type. The expression syntax follows:

```
collection_member_expression ::=
    {single_valued_cmr_path_expression |
    identification_variable | input_parameter}
    [NOT ] MEMBER [OF ] collection_valued_path_expression
```

If either the collection-valued or single-valued path expression is unknown, then the collection member expression is unknown. If the collection-valued path expression designates an empty collection, then the collection member expression is FALSE.

Functional Expressions

EJB QL includes several string and arithmetic functions, which are listed in the following tables. In Table 29–4, the start and length arguments are of type int. They designate positions in the String argument. The first position in a string is designated by 1. In Table 29–5, the number argument can be either an int, a float, or a double.

Table 29–4   String Expressions

Function Syntax	Return Type
CONCAT(String, String)	String
LENGTH(String)	int
LOCATE(String, String [, start])	int
SUBSTRING(String, start, length)	String

Table 29–5   Arithmetic Expressions

Function Syntax	Return Type
ABS(number)	int, float, or double
MOD(int, int)	int
SQRT(double)	double

NULL Values

If the target of a reference is not in the persistent store, then the target is NULL. For conditional expressions containing NULL, EJB QL uses the semantics defined by SQL92. Briefly, these semantics are as follows:

- If a comparison or arithmetic operation has an unknown value, it yields a NULL value.
- Two NULL values are not equal. Comparing two NULL values yields an unknown value.
- The IS NULL test converts a NULL persistent field or a single-valued relationship field to TRUE. The IS NOT NULL test converts them to FALSE.
- Boolean operators and conditional tests use the three-valued logic defined by Table 29–6 and Table 29–7. (In these tables, T stands for TRUE, F for FALSE, and U for unknown.)

Table 29–6 AND Operator Logic

AND	T	F	U
T	T	F	U
F	F	F	F
U	U	F	U

Table 29–7 OR Operator Logic

OR	T	F	U
T	T	T	T
F	T	F	U
U	T	U	U

Equality Semantics

In EJB QL, only values of the same type can be compared. However, this rule has one exception: Exact and approximate numeric values can be compared. In such a comparison, the required type conversion adheres to the rules of Java numeric promotion.

EJB QL treats compared values as if they were Java types and not as if they represented types in the underlying data store. For example, if a persistent field could be either an integer or a NULL, then it must be designated as an Integer object and not as an int primitive. This designation is required because a Java object can be NULL but a primitive cannot.

Two strings are equal only if they contain the same sequence of characters. Trailing blanks are significant; for example, the strings 'abc' and 'abc ' are not equal.

Two entity beans of the same abstract schema type are equal only if their primary keys have the same value. Table 29–8 shows the operator logic of a negation, and Table 29–9 shows the truth values of conditional tests.

Table 29–8 NOT Operator Logic

NOT Value	Value
T	F
F	T
U	U

Table 29–9 Conditional Test

Conditional Test	T	F	U
Expression IS TRUE	T	F	F
Expression IS FALSE	F	T	F
Expression is unknown	F	F	T

SELECT Clause

The SELECT clause defines the types of the objects or values returned by the query. The SELECT clause has the following syntax:

```
select_clause ::= SELECT [DISTINCT ] {select_expression
    |OBJECT( identification_variable) }

select_expression ::= single_valued_path_expression |
    aggregate_select_expression

aggregate_select_expression ::=
    {AVG |MAX |MIN |SUM |COUNT }( [DISTINCT ]
    cmp_path_expression) |
    COUNT ( [DISTINCT ] identification_variable |
    single_valued_cmr_path_expression)
```

Return Types

The return type defined by the SELECT clause must match that of the finder or select method for which the query is defined.

For finder method queries, the return type of the SELECT clause is the abstract schema type of the entity bean that defines the finder method. This abstract schema type maps to either a remote or a local interface. If the bean's remote home interface defines the finder method, then the return type is the remote interface (or a collection of remote interfaces). Similarly, if the local home interface defines the finder method, the return type is the local interface (or a collection). For example, the LocalPlayerHome interface of the PlayerBean entity bean defines the findAll method:

```
public Collection findAll() throws FinderException;
```

The EJB QL query of the findAll method returns a collection of LocalPlayer interface types:

```
SELECT OBJECT(p)
FROM Player p
```

For select method queries (except for aggregate function queries), the return type of the SELECT clause can be one of the following:

- The abstract schema of the entity bean that contains the select method.
- The abstract schema of a related entity bean. (By default, each of these abstract schema types maps to the local interface of the entity bean. Although it is uncommon, in the deployment descriptor you can override the default mapping by specifying a remote interface.)
- A persistent field.

The PlayerBean entity bean, for example, implements the ejbSelectSports method, which returns a collection of String objects for sport. The sport is a persistent field of the LeagueBean entity bean. See Example 11 (page 1022).

A SELECT clause cannot specify a collection-valued expression. For example, the SELECT clause p.teams is invalid because teams is a collection. However, the clause in the following query is valid because the t is a single element of the teams collection:

```
SELECT t
FROM Player p, IN (p.teams) AS t
```

For select method queries with an aggregate function (AVG, COUNT, MAX, MIN, or SUM) in the SELECT clause, the following rules apply:

- The select method must return a single object, primitive, or wrapper type that is compatible with the standard JDBC conversion mappings for the persistent field type.
- For the AVG, MAX, MIN, and SUM functions, if the select method return type is an object and the function returns no values, then the select method returns null. In this case, if the select method return type is a primitive, then the container throws the ObjectNotFoundException.
- For the COUNT function, the result of the select method must be an exact numeric type. If the function returns no values, the select method returns 0.

DISTINCT and OBJECT Keywords

The DISTINCT keyword eliminates duplicate return values. If the method of the query returns a java.util.Collection—which allows duplicates—then you must specify the DISTINCT keyword to eliminate duplicates. However, if the method returns a java.util.Set, the DISTINCT keyword is redundant because a java.util.Set cannot contain duplicates.

The OBJECT keyword must precede a stand-alone identification variable, but it must not precede a single-valued path expression. If an identification variable is part of a single-valued path expression, it is not stand-alone.

Aggregate Functions

The SELECT clause can contain an aggregate function with the following syntax:

```
aggregate_select_expression ::=
    {AVG |MAX |MIN |SUM |COUNT }( [DISTINCT ]
    cmp_path_expression) |
    COUNT ( [DISTINCT ] identification_variable |
    single_valued_cmr_path_expression)
```

Except for the COUNT function, the path expression argument for an aggregate function must terminate in a persistent field. For the COUNT function, the path expression argument can terminate in a persistent field, a relationship field, or an identification variable.

The arguments of the SUM and AVG functions must be numeric. The arguments of the MAX and MIN functions must be orderable: numeric, string, character, or date.

If the argument is empty, the COUNT function returns 0 and the other aggregate functions return NULL.

If the DISTINCT keyword is specified, duplicate values are eliminated before the aggregate function is applied. NULL values are always eliminated before the function is applied, whether or not the DISTINCT keyword is used.

ORDER BY Clause

As its name suggests, the ORDER BY clause orders the values or objects returned by the query. The syntax of the clause follows:

```
orderby_clause ::= ORDER BY orderby_item [, orderby_item]*

orderby_item ::= cmp_path_expression [ASC |DESC ]
```

If the ORDER BY clause contains multiple orderby_item elements, the left-to-right sequence of the elements determines the high-to-low precedence.

The ASC keyword specifies ascending order (the default), and the DESC keyword indicates descending order.

If the ORDER BY clause is used, then the SELECT clause must be one of the following:

- An identification variable x, denoted as OBJECT(x)
- A single_valued_cmr_path_expression
- A cmp_path_expression

If the SELECT clause is an identification variable or a single_valued_cmr_path_expression, then the orderby_item must be an orderable persistent field of the entity bean returned by the SELECT clause. If the SELECT clause is a cmp_path_expression, then the cmp_path_expression and the orderby_item must evaluate to the same persistent field of the same entity bean.

EJB QL Restrictions

EJB QL has a few restrictions:

- Comments are not allowed.

- To compare date and time values in an EJB QL query, use `long` primitives to represent the values as milliseconds. Do not use the `java.util.Date` and `java.sql.Time` objects in EJB QL comparisons.

- Because support for `BigDecimal` and `BigInteger` types is optional for EJB 2.1 containers, applications that use these types in EJB QL queries may not be portable.

- Currently, container-managed persistence does not support inheritance. For this reason, two entity beans of different types cannot be compared.

30

Transactions

A typical enterprise application accesses and stores information in one or more databases. Because this information is critical for business operations, it must be accurate, current, and reliable. Data integrity would be lost if multiple programs were allowed to update the same information simultaneously. It would also be lost if a system that failed while processing a business transaction were to leave the affected data only partially updated. By preventing both of these scenarios, software transactions ensure data integrity. Transactions control the concurrent access of data by multiple programs. In the event of a system failure, transactions make sure that after recovery the data will be in a consistent state.

What Is a Transaction?

To emulate a business transaction, a program may need to perform several steps. A financial program, for example, might transfer funds from a checking account to a savings account using the steps listed in the following pseudocode:

```
begin transaction
    debit checking account
    credit savings account
    update history log
commit transaction
```

Either all three of these steps must complete, or none of them at all. Otherwise, data integrity is lost. Because the steps within a transaction are a unified whole, a *transaction* is often defined as an indivisible unit of work.

A transaction can end in two ways: with a commit or with a rollback. When a transaction commits, the data modifications made by its statements are saved. If a statement within a transaction fails, the transaction rolls back, undoing the effects of all statements in the transaction. In the pseudocode, for example, if a disk drive were to crash during the `credit` step, the transaction would roll back and undo the data modifications made by the `debit` statement. Although the transaction fails, data integrity would be intact because the accounts still balance.

In the preceding pseudocode, the `begin` and `commit` statements mark the boundaries of the transaction. When designing an enterprise bean, you determine how the boundaries are set by specifying either container-managed or bean-managed transactions.

Container-Managed Transactions

In an enterprise bean with *container-managed transactions*, the EJB container sets the boundaries of the transactions. You can use container-managed transactions with any type of enterprise bean: session, entity, or message-driven. Container-managed transactions simplify development because the enterprise bean code does not explicitly mark the transaction's boundaries. The code does not include statements that begin and end the transaction.

Typically, the container begins a transaction immediately before an enterprise bean method starts. It commits the transaction just before the method exits. Each method can be associated with a single transaction. Nested or multiple transactions are not allowed within a method.

Container-managed transactions do not require all methods to be associated with transactions. When deploying a bean, you specify which of the bean's methods are associated with transactions by setting the transaction attributes.

Transaction Attributes

A *transaction attribute* controls the scope of a transaction. Figure 30–1 illustrates why controlling the scope is important. In the diagram, `method-A` begins a transaction and then invokes `method-B` of Bean-2. When `method-B` executes, does it run within the scope of the transaction started by `method-A`, or does it execute with a new transaction? The answer depends on the transaction attribute of `method-B`.

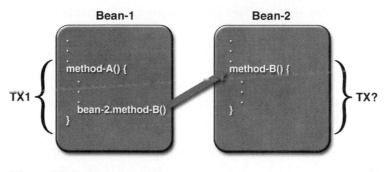

Figure 30–1 Transaction Scope

A transaction attribute can have one of the following values:

- Required
- RequiresNew
- Mandatory
- NotSupported
- Supports
- Never

Required

If the client is running within a transaction and invokes the enterprise bean's method, the method executes within the client's transaction. If the client is not associated with a transaction, the container starts a new transaction before running the method.

The Required attribute will work for most transactions. Therefore, you may want to use it as a default, at least in the early phases of development. Because transaction attributes are declarative, you can easily change them later.

RequiresNew

If the client is running within a transaction and invokes the enterprise bean's method, the container takes the following steps:

1. Suspends the client's transaction
2. Starts a new transaction
3. Delegates the call to the method
4. Resumes the client's transaction after the method completes

If the client is not associated with a transaction, the container starts a new transaction before running the method.

You should use the `RequiresNew` attribute when you want to ensure that the method always runs within a new transaction.

Mandatory

If the client is running within a transaction and invokes the enterprise bean's method, the method executes within the client's transaction. If the client is not associated with a transaction, the container throws the `TransactionRequired-Exception`.

Use the `Mandatory` attribute if the enterprise bean's method must use the transaction of the client.

NotSupported

If the client is running within a transaction and invokes the enterprise bean's method, the container suspends the client's transaction before invoking the method. After the method has completed, the container resumes the client's transaction.

If the client is not associated with a transaction, the container does not start a new transaction before running the method.

Use the `NotSupported` attribute for methods that don't need transactions. Because transactions involve overhead, this attribute may improve performance.

Supports

If the client is running within a transaction and invokes the enterprise bean's method, the method executes within the client's transaction. If the client is not associated with a transaction, the container does not start a new transaction before running the method.

Because the transactional behavior of the method may vary, you should use the `Supports` attribute with caution.

Never

If the client is running within a transaction and invokes the enterprise bean's method, the container throws a `RemoteException`. If the client is not associated with a transaction, the container does not start a new transaction before running the method.

Summary of Transaction Attributes

Table 30–1 summarizes the effects of the transaction attributes. Both the T1 and the T2 transactions are controlled by the container. A T1 transaction is associated with the client that calls a method in the enterprise bean. In most cases, the client is another enterprise bean. A T2 transaction is started by the container just before the method executes.

In the last column of Table 30–1, the word *None* means that the business method does not execute within a transaction controlled by the container. However, the database calls in such a business method might be controlled by the transaction manager of the DBMS.

Setting Transaction Attributes

Because transaction attributes are stored in the deployment descriptor, they can be changed during several phases of J2EE application development: enterprise bean creation, application assembly, and deployment. However, it is the responsibility of an enterprise bean developer to specify the attributes when creating the bean. The attributes should be modified only by an application developer who is assembling components into larger applications. Do not expect the person deploying the J2EE application to specify the transaction attributes.

You can specify the transaction attributes for the entire enterprise bean or for individual methods. If you've specified one attribute for a method and another for the bean, the attribute for the method takes precedence. When you specify attributes for individual methods, the requirements differ with the type of bean. Session beans need the attributes defined for business methods but do not allow them for the `create` methods. Entity beans require transaction attributes for the business, `create`, `remove`, and finder methods. Message-driven beans require transaction attributes (either `Required` or `NotSupported`) for the `onMessage` method.

Table 30–1 Transaction Attributes and Scope

Transaction Attribute	Client's Transaction	Business Method's Transaction
Required	None	T2
	T1	T1
RequiresNew	None	T2
	T1	T2
Mandatory	None	Error
	T1	T1
NotSupported	None	None
	T1	None
Supports	None	None
	T1	T1
Never	None	None
	T1	Error

Rolling Back a Container-Managed Transaction

There are two ways to roll back a container-managed transaction. First, if a system exception is thrown, the container will automatically roll back the transaction. Second, by invoking the setRollbackOnly method of the EJBContext interface, the bean method instructs the container to roll back the transaction. If the bean throws an application exception, the rollback is not automatic but can be initiated by a call to setRollbackOnly. For a description of system and application exceptions, see deploytool Tips for Entity Beans with Bean-Managed Persistence (page 937).

The source code for the following example is in the *<INSTALL>*/j2ee-tutorial14/examples/ejb/bank directory.

The transferToSaving method of the BankBean example illustrates the set-RollbackOnly method. If a negative checking balance occurs, transferToSaving invokes setRollBackOnly and throws an application exception (InsufficientBalanceException). The updateChecking and updateSaving methods update database tables. If the updates fail, these methods throw an SQLException and the transferToSaving method throws an EJBException. Because the EJBException is a system exception, it causes the container to automatically roll back the transaction. Here is the code for the transferToSaving method:

```
public void transferToSaving(double amount) throws
   InsufficientBalanceException  {

   checkingBalance -= amount;
   savingBalance += amount;

   try {
      updateChecking(checkingBalance);
      if (checkingBalance < 0.00) {
         context.setRollbackOnly();
         throw new InsufficientBalanceException();
      }
      updateSaving(savingBalance);
   } catch (SQLException ex) {
      throw new EJBException
         ("Transaction failed due to SQLException: "
         + ex.getMessage());
   }
}
```

When the container rolls back a transaction, it always undoes the changes to data made by SQL calls within the transaction. However, only in entity beans will the container undo changes made to instance variables. (It does so by automatically invoking the entity bean's ejbLoad method, which loads the instance variables from the database.) When a rollback occurs, a session bean must explicitly reset any instance variables changed within the transaction. The easiest way to reset a session bean's instance variables is by implementing the SessionSynchronization interface.

Synchronizing a Session Bean's Instance Variables

The SessionSynchronization interface, which is optional, allows you to synchronize the instance variables with their corresponding values in the database. The container invokes the SessionSynchronization methods—afterBegin, beforeCompletion, and afterCompletion—at each of the main stages of a transaction.

The afterBegin method informs the instance that a new transaction has begun. The container invokes afterBegin immediately before it invokes the business method. The afterBegin method is a good place to load the instance variables from the database. The BankBean class, for example, loads the checkingBalance and savingBalance variables in the afterBegin method:

```
public void afterBegin() {

    System.out.println("afterBegin()");
    try {
        checkingBalance = selectChecking();
        savingBalance = selectSaving();
    } catch (SQLException ex) {
        throw new EJBException("afterBegin Exception: " +
            ex.getMessage());
    }
}
```

The container invokes the beforeCompletion method after the business method has finished, but just before the transaction commits. The beforeCompletion method is the last opportunity for the session bean to roll back the transaction (by calling setRollbackOnly). If it hasn't already updated the database with the values of the instance variables, the session bean can do so in the before-Completion method.

The afterCompletion method indicates that the transaction has completed. It has a single boolean parameter whose value is true if the transaction was committed and false if it was rolled back. If a rollback occurred, the session bean can refresh its instance variables from the database in the afterCompletion method:

```
public void afterCompletion(boolean committed) {

    System.out.println("afterCompletion: " + committed);
    if (committed == false) {
```

```
    try {
       checkingBalance = selectChecking();
       savingBalance = selectSaving();
    } catch (SQLException ex) {
       throw new EJBException("afterCompletion SQLException:
    " + ex.getMessage());
    }
  }
}
```

Compiling the BankBean Example

To compile the classes and interfaces in the BankBean example, follow these steps:

1. In a terminal window, go to this directory:

   `<INSTALL>/j2eetutorial14/examples/ejb/bank/`

2. Start the PointBase server. For instructions, see Starting and Stopping the PointBase Database Server (page 28).

3. Create the database tables and data by typing

   `asant create-db_common`

4. Type the following command to build the enterprise bean's classes and interfaces:

   `asant build`

Packaging the BankBean Example

The BankBean session bean uses container-managed transactions. These steps assume that you are familiar with the steps needed to create and deploy an enterprise application using deploytool, as described in Chapter 24.

Creating the J2EE Application

Create a new application named BankApp in:

   `<INSTALL>/j2eetutorial14/examples/ejb/bank/`

Packaging the Enterprise Bean

1. Create a new enterprise bean in BankApp by selecting File→New→Enterprise Bean.

2. In the EJB JAR screen:

   a. Select Create New JAR Module in Application.

   b. Enter BankJAR under JAR Name.

   c. Click Edit.

   d. Navigate to *<INSTALL>*/j2eetutorial14/examples/ejb/bank/build/.

   e. Select Bank.class, BankBean.class, BankHome.class, and InsufficientBalanceException.class.

   f. Click Add.

   g. Click OK.

   h. Click Next.

3. In the General screen:

   a. Select BankBean under Enterprise Bean Class.

   b. Enter BankBean under Enterprise Bean Name.

   c. Select Stateful Session under Enterprise Bean Type.

   d. Select BankHome under Remote Home Interface.

   e. Select Bank under Remote Interface.

   f. Select Next.

4. Click Finish.

5. Select BankBean in deploytool's tree.

6. In the Resource Ref's tab:

   a. Click Add.

   b. Set the Coded Name to jdbc/BankDB.

   c. Set the JNDI Name to jdbc/ejbTutorialDB.

7. In the Transactions tab:

   a. Select Container-Managed under Transaction Management.

   b. Verify that getCheckingBalance(), getSavingBalance(), and transferToSaving() have the Required transaction attribute.

Packaging the Application Client

1. Create a new application client in BankApp by selecting File→New→Application Client.
2. In the JAR File Contents screen:
   a. Select BankApp under Create New AppClient Module in Application.
   b. Enter BankClient under AppClient Name.
   c. Click Edit.
   d. Navigate to *<INSTALL>*/j2eetutorial14/examples/ejb/bank/build/.
   e. Select BankClient.class.
   f. Click Add.
   g. Click OK.
   h. Click Next.
3. In the General screen:
   a. Select BankClient under Main Class.
   b. Select (Use container-managed authentication) under Callback Handler Class.
   c. Click Next.
4. Click Finish.

Specifying the Application Client's Enterprise Bean Reference

When it invokes the lookup method, BankClient refers to the home of an enterprise bean:

```
Object objref = initial.lookup("java:comp/env/ejb/
SimpleBank");
```

You specify this reference as follows:

1. In the tree, select BankClient.
2. Select the EJB Ref's tab.
3. Click Add.

4. In the Coded Name field, enter `ejb/SimpleBank`.

5. In the EJB Type field, select `Session`.

6. In the Interfaces field, select `Remote`.

7. In the Home Interface field, enter `BankHome`.

8. In the Local/Remote Interface field, enter `Bank`.

9. Click OK.

10. Select the line you just added.

11. Under Sun-specific Settings for `ejb/SimpleBank`, select JNDI Name.

12. In the JNDI Name field select, `BankBean`.

13. Select File→Save.

Deploying the J2EE Application

1. Select `BankApp` in `deploytool`.

2. Select Tools→Deploy.

3. Under Connection Settings, enter the user name and password for the Sun Java System Application Server Platform Edition 8.

4. Tell `deploytool` to create a JAR file that contains the client stubs:

   a. Check the Return Client JAR box.

   b. In the field below the checkbox, enter `<INSTALL>`/j2eetutorial14/ examples/ejb/bank/.

5. Click OK.

6. In the Distribute Module dialog box, click Close when the deployment completes successfully.

Running the Application Client

1. In a terminal window, go to the `<INSTALL>`/j2eetutorial14/ examples/ejb/bank/ directory.

2. Type the following command:

   `appclient -client BankAppClient.jar`

In the terminal window, the client displays these lines:

```
checking: 60.0
saving: 540.0
```

Methods Not Allowed in Container-Managed Transactions

You should not invoke any method that might interfere with the transaction boundaries set by the container. The list of prohibited methods follows:

- The `commit`, `setAutoCommit`, and `rollback` methods of `java.sql.Connection`
- The `getUserTransaction` method of `javax.ejb.EJBContext`
- Any method of `javax.transaction.UserTransaction`

You can, however, use these methods to set boundaries in bean-managed transactions.

Bean-Managed Transactions

In a *bean-managed transaction*, the code in the session or message-driven bean explicitly marks the boundaries of the transaction. An entity bean cannot have bean-managed transactions; it must use container-managed transactions instead. Although beans with container-managed transactions require less coding, they have one limitation: When a method is executing, it can be associated with either a single transaction or no transaction at all. If this limitation will make coding your bean difficult, you should consider using bean-managed transactions.

The following pseudocode illustrates the kind of fine-grained control you can obtain with bean-managed transactions. By checking various conditions, the pseudocode decides whether to start or stop different transactions within the business method.

```
begin transaction
...
update table-a
...
if (condition-x)
   commit transaction
else if (condition-y)
   update table-b
   commit transaction
else
   rollback transaction
   begin transaction
   update table-c
   commit transaction
```

When coding a bean-managed transaction for session or message-driven beans, you must decide whether to use JDBC or JTA transactions. The sections that follow discuss both types of transactions.

JDBC Transactions

A *JDBC transaction* is controlled by the transaction manager of the DBMS. You may want to use JDBC transactions when wrapping legacy code inside a session bean. To code a JDBC transaction, you invoke the `commit` and `rollback` methods of the `java.sql.Connection` interface. The beginning of a transaction is implicit. A transaction begins with the first SQL statement that follows the most recent `commit`, `rollback`, or `connect` statement. (This rule is generally true but may vary with DBMS vendor.)

The source code for the following example is in the `<INSTALL>`/j2ee-tutorial14/examples/ejb/warehouse/ directory.

The following code is from the `WarehouseBean` example, a session bean that uses the `Connection` interface's methods to delimit bean-managed transactions. The `ship` method starts by invoking `setAutoCommit` on the `Connection` object named `con`. This invocation tells the DBMS not to automatically commit every SQL statement. Next, the `ship` method calls routines that update the `order_item` and `inventory` database tables. If the updates succeed, the transaction is committed. If an exception is thrown, however, the transaction is rolled back.

```
public void ship (String productId, String orderId, int
quantity) {

   try {
      makeConnection();
      con.setAutoCommit(false);
      updateOrderItem(productId, orderId);
      updateInventory(productId, quantity);
      con.commit();
   } catch (Exception ex) {
       try {
          con.rollback();
          throw new EJBException("Transaction failed: " +
             ex.getMessage());
       } catch (SQLException sqx) {
          throw new EJBException("Rollback failed: " +
             sqx.getMessage());
       }
```

```
        } finally {
            releaseConnection();
        }
    }
}
```

Deploying and Running the WarehouseBean Example

WarehouseBean is a session bean that uses bean-managed, JDBC transactions. These steps assume that you are familiar with the steps needed to create and deploy an enterprise application using deploytool, as described in Chapter 25. To deploy and run the example, do the following.

Compiling the WarehouseBean Example

To compile the classes and interfaces in the WarehouseBean example, follow these steps:

1. In a terminal window, go to this directory:

   `<INSTALL>/j2eetutorial14/examples/ejb/warehouse/`

2. Start the PointBase server. For instructions, see Starting and Stopping the PointBase Database Server (page 28).

3. Create the database tables and data by typing

   `asant create-db_common`

4. Type the following command to build the enterprise bean's classes and interfaces:

   `asant build`

Packaging the WarehouseBean Example

The WarehouseBean session bean uses bean-managed transactions. These steps assume that you are familiar with the steps needed to create and deploy an enterprise application using deploytool, as described in Chapter 24.

Creating the J2EE Application

Create a new application named WarehouseApp in:

```
<INSTALL>/j2eetutorial14/examples/ejb/warehouse/
```

Packaging the Enterprise Bean

1. Create a new enterprise bean in WarehouseApp by selecting File→New→ Enterprise Bean.

2. In the EJB JAR screen:
   a. Select Create New JAR Module in Application.
   b. Enter WarehouseJAR under JAR Name.
   c. Click Edit.
   d. Navigate to <INSTALL>/j2eetutorial14/examples/ejb/warehouse/.
   e. Select Warehouse.class, WarehouseBean.class, and Warehouse-Home.class.
   f. Click Add.
   g. Click OK.
   h. Click Next.

3. In the General screen:
   a. Select WarehouseBean under Enterprise Bean Class.
   b. Enter WarehouseBean under Enterprise Bean Name.
   c. Select Stateful Session under Enterprise Bean Type.
   d. Select WarehouseHome under Remote Home Interface.
   e. Select Warehouse under Remote Interface.
   f. Select Next.

4. Click Finish.

5. Select WarehouseBean in deploytool's tree.

6. In the Transactions tab select Bean-Managed under Transaction Management.

7. In the Resource Ref's tab:
   a. Click Add.
   b. Double-click the Coded Name column for the row that was just created.

c. Enter `jdbc/WarehouseDB`.

d. Under Sun-specific Settings for `jdbc/WarehouseDB` in the JNDI Name field, select `jdbc/ejbTutorialDB`.

Packaging the Application Client

1. Create a new application client in `WarehouseApp` by selecting File→New→Application Client.

2. In the JAR File Contents screen:

   a. Select `WarehouseApp` under Create New AppClient Module in Application.

   b. Enter `WarehouseClient` under AppClient Name.

   c. Click Edit.

   d. Navigate to `<INSTALL>/j2eetutorial14/examples/ejb/warehouse/`.

   e. Select `WarehouseClient.class`.

   f. Click Add.

   g. Click OK.

   h. Click Next.

3. In the General screen:

   a. Select `WarehouseClient` under Main Class.

   b. Select (`Use container-managed authentication`) under Callback Handler Class.

   c. Click Next.

4. Click Finish.

Specifying the Application Client's Enterprise Bean Reference

When it invokes the `lookup` method, `WarehouseClient` refers to the home of an enterprise bean:

```
Object objref = initial.lookup("java:comp/env/ejb/
SimpleWarehouse");
```

You specify this reference as follows:

1. In the tree, select `WarehouseClient`.
2. Select the EJB Ref's tab.
3. Click Add.
4. In the Coded Name field, enter `ejb/SimpleWarehouse`.
5. In the EJB Type field, select `Session`.
6. In the Interfaces field, select `Remote`.
7. In the Home Interface field, enter `WarehouseHome`.
8. In the Local/Remote Interface field, enter `Warehouse`.
9. Click OK.
10. Select the line you just added.
11. Under Sun-specific Settings for `ejb/SimpleWarehouse`, select JNDI Name.
12. In the JNDI Name field, select `WarehouseBean`.
13. Select File→Save.

Deploying the J2EE Application

1. Select `WarehouseApp` in `deploytool`.
2. Select Tools→Deploy.
3. Under Connection Settings, enter the user name and password for the Application Server.
4. Tell `deploytool` to create a JAR file that contains the client stubs:
   a. Check the Return Client JAR box.
   b. In the field below the checkbox, enter `<INSTALL>`/j2eetutorial14/ examples/ejb/warehouse/.
5. Click OK.
6. In the Distribute Module dialog box, click Close when the deployment completes successfully.

Running the Application Client

1. In a terminal window, go to the `<INSTALL>`/j2eetutorial14/ examples/ejb/warehouse/ directory.

2. Type the following command:

```
appclient -client WarehouseAppClient.jar
```

In the terminal window, the client displays these lines:

```
status = shipped
```

JTA Transactions

JTA is the abbreviation for the Java Transaction API. This API allows you to demarcate transactions in a manner that is independent of the transaction manager implementation. The Application Server implements the transaction manager with the Java Transaction Service (JTS). But your code doesn't call the JTS methods directly. Instead, it invokes the JTA methods, which then call the lower-level JTS routines.

A *JTA transaction* is controlled by the J2EE transaction manager. You may want to use a JTA transaction because it can span updates to multiple databases from different vendors. A particular DBMS's transaction manager may not work with heterogeneous databases. However, the J2EE transaction manager does have one limitation: it does not support nested transactions. In other words, it cannot start a transaction for an instance until the preceding transaction has ended.

The source code for the following example is in the `<INSTALL>/j2eetutorial14/examples/ejb/teller/` directory.

To demarcate a JTA transaction, you invoke the `begin`, `commit`, and `rollback` methods of the `javax.transaction.UserTransaction` interface. The following code, taken from the `TellerBean` class, demonstrates the `UserTransaction` methods. The `begin` and `commit` invocations delimit the updates to the database. If the updates fail, the code invokes the `rollback` method and throws an `EJBException`.

```
public void withdrawCash(double amount) {

    UserTransaction ut = context.getUserTransaction();

    try {
        ut.begin();
        updateChecking(amount);
        machineBalance -= amount;
        insertMachine(machineBalance);
        ut.commit();
    } catch (Exception ex) {
```

```
        try {
           ut.rollback();
        } catch (SystemException syex) {
            throw new EJBException
                ("Rollback failed: " + syex.getMessage());
        }
        throw new EJBException
           ("Transaction failed: " + ex.getMessage());
    }
}
```

Deploying and Running the TellerBean Example

The TellerBean session bean uses bean-managed JTA transactions. These steps assume that you are familiar with the steps needed to create and deploy an enterprise application using deploytool, as described in Chapter 25. To deploy and run the TellerBean example, perform these steps.

Compiling the TellerBean Example

To compile the classes and interfaces in the TellerBean example, follow these steps:

1. In a terminal window, go to this directory:

   <INSTALL>/j2eetutorial14/examples/ejb/teller/

2. Start the PointBase server. For instructions, see Starting and Stopping the PointBase Database Server (page 28).

3. Create the database tables and data by typing

   asant create-db_common

4. Type the following command to build the enterprise bean's classes and interfaces:

   asant build

Packaging the TellerBean Example

The TellerBean session bean uses JTA transactions. These steps assume that you are familiar with the steps needed to create and deploy an enterprise application using deploytool, as described in Chapter 24.

Creating the J2EE Application

Create a new application named TellerApp in

    <INSTALL>/j2eetutorial14/examples/ejb/teller/

Packaging the Enterprise Bean

1. Create a new enterprise bean in TellerApp by selecting File→New→ Enterprise Bean.

2. In the EJB JAR screen:

   a. Select Create New JAR Module in Application.

   b. Enter TellerJAR under JAR Name.

   c. Click Edit.

   d. Navigate to <INSTALL>/j2eetutorial14/examples/ejb/teller/.

   e. Select Teller.class, TellerBean.class, and TellerHome.class.

   f. Click Add.

   g. Click OK.

   h. Click Next.

3. In the General screen:

   a. Select TellerBean under Enterprise Bean Class.

   b. Enter TellerBean under Enterprise Bean Name.

   c. Select Stateful Session under Enterprise Bean Type.

   d. Select TellerHome under Remote Home Interface.

   e. Select Teller under Remote Interface.

   f. Select Next.

4. Click Finish.

5. Select `TellerBean` in `deploytool`'s tree.

6. In the Transactions tab select Bean-Managed under Transaction Management.

7. In the Resource Ref's tab:

    a. Click Add.

    b. Double-click the Coded Name column for the row that was just created.

    c. Enter `jdbc/TellerDB`.

    d. Under Sun-specific Settings for `jdbc/TellerDB` in the JNDI Name field, select `jdbc/ejbTutorialDB`.

Packaging the Application Client

1. Create a new application client in `TellerApp` by selecting File→New→Application Client.

2. In the JAR File Contents screen:

    a. Select `TellerApp` under Create New AppClient Module in Application.

    b. Enter `TellerClient` under AppClient Name.

    c. Click Edit.

    d. Navigate to `<INSTALL>`/j2eetutorial14/examples/ejb/teller/.

    e. Select `TellerClient.class`.

    f. Click Add.

    g. Click OK.

    h. Click Next.

3. In the General screen:

    a. Select `TellerClient` under Main Class.

    b. Select (`Use container-managed authentication`) under Callback Handler Class.

    c. Click Next.

4. Click Finish.

Specifying the Application Client's Enterprise Bean Reference

When it invokes the `lookup` method, `TellerClient` refers to the home of an enterprise bean:

```
Object objref = initial.lookup("java:comp/env/ejb/
SimpleTeller");
```

You specify this reference as follows:

1. In the tree, select `TellerClient`.
2. Select the EJB Ref's tab.
3. Click Add.
4. In the Coded Name field, enter `ejb/SimpleTeller`.
5. In the EJB Type field, select `Session`.
6. In the Interfaces field, select `Remote`.
7. In the Home Interface field, enter `TellerHome`.
8. In the Local/Remote Interface field, enter `Teller`.
9. Click OK.
10. Select the line you just added.
11. Under Sun-specific Settings for `ejb/SimpleTeller`, select JNDI Name.
12. In the JNDI Name field, select `TellerBean`.
13. Select File→Save.

Deploying the J2EE Application

1. Select `TellerApp` in `deploytool`.
2. Select Tools→Deploy.
3. Under Connection Settings, enter the user name and password for the Application Server.
4. Tell `deploytool` to create a JAR file that contains the client stubs:
   a. Check the Return Client JAR box.
   b. In the field below the checkbox, enter `<INSTALL>/j2eetutorial14/examples/ejb/teller/`.

5. Click OK.

6. In the Distribute Module dialog box, click Close when the deployment completes successfully.

Running the Application Client

1. In a terminal window, go to the `<INSTALL>`/`j2eetutorial14/` `examples/ejb/teller/` directory.

2. Type the following command:

```
appclient -client TellerAppClient.jar
```

In the terminal window, the client displays these lines:

```
checking = 500.0
checking = 440.0
```

Returning without Committing

In a stateless session bean with bean-managed transactions, a business method must commit or roll back a transaction before returning. However, a stateful session bean does not have this restriction.

In a stateful session bean with a JTA transaction, the association between the bean instance and the transaction is retained across multiple client calls. Even if each business method called by the client opens and closes the database connection, the association is retained until the instance completes the transaction.

In a stateful session bean with a JDBC transaction, the JDBC connection retains the association between the bean instance and the transaction across multiple calls. If the connection is closed, the association is not retained.

Methods Not Allowed in Bean-Managed Transactions

Do not invoke the `getRollbackOnly` and `setRollbackOnly` methods of the `EJBContext` interface in bean-managed transactions. These methods should be used only in container-managed transactions. For bean-managed transactions, invoke the `getStatus` and `rollback` methods of the `UserTransaction` interface.

Summary of Transaction Options for Enterprise Beans

If you're unsure about how to set up transactions in an enterprise bean, here's a tip: In the bean's deployment descriptor, specify container-managed transactions. Then set the `Required` transaction attribute for the entire bean. This approach will work most of the time.

Table 30–2 lists the types of transactions that are allowed for the different types of enterprise beans. An entity bean must use container-managed transactions. With container-managed transactions, you specify the transaction attributes in the deployment descriptor and you roll back a transaction by calling the `set-RollbackOnly` method of the `EJBContext` interface or when a system-level exception is thrown.

A session bean can have either container-managed or bean-managed transactions. There are two types of bean-managed transactions: JDBC and JTA transactions. You delimit JDBC transactions using the `commit` and `rollback` methods of the `Connection` interface. To demarcate JTA transactions, you invoke the `begin`, `commit`, and `rollback` methods of the `UserTransaction` interface.

In a session bean with bean-managed transactions, it is possible to mix JDBC and JTA transactions. This practice is not recommended, however, because it can make your code difficult to debug and maintain.

Like a session bean, a message-driven bean can have either container-managed or bean-managed transactions.

Table 30–2 Allowed Transaction Types for Enterprise Beans

		Bean-Managed	
		---	---
Bean Type	**Container-Managed**	**JTA**	**JDBC**
Entity	Y	N	N
Session	Y	Y	Y
Message-driven	Y	Y	Y

Transaction Timeouts

For container-managed transactions, you control the transaction timeout interval by setting the value of the `timeout-in-seconds` property in the `domain.xml` file, which is in the `config` directory of your Application Server installation. For example, you would set the timeout value to 5 seconds as follows:

```
timeout-in-seconds=5
```

With this setting, if the transaction has not completed within 5 seconds, the EJB container rolls it back.

When the Application Server is first installed, the timeout value is set to 0:

```
timeout-in-seconds=0
```

If the value is 0, the transaction will not time out.

Only enterprise beans with container-managed transactions are affected by the `timeout-in-seconds` property. For enterprise beans with bean-managed JTA transactions, you invoke the `setTransactionTimeout` method of the `User-Transaction` interface.

Isolation Levels

Transactions not only ensure the full completion (or rollback) of the statements that they enclose but also isolate the data modified by the statements. The *isolation level* describes the degree to which the data being updated is visible to other transactions.

Suppose that a transaction in one program updates a customer's phone number, but before the transaction commits, another program reads the same phone number. Will the second program read the updated and uncommitted phone number, or will it read the old one? The answer depends on the isolation level of the transaction. If the transaction allows other programs to read uncommitted data, performance may improve because the other programs don't have to wait until the transaction ends. But there's a trade-off: if the transaction rolls back, another program might read the wrong data.

For entity beans with container-managed persistence, you can change the isolation level by editing the `consistency` element in the `sun-cmp-mapping.xml` file. These beans use the default isolation level of the DBMS, which is usually `READ_COMMITTED`.

For entity beans with bean-managed persistence and for all session beans, you can set the isolation level programmatically by using the API provided by the underlying DBMS. A DBMS, for example, might allow you to permit uncommitted reads by invoking the `setTransactionIsolation` method:

```
Connection con;
...
con.setTransactionIsolation(TRANSACTION_READ_UNCOMMITTED);
```

Do not change the isolation level in the middle of a transaction. Usually, such a change causes the DBMS software to issue an implicit commit. Because the isolation levels offered by DBMS vendors may vary, you should check the DBMS documentation for more information. Isolation levels are not standardized for the J2EE platform.

Updating Multiple Databases

The J2EE transaction manager controls all enterprise bean transactions except for bean-managed JDBC transactions. The J2EE transaction manager allows an enterprise bean to update multiple databases within a transaction. The figures that follow show two scenarios for updating multiple databases in a single transaction.

In Figure 30–2, the client invokes a business method in `Bean-A`. The business method begins a transaction, updates Database X, updates Database Y, and invokes a business method in `Bean-B`. The second business method updates Database Z and returns control to the business method in `Bean-A`, which commits the transaction. All three database updates occur in the same transaction.

In Figure 30–3, the client calls a business method in `Bean-A`, which begins a transaction and updates Database X. Then `Bean-A` invokes a method in `Bean-B`, which resides in a remote J2EE server. The method in `Bean-B` updates Database Y. The transaction managers of the J2EE servers ensure that both databases are updated in the same transaction.

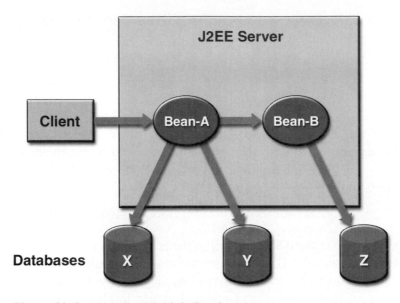

Figure 30–2 Updating Multiple Databases

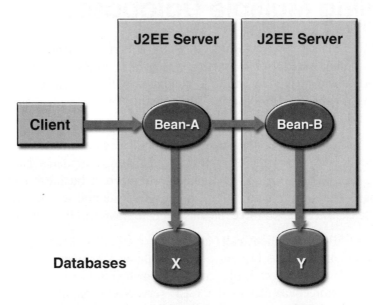

Figure 30–3 Updating Multiple Databases across J2EE Servers

Transactions in Web Components

You can demarcate a transaction in a Web component by using either the `java.sql.Connection` or `javax.transaction.UserTransaction` interface. These are the same interfaces that a session bean with bean-managed transactions can use. Transactions demarcated with the `Connection` interface are discussed in the section JDBC Transactions (page 1058), and those with the `UserTransaction` interface are discussed in the section JTA Transactions (page 1063). For an example of a Web component using transactions, see Accessing Databases (page 446).

31

Resource Connections

J 2EE components can access a wide variety of resources, including databases, mail sessions, Java Message Service objects, JAXR connection factories, and URLs. The J2EE platform provides mechanisms that allow you to access all these resources in a similar manner. This chapter describes how to get connections to several types of resources. Although the code samples in this chapter are from enterprise beans, they will also work in Web components.

JNDI Naming

In a distributed application, components need to access other components and resources such as databases. For example, a servlet might invoke remote methods on an enterprise bean that retrieves information from a database. In the J2EE platform, the Java Naming and Directory Interface (JNDI) naming service enables components to locate other components and resources. To locate a JDBC resource, for example, an enterprise bean invokes the JNDI `lookup` method. The JNDI naming service maintains a set of bindings that relate names to objects. The `lookup` method passes a JNDI name parameter and returns the related object.

JNDI provides a *naming context*, which is a set of name-to-object bindings. All naming operations are relative to a context. A name that is bound within a context is the JNDI name of the object. In Specifying a Resource Reference (page 1079), for example, the JNDI name for the JDBC resource (or data source) is `jdbc/ejbTutorialDB`. A `Context` object provides the methods for binding names to objects, unbinding names from objects, renaming objects, and listing the bindings. JNDI also provides subcontext functionality. Much like a directory in a file system, a *subcontext* is a context within a context. This hierarchical structure permits better organization of information. For naming services that support subcontexts, the `Context` class also provides methods for creating and destroying subcontexts.

For detailed information about JNDI, see *The JNDI Tutorial*:

```
http://java.sun.com/products/jndi/tutorial
```

Table 31–1 describes JNDI subcontexts for connection factories in the Application Server Platform Edition 8.

Note: To avoid collisions with names of other enterprise resources in the JNDI namespace, and to avoid portability problems, all names in a J2EE application should begin with the string `java:comp/env`.

Table 31–1 JNDI Subcontexts for Connection Factories

Resource Manager Type	Connection Factory Type	JNDI Subcontext
JDBC	`javax.sql.DataSource`	`java:comp/env/jdbc`
JMS	`javax.jms.TopicConnectionFactory` `javax.jms.QueueConnectionFactory`	`java:comp/env/jms`
JavaMail	`javax.mail.Session`	`java:comp/env/mail`
URL	`java.net.URL`	`java:comp/env/url`
Connector	`javax.resource.cci.ConnectionFactory`	`java:comp/env/eis`
JAXR Resource Adapter	`javax.xml.registry.ConnectionFactory`	`java:comp/env/eis/JAXR`

DataSource Objects and Connection Pools

To store, organize, and retrieve data, most applications use a relational database. J2EE components access relational databases through the JDBC API. For information on this API, see:

```
http://java.sun.com/docs/books/tutorial/jdbc
```

In the JDBC API, databases are accessed via `DataSource` objects. A `DataSource` has a set of properties that identify and describe the real world data source that it represents. These properties include information such as the location of the database server, the name of the database, the network protocol to use to communicate with the server, and so on. In the Application Server, a data source is called a JDBC resource.

Applications access a data source using a connection, and a `DataSource` object can be thought of as a factory for connections to the particular data source that the `DataSource` instance represents. In a basic `DataSource` implementation, a call to the `getConnection` method returns a connection object that is a physical connection to the data source.

If a `DataSource` object is registered with a JNDI naming service, an application can use the JNDI API to access that `DataSource` object, which can then be used to connect to the data source it represents.

`DataSource` objects that implement connection pooling also produce a connection to the particular data source that the `DataSource` class represents. The connection object that the `getConnection` method returns is a handle to a `PooledConnection` object rather than being a physical connection. An application uses the connection object in the same way that it uses a connection. Connection pooling has no effect on application code except that a pooled connection, like all connections, should always be explicitly closed. When an application closes a connection that is pooled, the connection is returned to a pool of reusable connections. The next time `getConnection` is called, a handle to one of these pooled connections will be returned if one is available. Because connection pooling avoids creating a new physical connection every time one is requested, it can help applications run significantly faster.

The Application Server is distributed with a connection pool named `PointBase-Pool`, which handles connections to the PointBase database server. In this book, all the code examples that access a database use `DataSource` objects that are mapped to `PointBasePool`.

Database Connections

The Application Server ships with a relational database product named Point-Base. The following material shows how the SavingsAccountBean example of Chapter 26 accesses a PointBase database. The SavingsAccountBean component is an entity bean with bean-managed persistence.

Session beans and Web components will use the same approach as Savings-AccountBean to access a database. (Entity beans with container-managed persistence are different. See Chapter 27.)

Coding a Database Connection

For the SavingsAccountBean example, the code that connects to the database is in the entity bean implementation class SavingsAccountBean. The source code for this class is in this directory:

```
<INSTALL>/j2eetutorial14/ejb/savingsaccount/src/
```

The bean connects to the database in three steps:

1. Specify the logical name of the database.
   ```
   private String dbName
       = "java:comp/env/jdbc/SavingsAccountDB";
   ```
   The java:comp/env portion of the logical name is the environment naming context of the component. The jdbc/SavingsAccountDB string is the *resource reference name* (sometimes referred to as the *coded name*). In deploytool, you specify the resource reference name and then map it to the JNDI name of the DataSource object.

2. Obtain the DataSource object associated with the logical name.
   ```
   InitialContext ic = new InitialContext();
   DataSource ds = (DataSource) ic.lookup(dbName);
   ```
   Given the logical name for the resource, the lookup method returns the DataSource object that is bound to the JNDI name in the directory.

3. Get the Connection object from the DataSource object.
   ```
   Connection con = ds.getConnection();
   ```

Specifying a Resource Reference

The application for the `SavingAccountBean` example is in the `SavingsAccount-App.ear` file, which is in this directory:

`<INSTALL>/j2eetutorial14/examples/ejb/provided-ears/`

For your convenience, the resource reference and JNDI names in `Savings-AccountApp.ear` have already been configured in `deploytool`. However, you may find it instructive to open `SavingsAccountApp.ear` in `deploytool` and follow these steps for specifying the resource reference.

1. In `deploytool`, select `SavingsAccountBean` from the tree.
2. Select the Resource Ref's tab.
3. Click Add.
4. In the Coded Name field, enter `jdbc/SavingsAccountDB`.
5. In the Type combo box, select `javax.sql.DataSource`.
6. In the Authentication combo box, select Container.
7. If you want other enterprise beans to share the connections acquired from the `DataSource`, select the Sharable checkbox.
8. To map the resource reference to the data source, enter `jdbc/ejbTutori-alDB` in the JNDI Name field.

If the preceding steps are followed, the Resource Ref's tab will appear as shown in Figure 31–1.

Creating a Data Source

In the preceding section, you map the resource reference to the JNDI name of the data source. The `deploytool` utility stores this mapping information in a deployment descriptor of `SavingsAccountBean`. In addition to setting the bean's deployment descriptor, you also must define the data source in the Application Server. You define a data source by using the Admin Console. To create the data source with the Admin Console, follow this procedure:

1. Open the URL `http://localhost:4848/asadmin` in a browser.
2. Expand the JDBC node.
3. Select the JDBC Resources node.

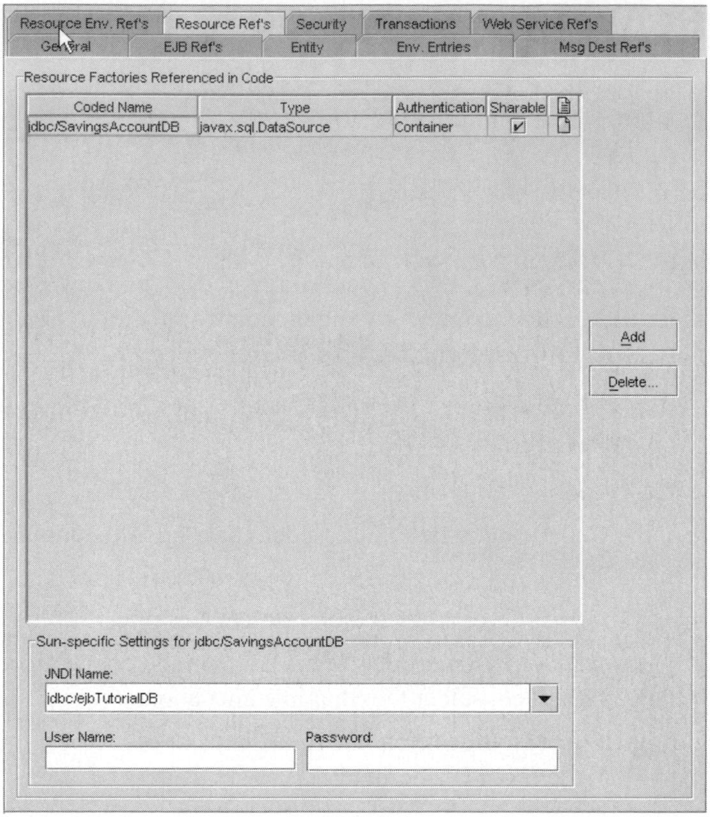

Figure 31–1 Resource Ref's Tabbed Pane of `SavingsAccountBean`

4. Click New.

5. Type `jdbc/ejbTutorialDB` in the JNDI Name field.

6. Choose `PointBasePool` from the Pool Name combo box.

7. Click OK.

8. Note that `jdbc/ejbTutorialDB` is listed under the JDBC Resources node.

Mail Session Connections

If you've ever ordered a product from a Web site, you've probably received an email confirming your order. The `ConfirmerBean` class demonstrates how to send email from an enterprise bean.

Note: The source code for this example is in this directory: *<INSTALL>*/j2ee-tutorial14/ejb/confirmer/src/.

In the sendNotice method of the ConfirmerBean class, the lookup method returns a Session object, which represents a mail session. Like a database connection, a mail session is a resource. In the Application Server, a mail session is called a JavaMail resource. As with any resource, you must link the coded name (mail/TheMailSession) with a JNDI name. Using the Session object as an argument, the sendNotice method creates an empty Message object. After calling several set methods on the Message object, sendNotice invokes the send method of the Transport class to send the message on its way. The source code for the sendNotice method follows.

```java
public void sendNotice(String recipient) {

    try {
        Context initial = new InitialContext();
        Session session =
            (Session) initial.lookup(
            "java:comp/env/mail/TheMailSession");

        Message msg = new MimeMessage(session);
        msg.setFrom();

        msg.setRecipients(Message.RecipientType.TO,
            InternetAddress.parse(recipient, false));

        msg.setSubject("Test Message from ConfirmerBean");

        DateFormat dateFormatter =
            DateFormat.getDateTimeInstance(
            DateFormat.LONG, DateFormat.SHORT);

        Date timeStamp = new Date();

        String messageText = "Thank you for your order." + '\n' +
            "We received your order on " +
            dateFormatter.format(timeStamp) + ".";

        msg.setText(messageText);
        msg.setHeader("X-Mailer", mailer);
        msg.setSentDate(timeStamp);
```

```
        Transport.send(msg);

    } catch(Exception e) {
        throw new EJBException(e.getMessage());
    }
}
```

Running the ConfirmerBean Example

Creating a Mail Session

To create a mail session in the Application Server using the Admin Console, follow these steps:

1. Open the URL `http://localhost:4848/asadmin` in a browser.
2. Select the JavaMail Sessions node.
3. Click New.
4. Type `mail/MySession` in the JNDI Name field.
5. Type the name of the host running your mail server in the Mail Host field.
6. Type the destination email address in the Default User field.
7. Type your email address in the Default Return Address field.
8. Click OK.
9. Note that `mail/MySession` is listed under the JavaMail Sessions node.

Deploying the Application

1. In `deploytool`, open the `ConfirmerApp.ear` file, which resides in this directory:

   `<INSTALL>/j2eetutorial14/examples/ejb/provided-ears/`

2. Verify the resource reference.

   a. In the tree, expand the `ConfirmerApp` node.

   b. Select the `ConfirmerBean` node.

   c. Select the Resource Ref's tab.

   d. Note the JavaMail resource reference for `mail/TheMailSession`.

3. Verify the mapping of the reference to the JNDI name.

   a. In the tree, select the `ConfirmerApp` node.

b. Click the Sun-specific Settings button.

c. Note the mapping of `mail/TheMailSession` (coded in `Confirmer-Bean.java`) to `mail/MySession`.

4. Deploy the `ConfirmerApp` application.

5. In the Deploy Module dialog box, do the following:

a. Select the Return Client JAR checkbox.

b. In the field below the check box, enter the following:

`<INSTALL>/j2eetutorial14/examples/ejb/confirmer`

Running the Client

To run the `SavingsAccountClient` program, do the following:

1. In a terminal window, go to this directory:

`<INSTALL>/j2eetutorial14/examples/ejb/confirmer/`

2. Type the following command on a single line:

`appclient -client ConfirmerAppClient.jar` *your_email_address*

3. The client should display the following lines:

```
. . .
Sending email to . . .
. . .
```

To modify this example, see the instructions in Modifying the J2EE Application (page 870).

URL Connections

A uniform resource locator (URL) specifies the location of a resource on the Web. The `HTMLReaderBean` class shows how to connect to a URL from within an enterprise bean.

Note: The source code for this example is in this directory: `<INSTALL>/j2eetutorial14/ejb/htmlreader/src/`.

The `getContents` method of the `HTMLReaderBean` class returns a `String` that contains the contents of an HTML file. This method looks up the `java.net.URL` object associated with a coded name (url/MyURL), opens a connection to it, and then reads its contents from an InputStream. Here is the source code for the getContents method.

```java
public StringBuffer getContents() throws HTTPResponseException
{

    Context context;
    URL url;
    StringBuffer buffer;
    String line;
    int responseCode;
    HttpURLConnection connection;
    InputStream input;
    BufferedReader dataInput;

    try {
        context = new InitialContext();
        url = (URL)context.lookup("java:comp/env/url/MyURL");
        connection = (HttpURLConnection)url.openConnection();
        responseCode = connection.getResponseCode();
    } catch (Exception ex) {
        throw new EJBException(ex.getMessage());
    }

    if (responseCode != HttpURLConnection.HTTP_OK) {
        throw new HTTPResponseException("HTTP response code: " +
            String.valueOf(responseCode));
    }

    try {
        buffer = new StringBuffer();
        input = connection.getInputStream();
        dataInput =
            new BufferedReader(new InputStreamReader(input));
        while ((line = dataInput.readLine()) != null) {
            buffer.append(line);
            buffer.append('\n');
        }
    } catch (Exception ex) {
        throw new EJBException(ex.getMessage());
    }
    return buffer;
}
```

Running the HTMLReaderBean Example

The coded name (url/MyURL) must be mapped to a JNDI name (a URL string). In the provided HTMLReaderApp application, the mapping has already been specified. The next section shows you how to verify the mapping in deploytool.

Deploying the Application

1. In deploytool, open the HTMLReaderApp.ear file, which resides in this directory:

   <INSTALL>/j2eetutorial14/examples/ejb/provided-ears/

2. Verify the resource reference.

   a. In the tree, expand the HTMLReaderApp node.

   b. Select the HTMLReaderBean node.

   c. Select the Resource Ref's tab.

   d. Note the URL resource reference for url/MyURL.

3. Verify the mapping of the reference to the JNDI name.

   a. In the tree, select the HTMLReaderApp node.

   b. Click the Sun-specific Settings button.

   c. Note the mapping of url/MyURL (coded in HTMLReaderBean.java) to this URL:

   http://localhost:8080/index.html

4. Deploy the HTMLReaderApp application.

5. In the Deploy Module dialog box, do the following:

   a. Select the Return Client JAR checkbox.

   b. In the field below the check box, enter the following:

   <INSTALL>/j2eetutorial14/examples/ejb/htmlreader

Running the Client

To run the HTMLReaderClient program, do the following:

1. In a terminal window, go to this directory:

   <INSTALL>/j2eetutorial14/examples/ejb/htmlreader/

2. Type the following command on a single line:

   ```
   appclient -client HTMLReaderAppClient.jar
   ```

3. The client should display the source of the HTML file at this URL:

   ```
   http://localhost:8080/index.html
   ```

Further Information

For information on creating JMS resources, see Creating JMS Administered Objects (page 1178). For information on creating JAXR resources, see Creating JAXR Resources (page 429).

32

Security

THE J2EE application programming model insulates developers from mechanism-specific implementation details of application security. The J2EE platform provides this insulation in a way that enhances the portability of applications, allowing them to be deployed in diverse security environments.

Some of the material in this chapter assumes that you understand basic security concepts. To learn more about these concepts, we recommend that you explore `http://java.sun.com/j2se/1.4.2/docs/guide/security/index.html` before you begin this chapter.

Overview

J2EE and Web services applications are made up of components that can be deployed into different containers. These components are used to build a multi-tier enterprise application. Security for components is provided by their containers. A container provides two kinds of security: declarative and programmatic security.

Declarative security expresses an application's security structure, including security roles, access control, and authentication requirements, in a form external to the application (in a deployment descriptor). *Programmatic security* is embedded in an application and is used to make security decisions. Programmatic security is useful when declarative security alone is not sufficient to express the security model of an application.

J2EE applications consist of components that can contain both protected and unprotected resources. Often, you need to protect resources to ensure that only authorized users have access. *Authorization* provides controlled access to protected resources. Authorization is based on identification and authentication. *Identification* is a process that enables recognition of an entity by a system, and *authentication* is a process that verifies the identity of a user, device, or other entity in a computer system, usually as a prerequisite to allowing access to resources in a system.

Authorization and authentication are not required for an entity to access unprotected resources. Accessing a resource without authentication is referred to as *unauthenticated* or *anonymous* access.

Realms, Users, Groups, and Roles

A J2EE user is similar to an operating system user. Typically, both types of users represent people. However, these two types of users are not the same. The J2EE server authentication service has no knowledge of the user name and password you provide when you log on to the operating system. The J2EE server authentication service is not connected to the security mechanism of the operating system. The two security services manage users that belong to different realms.

The J2EE server's authentication service includes and interacts with the following components:

- *Realm*: A collection of users and groups that are controlled by the same authentication policy.
- *User*: An individual (or application program) identity that has been defined in the Sun Java System Application Server Platform Edition 8.0. Users can be associated with a group.
- *Group*: A set of authenticated *users*, classified by common traits, defined in the Application Server.
- *Role:* An abstract name for the permission to access a particular set of resources in an application. A *role* can be compared to a key that can open a lock. Many people might have a copy of the key. The lock doesn't care who you are, only that you have the right key.

The J2EE server authentication service can govern users in multiple realms. In this release of the Sun Java System Application Server Platform Edition 8.0, the `file` and `certificate` realms come preconfigured for the Application Server.

When using the `file` realm, the server authentication service verifies user identity by checking the `file` realm. This realm is used for the authentication of all clients except for Web browser clients that use the HTTPS protocol and certificates.

A J2EE user of the `file` realm can belong to a J2EE group. (A user in the `certificate` realm cannot.) A *J2EE group* is a category of users classified by common traits, such as job title or customer profile. For example, most customers of an e-commerce application might belong to the CUSTOMER group, but the big spenders would belong to the PREFERRED group. Categorizing users into groups makes it easier to control the access of large numbers of users. The section EJB-Tier Security (page 1142) explains how to control user access to enterprise beans.

When the authentication service is using the `certificate` realm, certificates are used with the HTTPS protocol to authenticate Web browser clients. To verify the identity of a user in the `certificate` realm, the authentication service verifies an X.509 certificate. For step-by-step instructions for creating this type of certificate, see Understanding Digital Certificates (page 1115). The common name field of the X.509 certificate is used as the principal name.

Managing Users

To add authorized users to the Application Server, follow these steps:

1. Start the Application Server if you haven't already done so. Information on starting the Application Server is available in Starting and Stopping the Application Server (page 25).
2. Start the Admin Console if you haven't already done so. You can start the Admin Console by starting a Web browser and browsing to `http://localhost:4848/asadmin`. If you changed the default Admin port during installation, enter the correct port number in place of `4848`.
3. Enter the user name and password provided during installation.
4. Expand the Security node in the Admin Console tree.
5. Expand the Realms node.
6. Select the `file` realm.
7. Click the Manage Users button.
8. Click New to add a new user to the `file` realm.
9. Enter the correct information into the User ID, Password, and Group(s) fields. Click OK to add this user to the list of users in the `file` realm.
10. Click Logout when you have completed this task.

Setting Up Security Roles

When you design an enterprise bean or Web component, you should always think about the kinds of users who will access the component. For example, a Web application for a human resources department might have a different request URL for someone who has been assigned the role of admin than for someone who has been assigned the role of director. The admin role may let you view some employee data, but the director role enables you to view salary information. Each of these *security roles* is an abstract logical grouping of users that is defined by the person who assembles the application. When an application is deployed, the deployer will map the roles to security identities in the operational environment, as shown in Figure 32–1.

A J2EE group also represents a category of users, but it has a different scope from a role. A J2EE group is designated for the entire Application Server, whereas a role is associated only with a specific application in the Application Server.

To create a role for a Web application, see Setting Security Requirements Using deploytool (page 1095).

To create a role for a J2EE application, declare it for the application EAR file. For example, you could use the following procedure to create a role using deploytool:

1. Select an application.
2. In the Roles tabbed pane, click Add to add a row to the table.
3. In the Name column, enter the security role name—for example, bankCustomer.
4. Click the folded-paper icon to add a description of the security role—for example, Customer-of-Bank.
5. Click OK.

Before you can map the role to users or groups (see Mapping Roles to Users and Groups, page 1090), you must first create those users or groups (see Managing Users, page 1089).

Mapping Roles to Users and Groups

When you are developing a J2EE application, you don't need to know what categories of users have been defined for the realm in which the application will be run. In the J2EE platform, the security architecture provides a mechanism for automatically mapping the roles defined in the application to the users or groups defined in the runtime realm. After your application has been deployed, the administrator of the Application Server will map the roles of the application to the users or groups of the file realm, as shown in Figure 32–1.

Use deploytool to map roles defined for an application to J2EE users, groups, or both:

1. Add authorized users and groups to the file realm using the Admin Console as discussed in Managing Users (page 1089). You must define the users and groups for the Application Server before you can map them to application security roles.

2. Create or open the Web application in deploytool. Creating an application using deploytool is discussed in Packaging Web Modules (page 88).

3. Select the Web application in the deploytool tree. Select the Security tabbed pane. We use the Security tabbed pane to add a security constraint to the Web application. If you would like more information on security constraints, read Protecting Web Resources (page 1094). Click Add Constraint to add a security constraint to this application.

4. Click Add Collections to add a Web resource collection to this application.

5. Click Edit Roles to select which roles are authorized to access restricted parts of this application.

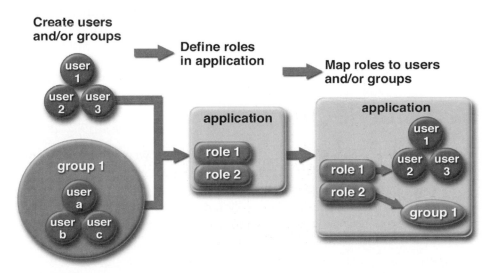

Figure 32–1 Role Mapping

6. Click Edit Roles in the Authorized Roles for Security Constraint dialog box.

7. Click Add to add a new role. Click in the cell that is created under Name. For this example, add the roles of CUSTOMER and MANAGER. Click OK to exit this dialog box.

8. Add both roles to the list of authorized roles by selecting each in turn and clicking Add.

9. Click OK to exit the Authorized Roles dialog box.

10. Select the General tabbed pane.

11. Select Sun-specific Settings.

12. To map the users defined for the Application Server to roles defined for this application, select User to Role Mapping from the View list.

13. Select a role name—for example, MANAGER—in the Roles pane. These are the role names you defined in the Authorized Roles for Security Constraint dialog box.

14. Click the Edit button under either Users or Groups. (If you do not see the users or groups that you defined for the Application Server, you may need to log on to the Admin Server before continuing.) Use this dialog box to select a specific user or group to map to the MANAGER role. Then click Add. If you selected a user, the name of the user will display in the Users Name pane when the MANAGER role is selected in the Role Name pane. If you selected a group, the name of the group will display in the Groups Name pane when the MANAGER role is selected. When you defined users using the Admin Console, you provided them with a name, password, and group. Any users assigned to the group selected in this step will have access to the restricted Web application.

Web-Tier Security

Security in a Web application is configured in the Web application deployment descriptor using deploytool. When the settings are entered in deploytool, they are saved to the deployment descriptor contained in the WAR. To view the generated deployment descriptor, choose Descriptor Viewer from deploytool's Tools menu. For more information on deployment descriptors, see Chapter 3.

After a WAR is created, select the Security tabbed pane to configure its security elements. See Setting Security Requirements Using deploytool (page 1095) for more information on using deploytool to accomplish these tasks:

- User authentication method: The User Authentication Method box on the Security tab of deploytool enables you to specify how the user is prompted to log in. If specified, the user must be authenticated before it can access any resource that is constrained by a security constraint. The User Authentication Method options are discussed in Understanding Login Authentication (page 1100).

- Security constraints: The Security Constraint option is used to define the access privileges to a collection of resources using their URL mapping. Security constraints are discussed in Protecting Web Resources (page 1094).

- Web resource collections: The Web Resource Collections option is part of a security constraint and describes a URL pattern and HTTP method pair that refers to resources that need to be protected. Web resource collections are discussed in Protecting Web Resources (page 1094).

- Network security requirement: The Network Security Requirement option is used to configure HTTP basic or form-based authentication over SSL. Select a network security requirement for each security constraint. Network security requirements are discussed in What Is Secure Socket Layer Technology? (page 1114).

- Authorized roles: The Authorized Roles section is used to specify which roles that have been defined for an application are authorized to access this Web resource collection. The roles defined for the application must be mapped to users and groups defined on the server. Authorized roles are discussed in Setting Up Security Roles (page 1090).

These elements of the deployment descriptor can be entered directly into the web.xml file or can be created using an application deployment tool, such as deploytool. This section describes how to create the deployment descriptor using deploytool.

Depending on the Web server, some of the elements of Web application security must be addressed in Web server configuration files rather than in the deployment descriptor for the Web application. This information is discussed in Installing and Configuring SSL Support (page 1114), Using Programmatic Security in the Web Tier (page 1098), and Setting Up Security Roles (page 1090).

Protecting Web Resources

You protect Web resources by specifying a security constraint. A *security constraint* determines who is authorized to access a *Web resource collection*, which is a list of URL patterns and HTTP methods that describe a set of resources to be protected. Security constraints are defined using an application deployment tool, such as `deploytool`, as discussed in Setting Security Requirements Using deploytool (page 1095) or in a deployment descriptor.

If you try to access a protected Web resource as an unauthenticated user, the Web container will try to authenticate you. The container will accept the request only after you have proven your identity to the container and have been granted permission to access the resource.

Security constraints work only on the original request URI and not on calls made via a `RequestDispatcher` (which include `<jsp:include>` and `<jsp:forward>`). Inside the application, it is assumed that the application itself has complete access to all resources and would not forward a user request unless it had decided that the requesting user also had access.

Many applications feature unprotected Web content, which any caller can access without authentication. In the Web tier, you provide unrestricted access simply by not configuring a security constraint for that particular request URI. It is common to have some unprotected resources and some protected resources. In this case, you will define security constraints and a login method, but they will not be used to control access to the unprotected resources. Users won't be asked to log on until the first time they enter a protected request URI.

In the Java Servlet specification, the request URI is the part of a URL *after* the host name and port. For example, let's say you have an e-commerce site with a browsable catalog that you would want anyone to be able to access, and a shopping cart area for customers only. You could set up the paths for your Web application so that the pattern `/cart/*` is protected but nothing else is protected. Assuming that the application is installed at context path `/myapp`, the following are true:

- `http://localhost:8080/myapp/index.jsp` is *not* protected.
- `http://localhost:8080/myapp/cart/index.jsp` *is* protected.

A user will not be prompted to log in until the first time that user accesses a resource in the `cart/` subdirectory.

To set up a security constraint, see the section Setting Security Requirements Using deploytool (page 1095).

Setting Security Requirements Using deploytool

To set security requirements for a WAR, select the WAR in the `deploytool` tree, and then select the Security tabbed pane. In the Security tabbed pane, you can define how users are authenticated to the server and which users have access to particular resources. Follow these steps:

1. Choose the authentication method. Authentication refers to the method by which a client verifies the identity of a user to a server. The authentication methods supported in this release are shown next and are discussed in more detail in Understanding Login Authentication (page 1100). Select one of the following authentication methods from the Authentication Method list:

   - None
   - Basic
   - Client Certificate
   - Digest
   - Form Based

   If you selected `Basic` or `Digest` from the list, click Settings to go to the User Authentication Settings dialog box and enter the realm name in the Realm Name field (valid choices include `file` and `certificate`). If you selected `Form Based`, click Settings to go to the User Authentication Settings dialog box and enter or select the values for Realm Name, Login Page, and Error Page.

2. Define a security constraint. In the Security Constraints section of the screen, you can define the security constraints for accessing the content of your WAR file. Click the Add Constraint button adjacent to the Security Constraints field to add a security constraint. Double-click the cell containing the security constraint to change its name. Each security constraint consists of the following pieces:

   a. A Web resource collection, which describes a URL pattern and HTTP method pair that refer to resources that need to be protected.

   b. An authorization constraint, which is a set of roles that are defined to have access to the Web resource collection.

   c. A user data constraint, which defines whether a resource is accessed with confidentiality protection, integrity protection, or no protection.

3. Define a Web resource collection for this security constraint. With the security constraint selected, click the Add Collections button adjacent to the Web Resource Collections field to add a Web resource collection to the security constraint. A Web resource collection is part of a security constraint and describes a URL pattern and HTTP method pair that refer to resources that need to be protected. Double-click the cell containing the Web resource collection to edit its name.

4. Edit the contents of the Web resource collection by selecting it in the list and then clicking the Edit Contents button. The Edit Contents dialog box displays. Use it to add individual files or whole directories to the Web resource collection, to add a URL pattern, or to specify which HTTP methods will be governed by this Web resource collection.

   a. Select the files and directories that you want to add to the Web resource collection in the top text field, and then click the Add button to add them to the Web resource collection.

   b. Add URL patterns to the Web resource collection by clicking Add URL and entering the URL in the edit field. For example, specify /* to protect all resources.

   c. Select the options from the HTTP Methods list that need to be added to the Web application. The options are `Delete`, `Get`, `Head`, `Options`, `Post`, `Put`, and `Trace`.

   d. Click OK to return to the Security tabbed pane. The contents of the Web resource collection display in the box beside the Edit Contents button.

5. Select the proper option from the Network Security Requirement list for this security constraint. The choices are `None`, `Integral`, and `Confidential`.

   a. Specify `NONE` when the application does not require a security constraint.

   b. Specify `CONFIDENTIAL` when the application requires that data be transmitted so as to prevent other entities from observing the contents of the transmission.

   c. Specify `INTEGRAL` when the application requires that the data be sent between client and server in such a way that it cannot be changed in transit.

   If you specify `CONFIDENTIAL` or `INTEGRAL` as a security constraint, that type of security constraint applies to all requests that match the URL patterns in the Web resource collection and not just to the login dialog box.

For further discussion on network security requirements, see What Is Secure Socket Layer Technology? (page 1114).

6. Select which roles are authorized to access the secure application. In the Authorized Roles pane, click Edit to specify which defined roles are authorized to access this secure application.

   Select the role for which you want to authorize access from the list of Roles, and click the Add button to add it to the list of Authorized Roles.

   If roles have not been defined for this application, click the Edit Roles button and add the roles for this application. If you add roles in this fashion, make sure to map the roles to the appropriate users and groups. For more information on role mapping, see Mapping Roles to Users and Groups (page 1090).

7. To add security specifically to a JSP page or to a servlet in the application, select the JSP page or servlet in the `deploytool` tree and select the Security tab. For more information on the options displayed on this page, see Declaring and Linking Role References (page 1098).

   You can view the resulting deployment descriptor by selecting the WAR file in the `deploytool` tree and then selecting Descriptor Viewer from the Tools menu.

Specifying a Secure Connection

When the login authentication method is set to BASIC or FORM, passwords are not protected, meaning that passwords sent between a client and a server on a non-protected session can be viewed and intercepted by third parties.

To configure HTTP basic or form-based authentication over SSL, specify CONFIDENTIAL or INTEGRAL as the network security requirement on the WAR's Security page in `deploytool`. Specify CONFIDENTIAL when the application requires that data be transmitted so as to prevent other entities from observing the contents of the transmission. Specify INTEGRAL when the application requires that the data be sent between client and server in such a way that it cannot be changed in transit.

If you specify CONFIDENTIAL or INTEGRAL as a security constraint, that type of security constraint applies to all requests that match the URL patterns in the Web resource collection and not just to the login dialog box.

If the default configuration of your server does not support SSL, you must configure it using an SSL connector to make this work. By default, the Sun Java System Application Server Platform Edition 8.0 is configured with an SSL connector. To set up an SSL connector on other servers, see Installing and Configuring SSL Support (page 1114).

Note: Good Security Practice: If you are using sessions, after you switch to SSL you should never accept any further requests for that session that are non-SSL. For example, a shopping site might not use SSL until the checkout page, and then it may switch to using SSL in order to accept your card number. After switching to SSL, you should stop listening to non-SSL requests for this session. The reason for this practice is that the session ID itself was not encrypted on the earlier communications. This is not so bad when you're only doing your shopping, but after the credit card information is stored in the session, you don't want a bad guy trying to fake the purchase transaction against your credit card. This practice could be easily implemented using a filter.

Using Programmatic Security in the Web Tier

Web-tier programmatic security consists of the following methods of the `Http-ServletRequest` interface:

- `getRemoteUser`: Determines the user name with which the client authenticated.
- `isUserInRole`: Determines whether a user is in a specific security role.
- `getUserPrincipal`: Returns a `java.security.Principal` object.

Your application can make security decisions based on the output of these APIs.

Declaring and Linking Role References

A *security role reference* allows a Web component to reference an existing security role. A security role is an application-specific logical grouping of users, classified by common traits such as customer profile or job title. When an application is deployed, roles are mapped to security identities, such as *principals* (identities assigned to users as a result of authentication) or groups, in the operational environment. Based on this, a user with a certain security role has associated access rights to a Web application. The link is the actual name of the security role that is being referenced.

During application assembly, the assembler creates security roles for the application and associates these roles with available security mechanisms. The assembler then resolves the security role references in individual servlets and JSP pages by linking them to roles defined for the application.

The security role reference defines a mapping between the name of a role that is called from a Web component using `isUserInRole(String name)` and the name of a security role that has been defined for the application. For example, the mapping of the security role reference `cust` to the security role with the role name `bankCustomer` is shown in the following example.

1. Select the Web component in the `deploytool` tree.
2. Select the Security tab.
3. Select Add Constraints and Add Collections to add a security constraint and Web resource collection. Adding a security constraint enables the Edit Roles button.
4. Select the Edit Roles button to open the Authorized Roles dialog box. Click the Edit Roles button to open the Edit Roles dialog box. Click Add to add an authorized role to this application.
5. Click in the edit box and enter a role—for example, `admin` or `loginUser`. If you haven't added any users, refer to Managing Users (page 1089) for information on how to do so. Select OK to close this dialog box.
6. Select the role you just added in the left pane, and click Add to add it to the list of authorized roles for this application. Click OK to close this dialog box. The role you added displays in the list of Authorized Roles on the Security tabbed pane.

Now that you've set up a role for this application, you map it to the list of users and groups set up for the Application Server. To do this, follow these steps:

1. Log on to the `localhost:4848` by double-clicking it in the `deploytool` tree. If you skip this step, the roles defined for the Application Server will not be displayed in subsequent steps.
2. Select the General tabbed pane.
3. Select Sun-specific Settings.
4. Select User to Role Mapping from the View list to map the users defined for the Application Server to roles defined for this application.

5. Select a role name in the Roles pane. These are the role names currently defined in the Authorized Roles for Security Constraint dialog box.

6. Click the Edit button under either Users or Groups. Use this dialog box to select a specific user or group to map to this role. Then click Add. If you selected a user, the name of the user will display in the Users Name pane when the role is selected in the Roles pane. If you selected a group, the name of the group will display in the Groups pane when that role is selected. When you defined users using the Admin Console, you provided them with a name, password, and group. Any users assigned to the group selected in this step will have access to the restricted Web application.

7. Select OK and then Close.

8. Select Save from the File menu to save these changes.

When you use the `isUserInRole(String role)` method, the String `role` is mapped to the role name defined in the Authorized Roles section of the WAR file's Security tabbed pane.

Understanding Login Authentication

When you try to access a protected Web resource, the Web container activates the authentication mechanism that has been configured for that resource. You can specify the following authentication mechanisms:

- HTTP basic authentication
- Form-based login authentication
- Client certificate authentication
- Mutual authentication
- Digest authentication

If you do not specify one of these mechanisms, the user will not be authenticated.

Using HTTP Basic Authentication

Figure 32–2 shows what happens if you specify *HTTP basic authentication*.

With basic authentication, the following things occur:

1. A client requests access to a protected resource.

2. The Web server returns a dialog box that requests the user name and password.

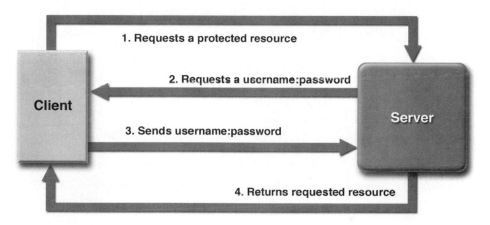

Figure 32–2 HTTP Basic Authentication

> 3. The client submits the user name and password to the server.
>
> 4. The server validates the credentials and, if successful, returns the requested resource.

HTTP basic authentication is not particularly secure. Basic authentication sends user names and passwords over the Internet as text that is uu-encoded (Unix-to-Unix encoded) but not encrypted. This form of authentication, which uses Base64 encoding, can expose your user names and passwords unless all connections are over SSL. If someone can intercept the transmission, the user name and password information can easily be decoded.

Example: Basic Authentication with JAX-RPC (page 1126) is an example application that uses HTTP basic authentication in a JAX-RPC service.

Using Form-Based Authentication

Figure 32–3 shows what happens if you specify *form-based authentication*, in which you can customize the login screen and error pages that an HTTP browser presents to the end user.

With form-based authentication, the following things occur:

> 1. A client requests access to a protected resource.
>
> 2. If the client is unauthenticated, the server redirects the client to a login page.
>
> 3. The client submits the login form to the server.
>
> 4. If the login succeeds, the server redirects the client to the resource. If the login fails, the client is redirected to an error page.

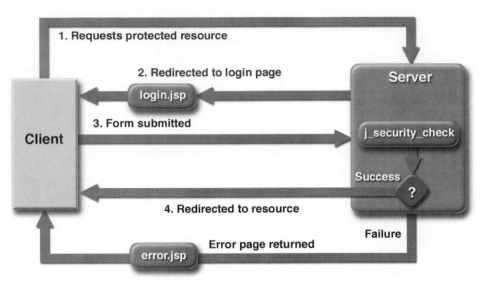

Figure 32–3 Form-Based Authentication

Form-based authentication is not particularly secure. In form-based authentication, the content of the user dialog box is sent as plain text, and the target server is not authenticated. This form of authentication can expose your user names and passwords unless all connections are over SSL. If someone can intercept the transmission, the user name and password information can easily be decoded.

Example: Using Form-Based Authentication (page 1105) is an example application that uses form-based authentication.

Using Client-Certificate Authentication

Client-certificate authentication is a more secure method of authentication than either basic or form-based authentication. It uses HTTP over SSL, in which the server and, optionally, the client authenticate one another using public key certificates. *Secure Socket Layer* (SSL) provides data encryption, server authentication, message integrity, and optional client authentication for a TCP/IP connection. You can think of a *public key certificate* as the digital equivalent of a passport. It is issued by a trusted organization, which is called a *certificate authority* (CA), and provides identification for the bearer.

If you specify client-certificate authentication, the Web server will authenticate the client using the client's *X.509 certificate*, a public key certificate that conforms to a standard that is defined by X.509 Public Key Infrastructure (PKI). Before running an application that uses SSL, you must configure SSL support on the server (see Installing and Configuring SSL Support, page 1114) and set up the public key certificate (see Understanding Digital Certificates, page 1115).

Example: Client-Certificate Authentication over HTTP/SSL with JAX-RPC (page 1133) describes an example application that uses client-certificate authentication.

Using Mutual Authentication

With *mutual authentication*, the server and the client authenticate each other. There are two types of mutual authentication:

- Certificate-based mutual authentication (see Figure 32–4)
- User name- and password-based mutual authentication (see Figure 32–5)

Figure 32–4 shows what occurs during certificate-based mutual authentication.

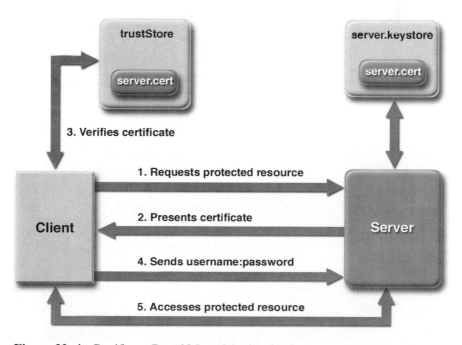

Figure 32–4 Certificate-Based Mutual Authentication

In certificate-based mutual authentication, the following things occur:

1. A client requests access to a protected resource.
2. The Web server presents its certificate to the client.
3. The client verifies the server's certificate.
4. If successful, the client sends its certificate to the server.
5. The server verifies the client's credentials.
6. If successful, the server grants access to the protected resource requested by the client.

Example: Client-Certificate Authentication over HTTP/SSL with JAX-RPC (page 1133) describes an example application that uses certificate-based mutual authentication.

Figure 32–5 shows what occurs during user name- and password-based mutual authentication.

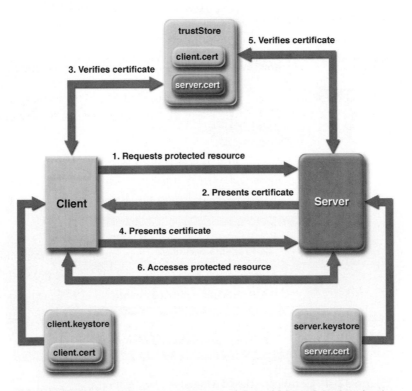

Figure 32–5 User Name- and Password-Based Mutual Authentication

In user name- and password-based mutual authentication, the following things occur:

1. A client requests access to a protected resource.
2. The Web server presents its certificate to the client.
3. The client verifies the server's certificate.
4. If successful, the client sends its user name and password to the server, which verifies the client's credentials.
5. If the verification is successful, the server grants access to the protected resource requested by the client.

Using Digest Authentication

Like HTTP basic authentication, HTTP digest authentication authenticates a user based on a user name and a password. However, the authentication is performed by transmitting the password in an encrypted form which is much more secure than the simple base64 encoding used by basic authentication. Because digest authentication is not currently in widespread use, there is no further discussion of it in this document.

Configuring Authentication

To configure the authentication mechanism that the Web resources in a WAR will use, select the WAR in the `deploytool` tree. Select the Security tabbed pane, and then proceed as follows:

1. Select one of the user authentication methods described earlier.
2. Specify a security realm. If omitted, the `file` realm is assumed. Select the Settings button beside the User Authentication Mechanism field to specify the realm.
3. If the authentication method is specified as form-based, specify a form login page and form error page. Select the Settings button beside the User Authentication Mechanism field to specify the login page and the error page to be used for form-based authentication.

Example: Using Form-Based Authentication

In this section, we discuss how to add form-based authentication to a basic JSP page. With form-based authentication, you can customize the login screen and error pages that are presented to the Web client for authentication of their user name and password. If the topic of authentication is new to you, please refer to the section Understanding Login Authentication (page 1100).

The example application discussed in this tutorial can be found in `<INSTALL>/ j2eetutorial14/examples/security/formbasedauth/`. In general, the following steps are necessary to add form-based authentication to a Web client. In the example application included with this tutorial, most of these steps have been completed for you and are listed here to show what needs to be done should you wish to create a similar application.

1. Map the role name to the appropriate users and groups defined for the Application Server. See Adding Authorized Users (page 1106) for more information on needed modifications.

2. Edit the `build.properties` file. The `build.properties` file needs to be modified because the properties in this file are specific to your installation of the Application Server and J2EE 1.4 Tutorial. See Building the Examples (page xli) for information on which properties need to be set.

3. Create the Web client. For this example, the Web client, a very simple JSP page, is already created. The client is discussed in Creating a Web Client for Form-Based Authentication (page 1107).

4. Create the login form and login error form pages. For this example, these files are already created. These pages are discussed in Creating the Login Form and Error Page (page 1107).

5. Add the appropriate security elements using `deploytool`. See Specifying Security Elements for Form-Based Authentication (page 1108) for information on which settings need to be made.

6. Build, package, deploy, and run the Web application (see Building, Packaging, Deploying, and Running the Form-Based Authentication Example, page 1109). You will use the `asant` tool to compile the example application and to run the client. You will use `deploytool` to package and deploy the server.

Adding Authorized Users

This example application will be configured to authorize access for users assigned to the role of `loginUser`. To specify which users can assume that role and can access the protected parts of the application, you must map this role to users and groups defined for the Application Server.

When the Application Server is started, it reads the settings in its configuration files. When a constrained resource is accessed, the Application Server verifies that the user name and password are authorized to access that resource before granting access to the requester. The roles that are authorized to access a resource are specified in the security constraint for that application.

Information for adding users to the Application Server is provided in Managing Users (page 1089). For this example, create a new user and assign that user to the group `loginUser`. For information about the steps required to map the user assigned to the *group* of `loginUser` as defined on the Application Server to the role of `loginUser` authorized to access this application, see Adding Security to the Form-Based Example (page 1110).

Creating a Web Client for Form-Based Authentication

The Web client is a standard JSP page. None of the code that adds form-based authentication to the example is included in the Web client. The information that adds the form-based authentication to this example is specified in the deployment descriptor, which is created with `deploytool`. The code for the JSP page used in this example, `formbasedauth/web/index.jsp`, is listed next. The running application is shown later in Figure 32–7.

```
<html>
<head><title>Hello</title></head>
<body bgcolor="white">

<img src="duke.waving.gif">
<h2>My name is Duke.</h2>
<h2><font color="black">Hello,
    ${pageContext.request.userPrincipal.name}!</font></h2>
</body>
</html>
```

Creating the Login Form and Error Page

When you create a form-based login mechanism, you must specify which JSP page contains the form to obtain the user name and password to verify access. You also must specify which page is displayed if login authentication fails. This section discusses how to create the login form and error page. Adding Security to the Form-Based Example (page 1110) discusses how to specify these pages when you are setting up form-based authentication.

The login page can be an HTML page, a JSP page, or a servlet, and it must return an HTML page containing a form that conforms to specific naming conventions (see the Java Servlet 2.4 specification for more information on these requirements). The content of the login form in an HTML page, JSP page, or servlet for a login page should be coded as follows:

```
<form method=post action="j_security_check" >
 <input type="text"  name= "j_username" >
 <input type="password"  name= "j_password" >
</form>
```

The full code for the login page used in this example can be found at *<INSTALL>/* j2eetutorial14/examples/security/formbasedauth/web/logon.jsp. An example of the running login form page is shown later in Figure 32–6.

The login error page is displayed if the user enters a user name and password combination that is not authorized to access the protected URI. For this example, the login error page can be found at *<INSTALL>*/j2eetutorial14/examples/ security/formbasedauth/web/logonError.jsp. Here is the code for this page:

```
<%@ taglib uri="http://java.sun.com/jsp/jstl/core"
    prefix="c" %>
<html>
<head>
<title>
    Login Error
</title>
</head>
<body>
    <c:url var="url" value="/index.jsp"/>
    <p><a href="${url}">Try again.</a></p>
</body>
</html>
```

Specifying Security Elements for Form-Based Authentication

To enable form-based authentication, you add the following elements to this application using deploytool.

- A security constraint, which is used to define the access privileges to a collection of resources using their URL mapping.

- A Web resource collection, which is used to identify a subset of the resources within a Web application to which a security constraint applies. In this example, by specifying a URL pattern of /*, we are specifying that all resources in this application are protected.
- An authorized roles list, which indicates the user roles that should be permitted access to this resource collection. In this example, it is users assigned the role of loginUser. If no role name is provided, no user is allowed to access the portion of the Web application described by the security constraint.
- A user authentication method, which is used to choose the form-based login method and configure parameters of the method. The login page parameter provides the URI of a Web resource relative to the document root that will be used to authenticate the user. The error page parameter requires a URI of a Web resource relative to the document root that sends a response when authentication has failed.

In the Application Server, these security elements are added to the application using deploytool, after the application has been packaged. Information on adding the security elements to this application using deploytool is discussed in Adding Security to the Form-Based Example (page 1110).

Building, Packaging, Deploying, and Running the Form-Based Authentication Example

To build, package, deploy, and run the security/formbasedauth example, which uses form-based authentication, follow these steps.

Building the Form-Based Authentication Example

1. Follow the instructions in Building the Examples (page xli).
2. Follow the instructions in Adding Authorized Users (page 1106).
3. Go to the *<INSTALL>*/j2eetutorial14/examples/security/formbased-auth/ directory.
4. Build the Web application by entering the following command at the terminal window or command prompt:

```
asant build
```

Packaging the Web Application

1. Start the Application Server if you have not already done so. For information on starting the Application Server, see Starting and Stopping the Application Server (page 25).

2. Start `deploytool`. Information on starting `deploytool` can be found in Starting the deploytool Utility (page 27).

3. Package the `formbasedauth` example using `deploytool` following these steps. More detail on packaging Web applications can be found in Packaging Web Modules (page 88).

   a. Select File→New→Web Component from the `deploytool` menu.

   b. Select Next from the Introduction page.

   c. Select the Create New Stand-Alone WAR Module radio button.

   d. In the WAR Location field, browse to the `<INSTALL>`/j2ee-`tutorial14/examples/security/formbasedauth/` directory and create the file `formbasedauth.war`. Give the WAR the name `FormBasedAuth`.

   e. Enter `/formbasedauth` in the Context Root field.

   f. Click Edit Contents to add the contents of the application to the WAR file. Select the `formbasedauth/` directory from the Starting Directory list. Select each of the files `index.jsp`, `logon.jsp`, `logonError.jsp`, and `duke.waving.gif` from the `build/` directory, and then click Add. Click OK to close this dialog box.

   g. Click Next.

   h. Select JSP.

   i. Click Next.

   j. Select `index.jsp` in the JSP File Name field.

   k. Click Next.

   l. Click Finish. The `FormBasedAuth` example displays in the `deploytool` tree.

   m. Select Save from the File menu to save the Web component.

Adding Security to the Form-Based Example

To add form-based authentication to your application, select the application in the `deploytool` tree and then follow these steps:

1. Select the Security tabbed pane.

2. Select `Form Based` in the User Authentication Method field.

3. Select the Settings button. Set the following properties in this dialog box:

    a. Set Realm Name to `file`.

    b. Select `logon.jsp` from the Login Page list.

    c. Select `logonError.jsp` from the Login Error Page list.

    d. Click OK.

4. Select Add Constraints to add a security constraint to this example.

5. Select Add Collections to add a Web resource collection to this example.

6. With the security constraint and Web resource collection selected, click the Edit Contents button.

7. In the Edit Contents dialog box, select Add URL Pattern. In the edit box, make sure that the URL pattern reads `/*`. Click OK to close this dialog box. Using a URL pattern of `/*` and selecting no HTTP patterns means that all files and methods in this application are protected and may be accessed only by a user who provides an authorized login.

8. Click OK.

9. Click Edit Roles on the Security tabbed pane and then Edit Roles again in the Authorized Roles dialog box. Click Add, and then enter the role `loginUser` in the Name column. This is the authorized role for this security constraint. Click OK to close this dialog box.

10. Select `loginUser` in the left pane and click Add to add it to the list of authorized roles for this application. Select OK to close this dialog box.

The next step is to map the authorized role of `loginUser`, as defined in the application, to the group of `loginUser` that is defined for the Application Server. To do this, follow these steps:

1. Select the General tabbed pane.

2. Click the Sun-specific Settings button.

3. In the Sun-specific Settings dialog box, select User to Role Mappings from the View list.

4. Select `loginUser` from the list of roles.

5. Click the Edit button under the Group box.

6. Select `loginUser` from the Available Groups list, and then click the Add button to map the role of `loginUser` (defined for the application) to the group of `loginUser` (defined for the Application Server). Click OK.

Note: If you don't see the list of users or groups that you defined using the Admin Console, connect to the Admin Server by double-clicking `localhost:4848` in the `deploytool` tree and entering your admin user name and password. If this is not the current target server, change to this server by selecting it and then selecting File→Set Current Target Server.

---

7. Click Close to return to the General tabbed pane.

8. Select File→Save to save these changes.

After all the security elements have been added, view the generated deployment descriptor by selecting Tools→Descriptor Viewer→Descriptor Viewer from the `deploytool` menu.

Deploying the Web Application

Deploy the Web application by following these steps:

1. Select the `FormBasedAuth` application in the `deploytool` tree.

2. Select Tools→Deploy.

3. Make sure the server is correct.

4. Enter your admin user name and password.

5. Click OK.

6. Click the Close button after the messages indicating successful completion are finished.

Running the Web Application

Run the Web client by entering the following URL in your Web browser:

```
http://localhost:8080/formbasedauth
```

The login form displays in the browser, as shown in Figure 32–6. Enter a user name and password combination that corresponds to the role of `loginUser`, and then click the Submit button.

If you entered `Debbie` as the name and if there is a user defined for the Application Server with the user name of `Debbie` that also matches the password you entered and is assigned to the group of `loginUser` that we mapped to the role of `loginUser`, the display will appear as in Figure 32–7.

Figure 32–6   Form-Based Login Page

Figure 32–7   The Running Form-Based Authentication Example

Note: For repetitive testing of this example, you may need to close and reopen your browser.

Using Authentication with SSL

Passwords are not protected for confidentiality with HTTP basic or form-based authentication, meaning that passwords sent between a client and a server on an unprotected session can be viewed and intercepted by third parties. To overcome this limitation, you can run these authentication protocols over an SSL-protected session and ensure that all message content is protected for confidentiality. To configure HTTP basic or form-based authentication over SSL, specify CONFI-DENTIAL or INTEGRAL as the network security requirement on the WAR's Security pane in deploytool. Read the section Specifying a Secure Connection (page 1097) for more information.

Installing and Configuring SSL Support

What Is Secure Socket Layer Technology?

Secure Socket Layer (SSL) technology allows Web browsers and Web servers to communicate over a secure connection. In this secure connection, the data that is being sent is encrypted before being sent and then is decrypted upon receipt and before processing. Both the browser and the server encrypt all traffic before sending any data. SSL addresses the following important security considerations.

- *Authentication*: During your initial attempt to communicate with a Web server over a secure connection, that server will present your Web browser with a set of credentials in the form of a server certificate. The purpose of the certificate is to verify that the site is who and what it claims to be. In some cases, the server may request a certificate that the client is who and what it claims to be (which is known as client authentication).

- *Confidentiality*: When data is being passed between the client and the server on a network, third parties can view and intercept this data. SSL responses are encrypted so that the data cannot be deciphered by the third party and the data remains confidential.

- *Integrity*: When data is being passed between the client and the server on a network, third parties can view and intercept this data. SSL helps guarantee that the data will not be modified in transit by that third party.

To install and configure SSL support on your stand-alone Web server, you need the following components. SSL support is already provided if you are using the

Application Server. If you are using a different Web server, consult the documentation for your product.

- A server certificate keystore (see Understanding Digital Certificates, page 1115).
- An HTTPS connector (see Configuring the SSL Connector, page 1122).

To verify that SSL support is enabled, see Verifying SSL Support (page 1122).

Understanding Digital Certificates

> **Note:** Digital certificates for the Application Server have been generated already and can be found in the directory *<J2EE_HOME>*/domains/domain1/config/. These digital certificates are self-signed and are intended for use in a development environment; they are not intended for production purposes. For production purposes, generate your own certificates and have them signed by a CA.

To use SSL, an application server must have an associated certificate for each external interface, or IP address, that accepts secure connections. The theory behind this design is that a server should provide some kind of reasonable assurance that its owner is who you think it is, particularly before receiving any sensitive information. It may be useful to think of a certificate as a "digital driver's license" for an Internet address. It states with which company the site is associated, along with some basic contact information about the site owner or administrator.

The digital certificate is cryptographically signed by its owner and is difficult for anyone else to forge. For sites involved in e-commerce or in any other business transaction in which authentication of identity is important, a certificate can be purchased from a well-known certificate authority (CA) such as VeriSign or Thawte.

Sometimes authentication is not really a concern—for example, an administrator may simply want to ensure that data being transmitted and received by the server is private and cannot be snooped by anyone eavesdropping on the connection. In such cases, you can save the time and expense involved in obtaining a CA certificate and simply use a self-signed certificate.

SSL uses *public key cryptography*, which is based on *key pairs*. Key pairs contain one public key and one private key. If data is encrypted with one key, it can be decrypted only with the other key of the pair. This property is fundamental to establishing trust and privacy in transactions. For example, using SSL, the server computes a value and encrypts the value using its private key. The encrypted value is called a *digital signature*. The client decrypts the encrypted value using the server's public key and compares the value to its own computed value. If the two values match, the client can trust that the signature is authentic, because only the private key could have been used to produce such a signature.

Digital certificates are used with the HTTPS protocol to authenticate Web clients. The HTTPS service of most Web servers will not run unless a digital certificate has been installed. Use the procedure outlined later to set up a digital certificate that can be used by your Web server to enable SSL.

One tool that can be used to set up a digital certificate is keytool, a key and certificate management utility that ships with the J2SE SDK. It enables users to administer their own public/private key pairs and associated certificates for use in self-authentication (where the user authenticates himself or herself to other users or services) or data integrity and authentication services, using digital signatures. It also allows users to cache the public keys (in the form of certificates) of their communicating peers. For a better understanding of keytool and public key cryptography, read the keytool documentation at the following URL:

```
http://java.sun.com/j2se/1.4.2/docs/tooldocs/solaris/
keytool.html
```

Creating a Server Certificate

A server certificate has been created already for the Application Server. The certificate can be found in the *<J2EE_HOME>*/domains/domain1/config/ directory. The server certificate is in keystore.jks. The cacerts.jks file contains all the trusted certificates, including client certificates.

If necessary, you can use keytool to generate certificates. The keytool stores the keys and certificates in a file termed a *keystore*, a repository of certificates used for identifying a client or a server. Typically, a keystore contains one client or one server's identity. The default keystore implementation implements the keystore as a file. It protects private keys by using a password.

The keystores are created in the directory from which you run keytool. This can be the directory where the application resides, or it can be a directory common to many applications. If you don't specify the keystore file name, the keystores are created in the user's home directory.

To create a server certificate follow these steps:

1. Create the keystore.
2. Export the certificate from the keystore.
3. Sign the certificate.
4. Import the certificate into a *trust-store*: a repository of certificates used for verifying the certificates. A trust-store typically contains more than one certificate. An example using a trust-store for SSL-based mutual authentication is discussed in Example: Client-Certificate Authentication over HTTP/SSL with JAX-RPC (page 1133).

Run `keytool` to generate the server keystore, which we will name `server-keystore.jks`. This step uses the alias `server-alias` to generate a new public/private key pair and wrap the public key into a self-signed certificate inside `server-keystore.jks`. The key pair is generated using an algorithm of type RSA, with a default password of `changeit`. For more information on key-tool options, see its online help at `http://java.sun.com/j2se/1.4.2/docs/tooldocs/solaris/keytool.html`.

Note: RSA is public-key encryption technology developed by RSA Data Security, Inc. The acronym stands for Rivest, Shamir, and Adelman, the inventors of the technology.

From the directory in which you want to create the keystore, run `keytool` with the following parameters. When you press Enter, `keytool` prompts you to enter the server name, organizational unit, organization, locality, state, and country code. Note that you must enter the server name in response to `keytool`'s first prompt, in which it asks for first and last names. For testing purposes, this can be `localhost`. The host specified in the keystore must match the host identified in the host variable specified in the `<INSTALL>/j2eetutorial14/examples/common/build.properties`.

1. Generate the server certificate.

```
<JAVA_HOME>\bin\keytool -genkey -alias server-alias
-keyalg RSA -keypass changeit -storepass changeit
-keystore keystore.jks
```

2. Export the generated server certificate in keystore.jks into the file server.cer.

   <JAVA_HOME>\bin\keytool -export -alias server-alias
   -storepass changeit -file server.cer -keystore keystore.jks

3. If you want to have the certificate signed by a CA, read Signing Digital Certificates (page 1118) for more information.

4. To create the trust-store file cacerts.jks and add the server certificate to the trust-store, run keytool from the directory where you created the key-store and server certificate. Use the following parameters:

   <JAVA_HOME>\bin\keytool -import -v -trustcacerts
   -alias server-alias -file server.cer
   -keystore cacerts.jks -keypass changeit
   -storepass changeit

   Information on the certificate, such as that shown next, will display.

   ```
   <INSTALL>/j2eetutorial14/examples/gs 60% keytool -import
   -v -trustcacerts -alias server-alias -file server.cer
   -keystore cacerts.jks -keypass changeit -storepass changeit
   Owner: CN=localhost, OU=Sun Micro, O=Docs, L=Santa Clara,
   ST=CA, C=US
   Issuer: CN=localhost, OU=Sun Micro, O=Docs, L=Santa Clara,
   ST=CA, C=US
   Serial number: 3e932169
   Valid from: Tue Apr 08
   Certificate fingerprints:
   MD5: 52:9F:49:68:ED:78:6F:39:87:F3:98:B3:6A:6B:0F:90
   SHA1: EE:2E:2A:A6:9E:03:9A:3A:1C:17:4A:28:5E:97:20:78:3F:
   Trust this certificate? [no]:
   ```

5. Enter yes, and then press the Enter or Return key. The following information displays:

   ```
   Certificate was added to keystore
   [Saving cacerts.jks]
   ```

Signing Digital Certificates

After you've created a digital certificate, you will want to have it signed by its owner. After the digital certificate has been cryptographically signed by its owner, it is difficult for anyone else to forge. For sites involved in e-commerce or any other business transaction in which authentication of identity is important, a certificate can be purchased from a well-known certificate authority such as VeriSign or Thawte.

As mentioned earlier, if authentication is not really a concern, you can save the time and expense involved in obtaining a CA certificate and simply use the self-signed certificate.

Using a Different Server Certificate with the Application Server

After you have created your own server certificate, had it signed by a CA, and are ready to use it with the Application Server, follow these steps. You will use `keytool` to import the certificate into `keystore.jks`.

1. Export the certificate into a certificate file using `keytool -export`:

   ```
   keytool -export [-v] [-rfc] [-alias <alias>] [-file <cert_
   file>]
   [-keystore <keystore>] [-storepass <storepass>]
   [-storetype <storetype>] [-provider <provider_class_name>]
   ```

   Here is an example:

   ```
   keytool -export -alias myalias -file
   _my_exported_file -keystore whereever_your_cert_resides.jks
   ```

2. Then use the `keytool -import` command to import it:

   ```
   keytool -import [-v] [-noprompt] [-trustcacerts] [-alias
   <alias>]
   [-file <cert_file>] [-keypass <keypass>]
   [-keystore <keystore>] [-storepass <storepass>]
   [-storetype <storetype>] [-provider <provider_class_name>]
   ```

   Here is an example:

   ```
   keytool -import -alias myalias -file _my_exported_file
   -keystore   domains/domain1/config/keystore.jks   -storepass
   changeit
   ```

Note: Your key/certificate password in `keystore.jks` should match your key-store.jks password. This is a bug. If there is a mismatch, the Java SDK cannot read the certificate and you get a "tampered" message.

Another option is to replace the existing `keystore.jks`. To do it this way, you must either change your keystore's password to the default password or change the default password to your keystore's password:

- Change your keystore's password to the default of `changeit`.
- Use the following as your system properties in the file `domain.xml`:

```
-Djavax.net.ssl.keystore=point_to_your_keystore
-Djavax.net.ssl.keyStorePassword=your_password
```

Creating a Client Certificate for Mutual Authentication

This section discusses setting up client-side authentication. When both server-side and client-side authentication are enabled, it is called mutual, or two-way, authentication. In client authentication, clients are required to submit certificates that are issued by a certificate authority that you choose to accept. From the directory where you want to create the client certificate, run `keytool` as outlined here. When you press Enter, `keytool` prompts you to enter the server name, organizational unit, organization, locality, state, and country code.

Note: You must enter the *server name* in response to `keytool`'s first prompt, in which it asks for first and last names. For testing purposes, this can be `localhost`. The host specified in the keystore must match the host identified in the `host` variable specified in the `<INSTALL>`/j2eetutorial14/examples/common/ `build.properties` file. If this example is to verify mutual authentication and you receive a runtime error stating that the HTTPS host name is wrong, re-create the client certificate, being sure to use the same host name that you will use when running the example. For example, if your machine name is duke, then enter duke as the certificate CN or when prompted for first and last names. When accessing the application, enter a URL that points to the same location—for example, `https:// duke:1043/mutualauth/hello`. This is necessary because during SSL handshake, the server verifies the client certificate by comparing the certificate name and the host name from which it originates.

To create a keystore named `client-keystore.jks` that contains a client certificate named `client.cer`, follow these steps:

1. Generate the client certificate.

```
<JAVA_HOME>\bin\keytool -genkey -alias client-alias -keyalg
RSA -keypass changeit -storepass changeit
-keystore keystore.jks
```

2. Export the generated client certificate into the file `client.cer`.

```
<JAVA_HOME>\bin\keytool -export -alias client-alias
-storepass changeit -file client.cer -keystore keystore.jks
```

3. Add the certificate to the trust-store file `<J2EE_HOME>/domains/domain1/config/cacerts.jks`. Run keytool from the directory where you created the keystore and client certificate. Use the following parameters:

```
<JAVA_HOME>\bin\keytool -import -v -trustcacerts
-alias client-alias -file client.cer
-keystore <J2EE_HOME>/domains/domain1/config/cacerts.jks
-keypass changeit
-storepass changeit
```

The `keytool` utility returns this message:

```
Owner: CN=J2EE Client, OU=Java Web Services, O=Sun, L=Santa
Clara, ST=CA, C=US
Issuer: CN=J2EE Client, OU=Java Web Services, O=Sun, L=Santa
Clara, ST=CA, C=US
Serial number: 3e39e66a
Valid from: Thu Jan 30 18:58:50 PST 2003 until: Wed Apr 30
19:58:50 PDT 2003
Certificate fingerprints:
MD5: 5A:B0:4C:88:4E:F8:EF:E9:E5:8B:53:BD:D0:AA:8E:5A
SHA1:90:00:36:5B:E0:A7:A2:BD:67:DB:EA:37:B9:61:3E:26:B3:89:
46:
32
Trust this certificate? [no]: yes
Certificate was added to keystore
```

For an example application that uses mutual authentication, see Example: Client-Certificate Authentication over HTTP/SSL with JAX-RPC (page 1133). For information on verifying that mutual authentication is running, see Verifying That Mutual Authentication Is Running (page 1124).

Miscellaneous Commands for Certificates

To check the contents of a keystore that contains a certificate with an alias `server-alias`, use this command:

```
keytool -list -keystore keystore.jks -alias server-alias -v
```

To check the contents of the `cacerts` file, use this command:

```
keytool -list -keystore cacerts.jks
```

Configuring the SSL Connector

An SSL connector is preconfigured for the Application Server. You do not have to configure anything. If you are working with another application server, see its documentation for setting up its SSL connector.

Verifying SSL Support

For testing purposes, and to verify that SSL support has been correctly installed, load the default introduction page with a URL that connects to the port defined in the server deployment descriptor:

```
https://localhost:1043/
```

The `https` in this URL indicates that the browser should be using the SSL protocol. The `localhost` in this example assumes that you are running the example on your local machine as part of the development process. The `1043` in this example is the secure port that was specified where the SSL connector was created in Configuring the SSL Connector (page 1122). If you are using a different server or port, modify this value accordingly.

The first time a user loads this application, the New Site Certificate or Security Alert dialog box displays. Select Next to move through the series of dialog boxes, and select Finish when you reach the last dialog box. The certificates will display only the first time. When you accept the certificates, subsequent hits to this site assume that you still trust the content.

Tips on Running SSL

The SSL protocol is designed to be as efficient as securely possible. However, encryption and decryption are computationally expensive processes from a performance standpoint. It is not strictly necessary to run an entire Web application over SSL, and it is customary for a developer to decide which pages require a secure connection and which do not. Pages that might require a secure connection include login pages, personal information pages, shopping cart checkouts, or any pages where credit card information could possibly be transmitted. Any page within an application can be requested over a secure socket by simply prefixing the address with `https:` instead of `http:`. Any pages that absolutely require a secure connection should check the protocol type associated with the page request and take the appropriate action if `https:` is not specified.

Using name-based virtual hosts on a secured connection can be problematic. This is a design limitation of the SSL protocol itself. The SSL *handshake*, where the client browser accepts the server certificate, must occur before the HTTP request is accessed. As a result, the request information containing the virtual host name cannot be determined before authentication, and it is therefore not possible to assign multiple certificates to a single IP address. If all virtual hosts on a single IP address need to authenticate against the same certificate, the addition of multiple virtual hosts should not interfere with normal SSL operations on the server. Be aware, however, that most client browsers will compare the server's domain name against the domain name listed in the certificate, if any (this is applicable primarily to official, CA-signed certificates). If the domain names do not match, these browsers will display a warning to the client. In general, only address-based virtual hosts are commonly used with SSL in a production environment.

Enabling Mutual Authentication over SSL

This section discusses setting up client-side authentication. As mentioned earlier, when both server-side and client-side authentication are enabled, it is called mutual, or two-way, authentication. In client authentication, clients are required to submit certificates that are issued by a certificate authority that you choose to accept. If you regulate it through the application (via the `Client-Certificate` authentication requirement), the check is performed when the application requires client authentication. You must enter the keystore location and password in the Web server configuration file to enable SSL, as discussed in Configuring the SSL Connector (page 1122).

Here are two ways to enable mutual authentication over SSL:

- *PREFERRED*: Set the method of authentication to `Client-Certificate` using `deploytool`. This enforces mutual authentication by modifying the deployment descriptor of the given application. By enabling client authentication in this way, client authentication is enabled only for a specific resource controlled by the security constraint. Setting client authentication in this way is discussed in Example: Client-Certificate Authentication over HTTP/SSL with JAX-RPC (page 1133).

- *RARELY*: Set the `clientAuth` property in the `certificate` realm to `true`. To do this, follow these steps:

  a. Start the Application Server if you haven't already done so. Information on starting the Application Server can be found in Starting and Stopping the Application Server (page 25).

b. Start the Admin Console. Information on starting the Admin Console can be found in Starting the Admin Console (page 27).

c. In the Admin Console tree, expand Security, then expand Realms, and then select `certificate`. The `certificate` realm is used for all transfers over HTTP with SSL.

d. Select Add to add the property of `clientAuth` to the server. Enter `clientAuth` in the Name field, and enter `true` in the Value field.

e. Click Save to save these new properties.

f. Log out of the Admin Console.

When client authentication is enabled in both of these ways, client authentication will be performed twice.

Verifying That Mutual Authentication Is Running

You can verify that mutual authentication is working by obtaining debug messages. This should be done at the client end, and this example shows how to pass a system property in `targets.xml` so that `targets.xml` forks a client with `javax.net.debug` in its system properties, which could be added in a file such as *<INSTALL>*`/j2eetutorial14/examples/security/common/targets.xml`.

To enable debug messages for SSL mutual authentication, pass the system property `javax.net.debug=ssl,handshake`, which will provide information on whether or not mutual authentication is working. The following example modifies the `run-mutualauth-client` target from the *<INSTALL>*`/j2eetutorial14/examples/security/common/targets.xml` file by adding `sysproperty` as shown in bold:

```
<target name="run-mutualauth-client"
description="Runs a client with mutual authentication over
SSL">
  <java classname="${client.class}" fork="yes" >
    <arg line="${key.store} ${key.store.password}
          ${trust.store} ${trust.store.password}
          ${endpoint.address}" />
    <sysproperty key="javax.net.debug" value="ssl,
          handshake" />
    <sysproperty key="javax.net.ssl.keyStore"
          value="${key.store}" />
    <sysproperty key="java.net.ssl.keyStorePassword"
          value="${key.store.password}"/>
    <classpath refid="run.classpath" />
  </java>
</target>
```

XML and Web Services Security

XML and Web services security can include transport-level security and message-level security. This section discusses transport-level security. Information about using message-level security may be included in future releases of The J2EE Tutorial.

Transport-level security is security addressed by the transport layer. Adding security in this way is discussed in the following example sections:

- Example: Basic Authentication with JAX-RPC (page 1126)
- Example: Client-Certificate Authentication over HTTP/SSL with JAX-RPC (page 1133)

Authentication verifies the identity of a user, device, or other entity in a computer system, usually as a prerequisite to allowing access to resources in a system. There are several ways in which this can happen. The following ways are discussed in this section.

One approach is that a user authentication method can be defined for an application in its deployment descriptor. When a user authentication method is specified for an application, the Web container activates the specified authentication mechanism when you attempt to access a protected resource. The options for user authentication methods are discussed in Understanding Login Authentication (page 1100). The example application discussed in Example: Basic Authentication with JAX-RPC (page 1126) shows how to add basic authentication to a JAX-RPC application. The example discussed in Example: Client-Certificate Authentication over HTTP/SSL with JAX-RPC (page 1133) shows how to add client-certificate, or mutual, authentication to a JAX-RPC application.

A second approach is that a transport guarantee can be defined for an application in its deployment descriptor. Use this method to run over an SSL-protected session and ensure that all message content is protected for confidentiality. The options for transport guarantees are discussed in Specifying a Secure Connection (page 1097). An example application that discusses running over an SSL-protected session is discussed in Example: Client-Certificate Authentication over HTTP/SSL with JAX-RPC (page 1133).

When running over an SSL-protected session, the server and client can authenticate one another and negotiate an encryption algorithm and cryptographic keys before the application protocol transmits or receives its first byte of data.

SSL technology allows Web browsers and Web servers to communicate over a secure connection. In this secure connection, the data is encrypted before being sent, and then is decrypted upon receipt and before processing. Both the browser and the server encrypt all traffic before sending any data. For more information, see What Is Secure Socket Layer Technology? (page 1114).

Digital certificates are necessary when running HTTP over SSL (HTTPS). The HTTPS service of most Web servers will not run unless a digital certificate has been installed. Digital certificates have been created already for the Application Server.

Example: Basic Authentication with JAX-RPC

In this section, we discuss how to configure JAX-RPC-based Web service applications for HTTP basic authentication. With *HTTP basic authentication*, the Web server authenticates a user by using the user name and password obtained from the Web client. If the topic of authentication is new to you, please refer to the section titled Understanding Login Authentication (page 1100). For an explanation of how basic authentication works, see Figure 32–2 (page 1101).

For this tutorial, we begin with the example application in `<INSTALL>/` `j2eetutorial14/examples/jaxrpc/staticstub/` and `<INSTALL>/` `j2eetutorial14/examples/jaxrpc/helloservice/` and add user name and password authentication. The resulting application can be found in the directories `<INSTALL>/j2eetutorial14/examples/security/basicauth/` and `<INSTALL>/j2eetutorial14/examples/security/basicauthclient/`.

In general, the following steps are necessary to add basic authentication to a JAX-RPC application. In the example application included with this tutorial, many of these steps have been completed for you and are listed here to show what needs to be done should you wish to create a similar application.

1. Add the appropriate security elements using `deploytool`. For this example, the security elements are added in the packaging and deployment phase. Refer to Adding Basic Authentication Using deploytool (page 1131) for more information.

2. If the default port value is changed from 8080, see Setting the Port (page 314) for information on updating the example files to reflect this change. The WAR files mentioned in this tutorial will not work if the port has been changed.

3. Edit the `<INSTALL>`/j2eetutorial14/examples/common/ `build.properties` file. The `build.properties` file needs to be modified because the properties in this file are specific to your installation. See Building the Examples (page xli) for information on which properties need to be set.

4. Set security properties in the client code. For the example application, this step has been completed. The code for this example is shown in Setting Security Properties in the Client Code (page 1127).

5. Build, package, deploy, and run the Web service. You will use the `asant` tool to compile the client and service, and `deploytool` to package and deploy the service. Instructions for this example can be found in Building, Packaging, Deploying, and Running the Example for Basic Authentication (page 1128).

Setting Security Properties in the Client Code

The source code for the client is in the `HelloClient.java` file of the `<INSTALL>`/j2eetutorial14/examples/security/basicauthclient/src/ directory. For basic authentication, the client code must set `username` and `password` properties. The `username` and `password` properties correspond to the `admin` group (which includes the user name and password combination entered during installation) and the role of `admin`, which is provided in the application deployment descriptor as an authorized role for secure transactions. (See Setting Up Security Roles, page 1090.)

The client sets the aforementioned security properties as shown in the following code. The code in bold is the code that has been added from the original version of the `jaxrpc/staticstub` example application.

```
package basicauthclient;

import javax.xml.rpc.Stub;

public class HelloClient {

    public static void main(String[] args) {

        if (args.length !=3) {
        System.out.println("HelloClient Error: Wrong
            number of runtime arguments!");
        System.exit(1);
        }
```

```
                String username=args[0];
                String password=args[1];
                String endpointAddress=args[2];

                // print to display for verification purposes
                System.out.println("username: " + username);
                System.out.println("password: " + password);
                System.out.println("Endpoint address = " +
                    endpointAddress);



        try {
          Stub stub = createProxy();
              stub._setProperty(
                javax.xml.rpc.Stub.USERNAME_PROPERTY,
                    username);
              stub._setProperty(
                javax.xml.rpc.Stub.PASSWORD_PROPERTY,
                    password);
              stub._setProperty
                (javax.xml.rpc.Stub.ENDPOINT_ADDRESS_PROPERTY,
                endpointAddress);

          HelloIF hello = (HelloIF)stub;
          System.out.println(hello.sayHello("Duke (secure)"));
          } catch (Exception ex) {
              ex.printStackTrace();
          }
        }

        private static Stub createProxy() {
           // Note: MyHelloService_Impl is implementation-specific.
           return (Stub)(new
                MyHelloService_Impl().getHelloIFPort());
        }
    }
```

Building, Packaging, Deploying, and Running the Example for Basic Authentication

To build, package, deploy, and run the security/basicauth example using basic authentication, follow these steps.

Building the Basic Authentication Service

1. Set up your system for running the tutorial examples if you haven't done so already by following the instructions in Building the Examples (page xli).

2. From a terminal window or command prompt, go to the *<INSTALL>*/ j2eetutorial14/examples/security/basicauth/ directory.

3. Build the JAX-RPC service by entering the following at the terminal window or command prompt in the basicauth/ directory (this and the following steps that use asant assume that you have the executable for asant in your path; if not, you will need to provide the fully qualified path to the executable). This command runs the target named build in the build.xml file.

   ```
   asant build
   ```

Packaging the Basic Authentication Service

You can package the basic authentication example using deploytool, or you can just open the WAR file located in the *<INSTALL>*/j2eetutorial14/examples/ security/provided-wars/basicauth.war file. This section shows the steps you use to package the JAX-RPC service. More detail on packaging JAX-RPC services can be found in Packaging the Service (page 318).

1. Start the Application Server if you haven't already done so. Instructions for starting the Application Server can be found in Starting and Stopping the Application Server (page 25).

2. Start deploytool if you haven't already done so. Information on starting deploytool can be found in Starting the deploytool Utility (page 27).

3. Select File→New→Web Component from the deploytool menu. The wizard displays the following dialog boxes.

   a. Introduction dialog box

      1. Read the explanatory text for an overview of the wizard's features.

      2. Click Next.

   b. WAR File dialog box

      1. Select the button labeled Create New Stand-Alone WAR Module.

      2. In the WAR Location field, enter *<INSTALL>*/j2eetutorial14/ examples/security/basicauth/BasicAuth.war.

3. In the WAR Display Field, enter `BasicAuth`.

4. In the Context Root field, enter `/basicauth-jaxrpc`.

5. Click Edit Contents.

6. From the Starting Directory list, select the `<INSTALL>/`
   `j2eetutorial14/examples/security/basicauth/` directory.

7. Select the `build/` subdirectory.

8. Click Add.

9. Click OK.

10. Click Next.

c. Choose Component Type dialog box

1. Select the Web Services Endpoint button.

2. Click Next.

d. Choose Service dialog box

1. In the WSDL File combo box, select `WEB-INF/wsdl/`
   `MyBasicHelloService.wsdl`.

2. In the Mapping File combo box, select `build/mapping.xml`.

3. Click Next.

e. Component General Properties dialog box

1. In the Service Endpoint Implementation combo box, select
   `basicauth.HelloImpl`.

2. Click Next.

f. Web Service Endpoint dialog box

1. In the Service Endpoint Interface combo box, select
   `basicauth.HelloIF`.

2. In the Namespace field, select `urn:Foo`.

3. In the Local Part field, select `HelloIFPort`. The `deploytool` utility
   will enter a default endpoint address URI in this dialog box. It must
   be updated later in this section.

4. Click Next.

5. Click Finish.

To access `MyHelloService`, the tutorial clients will specify this service
endpoint address URI:

`http://localhost:8080/basicauth-jaxrpc/hello`

The /basicauth-jaxrpc string is the context root of the servlet that implements MySecureHelloService. The /hello string is the servlet alias.

4. Specify the endpoint address as follows:

   a. In deploytool, select HelloImpl.

   b. Select the Aliases tab.

   c. In the Component Aliases table, add /hello. (Don't forget the forward slash.)

   d. On the Endpoint tab, select hello for the endpoint address in the Sun-specific Settings frame.

   e. Select File→Save.

Adding Basic Authentication Using deploytool

For HTTP basic authentication, the application deployment descriptor, web.xml, includes the information on who is authorized to access the application, which URL patterns and HTTP methods are protected, and what type of user authentication method this application uses. This information is added to the deployment descriptor using deploytool. Its contents are discussed in more detail in Web-Tier Security (page 1092) and in the Java Servlet specification, which can be browsed or downloaded online at http://java.sun.com/products/servlet/.

   1. Select the basic authentication example, BasicAuth, in the deploytool tree.

   2. Select the Security tabbed pane.

   3. Select Basic in the User Authentication Method field.

   4. Select Add Constraints to add a security constraint.

   5. Select Add Collection to add a Web resource collection.

   6. Select the Web resource collection from the list, and then select Edit Collections.

   7. Select Add URL Pattern. Enter /hello in the text field. Click OK.

   8. Select the HTTP GET and POST methods.

   9. Click OK to close the Edit Contents dialog box.

   10. Select Edit Roles on the Security tabbed pane to specify an authorized role for this application.

11. Click Edit Roles in the Authorized Roles dialog box to add an authorized user to this application. Click Add in the Edit Roles dialog box and add the Name of `admin`. Click OK to close this dialog box.

12. Select `admin` under the Roles In field, and then click Add to add it to the list of authorized roles for this application. Click OK to close the dialog box.

Note that the Authorized Roles list specifies `admin`, a group that was specified during installation. To map this role to a user, follow these steps.

1. Select the General tabbed pane.

2. Click the Sun-specific Settings button.

3. In the Sun-specific Settings dialog box, select User to Role Mappings from the View list.

4. Select `admin` from the list of roles.

5. Click the Edit button under the Users box.

6. Select `admin` from the Available Users list, and then click the Add button to map the role of `admin` (defined for the application) to the user named `admin` (defined for the Application Server). Click OK.

Note: If you don't see the list of users or groups that you defined using the Admin Console, connect to the Admin Server by double-clicking `localhost:4848` in the `deploytool` tree and entering your admin user name and password. If this is not the current target server, change to this server by selecting it and then selecting File→Set Current Target Server.

---

7. Click Close to return to the General tabbed pane.

8. Select Save from the File menu to save these settings.

Deploying the Basic Authentication Service

1. Start the Application Server if you have not already done so.

2. To deploy the WAR that contains the JAX-RPC service, select the `BasicAuth` application in the `deploytool` tree. Then select Tools→ Deploy.

3. Make sure the server is correct, `localhost:4848` by default.

4. Enter your admin user name and password.

5. Click OK.

6. Click the Close button after the messages indicating successful completion are finished.

Building and Running the Basic Authentication Client

To build the JAX-RPC client, do the following:

1. Enter the following command at the terminal window or command prompt in the `basicauthclient/` directory:

   ```
   asant build
   ```

2. Run the JAX-RPC client by entering the following at the terminal window or command prompt in the `basicauthclient/` directory:

   ```
   asant run
   ```

The client should display the following output:

```
Buildfile: build.xml

run-secure-client:
    [java] username: your_name
    [java] password: your_pwd
    [java] Endpoint address = http://localhost:8080/
basicauthjaxrpc/hello
    [java] Hello Duke (secure)

BUILD SUCCESSFUL
```

Example: Client-Certificate Authentication over HTTP/SSL with JAX-RPC

In this section, we discuss how to configure a simple JAX-RPC-based Web service application for client-certificate authentication over HTTP/SSL. *Client-certificate authentication* uses HTTP over SSL, in which the server and, optionally, the client authenticate one another using public key certificates. If the topic of authentication is new to you, please refer to the section titled Understanding Login Authentication (page 1100). For more information on how client-certificate authentication works, see Figure 32–4 (page 1103).

This example application starts with the example application in `<INSTALL>/j2eetutorial14/examples/jaxrpc/helloservice/` and adds both client and server authentication to the example. In SSL certificate-based basic authentication, the server presents its certificate to the client, and the client authenticates itself to the server by sending its user name and password. This type of authentication is sometimes called server authentication. Mutual authentication adds the dimension of client authentication. For mutual authentication, we need both the client's identity, as contained in a client certificate, and the server's identity, as contained in a server certificate inside a keystore file (`keystore.jks`). We also need both of these identities to be contained in a mutual trust-store (`cacerts.jks`) where they can be verified.

To add mutual authentication to the `<INSTALL>`/`j2eetutorial14/examples/` `jaxrpc/helloservice/` example, complete the following steps. In the example application included with this tutorial, many of these steps have been completed for you and are listed here to show what needs to be done should you wish to create a similar application.

1. Create the appropriate certificates and keystores. For this example, the certificates and keystores are created for the server as a generic `localhost` and are included with the Application Server. See the section Keystores and Trust-Stores in the Mutual Authentication Example (page 1135) for a discussion of how to create the client certificates for this example.

2. If the port value is changed from the default of `localhost:8080`, see Setting the Port (page 314) for information on updating the example files to reflect this change. The WAR files mentioned in this tutorial will not work if the port has been changed.

3. Edit the `build.properties` files to add the location and password to the trust-store, and other properties, as appropriate. For a discussion of the modifications that need to be made to `build.properties`, see Modifying the Build Properties (page 1135).

4. Set security properties in the client code. For the example application, this step has been completed. For a discussion of the security properties that have been set in `HelloClient`, see Setting Security Properties in the Client Code (page 1136).

5. Add the appropriate security elements using `deploytool`. The security elements are discussed in the section Enabling Client-Certificate Authentication for the Mutual Authentication Example (page 1137).

6. Build, package, and deploy the service, deploy the server, and then build and run the client (see Building, Packaging, Deploying, and Running the Mutual Authentication Example, page 1138). You will use the `asant` tool

to compile the client and service and to run the client. You will use `deploytool` to package and deploy the service.

Keystores and Trust-Stores in the Mutual Authentication Example

In this example, the keystore file (`keystore.jks`) and the trust-store file (`cacerts.jks`) have been created for the server as a generic `localhost` and are included with the Application Server in the directory *<J2EE_HOME>*/domains/domain1/config/. You must follow the instructions in Creating a Client Certificate for Mutual Authentication (page 1120) to create a client certificate and add it to the existing trust-store. You must create the client certificates in the directory *<J2EE_HOME>*/domains/domain1/config/, and you must restart the Application Server for the client certificate to be accessed by the application.

Modifying the Build Properties

To build and run the application with mutual authentication, we have set up the example so that some of the values are passed to the application from various `build.properties` files.

To run any of the examples, you must modify the `build.properties` file located in the *<INSTALL>*/j2eetutorial14/examples/common/ directory to provide your admin password and the location where the Application Server is installed. If you need more information, see Building the Examples (page xli).

For this example, the `build.properties` file that is specific to this application, *<INSTALL>*/j2eetutorial14/examples/security/common/build.properties, has been modified for you. This file provides specific information about the JAX-RPC examples to the `asant` targets we will be running later. This information concerns the location of the keystore and trust-store files and their associated passwords.

Make sure that the following properties exist and are correctly defined.

```
trust.store=${j2ee.home}/domains/domain1/config/cacerts.jks
trust.store.password=changeit
key.store=${j2ee.home}/domains/domain1/config/keystore.jks
key.store.password=changeit
```

Setting Security Properties in the Client Code

The source code for the client is in the `HelloClient.java` file of the `<INSTALL>`/j2eetutorial14/examples/security/mutualauthclient/src/ directory. For mutual authentication, the client code must set several security-related properties. These values are passed into the client code when the `asant build` and run tasks are executed.

- `trustStore`: The value of the `trustStore` property is the fully qualified name of the trust-store file: `<J2EE_HOME>`/domains/domain1/config/cacerts.jks.

- `trustStorePassword`: The `trustStorePassword` property is the password of the trust-store. The default value of this password is `changeit`.

- `keyStore`: The value of the `keyStore` property is the fully qualified name of the keystore file: `<J2EE_HOME>`/domains/domain1/config/keystore.jks

- `keyStorePassword`: The `keyStorePassword` property is the password of the keystore. The default value of this password is `changeit`.

- `ENDPOINT_ADDRESS_PROPERTY`: The `ENDPOINT_ADDRESS_PROPERTY` property sets the endpoint address that the stub uses to access the service.

The client sets the aforementioned security properties as shown in the following code. The code in bold is the code that has been added from the original version of the `jaxrpc/staticstub` example application.

```
package mutualauthclient;

import javax.xml.rpc.Stub;

public class HelloClient {

    public static void main(String[] args) {

        if (args.length !=5) {
        System.out.println("HelloClient Error: Need 5
          runtime arguments!");
        System.exit(1);
        }

        String keyStore=args[0];
        String keyStorePassword=args[1];
        String trustStore=args[2];
        String trustStorePassword=args[3];
        String endpointAddress=args[4];
```

```
            // print to display for verification purposes
             System.out.println("keystore: " + keyStore);
             System.out.println("keystorePassword: " +
                keyStorePassword);
             System.out.println("trustStore: " + trustStore);
             System.out.println("trustStorePassword: " +
                trustStorePassword);
             System.out.println("Endpoint address: " +
                endpointAddress);

        try {
           Stub stub = createProxy();
           System.setProperty("javax.net.ssl.keyStore",
              keyStore);
           System.setProperty("javax.net.ssl.keyStorePassword",
              keyStorePassword);
           System.setProperty("javax.net.ssl.trustStore",
              trustStore);
           System.setProperty("javax.net.ssl.trustStorePassword",
              trustStorePassword);
           stub._setProperty(
                 javax.xml.rpc.Stub.ENDPOINT_ADDRESS_PROPERTY,
                    endpointAddress);

           HelloIF hello = (HelloIF)stub;
           System.out.println(hello.sayHello("Duke! (secure!")));
           } catch (Exception ex) {
               ex.printStackTrace();
           }
        }

     private static Stub createProxy() {
        // Note: MyHelloService_Impl is implementation-specific.
        return (Stub)(new
              MySecureHelloService_Impl().getHelloIFPort());
     }
   }
```

Enabling Client-Certificate Authentication for the Mutual Authentication Example

The two ways of implementing client authentication are discussed in Enabling Mutual Authentication over SSL (page 1123). You can set client authentication for all applications (by specifying this in the deployment descriptor for the server) or for only a single application (by specifying this in the deployment descriptor for the application). For this example, we are enabling client authentication for this application only, so we specify the login authentication method as being Client Certificate. The steps for adding client-certificate authentication are shown in Adding Client-Certificate Authentication Using deploytool (page 1141).

For more information on login configuration options, read Understanding Login Authentication (page 1100).

The user authentication method specifies a client-certificate method of authentication in this example. For this authentication to run over SSL, you must also specify which type of transport guarantee to use. For this example, we have chosen CONFIDENTIAL, which is specified in the Network Security Requirement field on the Security tabbed pane in deploytool.

For more information on this type of constraint, read Specifying a Secure Connection (page 1097).

Building, Packaging, Deploying, and Running the Mutual Authentication Example

To build, deploy, and run the JAX-RPC service example with mutual authentication, follow these steps.

Building the Mutual Authentication Example

To compile the application files and copy them to the correct directories, run the asant build task. More information on what happens when the build task is called can be found in Building the Service (page 317).

1. If you haven't already done so, follow these steps for setting up the example.
   - Configuring the SSL Connector (page 1122)
   - Building the Examples (page xli)
2. Go to the <INSTALL>/j2eetutorial14/examples/security/mutualauth/ directory.
3. Build the JAX-RPC service by entering the following at the terminal window or command prompt in the mutualauth/ directory (this and the following steps that use asant assume that you have the executable for asant in your path; if not, you will need to provide the fully qualified path to the asant executable):

   ```
   asant build
   ```

4. Change to the directory *<INSTALL>*/j2eetutorial14/examples/
security/mutualauthclient/.

5. Build the JAX-RPC client by entering the following at the terminal window or command prompt:

```
asant build
```

Packaging the Mutual Authentication Example

You can package the mutual authentication example using deploytool, or you can open the WAR file located in the *<INSTALL>*/j2eetutorial14/examples/
security/provided-wars/mutualauth.war file. This section shows the steps you use to package the JAX-RPC service.

1. Start deploytool if you haven't already done so.

2. Select File→New→Web Component from the deploytool menu. The wizard displays the following dialog boxes.

   a. Introduction dialog box

      1. Read the explanatory text for an overview of the wizard's features.

      2. Click Next.

   b. WAR File dialog box

      1. Select the button labeled Create New Stand-Alone WAR Module.

      2. In the WAR Location field, enter *<INSTALL>*/j2eetutorial14/
examples/security/mutualauth/MutualAuth.war.

      3. In the WAR Display field, enter MutualAuth.

      4. In the Context Root field, enter /mutualauth-jaxrpc.

      5. Click Edit.

      6. In the tree under Available Files, locate the *<INSTALL>*/
j2eetutorial14/examples/security/mutualauth/ directory.

      7. Select the build/ subdirectory.

      8. Click Add.

      9. Click OK.

      10. Click Next.

   c. Choose Component Type dialog box

      1. Select the Web Services Endpoint button.

      2. Click Next.

d. Choose Service dialog box

1. In the WSDL File combo box, select `WEB-INF/wsdl/MySecureHelloService.wsdl`.

2. In the Mapping File combo box, select `build/mapping.xml`.

3. Click Next.

e. Component General Properties dialog box

1.In the Service Endpoint Implementation combo box, select `mutualauth.HelloImpl`.

2. Click Next.

f. Web Service Endpoint dialog box

1. In the Service Endpoint Interface combo box, select `mutualauth.HelloIF`.

2. In the Namespace field, select `urn:Foo`.

3. In the Local Part field, select `HelloIFPort`.

4. The `deploytool` utility will enter a default endpoint address URI in this dialog box. It must be updated later in this section. Click Next.

5. Click Finish.

To access `MyHelloService`, the tutorial clients will specify this service endpoint address URI:

`http://localhost:8080/mutualauth-jaxrpc/hello`

The `/mutualauth-jaxrpc` string is the context root of the servlet that implements `MySecureHelloService`. The `/hello` string is the servlet alias.

3. Specify the endpoint address as follows:

a. In `deploytool`, select `HelloImpl`.

b. Select the Aliases tab.

c. In the Component Aliases table, add `/hello`. (Don't forget the forward slash.)

d. On the Endpoint tab, select `hello` for the endpoint address in the Sun-specific Settings frame.

e. Select File→Save.

Adding Client-Certificate Authentication Using deploytool

For HTTP client-certificate authentication, the application deployment descriptor, `web.xml`, includes the information on who is authorized to access the application, which URL patterns and HTTP methods are protected, and what type of user authentication method this application uses. This information is added to the deployment descriptor using `deploytool`, and its contents are discussed in more detail in Web-Tier Security (page 1092) and in the Java Servlet specification, which can be browsed or downloaded online at `http://java.sun.com/products/servlet/`.

1. Select the `MutualAuth` example in the `deploytool` tree.
2. Select the Security tabbed pane.
3. Select Client Certificate in the User Authentication Method field.
4. Select Add Constraints to add a security constraint.
5. Select Add Collection to add a Web resource collection.
6. Select the Web resource collection from the list, and then select Edit Collections.
7. Select Add URL Pattern. Enter `/hello` in the text field. Click OK.
8. Select the HTTP `GET` and `POST` methods.
9. Click OK to close the Edit Contents dialog box.
10. Select `CONFIDENTIAL` under Network Security Requirement so that the application requires HTTP/SSL.
11. Select Save from the File menu to save these settings.

Deploying the Mutual Authentication Example

1. Deploy the JAX-RPC service by selecting the `mutualauth` example in the `deploytool` tree. Then select Tools→Deploy.
2. Make sure the server is correct. By default, this will be `localhost:4848`.
3. Enter your admin user name and password.
4. Click OK.
5. Click the Close button after the messages indicating successful completion are finished.

Running the Mutual Authentication Example

Enter the following command from the `mutualauthclient/` directory at the terminal window or command prompt to run the JAX-RPC client:

```
asant run
```

The client should display the following output:

```
Buildfile: build.xml

run-mutualauth-client:
    [java] keyStore: <J2EE_HOME>/domains/domain1/config/
cacerts.jks
    [java] keyStorePassword: changeit
    [java] trustStore: <J2EE_HOME>/domains/domain1/config/
keystore.jks
    [java] trustStorePassword: changeit
    [java] endpointAddress = https://localhost:1043/
secure-mutualauth/hello
    [java] Hello Duke (secure)

BUILD SUCCESSFUL
```

For information on verifying that mutual authentication is running, see Verifying That Mutual Authentication Is Running (page 1124).

EJB-Tier Security

The following sections describe declarative and programmatic security mechanisms that can be used to protect resources in the EJB tier. The protected resources include methods of enterprise beans that are called from application clients, Web components, or other enterprise beans.

You can protect EJB tier resources by doing the following:

• Declaring method permissions
• Mapping roles to J2EE users and groups

For information about mapping roles to J2EE users and groups, see Mapping Roles to Users and Groups (page 1090).

Declaring Method Permissions

After you've defined the roles (see Setting Up Security Roles, page 1090), you can define the method permissions of an enterprise bean. Method permissions indicate which roles are allowed to invoke which methods. You can define method permissions in various ways.

- You can apply method permissions to all the methods of the specified enterprise bean's home, component, and Web service endpoint interfaces.
- You can apply method permissions to the specified method of the enterprise bean. If the enterprise bean contains multiple methods having the same method name, the method permission applies to all the methods.
- If the enterprise bean contains multiple methods having the same method name but the methods have different method parameters (such as `create(a,b)` and `create(a,b,c)`), you can apply method permissions by specifying the method parameters.

In general, use `deploytool` to specify method permissions by mapping roles to methods:

1. Select the enterprise bean.
2. Select the Security tab.
3. Select the interface type (local, local home, remote, or remote home). The table displays methods contained in the selected interface. If no interfaces have been defined, the interface buttons will be disabled.
4. In the Method Permissions table, select Sel Roles in the Availability column.
5. Select a role's checkbox if that role should be allowed to invoke a method.

Configuring IOR Security

Enterprise beans that are deployed in one vendor's server product are often accessed from J2EE client components that are deployed in another vendor's product. Common Secure Interoperability version 2 (CSIv2), a CORBA/IIOP-based standard interoperability protocol, addresses this situation by providing authentication, protection of integrity and confidentiality, and principal propagation for invocations on enterprise beans, where the invocations take place over an enterprise's intranet.

CSIv2 configuration settings are specified in the Interoperable Object Reference (IOR) of the target enterprise bean. In the IOR security configuration dialog box, you can specify the security information for the IOR.

To get to the IOR security configuration dialog box, select the enterprise bean to which you want to add the settings in the `deploytool` tree view. From the General tabbed pane, select Sun-specific Settings. In the General subpane of the EJB Settings pane, press the IOR button.

In the Transport Configuration subpane are the following fields:

- The Integrity field specifies whether the target supports integrity-protected messages for transport.

- The Confidentiality field specifies whether the target supports privacy-protected messages (SSL) for transport.

- The Establish Trust In Target field specifies whether or not the target component is capable of authenticating to a client for transport. It is used for mutual authentication (to validate the server's identity).

- The Establish Trust In Client field specifies whether or not the target component is capable of authenticating a client for transport (target asks the client to authenticate itself).

In each of these fields, you can select whether the item is supported, required, or not activated (none).

In the As Context subpane, do the following:

1. Use the Required drop-down list to identify whether the authentication method specified is required to be used for client authentication. Setting this field to `True` indicates that the authentication method specified is required. Setting this field to `False` indicates that the method authentication is not required.

2. Use the Authorization Method drop-down list to authenticate the client. The only supported value is `USERNAME_PASSWORD`.

3. Use the Realm field to identify the realm in which the user is authenticated.

In the Duke's Bank example, the As Context setting is used to require client authentication (with user name and password) when access to protected methods in the `AccountControllerBean` and `CustomerControllerBean` components is attempted.

In the Sas Context subpane, use the Caller Propagation drop-down list to identify whether or not the target component will accept propagated caller identities.

In the Duke's Bank example, the Sas Context setting is set to Supported for the AccountBean, CustomerBean, and TxBean components, indicating that these target components will accept propagated caller identities.

Using Programmatic Security in the EJB Tier

Programmatic security in the EJB tier consists of the getCallerPrincipal and the isCallerInRole methods. You can use the getCallerPrincipal method to determine the caller of the enterprise bean and use the isCallerInRole method to determine whether the caller has the specified role.

The getCallerPrincipal method of the EJBContext interface returns the java.security.Principal object that identifies the caller of the enterprise bean. (In this case, a principal is the same as a user.) In the following example, the getUser method of an enterprise bean returns the name of the J2EE user that invoked it:

```
public String getUser() {
    return context.getCallerPrincipal().getName();
}
```

You can determine whether an enterprise bean's caller belongs to the Customer role.

```
boolean result = context.isCallerInRole("Customer");
```

Unauthenticated User Name

Web applications accept unauthenticated Web clients and allow these clients to make calls to the EJB container. The EJB specification requires a security credential for accessing EJB methods. Typically, the credential will be that of a generic unauthenticated user.

Application Client-Tier Security

Authentication requirements for J2EE application clients are the same as the requirements for other J2EE components. Access to protected resources in either the EJB tier or the Web tier requires user authentication, whereas access to unprotected resources does not.

An application client can use the Java Authentication and Authorization Service (JAAS) for authentication. JAAS implements a Java version of the standard Pluggable Authentication Module (PAM) framework, which permits applications to remain independent of underlying authentication technologies. You can plug new or updated authentication technologies under an application without making any modifications to the application itself. Applications enable the authentication process by instantiating a `LoginContext` object, which, in turn, references a configuration to determine the authentication technologies or login modules that will be used to perform the authentication.

A typical login module can prompt for and verify a user name and password. Other modules can read and verify a voice or fingerprint sample.

In some cases, a login module must communicate with the user to obtain authentication information. Login modules use a `javax.security.auth.callback.CallbackHandler` for this purpose. Applications implement the `CallbackHandler` interface and pass it to the login context, which forwards it directly to the underlying login modules. A login module uses the callback handler both to gather input (such as a password or smart card PIN) from users and to supply information (such as status information) to users. Because the application specifies the callback handler, an underlying login module can remain independent of the various ways applications interact with users.

For example, the implementation of a callback handler for a GUI application might display a window to solicit user input. Or the implementation of a callback handler for a command-line tool might simply prompt the user for input directly from the command line.

The login module passes an array of appropriate callbacks to the callback handler's `handle` method (for example, a `NameCallback` for the user name and a `PasswordCallback` for the password); the callback handler performs the requested user interaction and sets appropriate values in the callbacks. For example, to process a `NameCallback`, the `CallbackHandler` might prompt for a name, retrieve the value from the user, and call the `setName` method of the `NameCallback` to store the name.

EIS-Tier Security

In the EIS tier, an application component requests a connection to an EIS resource. As part of this connection, the EIS may require a sign-on for the requester to access the resource. The application component provider has two choices for the design of the EIS sign-on:

- In the container-managed sign-on approach, the application component lets the container take the responsibility of configuring and managing the EIS sign-on. The container determines the user name and password for establishing a connection to an EIS instance.
- In the component-managed sign-on approach, the application component code manages EIS sign-on by including code that performs the sign-on process to an EIS.

Container-Managed Sign-On

In container-managed sign-on, an application component does not have to pass any sign-on security information to the getConnection() method. The security information is supplied by the container, as shown in the following example.

```
// Business method in an application component
Context initctx = new InitialContext();

// Perform JNDI lookup to obtain a connection factory
javax.resource.cci.ConnectionFactory cxf =
    (javax.resource.cci.ConnectionFactory)initctx.lookup(
    "java:comp/env/eis/MainframeCxFactory");

// Invoke factory to obtain a connection. The security
// information is not passed in the getConnection method
javax.resource.cci.Connection cx = cxf.getConnection();
...
```

Component-Managed Sign-On

In component-managed sign-on, an application component is responsible for passing the needed sign-on security information to the resource to the `getConnection()` method. For example, security information might be a user name and password, as shown here:

```
// Method in an application component
Context initctx = new InitialContext();

// Perform JNDI lookup to obtain a connection factory
javax.resource.cci.ConnectionFactory cxf =
    (javax.resource.cci.ConnectionFactory)initctx.lookup(
        "java:comp/env/eis/MainframeCxFactory");

// Get a new ConnectionSpec
com.myeis.ConnectionSpecImpl properties = //..

// Invoke factory to obtain a connection
properties.setUserName("...");
properties.setPassword("...");
javax.resource.cci.Connection cx =
  cxf.getConnection(properties);
...
```

Configuring Resource Adapter Security

In addition to configuring the sign-on, you can configure the following security settings for the resource adapter:

- Authentication mechanisms
- Reauthentication support
- Security permissions

To configure these settings using `deploytool`, do the following:

1. Select the resource adapter file.
2. Select the Security tabbed pane.
3. In the Authentication Mechanisms pane, specify the authentication mechanisms that are supported by this resource adapter:
   a. Select Password to require a user name and password to connect to an EIS.

  b. Select Kerberos Version 5.0 to require the resource adapter to support the Kerberos authentication mechanism.

  You can select more than one mechanism or no mechanism. If you do not select one, no standard security authentication is supported as part of the security contract.

4. Select Reauthentication Supported if the resource adapter implementation supports performing reauthentication on an existing physical connection. Reauthentication is performed when an application server calls the `getConnection` method with a security context that is different from the one used to establish the connection. This information is for the resource adapter implementation and not for the underlying EIS instance.

5. In the Security Permissions pane, click Add to enter a security permission that the resource adapter needs to access system resources in the operational environment. You specify only those permissions that are not included in the default set (see section 11.2 of the Connector specification). For example, to allow the resource to look up the name of any remote host, add the following security permission:

```
permission java.net.SocketPermission *, "resolve";
```

For each security permission you add, click the column to the far right (labeled with a folded paper) to enter a description for the permission. To delete a security permission, select the permission in the table and click Delete.

Propagating Security Identity

When you deploy an enterprise bean or Web component, you can specify the security identity that will be propagated (illustrated in Figure 32–8) to enterprise beans invoked from within that component.

You can choose one of the following propagation styles:

- The caller identity of the intermediate component is propagated to the target enterprise bean. This technique is used when the target container trusts the intermediate container.

- A specific identity is propagated to the target enterprise bean. This technique is used when the target container expects access via a specific identity.

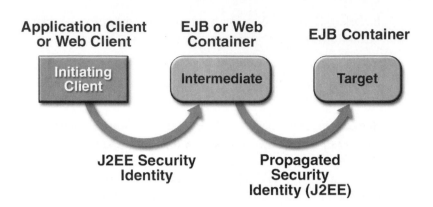

Figure 32–8 Security Identity Propagation

Configuring a Component's Propagated Security Identity

To configure an enterprise bean's propagated security identity, do the following:

1. Select the enterprise bean to configure.

2. In the Security Identity panel of the Security pane, select the security identity that will be propagated to the beans that this enterprise bean calls:

   a. If you want the principal of this enterprise bean's caller to be propagated to other beans that it calls, choose Use Caller ID.

   b. If you want a security identity other than the caller's identity propagated to other beans, choose Run As Role, select the role from the menu, and then select the User In Role from the available users in the selected role.

3. If the role that you want to use as the security identity is not in the list, click Edit Roles and add the role.

To configure a Web component's propagated security identity, do the following:

1. Select the Web component to configure.

2. In the Security Identity panel of the Security pane, select Use Caller ID if the caller ID is to be propagated to methods of other components called from this Web component. Otherwise, select Run As Role, and select a role from the list of known roles in the WAR file.

3. If the role that you want to use as the security identity is not in the list, click Edit Roles and add it.

Configuring Client Authentication

If an application component in an application client container accesses a protected method on a bean, use client authentication.

Trust between Containers

When an enterprise bean is designed so that either the original caller identity or a designated identity is used to call a target bean, the target bean will receive the propagated identity only; it will *not* receive any authentication data.

There is no way for the target container to authenticate the propagated security identity. However, because the security identity is used in authorization checks (for example, method permissions or with the `isCallerInRole()` method), it is vitally important that the security identity be authentic. Because there is no authentication data available to authenticate the propagated identity, the target must trust that the calling container has propagated an authenticated security identity.

By default, the Application Server is configured to trust identities that are propagated from different containers. Therefore, there are no special steps that you need to take to set up a trust relationship.

What Is Java Authorization Contract for Containers?

Java Authorization Contract for Containers (JACC) defines security contracts between the Application Server and authorization policy modules. These contracts specify how the authorization providers are installed, configured, and used in access decisions.

Further Information

- Java 2 Standard Edition, v1.4.2 security information at `http://java.sun.com/j2se/1.4.2/docs/guide/security/index.html`.

- Java Servlet specification, which can be browsed or downloaded online at `http://java.sun.com/products/servlet/`.

- Information on SSL specifications is available at `http://wp.netscape.com/eng/security/`.

- The API specification for Java Authorization Contract for Containers is available at `http://java.sun.com/j2ee/javaacc/`.

33

The Java Message Service API

THIS chapter provides an introduction to the Java Message Service (JMS) API, a Java API that allows applications to create, send, receive, and read messages using reliable, asynchronous, loosely coupled communication. It covers the following topics:

- Overview
- Basic JMS API concepts
- The JMS API programming model
- Writing simple JMS client applications
- Creating robust JMS applications
- Using the JMS API in a J2EE application
- Further information

Overview

This overview of the JMS API answers the following questions.

- What is messaging?
- What is the JMS API?
- When can you use the JMS API?
- How does the JMS API work with the J2EE platform?

What Is Messaging?

Messaging is a method of communication between software components or applications. A messaging system is a peer-to-peer facility: A messaging client can send messages to, and receive messages from, any other client. Each client connects to a messaging agent that provides facilities for creating, sending, receiving, and reading messages.

Messaging enables distributed communication that is *loosely coupled*. A component sends a message to a destination, and the recipient can retrieve the message from the destination. However, the sender and the receiver do not have to be available at the same time in order to communicate. In fact, the sender does not need to know anything about the receiver; nor does the receiver need to know anything about the sender. The sender and the receiver need to know only which message format and which destination to use. In this respect, messaging differs from tightly coupled technologies, such as Remote Method Invocation (RMI), which require an application to know a remote application's methods.

Messaging also differs from electronic mail (email), which is a method of communication between people or between software applications and people. Messaging is used for communication between software applications or software components.

What Is the JMS API?

The Java Message Service is a Java API that allows applications to create, send, receive, and read messages. Designed by Sun and several partner companies, the JMS API defines a common set of interfaces and associated semantics that allow programs written in the Java programming language to communicate with other messaging implementations.

The JMS API minimizes the set of concepts a programmer must learn in order to use messaging products but provides enough features to support sophisticated messaging applications. It also strives to maximize the portability of JMS applications across JMS providers in the same messaging domain.

The JMS API enables communication that is not only loosely coupled but also

- *Asynchronous*: A JMS provider can deliver messages to a client as they arrive; a client does not have to request messages in order to receive them.
- *Reliable*: The JMS API can ensure that a message is delivered once and only once. Lower levels of reliability are available for applications that can afford to miss messages or to receive duplicate messages.

The JMS specification was first published in August 1998. The latest version is Version 1.1, which was released in April 2002. You can download a copy of the specification from the JMS Web site: `http://java.sun.com/products/jms/`.

When Can You Use the JMS API?

An enterprise application provider is likely to choose a messaging API over a tightly coupled API, such as remote procedure call (RPC), under the following circumstances.

- The provider wants the components not to depend on information about other components' interfaces, so that components can be easily replaced.
- The provider wants the application to run whether or not all components are up and running simultaneously.
- The application business model allows a component to send information to another and to continue to operate without receiving an immediate response.

For example, components of an enterprise application for an automobile manufacturer can use the JMS API in situations like these:

- The inventory component can send a message to the factory component when the inventory level for a product goes below a certain level so that the factory can make more cars.
- The factory component can send a message to the parts components so that the factory can assemble the parts it needs.
- The parts components in turn can send messages to their own inventory and order components to update their inventories and to order new parts from suppliers.

- Both the factory and the parts components can send messages to the accounting component to update their budget numbers.
- The business can publish updated catalog items to its sales force.

Using messaging for these tasks allows the various components to interact with one another efficiently, without tying up network or other resources. Figure 33–1 illustrates how this simple example might work.

Manufacturing is only one example of how an enterprise can use the JMS API. Retail applications, financial services applications, health services applications, and many others can make use of messaging.

How Does the JMS API Work with the J2EE Platform?

When the JMS API was introduced in 1998, its most important purpose was to allow Java applications to access existing messaging-oriented middleware (MOM) systems, such as MQSeries from IBM. Since that time, many vendors have adopted and implemented the JMS API, so a JMS product can now provide a complete messaging capability for an enterprise.

Since the 1.3 release of the J2EE platform, the JMS API has been an integral part of the platform, and application developers can use messaging with J2EE components.

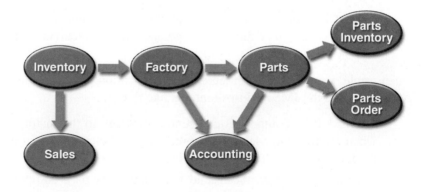

Figure 33–1 Messaging in an Enterprise Application

The JMS API in the J2EE platform has the following features.

- Application clients, Enterprise JavaBeans (EJB) components, and Web components can send or synchronously receive a JMS message. Application clients can, in addition, receive JMS messages asynchronously. (Applets, however, are not required to support the JMS API.)

- Message-driven beans, which are a kind of enterprise bean, enable the asynchronous consumption of messages. A JMS provider can optionally implement concurrent processing of messages by message-driven beans.

- Message send and receive operations can participate in distributed transactions, which allow JMS operations and database accesses to take place within a single transaction.

The JMS API enhances the J2EE platform by simplifying enterprise development, allowing loosely coupled, reliable, asynchronous interactions among J2EE components and legacy systems capable of messaging. A developer can easily add new behavior to a J2EE application that has existing business events by adding a new message-driven bean to operate on specific business events. The J2EE platform, moreover, enhances the JMS API by providing support for distributed transactions and allowing for the concurrent consumption of messages. For more information, see the Enterprise JavaBeans specification, v2.1.

At the 1.4 release of the J2EE platform, the JMS provider can be integrated with the application server using the J2EE Connector architecture. You access the JMS provider through a resource adapter. This capability allows vendors to create JMS providers that can be plugged in to multiple application servers, and it allows application servers to support multiple JMS providers. For more information, see the J2EE Connector architecture specification, v1.5.

Basic JMS API Concepts

This section introduces the most basic JMS API concepts, the ones you must know to get started writing simple JMS client applications:

- JMS API architecture
- Messaging domains
- Message consumption

The next section introduces the JMS API programming model. Later sections cover more advanced concepts, including the ones you need to write J2EE applications that use message-driven beans.

JMS API Architecture

A JMS application is composed of the following parts.

- A *JMS provider* is a messaging system that implements the JMS interfaces and provides administrative and control features. An implementation of the J2EE platform at release 1.3 and later includes a JMS provider.

- *JMS clients* are the programs or components, written in the Java programming language, that produce and consume messages. Any J2EE application component can act as a JMS client.

- *Messages* are the objects that communicate information between JMS clients.

- *Administered objects* are preconfigured JMS objects created by an administrator for the use of clients. The two kinds of JMS administered objects are destinations and connection factories, which are described in Administered Objects (page 1163).

Figure 33–2 illustrates the way these parts interact. Administrative tools allow you to bind destinations and connection factories into a JNDI namespace. A JMS client can then look up the administered objects in the namespace and then establish a logical connection to the same objects through the JMS provider.

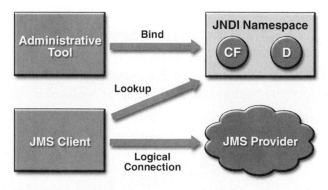

Figure 33–2 JMS API Architecture

Messaging Domains

Before the JMS API existed, most messaging products supported either the *point-to-point* or the *publish/subscribe* approach to messaging. The JMS specification provides a separate domain for each approach and defines compliance for each domain. A stand-alone JMS provider can implement one or both domains. A J2EE provider must implement both domains.

In fact, most implementations of the JMS API support both the point-to-point and the publish/subscribe domains, and some JMS clients combine the use of both domains in a single application. In this way, the JMS API has extended the power and flexibility of messaging products.

The JMS 1.1 specification goes one step further: It provides common interfaces that enable you to use the JMS API in a way that is not specific to either domain. The following subsections describe the two messaging domains and then describe this new way of programming using common interfaces.

Point-to-Point Messaging Domain

A point-to-point (PTP) product or application is built on the concept of message queues, senders, and receivers. Each message is addressed to a specific queue, and receiving clients extract messages from the queues established to hold their messages. Queues retain all messages sent to them until the messages are consumed or until the messages expire.

PTP messaging has the following characteristics and is illustrated in Figure 33–3.

- Each message has only one consumer.
- A sender and a receiver of a message have no timing dependencies. The receiver can fetch the message whether or not it was running when the client sent the message.
- The receiver acknowledges the successful processing of a message.

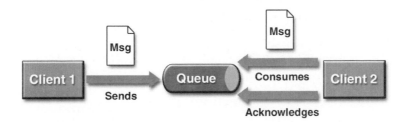

Figure 33–3 Point-to-Point Messaging

Use PTP messaging when every message you send must be processed success-fully by one consumer.

Publish/Subscribe Messaging Domain

In a publish/subscribe (pub/sub) product or application, clients address messages to a *topic*, which functions somewhat like a bulletin board. Publishers and sub-scribers are generally anonymous and can dynamically publish or subscribe to the content hierarchy. The system takes care of distributing the messages arriv-ing from a topic's multiple publishers to its multiple subscribers. Topics retain messages only as long as it takes to distribute them to current subscribers.

Pub/sub messaging has the following characteristics.

- Each message can have multiple consumers.
- Publishers and subscribers have a timing dependency. A client that sub-scribes to a topic can consume only messages published after the client has created a subscription, and the subscriber must continue to be active in order for it to consume messages.

The JMS API relaxes this timing dependency to some extent by allowing sub-scribers to create *durable subscriptions*, which receive messages sent while the subscribers are not active. Durable subscriptions provide the flexibility and reli-ability of queues but still allow clients to send messages to many recipients. For more information about durable subscriptions, see Creating Durable Subscrip-tions (page 1200).

Use pub/sub messaging when each message can be processed by zero, one, or many consumers. Figure 33–4 illustrates pub/sub messaging.

Programming with the Common Interfaces

Version 1.1 of the JMS API allows you to use the same code to send and receive messages under either the PTP or the pub/sub domain. The administered objects that you use remain domain-specific, and the behavior of the application will

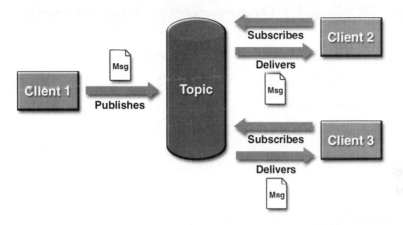

Figure 33–4 Publish/Subscribe Messaging

depend in part on whether you are using a queue or a topic. However, the code itself can be common to both domains, making your applications flexible and reusable. This tutorial describes and illustrates these common interfaces.

Message Consumption

Messaging products are inherently asynchronous: There is no fundamental timing dependency between the production and the consumption of a message. However, the JMS specification uses this term in a more precise sense. Messages can be consumed in either of two ways:

- *Synchronously*: A subscriber or a receiver explicitly fetches the message from the destination by calling the `receive` method. The `receive` method can block until a message arrives or can time out if a message does not arrive within a specified time limit.

- *Asynchronously*: A client can register a *message listener* with a consumer. A message listener is similar to an event listener. Whenever a message arrives at the destination, the JMS provider delivers the message by calling the listener's `onMessage` method, which acts on the contents of the message.

The JMS API Programming Model

The basic building blocks of a JMS application consist of

- Administered objects: connection factories and destinations
- Connections
- Sessions
- Message producers
- Message consumers
- Messages

Figure 33–5 shows how all these objects fit together in a JMS client application.

This section describes all these objects briefly and provides sample commands and code snippets that show how to create and use the objects. The last subsection briefly describes JMS API exception handling.

Examples that show how to combine all these objects in applications appear in later sections. For more details, see the JMS API documentation, which is part of the J2EE API documentation.

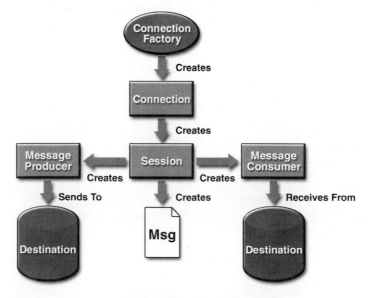

Figure 33–5   The JMS API Programming Model

Administered Objects

Two parts of a JMS application—destinations and connection factories—are best maintained administratively rather than programmatically. The technology underlying these objects is likely to be very different from one implementation of the JMS API to another. Therefore, the management of these objects belongs with other administrative tasks that vary from provider to provider.

JMS clients access these objects through interfaces that are portable, so a client application can run with little or no change on more than one implementation of the JMS API. Ordinarily, an administrator configures administered objects in a JNDI namespace, and JMS clients then look them up by using the JNDI API. J2EE applications always use the JNDI API.

With the Sun Java System Application Server Platform Edition 8, you use the Admin Console to create JMS administered objects in the form of resources. You can also use the asadmin command.

Connection Factories

A *connection factory* is the object a client uses to create a connection to a provider. A connection factory encapsulates a set of connection configuration parameters that has been defined by an administrator. Each connection factory is an instance of either the QueueConnectionFactory or the TopicConnection-Factory interface.

To learn how to use the Admin Console to create connection factories, see Creating JMS Administered Objects (page 1178).

At the beginning of a JMS client program, you usually perform a JNDI lookup of the connection factory. The connection factory itself is specific to one domain or the other. However, you normally cast and assign it to a ConnectionFactory object.

For example, the following code fragment obtains an InitialContext object and uses it to look up the QueueConnectionFactory and the TopicConnection-Factory by name. Then it assigns each to a ConnectionFactory object:

```
Context ctx = new InitialContext();

ConnectionFactory connectionFactory1 = (ConnectionFactory)
    ctx.lookup("jms/QueueConnectionFactory");

ConnectionFactory connectionFactory2 = (ConnectionFactory)
    ctx.lookup("jms/TopicConnectionFactory");
```

In a J2EE application, JMS administered objects are normally placed in the `jms` naming subcontext.

Destinations

A *destination* is the object a client uses to specify the target of messages it produces and the source of messages it consumes. In the PTP messaging domain, destinations are called queues. In the pub/sub messaging domain, destinations are called topics.

Creating destinations using the Application Server is a two-step process. You create a JMS destination resource that specifies the JNDI name of the destination. You also create a physical destination to which the JNDI name refers.

To learn how to use the Admin Console to create physical destinations and destination resources, see Creating JMS Administered Objects (page 1178).

A JMS application can use multiple queues or topics (or both).

In addition to looking up a connection factory in a client program, you usually look up a destination. Like connection factories, destinations are specific to one domain or the other. You normally assign the destination to a `Destination` object. To preserve the semantics of queues and topics, however, you cast the object to a destination of the appropriate type.

For example, the following line of code performs a JNDI lookup of the previously created topic `jms/MyTopic` and assigns it to a `Destination` object, after casting it to a `Topic` object:

```
Destination myDest = (Topic) ctx.lookup("jms/MyTopic");
```

The following line of code looks up a queue named `jms/MyQueue` and assigns it to a `Destination` object, after casting it to a `Queue` object:

```
Destination myDest = (Queue) ctx.lookup("jms/MyQueue");
```

With the common interfaces, you can mix or match connection factories and destinations. That is, you can look up a `QueueConnectionFactory` and use it with a `Topic`, and you can look up a `TopicConnectionFactory` and use it with a `Queue`. The behavior of the application will depend on the kind of destination you use and not on the kind of connection factory you use.

Connections

A *connection* encapsulates a virtual connection with a JMS provider. A connection could represent an open TCP/IP socket between a client and a provider service daemon. You use a connection to create one or more sessions.

Connections implement the Connection interface. When you have a ConnectionFactory object, you can use it to create a Connection:

```
Connection connection = connectionFactory.createConnection();
```

Before an application completes, you must close any connections that you have created. Failure to close a connection can cause resources not to be released by the JMS provider. Closing a connection also closes its sessions and their message producers and message consumers.

```
connection.close();
```

Before your application can consume messages, you must call the connection's start method; for details, see Message Consumers (page 1167). If you want to stop message delivery temporarily without closing the connection, you call the stop method.

Sessions

A *session* is a single-threaded context for producing and consuming messages. You use sessions to create message producers, message consumers, and messages. Sessions serialize the execution of message listeners; for details, see Message Listeners (page 1168).

A session provides a transactional context with which to group a set of sends and receives into an atomic unit of work. For details, see Using JMS API Local Transactions (page 1204).

Sessions implement the Session interface. After you create a Connection object, you use it to create a Session:

```
Session session = connection.createSession(false,
    Session.AUTO_ACKNOWLEDGE);
```

The first argument means that the session is not transacted; the second means that the session automatically acknowledges messages when they have been received successfully. (For more information, see Controlling Message Acknowledgment, page 1193.)

To create a transacted session, use the following code:

```
Session session = connection.createSession(true, 0);
```

Here, the first argument means that the session is transacted; the second indicates that message acknowledgment is not specified for transacted sessions. For more information on transactions, see Using JMS API Local Transactions (page 1204). For information about the way JMS transactions work in J2EE applications, see Using the JMS API in a J2EE Application (page 1212).

Message Producers

A *message producer* is an object that is created by a session and used for sending messages to a destination. It implements the MessageProducer interface.

You use a Session to create a MessageProducer for a destination. Here, the first example creates a producer for the destination myQueue, and the second for the destination myTopic:

```
MessageProducer producer = session.createProducer(myQueue);

MessageProducer producer = session.createProducer(myTopic);
```

You can create an unidentified producer by specifying null as the argument to createProducer. With an unidentified producer, you can wait to specify which destination to send the message to until you send a message.

After you have created a message producer, you can use it to send messages by using the send method:

```
producer.send(message);
```

You must first create the messages; see Messages (page 1169).

If you created an unidentified producer, use an overloaded `send` method that specifies the destination as the first parameter. For example:

```
MessageProducer anon_prod = session.createProducer(null);

anon_prod.send(myQueue, message);
```

Message Consumers

A *message consumer* is an object that is created by a session and used for receiving messages sent to a destination. It implements the `MessageConsumer` interface.

A message consumer allows a JMS client to register interest in a destination with a JMS provider. The JMS provider manages the delivery of messages from a destination to the registered consumers of the destination.

For example, you use a `Session` to create a `MessageConsumer` for either a queue or a topic:

```
MessageConsumer consumer = session.createConsumer(myQueue);

MessageConsumer consumer = session.createConsumer(myTopic);
```

You use the `Session.createDurableSubscriber` method to create a durable topic subscriber. This method is valid only if you are using a topic. For details, see Creating Durable Subscriptions (page 1200).

After you have created a message consumer, it becomes active, and you can use it to receive messages. You can use the `close` method for a `MessageConsumer` to make the message consumer inactive. Message delivery does not begin until you start the connection you created by calling its `start` method. (Remember always to call the `start` method; forgetting to start the connection is one of the most common JMS programming errors.)

You use the `receive` method to consume a message synchronously. You can use this method at any time after you call the `start` method:

```
connection.start();
Message m = consumer.receive();

connection.start();
Message m = consumer.receive(1000); // time out after a second
```

To consume a message asynchronously, you use a message listener, described in the next section.

Message Listeners

A *message listener* is an object that acts as an asynchronous event handler for messages. This object implements the `MessageListener` interface, which contains one method, `onMessage`. In the `onMessage` method, you define the actions to be taken when a message arrives.

You register the message listener with a specific `MessageConsumer` by using the `setMessageListener` method. For example, if you define a class named `Listener` that implements the `MessageListener` interface, you can register the message listener as follows:

```
Listener myListener = new Listener();
consumer.setMessageListener(myListener);
```

After you register the message listener, you call the `start` method on the `Connection` to begin message delivery. (If you call `start` before you register the message listener, you are likely to miss messages.)

When message delivery begins, the JMS provider automatically calls the message listener's `onMessage` method whenever a message is delivered. The `onMessage` method takes one argument of type `Message`, which your implementation of the method can cast to any of the other message types (see Message Bodies, page 1171).

A message listener is not specific to a particular destination type. The same listener can obtain messages from either a queue or a topic, depending on the type of destination for which the message consumer was created. A message listener does, however, usually expect a specific message type and format. Moreover, if it needs to reply to messages, a message listener must either assume a particular destination type or obtain the destination type of the message and create a producer for that destination type.

Your `onMessage` method should handle all exceptions. It must not throw checked exceptions, and throwing a `RuntimeException` is considered a programming error.

The session used to create the message consumer serializes the execution of all message listeners registered with the session. At any time, only one of the session's message listeners is running.

In the J2EE platform, a message-driven bean is a special kind of message listener. For details, see Using Message-Driven Beans (page 1214).

Message Selectors

If your messaging application needs to filter the messages it receives, you can use a JMS API message selector, which allows a message consumer to specify the messages it is interested in. Message selectors assign the work of filtering messages to the JMS provider rather than to the application. For an example of an application that uses a message selector, see A J2EE Application That Uses the JMS API with a Session Bean (page 1222).

A message selector is a String that contains an expression. The syntax of the expression is based on a subset of the SQL92 conditional expression syntax. The message selector in the example selects any message that has a NewsType property that is set to the value 'Sports' or 'Opinion':

```
NewsType = 'Sports' OR NewsType = 'Opinion'
```

The createConsumer and createDurableSubscriber methods allow you to specify a message selector as an argument when you create a message consumer.

The message consumer then receives only messages whose headers and properties match the selector. (See Message Headers, page 1170, and Message Properties, page 1171.) A message selector cannot select messages on the basis of the content of the message body.

Messages

The ultimate purpose of a JMS application is to produce and to consume messages that can then be used by other software applications. JMS messages have a basic format that is simple but highly flexible, allowing you to create messages that match formats used by non-JMS applications on heterogeneous platforms.

A JMS message has three parts: a header, properties, and a body. Only the header is required. The following sections describe these parts:

- Message headers
- Message properties (optional)
- Message bodies (optional)

For complete documentation of message headers, properties, and bodies, see the documentation of the Message interface in the API documentation.

Message Headers

A JMS message header contains a number of predefined fields that contain values that both clients and providers use to identify and to route messages. Table 33–1 lists the JMS message header fields and indicates how their values are set. For example, every message has a unique identifier, which is represented in the header field JMSMessageID. The value of another header field, JMSDestination, represents the queue or the topic to which the message is sent. Other fields include a timestamp and a priority level.

Each header field has associated setter and getter methods, which are documented in the description of the Message interface. Some header fields are intended to be set by a client, but many are set automatically by the send or the publish method, which overrides any client-set values.

Table 33–1   How JMS Message Header Field Values Are Set

Header Field	Set By
JMSDestination	send or publish method
JMSDeliveryMode	send or publish method
JMSExpiration	send or publish method
JMSPriority	send or publish method
JMSMessageID	send or publish method
JMSTimestamp	send or publish method
JMSCorrelationID	Client
JMSReplyTo	Client
JMSType	Client
JMSRedelivered	JMS provider

Message Properties

You can create and set properties for messages if you need values in addition to those provided by the header fields. You can use properties to provide compatibility with other messaging systems, or you can use them to create message selectors (see Message Selectors, page 1169). For an example of setting a property to be used as a message selector, see A J2EE Application That Uses the JMS API with a Session Bean (page 1222).

The JMS API provides some predefined property names that a provider can support. The use either of these predefined properties or of user-defined properties is optional.

Message Bodies

The JMS API defines five message body formats, also called message types, which allow you to send and to receive data in many different forms and provide compatibility with existing messaging formats. Table 33–2 describes these message types.

Table 33–2 JMS Message Types

Message Type	Body Contains
TextMessage	A `java.lang.String` object (for example, the contents of an Extensible Markup Language file).
MapMessage	A set of name-value pairs, with names as `String` objects and values as primitive types in the Java programming language. The entries can be accessed sequentially by enumerator or randomly by name. The order of the entries is undefined.
BytesMessage	A stream of uninterpreted bytes. This message type is for literally encoding a body to match an existing message format.
StreamMessage	A stream of primitive values in the Java programming language, filled and read sequentially.
ObjectMessage	A `Serializable` object in the Java programming language.
Message	Nothing. Composed of header fields and properties only. This message type is useful when a message body is not required.

The JMS API provides methods for creating messages of each type and for filling in their contents. For example, to create and send a `TextMessage`, you might use the following statements:

```
TextMessage message = session.createTextMessage();
message.setText(msg_text);      // msg_text is a String
producer.send(message);
```

At the consuming end, a message arrives as a generic `Message` object and must be cast to the appropriate message type. You can use one or more getter methods to extract the message contents. The following code fragment uses the `getText` method:

```
Message m = consumer.receive();
if (m instanceof TextMessage) {
  TextMessage message = (TextMessage) m;
  System.out.println("Reading message: " + message.getText());
} else {
  // Handle error
}
```

Exception Handling

The root class for exceptions thrown by JMS API methods is `JMSException`. Catching `JMSException` provides a generic way of handling all exceptions related to the JMS API. The `JMSException` class includes the following subclasses, which are described in the API documentation:

- `IllegalStateException`
- `InvalidClientIDException`
- `InvalidDestinationException`
- `InvalidSelectorException`
- `JMSSecurityException`
- `MessageEOFException`
- `MessageFormatException`
- `MessageNotReadableException`
- `MessageNotWriteableException`

- `ResourceAllocationException`
- `TransactionInProgressException`
- `TransactionRolledBackException`

All the examples in the tutorial catch and handle `JMSException` when it is appropriate to do so.

Writing Simple JMS Client Applications

This section shows how to create, package, and run simple JMS client programs packaged as stand-alone application clients. These clients access a J2EE server. The clients demonstrate the basic tasks that a JMS application must perform:

- Creating a connection and a session
- Creating message producers and consumers
- Sending and receiving messages

In a J2EE application, some of these tasks are performed, in whole or in part, by the container. If you learn about these tasks, you will have a good basis for understanding how a JMS application works on the J2EE platform.

This section covers the following topics:

- An example that uses synchronous message receives
- An example that uses a message listener
- Running JMS clients on multiple systems

Each example uses two programs: one that sends messages and one that receives them. You can run the programs in two terminal windows.

When you write a JMS application to run in a J2EE application, you use many of the same methods in much the same sequence as you do for a stand-alone application client. However, there are some significant differences. Using the JMS API in a J2EE Application (page 1212) describes these differences, and Chapter 34 provides examples that illustrate them.

The examples for this section are in the following directory:

`<INSTALL>/j2eetutorial14/examples/jms/simple/`

A Simple Example of Synchronous Message Receives

This section describes the sending and receiving programs in an example that uses the `receive` method to consume messages synchronously. This section then explains how to compile, package, and run the programs using the Application Server.

The following sections describe the steps in creating and running the example:

- Writing the client programs
- Compiling the clients
- Starting the JMS provider
- Creating JMS administered objects
- Packaging the clients
- Running the clients

Writing the Client Programs

The sending program, `src/SimpleProducer.java`, performs the following steps:

1. Retrieves command-line arguments that specify the destination name and type and the number of arguments:

   ```
   final int NUM_MSGS;
   String destName = new String(args[0]);
   String destType = new String(args[1]);
   System.out.println("Destination name is " + destName +
       ", type is " + destType);
   if (args.length == 3){
     NUM_MSGS = (new Integer(args[2])).intValue();
   } else {
     NUM_MSGS = 1;
   }
   ```

2. Performs a JNDI lookup of the `ConnectionFactory` and `Destination`:

   ```
   /*
    * Create a JNDI API InitialContext object if none exists
    * yet.
    */
   Context jndiContext = null;
   try {
     jndiContext = new InitialContext();
   ```

```java
  } catch (NamingException e) {
    System.out.println("Could not create JNDI API " +
      "context: " + e.toString());
    System.exit(1);
  }

  /*
   * Look up connection factory and destination.  If either
   * does not exist, exit.  If you look up a
   * TopicConnectionFactory instead of a
   * QueueConnectionFactory, program behavior is the same.
   */
  ConnectionFactory connectionFactory = null;
  Destination dest = null;
  try {
    connectionFactory = (ConnectionFactory)
      jndiContext.lookup("jms/QueueConnectionFactory");
    if (destType.equals("queue")) {
      dest = (Queue) jndiContext.lookup(destName);
    } else if (destType.equals("topic")) {
      dest = (Topic) jndiContext.lookup(destName);
    } else {
      throw new Exception("Invalid destination type" +
          "; must be queue or topic");
    }
  } catch (Exception e) {
    System.out.println("JNDI API lookup failed: " +
      e.toString());
    System.exit(1);
  }
```

3. Creates a Connection and a Session:

```java
Connection connection =
  connectionFactory.createConnection();
Session session = connection.createSession(false,
  Session.AUTO_ACKNOWLEDGE);
```

4. Creates a MessageProducer and a TextMessage:

```java
MessageProducer producer =
  session.createProducer(dest);
TextMessage message = session.createTextMessage();
```

5. Sends one or more messages to the destination:

```java
for (int i = 0; i < NUM_MSGS; i++) {
  message.setText("This is message " + (i + 1));
  System.out.println("Sending message: " +
    message.getText());
  producer.send(message);
}
```

6. Sends an empty control message to indicate the end of the message stream:

```
producer.send(session.createMessage());
```

Sending an empty message of no specified type is a convenient way to indicate to the consumer that the final message has arrived.

7. Closes the connection in a `finally` block, automatically closing the session and `MessageProducer`:

```
} finally {
    if (connection != null) {
        try {
            connection.close();
        } catch (JMSException e) {}
    }
}
```

The receiving program, `src/SimpleSynchConsumer.java`, performs the following steps:

1. Performs a JNDI lookup of the `ConnectionFactory` and `Destination`.

2. Creates a `Connection` and a `Session`.

3. Creates a `MessageConsumer`:

```
consumer = session.createConsumer(dest);
```

4. Starts the connection, causing message delivery to begin:

```
connection.start();
```

5. Receives the messages sent to the destination until the end-of-message-stream control message is received:

```
while (true) {
    Message m = consumer.receive(1);
    if (m != null) {
        if (m instanceof TextMessage) {
            message = (TextMessage) m;
            System.out.println("Reading message: " +
                message.getText());
        } else {
            break;
        }
    }
}
```

Because the control message is not a `TextMessage`, the receiving program terminates the `while` loop and stops receiving messages after the control message arrives.

6. Closes the connection in a `finally` block, automatically closing the session and `MessageConsumer`.

The `receive` method can be used in several ways to perform a synchronous receive. If you specify no arguments or an argument of 0, the method blocks indefinitely until a message arrives:

```
Message m = consumer.receive();

Message m = consumer.receive(0);
```

For a simple client program, this may not matter. But if you do not want your program to consume system resources unnecessarily, use a timed synchronous receive. Do one of the following:

- Call the `receive` method with a timeout argument greater than 0:
  ```
  Message m = consumer.receive(1); // 1 millisecond
  ```
- Call the `receiveNoWait` method, which receives a message only if one is available:
  ```
  Message m = consumer.receiveNoWait();
  ```

The `SimpleSynchConsumer` program uses an indefinite `while` loop to receive messages, calling `receive` with a timeout argument. Calling `receiveNoWait` would have the same effect.

Compiling the Clients

You can compile the examples using the `asant` tool, as described in Building the Examples (page xli).

To compile the examples, do the following:

1. In a terminal window, go to the following directory:
   ```
   <INSTALL>/j2eetutorial14/examples/jms/simple/
   ```
2. Type the following command:
   ```
   asant build
   ```

This command uses the `build.xml` file in the `simple` directory to compile all the source files in the directory. The class files are placed in the `build` directory.

Starting the JMS Provider

When you use the Application Server, your JMS provider is the Application Server. Start the server as described in Starting and Stopping the Application Server (page 25).

Creating JMS Administered Objects

Creating the JMS administered objects for this section involves the following:

- Starting the Admin Console
- Creating two connection factories
- Creating two physical destinations
- Creating two destination resources

If you built and ran the SimpleMessage example in Chapter 28 and did not delete the resources afterward, you need to create only half of these resources: those that involve topics.

To start the Admin Console, follow the instructions in Starting the Admin Console (page 27).

To create the connection factories, perform the following steps:

1. In the tree component, expand the Java Message Service node.
2. Select the Connection Factories node.
3. On the JMS Connection Factories page, click New. The Create JMS Connection Factory page appears.
4. In the JNDI Name field, type jms/QueueConnectionFactory.
5. Choose javax.jms.QueueConnectionFactory from the Type combo box.
6. Select the Enabled checkbox. The Admin Console appears as shown in Figure 33–6.
7. Click OK to save the connection factory.
8. Click New again.
9. In the JNDI Name field, type jms/TopicConnectionFactory.
10. Choose javax.jms.TopicConnectionFactory from the Type combo box.
11. Select the Enabled checkbox.
12. Click OK.

To create the physical destinations, perform the following steps:

1. Select the Physical Destinations node.
2. On the Physical Destinations page, click New. The Create Physical Destination page appears.
3. In the Physical Destination Name field, type PhysicalQueue.
4. Choose queue from the Type combo box.

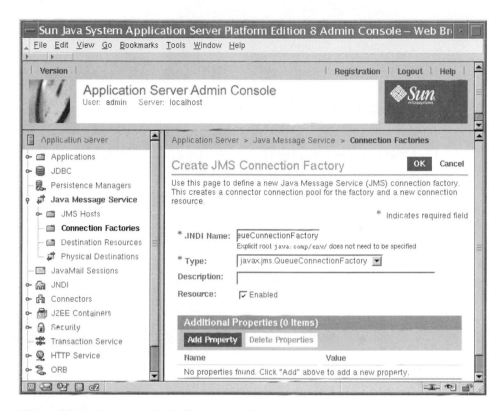

Figure 33–6   Creating a JMS Connection Factory

5. Click OK.

6. Click New again.

7. In the Physical Destination Name field, type `PhysicalTopic`.

8. Choose `topic` from the Type combo box.

9. Click OK.

To create the destination resources and link them to the physical destinations, perform the following steps:

1. In the tree component, expand Destination Resources.

2. On the JMS Destination Resources page, click New. The Create JMS Destination Resource page appears.

3. In the JNDI Name field, type `jms/Queue`.

4. Choose `javax.jms.Queue` from the Type combo box.

5. Select the Enabled checkbox.

6. Under Additional Properties, click Add.

7. Type `Name` in the Name field.

8. Type `PhysicalQueue` in the Value field.

9. Click OK.

10. Click New again.

11. In the JNDI Name field, type `jms/Topic`.

12. Choose `javax.jms.Topic` from the Type combo box.

13. Select the Enabled checkbox.

14. Under Additional Properties, click Add.

15. Enter `Name` in the Name field.

16. Enter `PhysicalTopic` in the Value field. The Admin Console appears as shown in Figure 33–7.

17. Click OK to save the resource.

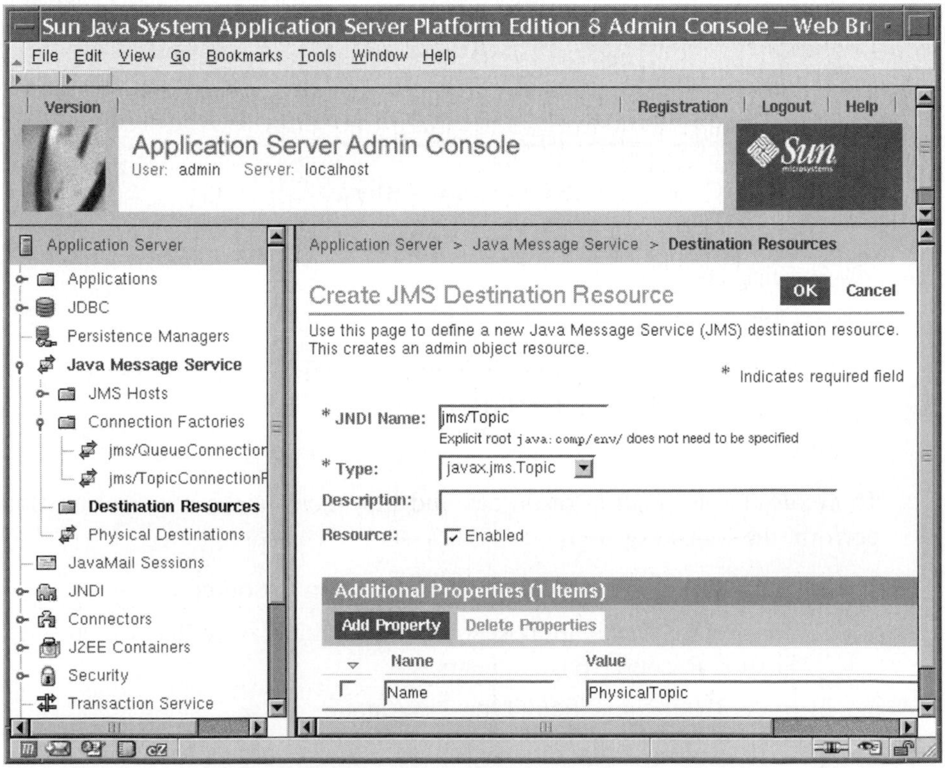

Figure 33–7 Creating a JMS Destination Resource

Packaging the Clients

The simplest way to run these examples using the Application Server is to package each one in an application client JAR file.

First, start `deploytool`:

- On Windows systems, choose Start→Programs→Sun Microsystems→J2EE 1.4 SDK→Deploytool.
- On UNIX systems, use the `deploytool` command.

Package the `SimpleProducer` example as follows:

1. Choose File→New→Application Client to start the Application Client wizard.
2. In the JAR File Contents screen, select the radio button labeled Create New Stand-Alone AppClient Module.
3. Click Browse next to the AppClient Location field and navigate to the `<INSTALL>/j2eetutorial14/examples/jms/simple/` directory.
4. Type `SimpleProducer` in the File Name field, and click Create Module File.
5. Verify that `SimpleProducer` appears in the AppClient Name field.
6. Click the Edit button next to the Contents text area.
7. In the dialog box, locate the `build` directory. Select `Simple-Producer.class` from the Available Files tree. Click Add and then OK.
8. In the General screen, select `SimpleProducer` in the Main Class combo box.
9. Click Next.
10. Click Finish.

Package the `SimpleSynchConsumer` example in the same way, except for the values listed in Table 33–3.

Table 33–3 Application Values for `SimpleSynchConsumer`

Wizard Field or Area	Value
File Name	`SimpleSynchConsumer.jar`
AppClient Name	`SimpleSynchConsumer`
Available Files class	`build/SimpleSynchConsumer.class`
Main Class	`SimpleSynchConsumer`

Running the Clients

You run the sample programs using the `appclient` command. Each of the programs takes command-line arguments: a destination name, a destination type, and, for `SimpleProducer`, a number of messages.

Run the clients as follows.

1. Run the `SimpleProducer` program, sending three messages to the queue `jms/Queue`:

   ```
   appclient -client SimpleProducer.jar jms/Queue queue 3
   ```

   The output of the program looks like this:

   ```
   Destination name is jms/Queue, type is queue
   Sending message: This is message 1
   Sending message: This is message 2
   Sending message: This is message 3
   ```

   The messages are now in the queue, waiting to be received.

2. In the same window, run the `SimpleSynchConsumer` program, specifying the queue name and type:

   ```
   appclient -client SimpleSynchConsumer.jar jms/Queue queue
   ```

   The output of the program looks like this:

   ```
   Destination name is jms/Queue, type is queue
   Reading message: This is message 1
   Reading message: This is message 2
   Reading message: This is message 3
   ```

3. Now try running the programs in the opposite order. Run the `SimpleSynchConsumer` program. It displays the queue name and then appears to hang, waiting for messages.

4. In a different terminal window, run the `SimpleProducer` program. When the messages have been sent, the `SimpleSynchConsumer` program receives them and exits.

5. Now run the `SimpleProducer` program using a topic instead of a queue:

   ```
   appclient -client SimpleProducer.jar jms/Topic topic 3
   ```

   The output of the program looks like this:

   ```
   Destination name is jms/Topic, type is topic
   Sending message: This is message 1
   Sending message: This is message 2
   Sending message: This is message 3
   ```

6. Now run the `SimpleSynchConsumer` program using the topic:

```
appclient -client SimpleSynchConsumer.jar jms/Topic topic
```

   The result, however, is different. Because you are using a topic, messages that were sent before you started the consumer cannot be received. (See Publish/Subscribe Messaging Domain, page 1160, for details.) Instead of receiving the messages, the program appears to hang.

7. Run the `SimpleProducer` program again in another terminal window. Now the `SimpleSynchConsumer` program receives the messages:

```
Destination name is jms/Topic, type is topic
Reading message: This is message 1
Reading message: This is message 2
Reading message: This is message 3
```

Because the examples use the common interfaces, you can run them using either a queue or a topic.

A Simple Example of Asynchronous Message Consumption

This section describes the receiving programs in an example that uses a message listener to consume messages asynchronously. This section then explains how to compile and run the programs using the Application Server.

The following sections describe the steps in creating and running the example:

- Writing the client programs
- Compiling the clients
- Starting the JMS provider
- Packaging the `SimpleAsynchConsumer` client
- Running the clients

Writing the Client Programs

The sending program is `src/SimpleProducer.java`, the same program used in the example in A Simple Example of Synchronous Message Receives (page 1174). You may, however, want to comment out the following line of code, where the producer sends a nontext control message to indicate the end of the messages:

```
producer.send(session.createMessage());
```

An asynchronous consumer normally runs indefinitely. This one runs until the user types the letter q or Q to stop the program, so it does not use the nontext control message.

The receiving program, `src/SimpleAsynchConsumer.java`, performs the following steps:

1. Performs a JNDI lookup of the `ConnectionFactory` and `Destination`.
2. Creates a `Connection` and a `Session`.
3. Creates a `MessageConsumer`.
4. Creates an instance of the `TextListener` class and registers it as the message listener for the `MessageConsumer`:

```
listener = new TextListener();
consumer.setMessageListener(listener);
```

5. Starts the connection, causing message delivery to begin.
6. Listens for the messages published to the destination, stopping when the user types the character q or Q:

```
System.out.println("To end program, type Q or q, " +
   "then <return>");
inputStreamReader = new InputStreamReader(System.in);
while (!((answer == 'q') || (answer == 'Q'))) {
   try {
      answer = (char) inputStreamReader.read();
   } catch (IOException e) {
      System.out.println("I/O exception: "
         + e.toString());
   }
}
```

7. Closes the connection, which automatically closes the session and `MessageConsumer`.

The message listener, `src/TextListener.java`, follows these steps:

1. When a message arrives, the `onMessage` method is called automatically.
2. The `onMessage` method converts the incoming message to a `TextMessage` and displays its content. If the message is not a text message, it reports this fact:

```
public void onMessage(Message message) {
   TextMessage msg = null;
```

```
    try {
      if (message instanceof TextMessage) {
        msg = (TextMessage) message;
        System.out.println("Reading message: " +
          msg.getText());
      } else {
        System.out.println("Message is not a " +
          "TextMessage");
      }
    } catch (JMSException e) {
      System.out.println("JMSException in onMessage(): " +
        e.toString());
    } catch (Throwable t) {
      System.out.println("Exception in onMessage():" +
        t.getMessage());
    }
  }
}
```

Compiling the Clients

Compile the programs if you did not do so before or if you edited `SimplePro-ducer.java` as described in Writing the Client Programs (page 1183):

```
asant build
```

Starting the JMS Provider

If you did not do so before, start the Application Server in another terminal window.

You will use the connection factories and destinations you created in Creating JMS Administered Objects (page 1178).

Packaging the SimpleAsynchConsumer Client

If you did not do so before, start `deploytool`.

If you did not package the `SimpleProducer` example, follow the instructions in Packaging the Clients (page 1181) to do so. Package the `SimpleAsynch-Consumer` example in the same way as `SimpleProducer`, except for the values listed in Table 33–4.

Table 33–4 Application Values for `SimpleAsynchConsumer`

Wizard Field or Area	Value
File Name	`SimpleAsynchConsumer.jar`
AppClient Name	`SimpleAsynchConsumer`
Available Files classes	`build/SimpleAsynchConsumer.class` `build/TextListener.class`
Main Class	`SimpleAsynchConsumer`

Running the Clients

As before, you run the sample programs using the `appclient` command.

Run the clients as follows.

1. Run the `SimpleAsynchConsumer` program, specifying the topic `jms/Topic` and its type.

   ```
   appclient -client SimpleAsynchConsumer.jar jms/Topic topic
   ```

   The program displays the following lines and appears to hang:

   ```
   Destination name is jms/Topic, type is topic
   To end program, type Q or q, then <return>
   ```

2. In another terminal window, run the `SimpleProducer` program, sending three messages.

   ```
   appclient -client SimpleProducer.jar jms/Topic topic 3
   ```

   The output of the program looks like this:

   ```
   Destination name is jms/Topic, type is topic
   Sending message: This is message 1
   Sending message: This is message 2
   Sending message: This is message 3
   ```

   In the other window, the `SimpleAsynchConsumer` program displays the following:

   ```
   Destination name is jms/Topic, type is topic
   To end program, type Q or q, then <return>
   Reading message: This is message 1
   Reading message: This is message 2
   Reading message: This is message 3
   ```

If you did not edit `SimpleProducer.java`, the following line also appears:

```
Message is not a TextMessage
```

3. Type Q or q to stop the program.

4. Now run the programs using a queue. In this case, as with the synchronous example, you can run the `SimpleProducer` program first, because there is no timing dependency between the sender and receiver:

```
appclient -client SimpleProducer.jar jms/Queue queue 3
```

The output of the program looks like this:

```
Destination name is jms/Queue, type is queue
Sending message: This is message 1
Sending message: This is message 2
Sending message: This is message 3
```

5. Run the `SimpleAsynchConsumer` program:

```
appclient -client SimpleAsynchConsumer.jar jms/Queue queue
```

The output of the program looks like this:

```
Destination name is jms/Queue, type is queue
To end program, type Q or q, then <return>
Reading message: This is message 1
Reading message: This is message 2
Reading message: This is message 3
```

6. Type Q or q to stop the program.

Running JMS Client Programs on Multiple Systems

JMS client programs using the Application Server can exchange messages with each other when they are running on different systems in a network. The systems must be visible to each other by name—the UNIX host name or the Microsoft Windows computer name—and must both be running the Application Server. You do not have to install the tutorial examples on both systems; you can use the examples installed on one system if you can access its file system from the other system.

Note: Any mechanism for exchanging messages between systems is specific to the J2EE server implementation. This tutorial describes how to use the Application Server for this purpose.

Suppose that you want to run the `SimpleProducer` program on one system, earth, and the `SimpleSynchConsumer` program on another system, `jupiter`. Before you can do so, you need to perform these tasks:

- Create two new connection factories
- Edit the source code
- Recompile the source code and update the client JAR files

Note: A limitation in the JMS provider in the Application Server may cause a runtime failure to create a connection to systems that use the Dynamic Host Configuration Protocol (DHCP) to obtain an IP address. You can, however, create a connection *from* a system that uses DHCP *to* a system that does not use DHCP. In the examples in this tutorial, earth can be a system that uses DHCP, and `jupiter` can be a system that does not use DHCP.

Before you begin, start the server on both systems:

1. Start the Application Server on earth and log in to the Admin Console.
2. Start the Application Server on `jupiter` and log in to the Admin Console.

Creating Administered Objects for Multiple Systems

To run these programs, you must do the following:

- Create a new connection factory on both earth and `jupiter`
- Create a destination resource and physical destination on both earth and `jupiter`

Create a new connection factory on `jupiter` as follows:

1. In the Admin Console, expand the Java Message Service node.
2. Select the Connection Factories node.
3. On the JMS Connection Factories page, click New. The Create JMS Connection Factory page appears.
4. In the JNDI Name field, type `jms/JupiterQueueConnectionFactory`.
5. Choose `javax.jms.QueueConnectionFactory` from the Type combo box.
6. Select the Enabled checkbox.
7. Click OK.

Create a new connection factory with the same name on `earth` as follows:

1. In the Admin Console, expand the Java Message Service node.
2. Select the Connection Factories node.
3. On the JMS Connection Factories page, click New. The Create JMS Connection Factory page appears.
4. In the JNDI Name field, type `jms/JupiterQueueConnectionFactory`.
5. Choose `javax.jms.QueueConnectionFactory` from the Type combo box.
6. Select the Enabled checkbox.
7. Click Add in the Additional Properties area. A Name/Value line appears.
8. In the Name field, type `MessageServiceAddressList`.
9. In the Value field, type the name of the remote system (whatever the real name of `jupiter` is). If the JMS service on the remote system uses a port number other than the default (7676), specify the port number also, using the syntax `sys-name:port-number`.
10. Click OK.

If you have already been working on either `earth` or `jupiter`, you have the queue on one system. On the system that does not have the queue, perform the following steps:

1. Use the Admin Console to create a physical destination named `Physical-Queue`, just as you did in Creating JMS Administered Objects (page 1178).
2. Use the Admin Console to create a destination resource named `jms/Queue` and set its `Name` property to the value `PhysicalQueue`.

When you run the programs, they will work as shown in Figure 33–8. The program run on `earth` needs the queue on `earth` only in order that the JNDI lookup will succeed. The connection, session, and message producer are all created on `jupiter` using the connection factory that points to `jupiter`. The messages sent from `earth` will be received on `jupiter`.

Running the Programs

These steps assume that you have the tutorial installed on only one of the two systems you are using.

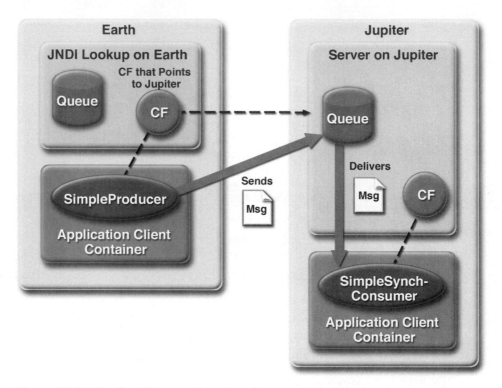

Figure 33–8 Sending Messages from One System to Another

To edit, update, and run the programs, perform the following steps on the system where you first ran them:

1. In both `SimpleProducer.java` and `SimpleSynchConsumer.java`, change the line that looks up the connection factory so that it refers to the new connection factory:

   ```
   connectionFactory = (ConnectionFactory)
       jndiContext.lookup("jms/JupiterQueueConnectionFactory");
   ```

2. Recompile the programs:

   ```
   asant build
   ```

3. In `deploytool`, choose Tools→Update Module Files to add the recompiled source files to the `SimpleProducer.jar` and `SimpleSynchConsumer.jar` files.

4. Save the changed JAR files.

5. Run `SimpleProducer` on earth:

   ```
   appclient -client SimpleProducer.jar jms/Queue queue 3
   ```

6. Run `SimpleSynchConsumer` on `jupiter`:

```
appclient -client SimpleSynchConsumer.jar jms/Queue queue
```

Because both connection factories have the same name, you can run either the producer or the consumer on either system.

For examples showing how to deploy J2EE applications on two different systems, see An Application Example That Consumes Messages from a Remote J2EE Server (page 1239) and An Application Example That Deploys a Message-Driven Bean on Two J2EE Servers (page 1246).

Deleting the Connection Factory and Stopping the Server

You will need the connection factory `jms/JupiterQueueConnectionFactory` in Chapter 34. However, if you wish to delete it, perform the following steps in the Admin Console:

1. Expand the Java Message Service node and click Connection Factories.
2. Select the checkbox next to `jms/JupiterQueueConnectionFactory` and click Delete.

Remember to delete the connection factory on both systems.

You can also use the Admin Console to delete the destinations and connection factories you created in Creating JMS Administered Objects (page 1178). However, we recommend that you keep them, because they will be used in most of the examples in Chapter 34. After you have created them, they will be available whenever you restart the Application Server.

Delete the class files for the programs as follows:

```
asant clean
```

If you wish, you can manually delete the client JAR files.

You can also stop the Application Server, but you will need it to run the sample programs in the next section.

Creating Robust JMS Applications

This section explains how to use features of the JMS API to achieve the level of reliability and performance your application requires. Many people choose to implement JMS applications because they cannot tolerate dropped or duplicate messages and require that every message be received once and only once. The JMS API provides this functionality.

The most reliable way to produce a message is to send a PERSISTENT message within a transaction. JMS messages are PERSISTENT by default. A *transaction* is a unit of work into which you can group a series of operations, such as message sends and receives, so that the operations either all succeed or all fail. For details, see Specifying Message Persistence (page 1197) and Using JMS API Local Transactions (page 1204).

The most reliable way to consume a message is to do so within a transaction, either from a queue or from a durable subscription to a topic. For details, see Creating Temporary Destinations (page 1199), Creating Durable Subscriptions (page 1200), and Using JMS API Local Transactions (page 1204).

For other applications, a lower level of reliability can reduce overhead and improve performance. You can send messages with varying priority levels—see Setting Message Priority Levels (page 1198)—and you can set them to expire after a certain length of time (see Allowing Messages to Expire, page 1198).

The JMS API provides several ways to achieve various kinds and degrees of reliability. This section divides them into two categories:

 • Using basic reliability mechanisms
 • Using advanced reliability mechanisms

The following sections describe these features as they apply to JMS clients. Some of the features work differently in J2EE applications; in these cases, the differences are noted here and are explained in detail in Using the JMS API in a J2EE Application (page 1212).

This section includes three sample programs, which you can find in the directory `<INSTALL>`/j2eetutorial14/examples/jms/advanced/src/, along with a utility class called `SampleUtilities.java`.

To compile the programs in advance, go to the `<INSTALL>`/j2eetutorial14/examples/jms/advanced directory and use the following `asant` target:

```
asant build
```

Using Basic Reliability Mechanisms

The basic mechanisms for achieving or affecting reliable message delivery are as follows:

- *Controlling message acknowledgment*: You can specify various levels of control over message acknowledgment.

- *Specifying message persistence*: You can specify that messages are persistent, meaning that they must not be lost in the event of a provider failure.

- *Setting message priority levels*: You can set various priority levels for messages, which can affect the order in which the messages are delivered.

- *Allowing messages to expire*: You can specify an expiration time for messages so that they will not be delivered if they are obsolete.

- *Creating temporary destinations*: You can create temporary destinations that last only for the duration of the connection in which they are created.

Controlling Message Acknowledgment

Until a JMS message has been acknowledged, it is not considered to be successfully consumed. The successful consumption of a message ordinarily takes place in three stages.

1. The client receives the message.
2. The client processes the message.
3. The message is acknowledged. Acknowledgment is initiated either by the JMS provider or by the client, depending on the session acknowledgment mode.

In transacted sessions (see Using JMS API Local Transactions, page 1204), acknowledgment happens automatically when a transaction is committed. If a transaction is rolled back, all consumed messages are redelivered.

In nontransacted sessions, when and how a message is acknowledged depend on the value specified as the second argument of the `createSession` method. The three possible argument values are as follows:

- `Session.AUTO_ACKNOWLEDGE`: The session automatically acknowledges a client's receipt of a message either when the client has successfully returned from a call to `receive` or when the `MessageListener` it has called to process the message returns successfully. A synchronous receive in an AUTO_ACKNOWLEDGE session is the one exception to the rule that message consumption is a three-stage process as described earlier.

In this case, the receipt and acknowledgment take place in one step, followed by the processing of the message.

- Session.CLIENT_ACKNOWLEDGE: A client acknowledges a message by calling the message's acknowledge method. In this mode, acknowledgment takes place on the session level: Acknowledging a consumed message automatically acknowledges the receipt of *all* messages that have been consumed by its session. For example, if a message consumer consumes ten messages and then acknowledges the fifth message delivered, all ten messages are acknowledged.

- Session.DUPS_OK_ACKNOWLEDGE: This option instructs the session to lazily acknowledge the delivery of messages. This is likely to result in the delivery of some duplicate messages if the JMS provider fails, so it should be used only by consumers that can tolerate duplicate messages. (If the JMS provider redelivers a message, it must set the value of the JMSRedelivered message header to true.) This option can reduce session overhead by minimizing the work the session does to prevent duplicates.

If messages have been received from a queue but not acknowledged when a session terminates, the JMS provider retains them and redelivers them when a consumer next accesses the queue. The provider also retains unacknowledged messages for a terminated session that has a durable TopicSubscriber. (See Creating Durable Subscriptions, page 1200.) Unacknowledged messages for a nondurable TopicSubscriber are dropped when the session is closed.

If you use a queue or a durable subscription, you can use the Session.recover method to stop a nontransacted session and restart it with its first unacknowledged message. In effect, the session's series of delivered messages is reset to the point after its last acknowledged message. The messages it now delivers may be different from those that were originally delivered, if messages have expired or if higher-priority messages have arrived. For a nondurable TopicSubscriber, the provider may drop unacknowledged messages when its session is recovered.

The sample program in the next section demonstrates two ways to ensure that a message will not be acknowledged until processing of the message is complete.

A Message Acknowledgment Example

The AckEquivExample.java program in the directory *<INSTALL>*/j2ee-tutorial14/examples/jms/advanced/src/ shows how both of the following two scenarios ensure that a message will not be acknowledged until processing of it is complete:

- Using an asynchronous message consumer—a message listener—in an AUTO_ACKNOWLEDGE session
- Using a synchronous receiver in a CLIENT_ACKNOWLEDGE session

With a message listener, the automatic acknowledgment happens when the onMessage method returns—that is, after message processing has finished. With a synchronous receiver, the client acknowledges the message after processing is complete. (If you use AUTO_ACKNOWLEDGE with a synchronous receive, the acknowledgment happens immediately after the receive call; if any subsequent processing steps fail, the message cannot be redelivered.)

The program contains a SynchSender class, a SynchReceiver class, an Asynch-Subscriber class with a TextListener class, a MultiplePublisher class, a main method, and a method that runs the other classes' threads.

The program uses the following objects:

- jms/QueueConnectionFactory, jms/Queue, and jms/Topic: resources that you created in Creating JMS Administered Objects (page 1178)
- jms/ControlQueue: an additional queue
- jms/DurableTopicConnectionFactory: a connection factory with a client ID (see Creating Durable Subscriptions, page 1200, for more information)

Use the Admin Console to create the new queue and connection factory as follows:

1. Create a physical destination of type queue with the name ControlQueueP.
2. Create a destination resource with the name jms/ControlQueue and type javax.jms.Queue. Add the property Name with the value ControlQueueP.
3. Create a connection factory with the name jms/DurableTopicConnectionFactory and type javax.jms.TopicConnectionFactory. Add the property ClientId with the value MyID.

If you did not do so previously, compile the source file:

```
asant build
```

To package the program, follow the instructions in Packaging the Clients (page 1181), except for the values listed in Table 33–5.

Table 33–5 Application Values for `AckEquivExample`

Wizard Field or Area	Value
AppClient Location	`<INSTALL>/j2eetutorial14/examples/jms/advanced`
File Name	`AckEquivExample.jar`
AppClient Name	`AckEquivExample`
Available Files classes	`build/AckEquivExample*.class` (7 files) `build/SampleUtilities*.class` (2 files)
Main Class	`AckEquivExample`

To run the program, use the following command:

```
appclient -client AckEquivExample.jar
```

The program output looks like this:

```
Queue name is jms/ControlQueue
Queue name is jms/Queue
Topic name is jms/Topic
Connection factory name is jms/DurableTopicConnectionFactory
  SENDER: Created client-acknowledge session
  SENDER: Sending message: Here is a client-acknowledge message
  RECEIVER: Created client-acknowledge session
  RECEIVER: Processing message: Here is a client-acknowledge
message
  RECEIVER: Now I'll acknowledge the message
PUBLISHER: Created auto-acknowledge session
SUBSCRIBER: Created auto-acknowledge session
PUBLISHER: Receiving synchronize messages from jms/
ControlQueue; count = 1
SUBSCRIBER: Sending synchronize message to jms/ControlQueue
PUBLISHER: Received synchronize message;  expect 0 more
PUBLISHER: Publishing message: Here is an auto-acknowledge
message 1
PUBLISHER: Publishing message: Here is an auto-acknowledge
message 2
SUBSCRIBER: Processing message: Here is an auto-acknowledge
message 1
PUBLISHER: Publishing message: Here is an auto-acknowledge
message 3
```

```
SUBSCRIBER: Processing message: Here is an auto-acknowledge
message 2
SUBSCRIBER: Processing message: Here is an auto-acknowledge
message 3
```

After you run the program, you can delete the physical destination `Control-QueueP` and the destination resource `jms/ControlQueue`.

Specifying Message Persistence

The JMS API supports two delivery modes for messages to specify whether messages are lost if the JMS provider fails. These delivery modes are fields of the `DeliveryMode` interface.

- The `PERSISTENT` delivery mode, which is the default, instructs the JMS provider to take extra care to ensure that a message is not lost in transit in case of a JMS provider failure. A message sent with this delivery mode is logged to stable storage when it is sent.

- The `NON_PERSISTENT` delivery mode does not require the JMS provider to store the message or otherwise guarantee that it is not lost if the provider fails.

You can specify the delivery mode in either of two ways.

- You can use the `setDeliveryMode` method of the `MessageProducer` interface to set the delivery mode for all messages sent by that producer. For example, the following call sets the delivery mode to `NON_PERSISTENT` for a producer:

  ```
  producer.setDeliveryMode(DeliveryMode.NON_PERSISTENT);
  ```

- You can use the long form of the `send` or the `publish` method to set the delivery mode for a specific message. The second argument sets the delivery mode. For example, the following `send` call sets the delivery mode for `message` to NON_PERSISTENT:

  ```
  producer.send(message, DeliveryMode.NON_PERSISTENT, 3,
      10000);
  ```

  The third and fourth arguments set the priority level and expiration time, which are described in the next two subsections.

If you do not specify a delivery mode, the default is `PERSISTENT`. Using the `NON_PERSISTENT` delivery mode may improve performance and reduce storage overhead, but you should use it only if your application can afford to miss messages.

Setting Message Priority Levels

You can use message priority levels to instruct the JMS provider to deliver urgent messages first. You can set the priority level in either of two ways.

- You can use the `setPriority` method of the `MessageProducer` interface to set the priority level for all messages sent by that producer. For example, the following call sets a priority level of 7 for a producer:

  ```
  producer.setPriority(7);
  ```

- You can use the long form of the `send` or the `publish` method to set the priority level for a specific message. The third argument sets the priority level. For example, the following `send` call sets the priority level for `message` to 3:

  ```
  producer.send(message, DeliveryMode.NON_PERSISTENT, 3,
      10000);
  ```

The ten levels of priority range from 0 (lowest) to 9 (highest). If you do not specify a priority level, the default level is 4. A JMS provider tries to deliver higher-priority messages before lower-priority ones but does not have to deliver messages in exact order of priority.

Allowing Messages to Expire

By default, a message never expires. If a message will become obsolete after a certain period, however, you may want to set an expiration time. You can do this in either of two ways.

- You can use the `setTimeToLive` method of the `MessageProducer` interface to set a default expiration time for all messages sent by that producer. For example, the following call sets a time to live of one minute for a producer:

  ```
  producer.setTimeToLive(60000);
  ```

- You can use the long form of the `send` or the `publish` method to set an expiration time for a specific message. The fourth argument sets the expiration time in milliseconds. For example, the following `send` call sets a time to live of 10 seconds:

  ```
  producer.send(message, DeliveryMode.NON_PERSISTENT, 3,
      10000);
  ```

If the specified `timeToLive` value is 0, the message never expires.

When the message is sent, the specified `timeToLive` is added to the current time to give the expiration time. Any message not delivered before the specified expiration time is destroyed. The destruction of obsolete messages conserves storage and computing resources.

Creating Temporary Destinations

Normally, you create JMS destinations—queues and topics—administratively rather than programmatically. Your JMS provider includes a tool that you use to create and remove destinations, and it is common for destinations to be long-lasting.

The JMS API also enables you to create destinations—`TemporaryQueue` and `TemporaryTopic` objects—that last only for the duration of the connection in which they are created. You create these destinations dynamically using the `Session.createTemporaryQueue` and the `Session.createTemporaryTopic` methods.

The only message consumers that can consume from a temporary destination are those created by the same connection that created the destination. Any message producer can send to the temporary destination. If you close the connection that a temporary destination belongs to, the destination is closed and its contents are lost.

You can use temporary destinations to implement a simple request/reply mechanism. If you create a temporary destination and specify it as the value of the `JMSReplyTo` message header field when you send a message, then the consumer of the message can use the value of the `JMSReplyTo` field as the destination to which it sends a reply. The consumer can also reference the original request by setting the `JMSCorrelationID` header field of the reply message to the value of the `JMSMessageID` header field of the request. For example, an `onMessage` method can create a session so that it can send a reply to the message it receives. It can use code such as the following:

```
producer = session.createProducer(msg.getJMSReplyTo());
replyMsg = session.createTextMessage("Consumer " +
  "processed message: " + msg.getText());
replyMsg.setJMSCorrelationID(msg.getJMSMessageID());
producer.send(replyMsg);
```

For more examples, see Chapter 34.

Using Advanced Reliability Mechanisms

The more advanced mechanisms for achieving reliable message delivery are the following:

- *Creating durable subscriptions*: You can create durable topic subscriptions, which receive messages published while the subscriber is not active. Durable subscriptions offer the reliability of queues to the publish/subscribe message domain.
- *Using local transactions*: You can use local transactions, which allow you to group a series of sends and receives into an atomic unit of work. Transactions are rolled back if they fail at any time.

Creating Durable Subscriptions

To ensure that a pub/sub application receives all published messages, use PERSISTENT delivery mode for the publishers. In addition, use durable subscriptions for the subscribers.

The `Session.createConsumer` method creates a nondurable subscriber if a topic is specified as the destination. A nondurable subscriber can receive only messages that are published while it is active.

At the cost of higher overhead, you can use the `Session.createDurableSubscriber` method to create a durable subscriber. A durable subscription can have only one active subscriber at a time.

A durable subscriber registers a durable subscription by specifying a unique identity that is retained by the JMS provider. Subsequent subscriber objects that have the same identity resume the subscription in the state in which it was left by the preceding subscriber. If a durable subscription has no active subscriber, the JMS provider retains the subscription's messages until they are received by the subscription or until they expire.

You establish the unique identity of a durable subscriber by setting the following:

- A client ID for the connection
- A topic and a subscription name for the subscriber

You set the client ID administratively for a client-specific connection factory using the Admin Console.

After using this connection factory to create the connection and the session, you call the `createDurableSubscriber` method with two arguments: the topic and a string that specifies the name of the subscription:

```
String subName = "MySub";
MessageConsumer topicSubscriber =
    session.createDurableSubscriber(myTopic, subName);
```

The subscriber becomes active after you start the `Connection` or `TopicConnection`. Later, you might close the subscriber:

```
topicSubscriber.close();
```

The JMS provider stores the messages sent or published to the topic, as it would store messages sent to a queue. If the program or another application calls `createDurableSubscriber` using the same connection factory and its client ID, the same topic, and the same subscription name, the subscription is reactivated, and the JMS provider delivers the messages that were published while the subscriber was inactive.

To delete a durable subscription, first close the subscriber, and then use the `unsubscribe` method, with the subscription name as the argument:

```
topicSubscriber.close();
session.unsubscribe("MySub");
```

The `unsubscribe` method deletes the state that the provider maintains for the subscriber.

Figures 33–9 and 33–10 show the difference between a nondurable and a durable subscriber. With an ordinary, nondurable subscriber, the subscriber and the subscription begin and end at the same point and are, in effect, identical. When a

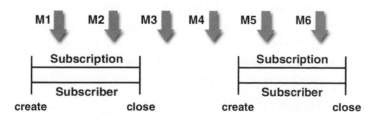

Figure 33–9 Nondurable Subscribers and Subscriptions

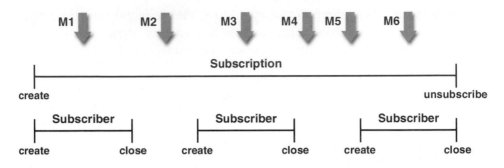

Figure 33–10 A Durable Subscriber and Subscription

subscriber is closed, the subscription also ends. Here, create stands for a call to Session.createConsumer with a Topic argument, and close stands for a call to MessageConsumer.close. Any messages published to the topic between the time of the first close and the time of the second create are not consumed by the subscriber. In Figure 33–9, the subscriber consumes messages M1, M2, M5, and M6, but messages M3 and M4 are lost.

With a durable subscriber, the subscriber can be closed and re-created, but the subscription continues to exist and to hold messages until the application calls the unsubscribe method. In Figure 33–10, create stands for a call to Session.createDurableSubscriber, close stands for a call to MessageConsumer.close, and unsubscribe stands for a call to Session.unsubscribe. Messages published while the subscriber is closed are received when the subscriber is created again. So even though messages M2, M4, and M5 arrive while the subscriber is closed, they are not lost.

See A J2EE Application That Uses the JMS API with a Session Bean (page 1222) for an example of a J2EE application that uses durable subscriptions. See A Message Acknowledgment Example (page 1194) and the next section for examples of client applications that use durable subscriptions.

A Durable Subscription Example

The DurableSubscriberExample.java program in the directory *<INSTALL>*/j2eetutorial14/examples/jms/advanced/src/ shows how durable subscriptions work. It demonstrates that a durable subscription is active even when the subscriber is not active. The program contains a DurableSubscriber class, a

MultiplePublisher class, a main method, and a method that instantiates the classes and calls their methods in sequence.

The program begins in the same way as any publish/subscribe program: The subscriber starts, the publisher publishes some messages, and the subscriber receives them. At this point, the subscriber closes itself. The publisher then publishes some messages while the subscriber is not active. The subscriber then restarts and receives the messages.

Before you run this program, compile the source file and create a connection factory that has a client ID. If you did not already do so in A Message Acknowledgment Example (page 1194), perform the following steps:

1. Compile the source code as follows:

   asant build

2. Create a connection factory with the name jms/DurableTopicConnectionFactory and type javax.jms.TopicConnectionFactory. Add the property ClientId with the value MyID.

To package the program, follow the instructions in Packaging the Clients (page 1181), except for the values listed in Table 33–6.

Use the following command to run the program. The destination is jms/Topic:

   appclient -client DurableSubscriberExample.jar

Table 33–6 Application Values for DurableSubscriberExample

Wizard Field or Area	Value
AppClient Location	<INSTALL>/j2eetutorial14/examples/jms/advanced
File Name	DurableSubscriberExample.jar
AppClient Name	DurableSubscriberExample
Available Files classes	build/DurableSubscriberExample*.class (5 files) build/SampleUtilities*.class (2 files)
Main Class	DurableSubscriberExample

The output looks something like this:

```
Connection factory without client ID is jms/
TopicConnectionFactory
Connection factory with client ID is jms/
DurableTopicConnectionFactory
Topic name is jms/Topic
Starting subscriber
PUBLISHER: Publishing message: Here is a message 1
SUBSCRIBER: Reading message: Here is a message 1
PUBLISHER: Publishing message: Here is a message 2
SUBSCRIBER: Reading message: Here is a message 2
PUBLISHER: Publishing message: Here is a message 3
SUBSCRIBER: Reading message: Here is a message 3
Closing subscriber
PUBLISHER: Publishing message: Here is a message 4
PUBLISHER: Publishing message: Here is a message 5
PUBLISHER: Publishing message: Here is a message 6
Starting subscriber
SUBSCRIBER: Reading message: Here is a message 4
SUBSCRIBER: Reading message: Here is a message 5
SUBSCRIBER: Reading message: Here is a message 6
Closing subscriber
Unsubscribing from durable subscription
```

Using JMS API Local Transactions

You can group a series of operations into an atomic unit of work called a transaction. If any one of the operations fails, the transaction can be rolled back, and the operations can be attempted again from the beginning. If all the operations succeed, the transaction can be committed.

In a JMS client, you can use local transactions to group message sends and receives. The JMS API `Session` interface provides `commit` and `rollback` methods that you can use in a JMS client. A transaction commit means that all produced messages are sent and all consumed messages are acknowledged. A transaction rollback means that all produced messages are destroyed and all consumed messages are recovered and redelivered unless they have expired (see Allowing Messages to Expire, page 1198).

A transacted session is always involved in a transaction. As soon as the `commit` or the `rollback` method is called, one transaction ends and another transaction begins. Closing a transacted session rolls back its transaction in progress, including any pending sends and receives.

In an Enterprise JavaBeans component, you cannot use the `Session.commit` and `Session.rollback` methods. Instead, you use distributed transactions, which are described in Using the JMS API in a J2EE Application (page 1212).

You can combine several sends and receives in a single JMS API local transaction. If you do so, you need to be careful about the order of the operations. You will have no problems if the transaction consists of all sends or all receives or if the receives come before the sends. But if you try to use a request/reply mechanism, whereby you send a message and then try to receive a reply to the sent message in the same transaction, the program will hang, because the send cannot take place until the transaction is committed. The following code fragment illustrates the problem:

```
// Don't do this!
outMsg.setJMSReplyTo(replyQueue);
producer.send(outQueue, outMsg);
consumer = session.createConsumer(replyQueue);
inMsg = consumer.receive();
session.commit();
```

Because a message sent during a transaction is not actually sent until the transaction is committed, the transaction cannot contain any receives that depend on that message's having been sent.

In addition, the production and the consumption of a message cannot both be part of the same transaction. The reason is that the transactions take place between the clients and the JMS provider, which intervenes between the production and the consumption of the message. Figure 33–11 illustrates this interaction.

The sending of one or more messages to one or more destinations by client 1 can form a single transaction, because it forms a single set of interactions with the JMS provider using a single session. Similarly, the receiving of one or more messages from one or more destinations by client 2 also forms a single transaction

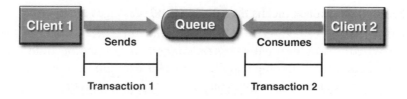

Figure 33–11 Using JMS API Local Transactions

using a single session. But because the two clients have no direct interaction and are using two different sessions, no transactions can take place between them.

Another way of putting this is that the act of producing and/or consuming messages in a session can be transactional, but the act of producing and consuming a specific message across different sessions cannot be transactional.

This is the fundamental difference between messaging and synchronized processing. Instead of tightly coupling the sending and receiving of data, message producers and consumers use an alternative approach to reliability, one that is built on a JMS provider's ability to supply a once-and-only-once message delivery guarantee.

When you create a session, you specify whether it is transacted. The first argument to the `createSession` method is a `boolean` value. A value of `true` means that the session is transacted; a value of `false` means that it is not transacted. The second argument to this method is the acknowledgment mode, which is relevant only to nontransacted sessions (see Controlling Message Acknowledgment, page 1193). If the session is transacted, the second argument is ignored, so it is a good idea to specify `0` to make the meaning of your code clear. For example:

```
session = connection.createSession(true, 0);
```

The `commit` and the `rollback` methods for local transactions are associated with the session. You can combine queue and topic operations in a single transaction if you use the same session to perform the operations. For example, you can use the same session to receive a message from a queue and send a message to a topic in the same transaction.

You can pass a client program's session to a message listener's constructor function and use it to create a message producer. In this way, you can use the same session for receives and sends in asynchronous message consumers.

The next section provides an example of the use of JMS API local transactions.

A Local Transaction Example

The `TransactedExample.java` program in the directory `<INSTALL>/j2eetutorial14/examples/jms/advanced/src/` demonstrates the use of transactions in a JMS client application. This example shows how to use a queue and a topic in a single transaction as well as how to pass a session to a message listener's constructor function. The program represents a highly simplified e-commerce application in which the following things happen.

1. A retailer sends a `MapMessage` to the vendor order queue, ordering a quantity of computers, and waits for the vendor's reply:

```
producer =
    session.createProducer(vendorOrderQueue);
outMessage = session.createMapMessage();
outMessage.setString("Item", "Computer(s)");
outMessage.setInt("Quantity", quantity);
outMessage.setJMSReplyTo(retailerConfirmQueue);
producer.send(outMessage);
System.out.println("Retailer: ordered " +
    quantity + " computer(s)");

orderConfirmReceiver =
    session.createConsumer(retailerConfirmQueue);
connection.start();
```

2. The vendor receives the retailer's order message and sends an order message to the supplier order topic in one transaction. This JMS transaction uses a single session, so we can combine a receive from a queue with a send to a topic. Here is the code that uses the same session to create a consumer for a queue and a producer for a topic:

```
vendorOrderReceiver =
    session.createConsumer(vendorOrderQueue);
supplierOrderProducer =
    session.createProducer(supplierOrderTopic);
```

The following code receives the incoming message, sends an outgoing message, and commits the session. The message processing has been removed to keep the sequence simple:

```
inMessage = vendorOrderReceiver.receive();
// Process the incoming message and format the outgoing
// message
...
supplierOrderProducer.send(orderMessage);
...
session.commit();
```

3. Each supplier receives the order from the order topic, checks its inventory, and then sends the items ordered to the queue named in the order message's `JMSReplyTo` field. If it does not have enough in stock, the supplier sends what it has. The synchronous receive from the topic and the send to the queue take place in one JMS transaction.

```
receiver = session.createConsumer(orderTopic);
...
inMessage = receiver.receive();
if (inMessage instanceof MapMessage) {
   orderMessage = (MapMessage) inMessage;
   // Process message
MessageProducer producer =
   session.createProducer((Queue)
      orderMessage.getJMSReplyTo());
outMessage = session.createMapMessage();
// Add content to message
producer.send(outMessage);
// Display message contents
session.commit();
```

4. The vendor receives the replies from the suppliers from its confirmation
   queue and updates the state of the order. Messages are processed by an
   asynchronous message listener; this step shows the use of JMS transactions with a message listener.

```
MapMessage component = (MapMessage) message;
...
orderNumber =
   component.getInt("VendorOrderNumber");
Order order =
   Order.getOrder(orderNumber).processSubOrder(component);
session.commit();
```

5. When all outstanding replies are processed for a given order, the vendor
   message listener sends a message notifying the retailer whether it can ful-
   fill the order.

```
Queue replyQueue =
   (Queue) order.order.getJMSReplyTo();
MessageProducer producer =
   session.createProducer(replyQueue);
MapMessage retailerConfirmMessage =
   session.createMapMessage();
// Format the message
producer.send(retailerConfirmMessage);
session.commit();
```

6. The retailer receives the message from the vendor:

```
inMessage =
   (MapMessage) orderConfirmReceiver.receive();
```

Figure 33–12 illustrates these steps.

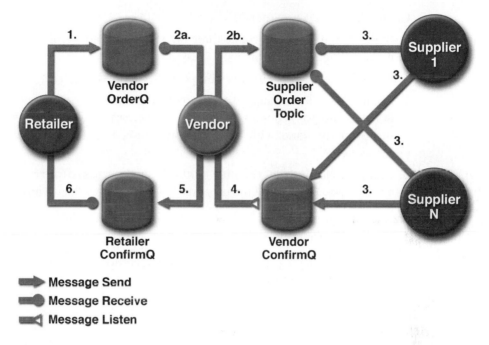

Figure 33–12 Transactions: JMS Client Example

The program contains five classes: `Retailer`, `Vendor`, `GenericSupplier`, `VendorMessageListener`, and `Order`. The program also contains a `main` method and a method that runs the threads of the `Retailer`, `Vendor`, and two supplier classes.

All the messages use the `MapMessage` message type. Synchronous receives are used for all message reception except for the case of the vendor processing the replies of the suppliers. These replies are processed asynchronously and demonstrate how to use transactions within a message listener.

At random intervals, the `Vendor` class throws an exception to simulate a database problem and cause a rollback.

All classes except `Retailer` use transacted sessions.

The program uses three queues named `jms/AQueue`, `jms/BQueue`, and `jms/CQueue`, and one topic named `jms/OTopic`. Before you run the program, do the following:

1. Compile the program if you did not do so previously:

```
asant build
```

2. Create the necessary resources:

   a. In the Admin Console, create three physical destinations of type `queue` named `AQueueP`, `BQueueP`, and `CQueueP`.

   b. Create a physical destination of type `topic` named `OTopicP`.

   c. Create three destination resources with the names `jms/AQueue`, `jms/BQueue`, and `jms/CQueue`, all of type `javax.jms.Queue`. For each, add the property `Name` with the value `AQueueP`, `BQueueP`, or `CQueueP`, respectively.

   d. Create a destination resource with the name `jms/OTopic` of type `javax.jms.Topic`. Add the property `Name` with the value `OTopicP`.

To package the program, follow the instructions in Packaging the Clients (page 1181), except for the values listed in Table 33–7.

Run the program, specifying the number of computers to be ordered. To order three computers, use the following command:

```
appclient -client TransactedExample.jar 3
```

The output looks something like this:

```
Quantity to be ordered is 3
Retailer: ordered 3 computer(s)
Vendor: Retailer ordered 3 Computer(s)
Vendor: ordered 3 monitor(s) and hard drive(s)
Monitor Supplier: Vendor ordered 3 Monitor(s)
Monitor Supplier: sent 3 Monitor(s)
  Monitor Supplier: committed transaction
  Vendor: committed transaction 1
Hard Drive Supplier: Vendor ordered 3 Hard Drive(s)
Hard Drive Supplier: sent 1 Hard Drive(s)
Vendor: Completed processing for order 1
  Hard Drive Supplier: committed transaction
Vendor: unable to send 3 computer(s)
  Vendor: committed transaction 2
Retailer: Order not filled
Retailer: placing another order
Retailer: ordered 6 computer(s)
Vendor: JMSException occurred: javax.jms.JMSException:
Simulated database concurrent access exception
```

Table 33–7   Application Values for `TransactedExample`

Wizard Field or Area	Value
AppClient Location	`<INSTALL>/j2eetutorial14/examples/jms/advanced`
File Name	`TransactedExample.jar`
AppClient Name	`TransactedExample`
Available Files classes	`build/TransactedExample*.class` (6 files) `build/SampleUtilities*.class` (2 files)
Main Class	`TransactedExample`

```
javax.jms.JMSException: Simulated database concurrent access
exception
        at TransactedExample$Vendor.run(Unknown Source)
  Vendor: rolled back transaction 1
Vendor: Retailer ordered 6 Computer(s)
Vendor: ordered 6 monitor(s) and hard drive(s)
Monitor Supplier: Vendor ordered 6 Monitor(s)
Hard Drive Supplier: Vendor ordered 6 Hard Drive(s)
Monitor Supplier: sent 6 Monitor(s)
  Monitor Supplier: committed transaction
Hard Drive Supplier: sent 6 Hard Drive(s)
  Hard Drive Supplier: committed transaction
  Vendor: committed transaction 1
Vendor: Completed processing for order 2
Vendor: sent 6 computer(s)
Retailer: Order filled
  Vendor: committed transaction 2
```

When you have finished with this sample application, use the Admin Console to delete the physical destinations `AQueueP`, `BQueueP`, `CQueueP`, and `OTopicP`, and the destination resources `jms/AQueue`, `jms/BQueue`, `jms/CQueue`, and `jms/OTopic`.

Use the following command to remove the class files:

```
asant clean
```

If you wish, you can manually remove the client JAR files.

Using the JMS API in a J2EE Application

This section describes the ways in which using the JMS API in a J2EE application differs from using it in a stand-alone client application:

- Using session and entity beans to produce and to synchronously receive messages
- Using message-driven beans to receive messages asynchronously
- Managing distributed transactions
- Using application clients and Web components

A general rule new in the J2EE 1.4 platform specification applies to all J2EE components that use the JMS API within EJB or Web containers:

> Any component within an EJB or Web container must have no more than one JMS session per JMS connection.

This rule does not apply to application clients.

Using Session and Entity Beans to Produce and to Synchronously Receive Messages

A J2EE application that produces messages or synchronously receives them can use either a session bean or an entity bean to perform these operations. The example in A J2EE Application That Uses the JMS API with a Session Bean (page 1222) uses a stateless session bean to publish messages to a topic.

Because a blocking synchronous receive ties up server resources, it is not a good programming practice to use such a `receive` call in an enterprise bean. Instead, use a timed synchronous receive, or use a message-driven bean to receive messages asynchronously. For details about blocking and timed synchronous receives, see Writing the Client Programs (page 1174).

Using the JMS API in a J2EE application is in many ways similar to using it in a stand-alone client. The main differences are in administered objects, resource management, and transactions.

Administered Objects

The J2EE platform specification recommends that you use `java:comp/env/jms` as the environment subcontext for JNDI lookups of connection factories and destinations. With the Application Server, you use `deploytool` to specify JNDI names that correspond to those in your source code.

Instead of looking up a JMS API connection factory or destination each time it is used in a method, it is recommended that you look up these instances once in the enterprise bean's `ejbCreate` method and cache them for the lifetime of the enterprise bean.

Resource Management

The JMS API resources are a JMS API connection and a JMS API session. In general, it is important to release JMS resources when they are no longer being used. Here are some useful practices to follow.

- If you wish to maintain a JMS API resource only for the life span of a business method, it is a good idea to close the resource in a `finally` block within the method.

- If you would like to maintain a JMS API resource for the life span of an enterprise bean instance, it is a good idea to use the component's `ejbCreate` method to create the resource and to use the component's `ejbRemove` method to close the resource. If you use a stateful session bean or an entity bean and you wish to maintain the JMS API resource in a cached state, you must close the resource in the `ejbPassivate` method and set its value to `null`, and you must create it again in the `ejbActivate` method.

Transactions

Instead of using local transactions, you use `deploytool` to specify container-managed transactions for bean methods that perform sends or receives, allowing the EJB container to handle transaction demarcation.

You can use bean-managed transactions and the `javax.transaction.User-Transaction` interface's transaction demarcation methods, but you should do so only if your application has special requirements and you are an expert in using transactions. Usually, container-managed transactions produce the most efficient and correct behavior. This tutorial does not provide any examples of bean-managed transactions.

Using Message-Driven Beans

As we noted in What Is a Message-Driven Bean? (page 838) and How Does the JMS API Work with the J2EE Platform? (page 1156), the J2EE platform supports a special kind of enterprise bean, the message-driven bean, which allows J2EE applications to process JMS messages asynchronously. Session beans and entity beans allow you to send messages and to receive them synchronously but not asynchronously.

A message-driven bean is a message listener that can reliably consume messages from a queue or a durable subscription. The messages can be sent by any J2EE component—from an application client, another enterprise bean, or a Web component—or from an application or a system that does not use J2EE technology.

Like a message listener in a stand-alone JMS client, a message-driven bean contains an `onMessage` method that is called automatically when a message arrives. Like a message listener, a message-driven bean class can implement helper methods invoked by the `onMessage` method to aid in message processing.

A message-driven bean, however, differs from a stand-alone client's message listener in the following ways:

- Certain setup tasks are performed by the EJB container.
- The bean class must implement certain interfaces and methods.

The EJB container automatically performs several setup tasks that a stand-alone client has to do:

- Creating a message consumer to receive the messages. Instead of creating a message consumer in your source code, you associate the message-driven bean with a destination and a connection factory at deployment time. If you want to specify a durable subscription or use a message selector, you do this at deployment time also.
- Registering the message listener. You must not call `setMessageListener`.
- Specifying a message acknowledgment mode. (For details, see Managing Distributed Transactions, page 1216.)

If JMS is integrated with the application server using a resource adapter, the JMS resource adapter handles these tasks for the EJB container. It creates a connection factory for the message-driven bean to use. You use an activation configuration specification to specify properties for the connection factory, such as a durable subscription, a message selector, or an acknowledgment mode. The examples in Chapter 34 show how the JMS resource adapter works in the Application Server.

Your message-driven bean class must implement the following in addition to the onMessage method:

- The javax.ejb.MessageDrivenBean and the javax.jms.Message-Listener interfaces.

- The ejbCreate method, which has the following signature:

```
public void ejbCreate() {}
```

  If your message-driven bean produces messages or does synchronous receives from another destination, you use its ejbCreate method to look up JMS API connection factories and destinations and to create the JMS API connection.

- The ejbRemove method, which has the following signature:

```
public void ejbRemove() {}
```

  If you used the message-driven bean's ejbCreate method to create a JMS API connection, you ordinarily use the ejbRemove method to close the connection.

- The setMessageDrivenContext method. A MessageDrivenContext object provides some additional methods that you can use for transaction management. The method has the following signature:

```
public void setMessageDrivenContext(MessageDrivenContext
    mdc) {}
```

The main difference between a message-driven bean and other enterprise beans is that a message-driven bean has no home or remote interface. Instead, it has only a bean class.

A message-driven bean is similar in some ways to a stateless session bean: Its instances are relatively short-lived and retain no state for a specific client. The instance variables of the message-driven bean instance can contain some state across the handling of client messages—for example, a JMS API connection, an open database connection, or an object reference to an enterprise bean object.

Like a stateless session bean, a message-driven bean can have many interchangeable instances running at the same time. The container can pool these instances to allow streams of messages to be processed concurrently. The container attempts to deliver messages in chronological order when it does not impair the concurrency of message processing, but no guarantees are made as to the exact order in which messages are delivered to the instances of the message-driven bean class. Because concurrency can affect the order in which messages are delivered, you should write your applications to handle messages that arrive out of sequence.

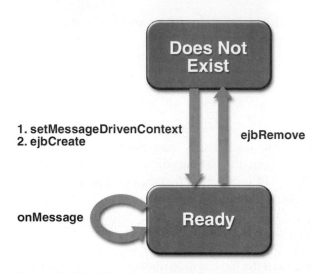

Figure 33–13 Life Cycle of a Message-Driven Bean

For example, your application could manage conversations by using application-level sequence numbers. An application-level conversation control mechanism with a persistent conversation state could cache later messages until earlier messages have been processed.

Another way to ensure order is to have each message or message group in a conversation require a confirmation message that the sender blocks on receipt of. This forces the responsibility for order back on the sender and more tightly couples senders to the progress of message-driven beans.

To create a new instance of a message-driven bean, the container instantiates the bean and then does the following:

- Calls the `setMessageDrivenContext` method to pass the context object to the instance
- Calls the instance's `ejbCreate` method

Figure 33–13 shows the life cycle of a message-driven bean.

Managing Distributed Transactions

JMS client applications use JMS API local transactions (described in Using JMS API Local Transactions, page 1204), which allow the grouping of sends and receives within a specific JMS session. J2EE applications commonly use distributed transactions to ensure the integrity of accesses to external resources. For example, distributed transactions allow multiple applications to perform atomic updates on the same database, and they allow a single application to perform atomic updates on multiple databases.

In a J2EE application that uses the JMS API, you can use transactions to combine message sends or receives with database updates and other resource manager operations. You can access resources from multiple application components within a single transaction. For example, a servlet can start a transaction, access multiple databases, invoke an enterprise bean that sends a JMS message, invoke another enterprise bean that modifies an EIS system using the Connector architecture, and finally commit the transaction. Your application cannot, however, both send a JMS message and receive a reply to it within the same transaction; the restriction described in Using JMS API Local Transactions (page 1204) still applies.

Distributed transactions within the EJB container can be either of two kinds:

- *Container-managed transactions*: The EJB container controls the integrity of your transactions without your having to call `commit` or `rollback`. Container-managed transactions are recommended for J2EE applications that use the JMS API. You can specify appropriate transaction attributes for your enterprise bean methods.

  Use the `Required` transaction attribute to ensure that a method is always part of a transaction. If a transaction is in progress when the method is called, the method will be part of that transaction; if not, a new transaction will be started before the method is called and will be committed when the method returns.

- *Bean-managed transactions*: You can use these in conjunction with the `javax.transaction.UserTransaction` interface, which provides its own `commit` and `rollback` methods that you can use to delimit transaction boundaries. Bean-managed transactions are recommended only for those who are experienced in programming transactions.

You can use either container-managed transactions or bean-managed transactions with message-driven beans. To ensure that all messages are received and handled within the context of a transaction, use container-managed transactions and specify the `Required` transaction attribute for the `onMessage` method. This means that if there is no transaction in progress, a new transaction will be started before the method is called and will be committed when the method returns.

When you use container-managed transactions, you can call the following `MessageDrivenContext` methods:

- `setRollbackOnly`: Use this method for error handling. If an exception occurs, `setRollbackOnly` marks the current transaction so that the only possible outcome of the transaction is a rollback.
- `getRollbackOnly`: Use this method to test whether the current transaction has been marked for rollback.

If you use bean-managed transactions, the delivery of a message to the `onMessage` method takes place outside the distributed transaction context. The transaction begins when you call the `UserTransaction.begin` method within the `onMessage` method, and it ends when you call `UserTransaction.commit` or `UserTransaction.rollback`. Any call to the `Connection.createSession` method must take place within the transaction. If you call `UserTransaction.rollback`, the message is not redelivered, whereas calling `setRollbackOnly` for container-managed transactions does cause a message to be redelivered.

Neither the JMS API specification nor the Enterprise JavaBeans specification (available from `http://java.sun.com/products/ejb/`) specifies how to handle calls to JMS API methods outside transaction boundaries. The Enterprise JavaBeans specification does state that the EJB container is responsible for acknowledging a message that is successfully processed by the `onMessage` method of a message-driven bean that uses bean-managed transactions. Using bean-managed transactions allows you to process the message by using more than one transaction or to have some parts of the message processing take place outside a transaction context. In most cases, however, container-managed transactions provide greater reliability and are therefore preferable.

When you create a session in an enterprise bean, the container ignores the arguments you specify, because it manages all transactional properties for enterprise beans. It is still a good idea to specify arguments of `true` and `0` to the `createSession` method to make this situation clear:

```
session = connection.createSession(true, 0);
```

When you use container-managed transactions, you usually specify the `Required` transaction attribute for your enterprise bean's business methods.

You do not specify a message acknowledgment mode when you create a message-driven bean that uses container-managed transactions. The container acknowledges the message automatically when it commits the transaction.

If a message-driven bean uses bean-managed transactions, the message receipt cannot be part of the bean-managed transaction, so the container acknowledges the message outside the transaction.

If the onMessage method throws a RuntimeException, the container does not acknowledge processing the message. In that case, the JMS provider will redeliver the unacknowledged message in the future.

Using the JMS API with Application Clients and Web Components

An application client in a J2EE application can use the JMS API in much the same way that a stand-alone client program does. It can produce messages, and it can consume messages by using either synchronous receives or message listeners. See Chapter 28 for an example of an application client that produces messages. For examples of using application clients to produce and to consume messages, see A J2EE Application That Uses the JMS API with an Entity Bean (page 1231) and An Application Example That Deploys a Message-Driven Bean on Two J2EE Servers (page 1246).

The J2EE platform specification does not impose strict constraints on how Web components should use the JMS API. In the Application Server, a Web component—one that uses either the Java Servlet API or JavaServer Pages (JSP) technology—can send messages and consume them synchronously but cannot consume them asynchronously.

Because a blocking synchronous receive ties up server resources, it is not a good programming practice to use such a receive call in a Web component. Instead, use a timed synchronous receive. For details about blocking and timed synchronous receives, see Writing the Client Programs (page 1174).

Further Information

For more information about JMS, see the following:

- Java Message Service Web site:
  `http://java.sun.com/products/jms/`
- Java Message Service specification, version 1.1, available from
  `http://java.sun.com/products/jms/docs.html`

34

J2EE Examples Using
the JMS API

THIS chapter provides examples that show how to use the JMS API within a J2EE application in the following ways:

- Using a session bean to send messages that are consumed by a message-driven bean using a message selector and a durable subscription
- Using an application client to send messages that are consumed by two message-driven beans; the information from them is stored in an entity bean
- Using an application client to send messages that are consumed by a message-driven bean on a remote server
- Using an application client to send messages that are consumed by message-driven beans on two different servers

The examples are in the following directory:

```
<INSTALL>/j2eetutorial14/examples/jms/
```

To build and run the examples, you will do the following:

1. Use the `asant` tool to compile the example
2. Use the Admin Console to create resources
3. Use `deploytool` to package and deploy the example
4. Use the `appclient` command to run the client

Each example has a `build.xml` file that refers to a `targets.xml` file and a `build.properties` file in the following directory:

> `<INSTALL>`/j2eetutorial14/examples/jms/common/

The following directory contains previously built versions of each application:

> `<INSTALL>`/j2eetutorial14/examples/jms/provided-ears/

If you run into difficulty at any time, you can open the appropriate EAR file in `deploytool` and compare that file to your own version.

See Chapter 28 for a simpler example of a J2EE application that uses the JMS API.

A J2EE Application That Uses the JMS API with a Session Bean

This section explains how to write, compile, package, deploy, and run a J2EE application that uses the JMS API in conjunction with a session bean. The application contains the following components:

- An application client that invokes an enterprise bean
- A session bean that publishes several messages to a topic
- A message-driven bean that receives and processes the messages using a durable topic subscriber and a message selector

The section covers the following topics:

- Writing the application components
- Creating and packaging the application
- Deploying the application
- Running the application client

You will find the source files for this section in the directory `<INSTALL>`/j2eetutorial14/examples/jms/clientsessionmdb/. Path names in this section are relative to this directory.

Writing the Application Components

This application demonstrates how to send messages from an enterprise bean—in this case, a session bean—rather than from an application client, as in the example in Chapter 28. Figure 34–1 illustrates the structure of this application.

The Publisher enterprise bean in this example is the enterprise-application equivalent of a wire-service news feed that categorizes news events into six news categories. The message-driven bean could represent a newsroom, where the sports desk, for example, would set up a subscription for all news events pertaining to sports.

The application client in the example obtains a handle to the Publisher enterprise bean's remote home interface, creates an instance of the bean, and then calls the bean's business method. The enterprise bean creates 18 text messages. For each message, it sets a `String` property randomly to one of six values representing the news categories and then publishes the message to a topic. The message-driven bean uses a message selector for the property to limit which of the published messages it receives.

Writing the components of the application involves the following:

- Coding the application client: `MyAppClient.java`
- Coding the Publisher session bean
- Coding the message-driven bean: `MessageBean.java`

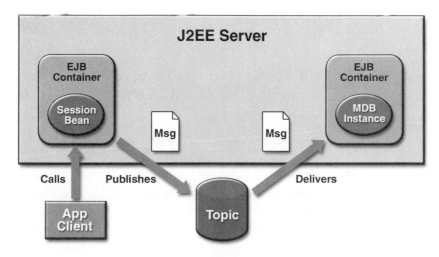

Figure 34–1   A J2EE Application: Client to Session Bean to Message-Driven Bean

Coding the Application Client: MyAppClient.java

The application client program, `src/MyAppClient.java`, performs no JMS API operations and so is simpler than the client program in Chapter 28. The program obtains a handle to the Publisher enterprise bean's remote home interface, using the JNDI naming context `java:comp/env`. The program then creates an instance of the bean and calls the bean's business method twice.

Coding the Publisher Session Bean

The Publisher bean is a stateless session bean that has one `create` method and one business method. The Publisher bean uses remote interfaces rather than local interfaces because it is accessed from the application client.

The remote home interface source file is `src/PublisherHome.java`.

The remote interface, `src/PublisherRemote.java`, declares a single business method, `publishNews`.

The bean class, `src/PublisherBean.java`, implements the `publishNews` method and its helper method `chooseType`. The bean class also implements the required methods `ejbCreate`, `setSessionContext`, `ejbRemove`, `ejbActivate`, and `ejbPassivate`.

The `ejbCreate` method of the bean class allocates resources—in this case, by looking up the `ConnectionFactory` and the topic and creating the `Connection`. The business method `publishNews` creates a `Session` and a `MessageProducer` and publishes the messages.

The `ejbRemove` method must deallocate the resources that were allocated by the `ejbCreate` method. In this case, the `ejbRemove` method closes the `Connection`.

Coding the Message-Driven Bean: MessageBean.java

The message-driven bean class, `src/MessageBean.java`, is identical to the one in Chapter 28. However, the deployment descriptor will be different, because instead of a queue the bean is using a topic with a durable subscription.

Creating and Packaging the Application

This example uses the topic named jms/Topic and the connection factory jms/TopicConnectionFactory, which you created in Creating JMS Administered Objects (page 1178). It also uses the connection factory jms/DurableTopicConnectionFactory, which you created in A Message Acknowledgment Example (page 1194) and A Durable Subscription Example (page 1202). If you deleted any of these objects, create them again.

Creating and packaging this application involve six steps:

1. Compiling the source files and starting the Sun Java System Application Server Platform Edition 8
2. Starting deploytool and creating the application
3. Packaging the session bean
4. Packaging the message-driven bean
5. Packaging the application client
6. Updating the JNDI names

Compiling the Source Files and Starting the Sun Java System Application Server Platform Edition 8

1. In the directory *<INSTALL>*/j2eetutorial14/examples/jms/client-sessionmdb, use the build target to compile the source files:
   asant build
2. Start the Application Server, if it is not already running.

Starting deploytool and Creating the Application

1. Start deploytool.
2. Choose File→New→Application.
3. Click Browse next to the Application File Name field, and use the file chooser to locate the directory clientsessionmdb.
4. In the File Name field, type ClientSessionMDBApp.

5. Click New Application.

6. Click OK.

Packaging the Session Bean

To package the session bean, perform the following steps:

1. Choose File→New→Enterprise Bean to start the Enterprise Bean wizard.

2. In the EJB JAR General Settings screen:

    a. Select Create New JAR Module in Application and verify that the application is `ClientSessionMDBApp`. In the JAR Name field, type `EBJAR`.

    b. Click the Edit button next to the Contents text area.

    c. In the dialog box, locate the `build/sb/` directory. Select `Publisher-Bean.class`, `PublisherHome.class`, and `PublisherRemote.class` from the Available Files tree. Click Add and then OK.

3. In the Bean General Settings screen:

    a. From the Enterprise Bean Class menu, choose `sb.PublisherBean`.

    b. Verify that the enterprise bean name is `PublisherBean` and that the enterprise bean type is Stateless Session.

    c. In the Remote Interfaces area, choose `sb.PublisherHome` from the Remote Home Interface menu, and choose `sb.PublisherRemote` from the Remote Interface menu.

After you finish the wizard, perform the following steps:

1. Click the `PublisherBean` node, and then click the Msg Dest Ref's tab. In the inspector pane:

    a. Click Add. A dialog box opens.

    b. Type `jms/TopicName` in the Coded Name field.

    c. Choose `javax.jms.Topic` from the Destination Type combo box.

    d. Choose Produces from the Usage combo box.

    e. Type `PhysicalTopic` in the Destination Name field.

2. Click the `PublisherBean` node, and then click the Resource Ref's tab. In the inspector pane:

    a. Click Add.

    b. Type `jms/MyConnectionFactory` in the Coded Name field.

    c. Choose `javax.jms.ConnectionFactory` from the Type menu.

    d. Choose `jms/TopicConnectionFactory` from the JNDI name combo box, and type `j2ee` in both the User Name and the Password fields.

3. Click the `PublisherBean` node, and then click the Transactions tab. In the inspector pane, select the Container-Managed radio button.

4. Click the `EBJAR` node, and then click the Message Destinations tab. In the inspector pane:

    a. Click Add.

    b. Type `PhysicalTopic` in the Destination Name field. When you press Enter, this name appears in the Display Name field, and `PublisherBean` appears in the Producers area.

    c. Type `jms/Topic` in the JNDI Name field.

Packaging the Message-Driven Bean

For greater efficiency, you will package the message-driven bean in the same JAR file as the session bean.

To package the message-driven bean, perform the following steps:

1. Choose File→New→Enterprise Bean to start the Enterprise Bean wizard.

2. In the EJB JAR General Settings screen:

    a. Select the Add to Existing JAR Module radio button, and verify that the module is `EBJAR (ClientSessionMDBApp)`.

    b. Click the Edit button next to the Contents text area.

    c. In the dialog box, locate the `build/mdb/` directory. Select `MessageBean.class` from the Available Files tree. Click Add and then OK.

3. In the Bean General Settings screen:

    a. From the Enterprise Bean Class menu, choose `mdb.MessageBean`.

    b. In the Enterprise Bean Name field, accept the default value, `MessageBean`.

    c. Verify that the enterprise bean type is Message-Driven.

4. In the Message-Driven Bean Settings screen:

    a. For the Messaging Service, accept the default, JMS.

    b. Choose `javax.jms.Topic` from the Destination Type combo box.

    c. Choose `PhysicalTopic` from the Target Destination Name combo box.

    d. Select the Durable Subscription checkbox. In the Subscription Name field, type `MySub`.

   e. In the Message Selector field, type the following:

```
NewsType = 'Sports' OR NewsType = 'Opinion'
```

   f. In the Connection Factory JNDI Name (Sun-specific) field, type the following:

```
jms/DurableTopicConnectionFactory
```

After you finish the wizard, perform the following steps:

1. Click the `MessageBean` node, and then click the Transactions tab. In the inspector pane, select the Container-Managed radio button.
2. Click the `EBJAR` node, and then click the Message Destinations tab and select `PhysicalTopic`. You will see that `MessageBean` now appears in the Consumers area.

Packaging the Application Client

To package the application client, perform the following steps:

1. Choose File→New→Application Client to start the Application Client wizard.
2. In the JAR File Contents screen:
   a. Verify that Create New AppClient Module in Application is selected and that the application is `ClientSessionMDBApp`.
   b. In the AppClient Name field, type `MyAppClient`.
   c. Click the Edit button next to the Contents text area.
   d. In the dialog box, locate the `build/client/` directory. Select `MyApp-Client.class` from the Available Files tree. Click Add and then OK.
3. In the General screen, choose `client.MyAppClient` in the Main Class combo box.

After you finish the wizard, click the EJB Ref's tab, and then click Add in the inspector pane. In the dialog box, do the following:

1. Type `ejb/remote/Publisher` in the Coded Name field.
2. Choose Session from the EJB Type combo box.
3. Choose Remote from the Interfaces combo box.
4. Type `sb.PublisherHome` in the Home Interface field.
5. Type `sb.PublisherRemote` in the Local/Remote Interface field.
6. In the Target EJB area, select JNDI Name and choose `PublisherBean` from the combo box.

Updating the JNDI Names

You need to update the JNDI name for the message-driven bean so that it specifies the destination it receives messages from and not the bean name.

1. Select `ClientSessionMDBApp` and click Sun-specific Settings on the General screen.

2. Type `jms/Topic` in the JNDI Name field for the `MessageBean` component.

Verify that the JNDI names for the application components are correct. They should appear as shown in Tables 34–1 and 34–2.

Table 34–1 Application Pane for `ClientSessionMDBApp`

Component Type	Component	JNDI Name
EJB	MessageBean	jms/Topic
EJB	PublisherBean	PublisherBean

Table 34–2 References Pane for `ClientSessionMDBApp`

Ref. Type	Referenced By	Reference Name	JNDI Name
EJB Ref	MyAppClient	ejb/remote/Publisher	PublisherBean
Resource	PublisherBean	jms/MyConnectionFactory	jms/TopicConnectionFactory

Deploying the Application

1. Choose File→Save to save the application.

2. Choose Tools→Deploy.

3. In the dialog box, type your administrative user name and password (if they are not already filled in).

4. In the Application Client Stub Directory area, select the Return Client Jar checkbox. If you wish to run the client in a directory other than the default, click Browse and use the file chooser to specify it.

5. Click OK.

6. In the Distribute Module dialog box, click Close when the process completes. You will find a file named ClientSessionMDBAppClient.jar in the specified directory.

Running the Application Client

To run the client, use the following command:

```
appclient -client ClientSessionMDBAppClient.jar
```

The program output in the terminal window looks like this:

```
Looking up EJB reference
Looked up home
Narrowed home
Got the EJB
To view the bean output,
 check <install_dir>/domains/domain1/logs/server.log.
```

The output from the enterprise beans appears in the server log (*<J2EE_HOME>*/domains/domain1/logs/server.log), wrapped in logging information. The Publisher session bean sends two sets of 18 messages numbered 0 through 17. Because of the message selector, the message-driven bean receives only the messages whose NewsType property is Sports or Opinion.

Suppose that the last few messages from the Publisher session bean look like this:

```
PUBLISHER: Setting message text to: Item 12: Business
PUBLISHER: Setting message text to: Item 13: Opinion
PUBLISHER: Setting message text to: Item 14: Living/Arts
PUBLISHER: Setting message text to: Item 15: Sports
PUBLISHER: Setting message text to: Item 16: Living/Arts
PUBLISHER: Setting message text to: Item 17: Living/Arts
```

Because of the message selector, the last messages received by the message-driven bean will be the following:

```
MESSAGE BEAN: Message received: Item 13: Opinion
MESSAGE BEAN: Message received: Item 15: Sports
```

If you like, you can rewrite the message selector to receive different messages.

Undeploy the application after you finish running the client.

A J2EE Application That Uses the JMS API with an Entity Bean

This section explains how to write, compile, package, deploy, and run a J2EE application that uses the JMS API with an entity bean. The application uses the following components:

- An application client that both sends and receives messages
- Two message-driven beans
- An entity bean that uses container-managed persistence

This section covers the following topics:

- Overview of the human resources application
- Writing the application components
- Creating and packaging the application
- Deploying the application
- Running the application client

You will find the source files for this section in the directory `<INSTALL>/ j2eetutorial14/examples/jms/clientmdbentity/`. Path names in this section are relative to this directory.

Overview of the Human Resources Application

This application simulates, in a simplified way, the work flow of a company's human resources (HR) department when it processes a new hire. This application also demonstrates how to use the J2EE platform to accomplish a task that many JMS client applications perform.

A JMS client must often wait for several messages from various sources. It then uses the information in all these messages to assemble a message that it then sends to another destination. The common term for this process is *joining messages*. Such a task must be transactional, with all the receives and the send as a single transaction. If not all the messages are received successfully, the transaction can be rolled back. For a client example that illustrates this task, see A Local Transaction Example (page 1206).

A message-driven bean can process only one message at a time in a transaction. To provide the ability to join messages, a J2EE application can have the message-driven bean store the interim information in an entity bean. The entity bean can then determine whether all the information has been received; when it has, the entity bean can create and send the message to the other destination. After it has completed its task, the entity bean can remove itself.

The basic steps of the application are as follows.

1. The HR department's application client generates an employee ID for each new hire and then publishes a message (M1) containing the new hire's name and employee ID. The client then creates a temporary queue, `Reply-Queue`, with a message listener that waits for a reply to the message. (See Creating Temporary Destinations, page 1199, for more information.)

2. Two message-driven beans process each message: One bean, `OfficeMDB`, assigns the new hire's office number, and the other bean, `EquipmentMDB`, assigns the new hire's equipment. The first bean to process the message creates an entity bean named `SetupOffice` to store the information it has generated. The second bean locates the existing entity bean and adds its information.

3. When both the office and the equipment have been assigned, the entity bean sends to the reply queue a message (M2) describing the assignments. Then it removes itself. The application client's message listener retrieves the information.

Figure 34–2 illustrates the structure of this application. Of course, an actual HR application would have more components; other beans could set up payroll and benefits records, schedule orientation, and so on.

Writing the Application Components

Writing the components of the application involves the following:

- Coding the application client: `HumanResourceClient.java`
- Coding the message-driven beans
- Coding the entity bean

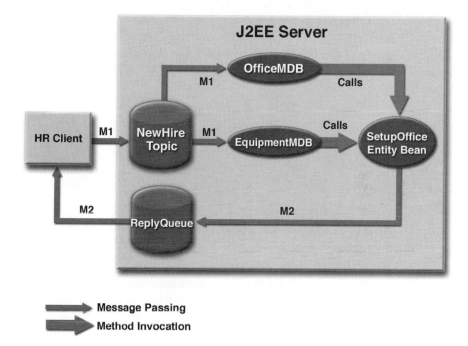

Figure 34–2   A J2EE Application: Client to Message-Driven Beans to
Entity Bean

Coding the Application Client: HumanResourceClient.java

The application client program, src/HumanResourceClient.java, performs the
following steps:

1. Uses the JNDI naming context java:comp/env to look up a Connection-
   Factory and a topic

2. Creates a TemporaryQueue to receive notification of processing that
   occurs, based on new-hire events it has published

3. Creates a MessageConsumer for the TemporaryQueue, sets the Message-
   Consumer's message listener, and starts the connection

4. Creates a MessageProducer and a MapMessage

5. Creates five new employees with randomly generated names, positions,
   and ID numbers (in sequence) and publishes five messages containing this
   information

The message listener, `HRListener`, waits for messages that contain the assigned office and equipment for each employee. When a message arrives, the message listener displays the information received and determines whether all five messages have arrived. When they have, the message listener notifies the main program, which then exits.

Coding the Message-Driven Beans

This example uses two message-driven beans: `src/ReserveEquipmentMsg-Bean.java` and `src/ReserveOfficeMsgBean.java`. The beans take the following steps.

1. The `ejbCreate` method gets a handle to the local home interface of the entity bean.

2. The `onMessage` method retrieves the information in the message. The `ReserveEquipmentMsgBean`'s `onMessage` method chooses equipment, based on the new hire's position; the `ReserveOfficeMsgBean`'s `onMessage` method randomly generates an office number.

3. After a slight delay to simulate real-world processing hitches, the `onMessage` method calls a helper method, `compose`.

4. The `compose` method either creates or finds, by primary key, the `SetupOffice` entity bean and uses it to store the equipment or the office information in the database.

Coding the Entity Bean

The `SetupOffice` bean is an entity bean that uses a local interface. The local interface means that the entity bean and the message-driven beans run in the same Java virtual machine (JVM) for maximum efficiency. The entity bean has these components:

- The local home interface, `SetupOfficeLocalHome.java`
- The local interface, `SetupOfficeLocal.java`
- The bean class, `SetupOfficeBean.java`

The local home interface source file is `src/SetupOfficeLocalHome.java`. It declares the create method, called `createLocal` (because the bean uses a local interface), and one finder method, `findByPrimaryKey`.

The local interface, `src/SetupOfficeLocal.java`, declares several business methods that get and manipulate new-hire data.

The bean class, `src/SetupOfficeBean.java`, implements the business methods and their helper method, `checkIfSetupComplete`. The bean class also implements the required methods `ejbCreateLocal`, `ejbPostCreateLocal`, `setEntityContext`, `unsetEntityContext`, `ejbRemove`, `ejbActivate`, `ejbPassivate`, `ejbLoad`, and `ejbStore`.

The only methods called by the message-driven beans are the business methods declared in the local interface, along with the `findByPrimaryKey` and `createLocal` methods declared in the local home interface. The entity bean uses container-managed persistence, so all database calls are generated automatically.

Creating and Packaging the Application

This example uses a connection factory named `jms/TopicConnectionFactory` and a topic named `jms/Topic`, both of which you created in Chapter 33. (See Creating JMS Administered Objects, page 1178, for instructions.) It also uses a JDBC resource named `jdbc/PointBase`, which is enabled by default when you start the Application Server.

Creating and packaging this application involve seven steps:

1. Starting the PointBase server
2. Compiling the source files
3. Creating the application
4. Packaging the entity bean
5. Packaging the message-driven beans
6. Packaging the application client
7. Updating the JNDI names

You can package the application yourself as an exercise. Use the `asant build` target to compile the source files.

This section uses the prepackaged EAR file to show how to create and package the application.

Examining the Application

1. In deploytool, open the ClientMDBEntityApp.ear file, which resides in the directory <*INSTALL*>/j2eetutorial14/examples/jms/provided-ears.

2. Expand the EBJAR node and select the entity bean SetupOffice.

   a. In the General tab, notice that the bean uses local interfaces.

   b. Click the Entity tab. The bean uses container-managed persistence.

   c. In the Entity screen, click the Sun-specific CMP Settings tab. The application uses the preconfigured jdbc/PointBase JDBC resource.

   d. Click the Resource Ref's tab. The bean uses the connection factory jms/TopicConnectionFactory to send reply messages to the application client. The bean does not specify any message destination references, however, because it uses a temporary destination for the reply messages. Notice that it uses a TopicConnectionFactory object, even though it is using the connection to send messages to a temporary queue.

3. Select either of the message-driven beans: EquipmentMDB or OfficeMDB. They are configured identically.

   a. Click the Message-Driven tab. The beans use the PhysicalTopic target destination and the connection factory jms/TopicConnectionFactory.

   b. Click the EJB Ref's tab. Both beans reference the entity bean using local references.

4. Select the HumanResourceClient node.

   a. Click the Resource Ref's tab. The client uses the connection factory jms/TopicConnectionFactory both to send messages to a topic and to receive messages from a temporary queue. The application looks up the coded name jms/MyConnectionFactory and casts the object to an object of type javax.jms.ConnectionFactory.

   b. Click the Msg Dest Ref's tab. The coded name jms/NewHireTopic refers to the target destination PhysicalTopic.

   c. Click the Message Destinations tab, and then click PhysicalTopic. The client appears in the Producers area, and the message-driven beans appear in the Consumers area. All of them refer to the JNDI name jms/Topic.

Table 34–3 Application Pane for `ClientMDBEntityApp`

Component Type	Component	JNDI Name
EJB	`EquipmentMDB`	`jms/Topic`
EJB	`OfficeMDB`	`jms/Topic`

Table 34–4 References Pane for `ClientMDBEntityApp`

Ref. Type	Referenced By	Reference Name	JNDI Name
Resource	`HumanResourceClient`	`jms/MyConnection-Factory`	`jms/TopicConnec-tionFactory`
Resource	`SetupOffice`	`jms/MyConnection-Factory`	`jms/TopicConnec-tionFactory`

5. Notice that for all the components, the Transactions tab is set to Container-Managed.

6. Select the `ClientMDBEntityApp` node and click the Sun-specific Settings button. On the JNDI Names screen, the JNDI name for the message-driven beans is the topic destination resource, `jms/Topic`.

Verify that the JNDI names for the application components are correct. They should appear as shown in Tables 34–3 and 34–4.

Deploying the Application

1. Start the PointBase server. For instructions, see Starting and Stopping the PointBase Database Server (page 28).

2. Save the application.

3. Deploy the application. Select the Return Client Jar checkbox.

You will find a file named `ClientMDBEntityAppClient.jar` in the provided-ears directory.

Running the Application Client

To run the client, use the following command:

```
appclient -client ClientMDBEntityAppClient.jar
```

The program output in the terminal window looks something like this:

```
PUBLISHER: Setting hire ID to 25, name Gertrude Bourbon,
position Senior Programmer
PUBLISHER: Setting hire ID to 26, name Jack Verdon, position
Manager
PUBLISHER: Setting hire ID to 27, name Fred Tudor, position
Manager
PUBLISHER: Setting hire ID to 28, name Fred Martin, position
Programmer
PUBLISHER: Setting hire ID to 29, name Mary Stuart, position
Manager
Waiting for 5 message(s)
New hire event processed:
  Employee ID: 25
  Name: Gertrude Bourbon
  Equipment: Laptop
  Office number: 183
Waiting for 4 message(s)
New hire event processed:
  Employee ID: 26
  Name: Jack Verdon
  Equipment: Pager
  Office number: 20
Waiting for 3 message(s)
New hire event processed:
  Employee ID: 27
  Name: Fred Tudor
  Equipment: Pager
  Office number: 51
Waiting for 2 message(s)
New hire event processed:
  Employee ID: 28
  Name: Fred Martin
  Equipment: Desktop System
  Office number: 141
Waiting for 1 message(s)
New hire event processed:
```

```
Employee ID: 29
Name: Mary Stuart
Equipment: Pager
Office number: 238
```

The output from the enterprise beans appears in the server log, wrapped in logging information. For each employee, the application first creates the entity bean and then finds it. You may see runtime errors in the server log, and transaction rollbacks may occur. The errors occur if both of the message-driven beans discover at the same time that the entity bean does not yet exist, so they both try to create it. The first attempt succeeds, but the second fails because the bean already exists. After the rollback, the second message-driven bean tries again and succeeds in finding the entity bean. Container-managed transactions allow the application to run correctly, in spite of these errors, with no special programming.

Undeploy the application after you finish running the client.

An Application Example That Consumes Messages from a Remote J2EE Server

This section and the following section explain how to write, compile, package, deploy, and run a pair of J2EE applications that run on two J2EE servers and that use the JMS API to interchange messages with each other. It is a common practice to deploy different components of an enterprise application on different systems within a company, and these examples illustrate on a small scale how to do this for an application that uses the JMS API.

However, the two examples work in slightly different ways. In this first example, the deployment information for a message-driven bean specifies the remote server from which it will *consume* messages. In the next example, the same bean is deployed on two different servers, so it is the client application that specifies the servers (one local, one remote) to which it is *sending* messages.

This first example divides the example in Chapter 28 into two applications: one containing the application client, and the other containing the message-driven bean.

This section covers the following topics:

- Overview of the applications
- Writing the application components
- Creating and packaging the applications
- Deploying the applications
- Running the application client

You will find the source files for this section in `<INSTALL>`/j2eetutorial14/ examples/jms/consumeremote/. Path names in this section are relative to this directory.

Overview of the Applications

Except for the fact that it is packaged as two separate applications, this example is very similar to the one in Chapter 28:

- One application contains the application client, which runs on the remote server and sends three messages to a queue.
- The other application contains the message-driven bean, which consumes the messages from the queue on the remote server.

The basic steps of the applications are as follows.

1. The administrator starts two J2EE servers, one on each system.
2. On the remote server, the administrator deploys the client application.
3. On the local server, the administrator deploys the message-driven bean application, which uses a connection factory that specifies the remote server where the client is deployed.
4. The client application sends three messages to a queue.
5. The message-driven bean consumes the messages.

Figure 34–3 illustrates the structure of this application. You can see that it is almost identical to Figure 28–1 (page 1004) except that there are two J2EE servers. The queue used is the one on the remote server; the queue must also exist on the local server for JNDI lookups to succeed.

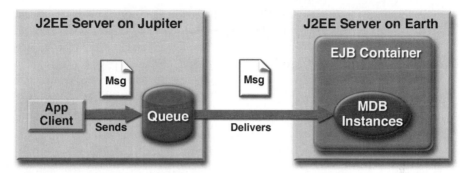

Figure 34–3   A J2EE Application That Consumes Messages from a
Remote Server

Writing the Application Components

Writing the components of the applications involves

- Coding the application client
- Coding the message-driven bean

The application client, `jupiterclient/src/SimpleClient.java`, is almost identical to the one in The Application Client (page 1004).

Similarly, the message-driven bean, `earthmdb/src/MessageBean.java`, is almost identical to the one in The Message-Driven Bean Class (page 1005).

The only major difference is that the client and the bean are packaged in two separate applications.

Creating and Packaging the Applications

For this example, the message-driven bean uses the connection factory named `jms/JupiterQueueConnectionFactory`, which you created in Creating Administered Objects for Multiple Systems (page 1188). Use the Admin Console to verify that the connection factory still exists and that its `MessageService-AddressList` property is set to the name of the remote system.

The application client can use any connection factory that exists on the remote server; you created `jms/JupiterQueueConnectionFactory` on that server, so you can use that. Both components use the queue named `jms/Queue`, which you created in Creating JMS Administered Objects (page 1178).

We'll assume, as we did in Running JMS Client Programs on Multiple Systems (page 1187), that the two servers are named `earth` and `jupiter`.

Creating and packaging this application involve five steps:

1. Compiling the source files
2. Creating the application
3. Packaging the application client
4. Packaging the message-driven bean
5. Verifying the JNDI names

You can package the applications yourself as an exercise. Use the `asant build` targets in the `jupiterclient` and `earthmdb` directories to compile the source files.

This section uses the prepackaged EAR files to show how to create and package the applications.

Which system you use to package and deploy the applications and which system you use to run the client depend on your network configuration—which file system you can access remotely. These instructions assume that you can access the file system of `jupiter` from `earth` but cannot access the file system of `earth` from `jupiter`. (You can use the same systems for `jupiter` and `earth` that you used in Running JMS Client Programs on Multiple Systems, page 1187.)

The Application Server must be running on both systems.

You can package both applications on `earth` and deploy them from there. The only action you perform on `jupiter` is running the client application.

Examining the Applications

1. In `deploytool`, on `earth`, open the two EAR files `JupiterClient-App.ear` and `EarthMDBApp.ear`, which reside in the directory `<INSTALL>/j2eetutorial14/jms/provided-ears`.

2. In `JupiterClientApp.ear`, select the application client node, `Simple-Client`.

   a. Click the Resource Ref's tab. The client uses the connection factory `jms/JupiterQueueConnectionFactory` to send messages to a queue. The application looks up the coded name `jms/MyConnectionFactory` and casts the object to an object of type `javax.jms.Connection-Factory`.

   b. Click the Msg Dest Ref's tab. The coded name `jms/QueueName` refers to the target destination `PhysicalQueue`.

   c. Click the Message Destinations tab, and then click `PhysicalQueue`. The client appears in the Producers area. It refers to the JNDI name `jms/Queue`.

3. In `EarthMDBApp.ear`, expand the `MDBJAR` node and select `MessageBean`.

   a. Click the Message-Driven tab. The bean uses the `PhysicalQueue` target destination and the connection factory `jms/JupiterQueueConnec-tionFactory`.

   b. Click the Transactions tab. The bean uses container-managed transactions.

4. Select the `MDBJAR` node, click the Message Destinations tab, and then click `PhysicalQueue`. The message-driven bean appears in the Consumers area. It refers to the JNDI name `jms/Queue`.

5. Select the `EarthMDBApp` node and click Sun-specific Settings on the General page. The JNDI name for the message-driven bean is the queue destination resource, `jms/Queue`.

The JNDI name for the `EarthMDBApp` application should appear as shown in Table 34–5. Only the Application pane has any content.

The JNDI name for the `JupiterClientApp` application should appear as shown in Table 34–6. Only the References pane has any content.

Table 34–5 Application Pane for `EarthMDBApp`

Component Type	Component	JNDI Name
EJB	MessageBean	jms/Queue

Table 34–6 References Pane for `JupiterClientApp`

Ref. Type	Referenced By	Reference Name	JNDI Name
Resource	SimpleClient	jms/MyConnectionFactory	jms/JupiterQueue-ConnectionFactory

Deploying the Applications

To deploy the `EarthMDBApp` application, perform the following steps:

1. Save the application.
2. Choose Tools→Deploy.
3. In the dialog box, choose the URI for `localhost` from the Server menu.
4. Type your administrative user name and password (if they are not already filled in) and click OK.
5. In the Distribute Module dialog box, click Close when the process completes.

Before you can deploy the `JupiterClientApp` application, you must add the remote server. On `earth`, perform the following steps:

1. Choose File→Add Server.
2. Type the name of the remote system in the Server Name field.
3. Click OK.
4. The server appears in the tree under Servers. Select it.
5. In the Connect to Server dialog box that appears, type the administrative user name and password for the server in the Connection Settings area, and click OK.

To deploy the `JupiterClientApp` application and save the client JAR file, perform the following steps:

1. Save the application.
2. Choose Tools→Deploy.
3. In the dialog box, choose the URI for the remote system (`jupiter`) from the Server menu:

   system-name:4848

4. Type your administrative user name and password (if they are not already filled in).

5. In the Application Client Stub Directory area, select the Return Client Jar checkbox.

6. Choose Browse to navigate to the directory on the remote system (jupiter) from which you will run the client. When you reach the directory, click Select, and then click OK.

7. Click OK.

8. In the Distribute Module dialog box, click Close when the process completes. You will find a file named `JupiterClientAppClient.jar` in the specified directory.

Running the Application Client

To run the client, perform the following steps:

1. Go to the directory on the remote system (jupiter) where you created the client JAR file.

2. Use the following command:

```
appclient -client JupiterClientAppClient.jar
```

On jupiter, the output of the appclient command looks like this:

```
Sending message: This is message 1
Sending message: This is message 2
Sending message: This is message 3
```

On earth, the output in the server log looks like this (wrapped in logging information):

```
In MessageBean.MessageBean()
In MessageBean.setMessageDrivenContext()
In MessageBean.ejbCreate()
MESSAGE BEAN: Message received: This is message 1
MESSAGE BEAN: Message received: This is message 2
MESSAGE BEAN: Message received: This is message 3
```

Undeploy the applications after you finish running the client.

An Application Example That Deploys a Message-Driven Bean on Two J2EE Servers

This section, like the preceding one, explains how to write, compile, package, deploy, and run a pair of J2EE applications that use the JMS API and run on two J2EE servers. The applications are slightly more complex than the ones in the first example.

The applications use the following components:

- An application client that is deployed on the local server. It uses two connection factories—one ordinary one and one that is configured to communicate with the remote server—to create two publishers and two subscribers and to publish and to consume messages.
- A message-driven bean that is deployed twice: once on the local server, and once on the remote one. It processes the messages and sends replies.

In this section, the term *local server* means the server on which both the application client and the message-driven bean are deployed (`earth` in the preceding example). The term *remote server* means the server on which only the message-driven bean is deployed (`jupiter` in the preceding example).

The section covers the following topics:

- Overview of the applications
- Writing the application components
- Creating and packaging the applications
- Deploying the applications
- Running the application client

You will find the source files for this section in `<INSTALL>`/j2eetutorial14/examples/jms/sendremote/. Path names in this section are relative to this directory.

Overview of the Applications

This pair of applications is somewhat similar to the applications in An Application Example That Consumes Messages from a Remote J2EE Server (page 1239) in that the only components are a client and a message-driven bean. However, the applications here use these components in more complex ways. One application consists of the application client. The other application contains only the message-driven bean and is deployed twice, once on each server.

The basic steps of the applications are as follows.

1. You start two J2EE servers, one on each system.

2. On the local server (`earth`), you create two connection factories: one local and one that communicates with the remote server (`jupiter`). On the remote server, you create a connection factory that has the same name.

3. The application client looks up the two connection factories—the local one and the one that communicates with the remote server—to create two connections, sessions, publishers, and subscribers. The subscribers use a message listener.

4. Each publisher publishes five messages.

5. Each of the local and the remote message-driven beans receives five messages and sends replies.

6. The client's message listener consumes the replies.

Figure 34–4 illustrates the structure of this application. M1 represents the first message sent using the local connection factory, and RM1 represents the first reply

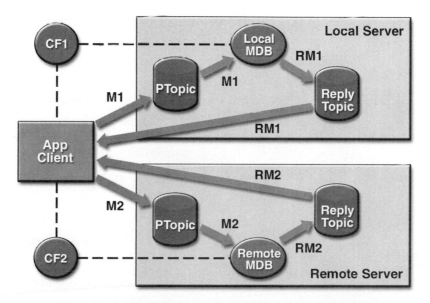

Figure 34–4 A J2EE Application That Sends Messages to Two Servers

message sent by the local MDB. M2 represents the first message sent using the remote connection factory, and RM2 represents the first reply message sent by the remote MDB.

Writing the Application Components

Writing the components of the applications involves two tasks:

- Coding the application client: `MultiAppServerClient.java`
- Coding the message-driven bean: `ReplyMsgBean.java`

Coding the Application Client: MultiAppServerClient.java

The application client class, `multiclient/src/MultiAppServerClient.java`, does the following.

1. It uses the JNDI naming context `java:comp/env` to look up two connection factories and a topic.
2. For each connection factory, it creates a connection, a publisher session, a publisher, a subscriber session, a subscriber, and a temporary topic for replies.
3. Each subscriber sets its message listener, `ReplyListener`, and starts the connection.
4. Each publisher publishes five messages and creates a list of the messages the listener should expect.
5. When each reply arrives, the message listener displays its contents and removes it from the list of expected messages.
6. When all the messages have arrived, the client exits.

Coding the Message-Driven Bean: ReplyMsgBean.java

The `onMessage` method of the message-driven bean class, `replybean/src/ReplyMsgBean.java`, does the following:

1. Casts the incoming message to a `TextMessage` and displays the text
2. Creates a connection, a session, and a publisher for the reply message

3. Publishes the message to the reply topic

4. Closes the connection

On both servers, the bean will consume messages from the topic `jms/Topic`.

Creating and Packaging the Applications

This example uses the connection factory named `jms/TopicConnectionFac-tory` and the topic named `jms/Topic`. These objects must exist on both the local and the remote servers. If you need to, you can create the objects there using the Admin Console, as described in Creating JMS Administered Objects (page 1178).

This example uses an additional connection factory, `jms/JupiterQueueConnec-tionFactory`, which communicates with the remote system; you created it in Creating Administered Objects for Multiple Systems (page 1188). Because connection factories are not specific to a domain (unless you are using a durable subscriber), you can use a `QueueConnectionFactory` object when you are sending messages to a topic. This connection factory needs to exist only on the local server.

Creating and packaging this application involve six steps:

1. Creating the connection factories
2. Compiling the source files
3. Creating the applications
4. Packaging the application client
5. Packaging the message-driven bean
6. Updating the JNDI names

You can package the applications yourself as an exercise. Use the `asant build` targets in the `multiclient` and `replybean` directories to compile the source files.

This section uses the prepackaged EAR files to show how to create and package the applications. You can use the systems `earth` and `jupiter` for the local and remote systems.

The Application Server must be running on both systems. You package, deploy, and run the application from the local system.

Examining the Applications

1. In `deploytool`, on the local system, open the two EAR files `MultiClientApp.ear` and `ReplyBeanApp.ear`, which reside in the directory `<INSTALL>/j2eetutorial14/jms/provided-ears`.

2. In `MultiClientApp.ear`, select the application client node, `MultiApp-ServerClient`.

   a. Click the Resource Ref's tab. The client looks up two connection factories and casts them to objects of type `javax.jms.ConnectionFactory`. The coded name `jms/ConnectionFactory1` refers to `jms/TopicConnectionFactory`, and the coded name `jms/ConnectionFactory2` refers to `jms/JupiterQueueConnectionFactory`.

   b. Click the Msg Dest Ref's tab. The coded name `jms/TopicName` refers to the target destination `PhysicalTopic`.

   c. Click the Message Destinations tab, and then click `PhysicalTopic`. The client appears in the Producers area. It refers to the JNDI name `jms/Topic`. This is the destination where messages are sent. Replies will come to a temporary destination.

3. In `ReplyBeanApp.ear`, expand the `MDBJAR` node and select `ReplyMsgBean`.

   a. Click the Message-Driven tab. The bean uses the `PhysicalTopic` target destination and the connection factory `jms/TopicConnectionFactory`.

   b. Click the Resource Ref's tab. The bean uses the connection factory `jms/TopicConnectionFactory` to send reply messages. The bean looks up the coded name `jms/MyConnectionFactory` and casts the object to an object of type `javax.jms.ConnectionFactory`. The bean does not look up a topic for the reply messages; instead, it uses the temporary topic specified in the incoming message's `JMSReplyTo` header field.

   c. Click the Transactions tab. The bean uses container-managed transactions.

4. Select the `MDBJAR` node, click the Message Destinations tab, and then click `PhysicalTopic`. The message-driven bean appears in the Consumers area. It refers to the JNDI name `jms/Topic`.

5. Select the `ReplyBeanApp` node and click Sun-specific Settings on the General page. The JNDI name for the message-driven bean is the topic destination resource, `jms/Topic`.

Verify that the JNDI names for the applications are correct.

The Application pane for `ReplyBeanApp` should appear as shown in Table 34–7.

Table 34–7 Application Pane for `ReplyBeanApp`

Component Type	Component	JNDI Name
EJB	ReplyMsgBean	jms/Topic

Table 34–8 References Pane for `ReplyBeanApp`

Ref. Type	Referenced By	Reference Name	JNDI Name
Resource	ReplyMsgBean	jms/MyConnection-Factory	jms/TopicConnec-tionFactory

Table 34–9 References Pane for `MultiClientApp`

Ref. Type	Referenced By	Reference Name	JNDI Name
Resource	MultiApp-ServerClient	jms/ConnectionFactory1	jms/TopicConnec-tionFactory
Resource	MultiApp-ServerClient	jms/ConnectionFactory2	jms/JupiterQueue-ConnectionFactory

The References pane for `ReplyBeanApp` should appear as shown in Table 34–8.

Select the `MultiClientApp` application and click the JNDI Names tab.

The JNDI names for the application should appear as shown in Table 34–9. Only the References pane has any content.

Deploying the Applications

To deploy the `MultiClientApp` application and the `ReplyBeanApp` application on the local server, perform the following steps for each application:

1. Save the application.
2. Choose Tools→Deploy.
3. In the dialog box, choose the URI for `localhost` from the menu:
   `localhost:4848`

4. Type your administrative user name and password (if they are not already filled in).

5. For the `MultiClientApp` application, select the Return Client Jar checkbox in the Application Client Stub Directory area. If you wish to run the client in a directory other than the default, click Browse and use the file chooser to specify it.

6. Click OK.

7. In the Distribute Module dialog box, click Close when the process completes. For the `MultiClientApp` application, you will find a file named `MultiClientAppClient.jar` in the specified directory.

Before you can deploy the `ReplyBeanApp` application on the remote server, you must add the remote server. If you did not do so before, perform the following steps:

1. Choose File→Add Server.

2. Type the name of the server in the Server Name field, and click OK.

3. The server appears in the tree under Servers. Select it.

4. In the dialog box that appears, type the administrative user name and password for the server in the Connection Settings area, and click OK.

To deploy the `ReplyBeanApp` application on the remote server, perform the following steps:

1. Save the application.

2. Choose Tools→Deploy.

3. In the dialog box, choose the URI with the name of the remote system from the menu.

4. Type your administrative user name and password (if they are not already filled in), and click OK.

5. In the Distribute Module dialog box, click Close when the process completes.

Running the Application Client

To run the client, use the following command:

```
appclient -client MultiClientAppClient.jar
```

On the local system, the output of the `appclient` command looks something like this:

```
Sent message: text: id=1 to local app server
Sent message: text: id=2 to remote app server
ReplyListener: Received message: id=1, text=ReplyMsgBean
processed message: text: id=1 to local app server
Sent message: text: id=3 to local app server
ReplyListener: Received message: id=3, text=ReplyMsgBean
processed message: text: id=3 to local app server
ReplyListener: Received message: id=2, text=ReplyMsgBean
processed message: text: id=2 to remote app server
Sent message: text: id=4 to remote app server
ReplyListener: Received message: id=4, text=ReplyMsgBean
processed message: text: id=4 to remote app server
Sent message: text: id=5 to local app server
ReplyListener: Received message: id=5, text=ReplyMsgBean
processed message: text: id=5 to local app server
Sent message: text: id=6 to remote app server
ReplyListener: Received message: id=6, text=ReplyMsgBean
processed message: text: id=6 to remote app server
Sent message: text: id=7 to local app server
ReplyListener: Received message: id=7, text=ReplyMsgBean
processed message: text: id-7 to local app server
Sent message: text: id=8 to remote app server
ReplyListener: Received message: id=8, text=ReplyMsgBean
processed message: text: id=8 to remote app server
Sent message: text: id=9 to local app server
ReplyListener: Received message: id=9, text=ReplyMsgBean
processed message: text: id-9 to local app server
Sent message: text: id=10 to remote app server
ReplyListener: Received message: id=10, text=ReplyMsgBean
processed message: text: id=10 to remote app server
Waiting for 0 message(s) from local app server
Waiting for 0 message(s) from remote app server
Finished
Closing connection 1
Closing connection 2
```

On the local system, where the message-driven bean receives the odd-numbered messages, the output in the server log looks like this (wrapped in logging information):

```
In ReplyMsgBean.ReplyMsgBean()
In ReplyMsgBean.setMessageDrivenContext()
In ReplyMsgBean.ejbCreate()
ReplyMsgBean: Received message: text: id=1 to local app server
```

```
ReplyMsgBean: Received message: text: id=3 to local app server
ReplyMsgBean: Received message: text: id=5 to local app server
ReplyMsgBean: Received message: text: id=7 to local app server
ReplyMsgBean: Received message: text: id=9 to local app server
```

On the remote system, where the bean receives the even-numbered messages, the output in the server log looks like this (wrapped in logging information):

```
In ReplyMsgBean.ReplyMsgBean()
In ReplyMsgBean.setMessageDrivenContext()
In ReplyMsgBean.ejbCreate()
ReplyMsgBean: Received message: text: id=2 to remote app server
ReplyMsgBean: Received message: text: id=4 to remote app server
ReplyMsgBean: Received message: text: id=6 to remote app server
ReplyMsgBean: Received message: text: id=8 to remote app server
ReplyMsgBean: Received message: text: id=10 to remote app server
```

Undeploy the applications after you finish running the client.

35

The Coffee Break
Application

This chapter describes the Coffee Break application, a set of Web applications that demonstrate how to use several of the Java Web service APIs together. The Coffee Break sells coffee on the Internet. Customers communicate with the Coffee Break server to order coffee online. There are two versions of the Coffee Break server that you can run: One version consists of Java servlets, JSP pages, and JavaBeans components; the second version uses JavaServer Faces technology as well Java servlets, JSP pages, and JavaBeans components. Using either version, a customer enters the quantity of each coffee to order and clicks the Submit button to send the order.

The Coffee Break does not maintain any inventory. It handles customer and order management and billing. Each order is filled by forwarding suborders to one or more coffee suppliers. This process is depicted in Figure 35–1.

Both versions of the Coffee Break server obtain the coffee varieties and their prices by querying suppliers at startup and on demand.

1. The Coffee Break servers use SAAJ messaging to communicate with one of the suppliers. The Coffee Break has been dealing with this supplier for some time and has previously made the necessary arrangements for doing request-response SAAJ messaging. The two parties have agreed to exchange four kinds of XML messages and have set up the DTDs those messages will follow.

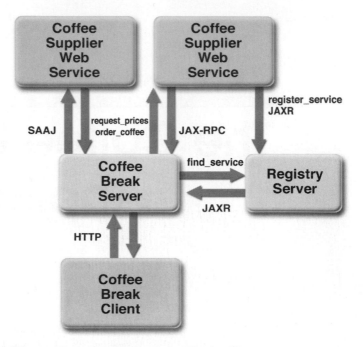

Figure 35–1   Coffee Break Application Flow

2. The Coffee Break servers use JAXR to send a query searching for coffee suppliers that support JAX-RPC to a registry server.

3. The Coffee Break servers request price lists from each of the coffee suppliers. The servers make the appropriate remote procedure calls and wait for the response, which is a JavaBeans component representing a price list. The SAAJ supplier returns price lists as XML documents.

4. Upon receiving the responses, the Coffee Break servers process the price lists from the JavaBeans components returned by calls to the suppliers.

5. The Coffee Break servers create a local database of suppliers.

6. When an order is placed, suborders are sent to one or more suppliers using the supplier's preferred protocol.

Common Code

The Coffee Break servers share the CoffeeBreak.properties file, which contains the URLs exposed by the JAX-RPC and SAAJ suppliers; the URLHelper

class, which is used by the server and client classes to retrieve the URLs; the
DateHelper utility class; and the following JavaBeans components:

- AddressBean: shipping information for customer
- ConfirmationBean: order id and ship date
- CustomerBean: customer contact information
- LineItemBean: order item
- OrderBean: order id, customer, address, list of line items, total price
- PriceItemBean: price list entry (coffee name and wholesale price)
- PriceListBean: price list

The source code for the shared files is in the *<INSTALL>*/j2eetutorial14/
examples/cb/common/src/com/sun/cb/ directory.

JAX-RPC Coffee Supplier Service

The Coffee Break servers are clients of the JAX-RPC coffee supplier service.
The service code consists of the service interface, the service implementation
class, and several JavaBeans components that are used for method parameters
and return types.

Service Interface

The service interface, SupplierIF, defines the methods that can be called by
remote clients. The parameters and return types of these methods are the Java-
Beans components listed in the preceding section.

The source code for the SupplierIF interface, which follows, resides in the
<INSTALL>/j2eetutorial14/examples/cb/jaxrpc/src/ directory.

```
package com.sun.cb;

import java.rmi.Remote;
import java.rmi.RemoteException;

public interface SupplierIF extends Remote {

   public ConfirmationBean placeOrder(OrderBean order)
      throws RemoteException;
   public PriceListBean getPriceList() throws RemoteException;
}
```

Service Implementation

The SupplierImpl class implements the placeOrder and getPriceList methods, which are defined by the SupplierIF interface. So that you can focus on the code related to JAX-RPC, these methods are short and simplistic. In a real world application, these methods would access databases and would interact with other services, such as shipping, accounting, and inventory.

The placeOrder method accepts as input a coffee order and returns a confirmation for the order. To keep things simple, the placeOrder method confirms every order and sets the ship date in the confirmation to the next day. The source code for the placeOrder method follows:

```
public ConfirmationBean placeOrder(OrderBean order) {

    Date tomorrow = DateHelper.addDays(new Date(), 1);
    ConfirmationBean confirmation =
      new ConfirmationBean(order.getId(),
        DateHelper.dateToCalendar(tomorrow));
    return confirmation;
}
```

The getPriceList method returns a PriceListBean object, which lists the name and price of each type of coffee that can be ordered from this service. The getPriceList method creates the PriceListBean object by invoking a private method named loadPrices. In a production application, the loadPrices method would fetch the prices from a database. However, our loadPrices method takes a shortcut by getting the prices from the SupplierPrices.properties file. Here are the getPriceList and loadPrices methods:

```
public PriceListBean getPriceList() {

    PriceListBean priceList = loadPrices();
    return priceList;
}

private PriceListBean loadPrices() {

    String propsName = "com.sun.cb.SupplierPrices";
    Date today = new Date();
    Date endDate = DateHelper.addDays(today, 30);

    PriceItemBean[] priceItems =
      PriceLoader.loadItems(propsName);
```

```
PriceListBean priceList =
   new PriceListBean(DateHelper.dateToCalendar(today),
      DateHelper.dateToCalendar(endDate), priceItems);

return priceList;
}
```

Publishing the Service in the Registry

Because we want customers to find our service, we publish it in a registry. When the JAX-RPC Web application is started and stopped, the context listener object ContextListener publishes and removes the service in the contextInitialized and contextDestroyed methods respectively.

The contextInitialized method begins by retrieving the registry and endpoint URLs and coffee registry properties. Both the context initializer and destroyer call the makeConnection method, which creates a connection to the registry server. See Establishing a Connection (page 394) for more information. To do this, it first specifies a set of connection properties using the registry URL retrieved from a context parameter. For the registry server, the query and publish URLs are actually the same.

```
Properties props = new Properties();
props.setProperty("javax.xml.registry.queryManagerURL",
   queryUrl);
props.setProperty("javax.xml.registry.lifeCycleManagerURL",
   publishUrl);
```

Next, the makeConnection method creates the connection using a connection factory it looks up using JNDI:

```
context = new InitialContext();
factory = (ConnectionFactory)
   context.lookup("java:comp/env/eis/JAXR");
factory.setProperties(props);
connection = factory.createConnection();
```

Next, the program instantiates a utility class named JAXRPublisher. To publish the service, the contextInitialized method invokes the executePublish method, which accepts as input connection, username, password, and endpoint. The username and password values are required by the registry server. The endpoint value is the URL that remote clients will use to contact our JAX-RPC service. The executePublish method of JAXRPublisher returns a key that uniquely identifies the service in the registry. The contextInitialized method saves this key in a text file named orgkey.txt. The contextDestroyed method reads the key from orgkey.txt so that it can delete the service. See Deleting the Service from the Registry, page 1263. The source code for the contextInitialized method follows.

```
public void contextInitialized(ServletContextEvent event) {
    String registryURL =
        context.getInitParameter("registryURL");
    String endpoint = URLHelper.getEndpointURL();

    ResourceBundle registryBundle = ResourceBundle.getBundle("
        com.sun.cb.CoffeeRegistry");

    String username =
        registryBundle.getString("registry.username");
    String password =
        registryBundle.getString("registry.password");
    String keyFile = registryBundle.getString("key.file");

    Connection connection = makeConnection(registryURL,
        registryURL);
    if (connection != null) {
    String key = publisher.executePublish(connection, username,
            password, endpoint);
    try {
        FileWriter out = new FileWriter(keyFile);
        out.write(key);
        out.flush();
        out.close();
    } catch (IOException ex) {
        System.out.println(ex.getMessage());
    }
    try {
        connection.close();
    } catch (Exception je) {}
    }
}
```

The JAXRPublisher class is almost identical to the sample program JAXRPublish.java, which is described in Managing Registry Data (page 404).

The executePublish method takes four arguments: the connection to the registry server, a user name, a password, and an endpoint. It begins by obtaining a

RegistryService object and then a BusinessQueryManager object and a BusinessLifeCycleManager object, which enable it to perform queries and manage data:

```
rs = connection.getRegistryService();
blcm = rs.getBusinessLifeCycleManager();
bqm = rs.getBusinessQueryManager();
```

Because it needs password authentication in order to publish data, the executePublish method then uses the username and password arguments to establish its security credentials:

```
PasswordAuthentication passwdAuth =
   new PasswordAuthentication(username,
      password.toCharArray());
Set creds = new HashSet();
creds.add(passwdAuth);
connection.setCredentials(creds);
```

It then creates an Organization object with the name JAXRPCCoffeeSupplier, and a User object that will serve as the primary contact. This code is almost identical to the code in the JAXR examples.

```
ResourceBundle bundle =
   ResourceBundle.getBundle("com.sun.cb.CoffeeRegistry");

// Create organization name and description
Organization org =
   blcm.createOrganization(bundle.getString("org.name"));
InternationalString s =
   blcm.createInternationalString
   (bundle.getString("org.description"));
org.setDescription(s);

// Create primary contact, set name
User primaryContact = blcm.createUser();
PersonName pName =
   blcm.createPersonName(bundle.getString("person.name"));
primaryContact.setPersonName(pName);
```

The executePublish method adds a telephone number and email address for the user, then makes the user the primary contact:

```
org.setPrimaryContact(primaryContact);
```

It gives JAXRPCCoffeeSupplier a classification using the North American Industry Classification System (NAICS). In this case it uses the classification "Other Grocery and Related Products Wholesalers."

```
Classification classification = (Classification)
  blcm.createClassification(cScheme,
    bundle.getString("classification.name"),
    bundle.getString("classification.value"));
Collection classifications = new ArrayList();
classifications.add(classification);
org.addClassifications(classifications);
```

Next, it adds the JAX-RPC service, called JAXRPCCoffee Service, and its service binding. The access URL for the service binding contains the endpoint URL that remote clients will use to contact our service:

```
http://localhost:8080/jaxrpc-coffee-supplier/jaxrpc

Collection services = new ArrayList();
Service service =
  blcm.createService(bundle.getString("service.name"));
InternationalString is =
  blcm.createInternationalString
  (bundle.getString("service.description"));
service.setDescription(is);

// Create service bindings
Collection serviceBindings = new ArrayList();
ServiceBinding binding = blcm.createServiceBinding();
is = blcm.createInternationalString
  (bundle.getString("service.binding"));
binding.setDescription(is);
binding.setValidateURI(false);
binding.setAccessURI(endpoint);
serviceBindings.add(binding);

// Add service bindings to service
service.addServiceBindings(serviceBindings);

// Add service to services, then add services to organization
services.add(service);
org.addServices(services);
```

Then it saves the organization to the registry:

```
Collection orgs = new ArrayList();
orgs.add(org);
BulkResponse response = blcm.saveOrganizations(orgs);
```

The `BulkResponse` object returned by `saveOrganizations` includes the `Key` object containing the unique key value for the organization. The `executePublish` method first checks to make sure that the `saveOrganizations` call succeeded.

If the call succeeded, the method extracts the value from the `Key` object and displays it:

```
Collection keys = response.getCollection();
Iterator keyIter = keys.iterator();
if (keyIter.hasNext()) {
  javax.xml.registry.infomodel.Key orgKey =
    (javax.xml.registry.infomodel.Key) keyIter.next();
  id = orgKey.getId();
  System.out.println("Organization key is " + id);
}
```

Finally, the method returns the string `id` so that the `OrgPublisher` program can save it in a file for use by the `OrgRemover` program.

Deleting the Service from the Registry

The `contextDestroyed` method deletes the service from the Registry Server. Like the `contextInitialized` method, the `contextDestroyed` method starts by fetching the registry URL and other values from the `CoffeeRegistry.properties` file. One these values, `keyFile`, is the name of the file that contains the key that uniquely identifies the service. The `contextDestroyed` method reads the key from the file, connects to the registry server by invoking `makeConnection`, and then deletes the service from the registry by calling `executeRemove`. Here is the source code for the `contextDestroyed` method:

```
public void contextDestroyed(ServletContextEvent event) {
  String keyStr = null;

  String registryURL =
    context.getInitParameter("registryURL");
```

```
        ResourceBundle registryBundle =
          ResourceBundle.getBundle("com.sun.cb.CoffeeRegistry");

        String username =
        registryBundle.getString("registry.username");
          String password =
          registryBundle.getString("registry.password");
        String keyFile = registryBundle.getString("key.file");

        try {
          FileReader in = new FileReader(keyFile);
          char[] buf = new char[512];
          while (in.read(buf, 0, 512) >= 0) { }
          in.close();
          keyStr = new String(buf).trim();
        } catch (IOException ex) {
          System.out.println(ex.getMessage());
        }

        JAXRRemover remover = new JAXRRemover();
        Connection connection = makeConnection(registryURL,
          registryURL);
        if (connection != null) {
          javax.xml.registry.infomodel.Key modelKey = null;
          modelKey = remover.createOrgKey(connection, keyStr);
          remover.executeRemove(connection, modelKey, username,
    password);
          try {
            connection.close();
          } catch (Exception je) {}
        }
      }
```

Instantiated by the contextDestroyed method, the JAXRRemover class contains the createOrgKey and executeRemove methods. It is almost identical to the sample program JAXRDelete.java, which is described in Removing Data from the Registry (page 411).

The createOrgKey utility method takes two arguments: the connection to the registry server and the string value extracted from the key file. It obtains the RegistryService object and the BusinessLifeCycleManager object, and then creates a Key object from the string value.

The executeRemove method takes four arguments: a connection, a user name, a password, and the Key object returned by the createOrgKey method. It uses the username and password arguments to establish its security credentials with the Registry Server, just as the executePublish method does.

The method then wraps the Key object in a Collection and uses the Business-LifeCycleManager object's deleteOrganizations method to delete the organization.

```
Collection keys = new ArrayList();
keys.add(key);
BulkResponse response = blcm.deleteOrganizations(keys);
```

The deleteOrganizations method returns the keys of the organizations it deleted, so the executeRemove method then verifies that the correct operation was performed and displays the key for the deleted organization.

```
Collection retKeys = response.getCollection();
Iterator keyIter = retKeys.iterator();
javax.xml.registry.infomodel.Key orgKey = null;
if (keyIter.hasNext()) {
  orgKey = (javax.xml.registry.infomodel.Key) keyIter.next();
  id - orgKcy.getId();
  System.out.println("Organization key was " + id);
}
```

SAAJ Coffee Supplier Service

In contrast to the JAX-RPC service, the SAAJ supplier service does not register in a publicly accessible registry. It simply implements the arrangements that the supplier and the Coffee Break have made regarding their exchange of XML documents. These arrangements include the kinds of messages they will send, the form of those messages, and the kind of messaging they will do. They have agreed to do request-response messaging using the SAAJ API (the javax.xml.soap package).

The Coffee Break servers send two kinds of messages:

- Requests for current wholesale coffee prices
- Customer orders for coffee

The SAAJ coffee supplier responds with two kinds of messages:

- Current price lists
- Order confirmations

All the messages they send conform to an agreed-upon XML structure, which is specified in a DTD for each kind of message. This allows them to exchange messages even though they use different document formats internally.

The four kinds of messages exchanged by the Coffee Break servers and the SAAJ supplier are specified by the following DTDs:

- `request-prices.dtd`
- `price-list.dtd`
- `coffee-order.dtd`
- `confirm.dtd`

These DTDs can be found at `<INSTALL>/j2eetutorial14/examples/cb/saaj/dtds/`. The `dtds` directory also contains a sample of what the XML documents specified in the DTDs might look like. The corresponding XML files for the DTDs are as follows:

- `request-prices.xml`
- `price-list.xml`
- `coffee-order.xml`
- `confirm.xml`

Because of the DTDs, both parties know ahead of time what to expect in a particular kind of message and can therefore extract its content using the SAAJ API.

Code for the client and server applications is in this directory:

```
<INSTALL>/j2eetutorial14/examples/cb/saaj/src/
```

SAAJ Client

The Coffee Break servers, which are the SAAJ clients in this scenario, send requests to their SAAJ supplier. The SAAJ client application uses the `SOAPConnection` method `call` to send messages.

```
SOAPMessage response = con.call(request, endpoint);
```

Accordingly, the client code has two major tasks. The first is to create and send the request; the second is to extract the content from the response. These tasks are handled by the classes `PriceListRequest` and `OrderRequest`.

Sending the Request

This section covers the code for creating and sending the request for an updated price list. This is done in the `getPriceList` method of `PriceListRequest`, which follows the DTD `price-list.dtd`.

The `getPriceList` method begins by creating the connection that will be used to send the request. Then it gets the default `MessageFactory` object so that it can create the `SOAPMessage` object `msg`.

```
SOAPConnectionFactory scf =
  SOAPConnectionFactory.newInstance();
SOAPConnection con = scf.createConnection();

MessageFactory mf = MessageFactory.newInstance();
SOAPMessage msg = mf.createMessage();
```

The next step is to access the message's `SOAPEnvelope` object, which will be used to create a `Name` object for each new element that is created. The `SOAPEnvelope` object is also used to access the `SOAPBody` object, to which the message's content will be added.

```
SOAPPart part = msg.getSOAPPart();
SOAPEnvelope envelope = part.getEnvelope();
SOAPBody body = envelope.getBody();
```

The file `price-list.dtd` specifies that the topmost element inside the body is `request-prices` and that it contains the element `request`. The text node added to `request` is the text of the request being sent. Every new element that is added to the message must have a `Name` object to identify it, and this object is created by the `Envelope` method `createName`. The following lines of code create the top-level element in the `SOAPBody` object body. The first element created in a `SOAPBody` object is always a `SOAPBodyElement` object.

```
Name bodyName = envelope.createName("request-prices",
  "RequestPrices", "http://sonata.coffeebreak.com");
SOAPBodyElement requestPrices =
  body.addBodyElement(bodyName);
```

In the next few lines, the code adds the element `request` to the element `request-prices` (represented by the `SOAPBodyElement requestPrices`). Then the code adds a text node containing the text of the request. Next, because there are no other elements in the request, the code calls the method `saveChanges` on the message to save what has been done.

```
Name requestName = envelope.createName("request");
SOAPElement request =
  requestPrices.addChildElement(requestName);
request.addTextNode("Send updated price list.");

msg.saveChanges();
```

With the creation of the request message completed, the code sends the message to the SAAJ coffee supplier. The message being sent is the `SOAPMessage` object `msg`, to which the elements created in the previous code snippets were added. The endpoint is the URI for the SAAJ coffee supplier, `http://localhost:8080/saaj-coffee-supplier/getPriceList`. The `SOAPConnection` object `con` is used to send the message, and because it is no longer needed, it is closed.

```
URL endpoint = new URL(url);
SOAPMessage response = con.call(msg, endpoint);
con.close();
```

When the `call` method is executed, the Application Server executes the servlet `PriceListServlet`. This servlet creates and returns a `SOAPMessage` object whose content is the SAAJ supplier's price list. (`PriceListServlet` is discussed in Returning the Price List, page 1274.) The Application Server knows to execute `PriceListServlet` because we map the given endpoint to that servlet.

Extracting the Price List

This section demonstrates (1) retrieving the price list that is contained in `response`, the `SOAPMessage` object returned by the method `call`, and (2) returning the price list as a `PriceListBean`.

The code creates an empty `Vector` object that will hold the `coffee-name` and `price` elements that are extracted from `response`. Then the code uses `response` to access its `SOAPBody` object, which holds the message's content. Notice that the `SOAPEnvelope` object is not accessed separately because it is not needed for creating `Name` objects, as it was in the previous section.

```
Vector list = new Vector();

SOAPBody responseBody =
  response.getSOAPPart().getEnvelope().getBody();
```

The next step is to retrieve the SOAPBodyElement object. The method get-ChildElements returns an Iterator object that contains all the child elements of the element on which it is called, so in the following lines of code, it1 contains the SOAPBodyElement object bodyEl, which represents the price-list element.

```
Iterator it1 = responseBody.getChildElements();
while (it1.hasNext()) {
  SOAPBodyElement bodyEl = (SOAPBodyElement)it1.next();
```

The Iterator object it2 holds the child elements of bodyEl, which represent coffee elements. Calling the method next on it2 retrieves the first coffee element in bodyEl. As long as it2 has another element, the method next will return the next coffee element.

```
Iterator it2 = bodyEl.getChildElements();
while (it2.hasNext()) {
  SOAPElement child2 = (SOAPElement)it2.next();
```

The next lines of code drill down another level to retrieve the coffee-name and price elements contained in it3. Then the message getValue retrieves the text (a coffee name or a price) that the SAAJ coffee supplier added to the coffee-name and price elements when it gave content to response. The final line in the following code fragment adds the coffee name or price to the Vector object list. Note that because of the nested while loops, for each coffee element that the code retrieves, both of its child elements (the coffee-name and price elements) are retrieved.

```
Iterator it3 = child2.getChildElements();
while (it3.hasNext()) {
  SOAPElement child3 = (SOAPElement)it3.next();
  String value = child3.getValue();
  list.addElement(value);
      }
    }
  }
```

The final code fragment adds the coffee names and their prices (as a PriceListItem) to the ArrayList priceItems, and prints each pair on a separate line. Finally it constructs and returns a PriceListBean.

```
ArrayList priceItems = new ArrayList();
for (int i = 0; i < list.size(); i = i + 2) {
  priceItems.add(
    new PriceItemBean(list.elementAt(i).toString(),
```

```
        new BigDecimal(list.elementAt(i + 1).toString())));
    System.out.print(list.elementAt(i) + "              ");
    System.out.println(list.elementAt(i + 1));
}

Date today = new Date();
Date endDate = DateHelper.addDays(today, 30);
Calendar todayCal = new GregorianCalendar();
todayCal.setTime(today);
Calendar cal = new GregorianCalendar();
cal.setTime(endDate);
plb = new PriceListBean();
plb.setStartDate(todayCal);
plb.setPriceItems(priceItems);
plb.setEndDate(cal);
```

Ordering Coffee

The other kind of message that the Coffee Break servers can send to the SAAJ supplier is an order for coffee. This is done in the placeOrder method of Order-Request, which follows the DTD coffee-order.dtd.

Creating the Order

As with the client code for requesting a price list, the placeOrder method starts by creating a SOAPConnection object, creating a SOAPMessage object, and accessing the message's SOAPEnvelope and SOAPBody objects.

```
SOAPConnectionFactory scf =
    SOAPConnectionFactory.newInstance();
SOAPConnection con = scf.createConnection();

MessageFactory mf = MessageFactory.newInstance();
SOAPMessage msg = mf.createMessage();

SOAPPart part = msg.getSOAPPart();
SOAPEnvelope envelope = part.getEnvelope();
SOAPBody body = envelope.getBody();
```

Next, the code creates and adds XML elements to form the order. As is required, the first element is a SOAPBodyElement, which in this case is coffee-order.

```
Name bodyName = envelope.createName("coffee-order", "PO",
    "http://sonata.coffeebreak.com");
SOAPBodyElement order = body.addBodyElement(bodyName);
```

The application then adds the next level of elements, the first of these being orderID. The value given to orderID is extracted from the OrderBean object passed to the OrderRequest.placeOrder method.

```
Name orderIDName = envelope.createName("orderID");
SOAPElement orderID = order.addChildElement(orderIDName);
orderID.addTextNode(orderBean.getId());
```

The next element, customer, has several child elements that give information about the customer. This information is also extracted from the Customer component of OrderBean.

```
Name childName = envelope.createName("customer");
SOAPElement customer = order.addChildElement(childName);

childName = envelope.createName("last-name");
SOAPElement lastName = customer.addChildElement(childName);
lastName.addTextNode(orderBean.getCustomer().getLastName());

childName = envelope.createName("first-name");
SOAPElement firstName = customer.addChildElement(childName);
firstName.addTextNode(orderBean.getCustomer().getFirstName());

childName = envelope.createName("phone-number");
SOAPElement phoneNumber = customer.addChildElement(childName);
phoneNumber.addTextNode(
    orderBean.getCustomer().getPhoneNumber());

childName = envelope.createName("email-address");
SOAPElement emailAddress =
    customer.addChildElement(childName);
emailAddress.addTextNode(
    orderBean.getCustomer().getEmailAddress());
```

The address element, added next, has child elements for the street, city, state, and zip code. This information is extracted from the Address component of OrderBean.

```
childName = envelope.createName("address");
SOAPElement address = order.addChildElement(childName);

childName = envelope.createName("street");
SOAPElement street = address.addChildElement(childName);
street.addTextNode(orderBean.getAddress().getStreet());
```

```
childName = envelope.createName("city");
SOAPElement city = address.addChildElement(childName);
city.addTextNode(orderBean.getAddress().getCity());

childName = envelope.createName("state");
SOAPElement state = address.addChildElement(childName);
state.addTextNode(orderBean.getAddress().getState());

childName = envelope.createName("zip");
SOAPElement zip = address.addChildElement(childName);
zip.addTextNode(orderBean.getAddress().getZip());
```

The element line-item has three child elements: coffeeName, pounds, and price. This information is extracted from the LineItems list contained in OrderBean.

```
for (Iterator it = orderBean.getLineItems().iterator();
     it.hasNext(); ) {
  LineItemBean lib = (LineItemBean)it.next();

  childName = envelope.createName("line-item");
  SOAPElement lineItem = order.addChildElement(childName);

  childName = envelope.createName("coffeeName");
  SOAPElement coffeeName =
     lineItem.addChildElement(childName);
  coffeeName.addTextNode(lib.getCoffeeName());

  childName = envelope.createName("pounds");
  SOAPElement pounds = lineItem.addChildElement(childName);
  pounds.addTextNode(lib.getPounds().toString());

  childName = envelope.createName("price");
  SOAPElement price = lineItem.addChildElement(childName);
  price.addTextNode(lib.getPrice().toString());
}

// total
childName = envelope.createName("total");
SOAPElement total = order.addChildElement(childName);
total.addTextNode(orderBean.getTotal().toString());
```

With the order complete, the application sends the message to the endpoint `http://localhost:8080/saaj-coffee-supplier/orderCoffee` and closes the connection.

```
URL endpoint = new URL(url);
SOAPMessage reply = con.call(msg, endpoint);
con.close();
```

Because we map the given endpoint to `ConfirmationServlet`, the Application Server executes that servlet (discussed in Returning the Order Confirmation, page 1279) to create and return the `SOAPMessage` object `reply`.

Retrieving the Order Confirmation

The rest of the `placeOrder` method retrieves the information returned in `reply`. The client knows what elements are in it because they are specified in `confirm.dtd`. After accessing the `SOAPBody` object, the code retrieves the `confirmation` element and gets the text of the `orderID` and `ship-date` elements. Finally, it constructs and returns a `ConfirmationBean` with this information.

```
SOAPBody sBody = reply.getSOAPPart().getEnvelope().getBody();
Iterator bodyIt = sBody.getChildElements();
SOAPBodyElement sbEl = (SOAPBodyElement)bodyIt.next();
Iterator bodyIt2 = sbEl.getChildElements();

SOAPElement ID = (SOAPElement)bodyIt2.next();
String id - ID.getValue();

SOAPElement sDate = (SOAPElement)bodyIt2.next();
String shippingDate = sDate.getValue();

SimpleDateFormat df =
   new SimpleDateFormat("EEE MMM dd HH:mm:ss z yyyy");
Date date = df.parse(shippingDate);
Calendar cal = new GregorianCalendar();
cal.setTime(date);
cb = new ConfirmationBean(id, cal);
```

SAAJ Service

The SAAJ coffee supplier—the SAAJ server in this scenario—provides the response part of the request-response paradigm. When SAAJ messaging is being used, the server code is a servlet. The core part of each servlet is made up of three javax.servlet.HttpServlet methods: init, doPost, and onMessage. The init and doPost methods set up the response message, and the onMessage method gives the message its content.

Returning the Price List

This section takes you through the servlet PriceListServlet. This servlet creates the message containing the current price list that is returned to the method call, invoked in PriceListRequest.

Any servlet extends a javax.servlet class. Being part of a Web application, this servlet extends HttpServlet. It first creates a static MessageFactory object that will be used later to create the SOAPMessage object that is returned.

```
public class PriceListServlet extends HttpServlet {
   static MessageFactory fac = null;

   static {
      try {
         fac = MessageFactory.newInstance();
      } catch (Exception ex) {
         ex.printStackTrace();
      }
   };
```

Every servlet has an init method. This init method initializes the servlet with the configuration information that the Application Server passed to it.

```
public void init(ServletConfig servletConfig)
    throws ServletException {
   super.init(servletConfig);
}
```

The next method defined in PriceListServlet is doPost, which does the real work of the servlet by calling the onMessage method. (The onMessage method is discussed later in this section.) The Application Server passes the doPost method two arguments. The first argument, the HttpServletRequest object req, holds the content of the message sent in PriceListRequest. The doPost method gets the content from req and puts it in the SOAPMessage object msg so that it can pass it to the onMessage method. The second argument, the Http-ServletResponse object resp, will hold the message generated by executing the method onMessage.

In the following code fragment, doPost calls the methods getHeaders and put-Headers, defined immediately after doPost, to read and write the headers in req. It then gets the content of req as a stream and passes the headers and the input stream to the method MessageFactory.createMessage. The result is that the SOAPMessage object msg contains the request for a price list. Note that in this case, msg does not have any headers because the message sent in PriceListRequest did not have any headers.

```
public void doPost(HttpServletRequest req,
    HttpServletResponse resp)
    throws ServletException, IOException {
  try {
    // Get all the headers from the HTTP request
    MimeHeaders headers = getHeaders(req);

    // Get the body of the HTTP request
    InputStream is = req.getInputStream();

    // Now internalize the contents of the HTTP request
    // and create a SOAPMessage
    SOAPMessage msg = fac.createMessage(headers, is);
```

Next, the code declares the SOAPMessage object reply and populates it by calling the method onMessage.

```
SOAPMessage reply = null;
reply = onMessage(msg);
```

If reply has anything in it, its contents are saved, the status of resp is set to OK, and the headers and content of reply are written to resp. If reply is empty, the status of resp is set to indicate that there is no content.

```
if (reply != null) {

    /*
     * Need to call saveChanges because we're
     * going to use the MimeHeaders to set HTTP
     * response information. These MimeHeaders
     * are generated as part of the save.
     */
```

```
            if (reply.saveRequired()) {
               reply.saveChanges();
            }

            resp.setStatus(HttpServletResponse.SC_OK);
            putHeaders(reply.getMimeHeaders(), resp);

            // Write out the message on the response stream
            OutputStream os = resp.getOutputStream();
            reply.writeTo(os);
            os.flush();
         } else {
            resp.setStatus(
               HttpServletResponse.SC_NO_CONTENT);
         }
      } catch (Exception ex) {
         throw new ServletException( "SAAJ POST failed: " +
            ex.getMessage());
      }
   }
}
```

The methods getHeaders and putHeaders are not standard methods in a servlet, as init, doPost, and onMessage are. The method doPost calls getHeaders and passes it the HttpServletRequest object req that the Application Server passed to it. It returns a MimeHeaders object populated with the headers from req.

```
static MimeHeaders getHeaders(HttpServletRequest req) {

   Enumeration enum = req.getHeaderNames();
   MimeHeaders headers = new MimeHeaders();

   while (enum.hasMoreElements()) {
      String headerName = (String)enum.nextElement();
      String headerValue = req.getHeader(headerName);

      StringTokenizer values =
         new StringTokenizer(headerValue, ",");
      while (values.hasMoreTokens()) {
         headers.addHeader(headerName,
            values.nextToken().trim());
      }
   }
   return headers;
}
```

The doPost method calls putHeaders and passes it the MimeHeaders object headers, which was returned by the method getHeaders. The method putHeaders writes the headers in `headers` to `res`, the second argument passed to it. The result is that `res`, the response that the Application Server will return to the method `call`, now contains the headers that were in the original request.

```
static void putHeaders(MimeHeaders headers,
    HttpServletResponse res) {

  Iterator it = headers.getAllHeaders();
  while (it.hasNext()) {
    MimeHeader header = (MimeHeader)it.next();

    String[] values = headers.getHeader(header.getName());
    if (values.length == 1)
      res.setHeader(header.getName(), header.getValue());
    else {
      StringBuffer concat = new StringBuffer();
      int i = 0;
      while (i < values.length) {
        if (i != 0) {
          concat.append(',');
        }
        concat.append(values[i++]);
      }
      res.setHeader(header.getName(), concat.toString());
    }
  }
}
```

The method `onMessage` is the application code for responding to the message sent by `PriceListRequest` and internalized into `msg`. It uses the static `Message-Factory` object `fac` to create the `SOAPMessage` object `message` and then populates it with the supplier's current coffee prices.

The method `doPost` invokes `onMessage` and passes it `msg`. In this case, `onMessage` does not need to use `msg` because it simply creates a message containing the supplier's price list. The `onMessage` method in `ConfirmationServlet` (see Returning the Order Confirmation, page 1279), on the other hand, uses the message passed to it to get the order ID.

```
public SOAPMessage onMessage(SOAPMessage msg) {
  SOAPMessage message = null;

  try {
    message = fac.createMessage();
```

```
SOAPPart part = message.getSOAPPart();
SOAPEnvelope envelope = part.getEnvelope();
SOAPBody body = envelope.getBody();

Name bodyName = envelope.createName("price-list",
   "PriceList", "http://sonata.coffeebreak.com");
SOAPBodyElement list = body.addBodyElement(bodyName);

Name coffeeN = envelope.createName("coffee");
SOAPElement coffee = list.addChildElement(coffeeN);

Name coffeeNm1 = envelope.createName("coffee-name");
SOAPElement coffeeName =
   coffee.addChildElement(coffeeNm1);
coffeeName.addTextNode("Arabica");

Name priceName1 = envelope.createName("price");
SOAPElement price1 = coffee.addChildElement(priceName1);
price1.addTextNode("4.50");

Name coffeeNm2 = envelope.createName("coffee-name");
SOAPElement coffeeName2 =
   coffee.addChildElement(coffeeNm2);
coffeeName2.addTextNode("Espresso");

Name priceName2 = envelope.createName("price");
SOAPElement price2 = coffee.addChildElement(priceName2);
price2.addTextNode("5.00");

Name coffeeNm3 = envelope.createName("coffee-name");
SOAPElement coffeeName3 =
   coffee.addChildElement(coffeeNm3);
coffeeName3.addTextNode("Dorada");

Name priceName3 = envelope.createName("price");
SOAPElement price3 = coffee.addChildElement(priceName3);
price3.addTextNode("6.00");

Name coffeeNm4 = envelope.createName("coffee-name");
SOAPElement coffeeName4 =
   coffee.addChildElement(coffeeNm4);
coffeeName4.addTextNode("House Blend");

Name priceName4 = envelope.createName("price");
SOAPElement price4 = coffee.addChildElement(priceName4);
price4.addTextNode("5.00");

message.saveChanges();
```

```
    } catch(Exception e) {
        e.printStackTrace();
    }
    return message;
}
```

Returning the Order Confirmation

ConfirmationServlet creates the confirmation message that is returned to the call method that is invoked in OrderRequest. It is very similar to the code in PriceListServlet except that instead of building a price list, its onMessage method builds a confirmation containing the order number and shipping date.

The onMessage method for this servlet uses the SOAPMessage object passed to it by the doPost method to get the order number sent in OrderRequest. Then it builds a confirmation message containing the order ID and shipping date. The shipping date is calculated as today's date plus two days.

```
public SOAPMessage onMessage(SOAPMessage message) {

    SOAPMessage confirmation = null;

    try {

        // Retrieve orderID from message received
        SOAPBody sentSB =
            message.getSOAPPart().getEnvelope().getBody();
        Iterator sentIt = sentSB.getChildElements();
        SOAPBodyElement sentSBE = (SOAPBodyElement)sentIt.next();
        Iterator sentIt2 = sentSBE.getChildElements();
        SOAPElement sentSE = (SOAPElement)sentIt2.next();

        // Get the orderID test to put in confirmation
        String sentID = sentSE.getValue();

        // Create the confirmation message
        confirmation = fac.createMessage();
        SOAPPart sp = confirmation.getSOAPPart();
        SOAPEnvelope env = sp.getEnvelope();
        SOAPBody sb = env.getBody();

        Name newBodyName = env.createName("confirmation",
            "Confirm", "http://sonata.coffeebreak.com");
        SOAPBodyElement confirm = sb.addBodyElement(newBodyName);
```

```
    // Create the orderID element for confirmation
    Name newOrderIDName = env.createName("orderId");
    SOAPElement newOrderNo =
        confirm.addChildElement(newOrderIDName);
    newOrderNo.addTextNode(sentID);

    // Create ship-date element
    Name shipDateName = env.createName("ship-date");
    SOAPElement shipDate =
        confirm.addChildElement(shipDateName);

    // Create the shipping date
    Date today = new Date();
    long msPerDay = 1000 * 60 * 60 * 24;
    long msTarget = today.getTime();
    long msSum = msTarget + (msPerDay * 2);
    Date result = new Date();
    result.setTime(msSum);
    String sd = result.toString();
    shipDate.addTextNode(sd);

    confirmation.saveChanges();

  } catch (Exception ex) {
    ex.printStackTrace();
  }
  return confirmation;
}
```

Coffee Break Server

The Coffee Break server uses servlets, JSP pages, and JavaBeans components to dynamically construct HTML pages for consumption by a Web browser client. The JSP pages use the template tag library discussed in A Template Tag Library (page 610) to achieve a common look and feel among the HTML pages, and many of the JSTL custom tags discussed in Chapter 14.

The Coffee Break server implementation is organized along the Model-View-Controller design pattern. The Dispatcher servlet is the controller. It examines the request URL, creates and initializes model JavaBeans components, and dispatches requests to view JSP pages. The JavaBeans components contain the business logic for the application; they call the Web services and perform computations on the data returned from the services. The JSP pages format the data stored in the JavaBeans components. The mapping between JavaBeans components and pages is summarized in Table 35–1.

Table 35–1 Model and View Components

Function	JSP Page	JavaBeans Component
Update order data	orderForm	ShoppingCart
Update delivery and billing data	checkoutForm	CheckoutFormBean
Display order confirmation	checkoutAck	OrderConfirmations

JSP Pages

orderForm

orderForm displays the current contents of the shopping cart. The first time the page is requested, the quantities of all the coffees are 0 (zero). Each time the customer changes the coffee amounts and clicks the Update button, the request is posted back to orderForm. The Dispatcher servlet updates the values in the shopping cart, which are then redisplayed by orderForm. When the order is complete, the customer proceeds to the checkoutForm page by clicking the Checkout link.

checkoutForm

checkoutForm is used to collect delivery and billing information from the customer. When the Submit button is clicked, the request is posted to the checkoutAck page. However, the request is first handled by the Dispatcher, which invokes the validate method of checkoutFormBean. If the validation does not succeed, the requested page is reset to checkoutForm, with error notifications in each invalid field. If the validation succeeds, checkoutFormBean submits suborders to each supplier and stores the result in the request-scoped OrderConfirmations JavaBeans component, and control is passed to checkoutAck.

checkoutAck

checkoutAck simply displays the contents of the OrderConfirmations JavaBeans component, which is a list of the suborders that constitute an order and the ship dates of each suborder.

JavaBeans Components

RetailPriceList

`RetailPriceList` is a list of retail price items. A retail price item contains a coffee name, a wholesale price per pound, a retail price per pound, and a supplier. This data is used for two purposes: it contains the price list presented to the end user and is used by `CheckoutFormBean` when it constructs the suborders dispatched to coffee suppliers.

`RetailPriceList` first performs a JAXR lookup to determine the JAX-RPC service endpoints. It then queries each JAX-RPC service for a coffee price list. Finally it queries the SAAJ service for a price list. The two price lists are combined and a retail price per pound is determined by adding a markup of 35% to the wholesale prices.

Discovering the JAX-RPC Service

Instantiated by `RetailPriceList`, `JAXRQueryByName` connects to the registry server and searches for coffee suppliers registered with the name `JAXRPCCoffeeSupplier` in the `executeQuery` method. The method returns a collection of organizations that contain services. Each service is accessible via a service binding or URL. `RetailPriceList` makes a JAX-RPC call to each URL.

ShoppingCart

`ShoppingCart` is a list of shopping cart items. A `ShoppingCartItem` contains a retail price item, the number of pounds of that item, and the total price for that item.

OrderConfirmations

`OrderConfirmations` is a list of order confirmation objects. An `OrderConfirmation` contains order and confirmation objects, as discussed in Service Interface (page 1257).

CheckoutFormBean

`CheckoutFormBean` checks the completeness of information entered into `checkoutForm`. If the information is incomplete, the bean populates error messages, and Dispatcher redisplays checkoutForm with the error messages. If the information is complete, order requests are constructed from the shopping cart and the information supplied to checkoutForm, and these orders are sent to each supplier. As each confirmation is received, an order confirmation is created and added to OrderConfirmations.

```java
if (allOk) {
  String orderId = CCNumber;

  AddressBean address =
    new AddressBean(street, city, state, zip);
  CustomerBean customer =
    new CustomerBean(firstName, lastName,
      "(" + areaCode + ") " + phoneNumber, email);

  for (Iterator d = rpl.getSuppliers().iterator();
      d.hasNext(); ) {
    String supplier = (String)d.next();
    System.out.println(supplier);
    ArrayList lis = new ArrayList();
    BigDecimal price = new BigDecimal("0.00");
    BigDecimal total = new BigDecimal("0.00");
    for (Iterator c = cart.getItems().iterator();
        c.hasNext(); ) {
      ShoppingCartItem sci = (ShoppingCartItem) c.next();
      if ((sci.getItem().getSupplier()).
          equals(supplier) &&
          sci.getPounds().floatValue() > 0) {
        price = sci.getItem().getWholesalePricePerPound().
          multiply(sci.getPounds());
        total = total.add(price);
        LineItemBean li = new LineItemBean(
          sci.getItem().getCoffeeName(), sci.getPounds(),
          sci.getItem().getWholesalePricePerPound());
        lis.add(li);
      }
    }

    if (!lis.isEmpty()) {
      OrderBean order = new OrderBean(address, customer,
        orderId, lis, total);

      String SAAJOrderURL =
        URLHelper.getSaajURL() + "/orderCoffee";
      if (supplier.equals(SAAJOrderURL)) {
        OrderRequest or = new OrderRequest(SAAJOrderURL);
        confirmation = or.placeOrder(order);
```

```
        } else {
          OrderCaller ocaller = new OrderCaller(supplier);
          confirmation = ocaller.placeOrder(order);
        }
        OrderConfirmation oc =
          new OrderConfirmation(order, confirmation);
        ocs.add(oc);
      }
    }
  }
```

RetailPriceListServlet

RetailPriceListServlet responds to requests to reload the price list via the URL /loadPriceList. It simply creates a new RetailPriceList and a new ShoppingCart.

Because this servlet would be used by administrators of the Coffee Break server, it is a protected Web resource. To load the price list, a user must authenticate (using basic authentication), and the authenticated user must be in the admin role.

JavaServer Faces Version of Coffee Break Server

JavaServer Faces is designed to provide a clean separation of the presentation layer and the model layer so that you can readily add JavaServer Faces functionality to existing applications. In fact, almost all of the original Coffee Break Server back-end code remains the same in the JavaServer Faces technology version of the server.

This section provides some details on how the JavaServer Faces version of the Coffee Break server is different from the non-GUI framework version. Like the non-GUI framework version of the Coffee Break server implementation, the JavaServer Faces Coffee Break server is organized along the Model-View-Controller design pattern. Instead of the Dispatcher servlet examining the request URL, creating and initializing model JavaBeans components, and dispatching requests to view JSP pages, now the FacesServlet (included with the

JavaServer Faces API), performs these tasks. As a result, the `Dispatcher` servlet has been removed from the JavaServer Faces version of the Coffee Break server. Some of the code from the `Dispatcher` has been moved to beans. This will be explained later in this section.

As with the non-GUI framework version of the Coffee Break server, the JavaServer Faces Coffee Break server includes JavaBeans components that contain the business logic for the application: they call the Web services and perform computations on the data returned from the services. The JSP pages format the data stored in the JavaBeans components. The mapping between JavaBeans components and pages is summarized in Table 35–2.

Table 35–2 Model and View Components

Function	JSP Page	JavaBeans Component
Update order data	`orderForm`	`CoffeeBreakBean`, `ShoppingCart`
Update delivery and billing data	`checkoutForm`	`CheckoutFormBean`
Display order confirmation	`checkoutAck`	`OrderConfirmations`

JSP Pages

orderForm

As in the non-GUI framework version of the Coffee Break server, the `orderForm` displays the current contents of the shopping cart. The first time the page is requested, the quantities of all the coffees are 0. Each time the customer changes the coffee amounts and clicks the Update button, the request is posted back to `orderForm`.

The `CoffeeBreakBean` bean component updates the values in the shopping cart, which are then redisplayed by `orderForm`. When the order is complete, the customer proceeds to the `checkoutForm` page by clicking the Checkout button.

The table of coffees displayed on the orderForm is rendered using one of the JavaServer Faces component tags, data_table. Here is part of the data_table tag from orderForm:

```
<h:dataTable id="table"
  columnClasses="list-column-center,list-column-right,
    list-column-center, list-column-right"
  headerClass="list-header" rowClasses="list-row"
  footerClass="list-column-right"
  styleClass="list-background-grid"
  value="#{CoffeeBreakBean.cart.items}" var="sci">
  <f:facet name="header">
    <h:outputText  value="#{CBMessages.OrderForm}"/>
  </f:facet>
  <h:column>
    <f:facet name="header">
      <h:outputText  value="Coffee"/>
    </f:facet>
    <h:outputText id="coffeeName"
      value="#{sci.item.coffeeName}"/>
  </h:column>
  ...
</h:dataTable>
```

When this tag is processed, a UIData component and a Table renderer are created on the server side. The UIData component supports a data binding to a collection of data objects. The Table renderer takes care of generating the HTML markup. The UIData component iterates through the list of coffees, and the Table renderer renders each row in the table.

This example is a classic use case for a UIData component because the number of coffees might not be known to the application developer or the page author at the time the application is developed. Also, the UIData component can dynamically adjust the number of rows in the table to accommodate the underlying data.

For more information on UIData, please see The UIData Component (page 686).

checkoutForm

checkoutForm is used to collect delivery and billing information for the customer. When the Submit button is clicked, an ActionEvent is generated. This event is first handled by the submit method of the checkoutFormBean. This method acts as a listener for the event because the tag corresponding to the submit button references the `submit` method with its `action` attribute:

```
<h:commandButton value="#{CBMessages.Submit}"
    action="#{checkoutFormBean.submit}"/>
```

The `submit` method submits the suborders to each supplier and stores the result in the request-scoped `OrderConfirmations` bean.

The `checkoutForm` page has standard validators on several components and a custom validator on the email component. Here is the tag corresponding to the `firstName` component, which holds the customer's first name:

```
<h:inputText id="firstName"
    value="#{checkoutFormBean.firstName}"
    size="15" maxlength="20" required="true"/>
```

With the `required` attribute set to `true`, the JavaServer Faces implementation will check whether the user entered something in the First Name field.

The `email` component has a custom validator registered on it. Here is the tag corresponding to the `email` component:

```
<h:inputText id="email" value="#{checkoutFormBean.email}"
    size="25" maxlength="125"
    validator="#{checkoutFormBean.validateEmail}"/>
```

The `validator` attribute refers to the `validateEmail` method on the `Checkout-FormBean` class. This method ensures that the value the user enters in the email field contains an @ character.

If the validation does not succeed, the `checkoutForm` is re-rendered, with error notifications in each invalid field. If the validation succeeds, `checkoutFormBean` submits suborders to each supplier and stores the result in the request-scoped `OrderConfirmations` JavaBeans component and control is passed to the `checkoutAck` page.

checkoutAck

`checkoutAck` simply displays the contents of the `OrderConfirmations` JavaBeans component, which is a list of the suborders constituting an order and the ship dates of each suborder. This page also uses a `UIData` component. Again, the number of coffees the customer ordered is not known before runtime. The `UIData` component dynamically adds rows to accommodate the order.

JavaBeans Components

The JavaBeans components in the JavaServer Faces version of the Coffee Break server are almost the same as those in the original version. This section highlights what has changed and describes the new components.

CheckoutFormBean

The validate method of the original version of the CheckoutFormBean checks the completeness of information entered into checkoutForm. Because JavaServer Faces technology automatically validates certain kinds of data when the appropriate validator is registered on a component, the validate method of checkoutFormBean is not necessary in the JavaServer Faces version of that bean.

Several of the tags on the checkoutForm page have their required attributes set to true. This will cause the implementation to check whether the user enters values in these fields. The tag corresponding to the email component registers a custom validator on the email component, as explained in checkoutForm (page 1286). The code that performs the validation is the validateEmail method:

```
public void validateEmail(FacesContext context,
    UIComponent toValidate) {
    String message = "";
    String email = (String) toValidate.getValue();
    if (email.indexOf('@') == -1) {
        toValidate.setValid(false);
        message = CoffeeBreakBean.loadErrorMessage(context,
            CoffeeBreakBean.CB_RESOURCE_BUNDLE_NAME,
                "EMailError");
        context.addMessage(toValidate.getClientId(context),
            new FacesMessage(message));
    }
}
```

As in the non-GUI framework version of the Coffee Break server, if the information is incomplete or invalid, the page is rerendered to display the error messages. If the information is complete, order requests are constructed from the shopping cart and the information supplied to checkoutForm and are sent to each supplier.

CoffeeBreakBean

CoffeeBreakBean is exclusive to the JavaServer Faces technology version of the Coffee Break server. It acts as the backing bean to the JSP pages. See Backing Bean Management (page 656) for more information on backing beans. Coffee-BreakBean creates the ShoppingCart object, which defines the model data for the components on the orderForm page that hold the data about each coffee. CoffeeBreakBean also loads the RetailPriceList object. In addition, it provides the methods that are invoked when the buttons on the orderForm and checkoutAck are clicked. For example, the checkout method is invoked when the Checkout button is clicked because the tag corresponding to the Checkout button refers to the checkout method via its action attribute:

```
<h:commandButton id="checkoutLink"
    value="#{CBMessages.Checkout}"
    action="#{CoffeeBreakBean.checkout}" />
```

The checkout method returns a String, which the JavaServer Faces page navigation system matches against a set of navigation rules to determine what page to access next. The navigation rules are defined in a separate XML file, described in the next section.

Resource Configuration

A JavaServer Faces application usually includes an XML file that configures resources for the application. These resources include JavaBeans components, navigation rules, and others.

Two of the resources configured for the JavaServer Faces version of the Coffee Break server are the CheckoutForm bean and navigation rules for the orderForm page:

```
<managed-bean>
  <managed-bean-name>checkoutFormBean</managed-bean-name>
  <managed-bean-class>
    com.sun.cb.CheckoutFormBean
  </managed-bean-class>
  <managed-bean-scope>request</managed-bean-scope>
    <managed-property>
      <property-name>firstName</property-name>
      <value>Coffee</value>
    </managed-property>
```

```
        <managed-property>
          <property-name>lastName</property-name>
          <value>Lover</value>
        </managed-property>
        <managed-property>
          <property-name>email</property-name>
          <value>jane@home</value>
        </managed-property>
        ...
      </managed-bean>

    <navigation-rule>
      <from-view-id>/orderForm.jsp</from-view-id>
      <navigation-case>
        <from-outcome>checkout</from-outcome>
        <to-view-id>/checkoutForm.jsp</to-view-id>
      </navigation-case>
    </navigation-rule>
```

As shown in the managed-bean element, the checkoutForm bean properties are initialized with the values for the user, Coffee Lover. In this way, the hyperlink tag from orderForm is not required to submit these values in the request parameters.

As shown in the navigation-rule element, when the String, checkout, is returned from a method referred to by a component's action attribute, the checkoutForm page displays.

Building, Packaging, Deploying, and Running the Application

The source code for the Coffee Break application is located in the directory <INSTALL>/j2eetutorial14/examples/cb/. Within the cb directory are subdirectories for each Web application—saaj, jaxrpc, server, and server-jsf— and a directory, common, for classes shared by the Web applications. Each subdirectory contains a build.xml and build.properties file. The Web application subdirectories in turn contain a src subdirectory for Java classes and a web subdirectory for Web resources.

Setting the Port

The JAX-RPC and SAAJ services in the Coffee Break application run at the port that you specified when you installed the Application Server. The tutorial examples assume that the Application Server runs on the default port, 8080. If you have changed the port, you must update the port number in the following files before building and running the examples:

- *<INSTALL>*/j2eetutorial14/examples/cb/common/src/com/sun/cb/
  CoffeeBreak.properties. Update the port in the following URLs:
  - endpoint.url=http://localhost:**8080**/jaxrpc-coffee-sup-
    plier/jaxrpc
  - saaj.url=http://localhost:**8080**/saaj-coffee-supplier
- *<INSTALL>*/j2eetutorial14/examples/cb/jaxrpc/config-wsdl.xml

Setting Up the Registry Server

The Coffee Break servers use a registry server to obtain information about the JAX-RPC service endpoint. Since the Application Server does not include a registry server, you must obtain one before you can run the application.

We recommend that you use the Registry Server provided with the Java Web Services Developer Pack (Java WSDP) 1.4, which you can download from http://java.sun.com/webservices/downloads/. To use the Java WSDP Registry Server, follow these steps:

1. Stop the Application Server.
2. Start the Java WSDP install program.
3. Choose the Custom install option.
4. When the install program requests that you choose which features to install, deselect everything except the Java WSDP Registry Server.
5. Select the Sun Java System Application Server Platform Edition 8 for the Web container. The Registry Server and its backing repository Xindice are installed into the Application Server as Web applications.
6. Start the Application Server.
7. Confirm that the Registry Server and Xindice Web applications are running using the Admin Console or deploytool.

Using the Provided WARs

The instructions that follow for packaging and deploying the Coffee Break Web applications assume that you are familiar with the deploytool procedures for packaging Web services and presentation-oriented Web applications described in previous chapters of the tutorial. If after following these procedures you have trouble deploying or running the application, you can use the WARs provided in <INSTALL>/j2eetutorial14/examples/cb/provided-wars/ to run the example. The provided WARs assume that Coffee Break supplier services are running on port 8080 and the registry server is running on port 8082. If the services are not running on port 8080, you won't be able to use these WARs. If the registry server is not running on port 8082, you can use the WARs but you must update the registryURL context parameter in the JAX-RPC service and Coffee Break server WARs.

Building the Common Classes

The Coffee Break applications share a number of common utility classes. To build the common classes, do the following:

1. In a terminal window, go to <INSTALL>/j2eetutorial14/examples/cb/ common/.
2. Run asant build.

Building, Packaging, and Deploying the JAX-RPC Service

To build the JAX-RPC service and client library and to package and deploy the JAX-RPC service, follow these steps:

1. In a terminal window, go to <INSTALL>/j2eetutorial14/examples/cb/ jaxrpc/.
2. Run asant build-registry and asant build-service. These tasks create the JAR file containing the JAXR routines and run wscompile and compile the source files of the JAX-RPC service.

   If you get an error, make sure that you edited the file <INSTALL>/ j2eetutorial14/examples/common/build.properties as described in Building the Examples (page xli).

3. Make sure the Application Server and Registry Server are started.

4. Start `deploytool`.

5. Create a stand-alone Web module named `jaxrpc-coffee-supplier` in `<INSTALL>/j2eetutorial14/examples/cb/jaxrpc/`.

6. Set the context root to `/jaxrpc-coffee-supplier`.

7. Add the content to the service.

   a. Add the `com` package, `Supplier.wsdl`, and `mapping.xml` under `<INSTALL>/j2eetutorial14/examples/cb/jaxrpc/build/server/` to the module.

   b. Navigate to `<INSTALL>/j2eetutorial14/examples/cb/jaxrpc/build/registry/dist/` and add `registry-org.jar`.

   c. In the Web module contents editor, drag the `com` directory (containing `sun/cb/SupplierPrices.properties`) from the context root to `WEB-INF/classes/`.

8. Specify Web Services Endpoint as the component type.

9. In the Choose Service dialog box (Define New Service):

   a. In the WSDL File combo box, select `WEB-INF/wsdl/Supplier.wsdl`.

   b. In the Mapping File combo box, select `mapping.xml`.

10. In the Component General Properties dialog box:

    a. In the Service Endpoint Implementation combo box, select `com.sun.cb.SupplierImpl`.

    b. Click Next.

11. In the Web Service Endpoint dialog box:

    a. In the Service Endpoint Interface combo box, select `com.sun.cb.SupplierIF`.

    b. In the Namespace combo box, select `urn:Foo`.

    c. In the Local Part combo box, select `SupplierIFPort`.

    d. Click Next.

12. Add the alias `/jaxrpc` to the `SupplierImpl` Web component.

13. Select the Endpoint tab, and then select `jaxrpc` from the Endpoint Address combo box in the Sun-specific Settings frame.

14. Add an event listener that references the listener class `com.sun.cb.ContextListener`.

15. Add a resource reference of type javax.xml.registry.Connection-Factory named eis/JAXR mapped to the JAXR connection factory eis/JAXR. If you have not already created the connection factory, follow the instructions in Creating JAXR Resources (page 429).

16. Add the context parameter that specifies the URL of the registry server. The parameter is named registryURL and the value is http://local-host:*port*/RegistryServer/, where *port* is the port at which the registry server is running.

17. Save the module.

18. Deploy the module.

19. Run asant build-client. This task creates the JAR file that contains the classes needed by JAX-RPC clients. The build-client task runs wscompile to generate the stubs and JavaBeans components.

20. Test that the JAX-RPC service has been deployed correctly by running the test programs asant run-test-order and asant run-test-price

Here is what you should see when you run asant run-test-price:

```
run-test-price:
run-test-client:
    [java] 07/21/03 08/20/03
    [java] Kona 6.50
    [java] French Roast 5.00
    [java] Wake Up Call 5.50
    [java] Mocca 4.00
```

Building, Packaging, and Deploying the SAAJ Service

To build the SAAJ service and client library and to package and deploy the SAAJ service, follow these steps:

1. In a terminal window, go to *<INSTALL>*/j2eetutorial14/examples/cb/saaj/.

2. Run asant build. This task creates the client library and compiles the server classes.

3. Make sure the Application Server is started.

4. Start deploytool.

5. Create a stand-alone Web module called saaj-coffee-supplier in *<INSTALL>*/j2eetutorial14/examples/cb/saaj/.

6. Set the context root to `/saaj-coffee-supplier`.

7. Add the `com` directory under `<INSTALL>`/j2eetutorial14/examples/ cb/saaj/build/server/ to the module.

8. Add the `ConfirmationServlet` Web component. Choose the Servlet component type.

9. Add the alias `/orderCoffee` to the `ConfirmationServlet` Web component.

10. Add the `PriceListServlet` Web component to the existing `saaj-coffee-supplier` WAR.

11. Add the alias `/getPriceList` to the `PriceListServlet` Web component.

12. Save the module.

13. Deploy the module.

14. Test that the SAAJ service has been deployed correctly by running one or both of the test programs `asant run-test-price` and `asant run-test-order`.

Building, Packaging, and Deploying the Coffee Break Server

To build, package, and deploy the Coffee Break server:

1. In a terminal window, go to `<INSTALL>`/j2eetutorial14/examples/cb/ server/.

2. Run `asant build`. This task compiles the server classes and copies the classes, JSP pages, and tag libraries into the correct location for packaging.

3. Make sure the Application Server is started.

4. Start `deploytool`.

5. Create a stand-alone Web module called `cbserver` in `<INSTALL>`/ j2eetutorial14/examples/cb/server/.

6. Set the context root to `/cbserver`.

7. Add the content to the Web module.

   a. Add all the JSP pages, `tutorial-template.tld`, and the `template` and `com` directories under `<INSTALL>`/j2eetutorial14/examples/cb/ server/build/ to the module.

   b. In the Web module contents editor, drag the `com` directory (containing `sun/cb/CoffeeBreak.properties`) from the context root to `WEB-INF/ classes/`.

c. Add the JAX-RPC client library in *<INSTALL>*/j2eetutorial14/ examples/cb/jaxrpc/dist/jaxrpc-client.jar to the module.

d. Add the SAAJ client library in *<INSTALL>*/j2eetutorial14/examples/cb/saaj/dist/saaj-client.jar to the module.

8. Create a Dispatcher Web component. Choose the Servlet component type.

9. Add the aliases /orderForm, /checkoutForm, and /checkoutAck to the Dispatcher component.

10. Add the RetailPriceListServlet Web component to the existing cbserver WAR.

11. Add the alias /loadPriceList to the RetailPriceListServlet component.

12. Add a resource reference of type javax.xml.registry.ConnectionFactory named eis/JAXR mapped to the JAXR connection factory eis/JAXR.

13. Add a JSP property group named cbserver. The property group applies to the URL pattern *.jsp. Add the include prelude /template/prelude.jspf.

14. Add a context parameter named javax.servlet.jsp.jstl.fmt.localizationContext and value com.sun.cb.messages.CBMessages.

15. Add the context parameter that specifies the URL of the registry server. The parameter is named registryURL and the value is http://localhost:*port*/RegistryServer/, where *port* is the port at which the registry server is running.

16. Specify a security constraint for RetailPriceListServlet.

a. Select Basic as the User Authentication Method.

b. Click Settings and enter file in the Realm Name field. Click OK.

c. Add a security constraint and a web resource collection. Use the default names provided by deploytool.

d. Add the URL /loadPriceList to the web resource collection.

e. Select the GET HTTP method.

f. Add the security role admin.

17. Map the admin role to the admin user.

18. Save the module.

19. Deploy the module.

Building, Packaging, and Deploying the JavaServer Faces Technology Coffee Break Server

To build, package, and deploy the JavaServer Faces technology version of the Coffee Break server, follow these steps:

1. In a terminal window, go to `<INSTALL>/j2eetutorial14/examples/cb/server-jsf/`.

2. Run `asant build`. This task compiles the server classes and copies the classes, JSP pages, tag libraries, and other necessary files into the correct location for packaging.

3. Make sure the Application Server is started.

4. Start `deploytool`.

5. Create a stand-alone Web module called `cbserver-jsf` in `<INSTALL>/j2eetutorial14/examples/cb/server-jsf/`.

6. Set the context root to `/cbserver-jsf`.

7. Add the content to the Web module.

   a. Add all the JSP pages, `coffeebreak.css`, `faces-config.xml`, `index.html`, and the `template` and `com` directories under `<INSTALL>/j2eetutorial14/examples/cb/server-jsf/build/` to the module.

   b. In the Web module contents editor, drag the `com` directory (containing `sun/cb/CoffeeBreak.properties`) from the context root to `WEB-INF/classes`.

   c. Drag `faces-config.xml` to the root of the `WEB-INF` directory.

   d. Add the JSF API library from `<J2EE_HOME>/lib/jsf-api.jar` to the module.

   e. Add the JAX-RPC client library in `<INSTALL>/j2eetutorial14/examples/cb/jaxrpc/dist/jaxrpc-client.jar` to the module.

   f. Add the SAAJ client library in `<INSTALL>/j2eetutorial14/examples/cb/saaj/dist/saaj-client.jar` to the module.

8. Create a `FacesServlet` Web component. Choose the Servlet component type.

   a. In the Load Sequence Position field on the Component General Properties dialog, enter 1.

9. Add the aliases `/faces/*` and `*.jsf` to the `FacesServlet` component.

10. Add a resource reference of type `javax.xml.registry.Connection-Factory` named `eis/JAXR` mapped to the JAXR connection factory `eis/JAXR`.

11. Add a JSP property group named `cbserver-jsf`. The property group applies to the URL pattern `*.jsp`. Add the include prelude `/template/prelude.jspf`.

12. Add the context parameter that specifies the URL of the registry server. The parameter is named `registryURL` and the value is `http://localhost:port/RegistryServer/`, where *port* is the port at which the registry server is running.

13. Save the module.

14. Deploy the module.

Running the Coffee Break Client

After you have installed all the Web applications, check that all the applications are running in deploytool or the Admin Console. You should see `cbserver`, `jaxrpc-coffee-supplier`, and `saaj-coffee-supplier` in the list of applications.

If you have installed the non-GUI framework version of the Coffee Break server, you can run the Coffee Break client by opening the Coffee Break server URL in a Web browser:

```
http://localhost:8080/cbserver/orderForm
```

If you have installed the JavaServer Faces technology version of the Coffee Break server, you can run the JavaServer Faces version of the Coffee Break client by opening this URL in a Web browser:

```
http://localhost:8080/cbserver-jsf/faces/orderForm.jsp
```

You should see a page something like the one shown in Figure 35–2.

After you have gone through the application screens, you will get an order confirmation that looks like the one shown in Figure 35–3.

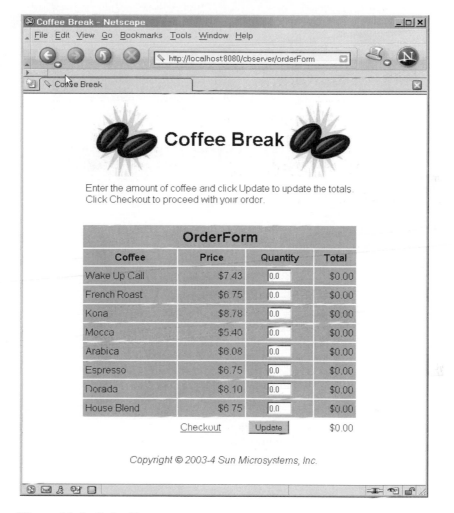

Figure 35–2 Order Form

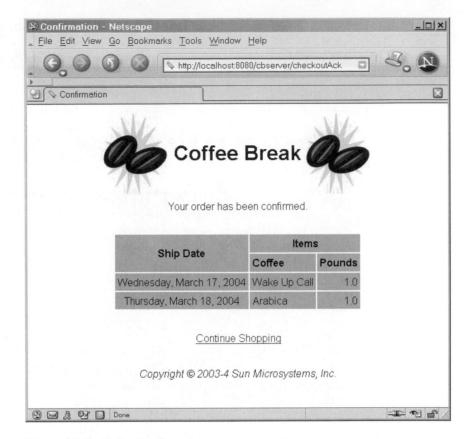

Figure 35–3   Order Confirmation

Removing the Coffee Break Application

To remove the Coffee Break application, perform the following steps:

1. Undeploy the JAX-RPC and SAAJ services and the Coffee Break server using deploytool or the Admin Console.
2. Stop the Application Server.

If you want to remove the build and dist directories, run ant clean in each directory, including <INSTALL>/j2eetutorial14/examples/cb/common/.

The Duke's Bank
Application

THIS chapter describes the Duke's Bank application, an online banking application. Duke's Bank has two clients: an application client used by administrators to manage customers and accounts, and a Web client used by customers to access account histories and perform transactions. The clients access the customer, account, and transaction information maintained in a database through enterprise beans. The Duke's Bank application demonstrates the way that many of the component technologies presented in this tutorial—enterprise beans, application clients, and Web components—are applied to provide a simple but functional application.

Figure 36–1 gives a high-level view of how the components interact. This chapter looks at each of the component types in detail and concludes with a discussion of how to build, deploy, and run the application.

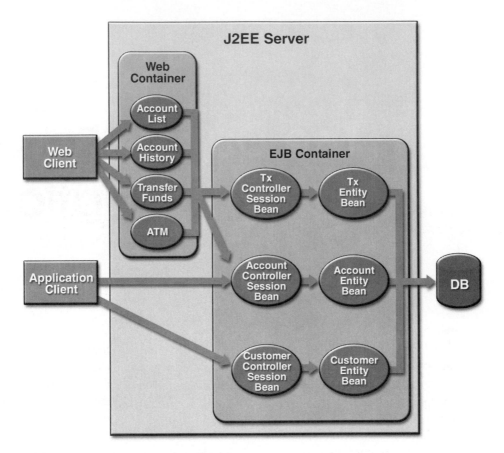

Figure 36–1 Duke's Bank Application

Enterprise Beans

Figure 36–2 takes a closer look at the access paths between the clients, enterprise beans, and database tables. As you can see, the end-user clients (Web and application clients) access only the session beans. Within the enterprise bean tier, the session beans are clients of the entity beans. On the back end of the application, the entity beans access the database tables that store the entity states.

Note: The source code for these enterprise beans is in the `<INSTALL>/`
`j2eetutorial14/examples/bank/src/com/sun/ebank/ejb/` directory.

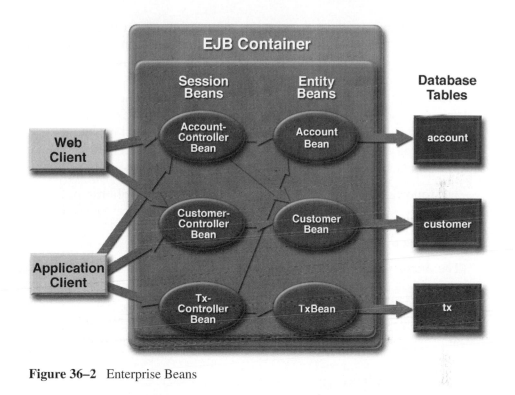

Figure 36–2 Enterprise Beans

Session Beans

The Duke's Bank application has three session beans: AccountControllerBean, CustomerControllerBean, and TxControllerBean. (Tx stands for a business transaction, such as transferring funds.) These session beans provide a client's view of the application's business logic. Hidden from the clients are the server-side routines that implement the business logic, access databases, manage relationships, and perform error checking.

AccountControllerBean

The business methods of the AccountControllerBean session bean perform tasks that fall into the following categories: creating and removing entity beans, managing the account-customer relationship, and getting the account information.

The following methods create and remove entity beans:

- createAccount
- removeAccount

These methods of the AccountControllerBean session bean call the create and remove methods of the AccountBean entity bean. The createAccount and removeAccount methods throw application exceptions to indicate invalid method arguments. The createAccount method throws an IllegalAccount-TypeException if the type argument is neither Checking, Savings, Credit, nor Money Market. The createAccount method also verifies that the specified customer exists by invoking the findByPrimaryKey method of the CustomerBean entity bean. If the result of this verification is false, the createAccount method throws a CustomerNotFoundException.

The following methods manage the account-customer relationship:

- addCustomerToAccount
- removeCustomerFromAccount

The AccountBean and CustomerBean entity beans have a many-to-many relationship. A bank account can be jointly held by more than one customer, and a customer can have multiple accounts. Because the entity beans use bean-managed persistence, there are several ways to manage this relationship. For more information, see Mapping Table Relationships for Bean-Managed Persistence (page 919).

In the Duke's Bank application, the addCustomerToAccount and removeCustomerFromAccount methods of the AccountControllerBean session bean manage the account-customer relationship. The addCustomerToAccount method, for example, starts by verifying that the customer exists. To create the relationship, the addCustomerToAccount method inserts a row into the customer_account_xref database table. In this cross-reference table, each row contains the customerId and accountId of the related entities. To remove a relationship, the removeCustomerFromAccount method deletes a row from the customer_account_xref table. If a client calls the removeAccount method, then all rows for the specified accountId are removed from the customer_account_xref table.

The following methods get the account information:

- getAccountsOfCustomer
- getDetails

The AccountControllerBean session bean has two get methods. The getAccountsOfCustomer method returns all of the accounts of a given customer by invoking the findByCustomer method of the AccountBean entity bean. Instead of implementing a get method for every instance variable, the Account-ControllerBean has a getDetails method that returns an object (Account-Details) that encapsulates the entire state of an AccountBean bean. Because it can invoke a single method to retrieve the entire state, the client avoids the overhead associated with multiple remote calls.

CustomerControllerBean

Because it is the AccountControllerBean enterprise bean that manages the customer-account relationship, CustomerControllerBean is the simpler of these two session beans. A client creates a CustomerBean entity bean by invoking the createCustomer method of the CustomerControllerBean session bean. To remove a customer, the client calls the removeCustomer method, which not only invokes the remove method of CustomerBean but also deletes from the customer_account_xref table all rows that identify the customer.

The CustomerControllerBean session bean has two methods that return multiple customers: getCustomersOfAccount and getCustomersOfLastName. These methods call the corresponding finder methods—findbyAccountId and findByLastName—of CustomerBean.

TxControllerBean

The TxControllerBean session bean handles bank transactions. In addition to its get methods, getTxsOfAccount and getDetails, the TxControllerBean bean has several methods that change the balances of the bank accounts:

- withdraw
- deposit
- makeCharge
- makePayment
- transferFunds

These methods access an AccountBean entity bean to verify the account type and to set the new balance. The withdraw and deposit methods are for standard accounts, whereas the makeCharge and makePayment methods are for accounts that include a line of credit. If the type method argument does not match the account, these methods throw an IllegalAccountTypeException. If a withdrawal were to result in a negative balance, the withdraw method throws an `InsufficientFundsException`. If a credit charge attempts to exceed the account's credit line, the `makeCharge` method throws an `Insufficient-CreditException`.

The `transferFunds` method also checks the account type and new balance; if necessary, it throws the same exceptions as the `withdraw` and `makeCharge` methods. The `transferFunds` method subtracts from the balance of one `Account-Bean` instance and adds the same amount to another instance. Because both of these steps must complete, the `transferFunds` method has a `Required` transaction attribute. If either step fails, the entire operation is rolled back and the balances remain unchanged.

Entity Beans

For each business entity represented in our simple bank, the Duke's Bank application has a matching entity bean:

- `AccountBean`
- `CustomerBean`
- `TxBean`

The purpose of these beans is to provide an object view of these database tables: `account`, `customer`, and `tx`. For each column in a table, the corresponding entity bean has an instance variable. Because they use bean-managed persistence, the entity beans contain the SQL statements that access the tables. For example, the `create` method of the `CustomerBean` entity bean calls the SQL `INSERT` command.

Unlike the session beans, the entity beans do not validate method parameters (except for the primary key parameter of `ejbCreate`). During the design phase, we decided that the session beans would check the parameters and throw the application exceptions, such as `CustomerNotInAccountException` and `Illegal-AccountTypeException`. Consequently, if some other application were to include these entity beans, its session beans would also have to validate the method parameters.

Because the entity beans always run in the same Java VM as their clients, the session beans, for improved performance the entity beans are coded with local interfaces.

Helper Classes

The EJB JAR files include several helper classes that are used by the enterprise beans. The source code for these classes is in the *<INSTALL>*/j2eetutorial14/examples/bank/src/com/sun/ebank/util/ directory. Table 36–1 briefly describes the helper classes.

Table 36–1 Helper Classes for the Application's Enterprise Beans

Class Name	Description
AccountDetails	Encapsulates the state of an AccountBean instance. Returned by the getDetails methods of AccountControllerBean and Account-Bean.
CodedNames	Defines the strings that are the logical names in the calls of the lookup method (for example, java:comp/env/ejb/account). The EJB-Getter class references these strings.
CustomerDetails	Encapsulates the state of a CustomerBean instance. Returned by the getDetails methods of CustomerControllerBean and Custom-erBean.
DBHelper	Provides methods that generate the next primary keys (for example, getNextAccountId).
Debug	Has simple methods for printing a debugging message from an enterprise bean. These messages appear on the standard output of the Application Server when it's run with the --verbose option and in the server log.
DomainUtil	Contains validation methods: getAccountTypes, checkAccount-Type, and isCreditAccount.
EJBGetter	Has methods that locate (by invoking lookup) and return home interfaces (for example, getAccountControllerHome).
TxDetails	Encapsulates the state of a TxBean instance. Returned by the get-Details methods of TxControllerBean and TxBean.

Database Tables

A database table of the Duke's Bank application can be categorized by its purpose: representing business entities and holding the next primary key.

Tables Representing Business Entities

Figure 36–3 shows the relationships between the database tables. The `customer` and `account` tables have a many-to-many relationship: A customer can have several bank accounts, and each account can be owned by more than one customer. This many-to-many relationship is implemented by the cross–reference table named `customer_account_xref`. The `account` and `tx` tables have a one-to-many relationship: A bank account can have many transactions, but each transaction refers to a single account.

Figure 36–3 uses several abbreviations. PK stands for primary key, the value that uniquely identifies a row in a table. FK is an abbreviation for foreign key, which is the primary key of the related table. Tx is short for transaction, such as a deposit or withdrawal.

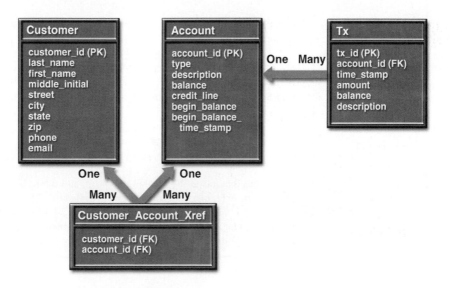

Figure 36–3 Database Tables

Tables That Hold the Next Primary Key

These tables have the following names:

- `next_account_id`
- `next_customer_id`
- `next_tx_id`

Each of these tables has a single column named `id`. The value of `id` is the next primary key that is passed to the `create` method of an entity bean. For example, before it creates a new `AccountBean` entity bean, the `AccountControllerBean` session bean must obtain a unique key by invoking the `getNextAccountId` method of the `DBHelper` class. The `getNextAccountId` method reads the `id` from the `next_account_id` table, increments the `id` value in the table, and then returns the `id`.

Protecting the Enterprise Beans

In the J2EE platform, you protect an enterprise bean by specifying the security roles that can access its methods. In the Duke's Bank application, you define two roles—`bankCustomer` and `bankAdmin`—because two categories of operations are defined by the enterprise beans.

A user in the `bankAdmin` role will be allowed to perform administrative functions: creating or removing an account, adding a customer to or removing a customer from an account, setting a credit line, and setting an initial balance. A user in the `bankCustomer` role will be allowed to deposit, withdraw, and transfer funds, make charges and payments, and list the account's transactions. Notice that there is no overlap in functions that users in either role can perform.

The system restricts access to these functions to the appropriate role by setting method permissions on selected methods of the `CustomerControllerBean`, `AccountControllerBean`, and `TxControllerBean` enterprise beans. For example, by allowing only users in the `bankAdmin` role to access the `createAccount` method in the `AccountControllerBean` enterprise bean, you deny users in the `bankCustomer` role (or any other role) permission to create bank accounts.

Application Client

Sometimes, enterprise applications use a stand-alone client application for handling tasks such as system or application administration. For example, the Duke's Bank application uses an application client to administer customers and accounts. This capability is useful in the event that the site becomes inaccessible for any reason or if a customer prefers to communicate things such as changes to account information by phone.

The application client shown in Figure 36–4 handles basic customer and account administration for the banking application through a Swing user interface. The bank administrator can perform any of the following functions by making menu selections.

Customer administration:

- View customer information
- Add a new customer to the database
- Update customer information
- Find customer ID

Account administration:

- Create a new account
- Add a new customer to an existing account

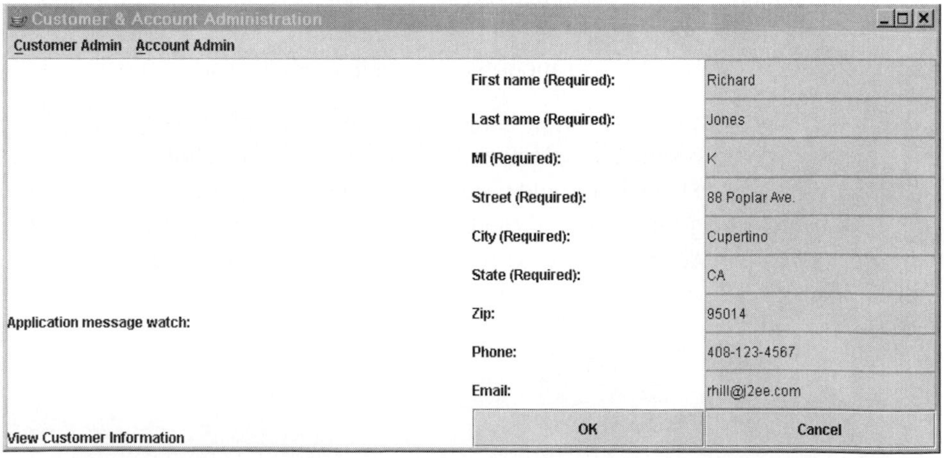

Figure 36–4   Application Client

- View account information
- Remove an account from the database

Error and informational messages appear in the left pane under Application message watch:, and data is entered and displayed in the right pane.

The Classes and Their Relationships

The source code for the application client is in the <INSTALL>/ j2eetutorial14/examples/bank/src/com/sun/ebank/appclient/ directory. The application client is divided into three classes: BankAdmin, EventHandle, and DataModel; the relationships among the classes are depicted in Figure 36–5.

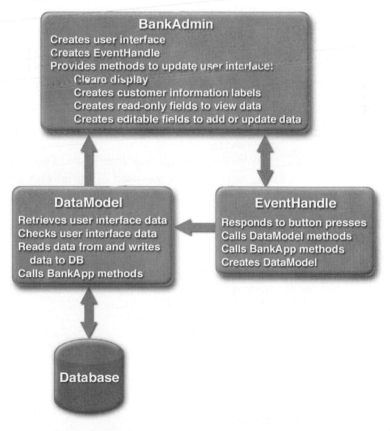

Figure 36–5 Relationships among Application Client Classes

BankAdmin builds the initial user interface, creates the EventHandle object, and provides methods for the EventHandle and DataModel objects to call when they update the user interface.

EventHandle listens for button clicks by the user, takes action based on which button the user clicks, creates the DataModel object, calls methods in the Data-Model object to write data to and read data from the enterprise beans, and calls methods in the BankAdmin object to update the user interface when actions complete.

DataModel retrieves data from the user interface, performs data checks, writes valid data to and reads stored data from the underlying database, and calls methods in the BankAdmin object to update the user interface based on the success of the database read or write operation.

BankAdmin Class

The BankAdmin class, which creates the user interface, is the class that contains the main method and provides protected methods for the other BankAdmin application classes to call.

main Method

The main method creates instances of the BankAdmin and EventHandle classes. Arguments passed to the main method are used to initialize a locale, which is passed to the BankAdmin constructor.

```
public static void main(String args[]) {
  String language, country;
  if(args.length == 1) {
    language = new String(args[0]);
    currentLocale = new Locale(language, "");
  } else if(args.length == 2) {
    language = new String(args[0]);
    country = new String(args[1]);
    currentLocale = new Locale(language, country);
  } else
    currentLocale = Locale.getDefault();
    frame = new BankAdmin(currentLocale);
    frame.setTitle(messages.getString(
      "CustAndAccountAdmin"));
    WindowListener l = new WindowAdapter() {
      public void windowClosing(WindowEvent e) {
```

```
        System.exit(0);
    }
};
frame.addWindowListener(1);
frame.pack();
frame.setVisible(true);
ehandle = new EventHandle(frame, messages);
System.exit(0);
    }
}
```

Constructor

The BankAdmin constructor creates the initial user interface, which consists of a menu bar and two panels. The menu bar contains the customer and account menus, the left panel contains a message area, and the right panel is a data display or update area.

Class Methods

The BankAdmin class provides methods that other objects call when they need to update the user interface. These methods are as follows:

- clearMessages: Clears the application messages that appear in the left panel
- resetPanelTwo: Resets the right panel when the user selects OK to signal the end of a data view or update operation
- createPanelTwoActLabels: Creates labels for account fields when account information is either viewed or updated
- createActFields: Creates account fields when account information is either viewed or updated
- createPanelTwoCustLabels: Creates labels for customer fields when customer information is either viewed or updated
- createCustFields: Creates customer fields when customer information is either viewed or updated
- addCustToActFields: Creates labels and fields when an add customer to account operation is invoked
- makeRadioButtons: Makes radio buttons for selecting the account type when a new account is created
- getDescription: Makes the radio button labels that describe each available account type

EventHandle Class

The EventHandle class implements the ActionListener interface, which provides a method interface for handling action events. Like all other interfaces in the Java programming language, ActionListener defines a set of methods but does not implement their behavior. Instead, you provide the implementations because they take application-specific actions.

Constructor

The constructor receives an instance of the ResourceBundle and BankAdmin classes and assigns them to its private instance variable so that the EventHandle object has access to the application client's localized text and can update the user interface as needed. The constructor also calls the hookupEvents method to create the inner classes to listen for and handle action events.

```
public EventHandle(BankAdmin frame, ResourceBundle messages) {
    this.frame = frame;
    this.messages = messages;
    this.dataModel = new DataModel(frame, messages);
    //Hook up action events
    hookupEvents();
}
```

actionPerformed Method

The ActionListener interface has only one method, the actionPerformed method. This method handles action events generated by the BankAdmin user interface when users create a new account. Specifically, it sets the account description when a bank administrator selects an account type radio button, and it sets the current balance to the beginning balance for new accounts when a bank administrator presses the Return key in the Beginning Balance field.

hookupEvents Method

The hookupEvents method uses inner classes to handle menu and button press events. An inner class is a class that is nested or defined inside another class.

Using inner classes in this way modularizes the code, making it easier to read and maintain. EventHandle inner classes manage the following application client operations:

- Viewing customer information
- Creating a new customer
- Updating customer information
- Finding a customer ID by last name
- Viewing account information
- Creating a new account
- Adding a customer to an account
- Removing an account
- Clearing data on Cancel button press
- Processing data on OK button press

DataModel Class

The DataModel class provides methods for reading data from the database, writing data to the database, retrieving data from the user interface, and checking that data before it is written to the database.

Constructor

The constructor receives an instance of the BankAdmin class and assigns it to its private instance variable so that the DataModel object can display error messages in the user interface when its checkActData, checkCustData, or write-Data method detects errors. The constructor also receives an instance of the ResourceBundle class and assigns it to its private instance variable so that the DataModel object has access to the application client's localized text.

Because the DataModel class interacts with the database, the constructor also has the code to establish connections with the remote interfaces for the CustomerController and AccountController enterprise beans, and the code to use their remote interfaces to create instances of the CustomerController and AccountController enterprise beans.

```
//Constructor
public DataModel(BankAdmin frame, ResourceBundle messages) {
  this.frame = frame;
  this.messages = messages;
//Look up and create CustomerController bean
  try {
    CustomerControllerHome customerControllerHome =
      EJBGetter.getCustomerControllerHome();
    customer = customerControllerHome.create();
  } catch (Exception namingException) {
    namingException.printStackTrace();
  }
//Look up and create AccountController bean
  try {
    AccountControllerHome accountControllerHome =
      EJBGetter.getAccountControllerHome();
    account = accountControllerHome.create();
  } catch (Exception namingException) {
    namingException.printStackTrace();
  }
}
```

Methods

The getData method retrieves data from the user interface text fields and uses the String.trim method to remove extra control characters such as spaces and returns. Its one parameter is a JTextfield so that any instance of the JText-field class can be passed in for processing.

```
private String getData(JTextField component) {
  String text, trimmed;
  if(component.getText().length() > 0) {
    text = component.getText();
    trimmed = text.trim();
    return trimmed;
  } else {
    text = null;
    return text;
  }
}
```

The checkCustData method stores customer data retrieved by the getData method, but first it checks the data to be sure that all required fields have data, that the middle initial is no longer than one character, and that the state is no longer than two characters. If everything checks out, the writeData method is called. If there are errors, they are printed to the user interface in the BankAdmin object. The checkActData method uses a similar model to check and store account data.

The createCustInf and createActInf methods are called by the EventHandle class to refresh the customer and account information display in the event of a view, update, or add action event.

Create Customer Information

For a view or update event, the createCustInf method gets the customer information for the specified customer from the database and passes it to the create-CustFields method in the BankAdmin class. A Boolean variable is used to determine whether the createCustFields method should create read-only fields for a view event or writable fields for an update event.

For a create event, the createCustInf method calls the createCustFields method in the BankAdmin class with null data and a Boolean variable to create empty editable fields for the user to enter customer data.

Create Account Information

For a view or update event, the createActInf method gets the account information for the specified account from the database and passes it to the createAct-Fields method in the BankAdmin class. A Boolean variable is used to determine whether the createActFields method should create read-only fields for a view event or writable fields for an update event.

For a create event, the createActInf method calls the createActFields method in the BankAdmin class with null data and a Boolean variable to create empty editable fields for the user to enter customer data.

Adding a customer to an account or removing an account events operate directly on the database without creating any user interface components.

Web Client

In the Duke's Bank application, the Web client is used by customers to access account information and perform operations on accounts. Table 36–2 lists the functions the client supports, the URLs used to access the functions, and the components that implement the functions. Figure 36–6 shows an account history screen.

Note: The source code for the Web client is in the `<INSTALL>`/j2eetutorial14/ examples/bank/src/com/sun/ebank/web/ and `<INSTALL>`/j2eetutorial14/ examples/bank/web/ directories.

Table 36–2 Web Client

Function	URL Aliases	JSP Pages	JavaBeans Components
Home page	`/main`	`main.jsp`	`CustomerBean`

Log on to or off of the application	`/logon`
	`/logonError`
	`/logoff`
		`logon.jsp`
		`logonError.jsp`
		`logoff.jsp`	

List accounts	`/accountList`	`accountList.jsp`	`CustomerBean`

List the history of an account	`/accountHist`	`accountHist.jsp`	`CustomerBean,`
			`AccountHistory-`
			`Bean`

Transfer funds between accounts	`/transferFunds` `/transferAck`	`transferFunds.jsp` `transferAck.jsp`	`CustomerBean,` `TransferBean`
Withdraw and deposit funds	`/atm` `/atmAck`	`atm.jsp` `atmAck.jsp`	`CustomerBean,` `ATMBean`
Error handling	`/error`	`error.jsp`	

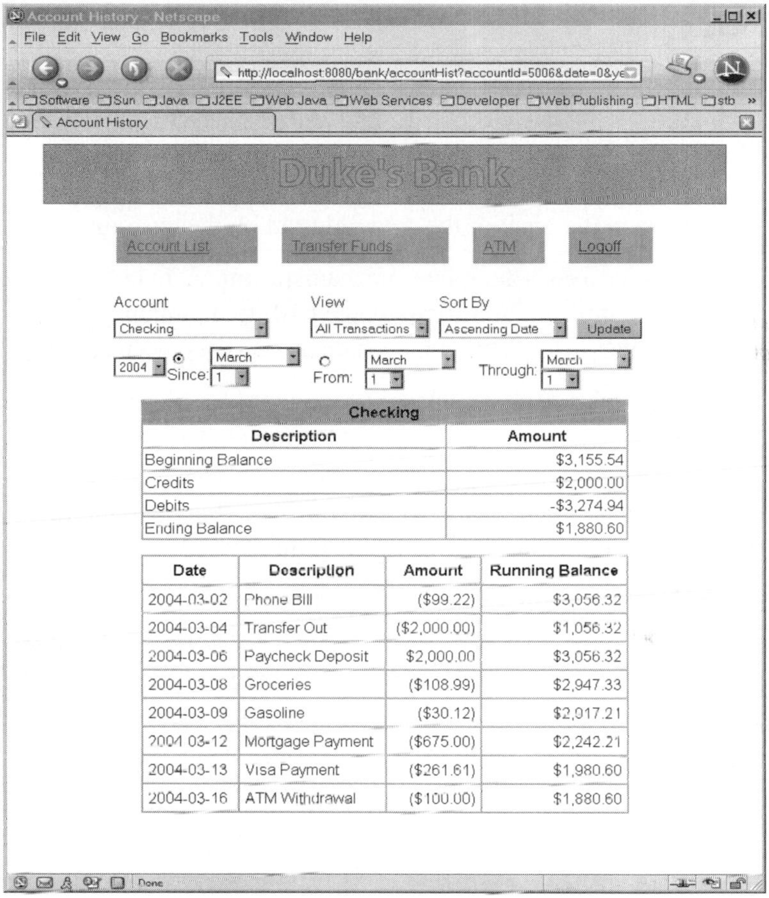

Figure 36–6 Account History

Design Strategies

The main job of the JSP pages in the Duke's Bank application is presentation. To achieve this, most dynamic processing tasks are delegated to enterprise beans, custom tags, and JavaBeans components.

In the Duke's Bank application, the JSP pages use enterprise beans to handle interactions with the database and rely on JavaBeans components for interactions with the enterprise beans. In the Duke's Bookstore application, discussed in

Chapters 11 to 22, the BookDB JavaBeans component acts as a front end to a database. In the Duke's Bank application, TransferBean acts as a facade to the TransactionControllerBean enterprise bean. However, the other JavaBeans components have much richer functionality. ATMBean invokes enterprise bean methods and sets acknowledgment strings according to customer input, and AccountHistoryBean massages the data returned from the enterprise beans in order to present the view of the data required by the customer.

The Web client uses a template mechanism implemented by custom tags (discussed in A Template Tag Library, page 610) to maintain a common look across all the JSP pages. The template mechanism consists of three components:

- template.jsp determines the structure of each screen. It uses the insert tag to compose a screen from subcomponents.
- screendefinitions.jspf defines the subcomponents used by each screen. All screens have the same banner, but different title and body content (specified in the JSP Pages column in Table 36–2, page 1318).
- Dispatcher, a servlet, processes requests and forwards them to template.jsp.

Finally, the Web client uses logic tags from the JSTL core tag library to perform flow control and tags from the JSTL fmt tag library to localize messages and format currency.

Client Components

All the JavaBeans components used in the Web client are instantiated by Dispatcher. The BeanManager and CustomerBean components are instantiated for the session and request, respectively. The other beans—AccountHistoryBean, TransferBean, and ATMBean—are instantiated depending on which request URL is being handled.

Responsibility for managing the enterprise beans used by the Web client rests with the BeanManager. It creates customer, account, and transaction controller enterprise beans and provides methods for retrieving the beans.

When instantiated by Dispatcher, the BeanManager component retrieves the home interface for each bean from the helper class EJBGetter and creates an instance by calling the create method of the home interface. Because these enterprise beans apply to a particular customer or session, Dispatcher stores a BeanManager as a session attribute.

```
public class BeanManager {
  private CustomerController custctl;
  private AccountController acctctl;
  private TxController txctl;
  public BeanManager() {
    if (custctl == null) {
      try {
        CustomerControllerHome home =
          EJBGetter.getCustomerControllerHome();
        custctl = home.create();
      } catch (RemoteException ex) {
        Debug.print("Couldn't create customer bean." +
          ex.getMessage());
      } catch (CreateException ex) {
        Debug.print("Couldn't create customer bean." +
          ex.getMessage());
      } catch (NamingException ex) {
        Debug.print("Unable to look up home: " +
          CodedNames.CUSTOMER_CONTROLLER_EJBHOME  +
          ex.getMessage());
      }
    }
  }
  public CustomerController getCustomerController() {
    return custctl;
  }
  ...
}
```

CustomerBean maintains the customer and account information for the current request. Although the customer is the same for each request, the account may change, so Dispatcher stores a CustomerBean as a request attribute.

```
public class CustomerBean {
  private BeanManager beanManager;
  private String customer;
  private String account;

  public AccountDetails getAccountDetails() {
  AccountDetails ad = null;
    try {
      ad = beanManager.getAccountController().
          getDetails(this.account);
    } catch (InvalidParameterException e) {
      ...
    return ad;
  }
```

```
public ArrayList getAccounts() {
  ArrayList accounts = null;
  try {
    accounts = beanManager.getAccountController().
      getAccountsOfCustomer(this.customer);
  } catch (InvalidParameterException e) {
    ...
  }
  return accounts;
}
```

The page fragment `template/links.jsp` generates the list of bank function links at the top of every page. Notice that the customer is retrieved from the `userPrincipal` object, which is set when the customer logs in (see Protecting the Web Client Resources, page 1325). After the customer is set, the page can retrieve from `CustomerBean` the collection of accounts for the customer. The collection is assigned to the `accounts` variable, and the first item in the collection is used as the default account ID for the ATM operation.

```
<%@ taglib uri="http://java.sun.com/jsp/jstl/core" prefix="c"
%>
<%@ taglib uri="http://java.sun.com/jsp/jstl/fmt" prefix="fmt"
%>
<jsp:useBean id="customerBean"
  class="com.sun.ebank.web.CustomerBean" scope="request"/>
<jsp:setProperty name="customerBean" property="customer"
  value="${pageContext.request.userPrincipal.name}"/>

<c:set var="accounts" value="${customerBean.accounts}" />
<c:forEach items="${accounts}" begin="0" end="0" var="ad">
  <c:set var="accountId" value="${ad.accountId}" />
</c:forEach>
<center>
<table border=0 cellpadding=10 cellspacing=25
  width=600 summary="layout">
  <tr>
    <c:url var="url" value="/accountList" />
    <td bgcolor="#CE9A00"><a href="${url}">
      <fmt:message key="AccountList"/></a></td>
    <c:url var="url" value="/transferFunds" />
    <td bgcolor="#CE9A00"><a href="${url}">
      <fmt:message key="TransferFunds"/></a></td>
    <c:url var="url"
      value="/atm?accountId=${accountId}&operation=0" />
    <td bgcolor="#CE9A00"><a href="${url}">
      <fmt:message key="ATM"/></a></td>
```

```
        <c:url var="url" value="/logoff" />
        <td bgcolor="#CE9A00"><a href="${url}">
          <fmt:message key="Logoff"/></a></td>
    </tr>
  </table>
</center>
```

Request Processing

All requests for the URLs listed in Table 36–2 are mapped to the dispatcher
Web component, which is implemented by the Dispatcher servlet:

```
public class Dispatcher extends HttpServlet {
  public void doPost(HttpServletRequest request,
    HttpServletResponse response) {
    ...
    String selectedScreen = request.getServletPath();
    ...
    if (selectedScreen.equals("/accountHist")) {
      ...
    } else if (selectedScreen.equals("/transferAck")) {
      String fromAccountId =
        request.getParameter("fromAccountId");
      String toAccountId =
        request.getParameter("toAccountId");
      if ( (fromAccountId == null) || (toAccountId == null)) {
        request.setAttribute("errorMessage",
          messages.getString("AccountError"));
        try {
          request.getRequestDispatcher(
            "/error.jsp").forward(request, response);
        } catch(Exception ex) {
        }
      } else {
        TransferBean transferBean = new TransferBean();
        request.setAttribute("transferBean",
          transferBean);
        try {
          transferBean.setMessages(messages);
          transferBean.setFromAccountId(fromAccountId);
          transferBean.setToAccountId(toAccountId);
          transferBean.setBeanManager(beanManager);
          transferBean.setTransferAmount(new
            BigDecimal(request.
              getParameter("transferAmount")));
          String errorMessage = transferBean.doTx();
```

```
            if (errorMessage != null) {
               request.setAttribute("errorMessage",
                  errorMessage);
               try {
                  request.getRequestDispatcher(
                     "/error.jsp").forward(request, response);
               } catch(Exception ex) {
               }
            }
         } catch (NumberFormatException e) {
            request.setAttribute("errorMessage",
               messages.getString("AmountError"));
            try {
               request.getRequestDispatcher(
                  "/error.jsp").forward(request, response);
            } catch(Exception ex) {
            }
         }
      }
      ...
      try {
         request.getRequestDispatcher(
            "/template/template.jsp").forward(request, response);
      } catch(Exception e) {
      }
   }
}
```

When a request is delivered, Dispatcher does the following:

1. Retrieves the incoming request URL and extracts the requested screen. Dispatcher performs business logic and updates model objects based on the requested screen.

2. Creates a JavaBeans component and stores the bean as a request attribute.

3. Parses and validates the request parameters. If a parameter is invalid, Dispatcher may reset the request alias to an error page. Otherwise, it initializes the JavaBeans component.

4. Calls the doTx method of the JavaBeans component. This method retrieves data from the enterprise beans and processes the data according to options specified by the customer.

5. Forwards the request to template.jsp.

As mentioned earlier, template.jsp generates the response by including the responses from subcomponents. The body subcomponent in turn usually retrieves data from the JavaBeans components initialized by Dispatcher.

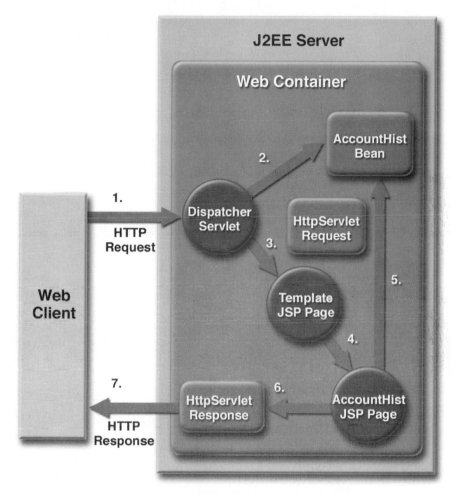

Figure 36–7 Web Component Interaction

Figure 36–7 depicts the interaction among these components.

Protecting the Web Client Resources

In the J2EE platform, you protect a Web resource from anonymous access by specifying which security roles can access the resource. The Web container guarantees that only certain users acting in those roles can access the resource. For the Web container to enforce the security constraint, the application must specify a means for users to identify themselves, and the Web container must support mapping a role to a user.

In the Duke's Bank Web client, you restrict all the URLs listed in Table 36–2 to the security role `bankCustomer`. The application requires users to identify themselves via the form-based login mechanism. When a customer tries to access a Web client URL and has not been authenticated, the Web container displays the JSP page `logon.jsp`. This page contains a form that requires a customer to enter an identifier and password.

```
<form action="j_security_check" method=post>
<table>
<tr>
  <td align="center" >
  <table border="0">
  <tr>
  <td><b><fmt:message key="CustomerId"/></b></td>
  <td>
    <input type="text" size="15" name="j_username">
  </td>
  </tr>
  <tr>
  <td><b><fmt:message key="Password"/></b></td>
  <td>
    <input type="password" size="15" name="j_password">
  </td>
  ...
</form>
```

Note that the action invoked by the form, `j_security_check`, is specified by the Java Servlet specification, as are the request parameters `j_username` and `j_password`. The Web container retrieves this information, maps it to a security role, and verifies that the role matches that specified in the security constraint. Note that in order for the Web container to check the validity of the authentication information and perform the mapping, you must perform these two steps when you deploy the application:

1. Add the customer's group, ID, and password to the default realm of the container using the Admin Console.

2. Map the `bankCustomer` role to the customer *or* the customer's group in `deploytool`.

After the customer has been authenticated, the identifier provided by the customer is used as a key to identify the customer's accounts. The identifier is retrieved from the request using the following expression:

```
${pageContext.request.userPrincipal.name}
```

Internationalization

The application client and Web client distributed with the Duke's Bank application are internationalized. All strings that appear in the user interfaces are retrieved from resource bundles. The administration client uses resource bundles named `AdminMessages_*.properties`. The Web client uses resource bundles named `WebMessages_*.properties`. Both clients are distributed with English and Spanish resource bundles.

The application client retrieves locale information from the command line. For example, to use the Spanish resource bundle, invoke the application this way:

```
appclient -client DukesBankAppClient.jar es
```

The administration client class `BankAdmin` creates a `ResourceBundle` that has a locale created from the command-line arguments:

```
//Constructor
public BankAdmin(Locale currentLocale) {
  //Internationalization setup
  messages = ResourceBundle.getBundle("AdminMessages",
    currentLocale);
```

The Web client `Dispatcher` component retrieves the locale (set by a browser language preference) from the request, opens the resource bundle, and then saves the bundle as a session attribute:

```
ResourceBundle messages = (ResourceBundle)session.
  getAttribute("messages");
  if (messages == null) {
    Locale locale=request.getLocale();
    messages = ResourceBundle.getBundle("WebMessages",
      locale);
    session.setAttribute("messages", messages);
  }
```

The Web client's JavaBeans components access localized messages using `messages.getString("key");`.

The Web client's JSP pages use the JSTL `fmt:message` tags to retrieve localized messages. You set the localization context of the JSTL `fmt` tag library as a context parameter when you package the Web client with `deploytool`.

For example, here is how `accountHist.jsp` generates the headings for the transactions table:

```
<td><center><b><fmt:message
    key="TxDate"/></b></center></td>
<td><center><b><fmt:message
    key="TxDescription"/></center></b></td>
<td><center><b><fmt:message
    key="TxAmount"/></b></center></td>
<td><center><b><fmt:message
    key="TxRunningBalance"/></b></center></td>
```

Building, Packaging, Deploying, and Running the Application

To build the Duke's Bank application, you must have installed the tutorial bundle as described in About the Examples (page xl). When you install the bundle, the Duke's Bank application files are located in the `<INSTALL>`/j2eetutorial14/ examples/bank/ directory:

```
/bank
    /provided-jars - packaged J2EE application containing
        the enterprise beans, and Web and application clients
    /sql - database scripts
    /src
        /com - component classes
            /sun/ebank/appclient
            /sun/ebank/ejb
            /sun/ebank/util
            /sun/ebank/web
    /web - JSP pages, images
```

After you compile the source code, the resulting files will reside in the `<INSTALL>`/j2eetutorial14/examples/bank/build/ directory.

Setting Up the Servers

Before you can package, deploy, and run the example, you must first set up the PointBase database server with customer and account data, and you must add some resources to the Application Server.

Creating the Bank Database

You create and enter data into the appropriate tables so that the enterprise beans have something to read from and write to the database. To create and populate the database tables, follow these steps:

1. Start the PointBase database server.
2. In a terminal window or command prompt, go to the `<INSTALL>/j2eetutorial14/examples/bank/` directory and execute the command `asant create-db_common`. This task invokes the PointBase console tool library to execute the SQL contained in `<INSTALL>/j2eetutorial14/examples/bank/sql/bank.sql`. The SQL statements in this file delete any existing tables, create new tables, and insert data. The first time the script is run the tables don't exist, so you will see SQL errors. You can just ignore them.

Creating the JDBC Data Source

The Duke's Bank enterprise beans reference the database having the JNDI name `jdbc/BankDB`. That JNDI name must be mapped to a JDBC data source in the Application Server. You create the data source using the Admin Console following the procedures described in Creating a Data Source (page 1079). When you create the JDBC data source, name it `jdbc/BankDB` and map it to `PointBasePool`.

Adding Users and Groups to the File Realm

To enable the Application Server to determine which users can access enterprise bean methods and resources in the Web client, add users and groups to the server's file security realm using the Admin Console following the procedures described in Managing Users (page 1089). Add the users and groups listed in Table 36–3.

Table 36–3 Duke's Bank Users and Groups

User	Password	Group
200	j2ee	bankCustomer
bankadmin	j2ee	bankAdmin

Compiling the Duke's Bank Application Code

To compile the enterprise beans, application client, and Web client, go to the `<INSTALL>`/j2eetutorial14/examples/bank/ directory of the tutorial distribution and execute the command `asant build`.

Packaging and Deploying the Duke's Bank Application

The instructions that follow for packaging and deploying Duke's Bank assume that you are familiar with the deploytool procedures for packaging enterprise beans, application clients, and Web applications described in previous chapters of the tutorial. If after following these procedures you have trouble deploying or running the application, you can use the EAR provided in `<INSTALL>`/ j2eetutorial14/examples/bank/provided-jars/ to run the example.

Packaging the Enterprise Beans

1. Invoke the Enterprise Bean wizard for each entity bean in Table 36–4. For each bean, select Bean-Managed Persistence as the persistence management type and `java.lang.String` as the primary key class.

   The first time you invoke the wizard, create an EJB JAR module named `DukesBankEJBJAR` in `<INSTALL>`/j2eetutorial14/examples/bank/. Add the `ejb` and `util` packages under `<INSTALL>`/j2eetutorial14/ examples/bank/build/com/sun/ebank/ to the JAR.

Table 36–4   Entity Beans

Entity Bean	Home Interface	Local Interface	Implementation Class
AccountBean	AccountHome	Account	AccountBean
CustomerBean	CustomerHome	Customer	CustomerBean
TxBean	TxHome	Tx	TxBean

2. For each entity bean, add a resource reference to a data source with coded name jdbc/BankDB. Set the Sun-specific JNDI name to jdbc/BankDB. Because you have already added the JDBC resource to the Application Server, you should select the name from the drop-down menu.

3. For each entity bean, set the transaction attributes for all methods to Required, except for the methods listed in Table 36–5, which should be set to Not Supported.

4. Invoke the Enterprise Bean Wizard for each of the stateful session beans in Table 36–6.

5. For each session bean, add a resource reference to a data source with coded name jdbc/BankDB. Set the Sun-specific JNDI name to jdbc/BankDB. Because you have already added the JDBC resource to the Application Server, you should select the name from the drop-down menu.

Table 36–5 Transaction Attribute Settings

Entity Bean	Tx Not Supported Methods
AccountBean	getCreditLine findByCustomerId findByPrimaryKey
CustomerBean	remove findByLastName findByPrimaryKey
TxBean	remove findByAccountId findByPrimaryKey

Table 36–6 Stateful Session Beans

Session Bean	Home Interface	Remote Interface	Implementation Class
AccountCon- trollerBean	AccountCon- trollerHome	AccountCon- troller	AccountController- Bean
CustomerCon- trollerBean	CustomerCon- trollerHome	CustomerCon- troller	CustomerController- Bean
TxController- Bean	TxController- Home	TxController	TxBean

Table 36–7 EJB References to Entity Beans

Session Bean	Coded Name	Entity Bean Name
AccountControllerBean	ejb/account ejb/customer	AccountBean CustomerBean
CustomerControllerBean	ejb/customer	CustomerBean
TxControllerBean	ejb/account ejb/tx	AccountBean TxBean

6. Add EJB references from the session beans to the local entity beans listed in Table 36–7.

7. Save the module.

Packaging the Application Client

1. Invoke the Application Client wizard.

   a. Create an application client module named DukesBankACJAR in `<INSTALL>`/j2eetutorial14/examples/bank/.

   b. Add the appclient, util, and ejb/exception packages and the ejb/*/*Controller* home and remote interfaces (AccountController, AccountControllerHome, CustomerController, CustomerControllerHome, TxController, TxControllerHome) under `<INSTALL>`/j2eetutorial14/examples/bank/build/com/sun/ebank/ to the JAR.

   c. Select appclient.BankAdmin as the application client main class.

2. Add EJB references to the session beans listed in Table 36–8.

3. Save the module.

Table 36–8 EJB References to Session Beans

Coded Name	JNDI Name of Session Bean
ejb/accountController	AccountControllerBean
ejb/customerController	CustomerControllerBean

Packaging the Web Client

1. Create a `Dispatcher` servlet Web component using the Web Component wizard. Create a new Web module containing the component `DukesBank-WAR` in `<INSTALL>`/j2eetutorial14/examples/bank/.

2. Add content to the Web module.

   a. Add the `web`, `util`, and `ejb/exception` packages and the `ejb/*/*Controller*` home and remote interfaces (`AccountController`, `AccountControllerHome`, `CustomerController`, `CustomerControllerHome`, `TxController`, `TxControllerHome`) under `<INSTALL>`/j2eetutorial14/examples/bank/build/com/sun/ebank to the module.

   b. Add the `template` directory, all the JSP pages, the `WebMessages*.properties` files and `tutorial-template.tld` under `<INSTALL>`/j2eetutorial14/examples/bank/build/ to the module.

   c. In the Web module contents editor, drag the files `WebMessages*.properties` from the context root to `WEB-INF/classes`.

3. Set the context root to `/bank`.

4. Add the `/accountHist`, `/accountList`, `/atm`, `/atmAck`, `/main`, `/transferAck`, `/transferFunds`, and `/logoff` aliases to the `Dispatcher` component.

5. Add EJB references to the session beans listed in Table 36–9.

6. Add a JSP property group named `bank`. The property group applies to the URL pattern `*.jsp`. Add the include prelude `/template/prelude.jspf`.

7. Add a context parameter named `javax.servlet.jsp.jstl.fmt.localizationContext` and value `WebMessages`.

Table 36–9 EJB References to Session Beans

Coded Name	JNDI Name of Session Bean
ejb/accountController	AccountControllerBean
ejb/customerController	CustomerControllerBean
ejb/txController	TxControllerBean

8. Add a security constraint.

    a. Select Form Based as the user authentication method. The authentication settings are `file` for the realm name, `/logon.jsp` for the login page, and `/logonError.jsp` for the error page.

    b. Add a security constraint and a Web resource collection. Use the default names provided by `deploytool`.

    c. Add the URL patterns `/main`, `/accountList`, `/accountHist`, `/atm`, `/atmAck`, `/transferFunds`, and `/transferAck` to the Web resource collection.

    d. Select the `GET` and `POST` HTTP methods.

    e. Add the security role `bankCustomer`.

9. Save the module.

Packaging and Deploying the Application

1. Create a J2EE application named `DukesBankApp` in `<INSTALL>/j2eetutorial14/examples/bank/`.

2. Add the `DukesBankACJAR` application client module to `DukesBankApp`.

3. Add the `DukesBankEJBJAR` EJB module to `DukesBankApp`.

4. Add the `DukesBankWAR` Web module to `DukesBankApp`.

5. Add the security roles `bankAdmin` and `bankCustomer`.

6. Add the following security settings for the enterprise beans.

    a. `AccountControllerBean`: In the Security tab, restrict access to users in the `bankAdmin` security role for the methods `setBalance`, `removeCustomerFromAccount`, `setCreditLine`, `setDescription`, `removeAccount`, `createAccount`, `addCustomerToAccount`, `setBeginBalance`, and `setType`. In the General tab, click the Sun-specific Settings button, and then click the IOR button in the General frame. In the As Context frame, set Required to `true`.

    b. `CustomerControllerBean`: In the Security tab, restrict access to users in the `bankAdmin` security role for the methods `getCustomersOfAccount`, `createCustomer`, `getCustomersOfLastName`, `setName`, `removeCustomer`, and `setAddress`. In the General tab, click the Sun-specific Settings button, and then click the IOR button in the General frame. In the As Context frame, set Required to `true`.

c. TxControllerBean: In the Security tab, restrict access to users in the bankCustomer security role for the methods getTxsOfAccount, make-Charge, deposit, transferFunds, withdraw, and makePayment.

7. Start the Application Server.

8. Map the bankCustomer role to the bankCustomer group.

9. Map the bankAdmin role to the bankAdmin group.

10. Save the application.

11. Deploy the application. In the Deploy DukesBankApp dialog box, select the Return Client Jar checkbox.

After you have packaged all the modules, deploytool should look like Figure 36–8.

Reviewing JNDI Names

With DukesBankApp selected, click the JNDI Names tab. The JNDI Name column is shown in Figure 36 9. The order may be a little different in your own environment.

A JNDI name is the name the Application Server uses to look up enterprise beans and resources. When you look up an enterprise bean, you supply statements similar to those shown in the following code.

```
try {
  customerControllerHome =
    EJBGetter.getCustomerControllerHome();
  customer = customerControllerHome.create();
} catch (Exception namingException) {
  namingException.printStackTrace();
}

public static CustomerControllerHome
  getCustomerControllerHome() throws NamingException {
  InitialContext initial = new InitialContext();
  Object objref = initial.lookup(
    CodedNames.CUSTOMER_CONTROLLER_EJBHOME);
```

The lookup takes place in the third line of code, in which the getCustomerControllerHome method of com.sun.ebank.utilEJBGetter is called. EJBGetter is a utility class that retrieves a coded JNDI name from com.sun.ebank.util.CodedNames.

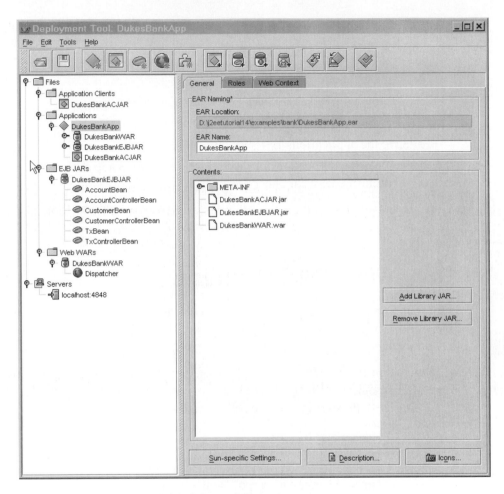

Figure 36–8 Duke's Bank Modules and Components

In this example, the application client is looking up the coded name for the Cus-tomerController remote interface. BankAdmin (the display name for the main class of the application client) references ejb/customerController, which is the coded name defined in CodedNames for the CustomerController remote interface.

The JNDI name is stored in the J2EE application deployment descriptor, and the Application Server uses it to look up the CustomerControllerBean bean. In Figure 36–9 you see that CustomerControllerBean is mapped to the same JNDI name as is ejb/customerController. It does not matter what the JNDI name is, as long as it is the same name for the remote interface lookup as you use

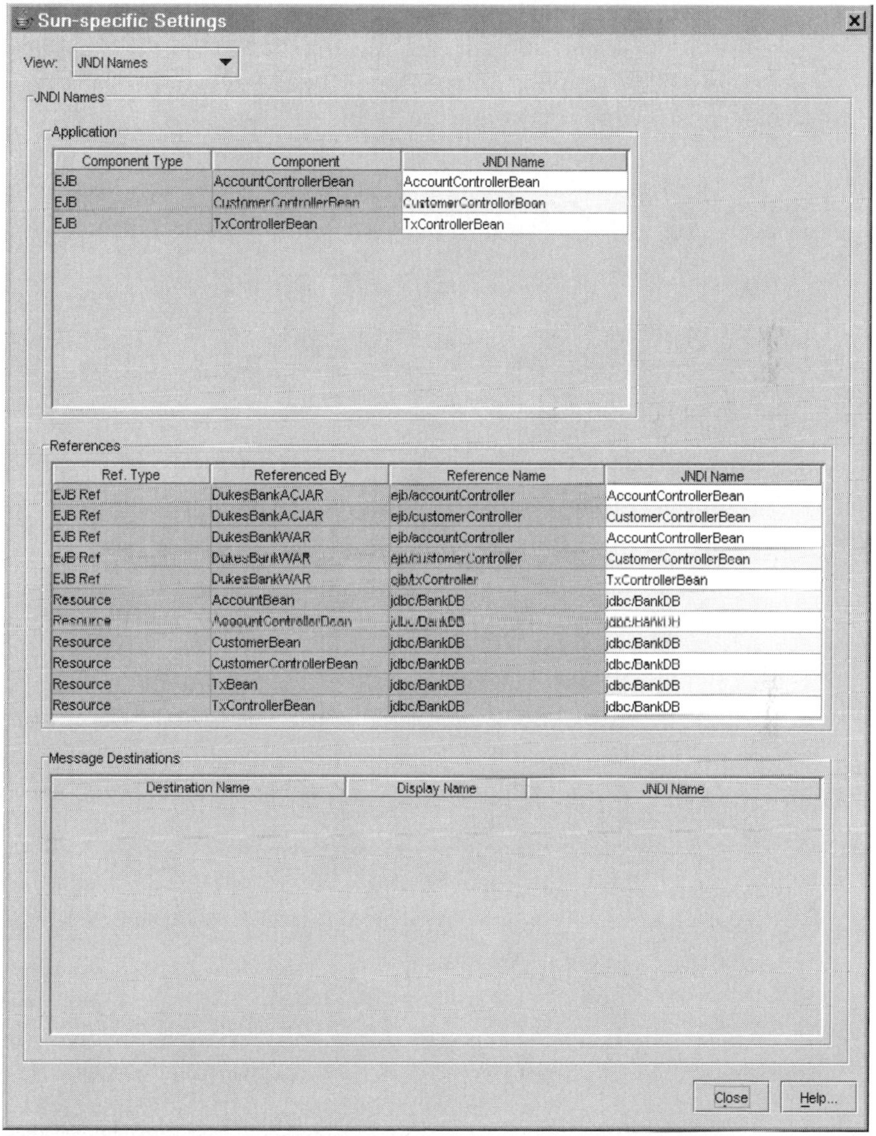

Figure 36–9 Duke's Bank JNDI Names

for its corresponding bean. So, looking at the table, you can say that the application client (BankAdmin) looks up the CustomerController remote interface, which uses the JNDI name of CustomerControllerBean, and the Application Server uses the CustomerControllerBean JNDI name to find the corresponding CustomerControllerBean object.

The other rows in the table have the mappings for the other enterprise beans. All of these beans are stored in the JAR file you added to the J2EE application during assembly. Their implementations have coded names for looking up either other enterprise beans or the database driver.

Running the Clients

Running the Application Client

To run the application client, follow these steps:

1. In a terminal window, go to <INSTALL>/j2eetutorial14/examples/bank/.
2. To run the English version of the client, execute the following command:
    ```
    appclient -client DukesBankAppClient.jar
    ```
    The DukesBankAppClient.jar parameter is the name of the application client JAR file returned when you deployed DukesBankApp.

3. To run the Spanish version, include the es language code:
    ```
    appclient -client DukesBankAppClient.jar es
    ```
4. At the login prompts, type bankadmin for the user name and j2ee for the password. The next thing you should see is the application shown in Figure 36–10.

Figure 36–10 BankAdmin Application Client

Running the Web Client

To run the Web client, follow these steps:

1. Open the bank URL, `http://localhost:8080/bank/main`, in a Web browser. To see the Spanish version of the application, set your browser language preference to any Spanish dialect.

2. The application will display the login page. Enter 200 for the customer ID and j2ee for the password. Click Submit.

3. Select an application function: Account List, Transfer Funds, ATM, or Logoff. When you have a list of accounts, you can get an account history by selecting an account link.

Note: The first time you select a new page, particularly a complicated page such as an account history, it takes some time to display because the Application Server must translate the page into a servlet class and compile and load the class.

If you select Account List, you will see the screen shown in Figure 36–11.

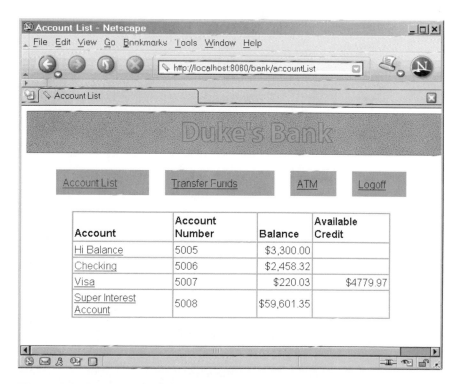

Figure 36–11 Account List

A

Java Encoding Schemes

This appendix describes the character-encoding schemes that are supported by the Java platform.

US-ASCII

US-ASCII is a 7-bit character set and encoding that covers the English-language alphabet. It is not large enough to cover the characters used in other languages, however, so it is not very useful for internationalization.

ISO-8859-1

ISO-8859-1 is the character set for Western European languages. It's an 8-bit encoding scheme in which every encoded character takes exactly 8 bits. (With the remaining character sets, on the other hand, some codes are reserved to signal the start of a multibyte character.)

UTF-8

UTF-8 is an 8-bit encoding scheme. Characters from the English-language alphabet are all encoded using an 8-bit byte. Characters for other languages are encoded using 2, 3, or even 4 bytes. UTF-8 therefore produces compact documents for the English language, but for other languages, documents tend to be half again as large as they would be if they used UTF-16. If the majority of a document's text is in a Western European language, then UTF-8 is generally a good choice because it allows for internationalization while still minimizing the space required for encoding.

UTF-16

UTF-16 is a 16-bit encoding scheme. It is large enough to encode all the characters from all the alphabets in the world. It uses 16 bits for most characters but includes 32-bit characters for ideogram-based languages such as Chinese. A Western European-language document that uses UTF-16 will be twice as large as the same document encoded using UTF-8. But documents written in far Eastern languages will be far smaller using UTF-16.

Note: UTF-16 depends on the system's byte-ordering conventions. Although in most systems, high-order bytes follow low-order bytes in a 16-bit or 32-bit "word," some systems use the reverse order. UTF-16 documents cannot be interchanged between such systems without a conversion.

Further Information

The character set and encoding names recognized by Internet authorities are listed in the IANA character set registry:

```
http://www.iana.org/assignments/character-sets
```

The Java programming language represents characters internally using the Unicode character set, which provides support for most languages. For storage and transmission over networks, however, many other character encodings are used. The Java 2 platform therefore also supports character conversion to and from other character encodings. Any Java runtime must support the Unicode transformations UTF-8, UTF-16BE, and UTF-16LE as well as the ISO-8859-1 character encoding, but most implementations support many more. For a complete list of the encodings that can be supported by the Java 2 platform, see

```
http://java.sun.com/j2se/1.4/docs/guide/intl/encoding.doc.html
```

B

XML and Related
Specs: Digesting the
Alphabet Soup

$\mathbf{T}$HIS appendix provides a high-level overview of the various XML-related acronyms and what they mean. There is a lot of work going on around XML, so there is a lot to learn.

The current APIs for accessing XML documents either serially or in random access mode are, respectively, SAX (page 1344) and DOM (page 1345). The specifications for ensuring the validity of XML documents are DTD (page 1346) (the original mechanism, defined as part of the XML specification) and various Schema Standards (page 1348) proposals (newer mechanisms that use XML syntax to do the job of describing validation criteria).

Other future standards that are nearing completion include the XSL (page 1347) standard, a mechanism for setting up translations of XML documents (for example to HTML or other XML) and for dictating how the document is rendered. The transformation part of that standard, XSLT (+XPath) (page 1347), is completed and covered in this tutorial. Another effort nearing completion is the XML Link Language specification (XML Linking, page 1350), which enables links between XML documents.

Those are the major initiatives you will want to be familiar with. This appendix also surveys a number of other interesting proposals, including the HTML-lookalike standard, XHTML (page 1351), and the meta-standard for describing the information an XML document contains, RDF (page 1351). There are also standards efforts that extend XML's capabilities, such as XLink and XPointer.

Finally, there are a number of interesting standards and standards proposals that build on XML, including Synchronized Multimedia Integration Language (SMIL, page 1353), Mathematical Markup Language (MathML, page 1353), Scalable Vector Graphics (SVG, page 1353), and DrawML (page 1353), as well as a number of e-commerce standards.

The remainder of this appendix gives you a more detailed description of these initiatives. To help keep things straight, it's divided into these topics:

- Basic Standards (page 1344)
- Schema Standards (page 1348)
- Linking and Presentation Standards (page 1350)
- Knowledge Standards (page 1351)
- Standards That Build on XML (page 1352)

Skim the terms once so you know what's here, and keep a copy of this document handy to refer to whenever you see one of these terms in something you're reading. Pretty soon, you'll have them all committed to memory, and you'll be at least "conversant" with XML.

Basic Standards

These are the basic standards you need to be familiar with. They come up in almost any discussion of XML.

SAX

The Simple API for XML was a product of collaboration on the XML-DEV mailing list rather than a product of the W3C. It's included here because it has the same "final" characteristics as a W3C recommendation.

You can think of SAX as a "serial access" protocol for XML that is ideal for *stateless* processing, where the handling of an element does not depend on any of the elements that came before. With a small memory footprint and fast execution speeds, this API is great for straight-through transformations of data into XML, or out of it. It is an *event-driven* protocol, because you register a handler with the parser that defines one callback method for elements, another for text, and one for comments (plus methods for errors and other XML components).

StAX

The Streaming API for XML is a Java "pull parsing" API. This API also acts like a "serial access" protocol, but its processing model is ideal for *state dependent* processing. With this API, you ask the parser to send you the next thing it has, and then decide what to do with what it gives you. For example, when you're in a heading element and you get text, you'll use one font size. But if you're in a normal paragraph and you get text, you'll use a different font size.

DOM

The Document Object Model protocol converts an XML document into a collection of objects in your program. You can then manipulate the object model in any way that makes sense. This mechanism is also known as the "random access" protocol, because you can visit any part of the data at any time. You can then modify the data, remove it, or insert new data.

JDOM and dom4j

Although the Document Object Model provides a lot of power for document-oriented processing, it doesn't provide much in the way of object-oriented simplification. Java developers who are processing more data-oriented structures—rather than books, articles, and other full-fledged documents—frequently find that object-oriented APIs such as JDOM and dom4j are easier to use and more suited to their needs.

Here are the important differences to understand when you choose between the two:

- JDOM is a somewhat cleaner, smaller API. Where coding style is an important consideration, JDOM is a good choice.
- JDOM is a Java Community Process (JCP) initiative. When completed, it will be an endorsed standard.
- dom4j is a smaller, faster implementation that has been in wide use for a number of years.
- dom4j is a factory-based implementation. That makes it easier to modify for complex, special-purpose applications. At the time of this writing, JDOM does not yet use a factory to instantiate an instance of the parser (although the standard appears to be headed in that direction). So, with JDOM, you always get the original parser. (That's fine for the majority of applications, but may not be appropriate if your application has special needs.)

For more information on JDOM, see `http://www.jdom.org/`. For more information on dom4j, see `http://dom4j.org/`.

DTD

The Document Type Definition specification is actually part of the XML specification rather than a separate entity. On the other hand, it is optional; you can write an XML document without it. And there are a number of schema standards proposals that offer more flexible alternatives. So the DTD is discussed here as though it were a separate specification.

A DTD specifies the kinds of tags that can be included in your XML document, along with the valid arrangements of those tags. You can use the DTD to make sure that you don't create an invalid XML structure. You can also use it to make sure that the XML structure you are reading (or that got sent over the Net) is indeed valid.

Unfortunately, it is difficult to specify a DTD for a complex document in such a way that it prevents all invalid combinations and allows all the valid ones. So constructing a DTD is something of an art. The DTD can exist at the front of the document, as part of the prolog. It can also exist as a separate entity, or it can be split between the document prolog and one or more additional entities.

However, although the DTD mechanism was the first method defined for specifying valid document structure, it was not the last. Several newer schema specifications have been devised. You'll learn about those momentarily.

Namespaces

The namespace standard lets you write an XML document that uses two or more sets of XML tags in modular fashion. Suppose for example that you created an XML-based parts list that uses XML descriptions of parts supplied by other manufacturers (online!). The price data supplied by the subcomponents would be amounts you want to total up, whereas the price data for the structure as a whole would be something you want to display. The namespace specification defines mechanisms for qualifying the names so as to eliminate ambiguity. That lets you write programs that use information from other sources and do the right things with it.

The latest information on namespaces can be found at `http://www.w3.org/TR/REC-xml-names`.

XSL

The Extensible Stylesheet Language adds display and transformation capabilities to XML. The XML standard specifies how to identify data, rather than how to display it. HTML, on the other hand, tells how things should be displayed without identifying what they are. Among other purposes, XSL bridges the gap between the two.

The XSL standard has two parts: XSLT (the transformation standard, described next) and XSL-FO (the part that covers *formatting objects*). XSL-FO lets you specify complex formatting for a variety of publications.

The latest W3C work on XSL is at `http://www.w3.org/TR/WD-xsl`.

XSLT (+XPath)

The Extensible Stylesheet Language Transformations standard is essentially a translation mechanism that lets you convert XML data into other forms—for example, into HTML. Different XSL transforms then let you use the same XML data in a variety of ways. (The XPath standard is an addressing mechanism that you use when constructing transformation instructions. You use it to specify the parts of the XML structure you want to transform.)

Schema Standards

A DTD makes it possible to validate the structure of relatively simple XML documents, but that's as far as it goes.

A DTD can't restrict the content of elements, and it can't specify complex relationships. For example, it is impossible to specify that a <heading> for a <book> must have both a <title> and an <author>, whereas a <heading> for a <chapter> needs only a <title>. In a DTD, you get to specify the structure of the <heading> element only one time. There is no context sensitivity, because a DTD specification is not hierarchical.

For example, for a mailing address that contains several parsed character data (PCDATA) elements, the DTD might look something like this:

```
<!ELEMENT mailAddress (name, address, zipcode)>
<!ELEMENT name (#PCDATA)>
<!ELEMENT address (#PCDATA)>
<!ELEMENT zipcode (#PCDATA)>
```

As you can see, the specifications are linear. So if you need another "name" element in the DTD, you need a different identifier for it. You could not simply call it "name" without conflicting with the <name> element defined for use in a <mailAddress>.

Another problem with the nonhierarchical nature of DTD specifications is that it is not clear what the comments are meant to explain. A comment at the top might be intended to apply to the whole structure, or it might be intended only for the first item. Finally, DTDs do not allow you to formally specify field-validation criteria, such as the 5-digit (or 5 and 4) limitation for the zipcode field.

Finally, a DTD uses syntax that is substantially different from that of XML, so it can't be processed by using a standard XML parser. This means that you can't, for example, read a DTD into a DOM, modify it, and then write it back out again.

To remedy these shortcomings, a number of standards have arisen that define a more databaselike, hierarchical *schema* that specifies validation criteria. The major proposals are discussed in the following sections.

XML Schema

XML Schema is a large, complex standard that has two parts. One part specifies structure relationships. (This is the largest and most complex part.) The other part specifies mechanisms for validating the content of XML elements by specifying a (potentially very sophisticated) *data type* for each element. The good news is that XML Schema for Structures lets you specify virtually any relationship you can imagine. The bad news is that it is very difficult to implement, and it's hard to learn. Most of the alternatives provide simpler structure definitions while incorporating XML Schema's data-typing mechanisms.

For more information on XML Schema, see the W3C specs XML Schema (Structures) and XML Schema (Data Types), as well as other information accessible at `http://www.w3c.org/XML/Schema`.

RELAX NG

Simpler than XML Structure Schema, Regular Language Description for XML (Next Generation) is an emerging standard under the auspices of OASIS (Organization for the Advancement of Structured Information Standards). It may also become an ISO standard in the near future.

RELAX NG uses regular-expression patterns to express constraints on structure relationships, and it uses XML Schema data-typing mechanisms to express content constraints. This standard also uses XML syntax, and it includes a DTD-to-RELAX converter. (It's "next generation" because it's a newer version of the RELAX schema mechanism that integrated TREX—Tree Regular Expressions for XML—a means of expressing validation criteria by describing a *pattern* for the structure and content of an XML document.)

For more information on RELAX NG, see `http://www.oasis-open.org/committees/relax-ng/`

SOX

Schema for Object-oriented XML is a schema proposal that includes extensible data types, namespaces, and embedded documentation.

For more information on SOX, see `http://www.w3.org/TR/NOTE-SOX`.

Schematron

Schema for Object-oriented XML is an assertion-based schema mechanism that allows for sophisticated validation.

For more information on the Schematron validation mechanism, see `http://www.ascc.net/xml/resource/schematron/schematron.html`.

Linking and Presentation Standards

Arguably the two greatest benefits provided by HTML are the ability to link between documents and the ability to create simple formatted documents (and, eventually, very complex formatted documents). The following standards aim to preserve the benefits of HTML in the XML arena and add new functionality.

XML Linking

These specifications provide a variety of powerful linking mechanisms and may well have a big impact on how XML documents are used.

XLink

> The XLink protocol is a specification for handling links between XML documents. This specification allows for some pretty sophisticated linking, including two-way links, links to multiple documents, expanding links that insert the linked information into your document rather than replace your document with a new page, links between two documents that are created in a third, independent document, and indirect links (so that you can point to an "address book" rather than directly to the target document; updating the address book then automatically changes any links that use it).

XML Base

> This standard defines an attribute for XML documents that defines a base address that is used when evaluating a relative address specified in the document. (So, for example, a simple file name would be found in the base address directory.)

XPointer

> In general, the XLink specification targets a document or document segment using its ID. The XPointer specification defines mechanisms for "addressing into the internal structures of XML documents," without requiring the author of the document to have defined an ID for that segment. To quote the spec, it

provides for "reference to elements, character strings, and other parts of XML documents, whether or not they bear an explicit ID attribute."

For more information on the XML Linking standards, see `http://www.w3.org/XML/Linking`.

XHTML

The XHTML specification is a way of making XML documents that look and act like HTML documents. Given that an XML document can contain any tags you care to define, why not define a set of tags that look like HTML? That's the thinking behind the XHTML specification, at any rate. The result of this specification is a document that can be displayed in browsers and also treated as XML data. The data may not be quite as identifiable as "pure" XML, but it will be a heck of a lot easier to manipulate than standard HTML, because XML specifies a good deal more regularity and consistency.

For example, either every tag in a well-formed XML document must have an end tag associated with it, or it must end in `/>`. So you might see `<p>...</p>`, or you might see `<p/>`, but you will never see `<p>` standing by itself. The upshot of this requirement is that you never have to program for the weird kinds of cases you see in HTML—where, for example, a `<dt>` tag might be terminated by `</DT>`, by another `<DT>`, by `<dd>`, or by `</dl>`. That makes it a lot easier to write code.

The XHTML specification is a reformulation of HTML 4.0 into XML. The latest information is at `http://www.w3.org/TR/xhtml1`.

Knowledge Standards

When you start looking down the road five or six years, and you visualize how the information on the Web will begin to turn into one huge knowledge base (the "semantic Web"). For the latest on the semantic Web, visit `http://www.w3.org/2001/sw/`.

In the meantime, here are the fundamental standards you'll want to know about.

RDF

Resource Description Framework is a standard for defining *meta*data: information that describes what a particular data item is and specifies how it can be used.

Used in conjunction with the XHTML specification, for example, or with HTML pages, RDF could be used to describe the content of the pages. For example, if your browser stored your ID information as `FIRSTNAME`, `LASTNAME`, and `EMAIL`, an RDF description could make it possible to transfer data to an application that wanted `NAME` and `EMAILADDRESS`. Just think: One day you may not need to type your name and address at every Web site you visit!

For the latest information on RDF, see `http://www.w3.org/TR/REC-rdf-syntax`.

RDF Schema

RDF Schema allows the specification of consistency rules and additional information that describe how the statements in a resource description framework (RDF) should be interpreted.

For more information on the RDF Schema recommendation, see `http://www.w3.org/TR/rdf-schema`.

XTM

XML topic maps are in many ways a simpler, more readily usable knowledge representation than RDF, and this standard is one worth watching. So far, RDF is the W3C standard for knowledge representation, but topic maps could possibly become the developer's choice among knowledge representation standards.

For more information on the XML Topic Maps standard, see `http://www.topicmaps.org/xtm/index.html`. For information on topic maps and the Web, see `http://www.topicmaps.org/`.

Standards That Build on XML

The following standards and proposals build on XML. Because XML is basically a language-definition tool, these specifications use it to define standardized languages for specialized purposes.

Extended Document Standards

These standards define mechanisms for producing extremely complex documents—books, journals, magazines, and the like—using XML.

SMIL

Synchronized Multimedia Integration Language is a W3C recommendation that covers audio, video, and animations. It also addresses the difficult issue of synchronizing the playback of such elements.

For more information on SMIL, see `http://www.w3.org/TR/REC-smil`.

MathML

Mathematical Markup Language is a W3C recommendation that deals with the representation of mathematical formulas.

For more information on MathML, see `http://www.w3.org/TR/REC-MathML`.

SVG

Scalable Vector Graphics is a W3C recommendation that covers the representation of vector graphic images. (Vector graphic images are built from commands that say things such as "draw a line (square, circle) from point xi to point m,n" rather than encoding the image as a series of bits. Such images are more easily scalable, although they typically require more processing time to render.)

For more information on SVG, see `http://www.w3.org/TR/SVG/`.

DrawML

Drawing Meta Language is a W3C note that covers two-dimensional images for technical illustrations. It also addresses the problem of updating and refining such images.

For more information on DrawML, see `http://www.w3.org/TR/NOTE-drawml`.

e-Commerce Standards

These standards are aimed at using XML in the world of business-to-business (B2B) and business-to-consumer (B2C) commerce.

ICE

Information and Content Exchange is a protocol for use by content syndicators and their subscribers. It focuses on "automating content exchange and reuse, both in traditional publishing contexts and in business-to-business relationships."

For more information on ICE, see `http://www.w3.org/TR/NOTE-ice`.

ebXML

The Electronic Business with XML standard aims at creating a modular electronic business framework using XML. It is the product of a joint initiative by the United Nations (UN/CEFACT) and the Organization for the Advancement of Structured Information Standards (OASIS).

For more information on ebXML, see `http://www.ebxml.org/`.

cxml

Commerce XML is a RosettaNet (`www.rosettanet.org`) standard for setting up interactive online catalogs for different buyers, where the pricing and product offerings are company-specific. cxml includes mechanisms to handle purchase orders, change orders, status updates, and shipping notifications.

For more information on cxml, see `http://www.cxml.org/`

UBL

Universal Business Language is an OASIS initiative aimed at compiling a standard library of XML business documents (purchase orders, invoices, etc.) that are defined with XML Schema definitions.

For more information on UBL, see `http://www.oasis-open.org/commit-tees/ubl`.

Summary

XML has become a widely adopted standard that is being used in a dizzying variety of application areas.

C

HTTP Overview

MOST Web clients use the HTTP protocol to communicate with a J2EE server. HTTP defines the requests that a client can send to a server and responses that the server can send in reply. Each request contains a URL, which is a string that identifies a Web component or a static object such as an HTML page or image file.

A J2EE server converts an HTTP request to an HTTP request object and delivers it to the Web component identified by the request URL. The Web component fills in an HTTP response object, which the server converts to an HTTP response and sends to the client.

This appendix provides introductory material on the HTTP protocol. For further information on this protocol, see the Internet RFCs: HTTP/1.0 (RFC 1945), HTTP/1.1 (RFC 2616). These can be downloaded from

```
http://www.rfc-editor.org/rfc.html
```

HTTP Requests

An HTTP request consists of a request method, a request URL, header fields, and a body. HTTP 1.1 defines the following request methods:

- GET: Retrieves the resource identified by the request URL
- HEAD: Returns the headers identified by the request URL
- POST: Sends data of unlimited length to the Web server
- PUT: Stores a resource under the request URL
- DELETE: Removes the resource identified by the request URL
- OPTIONS: Returns the HTTP methods the server supports
- TRACE: Returns the header fields sent with the TRACE request

HTTP 1.0 includes only the GET, HEAD, and POST methods. Although J2EE servers are required to support only HTTP 1.0, in practice many servers, including the Sun Java System Application Server Platform Edition 8, support HTTP 1.1.

HTTP Responses

An HTTP response contains a result code, header fields, and a body.

The HTTP protocol expects the result code and all header fields to be returned before any body content.

Some commonly used status codes include:

- 404: Indicates that the requested resource is not available
- 401: Indicates that the request requires HTTP authentication
- 500: Indicates that an error occurred inside the HTTP server that prevented it from fulfilling the request
- 503: Indicates that the HTTP server is temporarily overloaded and unable to handle the request

D

J2EE Connector
Architecture

THE J2EE Connector architecture enables J2EE components to interact with enterprise information systems (EISs) and EISs to interact with J2EE components. EIS software includes various types of systems: enterprise resource planning (ERP), mainframe transaction processing, and nonrelational databases, among others. The J2EE Connector architecture simplifies the integration of diverse EISs. Each EIS requires only one implementation of the J2EE Connector architecture. Because an implementation adheres to the J2EE Connector specification, it is portable across all compliant J2EE servers.

About Resource Adapters

A *resource adapter* is a J2EE component that implements the J2EE Connector architecture for a specific EIS. As illustrated in Figure D–1, it is through the resource adapter that a J2EE application and an EIS communicate with each other.

Stored in a Resource Adapter Archive (RAR) file, a resource adapter can be deployed on any J2EE server, much like the EAR file of a J2EE application. An RAR file may be contained in an EAR file, or it may exist as a separate file. See Figure D–2 for the structure of a resource adapter module.

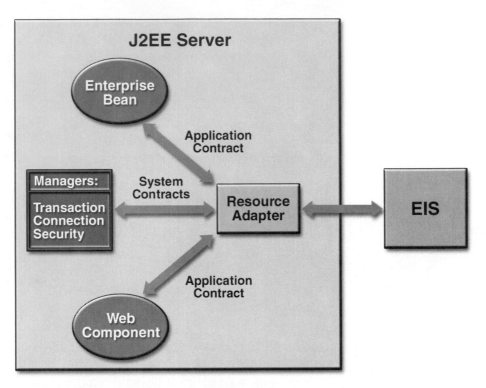

Figure D–1   Resource Adapter Contracts

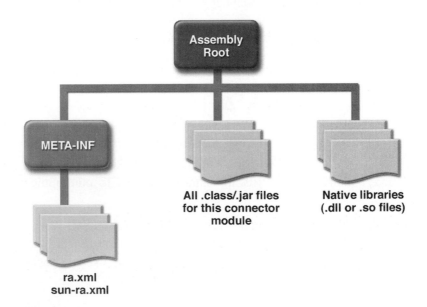

Figure D–2   Resource Adapter Module Structure

A resource adapter is analogous to a JDBC driver. Both provide a standard API through which an application can access a resource that is outside the J2EE server. For a resource adapter, the outside resource is an EIS; for a JDBC driver, it is a DBMS. Resource adapters and JDBC drivers are rarely created by application developers. In most cases, both types of software are built by vendors that sell products such as tools, servers, or integration software.

Resource Adapter Contracts

The resource adapter mediates communication between the J2EE server and the EIS via contracts. The application contract defines the API through which a J2EE component such as an enterprise bean accesses the EIS. This API is the only view that the component has of the EIS. The system contracts link the resource adapter to important services that are managed by the J2EE server. The resource adapter itself and its system contracts are transparent to the J2EE component.

Management Contracts

The J2EE Connector architecture defines system contracts that enable resource adapter life cycle and thread management.

Life-Cycle Management

The Connector architecture specifies a *life-cycle management contract* that allows an application server to manage the life cycle of a resource adapter. This contract provides a mechanism for the application server to bootstrap a resource adapter instance during the instance's deployment or application server startup. It also provides a means for the application server to notify the resource adapter instance when it is undeployed or when an orderly shutdown of the application server takes place.

Work Management Contract

The Connector architecture *work management contract* ensures that resource adapters use threads in the proper, recommended manner. It also enables an application server to manage threads for resource adapters.

Resource adapters that improperly use threads can create problems for the entire application server environment. For example, a resource adapter might create too many threads or it might not properly release threads it has created. Poor thread handling inhibits application server shutdown. It also impacts the application server's performance because creating and destroying threads are expensive operations.

The work management contract establishes a means for the application server to pool and reuse threads, similar to pooling and reusing connections. By adhering to this contract, the resource adapter does not have to manage threads itself. Instead, the resource adapter has the application server create and provide needed threads. When the resource adapter is finished with a given thread, it returns the thread to the application server. The application server manages the thread: It can return the thread to a pool and reuse it later, or it can destroy the thread. Handling threads in this manner results in increased application server performance and more efficient use of resources.

In addition to moving thread management to the application server, the Connector architecture provides a flexible model for a resource adapter that uses threads:

- The requesting thread can choose to block—stop its own execution—until the work thread completes.
- Or the requesting thread can block while it waits to get the thread. When the application server provides a work thread, the requesting thread and the work thread execute in parallel.
- The resource adapter can opt to submit the work for the thread to a queue. The thread executes the work from the queue at some later point. The resource adapter continues its own execution from the point it submitted the work to the queue, no matter of when the thread executes it.

With the latter two approaches, the resource adapter and the thread may execute simultaneously or independently from each other. For these approaches, the contract specifies a listener mechanism to notify the resource adapter that the thread has completed its operation. The resource adapter can also specify the execution context for the thread, and the work management contract controls the context in which the thread executes.

Outbound Contracts

The J2EE Connector architecture defines system-level contracts between a J2EE server and an EIS that enable outbound connectivity to the EIS: connection management, transaction management, and security.

The *connection management contract* supports connection pooling, a technique that enhances application performance and scalability. Connection pooling is transparent to the application, which simply obtains a connection to the EIS.

The *transaction management contract* between the transaction manager and an EIS supports transactional access to EIS resource managers. This contract lets an application server use a transaction manager to manage transactions across multiple resource managers. This contract also supports transactions that are managed inside an EIS resource manager without the necessity of involving an external transaction manager. Because of the transaction management contract, a call to the EIS may be enclosed in an XA transaction (a transaction type defined by the distributed transaction processing specification created by The Open Group). XA transactions are global: they can contain calls to multiple EISs, databases, and enterprise bean business methods. Although often appropriate, XA transactions are not mandatory. Instead, an application can use local transactions, which are managed by the individual EIS, or it can use no transactions at all.

The *security management contract* provides mechanisms for authentication, authorization, and secure communication between a J2EE server and an EIS to protect the information in the EIS.

Inbound Contracts

The J2EE Connector architecture defines system contracts between an application server and an EIS that enable inbound connectivity from an EIS: pluggability contracts for message providers and contracts for importing transactions.

Messaging Contracts

To enable external systems to connect to a J2EE application server, the Connector architecture extends the capabilities of message-driven beans to handle messages from any message provider. That is, message-driven beans are no longer limited to handling JMS messages. Instead, EISs and message providers can plug any message provider, including their own custom or proprietary message providers, into a J2EE server.

To provide this feature, a message provider or an EIS resource adapter implements the *messaging contract*, which details APIs for message handling and message delivery. A conforming resource adapter is assured of the ability to send messages from any provider to a message-driven bean, and it also can be plugged into a J2EE server in a standard manner.

Transaction Inflow

The Connector architecture supports importing transactions from an EIS to the J2EE server. The architecture specifies how to propagate the transaction context from the EIS. For example, a transaction can be started by the EIS, such as the Customer Information Control System (CICS). Within the same CICS transaction, a connection can be made through a resource adapter to an enterprise bean on the application server. The enterprise bean does its work under the CICS transaction context and commits within that transaction context.

The Connector architecture also specifies how the container participates in transaction completion and how it handles crash recovery to ensure that data integrity is not lost.

Common Client Interface

This section describes how components use the Connector architecture Common Client Interface (CCI) API and a resource adapter to access data from an EIS.

Defined by the J2EE Connector architecture specification, the CCI defines a set of interfaces and classes whose methods allow a client to perform typical data access operations. The CCI interfaces and classes are as follows:

- `ConnectionFactory`: Provides an application component with a `Connection` instance to an EIS.
- `Connection`: Represents the connection to the underlying EIS.
- `ConnectionSpec`: Provides a means for an application component to pass connection-request-specific properties to the `ConnectionFactory` when making a connection request.
- `Interaction`: Provides a means for an application component to execute EIS functions, such as database stored procedures.
- `InteractionSpec`: Holds properties pertaining to an application component's interaction with an EIS.
- `Record`: The superclass for the various kinds of record instances. Record instances can be `MappedRecord`, `IndexedRecord`, or `ResultSet` instances, all of which inherit from the `Record` interface.
- `RecordFactory`: Provides an application component with a `Record` instance.
- `IndexedRecord`: Represents an ordered collection of `Record` instances based on the `java.util.List` interface.

A client or application component that uses the CCI to interact with an underlying EIS does so in a prescribed manner. The component must establish a connection to the EIS's resource manager, and it does so using the ConnectionFactory. The Connection object represents the actual connection to the EIS and is used for subsequent interactions with the EIS.

The component performs its interactions with the EIS, such as accessing data from a specific table, using an Interaction object. The application component defines the Interaction object using an InteractionSpec object. When the application component reads data from the EIS (such as from database tables) or writes to those tables, it does so using a particular type of Record instance: either a MappedRecord, an IndexedRecord, or a ResultSet instance. Just as the ConnectionFactory creates Connection instances, a RecordFactory creates Record instances.

Note, too, that a client application that relies on a CCI resource adapter is very much like any other J2EE client that uses enterprise bean methods.

Further Information

For further information on the J2EE Connector architecture, see:

- J2EE Connector 1.5 specification
  http://java.sun.com/j2ee/connector/download.html
- The J2EE Connector Web site
  http://java.sun.com/j2ee/connector

Glossary

abstract schema

The part of an entity bean's deployment descriptor that defines the bean's persistent fields and relationships.

abstract schema name

A logical name that is referenced in EJB QL queries.

access control

The methods by which interactions with resources are limited to collections of users or programs for the purpose of enforcing integrity, confidentiality, or availability constraints.

ACID

The acronym for the four properties guaranteed by transactions: atomicity, consistency, isolation, and durability.

activation

The process of transferring an enterprise bean from secondary storage to memory. See *passivation*.

anonymous access

Accessing a resource without authentication.

applet

A J2EE component that typically executes in a Web browser but can execute in a variety of other applications or devices that support the applet programming model.

applet container

A container that includes support for the applet programming model.

application assembler

A person who combines J2EE components and modules into deployable application units.

application client

A first-tier J2EE client component that executes in its own Java virtual machine. Application clients have access to some J2EE platform APIs.

application client container

A container that supports application client components.

application client module

A software unit that consists of one or more classes and an application client deployment descriptor.

application component provider

A vendor that provides the Java classes that implement components' methods, JSP page definitions, and any required deployment descriptors.

application configuration resource file

An XML file used to configure resources for a JavaServer Faces application, to define navigation rules for the application, and to register converters, validators, listeners, renderers, and components with the application.

archiving

The process of saving the state of an object and restoring it.

asant

A Java-based build tool that can be extended using Java classes. The configuration files are XML-based, calling out a target tree where various tasks get executed.

attribute

A qualifier on an XML tag that provides additional information.

authentication

The process that verifies the identity of a user, device, or other entity in a computer system, usually as a prerequisite to allowing access to resources in a system. The Java servlet specification requires three types of authentication—basic, form-based, and mutual—and supports digest authentication.

authorization

The process by which access to a method or resource is determined. Authorization depends on the determination of whether the principal associated with a request through authentication is in a given security role. A security role is a logical grouping of users defined by the person who assembles the application. A deployer maps security roles to security identities. Security identities may be principals or groups in the operational environment.

authorization constraint

An authorization rule that determines who is permitted to access a Web resource collection.

B2B

Business-to-business.

backing bean

A JavaBeans component that corresponds to a JSP page that includes Java-Server Faces components. The backing bean defines properties for the components on the page and methods that perform processing for the component. This processing includes event handling, validation, and processing associated with navigation.

basic authentication

An authentication mechanism in which a Web server authenticates an entity via a user name and password obtained using the Web application's built-in authentication mechanism.

bean-managed persistence

The mechanism whereby data transfer between an entity bean's variables and a resource manager is managed by the entity bean.

bean-managed transaction

A transaction whose boundaries are defined by an enterprise bean.

binary entity

See *unparsed entity*.

binding (JavaServer Faces technology)

Wiring UI components to back-end data sources such as backing bean properties.

binding (XML)

Generating the code needed to process a well-defined portion of XML data.

build file

The XML file that contains one or more `asant` targets. A target is a set of tasks you want to be executed. When starting `asant`, you can select which targets you want to have executed. When no target is given, the project's default target is executed.

business logic

The code that implements the functionality of an application. In the Enterprise JavaBeans architecture, this logic is implemented by the methods of an enterprise bean.

business method

A method of an enterprise bean that implements the business logic or rules of an application.

callback methods

Component methods called by the container to notify the component of important events in its life cycle.

caller

Same as *caller principal*.

caller principal

The principal that identifies the invoker of the enterprise bean method.

cascade delete

A deletion that triggers another deletion. A cascade delete can be specified for an entity bean that has container-managed persistence.

CDATA

A predefined XML tag for character data that means "don't interpret these characters," as opposed to parsed character data (PCDATA), in which the normal rules of XML syntax apply. CDATA sections are typically used to show examples of XML syntax.

certificate authority

A trusted organization that issues public key certificates and provides identification to the bearer.

client-certificate authentication

An authentication mechanism that uses HTTP over SSL, in which the server and, optionally, the client authenticate each other with a public key certificate that conforms to a standard that is defined by X.509 Public Key Infrastructure.

comment

In an XML document, text that is ignored unless the parser is specifically told to recognize it.

commit

The point in a transaction when all updates to any resources involved in the transaction are made permanent.

component

See *J2EE component*.

component contract

The contract between a J2EE component and its container. The contract includes life-cycle management of the component, a context interface that the instance uses to obtain various information and services from its container, and a list of services that every container must provide for its components.

component (JavaServer Faces technology)

See *JavaServer Faces UI component*.

component-managed sign-on

A mechanism whereby security information needed for signing on to a resource is provided by an application component.

connection

See *resource manager connection*.

connection factory

See *resource manager connection factory.*

connector

A standard extension mechanism for containers that provides connectivity to enterprise information systems. A connector is specific to an enterprise information system and consists of a resource adapter and application development tools for enterprise information system connectivity. The resource adapter is plugged in to a container through its support for system-level contracts defined in the Connector architecture.

Connector architecture

An architecture for integration of J2EE products with enterprise information systems. There are two parts to this architecture: a resource adapter provided by an enterprise information system vendor and the J2EE product that allows this resource adapter to plug in. This architecture defines a set of contracts that a resource adapter must support to plug in to a J2EE product—for example, transactions, security, and resource management.

container

An entity that provides life-cycle management, security, deployment, and runtime services to J2EE components. Each type of container (EJB, Web, JSP, servlet, applet, and application client) also provides component-specific services.

container-managed persistence

The mechanism whereby data transfer between an entity bean's variables and a resource manager is managed by the entity bean's container.

container-managed sign-on

The mechanism whereby security information needed for signing on to a resource is supplied by the container.

container-managed transaction

A transaction whose boundaries are defined by an EJB container. An entity bean must use container-managed transactions.

content

In an XML document, the part that occurs after the prolog, including the root element and everything it contains.

context attribute

An object bound into the context associated with a servlet.

context root

A name that gets mapped to the document root of a Web application.

conversational state

The field values of a session bean plus the transitive closure of the objects reachable from the bean's fields. The transitive closure of a bean is defined in terms of the serialization protocol for the Java programming language, that is, the fields that would be stored by serializing the bean instance.

CORBA

Common Object Request Broker Architecture. A language-independent distributed object model specified by the OMG.

create method

A method defined in the home interface and invoked by a client to create an enterprise bean.

credentials

The information describing the security attributes of a principal.

CSS

Cascading style sheet. A stylesheet used with HTML and XML documents to add a style to all elements marked with a particular tag, for the direction of browsers or other presentation mechanisms.

CTS

Compatibility test suite. A suite of compatibility tests for verifying that a J2EE product complies with the J2EE platform specification.

data

The contents of an element in an XML stream, generally used when the element does not contain any subelements. When it does, the term *content* is generally used. When the only text in an XML structure is contained in simple elements and when elements that have subelements have little or no data mixed in, then that structure is often thought of as XML data, as opposed to an XML document.

DDP

Document-driven programming. The use of XML to define applications.

declaration

The very first thing in an XML document, which declares it as XML. The minimal declaration is `<?xml version="1.0"?>`. The declaration is part of the document prolog.

declarative security

Mechanisms used in an application that are expressed in a declarative syntax in a deployment descriptor.

delegation

An act whereby one principal authorizes another principal to use its identity or privileges with some restrictions.

deployer

A person who installs J2EE modules and applications into an operational environment.

deployment

The process whereby software is installed into an operational environment.

deployment descriptor

An XML file provided with each module and J2EE application that describes how they should be deployed. The deployment descriptor directs a deployment tool to deploy a module or application with specific container options and describes specific configuration requirements that a deployer must resolve.

destination

A JMS administered object that encapsulates the identity of a JMS queue or topic. See *point-to-point messaging system*, *publish/subscribe messaging system*.

digest authentication

An authentication mechanism in which a Web application authenticates itself to a Web server by sending the server a message digest along with its HTTP request message. The digest is computed by employing a one-way hash algorithm to a concatenation of the HTTP request message and the client's password. The digest is typically much smaller than the HTTP request and doesn't contain the password.

distributed application

An application made up of distinct components running in separate runtime environments, usually on different platforms connected via a network. Typical distributed applications are two-tier (client-server), three-tier (client-middleware-server), and multitier (client-multiple middleware-multiple servers).

document

In general, an XML structure in which one or more elements contains text intermixed with subelements. See also *data*.

Document Object Model

An API for accessing and manipulating XML documents as tree structures. DOM provides platform-neutral, language-neutral interfaces that enable programs and scripts to dynamically access and modify content and structure in XML documents.

document root

The top-level directory of a WAR. The document root is where JSP pages, client-side classes and archives, and static Web resources are stored.

DOM

See *Document Object Model*.

DTD

Document type definition. An optional part of the XML document prolog, as specified by the XML standard. The DTD specifies constraints on the valid tags and tag sequences that can be in the document. The DTD has a number of shortcomings, however, and this has led to various schema proposals. For example, the DTD entry `<!ELEMENT username (#PCDATA)>` says that the XML element called `username` contains parsed character data—that is, text alone, with no other structural elements under it. The DTD includes both the local subset, defined in the current file, and the external subset, which consists of the definitions contained in external DTD files that are referenced in the local subset using a parameter entity.

durable subscription

In a JMS publish/subscribe messaging system, a subscription that continues to exist whether or not there is a current active subscriber object. If there is no active subscriber, the JMS provider retains the subscription's messages until they are received by the subscription or until they expire.

EAR file

Enterprise Archive file. A JAR archive that contains a J2EE application.

ebXML

Electronic Business XML. A group of specifications designed to enable enterprises to conduct business through the exchange of XML-based messages. It is sponsored by OASIS and the United Nations Centre for the Facilitation of Procedures and Practices in Administration, Commerce and Transport (U.N./CEFACT).

EJB

See *Enterprise JavaBeans*.

EJB container

A container that implements the EJB component contract of the J2EE architecture. This contract specifies a runtime environment for enterprise beans that includes security, concurrency, life-cycle management, transactions, deployment, naming, and other services. An EJB container is provided by an EJB or J2EE server.

EJB container provider

A vendor that supplies an EJB container.

EJB context

An object that allows an enterprise bean to invoke services provided by the container and to obtain the information about the caller of a client-invoked method.

EJB home object

An object that provides the life-cycle operations (create, remove, find) for an enterprise bean. The class for the EJB home object is generated by the container's deployment tools. The EJB home object implements the enterprise bean's home interface. The client references an EJB home object to perform life-cycle operations on an EJB object. The client uses JNDI to locate an EJB home object.

EJB JAR file

A JAR archive that contains an EJB module.

EJB module

A deployable unit that consists of one or more enterprise beans and an EJB deployment descriptor.

EJB object

An object whose class implements the enterprise bean's remote interface. A client never references an enterprise bean instance directly; a client always references an EJB object. The class of an EJB object is generated by a container's deployment tools.

EJB server

Software that provides services to an EJB container. For example, an EJB container typically relies on a transaction manager that is part of the EJB server to perform the two-phase commit across all the participating resource managers. The J2EE architecture assumes that an EJB container is hosted by an EJB server from the same vendor, so it does not specify the contract between these two entities. An EJB server can host one or more EJB containers.

EJB server provider

A vendor that supplies an EJB server.

element

A unit of XML data, delimited by tags. An XML element can enclose other elements.

empty tag

A tag that does not enclose any content.

enterprise bean

A J2EE component that implements a business task or business entity and is hosted by an EJB container; either an entity bean, a session bean, or a message-driven bean.

enterprise bean provider

An application developer who produces enterprise bean classes, remote and home interfaces, and deployment descriptor files, and packages them in an EJB JAR file.

enterprise information system

The applications that constitute an enterprise's existing system for handling companywide information. These applications provide an information infrastructure for an enterprise. An enterprise information system offers a well-defined set of services to its clients. These services are exposed to clients as local or remote interfaces or both. Examples of enterprise information systems include enterprise resource planning systems, mainframe transaction processing systems, and legacy database systems.

enterprise information system resource

An entity that provides enterprise information system-specific functionality to its clients. Examples are a record or set of records in a database system, a business object in an enterprise resource planning system, and a transaction program in a transaction processing system.

Enterprise JavaBeans (EJB)

A component architecture for the development and deployment of object-oriented, distributed, enterprise-level applications. Applications written using the Enterprise JavaBeans architecture are scalable, transactional, and secure.

Enterprise JavaBeans Query Language (EJB QL)

Defines the queries for the finder and select methods of an entity bean having container-managed persistence. A subset of SQL92, EJB QL has extensions that allow navigation over the relationships defined in an entity bean's abstract schema.

entity

A distinct, individual item that can be included in an XML document by referencing it. Such an entity reference can name an entity as small as a character (for example, <, which references the less-than symbol or left angle bracket, <). An entity reference can also reference an entire document, an external entity, or a collection of DTD definitions.

entity bean

> An enterprise bean that represents persistent data maintained in a database. An entity bean can manage its own persistence or can delegate this function to its container. An entity bean is identified by a primary key. If the container in which an entity bean is hosted crashes, the entity bean, its primary key, and any remote references survive the crash.

entity reference

> A reference to an entity that is substituted for the reference when the XML document is parsed. It can reference a predefined entity such as < or reference one that is defined in the DTD. In the XML data, the reference could be to an entity that is defined in the local subset of the DTD or to an external XML file (an external entity). The DTD can also carve out a segment of DTD specifications and give it a name so that it can be reused (included) at multiple points in the DTD by defining a parameter entity.

error

> A SAX parsing error is generally a validation error; in other words, it occurs when an XML document is not valid, although it can also occur if the declaration specifies an XML version that the parser cannot handle. See also *fatal error*, *warning*.

Extensible Markup Language

> See *XML*.

external entity

> An entity that exists as an external XML file, which is included in the XML document using an entity reference.

external subset

> That part of a DTD that is defined by references to external DTD files.

fatal error

> A fatal error occurs in the SAX parser when a document is not well formed or otherwise cannot be processed. See also *error*, *warning*.

filter

> An object that can transform the header or content (or both) of a request or response. Filters differ from Web components in that they usually do not themselves create responses but rather modify or adapt the requests for a resource, and modify or adapt responses from a resource. A filter should not have any dependencies on a Web resource for which it is acting as a filter so that it can be composable with more than one type of Web resource.

filter chain

> A concatenation of XSLT transformations in which the output of one transformation becomes the input of the next.

finder method

A method defined in the home interface and invoked by a client to locate an entity bean.

form-based authentication

An authentication mechanism in which a Web container provides an application-specific form for logging in. This form of authentication uses Base64 encoding and can expose user names and passwords unless all connections are over SSL.

general entity

An entity that is referenced as part of an XML document's content, as distinct from a parameter entity, which is referenced in the DTD. A general entity can be a parsed entity or an unparsed entity.

group

An authenticated set of users classified by common traits such as job title or customer profile. Groups are also associated with a set of roles, and every user that is a member of a group inherits all the roles assigned to that group.

handle

An object that identifies an enterprise bean. A client can serialize the handle and then later deserialize it to obtain a reference to the enterprise bean.

home handle

An object that can be used to obtain a reference to the home interface. A home handle can be serialized and written to stable storage and deserialized to obtain the reference.

home interface

One of two interfaces for an enterprise bean. The home interface defines zero or more methods for managing an enterprise bean. The home interface of a session bean defines `create` and `remove` methods, whereas the home interface of an entity bean defines `create`, finder, and `remove` methods.

HTML

Hypertext Markup Language. A markup language for hypertext documents on the Internet. HTML enables the embedding of images, sounds, video streams, form fields, references to other objects with URLs, and basic text formatting.

HTTP

Hypertext Transfer Protocol. The Internet protocol used to retrieve hypertext objects from remote hosts. HTTP messages consist of requests from client to server and responses from server to client.

HTTPS

HTTP layered over the SSL protocol.

IDL

Interface Definition Language. A language used to define interfaces to remote CORBA objects. The interfaces are independent of operating systems and programming languages.

IIOP

Internet Inter-ORB Protocol. A protocol used for communication between CORBA object request brokers.

impersonation

An act whereby one entity assumes the identity and privileges of another entity without restrictions and without any indication visible to the recipients of the impersonator's calls that delegation has taken place. Impersonation is a case of simple delegation.

initialization parameter

A parameter that initializes the context associated with a servlet.

ISO 3166

The international standard for country codes maintained by the International Organization for Standardization (ISO).

ISV

Independent software vendor.

J2EE

See *Java 2 Platform, Enterprise Edition*.

J2EE application

Any deployable unit of J2EE functionality. This can be a single J2EE module or a group of modules packaged into an EAR file along with a J2EE application deployment descriptor. J2EE applications are typically engineered to be distributed across multiple computing tiers.

J2EE component

A self-contained functional software unit supported by a container and configurable at deployment time. The J2EE specification defines the following J2EE components:

- Application clients and applets are components that run on the client.

- Java servlet and JavaServer Pages (JSP) technology components are Web components that run on the server.

- Enterprise JavaBeans (EJB) components (enterprise beans) are business components that run on the server.

J2EE components are written in the Java programming language and are compiled in the same way as any program in the language. The difference between J2EE components and "standard" Java classes is that J2EE components are assembled into a J2EE application, verified to be well formed and in compliance with the J2EE specification, and deployed to production, where they are run and managed by the J2EE server or client container.

J2EE module

A software unit that consists of one or more J2EE components of the same container type and one deployment descriptor of that type. There are four types of modules: EJB, Web, application client, and resource adapter. Modules can be deployed as stand-alone units or can be assembled into a J2EE application.

J2EE product

An implementation that conforms to the J2EE platform specification.

J2EE product provider

A vendor that supplies a J2EE product.

J2EE server

The runtime portion of a J2EE product. A J2EE server provides EJB or Web containers or both.

J2ME

See *Java 2 Platform, Micro Edition*.

J2SE

See *Java 2 Platform, Standard Edition*.

JAR

Java archive. A platform-independent file format that permits many files to be aggregated into one file.

Java 2 Platform, Enterprise Edition (J2EE)

An environment for developing and deploying enterprise applications. The J2EE platform consists of a set of services, application programming interfaces (APIs), and protocols that provide the functionality for developing multitiered, Web-based applications.

Java 2 Platform, Micro Edition (J2ME)

A highly optimized Java runtime environment targeting a wide range of consumer products, including pagers, cellular phones, screen phones, digital settop boxes, and car navigation systems.

Java 2 Platform, Standard Edition (J2SE)

The core Java technology platform.

Java API for XML Processing (JAXP)

An API for processing XML documents. JAXP leverages the parser standards SAX and DOM so that you can choose to parse your data as a stream of events or to build a tree-structured representation of it. JAXP supports the XSLT standard, giving you control over the presentation of the data and enabling you to convert the data to other XML documents or to other formats, such as HTML. JAXP provides namespace support, allowing you to work with schema that might otherwise have naming conflicts.

Java API for XML Registries (JAXR)

An API for accessing various kinds of XML registries.

Java API for XML-based RPC (JAX-RPC)

An API for building Web services and clients that use remote procedure calls and XML.

Java IDL

A technology that provides CORBA interoperability and connectivity capabilities for the J2EE platform. These capabilities enable J2EE applications to invoke operations on remote network services using the Object Management Group IDL and IIOP.

Java Message Service (JMS)

An API for invoking operations on enterprise messaging systems.

Java Naming and Directory Interface (JNDI)

An API that provides naming and directory functionality.

Java Secure Socket Extension (JSSE)

A set of packages that enable secure Internet communications.

Java Transaction API (JTA)

An API that allows applications and J2EE servers to access transactions.

Java Transaction Service (JTS)

Specifies the implementation of a transaction manager that supports JTA and implements the Java mapping of the Object Management Group Object Transaction Service 1.1 specification at the level below the API.

JavaBeans component

A Java class that can be manipulated by tools and composed into applications. A JavaBeans component must adhere to certain property and event interface conventions.

JavaMail

An API for sending and receiving email.

JavaServer Faces

A framework for building server-side user interfaces for Web applications written in the Java programming language.

JavaServer Faces conversion model

A mechanism for converting between string-based markup generated by Java-Server Faces UI components and server-side Java objects.

JavaServer Faces event and listener model

A mechanism for determining how events emitted by JavaServer Faces UI components are handled. This model is based on the JavaBeans component event and listener model.

JavaServer Faces expression language

A simple expression language used by a JavaServer Faces UI component tag attributes to bind the associated component to a bean property or to bind the associated component's value to a method or an external data source, such as a bean property. Unlike JSP EL expressions, JavaServer Faces EL expressions are evaluated by the JavaServer Faces implementation rather than by the Web container.

JavaServer Faces navigation model

A mechanism for defining the sequence in which pages in a JavaServer Faces application are displayed.

JavaServer Faces UI component

A user interface control that outputs data to a client or allows a user to input data to a JavaServer Faces application.

JavaServer Faces UI component class

A JavaServer Faces class that defines the behavior and properties of a Java-Server Faces UI component.

JavaServer Faces validation model

A mechanism for validating the data a user inputs to a JavaServer Faces UI component.

JavaServer Pages (JSP)

An extensible Web technology that uses static data, JSP elements, and server-side Java objects to generate dynamic content for a client. Typically the static data is HTML or XML elements, and in many cases the client is a Web browser.

JavaServer Pages Standard Tag Library (JSTL)

A tag library that encapsulates core functionality common to many JSP applications. JSTL has support for common, structural tasks such as iteration and conditionals, tags for manipulating XML documents, internationalization and locale-specific formatting tags, SQL tags, and functions.

JAXR client

A client program that uses the JAXR API to access a business registry via a JAXR provider.

JAXR provider

An implementation of the JAXR API that provides access to a specific registry provider or to a class of registry providers that are based on a common specification.

JDBC

An API for database-independent connectivity between the J2EE platform and a wide range of data sources.

JMS

See *Java Message Service*.

JMS administered object

A preconfigured JMS object (a resource manager connection factory or a destination) created by an administrator for the use of JMS clients and placed in a JNDI namespace.

JMS application

One or more JMS clients that exchange messages.

JMS client

A Java language program that sends or receives messages.

JMS provider

A messaging system that implements the Java Message Service as well as other administrative and control functionality needed in a full-featured messaging product.

JMS session

A single-threaded context for sending and receiving JMS messages. A JMS session can be nontransacted, locally transacted, or participating in a distributed transaction.

JNDI

See *Java Naming and Directory Interface*.

JSP

See *JavaServer Pages*.

JSP action

A JSP element that can act on implicit objects and other server-side objects or can define new scripting variables. Actions follow the XML syntax for elements, with a start tag, a body, and an end tag; if the body is empty it can also use the empty tag syntax. The tag must use a prefix. There are standard and custom actions.

JSP container

A container that provides the same services as a servlet container and an engine that interprets and processes JSP pages into a servlet.

JSP container, distributed

A JSP container that can run a Web application that is tagged as distributable and is spread across multiple Java virtual machines that might be running on different hosts.

JSP custom action

A user-defined action described in a portable manner by a tag library descriptor and imported into a JSP page by a `taglib` directive. Custom actions are used to encapsulate recurring tasks in writing JSP pages.

JSP custom tag

A tag that references a JSP custom action.

JSP declaration

A JSP scripting element that declares methods, variables, or both in a JSP page.

JSP directive

A JSP element that gives an instruction to the JSP container and is interpreted at translation time.

JSP document

A JSP page written in XML syntax and subject to the constraints of XML documents.

JSP element

A portion of a JSP page that is recognized by a JSP translator. An element can be a directive, an action, or a scripting element.

JSP expression

A scripting element that contains a valid scripting language expression that is evaluated, converted to a `String`, and placed into the implicit `out` object.

JSP expression language

A language used to write expressions that access the properties of JavaBeans components. EL expressions can be used in static text and in any standard or custom tag attribute that can accept an expression.

JSP page

A text-based document containing static text and JSP elements that describes how to process a request to create a response. A JSP page is translated into and handles requests as a servlet.

JSP scripting element

A JSP declaration, scriptlet, or expression whose syntax is defined by the JSP specification and whose content is written according to the scripting language used in the JSP page. The JSP specification describes the syntax and semantics for the case where the language page attribute is `"java"`.

JSP scriptlet

A JSP scripting element containing any code fragment that is valid in the scripting language used in the JSP page. The JSP specification describes what is a valid scriptlet for the case where the language page attribute is `"java"`.

JSP standard action

An action that is defined in the JSP specification and is always available to a JSP page.

JSP tag file

A source file containing a reusable fragment of JSP code that is translated into a tag handler when a JSP page is translated into a servlet.

JSP tag handler

A Java programming language object that implements the behavior of a custom tag.

JSP tag library

A collection of custom tags described via a tag library descriptor and Java classes.

JSTL

See *JavaServer Pages Standard Tag Library.*

JTA

See *Java Transaction API.*

JTS

See *Java Transaction Service.*

keystore

A file containing the keys and certificates used for authentication.

life cycle (J2EE component)

The framework events of a J2EE component's existence. Each type of component has defining events that mark its transition into states in which it has varying availability for use. For example, a servlet is created and has its `init` method called by its container before invocation of its service method by clients or other servlets that require its functionality. After the call of its `init` method, it has the data and readiness for its intended use. The servlet's `destroy` method is called by its container before the ending of its existence so that processing associated with winding up can be done and resources can be released. The `init` and `destroy` methods in this example are callback methods. Similar considerations apply to the life cycle of all J2EE component types: enterprise beans, Web components (servlets or JSP pages), applets, and application clients.

life cycle (JavaServer Faces)

A set of phases during which a request for a page is received, a UI component tree representing the page is processed, and a response is produced. During the phases of the life cycle:

- The local data of the components is updated with the values contained in the request parameters.

- Events generated by the components are processed.

- Validators and converters registered on the components are processed.

- The components' local data is updated to back-end objects.

- The response is rendered to the client while the component state of the response is saved on the server for future requests.

local subset

That part of the DTD that is defined within the current XML file.

managed bean creation facility

A mechanism for defining the characteristics of JavaBeans components used in a JavaServer Faces application.

message

In the Java Message Service, an asynchronous request, report, or event that is created, sent, and consumed by an enterprise application and not by a human. It contains vital information needed to coordinate enterprise applications, in the form of precisely formatted data that describes specific business actions.

message consumer

An object created by a JMS session that is used for receiving messages sent to a destination.

message-driven bean

An enterprise bean that is an asynchronous message consumer. A message-driven bean has no state for a specific client, but its instance variables can contain state across the handling of client messages, including an open database connection and an object reference to an EJB object. A client accesses a message-driven bean by sending messages to the destination for which the bean is a message listener.

message producer

An object created by a JMS session that is used for sending messages to a destination.

mixed-content model

A DTD specification that defines an element as containing a mixture of text and one or more other element. The specification must start with #PCDATA, followed by diverse elements, and must end with the "zero-or-more" asterisk symbol (*).

method-binding expression

A JavaServer Faces EL expression that refers to a method of a backing bean. This method performs either event handling, validation, or navigation processing for the UI component whose tag uses the method-binding expression.

method permission

An authorization rule that determines who is permitted to execute one or more enterprise bean methods.

mutual authentication

An authentication mechanism employed by two parties for the purpose of proving each other's identity to one another.

namespace

A standard that lets you specify a unique label for the set of element names defined by a DTD. A document using that DTD can be included in any other document without having a conflict between element names. The elements defined in your DTD are then uniquely identified so that, for example, the parser can tell when an element <name> should be interpreted according to your DTD rather than using the definition for an element <name> in a different DTD.

naming context

A set of associations between unique, atomic, people-friendly identifiers and objects.

naming environment

A mechanism that allows a component to be customized without the need to access or change the component's source code. A container implements the component's naming environment and provides it to the component as a JNDI naming context. Each component names and accesses its environment entries using the java:comp/env JNDI context. The environment entries are declaratively specified in the component's deployment descriptor.

normalization

The process of removing redundancy by modularizing, as with subroutines, and of removing superfluous differences by reducing them to a common denominator. For example, line endings from different systems are normalized by reducing them to a single new line, and multiple whitespace characters are normalized to one space.

North American Industry Classification System (NAICS)

A system for classifying business establishments based on the processes they use to produce goods or services.

notation

A mechanism for defining a data format for a non-XML document referenced as an unparsed entity. This is a holdover from SGML. A newer standard is to use MIME data types and namespaces to prevent naming conflicts.

OASIS

Organization for the Advancement of Structured Information Standards. A consortium that drives the development, convergence, and adoption of e-business standards. Its Web site is `http://www.oasis-open.org/`. The DTD repository it sponsors is at `http://www.XML.org`.

OMG

Object Management Group. A consortium that produces and maintains computer industry specifications for interoperable enterprise applications. Its Web site is `http://www.omg.org/`.

one-way messaging

A method of transmitting messages without having to block until a response is received.

ORB

Object request broker. A library that enables CORBA objects to locate and communicate with one another.

OS principal

A principal native to the operating system on which the J2EE platform is executing.

OTS

Object Transaction Service. A definition of the interfaces that permit CORBA objects to participate in transactions.

parameter entity

An entity that consists of DTD specifications, as distinct from a general entity. A parameter entity defined in the DTD can then be referenced at other points, thereby eliminating the need to recode the definition at each location it is used.

parsed entity

A general entity that contains XML and therefore is parsed when inserted into the XML document, as opposed to an unparsed entity.

parser

A module that reads in XML data from an input source and breaks it into chunks so that your program knows when it is working with a tag, an attribute, or element data. A nonvalidating parser ensures that the XML data is well formed but does not verify that it is valid. See also *validating parser.*

passivation

The process of transferring an enterprise bean from memory to secondary storage. See *activation.*

persistence

The protocol for transferring the state of an entity bean between its instance variables and an underlying database.

persistent field

A virtual field of an entity bean that has container-managed persistence; it is stored in a database.

POA

Portable Object Adapter. A CORBA standard for building server-side applications that are portable across heterogeneous ORBs.

point-to-point messaging system

A messaging system built on the concept of message queues. Each message is addressed to a specific queue; clients extract messages from the queues established to hold their messages.

primary key

An object that uniquely identifies an entity bean within a home.

principal

The identity assigned to a user as a result of authentication.

privilege

A security attribute that does not have the property of uniqueness and that can be shared by many principals.

processing instruction

Information contained in an XML structure that is intended to be interpreted by a specific application.

programmatic security

Security decisions that are made by security-aware applications. Programmatic security is useful when declarative security alone is not sufficient to express the security model of an application.

prolog

The part of an XML document that precedes the XML data. The prolog includes the declaration and an optional DTD.

public key certificate

Used in client-certificate authentication to enable the server, and optionally the client, to authenticate each other. The public key certificate is the digital equivalent of a passport. It is issued by a trusted organization, called a certificate authority, and provides identification for the bearer.

publish/subscribe messaging system

A messaging system in which clients address messages to a specific node in a content hierarchy, called a topic. Publishers and subscribers are generally anonymous and can dynamically publish or subscribe to the content hierarchy. The system takes care of distributing the messages arriving from a node's multiple publishers to its multiple subscribers.

query string

A component of an HTTP request URL that contains a set of parameters and values that affect the handling of the request.

queue

See *point-to-point messaging system*.

RAR

Resource Adapter Archive. A JAR archive that contains a resource adapter module.

RDF

Resource Description Framework. A standard for defining the kind of data that an XML file contains. Such information can help ensure semantic integrity; for example, by helping to make sure that a date is treated as a date rather than simply as text.

RDF schema

A standard for specifying consistency rules that apply to the specifications contained in an RDF.

realm

See *security policy domain*. Also, a string, passed as part of an HTTP request during basic authentication, that defines a protection space. The protected resources on a server can be partitioned into a set of protection spaces, each with its own authentication scheme or authorization database or both.

In the J2EE server authentication service, a realm is a complete database of roles, users, and groups that identify valid users of a Web application or a set of Web applications.

reentrant entity bean

An entity bean that can handle multiple simultaneous, interleaved, or nested invocations that will not interfere with each other.

reference

See *entity reference*.

registry

An infrastructure that enables the building, deployment, and discovery of Web services. It is a neutral third party that facilitates dynamic and loosely coupled business-to-business (B2B) interactions.

registry provider

An implementation of a business registry that conforms to a specification for XML registries (for example, ebXML or UDDI).

relationship field

A virtual field of an entity bean having container-managed persistence; it identifies a related entity bean.

remote interface

One of two interfaces for an enterprise bean. The remote interface defines the business methods callable by a client.

remove method

Method defined in the home interface and invoked by a client to destroy an enterprise bean.

render kit

A set of renderers that render output to a particular client. The JavaServer Faces implementation provides a standard HTML render kit, which is composed of renderers that can render HMTL markup.

renderer

A Java class that can render the output for a set of JavaServer Faces UI components.

request-response messaging

A method of messaging that includes blocking until a response is received.

resource adapter

A system-level software driver that is used by an EJB container or an application client to connect to an enterprise information system. A resource adapter typically is specific to an enterprise information system. It is available as a library and is used within the address space of the server or client using it. A resource adapter plugs in to a container. The application components deployed on the container then use the client API (exposed by the adapter) or tool-generated high-level abstractions to access the underlying enterprise information system. The resource adapter and EJB container collaborate to provide the underlying mechanisms—transactions, security, and connection pooling—for connectivity to the enterprise information system.

resource adapter module

A deployable unit that contains all Java interfaces, classes, and native libraries, implementing a resource adapter along with the resource adapter deployment descriptor.

resource manager

Provides access to a set of shared resources. A resource manager participates in transactions that are externally controlled and coordinated by a transaction manager. A resource manager typically is in a different address space or on a different machine from the clients that access it. Note: An enterprise information system is referred to as a resource manager when it is mentioned in the context of resource and transaction management.

resource manager connection

An object that represents a session with a resource manager.

resource manager connection factory

An object used for creating a resource manager connection.

RMI

Remote Method Invocation. A technology that allows an object running in one Java virtual machine to invoke methods on an object running in a different Java virtual machine.

RMI-IIOP

A version of RMI implemented to use the CORBA IIOP protocol. RMI over IIOP provides interoperability with CORBA objects implemented in any language if all the remote interfaces are originally defined as RMI interfaces.

role (development)

The function performed by a party in the development and deployment phases of an application developed using J2EE technology. The roles are application component provider, application assembler, deployer, J2EE product provider, EJB container provider, EJB server provider, Web container provider, Web server provider, tool provider, and system administrator.

role mapping

The process of associating the groups or principals (or both), recognized by the container with security roles specified in the deployment descriptor. Security roles must be mapped by the deployer before a component is installed in the server.

role (security)

An abstract logical grouping of users that is defined by the application assembler. When an application is deployed, the roles are mapped to security identities, such as principals or groups, in the operational environment.

In the J2EE server authentication service, a role is an abstract name for permission to access a particular set of resources. A role can be compared to a key that can open a lock. Many people might have a copy of the key; the lock doesn't care who you are, only that you have the right key.

rollback

The point in a transaction when all updates to any resources involved in the transaction are reversed.

root

The outermost element in an XML document. The element that contains all other elements.

SAX

See *Simple API for XML*.

schema

A database-inspired method for specifying constraints on XML documents using an XML-based language. Schemas address deficiencies in DTDs, such as the inability to put constraints on the kinds of data that can occur in a particular field. Because schemas are founded on XML, they are hierarchical. Thus it is easier to create an unambiguous specification, and it is possible to determine the scope over which a comment is meant to apply.

Secure Socket Layer (SSL)

A technology that allows Web browsers and Web servers to communicate over a secured connection.

security attributes

A set of properties associated with a principal. Security attributes can be associated with a principal by an authentication protocol or by a J2EE product provider or both.

security constraint

A declarative way to annotate the intended protection of Web content. A security constraint consists of a Web resource collection, an authorization constraint, and a user data constraint.

security context

An object that encapsulates the shared state information regarding security between two entities.

security permission

A mechanism defined by J2SE, and used by the J2EE platform to express the programming restrictions imposed on application component developers.

security permission set

The minimum set of security permissions that a J2EE product provider must provide for the execution of each component type.

security policy domain

A scope over which security policies are defined and enforced by a security administrator. A security policy domain has a collection of users (or principals), uses a well-defined authentication protocol or protocols for authenticating users (or principals), and may have groups to simplify setting of security policies.

security role

See *role (security)*.

security technology domain

A scope over which the same security mechanism is used to enforce a security policy. Multiple security policy domains can exist within a single technology domain.

security view

The set of security roles defined by the application assembler.

server certificate

Used with the HTTPS protocol to authenticate Web applications. The certificate can be self-signed or approved by a certificate authority (CA). The HTTPS service of the Sun Java System Application Server Platform Edition 8 will not run unless a server certificate has been installed.

server principal

The OS principal that the server is executing as.

service element

A representation of the combination of one or more Connector components that share a single engine component for processing incoming requests.

service endpoint interface

A Java interface that declares the methods that a client can invoke on a Web service.

servlet

A Java program that extends the functionality of a Web server, generating dynamic content and interacting with Web applications using a request-response paradigm.

servlet container

A container that provides the network services over which requests and responses are sent, decodes requests, and formats responses. All servlet containers must support HTTP as a protocol for requests and responses but can also support additional request-response protocols, such as HTTPS.

servlet container, distributed

A servlet container that can run a Web application that is tagged as distributable and that executes across multiple Java virtual machines running on the same host or on different hosts.

servlet context

An object that contains a servlet's view of the Web application within which the servlet is running. Using the context, a servlet can log events, obtain URL references to resources, and set and store attributes that other servlets in the context can use.

servlet mapping

Defines an association between a URL pattern and a servlet. The mapping is used to map requests to servlets.

session

An object used by a servlet to track a user's interaction with a Web application across multiple HTTP requests.

session bean

An enterprise bean that is created by a client and that usually exists only for the duration of a single client-server session. A session bean performs operations, such as calculations or database access, for the client. Although a session bean can be transactional, it is not recoverable should a system crash occur. Session bean objects either can be stateless or can maintain conversational state across methods and transactions. If a session bean maintains state, then the EJB container manages this state if the object must be removed from memory. However, the session bean object itself must manage its own persistent data.

Simple API for XML

An event-driven interface in which the parser invokes one of several methods supplied by the caller when a parsing event occurs. Events include recognizing an XML tag, finding an error, encountering a reference to an external entity, or processing a DTD specification.

SGML

Standard Generalized Markup Language. The parent of both HTML and XML. Although HTML shares SGML's propensity for embedding presentation information in the markup, XML is a standard that allows information content to be totally separated from the mechanisms for rendering that content.

SOAP

Simple Object Access Protocol. A lightweight protocol intended for exchanging structured information in a decentralized, distributed environment. It defines, using XML technologies, an extensible messaging framework containing a message construct that can be exchanged over a variety of underlying protocols.

SOAP with Attachments API for Java (SAAJ)

The basic package for SOAP messaging, SAAJ contains the API for creating and populating a SOAP message.

SQL

Structured Query Language. The standardized relational database language for defining database objects and manipulating data.

SQL/J

A set of standards that includes specifications for embedding SQL statements in methods in the Java programming language and specifications for calling Java static methods as SQL-stored procedures and user-defined functions. An SQL checker can detect errors in static SQL statements at program development time, rather than at execution time as with a JDBC driver.

SSL

Secure Socket Layer. A security protocol that provides privacy over the Internet. The protocol allows client-server applications to communicate in a way that cannot be eavesdropped on or tampered with. Servers are always authenticated, and clients are optionally authenticated.

stateful session bean

A session bean with a conversational state.

stateless session bean

A session bean with no conversational state. All instances of a stateless session bean are identical.

system administrator

The person responsible for configuring and administering the enterprise's computers, networks, and software systems.

tag

In XML documents, a piece of text that describes a unit of data or an element. The tag is distinguishable as markup, as opposed to data, because it is surrounded by angle brackets (< and >). To treat such markup syntax as data, you use an entity reference or a CDATA section.

template

A set of formatting instructions that apply to the nodes selected by an XPath expression.

tool provider

An organization or software vendor that provides tools used for the development, packaging, and deployment of J2EE applications.

topic

See *publish-subscribe messaging system.*

transaction

An atomic unit of work that modifies data. A transaction encloses one or more program statements, all of which either complete or roll back. Transactions enable multiple users to access the same data concurrently.

transaction attribute

A value specified in an enterprise bean's deployment descriptor that is used by the EJB container to control the transaction scope when the enterprise bean's methods are invoked. A transaction attribute can have the following values: `Required`, `RequiresNew`, `Supports`, `NotSupported`, `Mandatory`, or `Never`.

transaction isolation level

The degree to which the intermediate state of the data being modified by a transaction is visible to other concurrent transactions and data being modified by other transactions is visible to it.

transaction manager

Provides the services and management functions required to support transaction demarcation, transactional resource management, synchronization, and transaction context propagation.

Unicode

A standard defined by the Unicode Consortium that uses a 16-bit code page that maps digits to characters in languages around the world. Because 16 bits covers 32,768 codes, Unicode is large enough to include all the world's languages, with the exception of ideographic languages that have a different character for every concept, such as Chinese. For more information, see `http://www.unicode.org/`.

Universal Description, Discovery and Integration (UDDI) project

An industry initiative to create a platform-independent, open framework for describing services, discovering businesses, and integrating business services using the Internet, as well as a registry. It is being developed by a vendor consortium.

Universal Standard Products and Services Classification (UNSPSC)

A schema that classifies and identifies commodities. It is used in sell-side and buy-side catalogs and as a standardized account code in analyzing expenditure.

unparsed entity

A general entity that contains something other than XML. By its nature, an unparsed entity contains binary data.

URI

Uniform resource identifier. A globally unique identifier for an abstract or physical resource. A URL is a kind of URI that specifies the retrieval protocol (`http` or `https` for Web applications) and physical location of a resource (host name and host-relative path). A URN is another type of URI.

URL

Uniform resource locator. A standard for writing a textual reference to an arbitrary piece of data in the World Wide Web. A URL looks like this: `protocol://host/localinfo` where `protocol` specifies a protocol for fetching the object (such as `http` or `ftp`), `host` specifies the Internet name of the targeted host, and `localinfo` is a string (often a file name) passed to the protocol handler on the remote host.

URL path

The part of a URL passed by an HTTP request to invoke a servlet. A URL path consists of the context path + servlet path + path info, where

- Context path is the path prefix associated with a servlet context of which the servlet is a part. If this context is the default context rooted at the base of the Web server's URL namespace, the path prefix will be an empty string. Otherwise, the path prefix starts with a / character but does not end with a / character.

- Servlet path is the path section that directly corresponds to the mapping that activated this request. This path starts with a / character.

- Path info is the part of the request path that is not part of the context path or the servlet path.

URN

Uniform resource name. A unique identifier that identifies an entity but doesn't tell where it is located. A system can use a URN to look up an entity locally before trying to find it on the Web. It also allows the Web location to change, while still allowing the entity to be found.

user data constraint

Indicates how data between a client and a Web container should be protected. The protection can be the prevention of tampering with the data or prevention of eavesdropping on the data.

user (security)

An individual (or application program) identity that has been authenticated. A user can have a set of roles associated with that identity, which entitles the user to access all resources protected by those roles.

valid

A valid XML document, in addition to being well formed, conforms to all the constraints imposed by a DTD. It does not contain any tags that are not permitted by the DTD, and the order of the tags conforms to the DTD's specifications.

validating parser

A parser that ensures that an XML document is valid in addition to being well formed. See also *parser*.

value-binding expression

A JavaServer Faces EL expression that refers to a property of a backing bean. A component tag uses this expression to bind the associated component's value or the component instance to the bean property. If the component tag refers to the property via its `value` attribute, then the component's value is bound to the property. If the component tag refers to the property via its `binding` attribute, then the component itself is bound to the property.

virtual host

Multiple hosts plus domain names mapped to a single IP address.

W3C

World Wide Web Consortium. The international body that governs Internet standards. Its Web site is `http://www.w3.org/`.

WAR file

Web application archive file. A JAR archive that contains a Web module.

warning

A SAX parser warning is generated when the document's DTD contains duplicate definitions and in similar situations that are not necessarily an error but which the document author might like to know about, because they could be. See also *fatal error, error*.

Web application

An application written for the Internet, including those built with Java technologies such as JavaServer Pages and servlets, as well as those built with non-Java technologies such as CGI and Perl.

Web application, distributable

A Web application that uses J2EE technology written so that it can be deployed in a Web container distributed across multiple Java virtual machines running on the same host or different hosts. The deployment descriptor for such an application uses the `distributable` element.

Web component

A component that provides services in response to requests; either a servlet or a JSP page.

Web container

A container that implements the Web component contract of the J2EE architecture. This contract specifies a runtime environment for Web components that includes security, concurrency, life-cycle management, transaction, deployment, and other services. A Web container provides the same services as a JSP container as well as a federated view of the J2EE platform APIs. A Web container is provided by a Web or J2EE server.

Web container, distributed

A Web container that can run a Web application that is tagged as distributable and that executes across multiple Java virtual machines running on the same host or on different hosts.

Web container provider

A vendor that supplies a Web container.

Web module

A deployable unit that consists of one or more Web components, other resources, and a Web application deployment descriptor contained in a hierarchy of directories and files in a standard Web application format.

Web resource

A static or dynamic object contained in a Web application that can be referenced by a URL.

Web resource collection

A list of URL patterns and HTTP methods that describe a set of Web resources to be protected.

Web server

Software that provides services to access the Internet, an intranet, or an extranet. A Web server hosts Web sites, provides support for HTTP and other protocols, and executes server-side programs (such as CGI scripts or servlets) that perform certain functions. In the J2EE architecture, a Web server provides services to a Web container. For example, a Web container typically relies on a Web server to provide HTTP message handling. The J2EE architecture assumes that a Web container is hosted by a Web server from the same vendor, so it does not specify the contract between these two entities. A Web server can host one or more Web containers.

Web server provider

A vendor that supplies a Web server.

Web service

An application that exists in a distributed environment, such as the Internet. A Web service accepts a request, performs its function based on the request, and returns a response. The request and the response can be part of the same operation, or they can occur separately, in which case the consumer does not need to wait for a response. Both the request and the response usually take the form of XML, a portable data-interchange format, and are delivered over a wire protocol, such as HTTP.

well-formed

An XML document that is syntactically correct. It does not have any angle brackets that are not part of tags, all tags have an ending tag or are themselves self-ending, and all tags are fully nested. Knowing that a document is well formed makes it possible to process it. However, a well-formed document may not be valid. To determine that, you need a validating parser and a DTD.

Xalan

An interpreting version of XSLT.

XHTML

An XML look-alike for HTML defined by one of several XHTML DTDs. To use XHTML for everything would, of course, defeat the purpose of XML, because the idea of XML is to identify information content, and not just to tell how to display it. You can reference it in a DTD, which allows you to say, for example, that the text in an element can contain <em> and <b> tags rather than being limited to plain text.

XLink

The part of the XLL specification that is concerned with specifying links between documents.

XLL

The XML Link Language specification, consisting of XLink and XPointer.

XML

Extensible Markup Language. A markup language that allows you to define the tags (markup) needed to identify the content, data, and text in XML documents. It differs from HTML, the markup language most often used to present information on the Internet. HTML has fixed tags that deal mainly with style or presentation. An XML document must undergo a transformation into a language with style tags under the control of a style sheet before it can be presented by a browser or other presentation mechanism. Two types of style sheets used with XML are CSS and XSL. Typically, XML is transformed into HTML for presentation. Although tags can be defined as needed in the generation of an XML document, a document type definition (DTD) can be used to define the elements allowed in a particular type of document. A document can be compared by using the rules in the DTD to determine its validity and to locate particular elements in the document. A Web services application's J2EE deployment descriptors are expressed in XML with schemas defining allowed elements. Programs for processing XML documents use SAX or DOM APIs.

XML registry

See *registry*.

XML Schema

The W3C specification for defining the structure, content, and semantics of XML documents.

XPath

An addressing mechanism for identifying the parts of an XML document.

XPointer

The part of the XLL specification that is concerned with identifying sections of documents so that they can be referenced in links or included in other documents.

XSL

Extensible Stylesheet Language. A standard that lets you do the following:

- Specify an addressing mechanism, so that you can identify the parts of an XML document that a transformation applies to (XPath).

- Specify tag conversions, so that you can convert XML data into different formats (XSLT).

- Specify display characteristics, such page sizes, margins, and font heights and widths, as well as the flow objects on each page. Information fills in one area of a page and then automatically flows to the next object when that area fills up. That allows you to wrap text around pictures, for example, or to continue a newsletter article on a different page (XSL-FO).

XSL-FO

A subcomponent of XSL used for describing font sizes, page layouts, and how information flows from one page to another.

XSLT

XSL Transformations. An XML document that controls the transformation of an XML document into another XML document or HTML. The target document often has presentation-related tags dictating how it will be rendered by a browser or other presentation mechanism. XSLT was formerly a part of XSL, which also included a tag language of style flow objects.

XSLTC

A compiling version of XSLT.

About the Authors

Java API for XML Processing

Eric Armstrong has been programming and writing professionally since before there were personal computers. His production experience includes artificial intelligence (AI) programs, system libraries, real-time programs, and business applications in a variety of languages. He is a contributor to *JavaWorld*. He wrote *The JBuilder2 Bible*, as well as Sun's Java XML programming tutorial. For a time, Eric was involved in efforts to design next-generation collaborative discussion/decision systems. His learn-by-ear, see-the-fingering music teaching program is currently on hold while he finishes a weight-training book. His Web site is http://www.treelight.com.

JavaServer Faces Technology and JavaServer Pages Documents

Jennifer Ball is a staff writer at Sun Microsystems, where she documents JavaServer Faces technology. Previously she documented the Java2D API, deploytool, and JAXB. She holds a master's degree in Interdisciplinary Computer Science from Mills College.

Web Applications and Technology

Stephanie Bodoff is a staff writer at Sun Microsystems. In previous positions she worked as a software engineer on distributed computing and telecommunications systems and object-oriented software development methods. Since her conversion to technical writing, Stephanie has documented enterprise application development methods, object-oriented databases, application servers, and Web technologies. She is a coauthor of *Designing Enterprise Applications with the Java™ 2 Platform, Enterprise Edition*, and *Object-Oriented Software Development: The Fusion Method*.

Security

Debbie Bode Carson is a staff writer with Sun Microsystems, where she documents the J2EE, J2SE, and Java Web Services platforms. In previous positions she documented creating database applications using C++ and Java technologies and creating distributed applications using Java technology.

Eric Jendrock is a staff writer with Sun Microsystems, where he documents the J2EE platform and Java Web Services. Previously, he documented middleware products and standards. Currently, he writes about the Java Web Services Developer Pack, the Java Architecture for XML Binding, and the J2EE platform and Web security.

Java API for RPC-based XML, Enterprise JavaBeans Technology

Dale Green is a staff writer with Sun Microsystems, where he documents the J2EE platform and the Java API for RPC-based XML. In previous positions he programmed business applications, designed databases, taught technical classes, and documented RDBMS products. He wrote the Internationalization and Reflection trails for *The Java™ Tutorial Continued*.

Ian Evans is a staff writer and editor at Sun Microsystems, where he documents the J2EE and Java Web Services platforms and edits the J2EE platform specifications. In previous positions he documented programming tools, CORBA middleware, and Java application servers, and taught classes on UNIX, Web programming, and server-side Java development.

Java API for XML Registries, SOAP with Attachments API for Java, Java Message Service API

Kim Haase is a staff writer with Sun Microsystems, where she documents the J2EE platform and Java Web Services. In previous positions she documented compilers, debuggers, and floating-point programming. She currently writes about the Java Message Service, the Java API for XML Registries, and SOAP with Attachments API for Java.

Index

The Java™ Series

ISBN 0-201-63456-2 ISBN 0-201-70433-1 ISBN 0-201-31005-8 ISBN 0-321-24575-X ISBN 0-201-70393-9 ISBN 0-201-48558-3

ISBN 0-201-74622-0 ISBN 0-201-75280-8 ISBN 0-201-76810-0 ISBN 0-201-31002-3 ISBN 0-201-31003-1 ISBN 0-201-48552-4

ISBN 0-201-71102-8 ISBN 0-201-70329-7 ISBN 0-201-30955-6 ISBN 0-201-31008-2 ISBN 0-201-78472-6 ISBN 0-201-78791-1

ISBN 0-201-31009-0 ISBN 0-201-70502-8 ISBN 0-201-32577-2 ISBN 0-201-43294-3 ISBN 0-201-91466-2

ISBN 0-321-19801-8 ISBN 0-201-74627-1 ISBN 0-201-70456-0 ISBN 0-201-77580-8 ISBN 0-201-78790-3

ISBN 0-201-77582-4 ISBN 0-201-91467-0 ISBN 0-201-70969-4 ISBN 0-321-17384-8

Visit www.awprofessional.com/javaseries for more information on these titles.

informIT

CD-ROM Warranty

Addison-Wesley and Sun Microsystems warrant the enclosed CD-ROM to be free of defects in materials and faulty workmanship under normal use for a period of ninety days after purchase (when purchased new). If a defect is discovered in the CD-ROM during this warranty period, a replacement CD-ROM can be obtained at no charge by sending the defective CD-ROM, postage prepaid, with proof of purchase to:

Disc Exchange
Addison-Wesley Professional
Pearson Technology Group
75 Arlington Street, Suite 300
Boston, MA 02116
Email: AWPro@aw.com

Addison-Wesley and Sun Microsystems make no warranty or representation, either expressed or implied, with respect to this software, its quality, performance, merchantability, or fitness for a particular purpose. In no event will Addison-Wesley, Sun Microsystems, their distributors, or dealers be liable for direct, indirect, special, incidental, or consequential damages arising out of the use or inability to use the software. The exclusion of implied warranties is not permitted in some states. Therefore, the above exclusion may not apply to you. This warranty provides you with specific legal rights. There may be other rights that you may have that vary from state to state. The contents of this CD-ROM are intended for personal use only.

Java[TM] 2 Platform, Enterprise Edition 1.4 SDK
Binary Code License Agreement

READ THE TERMS OF THIS AGREEMENT AND ANY PROVIDED SUPPLEMEN-TAL LICENSE TERMS (COLLECTIVELY "AGREEMENT") CAREFULLY BEFORE OPENING THE SOFTWARE MEDIA PACKAGE. BY OPENING THE SOFTWARE MEDIA PACKAGE, YOU AGREE TO THE TERMS OF THIS AGREEMENT. IF YOU DO NOT AGREE TO ALL OF THE TERMS OF THE AGREEMENT, DO NOT INSTALL, COPY OR OTHERWISE USE THE JAVA(TM) 2 PLATFORM, ENTER-PRISE EDITION 1.4 SDK ("SOFTWARE"). IF YOU ARE ACCESSING THE SOFT-WARE ELECTRONICALLY, INDICATE YOUR NON-ACCEPTANCE OF THE AGREEMENT BY SELECTING THE "REJECT" BUTTON OR OTHERWISE PRO-VIDING THE NEGATIVE RESPONSE REQUESTED. YOUR INSTALLATION, COPYING OR USE OF THE SOFTWARE INDICATES THAT YOU AGREE TO BE BOUND BY ALL THE TERMS OF THE AGREEMENT. If you are accepting the Agreement on behalf of a corporation, partnership or other legal entity, the use of the terms "you" and "your" in the Agreement will refer to such entity and the entity accepting the Agreement represents and warrants to Sun that it has sufficient permissions, capacity, consents and authority to enter into the Agreement. Sun Microsystems, Inc. Binary Code License Agreement ("BCL") THE TERMS OF THIS AGREEMENT AND ANY PRO-VIDED SUPPLEMENTAL LICENSE TERMS ARE COLLECTIVELY TERMED THE "AGREEMENT".

1. LICENSE TO USE. Sun grants you a non exclusive and non transferable license for the internal use only of the accompanying software and documentation and any error corrections provided by Sun (collectively "Software"), by the number of users and the class of computer hardware for which the corresponding fee has been paid.

2. RESTRICTIONS. Software is confidential and copyrighted. Title to Software and all associated intellectual property rights is retained by Sun and/or its licensors. Except as specifically authorized in any Supplemental License Terms, you may not make copies of Software, other than a single copy of Software for archival purposes. Unless enforcement is prohibited by applicable law, you may not modify, decompile, or reverse engineer Software. Licensee acknowledges that Licensed Software is not designed or intended for use in the design, construction, operation or maintenance of any nuclear facility. Sun Microsystems, Inc. disclaims any express or implied warranty of fitness for such uses. No right, title or interest in or to any trademark, service mark, logo or trade name of Sun or its licensors is granted under this Agreement.

3. LIMITED WARRANTY. Sun warrants to you that for a period of ninety (90) days from the date of purchase, as evidenced by a copy of the receipt, the media on which Software is furnished (if any) will be free of defects in materials and workmanship under normal use. Except for the foregoing, Software is provided "AS IS". Your exclusive remedy and Sun's entire liability under this limited warranty will be at Sun's option to replace Software media or refund the fee paid for Software.

4. DISCLAIMER OF WARRANTY. UNLESS SPECIFIED IN THIS AGREEMENT, ALL EXPRESS OR IMPLIED CONDITIONS, REPRESENTATIONS AND WARRANTIES, INCLUDING ANY IMPLIED WARRANTY OF MERCHANTABILITY, FITNESS FOR A PARTICULAR PURPOSE OR NON-INFRINGEMENT ARE DISCLAIMED, EXCEPT TO THE EXTENT THAT THESE DISCLAIMERS ARE HELD TO BE LEGALLY INVALID.

5. LIMITATION OF LIABILITY. TO THE EXTENT NOT PROHIBITED BY LAW, IN NO EVENT WILL SUN OR ITS LICENSORS BE LIABLE FOR ANY LOST REVENUE, PROFIT OR DATA, OR FOR SPECIAL, INDIRECT, CONSEQUENTIAL, INCIDEN-TAL OR PUNITIVE DAMAGES, HOWEVER CAUSED REGARDLESS OF THE THEORY OF LIABILITY, ARISING OUT OF OR RELATED TO THE USE OF OR INABILITY TO USE SOFTWARE, EVEN IF SUN HAS BEEN ADVISED OF THE POSSIBILITY OF SUCH DAMAGES. In no event will Sun's liability to you, whether in contract, tort (including negligence), or otherwise, exceed the amount paid by you for Software under this Agreement. The foregoing limitations will apply even if the above stated warranty fails of its essential purpose.

6. Termination. This Agreement is effective until terminated. You may terminate this Agreement at any time by destroying all copies of Software. This Agreement will termi-nate immediately without notice from Sun if you fail to comply with any provision of this Agreement. Upon Termination, you must destroy all copies of Software.

7. Export Regulations. All Software and technical data delivered under this Agreement are subject to US export control laws and may be subject to export or import regulations in other countries. You agree to comply strictly with all such laws and regulations and acknowledge that you have the responsibility to obtain such licenses to export, re-export, or import as may be required after delivery to you.

8. U.S. Government Restricted Rights. If Software is being acquired by or on behalf of the U.S. Government or by a U.S. Government prime contractor or subcontractor (at any tier), then the Government's rights in Software and accompanying documentation will be only as set forth in this Agreement; this is in accordance with 48 CFR 227.7201 through 227.7202-4 (for Department of Defense (DOD) acquisitions) and with 48 CFR 2.101 and 12.212 (for non-DOD acquisitions).

9. Governing Law. Any action related to this Agreement will be governed by California law and controlling U.S. federal law. No choice of law rules of any jurisdiction will apply.

10. Severability. If any provision of this Agreement is held to be unenforceable, this Agreement will remain in effect with the provision omitted, unless omission would frus-trate the intent of the parties, in which case this Agreement will immediately terminate.

11. Integration. This Agreement is the entire agreement between you and Sun relating to its subject matter. It supersedes all prior or contemporaneous oral or written communica-tions, proposals, representations and warranties and prevails over any conflicting or addi-tional terms of any quote, order, acknowledgment, or other communication between the parties relating to its subject matter during the term of this Agreement. No modification of

this Agreement will be binding, unless in writing and signed by an authorized representative of each party. For inquiries please contact: Sun Microsystems, Inc., 4150 Network Circle, Santa Clara, California 95054

Supplemental Terms for Java 2 Platform, Enterprise Edition 1.4 SDK

These terms and conditions for Java 2 Platform, Enterprise Edition 1.4 SDK supplement the terms of the Binary Code License Agreement ("BCL"). Capitalized terms not defined herein shall have the meanings ascribed to them in the BCL. These terms shall supersede any inconsistent or conflicting terms in the BCL.

1.License Grant

A. Internal Use and Development License. Subject to the terms and conditions of this Agreement and your complete acceptance of this Agreement, Sun grants to you a non-exclusive, non-transferable, royalty-free and limited license to:

(i) internally reproduce and use the binary form of Software; and

(ii) host Software for third parties, provided that you: (a) only permit access to Software subject to an agreement that protects Sun's interests consistent with the terms contained in this Agreement; and (b) agree to defend and indemnify Sun and its licensors from and against any damages, costs, liabilities, settlement amounts and /or expenses (including attorneys' fees) incurred in connection with any claim, lawsuit or action by any third party that arises or results from the hosting of Software. For the purposes of this section, internal use includes deployment of Software in a production environment.

B. Redistribution. This Agreement does not grant you the right to redistribute Software. Please refer to the following URL for information regarding the redistribution of Software if you are interested in redistribution:

http://sun.com/software/products/appsrvr/appsrvr_oem.html

2.Additional Use Conditions

A. Whenever you are explicitly permitted to copy or reproduce all or any part of Software, you shall reproduce and not efface any and all titles, trademark symbols, copyright symbols and legends, and other proprietary markings on or accompanying Software. You acknowledge and agree as between you and Sun that Sun owns the SUN, SOLARIS, JAVA, J2EE, JINI, FORTE, STAROFFICE, STARPORTAL and IPLANET- related trademarks, service marks, logos and other brand designations ("Sun Marks"), and you agree to comply with the Sun Trademark and Logo Usage Requirements currently located at http://www.sun.com/policies/trademarks. Any use you make of the Sun Marks inures to Sun's benefit.

B. Software may contain source code that is provided solely for reference purposes pursuant to the terms of this Agreement. Source code may not be redistributed unless expressly provided for in this Agreement.

C. "Bundled Software" means any and all additional software bundled with or embedded in the Software (including without limitation the Java Development Kit), if any, and delivered to you as part of the Software. You may not use any Bundled Software on a stand-alone basis or use any portion of the Bundled Software to interoperate with any program other than the Software. Except for this restriction and those found below, the use of each such bundled or embedded product shall be governed by its license agreement. If you desire to use such Sun or third party products on a stand-alone basis, you must purchase a separate license permitting such use.

D. You may copy and use the header files and class libraries ("Redistributables") solely to create and distribute programs to interface with Software APIs ("Programs") only as explicitly provided in Software documentation provided that you (i) distribute the Redistributables complete and unmodified and only bundled as part of your Programs, (ii) do not distribute additional software intended to replace any component(s) of the Redistributables, (iii) do not remove or alter any proprietary legends or notices contained in the Redistributables, (iv) only distribute the Redistributables subject to a license agreement that protects Sun's interests consistent with the terms contained in this Agreement, and (v) agree to defend and indemnify Sun and its licensors from and against any damages, costs, liabilities, settlement amounts and/or expenses (including attorneys' fees) incurred in connection with any claim, lawsuit or action by any third party that arises or results from the use or distribution of any and all Redistributables and/or Programs.

E. You may not modify the Java Platform Interface ("JPI" identified as classes contained within the "java" Package or subpackages of the "java" package), by creating additional classes within the JPI or otherwise causing the addition to or modification of the classes in the JPI. In the event that you create an additional class and associated API(s) which (i) extends the functionality of the Java platform, and (ii) is exposed to third party software developers for the purpose of developing additional software which invokes such additional API, you must promptly publish broadly an accurate specification for such API for free use by all developers. You may not create, or authorize your licensees to create additional classes, interfaces, or sub- packages that are in any way identified as "java", "javax", "sun" or similar convention as specified by Sun in any naming convention designation.

F. You shall have the sole responsibility to protect adequately and backup your data and/or equipment used in connection with the Software. You shall not claim against Sun or its licensors for lost data, re-run time, inaccurate output, work delays or lost profits resulting from your use of the Software.

G. Software contains application Testing software components ("Verifier") for your convenience. However, you may not use the Sun tagline "J2EE(TM) Verified" or similar phrase designated by Sun to indicate your application's satisfaction of the J2EE Application Verification Criteria ("verification Tagline") based on the use of Software or Verifier under this Agreement. To obtain the right to use a Verification Tagline, you must license the J2EE Application Verification Kit from Sun, pay applicable fees, and execute a separate trademark license for the Verification Tagline.

H. Refer to the appropriate version of the Java Runtime Environment binary code license (currently located at http://www.java.sun.com/j2se) for the availability of runtime code which may be distributed with your applications.

I. Termination for Infringement. Either party may terminate this Agreement immediately should any Software become, or in either party's opinion be likely to become, the subject of a claim of infringement of any intellectual property right.

J. You acknowledge that at your request or consent optional features of the Software may download, install, and execute applets, applications, software extensions, and updated versions of the Software from Sun ("Software Updates"), which may require you to accept updated terms and conditions for installation. If additional terms and conditions are not presented on installation, the Software Updates will be considered part of the Software and subject to the terms and conditions of the Agreement.

K. You acknowledge that, by your use of optional features of the Software and/or by requesting services that require use of the optional features of the Software, the Software may automatically download, install, and execute software applications from sources other than Sun ("Other Software"). Sun makes no representations of a relationship of any kind to licensors of Other Software. TO THE EXTENT NOT PROHIBITED BY LAW, IN NO EVENT WILL SUN OR ITS LICENSORS BE LIABLE FOR ANY LOST REVENUE, PROFIT OR DATA, OR FOR SPECIAL, INDIRECT, CONSEQUENTIAL, INCIDENTAL OR PUNITIVE DAMAGES, HOWEVER CAUSED REGARDLESS OF THE THEORY OF LIABILITY, ARISING OUT OF OR RELATED TO THE USE OF OR INABILITY TO USE OTHER SOFTWARE, EVEN IF SUN HAS BEEN ADVISED OF THE POSSIBILITY OF SUCH DAMAGES. Some states do not allow the exclusion of incidental or consequential damages, so some of the terms above may not be applicable to you.

L. You may not publish or provide the results of any benchmark or comparison tests run on Software to any third party without the prior written consent of Sun.

M. Additional copyright notices and license terms applicable to portions of the Software are set forth in the THIRDPARTYLICENSEREADME file. In addition to any terms and conditions of any third party opensource/freeware license identified in the THIRDPARTYLICENSEREADME file, the Disclaimer of Warranty and Limitation of Liability provisions in paragraphs 4 and 5 of the Binary Code License Agreement shall apply to all Software in this distribution.

Java[TM] 2 Platform, Enterprise Edition 1.4 Tutorial
Binary Code License Agreement
Copyright 1994-2004 Sun Microsystems, Inc.